SPECIAL PHYSICAL
EDUCATION

SPECIAL PHYSICAL EDUCATION

Adapted, Individualized, Developmental

Seventh Edition

JOHN M. DUNN

The University of Utah

Brown & Benchmark
PUBLISHERS

Madison, WI Dubuque Guilford, CT Chicago Toronto London
Mexico City Caracas Buenos Aires Madrid Bogotá Sydney

Book Team

Project Editor *Theresa Grutz*
Publishing Services Coordinator *Peggy Selle*
Proofreading Coordinator *Carrie Barker*
Production Manager *Beth Kundert*
Production/Costing Manager *Sherry Padden*
Production/Imaging and Media Development Manager *Linda Meehan-Avenarius*
Visuals/Design Freelance Specialist *Mary L. Christianson*
Marketing Manager *Pamela S. Cooper*
Copywriter *Sandy Hyde*

Basal Text *10/12 Times Roman*
Display Type *Times Roman*
Typesetting System *Macintosh™ QuarkXPress™*
Paper Stock *50# Restore Cote*
Production Services *Shepherd, Inc.*

Brown & Benchmark
PUBLISHERS

Executive Vice President and General Manager *Bob McLaughlin*
Vice President of Business Development *Russ Domeyer*
Vice President of Production and New Media Development *Victoria Putman*
National Sales Manager *Phil Rudder*
National Telesales Director *John Finn*

 A Times Mirror Company

The credits section for this book begins on page 617 and is considered an extension of the copyright page.

Cover design by Lesiak/Crampton Design Inc.

Cover illustration © Mary Thelan

Copyedited by Rose Kramer

Proofread by Sarah Greer Bush

Library of Congress Catalog Card Number: 95–81071

ISBN 0–697–12623–4

Printed in the United States of America by Times Mirror Higher Education Group, Inc., 2460 Kerper Boulevard, Dubuque, IA 52001

10 9 8 7 6 5 4 3 2 1

Dedication

The writing and revising of a textbook requires knowledge of the subject matter and a desire to communicate important and sometimes difficult concepts in a meaningful and interesting matter. Much of the training to accomplish this task is attributable to formal and informal study and a deep interest in the subject matter. Former professors and teachers are influential in helping to instill interest in the subject matter. Colleagues and students challenge and help to sustain one's interest in learning and communicating new information. And of course, the real teachers, individuals with disabilities, play a significant role in educating and challenging professionals. For all those who have contributed to furthering my understanding of physical activity, sport, fitness and movement, and the importance of these mediums for individuals with disabilities, especially Dr. J. Hubert Dunn and the late Dr. Hollis F. Fait, I dedicate this text.

Family and loved ones know and feel the rigors of living with the author of a text. The demands of time lines and associated stresses create challenging interactions for family members and require sacrifices. The fortunate ones, such as is the case with me, are supported by loving and caring individuals who understand, accept, and accommodate the pace and idiosyncracies associated with the struggling author and his moments of creativity. Without cooperation, encouragement, and sacrifices from Linda, Matthew, Michael, and Kerry Dunn, this text would not have been possible; to them I dedicate this text.

During the latter stages in the writing of this text, two people who played a significant role in my life and activities died. Jackie Dell Turner, my father-in-law, passed away unexpectedly in June of 1995. Jack was a person's person; he enjoyed meeting and talking with others, was well read and informed and genuinely interested in many diverse topics. He also was very fond of his grandchildren and spent many quality moments interacting with them and contributing to their early development. Although the two of us on occasions differed in our positions on various social issues, we shared a common concern for people who were in greatest need. Jack helped me to understand that while people's views on social policies might differ, this should not preclude a shared vision of how to achieve common goals that would be in the best interest of the larger society. For his many contributions to my family and me, I dedicate this text with thanks and pride to the memory of Jackie Dell Turner (March 18, 1924—June 18, 1995).

My mother's health deteriorated rapidly, leading to her death in January of 1995. While dealing with the enormous grief associated with losing a parent, there were numerous occasions to reflect on my early childhood and the love and support provided by so many—town residents and relatives—but none more important to me than my mother, Arah May Dunn Belbas. My mother, while not highly educated in the sense of degrees and formal education, was an avid reader and a highly intelligent individual. Her knowledge of history, facts, and language was impressive and inspiring. Mom also knew the value of work. She was an excellent employee; one of the "little" people who made others, including her children, appear larger. She took enormous pride in the accomplishments of her children, placing them, their lives, and families above all else. Throughout the writing of this revision, as is true with earlier editions, I was governed by my mother's work ethics, fortitude, pride, and desire to see a fine product to its completion. One of the pleasures of completing earlier revisions was sharing a copy of the final text with Mom. Although that will not be possible with this edition, I dedicate with love, pride and gratitude this book to the memory of my mother—Arah May Dunn Belbas (March 15, 1913—January 18, 1995).

John M. Dunn
January, 1996

Contents Overview

Contents

S E C T I O N

◆ Fundamentals ◆

SECTION

4

Activities and Programs

Preface

As the old man walked the beach at dawn, he noticed a young man ahead of him picking up starfish and flinging them into the sea. Finally catching up with the youth, he asked him why he was doing this.

The answer was that the stranded starfish would die if left until the morning sun.

"But the beach goes on for miles and there are millions of starfish," countered the other. "How can your effort make any difference?"

The young man looked at the starfish in his hand and then threw it to safety in the waves. "It makes a difference to this one," he said.

—Anonymous

In the development of the 7th edition of this text, many moments were spent reflecting on and incorporating newer concepts in the field of special education, specifically as related to physical education. Some of the current thinking in our profession focuses on exciting concepts such as full inclusion, transition, person first language, a broadening of the definition of disabilities, and the age of populations served. While these concepts and philosophies challenge consistency of thinking they have motivated professionals in adapted and special physical education throughout history. This stated very simply is the desire to be of service to those who frequently are in greatest need of the skills and talents that we offer. Thus the story of the starfish and the never-ending quest to make a difference—even in the life of only one individual—serves as the foundation and underlying philosophy of this text. Professionals in special and adapted physical education make a difference by helping individuals with disabilities realize the full spectrum of life's offerings.

The 7th edition of *Special Physical Education: Adapted, Individualized, and Developmental*, transmits, as did its predecessors, current research findings and the best practices to assist professionals in designing and implementing appropriate physical education programs for individuals with disabilities. To accomplish this it was necessary to draw upon the fields of adapted physical education, special education, psychology, medicine, physical therapy, occupational therapy, and therapeutic recreation to form a body of knowledge that is effectively integrated with educational theories and special methods and techniques for reaching those with disabilities. The goal was to provide technical information in a sensitive manner, emphasizing the roles of parents, teachers, and other professionals in responding to the motor and physical fitness needs of infants, children, and young adults with disabilities.

In the development of any text, critical decisions must be made regarding the amount of information to be provided. In the field of adapted physical education this challenge is exacerbated by the number of disabilities to be discussed, an expanding body of knowledge regarding special populations, best approaches to enhancing the lives of those with disabilities, and the increasing realization that much remains to be discovered and learned about the full potential of people with disabilities. The criterion used to select the disability populations discussed in this text was to identify those disorders that are most prevalent among infants, preschool, elementary, and secondary students. Similarly, careful decisions were made about teaching strategies, methods, sport, physical activities, and adaptations to include in the text. The guiding principle was to focus on content that would be most useful to the practicing teacher of physical education.

This edition has been organized into four major sections: Fundamentals; Managing the Learning Environment; Conditions Resulting in Enervated and Impaired Movement; and Activities and Programs. This organizational pattern has received very favorable comments from reviewers and users of the text. The approach is comprehensive but designed to allow for flexibility in use. For example, some instructors have chosen to use Section 4, Activities and Programs, as primarily supplementary material. Decisions such as these are related to the academic calendar, time allocated to a course in special or adapted physical education, and the intended audience. The organization of the text allows for use in various settings ranging from a preservice course in special (adapted) physical education for physical educators or special educators to an inservice course designed for various teachers of physical education, including elementary educators, special educators, and physical educators.

Each chapter of the 7th edition has been reviewed carefully and revised. The strategy was to not only update, but to add, rewrite, and omit, as necessary. This entailed careful review of the latest research and scholarship in the field of adapted physical education and related areas. In response to feedback from reviewers and users of the text, this revision is more heavily referenced than earlier editions with an expanded bibliography for each chapter. This was done to document selected content and to help students become familiar with additional sources of information. Careful attention was given to recent changes in legislation associated with P.L. 101–476, the Individuals with Disabilities Education Act, (IDEA). For example, the changes in Federal Legislation and their implications for adapted physical education have been incorporated throughout the text. Chapter 2, Developmental Patterns, was revised to provide additional information related to the needs of infants and toddlers. Several of the chapters on disabilities, including Chapter 17, Mental Retardation; Chapter 12, Sensory Impairments; Chapter 18, Learning Disabilities; and Chapter 19, Behavioral Disorders, were revised and rewritten. New information and the latest thinking regarding Motor Learning (Chapter 4), Inclusion (Chapters 5 and 6) and Assistive Devices (Chapter 8) were included in this edition.

Given the increasing attention on activities and adaptations for individuals with disabilities, the fourth section of the text, Activities and Programs, was revised thoroughly. The attention in this section was to provide not only the latest findings, but to share information that would be of practical use to teachers and populations served by these individuals. An increasing number of individuals with disabilities are finding that they can successfully participate in healthy and enjoyable activities. This edition should equip teachers with new ideas to help those with disabilities enjoy the full spectrum of activities associated with sport, fitness, and movement-related programs.

Much of the new information contained in this text was guided by the increasing attention given to professional standards and the expectations of teachers who are asked to provide instruction in physical education for those with disabilities. The National Consortium on Physical Education and Recreation for Individuals with Disabilities has undertaken a major effort, with the assistance of funds from the Office of Special Education and Rehabilitative Services, to identify the standards expected of professionals with training in adapted physical education. The author, as one of several professionals associated with this project, is intimately familiar with the work of the group and, where possible, has tried to include information in this revision which addresses the standards as identified by professionals working with infants, children, and youth with disabilities.

As in previous editions, a special effort was made to present concepts so that they could be easily understood and applied. This concern for the reader is evident in the number of photographs, illustrations, and tables found in the 7th edition. Use of the book is facilitated by the inclusion of objectives, summaries, and enhancing activities for each chapter. Instructors and students alike will find these features helpful in understanding the major concepts contained in each chapter. The Glossary, Appendixes, and Indexes have been updated to ensure that terms used in the book are clear and to assist in locating items or topics of interest.

The 7th edition of *Special Physical Education: Adapted, Individualized, and Developmental* continues the standards that have earned the text the reputation of being the most comprehensive adapted (special) physical education text available. This edition retains the best of the old ideas and presents new concepts that will serve as the foundation for future research, scholarship, and program development in physical education for individuals with disabilities.

A teacher's guide, introduced with the last revision of the text, has been revised and updated. Significant features of the guide include suggested class activities, chapter summaries, and an extensive data base of test questions. The test questions are included on a disk for use in preparing course examinations.

Finally, this revision is a tribute to the wisdom and creative genius of the text's original author, Hollis F. Fait. Although Hollis died at a much too early age, his presence is evident today and he is widely recognized as one of the field's true pioneers. Through the efforts of Dr. Hollis F. Fait, the field of adapted physical education is much stronger and valued more highly than when he published the first edition of this text in 1960. I trust that this revision will serve as a reminder of the significant influence of Hollis F. Fait, the innovativeness of his thoughts and ideas, and his continuing contributions to the education of professionals and, indirectly, to individuals with disabilities taught by professionals who know and apply the concepts described in this text.

Acknowledgments

The writing of a textbook requires the support and assistance of many individuals. Special gratitude is extended to the numerous professionals and colleagues who shared their expertise and offered advice and assistance. I am indebted, in particular, to the following people who reviewed the manuscript and offered valuable suggestions regarding this and earlier revisions: Virginia Atkins, California State University at Fresno; Paul Bishop, University of Nebraska at Kearney; Gail Dummer, Michigan State University; Leon Johnson, University of Missouri at Columbia; Luke Kelly, University of Virginia; and Michael Loovis, Cleveland State University.

The special talent of those individuals who helped to revise chapters for this edition is particularly appreciated: Dr. Virginia Atkins, California State University at Fresno for extensive revisions of *Individual Lifetime Activities, Dual Lifetime Sports, Team Games, and Competitive Sports for Athletes with Disabilities;* Dr. Pauli Rintala, University of Jyvaskyla in Finland, for his assistance in rewriting the chapters on *Cerebral Palsy, Orthopedic Disabilities* and *Muscular Weakness and Other Movement Disorders (Les Autres);* Dr. Lauren Lieberman, State University of New York at Brockport, for sharing her extensive knowledge and background in the rewriting of the chapter on *Sensory Impairments;* and to Steve Downs, Oregon State University, for his assistance with information on *Mental Retardation.* During the development of this text, several advanced graduate students provided thoughtful comments about services and programs for individuals with disabilities that added to the content of this edition. These individuals include: Dr. Georgia Frey, Texas A & M University; Dr. Laurie Zittel, Northern Illinois University; Dr. Manny Felix, University of Wisconsin at LaCrosse; Dr. Steve Skaggs, University of Texas at Pan American; and Dr. Cathy Houston-Wilson, State University of New York at Brockport. Special note is accorded to professionals who were so generous in sharing of resources: Dr. Lorraine Bloomquist, University of Rhode Island; Dr. Joe Winnick, State University at Brockport; Dr. Joe Huber, Bridgewater State College, and Dr. Gail Dummer, Michigan State University.

Appreciation is also extended to various professionals whose contributions enhanced the quality of earlier editions. Some of these include: Dr. John E. Billing, University of North Carolina at Chapel Hill; Drs. John and Priscilla Douglas, University of Connecticut; Dr. James W. Morehouse, Warner Pacific College and Dr. Sharon Schmidt, Hockaday School for Girls in Dallas, Texas. Much of their original work has been revised and updated in this edition and any errors or omissions that may appear in the text are the responsibility of the author, not of the original contributors.

To the individuals, schools, organizations, and publications that loaned photographs, illustrations, and materials go sincere thanks for their courtesy in making these items available. Deep appreciation is extended to Dr. Joe Huber, Director of the Children's Physical Development Clinic, Bridgewater State College; Dr. Monica Lepore, specialist in Adapted Physical Education, Westchester State University; Dr. Virginia Atkins, Professor of Physical Education, California State University, Fresno; Cliff and Nancy Crase, *Sports 'n Spokes;* and Dr. Hester Henderson, Associate Professor of Exercise and Sport Science, The University of Utah.

Tributes in this section could not end without acknowledging Ruth Bowman Overgaard, who contributed pictures and ideas to earlier editions. Ruth was one of my first graduate students; a bright and generous individual who made many contributions to her profession, including helping to establish the Portland Public School Motor Development Team. Ruth's life was much shorter than planned, but her contributions were enormous and will be remembered by me and the many others who were touched by her.

I would also like to acknowledge Oregon State University, the College of Health and Human Performance, and the Department of Exercise and Sport Science for providing an environment that encourages scholarly and creative activity. Two people in particular deserve accolades. Without the outstanding support of Karen Hayden, this text would not have been produced. Mrs. Hayden's technical skills, organizational talents, and humor made the impossible seem manageable. Dr. Jeff McCubbin, my colleague and friend, has been unwavering in his willingness to share ideas, and to provide counsel and support.

A work of this magnitude would not be possible without the support of my family. Thank you Linda, Matthew, Michael, and Kerry for unselfishly allowing "Dad" time to complete this revision. Your support and encouragement made the creative moments special and the down times bearable.

Fundamentals

The section is designed to help the reader to:

1 Understand and appreciate the influences that have shaped present-day physical education for students with disabilities.

2 Recognize and apply the developmental patterns of motor movement as they relate to the performance of the basic skills.

3 Apply motor learning concepts to the development of appropriate physical education experiences for special students.

4 Accept students with disabilities as individuals with unique physical, emotional, and social needs.

This initial section delineates the role of physical education in providing a special education service through presentation of certain basic information about the historical backgroud, the general patterns of growth and development, the nature of motor learning, and the psychology of the person with a disability.

CHAPTER
1

Historical Background

After studying this chapter, the reader should be able to:

1 Understand the evolution of programs and services for individuals with disabilities.

2 Recognize various terms that are used to refer to special populations and use these terms appropriately.

3 Analyze selected terms that have been developed to refer to physical activity programs for individuals with disabilities.

4 Identify factors that have contributed to a more positive understanding of persons with disabilities.

5 Analyze the role that governmental agencies have played in expanding services for individuals with disabilities.

6 Identify and explain the significance of federal legislation and the impact of this legislation on physical education and sport programs for individuals with disabilities.

7 Recognize significant events and people that have been instrumental in the evolution of physical education for those with disabilities.

8 Identify professional organizations that promote physical education and sport for individuals with disabilities and the role these organizations play in helping professionals.

Since the beginning of time there has been an interest in and fascination with human development and individual differences. This is reflected in the writings of the early religious prophets and documented as well by the actions of the kings and emperors of ancient time. The early attitude was one of describing differences that existed between individuals considered to be normal compared to those identified as atypical. Nowhere is this fascination with individual differences more real than when applied to those who possess some type of handicapping condition. Fortunately in recent years, with the passage of enlightened legislation such as Public Law 94-142, The Education for All Handicapped Children Act of 1975, as amended by Public Law 101-476, the Individuals with Disabilities Education Act, a concerted effort has been made to recognize not only differences but to accentuate as well similarities between individuals with and without disabilities. Within this chapter, information will be presented to assist readers in understanding the changing perspective that is occurring in society concerning those individuals with handicapping conditions and the importance of physical education in contributing to the lives of individuals with special needs. To help the reader understand this chapter and the rest of the book, selected terms will be defined before undertaking a discussion of the role of those with disabilities in society.

Not all physical educators working with students who have special educational needs approve the designation of all such individuals as handicapped. Some professionals believe the appellation should be limited to those persons who are adversely affected psychologically, emotionally, or socially by their disability. In this way, they explain, the word would properly reflect "an attitude of self-pity, feeling sorry for one's self, and despair" demonstrated by some individuals who have physical, mental, or emotional problems. Other terms, "impaired" and "disabled," are then applied only to those who have a physical disorder but who have made a satisfactory adjustment. Impaired is further defined as referring to those with "identifiable organic or functional disorders" and disabled as referring to those "who because of impairments are limited or restricted in executing some skills, performing tasks, or participating in certain activities." Substitution of the words "inconvenienced" or "exceptional" for "handicapped" is advocated by others in the field as having a less derogatory connotation.

The term "disabled" is used by the federal government under IDEA, to include individuals who are mentally retarded, hard of hearing, deaf, speech impaired, visually disabled, seriously emotionally disturbed, orthopedically impaired, other health impaired, deaf-blind, multidisabled, specific learning disabled, autistic, or traumatic brain injured. Traumatic brain injury and autism are new categories not previously specified under Public Law 94-142 (table 1.1). The author accepts this definition and will address each of these disabilities and their implications for developing movement skills. In addition, this book will include information about individuals with other disorders who require special considerations in physical education, such as those who are obese, low-fit, and awkward.

A number of different names are also given to the special educational provisions made in the physical education curriculum for those unable to profit from the offerings made to the student body. Among the terms used are "individualized," "therapeutic," "developmental," "remedial," and "adapted" physical education. The choice of names is determined largely by the emphasis and approach of the special program. The basic intent of all the programs is the same: the development of total well-being with specific emphasis upon the improvement of motor fitness and physical fitness through motor activity.

Individualized physical education refers to programs that respond to the unique needs of each individual. For students with disabilities this includes movement programs that respond to the physical, mental, and emotional needs of each individual through structured, success-oriented learning experiences.

Therapeutic physical education strives to rehabilitate through prescribed exercises those who have temporary disabilities.

Developmental physical education stresses the development of motor ability and physical fitness in those who are below the desired level.

Remedial physical education consists of programs designed to correct faulty movement patterns through selected activities.

Adapted physical education programs are those that have the same objectives as the regular physical education program, but in which adjustments are made in the regular offerings to meet the needs and abilities of exceptional students.

It should be explained here that *adapted* has also been widely used as a general term for all the programs directed toward students with deficiencies and disabilities. It is desirable, however, to avoid using the word in this all-inclusive sense, because it creates confusion with the more delimiting use of the term. A better umbrella term is *special physical education,* a term first promoted by Hollis Fait that has won wide acceptance in this country and abroad. Special physical education consists of programs designed to enhance the physical and motor fitness of persons with disabilities through modified and developmentally sequenced sport, game, and movement experiences individualized for each participant. The term "special physical education" is a particularly appropriate appellation because of its connotation of serving all students, meeting their individual needs through special provisions in the physical education program.

Table 1.1 *Disability populations recognized by IDEA*

Austism means a developmental disability significantly affecting verbal and nonverbal communication and social interaction, generally evident before age 3, that adversely affects a child's educational performance. Other characteristics often associated with autism are engagement in repetitive activities and stereotyped movements, resistance to environmental change or change in daily routines, and unusual responses to sensory experiences. The term does not apply if a child's educational performance is adversely affected primarily because the child has a serious emotional disturbance.

Deaf-blindness means concomitant hearing and visual impairments, the combination of which causes such severe communication and other developmental and educational problems that they cannot be accommodated in special education programs solely for children with deafness or children with blindness.

Deafness means a hearing impairment that is so severe that the child is impaired in processing linguistic information through hearing, with or without amplification, that adversely affects a child's educational performance.

Hearing impairment means an impairment in hearing, whether permanent or fluctuating, that adversely affects a child's education performance but that is not included under the definition of deafness in this section.

Mental retardation means significantly subaverage general intellectual functioning existing concurrently with deficits in adaptive behavior and manifested during the development period that adversely affects a child's educational performance.

Multiple disabilities means concomitant impairments (such as mental retardation-blindness, mental retardation-orthopedic impairment, etc.), the combination of which causes such severe educational problems that they cannot be accommodated in special education programs solely for one of the impairments. The term does not include deaf-blindness.

Orthopedic impairment means a severe orthopedic impairment that adversely affects a child's educational performance. The term includes impairments caused by congenital anomaly (e.g., clubfoot, absence of some member, etc.), impairments caused by disease (e.g., poliomyelitis, bone tuberculosis, etc.), and impairments from other causes (e.g., cerebral palsy, amputations, and fractures or burns that cause contractures).

Other health impairment means having limited strength, vitality or alertness, as due to chronic or acute health problems such as a heart condition, tuberculosis, rheumatic fever, nephritis, asthma, sickle cell anemia, hemophilia, epilepsy, lead poisoning, leukemia, or diabetes that adversely affects a child's educational performance.

Serious emotional disturbance is defined as follows: (i) The term means a condition exhibiting one or more of the following characteristics over a long period of time and to a marked degree that adversely affects a child's educational performance:

A. An inability to learn that cannot be explained by intellectual, sensory, or health factors
B. An inability to build or maintain satisfactory interpersonal relationships with peers and teachers
C. Inappropriate types of behavior or feelings under normal circumstances
D. A general pervasive mood of unhappiness or depression
E. A tendency to devlop physical symptoms or fears associated with personal or school problems

(ii) The term includes schizophrenia. The term does not necessarily apply to children who are socially maladjusted, unless it is determined that they have a serious emotional disturbance.

Specific learning disability means a disorder in one or more of the basic psychological processes involved in understanding or in using language, spoken or written, that may manifest itself in an imperfect ability to listen, think, speak, read, write, spell, or to do mathematical calculations. The term includes such conditions as perceptual disabilities, brain injury, minimal brain dysfuction, dyslexia, and developmental aphasia. The term does not apply to children who have learning problems that are primarily the result of visual, hearing, or motor disabilities, mental retardation, emotional disturbance, or enviornmental, cultural, or economic disadvantage.

Speech or language impairment means a communication disorder such as stuttering, impaired articulation, a language impairment, or a voice impairment that adversely affects a child's educational performance.

Traumatic brain injury means an acquired injury to the brain caused by an external physical force, resulting in total or partial functional disability or psychosocial impairment, or both, that adversely affects a child's educational performance. The term applies to open or closed head injuries resulting in impairments in one or more areas, such as cognition; language memory; attention; reasoning; abstract thinking; judgment; problem-solving; sensory, perceptual, and motor abilities; psychosocial behavior; physical functions; information processing; and speech. The term does not apply to brain injuries that are congenital or degenerative, or brain injuries induced by birth trauma.

Visual impairment including blindness means an impairment in vision that, even with correction, adversely affects a child's educational performance. The term includes both partial sight and blindness.

Note: The American Association of Mental Retardation adopted a revised definition of mental retardation which is discussed in chapter 17.

Role of Those with Disabilities in Society

Education for all is a basic tenet of our democratic faith, and the opportunity for each individual to develop optimum potential is a guiding principle of our educational system. In the progress toward equalized educational opportunities for all, individuals with disabilities have not always received due consideration. The development of special programs and methods of instruction and the integration of special students into the regular school programs have had to wait largely upon enlightened public opinion regarding students with disabilities and their special needs.

The first real public awareness in the United States of the problems of those who have disabilities came in the early years of this century, growing out of the tragic consequences of disease and war. In 1916 our country experienced an epidemic of infantile paralysis, and within the next few years the wounded returned from World War I. An aroused public's desire to help those with paralysis and veterans who were disabled forged a new attitude toward those with disabilities that spurred legislative and educational assistance.

Early Attitudes

To appreciate fully the new attitude and its ramifications, one must leaf back through the pages of history and appraise the prevailing attitude toward those perceived as disabled, as those perceptions are atypical in other times and places. In

Figure 1.1 Special physical education emphasizes experiences that are adapted, developmentally sequenced, and individualized for each participant.

primitive societies, children born with defects generally perished at an early age as a consequence of their inability to withstand the rigors of primitive man's strenuous existence. Even in the civilized societies of early Greece, the Spartan father of a child with a disabling condition was expected to carry the babe to the hills to be left to perish, whereas the Athenians, whom we generally consider to be more humanitarian than their Spartan neighbors, permitted such babies to die of neglect. During the days of the Roman Empire, babies with birth defects suffered a like fate.

Although some individuals with disabilities found social acceptance as court jesters during the Middle Ages, the prevailing attitude was one of superstition and fear. Physical and mental disabilities were believed to have been caused by Satan, and the afflicted were held to be sinful and evil. Hence, those with disabilities were either harshly treated or carefully avoided.

The humanistic philosophy that flowered in the period of the Renaissance undoubtedly softened the general attitude toward those with physical disabilities, but the gain in understanding of their problems did not extend to include treatment, care, and education. Some legislation to prevent conditions that might produce crippling injuries was passed during the Industrial Revolution, but beyond this, society lost sight of the conditions of those with disabilities in the tremendous technical advancement of the age.

Thus, it was not until the 1900s that social awareness of the problems of those with disabilities gained momentum in this country. This awareness resulted in the organization of conferences on the welfare of the child with a disability and in the opening of schools for children with orthopedic impairments and clinics and centers for their treatment.

World Wars I and II gave impetus to the development of the techniques of orthopedic surgery, which had already made important gains through the treatment of children with disabilities. From the treatment of war casualties, care was gradually expanded to include civilians with physical disabilities. Accompanying the physical reconditioning of seriously injured soldiers and civilians came a movement to rehabilitate those with disabilities, to help them become useful, self-sufficient citizens again.

There developed after World War I what were known at the time as curative workshops, in which patients were taught purposeful activities for their therapeutic value. This type of program is now known as occupational therapy, and it has as its goal the rehabilitation of patients through the teaching of skills by which they may become at least partially, if not totally, self-sustaining. Today there are also programs of physical therapy, therapeutic recreation, corrective therapy, and art, dance, and music therapies that endeavor to help those with disabilities reach maximum potential.

Funds for most early efforts to provide rehabilitation services for those with disabilities came from charity and fraternal organizations, private philanthropy, and community service organizations. A great deal was accomplished through the efforts of these groups, not the least of which was helping to arouse public concern for the needs and rights of those with serious disabilities including the blind, the deaf, and the otherwise disabled. As a result, states began to pass the legislation needed for a more complete program of care and rehabilitation of a heretofore largely neglected segment of our population. Today, states own and support hospitals and institutions at which adults and children can secure the kind of professional care and treatment their disabilities require. The states also assume a share of the responsibility for the educational and vocational needs of those with disabilities.

Governmental Assistance

Federal legislation was enacted following World War I to provide certain benefits to veterans with disabilities; these were supplemented by further legislation in 1943 to increase the scope of aid to the veterans of World War II. The legislation provided for the rehabilitation of soldiers with war disabilities under the supervision of the Veterans Administration.

The first law providing for assistance to civilians with disabling injuries was passed in 1920. Under its provisions, civilians injured in industrial accidents or due to certain other causes were entitled to vocational rehabilitation; they were to be returned to employment whenever possible. A subsequent law in 1943 provided for physical restoration as well as for vocational rehabilitation.

From the 1940s to the present there has been a steady growth of services to individuals with disabilities as the result of private, state, and federal assistance. Examples of the expanded services include research into the cause and cure of mental and physical diseases; better facilities and increased knowledge in detecting, diagnosing, and treating disabling conditions; vocational rehabilitation and training; job placement or replacement; and, in the case of veterans and the industrially disabled, compensation or disability allowances and pensions. Also during this time special hospitals and schools for certain types of individuals with disabilities were established throughout the country. These included hospitals or special homes for the physically disabled, convalescent, and aged; institutions for the mentally ill and emotionally disturbed; and schools for the blind, deaf, and mentally retarded. Efforts were also made to de-emphasize the role of state institutions by providing training for parents, thus enabling many to care for their children at home. Some states also provided funds to initiate group homes, creating living environments within the community for older adults who need assistance but not total care. A service of a different kind, but nonetheless important, was the legislative mandate that all new and remodeled public buildings must be made accessible to those with disabilities. Features such as ramps and elevators to replace stairs and corridors, and toilet facilities large enough to accommodate wheelchairs, enable individuals with disabilities to function much more independently.

Of special note is the emphasis during the 1960s on support for measures to improve education for children with disabilities. During this time the creation of the Bureau of Education for the Handicapped, now known as the Office of Special Education and Rehabilitative Services, is of singular importance. For the first time there existed at the federal level an agency with the sole purpose of administering programs and projects related to the education of students with disabilities. Another milestone of the period was the passage of an amendment to the Elementary and Secondary Education Act that provided funds to support research and demonstration projects in physical education and recreation for those with disabilities.

The 1970s saw the development of a different emphasis from that of the 1960s, this one focusing on restatement by the courts of the scope of the rights of all individuals with disabilities. Various civil and human rights, long denied them, were sought for people with disabilities in state and district courts across the country. An example is the "right of treatment," desperately needed on behalf of individuals in institutions for the mentally ill and mentally retarded, where a humane physical and psychological living environment is often lacking. By and large, the courts upheld the plaintiffs' quest to ensure equality under the law for those with disabilities in all areas of human endeavor.

Recent Federal Legislation

The legislative process has affirmed that individuals with disabilities may not be denied equal access to or services under any program that receives federal financial assistance. The rights of those with disabilities were firmly established with the passage of the Rehabilitation Act of 1973, Public Law 93-112. This law, popularly known as the Civil Rights Act for the Handicapped, is very broad, encompassing all aspects of the disabled person's life. The major concept of Public Law 93-112 may be summarized by explaining that individuals may not be discriminated against because of their disability.

The Rehabilitation Act of 1973, Section 504, reinforces the right of students with disabilities to participate in physical education by stating, "A recipient that offers physical education courses or that operates or sponsors intercollegiate, club, or intramural athletics shall provide to qualified handicapped students equal opportunities for comparable participation in these activities." This statement extends the concept of equal physical education opportunities beyond classroom instruction into the areas of intramurals and athletics. As will be discussed in chapter 30, *Competitive Sport for Athletes with Disabilities,* this means that those with disabilities may not be denied equal opportunity to participate on regular teams or comparable special teams.

To ensure that all children are secure in their right to quality education, Congress in the fall of 1975 approved passage of Public Law 94-142, the Education for All

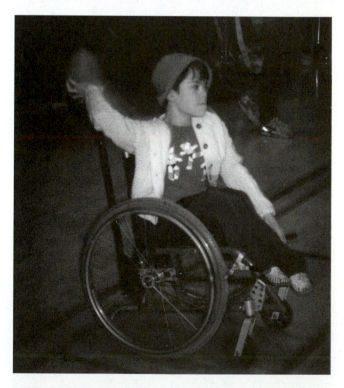

Figure 1.2 Students with disabilities can excel if provided with opportunities and support.

Handicapped Children Act. This law, which has been amended several times and is now known as the Individuals with Disabilities Education Act, Public Law 101-476, includes several provisions that are designed to enable students with disabilities to receive a free appropriate public education. An Individualized Educational Program (IEP) must be written specifically for the student with a disability by a team composed of parents, the child's teacher, a representative of the school, and, when appropriate, the child and other personnel as needed. The IEP team is also responsible for placing the student with a disability in educational programs that are as conducive to the individual's educational growth as is possible. For some students with disabilities, this may include placement in regular education; others may require more assistance and thus placement in a separate program. Obviously, there are many placement options available between regular education and special education. Public Law 94-142 emphasizes that, for each student with a disability, the environment that is least restrictive to the student's growth is the appropriate educational placement.

Concerning the provision of physical education, Public Law 94-142 is also very clear. The term special education ". . . means specially designed instruction, at no cost to the parent, to meet the unique needs of a handicapped child, including classroom instruction, instruction in physical education, home instruction, and instruction in hospitals and institutions." Public Law 94-142 defines physical education to mean "the development of physical and motor fitness; fundamental motor skills and patterns; and skills in aquatics, dance, and individual and group games and sports, including intramural and lifetime sports." The Rules and Regulations for Public Law 94-142 also stress that specially designed physical education services may be necessary for some students, and public schools must either provide this service or make arrangements for special programs through other public or private agencies.

Public Law 94-142 was amended in 1986 when Congress passed and President Reagan signed Public Law 99-457. This law, in addition to reaffirming the provisions of Public Law 94-142, extends special education services to include preschool students with disabilities. The intent of the law was to insure the availability of intervention programs and services at the earliest ages for children with disabilities, including infants and toddlers. Former Senator Lowell Weicker of Connecticut, the primary architect of Public Law 99-457, recognized that children with disabilities cannot wait until the school years to begin the process of developing skills necessary to function effectively within the mainstream of society.

Under Public Law 99-457, states were required by 1991 to provide special education and related services to children with disabilities who are three to five years old. Other provisions of the law specify that federal funds will be provided to assist states develop and implement services. States were also required to include instruction for parents as part of the

preschooler's individualized family service plan (IFSP). Public Law 99-457 also encourages states, through a discretionary grant program, to plan, develop, and implement a statewide, comprehensive, multidisciplinary, coordinated program of early intervention services to infants with disabilities, birth to age thirty-six months, and their families.

The emphasis that Public Law 99-457 places on the importance of early intervention services has been recognized by authorities in various fields as essential to insure that persons with disabilities are provided optimal opportunity to achieve at the highest possible level. The nature of the preschool child with a disability and the importance of physical and motor development will require the expertise of specialists including physical educators with specialized training. Information concerning the motor development needs of the preschool child will be discussed in chapter 2 and procedures for responding to these needs will be presented in chapters 5 and 6.

In the foregoing paragraphs we have attempted to understand individuals with disabilities and their position in society. We have seen how society's perception of those with disabilities has grown from the ancient practices of isolation, ridicule, and, in some cases, elimination of those who appeared different to the current acceptance of the right of all to a life that is as normal as possible. For those with disabilities, this means the right to receive an education, find employment, and live in a community, giving and sharing in all civic and governmental activities similar to all citizens. To achieve the highest level of self-realization possible is the ultimate goal for the highly motivated, regardless of whether one is disabled or not. Society's challenge for the future is to accept those who are different not as people with disabilities but as individuals who differ from others only to the extent of their disability.

Evolution of Special Physical Education

Although the special physical education program is a recently developed service for individuals with disabilities, it is interesting to note that an integral part of the program—the correction and improvement of motor functions of the body through exercise—is an ancient one. Pictures and records dating back 3,000 years before Christ have been found in China depicting the therapeutic use of gymnastics. In more recent times a system of medical gymnastics was developed in Sweden, by Per Henrick Ling, which was introduced in this country in 1884 and was widely in vogue. It was a system of calisthenics of precise, definite movements designed to produce a healthier body and improve posture. Because it was believed that exercise of this nature would be highly beneficial to school children, programs of calisthenics were widely introduced in the public schools of that period.

Adapted Physical Education

A department of corrective physical education was first established by Dudley Sargent at Harvard in 1879 with the objective of correcting certain pathological conditions. The idea of physical education as corrective exercise for bad postural habits and for the general improvement of health persisted until about the time of World War I. Then, following the development of successful physical therapy techniques for paralyzed and convalescent soldiers, the idea of corrective exercises for students with physical handicaps took hold. Soon, a number of colleges had established corrective classes for students who were unable to participate in the regular physical education program. Corrective physical education for the improvement of posture was de-emphasized generally, but a few schools continued to stress corrective exercises in their physical education classes.

Adapted physical education developed from the early corrective classes that were established specifically for those with disabilities. Gradually, over the years following World War I, the practice grew of assigning students with disabilities to corrective courses in order to protect their conditions from possible aggravation. As yet little consideration was given to the idea that students with disabilities could be taught to play modified forms of sports or games or that they could be integrated into regular classes for part of their instruction.

During the 1940s fundamental changes were initiated in physical education for students with disabilities in some universities and colleges. A recognition of the value of play as an educational tool to implement social, mental, and physical development became the philosophical basis of course offerings to those with disabilities. Calisthenics, gymnastics, and corrective exercises were supplanted in the course content by games, sports, and rhythmic activities modified to meet the individual needs of the students. In some schools special classes of adapted activities were developed for students with special needs; in other schools those who could participate with safety in some activities of the regular physical education classes began to receive as much instruction as their cases warranted in these regular classes.

Programs for Those with Physical and Mental Disabilities

Although physical education programs for those with disabilities were limited in number during the years from 1940 to 1960, a slow but steady increase was discernible. Almost all of the programs developed at this time were for the those with physical disabilities. Youngsters with mental disabilities and with abnormal behavior problems were generally not provided for unless they were in one of the few institutions that recognized the residents' need for a special kind of physical education program. Even in these institutions physical education was directed primarily toward those with adequate motor skills for sports participation.

Physical education for students with mental retardation began to receive attention early in the 1960s. The publication of the first textbook to discuss the need of students with mental retardation for adapted physical education, Fait's *Adapted Physical Education,* although not responsible for the upsurge of interest in providing for the physical and motor fitness needs of students with mental retardation, did chart the direction for the future development of such programs. Interest in the movement was fostered by the attention focused on it by the family of President John F. Kennedy; their concern was expressed by their active support of a number of projects to enhance the motor experiences of individuals with mental retardation.

The greatest impetus to the movement to provide quality physical education to serve the needs of those with disabilities has come from the establishment of federal funding for the promotion of research and training in physical education in colleges and universities. By the most recent count (Bokee, 1995), more than 40 institutions of higher learning receive grants either for research and demonstration projects related to the physical and motor needs of those with disabilities or for programs to prepare personnel to work with those with disabilities in physical education or recreation.

Figure 1.3 Society's perception of students with disabilities and their need for physical development has grown in recent years.

Some of the early program directors who, with the assistance of the federal government, developed programs to prepare adapted physical educators include Dr. Larry Rarick, University of California at Berkeley; Dr. Leon Johnson, University of Missouri at Columbia; Dr. Lane Goodwin, University of Wisconsin at LaCrosse; Dr. Lou Bowers, University of South Florida; Dr. Joe Winnick, State University of New York at Brockport; Dr. Claudine Sherrill, Texas Woman's University; Dr. David Auxter, Slippery Rock State College, Dr. Ernest Bunschuh, University of Georgia, and Dr. Hollis Fait, University of Connecticut.

The effect of increased knowledge and understanding that has resulted from these programs has been a commendable expansion in the number and quality of public school physical education programs for students with disabilities. New and more sophisticated methods and procedures for evaluating, planning, and teaching students with disabilities are replacing the "watered down" adaptations of physical education programs of the past. Students with disabilities who have had the advantage of a good physical education experience, one that served their special needs, have reaped benefits that supply the best possible indication of the importance and value of the federally funded programs.

Further evidence of the growth occurring in the field of physical education for those with disabilities is found in the number of specialized journals that have originated in recent years. The *Adapted Physical Activity Quarterly* (*APAQ*), published by Human Kinetics and nurtured by its first editor, Dr. Geoff Broadhead, prints current research findings and articles of general interest on various topics related to special populations. Dr. Greg Reid serves as the current editor of this excellent reference.

A journal that offers many excellent activity suggestions is *Palestra: The Forum of Sport and Physical Education for the Disabled*. This publication, begun in 1983, is edited by Dr. David Beaver of Western Illinois University.

Sports 'n Spokes, begun in 1975, is a valuable resource that provides helpful information on programs and activities for individuals with spinal cord injuries. *Sports 'n Spokes* is edited by Cliff Crase and published by Paralyzed Veterans of America.

Individualized Programming

Although educators of children with disabilities have long recognized the need to develop instructional programs that respond to individual needs, the movement to individualize instruction gathered momentum in the 1970s. The increased number of highly trained professionals in special physical education contributed to the growing awareness that movement experiences for students with disabilities must be personalized to maximize learning. Efforts to focus on individual needs received a boost in 1975 with the passage of Public Law 94-142 and its requirement that Individualized Educational Programs (IEPs) be developed for students with disabilities. Despite the fact that the logic of individualized instruction is obvious, in the past some physical educators dismissed this concept as an unrealistic goal. This response may be attributed in part to the common misconception that to individualize requires a pupil-teacher ratio of one to one. Although it is true that those with more severe disabilities might need one-to-one instruction, it is generally recognized today that many students with disabilities can receive individualized instruction in small and large groups.

Individualizing instruction for special students requires that physical educators attain some skills that have not traditionally been stressed in professional preparation programs. In addition to the skill of writing goals and objectives for the IEP and now the Individualized Family Service Plan under Public Law 99-457, the physical education instructor working with special students should be able to task-analyze (break skills down into smaller parts), manage behavior, evaluate student progress, train volunteers, work with parents, and serve as an interdisciplinary team member. Within the following chapters, these and many other skills will be presented to help physical educators provide effective individualized instruction for special students. Of course, many of these skills will also be helpful in working with all students regardless of ability level.

Fortunately many resources are available that have been developed to assist physical educators in responding to the activity needs of children with disabilities. These range from material found in several excellent adapted physical education texts to specific curricula that have been published. Wessel's I CAN program, developed primarily for children and adolescents with mental retardation, is an excellent example of a well-designed physical education curriculum that responds to individual needs. Other examples include Vodola's Project Active and Winnick and Short's Project Unique. The Project Active program is designed to be used with children experiencing various motor program difficulties, whereas the Project Unique program is specific to those with orthopedic and sensory impairments. Dunn, Morehouse, and Fredericks also have developed ideas on individualized instruction appropriate for students with severe disabilities. Resources that can be used to teach students with disabilities will be described in greater detail in chapter 6, *Teaching Special Physical Education.*

Individualized instruction builds upon the original concept of adapted physical education to produce special learning environments. Thus, the term "special physical education" is a contemporary title that emphasizes the value of adapting activities while stressing that modifications must be individualized and thus personalized to the needs of those with disabilities. It is in this way that physical education becomes special.

Professional Organizations and Physical Education for Individuals with Disabilities

Professional organizations have played an important role in helping physical educators serve students with disabilities. The type of assistance offered varies according to the organization but includes many possibilities, such as publishing journals and resource material; conducting annual meetings, workshops, and continuing education courses; certifying professionals; organizing legislative efforts; and serving as a catalyst to continually upgrade the general status of the profession and its professionals. Included within this section is a discussion of some of the more visible organizations that have been developed to promote physical education for students with disabilities. The address of each association is found in Appendix I.

American Alliance for Health, Physical Education, Recreation, and Dance

The American Alliance for Health, Physical Education, Recreation, and Dance (AAHPERD) is a 35,000-member organization of professionals concerned with the physical activity, health, and leisure needs of citizens within the United States. AAHPERD's commitment to those with disabilities is long-standing as evidenced by its formation in 1952 of the Therapeutics Council. The Council focused its early concerns on the rehabilitative needs of those with disabilities but broadened its mission in later years to include physical activity services for all disabled populations including the elderly. Perhaps the single most important effort by AAHPERD to promote services for those with disabilities occurred in 1965 when the Project on Recreation and Fitness for the Mentally Retarded was initiated through a grant by the Joseph P. Kennedy, Jr., Foundation. This project led to the development of AAHPERD's Unit on Programs for the Handicapped in 1968. Under its director, Dr. Julian Stein, the Unit on Programs for the Handicapped expanded its focus to include all special populations and developed numerous publications and resource materials. In 1975 a third organization, The Adapted Physical Education Academy, was formed by AAHPERD to focus primarily on school-age children with disabilities and their special physical education needs.

Although the Therapeutics Council, the Unit on Programs for the Handicapped, and the Adapted Physical Education Academy were successful in coordinating programs for the AAHPERD annual convention and in cooperating to develop guidelines for the preparation of specialists in adapted physical education, it became apparent to the leaders of the organizations that much duplication existed among the three groups. Therefore, representatives of the organizations proposed in 1985 that one organization be formed by AAHPERD to provide programs and services to assist professionals in responding to the physical activity needs of those with disabilities. Thus the Adapted Physical Activity Council was formed in 1985. This organization, housed within the Association for Active Lifestyles and Fitness of AAHPERD, has accepted as its primary purpose ". . . to advocate, promote, stimulate, and encourage programs for physical activity for special populations." The council provides AAHPERD and its members a unified base for cooperative interdisciplinary services for individuals with special needs.

For additional information write to the Council in care of AAHPERD at 1900 Association Drive, Reston, VA 22091.

National Consortium on Physical Education and Recreation for Individuals with Disabilities

In 1973, a small group of college and university adapted physical educators and therapeutic recreators met in Minneapolis, Minnesota, to discuss the feasibility of developing a new organization that would have as its sole purpose the promotion of physical education and recreation for those with disabilities. From this meeting the National Advisory Council on Physical Education and Recreation for Handicapped Children and Youth was formed. This organization was the forerunner to the present National Consortium on Physical Education and Recreation for Individuals with Disabilities (NCPERID). The Consortium is an organization of individuals with extensive backgrounds in the fields of adapted physical education and therapeutic recreation who agree with NCPERID's efforts to promote professional preparation programs and research in physical education and recreation for those with disabilities. In addition to conducting an annual meeting, NCPERID publishes a quarterly newsletter and supports legislative efforts on behalf of those with disabilities.

Related Therapy Organizations

The psychomotor needs of those with disabilities are so varied and intense that professionals from many fields can be called upon to assist physical educators in enhancing the performance capabilities of those with disabilities. Professionals from the fields of physical therapy and occupational therapy, for instance, are frequently employed by school districts to work with specialists in special physical education for the disabled as an interdisciplinary motor development team. Other professionals who are concerned with the rehabilitation and remediation of movement deficiencies include corrective therapists, dance therapists, and recreational therapists.

The various forms of therapy, with some exceptions such as dance therapy, can trace their origins to World Wars I and II, when individuals were trained to rehabilitate and prepare injured soldiers for new occupations, and to help them make the transition from hospital to home. In recent years, the types of therapeutic services offered have changed dramatically. Physical therapists, for instance, once were found only in treatment centers giving massages, hot and cold treatments, and a range of motion exercises. Today physical therapists can specialize in the treatment of young children and find employment in public schools.

Each of the therapies identified in this section has an active professional organization with a code of ethics and procedures for certifying and registering qualified therapists. Most of the therapy associations also have a professional journal that reports the latest research or motor treatment procedures for individuals with disabilities.

Specialists in physical education for those with disabilities realize that effective services for students with disabilities require cooperation and consultation with other experts in the field of motor development. An increasing number of physical educators are attending meetings sponsored by therapy organizations to pick up new ideas concerning treatment procedures. Therapists, too, have found meetings sponsored by physical educators helpful in enhancing their ability to provide effective services. Neither physical educators nor therapists desire to perform the others' responsibilities, but both groups are interested in improving the total services available to school-age children with disabilities. This effort can be accelerated by therapists and special physical educators who have the foresight to meet together in professional meetings and to read each others' professional journals.

Council for Exceptional Children

The national organization with which most special educators affiliate is the Council for Exceptional Children (CEC). Although the historical origin of the CEC can be traced to 1922, it was not until 1958 that the organization officially adopted its present name. Similar to the American Alliance for Health, Physical Education, Recreation, and Dance, the CEC provides many diverse services for its membership, such as holding an annual conference, sponsoring institutes, disseminating information, and publishing journals, including *Exceptional Children* and *Teaching Exceptional Children*. The primary focus of the CEC is the promotion of quality special education programs for exceptional students, including the talented and gifted.

In recent years, many physical educators have joined the CEC, leading to an increased awareness on the part of special educators and physical educators as to the contribution each profession can offer to students with disabilities. Fortunately, the Council for Exceptional Children is including more information about physical education in its publications and at its conferences. Through the efforts of specialists in adapted physical education, physical education has been identified as a section within CEC, thus allowing for greater visibility and expanded opportunities for programs at state, district, and national meetings.

Office of Special Education and Rehabilitative Services

The federal agency responsible for initiating, expanding, and monitoring services for students with disabilities is the Office of Special Education and Rehabilitative Services (OSERS). Prior to President Carter's creation of the Department of Education in 1980, OSERS was known from its inception in 1968 as the Bureau of Education for the Handicapped. Although OSERS is not a professional organization per se, it does sponsor many meetings and, consequently, opportunities for professionals from various disciplines to meet and share ideas about special education. One of OSERS's primary responsibilities through its Division of Personnel Preparation is to provide grants to colleges and universities for the training of professionals in special education and related services to work with students with disabilities. Funds for the training of physical educators to teach those with disabilities have increased significantly since 1968. Approximately two million dollars have been allocated yearly to train teachers in special physical education and to help general physical education personnel teach students with special needs. The Office of Special Education and Rehabilitative Services has significantly enhanced the quantity and quality of special physical education services available today.

Related Sport Organizations

Supported by the provisions of the Rehabilitation Act of 1973 and its emphasis on nondiscrimination in all facets of life, individuals with disabilities are striving to achieve success and recognition in all fields of endeavor, including sports. In 1970 specialized sport organizations such as the United States Association for Blind Athletes and the United States Cerebral Palsy Athletic Association were founded to provide and expand athletic experiences for participants with disabilities. These groups, with the assistance of organizations formed earlier such as the Special Olympics (1968) and the Wheelchair Sports USA, founded in 1959 as the National Wheelchair Athletics Association have been instrumental in enhancing the quality of training and coaching for athletes with disabilities. The spinoff of this effort has been to increase public awareness of the ability level of athletes with disabilities and to assist other service providers, including physical educators, in utilizing the valuable training materials generated by these specialized organizations. Chapter 30, *Competitive Sport for Athletes with Disabilities,* will provide information about these organizations and the exciting challenges created by segregated and integrated competition sport experiences for participants with special needs.

Summary

Within this chapter, a review of the origin of services for individuals with disabilities was provided from ancient times to the present. Careful review of the meaning of selected terms such as *handicapped, disabled,* and *impaired* were presented. Terms specific to physical education for individuals with disabilities, such as *adapted* and *special physical education,* were discussed, with the term *special physical education* proposed as the appropriate term to describe physical and motor fitness programs for students with disabilities.

Society and its view of those with disabilities was described. The favorable changes that are occurring in services and programs for those with disabilities and the important role the federal government plays in helping to make this possible were emphasized. Significant federal legislation, including Public Laws 94-142, 93-112, 99-457, and 101-476, and its relationship to physical education for students with disabilities were discussed.

Finally, the evolution of special physical education was traced from its beginning as primarily therapeutic and corrective exercises to its present status as an integral part of the services available to a large number of individuals with disabilities with a wide variety of disabilities.

Major professional organizations and the services they offer to physical educators interested in programs for those with disabilities were identified and described.

Selected Readings

American Alliance for Health, Physical Education, and Recreation. (1973). *Guidelines for professional preparation programs for personnel involved in physical education and recreation for the handicapped.* Washington, DC: Author.

American Alliance for Health, Physical Education, and Recreation. (1976). *Education of all handicapped children act: Implications for physical education. IRUC briefings.* Washington, DC: Author.

American Alliance for Health, Physical Education, and Recreation. (1976). *Physical education and recreation for impaired, disabled, and handicapped individuals . . . past, present and future.* Washington, DC: Author.

Assistance to states for education of handicapped children: Proposed rules, Department of Education. (1982, August 4). *Federal Register.*

Bokee, M.B. (1995). Fiscal year 1982 through 1995 adapted physical education and therapeutic recreation program analysis. Unpublished report. Office of Special Education and Rehabilitative Services, U.S. Dept. of Education.

Dunn, J.M., Morehouse, J.W., & Fredericks, H.D. (1986). *Physical education for the severely handicapped.* Austin, TX: Pro-Ed Publishers.

Education of handicapped children, part II, implementation of part B of the Education of the Handicapped Act, Department of Health, Education, and Welfare, Office of Education. (1977, August 23). *Federal Register.*

Education of the handicapped as amended by P.L. 99-457 and P.L. 99-372. (1986, November). *Education for the Handicapped Law Reporter.* Alexandria, VA.: CRR Publishing Co.

Sherrill, C. (1993). *Adapted physical education and recreation* (4th ed.). Dubuque, IA: Wm. C. Brown Publishers.

Turnbull, H.R., & Turnbull, A. (1978). *Free appropriate public education—law and implementation.* Denver: Love Publishing Company.

U.S. Department of Health, Education, and Welfare. *Basic education rights for the handicapped.* Washington, DC: U.S. Government Printing Office.

Vodola, T.M. (1974). *A.C.T.I.V.E. All Children Totally Involved Exercising.* Oakhurst, NJ: Township of Ocean School District.

Winnick, J.P., & Short, F.X. (1985). *Physical fitness testing of the disabled—Project Unique.* Champaign, IL: Human Kinetics Publishers.

Enhancing Activities

1. Interview a person with a disabling condition or a parent of a child with disabilities. Try to determine whether the individual feels that society's perception of those with disabilities has changed in recent years.

2. Review your state law to determine if services, including physical education programs, are provided for the preschool child with disabilities.

3. Explore with students or professionals from other fields (such as physical and occupational therapy) their views regarding physical education and its contributions to the development of children with disabilities.

4. Develop a list of prominent people including entertainers, athletes, and politicians who have a disabling condition. Select one and attempt to find information about how the disability has affected the person's life.

5. Review the local newspaper and assess its coverage of items related to persons with disabilities and programs. Is the reporting positive or negative in its views of those with disabilities?

6. Review your institution's library holdings to determine if journals such as *Adapted Physical Activity Quarterly* and *Palaestra* are included.

7. Obtain a copy of one of the issues of the *Federal Register* that describes one of the pieces of legislation discussed in this chapter.

8. Write to one of the professional organizations discussed in this chapter to obtain information about the organization, including services to professionals.

CHAPTER

2

Developmental Patterns

After studying this chapter, the reader should be able to:

1　Identify the importance of the Principles of Motor Development and Principles of Physical Growth as factors that help to explain the developmental patterns observed in children.

2　Recognize the developmental patterns associated with the periods of infancy, early childhood, and later childhood.

3　Appreciate the close and significant relationship among physical growth, motor development, and the social, emotional, and cognitive development of children.

4　Identify common reflexes observed in infants, their time of onset and integration, and their importance as early indicators of potential neurological problems.

5　Analyze the common movement patterns, forms of locomotion, and manipulative patterns associated with various ages and levels of performance.

6　Appreciate the wide range of individual difference found among children of similar ages.

In the growth of children from infancy to adolescence, certain discernible patterns of development occur roughly at each year of age. Consequently, at a certain chronological age a large majority of children demonstrate much the same physical development and similar intellectual and social traits. An understanding of the patterns of physical, intellectual, and social developments that are characteristic of each age group is extremely useful to teachers of children from nursery school to secondary school. Beginning with the period of adolescence, development becomes so highly individualized that patterns characteristic of specific age groups are no longer easily identifiable. During the early years, however, definite patterns in development are readily observed, and awareness of them will help the teacher serve the individual student more effectively; this is particularly true if the student has a disability.

As discussed in chapter 1, the need to provide early intervention services to infants and toddlers with suspected or diagnosed disabilities is receiving increased attention. Public Law 99-457, the Education for All Handicapped Children Amendment and Public Law 101-476, the Individual with Disabilities Education Act (IDEA), both highlight that preschool children (Part B, ages 3–5) and infants and toddlers (Part H, ages birth to 2) will benefit from early intervention services. Although the laws are not clear with respect to the types of services to be provided, most professionals recognize that motor development activities should play an integral part in services for preschool children, including infants and toddlers (Cowden and Eason, 1991; Haley and Baryza, 1990). Cowden and Eason (1991) have suggested that the adapted physical educator should play an integral part in the multidisciplinary services provided to infants, toddlers, and preschoolers and argue that individuals trained with these skills should be referred to as Pediatric Adapted Physical Educators. Regardless of the appropriate title selected or used, it is clear that professionals in physical education will play an increasingly important role in the education of infants, toddlers, and preschool children with disabilities. The information presented in this chapter provides a basic overview of developmental patterns and the relationship between early and later movement experiences and successes.

The patterns of development common to various age periods can be used by the teacher as criteria to evaluate the degree to which a disabling condition is affecting normal growth and development. In some instances, the disability will be seen to have interfered with the development of certain motor skills that most other children of the same age have developed; or it may be determined by a comparison with the pattern of social development typical of the age group that a child's social growth has been retarded by his or her attitude toward the disabling condition.

It should be noted at this point that significant differences in development can be expected among the students in any classroom where children are approximately the same age. Although children of a given age follow the same general developmental patterns, some progress at a faster or slower rate. The various aspects of physical development, such as height, weight, strength, and endurance, are generally, but not always, accelerated or retarded to the same degree. It is also usually true, but not always, that the rate of intellectual and social development parallels physical development. The exceptions can be found among children with and without disabilities. Account must be taken of the existence of the possible differences in rate of development when evaluating the effects of a disability upon development.

If, then, it is determined that a disabling condition is negatively influencing development, special steps can be taken to help the child improve. These might include selective exercises and activities to promote physical development if this is where the deficiency occurs; or if help is needed to overcome poor social development, attention can be directed toward instruction and increasing the opportunities for social interaction in group play. These are only two examples of the numerous ways in which the teacher can meet the special needs of students whose development has not kept pace with that of their peers; the subject of serving special needs is explored more fully in later chapters.

Familiarity with the developmental patterns also provides the teacher with a means of assessing progress toward achieving the degree of development that is common for a given age period. This is particularly helpful with young children who are difficult to test with standardized tools of evaluation. Although the comparison of a child's status of development with patterns that are generally characteristic of the age group is highly subjective and open to errors of misinterpretation, it is nevertheless a useful means of determining if and how much improvement has been made. It can be said of the method that its accuracy increases with experience in its use, thereby increasing its usefulness (King and Dunn, 1989).

It is often difficult to determine if a child with disabilities is ready to learn a new skill. Readiness is that state of development in which the child has acquired the physical, mental, and emotional capacity to comprehend the requirements of a task and to execute them. Because a disabling condition may so alter the responses of the child as to cause misdiagnosis of his or her readiness for new learning experiences, teachers need other means of making the determination. The patterns of development can provide one of the means, because they indicate the abilities and potentialities usually evident in those of the same age group, abilities that may well be present in the student with a disability as well.

When studying the developmental patterns presented on the following pages, it should be kept in mind that no single description of the characteristics for various age periods will fit every child of that age group. It is not likely that very many children will exhibit all of the patterns ascribed to their age group; it is possible that very few will evidence a particular pattern. Each child does, after all, grow and develop at his own individual rate, a rate that is influenced by factors such as inheritance, socioeconomic background, and educational environment.

Care should also be exercised to recognize that biology and environment play a significant role in the development of infants and children (Berman, 1993). Biology, to a large extent, is controlled by genetic factors. In the past, genetics has been recognized as an important, but little understood field. This is changing dramatically. In the past ten years, scientists have gone from mapping just a few human genes into mapping more than 1,900 genes (Van Dyke and Lin-Dyken, 1993). The implications of this for infants with disabilities is profound. What was once viewed as genetic and largely unknown is becoming more widely understood with the promise of major changes in the diagnosis, management, and possible treatment of children with developmental disabilities.

The environment in which infants and young children are raised is also becoming more widely understood and appreciated as to its importance in development. Included in environment are factors such as family relationships, cultural perspectives and child-rearing practices, poverty, and the availability of community resources.

Principles of Development

Investigators from several fields, including physical education, child development, medical sociology, and psychology, have identified some rather consistent, predictable developmental trends in children. Many of these trends will be discussed in this chapter. General principles have also been defined that help to explain some of these trends. The following principles will help professionals comprehend the process of motor development and guide them in developing appropriate movement experiences for youngsters with and without disabilities. This discussion will be grouped into two sections: *Principles of Motor Development* and *Principles of Physical Growth*.

Principles of Motor Development

Maturation

Early developmental patterns are generally dependent upon maturation. This means that certain physical and behavioral changes are primarily attributed to the innate process of growth rather than to the influence of the environment. The maturational concept suggests, therefore, that certain changes that are relatively independent of environmental influences occur as growth proceeds. Characteristics subject to the maturational process, such as early infant reflex patterns, will occur at broadly predictable periods of time in normal children. Close supervision of the child's development may detect significant delays in the maturational process, thus indicating a need for extensive effort to teach what normally occurs during the growth process.

Cephalocaudal (Head to Tail)

Development is not haphazard. In physical and motor development, two directional sequences have been noted. The first of these implies that muscular control and coordination advances in an orderly sequence from head to foot. In the initial stages of motor development, children gain control of the muscles that support the head and upper body before they gain control of the lower musculature. The progression in muscle control proceeds from the neck, to the back, lower back, upper leg, lower leg, and foot.

Proximodistal (Point of Origin to End)

The second of the directional sequences suggests that control of body parts proceeds from the center or torso to the periphery in a proximodistal fashion. Efforts to control the torso and shoulder, therefore, precede controlled movement of the elbow, wrist, and finger. In the lower half of the body, control of the hips precedes efforts to control the legs, feet, and toes. It is important to note that developmental principles of cephalocaudal and proximodistal, while generally recognized and accepted, have been challenged by some researchers (Allen and Capute, 1990). Some speculate, for instance, that head control may be functional first because it does not rely on the development of other body segments (Damiano, 1993).

Mass to Specific

An understanding of the proximodistal principle also suggests that motor function progresses from mass to specific. Therefore, control of gross motor movements will occur before fine motor movements. Skills that are simple and involve large muscles will be learned sooner than those that are refined and require the use of fine muscle movements. Drawing with a pencil is an example of a fine motor task that follows controlled movement of the shoulder, wrist, and hand.

Bilateral to Unilateral

After the age of four, children normally exhibit preference for conducting activities using one side of the body. Thus, a child may eat and draw with the right hand, kick a ball with the right foot, and use the right eye to look through a kaleidoscope. Until this preference is established, the child will do various activities with either hand. A recent concern of many specialists is that children be given the opportunity to explore activities bilaterally and that they not be forced into unilateral preference. Fortunately, parents and teachers have become more sensitive to the needs of left-handed children

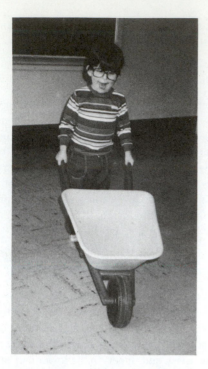

Figure 2.1 Pushing a wheelbarrow is an activity that develops bilateral coordination.

and are providing them with greater opportunities to exhibit their preference in a right-handed culture. Some children take longer to develop preference, or dominance, and some are ambidexterous. They may be able to write with either hand and perform physical tasks such as batting on either side.

Phylogenetic versus Ontogenetic

Changes in behavior that occur rather automatically as the individual grows are referred to as phylogenetic behavior. Grasping, reaching, crawling, and creeping are examples of behavior that fit into this category. Behavioral changes that depend primarily on learning and environmental influences are called ontogenetic behavior. Unlike phylogenetic behaviors, ontogenetic responses do not occur automatically but must be taught. Behaviors that are ontogenetic include such activities as throwing and catching and riding a bicycle.

Individual Development

A discussion of developmental patterns is incomplete without an emphasis on the uniqueness of each individual. Although there may be patterns that apply to the whole species, each child is different and thus the rate and speed at which certain movement patterns appear varies. These differences may be attributed to the combination of heredity and the environment in which the young child develops. The style in which children learn—auditory, kinesethetic, or visual, varies and is inclined to be genetically based. Awareness of

the individual difference principle will help teachers recognize that all children are not ready for the same experiences at the same age. For example, Thelen and her associates (1987) have identified "stereotypies" (i.e., flappings, swipings, and bouncings) of normal developing infants. These movements which occupy approximately 40 percent of the waking hours of the normal infant are important in the development of behaviors such as kneeling, standing, and sitting. Thelen further speculates that the stereotypies blend into and support appropriate voluntary movement. Unfortunately, infants exposed prenatally to drugs such as cocaine and marijuana do not exhibit the normal rhymicity seen in infants who are developing normally (Cratty, 1990).

Dynamic Systems Theory

Theorists in the area of motor development are suggesting that some of the commonly accepted principles of development have understated the importance of some factors in the development of infants and children. Dynamic systems theorists believe that the role of the central nervous system (CNS) in the control of coordinated movement should be deemphasized with greater attention placed on information in the environment and the dynamic properties of the body and limbs.

The key to understanding this approach is to accept the important connection between the person and the environment. While this relationship is generally recognized and supported by most developmental theorists, proponents of the dynamic systems theory argue that too much attention has been placed on the control center (CNS) and not enough on the importance of the interaction between the environment and the person. This, of course, has significant implications for motor programs for infants and toddlers. For example, proponents of the dynamic motor systems theory would argue that under traditional views of motor development, the inability to inhibit certain reflexes in a youngster with cerebral palsy would be discouraging and might either delay or inhibit the development of motor activity programs. Whitehall (1988) suggests that using a dynamic system perspective, movement patterns are not prescribed but emerge from interaction among body, task, and environment with little central input.

The implication of this, of course, is to suggest that the traditional strict reliance on a neuromaturational theory of development may be a disservice to infants and toddlers with developmental disabilities. This is not to suggest however that the traditional principles of development are unimportant, but it does mean that professionals should continually be open to new ideas and, most importantly, recognize the specific needs of the infant and the relationship between environmental stimuli and self-initiated movement.

Finally, all the answers to the best approaches to the developmental needs of individuals with disabilities and the appropriate remedial practices are not known. Thus professionals will need to seek and be open to new ideas and suggestions for working with this population. Chapter 21 will provide additional suggestions and activities that have been found to be helpful in working with infants and toddlers. A more thorough discussion of dynamic systems theory will be found in chapter 3.

Principles of Physical Growth

Although there are principles associated with growth, it must be stressed that growth is not smooth. As is very clear in assessing height, most individuals experience growth spurts. In addition each aspect of development has its own pattern of development. Whereas the child may experience rapid increase in height early, the growth curve slows and then increases rapidly (spurts) later. Sexual development, in contrast, is very slow and gradual until adolescence with significant increases associated with puberty.

As children grow and become taller and heavier, their ability to perform various motor skills also changes. This relationship is clearly seen in the observation of a young student who, through growth and practice, develops sufficient strength to shoot a basketball successfully at a ten-foot-high goal. Several of the factors affecting physical growth have been identified by J. M. Tanner (1978). These factors, which exert an influence on the performance of motor skills throughout the lifetime of an individual, are briefly discussed here.

Genetic Aspects of Growth

Heredity plays a very important part in determining the size of the offspring. Although the relationship is not perfect, several investigators have noted that the height of the child is related to the height of the parent. Thus, if both parents are tall, their children tend to be tall (Malina, Mueller, and Holman, 1976). Similarly, small parents tend to have small children. Correlations between parents and their children for other bodily measures exist but are not as significant as the height variable.

Effect of Health Status

Critical to the development of children is their health status at the time of birth. Factors arising from complications during delivery (e.g., absence of oxygen) can result in long-term cognitive, motor, and physical delays, including decreases in size and weight. Information is also available that drug-stressed babies are also likely to have motor and growth development problems including diminished height and weight and skeletal deformities. Unfortunately, available data suggest that over one million women of childbearing age are using one or more of four drugs—alcohol, marijuana, cocaine, and nicotine.

Effects of Nutrition on Growth

Good nutrition is essential to assist children in growing to their full potential. Tanner (1978) observed that chronic malnutrition during most or all of early childhood will result in smaller adults. Acute starvation for a short period of time will not, however, significantly alter potential growth, although the immediate effect is that the child's growth slows down.

Children from low-income homes, in which adequate nutrition is less likely, tend to be shorter and lighter than those from homes in which the family income is average to above average. The most notable retardation in growth for children who are poorly nourished occurs in their width. Children from deprived homes, therefore, tend to have a more linear body composition than do those from more affluent homes.

Differences between Races

Racial characteristics account for some of the differences in size, tempo of growth, and bodily shape that have been observed. In a study of the major population groups—European, African, and Asiatic—P. B. Eveleth and J. M. Tanner (1976) noted that the heights of European and African American boys are similar but that African American girls are slightly taller than European girls. Both sexes of the Asiatic group were shorter than either the European or African groups.

Effects of Disease

The frequency and acuteness of disease are factors that may slow the growth pattern. In well-nourished children, however, the slow period is often followed by a growth spurt when the illness is cured.

Psychosocial Stress

Severe stress, such as the emotional reaction to acute and chronic disease, has been found to retard growth temporarily. Once the stress is alleviated, the growth process will usually experience a catch-up phase. Effects of poverty on growth are currently being studied. Psychosocial dwarfism has been identified in some children who experience severe stress.

Number of Children

Although birth order does not affect the ultimate height of the adult, younger children in a family tend to grow at a slower rate. This means that children who are born first tend to be taller at various age levels than their younger brothers and sisters. This difference, however, frequently diminishes or reverses itself as children reach adulthood.

Secular Trend

The familiar statement that children appear to be getting bigger is a well-documented fact. Children born today are taller and heavier. This trend is consistent throughout childhood and adolescence. The reason for this is most likely an interaction between heredity and the environment in which the child is being raised.

Infant (Zero to Two Years)

The ability to participate in games, exercise, and activities of daily routine is important throughout life. The foundation to enjoyment of a happy, physically active life is determined in the early years of life. Within this section, the development of the individual during the first two critical years of life, the infant period, will be discussed.

Physical Growth

The average full-term baby weighs 7½ pounds and is approximately twenty inches long. One fourth of the baby's length is attributed to the head, with the trunk size accounting for slightly more of the remaining length than the lower extremities. As the baby grows during the first six months of life, these proportions remain constant. After approximately six months of age, however, the relationship of body proportions begins to change: the growth of the head slows and a rapid increase occurs in the growth of the extremities, with the rate of development of the trunk remaining constant. As the infant approaches two years of age, the relationship of the lower limbs and trunk are approximately equal. This adjustment in growth equips the two-year-old with the body size and proportion needed to successfully undertake the various locomotor skills.

Infant Reflexes

The earliest movements that can be observed in the infant are reflexes. These actions are involuntary behaviors elicited by various types of external stimuli. Physicians and specialists in motor and child development are interested in observing reflexes as a method of assessing the child's nervous system. An absent reflex or one that persists for too long may be an indication of neurological impairment. For educators working with young students with disabilities, familiarity with some of the more common infant reflexes is essential.

Moro and Startle Reflexes The Moro and startle reflexes in infants can be elicited in several ways, such as placing the infant on its back and tapping on the abdomen or moving the head quickly. The response may even be self-induced by a loud noise or the infant's own cough or sneeze. In the Moro reflex there is sudden extension of the arms and legs with spreading of the fingers and the toes (figure 2.2).

The action is usually more vigorous in the upper extremities than the lower extremities. The startle reflex is similar to the Moro reflex except that it involves flexion of the limbs without prior extension. The Moro reflex is normally present at birth and evident during the first three months of life. If the Moro reflex persists much after the sixth month of life, it may be an early warning of developmental delay. The startle reflex is present at birth and persists in an integrated fashion throughout life.

Search and Sucking The search and sucking reflexes are present in all normal newborns. These reflexes are essential to enable the newborn to obtain nourishment from its mother. The search reflex may be initiated by stimulating the infant's cheek and observing if the infant turns the head toward the source of stimulation. Stroking the area above or below the lips or placing a finger or nipple in the mouth will initiate the sucking reflex. The sucking reflex generally disappears by the end of the third month but persists throughout life as a voluntary response. The search reflex may persist beyond the first year of life. In some newborns the suck is not fully developed and intervention must be directed toward stimulating this reflex.

Symmetrical Tonic Neck Reflex This reflex is elicited by extension and flexion of the head and is characterized by two distinct patterns. When the head is flexed, the arms go into flexion and the legs into extension. When the head is extended beyond the midline, the arms go into

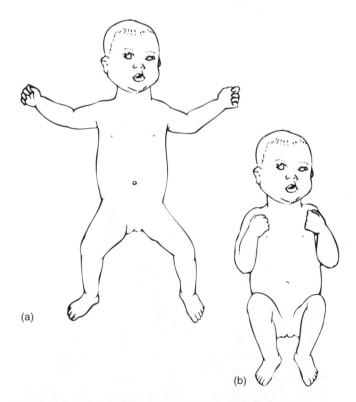

(a)

(b)

Figure 2.2 The (a) Moro reflex extension phase. (b) Flexion phase.

extension and the legs into flexion. The symmetrical tonic neck reflex is present at birth and its primary function is to help the infant develop extension patterns. Normally, the reflex is repressed between the fourth and sixth months.

Asymmetrical Tonic Neck Reflex The apparent purpose of this reflex is to aid in the development of extension patterns. The reflex is elicited by rotation of the head to either side. When the head is turned, the arm and leg on the side of the body to which the face is turned are extended and the limbs on the opposite side are flexed. Usually the asymmetrical tonic neck reflex disappears four to six months after birth.

Palmar or Grasp Reflex Pressing against or stroking the palm of the infant elicits a grasp reflex. Hyperextending the baby's wrist will also produce this reflex. The palmar reflex response is strongest at about the third month of life, becomes weaker by the sixth month of life, and disappears completely by the end of the first year. Delays in motor development may be apparent if this reflex persists after the first year.

Babinski and Plantar Grasp Reflexes The Babinski reflex is elicited by stroking the sole of the foot of the newborn. The pressure causes an extension of the toes. Persistence of this reflex beyond the sixth month may be an indication of a neurological difficulty.

The plantar grasp reflex is elicited by pressing against the infant's foot directly below the toes (figure 2.3). The pressure causes the toes to contract. The plantar grasp reflex is usually present about the fourth month and persists to approximately the twelfth month. Persistence of the plantar grasp reflex beyond this point may interfere with the infant's early attempts at standing and walking.

Labyrinthine Righting Reflex This reflex is important in helping the infant assume an upright head and body posture. The labyrinthine righting reflex can be initiated by holding the infant upright, then tipping the body forward. The infant's head will go back in an attempt to maintain an upright position. Angling the infant to the right or left will also initiate this response. The head will tend to move so as to maintain an upright position. The reflex may first appear at two months and becomes increasingly stronger until the fifth or sixth month, when it disappears.

Parachute and Propping Reflexes The parachute and propping reactions may be elicited in several ways. Basically both types of reaction by the infant are efforts to protect against sudden shifts in directions. As noted in figure 2.4, the infant, when tilted forward from a held position (the forward parachute), extends the arms as a protective mechanism. This same response may be obtained by holding an infant in an upright vertical position and lowering the infant quickly toward the ground. As indicated in figure 2.4, the infant's lower limbs extend, tense, and abduct. Propping reflexes may be observed by moving the infant off balance from a sitting position either forward or backward.

The parachute and propping responses occur at different stages in the infant's development. The forward and downward parachute reactions begin to occur around the fourth month. The sideways propping response is usually observed about the sixth month with the backward propping response occurring between the tenth and twelfth month. Each of these reflexes tends to persist beyond the first year and play an important role in assisting the infant in learning to walk.

Righting Reflexes of the Head and Body Within the first year of life, the infant has two involuntary reactions that help it to maintain a comfortable position in the crib. The first of these, the neck-righting reflex, is elicited by turning the head as the infant is on its back. The trunk will reflexively turn in the same direction. Likewise, if the hips are turned while the infant is in a prone position, the head will follow in the same direction.

Crawling Reflex The crawling reflex can be observed by placing the infant in a prone position on the floor and applying pressure to the sole of one foot. The infant will return the pressure by pushing with the affected foot while doing an extensor thrust with the nonaffected leg. Reflexive movement will occur, which resembles that of crawling. The

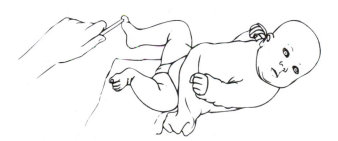

Figure 2.3 The plantar grasp reflex.

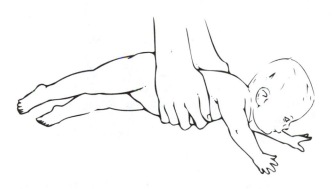

Figure 2.4 The parachute reflex.

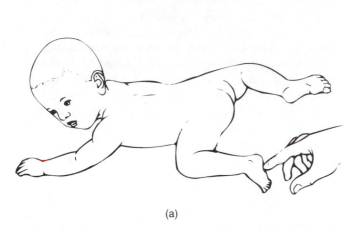

(a)   (b)

Figure 2.5 (a) The crawling reflex. (b) The primary stepping reflex.

crawling reflex is generally present at birth and disappears around the third or fourth month. The delay between reflexive crawling and voluntary crawling is approximately four months with most infants crawling around the seventh month.

Stepping Reflex Many parents become excited when they see their one-month-old baby make a response that looks very much like the taking of steps. This action is very normal and can be elicited in infants as young as two weeks by holding the baby in an upright position with the feet touching a level horizontal surface. The walking pattern is very immature and involves only the action of the legs and knees. The stepping reflex normally disappears by the end of the fifth month.

Early Voluntary Movement Patterns

The precise process by which reflex actions are phased out and replaced by voluntary movements is not clearly understood. This is due, in part, to the differences found within individuals as well as to the lack of definitive timeliness indicating when reflexes will normally appear and disappear. Nevertheless, professionals interested in the motor performance of those with disabilities find it helpful to study the relationship between reflex action and voluntary movement. For instance, familiarity with the walking reflex will help movement specialists explain to parents that although it appears their child with developmental disabilities is ready to walk, the necessary voluntary responses may not be present. Also, for those working with children with developmental disabilities, it is useful to understand the relationship between the failure of infant reflexes to disappear in those

who have cerebral palsy and the motor problems these individuals experience. (For further discussion, see chapter 10.)

Within this section, six voluntary movement patterns developing before the age of two will be discussed. As a word of caution it is important to emphasize that although we expect children at twenty-four months to have developed in a similar manner, differences in the rate of change and the quality of movement will be noted.

Postural control and locomotion are two movement problems that the newborn must resolve. Postural control refers to the ability of the infant to develop head control, sit without support, and pull to a standing position. Locomotion includes the prewalking skills of rolling, crawling, and creeping as well as the notable achievement of walking alone.

In figure 2.6, progressions of change in postural control are reported for head control, sitting alone, and standing. The progressions are based on the normative data developed by Bayley (1969) and by Frankenburg and Dodds (1991). As noted in figure 2.6, head control, or the ability to keep the head steady, without support, while being moved is achieved at approximately two months. Improvements in head control may also be noted when the infant's head does not lag while being pulled from a supine position. The movement behavior of sitting without support is generally achieved by five months, which indicates a basic control of head and trunk although only in a stationary position. As infants progress they develop the movement capability of getting to a sitting position from a supine or prone position. This means that by seven months the infant can change body position rather than being limited to the sitting position in which they are placed. As the ability to sit with no support is developed, the infant learns to do other things, including manipulating objects, while seated.

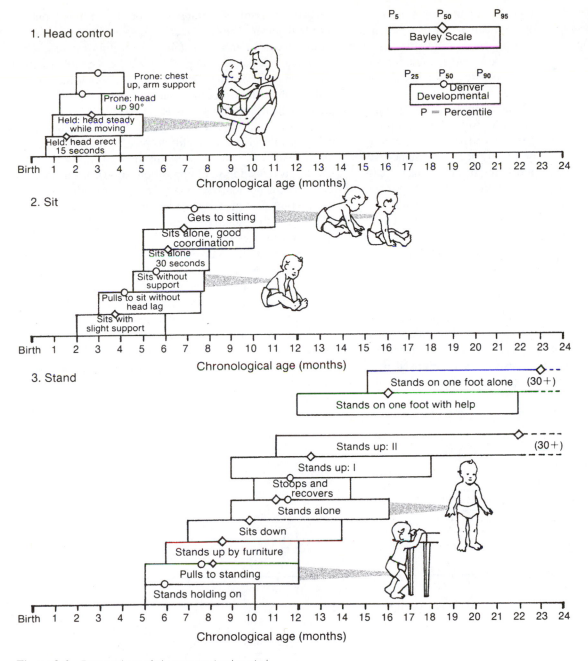

Figure 2.6 Progressions of change: postural control.

(Reprinted with permission of Macmillan Publishing Company from *Movement Skill Development* by Jack Keogh and David Sugden. Copyright © 1985 by Macmillan Publishing Co.)

The third progression in postural control is for the infant to pull to a standing position. As noted in figure 2.6, this is generally achieved by approximately seven to eight months of age. In developing this movement behavior, infants combine the skills of sitting without support, reaching, and pulling. As the infant becomes more and more accustomed to standing with support (by holding onto furniture, etc.) the necessary postural control to stand alone emerges. The ability to stand alone, normally seen at approximately eleven months, prepares the infant for walking.

Locomotion

During the first six months of life, infants experience much development but they are not very mobile. A typical newborn moves arms, legs, and head a great deal but full understanding of all this movement is not known. When placed prone or supine, the infant will remain in that position with little change in direction or location. This begins to change at approximately four months of age when the infant learns to move from the side to the back and back to side. The first progression of change in locomotion, rolling over, is not achieved until six months of age. This voluntary movement is believed to be triggered by a sequence of reflex actions. The infant lying supine in the crib focuses on and follows an object with the eyes. Thus, the head turns, initiating the body righting reflex. The body turns in the same direction as the head, resulting in a roll over.

As indicated in figure 2.7, the infant begins at approximately seven months of age to move forward from a prone position. Crawling is the term used to indicate this early movement response. Crawling usually occurs spontaneously when infants are placed in front-lying positions for increasing periods of time. For some newborns with rigid musculature or who show signs of other medical distress the supine lying position may increase extension. Therefore, health care providers, parents, and others working with the infant, may find the side-lying position more desirable.

Reach and Grasp

The development of hand control is very important in the early months of life. In the first weeks of life infants often hold their fingers together in a fist and, when touched, close the fist tighter, similar to a grasp. This is followed by a period in which the hands are open much of the time. In the second month of life infants develop the ability to put the hands together. The first successful reach and grasp of an object occurs at approximately three to four months, when the infant reaches for and picks up a cube. The first grasp of the cube is normally awkward with the infant holding the cube in the palm using the fingers. It is not until five to six months that the infant progresses to thumb opposition, where the thumb opposes the fingers to pick up an object. As the infant develops, the ability to pick up smaller objects is facilitated by the thumb working in opposition to the fingers. This refined form of opposition, known as the neat pincer grasp, is normally seen at nine to ten months. Development of the neat pincer grasp is important because it allows the fingers and thumb to work together in the manipulation of small and large objects.

The release of an object, normally seen at eight months, is another important landmark in being able to successfully manipulate objects. The initial release is crude in that the hand is opened and the object dropped. From this beginning, however, the important manual dexterity tasks, such as placing items in containers, begin to develop. Infants learn by the second year of life to make horizontal and vertical lines, color on paper, turn the pages of a book and stack six to eight cubes.

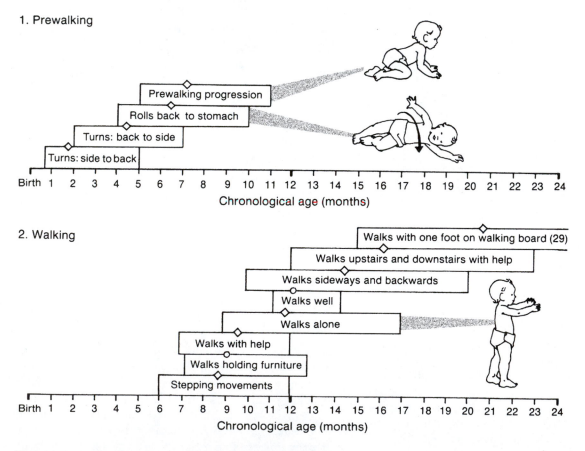

Figure 2.7 Progressions of change: locomotion.

(Reprinted with permission of Macmillan Publishing Co. from *Movement Skill Development* by Jack Keogh and David Sugden. Copyright © 1985 by Macmillan Publishing Co.)

*Crawling** This early movement pattern usually occurs spontaneously when infants are placed in front-lying positions for increasing periods of time. From this position it is natural for the infant to look up and eventually reach for items. Movement occurs when both arms are used to reach for an item. When this happens, the head and chest will fall toward the floor, with the infant sliding forward. From this primitive beginning a more concerted effort is developed to use the arms systematically as an aid in crawling.

The rate at which children learn to crawl is highly dependent on individual development. Most, however, crawl at about the seventh month.

*Creeping** Creeping, a more sophisticated form of locomotion than crawling, requires that the infant use the hands and knees for support. From this position, the mature creeping pattern requires that the infant move the arms and legs in a contralateral pattern. Thus, as the left arm moves forward so does the right leg. Early efforts to creep are not always this efficient. Some infants move only one limb at a time followed by a hesitation before the next limb is moved. Approximately 20 percent of all infants move the same side arm and knee forward when creeping. The infant who creeps using a unilateral rather than a contralateral (opposite leg and arm move in motion) pattern may or may not experience future problems. As the child develops, further observations should be made to determine if other opposition problems exist. Development of creeping skills occurs at ten to eleven months of age.

Figure 2.8 Young children with developmental disabilities require special activities to help them develop basic locomotor patterns.

---

*Creeping and crawling are defined as synonymous terms; however, a distinction is made here for purposes of the discussion.

*Walking** There is a great deal of variation among infants as to the age at which independent walking begins. Some infants walk as early as nine months, whereas others may not walk until eighteen months. Both early and late responses may be normal, depending on the individual's experiences and level of maturation.

The development of the locomotor skill of walking is generally believed to follow from crawling and creeping. As proficiency in these skills increases, efforts to gain an upright posture will become more evident as the infant moves around the environment, using objects such as tables and chairs for aids in standing. The first attempts at walking involve standing and moving from one handhold to another and are referred to as cruising. Many children use a table or chair as their support. Early attempts to step away from the handhold are frequently unsuccessful. This explains why some infants revert to creeping, which seems at the time to be a more efficient form of locomotion. Infants soon discover, however, the numerous advantages of walking.

There are various stages through which individuals progress as they move from an immature pattern to an integrated, efficient walking motion. Initially, the infant walks with a wide base of support in a flat-footed manner with the toes turned out. In addition, the arms tend to be held in an on-guard position. Little evidence of extension in the hip, leg, and ankle of the new walker is noted. A graphic representation of the walking pattern of an infant is presented in figure 2.9.

The walking pattern of young children becomes more refined as they become stronger and gain additional practice. When this occurs, the individual assumes a narrower gait, with the feet placed straight ahead and with a heel-to-toe step. The arms also swing forward and backward in opposition to the legs. The walking gait generally matures in infants between eleven and eighteen months of age.

*Striking** Striking in its earliest form develops from an overarm action that occurs in the anteroposterior (front-to-back) plane. The infant uses a hand as an implement to strike at suspended objects; this strike is usually restricted to a push rather than an actual hit. By twenty-two months, the child may still utilize an overarm striking pattern with an implement such as a small lightweight paddle. The striking action is still confined to extension of the forearm, and the child may exhibit one step forward. Mature striking movements do not occur until after the age of six or seven years.

Social Development

Interaction with the caregiver and the world begins at birth. Each newborn is unique in the need for sleep and alertness as well as the capacity for interaction. Brazelton, a leading pediatrician at Harvard University, developed the Brazelton Neonatal Behavioral Assessment Scale (1979) to rate the state and interaction capacity of the infant. Based on his

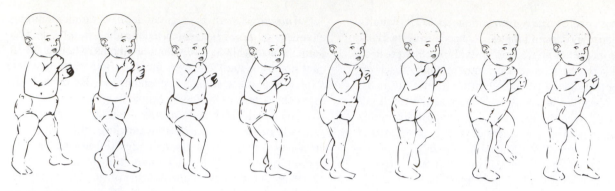

Figure 2.9 Early walking pattern of a 14½-month-old infant. Note the high arm position, flat foot contact, and general tentative nature of the walking pattern.

(Adapted from Wickstrom, Ralph L.: *Fundamental Motor Patterns*, 3d ed., Philadelphia, Lea and Febiger, 1983.)

work, it is clear that some infants initiate chance interactions with their caregiver. For some newborns, the interaction will be more subdued due to a greater need to control environmental stimulation. Caregivers need to be cognizant of the wide range of infant behavior and avoid feelings of rejection if the infant does not respond to adult initiated interaction.

Although the primary development during the infant period is in the motor domain, evidence of social growth and change may also be documented. Some of the earliest forms of social expression are the facial gestures seen in infants. Imitative smiling in response to a familiar face may occur as early as the first month of life.

Early forms of social interaction may also be observed in the play behavior of infants. For instance, most young children have enjoyed the games of pat-a-cake and peek-a-boo by ten months of age. However, parallel play, in which two infants do the same thing at the same time but not in direct contact with one another, is the preferred play pattern of the very young.

Early Childhood (Two to Six Years)

The early childhood period, ages two to six, is another exciting time in the developmental process of the young. During this time frame, children build upon and expand their walking ability into a variety of other locomotor activities. The foundation for the later refinement of manipulative skills, throwing, catching, and striking, is also established in the early childhood years. Social interaction becomes more complex, with the preschool child engaging in a variety of simple games. Within this section, the physical growth, locomotor activity, and social development of the young child will be presented.

Physical Growth

The rapid gains in weight and height associated with the period of infancy taper off and slow down during the period of early childhood. From ages two to six a relatively uniform process of growth is observed, with the rate of gain in height nearly double that in weight. Body proportions also change, with the lower limbs growing rapidly in proportion to the trunk length. Thus, the young child loses the round, stocky body build characteristic of the infant and becomes more rectilinear in appearance. Few differences in growth between the sexes are noted during this time. Boys tend to be somewhat taller and heavier, but the proportional rate of growth remains similar for both sexes during this time.

Brain growth is about 75 percent complete by age three and nearly 90 percent by age six. The increase in myelin, a fatty substance around the neurons, permits the transmission of nerve impulses. It is important to note that with myelination (the development of myelin), children perform at higher levels both motorically and cognitively.

Similar to the brain, the sensory apparatus is still developing during early childhood. The eyeball does not reach its full size until age twelve with the macula being incomplete in its development until age six. This accounts for the hyperopia (farsightedness) generally associated with young children.

Locomotor Activity

As children become more proficient in their walking ability, they will begin to explore other forms of locomotion, such as walking sideways and, eventually, backward. Children will also learn that they can walk quickly and, as they gain additional strength, will initiate other exciting movement patterns, including running, climbing, jumping, hopping, galloping and skipping. These patterns of locomotion are discussed in the following paragraphs.

Running The initial running pattern of young children is characterized by unstable and uncoordinated movements. As the young become more proficient in their walking ability, they tend to walk faster. The increased rate at first creates a problem because of insufficient balance. For this reason, many young children move from a mature walking pattern to a somewhat immature running pattern, in which the feet are turned out and the arms are held away from the body. From ages two to six, however, observable changes take place in the running pattern. Some of the more observable changes, as indicated in figure 2.10, include the following:

1. The stride lengthens as the amount of time in the flight phase increases.
2. The trailing foot is higher in the recovery phase and is swung forward faster and higher.
3. The arms are held higher and used more effectively as they move in opposition to the legs.
4. The amount of forward lean increases (McClenaghan and Gallahue, 1978).

Climbing   Once an independent walking pattern has been established, a young child may attempt to climb stairs in an upright position. Ascending a flight of stairs is negotiated sooner than the upright descent. A child will successfully ascend a flight of stairs, with alternate foot placement, between twenty-nine and forty-one months. Descending stairs proficiently may occur between forty-eight and fifty-five months.

Jumping   A jump is the act of propelling the body off the ground by extending one or both legs followed by a landing on one or both feet. This form of locomotion requires greater strength, coordination, and balance than are needed for running or walking. For this reason, jumping is viewed as a more difficult skill but is a locomotor pattern that most young children can master. Jumping is usually perceived as a very exciting skill by preschool children. The various types of jumps—vertical, horizontal, from objects, to objects, and over objects—all present different challenges to the young.

Although it is beyond the scope of this chapter to analyze the developmental phases of the various jumps, valuable information can be presented concerning the progressive difficulty of different forms of the jump. This information will help teachers of children with disabilities properly sequence instruction for students who have difficulty with jumping. From an analysis of table 2.1, it becomes clear that for many children a jump down from one foot is an easier skill than a jump up. Jumping in the vertical plane is less difficult than horizontal jumping.

Most children will master the sequence in table 2.1 by five years of age. Further improvement in jumping performance will thus be found in the height and distance of the jump.

Hopping   Hopping is a locomotor skill similar to jumping but more difficult in that it requires a one-foot take-off and landing on the same foot. Children do not hop successfully until they have gained sufficient strength and the necessary balance skills. By age four, however, most children can hop from four to six steps on their preferred foot. Rapid gains in the ability to hop greater distances and at faster rates of speed are made between the ages of four and six. Girls generally become more proficient hoppers at an earlier age than boys do, although there is wide variation in the ability to perform this skill within both sexes.

Galloping and Skipping   The skills of galloping and skipping are more advanced movement patterns that usually appear after children have learned to run, jump, and hop. Although galloping and skipping include variations of locomotor skills already learned, they are more difficult because of the balance and the movement sequences that must be learned.

Galloping, which includes the skills of walking and leaping, is a popular skill among children as young as four years. Proficiency in this pattern, however, is usually not observed until children reach the age of six. Skipping, a movement that includes a step and a hop on one foot followed by the same pattern on the opposite side, appears a little later than galloping. It is not until the age of six that children can accomplish this task with some degree of proficiency. Even at this age the variation in performance among children is great.

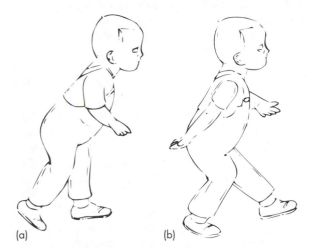

(a)   (b)

Figure 2.10   The running pattern of children varies. The arm and leg action of student (b) is more mature than that of student (a).

Table 2.1   *Jumping*

Types of Jumps Achieved by Children in Terms of Progressive Difficulty

Jump down from one foot to the other foot.
Jump up from two feet to two feet.
Jump down from one foot to two feet.
Jump down from two feet to two feet.
Run and jump forward from one foot to the other.
Jump forward from two feet to two feet.
Run and jump forward from one foot to two feet.
Jump over object from two feet to two feet.
Jump from one foot to same foot rhythmically.

(Wickstrom, 1983)

During infancy and the early childhood years, considerable energy is exerted by the young to explore their environment. At first, these efforts are restricted to simply observing. With increasing age, however, children become more mobile and quickly learn to interact with various objects. As infants develop the ability to reach, grasp, and release, they learn to play with blocks, rattles, and many other toys. Voluntary control of these basic manipulative abilities leads to refined patterns enabling children to throw, catch, kick, and strike.

Throwing   Any activity that requires using one or two arms to thrust an object into space falls into the general category of throwing. Although this definition is very broad and includes all of the major forms of throwing, only the developmental pattern of the overarm motion, the most commonly used motion, will be discussed here.

Sufficient evidence is available to document that children's throwing ability improves from infancy through childhood. Changes have been noted in the accuracy, distance, and form used by children of various ages. As distance and accuracy are dependent on the form used, the pattern of development of the throwing action is of primary importance. In 1938, Monica R. Wild conducted a thorough investigation of the developmental pattern of throwing. Although her work is dated, the developmental stages proposed by Wild are generally accepted today. The four stages she identified are summarized as follows:

Stage I. Children ages two and three years throw primarily with a forearm motion with no rotation of the body. The feet remain stationary throughout the throw but there is a slight forward body sway.

Stage II. As children become older, 3½ to 5 years of age, several important changes occur in their throwing pattern. These changes include rotation of the body first to the right as the ball is brought backward and then to the left as the ball is delivered by the right hand. In preparation for the throw, the ball is brought backward further and held with a cocked wrist. The throwing arm also swings forward in an oblique horizontal plane. Similar to Stage I, the feet remain stationary.

Stage III. This stage, normally observed in children five and six years of age, is marked because of the addition of a forward step with the leg on the same side of the body as the throwing arm. Forward form is added to the throw by the shifting of weight that occurs during the step.

Stage IV. The final stage, the mature throw, is normally achieved by boys 6½ years of age, with girls generally acquiring this pattern slightly later, unless they have had as much opportunity to observe and practice as the boys have, in which case they develop the pattern at the same age. In this stage the arm and trunk rotate backward in preparation for the throw. A contralateral step is then taken moving the body weight forward followed by rotation of the hips, trunk, and shoulder. The addition of opposition, coupled with the wider base of support, permits the throw to be completed with greater force.

Catching   Stopping the momentum of and controlling a thrown object using the arms and hands is referred to as catching. This skill, similar to those previously discussed, follows a developmental trend. As children become older, they become more proficient catchers. McClenaghan and Gallahue (1978) have identified three stages children experience as they learn to catch.

In the initial stage, children less than 3½ years of age frequently avoid the thrown ball by turning the head or holding the arms in extension. Young children also tend to hold the palms up and try to trap the ball against the chest. During the second stage, the elementary level, children of approximately four years of age learn to follow the ball with the eyes. The earlier tendency to avoid the ball also disappears in this stage, although they tend to close the eyes when the ball is about to make contact with the hands. Other changes include the position of the palms, which are held perpendicular rather than up as in the first stage. A mature catching pattern, the third stage, is achieved by many children at approximately six years of age. During this stage children track the ball from the time of release to when it is caught. The arms are held in a ready position, with the elbows flexed and the hands in a cupped position. As the ball is caught the arms give to help absorb the ball's momentum. These stages are presented in figure 2.11.

Kicking   Kicking is a manipulative pattern in which the foot is used to impart force to a ball. Although children as young as twenty-four months can kick, there have been few efforts to analyze the development of the kicking pattern. McClenaghan and Gallahue (1978) have reviewed the available information and identified three progressive stages young children exhibit as they learn to kick.

In stage one, the ball is kicked with a straight leg action with little arm and trunk action. Little force is imparted to the ball because there is no backward movement of the kicking leg prior to the kick and the follow-through is limited. During the elementary stage, the arms are held outward for stability. The straight-leg kicking action observed in the first stage is replaced by a flexed knee position with the leg "uncocking" and extending forward to hit the ball. The beginning of a follow-through is also present during this stage. During the last stage, the mature kicking pattern emerges. In general, more total body action is found in this stage. The arms swing in opposition to each other during the kick. Length of the leg swing increases with a larger backswing and a higher follow-through. During the follow-through, the trunk flexes at the waist with the support foot raising to its toes. These stages are presented in figure 2.12.

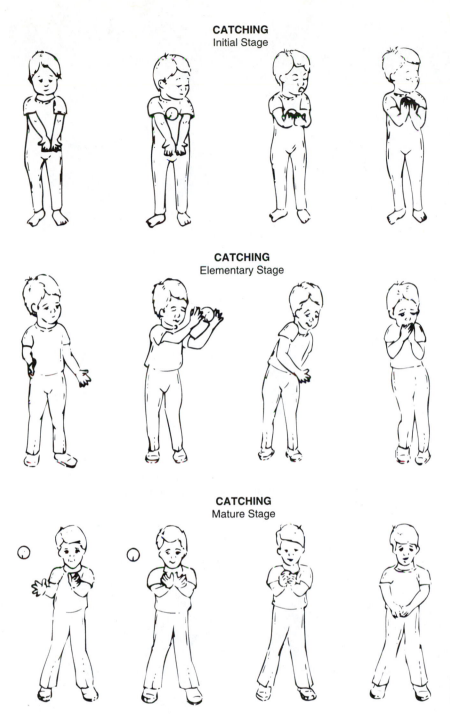

CATCHING
Initial Stage

CATCHING
Elementary Stage

CATCHING
Mature Stage

Figure 2.11 Catching (initial stage, elementary stage, mature stage).

Striking In general, well-defined sidearm striking patterns will be utilized by children beginning at approximately three years of age. Legs and lower body portion are used in a mature striking pattern after the age of six or seven.

Social Development

The early childhood period is a time of rapid change in the social development of the young. From ages three to six, children move from a preference for parallel play to an inter-

est in small group activities and games with simple rules. Changes are also noted in social behavior. Whereas two- and three-year-olds are very possessive of their play items and intolerant of others who intrude into their play space, five- and six-year-olds are more tolerant and show early interest in cooperative activities. Early attempts at leadership may also emerge in four- and five-year-olds.

The relationship between motor performance and social development is very important for the preschool child. Efforts to seek and gain approval occur frequently for the

KICKING
Initial Stage

KICKING
Elementary Stage

KICKING
Mature Stage

Figure 2.12 Kicking (initial stage, elementary stage, mature stage).

young as they utilize various movement patterns. Because motor skills are highly visible, they can easily be reinforced by the observant parent. The relationship of success in motor skills followed by parental praise encourages the child to explore other skills. Of course, the absence of success in play and game skills will lead to avoidance of these activities by young children, underlining the importance of structuring skills to ensure positive experiences.

Later Childhood (Seven to Twelve Years)

Children ages seven to twelve are provided many opportunities to utilize the movement skills that were developed during the early childhood years. As children enter school, their environment expands and the basic movement patterns are used continuously in various interactions with their peers. The combined effects of experience, age, and maturation improve dramatically the elementary-school-age child's motor performance. In this section some of these changes will be discussed.

Physical Growth

Changes in height and weight in the age period from six to twelve are relatively slow and constant in comparison with the early childhood and adolescent periods. During this time, therefore, children are provided an excellent opportunity to refine and expand the basic movement patterns that they have established during the early childhood period.

Differences in the pattern of growth rate for boys and girls may also be detected during the later childhood period. In general, gender differences in height and weight are not significant until after approximately age ten, when girls reach puberty and achieve a size advantage that is apparent until about age fourteen. The hip-shoulder ratio for boys and girls also changes during this time, with the shoulder being wider than the pelvis for boys and the pelvis being wider than the shoulder for girls. The leg length of boys and girls also increases in proportion to the size of the trunk. This is particularly true for boys, so that by late childhood boys generally have legs proportionally longer than those of girls, which was not the case during infancy and early childhood.

Refinement of Movement Patterns

Development of the basic locomotor and manipulative patterns occurs primarily in early childhood. As previously discussed, children learn the process of how to perform essential skills at very early ages. Many changes in skill performance occur during the early years. For example, the process that six-year-old children use to throw a ball is vastly different and more efficient than the process exhibited by a three-year-old. Continued refinement of the skills learned in early childhood occurs between the ages of six and twelve years, the later childhood period. Improved performance is noted in this age group because of several factors, including maturity, practice, and changes in size. This last factor, size, is particularly important. Bigger and stronger children are capable of performing many movement patterns more efficiently and effectively than can younger children.

The increase in functional complexity, noted in seven- to twelve-year olds, is attributed primarily to two different, but related processes—differentiation and integration (Gallahue and Ozmun, 1995). Differentiation is the gradual progression of movement patterns demonstrated by infants to the more refined movement patterns of children. Integration refers to the coordinated interaction of muscle and sensory systems. The relationship of the two processes is illustrated by the efforts of a young child to catch a ball. Early efforts rely primarily on corralling the ball and progresses only when the more mature visually guided reaching and grasping behavior is evident. This differentiation in the use of the arms, hands, and fingers followed by integration of the eyes and hands is crucial to success with hand-eye coordination tasks and to normal development. The intent of this section is to discuss how the skills learned in early childhood are further developed and refined in later childhood.

Figure 2.13 The initial stages of catching a ball are exhibited by this youngster.

Jumping The improvement children ages seven to twelve make in both a vertical jump and a jump for distance is illustrated in figures 2.14 and 2.15. With respect to the vertical jump, boys and girls compare favorably until age seven, after which boys tend to excel. Both sexes, however, improve dramatically in their vertical jump ability. A similar pattern is observed when analyzing boys' and girls' ability to perform a standing long jump. Until the age of seven both sexes perform equally. After this time both groups improve dramatically, with the boys achieving at a higher level.

Running The speed at which young children can run a short distance has frequently been used as an indication of running efficiency. As indicated in figure 2.16, improvements in running speed occur as children grow older. For boys this trend continues into adolescence. The rate at which girls can run short distances peaks at approximately twelve years of age, unless the girls are unusually active or involved in running programs.

Throwing As children emerge from the early childhood period, most can throw using a reasonably mature movement pattern. During the next few years, significant gains are made in the distance and accuracy with which children seven to twelve years of age can throw a ball. Figure 2.17 illustrates that improvements in throwing distance occur in a linear fashion for both boys and girls, with boys achieving at a higher performance level than girls at each age. This gender difference may be attributed to the superior arm-shoulder strength of boys and the more frequent exposure of boys to throwing tasks. Data obtained in the future, after girls have participated more widely in throwing experiences similar to those of boys, may indicate that the differences shown in data collected before 1980 are due more to experience than innate differences between the sexes.

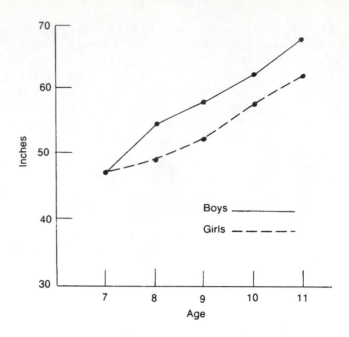

Figure 2.15 Standing long jump performance by age and sex.

(Adapted from Cratty, Bryant J.: *Perceptual and Motor Development in Infants and Children,* 2d ed. Englewood Cliffs, NJ, Prentice-Hall, Inc., 1979, p. 207; and Keogh, J. F.: *Motor Performance of Elementary School Children,* Monograph, University of California, Los Angeles, Physical Education Department, 1965.)

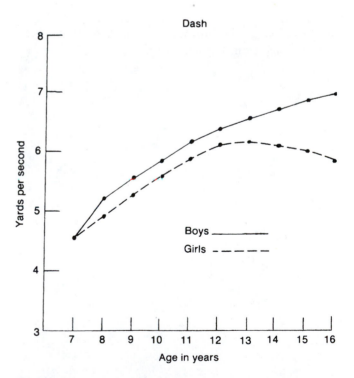

Figure 2.16 Running speed by age and sex.

(Adapted from Espenchade, Anna S., and Eckert, Helen M.: *Motor Development,* 2d ed. Columbus, OH, Charles E. Merrill Publishing Co., 1980; and Johnson, Warren R. (Ed.): *Science and Medicine of Exercise and Sports,* 1960.)

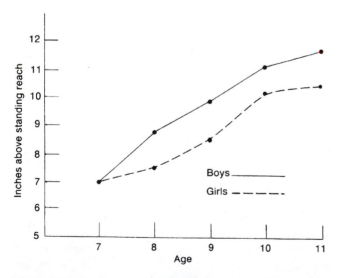

Figure 2.14 Vertical jump performance by age and sex.

(Adapted from Cratty, Bryant J.: *Perceptual and Motor Development in Infants and Children,* 2d ed. Englewood Cliffs, NJ, Prentice-Hall, Inc., 1979, p. 206; and Johnson, R. D.: "Measurements of Achievement in Fundamental Skills of Elementary School Children." *Research Quarterly,* 33:94–103, 1962.)

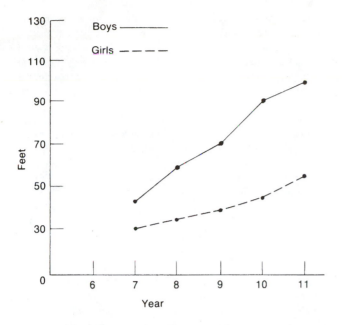

Figure 2.17 Throwing distance by age and sex.

(Adapted from Cratty, Bryant J.: *Perceptual and Motor Development in Infants and Children,* 2d ed., Englewood Cliffs, NJ, Prentice-Hall, Inc., 1979, p. 216; and Keogh, J. F.: *Motor Performance of Elementary School Children.* Monograph, University of California, Los Angeles, Physical Education Department, 1965.)

The accuracy with which older children can throw also improves in a linear fashion. Improvement in performance for girls tends to level off after age nine. Boys, however, plateau at approximately age eleven.

Catching Although few intensive studies have been conducted to analyze the developmental catching patterns of children ages six to twelve, most recognize that with increasing age, children become more proficient in this skill. Catching is more difficult for children to master than throwing. Six-year-olds find catching a ball from a bounce easier than receiving a ball in flight. Similarly, larger balls are easier for the young to catch than are smaller balls. By age twelve, however, most children can catch "on the fly" balls as small as a tennis ball with little difficulty.

Striking Progress in the development of an effective striking pattern is indicated by the changes observed in patterns used at successive ages. These changes involve greater freedom or more definite use of body parts in the swing, the forward step, the hip and trunk rotation preceding the action of the arms in the swing, and the uncocking of the wrists during the swing. These changes begin to occur after 6½ years, and it may be as long as two years before the child is capable of making mature striking movements.

Dribbling Dribbling an object is a movement pattern that most children are exposed to and practice, yet it has not been studied extensively. Deach (1950), after studying children ages two to six, identified four stages of development.

Stage 1 was a two-handed downward or diagonally forward overhand throw with no attempt to follow the ball. Stage 2 was an attempt to catch the ball after a single bounce. Stage 3 was an attempt to catch the ball after a single bounce, using one or more overhand swings with an outstretched arm. Stage 4 was a series of successive hits using a bent arm and palm/finger contact. In the final stage, the mature form is a rhythmic and a well coordinated series of pushes. Gallahue has identified the following elements as constituting the mature stage of dribbling:

Feet placed in narrow stride position, with foot opposite dribbling hand forward
Slight forward trunk lean
Ball held waist high
Ball pushed toward ground, with follow-through of arm, wrist, and fingers
Controlled force of downward thrust
Repeated contact and pushing action initiated from the fingertips
Visual monitoring not necessary
Controlled directional dribbling

The difficulty of the task of dribbling is compounded when the child moves while dribbling as contrasted to a stationary dribble. Dribbling while moving is a refined skill that should be introduced only after the child has successfully demonstrated the ability to perform a stationary dribble. This level of performance is normally not achieved prior to seven years of age.

Interest and Motor Activity

Children's interest in motor activities expands dramatically during the ages of six to twelve. This is the period in which children move from participation in simple games and relays to lead-up activities for various sport experiences to membership in organized teams. Participation in school physical education classes as well as involvement in community-sponsored programs helps to nurture this interest in motor activity.

The primary educational emphasis during this critical time should be to expose children to a wide variety of activities and to create successful learning experiences. Curricular experiences that are limited to the popular fall, winter, and spring sports repeated year after year contribute little to the educational growth of young children. Likewise, educational programs directed toward "playing the game" without first attempting to improve and refine the basic skills creates an environment loaded with failure. A concerted effort, therefore, must be made to expose children to developmentally sequenced motor activities so that all children, including those with disabilities, can grow and benefit. Without such a system, children's interest in motor activity will decline, and withdrawal will be likely, particularly for those who feel they are not proficient.

Social relationships and skills are widely extended during the six-to-twelve age period. Educators recognize that social growth, like physical growth, must be fostered through a developmental framework. At various stages the social needs of children change. Six-year-old children, for instance, prefer small group activities, whereas twelve-year-olds seek identification with a group or club. Educational experiences should build upon these needs and be structured to foster social growth.

Individual differences in behavior patterns are observed during the ages of seven to twelve. It is difficult, therefore, to predict how the social behavior of a nine-year-old differs from that of an eleven-year-old. For instance, although it is generally recognized that eleven-year-olds enjoy team games, not all children of this age are socially mature enough to engage in team play. To force such children to participate in group games would be wrong and a violation of the principle of readiness. It should be noted that differences in behavior patterns are varied regardless of ability or disability. The development of social skills by children with disabilities may lag behind that of their nondisabled peers. However, this need not be the case if adequate and appropriate opportunities are provided for the social development of the students with disabilities.

One area of certainty is that children need and seek approval. The basic desire to feel important, wanted, and accepted is a primary need of children ages six to twelve. Teachers must strive to ensure that each child is systematically recognized and valued as a unique individual.

Summary

An understanding of the patterns of development common to infants and children provides the physical educator with a means of assessing progress toward achieving the degree of development that is common for a given age period. This information can be very helpful as criteria to evaluate the degree to which a disabling condition is affecting normal growth and development. Development follows certain motor development and physical growth principles. There is an important distinction between voluntary and involuntary movement. The earliest movements that can be observed in the infant are reflexes. These actions are involuntary behaviors elicited by various types of external stimuli. An absent reflex or one that persists for too long may be an indication of neurological impairment. The precise process by which reflex actions are phased out and replaced by voluntary movements is not clearly understood. This is due, in part, to the differences found among individuals as well as to the lack of definitive timeliness dictating when reflexes will normally appear and disappear.

Postural control and locomotion are two movement problems that the infant must master. The ability to develop head control, sit without support, pull to a standing position, and perform selected locomotor acts such as rolling, crawling, and creeping is essential for later success in more refined movement patterns. Some of our limitations in determining with precision the initiation or absence of voluntary motor control may be attributed to an incomplete understanding of child development. Some have suggested that the reliance on a strict neuromaturational model with its motor control center approach to development may be too limiting in its view and appreciation for the environment and other factors important in the process of acquiring information. Much of the new view of development is being proposed by proponents of the dynamic systems theory.

In early childhood, ages two to six, children build and expand upon earlier development and establish the foundation for later refinement of locomotor and manipulative skills. This period, with its relatively uniform process of growth, allows for a great deal of movement exploration.

During later childhood, ages seven to twelve, the child is provided many opportunities to utilize the movement skills that were developed during the early childhood years. The combined effects of experience, age, and maturation dramatically improve the elementary-school-age child's performance. During this time frame children become more proficient in their locomotor and manipulative patterns, shifting to more refined movement patterns. Differences in the pattern of growth rate for boys and girls may also be detected during the later childhood period.

Paralleling the motor and physical development of infants and children is their emotional, social, and intellectual development. Change in the rate of development in these areas must be considered when evaluating the effects of a handicapping condition upon development.

Selected Readings

Allen, M.C., & Capute, A.J. (1990). Tone and reflex development before term. *Journal of Pediatrics,* supplement, 393–398.

Bayley, N. (1969). *Bayley scales of infant development.* The Pyschological Corporation. New York: Harcourt, Brace, Jovanovich, Inc.

Berman, B.D. (1993). Difficult and challenging behaviors in young children: A neurodevelopmental perspective for assessment and intervention. *Infants & Young Children: An Interdisciplinary Journal of Special Care Practices, 6*(1), 26–34.

Brazelton, T.B., Als, A., Tronick, E., & Lester, B.M. (1979). Specific neonatal measures: The Brazelton Neonatal Behavior Assessment Scale. In J. Osofsky (Ed.), *The Handbook of Infant Development.* New York: John Wiley and Sons, Inc.

Corbin, C.B. (Ed.). (1980). *A textbook of motor development* (2d ed.). Dubuque, IA: William C. Brown Publishers.

Cowden, J.E., & Eason, B.L. (1991). Pediatric adapted physical education for infants, toddlers, and preschoolers: Meeting IDEA-H and IDEA-B challenges. *Adapted Physical Activity Quarterly, 8,* 263–279.

Cratty, B.J. (1979). *Perceptual and motor development in infants and children* (2d ed.). Englewood Cliffs, NJ: Prentice-Hall, Inc.

Cratty, B.J. (1990). Motor development of infants subject to maternal drug use: Current evidence and future research strategies. *Adapted Physical Activity Quarterly, 8,* 263–279.

Damiano, D. (1993). Challenging current concepts in motor development. Unpublished paper, University of Virginia, 1–23.

Deach, D. (1950). *Genetic development of motor skills in children two through six years of age.* Unpublished doctoral dissertation. Ann Arbor, University of Michigan.

Dunn, J.M. (Ed.) (1991, August). PL 99–457, Challenges and opportunities for physical education. *Journal of Physical Education, Recreation, and Dance,* 33–48.

Espenchade, A.S., & Eckert, H.M. (1980). *Motor development* (2d ed.). Columbus, OH: Charles E. Merrill Publishing Co.

Eveleth, P.B., & Tanner, J.M. (1976). *Worldwide variation in human growth.* London: Cambridge University Press.

Frankenburg, W.K., & Dodds, J.B. (1991). *The Denver II developmental screening test.* Denver, CO: University of Colorado Medical Center.

Gallagher, J.J., Trohanis, P.L., & Clifford, R.M. (1989). *Policy implementations and PL 99–457.* Baltimore, MD: Paul H. Brookes Publishing Co.

Gallahue, D.L. (1982). *Understanding motor development in children.* New York: John Wiley and Sons, Inc.

Gallahue, D.L., & Ozmun, J.C. (1995). *Understanding motor development* (3d ed.). Madison, WI: Brown and Benchmark.

Garwood, S.G. (1979). *Educating young handicapped children: A developmental approach.* Germantown, MD: Aspen Systems Corporation.

Haley, S.M., & Baryza, M.J. (1990). A hierarchy of motor outcome assessment: Self-initiated movements through adaptive motor function. *Infants and Young Children, 3*(2),1–14.

Haskell, S.H. (1977). *The education of motor and neurologically handicapped children.* New York: John Wiley and Sons, Inc.

Holle, B. (1976). *Motor development in children normal and retarded.* Boston: Blackwell Scientific Publications.

Keogh, J., & Sugden, D. (1985). *Movement skill development.* New York: MacMillan Publishing Co.

King, C.M., & Dunn, J.M. (1989). Classroom teachers' accuracy in observing students' motor performance. *Adapted Physical Activity Quarterly, 6*(1), 52–57.

Malina, R.M., Mueller, W.H., & Holman, J.D. (1976). Parent-child correlations and heritability of stature in Philadelphia black and white children 6 to 12 years of age. *Human Biology, 48,* 475–496.

McClenaghan, B.A., & Gallahue, D.L. (1978). *Fundamental movement: A developmental and remedial approach.* Philadelphia: W. B. Saunders Co.

Pangrazi, R.P., & Dauer, V.P. (1981). *Movement in early childhood and primary education.* Minneapolis, MN: Burgess Publishing Co.

Rarick, G.L., et al. (1976). *The motor domain and its correlates in educationally handicapped children.* Englewood Cliffs, NJ: Prentice-Hall, Inc.

Ridenour, M.V. (Ed.). (1978). *Motor development: Issues and application.* Princeton, NJ: Princeton Book Company.

Tanner, J.M. (1978). *Foetus into man.* Cambridge, MA: Harvard University Press.

Thelen, E., Kelso, J.A.S., & Fogel, A. (1987). Self-organizing systems and infant motor development. *Developmental Review, 7,* 39–65.

Van Dyke, D.C., & Lin-Dyken, D.C. (1993). The new genetics, developmental disabilities, and early intervention. *Infants and Young Children, 5*(4), 8–19.

Whitehall, J. (1988). *A dynamical systems approach to motor development: Applying new theory to practice.* Paper presented at the International Early Childhood Physical Education Conference, Washington, DC.

Wickstrom, R.L. (1983). *Fundamental motor patterns* (3d ed.). Philadelphia: Lea and Febiger.

Wild, M.R. (1938). The behavior pattern of throwing and some observations concerning its course of development in children. *Research Quarterly, 9,* 20–24.

Winnick, J.P. (1979). *Early movement experiences and development: Habilitation and remediation.* Philadelphia: W. B. Saunders Co.

Enhancing Activities

1. Observe a therapist or physician evaluate an infant for the presence or absence of selected reflexes.

2. Review a motor development test, such as The Milani Comparetti Motor Development Screening Test or the Denver II, to enhance one's understanding of the nature of the test and the type of test items used to evaluate motor development.

3. Videotape children of different ages and analyze the tapes for purposes of comparing the developmental patterns of children of various ages.

4. Select a specific manipulative pattern (e.g., catching) and test a child to assess the individual's performance level—initial, elementary, or mature.

5. Compare and contrast the movement patterns of a young child with a neurological impairment to that of a nondisabled child of the same age. Develop a list of the similarities as well as the differences.

6. Describe differences in age-related performance of the following locomotor and manipulative patterns: running, climbing, jumping, skipping, throwing, catching, kicking, and striking.

CHAPTER

3

Motor Learning and Perception

◆ —— **CHAPTER OBJECTIVES** —— ◆

After studying this chapter, the reader should be able to:

1 Identify and describe the theories of learning.

2 Discuss the theories of learning and their application to motor learning.

3 Describe and discuss Thorndike's laws of effect, readiness, and exercise.

4 Explain the impact of Thorndike, Skinner, Tolman and Weiner.

5 Explain the laws of proximity, similarity, and closure and their relevance to the process of learning.

6 Identify and explain the various systems used to classify motor skills.

7 Recognize the commonly accepted motor skill tenets and their application to the teaching of students with disabilities.

8 Appreciate the value of recently developed motor learning theories and their potential application to individuals with disabilities.

9 Compare and contrast the views of the following perceptual-motor theorists: Kephart, Getman, Doman and Delacato, Barsch, Frostig, and Ayres.

10 Identify and describe the components of perception and their importance in the learning of various motor skills.

11 Explain how perception is developed.

12 Define the following terms and expressions: directionality, laterality, servomechanism, shaping, closed-loop, open-loop, figure-ground, body awareness, visual acuity.

Motor learning refers to the acquisition of skills involving muscular movement. The skills of movement with which physical educators have been traditionally concerned are gross motor in nature, *gross motor movements* being defined as those requiring vigorous action and big muscle-group contraction, for which a fairly large amount of space is needed. This definition is not meant to imply that fine motor skills are not utilized in physical education activities; fine motor skills are nearly always involved, but usually as part of a larger body movement that is predominately gross motor. In the gross motor skill of throwing, this is illustrated by the involvement of the fine motor movement of the fingers to grasp the ball as part of the total movement.

Motor Learning Theories

Much of our understanding of how movement skills are learned is based on various theories of learning. While much useful information can be obtained by understanding the theories of learning, it must be emphasized that learning theories are based on verbal learning, and therefore these principles cannot always be directly applied to motor learning. Within this section, the theoretical approaches that seem to have had the most influence on our understanding of behavior in general and motor skills in particular will be discussed. The learning theories to be reviewed will be grouped under the heading of Behavior theories, Cognitive theories, and Man/Machine theories. Those who wish to study these theories in depth should refer to a psychology text on learning.

Behavior Theories

The earliest theory of learning, introduced around the turn of the century, was *behaviorism*. This approach, which was based on the work of Edward Thorndike and J.B. Watson, is associated with the names of several well-known psychologists including Pavlov, Hull, and Skinner. The behaviorists are generally concerned with how two events that an individual perceives as occurring close together in time become associated. This approach is concerned with the individual's behavior (or response) and the events (or stimuli) that produced the behavior. For this reason, behaviorism is frequently referred to as the stimulus-response approach.

One of the earliest behaviorists, Pavlov, suggested that learning is the process of building conditioned reflexes through the substitution of one stimulus for another. His famous experiment in which a dog was conditioned to salivate at the sound of a bell provided early evidence of the ability to pair a conditioned stimulus, the bell, with an unconditioned stimulus, the food, to produce a particular response, salivation.

An early behaviorist who had a profound influence on education was Thorndike. He emphasized learning as a strengthening of the bond, or association, between a particular

stimulus and response. Thorndike's research led to the development of several "laws" that are still recognized today. These include:

> the *Law of Readiness,* which emphasizes the idea
> of being prepared to learn (in the mood) and the
> importance of developmental readiness in children;
> the *Law of Effect,* which stresses that students
> will repeat responses that are satisfying, thus
> strengthening the relationship between the
> stimulus and the response;
> the *Law of Exercise,* which is divided into the *Law of
> Use* and the *Law of Disuse.* The effect of these laws
> stated in very straightforward terms is that skills
> will only be retained if they are used.

Perhaps the best known of all the behaviorists is B.F. Skinner, whose work led to the formulation of many principles related to the use of rewards and reinforcement in the shaping of behavior. Unlike Thorndike, who focused on the S-R bond, Skinner stressed the importance of reinforcing the response itself and its probability of occurrence. A central component of Skinner's theory is *shaping,* which involves the gradual molding of the desired behavior. The application of shaping to instructional settings is commonly referred to as behavior modification. This approach has been successfully employed in physical education programs for students with disabilities. The use of this approach requires the teacher to (1) set goals to be achieved; (2) pretest to establish the current ability level; (3) set up the environment so as to remove irrelevant stimuli and center the learner's attention on the task; (4) shape a slow, step-like progression of intermediate goals leading toward the final goal; and (5) reinforce correct responses with appropriate rewards at all stages.

The influence of the behaviorists and their theories has had a profound impact on education, including the teaching of motor skills. As will be emphasized in other chapters within this text, an understanding of behaviorism and its correct application is important in developing positive learning environments for students with disabilities.

Cognitive Theories

The cognitive theorists developed primarily as an alternative to the behaviorists. Whereas behaviorists were primarily concerned with the environment and its influence on behaviors, the cognitive theorists stressed the importance of an individual's interpretation of the environment. The supporters of the cognitive approach argued that learning is not a trained or paired response to a stimulus but involves cognition—the process of knowing—which involves both awareness and judgment. Both theories emphasize, however, that reinforcement, repetition, and perception are relevant to learning. As will be explained later, the difference between the behaviorists and the cognitive theorists is mainly one of emphasis.

Gestalt theory was one of the earliest and best known of the cognitive theories. The supporters of this approach, known as *Gestaltists,* were interested in problem-solving, perception, and other processes that individuals use in order to develop appropriate behaviors in response to situations. They were concerned about how individuals abstract meaningful relationships from the environment and use this information to solve problems.

The Gestaltists, with their interest in perception and the organization of sensory data, developed several laws to explain the cognitive process. Three of the laws, proximity, similarity, and closure, are particularly relevant to the process of learning.

The *law of proximity* refers to the grouping of stimuli that are close together in time or space. From a learning standpoint this suggests that instructional material should be organized into modules or groups.

The *law of similarity* suggests that students find homogenous groups easier to identify than heterogenous groups. The implication of this law is that teachers must organize materials so that they are logical and related.

The *law of closure* emphasizes that some learners, if given part of the information, may be able to provide the rest of the response. The value of this law is very apparent when working with students who have sensory or cognitive impairments. Emphasis must be placed on providing verbal and sensory cues that are appropriate and challenging to the individual.

The relationship between the behaviorists and cognitive theorists was emphasized in the work of E.C. Tolman, published in 1934. Although a proponent of the cognitive approach, Tolman emphasized that initial learning is based on a mental trial-and-error process and therefore involves stimulus-response associations. He believed that beyond initial learning, the learner organizes the stimuli to form a cognitive map that provides cues for future repetitions. Tolman's views provide a valuable link between the theories of behaviorism and cognition. The implications of this for teaching motor skills to those with disabilities suggests that for initial learning, particularly with low-functioning individuals, the use of a behavioral approach is appropriate, but when possible students should be challenged to recognize and understand the principles employed in performing a motor skill.

Man/Machine Theories

The technological advances made during and following World War II led to a wealth of new ideas and approaches for studying human behavior. The development of the computer, a primary example of the "machine age," helped to make this possible. Using the computer as a mode for simulating how individuals receive and process information, the man/machine theorists combined elements of both the behaviorists and the cognitive theorists. Similar to the behaviorists,

they were interested in observable behavior and like the cognitive theorists, they were interested in understanding how information was processed in the brain.

One of the first of the man/machine theories, *cybernetics,* was developed by N. Weiner in 1961. Cybernetics means self-guidance and control of one's own behavior. Proponents of this approach believe that learning is determined by the sensory effects of the movement that accompanies a response. Similar to a computer, an individual accepts stimuli (input) and responds to stimuli (output) and has an internal mechanism (brain) to control and store information. While the cybernetics approach accepts the computer model, emphasis is placed on the role of feedback in which some output is stored and some is fed back into the system. The cybernetics model may be described as a *servomechanism,* or closed-loop system. As illustrated in figure 3.1, in a servomechanism or closed-loop system, there is a direct link between output and input based on continual feedback.

Information theory, another example of a man/machine theory, is concerned with the amount of information an individual can process. The early work in information theory was based primarily on probability theory. Using this approach, analyses were undertaken to assess how much information was needed to solve selected problems. Simulations were developed using the computer as a model with its ability to be programmed to make yes–no responses.

The work in information theory has been expanded today to focus on how people receive information, attend to it, organize, process, and store information, and ultimately develop a plan of action. As suggested earlier, there is a great deal of interest in how much information can be handled; or stated in computer language, what is the channel capacity. Information theory, therefore is concerned with very pertinent questions related to the teaching of motor skills: When is the system overloaded or underloaded? And what is the optimum amount and type of information for efficient and effective learning? These are obviously questions of fundamental importance when teaching students with disabilities.

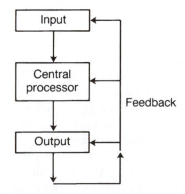

Figure 3.1 The servomechanistic model approach emphasizes the role of feedback for controlling ongoing activity. If the activity is terminated, feedback information can be stored in memory for future usages.

An information theory model is presented in figure 3.2. Similar to the cybernetics model, the information theory model stresses the importance of input, central processor (central nervous system), and output. The information theory model focuses on the capacity of the individual to process information, whereas the cybernetics model emphasizes the importance of feedback.

The last man/machine theory, *hierarchical control,* builds on the cybernetic and information theories by stressing the role of the central processes in controlling and directing movement. Humans, similar to computers, use programs (plans of action) to execute basic or routine patterns. These basic programs are deemed to be lower order and can be combined with other basic programs to produce more complex or higher-order programs. For the beginner, it will be necessary to become proficient with lower-order programs before combining lower-order programs into more complex or higher-order programs. As skill increases, the process of selecting routines will improve. The relationship between lower-order and higher-order programs serves to explain the seemingly automatic responses observed in highly skilled performers. A model of hierarchical control is presented in figure 3.3. The process of distinguishing lower-order from higher-order programs can be facilitated by the use of task analysis, which will be described later in this chapter.

The theories of motor learning described in this section are all evident to a certain degree in physical education programs for students with disabilities. For some individuals with severe and profound disabilities, particularly those with mental retardation, the use of a behavioral approach is appropriate. Problem-solving methods and efforts to encourage creativity (cognitive approach) are frequently observed in physical education programs for individuals with various disabilities including the sensory and orthopedically impaired. Recent efforts to explain human behavior through the use of computers have helped to explain and support

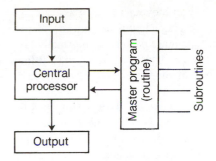

Figure 3.3 The hierarchical control model approach describes central control properties with master, or executor, routines and subroutines. Behavioral control is expressed in a hierarchical fashion: as skill increases, the type and level of control changes.

some of the instructional approaches used with students with disabilities. For example, channel capacity discussed in relation to information theory provides helpful information when deciding how best to present information to a student with mental retardation. Likewise, the distinction between lower-order and higher-order programs stressed in the concept of hierarchial control emphasizes the need to master appropriate developmental activities before undertaking complex skills. Other examples of the relationship between the motor learning theories and teaching students with disabilities will be covered in the section Motor Skill Tenets, as well as included, where appropriate, throughout the text.

Classification of Motor Skills

In an effort to impose some order on the many different types of motor skills, several classification systems have emerged. Familiarity with the classification systems, or taxonomies, as they are sometimes called, is important for several reasons. First, they provide a means of bringing some order to the very diverse field of motor skills. Second, knowledge of the classification systems helps teachers to recognize the similarities as well as the differences in respective skills. This information is very important in developing appropriate motor learning experiences for students with disabilities. Using the following classification systems will allow the teacher to make informed decisions about the level of difficulty and complexity of various skills.

Gross and Fine Motor Skills As stated in the introduction to this chapter, physical educators have frequently referred to motor skills as either gross or fine. Unfortunately, there is no standard criterion by which to identify a skill using these terms. Cratty (1979) suggests that motor skills might be placed on a continuum, from the fine to the gross, with a classification made with reference to the size of the muscle involved, the amount of force applied, or to the magnitude of space in which the movement is carried out.

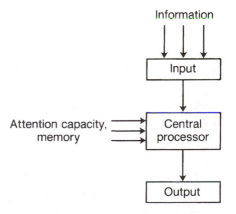

Figure 3.2 The information processing model approach calls to our attention the kinds of processes that are internally activated to organize information, leading to appropriate decisions and effective movements.

Total-body and multilimb movements such as walking, swimming, jumping, and serving a tennis ball are considered gross motor skills. Actions that are performed by small muscles, especially of the fingers and hand, are referred to as fine motor skills and frequently involve eye-hand coordination.

Discrete, Serial, and Continuous Skills This classification describes a continuum on which some skills have a distinct beginning and end and some skills involve a continuous or repetitive series of movements. Discrete skills involve only a single exertion, such as shooting an arrow or throwing a baseball. A skill is serial in nature when the beginning and ending components can be identified, but events follow each other in sequence, such as a gymnastics routine on the parallel bars. Continuous skills refer to those tasks that are repetitive in nature, such as running, walking, and swimming.

Open and Closed Skills In 1957, the British psychologist E.C. Poulton suggested that skills might be classified as either open or closed, depending upon the extent to which the performer must conform to a standard sequence of movement and the extent to which effective performance depends on environmental events. For example, diving is a closed skill because the required movement is consistent and the environment is fixed. However, tennis is an open skill. The game situation is constantly changing, and thus the individual playing tennis must respond within an unpredictable environment.

Variations on the open and closed classification system have been proposed by various individuals. B.N. Knapp in 1963 suggested the idea of a continuum from motor skills that are predominantly habitual to those that are predominantly perceptual. A.M. Gentile and her colleagues in 1975 believed that the type of movement should also be considered. In their model, type of movement was subdivided into (a) total body stability or total body movement and (b) movement of the limbs for changing or maintaining the position of objects in space (table 3.1).

The work of Gentile and her associates has been clarified and expanded by others. In table 3.2, Magill (1993) provides an excellent example of the four way classification system (response variability by environmental conditions) proposed by Gentile et al. Figure 3.4 extends the example in relationship to open and closed skills.

Theories of Movement Control The nature of open and closed skills has generated a great deal of attention in helping to explain how individuals control movement. Adams (1971) proposed the first model which addressed this critical question. His approach, which today is perceived as somewhat incomplete, focused on closed-loop skills. Adams, while recognizing that his theory was limited, believed it was important to establish a framework useful for understanding movement control by focusing on simple skills.

Adams reasoned that every closed-loop system must have a reference mechanism that can be used to assess the status of a movement being made. In Adams' theory this is known as the perceptual trace. Essentially, the perceptual trace is responsible for comparing feedback about what the movement is currently like with what it should be like. If error is detected, a command is sent to stop the movement. The goal of practice is to make sure that the perceptual trace gets stronger, thus allowing the individual to advance to the motor stage of learning where the movement can be made automatically.

Although Adams' theory focused on a closed-loop approach to control, it is clear that imbedded within the theory is information related to an open-loop process. The Adams theory suggests that it is the open-loop, specifically the memory trace, that is responsible for initiating the movement in contrast to terminating the movement which is left to the closed-loop.

In 1975, Schmidt identified limitations in the Adams theory and proposed an alternative theory of motor control and learning which today is known as Schmidt's schema theory (1982). According to this theory, the performer

Table 3.1   *Taxonomy based upon environmental and movement requirements*

| | Nature of Movement Required by Task | | | |
| | Total Body Stability | | Total Body Transport | |
Nature of Environmental Control	No LT/M	LT/M	No LT/M	LT/M*
Closed (spatial control: stationary environment)	Sitting Standing	Typing Writing	Walking Running	Carrying or handling objects during locomotion Javelin throw
Open (temporal/spatial control: moving environment)	Standing on a moving train Log rolling Riding an escalator	Reading a newspaper on a moving train	Walking in a moving train Dancing with a partner	Running and catching a moving object Throwing on the run Dribbling in basketball

*LT/M = Independent limb transport and manipulation, usually involving maintaining or changing the position of objects in space.

Table 3.2   *A 2 × 2 diagram representing the four-category classification system.*

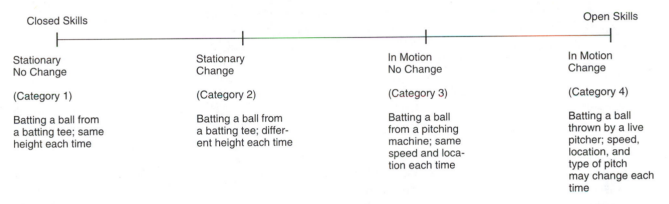

	Response-to-Response Variability	
	No Change	**Change**
Stationary	**Category 1** The object of the response remains stationary, and there is no change in response requirements from one response to the next.	**Category 3** The object of the response remains stationary, and the response requirements change from one response to the next.
In Motion	**Category 2** The object of the response is in motion, and there is no change in the response requirements from one response to the next.	**Category 4** The object of the response is in motion, and the response requirements change from one response to the next.

(Environmental Conditions)

Closed Skills   Open Skills

Stationary No Change	Stationary Change	In Motion No Change	In Motion Change
(Category 1)	(Category 2)	(Category 3)	(Category 4)
Batting a ball from a batting tee; same height each time	Batting a ball from a batting tee; different height each time	Batting a ball from a pitching machine; same speed and location each time	Batting a ball thrown by a live pitcher; speed, location, and type of pitch may change each time

Figure 3.4   The four categories from the Gentile et al., system placed on a continuum having closed- and open-skill categories as its extremes. Four different types of ball-batting tasks are presented to show how the categories are different.

solves motor problems by responding to a motor schema, which is an abstraction of four sources of information: (1) the desired outcome of the movement; (2) the initial conditions, or physiological and postural readiness for the movement; (3) knowledge of past actual outcomes of similar movements; and (4) knowledge of past actual sensory consequences of similar movements. Schmidt theorizes that the motor schema is developed as the student discovers the relationship among these sources of information. The motor schema can be characterized as a set of rules that generate instructions for producing movement.

Schmidt proposed two motor control components. The first is the generalized motor program that is the general memory representation of the action to be controlled. Stated simply, this program is responsible for controlling general actions, such as throwing, kicking, walking, and running.

The second component is the motor response schema that is responsible for the specific rules governing an action in a given situation. In practical terms, this suggests that with practice the learner abstracts different pieces of information from every action related to a motor skill. For example, with experience and practice, the learner acquires sufficient information to use the skill of kicking successfully in a variety of situations and conditions.

While the applied aspects of Schmidt's theory appear very promising, the research carried out with special populations has been limited and restricted primarily to individuals classified as mentally retarded (Poretta, 1982; Del Rey and Stewart, 1989). Eidson and Stadulis (1991) suggest that while Schmidt's schema theory seems quite useful for motor skills that are closed, its applicability for tasks that have complex generalized demands must be viewed cautiously.

The practical significance of this suggests that in teaching complex skills (i.e., skills with high environmental demand) the traditional approach of breaking the skill down and employing repetitive practice sessions may still be the best approach.

In recent years a new theory of motor control, dynamic systems theory, has been introduced as an alternative to the theories of Schmidt and Adams. The chief proponents of dynamic systems theory as applied to special physical education include Bev and Dale Ulrich of Indiana University and Martin Block from the University of Virginia.

Dynamic systems theory, as introduced in chapter 2, deemphasizes the influence of a central control center and emphasizes the role of information in the environment and the dynamic properties of the body and limbs. Perception and action are closely connected so that the execution of motor skills is dictated by the relationship between perceptual information and the motor system. This suggests, therefore, that unlike Adams and Schmidt, who recognized the importance of a command control center in the execution of motor skills, dynamic systems theorists argue that skilled action is controlled by the nervous system. Specifically, muscles and joints function as "collectives" so that an action can be carried out according to the dictates of the situation (Magill, 1993). The collectives, known as coordinative structures or action units, are developed through practice or experience, or may exist naturally. An example would be the young child who hits a ball from a batting tee. Given earlier practice, the youngster uses coordinative structures (joints and muscles), developed through earlier experience, to swing the bat, recognizing changes that might occur in the environment (e.g., height of ball, size of ball etc.). The command for this action rather than coming from a central executive is self organized according to a coordinative structure. The muscles and joints used to swing the bat are constrained to work together with the understanding that changes in the environment may dictate further refinements in the skill. As Whitehall (1988) has emphasized, the dynamic systems theory contends that patterns are not prescribed but emerge from interaction among body, task, and environment with little central input. It is important to note that while dynamic systems theorists deemphasize the importance of the central command center, they do recognize that commands can come from the central center. However, they also articulate clearly that the commands can come from various sources within and external to the person.

The various theories reviewed here offer much promise for improving the motor and physical activity programs provided to infants, children, and youth with disabilities. Our understanding of mechanisms that control movement is expanding at a dramatic rate and while the work of Adams, Schmidt, and proponents of the dynamic systems theory might seem contradictory, collectively these efforts represent a significant breakthrough in our understanding of how individuals with disabilities acquire motor skills. Adams and

Schmidt, for example, explain nicely the relationships inherent in a hierarchial system. A command is given and, following a very short period of time, action occurs. Feedback is provided as to the outcome of the action and, where necessary, corrections are made. The dynamic systems theorists, while recognizing the work of Adams and Schmidt, argue that there is more than one control center and specifically emphasize the importance of the joints and muscles and the environment in expanding the ability to perform motor skills.

Unfortunately, the available literature concerning the application of these theories to individuals with disabilities is very limited. However, it is clear that the information presented holds much promise for improving our understanding of how individuals acquire information. The dynamic systems theory, in particular, speaks to some of the practical challenges encountered by many teachers of adapted physical education. For example, many teachers have recognized that our traditional views of motor learning (i.e., a linear acquisition of skills in a building block arrangement) do not seem to hold true for individuals with disabilities. Specifically, at times it appears that some children learn skills out of sequence, making greater gains in some areas and less than expected improvements in others. The approach and explanation to this problem varies. Some teachers emphasize, correctly so, the uniqueness of each student with a disability and provide a rich and challenging curriculum. Others, however, seem to stall and spend more time on trying to "catch-up" those areas which seem to be lagging behind or conclude that the neuromaturational delay is too great and move to different skills. The dynamic systems theory offers the possibility that we need to be consistently conscious of the dynamic aspect of learning and the relationship between the central command center, other command centers located in the joints and muscles, and the environment. This theory helps to balance the relationship between the central nervous system and other important ecological variables in the learning environment. In summary, dynamic systems theory offers much promise as a foundation upon which to build exciting and relevant physical education programs for students with disabilities.

Motor Skill Tenets

The research and empirical evidence produced by the serious study of the phenomenon of movement has established certain tenets that are useful to the physical educator in teaching motor skills. Those most relevant to the purpose of this book are reviewed in the following paragraphs.

The ability to learn a motor skill is influenced by growth and maturation. A child normally can learn a specific motor activity when she or he has achieved the actual physical growth required to accomplish the movement. Motor readiness is affected not only by physical size but also by the level of maturation of the neuromuscular system. Maturation occurs as a result of experience and physiological changes that are produced naturally as age increases.

To determine the readiness of a child with a disability to learn, the teacher must be very sensitive to the child's reaction to the learning of motor movement. Pressuring the child to learn an activity when it is not possible for him or her to do so is detrimental to the child's well-being. On the other hand, it is necessary to encourage the child to explore his or her motor potential by trying to achieve various motor feats. The teacher must work out a procedure that will encourage but not pressure the child. Toward this end, it is useful to evaluate the motor achievements of the child with a disability by making a comparison of his or her motor development with that of nondisabled youngsters in the same age group (described in chapter 2) and by careful assessment of the child's mental, emotional, and physical limitations.

The best way to perform any given skill is dictated by mechanical and physiological principles of movement. Application of the principles of movement ensures the most effective performance, regardless of anatomical and physiological differences in body structure. When a child's physical structure deviates markedly from normal, the most acceptable means of performing a skill is usually not appropriate. The child with a disability will need to be encouraged to explore so that he or she can find the best way to perform the skill in question, using the principles of movement as a guide.

A new skill is learned through reinforcement and repetition. Reinforcement refers to any condition or event following a response that increases the probability that the response will be repeated. The instructor must determine the type of reinforcement that produces the best learning in any situation and then utilize that reinforcement. It should be noted that the child's knowledge that a certain effort by him or her produces a desired result is also a type of reinforcement, and the one that in the long run is probably the most effective. However, because many individuals with mental retardation are unable to understand the final consequence of an act, immediate goals must be stressed and reinforcement must be immediate and extrinsic; mastery of several parts of the whole is too abstract a concept for most of these children.

Repetition of motor movement tends to establish that movement as part of an individual's repertoire of movements. Therefore, repeated performance of the new skill should be encouraged by the teacher. To effect and establish improvement in the quality of the movement, however, the performer must be aware of what she or he is working toward and how to achieve it and, in general, must be motivated to improve.

Practice alone does not lead to improved performance. If the teacher is not careful, errors may be practiced or boredom from mere repetition may occur. Practice sessions should be structured to develop the youngster's attention to relevant cues. In addition, the time devoted to practice should be of sufficient duration and quality to ensure the development of skill.

A child progresses in the learning of movement at a specific rate that is uniquely his or her own. The teacher should determine as early as possible the learning pace of students and take that into consideration in setting goals for them. It must be kept in mind that individuals may learn different activities at different rates; for example, a child may rapidly learn to throw but have a more difficult time learning to kick a ball. The rate of motor learning for those with normal intelligence shows very little relationship to intelligence as measured by an IQ test. However, there is a fairly high relationship between speed of learning and intelligence when the IQ falls below seventy, particularly if it is lower than sixty. Some relationship also exists, although it is relatively limited, between motor ability and intelligence below the IQ of seventy.

Emotion affects the process of learning motor skills. Extreme emotional reactions are known to be detrimental to learning. Even though emotional responses to anxiety, fear, and humiliation may not be expressed overtly, these responses may be a strong deterrent to learning. It is incumbent upon the teacher to create an emotional atmosphere that is conducive to learning, taking into consideration that individuals may respond differently to the same situation. The teacher must be alert to the characteristic emotional responses of each student in order to develop the best possible climate for learning.

Confusion often exists concerning the effects of emotions on the learning of motor skills, arising from the fact that ability to perform physically is increased under stress in an emotional situation. The reaction of the body to a highly emotional situation that permits the exertion of great physical effort is one that occurs after a skill has been learned. During the time that a skill is being learned, extreme emotion is actually detrimental to the learning process.

The learning of motor skills is specific; that is, the learning of one skill does not necessarily improve performance in another. Transfer of the learning of one skill to the learning of another skill can occur but it is not automatic. The transfer occurs only under certain circumstances: (1) when two activities have identical elements and (2) when a principle learned in one situation can be generalized and applied in another situation. The teacher can help students make a transfer in learning by creating opportunities for the development of meaningful generalizations, providing practice in applying the generalizations in actual situations, pointing out the likenesses between activities in which transfer can occur, and providing a variety of different kinds of motor activities so that the possibility of transfer from one activity to another is increased.

A performer's learning ability is enhanced when he or she succeeds at a specific task. "Nothing succeeds like success" is as true for motor skill performance as for any other endeavor. Hence, the teacher should choose activities for the student with disabilities that can be achieved with some degree of success (figure 3.5). A complex task may be broken down into parts to encourage quick success in the learning of one or more segments before they are combined in the performance of the whole task. The student should be kept informed of his or her progress and be praised for any improvement, regardless of how small or unimpressive it is. In table 3.3, an example of a task analysis for the skill of throwing a ball underhand is presented. At each level from Phase I to Phase VI the skill becomes increasingly complex. For some students, beginning instruction at Phase VI may be appropriate; for others, instruction at an earlier phase or step may be necessary. Presenting a skill in this manner assists students in seeing that they can be successful even though they may not have mastered the entire task.

The kind and amount of praise given must be in keeping with the child's maturation and level of ability. For a child who has much success, the praise may be minimal for small successes or may be reserved entirely for greater achievements. But a child whose improvement is slow and

Figure 3.5 Motor activities should be chosen that are challenging, fun, and allow for success.

Table 3.3 *Example of a task analysis for the underhand throw*

Terminal Objective:	The student, standing, will perform an underhand throw swinging the arm backward and then forward while stepping forward simultaneously with the opposite foot and releasing the ball at the end of the swing in a manner that causes the ball to fly in the direction of the target.
Phase I	The student, standing 5 feet from the target, will swing the arm backward and then forward, releasing the ball at the end of the swing in the direction of the target. The teacher will physically assist the student to bring his or her arm back and then forward.
Phase II	The student, standing 5 feet from the target, will swing the arm backward and then forward, releasing the ball at the end of the swing in the direction of the target. The teacher will assist the student to bring his or her arm back.
Phase III	The student, standing 5 feet from the target, will independently swing the arm backward and then forward, releasing the ball at the end of the swing in the direction of the target.
Phase IV	The student, standing 5 feet from the target with one foot forward, one foot back, and knees bent, will swing the arm forward, releasing the ball at the end of the swing and in the direction of the target.
Phase V	The student, standing 5 feet from the target and with knees bent, will swing the arm backward and forward, releasing the ball at the end of the swing and in the direction of the target while the teacher is pushing the student's opposite foot forward simultaneously with swing.
Phase VI	The student, standing, will perform an underhand throw, swinging the arm backward and then forward while stepping forward simultaneously with the opposite foot and releasing the ball at the end of the swing in a manner that causes the ball to fly in the direction of the target. The following steps apply to Phase VI. *Steps:* 1. 7 feet 2. 15 feet

whose achievement is small needs to know that he or she has been successful when something has been done well, and he or she must be assured that others recognize and appreciate his or her accomplishment. The task-analysis process complements this need.

A performer learns faster when practice sessions are separated by adequate periods of rest. Children learn faster when their interest is high. Long practice sessions tend to dull this interest. To prevent the detrimental effect of loss of interest, the teacher should keep instructional periods short and change activities frequently, stopping for periods of rest when interest begins to wane.

Fatigue detracts from the learning process. Children with physical disabilities often tire more easily than do the nondisabled, and the teacher must be continuously alert to signs of fatigue during the teaching of a physical activity to those with physical disabilities. Fatigue is also a factor in learning for youngsters with mental retardation. If, as is often the case, these children are in poor physical condition, they will tire easily from physical exertion. In addition, they usually exhibit short attention spans. Therefore, the teacher will need to provide frequent periods of rest and to change the type of activity often to achieve peak learning potential.

A motor skill that is overlearned will be retained for a longer period of time. Overlearning can be defined as the process of repeating a task until its performance is automatic, that is, without conscious effort being exerted to accomplish the task. When a motor skill is overlearned, the length of retention time is very high, sometimes lasting a lifetime. A good example is bicycling, a skill that is overlearned by youngsters through constant repetition during the years when bicycling is most popular. In their adult years, these people can, after many years of not riding, mount a bike and ride without any loss of skill.

The point at which skill is overlearned varies with each individual. Children who are mentally retarded will require many more repetitions in performing a skill to reach the point of overlearning than will those who are not mentally retarded.

Gross motor skills and continuous tasks have been found to be retained longer and more effectively than other types of learning material. In addition, for material that is serially learned, that which is learned first is retained best; the last learned is mastered second best; whereas the middle part is last to be retained.

Retention of movement is greater when it has a natural relationship to other movements. The movements of skipping provide a good illustration. Although the hop is often taught to youngsters as a component of the total movement, the ability to perform the hop will be retained longer if it is related to and practiced with the other movements of the skip. Many physical skills have this kind of interrelationship of movements that form a definite rhythmic pattern of performance. Teaching the movements in their natural pattern ensures longer retention than teaching them in isolation.

Students with disabilities learn motor skills in accordance with the same motor learning principles as nondisabled students, but may take longer. Because some students with a disability learn more slowly than do nondisabled students, they require more extensive and intensive motor skill instruction to compensate for their slower learning rates. This implies that educational gains for those with disabilities will be greatest when teachers work cooperatively with parents, encouraging them to reinforce at home those skills that have been learned at school.

While the learning of motor skills is a continuous process, stages in the learning of motor skills have been identified. P.M. Fitts and M.I. Posner in 1967 identified these to be the cognitive, associative, and autonomous phases. The cognitive phase occurs early in learning as the student makes attempts at understanding the nature of the activity to be learned. The student has to understand the purpose of the motor skill and devise strategies for performing the skill. During this phase the student is also expected to respond to verbal information and to translate this into action. For many children, particularly those with a cognitive or learning problem, the ability to understand and translate the meaning of "adult" words can be a problem.

The second stage, the associative phase, requires the student to translate and put into action the information learned in the cognitive phase. Success at this stage requires the teacher to implement the right practice conditions to promote the learning of the activity.

The third and final stage in motor learning is the autonomous phase. In this phase the skill, through practice and repetition, has been refined to the point that it is automatic. Because little conscious control over the movement is required, the performer is free to attend to other things simultaneously. This explains why a basketball player can dribble a ball while at the same time contemplating strategy that will lead to the scoring of a basket.

An understanding of the stages of learning helps to explain why some students with disabilities require special and individualized attention. Helping students to understand the skill (cognitive phase) and perform the skill (associative phase) will require additional instructional and practice time. Later in this book, the specialized skills teachers can use to assist students will be discussed.

A word of caution concerning the Motor Tenets discussed in this section seems appropriate. Unfortunately little research in the area of motor learning has actually been conducted with populations that are disabled. Therefore, the instructional practices that are applied to students with disabilities are based on research conducted with nondisabled populations. While this is logical, because those with disabilities are more similar than dissimilar to the nondisabled, additional research in this area would serve to enhance our understanding of those motor learning principles that appear appropriate for both the populations with and without disabilities.

Perceptual-Motor Learning

In the 1960s, a number of men and women in the physical education profession directed their attention to an aspect of motor learning that had not been previously emphasized or thoroughly examined: the perceptual process that occurs while performing a motor skill. The interest was triggered by the earlier publication of the theories and experimental work in perceptual-motor learning by two men: Newell C. Kephart, a psychologist, and Gerald N. Getman, an optometrist. Kephart's book, *The Slow Learner in the Classroom,* appeared in 1960, and two years later Getman published *Improve Your Child's Intelligence.* In the decade after their publication, both books were widely read, and they had tremendous influence on the development of perceptual-motor programs in the physical education curriculum. The books were followed by works by such prominent perceptual-motor theorists and practitioners as Jean Ayres, Ray H. Barsch, and Marianne Frostig, and by some who are lesser known.

Although differences of opinion existed among these people about other aspects of perceptual-motor learning, they were in agreement that perception is the recognition and interpretation of stimuli received by the brain from the sense organs in the form of nerve impulses, and that a motor response to the interpretation is perceptual-motor. Today this definition is accepted universally.

Movement and Perception

The early theorists also agreed that movement is an important key in the development of perception; that understanding the concept of left and right (laterality) is vital to the process of moving the eyes left to right in reading; and that improvement in eye-hand coordination is related to the perceptual concept involved in eye-hand coordination and is critical in learning to write. Kephart considered movement the basis of intellectual development. Others of this group believed that the learning involved in perceiving and interpreting perception in movement is automatically transferred to perceptual learning in academic activities, particularly reading and writing. A review of the beliefs espoused by major perceptual-motor theorists is presented in the following paragraphs.

Newell C. Kephart

One of the early perceptual-motor theorists, Newell Kephart proposed that the inadequate development of certain motor skills may tend to inhibit the development of later, more complex skills. Infants first learn, according to Kephart, through the medium of movement. As they explore and locate objects, higher levels of learning become possible through feeling and manipulating these unknown objects. This latter process of matching the perceptual system with the motor system was referred to by Kephart as the perceptual-motor match. In the modern mechanistic world, Kephart warned, many of the opportunities to explore the environment are reduced and thus children have fewer opportunities to develop perceptual-motor matches. For instance, children no longer play with kitchen items such as coffee pots because many of these items are now electric, expensive, and off-limits. Kephart believed that without opportunities to match perceptual and motor data, later difficulties with academic skills such as reading and writing would occur. Remediation for Kephart, therefore, meant that instead of working on reading skills for the youngster with a reading difficulty, efforts should be directed toward treating the basic skills, motor and visual training, upon which reading skills are built. It is this focus on teaching generalization rather than highly specific skills

that made Kephart's approach different from those of earlier educators. Although the research results on the effectiveness of his program are contradictory, recent findings have not supported Kephart's generalization theory.

Gerald N. Getman

Getman's training as an optometrist led him to explore the relationship between intellectual development and visual development. For Getman, a child's growth, behavior, and cognitive development conform to a basic sequence of visually related development. Distinction is made by Getman between sight and vision. Sight is considered to be simply the basic biological response of the eye to light. Vision, by contrast, is the interpretation of what is seen. The importance Getman attaches to visual perception is repeatedly emphasized throughout his writings by statements such as "vision is intelligence."

Getman's support for motor activity is found in the six-stage training program he recommends. These stages include:

I. General Motor Patterns (basic movement skills such as creeping, crawling, and walking)
II. Special Movement Patterns (eye-hand coordination)
III. Eye Movement Patterns (matched movement for both eyes)
IV. Visual Language Patterns (effective communication patterns)
V. Visualization Patterns (visual memory skills)
VI. Visual Perceptual Organization (relationship of vision to other perceptual modalities)

Concern has been expressed regarding various aspects of Getman's work. The criticism generally focuses on two points: the strong emphasis placed by him on visual perception and the lack of scientific evidence to support his theory.

Doman and Delacato

One of the most controversial theories proposed concerning the development of perception and its relationship to the motor area was advanced in the late 1950s by Robert and Glen Doman and Carl Delacato. These three professionals, representing the fields of education, physical therapy, and physical medicine, believe that many perceptual, motor, and cognitive disabilities stem from inadequate neurological organization. According to them, neurological development follows the biogenetic postulate that ontogeny recapitulates phylogeny. This means that individual human development repeats the pattern of human evolutionary development. If individuals do not follow the sequential continuum of neurological development, Doman and Delacato hypothesized, they will exhibit problems of mobility and communication. The development of the brain, therefore, is of central concern to the Doman-Delacato team. They have traced the phylogenetic development of the brain from the lowest level of living vertebrae to humans. If injury to the brain occurs at any level of development, the child will show evidence of neurological dysfunction. According to the theory of neurological organization, never are all the cells of the brain damaged; those that remain intact can be trained to perform the functions of those that are damaged. Doman and Delacato, therefore, have proposed a treatment technique in which the brain is "patterned" through the active and passive manipulation of the arms, legs, and head. In short, they attempt to restructure the organization of the developing nervous system.

The premise of the Doman-Delacato theory, neurological organization, and their treatment effect have been heavily criticized by both the medical and the education field. Although their approach has received some favorable reviews by parents of brain-injured children, experimental studies have not supported their program.

Ray H. Barsch

Ray Barsch's support for perceptual-motor programs was expressed in his Theory of Movigenics. This theory relates learning to efficient movement patterns. As one moves more efficiently, the perceptual processes are enhanced, which Barsch theorizes contributes to intellectual development. His educational philosophy, therefore, relies heavily on a "physiologic" approach in contradistinction to the more traditional or psychiatric approach. This belief is expressed clearly in Barsch's Movigenic Curriculum, which emphasizes twelve dimensions of learning. Three of the dimensions, muscular strength, dynamic balance, and motor planning, highlight the importance Barsch places on movement. Like the approaches of authors previously discussed in this chapter, Barsch's approach is essentially nonlanguage, with the primary emphasis being on perceptual-motor learning. Unfortunately, few studies are available that either support or refute Barsch's work. It seems clear today, however, that a student with a language disorder will benefit from a program specifically designed to enhance language development, not motor development.

Marianne Frostig

Marianne Frostig, working with several of her associates, in 1964 proposed a visual perceptual training program. The intent of the program was to assist young children with visual perception problems, including those who are deaf, blind, mentally retarded, and have poor reading readiness skills. According to Frostig, visual perception is the ability to recognize and interpret visual stimuli by associating them with previous experiences. The Frostig program focuses on five perceptual skills: figure-ground perception, perception of position in space, perception of spatial relationships, perceptual constancy, and visual-motor coordination. As suggested by the title of the perceptual skill, movement plays an important part in the Frostig program. In a book written by Frostig and Maslow, *Movement Education: Theory and Practice,* movement experiences are viewed as essential to serve as a foundation for later perceptual skills. Activities are proposed to develop visual-motor coordination, manipulation, body awareness, and the basic movement skills of coordination, agility, balance, flexibility, strength, speed, and endurance. Frostig and her associates do not identify with a particular developmental theory. Instead, they have remained eclectic, selecting elements from various educational viewpoints.

Jean Ayres

Jean Ayres, an occupational therapist, believes that perceptual and academic skills improve through participation in sensory-motor experiences. She supports this view by explaining that the development of higher brain cells is dependent on the function of lower brain cells. Ayres suggests, therefore, that students with learning difficulties will respond positively to sensory-motor treatment programs because kinesthetic, vestibular, and tactile stimulation affect the brain stem and enhance cortical function. The ultimate goal of the Ayres program is to improve sensory-motor integration, enabling the central nervous system to achieve a higher functioning state, improving both motor and academic skills.

In reviewing the work of Ayres, Cratty questions the quality of research studies conducted to support her beliefs. Furthermore, he notes that data from Ayres' research shows that academic learning and reading proficiency appear to function *independently* of sensory-motor integration. Cratty (1980) concludes that until additional evidence is available to support Jean Ayres' sensory-motor model, teachers and therapists should employ sensory integration techniques cautiously.

Physical educators concerned with methods and techniques of teaching motor movements were quick to incorporate the perceptual-motor concepts established by Kephart and others into their practices and procedures. Programs of perceptual-motor skills were rapidly established in schools, particularly at the elementary level, or were incorporated into the existing physical education curricula. It is understandable that many practitioners were drawn to the theories espoused by the early perceptual-motor advocates, because the importance placed on motor development greatly enhances the role of physical education—does, in fact, make the teaching of physical education activities basic to the learning of many fundamental academic skills.

Many of the concepts that served as the bases for these perceptual-motor programs are in serious question today. Because the concepts were largely unsubstantiated by objective research, some ran counter to conclusions from research evidence that were even then well-established. Others of these concepts have been refuted by recent research findings.

Research has established that the learning of motor skills is specific. This applies also to perceptual-motor movement, because perception is involved in all voluntary muscular movement except reflex action. There is very little evidence to indicate a direct relationship between learning specific perceptual-motor skills and learning to read and write.

Although researchers have found that many of the motor activities that were devised to improve perception in academic endeavors are not successful in this purpose, they are useful in developing the motor skills involved in the activities. Perception and interpretation of stimuli in the performance of the particular skills also may be improved. Although transfer of neither the motor skills nor the perceptual-motor responses to other activities occurs, the capacity of the child in both areas is improved and is thus likely to enhance his or her future performances.

There is little doubt that perception is of vital importance to volitional movement. Emphasis in teaching directed toward perception in movement is of value in improving faulty perception in movement.

Components of Perception

When the word *perception* is used, most people think of visual perception. This is somewhat understandable because vision is the dominant sense in most people. However, as indicated in figure 3.6, vision is not the only source of sensory input. Information can be received through the channels of sound (auditory), touch (tactile), smell (olfactory), taste (gustatory), awareness of body position (kinesthetic), as well as sight (visual). In complex motor activity, the senses are used in an integrated manner to allow for efficient movement. In the game of basketball, for instance, players use vision to shoot a basket, sound to hear the referees and their teammates, touch to feel the ball, and kinesthetic sense to recognize their body position in relation to other players and the basket. As will be discussed in the chapters devoted to specific disabilities, students who do not have the use of some of the basic senses—for example, those who are deaf or blind—can participate successfully in various activities by relying on the other senses and, when necessary, through modifying the activity.

In the following section, the perceptual modalities and their component parts will be identified.

Visual Perception

Effective control of the visual system, or seeing what one wants, when one wants to see it, involves utilization of several skills that develop during childhood. For instance *visual acuity,* the ability to see objects clearly, improves until age ten when maximum acuity is attained for most children. *Perceptual constancy,* the ability to determine if different

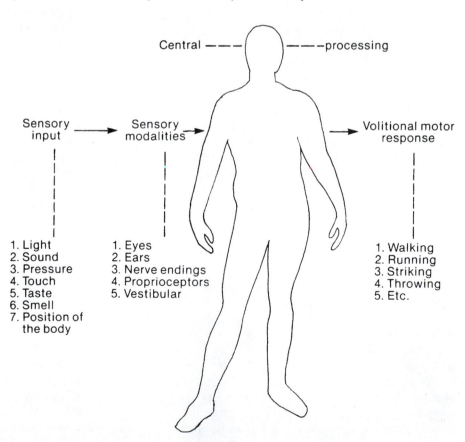

Figure 3.6 Overview of perceptual-motor system.

Figure 3.7 Catching a ball requires visual tracking skills.

objects are the same size, shape, and color, is also a necessary visual perceptual skill. Although infants appear to have some perceptual constancy skills, this trait follows a developmental course that extends through childhood. *Depth perception,* an important visual skill, is closely related to perceptual constancy. This skill involves perceiving three dimensions in proper perspective and having awareness of distance between objects or points. Scientists cannot agree whether depth perception is present in infants or is a developed skill. *Visual figure-ground* is a perceptual skill that involves distinguishing a figure from its background. Although it is generally recognized that form discriminations are among the first made by children, complete figure-ground mastery is slow to develop and normally continues to develop into adolescence. The ability to perceive a moving object is commonly referred to as *visual tracking.* Although infants as young as one month perceive and follow large objects, this trait continues to improve through the childhood years. As children become older and more experienced, the ability to track small objects moving at a rapid pace is remarkable.

Although the components of the visual perceptual system have been discussed separately, they work in an integrated fashion. For instance, successfully hitting a pitched ball requires that the ball can be seen clearly (visual acuity), followed as it leaves the pitcher's hand (visual tracking), and detected from among the many items in the background, such as the pitcher and fans (visual figure-ground). For some

students, the young and those with disabilities, the visual perceptual requirements of many skills may be too great, requiring that appropriate modifications be made. In the example given before, a simple modification would be to hit a stationary ball from a batting tee rather than a pitched ball, thus eliminating the visual process of tracking.

Auditory Perception

Auditory perception, similar to visual perception, consists of many identifiable subskills. Some of these subskills include *awareness,* the ability to indicate that there is sound or no sound; *discrimination,* the ability to discriminate between different tones and frequencies of sounds; *direction,* the ability to determine the direction from which sound is coming; and *figure-ground,* the ability to distinguish a specific sound or sound pattern from other noises occurring at the same time.

Very few studies have analyzed the process of auditory development. It does appear clear, however, that infants are sensitive to sound from birth onward. Furthermore, infants appear to respond more favorably to low-pitched sounds rather than to high-pitched sounds.

Simple observation indicates that sound is an integral part of many of our games and physical education activities. Teammates' shouting, spectators' noise, and the teacher's whistle are only a few of the many sounds found within the gymnasium. If there are students who cannot perceive auditorially, as is true with students who are deaf and hearing-impaired, the teacher must rely on the other sensory systems to ensure positive learning experiences.

Kinesthetic Perception

Visual and auditory perception enables humans to receive, organize, integrate, and interpret a vast mount of never-ending stimuli. Such is also the case with kinesthetic perception. Instead of using an eye or an ear to receive information, the kinesthetic system utilizes proprioceptors located in tissues surrounding and adjacent to joints and in joint capsules. Whereas eyes and ears help people to remember a sight or sound, proprioceptors help us remember a movement or body position. This is a valuable system, one that is constantly used in the teaching and learning of many movement skills. Three skills that are closely related to kinesthetic perception—balance, body awareness, and laterality—will be discussed here.

Balance, the ability of the individual to position the body in response to the effects of gravity, is controlled in part by the *vestibular system.* This system, located in the inner ear, is a very important mechanism in helping individuals maintain balance in both a stationary and a static position, or when changing body positions. The latter type of balance is referred to as dynamic balance. Some individuals with hearing impairments have a defective vestibular system and they require a wide base of support to maintain balance when they walk.

Body awareness refers to an understanding of the position of the body in space and the relationship of body parts to each other and to external objects. Newborns are not capable of perceiving much about their environment. As children grow, they become aware of their capability of moving their extremities, head, and trunk. Later on, children learn labels and associate particular terms with various body parts. The labeling of body parts is one of the first body awareness characteristics a child develops. DeOreo and Williams (1980) indicate that at the age of five years, 55 percent of children accurately label their body parts. Linear improvements are found until age twelve, at which point there is 100 percent accuracy.

Two other important areas in the development of body awareness are knowledge of what the body parts can do and knowledge of how to make the body parts move efficiently. Knowledge of what the body parts can do refers to the child's ability to recognize the parts of a motor act and the body's potential for performing it. For example, children should be able to identify the correct body part when asked to respond to the following statements: I see with my . . . ; I talk with my . . . ; I snap my . . . , etc. The third area, knowledge of how to make the body parts move efficiently, refers to the ability to organize the body parts for a particular motor act and the actual performance of the act. For example, the child, when asked, should be able to: Touch the nose to the shoulder; touch the elbow to the knee; click the heels and arch the back.

An important aspect of the development of body awareness is the concept of *laterality.* This means simply that children develop an ability to distinguish between the two sides of the body. This trait is developed in children by the age of three to four. Although they may not be able to correctly apply the label left or right, young children do understand that they have two feet, two hands, and two eyes and that they are on two different sides of the body. Laterality is considered by many as the foundation for the development of other body awareness characteristics.

Sensory dominance, the preferential use of one eye, hand, and foot over the other, is closely related to the development of laterality. Individuals who develop a preference for the use of the eye, hand, and foot on the same side of the body are said to have pure dominance. Those who happen to have one of the preferred body parts on the opposite side of the body have mixed dominance. Children normally exhibit a hand preference by age four and foot preference by age five. Eye preference appears later, and in some instances, a pure preference for one eye over the other apparently never fully develops. Preferential use of the eye and hand on the same side of the body shows a definite developmental trend with age. The eye-hand preference of five- and six-year-olds has a trend toward being mixed, whereas the eye-hand preference of nine- to eleven-year-olds has a trend toward pure preference.

Directionality is a kinesthetic sense that is also closely related to laterality. The ability to identify and relate objects and their positions to one another without the use of one's own body is referred to as directionality. More simply stated, directionality is evident when a child can indicate that an object in the room is to the right of a second object in the room without using his or her own body as a reference system. Children who have difficulty with directionality find it necessary to position their body between the two objects before they can indicate which is to the left or right of the other. Some educators also have speculated that incomplete development of directionality leads to a variety of learning disorders, such as the inability to distinguish between the letters b and d. Although this hypothesis appears plausible, there are few available studies to support or refute this contention.

Tactile, Gustatory, and Olfactory Perception

Tactile perception refers to the ability to interpret sensations by touching or feeling. This perception is used in learning many movement skills. Through experience, children quickly learn to distinguish between a hard and a soft ball, and between rough and smooth running surface textures. Tactile sensation is of paramount importance to certain students with disabilities, such as individuals without sight who frequently learn to perform various activities by feel. For example, a person who is visually impaired performing the basic skill of walking uses a cane to feel the sidewalk in contrast to other areas such as curbs and grass. Youngsters who are mentally retarded, too, learn many concepts such as smooth and rough by holding, feeling, and manipulating objects of various textures.

Very little is known about the development of taste and smell in children. Children do have a larger distribution of taste buds in their mouths than do adults, but it is not known whether children have a greater sensitivity to taste. With respect to smell, it is clear that young infants recognize pleasant from unpleasant odors, but precisely how this perceptual process develops is not clearly known. Movement skills generally do not require a highly refined taste or smell sensory input system.

Development of Perception

The Gestalt psychologists of the early 1900s felt that perception was not learned but was instead a factor of maturation. They reasoned that perception matured at a predetermined rate and experiences had little influence on the development. However, research accomplished since the early 1900s provides sufficient evidence to reject that theory. Today's evidence does support the concept that the process of perceiving can be improved through certain educational procedures. Perception does not necessarily improve automatically as the result of engaging in a given activity, however. Some children, through participation in an activity that involves the utilization of a specific sense, learn by themselves through trial and error to make an appropriate motor match with the sensory input. Others, because of learning disabilities, do not; they require specific assistance in interpreting sensory input and reacting to it with a suitable motor response.

Block (1993) and Burton (1987) suggest that for some children, including those with various disabilities, movement problems might, in some cases, be related to a deficit in perceiving what the environment affords for action. This difficulty which has been labeled as "affordance" suggests that children with disabilities may over- or underestimate their ability related to various tasks (e.g., distance that can be jumped) or they may misread the environment and use contextually inappropriate movements. For example, an object such as a ball might afford throwing, kicking, or bouncing, depending upon the expectation and environmental constraints. For the child with an affordance problem, the concern, of course, is that the child might be misjudged (i.e., viewed as not possessing the skill) when the problem may be related to an inability to properly read the environment. In some cases the individual may be confused by the environment and not perform at all or "read" the environment to call for an action different than that intended.

The human body perceives through different sense modalities. Each modality is different in function, providing a specific type of stimulation. The modalities that are usually involved in increasing the sensitivity and in improving the interpretation and reaction to the interpretation are sight, hearing, touch and pressure, and kinesthesis (the sensation of the location of body parts and of movement in muscles, tendons, and joints).

Children with learning disabilities cannot organize a sufficient amount of sensory information at one time to enable them to make an effective motor response. The amount of sensory stimuli directed at children with learning disabilities must be reduced to that which the child is able to absorb. The task at hand may be made simpler by breaking it down into its components, thereby reducing the inputs of many different sensory stimuli at one time. This does not mean that various methods of providing sensory information should not be utilized. If the teacher finds that the student is not assimilating the information from one source of sensory input, other sources should be tried. For example, a child may not learn how to perform a skill by watching a demonstration, but may get the idea when manual kinesthesis is used to lead the child through the required movements.

Although it is not established clearly how sensory interpretation and response to interpretation can be improved, it is generally conceded that practice in utilizing the senses and responding to the interpretation of the sense perceptions has value in effecting improvement of the process. The practice has to include cognition or conceptualization of the process of perception-interpretation; that is, there has to be an analysis of the deficient perception supplemented by analysis of the perception of the normally functioning senses to arrive at an interpretation that will produce the

desired result. For example, children with problems of visual discrimination in size must use the normal perceptions from senses other than sight to evaluate the size of the object they are looking at. They then compare the result with the visual input they receive ordinarily and make the necessary adjustments to achieve agreement between the visual input and the input from the other senses. Much practice in simple repetitive exercises designed specifically for the deficiency is required to improve the interpretation of the stimuli.

Much the same procedure is utilized with children who have problems in reacting with appropriate motor movement to a sensation. For example, a child who cannot balance well on the balance beam must first analyze the sensations received just before losing balance. Then, through experimentation the child must discover the movements of the body that eliminate those sensations. Practice in consciously substituting these for the unsatisfactory movements will eventually result in an automatic response of the muscles to maintain balance when a fall is imminent. Examples of activities designed to enhance the perceptual process are found in table 3.4.

In utilization of motor activities to enhance the perceptual process, one must keep in mind that some of these movements require complex muscular coordination, as in throwing or kicking a ball, and others require intellectual recall, as in naming the body parts, and hence are relatively specific—not automatically transferred to the performance of other activities of coordination or intellectual recall. It is not known how general the perceptual processes are. For example, there is insufficient evidence to determine how

Table 3.4 *Examples of activities to enhance the perceptual process*

Perceptual Area	Task
Visual	
Tracking	Watch a swinging, suspended ball.
Constancy	Reproduce on a chalkboard a shape that is provided by the teacher.
Depth perception	Throw a ball to the near basket rather than to the far basket.
Figure-ground	Kick a ball to a student standing in front of other children.
Auditory	
Direction	Point to the direction of a sound, e.g., a whistle.
Discrimination	Identify which bouncing ball sounds soft and which one sounds loud.
Figure-ground	Recognize the teacher's voice from among many voices in a crowded gymnasium.
Kinesthetic	
Body awareness	Touch and say the name of the body part located on a partner.
Laterality	Bend the body to the right (left) while in a standing position.
Directionality	Throw a ball from an off-center location to the right or left into a basket in the center of the room.

readily the learned ability to determine the figure-ground relationship in one situation is transferred to another.

Because of the specificity of coordination and the possibility that perceptual processes also may be somewhat specific, a large number of experiences in sorting figure-ground relations and reacting in various situations are necessary to establish a general ability to distinguish a figure from its background. This would be true not only in the example given for a figure-ground recognition activity but also for all of the perceptual processes. The activities given in table 3.4 are only examples to provide information on the types of activities that may stimulate various perceptual processes.

Impairment of Perception

Research has not supplied the educator with all the answers concerning the nature of perception and its relationship to movement. It is postulated that the perceptual difficulties discussed previously may be caused by brain injuries or by malfunction of the portion of the nervous system that interprets perception.

It is possible that such injury or malfunction occurs in one phase of perception but that other phases may be unimpaired. Application of this concept can be very helpful when teaching students with various disabilities. For example, for individuals with visual and hearing impairments, the primary deficits will occur in sensory input. Individuals who are mentally retarded will normally experience problems with interpreting input as well as processing of information. Impairment in the kinesthetic sense, as a result of muscular or nerve damage, will create unique challenges for those with orthopedic or neuromuscular disorders. Training the malfunctioning phase of perception or substituting another sensory organ for the one that is not functioning properly may help to overcome the motor problem that the perception problem creates.

However, in cases where no specific problem exists but where there is a nonspecific form of poor motor function, can the blame be placed upon any one perceptual area of malfunctioning? Probably not; it is reasonable to expect that the quality of motor ability fits a normal bell-shaped curve the same way it is supposed that intelligence does. If this is the case, it can be assumed that low general motor ability, or a large portion of it, is not caused by an organic lesion or malfunctioning of the nervous system but that the ability to learn motor movement is inherent within the neuromuscular system. The author feels that a large number of nonspecific awkward children fall into this category.

The Awkward Child

Children who demonstrate characteristics of nonspecific awkwardness do not necessarily respond positively to perceptual-motor activities designed for children with perceptual disabilities. Motor awkwardness appears to be general in nature;

however, in close observation of awkward children it can usually be noted that the awkwardness occurs in some specific movements and not in others. The awkwardness may, for example, appear in the skills of jumping, hopping, and skipping but not in throwing and catching.

To effect remediation of motor awkwardness in the specific skills in which it occurs, the first step is to determine the reason for the awkwardness. To make such a determination in the case of awkwardness in running, for example, the teacher observes the child running and watches for such faults as (1) failure to coordinate the arm and leg movements, (2) failure to swing the leg straight forward in each stride, and (3) twisting of the trunk from side to side with each stride. (For description and techniques of such an evaluation, see chapter 7.) After identification of the movement fault or faults that produce awkwardness in performing the skill, the child is taught how to overcome the problem and achieve a well-coordinated performance. Such instruction is much the same as that used to help any child break the habits of ineffective skill performance and achieve more efficient and graceful movement.

Unfortunately, although much has been written about awkwardness and related coordination problems, few serious efforts have been made to develop appropriate remediation programs (Burton, 1990). While it is outside the parameters of this chapter to provide a complete description of a remediation program, an example might prove helpful.

A useful framework for helping children with coordination problems has been proposed by Burton (1990). In his instructional hierarchy (figure 3.8), the child unable to coordinate the arms and legs while doing a jumping jack would be moved from level 3 to level 2 to work on between limb coordination. Suggested activities would include anything that required using between limbs together (e.g., two arms or two legs or the arm and leg on the same side). The movements should be done using the same (in-phase) or opposite (out-of-phase) movements. To make the skill easier, the movements should be executed first using as simple

Instructional Hierarchy for Working with Persons Who Have Movement Coordination Problems

Coordination level	Program focus
3 Between limb pairs (total body)	Coordination ⇄ Control
2 Between limb (within limb pairs)	Coordination ⇄ Control
1 Between joints (within limb	Coordination → Control

Figure 3.8 *Knowledge of the instructional hierarchy helps teachers ensure student success.*

(Note: From "Applying Principles of Coordination in Adapted Physical Education" by Allen Burton. *Adapted Physical Activity Quarterly* (Vol. 7, No. 2), p. 136, © 1990 by Human Kinetics Publishers.)

a position as possible (e.g., in a supine position). The relevant parameters (e.g., distance, time, and speed) should be varied to insure success. However, if the child is unsuccessful at level 2, then he/she would be moved to level 1, between joints. At this level, possible activities might include anything that required use of only one arm or leg (e.g., throwing, striking). As success is achieved at level 1, the youngster would be advanced to level 2. It is important to emphasize that the tasks should be varied incorporating the appropriate parameters and aids (e.g., use of weights or cues [ribbon] on the arms or legs may be helpful). The goal is to provide a program with clearly stated goals and instructional techniques that are reinforcing and creative.

Summary

Within this chapter information has been presented concerning motor learning and perception and their importance to an understanding of how individuals acquire skills. Various theories of learning and movement control were reviewed with the recognition that aspects of each theory have some application in the teaching of motor skills to students with disabilities. There are also overlap and common elements among the various theories of learning.

Motor skill tenets were identified to assist the reader in recognizing some of the applied aspects of information that have been derived through a study of motor learning. Special attention was directed toward the importance of success, reinforcement, practice, and feedback in the teaching and retention of a motor skill. Information about how skills can be classified was included to emphasize the similarities and differences related to various skills. Knowledge in this area will lead to a better understanding of task complexity and the appropriateness or inappropriateness of introducing selected skills, depending upon the student's background and readiness.

Due to the continuing interest in perceptual motor programs, the theories of prominent individuals were reviewed. Although these theorists have aided in a significant way our understanding of the importance of motor activity in the lives of infants and children, including the child with a disability, there is insufficient research to support the various claims made by proponents of these programs.

The components of perception, including how perception is developed, were reviewed. Knowledge in this area serves to underline the importance of perception in the acquisition of knowledge, including motor skills. Although it is obvious that many have experienced the loss of one of the senses, innovative ways have been developed to help individuals to compensate successfully.

Finally, the chapter should serve to highlight that although information concerning motor learning and perception has been generated, little research is available that specifically applies to individuals with disabilities. Until such time as a more adequate research base exists, teachers will apply the known information cautiously, using experience and common sense as guides.

Selected Readings

Adams, J.A. (1971). A closed-loop theory of motor learning. *Journal of Motor Behavior, 3,* 111–149.

Arnheim, D.D., & Sinclair, W.A. (1979). *The clumsy child* (2d ed.). St. Louis: C.V. Mosby Co.

Block, M.E. (1993). Can children with mild mental retardation perceive affordances for action? *Adapted Physical Activity Quarterly, 10*(2), 137–145.

Burton, A.W. (1987). Confronting the interaction between perception and movement in adapted physical education. *Adapted Physical Activity Quarterly, 4,* 257–276.

Burton, A.W. (1990). Applying principles of coordination in adapted physical education, *Adapted Physical Activity Quarterly, 7,* 126–142.

Corbin, C.B. (Ed.). (1980). *A textbook of motor development* (2d ed.). Dubuque, IA: Wm. C. Brown Publishers.

Cratty, B.J. (1979). *Perceptual and motor development in infants and children* (2d ed.). Englewood Cliffs, NJ: Prentice-Hall, Inc.

Cratty, B.J. (1980). *Adapted physical education for handicapped children and youth.* Denver: Love Publishing Co.

Delacato, C.H. (1963). *The diagnosis and treatment of speech and reading problems.* Springfield, IL: Charles C. Thomas.

Del Rey, P., & Stewart, D. (1989). Organizing input for mentally retarded subjects to enhance memory and transfer. *Adapted Physical Activity Quarterly, 6,* 247–254.

DeOreo, K., & Williams, H. (1980). Characteristics of kinesthetic perception. In C.B. Corbin (Ed.), *A textbook of motor development.* Dubuque, IA: Wm. C. Brown Publishers.

Dummer, G.M. (1985). Developmental differences in motor schema formation. In J. Humphrey & J. Clark (Eds.), *Current selected research in motor development* (chapter 11). Princeton, NJ: Princeton Books.

Dunn, J.M., & Fredericks, H.D. (1985). Behavior management applied to mainstreaming in physical education. *Adapted Physical Activity Quarterly, 4,* 338–346.

Eidson, T.A., & Stadulis, R.E. (1991). Effects of variability of practice on the transfer and performance of open and closed motor skill. *Adapted Physical Activity Quarterly, 8,* 342–356.

Fitts, P.M., & Posner, M.I. (1967). *Human performance.* Belmont, CA: Brooks/Cole Publishing.

Frostig, M., & Maslow, P. (1970). *Movement education: Theory and practice.* Chicago: Follett Publishing Co.

Gallahue, D.L. (1982). *Understanding motor development in children.* New York: John Wiley and Sons, Inc.

Gentile, A.M., Higgins, J.R., Miller, E.A., & Rosen, B.M. (1975). *The structure of motor tasks.* Quebec City: Movement 7.

Kephart, N.C. (1971). *The slow learner in the classroom* (2d ed.). Columbus, OH: Charles E. Merrill Publishing Co.

Kerr, R. (1982). *Psychomotor learning.* Philadelphia: Saunders College Publishing.

Magill, R.A. (1993). *Motor learning concepts and applications.* Dubuque, IA: Brown and Benchmark.

Poretta, D.L. (1982). Motor schema formation by EMR boys. *American Journal of Mental Deficiency, 87,* 164–172.

Poulton, E.C. (1957). On prediction in skilled movement. *Psychological Bulletin, 54.*

Project Beacon: Perceptual-motor activities handbook. (1977). Fairfax, VA: Fairfax County Public Schools.

Sage, G. H. (1984). *Motor learning and control.* Dubuque, IA: Wm. C. Brown Publishers.

Schmidt, R.A. (1975). A schema theory of discreet motor skill learning. *Psychological Review, 82,* 225–260.

Schmidt, R.A. (Ed.). (1982). *Motor control and learning.* Champaign, IL: Human Kinetics Publishers.

Singer, R.N. (1982). *The learning of motor skills.* New York: Macmillan Publishing Co.

Skinner, B.F. (1938). *The behavior of organisms: An experimental analysis.* New York: Appleton-Century-Crofts.

Tolman, E.C. (1934). Theories of learning. In F.A. Moss (Ed.), *Comparative psychology.* Englewood Cliffs, NJ: Prentice-Hall.

Weiner, N. (1961). *Cybernetics.* New York: The M.I.T. Press and John Wiley and Sons, Inc.

Wertheimer, M. (1961). Psychomotor coordination of audio-visual space at birth. *Science, 134,* 1692–1693.

Whitehall, J. (1988). A dynamical systems approach to motor development: Applying new theory to practice. Paper presented at the International Early Childhood Physical Education Conference, Washington, DC.

Williams, H.G. (1983). *Perceptual and motor development.* Englewood Cliffs, NJ: Prentice-Hall, Inc.

Williams, H.G. (1986). Development of sensory-motor functioning in young children. In V. Seefeldt (Ed.), *Physical activity and well-being* (pp. 105–122). Reston, VA: American Alliance for Health, Physical Education, Recreation, and Dance.

Zaichkowsky, L.D., Zaichkowsky, L.B., & Martinek, T.J. (1980). *Growth and development.* St. Louis: C.V. Mosby Co.

Enhancing Activities

1. Decide whether the following motor skills should be classified as open or closed; gross or fine; continuous or discrete: archery, soccer, bowling, walking, and typing. Identify other skills and challenge your classmates to classify the skills.

2. Interview other professionals such as physical therapists, occupational therapists, reading specialists, and special educators to obtain their views regarding perceptual-motor programs.

3. Review table 3.3 and identify other examples of activities to enhance the perceptual process.

4. Select a novel motor skill, such as tossing a tennis ball backward over the shoulder, and teach the skill to a child using the motor skill tenets listed in the chapter. For example, emphasize success, reinforcement, length of practice sessions, and retention of the skill.

5. For the following populations, identify perceptual and motor learning mechanisms that can be employed to help them compensate for their disabilities: visual impairment, orthopedic impairment, learning disability, and cerebral palsy.

6. Utilizing the theories of learning described earlier, explain how the process for teaching a motor skill might vary when employing a behavioral approach compared with a cognitive approach.

7. Develop a list of the italicized terms in this chapter, and for each term write a definition.

CHAPTER

4

Understanding Individuals
with Disabilities

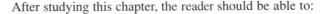

◆ CHAPTER OBJECTIVES ◆

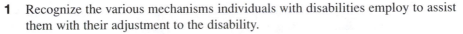

After studying this chapter, the reader should be able to:

1   Recognize the various mechanisms individuals with disabilities employ to assist them with their adjustment to the disability.

2   Appreciate the importance of others, namely parents, siblings, peers, and teachers, in helping the individual with a disability to adjust.

3   Identify and utilize various activities that teachers can use to help nondisabled students increase their sensitivity to their peers who have disabilities.

4   Define and utilize the following terms: sublimation, compensation, identification, projection, escape, rationalization, and repression.

5   Compare and contrast the effects of a mild versus severe disability on the adjustment of the individual with the disability, as well as the adjustment of the person's family.

6   List and discuss various strategies employed by parents to accept and integrate a child with a disability into the family.

7   Identify and explain the response commonly experienced by parents upon learning that their child has a disability.

8   Analyze the impact of a child with a disability on the organizational structure of the family.

Success in working with individuals with disabilities is dependent upon understanding their special problems. It is significant that for many individuals with a disability, the most difficult problems are psychological in nature rather than physical. Ways have been found to reduce, if not actually eliminate, the physical pain of a disability. Many mechanical devices have been created and methods of rehabilitation developed to assist the person with a disability in achieving more normal use of the body. Medical treatment and the careful regulation of diet and activity enable many individuals disabled by functional diseases to lead normal lives in many respects. But regardless of how nearly normal body function and physical performance may be, the presence of the disability creates the potential for many psychological problems. Such problems have their origin in both the individual's reactions to the disabling condition and the responses of others to it.

Satisfactory resolution of these problems to achieve a desirable level of adjustment is often difficult and may constitute the major obstacle in the total education of the person with a disability.

Factors Affecting Adjustment

Satisfactory solutions are achieved through the process of adjustment, a term used to describe the changes an individual undergoes in order to adapt to the environment. Adjustment begins at the moment of birth and is a continuous process throughout life. Certain innate factors, the result of inheritance, influence the kind of adjustment that is made in response to the stimuli of the environment. These factors are intelligence, physical appearance, temperament, and degree of disability.

Intelligence

The degree of native intelligence determines the amount and quality of the direction and control of behavior. A more intelligent child is better able to direct and control personal behavior. Greater ability to reason enables the results of certain actions to be anticipated and acted upon accordingly. Because of the greater depth of understanding, the more intelligent child is less likely to resort to undesirable behavior to achieve ends. Children who are mentally retarded are often able to learn socially acceptable behavior, but in new and unexpected circumstances they are unable to apply the learned behavior.

Physical Appearance

Physical appearance is an important factor in the development of behavior tendencies because of the responses of others to physical characteristics such as body build, facial features, and obvious deformities. We are aware that even such slight deviations as more-than-average height or weight cause others to respond with a certain amount of teasing or even ridicule. Greater deviations from normal cause more intense responses, even to the extent of casting the one who deviates in an inferior social role.

Temperament

Behavior tendencies are also influenced by what is generally called temperament but which scientific evidence indicates is actually glandular function. Although the precise functioning of all the glands is not presently known, it is known that the personality of an individual is affected if certain imbalances or malfunctions occur in the various glands. For example, less than normal activity of the thyroid gland influences certain metabolic changes that produce laziness, dullness, and depression, whereas, in contrast, an overactive thyroid causes an individual to be very active, tense, and restless.

Degree of Disability

Attention recently has been focused on the extent or degree of disability and its effect on adjustment. Although more research is needed in this area, some of the common assumptions of the past are now being seriously questioned. For instance, it was once widely accepted that the greater a person's disability, the more difficult it is for the individual to accept it or to achieve proper adjustment. Some have recently argued, however, that a person who is nearly "normal" in appearance and function may have a more difficult time adjusting than one who has a severe disability. Those who support this position postulate that an individual with a more severe disability recognizes that the disability is obvious to all and accepts his or her position, whereas the individual with a mild disability may try to hide or deny the disability. Future research will help to clarify this phenomenon. Until then it seems apparent that one should not assume that the mildly disabled will have fewer adjustment problems than those who are severely disabled.

Environmental Influence

A continual interplay exists between the conditions arising from these innate factors and the conditions of the environment—the attitudes and responses of others. Society tends to react in definite ways to any deviation from the norm. Sometimes the reaction is one of ridicule, curiosity, or maudlin sympathy; in the case of those close to the person with a disability, the reaction is often one of indulgence or overprotectiveness. The combined reactions of those in the social environment toward the one who deviates mentally or physically from the norm greatly influence that individual's adjustment. The responses of parents, peers, siblings, and teachers can significantly contribute toward a favorable social environment for the student with a disability.

Parent Reaction

Raising a child is recognized by most as a rewarding, but difficult and challenging task. As reported by Glass (1983), few couples are prepared for the realities of parenthood and the birth of a first child can be ". . . one of the most significant and stressful life events experienced by individuals." The birth of the first and subsequent children affects the marital relationship, economic status and social status of a couple in very significant ways, some of which may be viewed by the couple as positive or negative. Whatever negative aspects may occur, they are usually overshadowed by the excitement of the baby and the infant's first responses such as the first smile and first sound.

In contrast, the experiences for parents of abnormal babies, particularly when the severity of the disability is apparent at birth, can be devastating. The birth of a child with a severely disabling condition places the parents in a very awkward position. While it is customary in our society to respond positively to the birth of an infant, society views the birth of an infant with a disability negatively. Awareness of society's perception adds stress to an already stressful situation for the parents and may interfere with the marital relationship. In addition the parents may be faced with extra hospital and medical costs and in some cases extensive and extended medical treatment and further bills. Given these stresses and the sudden time frame in which they occur, it is understandable that there are commonalities among parents to the initial impact of the birth of a child who is disabled. Among the most frequently identified responses are shock, denial, and grief.

When the infant's disability is apparent at birth, the initial parent reaction may be overwhelming. The stage of shock is likely to encompass feelings of anxiety, guilt, numbness, confusion, helplessness, anger, and despair. Unfortunately, it is at this time that many parents fail to receive the support they need or, in some cases fail to comprehend the assistance that is available. Some parents avoid family and friends because of their own shame and uncertainty, as well as others' reactions.

The response of some parents to the birth of a child with a disability is to deny that a problem exists. These parents frequently suggest that the apparent delay is just that and as the child develops the deficits will be outgrown. For some, the denial process will involve obtaining additional professional opinions, hoping to find confusion and disagreement among the "experts." Although many parents overcome the denial stage, a conscientious effort must be made to minimize the length of this stage so that the child will receive the necessary treatment as soon as possible.

Parents of newborn children who are disabled experience grief for two reasons. First, there is grief associated with the loss of the expected normal child. Second, the parents need time to adjust to the child actually born to them. In this latter situation, some parents grieve because of their fear that their child will die. Kübler-Ross (1970) has described a grieving process that is frequently used to predict the stages that parents of infants who are disabled will experience. The stages—denial, anger, bargaining, depression, and acceptance—are described in figure 4.1. As indicated in figure 4.1, many parents of children with severe disabilities accept and love their infant. Reaching the stage of acceptance, however, may take a long time. Gath (1977) noted in a study of parents of newborn Down syndrome babies that all the parents experienced grief at the time of birth and that 90 percent still showed signs of grief two years later.

As children with disabilities grow and enter childhood and then adolescence, their parents will continue to be faced with many adjustments. This is particularly so for parents of children with severe disabilities. The realization for some that their child will not achieve sufficient independence to leave home will require an alteration in the normal family life cycle. The nature of the impact relates to expectations, family reorganization, prolonged and intensive care, provision of services, and fear of the future.

In a culture that is very conscious of chronological age, it is understandable that parents of children with severe disabilities are reminded at selected intervals of the child's life that their youngster is less than perfect. These include the expected milestones such as walking at age fourteen months and riding a bike at age five as well as socially imposed norms such as driving a car at age sixteen and eventually leaving home. Many parents indicate that they are at a loss to really know what to expect. For this reason many parents have found that observation of other children with the same disability as that of their child helps them to form reasonable expectations. Joining parent groups also provides an opportunity to share information about development in light of the child's disability.

The presence of a child with severe disabilities also has an impact on the family and its organizational pattern. In our society parents normally formulate certain expectations for their children based on the order in which they are born. The parents' perception of the child changes as the youngster becomes older and assumes more responsibility within and outside the home. The organizational structure of the family with a child with a severe disability, however, is altered to accommodate the child's slower rate of development. In some families, the child with a severe disability is always perceived to be the youngest regardless of the child's age and order of birth.

Parents of children with severe disabilities recognize that many of the tasks associated with infancy, such as feeding, dressing, and diapers, are extended for a longer period of time or may remain indefinitely. The parenting responsibilities associated with infancy are never easy and may be

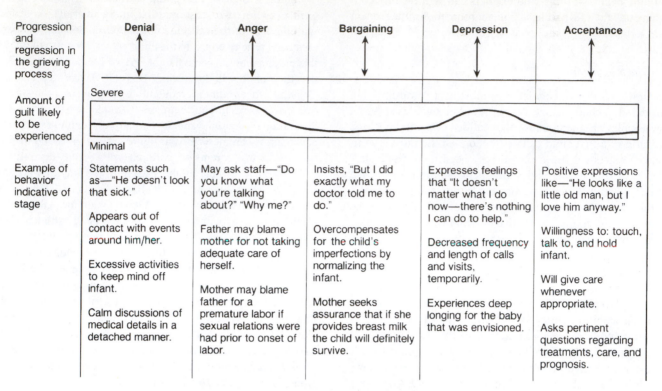

Figure 4.1 Components of the grieving process continuum.

(Source: Opirhory, G. & Peters, G. A. Counseling intervention strategies for families with the less than perfect newborn. *The Personnel and Guidance Journal, 60* (8), 1982, 451–455. Copyright AACD. Reprinted with permission. No further reproduction authorized without further permission of AACD.)

overwhelming when there appears to be no end in sight. Age of the parents, too, becomes a factor as they reach middle age. The prolonged and intensive care needed by some children with severe disabilities requires additional time as well as physical and fiscal responsibility.

The nature of the disability will require the provision of services beyond those normally provided for nondisabled children. In addition to medical costs, children with severe disabilities will require the assistance of other specialists including physical and occupational therapists, speech and language specialists, vocational trainers, and counselors. Parents will need assistance in identifying the services needed and finding appropriate service providers. Obtaining the necessary medical assistance can also be a challenge. Many parents experience frustration when attempting to find medical specialists such as dentists, ophthalmologists, and audiologists who are comfortable in treating a child or adolescent with a severe disability.

Perhaps the major impact facing parents of a child with a severe disability is the fear of the future. This fear response is heightened as the child grows and the parents are faced with concerns about their own health and provisions for their son or daughter after their death. Alternative placements, including group homes and institutions, place additional stress on the parents and the major decisions that confront them. It is not surprising that parents of children with severe disabilities experience greater parent burnout and more isolation than other parents. Divorce rates for parents of children with severe disabilities have been reported to be twice that of the national average.

Although research exists concerning parents of children with severe disabilities, little information is available concerning parents of children with mild disabilities. There is some evidence to suggest that the parent-child relationship for the child with a mild handicap may be more disturbed than that of the youngster with a severe disability. The impact felt by the family may be attributed to several factors including identification, type of disability, cause of the disability, and treatment.

Unlike the child with a severe disability, the child with a mild disability may not be discovered until later in life, normally during the first year of school. This discovery may come as a surprise to parents or it may serve as an affirmation of their own concern about the child's development. Parent response, therefore, may range from anger to relief. One of the advantages of later identification is that the family has formed a close tie to the child and the child has been accepted as a member of the family without the label of disabled.

The type of disability is also an important factor in determining the impact of a child with a mild disability on parents. In general, society tends to be more accepting of visible disabilities such as physical and sensory impairments and less accepting of hidden disabilities such as learning and emotional impairments. The use of labels such as *retarded* are normally difficult to accept and may generate various defense mechanisms. Children with learning disabilities create unique problems for the parents as they struggle to understand the nature of this disability and its implications.

Many parents are concerned with the cause of the disability. This can be a very frustrating search because for several of the major learning disorders, including learning disabilities, mental retardation, and emotional disturbances, the exact or precise cause is usually unknown. Some parents believe that they are the cause of their child's disability. They may go to extremes in their thinking regarding this, associating some event (dropping the child, for example) as the probable cause. Some may believe the cause is due to their own use and misuse of alcohol or stimulants. Parents of children with emotional disturbances may accept major responsibility because of the widespread belief that parents, at least in part, contribute to the development of the child's emotional problems. Some parents have begun to speak out on this issue, arguing that there are few studies available to support this claim.

The impact of raising a child with a mild disability can be lessened for many parents if they know that treatment, including education, is available to assist their offspring. In this respect parent groups have become essential in assisting new parents to interpret professional recommendations, retrieve information, and secure needed services. The impact of raising a child with a mild disability can be minimized if quality services, including education, provided by caring professionals are available.

Given the above, it should not be surprising to note that families with special needs children are more likely to experience characteristics associated with dysfunctional families (Daniels-Mohring and Lambie, 1993). Some of the signs of this include a tendency to be overprotective to the child with special needs; lack of conflict resolution with all family members; an imbalance in the amount of support provided by primary caregivers; and marital relationships that become subordinate to parental roles.

Although the challenges associated with raising a child with a disability are significant, many parents find genuine joy and satisfaction in raising their child. Some parents employ coping strategies to assist them in their relationship with their youngster. For example, some parents learn to accept their child with a disability by altering their expectations. Instead of continually comparing their youngster to selected developmental scales, they begin to accept and appreciate the individual progress made by their child. Parents also learn to cope by seeking solutions to the problems their children are encountering. The emphasis is not on fixing or correcting the child but instead focuses on a healthy concern that the youngster receive the best treatment and education possible. Some parents find it helpful to learn as much as they can about their child's disability and in a sense become an authority regarding the condition. In some instances the interest of the parent has led to formal education and a profession in a related area. Lindemann and Lindemann (1988) suggest that the key to raising a child with a disability is for each member of the family to maintain some personal identity, activities, and interests. If this is done, the final result will be a family in which the presence of the child with a disability, brother or sister, will enrich the lives of all.

There are, of course, some coping patterns that are more negative in their effects on the child. Some parents may choose to overprotect their children in an effort to insulate and isolate the youngster from situations that entail risk and possible failure. Withdrawal is a strategy some parents employ to avoid discussions about their children as well as situations in which the child's presence might lead to questions or comments from others including friends, family, and strangers.

The process of accepting and integrating a child with a disability into the family has been associated with three patterns of adaptation: rejection, acceptance, and adjustment.

Parental rejection of children with disabilities, similar to some of the negative coping patterns identified previously, is usually a temporary stage some parents experience as part of the process of adapting to their child with a disability. Rejection may be due to several factors. Schulz (1982) has summarized the factors as follows:

The parents view the child as a physical and psychological extension of themselves. For these parents, when the child does something good it is viewed as a positive reflection on one or both of the parents. Conversely, if the child does something bad, including those things over which the youngster may not have any control such as experiencing difficulty talking, the parents may feel that this is a negative reflection on them.

Parents are repulsed by the abnormal appearance of the child. Some parents avoid taking their children to public places because they feel uncomfortable with the stares and insensitive questions from people. The danger of this pattern, of course, is that the child, particularly during the formative years, may sense the parents' concern and in a way become more disabled than can be explained by the nature of the organic condition.

Serious behavior problems contribute to parental stress and rejection. Aggressive behavior and other problems can be very difficult for parents to accept and respond to in a mature manner. This difficulty can be magnified many times when the youngster does something inappropriate in a public place. Today there are many sources parents can turn to for assistance in dealing with aggressive and inappropriate behavior.

Parents receive ambiguous information from professionals. Unfortunately, the stresses of raising a child with a disability can be compounded when uncertainty exists about the nature or degree of the child's disabling condition. In these instances, parents, particularly those with children with learning disabilities, fluctuate between being overprotective and rejecting.

There are other reasons some parents reject a child who is disabled. Some parents set unrealistic goals or conversely communicate to the child that the youngster is incapable of accomplishing anything. Fortunately for most parents and the children with disabilities they are raising, rejection, when it does occur, is usually a temporary state that ultimately will be replaced by acceptance and adjustment.

If the parents were well adjusted in their personal lives and marital relations prior to the birth of a child with a disability, it is very likely that they will overcome any initial trauma associated with the birth and become very accepting and loving parents. Although acceptance is a difficult term to define, Robinson and Robinson (1976) suggested that it refers to warm respect ". . . for the child as he is, appreciation of his assets, tolerance for his shortcomings, and active pleasure in relating to him." Acceptance is something that parents of children with and without disabilities strive to incorporate into their roles as parents. Seligman (1979) suggests that teachers can determine acceptance of a child with a disability when the parents:

1. are willing to attend parent-teacher conferences;
2. are able to discuss the child's shortcomings with relative ease;
3. can abandon overprotective or unduly harsh behavioral patterns toward their child;
4. are able to collaborate with the teacher to make realistic short- and long-term plans;
5. become involved in advocacy functions and parent groups, but not at the expense of interaction with the child;
6. pursue their own interests unrelated to the child, again not to the exclusion of the child;
7. can discipline appropriately without undue guilt feelings.

In the process of adaptation it is also important that parents accept themselves as good parents and that they reinforce their own efforts to raise a child with a disability.

In the stage of adjustment, parents of children with disabilities come to realize that their efforts to raise these children will require many of the same skills they employ in dealing with other challenges in their lives. The adjustments may require a refocus of the parents and their emotional responses. A positive sign of adjustment is when the parents realize that others in their lives, including themselves and other children, if any, may need special attention and that the needs of their child are not the only priority. Other positive indicators relate to the parents' efforts to remain socially active. This will require the parents to find or develop support systems they can use for temporary babysitting or child care. Some parents, too, realize that it may be essential to obtain assistance in doing daily household chores. The adjustment, therefore, may involve money as well as time. Fortunately, there is a growing responsiveness in our society to the need for assistance to parents who have children with severe disabling conditions.

The recent emphasis on parent involvement in the education of children with disabilities was communicated clearly with the emphasis on the role of parents in both the Individualized Educational Plan (IEP) and the Individualized Family Service Plan (IFSP) (PL 94-142; PL 99-457; and PL 101-476). This has generated new enthusiasm for the partnership that should exist between home and school in the education of all children, particularly those students with special needs. Parents of children with disabilities have communicated, too, that they want to be partners, that they need assistance, and they want their input to be taken seriously. For future physical educators, this means that additional opportunities to meet and work with parents of children with disabilities should be given top priority. Future educators must also provide information and listen. The expectations of teachers were nicely summarized by one parent who reported, ". . . Let us process our grief over the fact that our children are not perfect. Give us information about our children's disabilities. And give us cautious 'optimism.' Let us know the potential range of limitations their disabilities may present, but let us also know what these special children may also be able to do. Allow us faith and belief in the future. And you professionals, 'just be human'" (Royeen, 1992 p. 66–67).

Sibling Reaction

In recent years additional attention has focused on the reaction and needs of siblings of individuals with disability. Not surprisingly, the reaction of many siblings to their brother or sister is determined to a large extent by the reaction of their parents. Young children, in particular, usually follow the example set by their parents. During the teen years the need to be accepted and liked by others is very important. Teenagers strive to be part of the norm and to be accepted. Having a sibling with a disability is different and may lead to embarrassment if their friends make insensitive remarks. Some young people avoid confrontations by not bringing their friends home and by avoiding family outings to public places.

Guilt, too, is a reaction experienced by many siblings. This is normally associated with their negative feelings toward the sibling who is disabled. Some also experience guilt because they are not disabled.

Fear is also a reaction of many siblings of children with disabilities. Younger siblings may fear that they, too, will become disabled. Older siblings may fear that someday they will become the parent of a child with a disability or that they will be expected to care for their brother or sister after the death of the parents.

Resentment appears to be the most pervasive reaction of siblings. This may be attributed to several factors, including neglect because of the excessive amount of time the parents seem to spend with the disabled sibling. Some siblings resent the amount of time that they are asked to contribute to the care of the child with a disability. Young people, too, may see their sibling with a disability as a drain on the financial resources of the family, which seems to interfere with the family's ability to buy selected items.

Although many siblings have spoken very positively about life with a brother or sister with a disability, studies are mixed on the effects of being raised with a sibling with a disability. One thing does appear clear: Siblings of children who are disabled need information. They need to know about the sibling's disability and how to explain the disability to their friends. Young children need basic answers to questions such as, How did this happen? Will it happen to me? They also need support, encouragement, and reinforcement for their accomplishments. Finally, siblings of children with a disability need to be recognized without continual reference to their disabled sibling. Sensitive teachers can be very helpful in assisting the sibling to make a positive adjustment.

Peer Reaction

In recent years, more students with disabilities are receiving their instructional program in the mainstream of education. When students are properly placed, individuals with and without disabilities benefit from the opportunity to interact. Teachers have learned from experience that a favorable classroom environment requires that students become more sensitive to the needs of their fellow students. Even children with minor differences, such as those who are overweight or wear glasses, find it embarrassing to be called names, such as "fat" or "four-eyes." Obviously, to be labeled a "retard" or "deaf and dumb" can be devastating to a person attempting to secure a place in the educational mainstream. Such examples are not without support, as there is some evidence to suggest that students without disabilities have many misconceptions about their peers with disabilities.

The results of surveys provide clear direction for public schools and teachers. Acceptance of students with disabilities and the concept of integration are not enough. Schools must assist students without disabilities to improve their knowledge of disabling conditions and persons who have various diseases. To do otherwise may create a situation in which initial acceptance may lead to avoidance and rejection if understanding and expectations are not emphasized from the start. Direct contact is of critical importance in improving understanding between groups of people. In addition, planned educational experiences should be undertaken to assist students without disabilities to relate in a positive way to peers with disabilities. Later in this chapter specific suggestions to help the teacher accomplish this goal will be presented.

Teacher Reaction

A positive and accepting teacher attitude toward the student with a disability is essential for creating a favorable learning experience. The manner in which the teacher responds to the special student communicates much to the student and his/her peers. If the teacher appears apprehensive and fearful, it is likely that other students will follow this lead. Teachers, therefore, must analyze carefully their own attitudes toward those who are disabled. Some teachers have recognized that they, like many others, are afraid of the student with special needs. Other common responses include a tendency to underestimate the student's capabilities, to worry unnecessarily about liability, and to be sympathetic and overprotective. Teachers who recognize these feelings are in an excellent position to undertake special projects to improve their understanding. For instance, one can read about the etiology of the student's disability, observe other children with similar disabilities, talk with other teachers who have worked with the student, observe the student in various settings, develop a list of the student's *abilities,* and talk with the parents. Teachers may also find it necessary to enroll in graduate courses or inservice workshops to receive more formal training in the field of adapted physical education. Many of these courses provide opportunities for the teacher to work in a practicum setting with special students under the guidance of an experienced teacher. As teachers become more familiar with the needs of students with disabilities, they will learn the subtle but important distinction between empathy and sympathy; the student needs understanding but not sorrow. Teachers will also learn to become more sensitive; to view the student not as a disabled individual but as an individual who has a disability, with abilities that are far greater in number than his or her disabilities.

A number of investigators (Jansma and Schultz, 1982; Patrick, 1987; Rowe and Stutts, 1987; Tripp, 1988; Stewart, 1988, 1990; Rizzo, 1984; Rizzo and Wright, 1988; and Rizzo and Vispoel, 1991, 1992) have analyzed various factors related to the attitude of physical educators toward teaching students with disabilities. Research findings suggest that the attitude of physical education teachers toward working with those students with disabilities can be improved if coursework and inservice experiences provide information about the nature of various disabilities. In addition, the attitude of teachers can be positively affected if teachers are provided supervised practicum experiences to work directly with students with disabilities. Innovative work by Rizzo and Vispoel (1991; 1992) highlights that the attitude of physical educators varies according to the type of disability. They have noted, for instance, that students with behavior disorders

Figure 4.2 Providing physical education opportunities for children with disabilities has helped teachers recognize the many similarities students with and without disabilities share.

Ways of Making Adjustments

Adjustment to the problems presented by a disabling condition may be made in several recognized ways. The mechanisms employed are not relegated only to those with disabilities; they are used by everyone in seeking satisfactory adjustment. There is, however, a tendency for those with disabilities to resort to the use of certain of these mechanisms more frequently and with greater intensity; as a consequence, they become unacceptable means of adjustment. Some of the mechanisms include:

1. *Sublimation*—the replacement of a desire or impulse that cannot be satisfied with one that can be fulfilled.
2. *Compensation*—an attempt to offset some shortcoming or limitation by developing some special talent or ability.
3. *Identification*—the conscious or unconscious assuming of the attitudes, manners, and so forth, of another admired individual or group.
4. *Projection*—placing the blame on others for one's own shortcomings.
5. *Escape*—an attempt to avoid reality by escaping from it in daydreams or fantasy.
6. *Rationalization*—the substitution of reasons other than the real ones for a certain act.
7. *Repression*—the unconscious inhibition of unpleasant memories.

Sublimation

Most people realize that not all desires and impulses can be satisfied in their original form, perhaps because of social disapproval, personal limitations, or other restrictions; then the original desire or impulse is replaced by another that is

tend to be perceived less positively than individuals with learning disabilities or mental retardation (Rizzo and Vispoel, 1992). This suggests, therefore, that greater emphasis may need to be placed on selected skills (e.g., behavior management) to insure that teachers feel adequately prepared and positive about providing services for all students.

Most important, teachers will come to appreciate the challenge of adapting games and activities so that the student with a disability will benefit from and appreciate the many positive experiences inherent in the physical education class.

There must be continuous interplay among parents, peers, and teachers to create a favorable social environment for the student with a disability. Teachers and parents, in particular, must communicate to ensure that the special student adjusts favorably. Cooperative planning and frequent interaction help parents and teachers maximize the assistance available to the young person with a disability.

Figure 4.3 Encouragement and positive reinforcement are essential in the development of skills.

capable of being fulfilled. In other words, the mechanism of sublimation is used to achieve adjustment. The person with a disability must necessarily make many more such substitutions than the nondisabled. An individual's problem is further complicated if the disability restricts the choice of substitutes.

Compensation

Everyone uses compensation as an adjustment mechanism, either consciously or unconsciously, to build up or maintain self-esteem. Individuals with orthopedic disabilities often develop special talents or abilities to offset their limitations in physical performance. A partially sighted boy, for example, may work very hard to develop a musical talent for playing the piano to compensate for his inability to perform the athletic skills that win esteem from his peers.

Identification

Identification is a frequently employed mechanism, particularly by children and adolescents who like to identify themselves with teachers, adult friends, movie stars, and athletic heroes. The child with a disability is particularly likely to identify with an individual who represents all the things he or she is not and cannot be. The danger in overuse of identification is that the activity and achievements of the one who is the object of the identification will provide the identifier with so much satisfaction that he or she will not attempt to achieve anything independently.

Projection

Projection might be said to be a negative application of the identification mechanism, for here the individual attributes to others activities and attitudes for which he or she is responsible but unwilling to accept responsibility. An example of a normal youngster's projection mechanism is the child, late for class, offering the excuse that his or her mother forgot to set the alarm clock. Projection is essentially a means of adjustment in which others are blamed for one's personal failures. A person unable to make satisfactory progress in mastering locomotion with crutches or prosthesis may lay the blame on the doctors for a poor fit, rather than accepting responsibility for the failure.

Escape

Avoiding difficult situations or problems by escaping into daydreams or fantasy is fairly common in all youngsters, not just those with disabilities; however, the latter are likely to resort to this kind of escape more frequently. A person with a disability—one who is deaf, for example—finding the demands of his or her environment too great and the failure to meet them too frequent is likely to withdraw from social contacts and to escape to a dream world to gain the satisfaction he or she cannot otherwise achieve.

Rationalization

Rationalization is another commonly employed mechanism. When the real reasons for certain behavior cannot be expressed because they are not socially acceptable, other reasons that will be accepted are substituted. The need to substitute a more acceptable explanation for the action usually indicates a self-dissatisfaction with the action and the adjustment. Environmental demands on the individual that exceed his or her physical and mental capabilities often cause the individual to find excuses for his or her limitations. Thus, the person who does not measure up often resorts to rationalization.

Repression

Repression of unpleasantness, of places and people that are feared or disliked, is not a conscious act. It does, however, prompt peculiar behavior, because the individual tries to avoid things, places, and people that call forth an association with the repressed memory. The child with mental and physical disabilities who was ridiculed at the beach may thereafter exhibit great fear of going into the water. He or she will attribute the fear and dislike of the water to something tangible, such as the water being too cold, but the actual reason, an unpleasant experience with those who teased and laughed, will be repressed in the subconscious mind.

People do not usually consciously select a special adjustment mechanism; rather, they are confronted by a situation and attempt to make an adjustment that is satisfying. If they succeed they are likely to use the same mechanism when confronted by a similar situation. If the mechanism does not actually solve the problem, it is, of course, not an acceptable means of adjustment. It may actually become harmful if it is used so frequently that an individual ceases to try to find a more satisfactory mechanism.

Developmental Stages of Adjustment

Bardach (1979) has proposed that there are developmental stages of adjustment experienced by individuals with disabilities. The stages that will be discussed here apply to those who have an acquired rather than a congenital loss. There is little known about the psychological adjustment process of those born with a disability.

The first stage of adjustment for the individual with a disability is denial. As is frequently the case when an individual receives disturbing news, the first reaction is to deny or repress the truth. This is a natural response and one that has therapeutic value in helping the person to avoid being overwhelmed by the tragedy. Over time, as the person engages in more activity, he or she gains self-confidence and comes to accept rather than to deny the truth.

This second stage, acceptance of the disability, may be accompanied by depression. Individuals become depressed when they lose something of value. The permanent movement restrictions, for example, associated with some disabilities are viewed as significant losses. Mourning is also frequently associated with the depression found among people with disabilities in the acceptance stage. Both of these emotional responses are healthy signs, indicating that the person is learning to cope with his or her disability. Another response found in this second stage is self-pity. Bardach explains that this response is associated with the discrepancy among the things the individual wants to do, is able to do, and is allowed to do. Self-pity, like depression and mourning, is a positive sign that the person is beginning to recognize his or her real strengths and limitations contrasted to perceived strengths and limitations.

The rate at which an individual with a disability moves to a full and complete acceptance of his or her condition is dependent upon two factors. The first relates to the extent of the disability. If the disability is such that the person must make extensive changes in life style, including such things as vocational choice and mobility training, adjustment may be prolonged. Closely related to this factor is the personal value that the individual associates with the loss. This second factor is difficult to analyze because of its close association with self-image. For the person who has always considered himself/herself to be totally self-sufficient, paralysis due to a traumatic injury may have a profound effect, delaying the adjustment process.

The Effects of Specific Disabilities

The nature of the limitation or the extent of disability appears to have no significant influence on the adjustment mechanism used. Observations of those with disabilities have revealed no definite personality traits inevitably arising from a particular disability, with the possible exception of cerebral palsy (discussed in chapter 10). However, subjective observations of disability groups have led some authorities to conclude that the problems presented to individuals by a major disability, such as blindness, deafness, or severe mobility impairment, are so similar for each person that certain common behavior tendencies are observable. Undoubtedly, innate personality factors lead to differences in adjustment, even among those with similar disabilities. An individual who is by temperament an active, aggressive person is more likely to seek adjustment through action and to achieve it in a satisfactory way, such as compensation, whereas one who is by temperament quiet and retiring is more likely to seek adjustment in less active ways, such as, perhaps, in daydreaming.

The Role of the Teacher

The environment of the individual with a disability does, as was suggested, play an important role in adjustment. Because any disabling condition reduces the social interaction between the person and his or her environment, the environment cannot make the same contribution that is possible with nondisabled people. Nevertheless, the help and understanding of those in the person's environment make a tremendous difference in the quality of the adjustment. No one develops a socially acceptable personality and becomes well adjusted entirely by personal efforts; individuals must have the help of family, friends, teachers, and classmates.

We are primarily concerned here with the role of teachers in promoting a good environment for the wholesome personality development of the child with a disability. Any educational endeavor to help the child make a more satisfactory adjustment must include the promotion of better understanding among the children with whom the child with a disability comes in daily contact in the classroom and on the playground. These children constitute the greater portion of the child's social environment. If they can be given a fuller understanding of the role that society forces on the

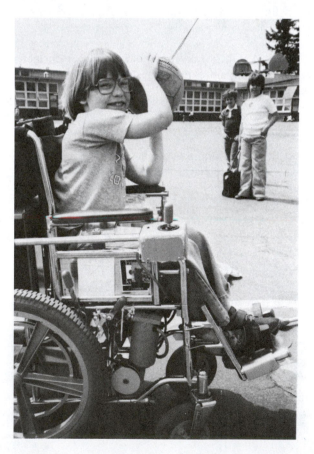

Figure 4.4 Teachers have a responsibility to help students appreciate the ability of their peers.

disabled, if they can acquire respect for a person with a disability as an individual rather than as a deviate, many of the difficulties imposed by the disability can be alleviated.

In developing a favorable climate in the classroom for the acceptance of students with disabilities, the teacher may discuss with the students the reasons for liking and disliking certain people. The importance that is sometimes attached to attractive physical appearance may be pointed out and contrasted with more meaningful personal attributes. The teacher might emphasize that performing to the best of one's ability is just as admirable and worthy of respect as being the most outstanding performer. Attention should be directed toward the concept that one does not have to excel in popular spectator sports such as football and basketball; success, according to one's ability, in an adapted game of beep baseball is of no less significance than success in the more popular games. Specific activities that teachers can undertake to help students increase their sensitivity to their the peers are presented in the following paragraphs.

Invite People with Disabilities to Speak to Students

All too frequently there is a tendency to generate good ideas and to develop plans of action without first involving those people who are affected by the decisions. People with disabilities have much to offer in any discussion about the nature, severity, or effects of various impairments. Some people with disabilities feel very comfortable addressing groups and explaining such interesting information as the process blind people use to prepare a meal or to walk down a sidewalk. As one would expect, not all people with disabilities enjoy addressing large or even small groups. For this reason and because of the candidness of students' questions, the selection of speakers should be done carefully. Most professional advisory groups, such as the United Cerebral Palsy Association and the local Association for Retarded Citizens, have lists of speakers who are qualified to address student groups and are interested in doing so.

Interview People with Disabilities

The interview is an activity suitable for older, more mature students. The specific assignment is to locate a person with a disability and then to ask a series of questions relative to the effects of the individual's disability on performance of daily living activities. The questions should be general, with the primary goal being to encourage interaction of people with and without disabilities. Most students who undertake this exercise find varied responses by people with disabilities to the interview process—some are enthusiastic, some agree reluctantly, and some firmly reply no.

Obtain Films and Books That Provide Information about People with Disabilities

Today many excellent resources are available at reasonable cost. For example, the humorous film *What Do You Do When You See A Blind Person?* may be obtained free or for a nominal charge from the State Commission for the Blind. Likewise, a *School Alert Kit,* which presents an enlightened discussion of epilepsy, may be obtained free by contacting the local chapter of the Epilepsy League of America. A partial list of books, films, and agencies of and for those with disabilities is found in Appendix II.

Obtain Appliances, Assistive Devices, and Equipment That Assist Persons with Disabilities to Function in Society

Opportunities for young people to explore the function and operation of wheelchairs, for instance, can prove to be a very interesting experience. With the help of individual Braille alphabet cards, supplied by the American Foundation for the Blind, students can be given basic lessons in reading and writing Braille. Older youngsters can use these cards to create and decipher jokes written in Braille. Young children can use their pencil erasers to form Braille impressions on sheets of aluminum foil and then try to decipher each other's messages. Similar valuable and enjoyable experiences can be created to illustrate the use of other devices such as hearing aids, canes, and walkers.

Simulate Disabling Conditions

Individuals of all ages are intrigued with opportunities to experience what it might be like to be disabled. Although such activities never fully simulate a disability, they do provide additional understanding and serve as the basis for some quality discussions. A few simulation exercises that have successfully been used include:

1. Permitting students to serve as guides for their blindfolded classmates. For a demonstration of the correct procedure for serving as the sighted guide the students should observe the film *What Do You Do When You See a Blind Person?,* which may be obtained from the State Commission for the Blind. Then, the students should attempt specific tasks while blindfolded, such as throwing a ball at a sound and identifying different objects by touch, and perform movement activities, such as hitting a ball and swinging a golf club. Finally, students should take turns assisting each other to perform the activities while simulating blindness.

2. Utilizing wheelchairs borrowed from hospitals and community agencies, permit students the experience of sitting in and operating a wheelchair. As with the

simulation of visual impairments, encourage the participants to perform routine physical activities, such as shooting a basketball or serving a volleyball. Students should also be asked to dress and undress for activity and to use the washroom. Many young people find that this experience helps them become more appreciative of the skill and ease with which wheelchair users can move. Novice wheelchair users also quickly become aware of the frustrations that can be generated by the inaccessible architectural features found in many public buildings.

3. Students can also be asked to perform various tasks utilizing only one arm or leg. Assistive devices such as canes, walkers, and braces can be borrowed to allow opportunities to simulate disorders, such as amputations and cerebral palsy. Using a crutch instead of a foot to kick a ball provides the student with a different perspective concerning the ability of a peer. Swinging a bat with only one arm helps the nondisabled student appreciate the special skill and strength a student with an amputated arm must develop to participate in a game of softball. Examples such as these in which students participate in a game or sport while simulating the loss of an arm or leg contribute to an awareness of the unique talents that individuals with disabilities develop.

Space does not permit discussion of other simulated experiences that can be undertaken. Those identified, however, do serve as examples that can be expanded or changed to fit the needs of various student groups.

Essential to the entire process of simulation is the opportunity to hold discussions after the experiments. Questions that may be asked include, "How did it feel to be blindfolded?" "Was your guide helpful?" "Did people stare at you in your wheelchair?" "Were buildings difficult to enter?" Discussions about such questions are a must to help clarify young people's feelings and concerns. Not all of the answers are available, but the process should serve to make students more empathetic toward people with disabilities and should thus assist in the integration of children with disabilities into the mainstream of physical education. With empathy comes understanding and with understanding the process of successful mainstreaming begins.

Reverse Mainstreaming

A process that is very helpful to many teachers who are preparing for the first time to introduce children with disabilities into a regular education class is to identify a small number of select nondisabled students to serve as aides in a special physical education class. This approach, which is frequently referred to as reverse or counter mainstreaming,

has many advantages. It allows students with disabilities the opportunity to benefit from peer interaction in a setting with which they are familiar as well as providing them with an opportunity to enhance their skill level before integrating into the regular class. Nondisabled students benefit from this arrangement, as it affords them the experience of interacting in an environment that is different from that to which they are accustomed. This new sensitivity will assist them to better comprehend the feelings students with disabilities have as they enter the regular physical education class. Many teachers have found reverse mainstreaming helpful because it allows them to observe children with and without disabilities interact. Discussion sessions should be held with both groups of students to respond to questions and concerns they may have. These sessions generate information that will assist the teacher to lay the foundation for successful integration of students with disabilities into the physical education mainstream.

Reverse mainstreaming, with its emphasis on direct contact between children with and without disabilities, is an effective mechanism to facilitate attitudinal change. It should be stressed, however, that these experiences are most beneficial with young children who are less likely to have developed fixed attitudinal responses to those who deviate from the norm. Initial efforts should also be structured and directed toward exposing students to individuals with mild and moderate disabilities before moving to those who are severely mentally retarded and emotionally disturbed.

The activities that have been described will do much to eliminate the wall of isolation with which many youngsters with disabilities have had to contend. Integrating those with disabilities may at first require additional planning time. Dividends, however, will be evident as youth with and without disabilities grow in their awareness and appreciation of individual differences. Mainstreaming programs offer hope that more children will learn to recognize others' abilities rather than their disabilities.

In addition to helping others understand and accept people with disabilities, an educational program should be directed toward helping these youngsters develop skills and abilities to offset their shortcomings, and to find satisfactory substitutes for the desires they cannot fulfill and the activities they cannot perform. In these ways those with disabilities may overcome the fear, shame, and social inadequacies that cause them to seek refuge in escape, projection, and other unacceptable behavior. The special physical education program can make significant contributions to the total educational program by helping those with disabilities to develop better motor skills, improve body mechanics, increase physical fitness, and enhance body image. The special contributions of various kinds of physical education activities will be presented in the chapters dealing with the specific types of disabilities.

Summary

How an individual reacts to a disability has much to do with the person's long-term adjustment. Psychological problems, when they do occur, have their origin in both the individual's reaction to the disabling condition and the response of others to it.

There are many factors that affect the individual's adjustment. These include the individual's intelligence, temperament, degree of disability, and physical appearance. Individuals with disabilities, similar to the nondisabled, use various mechanisms to adjust to their disability. These mechanisms, which include sublimation, compensation, identification, projection, escape, rationalization, and repression, are acceptable unless the individual resorts to these mechanisms too frequently and too intensely. Unfortunately some individuals with disabilities rely on these mechanisms more than they should.

The reactions of others have much to do with the ability of an individual with a disability to develop normally and lead a happy life. Key individuals in this respect include parents, siblings, peers, and teachers. Raising a child with a disability can be a very demanding task. For many parents integrating and accepting a child with a disability will take time. Some parents experience a grieving phase before they accept and make the necessary adjustments in their lives to fully integrate the child into the family unit.

Siblings and peers, too, play an important role in the life of an individual with a disability. A conscientious effort must be made to insure that friends and siblings understand the child's disability, including areas of limitations and strengths. The goal is to improve their understanding and sensitivity toward the needs of those with a disability. Siblings and peers will normally follow the lead of other adults, primarily parents and teachers, as they improve their understanding and acceptance of a child with a disability.

There are many techniques that teachers can employ to help young people become more empathetic and sensitive to the needs of their disabled peers. These include inviting people with disabilities to class, interviewing individuals with disabilities, and simulating disabling conditions. Some children will benefit, too, from the opportunity to work with students in special classes. This approach, frequently referred to as reverse mainstreaming, creates opportunities for nondisabled students to help and be helped as they learn and work with their disabled peers.

The underlying theme throughout this chapter is that individuals with disabilities are more similar than dissimilar to nondisabled people. While they may have some special adjustment problems, these difficulties can be minimized in an environment that is supportive and appreciative of individual needs and rights.

Selected Readings

Auxter, D., & Pyfer, J. (1985). *Adapted physical education and recreation.* St. Louis: Times Mirror/Mosby.

Bardach, J.L. (1979). Psychological adjustment of handicapped individuals and their families. *Awareness Papers.* Washington, DC: White House Conference on the Handicapped.

Bolton, B. (1976). *Psychology of deafness for rehabilitation counselors.* Baltimore: University Park Press.

Cruickshank, W.M. (Ed.). (1980). *Psychology of exceptional children and youth* (4th ed.). Englewood Cliffs, NJ: Prentice-Hall, Inc.

Daniels-Mohring, D., & Lambie, R. (1993). Dysfunctional families of the student with special needs. *Focus on Exceptional Children, 25*(5), 65–67.

DeLoach, C., & Greer, B.G. (1981). *Adjustment to severe physical disability: A metamorphosis.* New York: McGraw-Hill Book Co.

Faerstein, L.M. (1981). Stress and coping in families of learning disabled children: A literature review. *Journal of Learning Disabilities, 14*(7), 420–423.

Dunn, J.M., & Boarman, A.M. (1979). A need: Better understanding of people with special needs. *Campfire Leadership*, Winter 6–9.

Featherstone, H. (1980). *A difference in the family.* New York: Penguin Books.

Garrison, K.G., & Magoon, R.A. (1972). *Psychology: An interpretation of psychology and educational practices.* Columbus, OH: Charles E. Merrill Publishing Co.

Gath, A. (1977). The impact of an abnormal child upon the parents. *American Journal of Psychiatry, 130,* 405–410.

Glass, J. (1983). Pre-birth attitudes and adjustment to parenthood: When 'preparing for the worst' helps. *Family Relations, 32*(3) 377–386.

Hardman, M.L., Drew, C.J., & Egan, M.W. (1984). *Human exceptionality.* Boston: Allyn and Bacon, Inc.

Jansma, P., & Schultz, B. (1982). Validation and use of a mainstreaming attitude inventory with physical educators. *American Corrective Therapy Journal, 36,* 150–158.

Kirtley, D.D. (1975). *The psychology of blindness.* Chicago: Nelson-Hall Publishers.

Kübler-Ross, E. (1970). *On death and dying.* New York: MacMillan.

Lindemann, J.D., & Lindemann, S.J. (1988). *Growing up proud: A parent's guide to the psychological care of children with disabilities.* New York: Warner Books Inc.

Lindgren, H. (1969). *Psychology of personal development.* New York: American Book Co.

Marion, R.L. (1981). *Educators, parents and exceptional children.* Rockville, MD: Aspen Systems Corp.

Miller, A.G., & Sullivan, J.V. (1982). *Teaching physical activities to impaired youth.* New York: John Wiley and Sons, Inc.

Patrick, G. (1987). Improving attitudes toward disabled persons. *Adapted Physical Activity Quarterly, 4,* 316–325.

Rizzo, T.L. (1984). Attitudes of physical educators toward teaching handicapped pupils. *Adapted Physical Activity Quarterly, 1,* 263–274.

Rizzo, T.L., & Wright, R.G. (1988). Selected attributes related to physical educators' attitudes toward teaching students with handicaps. *Mental Retardation, 26,* 307–309.

Rizzo, T.L., & Vispoel, W.P. (1991). Physical educators' attributes and attitudes toward teaching students with handicaps. *Adapted Physical Activity Quarterly, 8,* 4–11.

Rizzo, T.L., & Vispoel, W.P. (1992). Changing attitudes about teaching students with handicaps. *Adapted Physical Activity Quarterly, 9,* 54–63.

Robinson, N.M., & Robinson, H.B. (1976). *The mentally retarded child.* New York: McGraw-Hill, Inc.

Ross, A.O. (1964). *The exceptional child in the family.* New York: Grune and Stratton.

Rowe, J., & Stutts, R.M. (1987). Effects of practica type, experience and gender on attitudes of undergraduate physical education majors toward disabled persons. *Adapted Physical Activity Quarterly, 4,* 268–277.

Royeen, C.B. (1992). A glimpse of the human experience: Parenting infants and toddlers who are disabled. *Infants and Young Children, 5*(2), 65–67.

Schulz, J.B. (1982). A parent views parent participation. *Exceptional Education Quarterly, 3*(2), 17–24.

Seligman, M. (1979). *Strategies for helping parents of exceptional children.* New York: The Free Press.

Seligman, M. (1983). Siblings of handicapped persons. In M. Seligman (Ed.), *The family with a handicapped child.* New York: Grune and Stratton.

Sherrick, C.E., Swets, J.A., & Elliott, L.L. (1974). *Psychology and the handicapped child.* Washington, DC: U.S. Dept. of Health, Education, and Welfare.

Shontz, F.C. (1980). Theories about the adjustment to having a disability. In W.M. Cruickshank (Ed.), *Psychology of exceptional children and youth* (4th ed.). Englewood Cliffs, N.J.: Prentice-Hall, Inc.

Stewart, C.G., (1988). Modification of student attitudes toward disabled peers. *Adapted Physical Activity Quarterly, 5,* 44–48.

Stewart, C.G. (1990). Effects of practica type in preservice adapted physical education curriculum on attitudes toward disabled populations. *Journal of Teaching in Physical Education, 10,* 76–83.

Tew, B.J., Payne, H., & Lawrence, K.M. (1974). Must a family with a handicapped child be a handicapped family? *Developmental Medicine and Child Neurology, 16,* 95–98.

Tripp, A. (1988). Comparison of attitudes of regular and adapted physical educators toward disabled individuals. *Perceptual and Motor Skills, 66,* 425–426.

Turnbull, A.P., & Brotherson, J.J. (1984). *Assisting parents in future planning.* Papers presented at the CEC 62d Annual Conference, Washington, DC.

Zuk, G.H. (1962). The cultural dilemma and spiritual crisis of the family with a handicapped child. *Exceptional Children, 28*(8), 405–408.

Enhancing Activities

1. Develop a list of indicators that might suggest whether a child has accepted his or her disability. A similar list could be developed for parents of the child. Include input from individuals with disabilities and parents in developing the lists.

2. Review with an individual with disabilities the defense mechanisms described in the chapter. Obtain his or her views concerning the psychological adjustments imposed by a disability.

3. Develop a list of various support organizations and groups within the community that offer services to individuals with disabilities and/or their families. Identify the services provided.

4. Conduct an interview with the parents of a person with a disability. Review with them figure 4.1 and ask whether they agree or disagree with the grieving process as described. Try to obtain the input of parents of children with various types of disabilities and levels of severity.

5. Interview students on the college campus to obtain their views of individuals with disabilities. Does their response vary as to the type of disability, such as visual impairment contrasted to orthopedic impairment? If you know them well ask how they would respond if they were to be the parent of a child with a disability.

6. Review the list of activities identified in the chapter to help students increase their sensitivity toward those with disabilities. Think of other suggestions that could be added to the list.

Managing
the Learning
Environment

The section is designed to help the reader to:

1   Organize and provide special physical education services that emphasize desirable instructional and placement practices consistent with federal regulations.

2   Utilize effective and contemporary instructional methods in the delivery of appropriate physical education services to students with disabilities.

3   Analyze screening instruments and evaluation tools to determine their appropriateness for use with special populations.

4   Recognize the various assistive devices used by individuals with disabilities and the effect these devices may have on the instructional program.

The chapters in this section are concerned with the practical aspects of providing a good physical education program for students with disabilities. Ideas are suggested for effective planning and operation of the program and for instructional and evaluative procedures that foster motor learning.

CHAPTER

5

Organization and Administration of Special Physical Education

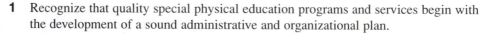

CHAPTER OBJECTIVES

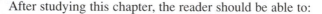

After studying this chapter, the reader should be able to:

1 Recognize that quality special physical education programs and services begin with the development of a sound administrative and organizational plan.

2 Comprehend the importance of federal, state, and local policy in influencing the depth and breadth of special education services to be provided.

3 Learn the procedures one can employ to identify the variety of students eligible to receive special physical education services.

4 Analyze the elements used in developing a special physical education plan for a school district and the relationship of the plan to the quality and quantity of services provided.

5 List the participants required by federal law to participate in the Individualized Education Program developed for each child with a disability and the content required in each program.

6 Appreciate the importance of having special physical education students receive appropriate instruction by qualified personnel.

7 Identify the various placement options that should be available to insure that students with disabilities receive physical education instruction in an educational environment conducive to their needs.

8 Recognize the important role that allied health personnel, parents, and school administrators play in determining the extent to which physical and motor fitness programs will be provided for students with special needs.

Organizing and administering a special physical education program requires a concerted effort to develop policies and procedures that fulfill the needs of students within the guidelines of federal and state statutes. Unlike practices of the past, when individuals were assigned to special classes because it seemed right, teachers and administrators are now required to carefully document all educational decisions relating to the student with a disability. This has created a new era in public education, one in which parents, teachers, administrators, and allied health professionals work together to plan appropriate physical and motor fitness programs for students with disabilities. Although it is generally true that cooperative decisions require more planning time, once the final educational program is developed, the chances of its being a successful and beneficial experience are greatly enhanced.

Providing for the physical education needs of students with disabilities requires that a specific individual be assigned the responsibility of serving as a special physical education coordinator. Large school systems may assign a full-time person to the position; smaller schools may find this assignment only requires a part-time appointment. Some districts may choose to assign this responsibility to the director of special education. It is of critical importance, however, that someone with an interest and preferably additional training in the field of physical education for individuals with disabilities be assigned the responsibility of coordinating the special physical education program.

The 1990s are an exciting transition time in the history of special physical education. Both the quantity and the quality of services available have expanded in a significant fashion. The challenges have resulted in a rethinking of some past administrative positions. Although change is good, planned change is better. Determining the need for change and planning ways to make changes where necessary are the subject of this chapter.

Preliminary Considerations

An important design feature in any organizational effort is a review of the present situation prior to initiating change. This simply means that an analysis should be made of the physical education experiences now available to the special student. The results may reveal several things: that the program offerings are limited; that they are good for some, but not all, disability populations; or that no program is available. Other information may be needed to provide reasons for the lack of opportunities or limited opportunities now available. For example, a survey of equipment and facilities may indicate inadequacies that limit the scope of the program. Regardless of the information obtained, the special physical education coordinator, by analyzing present conditions and practices, establishes a baseline from which future program growth can be compared.

Review State and Local Policies

A careful investigation should be undertaken of state and local codes concerning the provisions of physical education. These can be obtained by contacting the State Department of Education and local school district headquarters. This information will be useful in developing a complete and accurate statement regarding physical education requirements. Information of this nature, as will be discussed later, is helpful in assisting key school administrators and school board members to recognize the discrepancies that sometimes exists between the program available to the nondisabled and that available to students with disabilities. Items to be reviewed include the number of class meetings and instructional minutes required per week, years of required instruction, and necessary qualifications of the teacher.

Review Federal Policies

The Education for All Handicapped Children Act of 1975, P.L. 94-142, as amended by P.L. 99-457 and P.L. 101-476 and the Rehabilitation Act of 1973, P.L. 93-112, provide clear directives to school administrators concerning physical education experiences for students with disabilities. For example, the Federal Rules and Regulations for P.L. 101-476 establishes guidelines for the provision of physical education and emphasizes the importance of placement in the least restrictive environment. Concepts such as full inclusion, the regular education initiative, and programming for preschool students, P.L. 99-457, emphasize clearly the responsibility to provide appropriate services for infants and toddlers with disabilities. A thorough understanding of the federal requirements will enable the special physical education advocate to communicate objectively and factually with administrators and other interested citizens.

Interact with Administrators and Consumers

A second major step in the development of a special physical education plan is to hold a series of preliminary discussions with school administrators, parents, and consumer groups. The purpose of these meetings is to share information concerning the status of the present physical education program for infants, toddlers, and students with disabilities and to indicate a willingness to review and, where necessary, revise, improve, and expand the present offerings. It is not essential at this point to have a detailed plan of action developed. Instead, the discussion should focus on obtaining input and support from key groups. Administrative approval, for instance, is essential if the plan that is eventually developed is to be accepted. Assistance can also be provided by administrators who have dealt with similar efforts to evaluate and improve educational programs. Of primary importance is the enlightenment of school administrators regarding present practices and the extent to which the physical education program for those with disabilities complies with state and federal requirements.

Because every school and school district is administered differently, it is difficult to describe in detail the role of central administrators and their relationship to special physical education. Normally, however, efforts should be made to talk with the directors of physical education and special education and the curriculum coordinator. These individuals are the ones most likely to be charged with the responsibility of supervising the motor and physical fitness needs of students with disabilities. Once understanding is developed among this small number, administrative support will eventually spread to include building principals, superintendents, and, ultimately, the school board. Failure to obtain the support of key administrators may require direct interaction with the district's Superintendent of Public Instruction and, if necessary, the chair or president of the Board. Input from parents, as discussed in the next paragraph, can also be helpful in obtaining administrative support.

Early efforts also should be made to interact with parents and representatives of advocacy groups to obtain their assistance in organizational efforts to develop a special physical education plan. Parents, for instance, can be asked to react to and evaluate the present program and to recommend potential changes. Obtaining input from parents can be a sensitive undertaking because their wishes may be in conflict with present school practice. Parents also may not have sufficient background information concerning the school's rationale for the present program. For these reasons it is best to have an administrator, such as a director of physical education or a principal familiar with physical education, coordinate the parent meeting. Using a school administrator also avoids placing teachers in a position where they might be perceived as encouraging parents to challenge school policy. Fortunately, many administrators have realized recently that involving parents in early discussions concerning program changes not only encourages valuable input but also prevents the embarrassing situation that could result from the development of a program with weaknesses that could have been avoided if the perceptions of the parents of students with special needs had been solicited.

The meeting with parents should be structured to provide information about the program presently offered and some preliminary ideas about future directions. Parents should be encouraged to ask questions and to offer feedback and suggestions. The intent of the meeting is to enlist parent support and cooperation. Some parents may be hesitant to express themselves or may feel negatively toward the school system. Parents should be encouraged to ask questions and offer suggestions, even if the comments are not favorable.

Obtaining the advice of other consumers, such as advocacy groups for and of those with disabilities, is also a necessity. Not only can members of these groups be called upon to react to present and future plans, but they also can offer technical assistance with such problems as facility accessibility, which can be very helpful to school personnel. Obviously the views *of* people with disabilities are essential in any program designed *for* those with disabilities. A special physical education advisory group composed of administrators, parents, and individuals with disabilities as well as teachers provides a format for obtaining continuous input as the school's special physical education plan progresses.

Cooperate with Allied Health Personnel

Quality instruction in physical education for students with disabilities will occur only if the best available resources are used wisely. This concept is true whether one is talking about equipment, facilities, or personnel. It is this latter area that is of greatest concern in this section. Fortunately, physical educators recognize today that other professionals share their concern about the motor and physical fitness needs of the special students. Physicians and nurses, for instance, have an interest in the student's total health, including the individual's motor development. Specialized medical personnel such as neurologists study motor responses as a guide to evaluating the neurological system. Physical and occupational therapists work to enhance motor performance in a variety of ways, including posture exercises, fine and gross motor development, and specialized techniques designed to enhance movement capabilities. It is essential that physical educators work with these professionals to provide coordinated psychomotor programming for the student with special needs.

Working with Physicians

The special physical education program coordinator should meet with the local medical society prior to or immediately after initiating the special physical education program. The purpose of this meeting would be to share with physicians the goals of the special program and its relationship to federal and state statutes. Efforts should also be made to enlist the support of the medical groups and to emphasize the necessity of coordinated and cooperative efforts. Special care should be taken to speak about the new emphasis on individualized and personalized instruction in physical education. This approach should help to dispel any misconceptions the medical doctor may have about physical education. It is important to remember that some physicians' concepts of physical education may be limited to their own experiences as students. If those experiences consisted primarily of forced mass calisthenics, it is understandable that these doctors may be less than enthusiastic about permitting a student with a heart disorder, for example, to participate in physical education.

A point that must be emphasized with the medical community is that students with disabilities *will* participate in physical education classes. If necessary, specially designed classes will be developed to respond to individual needs. Physicians should be encouraged, therefore, to work with the school to identify an appropriate placement. The past practice of excusing students for a variety of medical reasons must be avoided. The recent emphasis, too, on the school's responsibility in the education of preschool children with disabilities (P.L. 99-457) provides additional reasons for close cooperation and articulation between school personnel and allied health personnel.

Every effort must be made to ensure that the student with special needs is not denied equal access to a full and appropriate education. For the coordinator of special physical education this means that a concerted effort must be undertaken to emphasize the school's commitment to quality physical education programs for the special student consistent with the medical information available. To achieve this end, most school systems ask the family physician to complete a medical referral form. An example form is presented in figure 5.1.

OFFICE OF THE LOS ANGELES COUNTY
SUPERINTENDENT OF SCHOOLS

PHYSICAL EDUCATION MEDICAL REFERRAL

Dear Physician:

All pupils enrolled in the public schools in the State of California are entitled to a physical education program designed to meet their specific needs. Many pupils enrolled in programs in Los Angeles County may have physical, mental, emotional or language related conditions which may prevent them from participating safely, successfully, or with personal satisfaction in a regular physical education class. It is the desire of the Office of the Los Angeles County Superintendent of School to provide a specialized physical education program for these children. To identify the specific needs of each pupil, the physician, parent, and school personnel must work cooperatively. Will you please take a few moments of your time to provide us with the information listed below so that we can plan an appropriate program for this child.

pupil's name	birth date	height	weight

parent's name	address	telephone

DIAGNOSIS

(Please indicate the type and extent of disability in the appropriate category and any recommendations pertaining to each)

Neurological Disorder (seizures, medication, hyperactivity, coordination problems, etc.)

Heart and Lung Condition

Orthopedic Condition (Indicate area and extent of disability)

Language Problems

Hearing Problems

Vision Problems

Emotional Problems

Other Problems

REMARKS _____

The period of disability shall be _____ weeks, _____ months _____ school year.

M.D.

Date	Physician's Signature	Physician's Name Typed

RETURN FORM TO:

Figure 5.1 Sample medical referral form.

(Courtesy of the Office of the Los Angeles County Superintendent of Schools, Division of Special Education.)

ADAPTED PHYSICAL EDUCATION ACTIVITY GUIDE

Pupil _____ Date _____

School _____ Teacher _____

Adapted Physical Education

I. MOVEMENTS	OMIT	MILD*	MODERATE**	UNLIMITED	REMARKS
Bending					
Climbing					
Hanging					
Jumping					
Kicking					
Lifting					
Pulling					
Pushing					
Running					
Stretching					
Throwing					
Twisting					

II. EXERCISE	OMIT	MILD*	MODERATE**	UNLIMITED	REMARKS
Abdominal					
Breathing					
Head					
Neck					
Trunk					

	R	L	R	L	R	L	R	L
Arm								
Foot								
Knee								
Leg								

III. ACTIVITIES	YES	NO	REMARKS
Running games			
Games—standing but no running or jumping			
Sitting games			

*Very little activity
**Half as much as the unlimited program

COMMITTEE RECOMMENDATIONS

Recommended until _____ 19_____

Comments:

Figure 5.1—*Continued*

The School Nurse

Many school systems, though not all, employ school nurses. The availability of such a person is helpful to the coordinator of special physical education in making interpretations of the medical information provided by the physician. A school nurse is also valuable in developing parental understanding of the importance of exercise and activity in the rehabilitative process for students with temporary disabilities. Maintaining medical records and communicating with physicians are other helpful services that the school nurse can provide.

Physical and Occupational Therapists

Physical educators have long recognized the importance of therapists in the habilitation and rehabilitation of those with disabilities. The role of physical and occupational therapists, in particular, as school-related service providers has been strengthened through Public Law 94-142, as amended in Public Law 101-476. Physical educators are in an excellent advocacy position to support the provision of therapy services for students who can benefit from these programs. The role of therapy is to supplement and not to supplant the special physical education program.

Conversely, physical educators should emphasize their educational role, leaving therapeutic programming to therapists. Although it is apparent that programs focusing on the psychomotor domain will have obvious overlaps, a definite line must be drawn between therapy and physical education. Therapy is defined as the treatment of disease and disorder, and therapeutic exercises are prescribed physical activities for specific corrective purposes, such as restoring normal alignment or function. Physical education, on the other hand, refers to the learning of sport and physical recreational skills and their concomitant learnings.

Identifying Students for Special Physical Education

Organizing and administering a special physical education program requires that students with special motor and physical fitness needs be identified. In some instances, it will be obvious that a student needs a special program. For others, however, a motor deficiency may not be apparent without the use of a formal survey of the student's motor and physical fitness capabilities. To accomplish the identification of students for whom a special physical education program is desirable, the following steps can be employed.

Review the Special Education Roster

Every student who has been identified as a qualified student with a disability under the provisions of Public Law 101-476 must be provided with a physical education program. This means, therefore, that the special education records of students who have been certified as having a disability under one of the following categories should be reviewed carefully to assess the students' needs for special activity programs: mental retardation, serious emotional disturbance, deafness, blindness, hardness of hearing, multidisabled, orthopedic impairment, specific learning disability, speech impairment, visual disability, other health impairments, autism, and traumatic brain injury. A word of caution: It is important to remember that because a student is recognized as an individual with a disability does not necessarily mean the student needs a special physical education program. Many students with speech impairments, for instance, will find the physical education program, without modification, suitable for their needs.

Screen Students for Special Physical Education Needs

The author recently assisted a school system in screening all of its third, seventh, and ninth graders, as well as students who had previously been identified as needing special services. This process involved selecting a screening instrument, establishing a date and time, "inservicing" teachers and volunteers to administer the various items, and specifying the location of test stations within the gymnasium. Utilizing the short form of the Bruininks-Oseretsky Test of Motor Proficiency, more than three-hundred students were assessed in approximately six hours.

One of the most significant findings from this survey was that approximately one-third of the thirty-nine P.L. 101-476 students screened scored at a level that indicated that they probably did not need a special program. These students scored above the third stanine on the Bruininks-Oseretsky Test of Motor Proficiency and did not display social or emotional problems that would interfere with their successful integration into regular physical education with modification. Of significance, too, is the finding that approximately 10 percent of the nondisabled students scored at a level that suggested that they could benefit from a program with specialized objectives. This example underlines the importance of recognizing that within every school system there are students who, although technically not qualified as having a disability, need and can benefit from a special physical education program. Examples of students found in this group include those who are obese, awkward, or uncoordinated. These individuals frequently find themselves unable to keep up with other students or execute well the tasks expected of them. For this reason, it is important that a school employ an annual screening program to identify students suspected of having motor proficiency problems. Identification of those suspected of having movement difficulties should be confirmed, with permission of parents, through more elaborate assessment procedures.

The programs and services offered these students should be similar to those offered students whose disability qualifies them under P.L. 101-476. While this normally will require additional costs, the amount will be minimal in relation to the benefits to the affected students. The appreciation expressed by parents will go a long way in helping the school board and administrators justify the necessary expenditure. Additional information on evaluation procedures, including the difference between screening and assessment, may be found in chapter 7.

Serve Students with Temporary Disabilities

Occasionally students will suffer an injury or illness that may appear to preclude their continued participation in the physical education class. The student will usually bring a note from home or the family physician requesting excuse from class until some later date. In such cases it is important that the physical educator ascertain, to the greatest extent possible, through communication with the home and physician the precise number of days the student will be absent. If the response is sixty consecutive calendar days or more, then the student should be treated as a student with a disability in accordance with the requirements of Public Law 101-476. This practice is in agreement with the requirement that a student who will be excused for sixty calendar days from a school activity because of illness or injury not be denied his constitutional right to a free and appropriate public education.

Regardless of whether the absence is permanent, more than sixty calendar days, or temporary, every effort should be made to identify an alternative educational experience for the individual. For some students this will mean continued participation in the regular class, with restrictions where necessary. In some cases, such as when a child has a broken extremity, it may be necessary to have the student transfer temporarily to an alternate class. If transferring is not possible, other options, such as developing a before-school program, may be necessary. Individual student contracts also may be drawn up that clearly specify expected student outcome in a self-directed program. Some school personnel have responded to the needs of the student with a temporary disability by assigning the individual a project that relates to the disability, such as selected readings concerning injuries to the knee.

It becomes apparent that physical education is such a broad area, involving attitude formation, skill development, and knowledge acquisition, that to excuse students from this important aspect of the educational process is a disservice to them. Many school districts have found it necessary to review and, where necessary, revise their policies regarding medical excuses from physical education classes. In many instances allied health professionals, including physicians, have been very helpful in developing a policy that is sensitive to the educational and medical needs of students.

Writing the Special Physical Education Plan

Following the meetings and discussions held with administrators, parents, medical representatives, and advocates for people with disabilities, an effort should be made to analyze the information gathered and to develop a written plan that addresses the specific needs of the school system. An organizational undertaking of this nature is extremely important because it provides a course of action by which the future growth and development of the program can be evaluated. The author of this plan should work in close concert with the special physical education advisory committee to ensure that the final document meets with approval. Some of the content areas that should be included in the plan are discussed here.

Philosophical Statement on the School's Commitment to Individuals with Disabilities

This statement should be a short, succinct observation that the school system is committed to the concept of quality education for *all* students. Such an observation would normally be provided in all of the school system's publications or instructional materials.

Goals and Objectives of the Special Physical Education Program

An important aspect of the special physical education plan is the section that identifies the goals and objectives of the program. An overview of Public Law 101-476 and its mandate that physical education be provided for special students should be included as an introduction to this section. Special attention should be focused on the guidelines for physical education found within Public Law 94-142 as amended by Public Law 101-476 and its relationship to the school system's special physical education goals and objectives. Also, it is important to emphasize that physical education for those with disabilities is important because of its contributions to physical fitness, motor fitness, fundamental motor skills, and skills in individual and group games and sports.

Goal statements are broad observations. For instance, it might be stated that the special physical education program is designed to assist students with special needs to achieve physical, mental, emotional, and social growth commensurate with their abilities through planned experiences individualized to their specific needs. Program objectives, however, are more specific. Some examples include the following: Provide students with opportunities to learn and to participate in a number of appropriate game and sport activities; develop physical fitness experiences that enable students to maximize their physical capabilities; enhance the motor development of students so that they can safely and successfully participate in the activities of daily living; and so on.

There are many other examples of program objectives that could be included here. No attempt has been made to develop an extensive list because the variables found within each school and school district are such that specific program goals and objectives are best developed by local school personnel. It is necessary to emphasize, too, that the discussion presented in this section focuses on program goals and objectives. In chapter 6, the development of program goals and objectives for individual students will be discussed.

Administrative Organization of the Program

An important discussion that must be included in the special physical education plan is the administrative pattern to be used in managing the program. It is difficult to recommend a specific management plan because schools vary greatly in their organizational setup due to such variables as enrollment size, philosophy of education, and region of the country. Nevertheless, the plan should address some important administrative concepts.

Of greatest concern is the need to identify one person who will be ultimately responsible for the program. As the program administrator, this person would be responsible for directing the program; working with parents and community groups; providing inservice training for teachers; developing screening, assessment, and placement procedures; recruiting and training volunteers; and ordering equipment and curricular materials. This individual may be identified by one of several titles, including *special physical education coordinator, special physical education director,* or *consultant for special physical education.*

The relationship of this individual to teachers and other administrators must also be clarified. In figure 5.2, an administrative pattern that has been used successfully by many school systems is presented. In this design the administrator is responsible to both the director of physical education and the director of special education. With large school systems, the program administrator coordinates with each of the schools through a special physical education facilitator, who is responsible for coordinating the program at the building level. In smaller districts, this responsibility may have to be assumed by the special education or physical education director or in the case of very small districts directly by the special education or physical education teacher.

Procedures for Providing Services

A section within the plan should be devoted to procedures for providing services to students with disabilities. The discussion should be directed toward an overview of

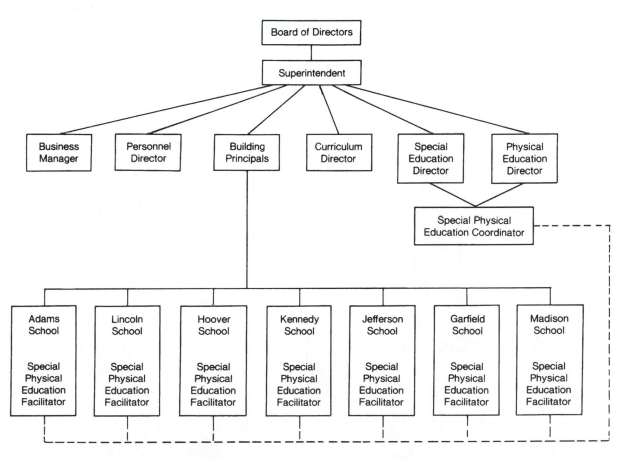

Figure 5.2 Administrative pattern showing the relationship of the special physical education coordinator within the administrative hierarchy.

organizational procedures that covers identification through implementation of a special program for an individual student rather than a discussion on teaching methodology. This latter information is important and should be covered in materials used for inservice sessions with teachers.

Although exact policies vary among school systems, there are some general guidelines that schools use in providing special educational services. In figure 5.3, a schematic is presented that covers the important elements in delivering services to students with disabilities. A discussion of each of these seven steps will be presented as a guide in helping to develop a plan for other districts.

In Step I, teachers should understand that they have a right and an obligation to refer students who are not learning, whether it be in the classroom or in the physical education environment. An example of a referral form is presented in figure 5.4. Information in the special physical education plan should indicate to the teacher where the referral form should be sent. Parents also may refer a son or daughter if they suspect a problem exists. "Childfind" is the term used when children who are suspected of having a disability are identified and referred for further assessment by school personnel or members of the community at large.

In Step II, the referral is reviewed by a committee that should consist of representatives from physical education,

special education, and the administration. In those districts where representatives of physical education are not included on the referral committee or it is not feasible for a representative from physical education to attend all of the meetings, special education personnel can be provided with information to insure that the physical education needs of students are addressed.

This committee reviews the reason for the referral plus other available information on the student. It is not uncommon, for instance, to have referrals from several teachers, including the instructor of physical education. Several options are available to the committee. It might, for instance, decide that the student may have a disability and should be formally assessed to verify whether the student does have special needs. The committee could also decide that the student's needs are well within the normal range and that assistance should be provided to the teacher to create a more favorable learning environment, or that possibly the student should be transferred to a different class.

In Step III, assessment, it is necessary to have signed parental permission prior to assessing the student to determine his or her eligibility as a learner with special needs. Without such permission, diagnostic tests cannot be administered unless the school district wishes to legally challenge the parents' decision. Fortunately, most parents are cooperative

PROCESS FOR PROVIDING SPECIAL EDUCATION SERVICES

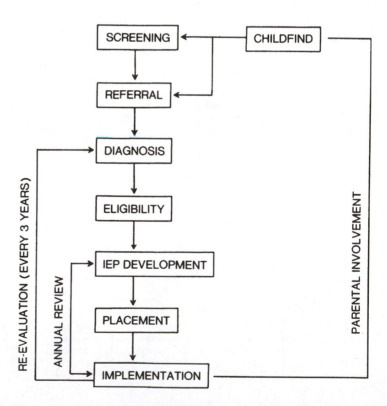

Figure 5.3 A schematic of the procedural steps used to deliver special physical education services.

(Courtesy of the Oregon Department of Education, Salem, Oregon.)

FAIRPLAY PUBLIC SCHOOLS
ADAPTED PHYSICAL EDUCATION PROGRAM

RECOMMENDATION
FOR REFERRAL

_____   _____
Pupil's Name   Birthdate

Some pupils in regular classes find it difficult, if not impossible, to safely and successfully participate in regular physical education. This may be due to low fitness, poor coordination, sensory problems, orthopedic conditions, low emotional tolerance, language disabilities, etc.

In recommending this pupil, please consider the above areas and provide us with your impressions of the child's level of function and the reason(s) for your referral.

By_____
        name and position

School_____

Date_____

Figure 5.4 Adapted physical education referral form.

(Adapted from the Office of the Los Angeles County Superintendent of Schools, Division of Special Physical Education.)

and desirous of obtaining as much information about their child as possible. Care should be taken to ensure that the assessment procedure is formalized and that accurate and valid information is obtained. The assessment procedures should be sufficiently comprehensive so as to diagnose and appraise a student's suspected disability. Regardless of whether the referral is initiated by a physical education teacher or by an instructor of another discipline, it is essential that information on the student's motor and physical fitness levels is obtained. Chapter 7 contains an in-depth discussion on procedures for evaluating the motor performance of the student with a disability.

Following assessment, the next step is to review the assessment data to determine whether the student is eligible as a student with a disability under the provision of Public Law 101-476. Both federal and state law must be reviewed to determine whether the student is legally qualified. Many schools have recognized, too, that although some students may not technically meet the criteria, it may still be best to meet with the parents and develop a special physical education plan. This is particularly true in physical education, where students who are awkward or obese, for example, may not technically qualify for services but nonetheless need assistance. School systems normally may not claim reimbursement for serving students who fail technically to qualify, but they do gain the respect and appreciation of many parents and students.

Developing the student's Individualized Education Program (IEP), Step V, is the core of the entire process of providing special educational services including physical education. In writing the special physical education plan it is important to alert teachers and administrators to some important concepts. First, it is necessary to emphasize that at every IEP meeting a discussion must be held to determine whether or not the student needs special physical education services. The response to this question is dependent upon the assessment information available and determines whether special goals and objectives need to be written or whether the student is capable of receiving instruction in the regular physical education program. A second point to emphasize is that the composition of the IEP team must by legal definition include the following:

1. A representative of the public agency, other than the child's teacher, who is qualified to provide, or supervise the provision of, special education
2. The child's teacher
3. One or both of the child's parents
4. The child, whenever appropriate
5. Other individuals at the discretion of the parents or agency

It is the responsibility of the school to formally notify the parents of the meeting and to schedule the meeting at a place and time that is convenient for them. Although P.L. 101-476 does not stipulate that a physical education teacher must be part of the IEP team, input from a person with training in this area is essential to assist the team in reaching an informed decision about the student's physical education needs. Schools have responded to this need in two ways. Some have elected to keep the IEP team small by having pre-IEP meetings at which personnel from various academic areas, including physical education, provide input on their perspectives of the student's needs. Other schools have elected to add a physical education teacher to the team, particularly for those students whose motor and physical fitness needs are great. Under Public Law 99-457, the provisions of special education services were extended to toddlers (3–5 years of age) and infants (0–2 years of age). Instead of an IEP, a very similar plan for infants and toddlers, referred to as an Individualized Family Services Plan (IFSP), must be developed. Information regarding the IFSP is found in chapters 6 and 21. Both systems seem to work equally well. The important element is that the IEP or IFSP team makes critical decisions that affect the quality of the physical education services provided.

Within the plan, a review of the content each IEP must address should also be stated. According to Public Law 101-476, the IEP must include:

1. A statement of the child's present levels of educational performance;

2. A statement of annual goals, including short-term instructional objectives;
3. A statement of the specific special education and related services to be provided to the child, and the extent to which the child will be able to participate in regular educational programs;
4. The projected date for initiation of services and anticipated duration of such services;
5. Appropriate objective criteria and evaluation procedures and schedules for determining, on at least an annual basis, whether instructional objectives are being achieved; and
6. A statement of the needed transition services no later than age 16 and annually thereafter.

A representative copy of an IEP form is shown in figure 5.5. In chapter 6, information on writing individual student goals and objectives will be presented.

Step VI focuses on the various aspects involved in implementing the IEP. Information should be provided in the special physical education plan to help teachers locate information that can be used to offer quality instruction. Curricular resources, including books, films, and instructional guides, should be identified along with procedures for efficiently obtaining these materials. A statement should be included in the plan concerning future inservice activities and the need to help teachers improve their competence in meeting special needs of the students. Additional information on improving teacher competence and using effective teaching strategies with students who are disabled will be presented later in the book.

A necessary step in the implementation of each IEP is to identify an appropriate placement for the special student. Procedurally, it is important to remind school personnel that changes in the educational placement of children with disabilities are not permissible without parent input and an IEP that documents the appropriateness of the change. This approach ensures that a team effort has been used to identify the best educational setting for the student. A section within this chapter is devoted to a discussion on physical education placement options for the special student.

Determining Program Costs

Every program has associated with it a number of costs that can be attributed to specific items. It is important that these costs are identified and documented for the special physical education programs. This information can be obtained by reviewing the school district's budget document, which is usually available to all school personnel as well as the general public. Items frequently specified in school budgets are personnel costs, including fringe benefits, equipment, travel, supplies, and communication expenses. The special physical education budget may also include other items, such as funds for consultants and released time for teachers to benefit from inservice experiences. Regardless of the number of

Date Initialized by District ____________________
Mo Day Yr

Individual Education Program

Name ____________________ Area ____________________

Transition Service ____________________

Present Level of Educational Performance

Student's Preferences, Interests, Needs Regarding Transition

Annual Goal

Short-term Objective(s)	Criteria	Evaluation Procedures	Schedule for Review	Progress/ Date Achieved

Form 581-5148T-X(New11/92) page 2 Page of

Figure 5.5 Sample individualized education program form.
(Courtesy of the Oregon Department of Education, Salem, Oregon.)

Individual Education Program

Student's Name _____

Last   First   MI

Birth Date (mo/day/yr) _____ Age _____

Date Special Education
Eligibility Established (mo/day/yr) _____

Date of Initial IEP (mo/day/yr) _____

Date of IEP Meeting (mo/day/yr) _____

Next Annual Review
Due Date (mo/day/yr) _____

Three-year Reevaluation
Due Date (mo/day/yr) _____

Student ID#/SS# _____

Grade _____

Attending School _____

Address _____

City, Zip _____

Participants in IEP Meeting

Student's Teacher _____

District Representative/Title _____

Parent(s) _____

Student, When Appropriate _____

Other/Title _____

Other/Title _____

Other/Title _____

High School Only (graduation information) ⑫

Diploma   ☐ Standard   ☐ Other _____

Current Number of Credits Toward Graduation _____

Number of Credits Required _____

Projected Graduation Date _____

Special Education Services to Be Provided

	Amount of Service (per day/week, etc.)	Projected Dates of Initiation	Anticipated Duration of Services	Provider: LEA, ESD, Regional Program or Other	Extended School year Services
Specially Designed Services					
☐ Reading	_____	_____	_____	_____	_____
☐ Math	_____	_____	_____	_____	_____
☐ Written Language	_____	_____	_____	_____	_____
☐ Physical Education	_____	_____	_____	_____	_____
☐ Behavioral	_____	_____	_____	_____	_____
☐ Speech/Language	_____	_____	_____	_____	_____
☐ Vocational Education	_____	_____	_____	_____	_____
☐ Transition Services	_____	_____	_____	_____	_____
☐ Other	_____	_____	_____	_____	_____
Related Services					
☐ Transportation	_____	_____	_____	_____	_____
☐ Counseling	_____	_____	_____	_____	_____
☐ Physical Therapy	_____	_____	_____	_____	_____
☐ Occupational Therapy	_____	_____	_____	_____	_____
☐ Psychological	_____	_____	_____	_____	_____
☐ Speech/Language	_____	_____	_____	_____	_____
☐ Audiology	_____	_____	_____	_____	_____
☐ School Health Services	_____	_____	_____	_____	_____
☐ Social Work	_____	_____	_____	_____	_____
☐ Recreation	_____	_____	_____	_____	_____
☐ Educational Interpreter	_____	_____	_____	_____	_____
☐ Assistive Technology	_____	_____	_____	_____	_____
☐ Transition Services	_____	_____	_____	_____	_____
☐ Other	_____	_____	_____	_____	_____

Extent of Participation in Regular Education _____% of time spent in regular education program _____
OR list academic and nonacademic classes and activities _____

Form 581-5148T-X (New11/92) page 1   Page 1 of _____

Figure 5.5—*Continued*

budget items, it is necessary not only to specify an amount per item but also to explain and justify all expenditures. For instance, to request dollars for inservicing staff without documenting the need for this service and providing a detailed inservice plan is not a desirable practice. A full explanation and justification of costs will help all superiors, including the superintendent and the school board, to understand the rationale for specific budget items and their relationship to the total program.

An intensive study also should be made of the State Department of Education procedure for reimbursing the school for costs incurred in providing special education services. Some states have rightfully recognized that physical education programs for students with disabilities are special education services and thus eligible for reimbursement. The State of Oregon, for instance, will reimburse its school districts for approximately 15 percent of excess costs for providing physical education for eligible students, if the students receiving the instruction have IEPs that support the need for specialized programs and the instruction is provided by a qualified physical education teacher.

Evaluating the Program

An important element to include in the program plan is a discussion of the evaluative procedures to be used to assess the effectiveness of the program. Information should be obtained to determine both the quantity and the quality of the program. For instance, records helpful in assessing the quantity of the program include number of students referred, number served, and the placement settings in which the services were provided. A random selection of students in the program and a review of their IEPs help to determine the quality of the program. For example, a review of the motor and physical fitness assessment data and its relationship to the goals and objectives developed for individual students will be helpful. In addition, the student's IEP for the present year can be compared with those of previous years to determine the extent to which educational gains have been made. A random survey of parents and students to obtain their reaction to the program will also help to determine the overall impact of the program.

In formulating the special physical education plan it is important to solicit input from others. Special efforts should be made to meet periodically with the directors of physical education and special education to seek their advice and to ask them to respond to sections of the plan as it is developed. The special physical education advisory committee can also be asked to respond to the content of the plan. Some committee members may express an interest in helping to develop certain components of the plan. The more people involved in the development of the plan, the greater the chances the document will be accepted once written.

Inservice Teachers

A very basic and essential aspect of a school district's effort to organize and administer a special physical education program is the involvement of personnel in the program who possess sufficient skills to teach students with disabilities. Although some districts may employ specialists in physical education, frequently these individuals spend the majority of their time consulting with teachers, developing and administering programs, and providing direct services to those with severe and profound disabilities. In most school districts, the primary implementor of physical education services, will be the physical education or classroom teacher.

For this reason, it is essential that a concerted effort be made to provide these individuals with quality inservice education experiences. Skill development is needed to ensure that appropriate physical education programs are implemented for special students. Information concerning screening procedures, assessment, placement, behavior management, and many other topics must be dealt with to enable the teachers of physical education to meet the requirements of Public Law 101-476. Extensive work also must focus on attitudes, value clarification, and the concept of normalcy to assist teachers in overcoming any apprehension that may be evident. Specific competencies that teachers who instruct students with special needs should possess will be discussed in chapter 6.

The need to upgrade the skills of personnel who are working with the students with disabilities in educational settings has been identified by the United States Office of Special Education and Rehabilitative Services (OSERS) as a priority training need. Thus, many university and college departments of physical education and some local school districts have received federal funding to provide special inservice training for teachers who teach students with disabilities. Consequently, more and more personnel are benefitting from the opportunity to improve their special physical education skills. Additionally, the process of providing information about physical education for students with disabilities to teachers has been refined and improved through experience. Indicated below are some recommendations that inservice providers can follow to develop quality training experiences for teachers to improve their competency in working with special students.

1. Provide information consistent with the requirements of federal and state statutes. Obviously, all relevant inservice experiences must provide information that conforms to the guidelines of the Individuals with Disabilities Education Act of 1990 and Section 504 of the Rehabilitation Act of 1973.

2. Address the state's plan for a comprehensive system of personnel preparation. The scarcity of financial

resources mandates that duplication of training efforts must be minimized. Most states today have a statewide personnel planning system. All agencies and personnel planning to provide inservice training would be wise to coordinate their efforts with the state personnel plan.

3. Reflect cooperative planning among local education agencies, state education agencies, and institutions of higher education. For optimal training models, the resources, knowledge, and experience of various agencies must be pooled to realistically perceive and deliver appropriate training.

4. Include representatives of training audiences in inservice planning. Inservice experiences designed to "do" something to trainees without involving such personnel in the formulation of the educational plan are often doomed to failure. Assumptions about training needs can be confirmed or modified through various needs-assessment processes. Inclusion of trainees and trainers in the planning stages creates an environment of sharing rather than the polar positions of giving and receiving. An example of a needs-assessment form is found in figure 5.6.

5. Provide for follow-up training. Documentation of skills developed through training should be monitored by following up trainees' classes. Efforts must be expended to ensure that skills developed are transferable and can be generalized to classroom use. On-site follow-up training can help to assure training that will have an impact.

6. Focus on the trainer-of-trainers, or multiplier, concept. The large number of personnel to receive inservice training requires that efforts be made to develop procedures for training a cadre of trainers. Successful inservice models have been developed in which select peers from various school districts are trained to provide inservice training for their respective colleagues.

7. Disseminate inservice plans and outcomes. The sharing of successful and unsuccessful training models serves as a vehicle to assist all inservice practitioners in refining training procedures and programs.

8. Incorporate administrators in training programs. Focusing on the inservice needs of regular educators without inservicing administrators frequently creates an environment in which the teachers' desire to provide appropriate physical education experiences is stymied because of administrative nonsupport. Many of the requirements of P.L. 101-476 necessitate changes that may require changes in school policies beyond the direct control of the classroom teacher.

9. Evaluate inservice training activities. Documentation of changes in such variables as attitude, skill, and knowledge must be determined for each trainee. Actual performance of teachers within the gymnasium as well as performance of children taught by trainees should be monitored. Anonymous reaction of trainees to the performance of trainers is also essential. The inservicing of teachers can be done in several ways. Some districts have chosen to employ an outside consultant who works under contract to provide the needed training. Other districts may choose to utilize one of their own staff members to conduct the inservice seminars. This last approach has many advantages including familiarity with the district. In addition, within-district inservice providers usually are perceived as credible professionals who have firsthand appreciation for the challenges associated with developing and implementing new teaching skills.

Placing the Student with a Disability

Providing appropriate physical education for students with disabilities requires that a decision be made concerning the educational setting in which individual students should be placed. This decision is an important aspect of the IEP team's deliberations and should be based on a careful study of the student's present motor and physical fitness performances. Other variables that enter into the decision include the student's cognitive level, socioemotional skills, and past physical education class experiences. Placement is made in reference to each individual student and not as part of a blanket decision that involves a class of children such as all classified as moderately mentally retarded.

Since the passage of P.L. 94-142 in 1975, there has been considerable discussion and professional debate regarding the appropriate educational setting or placement for the student with a disability. Until recent time, special educators relied on a placement concept referred to as the cascade system (figure 5.7). This approach, proposed in the 1960s, suggests that the educational needs of children with disabilities require a variety of settings ranging from full-time placement in a special school to placement in the regular classroom. Adapted physical education professionals emulated this model and developed several placement options specific to physical education. The most current representation of the model applied to physical education was proposed by Aufsesser (1991) (figure 5.8). In these models, the basic concept is that students with disabilities can learn and be successful, but the educational setting would vary depending upon the disability level of the individual. The desired goal, of course, was to mainstream or place students with disabilities with their nondisabled peers. When mainstreaming was not

Needs Assessment for Inservice in Adapted Physical Education

You are asked to evaluate how you feel about your own preparation to teach physical education to children with disabilities. Please read the following questions and respond utilizing a #2 soft pencil on the attached IBM card. Your responses will be anonymous.

Professional Information
1. I have completed the following degree
   A. Bachelors
   B. Masters
   C. Masters plus 30 hours
   D. Doctorate
   E. Other

2. My current position is
   A. Physical education teacher
   B. Special education teacher
   C. Regular education teacher
   D. Administration
   E. Other

3. I am employed at the
   A. Elementary school level
   B. Intermediate school level
   C. High school level
   D. District wide level
   E. Other

4. I have been teaching for
   A. 1–2 years
   B. 3–5 years
   C. 6–10 years
   D. 11–15 years
   E. More than 15 years

5. I prefer the inservice training to be
   A. Held during the school day and receive no course credit.
   B. Held during my own time and receive course credit.
   C. Held one evening and be released the following entire day for the remainder of the training.

Professional Preparation
Please read the following statements. Drawing on your own past experiences and present information, please react selecting A, B, C, D, and/or E according to need.

   A. Have adequate information
   B. Have some information and know where to get more.
   C. Have little or no information
   D. Need help and am willing to participate
   E. Does not apply and do not want help in this area.
6. Comprehending P.L. 97-157 and P.L. 101-476 of the Rehabilitation Act of 1973.
7. Comprehending P.L. 101-476 as it relates to physical education.
8. Understanding and outlining your district's referral system.
9. Understanding the physical educator's role on the IEP team.
10. Listing the components of the IEP process.
11. Leading an IEP meeting and following an acceptable format.
12. Working with adapted physical educators and special educators.
13. Locating aides to assist in conducting the physical education program.
14. Training aids to assist with the adapted physical education program.
15. Knowing where established adapted physical education programs are and understanding how they function.

16. Developing appropriate classroom management and organization.
17. Developing reasonable expectations for students with disabilities.
18. Understanding specific mental and physical disabling conditions. List those conditions on which you need more information.
19. Adapting equipment to complement a child's performance.
20. Integrating children with disabilities into the physical education program.
21. Interacting and communicating with parents about physical education.
22. Interacting with and educating physicians about physical education.
23. Dealing with prostheses (eye-glasses, hearing aids, braces).
24. Identifying community-based resources.

Looking at Behavior
25. Utilizing behavior management techniques in physical education environments.
26. Defining and describing behavior.
27. Evaluating behavior.

Surveys, Tests, Assessment and Evaluation
28. Developing your own screening tools.
29. Identifying established tools to be used.
30. Locating efficient and appropriate tools for assessment.
31. Assessing the disabled child's needs.
32. Recognizing normal and abnormal motor development.
33. Utilizing the motor and physical fitness sections of the student progress record.
34. Interpreting norms, reliability, and validity.
35. Analyzing and interpreting tests for diagnostic purposes.

Curriculum Development
36. Writing IEPs.
37. Assessing physical education skills.
38. Stating long term physical education goals.
39. Stating short term physical education goals.
40. Identifying placement options in physical education.
41. Prescribing appropriate physical education experiences.
42. Defining the scope and sequence for the physical education program.
43. Identifying resource materials.
44. Interpreting the "I Can" curriculum developed for special populations.
45. Completing a task analysis for any general physical education skill.
46. Discovering more about commercial materials and adapting them for instruction.
47. Developing individualized learning modules.
48. Determining the pupil's levels of performance.
49. Programming changes needed to better serve the impaired student.
50. Developing a sensitivity towards others.
51. Teaching to inclusion rather than exclusion.

Developed by:
John M. Dunn
Jim W. Morehouse
202 WB
Oregon State University
Corvallis, Oregon 97331

Figure 5.6 Inservice needs-assessment form.

(Courtesy of Oregon State University, John M. Dunn and James W. Morehouse, Project PELRA.)

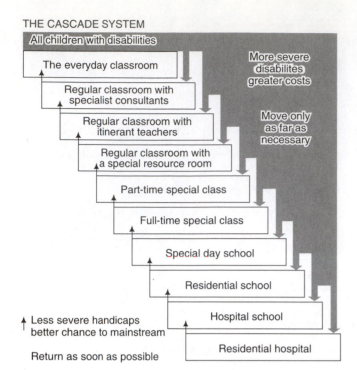

Less severe handicaps
better chance to mainstream

Return as soon as possible

Figure 5.7 The cascade system.

possible, educators then reasoned that the goal was to place the student in the educational environment that was least restrictive.

Recently, many have argued that students with disabilities, regardless of the level of severity of the disabling condition, should be educated in the regular educational setting. Madeline Will, former Assistant Secretary for the Office of Special Education and Rehabilitative Services, coined the phrase "Regular Education Initiative" (1986) to clearly emphasize that students with disabilities, with few exceptions, belonged in regular classrooms in public schools. Will also emphasized that the current dual system of regular and special education needed to change and proposed that regular educators, with assistance, could provide for the educational needs of most special students.

Block and Krebs (1992), using many of the principles proposed by Will and others, have proposed a new model for meeting the physical education needs of students with disabilities. In their model, Block and Krebs argue that the emphasis should move from a continuum of placements as presented in figure 5.8 to a continuum of support as proposed in figure 5.9. The major concept behind the new model is that with proper support and services all students can receive appropriate and successful education within the regular education environment. It should be noted, however, that there is overlap and similarity between figures 5.8 and 5.9. For example both models recognize that the needs of students with severe disabilities may require some part-time placement in adapted physical education or the provision of adapted physical education in special schools. Even in these settings, however, there would be opportunities for students with disabilities to interact in educational environments with nondisabled youngsters. In the Block and Krebs model (see figure 5.9), even in special schools, Level 5 students with severe disabilities would interact with nondisabled children through reverse mainstreaming, the integration of nondisabled students into special schools or classes.

Levels 1, 2, and 3 in figure 5.9, differ in the amount of support that needs to be provided to the regular physical educator or assistance that the student with disabilities might require. For example, in Level 2, the regular physical education teacher is responsible for providing instruction for the student with a disability, but has access to an adapted physical education consultant for various purposes including expertise and information regarding curricular and activity modifications, behavior management, IEP development, and other services. The regular physical education teacher

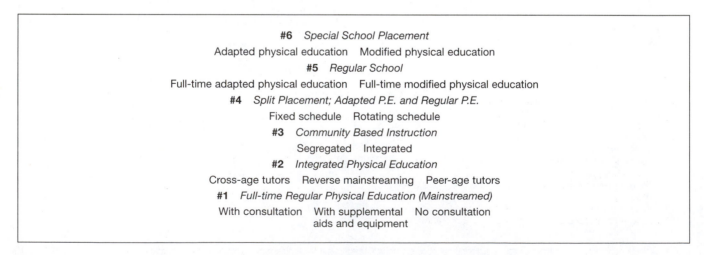

Figure 5.8 Least restrictive environment options in physical education (adapted from Aufsesser, 1991).

(Note: From "An Alternative to Least Restrictive Environments: A Continuum of Support to Regular Physical Education" by Martin E. Block and Patricia L. Krebs, *Adapted Physical Activities Quarterly* (Vol. 9, No. 2), p. 101. Copyright Human Kinetics Publishers. Reprinted by permission.)

LEVEL 1:   No Support Needed
             1.1 Student can make necessary modifications on his/her own
             1.2 RPE teacher feels comfortable working with student
LEVEL 2:   APE Consultation
             2.1 No extra assistance needed
             2.2 Peer tutor watches out for student
             2.3 Peer tutor assists student
             2.4 Paraprofessional assists student
LEVEL 3:   APE Direct Service in RPE 1–2 Times/Wk
             3.1 Peer tutor watches out for student
             3.2 Peer tutor assists student
             3.3 Paraprofessional assists student
LEVEL 4:   Part-time APE and Part-time RPE
             4.1 Flexible schedule with reverse mainstreaming
             4.2 Fixed schedule with reverse mainstreaming
LEVEL 5:   Reverse Mainstreaming in Special School
             5.1 Students from special school go to regular school for RPE
             5.2 Nondisabled students go to special school for RPE
             5.3 Students with and without disabilities meet in community for recreation training

Figure 5.9   A continuum of support to regular physical education (support from peers, volunteers, and paraprofessionals also should be provided in Levels 4 and 5).

(Note: From "An Alternative to Least Restrictive Environments: A Continuum of Support to Regular Physical Education" by Martin E. Block and Patricia L. Krebs, *Adapted Physical Activities Quarterly* (Vol. 9, No. 2), p. 104. Copyright Human Kinetics Publishers. Reprinted by permission.)

also has access to peer tutors and professionals to assist with instruction and to help with other tasks, including activity modifications. Webster (1987) and Houston-Wilson (1993) have documented that with training, peer tutors can be very successful in helping students with disabilities in the physical education class.

One of the primary concerns of many regular physical educators is the lack of available time to plan and/or provide for the special physical education needs of selected students. Some school systems have responded to this need by releasing physical education teachers from other responsibilities. Duties that are noninstructional in nature, such as hall supervision and lunchroom monitoring, can normally be reassigned without great difficulty. Of course to provide adapted physical education services as suggested in figure 5.9, Level 4, it may be necessary to reschedule the physical educator's teaching assignments to include responsibility for an adapted physical education class, at least part-time.

It should be emphasized that the type of service and placement desirable for a child in one academic area is not necessarily the same as for other areas of programming. A child who requires special assistance for some educational services, such as reading and math, may be able to successfully participate in a regular physical education program with little or no special services. Likewise, some students, such as the individual with severely involved cerebral palsy, may need little classroom assistance but may require specially designed physical education services. Individual differences must always be considered in determining appropriate placements. While some placement options may appear elaborate they are not. Implementation of the options as presented, or variations of the options, are clearly within the realm of school districts committed to the concept of

Figure 5.10   Physical education activities are defined broadly under federal legislation.

helping students achieve in the educational environment most conducive to their needs. As discussed earlier, parents and advisory groups can be very helpful in lobbying for the appropriate placement options and level of support.

Recruiting and Training Volunteers

Providing appropriate physical education services for the student with special needs, particularly those with severe disabilities, frequently requires that the amount of instructional time available for the student be increased. School districts have traditionally responded to this need by hiring more teachers or by rearranging the teacher's schedule so that non-teaching assignments are replaced by time allocated to instruct the special student. Some school personnel have recognized recently, however, that a third option for increasing the amount of instruction and practice time for students with disabilities is to recruit and train volunteers.

The availability of volunteers is quite good in most communities and is limited only by one's imagination when seeking them out. Volunteers can be recruited from a number of sources: community organizations, foster grandparent groups, parent-teacher organizations, and colleges, just to name a few. The public schools, too, are a valuable source of volunteers. Students of all ages, from high school to grade school, have been used within schools to serve as effective volunteers for their peers. In recruiting from any of these groups it is necessary to meet with the community or student organizations to describe the type of individuals with whom the volunteer will be working and specifically what the volunteer will be doing. Expectations of the volunteer must also be clearly established. Having the individual sign an informal contract is helpful in ensuring that the volunteer understands the terms of agreement.

Recruiting persons to help is valuable only to the extent that the volunteers are trained to perform tasks that can assist the teacher. It is recommended, therefore, that a training program be conducted for the volunteers to help them serve as an effective aide to the teacher. The type of information presented should include the goals of the special physical education program, how to work with the special student, procedures for reinforcing student's performance, how to record data, where to obtain equipment and supplies, and the role of the volunteer. The training session should also provide each volunteer with practical opportunities to work with a special student. The length of the training session varies depending upon the background of the volunteer and the role assigned to her or him. Some school systems provide short sessions of two hours; others have developed in-depth experiences that extend through a ten-week, twenty-hour program. It cannot be too strongly stressed that a volunteer should not be assigned to work with a student with a disability unless the school system feels that the individual is capable of following the directions of the teacher.

The role that the volunteer assumes is dependent upon the individual's background, training, and ability. Specific assignments are left to the discretion of the teacher. In some cases, the assigned tasks may be limited to procuring equipment and supplies, videotaping, officiating, helping to keep score, and other useful work but without direct involvement with students. Other volunteers, however, may be asked to help the teacher provide direct instruction in a one-to-one or small group situation. The information presented, and the way it is presented, is the responsibility of the teacher. This means that the teacher must be well organized and able to communicate effectively with the volunteer. It is also the responsibility of the teacher to frequently observe the volunteer to ensure that the instructional process is implemented in an acceptable fashion.

Recruiting and training volunteers and monitoring their progress is a role that is new for some physical education teachers. To use volunteers effectively, it is necessary for the teacher to give extra time to supervising and encouraging those who are offering their help. However, the assistance that volunteers offer more than compensates for the effort that must be expended to initiate and maintain a volunteer program.

Special Health and Safety Needs of Students with Disabilities

Because of their disabling conditions, special education students sometimes require unique health and safety considerations. For example, many special students lack endurance and strength, particularly in the early months of instruction, and must be protected from overexertion. Students should be made aware of their tolerance levels and educated to exercise caution for their own protection. Although some of the enrolled students will shun physical activity because of the sheltered life they have led as children with disabilities, others will be so enthused with the opportunities to participate in the activities being taught them that they will fail to regard the safety precautions. They will require supervision and direction until they become fully aware of the importance of taking the necessary precautionary measures. The poorly coordinated ones will not be adept at avoiding accidents, and they may be more prone to falling and stumbling and less adroit at catching and dodging thrown objects.

Certain students are highly susceptible to infection. Even a small cut or scratch can be potentially serious to a diabetic, for example. Other students may have other hygienic problems. For still others the problems will be related to dietary needs; the obese, the poorly coordinated, and the chronically fatigued may have problems essentially dietary in nature. All of these must be given consideration in planning the program for special students.

Students with disabilities should be taught to assume responsibility for their own health and safety. The teacher must, of course, provide the best possible environment for learning the necessary protective measures. This will include not only good program planning and superior teaching methods but also safe, clean equipment and facilities. Teachers should be trained in first aid and cardiopulmonary resuscitation (CPR), including appropriate responses to situations such as seizures and diabetic shock. Teachers should also be aware of students on medication and should be alert for symptoms of toxic effects.

There is always some hazard for students with disabilities who engage in play with nondisabled peers. They may not be able to move quickly enough to avoid collision, or they may not see a thrown ball until it is too late to dodge it. Then, too, in their desire to compete successfully, they may overexert themselves or take unnecessary risks that result in accidents. Every precaution should be taken to reduce the possibilities of accidental injuries by removing all physical hazards, such as nonessential playing equipment and unnecessary barriers and obstructions, from the playing area. Specific safety measures that should be observed for each kind of disabling condition will be suggested in subsequent chapters. In addition to these, however, the teacher should instill in the class respect for the playing courtesies of the game and a sportsmanlike regard for the abilities and limitations of others.

Liability

It is not only the moral responsibility but also the legal responsibility of the special physical education teacher to exercise all precautions necessary to avoid accidents and injury and to protect the welfare of the students involved. Statistics indicate that more accidental injuries occur in physical education classes than in any other area of school life. There are also more damage suits involving injury in physical education classes than there are in other classes or school activities. Although statistics are incomplete concerning the frequency of accidental injury in special physical education programs, there is evidence to indicate that the percentage of injuries is considerably less than that in the regular physical education program. This is probably due to the greater precautions exercised by teacher and students alike.

Regardless of the fact that injuries to special students are less likely to occur, the teacher must remember that he or she is liable for damage if negligence is shown to be the cause of injury. State laws governing negligence vary from state to state, but generally, negligence is said to occur when the teacher has not fulfilled his or her duty or when actions that were obviously wrong or were not those of a reasonably prudent person directly contributed to the injury.

A prudent person is considered to be one who is able to see the harmful consequences of a specific situation and who makes adjustments to prevent them from occurring. Common situations that frequently cause accidents are as follows: (1) defective equipment and unsafe facilities; (2) allowing or encouraging students to take unreasonable risks; (3) inadequate supervision and poor instruction; and (4) poor selection of activities in relation to the student's limitations.

The teacher should be constantly aware of the state of repair of all equipment and facilities. He or she should refrain from using potentially hazardous equipment and facilities until proper repairs can be made. Care should be taken not to allow students to take unnecessary risks in performance or to encourage them in excessive effort that may result in injury to them. Students in competitive situations should be closely observed for signs of overexertion in the effort to win. Extreme fatigue may lead to injury, and the teacher should watch constantly to see that the student does not exceed his or her tolerance level to exercise or become so fatigued that control over movements is lost.

Accidents frequently occur when there is inadequate supervision and poor instruction. A teacher is considered legally responsible for the improper conduct of the students when such conduct leads to an accident during physical education instruction and also for the injury of one member of the class by another. Inadequate preparation of the student for motor performance is another frequent cause of accidental injury. Failure to prepare the student with appropriate lead-up skills prior to performance of a complex skill is evidence of negligence.

Summary

Efforts to develop appropriate physical education programs for students with disabilities requires the development of a plan of action to ensure that the needed services are provided. The cornerstone of any plan, particularly one related to school systems, is a clear understanding of school district policy and its relationship to State and Federal requirements. Fortunately P.L. 94-142, P.L. 93-112, P.L. 99-457 and P.L. 101-476 are clear in their directive that physical education services for students with disabilities will be provided. The laws also specify procedures that should be followed from identification to placement of the student with special needs. The task for many of today's professionals is to review and revise, where needed, local school district policy and practice so that it complies with federal and state requirements. Success in this area will require that school administrators and officials are cognizant of the laws and the extent to which the district complies with the requirements. In large school districts, such an undertaking may be relegated to a specific individual such as a special physical education coordinator or facilitator. Smaller school districts may assign this responsibility to the director of special education or director of physical education. Regardless of who is given the responsibility, obtaining the support, philosophical and economical, of the administration is essential.

In addition to school administrators, parents, advocates for those with disabilities, and professionals such as allied health personnel can be very effective in lobbying for needed services. These individuals can help in articulating the value of the program. They also can offer valuable input into the organization of the special physical education program.

The success of any instructional program is dependent upon the quality of the personnel delivering the needed services. An essential component, therefore, in the organization of the special physical education program is to develop a strategy for utilizing quality personnel. Given the desirability of placing students with special needs in the regular physical education program, a program should be initiated to provide inservice education for personnel who need assistance in teaching those students. Efforts should also be directed toward recruiting and training volunteers. These individuals, if properly selected and trained, can be indispensable in helping physical education teachers create a positive learning experience for students with and without disabilities.

The organizational quality of any program is measured by its ability to provide quality services. The ultimate measure, therefore, has to do with student outcomes, the quality and quantity of change in student behavior. Desirable outcomes come from good plans. Efforts must be made to ensure that students with disabilities are identified and needed services provided in the appropriate educational setting. Good planning requires coordination with parents, professionals, advocates, and other teachers. These individuals collectively can help to plan for and support the implementation of special physical education services.

Selected Readings

American Alliance for Health, Physical Education, Recreation, and Dance. (1976). *Adapted physical education guidelines*. Washington, DC: Author.

Aufsesser, P.M. (1991). Mainstreaming and the least restrictive environment: How do they differ? *Palaestra, 7*(2), 31–34.

Block, M.E., & Krebs, P.L. (1992). An alternative to least restrictive environments: A continuum of support to regular physical education. *Adapted Physical Activity Quarterly, 9,* 97–113.

Brown, L., Schwarz, P., Udvari-Solner, A., Kampschroer, E.F., Johnson, F., Jorgensen, J., & Grunewald, L. (1991). How much time should students with severe intellectual disabilities spend in regular education classrooms and elsewhere? *Journal of the Association for Persons with Severe Handicaps, 16,* 39–47.

Bruininks, R.H. (1978). *Bruininks-Oseretsky test of motor proficiency*. Circle Pines, MN: American Guidance Service, Inc., 1978.

Department of Education. (1981, January 19). Assistance to states for education of children with disabilities: Interpretation of the Individualized Education Program (IEP). *Federal Register.* Washington, DC: Author.

Department of Education. (1982, August 4). Assistance to states for education of children with disabilities: Proposed rules. *Federal Register.* Washington, DC: Author.

Department of Education, Office of Special Education, Division of Personnel Preparation. (Fiscal Year 1983). *Grant application packet for federal assistance*. Washington, DC: Author.

Department of Health, Education, and Welfare, Office of Education. (1977, August 23). Education of handicapped children, part II, implementation of part B of the education of the Handicapped Act. *Federal Register.* Washington, DC: Author.

Dunn, J.M., & Craft, D. (1985). Mainstreaming theory and practice. *Adapted Physical Activity Quarterly, 2,* 273–276.

Dunn, J.M. (1979). *Adaptive physical education: A resource guide for teachers, administrators, and parents*. Salem, OR: Oregon Mental Health Division.

Dunn, J.M., & Harris, J.L. (Eds.). (1979). *Physical education for those with disabilities: Meeting the need through inservice education*. Washington, DC: Hawkins and Associates.

Houston-Wilson, C.H. (1993). The effect of untrained and trained peer tutors on the Opportunity to Respond (OTR) of students with developmental disabilities in integrated physical education classes. Unpublished Doctoral Dissertation. Oregon State University.

The National Association for Physical Education of College Women and The National College Physical Education Association for Men. (1976). *Mainstreaming Physical Education* (Briefings 4). N.p.

Office of the Los Angeles County Superintendent of Schools, Division of Special Education. (1979). *Process for identification, assessment, planning, and placement of individuals with exceptional needs into physical education*. Downey, CA: Author.

Shivers, J.S., & Fait, H.F. (1975). *Therapeutic and adapted recreational services*. Philadelphia: Lea and Febiger.

Webster, G. (1987). Influence of peer tutors upon academic learning time—physical education of mentally handicapped students. *Journal of Teaching in Physical Education, 6,* 393–403.

Will, M.C. (1986). Educating children with learning problems: A shared responsibility. *Exceptional Children, 52,* 411–416.

Enhancing Activities

1. Attend a meeting of a local school board to obtain an understanding of how the board receives citizen input and makes decisions.

2. Contact a local school district to obtain a copy of its budget for the fiscal year. Review the costs associated with their physical education and special education programs. Specific budget items to review include the following: personnel costs, including teacher and clerical salaries; associated fringe benefit costs, such as medical and dental benefits; equipment; supplies; and travel. Compute a per diem cost for students in special education programs. Compare this value to the per diem cost for a student in the regular educational program.

3. Conduct an interview with a local school district administrator to obtain his or her understanding and interest in physical education programs for students with disabilities. Solicit information concerning the administrator's philosophy about special education programs and services.

4. Meet with physical education teachers to obtain their views concerning special physical education programs. Ask selected teachers to complete figure 5.6, Needs Assessment for Inservice in Adapted Physical Education, and analyze the results.

5. Develop a plan of action for implementing a progressive physical education program for students with disabilities in a local school system. Given the number of teachers, students, and students needing special services, suggest some administrative options for developing needed programs.

6. Contact local officials including parents, physicians, and advocates for students with disabilities to obtain their views concerning the need for and desirability of special physical education services.

7. Develop an outline of the information you would present, if asked, to a group of parents concerning the value of physical education programs for students with disabilities.

CHAPTER
6

Teaching Special
Physical Education

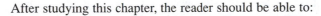

CHAPTER OBJECTIVES

After studying this chapter, the reader should be able to:

1 Recognize and appreciate the attributes and professional qualifications of teachers of special physical education.

2 Identify and describe the components of the Individualized Education Program (IEP) and the Individualized Family Service Plan (IFSP).

3 List the persons required to participate in the IEP/IFSP meeting and the rationale for their inclusion.

4 Discuss the importance of the IEP/IFSP and its relationship to quality education for students with disabilities.

5 Recognize the similarities and differences between the IEP and IFSP.

6 Identify, analyze, and apply selected principles of movement toward the education of students with disabilities.

7 Recognize the value of task analysis as an educational approach in teaching physical education to students with disabilities.

8 Describe the various approaches that can be employed to prevent and alleviate inappropriate behavior.

9 Recognize various medications used by students with disabilities and their effects on motor performance.

10 Compare and contrast various teaching methods and their application to students with disabilities.

It is the function of the teacher to provide a good learning situation. As a consequence, certain changes occur in the student. In physical education the most obvious changes will undoubtedly be the improvement of motor skills and a higher level of physical fitness. This will be evident not only in the success with which the students participate in games and physical education activities but also in general movement pattern improvement. Another desirable change that will occur, but that is likely to be less obvious to an untrained observer, is the student's increased understanding and appreciation of his or her personal limitations and attributes. This manifests itself in an improved attitude toward self and toward others. For many individuals with disabilities who suffer serious personality maladjustments, this is the first long step toward better adjustment and the development of more wholesome personality traits.

In order to provide the kind of learning situation that makes these desired results possible, the teacher needs both knowledge and training as well as certain special qualities of character and personality. Because of the specific challenges that a physical or mental disability creates for an individual, a teacher of students with disabilities must possess certain attributes beyond those generally required of a teacher of nondisabled individuals.

It is precisely this last point that has caused a great deal of frustration in today's public schools. Like teachers in other fields, physical education teachers often feel inadequate when faced with the prospect of teaching students with disabilities. Although this is an understandable response, it is one that is perhaps too readily accepted. Students with disabilities, as was stressed in chapter 4, are more similar to than different from those without disabilities. Therefore, many of the basic techniques that all good teachers of physical education use can be applied successfully in teaching the special population. The purpose of this chapter is to review and reinforce some of the educational concepts that apply to all students and to highlight, where necessary, additional or new skills that teachers will find helpful in working with individuals with disabilities, particularly those students who have severe disabilities.

Attributes of the Teacher of Special Physical Education

Perhaps the single most important attribute the teacher of students with disabilities can possess is emotional maturity. Emotional maturity is the ability to solve problems and adjust to the circumstances without undue emotional involvement. The teacher of the disabled must be a stabilizing influence, must represent to the students the ultimate in successful adjustment. A teacher who is unable to resolve personal psychological problems is not likely to be able to assist students in solving their problems. Behavior on the part of a teacher that is particularly immature may even contribute to the

maladjustment of students, rather than help them make satisfactory adjustments to their disability.

Patience and a sense of humor are indispensable qualities in any good teacher. Those who work with students with disabilities need to be endowed with a generous portion of each, for progress often proceeds very, very slowly. When the results of long hours of work do manifest themselves, however, they are extremely rewarding to the student and to the teacher. Equally important is the quality of sensitivity. This entails a recognition of the individual with a disability as a person, one who has special needs but not necessarily one who is special. People with disabilities appreciate efforts to help them learn but they also wish to be independent, self-sufficient, and, to the greatest extent possible, "normal." The special physical education teacher needs to be sensitive to this desire and respond to it by providing a quality program without fanfare or unnecessary focusing of attention on the student with a disability.

Creativity is yet another desirable quality in the teacher of those who deviate from the norm, for it may be necessary for the instructor to improvise equipment as well as techniques for performing skills. When facilities and equipment for the teaching of adapted activities are limited, the imaginative teacher adjusts and modifies the available facilities and equipment to fit the requirements of the program. The creative teacher meets the challenge of an unusual handicapping condition by devising suitable adaptations of the activities to meet the needs of the particular individual. Moreover, the teacher who is imaginative and creative is far better able to encourage and promote creativity in those whom he or she teaches. Creativity can be so easily stifled in physical education because of the tendency to enforce conformity in order to impress patterns in skill performance upon children.

Organizational ability is essential in the good physical education teacher. Regardless of the method of teaching used, carefully planned class procedures and well-organized class activities are time and energy savers. They make achievement of the desired goal easier and more certain. Class instruction left entirely, or even partially, to chance results in wasted time and motion, in poor learning, and in poor teaching.

A positive attitude toward students with disabilities is an indispensable teacher attribute. The teacher must be sensitive and empathetic but not overly solicitous. Students who are disabled deserve equal treatment and modifications, where appropriate, in instruction, activity, and equipment. Most students and their parents do not seek or expect special treatment beyond that which is necessary to create an equitable learning experience.

Unfortunately this is apparently not well understood by many teachers of physical education. Recent studies suggest that the attitude of physical education teachers toward those with disabilities is not positive. Some researchers have suggested that this may be due to insufficient coursework and field experience focusing on the needs of students with disabilities. Rizzo (1984) found that physical education teachers were more positive in their attitude toward teaching those with mental retardation than physical disabilities. He also suggested that the attitude of physical education teachers was less positive as the grade level advanced, with high school teachers less favorable in their attitudes toward teaching students with disabilities than elementary or intermediate teachers. Through additional studies, Rizzo and Vispoel (1991) have also found that physical education teachers have more favorable attitudes toward teaching students with learning disabilities in mainstreamed physical education classes in contrast to students with behavior disorders or mental retardation. A particularly encouraging finding of Rizzo's work is that a teacher's perception of competence has much to do with the teacher's attitude toward teaching individuals with disabilities. This suggests, therefore, that the attitude of teachers toward students with disabilities can be improved if provided coursework and structured practicum experiences.

It is hoped that coursework, the media, printed material, including this text, and the significant achievements of individuals with disabilities will help future generations of physical educators to recognize, appreciate, and accept the challenges and rewards associated with teaching students with disabilities. Most educators who have taught those with disabilities recognize that the energy expended is returned many times over.

Professional Qualifications of the Teacher of Special Physical Education

Regarding the qualifications a teacher needs in order to instruct adapted activities, it should be said that the background subject areas are essentially the same as those for physical education. A thorough knowledge of sport and game skills is very important, as is a sound understanding of the nature of the human body and its response to exercise. Training in methods of teaching and the psychology of learning, including motor learning, is very necessary.

In addition to knowledge pertaining to physical education generally, the teacher should acquire some specific information about the causes, nature, and psychological implications of the various disabilities. It is necessary to understand the effects of exercise upon these conditions and how sports and games may be utilized to improve the social and emotional as well as the physical well-being of individuals with disabilities. The teacher must also have a basic knowledge of emergency treatment of minor injuries and, most particularly, the practices that are applicable to certain disabilities, such as the emergency care to be administered to an indivdual experiencing a seizure or insulin shock.

In recent years, some states have developed standards and certification procedures for teachers of adapted physical education. Although there is not universal agreement among state education officials, administrators, and professionals about the number of hours and courses that should be required for a certificate, there is a growing interest in identifying the competencies that these professionals should possess.

It is clear that simply selecting more experienced teachers to serve as the teacher of students with disabilities will not guarantee success. Vogler, et al. (1992) report that there is no reason to believe that mainstreamed students will benefit more in physical education from experienced as contrasted to novice teachers. Their work suggests that teachers need specific expertise or experience to be successful in providing appropriate physical education programs for students with disabilities. For this and many other reasons, the Physical Activity Council of the American Alliance for Health, Physical Education, Recreation, and Dance (AAHPERD) developed guidelines identifying the competencies that representatives of this organization believe are important. The competencies identified are, for the most part, limited to those with direct relationship to teaching students with disabilities in regular physical education classes or those that would serve as the basic foundation for the more specialized competencies of the adapted physical education specialist. A modified list of competencies identified by AAHPERD for both the generalist and the specialist is presented in table 6.1.

Dempsey (1987) surveyed selected higher-education professors and specialists in adapted physical education to rate the competencies as to their importance. The study was designed to validate the competencies and to compare the observations of knowledgeable university professors to those of public school specialists in adapted physical education. Both groups were in agreement that the competencies were appropriate. In addition, the two groups were comparable in their overall ratings of each of the competency statements. While differences were noted, there was general consensus with both groups that the competencies were appropriate for the training of specialists in adapted physical education.

Suphawibul (1990), in a study similar to that of Dempsey's, using a sophisticated culturally-sensitive translation of the competencies, found that Thai physical educators, both university adapted physical educators and practicing teachers, agreed that the AAHPERD competencies were appropriate for Thailand.

A review of table 6.1 indicates that the primary difference between the competency level of the regular physical education teacher (generalist) and that of the special physical educator (specialist) is one of degree. Obviously both groups are expected to be knowledgeable with respect to the physical education needs of individuals with disabilities and receptive to providing needed services. It is recognized, however, that the generalist is not as knowledgeable about disabilities nor as experienced in working with those with disabilities. There also is a difference in the role of the generalist and specialist. Whereas the regular physical educator

Table 6.1 *Competencies for the generalist in physical education and the specialist in special physical education**

Competency	Generalist	Specialist
1.0 Biological Foundations		
1.1 Kinesiology	Demonstrate understanding of functional anatomy and its relationship to individuals with or without disabilities.	Demonstrate proficiency in evaluating and analyzing motor performance in terms of motor dysfunction and in applying biomechanical principles that affect motor functioning to posture and to neurological, muscular, and other specific health needs.
1.2 Physiology of Exercise	Demonstrate ability to design and conduct physical education programs that adhere to sound physiological principles.	Demonstrate ability to design and conduct physical education programs for individuals with disabilities that adhere to sound physiological principles.
1.3 Physiology and Motor Functioning	Demonstrate understanding of anatomical and physiological deviation and the effects such deviations have on motor performance.	Demonstrate the ability to apply an understanding of physiological motor characteristics for individuals with physical, mental, sensory, neurological, and other specific health needs to programs designed to improve the motor performances of these individuals with disabilities.
2.0 Sociological Foundations		
2.1 Sport, Dance, Play	Demonstrate understanding of the ethnic, social, and cultural aspects of sport, dance, and play and the importance of these in the lives of all, including the disabled.	Demonstrate the ability to analyze the significance of sport, dance, and play in the lives of individuals with disabilities.
2.2 Cooperative/Competitive Activities	Demonstrate understanding of the potential of cooperative/competitive activities for human interaction and social behavior and knowledge of organizations that conduct appropriate activities for the disabled.	Demonstrate ability to apply understanding of the potential for human interaction and social behavior occurring in cooperative/competitive activities for individuals with disabilities; cooperate with organizations that conduct adapted sport, dance, and play programs for individuals with disabilities.
2.3 Social Development	Demonstrate understanding of social learnings involved in experiencing human movement and its effects on perception, motivation, and personality for individuals with and without disabilities.	Demonstrate ability to apply understanding of the potential that sport, dance, and play provide for social interactions among individuals with and without disabilities.
3.0 Psychological Foundations		
3.1 Human Growth and Development	Demonstrate understanding of human growth and development, including how deviation in normal growth and development can result in disabilities and atypical motor development.	Demonstrate ability to apply understanding of deviations in human growth and development and atypical motor development to assist individuals with physical, mental, sensory, neurological, and other specific health needs.
3.2 Motor Learning	Demonstrate proficiency in applying principles of motor learning to teaching and learning motor skills.	Demonstrate ability to apply principles of motor learning, including motivation techniques, to the teaching and learning of motor skills by individuals with disabilities.
3.3 Self-Concept and Personality Development	Demonstrate ability to help students with and without disabilities develop positive self-concepts and overcome attitudinal barriers that can affect interpersonal relationships and development of positive self-concepts.	Demonstrate ability to apply skills and techniques in the teaching of physical and motor skills to assist individuals with disabilities to overcome attitudinal barriers that can affect interpersonal relationships and development of positive self-concepts.
3.4 Management of Behavior	Demonstrate an understanding of principles of motivation as they affect human behavior and promote motor performance and apply various methods for developing appropriate student behavior.	Demonstrate ability to apply appropriate techniques for managing behavior, including techniques of motivation to enhance acceptable behavior and promote motor performance.

*Adapted from a statement prepared by the American Alliance for Health, Physical Education, Recreation, and Dance, 1980.

Table 6.1—*Continued*

Competency	Generalist	Specialist
4.0 Historical and Philosophical Foundations		
4.1 Historical Development	Demonstrate understanding of the historical development of physical education, including the role and significance of professional organizations in the development of professional standards and ethics.	Demonstrate understanding of the historical development of adapted physical education, including the role and significance of professional and voluntary organizations in the development of professional standards and ethics related to adapted physical education.
4.2 Philosophical Development	Demonstrate understanding of the philosophies of physical education, current issues, and emerging trends in physical education and identify ways that individuals realize and express their individualities and uniquenesses through physical education, sport, dance, and play.	Demonstrate understanding of the philosophies of adapted physical education, current issues, and trends in adapted physical education and identify ways individuals with disabilities realize and express their individualities and uniquenesses through physical education, sport, dance, and play programs.
5.0 Assessment and Evaluation		
5.1 Program Goals and Objectives	Demonstrate understanding of goals and objectives of physical education, including programs and activities for individuals with disabilities.	Demonstrate ability to develop instructional objectives that lead to fulfillment of physical education goals in psychomotor, affective, and cognitive domains by individuals with disabilities.
5.2 Screening and Assessment	Demonstrate ability to select, construct, and administer various assessment instruments for measuring physical and motor performance.	Demonstrate proficiency in using appropriate instruments to assess and interpret the motor performances of students with disabilities.
5.3 Evaluation	Demonstrate proficiency in using appropriate evaluative procedures to determine student progress.	Demonstrate proficiency in applying appropriate instruments and evaluative procedures to determine student progress in adapted physical education.
6.0 Curriculum Planning, Organization, and Implementation		
6.1 Program Planning	Demonstrate ability to plan instructional programs that emphasize physical and motor fitness development.	Demonstrate ability to plan individual physical education programs that are adapted to individual student needs based on goals and objectives established by an interdisciplinary team.
6.2 Individual Instruction	Demonstrate ability to apply strategies for individualized instruction in regular physical education settings based on student's current level of performance.	Demonstrate ability to implement appropriate physical education programs for individuals with disabilities based on each student's current level of performance using appropriate strategies, including task-analysis techniques.
6.3 Program Implementation	Demonstrate understanding of role and significance of physical educators as members of interdisciplinary teams.	Demonstrate ability to function effectively as a member of an interdisciplinary team using appropriate techniques for facilitating interdisciplinary communication among all persons working with individuals who are disabled.
6.4 Safety Considerations	Demonstrate knowledge of specific safety considerations for individuals with disabilities as they participate in physical education, sport, dance, and play activities.	Demonstrate understanding of scientific bases for specifically contraindicated exercises and activities, including transfer techniques for individuals with disabilities.
6.5 Health Considerations	Demonstrate knowledge of special health considerations when individuals with disabilities participate in physical education, sport, dance, and play activities.	Demonstrate understanding of the effects of medication, fatigue, illness, posture, and nutrition on the mental, physical, and motor performances of individuals with disabilities.

should be competent to teach those with mild and moderate disabilities, the special physical educator has primary responsibility for structuring and ensuring that those with severe disabilities receive appropriate instruction in physical education. In addition, the special physical educator frequently is asked to provide indirect service to the student with disabilities by serving as a consultant to other physical education teachers. In this latter role, the special physical educator frequently serves as a member of the school system's special education staff, performing many services such as assessing the motor and physical fitness levels of students with disabilities, assisting with the writing of the Individualized Education Program (IEP), recommending placement options, providing teaching suggestions to physical educators, recruiting and training volunteers, and informing other teachers about the motor and physical fitness needs of the disabled.

The precise role of the special physical educator is dependent upon many factors, including the size of the school system, the number and type of special students, and the extent to which the regular physical educators are available and prepared to provide programs for students with special needs. A schematic of the role relationship responsibility between the general and special physical educator is presented in figure 6.1. Placement of the *X*s in figure 6.1 denotes who has primary responsibility for the specific function. An *X* placed somewhere between the regular physical educator and special physical educator emphasizes that many responsibilities are shared, with one party assuming a greater degree of responsibility. The functions and responsibilities of both professional groups are important in providing appropriate physical education services to the special student.

The most ambitious effort to date to identify the skills needed by professionals to be qualified to deliver special physical education services is the National Standards Project directed by Luke E. Kelly. This project, funded by the Office of Special Education and Rehabilitative Service, is designed to identify the content that specialists in adapted physical education sould possess to teach students with disabilities. The work thus far has led to the identification of a knowledge base which is grouped into fifteen content areas or standards (Kelly, 1995). The standards include:

Human Development
Motor Behavior
Exercise Science
Measurement and Evaluation
History and Philosphy
Unique Attributes of Learners
Curriculum Theory and Development
Assessment
Instructional Design and Planning
Teaching
Consultation and Staff Development
Program Evaluation

Continuing Education
Ethics
Communication

The ultimate goal of the National Standards Project is to create a valid examination that can be taken by professionals to demonstrate they possess the knowledge to be effective as practitioners. Given the wide support for the project from both university personnel and physical education teachers, it is probable that the National Standards Project will enhance the overall quality of services provided to individuals with disabilities.

Developing Individualized Education Programs (IEPs)

One of the significant features of P.L. 101-476 and its historic predecessor P.L. 94-142 is the requirement that an IEP be developed for each student with disabilities. There are two main parts of the IEP requirement as described in P.L. 101-476 and the regulations that accompany this law: (1) the IEP meeting(s), at which parents and school personnel jointly make decisions about a child's educational program and (2) the IEP document itself, which is a written record of the decisions reached at the meetings.

Purposes of the IEP

The IEP process is designed to accommodate a number of important functions. Some of these, as identified by the federal government, are indicated in the following paragraphs (Federal Register: Part XII, January 14, 1981, p. 5460).

The IEP meeting serves as a communication vehicle between parents and school personnel, thus allowing them as equal participants to jointly decide the student's educational needs and to identify the necessary special education and related services. The IEP meeting also helps to resolve potential differences between parents and school officials concerning the educational programs as well as anticipated outcomes.

A practical purpose of the IEP is to identify in writing the resources necessary to enable the student to benefit from the educational program that has been developed. Furthermore, the IEP is a management tool that is used to ensure that each student with a disability is provided special education and related services appropriate to the student's special learning needs.

The IEP also may be used as a compliance or monitoring device. Local school personnel as well as State Department of Education officials can review individual IEPs to determine whether a student is receiving the educational program agreed to by the parents and the school. An evaluation of the student's progress toward meeting the stated educational goals and objectives is also possible by periodically examining the IEP.

Degree of Responsibility for Various Special Physical Education Functions

FUNCTIONS	Regular Physical Educator	Special Physical Educator
Screen	X	
Assess	X	
Write IEPs/IFSPs	X	
Recommend Placement	X	
Recruit Volunteers	X	
Train Volunteers		X
Serve on Multidisciplinary Team	X	
Inservice Teachers		X
Implement Program/Mildly Handicapped	X	
Implement Program/Moderately Handicapped	X	
Implement Program/Severely Handicapped		X
Consult with Teachers		X

Figure 6.1 Schematic of the shared responsibilities of special and regular physical educators of students with disabilities.

IEP Team Members

Although the exact composition of the IEP team will vary from one school system to the next, P.L. 101-476 specifies that certain participants must be included in all IEP discussions. School officials are responsible for ensuring that the following participants are present at the IEP meeting:

1. *A representative of the public agency, other than the child's teacher, who is qualified to provide, or supervise the provision of, special education.* Various individuals, including building principals, counselors, and special education administrators, normally are selected to fulfill this role. The key factor is that the person selected must be thoroughly familiar with the local school's special education program, and federal and state law.

2. *The child's teacher.* Obviously, the person selected to fill this role is the teacher who has the most contact with the student. Depending upon the situation, this can be the regular classroom teacher, a special educator, or a specialist such as a speech therapist or physical educator. Of primary importance is that the person selected to fill this role cannot also serve as the school's representative to the team, as identified in point 1 above.

3. *One or both of the child's parents.* As discussed earlier, one of the basic premises of P.L. 101-476 is that parent input into the IEP plan is considered extremely important. For this reason, school systems should take whatever steps are necessary to ensure that parents are involved in the IEP deliberations. This means scheduling the meeting at a time convenient for parents as well as informing parents of their right to disagree with the recommended Individualized Education Program.

Some parents also may require the assistance of an interpreter if they are deaf or their native language is one other than English. Regardless of the provisions made to solicit parent input, a small percentage of parents will elect not to become involved in the IEP process. In these cases, the IEP meeting may still be held but school officials should be prepared to document, if asked, their attempts to solicit parent input. In some cases the State Department of Education will appoint surrogate parents for students living in state institutions whose parents are deceased, unknown, or express no interest in their child's welfare.

4. *The child, where appropriate.* Students with disabilities, like their nondisabled peers, frequently have helpful comments to make about the educational experiences that are to be provided for them. It is for this reason P.L. 101-476 emphasizes the importance of student input. The final decision as to whether the student will participate as a member of the IEP team rests with the parents, except in cases where the student is of majority age. Although P.L. 101-476 is not clear on this point, many schools have elected to invite the student of majority age as well as the student's parents.

5. *Other individuals, at the discretion of the parents or agency.* This last category for membership on the IEP team simply indicates that both the local school and the parents have the right to invite others to participate as members of the IEP team. For the school this means that on occasion it may be desirable to have additional school personnel involved in the IEP deliberations. Likewise, parents may feel the need to be accompanied by a relative or friend who is more knowledgeable about education and its relationship to their student. In some instances, parents have also felt it necessary to be accompanied by legal representation. The important point is that both the parents and the school may invite others to participate without asking the other party's permission.

The members identified previously are charged with the responsibility of developing an appropriate educational program for each special student. To accomplish this task requires that the team meet at least annually and more frequently if necessary. Because physical education is an integral part of special education, the IEP team must also decide on the type of physical education program to require. This is a critical decision that, if not handled properly, can result in inappropriate physical education services for the special education student. Some of the potential difficulty arises because of the composition of the team and the absence of a person knowledgeable about the area of physical education. Some school systems have resolved this problem by inviting a representative of physical education to serve on the IEP team, particularly for the student with more severe disabilities. Other school systems, desiring to keep the official IEP team small, have used pre-IEP meetings to obtain the input of specialists such as physical educators. Either system seems to work well. The important point is that the IEP team, as will be discussed next, makes critical decisions that affect the quality of physical education services that are eventually implemented.

Content of the IEP

The IEP document is an important source of information that specifies the special education programs and services to be provided the student. Each IEP must include the following information:

1. A statement of the child's educational performance;
2. A statement of annual goals, including short-term instructional objectives;
3. A statement of the specific special education and related services to be provided to the child and the extent to which the child will be able to participate in regular educational programs;
4. The projected dates for initiation of services and the anticipated duration of the services;
5. Appropriate objective criteria and evaluation procedures and schedules for determining, on at least an annual basis, whether the short-term instructional objectives are being achieved; and
6. A statement of the needed transition services for students beginning no later than age sixteen and annually thereafter (and when determined appropriate for the individual, beginning at age fourteen or younger), including, when appropriate, a statement of the interagency responsibilities or linkages (or both) before the student leaves the school setting.

A careful analysis of these elements is critical to the development of a meaningful IEP. Information on physical education must be included in the student's IEP. In the following paragraphs, information on physical education and its relationship to the content of the IEP will be discussed.

Present Level of Educational Performance

"Present level of educational performance," as the title implies, simply means those physical education skills the student presently possesses. To ascertain this information requires that an appropriate assessment be conducted to determine the student's physical and motor fitness levels. Without this information the school representatives will be at a disadvantage at the IEP meeting when called upon to make recommendations concerning the student's special physical education needs.

Assessment information about the special student's motor ability may be derived from a variety of sources. Some of these are as follows:

School Records

What physical education skills has the student previously been taught? How did the student do? Were any behavior problems observed? Did the student attend class on time? Were dressing and undressing before and after class a positive or problem area? Information such as this, which should be easily obtained from school records, is very helpful to the IEP team.

Norm-Referenced Tests

Comparing the performance of a student to the performances of a group of similar individuals is referred to as a norm-referenced comparison. *Project Unique* is an example of a nationally norm-referenced test. There is considerable value in being able to compare a student's performance to age-equivalent peers with similar disabilities. Norm-referenced tests help the teacher to determine the student's present level of performance, but they do little to identify an acceptable criterion level of performance.

Criterion-Referenced Tests

This type of test helps the IEP team to determine how a student's performance compares to a defined standard. Normally, the utilization of this approach requires the availability of a curriculum that is sequenced and in which tasks such as throwing a ball are broken down into smaller steps. An excellent example of this approach is the *I CAN* program, a set of physical education curricular materials that promote the concept of systematic teaching based on a criterion-referenced assessment procedure.

The use of both norm-referenced and criterion-referenced tests is discussed more fully in chapter 7.

Observations

Physical educators may find it necessary from time to time to use a readily available assessment tool, their own powers of observation, to document the need for special physical education services. Not all youngsters can be effectively evaluated by norm- or even criterion-referenced assessment procedures. Students with cerebral palsy, orthopedic impairments, and multiple disabilities are examples of the types of special populations that may require teachers to rely primarily on their observational skills to assess performance levels. Teachers who may be apprehensive about their ability to observe accurately can videotape examples of the student's movement skills to share with others at the IEP meeting. Such a procedure frequently provides valuable information to assist the rest of the team to focus on the individual's physical education needs.

The assessment process is the seed from which the individualized education program develops. Without accurate and adequate information, conclusions may be drawn that will result in inappropriate goals and objectives as well as inappropriate program placement. Additional information on evaluation procedures will be presented in chapter 7.

Goals and Objectives

The goals and objectives become the guideposts for determining whether the student with a disability is benefiting from the educational program developed by the IEP team. Goals provide direction and serve as a means to communicate to the child and members of the team that a particular area such as cardiorespiratory endurance needs work. The following are examples of physical education goals:

Joe will improve his overhand throw.
Mary will improve her performance on the 600-yard walk-run test.
Matthew will learn to skip.

For each of these goals, objectives should be developed that define more precisely the behaviors that will be taught the student. Essentially, each objective should specify the behavior, the conditions under which the behavior is to be performed, and the level of criteria accepted as appropriate. Using the first goal, objectives for teaching Joe the overhand throw, stated in behavioral terms, might include:

1. Using a tennis ball, Joe will throw the ball overhand and hit a four-foot by four-foot target ten feet away eight out of ten times;
2. Using a tennis ball, Joe will throw the ball overhand and hit a four-foot by four-foot target twenty feet away eight out of ten times;
3. Using a tennis ball, Joe will throw the ball overhand and hit a two-foot by two-foot target ten feet away eight out of ten times;
4. Using a tennis ball, Joe will throw the ball overhand and hit a two-foot by two-foot target twenty-five feet away eight out of ten times.

Depending on the particular student, the objectives might vary in a number of ways such as in the size of target or distance to target, as well as in the accuracy expected. For some students, the objective might focus simply on the throwing pattern.

One need only develop a sufficient number of objectives for each goal to indicate to other members of the team the process and level of behavior deemed appropriate. Many educators are now developing their objectives, including the number, to correspond with the school's grading periods. Therefore, if a school has six grading periods, six objectives would be proposed for each goal. For each objective, a projected date for reaching the specified criterion must be provided.

Special Education and Related Services

Public Laws 94-142 and 101-476, as discussed previously, identify physical education as a special education service. The primary concern in this section is, therefore, devoted to the type of physical education program to be provided. Specifically, the question of whether the student with a disability requires special physical education must be discussed. If the student's present level of educational performance, including motor, cognitive, and affective, is acceptable, the student is placed in the regular physical education program and expected to learn at a rate equivalent to that of other nondisabled peers. For some students, however, it will be obvious that deficiencies exist in their motor-skill level that will require special physical education services. As discussed in chapter 5, requests for special assistance do not eliminate the possibility of placing the student in the regular physical education class. Some individuals, for example, may simply need the assistance of an aide or volunteer. Of course, students with more severe disabilities may require help that can best be met in a special physical education experience. If so, services of this nature must be provided.

Physical educators will need to utilize the services of other related professionals to best fulfill the physical education needs of some students. Related services include, but are not limited to, the following:

speech therapy
physical therapy
occupational therapy
work experience
medical service
social services
transportation
recreation

Obviously, physical educators and the students they teach would benefit from the assistance of many of the professionals identified here. For instance, many individuals with Down syndrome experience congenital cardiovascular system problems; engaging such children in active movement skills without the consultation and advice of a physician would be inappropriate.

Educators should be cautioned to remember, however, that related services are *related* and should not be used to supplant physical education programs. Physical therapy, for instance, is a valuable and necessary service for many students with disabilities. However, justifying physical therapy as a replacement for a physical education program places too much emphasis on the commonality of the shared word "physical" and does a disservice to professionals in physical therapy and physical education and to the student who can benefit from both programs.

Time Line for Service

Each IEP is normally written to cover a time period of up to twelve months. For each goal and objective, a time line is established that provides a general estimate of when the student should achieve a particular goal. It is generally recognized that predicting when a "milestone" is to be reached is very difficult. Some students, for instance, reach the objectives much sooner than expected, whereas others achieve few, if any, of the stated objectives. When the teacher sees unusual deviations from the projected time line, it is best to request that the school personnel call for an IEP meeting to identify, with parent consultation, new goals and objectives or more realistic time lines for those previously developed.

Evaluation Procedures

The Individualized Education Program must include a plan that specifies the procedure to be used to evaluate the student's progress. This review must be done at least annually.

Many school systems have responded to this requirement by indicating the extent to which the student has achieved the goals and objectives specified in the IEP. It should be emphasized, however, that the IEP is not a performance contract that imposes liability on a teacher or public agency if a student does not meet the IEP objectives. According to the Rules and Regulations for Public Law 94-142, "While the agency must provide special education and related services in accordance with each handicapped child's IEP, the Act does not require that the agency, the teacher, or other persons be held accountable if the child does not achieve the growth projected in the written statement" (1981).

Transition Services

The concept of transition services was added when amendments to P.L. 94-142 were added in P.L. 101-476. Specifically, the Individuals with Disabilities Education Act (IDEA) provided a definition of transition services and added transition services to students' IEPs. Specifically, transition services means a coordinated set of activities for a student, which promotes movement from school to postschool activities including postsecondary education, vocational training, integrated employment, continuing and adult education, adult services, independent living, or community participation. The goal, of course, is to ensure that students and other community resources are fully integrated to the extent that students with disabilities can move easily from the school setting to other environments, including those used for various recreational pursuits. Physical educators, thus, are expected to be cognizant of procedures for ensuring that skills and activities learned in the school setting can be generalized easily and successfully into other settings (e.g., community fitness centers, roller skating rinks, swimming pools, etc.).

IDEA also made it clear that cooperating and participating agencies are responsible for providing services identified within the IEP. Specifically, the law states that where a participating agency, other than the educational agency, fails to provide agreed upon services, the educational agency shall reconvene the IEP team to identify alternative strategies to meet the transition objectives. This, of course, places the school in a unique position to not only work cooperatively with participating agencies, but also to monitor the quality of their services.

Individualized Family Service Plan

Closely related to the IEP, is the Individualized Family Service Plan (IFSP) mandated by P.L. 99-457, the Education of the Handicapped Act Amendments of 1986. Part H of this law extends previous legislation to include services for the youngest members of society (infants and toddlers) and their parents. Specifically, the law reaffirms the rights of children with disabilities ages three through five years under P.L. 101-476 and provides a new state grant program for infants and toddlers with disabilities up to two years old (Dunn, 1991). One of the critical aspects of P.L. 99-457 is the IFSP. The major components of the IFSP include:

1. A statement of the child's present levels of development (cognitive, motor, speech/language, psychosocial, and self help);
2. A statement of the family's strengths and needs relating to enhancing the child's development;
3. A statement of major outcomes expected to be achieved for the child and family;
4. The criteria, procedures, and timelines for determining progress;
5. The specific early intervention services necessary to meet the unique needs of the child and family including the method, frequency, and intensity of service; and
6. The projected dates for the initiation of services and expected duration.

While it is clear that there are many similarities between the IEP and IFSP, there are also some differences. First, the IFSP is family-centered with as much commitment and emphasis placed on the family as the individual child. As Deal, Dunst, and Trivett (1989) stated, "Major emphasis is placed on both enabling and empowering families. Enabling families means creating opportunities for family members to become more competent and self-sustaining with respect to their abilities to mobilize their social networks, to get needs met and attain desired goals . . . . Empowering families means carrying out interventions in a manner in which family members acquire a sense of control over their own development course as a result of their effort to meet needs" (p. 33). Second, the IFSP is designed to make certain that for the infant (0–2) that there is a transition plan to ensure a smooth integration into the school at age three. Additional information about the motor development and activity needs of infants and toddlers will be presented in chapter 21.

Systematic Approaches to Teaching

In recent years, there has been much greater emphasis placed on the systematic analysis of instruction. Much of this is attributed to growing recognition that selected process variables such as the amount of time spent in the academic or instructional environment and the number of opportunites to respond or perform is very important to the success of the learner. Many believe that a measure of the amount of learning time (frequently referred to as academic learning time, ALT) suggests that increases in on-task time leads to educational gain. For students with disabilities, it is clear that the efficient use of instructional time is critical. DePaepe (1985) for instance found that with the assistance of peer tutors the

ALT time in physical education was greatly enhanced. Webster (1987), too, suggested that peer tutors were effective in increasing the amount of ALT in physical education.

Other investigators have suggested that the frequency with which students have an opportutity to respond (OTR) in physical education may be as important as the amount of on-task instructional time. Houston-Wilson (1993), for instance, found that trained peer tutors were very effective in helping students with developmental disabilities increase their OTR in physical education.

Both ALT-PE and OTR-PE offer excellent methods for assessing important process variables (instructional time and frequency of response) which are vital to achieving desired learning objectives for students with disabilities.

Analyzing and Applying Principles of Movement

In teaching motor skills to those with disabilities, the teacher must understand and develop the ability to analyze the movements made by the student and to apply the mechanical principles of movement to achieve the most effective performance possible for the particular student. Analysis of movement consists of determining which essential parts of the body are involved in a given movement and how these parts relate to each other in the performance of the movement. Knowledge of anatomy and kinesiology is, of course, extremely useful in making an accurate analysis.

Every individual differs from every other anatomically, physiologically and neurologically; therefore, the best way to perform a movement varies to some extent for each person. Persons with disabilities, because their differences are increased by their particular conditions, will usually vary to a much greater extent. Consequently, the best way for each student to perform a particular skill can be most effectively determined by analyzing his or her movements in order to understand how he or she moves and then, by applying the principles of movement, to discover the most efficient and effective way to utilize the movements in the performance of the skill.

All movements, including human movements, are regulated by the laws of motion. In human movements, the chief elements are those related to maintaining equilibrium and stability.

Principles of Stability

Achieving stability is important in all action as well as in all stationary positions. The successful performance of such activities as standing, sitting, running, jumping, and bouncing requires some degree of stability. In maintaining stability, the body is governed by certain principles:

1. When the center of gravity is lowered, greater stability is achieved.

2. The larger or wider the base of the support, the greater the stability.
3. When the center of gravity is over the base, stability is greater.

When the body is lowered, as in bending the knees, the center of gravity is lowered, thereby providing more stability. In activities in which force must be received, such as catching a fast ball, greater stability can be created by lowering the body, thereby making it more capable of receiving the force without losing balance. Balance is more easily maintained in a sitting position than standing; hence, one who is on crutches may increase stability by sitting to play some types of games, such as bowling or shuttle badminton, rather than trying to balance with crutches in the erect position.

A larger base allows a greater range of body movement before the center of gravity moves beyond the base to cause the loss of balance. This is particularly evident in walking a narrow beam; maintaining balance in this kind of activity is difficult because the base of support is relatively small. In movement that requires a stable base, spreading the feet creates a larger base. A case in point is when a person balances with a cane; the triangle made by the feet and the cane affords more support as the size of the triangle is increased.

It should be noted that a wide base does not always create the most efficient position. If the stance is so wide that the legs are at an extreme angle to the ground, muscular efficiency is decreased so that, actually, any advantage created for maintaining balance by a wide base is nullified by the decrease in the muscular efficiency of the legs used in maintaining balance.

When the center of gravity is near the center of the base, greater stability is created. Many directions for performing skills include a suggestion to distribute the weight evenly in order to give better balance to the body. Such distribution brings the center of gravity to the center of the base. If the participant must make a quick move or start in a specific direction, he or she leans the body in that direction so that the balance is easily disturbed by the shifting of weight. In starting a race, the body is leaned forward and the center of gravity falls near the front of the base. In running rapidly, the center of gravity falls in front of the base so that, in a sense, the body falls forward and the legs "run up under the body." When slowing from a fast pace, the body is straightened so that the center of gravity is brought back near the center of the base.

Principles of Moving the Body

The movement of the human body or any part of it is governed by these laws of motion:

1. An object at rest will remain at rest, or if in motion will remain in motion at the same speed in a straight line unless acted upon by a force.

2. When a body is acted upon by a force, its resulting change of speed is directly proportional to the force and inversely proportional to the mass.
3. For every action, there is an equal and opposite reaction.

The tendency of the body to remain either stationary or in motion is known as inertia. The more the object weighs, the more force is required to overcome its inertia. Also, the faster the movement of the object, the greater the difficulty in overcoming its inertia. In initiating movement, the inertia is overcome by use of force. Once an object is moving, less force is required to keep it moving. In propelling a wheelchair, for example, less energy is required to push it after it is moving than to bring it into motion. The same is true of the body. An individual attempting to move from a sitting position to a standing position will find it much easier to complete the movement entirely than to stop halfway and then continue rising.

If unequal forces are applied to two objects of equal mass, the object to which the greater force is applied will move at a greater speed. If equal forces are applied to two masses of different sizes, the larger mass will move at a slower rate. For example, if two girls are batting balls and one of the girls consistently hits the ball with more force, her ball will travel much farther; however, if the girls are hitting with equal force but one has a heavier ball, the heavier ball will travel a shorter distance than the lighter ball.

The equal and opposite reaction is perhaps most easily illustrated by the swimmer pushing backward against the water—the water moves backward as the swimmer moves forward. This reaction is not so obvious when the performer pushes against a large solid object, such as a wall or the ground, because of the large size of the object in relation to the performer who is exerting force against it; movement of the large object is insignificant in relation to the movement of the performer and, therefore, is not noticed.

When the body is not supported by a surface but is in the air, the equal and opposite reaction occurs within the body itself. For example, when one jumps from a diving board with the arm extended to the side, and then swings that arm to the front of the body, the entire body will turn in the direction opposite to that in which the arm is moving. The speed of the turn is increased if the extended arm is bent as it is brought to the front. The rotary motion of turning is accelerated by shortening the radius of the body when the arm is brought close to the body. Conversely, the rotary motion is decreased when the radius of the moving body is increased. Application of this principle is, as should now be apparent, very important in diving and tumbling activities.

Still another factor that must be considered when absorbing force is the relationship of the force to the size of the area that bears the brunt of the impact. Force concentrated on a small area of body surface is likely to cause more serious injury than the same amount of force spread over a larger area. For this reason, injury is more likely in a fall in which the weight is taken on one foot than when the weight is distributed equally on both feet.

In catching an object, both factors (absorbing the force over a longer time and spreading the force over a larger area while receiving it) are important for the safety and success of the performer. Consequently, to catch a ball that has been thrown hard, the elbows are bent to help absorb the force; to catch large balls, the body is leaned backward as the ball is caught. A baseball glove helps to disperse the impact of the ball over a large area of the hand as well as to lengthen the time it takes the ball to slow down. The padding acts as a cushion that reduces the force over a longer period of time.

In many instances, individuals with disabilities, especially orthopedic and neurological impairments, will not be able to perform the movements described in the principles of absorbing force. In these cases, it is necessary to first determine if participation in the movements is contraindicated. If not, an analysis of those movements that can be performed should be made in order to determine what movements may be substituted for the lost movements. For example, a person who lacks the ability to bend the knees to lower the body closer to the ground while falling may use the arms to help absorb the force of the fall. The arms are slightly bent to take the force of the fall, and the body is lowered quickly to the ground to increase the distance over which kinetic energy is lost.

Principles of Imparting Force to an Object

Many of the activities in physical education require the projection of a ball or an object into the air. In throwing a ball there are three main concerns: (1) the speed of the throw, (2) the distance, and (3) the direction in which the ball will travel.

The speed and the distance that the ball is thrown are dependent upon the speed at which the hand was traveling at the moment of release. The speed that the hand can acquire depends upon the distance it travels before the ball is released. Therefore, it is advantageous to make the backswing of the throwing movement as long as possible by rotating the body, shifting the weight, and taking a step. The use of these movements to create distance is effective only if they are synchronized, so that each one is added to the preceding movement to take advantage of the momentum already created.

The distance that the ball will travel depends not only on the force exerted in the throwing but also on the angle at which it is released. As soon as the ball leaves the hand, gravity has a tendency to pull it downward. The pull of gravity becomes more noticeable as the ball is slowed by the resistance of the air. A greater distance can be obtained if the ball is thrown upward as well as forward because the ball will stay in the air longer and, hence, travel farther. The throwing angle that gains the most distance is approximately forty-five degrees.

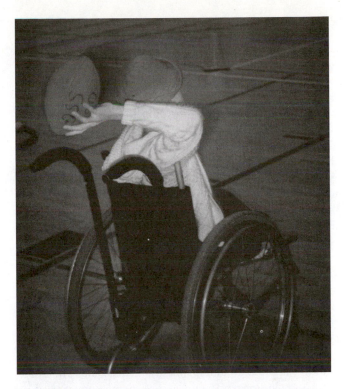

Figure 6.2 When mobility is impaired, principles of imparting force to an object must be modified.

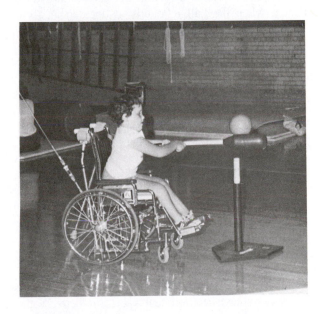

Figure 6.3 Activities may be modified in several ways to ensure that the student will be successful in imparting force to an object.

The follow-through is an important part of the throw. Stopping the movement immediately after the release of the ball tends to produce a short, jerky movement throughout the total throw and affects the direction and distance of the throw. Furthermore, stopping the throw abruptly may cause injury to the arm because the muscles that must contract for the throw may be damaged by the tremendous force exerted in the opposite direction.

The direction in which the ball travels depends upon the direction in which the force was applied at the moment of release. In most throwing, the hand describes an arc in the throwing process; when the ball is released, it goes off at a tangent to the arc described by the hand. The release of the ball must be timed so that the tangent is in the desired direction. It is easier to release the ball at the correct time when the hands are moved in a flatter arc at the time of the release. A ball that is too large to hold in the fingers and must be held in the palm is more difficult to release at the right time than one held in the fingers. Keeping the palm of the hand directly behind the ball as it moves in the desired direction will keep the ball moving in that direction.

The direction of flight may be influenced by winds as well as by any spin that is placed on the ball when it is released. A spin to the right causes the ball to curve to the right; a spin to the left causes it to curve to the left.

When an implement such as a bat or a racket is used to apply force to an object, the implement becomes an extension of the arm. The arm in throwing or batting is a lever; with the addition of an implement, the resistance arm of the lever becomes longer. Hence, greater momentum can be created. When a bat is swung in an arc, the end of the bat is moving much faster than the hands that are holding it. Consequently, when the ball rebounds, it does so at a much faster rate than if the bat were only moving at the speed of the hands.

The direction the ball travels is even more difficult to control when using an implement than when throwing. The angle of the ball as it leaves the striking surface is determined by the angle at which it hits the surface. The ball will bounce from the object at an angle opposite to that at which it struck; so, in batting a ball the bat must strike the ball at an angle opposite the direction of the intended flight of the ball. To cause the ball to rebound in the same direction that it came from, it must strike the implement at right angles.

There is no agreement among teachers on the value of teaching the principles of movement to participants before they engage in performance of skills. Research studies have not helped to clarify the issue. Some studies have indicated that students perform better when they are taught the mechanical principles before attempting performance; other studies have shown that students perform better without having been exposed to such knowledge. Whether participants profit from instruction in principles of movement appears to be dependent upon how the information is presented. The following suggestions are offered as ways in which maximum benefit may be gained from the teaching of the principles to students before their participation in motor activities:

1. Select the principles to be taught in relation to the ability of the students to understand them.

2. Simplify the presentation, when necessary, to fit the situation and the ability of the students to comprehend.

3. Avoid belaboring the obvious—do not offer explanations when the concept is already well understood by the participants.

4. Avoid lengthy sessions of discussion.

5. Integrate the teaching of principles with the teaching of a skill or movement.

In the author's work with students with orhopedic disabilities, the students have shown themselves to be more capable of experimenting intelligently to find the best kind of movement to fit their needs and abilities if they have some understanding of movement principles. Consequently, it is recommended that the principles be taught to students with disabilities with close adherence to the previous suggestions.

Task Analysis

Because learning motor skills is more challenging for students with disabilities, it is essential that activities be taught in a systematic way, starting with easier and then moving to more difficult components of an activity. To accomplish this goal, many teachers use a process referred to as task analysis, a technique in which the components of an activity are identified and then ordered according to their level of difficulty. Each component is then broken down into smaller

Figure 6.4 The analysis of movement principles must be individually applied to individuals with disabilities.

instructional units so that students will be taught at a level where they can achieve initial success before moving to more advanced levels. For example, the skill of roller skating is a complex motor activity comprised of many essential components. To successfully roller skate, students must be able to stand, walk, glide, stop, and turn on skates. After the components are identified, they should be ordered from least to most difficult. Using the roller skating example, standing on skates obviously would be taught prior to turning on skates. The next step, breaking the components into smaller instructional phases, is the heart of the task analysis process. For instance, the component of walking on skates might be taught as follows:

Selected Component: Walk on Skates

PHASE I: Walk on carpet squares attached to feet for ten feet
PHASE II: Walk on wood blocks attached to feet for ten feet
PHASE III: Walk on one skate, with a block under the other foot for ten feet
PHASE IV: Walk on two skates on a shag rug for a distance of ten feet
PHASE V: Walk on two skates on a shag rug for a distance of twenty feet
PHASE VI: Walk on two skates on an indoor carpet for a distance of twenty feet
PHASE VII: Walk on two skates on a gymnasium floor for a distance of twenty feet

The following steps apply to Phases IV–VII:

Step 1:   With teacher assistance
Step 2:   With assistance of an object such as a chair, rope, walker, and so on
Step 3:   Without assistance

There are several important features of the task-analysis process that must be emphasized. First, this procedure permits both the teacher and the student to see progress. For some students, the activity of roller skating will be extremely frustrating unless the activity is broken down into some smaller meaningful steps. For both student and teacher, many successful experiences will be shared as the student masters various tasks, then components, and finally the entire activity.

A second positive aspect of task-analyzing skills is that teachers quickly realize that they have more options available to them than they might have initially recognized. Breaking any component of an activity into smaller instructional packages will help the teacher to stretch his or her imagination to try new and creative methods of helping students learn. For instance, in the roller skating example, the use of carpet of varying textures is an idea generated by a teacher who was convinced that there had to be a way to increase friction and thus reduce the free roll of the skates. Other teaching ideas might include using old skates with

rusted, immovable wheels or having students walk on skates surrounded by a tall box for support.

The task-analysis process also lends itself as a valuable tool for helping to evaluate the students' accomplishments. Figure 6.5 illustrates the relationship between the students' accomplishments and the amount of time required at each phase. In this example, the phase must be performed correctly for two consecutive days before moving to the next phase. Some teachers might prefer that the student have three or four consecutive days with an X before moving to the next phase. These are decisions that the teacher makes for each individual student based on a variety of factors.

Figure 6.5 also identifies another positive feature of task analysis: Breaking skills down and charting student progress helps teachers make sound educational decisions. For instance, in figure 6.5, it appears that the student is having difficulty learning Phase IV, Step 2. What this suggests to the teacher is that the distance between Steps 1 and 2 of Phase IV is too great for this student. Therefore, it will be necessary to branch this specific task. For example, Phase IV, Step 1 requires that the student walk on two skates on a shag rug for a distance of ten feet with teacher assistance. Although the student is able to successfully complete this task, the next phase and step are apparently too difficult. In analyzing Phase IV, Step 2, the only difference in this task from the preceding one is that the student must do the task with the assistance of an object instead of a teacher. In inserting a branch into this program, several options could be employed. For instance, the teacher might want to monitor the amount of assistance, slowly fading from two-hand assistance to one-hand assistance prior to going to Phase IV, Step 2. In this example, the use of various amounts of teacher assistance would be identified as branches and added to the student's Task Analysis Evaluation Sheet. This example suggests, too, that despite the fact that an activity can be broken into components and in turn into tasks, not all students learn tasks or the components in the same order. Therefore, although a task-analyzed physical education curriculum is helpful, no sequenced curriculum will ever be developed that can be applied universally to all students. The task-analysis approach is essential, however, as an aid to assist teachers in becoming sensitive to individual students' learning needs by creating positive and successful educational experiences.

While task analysis continues to be a very effective instructional approach, particularly for individuals with severe disabilities (Dunn, Morehouse, Fredericks, 1986), Davis and Burton (1991) caution that this approach is not without limitations. They argue that traditional approaches to task analysis have focused too much on the task and not enough on the performer or the environment in which the task is to be performed. Building on the work of others, namely Gibson (1979) and Newell (1986), Burton and Davis offer a new approach to task analysis, known as Ecological Task Analysis. The ecological approach to task analysis,

TASK ANALYSIS EVALUATION SHEET

Component __WALK ON SKATES__

Student's Name _____

Starting Date _____

Ending Date _____

Date

PHASES	3/11	3/12	3/13	3/14	3/15	3/16	3/17	3/18	3/19	3/20	3/21	3/22	3/23	3/24	3/25	COMMENTS
I	O	X	X													
II			X	O	X	X										
III							O	X	X							
IV (1)										X	X					
IV (2)												O	O	O		
IV (3)																
V (1)																
V (2)																
V (3)																
VI (1)																
VI (2)																
VI (3)																
VII (1)																
VII (2)																
VII (3)																

Figure 6.5 Example of a task analysis evaluation sheet for monitoring student progress.

depicted in figure 6.6, focuses on the environment, the performer as well as the task that is to be learned. Burton and Davis argue that the primary difference between the ecological and regular approach to task analysis is that the "wholeness" of the skill to be learned is not divided into small parts such that the meaning of the skill is lost. Proponents of this approach, therefore, would argue that task sequences may vary considerably depending on the performer and environmental constraints. An application of the ecological approach would lead the teacher, therefore, to practice the "goal" of the task; e.g., locomotion using related movement skills such as rolling, creeping, etc. in various settings or environments. The "correctness" of the response is based on the performer's perception of the task, the environment and his or her personal attributes. In this respect, the ecological approach does not rely on the anatomical approach commonly used in many traditional approaches to task analysis.

While the ecological task analysis approach appears to be consistent with what proponents of task analysis have

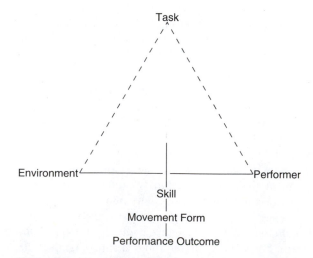

Figure 6.6 Task analysis helps to understand the relationship among the environment, skill, and performer.

long proposed, the ecological approach emphasizes correctly the need to focus on the learner and not the task and to emphasize the teaching and learning of skills in various environments. Ecological task analysis also holds much promise for directing future research efforts because of its sound theoretical premise and relationship to new research in motor development, including dynamic systems theory discussed earlier in chapter 3.

Motivating the Student with a Disability

Motivation cannot be thought of as a direct cause of all behavior. It is simply a concept that is used to explain why human behavior occurs. Wloodkowski (1977) states that most psychologists and educators use the word motivation "to describe those processes that can (a) arouse and instigate behavior, (b) give direction or purpose to behavior, (c) continue to allow behavior to persist, and (d) lead to choosing or performing a particular behavior."

Various theoretical concepts exist as the basis for ways to motivate behavior. Theorists of the different concepts have their own body of research to support and their own vernacular to express the ideas and methods particular to their theories about motivation. However, the theories do overlap, so that it is possible to utilize methods advocated by different theories in combination to produce the best results in motivating the learner. Also, certain concepts of various theoretical bases appear to be more effective in motivating some individuals than do others.

The last point can best be illustrated by the theories of humanism and behaviorism, the two theories most commonly utilized by educators. Basic to the humanistic approach is the idea that a reasoning process must be evoked in the learners so that they arrive at decisions that are best for themselves as individuals and for the society in which they live, and then act upon the decisions accordingly. Intrinsic rewards rather than extrinsic ones are used to motivate and reinforce learning. The behavioristic approach emphasizes extrinsic rewards and relies primarily on manipulation of the external environment to produce the desired behavior. There is more concern for the outcome, rather than the means by which the outcome is achieved, than is the case with humanism.

Experience with learners of various levels of intelligence confirms that development of a reasoning process that enables a person to make a decision with respect to the most desirable behavior is dependent upon the capacity to reason and possess an adequate degree of emotional stability. Hence, motivational methods of humanism have not proved to be as effective with those who are mentally retarded and emotionally disturbed as the methods of the behaviorists have.

Researchers have found the use of extrinsic rewards to be very effective in producing desired behavior in those with mental and emotional disabilities. However, the preponderance of research indicates that although extrinsic

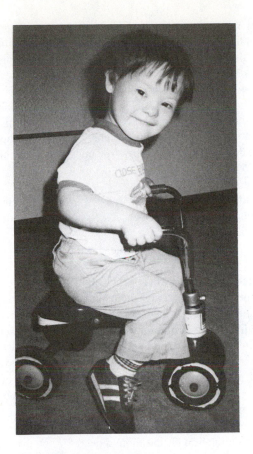

Figure 6.7 Learning to ride a push toy can be a very satisfying and rewarding experience.

rewards can be quite effective in altering behavior temporarily in a controlled setting, such rewards are less influential in effecting changes of a permanent nature outside the nonreinforcing environment. Individuals who are capable of reasoning at an adequate level appear to develop a more lasting positive behavior pattern when they achieve an understanding of the values of conduct and develop appropriate levels of self-esteem, aspiration, and achievement. This statement is not to be construed to mean these attainments should not be sought with those with behavior disorders and severe mental retardation; rather, the intent is to indicate that the use of intrinsic rewards is not always as effective with these individuals as it is with their nondisabled counterparts. (The technique of using these procedures will be discussed in chapter 20, as well as later in this chapter.)

Self-Esteem and Level of Aspiration

There is evidence to indicate that persons strive to behave in a manner that is consistent with how they look at themselves. Some individuals develop concepts about themselves that lead them to look for ways to be successful, whereas the concepts of others appear to cause them to actually avoid success. Seligman (1975) contends that the relationship between negative student self-esteem and motivation is a "learned helplessness." Children learn to try not to succeed because they believe they are unable to do anything right, so why make the attempt?

Closely associated with self-esteem is level of aspiration. Those who have low self-esteem generally set relatively low goals if they set goals at all. Without appropriate goals individuals do not perform effectively and learning is hampered.

Children with the ability to understand should be appraised of the relationship of self-esteem and level of aspiration to achievement. They should be helped to realistically judge their abilities and assisted in setting their goals high enough to produce the best efforts and optimum results.

Need for Achievement

Investigators of motivation have found that the need for achievement is an important factor in motivation. Alschuler (1973) and Wloodkowski (1977) have found that individuals with high achievement motivation tend to exhibit certain characteristics: (1) interest in excellence for its own sake rather than the reward it brings, (2) preference for assuming personal responsibilities for the outcomes of their efforts, (3) setting of goals after considering the probabilities of success of a variety of alternatives, (4) greater concern with the medium-to long-range future than persons with low achievement and motivation. To promote a need for achievement in students who lack it, teachers should encourage the development of these characteristics.

Excellence for Its Own Sake

The teacher can contribute to an attitude of striving for excellence and to an appreciation of accomplishment rather than concentrating on the extrinsic reward success will bring. Emphasis should be placed upon the instability of the extrinsic reward as compared to sound accomplishments that will lead to further success. Extrinsic rewards to encourage achievement should only be used in those classes and with those individuals who are incapable of understanding the limitations of these rewards and so need them as motivation to achieve a desired result. In many cases competition with others has value in promoting the striving for excellence. When the emphasis is only upon beating someone else regardless of the quality of performance, however, competition actually becomes detrimental to establishing the concept of excellence for its own sake.

Taking Personal Responsibility for the Outcome

When possible, the student should be helped to make sense out of experiences by attempting to conceptualize what happened and why it happened. Analyzing the experience and its results will help develop an understanding of what could have been done differently and how the results could have been changed. The student must be made to understand, if possible, that one's actions produce results and one must be responsible for the results. However, knowing the cause of the results will enable the student, in most cases, to take more appropriate action to gain better results.

Setting Goals

All children, regardless of age or mental capacity, set goals. Some of these goals may be very simple and short term. As soon as children are capable of doing so, they should begin to set long-term goals. Teachers can offer assistance in this by helping children to understand the reasons they really wish to achieve a goal and the effort required to reach the goal. Children also need help in analyzing their abilities in order to determine the possible level of achievement.

The setting of instructional objectives by the teacher can help motivate as well as give the student insight into the process of setting goals. It is argued by some that behavioral objectives are more effective than instructional objectives in motivating learning because the learners are able to anticipate the results of their actions. Regardless of the type, well-thought-out objectives, explained by the teacher to the students, will help them with their own goal setting, as well as motivate them to achieve the goals the teacher has set.

Preventing Behavior Problems

Students with disabilities, similar to those without disabilities, present behavior problems from time to time. These can range from minor problems, such as fidgeting in class and becoming unnecessarily upset over losing, to more serious problems such as aggressive or disruptive behavior. The goal of all teachers is to minimize behavior problems by creating a positive teaching and learning environment. Ackerman and Dummer (1982) have suggested the following strategies to help teachers reinforce desirable behaviors and to prevent behavior problems.

Structuring the Physical Environment

Before children enter an instructional environment they should know what they are expected to do, where they should go, and what to do when they get there. The room should be organized with activity areas and equipment clearly marked. Activity stations, for instance, can be lettered or numbered to help students who have difficulty following directions.

Modeling

Teachers must serve as effective models for their students. All students, including those with disabilities, look to the teacher as a standard for proper conduct. Teachers, therefore, must be particularly careful in their comments about other students and the manner in which they provide feedback or correction. A favorable response by a teacher to an overweight student, who although lacking in skill tries hard, can serve as an effective catalyst for acceptance of the student by others. Teachers also can serve as effective models by dressing appropriately for the activity, participating in the activity, and allowing students to challenge ideas without becoming defensive or negative.

Reinforcing Desirable Behavior

The sensitive teacher of students with disabilities seeks every possible opportunity to provide positive reinforcement. Using techniques such as verbal praise and public recognition increases the likelihood that appropriate behaviors will be exhibited again in future class sessions. The use of positive reinforcement can be infectious. In classes where this approach is consistently used, students will reciprocate by reinforcing the teacher and other students, as appropriate.

Regulated Permission

There are times when it is desirable to permit exceptions or deviations in the normal class routine for a student who is having difficulty. For example, a student who finds it exceptionally difficult to stand in line before returning to the classroom could be assigned the responsibility of gathering and returning equipment to the proper area. This same concept pertains to the student who comes to the gymnasium angry about something that happened earlier in the day. There are times when the teacher can avoid major confrontations by altering the student's program to allow time to regain composure. The use of this strategy will require that the teacher speak with the student about the exception and the circumstances that led to the exception. Care must be exercised to avoid a situation in which the student expects exceptions as a matter of routine.

Developing, Stating, and Enforcing Consequences

Students need to know that there are rules, standards of behavior, and consequences for inappropriate behavior. The rules must be clear and reasonable and the consequences appropriate to the infraction. Most importantly, the teacher needs to help the student understand that the consequence is related to a rule violation and not designed to suggest that the teacher dislikes the student. The message must be, "I dislike what you did," rather than, "I dislike you."

Student and Teacher Contracts

There are times when it is desirable for the teacher and student to develop a contract as part of a conference in which a problem is acknowledged, expected behaviors are identified, and rewards and consequences are specified. This approach has been effectively used with students with behavior disorder. Effective contracts require student input to insure that the expected behavior and consequences are clear and obtainable. Contracts have been used to motivate students to reduce weight, for example, or to reduce inappropriate behavior such as objectionable language and negative comments about another student.

Dealing with Atypical Behavior

There are times when the intensity, frequency, and duration of a student's behavior may be so severe that it is clearly atypical. For example, individuals who persist in being abusive to themselves or others normally require assistance beyond that designed to prevent behavior problems.

One of the primary concerns facing today's teacher is how to deal with inappropriate student behavior. This is particularly true for teachers who work with disruptive, aggressive, and self-destructive individuals. It is very difficult to teach motor skills to students who are constantly abusing themselves or their peers.

Although various strategies may be used in dealing with atypical behavior, the approach offered here is based largely on the theory and techniques of behaviorism, which has been shown to be the most effective way to deal with extremely antisocial behavior by individuals who are mentally retarded and emotionally disturbed. Suggestions for reducing antisocial behavior reflect primarily behavioral techniques, although the author does borrow from other theoretical concepts when appropriate. The technical vocabulary used in this section is chiefly that of the behaviorists (Dunn and French, 1982; Dunn and Fredericks, 1985). The primary focus will be on helping teachers apply their knowledge of learning theory to students with behavior problems.

Laying the Foundation

Prior to initiating any effort to help a student overcome a behavior problem, it is essential that the teacher talk first with the school administration to determine if other teachers have noted similar concerns and what, if anything, has been done to remediate the problem. Efforts should also be made to contact the student's parents. For students previously identified as having a disability, it may be necessary to request an IEP meeting. Meeting with the parents provides an excellent opportunity to explain to them the nature of the problem from the teacher's perspective and to ask if the parents have noted similar problems. Conversing with parents also helps the teacher and school officials clarify whether the parents are aware of any specific reason that may account for the abnormal behavior.

Every effort should also be made to enlist the support of fellow teachers and special personnel such as counselors and school psychologists. Their knowledge and wealth of experience will contribute much to the success of any efforts to help the student with a behavior problem. When a plan of action is developed for dealing with the student's behavior, the cooperation of parents, school officials, and colleagues is necessary to ensure that a conscientious effort is undertaken to respond to the student's behavior problems in a consistent manner.

Identifying Inappropriate Behavior

A concise description of what the teacher believes to be inappropriate behavior must be supplied. The importance of this process cannot be overemphasized because it is the foundation of the other steps to dealing with atypical behavior. To emphasize this point, let us assume that a basketball coach explains to one of the players that the youngster's lay-up shot is poor. Upon hearing this remark, the player asks, "Coach, what do you mean by poor? What am I doing wrong?" Faced with this question, the experienced coach will explain in descriptive terms the weakness of the player's shot, such as wrong foot take-off, wrong hand, improper eye placement, and so on. The same sort of specific description of inappropriate behavior is also required of teachers.

Teachers sometimes make broad sweeping statements about students and their behavior, such as, "Tom is bad." To deal with this behavior, however, the teacher will have to clearly identify the behavior—hitting other children and throwing objects, for example—that has led to the conclusion that Tom is bad. Teachers should strive to state the questionable behavior in descriptive terms that can be observed and measured by others. Inappropriate behavior can be measured only if the criterion of inappropriateness is clearly stated. Once teachers have made this initial step, they are in a position to systematically deal with the identified behavior and to evaluate the results of their attempts.

Establishing a Baseline

Once a specific behavior has been identified, it becomes necessary to measure the frequency of the behavior's occurrence. The recording of the behavior's frequency prior to initiating a plan for remediation helps to establish a baseline that can be referred to later as continuous and final measures are taken. It is through this procedure that the effects of the behavior program can be evaluated.

Although there is some controversy regarding the most accurate means of charting behavior, it is generally concluded that the most practical method for teachers is to simply count the occurrence of a behavior per unit of time. For the sake of convenience, the suggested procedure calls for the teacher to mark on a conveniently located card the number of times the inappropriate behavior appears.

Before the teacher establishes a baseline, the behavior should be observed each day at various times and under different circumstances for at least a week. At the end of this period, the tabulations per day are added and averaged, thus resulting in a behavior baseline value.

Developing a Plan of Action

The exact process that a teacher uses to decrease the frequency of an undesirable behavior depends on many factors. The uniqueness of the individual and the specific behavior to be remediated are simply two of the important variables that must be incorporated into a plan of action. Of course, the more severe the behavior problem, the greater the need for a well-developed strategy. In developing a specific plan, teachers are encouraged to use the assistance of specialists within their school system, such as school psychologists and behavior-management consultants, to help them with this important task. Indicated here are some general concepts to help teachers improve their understanding of how to deal with inappropriate behavior. For sake of clarity, the following techniques will be described and discussed separately; however, frequently these techniques are utilized together in various combinations.

Positive Reinforcement

Positive reinforcement is defined as any pleasant event that follows a behavior and strengthens the future frequency of that behavior. This technique is generally recognized as the most powerful tool for increasing selected behaviors. Children and adults, with and without disabilities, all respond favorably to positive reinforcement; people continue to do those activities for which reinforcement is provided. The key to this system, then, is the identification of appropriate reinforcers. It must be emphasized at this point that an event that follows a response is not a reinforcer unless it increases the frequency of a specified response. Educators are often tempted to identify certain items, such as ice cream, candy, trinkets, and so forth, as reinforcers. This is an unwise procedure, however, because students are not all the same and they therefore obviously do not all value similar items.

The basic or primary reinforcers used with children with disabilities include the categories of consumables (ice cream, candy, food treats); manipulatables (toys, trinkets, hobby items); visual and auditory stimuli (films, records, and animations); and social stimuli (verbal praise and attention). Although some students, specifically the seriously emotionally disturbed, require basic reinforcers, the goal of the positive reinforcement procedure is to help students learn to respond to natural forms of social praise. Many teachers have found it useful to implement a positive reinforcement procedure that employs a token system (Bennett et al., 1989). A token is a tangible item having no value of its own that is given for acceptable behavior to be exchanged at a later time for an item of value. The use of a token system has many advantages. It permits students to exchange tokens for items that personally appeal to them at a time mutually convenient for both teacher and student. Physical

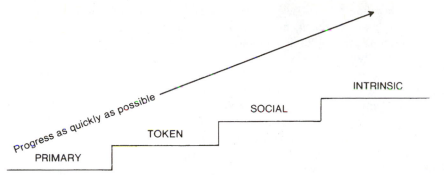

Figure 6.8 Hierarchy of the reinforcement system.

education teachers have found the token system a practical and manageable system. In figure 6.8 a schematic of a reinforcement hierarchy is presented. Although the ultimate goal is to have students respond to an intrinsic reward, this is not always possible.

Once the positive reinforcement system has been identified it is necessary next to decide on a reinforcement schedule. When the teacher is initially attempting to establish a behavior—to increase the student's compliance, for example—it is generally best to reinforce the student every time the desired response is made. This is called a continuous reinforcement schedule. Gradually, the teacher may introduce a fixed ratio schedule where a reinforcer is provided every three times the student demonstrates compliant behavior. Later, as the behavior is established, the continued permanency of the behavior is ensured by introducing a variable ratio schedule. Therefore, the behavior may be reinforced on the average of one out of every three, four, five or more times it appears. Changing reinforcement schedules, however, must be done carefully. Generally, it is best to consult with other school specialists before initiating a reinforcement schedule change.

Modeling

Frequently, children demonstrate inappropriate behavior because they do not know or have forgotten the proper way to behave. In an attempt to increase the student's repertoire of desirable behaviors, the behavior of others can often be utilized as examples of the types of behavior that should be exhibited. This system, whereby appropriate behavior is demonstrated for the student, is referred to as modeling.

The utilization of models is not a new concept for physical educators. For example, the teaching of most sport skills is greatly enhanced if either the teacher or a student leader can effectively demonstrate (model) the skill being taught.

Modeling has been successfully employed with special students. It is a particularly effective technique to use in a mainstreamed physical education class. For example, the teacher who is working on having children attend for longer periods of time to specific motor skill tasks can reward a student who is practicing by saying, "John, I like the way you are working hard." The strategy, of course, is to always speak loudly and enthusiastically while standing close to the student who needs to work harder. In some cases, it may also be necessary to be more direct by saying, "Mary, have you watched how hard John is working?" The message to the student is that if you work hard, the teacher will provide some strong positive verbal reinforcement. It is essential, therefore, that the teacher immediately reward the students who suddenly decide that they, too, would like some attention from the teacher. Various situations will arise when the student with a disability also can serve as the model, thus helping others to recognize that effort, and not perfection, is the name of the game.

The conduct of teachers, too, can often serve as a model for youngsters. Therefore, teachers should conduct themselves in a manner consistent with the behavior expected of their students. To do otherwise would be hypocritical.

Extinction

If a behavior has been learned under conditions of positive reinforcement, it follows logically that the particular behavior can be unlearned by withdrawing the reinforcer. This technique of gradually decreasing a previously reinforced behavior by withholding the reinforcer is known as extinction. Take, for example, the young child who insisted upon wandering around the gymnasium while the other children engaged in activities directed by the teacher. The teacher's natural reaction, upon seeing this student's purposeful attempt not to be part of the group, was to go to the student and lead him back to the group. This sequence of behavior, the child leaving and the teacher retrieving him, happened several times over a two-day period before it occurred to the teacher that by always retrieving the student, he was in effect positively reinforcing the youngster's behavior. The teacher also noted that although the gymnasium doors were open, the child never attempted to leave. Therefore, the teacher elected to focus his direct attention on the children who were participating and to ignore the child who was aimlessly walking around the gym. To the teacher's delight, by reinforcing the children who were in the right spot at the right time and by watching the nonjoiner for safety purposes only, the wandering student soon became more and more interested in the group experiences. The strategy of ignoring the child and then reinforcing him when he did participate was a successful technique for extinguishing an undesirable behavior.

Although the previous example concisely describes the extinction technique, rarely does this procedure work as effectively or as efficiently as indicated in the example. Sometimes the teacher utilizing this technique has difficulty extinguishing a behavior problem for two reasons: (1) Identification of all the reinforcers that are maintaining a behavior is difficult, and (2) even if the reinforcers can be identified, it is virtually impossible to control all of them. For instance, many people other than teachers, such as classmates, siblings, parents, and neighbors, reinforce student behavior; obviously, to manage the actions of all of these individuals would be a difficult task.

Physical educators who utilize extinction for the first time should be aware of additional concerns. First, when the extinction plan is initiated, the immediate reaction of many students will be to increase their level of undesirable activity. So by not attending to a child's use of abusive language, for instance, the youngster's cursing may at first become louder and more frequent. Second, the length of time required to completely diminish a behavior by the use of extinction alone may weaken the will of even the most patient teacher. Third, it is recommended that this procedure not be employed with certain behaviors exhibited by students who are emotionally disturbed, particularly self-destructive behaviors. Finally, although there is some research that would indicate that extinction alone may be used to reduce undesirable behavior, most authorities agree that extinction should be combined with other techniques, specifically positive reinforcement, to be most economical and efficient in producing changes in behavior.

Time-Out

The behavior of some students, particularly those with severe behavior disorders, will be disturbing and harmful to themselves as well as to others. When confronted with behavior problems that can be dangerous, teachers often rely upon a technique called time-out. Basically, this procedure involves removing the student quietly and gently from the room to a designated time-out area. During this transfer from the classroom, the teacher should make every effort not to positively reinforce the student's behavior by chastisement. The purpose of time-out is to remove the student from a setting that appears to possess positively reinforcing elements. Time-out also provides the student with an opportunity to recover composure in a quiet, private area. As soon as the undesirable behavior stops, the student should be permitted to return to class.

Many classrooms for students with severe behavior problems contain a specially designated time-out area. Generally, the time-out area is plain and free from distractions. Physical educators, because of their utilization of both indoor and outdoor facilities, may find it necessary to design their own time-out areas in each facility. Before employing a time-out procedure it is essential that the teacher review with school administrators and parents precisely the conditions under which the system will be employed.

Beyond the formal techniques of positive reinforcement, modeling, extinction, and time-out, there are some informal approaches teachers can use to deal with undesirable behavior. Ackerman and Dummer (1982) have identified several of these, three of which will be briefly described: signal interference, proximity control, and humor.

Teachers employ a variety of signals that communicate to students approval or disapproval for selected behaviors. Some of the nonverbal techniques that can be employed include: eye contact, hand gestures, snapping fingers, frowning, or various body postures. These signals, if employed before the behavior gets out of control, can be very effective in stopping or minimizing the intensity of the inappropriate behavior.

A very old but effective strategy to use when a teacher senses that a student's behavior is beginning to deteriorate is for the teacher to move close to the child. This action, when done in a noncombative way, serves to remind the student of the behavioral expectations for the class. The close presence of the teacher may assist the student in regaining self-control and/or ceasing the undesirable behavior.

Most teachers are aware that humor can be very effective in defusing a tense situation. A funny comment by the teacher creates the opportunity for the student to gain self-control and time for the teacher to think before removing the student or using some other behavioral strategy. Of course, care must be exercised to avoid ridicule or sarcasm. The humor must be in good taste and appropriate to the situation.

Medication and the Student with a Disability

The use of prescribed medication as an aid in the management of learning, behavior, and convulsive disorders is known as drug therapy. This treatment approach is used with students of various disabilities, including those with learning disabilities, mental retardation, behavior disorders, epilepsy, and cerebral palsy. Students with learning disabilities, for instance, are sometimes provided medication to manage such behaviors as short attention span, tendency to be distracted, restlessness, tantrums, and poor muscle coordination. Although exact figures are unavailable, it is clear that a large number of students are on medication for various disorders, including hyperactivity, behavior problems, and epilepsy.

Although the decision as to the type of medication and dosage is a medical decision, educators are interested in drugs and the role of the school in drug treatment. Teachers recognize, for example, that if a particular drug treatment is successful, the probability that a student will benefit from educational programs is greatly enhanced. If, however, a particular medication does not seem to have an effect on the student's behavior, then this information needs to be shared with the student's physician. Fortunately, an increasing number of physicians are becoming aware of the remarkable sensitivity teachers have concerning drug treatment programs. Sleator and Sprague (1978) believe that drug treatment programs will not be effective unless physicians routinely obtain input from teachers about the student's performance. Some educators and physicians have developed a close relationship in which information about drug treatment programs and their effects are exchanged. Kennedy, Terdal, and Fusetti (1993) note that blood studies, laboratory studies, and neurological teams are not as helpful in evaluating the effectiveness of medications as behavior ratings by parents, caregivers, and teachers.

Physical education teachers must also recognize that some drugs have side effects that may improve or impair the student's motor performance. Discussion about a student's educational progress in physical education, therefore, may be misleading unless information concerning the individual's medication is available. Awareness of this information may also explain any sudden or unusual change in behavior. Drug treatment is an important variable that must be combined with other information to help teachers make wise educational decisions.

Category of Drugs

Various terms are used to describe drugs. Drugs may be referred to by their generic names or their trade names. For example, Dilantin, a trade name for a drug used as an anticonvulsant in grand mal epilepsy, is known by its generic name as phenytoin sodium. The generic name is normally used in medical literature and by scientists throughout the world. The trade name, however, is a registered trademark that may vary from country to country.

Two major categories are used to identify the drugs frequently used in treating childhood disorders. These are psychotropic and anticonvulsant, or antiepileptic, drugs (Gadow, 1979). Drugs that are prescribed primarily for their effects on mood, behavior, and cognitive processes are known as psychotropic drugs. As the name implies, anticonvulsant drugs are used in the treatment of convulsive disorders.

Psychotropic drugs are commonly divided into six categories: stimulants, major tranquilizers, minor tranquilizers, antidepressants, hypnotics, and sedatives.

Stimulants

Stimulants are very popular psychotropic drugs frequently used in the treatment of hyperactivity. Ritalin, Dexedrine, and Cylert are drugs commonly found in this group. Stimulants are also occasionally used in the treatment of epilepsy and may be used to control drowsiness, which is a side effect of some anticonvulsant drugs.

Major Tranquilizers

Mellaril, Thorazine, and Haldol are the major tranquilizers most frequently used with children. These drugs are prescribed to control a variety of behaviors, including hyperactivity, aggressiveness, and self-destructiveness. Major tranquilizers are used more with those with mental retardation and behavior disorders than other disability populations.

Minor Tranquilizers

Minor tranquilizers are used primarily to control anxiety. Common drugs included in this category are Valium, Librium, Clonopin, and Tranxene. All of these drugs have anticonvulsant properties. Valium and Clonopin are also used to control seizures in epilepsy. Students with cerebral palsy are sometimes administered Valium as an aid in relaxing the skeletal muscles.

Antidepressants

One of the primary categories of antidepressant drugs is the monoamine oxidase inhibitors that are used primarily with adults to treat depression. The other category of antidepressant drugs is referred to as the tricyclics. The use of the name "antidepressants" to describe the variety of drugs included in this category is misleading when applied to children. Tofranil, for example, the most frequently prescribed tricyclic, is used primarily in the treatment of enuresis (bed wetting) and hyperactivity.

Sedatives and Hypnotics

Combining these two drug types for discussion is logical because both are used to help people relax. Sedatives are used to calm, whereas hypnotics help people sleep. Some sedatives, however, if administered in higher doses, will induce sleep. Barbiturates, a classification of hypnotics, have anticonvulsant properties. Phenobarbital and Mebaral, both barbiturates, are used to treat epilepsy in children.

The second major category of drugs used with children is anticonvulsant drugs. Because many psychotropic drugs have anticonvulsant properties, there is considerable overlap between drugs in the psychotropic and anticonvulsant categories. To avoid this confusion, only those drugs that are used to control convulsive disorders will be discussed here.

Anticonvulsant drugs are particularly effective in controlling epileptic seizures. Fifty percent of children with epilepsy will not experience epileptic seizures if treated with drugs. Only a very small percentage of children with epilepsy will not be helped through a drug treatment program.

The types of epilepsy described in chapter 16 respond differently to the various anticonvulsant drugs. Grand mal seizures, for instance, are treated with various drugs, including phenobarbital, Dilantin, Mebaral, and Mysoline. Zarontin, a drug of little value in the treatment of grand mal, is an effective agent in the control of petit mal seizures.

Medication Side Effects

Although drug treatment has been widely accepted as an effective treatment approach for various childhood disorders, it is important that teachers be aware of possible side effects that may occur as the result of a particular drug. For example, Ritalin, the most frequently prescribed drug for hyperactivity, has been shown to be effective in improving hyperactive children's motor performance (Lere, Lere, and Artner, 1977), cognitive levels (Sprague and Sleator, 1975), behavior (Gadow, 1977), and school achievement (Gittelman-Klein et al., 1976).

It is also clear that with some drugs detrimental side effects may occur in some children. These may be temporary or long-term problems. Using Ritalin again as an example, the most common side effects observed during the early stages of treatment with this drug are insomnia and loss of appetite. Other side effects that may be observed include headaches, nausea, moodiness, and irritability. These side effects may disappear as children develop a tolerance for Ritalin. In some instances a change in the amount or type of medication may also be necessary.

The use of Ritalin also has been shown to be associated with some potential long-term health concerns. These include the possibility of an increase in blood pressure and heart rate (Ballard et al., 1976), as well as a decrease in height and growth rates (French and Jansma, 1981). Insufficient data are available, however, to conclude that these findings apply to all users of Ritalin. Further studies are needed to evaluate the effects of several variables, such as dosage levels, length of treatment, and individual differences. Some have noted, for instance, that the retarded weight and height growth observed in some Ritalin users is temporary and when the treatment is ended, normal growth rates will be achieved (Roche et al., 1979).

Knowledge of which medication students are taking is helpful in developing physical education programs. Teachers who are aware of this information can communicate with parents and physicians concerning any unusual behavior that may be observed. Teachers might also be less likely to err in assessing the student's motor performance. Assessment information taken during a change in drug treatment, for instance, could alter the student's motor performance and mask the individual's true capability. Major tranquilizers, for example, are frequently used to treat children with mental retardation who are hyperactive, aggressive, or self-abusive. Unfortunately, major tranquilizers such as Haldol and Mellaril also affect the extrapyramidal tract, which coordinates motor activities—especially walking, posture, muscle tone, and patterns of movement. This problem can be corrected by taking a second prescribed drug or by attempting to alter the recommended dosage. The physical education teacher will obviously be at a major disadvantage in determining the student's present and potential motor ability until the adverse reaction is treated.

Awareness of the side effects of drugs is also essential in preparing a physical education experience that is safe for the student. The side effects of some medications may cause problems such as drowsiness, balance dysfunction, and lack of muscle coordination. These problems not only interfere with the student's performance but also can lead to unsafe activity experiences for the students. Asking a student who is experiencing a drug-related problem with balance to perform gymnastic stunts involving height is an unsafe practice.

Indicated in table 6.2 are some of the common medications used with children with disabilities, their generic names, purpose(s), and side effect(s). This information is included primarily to alert teachers to the need to obtain information about medication and its positive uses and to be aware of adverse side effects that may occur. Two excellent references that teachers should consult for additional information about drugs are *Children on Medication* by Gadow (1979) and the *Physicians' Desk Reference* (1995), published annually. Both of the publications are included in the reference list at the end of this chapter.

Teaching Methods

A method of teaching is a general procedure used by the teacher to help the student understand and apply the information that is being presented. In physical education, the methods most commonly used are the direct or traditional method, the indirect or problem-solving method, and a synthesis of both. The direct method has been most frequently utilized by teachers in the past. The problem-solving method has come into use fairly recently and is rapidly gaining popularity. A synthesis of the two is not generally recognized as a method, although it is widely practiced; for this reason and for others that will be discussed later, the author includes it as one of the methods of teaching physical education.

Techniques of teaching may be defined as special ways the teacher handles instructional problems efficiently and deals effectively with the varied responses of different children. Teaching techniques used by physical education teachers are of three general types: verbalization, visualization, and kinesthesis. Any of the techniques may be used with any method of teaching. Before examining how they are used with a specific teaching method, the various techniques will be described to provide the background necessary for understanding the use of the terms in the later discussion.

Verbalization

Verbalization refers to the use of the spoken word in the process of teaching. Describing a skill or explaining the strategy of a play vocally is an example of the use of the technique. The oral presentation of a motor problem to be solved is included in this category. Oral reports and class discussions are other examples of utilizing verbalization in classroom teaching, although their use is more limited in the teaching of physical education than in other types of classes. Some concepts can only be put across to students by means of verbalizing them: their presentation cannot be clearly made in any other way. For example, in the demonstration of a skill, verbalization is frequently employed to clarify a concept that could not be clearly identified without the use of a descriptive oral explanation. This technique also has obvious advantages for certain populations, such as those with visual impairments.

Visualization

Visualization is a technique that employs the visual attention of the students. Included under this general heading are demonstrations, motion pictures, filmstrips, videotapes, posters and pictures, diagrams, and the printed word.

Demonstration is a most effective tool, particularly when used with the traditional method of teaching. In a good demonstration, the skill is executed in perfect form one or more times, depending upon its complexity. The students then attempt to execute the skill by duplicating the movements they have observed. The teacher may need to simulate

Table 6.2 *Common medications used with children with disabilities**

Trade Name	Generic Name	Purpose	Possible Side Effects**
Ritalin	methylphenidate hydrochloride	Adjunctive therapy used with children who experience moderate to severe distractibility, short attention span, hyperactivity, emotional lability, and impulsivity.	Loss of appetite, abdominal pain, weight loss, insomnia, and tachycardia. Long-term effect may have implications for the cardio-vascular system and growth rate.
Dexedrine	dextroamphetamine sulfate	Same as Ritalin.	Palpitation, tachycardia, elevation of blood pressure, overstimulation, dizziness, insomnia, tremors, headache, gastrointestinal disturbances. Anorexia nervosa and weight loss may occur.
Cylert	pemoline	Same as Ritalin.	Insomnia, weight loss, anorexia, stomach ache, skin rashes, irritability, mild depression, nausea, dizziness, headache, drowsiness, and hallucinations.
Mellaril	thioridazine hydrochloride	Management of psychotic disorders, including severe behavioral problems in children marked by combativeness and/or explosive hyperexcitable behavior. May be used in the short-term treatment of hyperactivity.	Drowsiness, dryness of mouth, blurred vision, constipation, nausea, vomiting, diarrhea. Changes in electrocardiogram readings have been reported.
Thorazine	chlorpromazine hydrochloride	Management of psychotic disorders. For the control of moderate to severe agitation, hyperactivity, or aggressiveness in disturbed children.	Drowsiness, jaundice, constipation, occular changes, motor restlessness, and photosensitivity. Electrocardiogram changes have been noted.
Haldol	haloperidol	Management of psychotic disorders. Used in the treatment of severe behavioral problems in children of combative, explosive hyperexcitabilty. Useful in the treatment of short-term hyperactivity.	Neuromuscular reactions with Parkinson-like symptoms, insomnia, restlessness, anxiety, confusion, vertigo, grand mal seizures, lethargy, euphoria. Increased depth of respiration, nausea, and vomiting have been reported.
Valium	diazepam	Used with children in the treatment of epilepsy and as a skeletal muscle relaxant for cerebral palsy.	Drowsiness, fatigue, and ataxia are the most commonly reported side effects. Less frequently reported effects include confusion, depression, slurred speech, vertigo, constipation, cardiovascular collapse, blurred vision.
Tofranil	imipramine hydrochloride	Recommended for treatment of depression and childhood enuresis.	In enuretic children the most common adverse reactions are nervousness, sleep disorders, tiredness, and gastrointestinal disturbances. Other possible adverse reactions include constipation, convulsions, anxiety, uncoordination, ataxia, allergic responses, and jaundice.
Dilantin	phenytoin sodium	Indicated for the control of grand mal and psychomotor seizures.	Nystagmus, ataxia, slurred speech, and mental confusion are the most common side effects. Other effects reported include dizziness, insomnia, motor twitchings, headache, nausea, and constipation.

*Adapted from information found in Charles E. Baker, Jr., (Pub.): *Physicians' Desk Reference,* 42d ed. Oradell, NJ, Medical Economics Co., Litton Division, 1988.
**The side effects reported here are those most likely to have implications for physical education programming.

Table 6.2—*Continued*

Trade Name	Generic Name	Purpose	Possible Side Effects**
Zarontin	ethosuximide	Recommended for the treatment of petit mal seizures.	Gastrointestinal symptoms occur frequently and include anorexia, vague gastric upset, nausea, vomiting, cramps, weight loss, and diarrhea. Drowsiness, headache, dizziness, euphoria, hyperactivity, fatigue, and ataxia have also been reported.
Luminal	Phenubarbital	Recommended for treatment of seizures.	Hyperactivity, nystagmus, and a stumbling gait.
Myosoline	Primidone	Same as Luminal.	Hyperirritability, drowsiness, stumbling gait, nausea, vomiting, mild anemia.
Depakene (Depakole)	Valproic Acid	Used in treatment of myoclonic, petit mal, and grand mal seizures.	Nausea, vomiting, double vision, incoordination, muscle weakness.
Clonopin	Clonazepam	Recommended in treatment of akinetic and petit mal seizures.	Drowsiness, stumbling gait, loss of appetite.

*Adapted from information found in Charles E. Baker, Jr., (Pub.): *Physicians' Desk Reference,* 42d ed. Oradell, NJ, Medical Economics Co., Litton Division, 1988.
**The side effects reported here are those most likely to have implications for physical education programming.

the disability of the student being taught in order to give a meaningful demonstration. Even if it proves impossible for the teacher to duplicate exactly the adjustment that must be made by the student, the demonstration is still useful to the student with a disability because it will help to identify the objective of the movement and by doing this will provide the insight the student needs into how to best achieve similar results for himself or herself through experimentation.

Movies, filmstrips, and *videotapes* are effective for showing the proper techniques of performing skills. Many of these have a certain limitation for use in the special class, however, because they show how the skills are performed by individuals who do not have the disabilities that these students must circumvent in their performances. But if the teacher is prepared to describe possible adaptations of the skills for the students watching the film, a very effective teaching situation can be developed. Alert students with active minds and imaginations also may be assigned to watch the films and plan possible adaptation of the skills. These can then be discussed with the teacher and tried out under his or her supervision, or they can be set up as problems to be solved by the student. Teachers should be alert for films and tapes that show exercise and activity as performed by individuals with disabling conditions.

Showing films often constitutes a considerable problem because they must be shown in a darkened room. Then, too, setting the film up takes time so that if the film is lengthy, most or all the period is taken up with watching the film and discussing it at its conclusion. This means that the students are denied valuable active participation for that period. Consequently, films should be used judiciously in the special program. Videotapes, which can be stopped, slowed, or "frozen," have become very popular as an instructional aid. With the use of a portable video cassette recorder (VCR), many teachers now are able to incorporate the videotape into their instruction, including the use of the VCR in an activity area. Students are thus able to see the tape and practice, alternating back and forth as necessary.

Still pictures, posters, and *diagrams* may be used effectively to illustrate correct skill techniques. Pictures of non-handicapped performers executing the skills are less desirable than ones in which an adapted technique is illustrated, but they are nevertheless extremely useful. Diagrams of plays on the blackboard are used to good advantage in teaching students with disabilities who may be less familiar with the strategy of games than are other students who have participated in sports more widely.

The use of *the printed word* is a technique that has been largely overlooked as an effective teaching tool in physical education. Textbooks, pamphlets, and other written materials can be particularly advantageous in the special class in a dual program situation. Depending upon their reading level, students in the special class can use the written materials to answer questions that may arise when the teacher is not available. Students with disabilities who know little about a particular activity may be assigned to read about it before work in that activity begins so they will be familiar with the terminology and the general performance of the activity.

There are many textbooks available, some designed especially for a comprehensive activity course in physical education and others devoted entirely to the skills and strategy of a particular sport or recreational activity. Most of these are suitable for use by high school students. They are directed chiefly toward the nondisabled, but the student with a disability may still utilize much of the instruction. For example, in teaching weight-lifting to a student who suffers a chronic dislocation of the shoulder, the instructor might direct the student to read about all of the lifts except those that bring the arms higher than the shoulders—the only lifts the student could not perform.

Textbooks designed for activity classes usually offer a brief history of the game and stress the care of equipment and the playing courtesies, all of which are essential if the student is to attain the fullest possible understanding and appreciation of the activity. Although effective and well-organized teachers can manage to bring this additional information to their classes, their jobs are made considerably easier by the use of a textbook. Moreover, by assigning the students to acquire this information from books, a little more time is gained for working with individual students.

Worksheets are helpful to students who are working by themselves. An example of the kind of worksheet that may be used is given in figure 6.9. A photocopied form such as this will aid students in determining the cause of their skill faults, and also will show their progress.

Kinesthesis

The use of kinesthesis refers to the involvement of muscular activity in the teaching-learning situation. When students attempt to perform a skill and must make an adjustment in stance or grip because it doesn't feel right, they are making use of kinesthesis. Of course, in the case of beginners, students will not know how the correct form feels. In fact the correct form may feel more awkward than the incorrect. This is often the case in assuming the grip of a golf club or in making an overhand throw. It is only after students begin to associate the desired result with the correct form that they will begin to "feel right" about their performance.

In a sense, the adjustment that students make when their muscular movements have not achieved satisfactory results

Practice Guide

Techniques	Common Errors	My Errors
Grip	Gripping too high on the handle	
Strokes in General	Standing too close to the bird while stroking Failure to use the wrist in the stroke Failure to place the shot away from the opponent Telegraphing shots or using strokes in a specific pattern	
Overhead Stroke	Allowing the bird to drop too low before stroking	
Forehand Stroke	Failure to hit the bird up when it has dropped lower than the net	
Backhand Stroke	Failure to abduct the wrist in the back-swing and snap the wrist forward as the swing comes forward	
Serve	Failure to watch the bird while serving Failure to use the wrist in stroking Repeatedly serving to the same spot Moving the feet during the serve Holding the bird too close to the body; this causes the bird to go into the net Setting up the bird for the opponent which may be caused by holding the bird away from the body or by not using enough or too much wrist in the stroke	
Net Shots	Hitting net shots too high	
Drives	Hitting up on the bird	
Court Positions	Failure to return to the proper position after stroking the bird Encroaching on partner's court area Backing up for deep shots instead of pivoting and running back	

Figure 6.9 Practice guide for badminton.

is a phase of kinesthesis. Adjusting the serve in table tennis after the ball has fallen short of the net is a learning related to kinesthesis. Of course, the eyes tell the player that the serve was no good, but the adjustment in the muscular movement made to perform the skill more accurately is kinesthetic in nature.

Attempts to correct errors in order to achieve a more satisfactory performance are referred to as exploratory kinesthesis. Such exploration is an integral phase of the learning of any new activity and is particularly to be fostered among students who are disabled.

Still another phase of teaching that employs kinesthesis is that of actually leading the student's hand, arm, or part of the body involved in the activity through the performance of the skill. This technique is called manual kinesthesis (figure 6.10). It is extremely helpful to students who have failed to grasp the fundamentals through exploration, visualization, or verbalization. With students who have sensory deviations, as in the case of blindness, the technique is invaluable. It would be practically impossible, for example, to teach a boy who is blind to catch or throw a ball unless his hands were led through the movements by his instructor. Some students, particularly the blind, find a process known as reverse

Figure 6.10 Manual kinesthesis is helpful to a student unable to grasp the fundamentals of performing a skill.

manual kinesthesis also effective. In this technique, the student holds on to the instructor as the instructor executes the task. For example, the teacher permits the student to get the feel of a golf swing by having the student stand behind the instructor and hold on to the instructor's hands. Blind students learn much by feeling the movements involved in successful execution of a task.

Direct or Traditional Method

Basically, in the direct method the teacher selects the activity or skill to be learned and instructs the participants by describing the skill or by using one of the visual techniques to show how the skill is performed. The participants then attempt the skill, and the teacher assists each student in making the adjustments in movement necessary to perform the skill according to the prescribed standards.

The procedure is often described as consisting of the 3 Ds: Demonstration, Diagnosis, and Direction. The 3 Ds are discussed in the following paragraphs as they apply to the teaching of the students with disabilities.

Various techniques of *demonstration* have already been described. To present to students with disabilities the best method of performing a skill will require considerable insight and imagination on the part of the instructor. Teachers must try to put themselves in the place of the awkward child who has difficulty learning to skip or the student who is blind who desires to become a wrestler. At times it may be helpful for the teacher to attempt the skill simulating the disability, as, for example, attempting the side stroke in swimming without using one of the legs so as to demonstrate more clearly for the student who has lost a leg. Not all disabilities can be simulated successfully: loss of both arms, for instance, seriously affects the balance of the body, and in the attempt to perform a skill without the use of arms, the instructor will not be confronted with the same problem of balance as the armless student. Consequently, the teacher's demonstration will be limited in its value to the student except to the extent that it gives insight into the movement. The demonstration must, therefore, be supplemented with analysis of the student's movements as the skill is attempted.

We have just spoken of the need for *diagnosis* of the skill performance in the case of a student for whom a demonstration is not entirely satisfactory. Diagnosis goes beyond this, however; it is an integral factor in teaching skill improvement. Every good physical educator becomes an expert in diagnosing or analyzing learning difficulties and in giving clear, explicit directions to students to enable them to acquire a new pattern of movement.

It is not enough for the teacher to show a learner how to do the skill and to diagnose the student's learning difficulties; the instructor must also direct the student in overcoming his or her difficulties. *Direction* is extremely important in the teaching of students with disabilities, for these students want intensely to succeed in performing the skill, and the more quickly any learning difficulties can be overcome the sooner the skill can be mastered.

The techniques that are utilized by the teacher are dependent upon the circumstances and the objectives that are sought. Beginning teachers must choose their techniques on the basis of what they know about the needs of students with disabilities and on their prediction of the success a particular technique will have in accomplishing the changes they hope will be effected in the students. In addition, they may utilize the suggestions for performing sports skills in chapters 23 to 26 as a springboard for exploration and experimentation to determine the best teaching techniques for each individual student.

Problem-Solving or Indirect Method

In the problem-solving method, the teacher presents a motor task in the form of a problem to be solved by the students in the class. Basically, the problems are offered as a guide to the students to help them discover the movements their bodies are capable of and how they may control these movements to accomplish a specific goal. The method is very effective in teaching sports skills, particularly to those who have orthopedic and neurologic disabilities, because it necessitates experimentation with movement to determine the best way to perform the skill within the limitations imposed by the disability.

The nature of the problem to be solved by the students is determined by their level of maturation, past experiences, and the medical limitations established by the physician. It is very important that both the teacher and the student understand the kinds of activities and specific movements that are contraindicated by a student's disability so that he or she will not attempt anything that may be harmful during exploration of various movements in the attempt to solve the problem.

To use the problem-solving method effectively, the teacher must decide not only the general area of motor learning to be examined but also the kind of problem that will evoke most effectively the exploration of the selected area. Problems in motor movement may take two forms:

1. *A Single Problem.* The single problem consists of a simple motor task to be solved by the individual student. For example, the boy on crutches could be given the problem: Can you balance your body with the use of only one crutch? All problems should be organized and stated in such a way that, when they are resolved, the student will have gained a fuller understanding of how the body can be controlled in movement and the extent and kinds of movement the body is capable of performing.
2. Sequence of Subproblems Leading to the Answer of a Major Problem. This approach has been described as *guided discovery* or *independent discovery,* depending upon the role the teacher plays.

In guided discovery, the teacher presents the major problem to the participants and then guides them toward a solution by posing subproblems that, when solved, will provide answers that lead to the resolution of the major problem. An example that illustrates the procedure follows:

Major problem (For students who have the use of only one arm): How can a golf ball be stroked most effectively by using one arm to hold the club?

Subproblems:

1. How should the grip be taken on the club to get the firmest hold?
2. Where on the club should the grip be taken to achieve the best leverage and the best control?
3. Which movement produces the most power in hitting the ball, a forward or a backward movement?*
4. Is it now necessary to adjust the grip to execute the stroke with optimum power and control?

Effectively conducted guided discovery should lead to independent discovery. Independent discovery, as the name implies, is a form of problem-solving that requires the student to work independently in the search for the solution to the motor problem. The major problem is divided into subproblems by the student, who develops them so they will lead to the solution of the major problem. The student then experiments with each subproblem until he or she has worked out a satisfactory solution to each one. The solutions are then combined to provide the answer to the major problem.

In many situations involving a student with a disability, independent discovery will need to be a cooperative endeavor between the student and the teacher. For example, solving the problem of how a student with an amputated hand can swim the crawl stroke will require the student to try various positions and movements. The teacher will observe and, applying knowledge of mechanical analysis, suggest additional variations with which the student may experiment. Following this pattern of cooperative effort between student and teacher, a solution will eventually be discovered.

Synthesis of Methods

In actual practice, many physical education teachers combine the problem-solving and traditional methods of teaching. The author believes such a synthesis is a highly effective way of teaching youngsters with disabilities. It unites the best of each method and permits flexibility so that the teacher can choose the method best suited to a specific situation and to personal talents and abilities.

A synthesis of the two methods is likely to be more effective in helping students to achieve the objectives of the program than the exclusive use of either method may be. It allows students to be creative and experimental and

---

*The teacher should be aware that when using the right arm to stroke the ball with a backward movement, a left-handed club is used; when making a forward stroke, a right-handed club is used.

impresses upon them the possibilities of movement their bodies can achieve. It will encourage them to think reflectively and to apply the process of logical reasoning in solving the problem. But if, at any time, the teacher should sense a lack of security among the students with the problem-solving method, or confusion arising from failure to solve the motor task, the instructor can shift to the more direct approach. When time is a factor in developing a phase of the program, certain aspects of the motor problem being considered can be taught with the traditional techniques, since they generally require less time. Review of formally learned skills and evaluation of performance may also generally be more efficiently handled by traditional methods.

Summary

Physical education teachers of students with disabilities utilize many of the same attributes helpful in teaching any student: namely patience, creativity, a sense of humor, and an appreciation for individual differences. These attributes, combined with the unique professional qualifications identified by professional organizations, equip today's physical educator with the necessary skills and knowledge to provide effective instruction for students with disabilities. Successful teachers know that they must have a thorough understanding of federal and state legislation pertaining to the disabled. This information will be valuable in insuring that Individualized Education Programs (IEPs) include instruction in physical education with appropriate goals and objectives. The Individualized Family Service Plan (IFSP) addresses the motor needs of infants and toddlers. Physical education teachers should also have an appreciation of the least restrictive environment and the importance of creating opportunities for students with and without disabilities to interact.

One of the specialized skills the teacher of special physical education should possess is the ability to analyze and apply the principles of movement to students with disabilities. A strategy that can be very helpful in this respect is task analysis, a process by which the components of an activity are identified and then ordered according to their level of difficulty. Teachers should also know how to motivate students and create positive learning environments. An understanding of the process to use when inappropriate behavior occurs is also essential. Knowledge of various medications and their effects on students will help in establishing meaningful assessment data and establishing appropriate baselines.

Teachers of special physical education should be familiar with direct and indirect teaching methods and the appropriateness of these when combined with the techniques of verbalization, visualization, and kinesthesis. As the appreciation for these and other skills helpful in teaching increases, the teacher's sensitivity toward the needs of the student with a disability will deepen. There also will be a growing awareness, however, that good teaching is good teaching and that students with disabilities, like students without disabilities, respond to a concerned and knowledgeable teacher.

Selected Readings

Ackerman, V., & Dummer, G. (1982). *Behavior management in physical education: A handbook for teachers.* Maryland State Department of Education and Towson State University. (*Note: These two organizations published the manuscript.)

Alschuler, A. (1973). *Developing achievement motivation in adolescents.* Englewood Cliffs, NJ: Educational Technology Publications.

Baker, C.E., Jr. (1988). *Physicians' desk reference* (42d ed.). Oradell, NJ: Medical Economics Company, Litton Division.

Ballard, J.E., Boileau, R.A., Sleator, E.K., Majjey, B.A., & Sprague, R.L. (1976). Cardiovascular responses of hyperactive children to methylphenidate. *Journal of the American Medical Association, 236,* 2870–2874.

Bennett, F., Eisenman, P., French, R., Henderson, H., & Shultz, B. (1989). The effect of a token economy on the exercise behavior of individuals with Down Syndrome. *Adapted Physical Activity Quarterly, 6,* 230–246.

Davis, W., & Burton, A. (1991). Ecological Task Analysis: Translating Movement Behavior Theory Into Practice. *Adapted Physical Activity Quarterly, 8,* 154–157.

Deal, A., Dunst, C., & Trivett, C. (1989). A flexible and functional approach to developing individualized family support plans. *Infants and Young Children: An Interdisciplinary Journal of Special Care Practices, 1*(4), 32–43.

Dempsey, S. (1987). *A comparison of college/university professors and specialists in adapted physical education in their perception of the importance of a specified set of professional competencies.* (Doctoral dissertation.)

DePaepe, J.L. (1985). The influence of three least restrictive environments on the content motor ALT and performance of moderately mentally retarded students. *Journal of Teaching in Physical Education, 3,* 34–41.

Department of Education. (1981, January 19). Part XII, assistance to states for education of handicapped children; interpretation of the Individualized Education Program (IEP). *Federal Register.* Washington, DC: Author.

Department of Health, Education, and Welfare, Office of Education. (1977, August 23). Education of handicapped children, Article II, implementation of Part B of the Education of the Handicapped Act. *Federal Register.* Washington, DC: Author.

Dunn, J.M. (1979). *Adaptive physical education: A resource guide for teachers, administrators, and parents.* Salem, OR: State of Oregon, Mental Health Division.

Dunn, J.M. (1991). P.L. 99-457: Challenges and Opportunities for Physical Education. *Journal of Physical Education, Recreation, and Dance, 47,* 33–34.

Dunn, J.M., & Fredericks, H.D.B. (1985). The utilization of behavior management in mainstreaming in physical education. *Adapted Physical Activity Quarterly, 4*(2), 338–346.

Dunn, J.M., & French, R. (1982). Operant conditioning: A tool for special educators in the 1980s. *Exceptional Education Quarterly, 3*(1), 42–53.

Dunn, J.M., Morehouse, J.W., and Fredericks, H.D. (1986). *Physical education for the severely handicapped.* Austin, TX: Pro-Ed Publishers.

Fait, H.F. (1976). *Experiences in movement: Physical education for the elementary school child* (3d ed.). Philadelphia: W. B. Saunders Co.

French, R., & Jansma, P. (1981). Medication, learning disabilities, and physical education. *American Corrective Therapy Journal, 35,* 26–30.

Gadow, K.D. (1977, April). *Psychotropic and anticonvulsant drug usage in early childhood special education programs III. A preliminary report: Parent interviews about drug treatment.* Paper presented at the Annual Meeting of The Council for Exceptional Children, Atlanta, GA. (ERIC Document Reproduction Service No. ED 139 182.)

Gadow, K.D. (1979). *Children on medication: A primer for school personnel.* Reston, VA: The Council for Exceptional Children.

Geddes, D. (1981). *Psychomotor individualized educational programs.* Boston: Allyn and Bacon, Inc.

Gibson, J.J. (1979). An ecological approach to visual perception. Boston: Houghton Mifflin.

Gittelman-Klein, R., Katz, S., Klein, D.F., Abikoff, H., Gloisten, A.C., & Kates, W. (1976). Relative efficacy of methylphenidate and behavior modification in hyperkinetic children: An interim report. *Journal of Abnormal Child Psychology, 4,* 361–379.

Houston-Wilson, C. (1994). *The effect of untrained and trained peer tutors on the motor performance of students with developmental disabilities in integrated physical education classes.* Unpublished doctoral dissertation, Corvallis, Oregon: Oregon State University.

Kelly, L.E. (1995). *Adapted physical education national standards.* Champaign, IL: Human Kinetics Publishers.

Kennedy, P., Terdal, L., & Fusetti, L. (1993). *The Hyperactive Child Book.* New York, NY: St. Martin's Press, p. 276.

Lere, R.J., Lere, P.M., & Artner, J. (1977). The effects of methylphenidate on the handwriting of children with minimal brain dysfunction. *Journal of Pediatrics, 91,* 127–132.

Londeree, B., & Johnson, L.E. (1976). *Motor fitness test for the moderately mentally retarded.* Washington, DC: AAHPERD.

Newell, K.M. (1986). Constraints on the Development of Coordination. In M.G. Wade & H.T.A. Whiting (Eds.), *Motor Development in Children: Aspects of coordination and control* (pp. 341–360). Dordrecht: Martinus Nijhoff.

Rizzo, T. (1984). Attitudes of physical educators toward teaching handicapped pupils. *Adapted Physical Activity Quarterly, 1*(4) 267–274.

Rizzo, T.L., & Vispoel, W.P. (1991). Physical educators' attributes and attitudes toward teaching students with handicaps. *Adapted Physical Activity Quarterly, 8*(1), 4–11.

Roche, A.F., Lipman, R.S., Overall, J.E., & Hung, W. (1979). The effects of stimulant medication on the growth of hyperkinetic children. *Pediatrics, 63* (6):847–850.

Seligman, M. (1975). *Helplessness.* San Francisco: Freeman Press.

Sherrill, C. (1993). *Adapted physical education and recreation* (4th ed.). Dubuque, IA: Wm. C. Brown Publishers.

Sleator, E.K., & Sprague, R.L. (1978). Pediatric pharmacotherapy. In W.G. Clark & J. del Guidice (Eds.), *Principles of psychopharmacology* (2d ed.). New York: Academic Press.

Sprague, R.L., & Sleator, E.K. (1975). What is the proper dose of stimulant drugs in children? *International Journal of Mental Health, 4,* 75–104.

Suphawibul, M. (1990). *Competencies for adapted physical educators in Thailand.* Unpublished dissertation. Oregon State University.

Turnbull, A.P., Strickland, B., & Brantley, J.C. (1978). *Developing and implementing IEPs.* Columbus, OH: Charles E. Merrill Publishing Co.

Vogler E.W., van der Mars, H., Cusimano, B., & Darst, P. (1992). Experience, expertise, and teaching effectiveness with mainstreamed and nondisabled children in physical education. *Adapted Physical Activity Quarterly, 9*(4), 316–329.

Webster, G.E. (1987). Influence of peer tutors upon academic learning time—physical education of mentally handicapped students. *Journal of Teaching in Physical Education, 1,* 393–403.

Wessel, J. (1976). *I CAN program.* Northbrook, IL: Hubbard Scientific Company.

Winnick, J., & Hurwitz, J. (Eds.). (1979). *The preparation of regular physical educators for mainstreaming.* Brockport, NY: SUNY Press.

Wloodkowski, R.W. (1977). *Motivation.* Washington, DC: National Education Association.

Enhancing Activities

1. Develop a task analysis for a selected activity and utilize the analysis with a student who has a disability.

2. Contact a local school district and ask permission to observe an IEP meeting. Obtain the IEP forms used by the district and develop an IEP for a selected student.

3. Interview physical education teachers to obtain their views and perspectives on teaching students with disabilities. Do they tend to be generally positive or negative in their attitude toward the disabled?

4. Obtain a copy of the *Physicians' Desk Reference* and review information on one of the medications found in table 6.2.

5. Review the competencies identified in table 6.1 to determine how many of these you now possess.

6. Observe a physical education class and tally how many positive versus negative comments are made by the teacher and the students in the class. Focus on any student that appears to be exhibiting inappropriate behavior. Analyze the situation to see what changes you might recommend in the teaching environment.

CHAPTER 7

Evaluation

After studying this chapter, the reader should be able to:

1 Appreciate the need to evaluate the motor performance of students with disabilities and the benefits ranging from student screening to communication between home and school.

2 Comprehend the federal requirements of P.L. 101-476 related to the evaluation of students with disabilities, including assessment of the motor domain.

3 Identify the general and specific types of motor performance tests.

4 Explain the similarities and differences among the following types of tests and provide an example of each: developmental scales; motor skill tests; perceptual-motor tests; motor ability tests; and physical fitness tests.

5 Explain the differences and similarities between norm-referenced and criterion-referenced tests and the appropriate use of each.

6 Locate and retrieve sources of information about various tests that can be used to assess the motor and physical fitness performance of students with disabilities.

7 Define and apply various terms such as *validity, reliability, standard error of measure,* and *standard score,* which are used in describing and analyzing tests of physical fitness and motor performance.

8 Identify and discuss the process and elements to be used in selecting motor and physical fitness tests to employ with students with disabilities.

9 Analyze tests to ensure that the statistical properties of a test are such that the test is appropriate for use with students with disabilities.

10 Identify and discuss issues pertinent to the evaluation of the motor and physical fitness performance of students with disabilities.

Implicit in the term *special physical education* is the mandate to provide students with a physical education experience that is of greatest benefit to them as individuals. Good decisions concerning how to provide the best possible physical education program to students are based on sound evaluation of their individual needs and abilities. Periodically, evaluation must also be made to determine the amount of improvement that has occurred and to discover the kinds of activities and kinds of procedures and techniques in teaching that are proving most effective.

Both written and motor tests are utilized in physical education. However, because fundamentals of developing, administering, and interpreting such tests are established in courses of measurement and evaluation required of physical education majors, written tests will not be discussed and only such information as is germane to evaluating motor ability of those with disabilities will be presented in this chapter.

Need for Evaluation

There are many reasons why students with disabilities benefit from a physical education program that includes a strong evaluation component. One of the obvious reasons is that evaluation helps teachers and students recognize progress and in turn permits an effective exchange of communication between the school and home. Teachers also can use the results of student progress to analyze their own effectiveness as well as their methods of instruction and the curricular materials that they have utilized. The values of evaluation are so numerous and varied that students must be evaluated in a variety of educational areas, including motor performance. In the following paragraphs some of the benefits derived from evaluation will be examined.

Screening

One of the primary aspects of an evaluation program is screening for students who have physical and motor fitness deficiencies. Through this process, individuals who have specific needs can be identified. Additional tests can then be administered to confirm or refute the findings of the screening process. To be effective, the screening procedure must be efficient, time-effective, and highly reliable to identify students most needing assistance.

Some school systems use standardized screening instruments to assess the students' performance in various areas. The McCarthy Screening Test, for example, evaluates children ages five years or older in their right-left orientation, verbal memory, "draw-a-design," numerical memory, conceptual grouping, and leg coordination. School systems may prefer to develop instruments specifically for their own school and student population. Table 7.1 is an example of a screening instrument for identifying students with gross-motor problems, which was developed by the Portland, Oregon, School District's Motor Development Team.

Establish Eligibility for Special Physical Education Service

A second purpose of an evaluation program is to establish which students are eligible for special physical education services. Students identified as potential candidates through the screening process are referred for further evaluation to confirm the results of the screening. Additional tests are conducted, when necessary, to determine whether the student qualifies for special education services. Further testing also helps to pinpoint the student's specific strengths and weaknesses and the individual's particular educational needs. It is at this stage that the question of whether the student's motor skill level warrants special physical education services is answered. Moreover, it is necessary and consistent with the intent of Public Law 101–476 to assess the student's motor skills so that an objective decision can be made about the student's physical education needs.

Develop Individualized Physical Education Programs

The additional evaluative information generated when determining the student's eligibility for special physical education services is helpful in developing individualized programs. This aspect of the evaluation program assists in translating the assessment results into a meaningful program. Annual instructional goals and objectives that reflect the student's strengths and weaknesses can be developed to serve as the foundation upon which a physical education program, specific to the needs of the students, can be built.

Analyze Educational Progress

A periodic review of the annual goals and objectives coupled with further evaluation provides a mechanism whereby the effectiveness of the physical education experience can be determined. This aspect of the evaluation program is essential. Information obtained through this process informs the teacher and student about the extent to which educational progress has occurred. Areas where significant gains were made as well as areas where the instructional gains were minimal can also be identified. Teachers, therefore, can begin to systematically analyze their instructional process. A lack of student progress may lead a teacher to conclude that a specific instructional methodology is not appropriate for a given student. Questions can also be raised about the educational material utilized or the environment in which the experience was provided.

Table 7.1 *PPS/Motor Development Team Screening Report*

Student's Name: _____ Sex: M _____ F _____ Screening Date: _____

PPS/ID#: _____ Date of Birth: _____

School: _____ Chronological Age: _____

Tested By: _____ Physician: _____

Based on the results of the Portland Public Schools MDT Screening Tool, _____ is functioning at the following levels for fine and gross motor skills.

Skill: **Motor Ability:**

1. Running _____

2. Jumping _____

3. Hopping _____

4. Skipping _____

5. Throwing _____

6. Catching _____

7. Kicking _____

8. Static Balance _____

9. Dynamic Balance _____

10. Posture _____

11. Directionality _____

12. Prone Extension _____

13. Total Flexion Pattern _____

14. Writing: Name and Alphabet _____
         (90 second limit)

15. Design Duplication _____

16. Scissors _____

17. Bead Stringing _____

18. Pellets (optional) _____

19. Draw-A-Person _____

Summary:

_____

_____

_____

_____

_____

_____

_____

_____

_____

                                              _____
                                                          (MDT Member)

Review Curricular Effectiveness

Evaluation of student progress has many curricular ramifications. For instance, the lack of improvement in a student's physical fitness program may be due to the insufficient time allocated for the program. Likewise, some students may not progress because the curricular sequences are too difficult, requiring that skills be further task-analyzed and broken down into smaller steps. Evaluation results also can help to analyze the effectiveness of educational experiences in alternative placements. A review of the progress of a student who has recently been integrated into a regular physical education class can only be effectively conducted if sufficient evaluative data are available.

Communication between Home and School

Communication with students and their parents is greatly enhanced if there is a well-developed evaluation plan available. Teachers, naturally, feel more comfortable talking about a student's achievement if some objective data are available to support their position. Parents and students also more readily accept input if they feel teachers are attempting to be

Table 7.1—*Continued*

MDT/Screening Tool:

Student Name: _____

Date: _____ DOB: _____

School/Class: _____

Teacher: _____

MDT Examiner: _____

Diagnosis: _____

Muscle Tone: Floppy, tight, asymmetrical, unusual movement, unremarkable

		Developmental Age
	Walking without assistance	2
Running	Runs smoothly without proper arm usage	3/4
	Arm and leg opposition, small ROM	5
	Mature rhythmic arm and leg opposition	7
Jumping	Jumps forward without assistance	4
	Jumps forward over 30"	5
	Jump rope continuously, own rope 5 times	7/8
Hopping		R/L
	Hops 5 consecutive times on one foot	4
		R/L
	Hops forward 15'–20'	5/6
	Hops with accuracy	6.6
Skipping	Gallop with same lead foot	4
	Gallop/change lead foot	5/6
	Skips forward rhythmically 10 skips	5/6
Throwing		R/L
	Throws tennis ball overhand 4'	2½
	Push pass (8½" ball) 8'	4
	Throws tennis ball—unilateral	5
	Throws tennis ball—bilateral	6
	Overhand softball throw 50'	10
Catching		R/L
	Catch bounced ball with arm and body	3/4
	Catch thrown ball with both hands	5/6
	Catch tennis ball, 2 hands/1 hand	8/9
Kicking	Kicks a ball forward (immature)	3/4
	Kicks ball forward (mature)	5/6
	Punts a ball	7/8
		R/L
	Kicks a ball with accuracy	9
Balance		R/L
	Stand on one foot, arms folded 2 seconds	3/4
		R/L
	Stand on one foot, hands on hips 10 seconds	5
	Stand on one foot, arms folded, eyes closed	R/L
	5 seconds	7
	Walks 10'2" line	3/4
	Walks backward-heel-toe	4.8
Posture	Standing forward:	
	Standing backward:	
	Standing sideways:	
	Kneeling on hands and knees:	

Body Control	Directionality: FB/OUAT/LR 18/5/10	
	*Prone Extension: (seconds)	
	Degree of Effort: HI MED LOW	
	Total Flexion Pattern: (seconds)	
	Degree of Effort: HI MED LOW	
Writing	Alphabet/Name (90 seconds)	
	Pencil Grasp R/L	
	Desk Posture	
	Design duplicating—cannot erase (see instructions)	
Scissors	Cuts paper without turning scissors or tearing paper R/L	3
	Cuts on line without tearing and within ¼" of line R/L	4/5
	Cuts around 4" circle with little space showing	7/8
	Bead Stringing (40 seconds)	
Optional	10 pellets in container 25–30 seconds R/L	3/4
	10 pellets in container 18–25 seconds	5/6
	Scribble, make vertical lines or circle	3/4
	Mouth, nose and eyes/or body, arms, legs	5/6

Comments:

* 5 and under: half the pattern
6 and above: hold entire pattern for half the time

objective rather than subjective in their remarks. An evaluation plan helps the communication process because parents recognize and appreciate efforts to determine progress in their children's performance. Educational accountability requires that there be an evaluation plan to show student progress from year to year.

Evaluation is a valuable process whereby teachers, students, parents, and administrators can systematically analyze the effects of instruction. To maximize the benefits of education for each special student requires that certain variables, such as the amount of instruction time, placement setting, nature of the activity, and number of aides or volunteers, be monitored closely. Evaluative data are essential, therefore, to help school personnel and parents recognize that changes in these or other variables may have an effect on the student's progress.

Evaluation and Legal Requirements

The Education for All Handicapped Children Act of 1975 emphasized the importance of the evaluation process in the delivery of educational services to students with disabilities. The law established a framework in which evaluation became the key to the type of program provided and a reference point for educational outcomes. As discussed in earlier chapters, P.L. 94-142 has been amended several times (the most recent being the P.L. 101-476, The Individuals with Disabilities Education Act) but the essential provisions of the law remain unchanged. It is important that all educators, including teachers of physical education have a clear and comprehensive understanding of federal law for students with disabilities and the provisions related to evaluation.

In the following paragraphs, information will be provided to assist the teacher in understanding the requirements that must be adhered to in the process of assessing the special education student. Table 7.2 identifies some of the safeguards of federal law against assessment abuse.

Screening and Identification

Every state is required to develop a plan for identifying, locating, and evaluating all students with disabilities within the state. Most State Departments of Education work in cooperation with local education agencies to implement a plan for screening school-age students in order to identify individuals with disabling conditions. Identifying students with suspected problems also applies to the area of physical education, where students should be routinely and systematically screened. Teachers have a right and responsibility to refer those students whose motor and physical fitness levels deviate significantly.

The screening plan employed by most school systems involves a variety of procedures. Standardized tests are used

Table 7.2   *Safeguards of federal legislation against assessment abuses*

Past Abuses	Safeguards
Students evaluated for special education without notice to parents or parental consent	Prior written notice must be given to parents before evaluation; parents must give consent before evaluation [121a.504]*
Culturally biased tests used in evaluation	Tests must be selected and administered so that they are not racially or culturally discriminatory [121a.530]
Non-English-speaking students assessed in English	Tests must be provided and administered in the child's native language or other mode of communication, if feasible [121a.532]
Tests administered by untrained or poorly trained personnel	Trained professionals must administer tests according to the test instructions [121a.532]
Poor-quality assessment instruments used for evaluation	Tests must have been validated for the specific purpose for which they are used [121a.532]
Tests used that penalized individuals with disabilities	Tests must be selected so that they do not discriminate against the individual on the basis of disability (unless their purpose is the identification of the disabling condition) [121a.532]
Placement in services based solely on IQ scores	No one procedure may be used as the sole criterion for determination of the educational program [121a.532]; tests selected for use in evaluation must include not merely those that yield a single general IQ score [121a.532]
Placement decisions made without a complete evaluation of the individual	Individuals must be assessed in all areas related to the suspected disability (e.g., health, vision, hearing, social and emotional status, general intelligence, academic performance, communicative status, motor ability) [121a.532]; information from a variety of sources (aptitude and achievement tests, teacher recommendations, physical condition, social and cultural background, adaptive behavior) must be documented and carefully considered [121a.533]

*The numbers in brackets refer to a section of the *Code of Federal Regulations;* 45 CFR 121a contains regulations promulgated under the Education of the Handicapped Act (P.L. 91–320), as amended by the Education of All Handicapped Children Act (P.L. 94-142) and the Individuals with Disabilities Education Act, (PL 101-476).

as well as other informal techniques, such as teacher check-lists and observation of student performance. School records may also be consulted as a source of information.

Due Process

Federal law ensures that children with disabilities and their parents are guaranteed procedural safeguards. This protection, commonly known as due process, means that parents and their children will be informed of their rights, with the provision that they may challenge educational decisions that they feel are unfair. Informing the parents of their rights is an important process that must be administered in an organized and systematic manner. For this reason, most local education agencies assign this responsibility to an administrator, normally the Director of Special Education. What will follow, therefore, is a summary of some of the important due process considerations.

Permission Prior to Assessment

A written notice must be given to the parents indicating that their child has been referred and that the school requests permission to conduct an evaluation for the purpose of determining whether the child requires special education services. Parents must give written permission before the evaluation can be conducted. The letter sent to the parents seeking permission to evaluate must include a reason for the evaluation and a list and description of the tests to be used. A copy of the parents' rights must also be included. Figure 7.1 is an example of a form that includes the necessary information.

    The school is responsible for documenting that permission to test was obtained. Furthermore, all communication with the parents must be clearly presented and, if necessary, in the native language of the parents.

Results of the Assessment

The results of all tests conducted with the student must be interpreted in a meeting with the parents. Persons who are knowledgeable about the tests administered must be available to respond to any questions the parents may have about the test process or the obtained results. Finally, the parents must be told whether their child has a condition that qualifies under P.L. 101-476 and, if so, what special education and related services will be provided.

Outside Evaluation

If the parent wishes, an independent evaluation of the student can be conducted to confirm or refute the findings of the local school. The school system is legally responsible for providing a list of persons or agencies who can conduct the necessary evaluations. The parents must pay for the independent evaluation unless the results obtained differ from the information previously provided by the school system, in which case the cost is borne by the school district.

Hearings

If the parents and the school system cannot agree on the evaluation findings, efforts to mediate the differences should be undertaken. This process normally requires that both sides review their positions and continue to talk and negotiate in an effort to resolve the differences. When mediation fails, an impartial hearing officer is appointed to hear both parties, review the available information, and render a decision. Although not necessary, both the parents and the school system may elect to be represented by legal counsel during a hearing.

    The hearing officer's decision is final unless an appeal is filed with the State Department of Education. When this occurs, the State Department of Education is the final authority. Either party has the right to initiate civil action if it feels the final decision rendered by the Department of Education is inappropriate.

Confidentiality of Records

Only parents of the special education student and authorized school personnel are permitted to review the student's records. This confidentiality clause includes all available evaluation information. Other persons who request to review the file may do so only after the parents have given written permission. The names, dates, and purposes for which the file was reviewed by persons other than the parents or authorized school personnel must also be maintained.

    When the school system determines that certain information is no longer pertinent or helpful, the material may be destroyed if the parents are notified and they agree with the decision.

Standards for Evaluation

The legal requirements of P.L. 101-476 not only help to ensure that an evaluation process will be utilized but also help to establish standards that must be adhered to in the evaluation process. This is a marked departure from some of the past practices in which the label of handicap was primarily related to the student's intelligence quotient without concern for the performance capabilities of the student in other areas. Specific provisions of P.L. 101-476 related to standards for test selection, administration, and test examiner are presented here.

Test Selection

The instruments used to gather evaluative data must be valid tools designed to reflect the student's aptitude or achievement level, or whatever other factors the test purports to measure, rather than reflecting the student's impaired

Dear _____ :   Date _____

We would like to inform you that your child, _____, is being referred for individual testing which will help us in his/her educational planning. Following is a description of any records, reports, or previously administered tests which were used as a basis for recommending this evaluation: _____

_____

The following options for dealing with the above concerns were considered and rejected for the reasons specified: _____

_____

The evaluation procedures and/or tests will include the areas checked below:

☐ **ACADEMIC ACHIEVEMENT**
Assessment of basic skill development measuring current achievement in reading, mathematics, spelling and other areas as appropriate.

☐ **BEHAVIOR AND/OR PERSONALITY**
Assessment of current emotional/social development, adaptive behavior or personality.

☐ **COMMUNICATION DEVELOPMENT**
Assessment of current communication skills including the ability to use speech and/or language clearly and appropriately.

☐ **HEARING**
Assessment including air and bone conduction pure-tone audiometry and discrimination tests as appropriate.

☐ **INTELLECTUAL DEVELOPMENT**
Assessment of general intelligence measuring current verbal and/or non-verbal intellectual functioning.

☐ **PHYSICAL**
Assessment of coordination of body movements in small and large muscle activities.

☐ **OTHER** _____
(Specify areas)

Following is a description of any other factors which are relevant to the proposed testing: _____

_____

An explanation of your rights regarding the identification, evaluation, and placement of your child according to State Administrative Rules is on the reverse side of this form.

Since State Law requires that the district receive written consent before proceeding with testing, please sign this permission form and return it as soon as possible. If you have any questions, please feel free to contact me.

| _____ | _____ | _____ |
| Name/Title | Telephone | Date |

I understand and agree to the above described individual testing or other evaluation. I also understand that the granting of consent is voluntary and may be revoked at any time. I have received a copy of my rights.

Permission is *given* to conduct the evaluation as described _____ _____
                                                                                          Parent/Guardian   Date

Permission is *denied* to conduct the evaluation as described _____ _____
                                                                                          Parent/Guardian   Date

PLEASE RETAIN GOLDENROD PARENT COPY FOR YOUR RECORDS
Please return other copies to: _____   _____
                                        Name/Title   Location

Figure 7.1 Parental consent for evaluation form.

sensory, manual, or speaking skills. It is also essential that more than one test procedure be utilized to determine the student's educational status. This means that more than one test instrument is necessary and that formal as well as informal evaluation techniques are desirable. Total reliance on norm-referenced tests alone, for example, will not provide meaningful motor fitness test scores for students with severe and/or multiple disabilities.

Test Administration

Many students with disabilities have communication problems. For this reason, it is important that tests be administered in such a way that they measure the students' ability rather than their communication skills. Adaptations in test protocol may be necessary, therefore, for students who have visual and hearing impairments. Students whose native language is other than English will also require special attention to be certain that tests do not discriminate because of a language barrier. The important concern is that the test measure the students' motor abilities and performance levels rather than measure their communication and language skills.

Test Examiners

Public Law 101-476 emphasizes the importance of a multidisciplinary team approach to assessment. Incorporating the expertise of several professionals increases the probability that an accurate evaluation relevant to the student's educational needs will be made. Professionals involved in the assessment process must be trained and qualified to administer tests and interpret test results. Whereas federal law emphasizes the importance of qualified test administrators, it does not specify, for instance, the qualifications necessary to administer tests of motor ability. These decisions must be made by local school systems. Assigning this responsibility to special physical educators is logical because of their expertise, as well as their ability to relate test results to the educational programming available in the physical education setting. Some of the safeguards against assessment abuses are summarized in table 7.2.

Motor Performance Tests

General Types

Several procedures may be used to assess the motor performance of students with disabilities. In the following section, some of the more commonly used procedures are presented. As will be discussed, each of the assessment procedures is valuable in a comprehensive approach to evaluating the motor characteristics of the students with special needs.

Norm-Referenced Tests

In the past, most physical education tests were of a kind now called norm-referenced tests. This type of evaluation procedure consists of developing a test and then administering it to a randomly selected group of individuals. The test results become the criteria against which subsequent test takers can compare individual performances and also determine how each student stands in relationship to the others. The comparisons help the teacher to identify students who are in need of special physical education assistance.

In the examiner's manual, which accompanies norm-referenced tests, information about the test's validity, reliability, and objectivity is presented. The directions for administering, scoring, and interpreting the tests also are provided so that the test procedure is standardized. Also found in the test manual are tables and graphs that express the normative data as standard scores, such as age equivalents or percentages, and so on, thus permitting comparisons with others of similar age.

Criterion-Referenced Tests

Other types of referenced evaluation are the criterion-referenced and domain-referenced tests, both of which are well suited to evaluation in physical education. In the criterion-referenced test, a criterion or level of mastery of certain information or skills is arbitrarily established for each item of the test or for the test as a whole. The score achieved by the test taker, then, describes how well the criterion was met. A domain-referenced test, because it also utilizes a criterion, is often thought to be the same as the criterion-referenced test; there is a basic difference, however. The process of establishing a domain is distinctly different from setting a criterion. For example, to establish a domain in a motor activity, the teacher must visualize a pattern of movement rather than a specific isolated movement. In the activity of running, the total pattern of movement is the domain; the movement of picking up one foot and putting it in front of the other foot is a vital part of the domain but not the domain itself. After the domain has been determined, the test maker must decide which components of the domain or pattern are to be examined. For each criterion set, the evaluation of how well the pattern is performed is based on the level of mastery of the components. A domain need not be limited to a pattern of movement; it may be any general skill, which can be composed of more than one component.

Task Analysis

This evaluative procedure is closely related to the criterion-referenced process. With task analysis, the components of a specific task are identified and then arranged from least complex to most complex. Students are evaluated to determine whether they can master the final, most difficult, step of the task. The last step may be thought of as the criterion, and in this respect, the task-analysis evaluation approach is identical to the criterion-referenced procedure. If, however, the student cannot master the final step, the evaluation continues to determine the parts of the task that the student can perform. Evaluation using a task-analyzed approach provides a great deal of useful information for later instruction.

Recent analysis of the value of task-analytic evaluation procedures has been challenged and strengthened by the work of Davis and Burton (1991). They have argued correctly that teachers need to be very careful about developing a sequence of a specific skill (e.g., catching) and then assuming that all learners will master the skill following precisely the order of subtasks as defined. The traditional task-analytic approach, which normally uses either an anatomical or developmental perspective, if used rigidly, places too much emphasis on the sequence of the skill and fails to adequately consider individual variation found within groups of learners. Davis and Burton recommend that the traditional approach to task analysis be modified to recognize that the capability of the performer varies due to individual and environmental constraints. For example, the approach used by a student with cerebral palsy to catch a ball will be different than a student without a neurologic disability. Likewise, environmental constraints (e.g., the size of the ball and elements such as wind) should be considered in assessing the performance of any student. In using task-analytic procedures, it is important also to make sure that the parts (subtasks) of the skill are similar to the "whole" task so that the desired goal "catch a ball" is clear. Some of the new thoughts and arguments regarding task-analytic assessment approaches have helped to reinforce the need to always be attentive to individual differences and focus on what students *can* do as well as areas needing further work. As noted in figure 7.2, the relationship between assessment and instruction using an ecological task-analytic approach should be dynamic and interactive.

Observation

All evaluation techniques involve observation. What is meant by the use of the term here, however, is a greater reliance on technology to capture the student's performance for later review and study. Videotapes are finding increasing use today as aids in recording motor performance. This process permits the evaluator to enlist the aid of other professionals to analyze the student's skill level. Some individuals, such as those with cerebral palsy and various orthopedic impairments, who are difficult to assess with traditional instruments, can be effectively evaluated through the use of a visual recording of their effort. Further recording of their performance at periodic intervals provides an effective means of evaluating skill improvement over time. Parents, too, find a visual recording of their youngster's motor skills a helpful process in assisting them to recognize the importance of physical education and its contribution to total development.

As noted in chapter 6, two processes which lend themselves nicely to evaluation of individual performance include academic learning time (ALT) and opportunity-to-respond (OTR). Both of these variables have been shown to be related to student performance (Houston-Wilson, 1993). Using opportunity to respond as an example, Houston-Wilson found that the use of trained peer tutors was effective in assisting students with developmental disabilities learn discrete motor skills. This point is illustrated by analyzing the performance of one of the students in the Houston-Wilson study. As noted in figure 7.3, a definite improvement in performance with the use of a trained peer tutor was observed. Graphic presentations such as these provide meaningful information for parents and surrogates and assist them to recognize the capability and talent of their students.

King and Dunn (1991) report that with proper training, teachers can be used effectively to observe and report the performance of students who are performing at a high or low level. Visual recording of the student's performance, including a thoughtful analysis provided by the teacher, in combination with other sources of valid test data, provides a powerful and helpful communication device between the school and home.

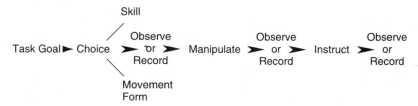

Figure 7.2 Ecological task-analysis model for assessment and instruction of movement tasks.

(From Davis, W. E., & Burton, A. W. (1991). Translating movement behavior theory into practice. *Adapted Physical Activity Quarterly, 8*(2), 167.)

Steps:
1. Select and present the task goal—one of the functional movement categories. Structure the environment and provide verbal and other cues to the student that allow for an understanding of the task goal.

2. Provide choices—have the student practice the task, allowing him/her to choose the skill and the movement form. Observe and/or record the skill choice and movement form in qualitative measures and the performance outcome in quantitative or qualitative measures.

3. Identify the relevant task dimensions and performer variables. Manipulate one or two task dimensions to find the optimal performance level. Observe and/or record the skill choice, movement form, and performance outcomes in qualitative and/or quantitative measures, and compare results with previous measures.

4. Provide direct instruction in skill selection and movement form. Manipulate task variable to challenge the student. Observe and/or record the skill choice, movement form and performance outcomes in qualitative and or quantitative measures, and compare results with previous measures.

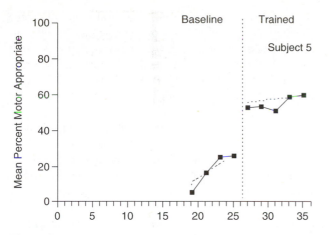

Figure 7.3 A visual analysis (OTR) of the effect of a trained peer tutor on the motor performance of a student with a developmental disability.

(Adapted from: Houston-Wilson, C. (1993). The effect of untrained and trained peer tutors on the motor performance of students with developmental disabilities in integrated physical education classes. Ph.D. dissertation, Oregon State University, Corvallis, OR.)

Self-Evaluation

Self-evaluation is an important skill and every student should be encouraged to develop the ability to evaluate his or her own progress toward achieving the objectives of the program. Self-evaluation of the kind involved in problem-solving can, and should, be more widely used by teachers of special students regardless of the method of teaching used. To institute self-evaluation in a more traditional program, the teacher must be certain that the objectives are clearly recognized by the students; involving them in setting up the objectives is an especially good way of accomplishing this.

Once the objectives have been identified, the student is then provided with a checklist on which selected objectives are listed for the student to accomplish in a given unit of time. The decision as to whether the objective has been met is made by the student based on the criterion identified for each objective. Although various rating scales can be used, a popular system is to have the student place a plus sign by those objectives that are completed and a check by those requiring more teacher assistance. A zero suggests that more practice is required. Self-evaluation techniques are not as structured as other assessment procedures, but they supply valuable information that can be used for individual programming.

Interviews

An increasingly popular evaluation tool is the use of interviews to obtain information about a student's motor performance capabilities. This technique can be used with many people, but it has been restricted primarily to use with parents and students. In each situation, the questions used should be individually developed for the specific student.

Parents can be asked questions related to the individual's developmental history. Information about motor tasks

their child accomplished at specific ages can be very useful. This information is helpful in planning for those with congenital disabilities as well as for those individuals who have developed a disabling condition.

Students should be interviewed to obtain their perceptions of their physical fitness levels and motor performance capabilities. Students' views as to the value of physical education and their activity preferences provide information that can make the difference between eliciting either a positive or a negative response to the physical education experience. The input of students at the Individualized Education Program (IEP) meeting can be a valuable addition to the team and, when possible, should be encouraged. An interview with the student prior to the meeting helps the student to focus his or her thoughts for more effective input.

Specific Types

Ulrich (1985) conducted a survey to determine the assessment practices of adapted physical education teachers in the United States. One of the questions asked of the 251 respondents was to identify the tests that they most frequently used. The results of Ulrich's findings are reported in table 7.3. Although it is beyond the scope of this text to discuss each of the tests, examples of some of the tests will be presented in this section. The tests identified in table 7.3 may be categorized into five different areas: developmental scales; motor ability tests; motor skill tests; perceptual-motor tests; and physical fitness tests. Tests are designed and constructed to perform specific purposes and functions. In this section, various types of tests that have been used to measure different aspects of motor performance will be reviewed.

Table 7.3 *Standardized tests used in adapted physical education*

Test	Frequency
Bruininks-Oseretsky Test of Motor Proficiency (short form)	90
AAHPERD Special Fitness Test for Mildly Mentally Retarded	45
Brigance Diagnostic Inventory for Early Development	40
Hughes Basic Gross Motor Assessment	31
Project ACTIVE	30
Purdue Perceptual Motor Survey	22
I CAN Curriculum Assessment	21
Ohio State University Scale of Intra-Gross Motor Assessment	16
AAHPERD Youth Fitness Test	16
Denver Developmental Screening Test	12
AAHPERD Fitness Test for Moderately Retarded	10
Southern California Sensory Integration Test	9
The Early Intervention Developmental Profile	7

Source: Ulrich, Dale, Department of Physical Education, Indiana University, 1985.

Developmental Scales

Educators for many years have been interested in a basic question: At what age do children exhibit certain motor characteristics? The work of Shirley, Bayley, and Gesell generally is recognized for its significant contribution in establishing developmental progressions that are useful in evaluating a child's acquisition of a specific skill compared to the average chronological age at which other children acquire the skill. In recent years, the revised Denver Developmental Scale, the Denver II, has become a popular instrument to use in screening young children for evidence of developmental delays. A review of the scale, which appears in figure 7.4, identifies items that are used to evaluate children from zero to six years of age in fine motor, gross motor, social, and language skills. Although helpful information can be obtained with the use of developmental scales, the results must be interpreted carefully because of the difficulty of obtaining accurate test information with young children as well as the diverse and unique growth pattern exhibited by some children. For example, infants prenatally exposed to drugs have been assessed using the Motor Assessment of Infants (MAI) which was found to be more sensitive in identifying infants at risk for motor problems.

Motor Ability Tests

Tests of motor ability are designed to provide information about a student's motor capabilities in comparison to individuals of similar age and gender. This type of test is based on the assumption that there are underlying abilities that determine a student's motor performance. In addition it is assumed that these abilities can be identified and measured by specific motor tasks. Motor ability tests are usually standardized with normative scores provided. Werder and Kalakian (1985) have identified the following as reasons for administering motor ability tests:

1. To determine general motor deficiency
2. To determine motor deficiencies in specific subtest areas
3. To provide empirical data to meet criteria for placement into a special physical education program
4. To determine relative areas of strengths and weaknesses in motor ability
5. To predict success in physical education programs

As indicated in table 7.3, the Bruininks-Oseretsky Test of Motor Proficiency is a popular test of motor ability. The test is designed to assess eight factors: running speed during a shuttle run; selected types of balance; bilateral coordination movements; strength and endurance of selected muscle groups; different types of upper-limb coordination, including visual tracking; specific types of visual-motor control; upper-limb speed and dexterity in various movements; and response speed. The complete test battery provides three estimates of motor ability: a gross motor composite score, a

fine motor composite score, and a general index of motor proficiency. A shorter version of the test can be used in screening when a brief overview of motor ability is desired. The complete battery, which consists of forty-six separate items, requires approximately sixty minutes to administer, whereas the fourteen-item short form can be completed in about twenty minutes.

Although motor ability tests such as the Bruininks-Oseretsky are helpful in identifying students with motor deficiencies, their use in a before-and-after design as a means of measuring individual student growth and progress over a period of time is limited. Before-and-after measures, using a general motor ability test, ignore the research literature available on transfer of learning. Changes in the student's score will not occur unless by chance, or unless there is practice of the items of the test or of items of sufficient similarity to permit a generalization to be made about one skill that can then be transferred to the performance of a test item.

Many professionals who obtain pre- and post-measures with motor ability tests frequently become concerned because they do not find any student improvement. This does not mean, however, that the students did not improve in specific skills, but rather that general tests are frequently unable to detect the individual progress in overall motor ability. This difficulty could be resolved by providing a program that emphasizes the various items found on the motor ability test. For the most part, however, teaching the test items of the test would result in a sterile physical education program and would provide little gain in improving overall motor skill development. One solution to this dilemma is to supplement motor ability tests with information derived from tests of motor skills. As will be explained in the next section, these tests focus on specific skills and utilize a criterion-referenced format.

Motor Skill Tests

Although motor ability tests are helpful in identifying students who can benefit from the special physical education program, additional information is needed to assess the degree to which the student progresses in the instructional program. Parents, students, and teachers are all interested in the basic question of whether there is change in the student's motor performance. This implies, therefore, that a system should be implemented in which the student's progress is monitored at regular intervals to detect improvement in performance. Measures are taken on motor skills that are important and basic in the life function and play of children. These essential skills, as discussed earlier, are referred to as basic skills.

Behavioral Objective-Type Tests

A very effective measuring device for evaluating basic motor skills is the behavioral objective. A behavioral objective is a statement describing the skills to be learned in terms

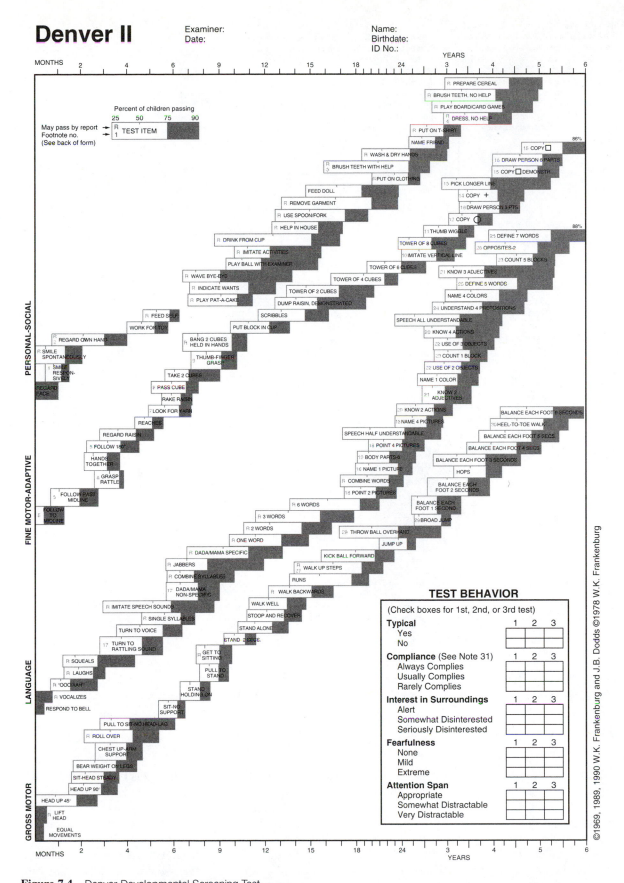

Figure 7.4 Denver Developmental Screening Test.

(Courtesy of William K. Frankenburg and Josiah B. Dodds, University of Colorado Medical Center, Boulder, Colorado.)

1. Try to get child to smile by smiling, talking or waving to him. Do not touch him.
2. When child is playing with toy, pull it away from him. Pass if he resists.
3. Child does not have to be able to tie shoes or button in the back.
4. Move yarn slowly in an arc from one side to the other, about 6" above child's face. Pass if eyes follow 90° to midline. (Past midline; 180°)
5. Pass if child grasps rattle when it is touched to the backs or tips of fingers.
6. Pass if child continues to look where yarn disappeared or tries to see where it went. Yarn should be dropped quickly from sight from tester's hand without arm movement.
7. Pass if child picks up raisin with any part of thumb and a finger.
8. Pass if child picks up raisin with the ends of thumb and index finger using an over hand approach.

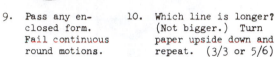

9. Pass any enclosed form. Fail continuous round motions.	10. Which line is longer? (Not bigger.) Turn paper upside down and repeat. (3/3 or 5/6)	11. Pass any crossing lines.	12. Have child copy first. If failed, demonstrate

When giving items 9, 11 and 12, do not name the forms. Do not demonstrate 9 and 11.

13. When scoring, each pair (2 arms, 2 legs, etc.) counts as one part.
14. Point to picture and have child name it. (No credit is given for sounds only.)

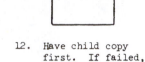

15. Tell child to: Give block to Mommie; put block on table; put block on floor. Pass 2 of 3. (Do not help child by pointing, moving head or eyes.)
16. Ask child: What do you do when you are cold? ..hungry? ..tired? Pass 2 of 3.
17. Tell child to: Put block on table; under table; in front of chair, behind chair. Pass 3 of 4. (Do not help child by pointing, moving head or eyes.)
18. Ask child: If fire is hot, ice is ?; Mother is a woman, Dad is a ?; a horse is big, a mouse is ?. Pass 2 of 3.
19. Ask child: What is a ball? ..lake? ..desk? ..house? ..banana? ..curtain? ..ceiling? ..hedge? ..pavement? Pass if defined in terms of use, shape, what it is made of or general category (such as banana is fruit, not just yellow). Pass 6 of 9.
20. Ask child: What is a spoon made of? ..a shoe made of? ..a door made of? (No other objects may be substituted.) Pass 3 of 3.
21. When placed on stomach, child lifts chest off table with support of forearms and/or hands.
22. When child is on back, grasp his hands and pull him to sitting. Pass if head does not hang back.
23. Child may use wall or rail only, not person. May not crawl.
24. Child must throw ball overhand 3 feet to within arm's reach of tester.
25. Child must perform standing broad jump over width of test sheet. (8-1/2 inches)
26. Tell child to walk forward, heel within 1 inch of toe. Tester may demonstrate. Child must walk 4 consecutive steps, 2 out of 3 trials.
27. Bounce ball to child who should stand 3 feet away from tester. Child must catch ball with hands, not arms, 2 out of 3 trials.
28. Tell child to walk backward,  toe within 1 inch of heel. Tester may demonstrate. Child must walk 4 consecutive steps, 2 out of 3 trials.

DATE AND BEHAVIORAL OBSERVATIONS (how child feels at time of test, relation to tester, attention span, verbal behavior, self-confidence, etc,):

Figure 7.4—*Continued*

that make possible an easy determination of whether or not the skill has been accomplished. For example, a behavioral objective for a specific type of balance might be: "Walk the total length of a balance beam that is six feet long, four inches wide, and two inches high." The statement clearly establishes the instructional objective, and the teacher knows the objective is met when the student is able to perform the skill described. The evaluation in the behavioral objective is explicitly a test of a specific skill; in this instance, it is a measure of a type of balance. The results of the test provide information only about a specific kind of balance skill: walking on a balance beam. No information is provided about the ability to balance on the hands, or head, or to perform other activities requiring a specific kind of balance. Information is also specific to a particular student and is, therefore, criterion-referenced. The *ABC program,* developed by Janet

Wessel is an excellent example of an instructional system for students with special needs that incorporates a behavioral objective-type of evaluation system. The OSU Data Based Gymnasium (1986), a program using a similar format, has been successfully employed with students with severe disabilities.

Specific Motor Skill Tests

Utilizing the concept of behavioral objectives, tests can be developed to evaluate the quality of performance in motor skills of every kind. For example, a test can be made to determine how efficiently and effectively a student can make an overhand throw. The test would need to give consideration to the components of the throw: for example, "the arm was brought back behind the shoulder, a step was made with the opposite foot as the throw was made, the elbow was preceded by the upper arm, the wrist was snapped when the ball was released," and so forth. Such a test provides information about the effectiveness of the specific movements of the throw. It does not provide much information about total coordination of the arm muscles in any other motor skill that is not similar to overhand throwing. Tests of this kind can be used to tell a good deal about the motor ability of a student, however, especially if the skills to be tested are basic skills frequently used in the student's everyday life. Skills such as walking, running, throwing, catching, striking, and kicking can be labeled as basic skills for most children because of their frequency of use in play and in everyday activities.

In designing a test to evaluate the components of a skill such as the overhand throw, it is necessary to task-analyze the movements required to perform effectively. The analysis is based upon the principles of movement—for example, the use of various parts of the body to apply force over a long period of time. To be able to teach and evaluate movement, one has to know how the movement is most effectively performed. Also, consideration must be given to the physical capacity of the individuals being tested. The overhand throw test, for example, must be modified for those under the age of six. Most children younger than six lack the maturity required to perform this skill in the most efficient way. The test would require further modification if it were to be used with students with orthopedic disabilities.

To make adaptations, an assessment must first be made of the child's limitations and potentialities. For example, if the individual is partially paraplegic, consideration must be given to the potential for movement in the arms. It may be found that flexion and extension of the fingers are possible but only flexion remains in the lower arms (i.e., the biceps are functional but not the triceps). Throwing a ball in the usual way is impossible because of the inability to extend the arm; however, a throw over the shoulder is possible. Analysis of the movements involved in throwing a ball over the shoulder produces these components in the performance of the best possible over-the-shoulder throw: (1) good grasp of the object, (2) hyperextended wrist at the start, (3) sharp contraction of the biceps, (4) sharp flexion of the wrist, and (5) release of the ball at the proper time so that it is propelled in a straight line.

The Test of Gross Motor Development (TGMD) developed by Ulrich (1985) is an excellent example of a well-developed motor skill test. The purpose of the TGMD is to identify children ages three to ten who are significantly behind their peers in the execution of gross motor skill patterns. Two subtests, locomotion and object control, assess different aspects of gross motor development. The gross motor patterns of the run, gallop, hop, leap, horizontal jump, skip, and slide comprise the test items in the locomotion subtest. Included in the object control subtest are the motor patterns of the two-hand strike, stationary bounce, catch, kick, and overhand throw. The results of the test provide both criteria and norm-referenced assessment data. The test is easy to administer with the equipment, directions, and performance criteria for each skill clearly identified. Some sample items from the TGMD are found in table 7.4. The TGMD is probably the most commonly used test today to assess the motor performance of children with disabilities.

Perceptual-Motor Tests

The best known of the perceptual-motor tests is the Purdue Perceptual-Motor Survey (PPMS). This test, designed to be administered to children ages six to ten, measures perceptual-motor abilities in five areas. The areas and the behaviors assessed in each area include the following:

1. Balance and posture: walking a balance beam and jumping
2. Body image and differentiation: identification of body parts, imitation of movement, obstacle course, Kraus-Weber, and "angels in the snow"
3. Perceptual-motor match: drawing a circle, drawing two circles simultaneously, drawing a lateral line, and drawing two straight vertical lines simultaneously
4. Ocular control: movement of eyes following a flashlight, and convergence on objects
5. Form perception: copying seven geometric forms

Roach and Kephart (1969), the test developers, emphasize that the test was not designed to diagnose but rather to allow the clinician to observe perceptual-motor behavior in a series of behavioral performances. The scoring procedures for the test battery are subjective and qualitative. An example of the test form is provided in figure 7.5. Given the nature of the scoring system, primarily a checklist, and the limited information regarding the validity of the PPMS, the instrument should be used cautiously and as a supplement to other assessment data.

Other perceptual-motor tests commonly used by educators include the Southern California Test of Sensory Integration and Cratty's Six-Category Gross Motor Test.

Table 7.4 *Sample items from Test of Gross Motor Development*

Locomotor Skills					
Skill	*Equipment*	*Directions*	*Performance Criteria*	*1st*	*2nd*
Run	50 feet of clear space, colored tape, chalk, or other marking device	Mark off two lines 50 feet apart Instruct student to "run fast" from one line to the other	1. Brief period where both feet are off the ground 2. Arms in opposition to legs, elbows bent 3. Foot placement near or on a line (not flat-footed) 4. Nonsupport leg bent approximately 90 degrees (close to buttocks)		
Gallop	A minimum of 30 feet of clear space	Mark off two lines 30 feet apart Tell student to gallop from one line to the other three times Tell student to gallop, leading with one foot and then the other	1. A step forward with the lead foot followed by a step with the trailing foot to a position adjacent to or behind the lead foot 2. Brief period where both feet are off the ground 3. Arms bent and lifted to waist level 4. Able to lead with the right and left foot		
Hop	A minimum of 15 feet of clear space	Ask student to hop 3 times, first on one foot and then on the other	1. Foot of nonsupport leg is bent and carried in back of the body 2. Nonsupport leg swings in pendular fashion to produce force 3. Arms bend at elbows and swing forward on take off 4. Able to hop on the right and left foot		
Leap	A minimum of 30 feet of clear space	Ask student to leap Tell him/her to take large steps leaping from one foot to the other	1. Take off on one foot and land on the opposite foot 2. A period where both feet are off the ground (longer than running) 3. Forward reach with arm opposite the lead foot		
Horizontal Jump	10 feet of clear space, tape or other marking devices	Mark off a starting line on the floor, mat, or carpet Have the student start behind the line Tell the student to "jump far"	1. Preparatory movement includes flexion of both knees with arms extended behind the body 2. Arms extend forcefully forward and upward, reaching full extension above head 3. Take off and land on both feet simultaneously 4. Arms are brought downward during landing		

Source: Ulrich, Dale, Department of Physical Education, Indiana University, 1985.

Many of the perceptual-motor ability tests were developed by special educators, whereas the older motor performance tests were developed by people with training in physical education. The two groups frequently use different constructs and different groupings of skills in developing their tests. Vocabularies differ, as does the use of terms. Special educators often use a single term to encompass several components that have traditionally been identified by two or more terms by physical educators. For example, "bilateral integration," a term popularized by special educators to describe a smooth working together of the right and left sides of the body, includes the traditional physical education concepts of agility and specific kinds of coordination.

Unfortunately, the tests developed by special educators often have ignored the research performed by those in physical education that provides evidence of the specificity of

Perceptual-Motor Survey

Name _Jim Smith_ Address _447 N. Elm_
Date of Birth _9/7/78_ Sex _M_ Grade _5th_
Date of Exam _10/10/88_ Examiner _JJ_ School _Hansen_

		Score 1	2	3	4
Balance and Posture	Walking board: Forward			X	
	Backward		X		
	Sidewise	X			
	Jumping			X	
Body Image and Differen-tiation	Identification of body parts				X
	Imitation of movement			X	
	Obstacle course		X		
	Kraus-Weber				X
	Angels-in-the-snow		X		
Perceptual-Motor Match	Chalkboard Circle		X		
	Double circle	X			
	Lateral line		X		
	Vetical line			X	
	Rhythmic writing Rhythm	X			
	Reproduction		X		
	Orientation	X			
Ocular Control	Ocular pursuits Both eyes		X		
	Right eye	X			
	Left eye	X			
	Convergence		X		
Form Perception	Visual achievement forms Form	X			
	Organization			X	

Figure 7.5 Purdue Perceptual-Motor Survey record form.

(Reprinted with permission of Macmillan Publishing Co. from *Assessment in Adapted Physical Education* by Werder and Kalakian. Copyright © 1985 by Macmillan Publishing Co.)

motor skills; hence, special educators have made greater claims for the validity of their tests as measurements of perceptual-motor ability than evidence would warrant. The perceptual-motor tests are valuable educational tools, but they do not provide the overall measurement of motor ability that is often claimed. Rather, they offer information concerning the ability to perform a specific motor skill.

Physical Fitness Tests

Tests of physical fitness are designed to assess the health-related aspects of a student's performance. The five areas most fitness tests attempt to assess are muscular strength, muscular endurance, cardiovascular endurance, flexibility, and body composition. Although many tests of physical fitness are available, few tests have been specifically developed for individuals with impairments. Exceptions to this statement include the AAHPERD Special Fitness Test for the Moderately Mentally Retarded, the AAHPERD Youth Fitness Test for the Mildly Mentally Retarded, and Buell's Test for blind and partially sighted.

Unfortunately, some physical educators have taken the position that any valid test of physical fitness can be used to assess the fitness level of students with disabilities. For example, the AAHPERD Health Related Fitness Test has been used to test the fitness level of many special students. This test has not been validated for use with any special population. Caution must be exercised in utilizing any test that has not been validated for use with specific populations. Traditional tests of cardiovascular endurance, in particular, have not been used successfully with individuals with selected disabilities. Pizarro (1990) and Baumgartner and Horvat (1991) indicated that field tests that assess endurance must be interpreted carefully when used with individuals with mental retardation. Fernhall and Tymeson (1988) noted, however, that the 1.5 mile could be used successfully with adults who are mildly mentally retarded. Rintala et al. (1992) found that the Rockport Walking Test could be used successfully as a measure of predicted cardiorespiratory fitness with adult moderately mentally retarded men. Rintala et al. questioned the use of running tests with this population, explaining that the running cadence and pace is a problem. Although less is known about the validity and reliability of other health related fitness tests for populations with disabilities, Pizarro (1990) found that the modified sit-up test, sit and reach, and skinfold measure used in AAHPERD's Health Related Fitness Test, with modifications, were reliable for individuals with mild and moderate levels of mental retardation. In an effort to address this problem as well as provide norms for individuals with sensory and orthopedical disabilities, Winnick and Short (1985) developed a fitness test for individuals with orthopedic and sensory disabilities that incorporates, with modifications, many of the items found in the Health Related Fitness Test. A summary of this test follows.

Project Unique is a test of physical fitness that was designed for use with children and youth ages ten to seventeen. The test is the outgrowth of an extensive field study in which 3,914 youngsters from twenty-three states and the District of Columbia were assessed. Youngsters and individuals with visual, auditory, and orthopedic impairments as well as those without disabilities were included in the study. The test items for all populations, with modifications where appropriate, are identified in table 7.5. Norms are provided that can be used to compare a student's performance with other youngsters with similar disabilities as well as individuals without disabilities of similar age and gender. Project Unique is an excellent example of a physical fitness test based on current information with practical and valuable application to special populations.

The efforts of Winnick and Short (1994) to develop procedures for assessing the fitness levels of individuals with disabilities has resulted in a new project known as Project Target. This project, funded by the Office of Special Education and Rehabilitative Services, has been designed to establish and validate criterion-referenced physical fitness test items and standards for adolescents with selected disabilities. It is hoped that these standards will provide targets for youngsters with disabilities in attaining healthful living through physical fitness activity. Once these targets are established, a program of physical fitness is to be developed to help youngsters with disabilities reach them. Although Project Target is at an early stage in its development, the goal is to develop a specific physical fitness test with items modified, as needed, for individuals with disabilities and to recommend criterion-referenced test items and standards to currently existing tests such as Physical Best (Palestra, 1994).

Table 7.5　*An outline of Project UNIQUE physical fitness test items according to major participant groups*

Test Items	Normal, Auditory Impaired, Visually Impaired[a]	Cerebral Palsy[a]	Paraplegic Wheelchair Spinal Neuromuscular[a]	Congenital Anomaly/ Amputee[a]
Body Composition Skinfolds	X	X	X	X
Muscular Strength and Endurance				
Grip Strength (Strength)	X[b]	X[c,f]	X[g,h]	X[b,j]
50-Yard/Meter Dash (Power-Speed)	X	X[d]	X[d]	X
Sit-Ups (Power-Strength)	X	—	—	X[i]
Softball Throw for Distance				
(Power-Strength)	—	X[e]	sub.[g,h]	sub.[i]
Flexibility				
Sit and Reach	X	X	—	X
Cardiorespiratory Endurance				
Long Distance Run	X	X	X	X

[a]Items may require modification or elimination for selected group subclassifications (see test administration section).
[b]The broad jump may be substituted for grip strength tests as a measure of strength for these groups.
[c]Grip strengths measure power-strength for males with cerebral palsy.
[d]The dash measures power-endurance for individuals in this group.
[e]The softball throw is recommended for females only as a measure of power-strength.
[f]The arm hang may be substituted for grip tests for males.
[g]The arm hang or softball throw for distance may be substituted for grip strength measures (strength factor) for males.
[h]The softball throw for distance may be substituted for grip strength measures (strength factor) for female participants.
[i]The softball throw for distance may be substituted for sit-ups (as a power-strength factor) in cases where the sit-up would be considered inappropriate.
[j]Males may substitute the arm hang for grip tests (strength factor).
Source: Winnick, J., & Short, F. (1985). Physical fitness testing of the disabled (p. 7). Champaign, IL: Human Kinetics Publishers.

Issues in Evaluation

Physical educators are confronted with several issues in their efforts to select the best procedure for evaluating the motor performance levels of students with disabilities. In the following paragraphs, some of the more critical issues will be discussed to assist the teacher in understanding some of the important factors that must be considered in selecting appropriate tests.

Motor Fitness versus Physical Fitness

Many of the tests developed in the past to evaluate students in physical education have combined tests of motor fitness and physical fitness into a single test battery. Analyzing student performance with this type of test is difficult and frustrating because of the uncertainty about whether the students' performance should be attributed to their motor fitness or physical fitness levels. The issue is not whether one should assess the students' motor fitness levels in contrast to their physical fitness levels, but rather that the distinction between motor fitness and physical fitness is recognized. Physical fitness is related to the concept of health and includes the five generally accepted areas of physical fitness: cardiorespiratory endurance, flexibility, muscular strength, muscular endurance, and body composition. Motor fitness, however, is related to the students' motor skill performance and includes those factors believed important (e.g., reaction time, balance, coordination, and agility) in the development of various motor tasks.

Norm-Referenced versus Criterion-Referenced

Specialists in the education of children with disabilities struggle with the issue of whether it is best to evaluate the student with norm-referenced or criterion-referenced instruments. In reality, this is a minor point that can be clarified easily once the use of each test is understood. Norm-referenced tests are helpful in screening for motor problems, in comparing students, in program evaluation, and in the placement of students. Criterion-referenced tests are valuable as aids in assessing student progress and for making day-to-day instructional decisions about individual students. As Davis explains it, "A major advantage of the criterion-reference test is that it accommodates an individualized approach to testing and programming more than the norm-referenced approach" (Davis, 1984). Some criterion-referenced tests also may be utilized as a screening test. This is true, for example, with the TGMD discussed previously. Because the criterion is the most effective movement for performing the basic skills, students who cannot accomplish one or more of the skills with maximum efficiency in accordance with their capabilities are immediately identified as needing work to improve the skills in which they are deficient. Inability to effectively execute a large number of basic skills is indicative of the need for special help.

Generality versus Specificity in Evaluation

Whether a general motor ability test can be used to evaluate students is a question that has generated a great deal of discussion. Some feel that tests that measure constructs such as motor ability and intelligence are limited in their usefulness and may provide misleading information. Even tests that measure components within the domain of motor ability, such as balance, are perceived by some as being too general. For example, the ability to do a handstand does not provide an indication of the ability to balance the body while standing on one foot with the eyes closed. To assume that an evaluation of either skill measures the other is incorrect, as is the assumption that a measurement of either evaluates total balancing skill.

Those who accept the concept that motor evaluation is specific argue that assessments should be made of the specific motor skills that are the foundation of general motor ability. These foundation skills are those often referred to as the basic skills: the skills that are used most frequently and are most important in the daily life functions and play of children. The specific skills that constitute the basic areas will vary in different environments and also may be quite different from one student to the next. For example, in a society devoid of dancing and games that utilize skipping and galloping, the skills of skipping and galloping would not be basic for children. Walking and running are not basic skills for a student who uses a wheelchair. For such a child, the skill of propelling would be a basic skill; for others it would not be. Obviously, for students with disabilities, tests of basic skills provide a meaningful indicator of their progress toward individually designed goals. General tests of motor ability, although valuable as screening tools, must be used with caution when serving as precise indicators of the motor performance of students with disabilities.

Process versus Product

Process and product evaluation both have been widely used with students. Those who favor the process system argue that the most important aspect of student performance relates to the mechanics or the process of how the skill is executed. For example, in the skill of throwing a ball, students would be evaluated on their ability to grasp the ball, step with the correct foot, look at the target, use an overhand motion, rotate the body, and follow through. Evaluators using the product approach focus on the results of the throw. Therefore, the primary measures would be how far the ball was thrown and with what degree of accuracy.

Both process and product evaluation are important and should be used for specific purposes. The process system is helpful in working with novice performers and for incorporating evaluation into the process of teaching, particularly when used with a task-analyzed curriculum or for employing the ecological task analysis approach recommended by Davis and Burton (1991). Product evaluation is helpful in obtaining an overview of the student's ability to perform specific motor tasks and for comparing students.

Selecting Tests to Evaluate Motor Behavior

Due to the large number of tests available that purport to measure motor performance or some aspect of this construct, it is essential that educators evaluate the various instruments carefully. Presented in this section is a discussion of the test qualities that should be considered prior to selecting instruments to evaluate motor performance.

Purpose of the Test

A fundamental question that must be asked when surveying the various motor tests is, What is the purpose of the test? For example, is the instrument designed as a screening tool or is the intent of the test to evaluate changes in motor performance? Is it a test of motor fitness, physical fitness, or both? These and many other questions related to the test's purpose should be analyzed.

The important concept is that a test should be used only for the purpose for which it was developed. Using a test of general motor ability as an instrument for assessing student change in motor performance is not acceptable. Likewise, using most criterion-referenced tests of basic motor skills as the sole instrument for comparing the performance of various students also has limitations.

Standardization and Normative Scores

Standardization refers to the process of administering a test in a systematic and consistent way to a large sample of individuals. The test developer must demonstrate that the standardization group is representative. This means that the group should have the same proportion of demographic variables as the national population or as the subpopulation with whom the instrument is to be used. Project Unique is an example of a physical fitness test that used a systematic sampling procedure to ensure that selected disability populations were adequately represented by geographic regions. Other important factors that must be considered in assessing a test's standardization sample is the currency of the sample—whether the sample represents a recent census report and sample size. Generally speaking, the larger the sample size, the more likely it is to be representative of the specific population.

Normative scores, based on the group used to standardize the test, are usually reported as standard scores, percentile ranks, and age or grade norms. These scores are used to describe the distance of a student's test score from the mean in terms of standard deviations. Examples of standard scores are T scores and z scores. T scores have a mean of fifty and a standard deviation of ten, whereas the mean for the z score is zero with a standard deviation of one. Stanine scores also are frequently used as standard scores. Stanine scores have a mean of five and a standard deviation of two. Percentiles are also frequently used in physical education to report student scores. A percentile tells the percentage of a norm group that falls at or below a specific score. Age and grade norms are derived by computing the average raw scores made by students of a given age or particular grade level. Many tests provide several normative scores, allowing the teacher to decide which scores would be appropriate for different occasions. For example, student scores on The Bruininks-Oseretsky Test of Motor Proficiency may be reported as standard scores, percentiles, stanines, or age equivalents. Whereas parents may be interested in percentiles and age equivalents, school administrators will probably focus closely on the standard scores and stanines.

Statistical Properties

Test developers must provide statistical information to help prospective users determine if the test is designed in conformity with accepted educational measurement procedures. Some important statistical properties include the test's validity, reliability, and objectivity. These and the procedures used to score the test will be reviewed in the following paragraphs.

Test Validity

A test is considered valid when it measures what it purports to measure. Although this is a clear statement and a reasonable expectation, it is, unfortunately, not always easy to establish validity. Procedures used to establish validity of motor tests include content validity, criterion-related validity, and construct validity.

Content Validity This term refers to a process whereby the content of a particular body of information is defined and a test constructed to measure the extent to which students have acquired the necessary information. For example, a test could be developed to measure a special student's ability to perform the tasks involved in a game such as kickball. The content, or the skills in kickball, would first be identified, and then certain aspects of the various skills would be selected for purposes of testing the individual. The test is valid if it measures those aspects of the skill that are most important. Logic is an important process in establishing content validity. This means that statements must be provided by the test developer that demonstrate that the test items selected are representative of the larger area from which they were developed and that a logical procedure was used to select the appropriate items.

Criterion-Related Validity This type of validity refers to the extent to which a test is related to an external criterion. For example, some tests of cardiorespiratory endurance, such as Cooper's Twelve Minute Run Test (1970), are validated by comparing the individual's running performance over a specified distance to the amount of oxygen that an individual can utilize while running on a treadmill. If individuals who consistently perform well on the criterion (i.e., they have a large oxygen intake capacity) run the specified distance quicker than those who have a small oxygen capacity, one may argue that the test has criterion-related validity. For example, Rintala et al. (1992) validated the Rockport Walking Test as a measure of cardiorespiratory fitness by comparing the performance of men with mental retardation as to their peak maximal oxygen uptake using a treadmill and standardized laboratory procedures.

Other examples of criteria against which a new test can be compared include teacher evaluations, parent expectations, performance on other tests, and success in school.

Construct Validity   Unlike content or criterion-related validity, construct validity is used when the quality to be measured is difficult to define. Items such as intelligence and motor ability are examples of constructs that investigators have historically attempted to define and measure. The process used in construct validity involves defining the construct and then comparing the test performances of individuals who represent extremes on the particular construct. A test of intelligence, for instance, could compare test scores of individuals with different levels of intelligence, including the mentally retarded. Rarick's (1977) effort to identify the factor structure of motor abilities of individuals with moderate mental retardation is an excellent example of construct validity.

Effects on Validity   It is important to recognize that tests are valid only under certain conditions and for specific populations. A test designed to be individually administered, for example, loses its validity when the conditions are altered by administering the test to the entire class. Likewise, a test that has validity when used with students without disabilities may not remain valid when given to students with special needs, because this is not the population for which the test is intended. In essence, then, a test that is valid when given under the conditions intended for testing students *without* disabilities may not be appropriate for testing those *with* disabilities. This is an important consideration that must be weighed carefully in the selection of tests to be administered to any special population.

Test Reliability

A test is reliable if it consistently measures those variables it is designed to measure. Reliability is frequently determined for physical and motor fitness tests by comparing the scores of students from trial to trial or day to day. If students perform in a similar manner on the same test each time it is given under like conditions, the test is considered to be a reliable measure.

An important factor in establishing test reliability is the development of specific instructions for how the test should be administered. Special adaptations for students with disabilities should also be specified. Frequently, it is necessary to establish reliability for tests that have been modified for use with students with disabilities. With some special populations, particularly the mentally retarded, the variability evident in the students' responses is so great that special efforts will be necessary to obtain an acceptable level of reliability.

An attempt must also be made to ensure that the conditions under which the test is given are similar to the conditions intended for administration of the test. Changing the procedures for administering the test or conducting the test in a different type of environment may alter its results. Also, students may not perform in a consistent manner because of such factors as the effects of fatigue or warm-up or the degree of motivation, thereby affecting the outcome of the test. An excellent discussion of the implications of testing the motor performance of special populations is reported by Stewart, Dummer, and Haubenstricker (1990). Although their discussion is specific to the deaf, the general concepts presented, including the dangers of administering and interpreting test results from invalid tests, are applicable to many individuals and populations with disabilities.

One of the primary reasons for determining a reliability coefficient is to use it in estimating the test's standard error of measurement (SEM). The SEM is actually the standard deviation of the error distribution around a true score and may be computed using the following formula:

$$SEM = \sqrt{1 - r}$$

where 1 is a constant and r represents the reliability coefficient

The SEM establishes the limits that anyone can place on a particular test score. For example, if a student achieves a standard score of 42 on the Bruininks-Oseretsky Test of Motor Proficiency and we know that this test has an SEM of 4.0, the student's true score 68 percent of the time would be somewhere between 38 and 46.

Objectivity

A special form of reliability is objectivity. This measure relates to how well different test examiners can give the same test to the same individuals and obtain similar results. Objectivity is a factor that must be considered in test selection. Tests that require special training to administer and score will obviously not be objective unless all individuals who give the test have developed the appropriate test examiner skills.

Scoring

The procedure used to score tests is a variable that should be studied when reviewing different tests. Some tests generate only a raw score reflecting the student's actual performance; other instruments allow for scores to be converted for comparative purposes. Norm-referenced tests, for instance, will frequently report scores as standard percentiles, which permits comparisons between students. Some tests identify specific criteria that must be met on individual tasks and then each test item is scored on a pass–fail scale. The percentage achieved on a specific criterion is yet another scoring system incorporated into some tests. The test reviewer must decide whether the scores to be obtained provide the type of information desired.

Ecological Validity

Several authorities have suggested that tests used to assess the performance of individuals with disabilities should be ecologically valid (Davis and Burton, 1991; Zittel, 1994). This suggests that the test should be sensitive to the child's comfort level and be administered in an enviroment familiar to the individual. This is especially true for preschool children with special needs and individuals with moderate to severe levels of mental retardation. Administering a test in a familiar environment by an examiner known to the student helps to ensure that the test results more accurately represent the individual's true ability. A good example of an ecologically valid instrument is the I Can Pre-Primary Motor and Play Skills (Wessel, 1980). With this test battery, the test is administered by a caregiver in a familiar setting, using material known to the child.

Independent Test Reviews

The process of selecting a test and assessing its quality has been made easier by the availability of selected references. *The Buros Mental Measurement Yearbook,* for example, provides concise reviews of many tests including some commonly employed with handicapped students. The reviews are conducted by knowledgeable individuals who are asked to provide an objective and independent review of various properties associated with the tests. Reviews of tests also may be found in selected professional journals. *The Adapted Physical Activity Quarterly* frequently publishes reviews or papers that critique selected tests. An excellent example is the paper authored by Zittel (1994) in which she analyzed nine gross motor assessment instruments frequently used with preschool children.

Sources such as these are extremely useful in helping professionals to make informed decisions about the quality and usefulness of a test. This information adds credibility to the test ultimately selected for use with special populations.

Brown and Bryant (1984) have developed a consumer's guide for professionals to assist them in the process of selecting tests. A sample of the guide may be found in figure 7.6. The guide summarizes in a formal way, using a checklist format, many of the test properties that have been discussed in this chapter.

Administrative Factors

The ease with which a test may be given is an important consideration in determining its usefulness in the school setting. Significant factors relate to the amount of time required for administration as well as the facilities and equipment needed.

Time

Tests of motor fitness vary considerably in the amount of time required to administer them. Some require only a few minutes, whereas others involve several test sessions over a two-day period. If a test is long but provides needed information, then it should be used. Motor tests designed primarily as screening instruments to identify students who may need further evaluation must be constructed so that they are time efficient, thus increasing the probability of their widespread use.

Caution must be exercised when attempting to shorten the necessary testing time by evaluating a group of students together. The performance of some students is dramatically affected when peers are permitted to observe their motor skill evaluation.

Facilities and Equipment

The examiner's manual that accompanies most tests provides information about space requirements and necessary equipment. Fortunately, most motor skill tests are developed to be used in school settings, and thus, the test developers recognize the space and equipment limitations with which some school systems must deal. There are, however, a few tests that, if used, involve the purchase of specialized equipment. Although the costs may be justified because of the type of information provided by a specific test, the budgetary impact of the purchase should be considered prior to incorporating this test into the physical education evaluation program.

The materials and equipment in some test kits may be reproduced with the permission of the publisher. Making duplicate copies of test material is a practical way to reduce costs while making the tests readily available throughout a school or school system.

Test Examiner

Each test should be reviewed carefully to determine the level of training required for potential users of the test. Despite the fact that many of the motor performance tests can be routinely administered and evaluated by personnel with preparation as physical educators, some do require additional expertise. This is particularly true of some of the tests designed to measure certain elements of perceptual-motor skills.

A Consumer's Guide to Tests in Print

Test Name (Date of Publication): _____
Test Author(s): _____
Publisher, City, State: _____

Test Score Being Reviewed: _____
Content Area: _____

Administration:
1. Administration:
   ☐ Group or individual
   ☐ Individual only
   ☐ Group only

2. Administration requires terms of:
   ☐ 14 minutes or less
   ☐ 15-29 minutes
   ☐ 30-59 minutes
   ☐ 60 minutes or longer
      ☐ Other:_____

3. Administration is:
   ☐ Timed
   ☐ Untimed
   ☐ Both timed and untimed

Scoring:
1. Scoring is:
   ☐ Computer only
   ☐ Manual only
   ☐ Both computer and manual

2. Scores are interpreted in:
   ☐ Age equivalents
   ☐ Grade equivalents
   ☐ Percentile ranks
   ☐ Standard scores

Age/Grades for Intended Use:
☐ Preschool (0 through 5 years or through kindergarten)
☐ Primary (6 through 8 years or grades 1–3)
☐ Elementary (9 through 11 years or grades 4–6)
☐ Junior High (12 through 14 years or grades 7–9)
☐ Senior High (15 through 18 years or grades 10–12)
☐ Adult (19 years or greater)

Examiner Characteristics:
☐ The test is administered easily after reading the manual.
☐ Administration requires special training beyond familiarity with the manual.
☐ Administration is restricted to certified examiners, examiners with specific licenses, or examiners who have completed supervised practice with the instrument.

Format Characteristics:
Format requires the subject to:
1. Input:
   ☐ Listen
   ☐ Read print
   ☐ Look at stimuli (pictures, objects)
   ☐ Understand sign language
   ☐ Read braille
      ☐ Other:_____
      ☐ Draw
      ☐ Write print
      ☐ Write braille
      ☐ Use sign language
      ☐ Other: _____

2. Output:
   ☐ Speak, minor (yes/no, one word responses)
   ☐ Speak, major (phrases, sentences required)
   ☐ Manipulate objects
   ☐ Mark answer sheet
   ☐ Point

Figure 7.6   Reviewer's evaluation form.

(Adapted from Brown, L., & Bryant, B.R., "A Consumer's Guide to Tests in Print" in *Remedial and Special Education, 5*(1), 57.)

Section II: Standardization and Normative Scores

A. Normative Scores
☐ No normative scores are reported or only age/grade equivalent scores are available.
☐ Percentile ranks are reported.
☐ Standard scores are reported.

B. Size of the Standardization Group
☐ The size of the standardization group is not specified or does not meet the criteria below.
☐ The standardization group contains 75-90 subjects in most chronological age intervals or academic grade levels for which a normative table is presented; in addition, there are 750-999 subjects in the total group.
☐ The standardization group contains 100 or more subjects in each chronological age interval or academic grade level for which a normative table is presented; in addition, there are 1,000 or more subjects in the total group.

C. Demographic Characteristics of the Standardization Group
☐ The characteristics of the standardization group are not specified or are not representative of the appropriate population.
☐ The characteristics of the standardization group correspond approximately to the census data for a specified region or population on at least three of the following: sex, domicile (urban/suburban/rural), socioeconomic status, geographic region, and race/ethnicity.
☐ The characteristics of the standardization group correspond approximately to national census data on at least three of the following: gender, domicile (urban/suburban/rural), socioeconomic status, geographic region, and race/ethnicity.

D. Recency of Test Standardization
Standardization was completed in:
☐ 1968 or before.
☐ 1969-1978.
☐ 1979 or after.
If no standardization date is given, use the test publication date.

Section III: Reliability

A. Internal Consistency Reliability
Internal consistency reliability is:
☐ not reported or is below .80 at most ages.
☐ between .80 and .89 at most ages.
☐ .90 or above at most ages.

B. Stability Reliability
Stability reliability is:
☐ not reported or is below .80 at most ages.
☐ between .80 and .89 at most ages.
☐ .90 or above at most ages.

Section IV: Validity

Validity is:
☐ not reported: or validity studies are not acceptable in design or significance of results.

Figure 7.6—*Continued*

Special qualifications are also necessary to administer tests to some students with disabilities. For instance, personnel who test students with hearing disabilities will need sufficient signing skills to communicate effectively so that the results will not be invalid. Likewise, examiners of individuals who are mentally retarded should have sufficient training to ensure that a given test is assessing the student's motor rather than cognitive level.

The quality of information obtained through the evaluation process is closely related to the skills of the examiner.

Every effort must be made to utilize personnel who have a thorough background in physical education and who are knowledgeable about appropriate motor tests and their use with special populations.

Although it is beyond the scope of this book to discuss all of the motor tests that have been used with students with disabilities, table 7.6 provides basic information about some of the instruments that have not been discussed elsewhere in the chapter. The tests listed are limited to measures of motor fitness. Tests of physical fitness will be presented in chapter 27.

Table 7.6 *Additional tests of motor performance**

Name	Purpose	Population	Components Measured
Basic Motor Ability Tests (Arnheim and Sinclair, 1974)	Screening test of motor ability	Children 4–12 years of age	Small and large muscle control, static and dynamic balance, eye-hand coordination, flexibility
Body Image Screening Test for Blind Children (Cratty, 1971)	Screening instrument for evaluating child's understanding of body parts and position	Blind children. With modifications the test can be used with deaf, sighted, and children with mental retardation	Body planes, body parts, body movements, laterality, and directionality
Brigance Diagnostic Inventory of Early Development (Brigance, 1978)	Assessment and screening tool to determine children's performance levels	General population including students with disabilities from birth to 6 years of age	(Motor aspect of the test): Standing, walking, stair climbing, running, jumping, hopping, kicking, balance board, catching, rolling/throwing, ball balance, rhythm, wheel toys
Cratty Six Category Gross Motor Test (Cratty, 1969)	Screening test for motor functioning	Nondisabled 4–11; EMR 5–12; and TMR 5–24 years of age	Body perception, gross agility, balance, locomotor agility, ball throwing, ball tracking
Godfrey-Kephart Movement Pattern Checklist—Short Form (Godfrey and Kephart, 1969)	Screening instrument presented as a checklist	Children with and without disabilities	Walk, run, crawl, jump, hop, skip, climb, roll, slide, stand, sit, throw, catch, hit, kick, push, pull, carry
Hughes Basic Gross Motor Assessment (Hughes, 1979)	Evaluation of gross motor function	Children 5 years 6 months to 12 years 5 months believed to have minor motor dysfunction	Eight subtests of static balance, jumping, walking, hopping, skipping, throwing, ball handling
Milani Comparetti Motor Development Screening Test (Trembath, 1977)	Screening instrument for assessing the neurodevelopment of children	Children from 0–2 years of age	Postural control, active movement, primitive reflexes, righting, parachute, tilting reactions
Motor Assessment of Infants (MAI) (Chandler, Andrews and Swanson, 1980)	Systematic assessment of early motor behaviors	Infants 0–12 months of age	Muscle tone, primitive reflexes, automatic reactions, and volitional movement
Motor Proficiency Assessment (Rarick and McQuillan, 1977)	Screening test of motor ability	Students with mild and moderate mental retardation	Body fat/dead weight, fine visual-motor coordination, balance, upper limb-eye coordination, arm strength, spinal flexibility, leg-power coordination
Move-Grow-Learn: Movement Skills Survey (Orpet and Heustis, 1971)	Survey designed to help teachers observe motor skills	Not specified. Test is normally used with elementary school-age children	Coordination and rhythm, agility, flexibility, strength, speed, balance, endurance, body awareness
Ohio State University SIGMA (Loovis and Ersing, 1979)	Criterion-referenced test of basic motor skill patterns	General population	Walking, stair climbing, running, throwing, catching, kicking, jumping, hopping, striking, ladder climbing
Peabody Developmental Motor Scale	Criterion-referenced developmental profile to assess student's current functioning level	Children up to 7 years of age	Large number of items for measurement of gross and fine motor skills

*See Selected References for information on publishers of the tests.

Table 7.6—*Continued*

Name	Purpose	Population	Components Measured
AHHPERD Youth Fitness Test for the Mildly Mentally Retarded (AAHPERD, 1976)	A physical fitness test battery designed for mildly mentally retarded youth	Students 8–18 years of age	Arm-shoulder-girdle strength; efficiency of abdominal and hip flexor muscles; speed and agility; explosive muscle power; skill and coordination; cardiovascular efficiency
I CAN Program (Wessel, 1976)	A systematic physical education curriculum incorporating assessment as part of the curriculum	Preschool to secondary students with disabilities	Aquatics, body management, health and fitness, fundamental skills
OSU Data Based Gymnasium (Dunn, Morehouse, Fredericks, 1986)	A systematic physical education curriculum for the severely disabled, incorporating assessment as essential to the curriculum	School-age students who are severely disabled	Movement concepts, basic skills, physical fitness, sport-leisure skills
Project Active (Vodola, 1975)	A comprehensive adapted and developmental physical education program	School-age populations with focus on mentally retarded, learning disabled, and emotionally disturbed	Gross body coordination, balance/postural orientation, eye-hand coordination, eye-hand accuracy, eye-foot accuracy
Project Unique (Winnick and Short, 1985)	Test of physical fitness for youth without disabilities and those with sensory and orthopedic disabilities	Youth, 10–17 years of age with sensory and orthopedic disabilities	Body composition, dynamic strength, agility, static balance, flexibility, muscular strength, cardiorespiratory endurance
Southern California Sensory Integration Test (Ayres, 1980)	Intended to measure sensory integrative dysfunction in underlying neural systems	Children 3 years of age to adults with perceptual difficulties	17 subtests including space visualization, figure-ground perception, kinesthesia, manual form perception, finger identification grapethesia, motor accuracy
Fait Physical Fitness Battery for Mentally Retarded Children (Fait, 1972)	Test of physical fitness	Children and adults 9–20 years of age; mildly and moderately retarded	Speed, aquatic muscular endurance, dynamic muscular endurance, balance, agility, cardiorespiratory endurance
Bruininks-Oseretsky Test of Motor Proficiency (Bruininks, 1978)	Test designed to assess motor functioning; both a long and short form have been developed	Children 4.5–14.5 years of age. May be used with students with and without disabilities	Static balance, dynamic balance, coordinated movements, strength, visual–motor coordination, response speed, visual–motor control, upper-limb speed and precision
AAHPERD Motor Fitness Testing Manual for the Moderately Mentally Retarded (Johnson and Londeree, 1976)	Test of physical and motor fitness for youth with moderate retardation	6–19 years of age; moderately mentally retarded	Cardiorespiratory endurance, abdominal endurance, arm and shoulder strength and endurance, explosive leg strength, speed and agility

Summary

Quality physical education programs require that, periodically, appropriate measures be taken to assess the effectiveness of the educational experience. Given this information, sound decisions can be made regarding modifications, if any, that should be made in the program. Recognizing the value of evaluation, the framers of P.L. 101-476, Individuals with Disabilities Education Act, mandated that comprehensive assessments, including measures of the student's motor performance, be an integral part of the services provided for children with disabilities. Federal statute requires that screenings be conducted to ensure that all students requiring assistance are identified. P.L. 101-476 also states that no child can be identified as disabled unless a thorough, nonbiased assessment is conducted. Besides screening and determining eligibility for special education services, evaluation is also helpful in formulating goals and objectives for the Individualized Education Program and for reviewing student progress toward meeting the IEP goals.

Evaluations of the motor fitness and physical fitness of students with disabilities should be comprehensive and should include, where possible, both criterion and norm-referenced measures. Normative data provides meaningful information concerning the youngster's performance compared to similar students. Because of the diverse nature and needs of students with disabilities, it is not always possible or desirable to use a norm-referenced test. In these instances, criterion-referenced measures that compare the child's performance to predetermined criteria are very helpful.

Various types of tests can be used to evaluate motor performance. These include developmental scales, and tests designed to measure motor ability, motor skills, perceptual-motor skills, and physical fitness. Within the chapter, a number of the popular tests used in special physical education programs are identified and described. In selecting a test it is important to identify tests that adhere to high standards of test construction. The purpose of the test and its statistical properties, validity, and reliability should be analyzed carefully.

Although there are some excellent tests that can be used in the special physical education program, teachers must be careful to use tests only for the purposes for which they were originally intended. This includes, too, special care to ensure that tests are ecologically valid and responsive to performer and environmental constraints. Professionals must also be cognizant of the various issues in evaluation, and must be conversant with the latest findings regarding the administration and interpretation of test results. Most importantly, teachers must recognize that good evaluation enhances the instructional process and helps in making wise educational decisions. Without an effective evaluation program, communication with parents and other professionals will be limited and issues of accountability and quality of service will surface. Evaluation takes time, but the effort is essential for determining student progress and for assessing the overall effectiveness of the special physical education program. A good evaluation system is the cornerstone of a quality special physical education program.

Selected Readings

American Alliance for Health, Physical Education, Recreation, and Dance (AAHPERD). (1976). *Testing for impaired, disabled, and handicapped individuals.* Washington, DC: Author.

Arnheim, D.D., & Sinclair, W.A. (1979). Basic motor ability test. In *The clumsy child.* St. Louis: C.V. Mosby Co.

Ayres, J. (1980). *Southern California Test of Sensory Integration.* Los Angeles: Western Psychological Services.

Baumgartner, T., & Horvat, M. (1991). Reliability of field based cardiovascular fitness running tests for individuals with mental retardation. *Adapted Physical Activity Quarterly, 8,* 107–114.

Bayley, N. (1969). *Bayley scales of infant development.* The Psychological Corporation. New York: Harcourt, Brace, Jovanovich, Inc.

Bowman, R.A., & Dunn, J.M. (1982). Effect of peer presence on psychomotor measures with educable mentally retarded children. *Exceptional Children, 48*(5), 449–451.

Brigance, A.H. (1978). *Brigance diagnostic inventory of early development.* North Billerica, MA: Curriculum Associates, Inc.

Brown, L., & Bryant, B.R. (1984). A consumer's guide to tests in print: The rating system. *Remedial and Special Education, 5*(1), 55–61.

Bruininks, R.H. (1978). *Bruininks-Oseretsky test of motor proficiency.* Minneapolis: American Guidance Service.

Buros, O.K. (1985). *Mental measurement yearbook* (9th ed.). Highland Park, NJ: Gryphon Press.

Chandler, L.S., Andrews, M.S., & Swanson, M.W. (1980). *Movement assessment of infants: A manual.* Rolling Bay, WA: Movement Assessment of Infants.

Cooper, K.H. (1970). *The new aerobics.* New York: M. Evans and Company, Inc.

Cratty, B.J. (1969). Cratty six-category gross motor test. In B.J. Cratty (Ed.), *Motor activity and the education of retardates.* Philadelphia: Lea and Febiger.

Cratty, B.J. (1971). Body-image screening test for blind children. In B.J. Cratty (Ed.), *Movement and spatial awareness in blind children and youth.* Springfield, IL: Charles C. Thomas.

Criterion-referenced physical fitness standards for adolescents with disabilities (1994). *Palaestra, 10,* p. 55.

Davis, W.E. (1984). Motor ability assessment of populations with handicapping conditions: Challenging basic assumptions. *Adapted Physical Activity Quarterly, 1,* 125–140.

Davis, W., & Burton, A. (1991). Ecological task analysis: Translating movement theory behavior into practice. *Adapted Physical Activity Quarterly, 8,* 154–177.

Department of Health, Education and Welfare, Office of Education. (1977, August 23). Education of handicapped children, part II, implementation of part B of the Education of the Handicapped Act. *Federal Register.* Washington, DC: Author.

Dunn, J.M., Morehouse, J.W., & Fredericks, H.D. (1986). *Physical education for the severely handicapped.* Austin, TX: Pro-Ed Publishers.

Fait, H. (1982). Evaluation of motor skills of the handicapped: Theory and practice. *Practical Pointers.* Washington, DC: American Alliance for Health, Physical Education, Recreation, and Dance, 5(8).

Fernhall, B., & Tymeson, G. (1988). Validation of cardiovascular fitness field tests for adults with mental retardation. *Adapted Physical Activity Quarterly, 5,* 49–55.

Frankenburg, W.K., & Dodds, J.B. (1991). *The Denver II developmental screening test.* Denver, CO: University of Colorado Medical Center.

Godfrey, B.B., & Kephart, N.C. (1969). Godfrey-Kephart movement pattern checklist—Short form. *Movement Patterns and Motor Education.* New York: Appleton-Century-Crofts.

Hammill, D., Brown, L., & Bryant, B.R. (1986). *A consumer's guide to tests in print.* Austin, TX: Pro-Ed Publishers.

Houston-Wilson, C. (1993). The effect of untrained and trained peer tutors on the Opportunity to Respond (OTR) of students with developmental disabilities in integrated physical education classes. (Unpublished dissertation). Oregon State University.

Hughes, J. (1979). *Hughes basic gross motor assessment.* Denver, CO: Office of Special Education, Denver Public Schools.

King, C.M., & Dunn, J.M. (1991). Classroom teachers' accuracy in observing students' motor performance. *Adapted Physical Activity Quarterly, 6,* 52–57.

Londeree, B., & Johnson, L.E. (1976). *Motor fitness test for the moderately mentally retarded.* Reston, VA: AAHPERD.

Loovis, E.M., & Ersing, W.F. (1979). Ohio State University SIGMA. In *Assessing and programming gross motor development for children.* Cleveland Heights, OH: Ohio Motor Assessment Associates.

McLoughlin, J.A., & Lewis, R.B. (1986). *Assessing special students.* (2d ed.). Columbus, OH: Charles E. Merrill Publishing Co.

Ness, R. (1974). *The standardization of the basic movement performance profile for profoundly retarded institutionalized residents.* (Unpublished dissertation). North Texas State University, Denton, TX.

Oregon Department of Education. (1981). *Adapted physical education in Oregon schools.* Salem, OR: Author.

Orpet, R.E., & Heustis, T.L. (1971). *Move-grow-learn movement skills survey.* Chicago: Follet Publishing Co.

Peabody Developmental Motor Scales. (1974). IMRID Behavioral Science Monograph No. 25, George Peabody College, Nashville, TN.

Pizarro, D.C. (1990). Reliability of the health related fitness test for mainstreamed educable and trainable mentally handicapped adolescents. *Adapted Physical Activity Quarterly, 7,* 240–248.

The Psychological Corporation. (1978). *McCarthy screening test.* New York: Harcourt, Brace, Jovanovich, Inc.

Rarick, G.L., & McQuillan, J.P. (1977). Motor proficiency assessment. In *The factor structure of motor abilities of trainable mentally retarded children: Implications for curriculum development.* Berkeley, CA: Department of Physical Education, University of California, Berkeley.

Rintala, P., Dunn, J., McCubbin, J., & Quinn, C. (1992). Validity of a cardiorespiratory fitness test for men with mental retardation. *Medicine and Science in Sports and Exercise, 24*(8), 941–945.

Roach, C., & Kephart, N.C. (1969). *The Purdue perceptual motor survey tests.* Los Angeles: Western Psychological Series.

Seaman, J. (Ed.). (1988). Testing the handicapped: A challenge by law. *Journal of Physical Education, Recreation and Dance, 59* (1).

Stewart, D., Dummer, G., & Haubenstricker, J. (1990). Review of administration procedures used to assess the motor skills of deaf children and youth. *Adapted Physical Activity Quarterly, 7,* 231–239.

Trembath, J. (1977). *The Milani-Comparetti motor development screening test.* Omaha, NE: Meyer Children's Rehabilitation Institute, University of Nebraska Medical Center.

Ulrich, D.A. (1985, August). *Current assessment practices in adapted physical education: Implications for future training and research activities.* Paper presented at the annual meeting of the National Consortium on Physical Education and Recreation for the Handicapped, New Carollton, MD.

Ulrich, D.A. (1985). *Test of gross motor development.* Austin, TX: Pro-Ed Publishers.

Vodola, T. (1976). *Project ACTIVE maxi-model: Nine training manuals.* Oakhurst, NJ: Project ACTIVE.

Werder, J.K., & Kalakian, L.H. (1985). *Assessment in adapted physical education.* Minneapolis, MN: Burgess Publishing Co.

Wessel, J. (1980). *I Can pre-primary motor and play skills.* East Lansing, MI: Field Service Unit in Physical Education and Recreation for the Handicapped.

Wessel, J.A. (1976). *I CAN.* Northbrook, IL: Hubbard Publishing Company.

Winnick, J.P. (1979). *Early movement experiences and development: Habilitation and remediation.* Philadelphia: W. B. Saunders, Co.

Winnick, J., & Short, F. (1994). Project Target. Paper presented at the annual meeting of the National Consortium for Physical Education and Recreation for Individuals with Disabilities, Washington, DC, July, 1994.

Winnick, J.P., & Short, F.X. (1985). *Physical fitness testing of the disabled: Project Unique.* Champaign, IL: Human Kinetics Publishers.

Zittel, L. (1994). Gross motor assessment of preschool children with special needs: Instrument selection considerations. *Adapted Physical Activity Quarterly, 11,* 245–260.

Enhancing Activities

1. Obtain a copy of the O.K. Buros Mental Measurement Year Book on your next visit to the library. Review this reference to see if one of the tests identified in table 7.6 is described.

2. Administer one of the tests identified in table 7.3 to a child with a disability.

3. Interview a parent and a teacher to obtain their views regarding evaluation. Discuss with them the value of norm-referenced versus criterion-referenced tests. Try to solicit their views on other issues related to evaluation.

4. Obtain a copy of the October 23, 1977, *Federal Register* and review those sections of P.L. 101-476 pertaining to the evaluation of students with disabilities.

5. Using the guide for evaluating tests found in figure 7.4, select one of the tests identified in table 7.6 and conduct a review of the test and its various properties.

6. Provide examples of test procedures that appear to be ecologically sensitive to variations.

CHAPTER

8

Assistive Devices

After studying this chapter, the reader should be able to:

1 Appreciate the various assistive devices and their importance in enhancing the functioning ability of individuals with disabilities.

2 Increase knowledge of the wheelchair and how its design has been modified to respond to the sport interests and needs of athletes with disabilities.

3 Recognize the variety of mobility devices that are available to help the child with a disability to benefit from and enjoy the pleasure of moving.

4 Understand some of the technical terms used to describe prosthetic and orthotic devices and mobility aides including wheelchairs.

5 Recognize the procedures and skills required to operate standard and powered wheelchairs.

6 Apply selected principles in assisting those with various mobility devices to use the device properly (for example, putting on and taking off braces, transferring into and out of a chair).

7 Identify different types of braces that have been used in the treatment of spinal deformities, and list some of the advantages associated with each.

8 Locate sources that can be utilized to obtain additional information about assistive devices.

Natural arm and leg movements that have been lost through injury or illness can often be compensated for, to some degree, by the use of assistive devices. The term assistive devices is applied to a variety of contrivances that assist, substitute for, or facilitate movement of the limbs. These devices range in complexity from the simple cane, which provides support in balancing the body, to artificial hands, the fingers of which are powered by small concealed batteries that enable the user to duplicate many actions of the real hand.

Among the children for whom the special physical education teacher must plan an appropriate program will be some who use assistive devices. Consequently, some information about the devices and their operation is important. Knowledge of the function of the specific device is helpful in understanding the movement problem imposed by the disability and in understanding the way and extent to which the device helps to overcome the problem. This insight facilitates analysis of the motor skills that are possible with the device so that appropriate physical education activities can be more readily selected and successfully presented.

Acquaintance with the operation of assistive devices is useful when the user requires assistance in transferring to or from the device as, for example, in moving from the wheelchair to a gymnasium mat on the floor. Understanding the techniques of effecting the transfer increases the efficiency and safety of the operation. Lack of such knowledge may, in addition to decreasing the effectiveness of the transfer, actually bring about fear or pain in the one being moved.

Information about the operation of assistive devices is also useful when assistance is required in removing and replacing them. The various braces and harnesses that are used to support the trunk or to hold artificial limbs in place are usually removed for certain types of physical activity. Safe, painless assistance in taking off and putting on the device is more likely to occur if the techniques of the operation are understood.

Locking mechanisms are provided on some devices to create stability or immobility when desired. An understanding of these and of how they function is important so that one may properly assist a user of such a device who doesn't understand how to operate the lock.

Mobility Devices

The most common of the assistive devices are those used to aid in mobility and will, in this discussion, be referred to as mobility devices. They include canes, crutches, walkers, scooters, and adapted tricycles and bicycles.

The simplest of these ambulatory devices is the cane. It is used primarily to help maintain body balance while standing or walking. The cane achieves this function by widening the base of support, thereby providing greater stability. Pressure on the cane reduces the weight-bearing strain on the involved limb (the leg, foot, or both of these).

The cane may be of the straight wooden variety with the handle being one of the various types available to accommodate different needs and preferences. A type of cane that is very popular is the folding cane which, as the name implies, can be folded when not in use. The folding cane and variations such as the adjustable type are very convenient to store, which is important when travelling (figure 8.1). The easy up cane (figure 8.1) is equipped with a second handle that enables the user to rise more easily from a seated position. Although the C-curved handle is the most popular design, it is not always comfortable for everyone. For this reason, some prefer to cushion the handle by wrapping it with foam or rubber. For safety's sake, the cane should have a rubber tip that prevents slipping. An ice gripper cane tip (figure 8.2) is a helpful device when walking outdoors in the winter. Proper length is important for effective and comfortable use: The cane should be long enough to allow the elbow to be flexed slightly when the tip is resting on the ground about six inches away from the side of the foot.

Those who have severe problems in balance may need more assistance than the common straight cane offers. For such individuals there is a metal cane with four feet at its base; hence its name of *quad cane*. Quad canes vary in width and in style of handle. Although somewhat awkward to use, these canes do provide substantial stability and permit ambulation by those who would experience great difficulty in walking with a regular cane.

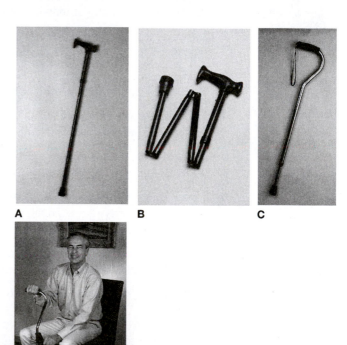

Figure 8.1 Folding cane—extended (*A*), folded (*B*). Adjustable cane (*C*). Easy-up cane (*D*).

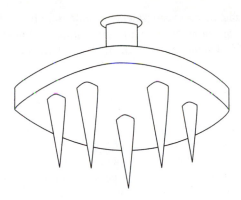

Figure 8.2 To prevent slipping, ice grippers are attached to the end of a cane.

For most efficient use, the cane is held in the hand opposite the involved limb and is brought forward as this limb is moved forward. The cane must be held close enough to the body to prevent leaning the body toward it, as this adversely affects balance. For the same reason, the cane should be advanced the same distance as the involved limb.

To prevent accidents on the floor of the playroom or gymnasium care must be taken to remove obstacles and to keep the floor dry and skid-proof. Taking care to avoid collision with those using canes must be instilled in players whose mobility is unencumbered.

Crutches

Crutches are ambulatory devices that offer more stability than canes. Several types of crutches are currently available.

The most common and most simple are made of wood with double uprights, an underarm bar, and a hand piece, which is adjustable to the length of the arm. In use, the crutches are placed under the arms, and the hands on the hand pieces, where pressure is exerted to move the body. The top of the crutch is placed approximately two inches short of the axilla (armpit) and should be well padded to avoid injury to the radial nerve of the arm.

Other types of crutches are made of metal and consist of a single vertical upright with a support for the forearm. Adjustment of these is accomplished by depressing a button on the lower part of the crutch. Three of the commonly used metal crutches are the forearm crutch, the underarm crutch, and the platform crutch (figure 8.3). With the forearm crutch, the cuff for the forearm may be either fixed or hinged. Hinged cuffs make it easier for the user to open a door or avoid injury in the case of a fall. Underarm crutches are similar to forearm crutches but instead of cuffs, they have extensions that fit under the arms. They can be used safely with the handle pointing forward or backward. Individuals with triceps brachii weakness find the underarm crutches to offer greater support. The platform crutch or gutter forearm cane allows weightbearing on the whole forearm when the elbow is flexed to ninety degrees. These crutches are very helpful to the individual with weak or painful wrists.

All crutches, whether wooden or metal, should be equipped with broad rubber tips to prevent slipping. Because the tips become worn with use, they should be inspected frequently and replaced promptly, when necessary. The safety precautions recommended for participants using canes on the playing floor also apply to those with

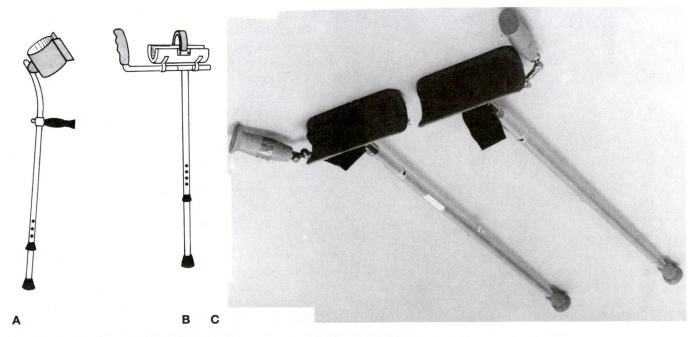

Figure 8.3 (A) Löfstrand crutch. (B) Forearm support crutch. (C) Platform crutch.

crutches. Assistance may be given to a weak or unskilled user of crutches by grasping his or her belt at the back with one hand.

As an additional safety measure, as well as for program planning purposes, it is desirable for the special physical educator to be aware of the various gaits taught by physical therapists to those who use crutches. The placement of the feet and crutches for each of four crutch walking gaits is illustrated in figure 8.4 *A* to *D*. The gait is determined by the individual's physical condition and ability to take steps. The speed at which the crutch user wishes to move is another factor in determining the choice of gait, provided the individual has the strength and endurance for faster speed. With this information, the teacher can select suitable activities and make appropriate adaptations with the assurance that they can be performed safely and effectively by participants on crutches.

Walkers

A walker is a four-legged stand with a hand railing that extends across the front and to the sides of the body (figure 8.5 *A, B, C, D* and *E*). It offers a wide base of support and affords greater security than do either canes or crutches. Hence the walker is greatly preferred by persons who have poor vision as well as lack of strength and balance.

The types of walkers shown in the illustration include two of the basic styles—the pick-up and the rolling walker. The techniques for using either are similar. The user grasps the railing, which should be at a height that allows the elbows to be slightly flexed, and lifts or pushes the walker forward a short distance. Then, one or more steps are taken, depending on ability, and the process is repeated.

The pick-up walker is recommended for those who need more support than is provided by the quad cane but who lack the balance required for the successful use of crutches. Individuals who do not have the strength to lift the pick-up walker or who have arm or hand problems that interfere with lifting employ the rolling walker. To accommodate persons who cannot stand but are able to use their feet, there is a rolling walker with a seat. Such a walker might be used by someone during convalescence from hip surgery until the hip is permitted to bear weight.

The forearm support walker (see figure 8.5 *C*), which consists of a metal frame with attached casters, provides some trunk support and good upper-limb support. This device can be particularly helpful to the older, weak child who has painful hands and wrists or those with poor coordination.

Several safety measures need to be observed in the use of both kinds of walkers. The rolling walker should be equipped with a hand brake to prevent unexpected rolling and loss of balance. If there is no brake, the walker should be stabilized by backing it against a wall. When moving the body between a chair and walker, the arms of the chair should be used for support; an uneven distribution of weight on the walker may cause it to move or tip. A pick-up walker should be set down so that all the legs touch the surface at the same time. It should be lifted using the arms, with the body's weight forward rather than by bending and straightening the back, which may cause so much backward lean that the body loses its balance. Many of these needs have been addressed through new designs, such as the gait trainer and mobile stander (see figure 8.5 *D* and *E*). Both units provide needed stability and support.

Baskets, trays, or pouches can be attached to the walker and crutches to help the user to transfer items from one location to another (figure 8.6). In a physical education unit on throwing, for instance, the student can use these aids to hold

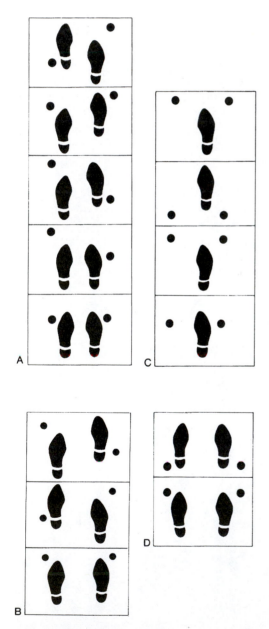

Figure 8.4 (*A*) Four point gait. (*B*) Two point gait. (*C*) Three point gait. (*D*) Swing through gait.

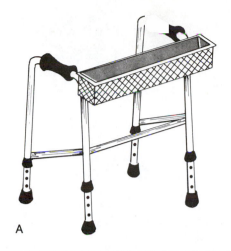

A

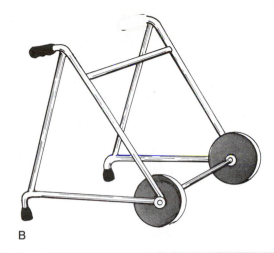

B

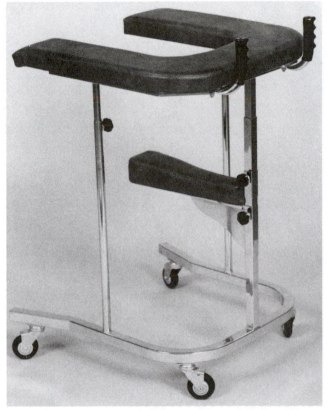

C

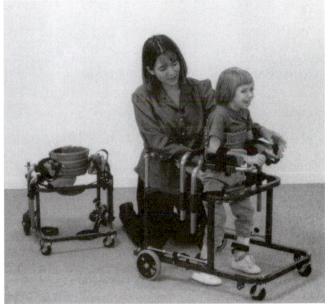

D

E

Figure 8.5 (*A*) Pick-up walker. (*B*) Rolling walker. (*C*) Forearm support walker. (*D*) Rifton Pediatric Gait Trainer. (*E*) Taylor Made Mobile Stander.

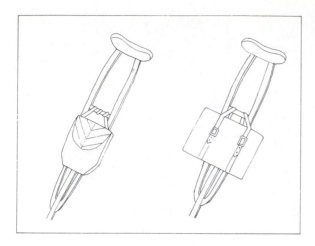

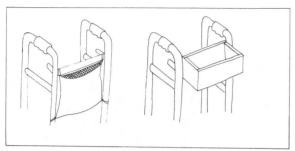

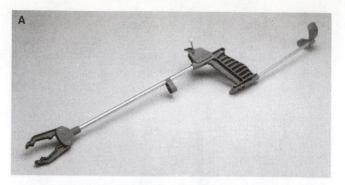

Figure 8.7 Winchester Reacher (*A*). Omnigrip Reachers (*B*). Both devices are helpful in extending the reach of the individual whose mobility is impaired.

Figure 8.6 Bags, pouches, and baskets attached to crutches and wheelchairs assist students to hold or transfer equipment used in physical education.

items such as balls and bean bags. Hand reachers such as the Winchester and Omnigrip (figure 8.7 *A* and *B*) are very helpful in assisting those with mobility impairments reach and pick up items. These units can be conveniently attached to a walker or wheelchair.

Adapted Tricycles and Bicycles

Several innovative and functional adaptations of bicycles and tricycles have been proposed in recent years. These efforts have assisted many youngsters with disabilities in improving their mobility and independence through an age-appropriate and socially acceptable medium. The pleasure generated through learning to ride a tricycle or bicycle is a powerful motivator that can be used to increase overall fitness and functional health.

Although elaborate adaptations in tricycles and bicycles have been proposed, some modifications can be done with minimal cost and alterations. For example, wooden blocks with velcro can be attached to the pedals to help the child with spasticity to keep the feet from slipping. Additional support through the use of a back rest, chest strap, or pelvic strap can aid the child with poor trunk balance. Handlebar posts also can be attached to aid the youngster with spasticity maintain trunk and limb position (figure 8.8). Older

Figure 8.8 Adapted tricycle with handlebar posts.

students who have good trunk control may find that an adult tricycle can be used without any modifications. The adult tricycle has enjoyed renewed popularity in recent years.

Many adaptations can be made to the standard bicycle to allow students with various disabilities to ride for enjoyment and as a form of mobility. For some students minor adjustments may be all that is necessary. The three-wheel cycle in figure 8.9 can aid mobility.

Figure 8.9 The use of a three-wheel hand crank cycle aids in mobility.

Figure 8.11 Tara cycle.

A

Figure 8.10 Shadow Cycle-One by Quickie converts an existing wheelchair into a high performance hand cycle.

B

Figure 8.12 Sloat cycle. (*A*) Low and (*B*) high profiles.

A relatively new design (figure 8.10) converts a wheelchair to a hand driven cycle. Many wheelchair users have found this to be a mobility device that offers a desirable alternative to the normal mode of transportation. The cycle can be easily attached and is transportable in the trunk of a car.

Other devices can be used as forms of self propulsion. Two of these, the Tara cycle and the Sloat cycle, are presented in figures 8.11 and 8.12. The Tara cycle, with its molded plastic seat, safety belt, and totally enclosed sprocket and chain, is ideally suited as a means of recreational mobility for the child with lower limb weakness or paralysis. The Sloat cycle is a hand-cranked cycle suitable for individuals who are paraplegic or those with spina bifida. The unit has good back support and an extended seat for leg and foot support. Similar units, including the Jansen handcycles, have been produced by other companies.

Scooter Boards

The scooter board is a flat board to which four caster wheels are attached for easy movement. Either a sitting or prone lying position may be taken on the board; propulsion is created by pushing the hands against the floor. Commercial scooter boards are usually approximately fourteen by eighteen inches in size, but larger ones can be easily constructed in the home or school workshop.

Scooter boards, particularly those of longer length, provide an excellent means of mobility to the youngster who cannot stand or who is unable to move about with any degree of speed and security. Those who are unable to sit on the board may lie on it. Use of the scooter board greatly extends the opportunities for participation in physical education activities for those with disabilities of the lower extremities. In many games, movement on the scooter can be substituted for walking and running. Various scooter boards, each designed to facilitate different forms of movement, are found in figure 8.13.

A variation of the scooter board is the Y cart (figure 8.14), so named because its design places the child in an abducted leg position. The child lies on the Y cart in a prone position, using the hands for propulsion.

The caster cart is another mobility device that can be effectively used by some children as a substitute for crawling. The cart's low center of gravity and big wheels (figure 8.15) allow for easy maneuvering. Children who have limited mobility are thus able to move and explore their environment.

Figure 8.14 Y cart.

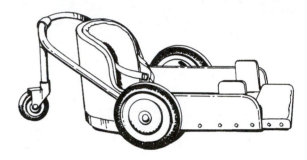

Figure 8.15 Caster cart, Mark 1 design.

The chief safety precaution in the use of scooter boards during physical education activities is to avoid injuries to the fingers. Participants should be warned to remove their hands from the floor and not to grasp the edge of the scooter when other scooters approach them, to avoid the possibility of the fingers and hands being run over or crushed between colliding scooters.

Wheelchairs

The wheelchair provides a means of locomotion for those who are so severely immobilized by their condition that they cannot stand or walk efficiently, even with the aid of the mobility devices described in the preceding sections. There are many types of wheelchairs available; they are commonly constructed with two large wheels in back and two smaller caster wheels in front. Attached to the larger wheels are slightly smaller wheels that are not in contact with the ground: These are called hand rims and are used for propelling the wheelchair by hand. Other equipment may include adjustable foot rests, movable leg rests, brakes to lock the large wheels, arm rests that may be detachable, and

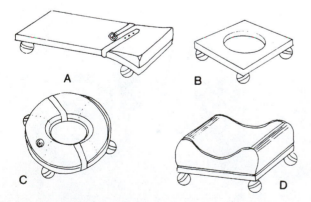

Figure 8.13 Scooter boards designed to assist the student with a disability move.

A

B

C

D

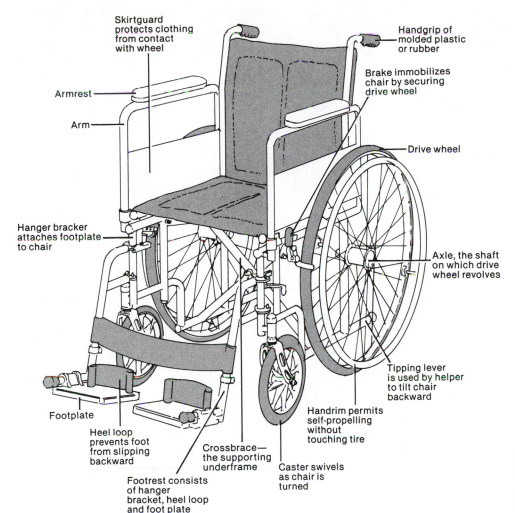

Skirtguard
protects clothing
from contact
with wheel

Handgrip of
molded plastic
or rubber

Armrest

Brake immobilizes
chair by securing
drive wheel

Arm

Drive wheel

Hanger bracker
attaches footplate
to chair

Axle, the shaft
on which drive
wheel revolves

Footplate

Tipping lever
is used by helper
to tilt chair
backward

Heel loop
prevents foot
from slipping
backward

Handrim permits
self-propelling
without
touching tire

Crossbrace—
the supporting
underframe

Footrest consists
of hanger
bracket, heel loop
and foot plate

Caster swivels
as chair is
turned

Figure 8.16 The wheelchair and its standard parts.

(Courtesy of Hale, G., & Barr, P. *The Source Book for the Disabled.* New York, Paddington Press Ltd., 1979.)

handles for use by a helper in pushing the wheelchair. The location of these and other items is presented in figure 8.16.

One type of wheelchair is lightweight and collapsible for easy transportation in the car by those who are able to drive. The wheelchair for the amputee is designed with the rear axle displaced posteriorly to compensate for the lack of weight in the lower limbs (figure 8.17).

In the physical education class, when the wheelchair user is engaged in any activity in which safety might be jeopardized by sudden rolling of the chair, the brake must be set. The teacher should always check to see that this is done (figure 8.18).

Help may be needed to negotiate curbs and stairs of one or two steps (more steps should not usually be attempted). To give safe assistance in going up, the teacher should stand behind the chair with the front of the chair toward the curb or steps and tilt the chair until the small wheels rest on the level surface when the wheelchair is pushed forward (figure 8.19). The procedure is reversed when going down the curb

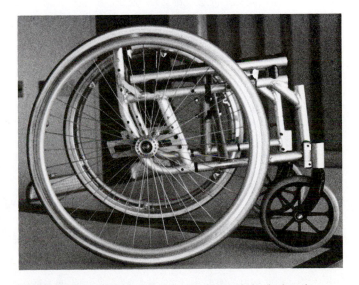

Figure 8.17 Amputee wheelchair. The rear axle is displaced posteriorly to compensate for the lack of weight of the user's lower limbs.

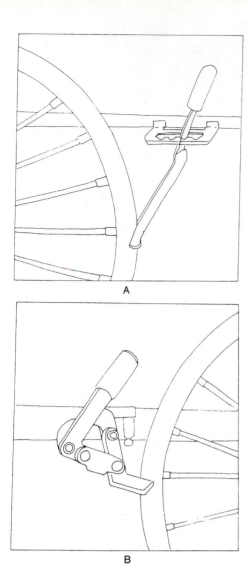

Figure 8.18 Standard wheelchair brakes. In (*A*) the lever type permits various amounts of pressure to be applied to the tire. The toggle-type brake in (*B*) has only off and on positions.

always be below the chair. Thus, in moving down the incline, the chair is turned and slowly pulled backward. It is tilted to place the weight on the large wheels. If the person being moved has sufficient strength and the incline is steep, he or she may exert pressure against the hand rims to help retard the speed of movement. In moving up the incline, the chair is pushed forward and tilted to bring the weight onto the large wheels. If possible, the occupant of the chair can assist by pushing on the hand rims to aid the forward movement. Additional tips for handling a wheelchair are presented in table 8.1.

When lifting someone who cannot move himself or herself from the chair to a mat for activity, the following procedure is suggested. The wheelchair is moved close to the edge of, or even onto, the mat. The wheels are locked and checked to see if they are secure. If the person being assisted is able to rise and stand, the arms of the chair are not detached but the foot and leg rests are moved aside. The helper stands to one side of the chair and lifts up on the torso under the arms of the person in the chair, who assists by pushing on the armrests. The helper then reaches down with one hand to release the lock on the side where he or she is standing and swings the chair away in order to move behind the wheelchair's occupant to give support to the torso while lowering the occupant to the mat. The process is reversed to place the individual back into the chair.

Table 8.1 *Tips for handling a wheelchair**

A. Folding a Wheelchair
   Remove the seat cushion
   Pull upward on the seat fabric at the center, front, and back
B. Opening a Wheelchair
   Place fingers toward the middle of the seat
   Press with the heels of the hands on the two sides of the seat
C. Putting a Wheelchair into a Car Trunk
   Position the folded wheelchair close to and parallel with the trunk
   Grasp struts of chair with one hand well forward, the other well back
   Lift the chair vertically
   Balance the chair on the edge of the trunk
   Tip the chair to a horizontal position
   Slide it into the trunk
D. Pushing a Wheelchair Down a Curb
   Tip the chair backward by placing a foot on the tipping lever and, holding the handgrips firmly, lower the chair down the curb
   Position the rear wheels so they hit the ground at the same time
E. Pushing a Wheelchair Up a Curb
   Place foot on tipping lever and lift the chair off its front wheels
   Move the front wheels onto the curb carefully to ensure that the wheels are even and on the curb
   Lift the back wheels and while moving the front wheels forward move the back wheels onto the curb. If a second helper is available, the lift may be accomplished by each person grasping one handle of the wheelchair and arm rest and lifting together

---

*Adapted from Hale, G., & Barr, P. (1979). The Source book for the disabled (p. 21). New York: Paddington Press Ltd. These concepts apply to most wheelchairs.

or steps (figure 8.20). The chair is turned so the person seated in it faces away from the curb or steps. The rear wheels are pulled back until the front wheels reach the edge of the step or curb and then the chair is slowly lowered to the surface. The backward pull continues until the front wheels can be lowered. The wheelchair also can be moved down with the person seated in it facing forward rather than backward. This requires more skill to ensure the occupant's safety. If the tilt of the chair is not maintained so the rear wheels touch ground first, the occupant will be dumped out of the wheelchair.

Because many wheelchairs have detachable armrests to facilitate movement in and out of the chair, assistance given by grabbing this part of the chair will usually result only in pulling the chair arms off. Instead, the hold should be taken on the leg or wheel. When going down or up a hill or ramp, the one who is helping to move the wheelchair should

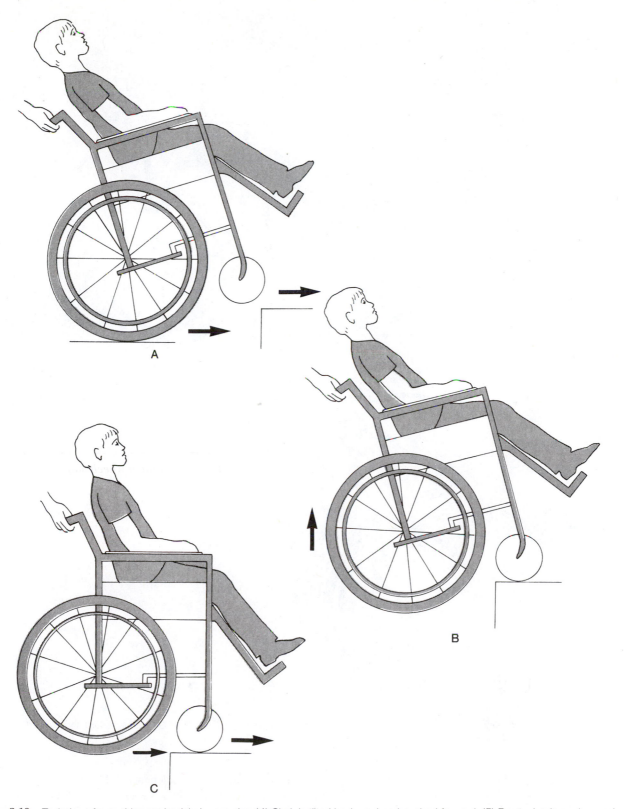

Figure 8.19 Technique for pushing a wheelchair up curbs. (*A*) Chair is tilted backward and pushed forward. (*B*) Front wheels are lowered onto curb and back wheels are lifted. (*C*) Back wheels are pushed onto curb.

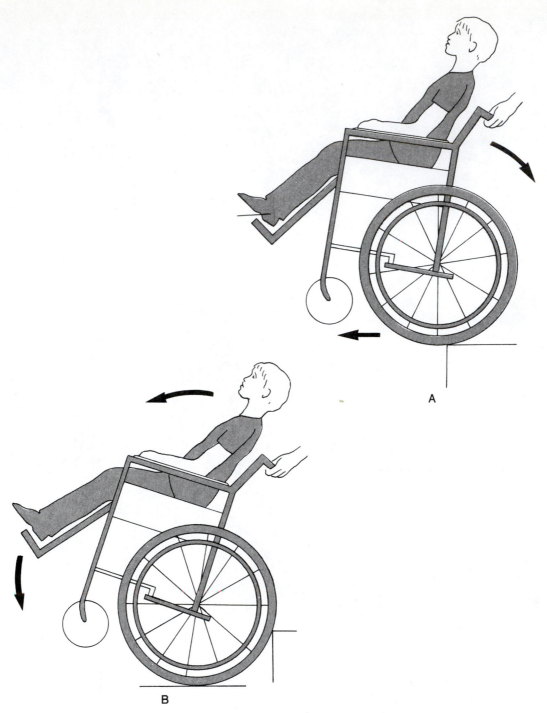

Figure 8.20 Technique for moving a wheelchair down curbs while occupant faces forward. (*A*) Chair is tilted backward and pushed slowly forward. (*B*) Back wheels are lowered slowly to the floor, followed by lowering the front wheels.

If the person in the chair is unable to assist in any way, two helpers will be needed. One stands on each side of the wheelchair, from which the armrests have been removed, and slides the hand that is nearer the front under the thighs of the occupant of the chair. The hands grasp each other under the thighs. The other hands are gently pushed behind the occupant's back and clasped together at about the level of the lumbar area. The occupant is then lifted up and

forward from the wheelchair and lowered to the mat. If the person in the wheelchair is small, one helper can manage the lift by using the same points of support. To return the wheelchair user to the chair, the procedure is reversed.

Wheelchair users who are severely impaired and lack the strength to self-propel the chair have found the powered chair to be very helpful. These units, normally powered by batteries similar to those found in automobiles, are manipulated by electronic control systems. The control unit can be attached to the arm of the chair or mounted in front of the seat. For individuals who are severely restricted in their mobility, systems can be designed to allow the person to control the chair by use of body parts, including the head or eyes.

Although it is not uncommon to see a motorized wheelchair, few people have had the opportunity to sit in one of the chairs and utilize the control system. Teachers working with students who have a motorized chair should sit in the chair (or if the chair is too small stand next to it) and operate the control system. By knowing how to operate the chair, the teacher will be better prepared to help the student to use the chair properly and safely. Teachers will also quickly recognize that while the motorized chair is a functional device, it is also very heavy, weighing from seventy-five to eighty-five pounds without the batteries. Folding the chair is impossible without removing the batteries. For this reason, students in motorized chairs must be transported by a special van or bus.

Fraser and Hensinger (1983) advocate that the student should not be permitted to independently use the powered chair at school until he or she has passed a user's test. The recommended test consists of the following six skill levels:

1. *Basic operation.* Basic operation includes turning the control switch on and off, and moving the chair forward, forward right, forward left, backward, backward right, and backward left for a short distance (less than three feet).
2. *Half turns.* Half turns involve maneuvering the chair 90 degrees right or left and then continuing forward for a short distance (less than three feet).
3. *Full turns.* Full turns (180 degrees) require reversal of direction by pivoting the chair right or left and then continuing forward in one sustained motion.
4. *Obstacle course.* The obstacle course requires that the student maneuver the wheelchair in a hallway or classroom, avoiding both stationary obstructions (trash baskets, chairs) and moving objects (people, other wheelchairs).
5. *Doorways.* The student must maneuver through a series of doorways, approaching from straight ahead, right, and left. The student first learns to drive the chair through wide or double doorways, then advances to narrow or single doorways.
6. *Ramps.* The student must climb and descend short ramps. This is the most difficult wheelchair training task because it requires that the student judge distance on an inclined or declined narrow surface.

Fraser and Hensinger (1983) recommend that students who pass level four can drive within the classroom. Success at level five qualifies the student to use the motorized chair within the school building. Those who pass level six can use the chair for driving within or outside the school building. Similar "driving" tests should be developed and used with students in self-propelled wheelchairs. Activities such as these are very appropriate to include within the physical education curriculum.

Recent variations in wheelchair design have helped many wheelchair users to improve their performance in athletic activities. The improvements have been so dramatic that the wheelchair athlete of today would no more consider playing basketball in a "street" chair than a runner would consider competing in street shoes. Many examples of excellent sport chairs have been designed and are commercially available. *Sports 'n Spokes,* the magazine for wheelchair sports, publishes an annual survey of sport wheelchairs. The number and variety of wheelchairs produced today has increased dramatically. For ease of use, *Sports 'n Spokes* groups wheelchairs by type of use: Everyday, Sport, Junior, and Racing. Wheelchair manufacturers also are expected to meet selected standards as determined by the American National Standards Institute (ANSI). The eighteen standards developed by ANSI are test procedures designed to produce objective information about wheelchairs. The standards, while voluntary, have been adopted by the Department of Veterans Affairs and are increasingly playing a significant role in shaping the design and manufacturing of wheelchairs. For additional information about the standards and an example of their application to a wide variety of wheelchairs, the reader is referred to an article by Axelson (1994). The availability of a wide selection of wheelchairs, while desirable, requires that today's consumer become very familiar with wheelchairs, their design features, measurements, and materials used in their construction. Some examples of sport wheelchairs are found in figure 8.21. Although it is beyond the scope of this book to describe all of the features found in today's sport chairs, some of the pertinent concepts will be discussed.

One of the first features that is very apparent in sport chairs is that they are lightweight, stable, and highly maneuverable. Weight is reduced by the use of lighter upholstery, elimination of armrests and brakes, and the substitution of a simple foot bar for footplates. Lightweight alloys are used in the construction of the frame. To increase the stability of the sports chair, the drive wheels are *cambered*—angled in at the top. Cambered wheels also permit an easier pushing angle, allow quicker turning, reduce contact between the arm and the wheel, and protect the athlete's hand during contact in close play. The tires, because they are pneumatic rather than solid, are lighter, roll better, and provide some cushion.

The design of sport chairs also varies according to the specific sport. Sport chairs used in basketball, for example, have solid front casters that provide quick turning capability. They are also equipped with a front roll-bar which prevents damage to the gymnasium floor when the chair tips forward. Roll-bars also prevent the chair from folding in case of a spill. Plastic discs, known as spoke protectors, are attached to the drive wheels to keep the foot rests of opposing players

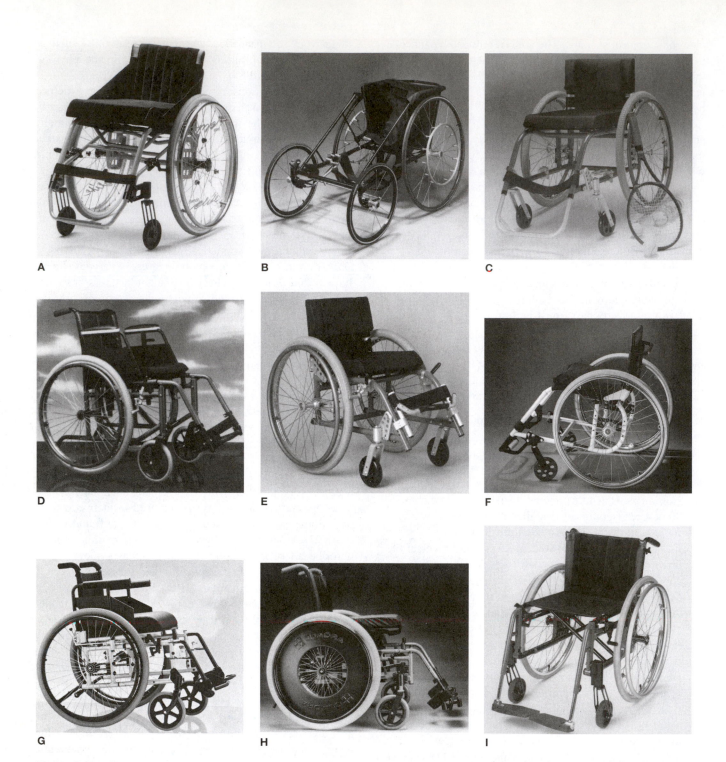

Figure 8.21   (*A*) Swede Flite by ETAC USA offers easy handling for day-to-day use. (*B*) Shadow Racer by Magic in Motion, Inc. is a specialty racing wheelchair for track and road. (*C*) Quickie 1 Adult by Motion Design, Inc. may be used for various sports, including tennis. (*D*) Express by Ortho-Kinetics is a lightweight, multipurpose chair which may be used for various recreational activities. (*E*) Quickie 1 Kids by Motion Design, Inc. is a rigid frame model. (*F*) Shadow One by Magic in Motion, Inc. is a rigid frame wheelchair for everyday and sport use. (*G*) Ultralite XP by Everest and Jennings is a lightweight wheelchair that may be used for everyday purposes. (*H*) Carrera by Ortho-Kinetics is a rigid frame chair used for various sports, including basketball and roadracing. (*I*) Swede Cross by ETAC USA has endless combinations to satisfy individual needs.

from breaking spokes during close play. Sport chairs used in basketball have large hand rims, which allow for quick acceleration. For further information on the modification and maintenance of wheelchairs for basketball, the reader should consult the book by Owen (1982), *Playing and Coaching Wheelchair Basketball.*

The design of the sport chair is critical for the athlete interested in track or road racing. In contrast to the typical sport chair used for basketball, the track racing chair must be as light as possible. The seat should be as low as possible to reduce the center of gravity, thereby improving stability and reducing wind resistance. Speed is enhanced by the use of large racing tires and small hand rims. The maneuverability of the racing chair is improved by the use of front caster steering devices. Tires for the front casters are pneumatic for easier rolling. The seated position of the athlete in a racing chair is different from that found in the standard wheelchair or sport chair. Instead of assuming a parallel seated position, the wheelchair racer sits with the buttocks lower than the thighs. The exact position is determined individually, according to the athlete's disability and preference. The low seated position combined with cambered wheels permits the longest force application time on the hand rims during the push phase of propulsion as well as maximum trunk thrust (American Academy of Orthopedic Surgeons, 1985). This human design feature, combined with the other adjustments in the sport chair, is producing phenomenal road racing times.

Not all adjustments to the sport chair need to be as dramatic as that found in the chair of the serious wheelchair racer. Tennis enthusiasts require only that the standard sport chair have a back which is lowered or removed so that they can make a complete swing in the forehand and backhand strokes. Table tennis and bowling enthusiasts will be able to use the sport chair without significant modifications. Some participants, depending on their ability level and personal goals, may choose to use their street wheelchair with some selected modifications, such as pneumatic tires and removal of the skirt guard.

The design of the sport chair has so many desirable features, including maneuverability, stability, and transportability, that more and more individuals are using the sport chair as a street chair. The multiple use of the sport chair has been good news for the economically conscious wheelchair user. Parents of children with disabilities have found the sport chair to be a good investment, particularly because of its advantages and multiple uses.

Maintenance of the wheelchair is very important to ensure that it functions properly and safely. The best reference for maintaining the chair is the manufacturer's manual that comes with the chair. The upholstery of the chair should be vacuumed frequently and washed as necessary with a mild soap and water. Several parts of the chair should be checked weekly. These include the spokes, tires, hand rims, axle, wheel rims, and footrest adjustments. The person

Figure 8.22 The Iron Horse enables the user to enjoy fly fishing.

inspecting the wheelchair should look for damage to parts and ensure that the parts requiring adjustment, such as the footrests, maintain their proper fit. Some parts of the wheelchair, primarily the bearings and axles, will require lubrication on a routine schedule as suggested by the manufacturer. Special efforts should be made to avoid damage to the chair such as that caused by rain, slush, and salt. The chair should never be taken into a shower. Some school districts have responded to this potential problem by purchasing a chair that is used solely as a shower chair. The student transfers to this chair prior to taking a shower.

Users of motorized wheelchairs should follow these same general maintenance guidelines. In addition, special care should be taken to keep the batteries in proper working order. This will entail keeping the battery fully charged and checking the water level of the battery. Some of the new batteries are sealed units that do not require periodic checking.

Prostheses

An artificial substitute for any part of the body is called a prosthesis. The development of prosthetic devices has made enormous progress in recent years so that it is now possible to provide artificial parts that closely resemble the actual body segment in function and in cosmetic appearance. Although prostheses offer many advantages, including improved functioning ability (reaching and grasping, for instance), there are disadvantages associated with the use of prosthetic appliances. A prosthesis is usually heavy, requires extra paraphernalia, and offers no sensory feedback from pain, touch, or proprioception. The teacher will need to be sensitive to these features when developing appropriate movement experiences for the youngster with a prosthetic device.

There are prostheses for various parts of the body, but the most important to this discussion are those for the lower and upper limbs. The loss of all or part of a limb is most often due to surgical amputation required by injury or disease. A less frequent cause is congenital amputation, a term meaning that a segment is missing at birth.

Leg Prostheses

The type of prosthesis provided for a lower limb depends upon the level of amputation, the place on the leg where the amputation occurs. If the level of amputation is below the knee joint but above the ankle, either a conventional below-the-knee prosthesis or the PTB (patellar tendon bearing) prosthesis is used. The former type has a tight corset that is laced around the thigh just above the knee (figure 8.23 *A*). With the PTB the stump is encased in a thin-walled plastic shank and is held in place by a strap secured above the knee (figure 8.23 *B*). The artificial foot may have a simulated ankle joint or it may be a solid foot device with a rubber heel that creates the appearance of ankle action in movement.

In amputation of the foot at the ankle, called Syme's amputation, the usual prosthesis is the Canadian-type Syme prosthesis, shown in figure 8.24. It does not have an ankle joint and is constructed so that the socket will bear the weight either on the distal portion (end) of the stump or on the distal and proximal rim (sides) of the stump. It is held in place by the contour of the leg after the door on the side of the prosthesis has been strapped shut.

A leg that has been amputated above the knee can be equipped with a prosthesis that has an artificial knee joint and a socket for insertion of the stump. Mechanical aids that operate either manually or automatically to lock the knee for standing may be added, if required, to stabilize the knee. The prosthetic device can be held in place in several possible ways. One of these ways is suction; the socket is so constructed in relationship to the stump that, when the stump is inserted, suction is created to hold it securely in the socket while walking. Special valves control the amount of suction.

Figure 8.24 *Canadian-type Syme prosthesis.*

A sock, which is usually worn over the stump, is omitted with this type of prosthesis. The prosthesis can also be held in place by means of suspenders or a pelvic belt. The suspenders pass over the shoulder to hold the prosthesis on the stump. The pelvic belt, sometimes referred to as a Silesian bandage, encircles the pelvic area to secure the prosthesis.

If the level of amputation is such that no thigh remains, a more elaborate prosthetic device that resembles a tilt table is used. The hip is fitted into the socket and held in place by a harness that resembles a girdle. The socket in articulation with the lower part of the device, creates a table-like hip joint with a lock that stabilizes the hip for standing and walking and unlocks for sitting.

To ensure safety and enjoyment in physical education activities by students wearing leg prostheses, the teacher must understand the leg and trunk movements necessary to achieve locomotion. With this in mind, it is possible to analyze the total movements required to perform a skill and to determine the modifications or adaptations that will be necessary for successful participation by the student.

The teacher also should learn how the locking mechanism of the student's prosthesis operates and how to remove and put on the prosthetic device. Then, if assistance is needed, the teacher will know how to proceed. Small children and those with mental retardation or cerebral palsy are particularly likely to need such help.

It is important to remember that the artificial limb should not get wet, because this causes deterioration of rubber and leather parts. If the prothesis does become wet, it should be removed and thoroughly dried with a cloth. A stump sock that has become damp from perspiration should be changed.

The skin at the stump's surface is very susceptible to injury and slow to recover due to poor circulation in the area. Consequently, any blisters, calluses, or sores noted by the teacher while helping a child with his or her prosthesis

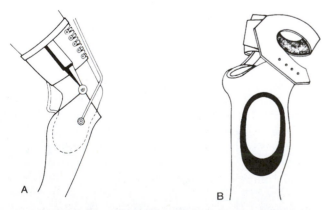

Figure 8.23 *(A)* Conventional below-the-knee prosthesis. *(B)* Patellar tendon bearing prosthesis.

should be reported to the proper personnel so that medical attention and adjustment of the prosthesis can be secured, if necessary.

Arm Prostheses

Arm prostheses are of two types: a cosmetic prosthesis, which is a dress hand or arm designed for appearance and not for use, and a work prosthesis, which is designed to enable the wearer to perform various tasks. The work prosthesis is usually fitted with a split utility hook that substitutes effectively for the hand in the performance of various jobs. When the fingers or thumb are missing, a prosthesis can be utilized that substitutes only for the missing digits.

Some arm prostheses are rigged with steel cables and a shoulder harness so that the wearer, by moving the shoulder, can manipulate the utility hook constructed for grasping. A similar arrangement is used with a prosthesis designed to enable the shoulder to flex and the artificial elbow joint to extend, in the case of amputation above the elbow.

When the arm is amputated below the shoulder, one of two different kinds of prostheses is used: the long below-elbow prosthesis (figure 8.25 A), designed for use with long stumps, and the standard above-elbow prosthesis, for shorter stumps (figure 8.25 B). In disarticulation at the shoulder, the prosthesis is constructed to encase the shoulder area; the simulated upper arm has joint action at the shoulder and at the elbow, and the split hook attaches to the simulated lower arm (figure 8.25 C). Operation is made possible by an electric device powered by a small battery. A similar device is used for manipulation of joints and utility hooks in other prostheses. The devices are activated by movement of the

shoulders or, in some cases, by controls inserted in the shoe that respond to pressure from the heel and toes.

In recent years there has been significant interest in developing upper arm protheses that are externally powered. In one system, referred to as the myoelectric prosthesis, small electrodes are placed on the stump so that electrical activity produced by muscular action can be detected. These signals, usually from isometric muscle contractions, are amplified and used to modulate the action of a "hand" battery operated motor that activates the terminal device. Depending on the amputation level and the availability of signal sites, these signals can also activate the wrist rotator and/or the elbow unit (Mensch, 1990). Some individuals with an upper arm amputation may be fitted with a switch control system. With this prosthetic device the movement of the stump controls the functioning of an electric motor through force exerted on single- or double-action switches. For example, with a single-action control switch, the one movement (e.g., protraction) is used to close the prosthetic hand and another movement (e.g., retraction) is used to open the hand.

Students with arm prostheses are trained by specialists in the use of the device. Once the basic skills have been established, those with amputations may be interested in extending the possible uses of their prostheses to include the motor skills of games and sports. Some possibilities that have been worked out by physical education teachers are described in detail in section 4 of this book; others can be developed by the teacher working with the individual student. The chief precaution that must be exercised is the prevention of misuse that will damage the prosthesis, as would be the case if it became wet and was not dried properly or if excessive force were exerted with it.

Individuals with recent amputations may need remedial posture exercises, which can be provided as part of their physical education program. After the loss of an arm or leg, the body tends to compensate for the lost weight by realignment that distributes the weight more evenly over the remaining segments of the body. This often results in poor posture that is usually less efficient and that is likely to cause other problems, such as back pain. Students with misalignment due to arm or leg amputation will profit from a posture improvement program appropriate to their individual needs, as discussed in chapter 28.

Orthotic Devices for Lower Limbs

An *orthosis* is a device that is applied to a segment of the body for support or immobilization, to prevent or correct a deformity, or to assist or restore function. The need for its use is indicated by pain, weakness, or paralysis in the particular part of the body. Orthoses can be applied to the spinal column and to both upper and lower limbs. Abbreviations such as AFOs (ankle-foot-orthoses) and KAFOs (knee-ankle-foot orthoses) are frequently used to refer to orthoses.

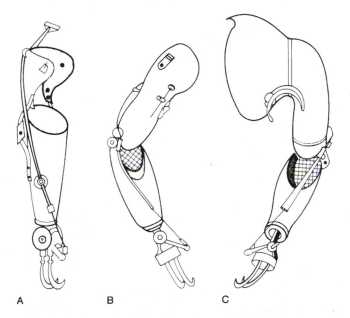

A   B   C

Figure 8.25 (*A*) Long below-elbow prosthesis. (*B*) Standard above-elbow prosthesis. (*C*) Arm prosthesis for disarticulation at the shoulder.

Our concern here is with orthoses used as braces on the lower limbs to give support to body weight, to decrease pain, or to aid ambulation.

Braces are referred to as supportive, corrective, protective, or dynamic, according to their function. A supportive brace stabilizes a specific part of the body, such as a painful joint. A corrective brace encourages changes in the structure, position, or function of the body, as would be the case when a brace is applied in the treatment of a clubfoot. Protective bracing affords protection from further injury to the body or prevents greater deformity. Dynamic bracing is utilized when there is a need to mobilize a body part or to aid weakened muscles, as in the loss of leg muscle strength due to poliomyelitis. Such braces utilize springs and cables or elastic bands to provide the required force to assist movement.

A full leg brace commonly consists of a shoe, a stirrup to which the uprights to the shoe are attached, uprights that support the total brace and run parallel to the length of the brace, knee joints in the upright to allow movement of the knee, and a weight-bearing band or ring at the top of the brace that comes to the very top of the thigh. Knee joints may operate freely or be provided with locks. There are many different types of locks in use. One of the most common is the drop ring lock, which locks automatically when the brace is straightened but must be unlocked manually. Another commonly used locking device is the automatic lock. It locks when the knee is straightened, and holds against a moderate amount of force but unlocks when the knee is bent forcefully.

In recent years there have been many excellent advances in orthotics. The beneficiaries of many of the new designs have been young children. In the following paragraphs some of the devices commonly used with children will be described. Examples of these orthotics appear in figure 8.26.

The Swivel Walker

The swivel walker, a rigid body brace mounted on swiveling feet, is used to encourage early standing and walking without crutches or a walker. This brace is used primarily with children who have myelomeningocele. Walking is possible with this brace by shifting the body weight from side to side. As weight is shifted to one side, the opposite foot plate rises and rotates forward. One of the limitations of the swivel walker is that there are no locks at the hips or knees; thus, sitting is not possible.

The Parapodium

The parapodium, like the swivel walker, is used primarily for children with myelomeningocele. The device is used for standing and walking. Although a shifting-from-side-to-side gait may be used, some children walk with the parapodium using a walker or crutches. When this latter approach is used, a swing-through gait pattern is employed. One of the advantages of the parapodium is that the device has hip and knee locks that allow the user to sit.

The Reciprocating Gait Orthosis (RGO)

The RGO is a lightweight orthosis that permits a reciprocal gait via a cable coupling system that supplies trunk and limb support for the child with paraplesia, including those with high spinal level myelomeningocele. The advantage of this unit over the swivel walker and the parapodium is that it permits independent leg motion (reciprocal walking) with a walker or crutches.

The Hip-Knee-Ankle-Foot Orthosis (HKAFO)

The HKAFO consists of long leg braces with a pelvic band. This device, which usually attaches to high-top shoes, is used for children with a variety of disabilities to stretch muscles or to assist in standing and walking. When ambulating with the HKAFO, the knees are usually locked and a swing-through or reciprocal gait pattern is used.

The Knee-Ankle-Foot Orthosis (KAFO)

This assistive device is similar to a HKAFO, but without the pelvic band. The KAFO is used for stretching and as an aid in walking. One of the advantages of the KAFO is that it may be made of either metal or plastic. While plastic braces are lighter and more cosmetically appealing, the metal braces can be adjusted and lengthened more easily.

The Ankle-Foot Orthosis (AFO)

The AFO is used with children who have muscular control at the hip and knee but not at the ankle. The AFO, also known as a short leg brace, can be either metal or plastic. Reciprocal walking, with or without crutches or a walker, is common with these braces.

Twister Cables

The twister device consists of a pelvic band with hip joints and a metal stirrup applied to the shoe. Although the device is designed to control inward or outward rotation of the legs, its effectiveness has been questioned.

Another area in which lower-limb orthotic devices have been widely applied is in the treatment of Legg-Calvé-Perthes disease (discussed in chapter 9). Orthoses used in the treatment of this disease must provide for abduction and internal rotation at the hip as well as cover for the femoral head. One type of leg abduction brace allows no flexion of the knee; another permits knee flexion. The most common of the former type is the Newington ambulatory splint, shown in figure 8.27. Both legs are encased so that no knee action is possible. An abduction bar between the legs at the ankles keeps the legs apart and slightly rotated inward. The brace is used at any time the legs must bear weight. It may be removed for swimming. Walking is possible while wearing the brace with the use of Canadian crutches; the technique is to twist the body to move one leg forward with the help of the crutches and then repeat the action on the other side.

Of the abduction braces that allow knee action, the most commonly used are the Craig bar and the Toronto brace. The former is an abduction bar attached to high-top shoes to keep the legs apart. The Toronto brace is similar to the Newington splint except that it has a pivotal hinge in the center of the abduction joint that allows a step to be taken forward without pivoting on the opposite foot and also enables the bending of the knees. Both kinds of braces are removed for swimming.

The Scottish Rite orthosis is a device that was developed to aid in the treatment of Legg-Calvé-Perthes disease. Unlike the Toronto or Newington orthoses, this orthotic device permits freedom of knees, feet, and ankles and can be

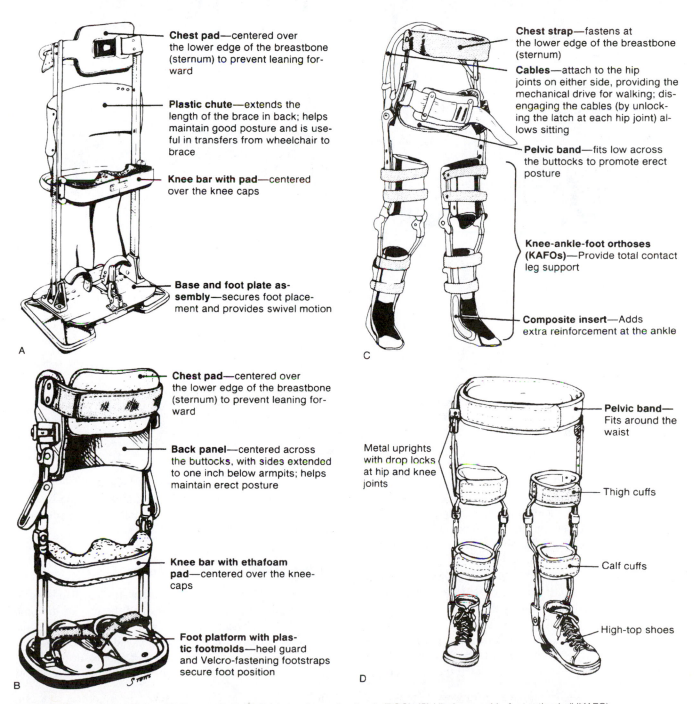

Figure 8.26 *(A)* Swivel walker. *(B)* Parapodium. *(C)* Reciprocating gait orthosis (RGO). *(D)* Hip-knee-ankle-foot orthosis (HKAFO). *(E)* Knee-ankle-foot orthosis (KAFO). *(F)* Ankle-foot orthosis (AFO). *(G)* Twister cables with pelvic band and short leg braces.

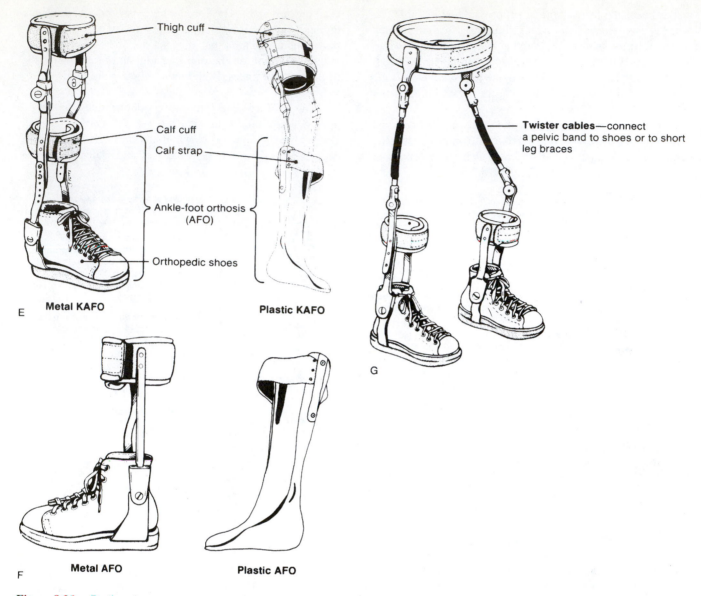

Figure 8.26—*Continued*

applied outside the clothing so that wearing clothes, including boots, is no problem. As can be seen in figure 8.28, the orthotic is much lighter and simpler in design compared to the Toronto and Newington braces. However, concern has been expressed regarding the ability of the Scottish Rite brace to maintain internal rotation.

Wearers of braces who are able to attend school will have been taught the care and use of their devices by medical personnel involved with their treatment. So, unless the student is very young or unable to communicate effectively, the teacher will not need to give much assistance to those with braces. Nevertheless, it is well to be familiar with the locking mechanism and the way in which the brace comes

off and is put on in order to be of help if aid is needed. Awareness of the movement possibilities with the brace is essential to the development of suitable physical education activities for the student with a brace.

Orthotic Devices for Upper Limbs

The type of orthotic device used for the arms and hands varies according to the purpose it serves and the part of the limb involved. The physical educator will likely encounter some devices or braces for the upper limbs, and will need to know about them so as to develop special programs for those who wear them. These are discussed in the paragraphs that follow.

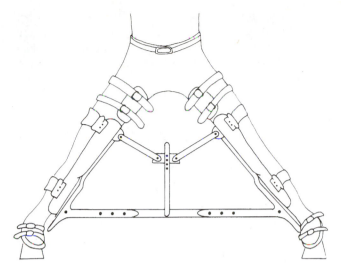

Figure 8.27   Newington ambulatory splint.

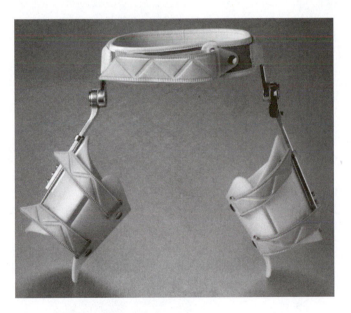

Figure 8.28   Scottish Rite orthosis.

Hand Opponens Orthosis

Hand opponens is the name given to any of several muscles of the hand that bring the fingers together in such a way as to form a cup in the palm of the hand. The hand opponens orthosis is designed to maintain correct thumb and palm position (figure 8.29) in a hand that is paralyzed. Attachments can be added to the brace to provide wrist support and better prehension (grip).

Reciprocal Wrist-Extension Finger-Flexion Orthosis

This is a device used by those with paralysis of all four limbs (quadriplegia) who have some movement of the wrist

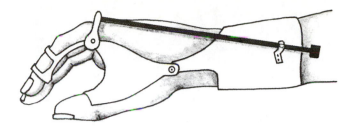

Figure 8.29   Hand opponens orthesis.

extensor muscles. The orthotic device is fitted to the wrist and hand to enable greater control and movement. Basically, the brace's function is to hold the fingers partially flexed with the thumb in the grasping position. A connective device from the fingers to above the wrist aids the fingers and thumb in grasping when the wrist is extended. With this orthosis, individuals with quadriplegia are able to work the lever of a motorized wheelchair, which they might not otherwise be able to do. Some may even be able to write with the aid of the device.

Feeders

Feeders are devices that support the hand and lower arm to allow self-feeding. There are two basic types of feeders: suspension and supportive. With the former, the arm is supported by an overhead bar; the latter consists of a swivel arm with ball bearings. Both types have a metal trough in which the arm rests. The design is such that the slightest movement of the body or shoulder will result in useful motion, enabling individuals using the device to extend and flex the arm and so feed themselves. Feeders have been utilized by physical educators to enable students who require the devices to achieve the arm movements needed to play a modified form of table tennis. With adaptations, light batting activities as well as those in which a light object is propelled forward may also be accomplished.

Cable-Controlled Hook Brace

This assistive device for those with flaccid or paralyzed hand muscles consists of a split hook positioned on a brace attached around the wrist. The split hook is located in the palm of the hand between the thumb and the index finger. A cable is connected to a shoulder harness so that the hook can be opened or closed by movement of the shoulder.

Shoulder Suspension Device

The shoulder suspension device is designed to support a weakened shoulder girdle. The device holds the arm up so that the shoulder joint is not required to support the weight of the arm. It is often used with other devices that enable the arm to function; one such device is the forearm cuff shown

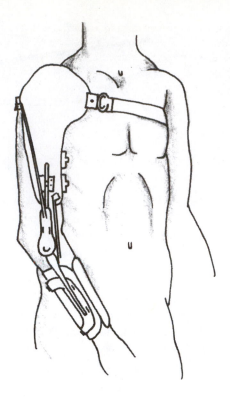

Figure 8.30 Shoulder suspension device with a forearm cuff.

in figure 8.30. In the illustration, the shoulder suspension device is used with a cuff that encircles the forearm and has a movable elbow unit. Rubber bands attach to the cuff and shoulder suspension device to aid in elbow flexion.

Back Braces

There are numerous kinds of back braces but all are designed chiefly to support the back and relieve pain, to protect the back from further injury, or to effect correction of the positioning of the spine. In relieving back pain the main purpose of the back braces, with the exception of the hyperextension braces, is to compress the abdominal area and to decrease lumbar lordosis (abnormal curve in the small of the back). The braces most often used for this purpose are corsets, rigid braces, belts, and molded jackets.

The corset is a garment with longitudinal metal stays. It is worn around the trunk, generally at the region between the groin area and ribs, chiefly to treat low back pain. The rigid brace is used for pains in various areas of the back. It is sometimes called the chair-back brace because it has a rigid brace in the back. Although there are many variations, the brace usually consists of a hip band and a chest band joined together with two metal uprights on each side of the spinal column.

There are several different kinds of belts. The trochanteric belt is a two- to three-inch-wide band worn around the pelvis. It is often used for support after a pelvic fracture. The sacroiliac and lumbosacral belts are also bands, but they are larger in width. The sacroiliac belt ranges

in width from four to six inches, while the lumbosacral belt is eight to sixteen inches wide. Both belts are worn around the lower back and are useful in preventing low back pain associated with spinal disc (cartilage between vertebrae) disorders. Molded jackets are constructed of heavy material to fit the contour of the body. The jacket exerts equal pressure through the trunk and so is useful in providing back support for very old or debilitated persons.

Braces for Repositioning the Spine

Various types of braces are used to place pressure on the spine in order to increase or decrease the anterior-posterior curves or to straighten the lateral curvature of the spine. Bracing for scoliosis is utilized more frequently than is other bracing for repositioning the spine.

Basically, there are two types of braces used in spinal bracing: CTLSO (cervical-thoracic-lumbar-sacral orthosis) and TLSO (thoracic-lumbar-sacral orthosis). The Milwaukee brace is the most common CTLSO brace used in the treatment of scoliosis (discussed in chapter 9). It consists of pads, straps, and metal strips designed to place pressure to the scoliotic curve at the neck and hip in one direction and at the convex side in the other (figure 8.31). The neck pad and neck ring exert pressure on the neck; the ring is hinged in front and fastens in the back. One of the posterior (back) uprights is attached to the thoracic pad by a snap and exerts force against the curve. The uprights are attached anteriorly to the pelvic girdle. A strap tightens and holds the pelvic girdle securely.

Although the Milwaukee brace has been reported to be successful in treating spinal deformities, there are disadvantages associated with the use of the brace. Some have

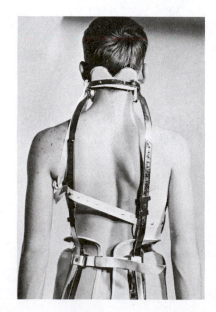

Figure 8.31 Milwaukee brace.

cautioned that it is important to emphasize that the brace controls the curve; it does not correct the curve. Others have cautioned that the brace is not well accepted by some teenagers and physicians (American Academy of Orthopedic Surgeons, 1985). The visibility of the brace, particularly the neck ring, places the teenager in the position of being "different" at an important phase of life. For this reason some physicians prefer the use of underarm orthoses. These devices extend from the thorax to the sacrum and thus are thoracic-lumbar-sacral orthosis or TLSOs. Although there are several models available, they can generally be divided into the prefabricated and the custom-fabricated designs.

The Milwaukee brace must be worn at all times, except for swimming or special exercise. Youngsters wearing the brace can participate in vigorous play, including such games as basketball, tennis, and soccer.

The science of spinal bracing has benefited in recent years from the introduction of new materials and a growing knowledge of their most effective use. Plastics have become very popular as a substance used in bracing. Their primary advantages are lighter weight, strength, appearance, impermeability to liquids, and easy conformity to the body. The Boston-Hall brace, a modular prefabricated plastic girdle, has received wide use with young patients evidencing a mild form of scoliosis.

Summary

Within this chapter a variety of assistive devices have been presented. Some of the devices assist in mobility, such as canes, crutches, walkers, scooters, and modified bicycles and tricycles. The wheelchair, a popular and necessary mobility device for some, was described in detail. Similarities and differences between the standard, powered, and sport chairs were discussed with an appreciation for modifications in the chair design that have been generated by the needs of athletes who use wheelchairs. Information about the use of the wheelchair and techniques for moving the chair were discussed. Teachers are encouraged to be conversant with terms used to describe the parts of the wheelchair as well as other assistive devices.

Examples of the more commonly used prosthetic and orthotic devices and how these units function were presented. A special focus was directed toward the body braces commonly used with young children. For example, braces helpful in walking, such as the swivel walker and reciprocating gait orthosis, were described. Because of their common use, braces such as the Milwaukee and Boston systems were described as aids in the treatment of spinal deformities, primarily scoliosis.

While the information presented in this chapter is helpful and important for the teacher of physical education, there obviously are many more assistive devices that have not been included. Some of these, specifically those related to physical education and sport, will be incorporated into sections 3 and 4 of this text. The important thing to remember is that assistive devices are aides for improving mobility and the level of functioning. They are helpful to the extent that knowledgeable professionals can incorporate assistive devices into the instructional unit. This may require using a device that is commercially available or it may be necessary to modify a product or fabricate something that is new. The goal is to use whatever is necessary to help the student with a disability to enjoy physical education as well as receive the benefits of instruction.

Selected Readings

Adams, R. C., & McCubbin, J. A., (1991). *Games, sports, and exercises for the physically handicapped* (4th ed.). Philadelphia: Lea and Febiger.

American Academy of Orthopedic Surgeons. (1985). *Atlas of orthotics* (2d ed.). St. Louis: C. V. Mosby Co.

Axelson, P. (1994). Chairs, chairs, everywhere. *Sports 'n Spokes, 19*(6), 15–63.

Basmajian, J. V., & Wolf, S. L. (1990). Therapeutic Exercise. (5th ed.). Baltimore: Williams and Wilkins.

Blackman, J. A. (1984). *Medical aspects of developmental disabilities in children birth to three*. Rockville, MD: An Aspen Publication.

Bromley, I. (1981). *Tetraplegia and paraplegia: A guide for physiotherapists* (2d ed.). New York: Churchill Livingstone.

The care and feeding of a wheelchair. (1979). Portland, OR: Medical Equipment Distributors, Inc.

Christopherson, V. A., Coulter, T. P., & Walanin, M. O. (1974). *Rehabilitation nursing perspectives and applications*. New York: McGraw-Hill Book Co.

Fraser, B. A., & Hensinger, R. N. (1983). *Managing physical handicaps*. Baltimore, MD: Paul H. Brookes Publishing Company.

Gilbert, A. E. (1973). *You can do it from a wheelchair*. New Rochelle, NY: Arlington House, Pub.

Hale, G., & Barr, P. (1979). *The source book for the disabled*. New York: Paddington Press Ltd.

Krusen, F. H., Kottke, F. J., Stillwell, G. K., & Lehmon, J. F. (Eds.). (1971). *Handbook of physical medicine and rehabilitation* (2d ed.). Philadelphia: W. B. Saunders Co.

Mensch, G. (1990). Exercise for Amputees, Chapter 13 in Basmajian. J. V. & Wolf, S. L. *Therapeutic exercise* (5th ed.). Baltimore: Williams and Wilkins, 251–278.

Nash, C. L. (1980). Current concepts review scoliosis bracing. In *The Journal of Bone and Joint Surgery, 62*, 848–852.

Nesbitt, J. A. (Ed.). (1986). *The international directory of recreation-oriented assistive device sources*. Marina del Ray, CA: Lifeboat Press.

Owen, E. (1982). *Playing and coaching wheelchair basketball*. Urbana, IL: University of Illinois Press.

Rose, G. K. (1986). *Orthotics: Principles and practice*. London: William Heinemann Medical Books.

Stryker, R. P. (1977). *Rehabilitative aspects of acute and chronic nursing care*. Philadelphia: W. B. Saunders Co.

Enhancing Activities

1. Visit a local orthopedic appliance store to review various models and types of assistive devices including canes, crutches, walkers and wheelchairs.

2. Obtain a standard wheelchair and experience sitting in and using the wheelchair. Use the chair to move around campus as well as in the community. While this activity does not provide a realistic picture of what wheelchair users experience, it will improve sensitivity to the need for the removal of architectural barriers.

3. Attend a wheelchair athletic event and observe the various models and types of chairs used. Interview an athlete to obtain his or her views on the essential features of a good sport chair.

4. Interview an adult who has used a wheelchair for many years. Obtain his or her views on wheelchair designs and modifications that they have found desirable and helpful.

5. Interview a parent of a youngster who has used one of the assistive devices described in this chapter. Ask the parent why they chose the device and how effective the apparatus was in improving mobility.

6. Review selected references, particularly the *Atlas of Orthotics*, to obtain additional information on the various orthoses that have been designed and prescribed for treatment.

Conditions Resulting in Enervated and Impaired Movement

The section is designed to help the reader to:

1 Recognize the cause and characteristics of the disabling conditions found in the school setting.

2 Appreciate students with disabilities as unique individuals with specific needs that are different in some ways but similar in other ways to those of their nondisabled peers.

3 Individualize instruction in the physical education program consistent with the developmental needs of students with various disabling conditions.

4 Recognize the breadth and depth of special physical education services that range from instruction in regular programs to special classes and include programs for those with mild as well as severe disabilities.

Discussed in this section are disorders that occur so commonly in school-age children that physical educators are very likely to find students with these conditions in their classes. The chapters on the various kinds of disorders briefly describe the etiology and pathology, discuss special considerations in planning the program, and suggest kinds of activities that may be offered.

CHAPTER
9

Orthopedic Disabilities

◆━━━━━━━━━━━━━━━━━━━━━━━━━━━━━━◆
CHAPTER OBJECTIVES
◆━━━━━━━━━━━━━━━━━━━━━━━━━━━━━━◆

After studying this chapter, the reader should be able to:

1 Recognize the various types of orthopedic disabilities and their implications for planning appropriate physical education activities and programs.

2 List the common causes and characteristics of the following orthopedic impairments: spinal cord injuries, Legg-Calvé-Perthes disease, Osgood Schlatters disease, congenital hip dislocation, spina bifida, burns, osteochondrosis, scoliosis, and amputations.

3 Analyze the spinal cord and the muscle impairments that accompany injuries at different levels of the spinal cord.

4 Appreciate and be sensitive to the various techniques used to assist those with bowel- and bladder-control problems and the implications of these related to physical education.

5 Understand the function and importance of various orthotic and bracing techniques in the treatment of impairments such as scoliosis, congenital hip dislocation, Legg-Calvé-Perthes disease, amputations, and burns.

6 Appreciate the importance of a comprehensive school screening program for detecting the presence of deviations in the spinal column.

7 Understand the important role physical activity, including sport, plays in helping individuals with orthopedic impairments develop to their full potential.

8 Develop appropriate program and activity modifications for individuals with various orthopedic impairments.

9 Recognize some of the unique physiological and biomechanical characteristics of those with orthopedic impairments and the implications of these in developing conditioning programs for optimal training levels.

Orthopedic is derived from the Greek words meaning "to straighten the child," and in modern usage is applied both to a specific type of disability and to the branch of medicine concerned with its prevention and treatment. An orthopedic disability is one that does not allow the individual to properly perform the motor and locomotor functions of the body and limbs. Such disabilities affect the functions of the bones, joints, and tendons.

The public attitude toward individuals with orthopedic disabilities has changed immensely since the Middle Ages, when the only hope one had of acceptance within the society was to become a court jester. Today the individual with an orthopedic disability has opportunities for treatment, rehabilitation, gainful employment, and social acceptance far beyond the dreams of even the most imaginative court jester. Although much remains to be done, especially in equalizing social and employment opportunities, those with orthopedic disabilities have, over the years, generally suffered less from a lack of public understanding of their needs and problems than have most other populations with disabilities.

Care for children with orthopedic disorders was extremely limited until the nineteenth century, when the work of several prominent orthopedic surgeons in England, continental Europe, and the United States began to direct attention to the prevention and remedial treatment for crippling conditions. Concern about the plight of children with orthopedic disabilities remained almost entirely medical until the closing years of the century, when the increasing number of such children aroused interest in adequate educational provisions for them. Special schools for "crippled" children were established, as were special classes within the public schools. Currently, students with orthopedic disabilities are mainstreamed, when appropriate, into the regular classes of the public schools, including classes in physical education. A number of hospital programs for children with orthopedic disorders exist throughout the country, and these provide educational instruction as well as medical and therapeutic treatment. However, advanced treatment techniques and the desire to return children to their homes as quickly as possible have greatly reduced the actual time the children spend in the hospital. The result is that more students receive their education in the public schools than in the hospitals.

Because of the lack of uniformity in defining the conditions of crippling and orthopedic disabilities, statistics of incidence are neither very meaningful nor very accurate. The number can be doubled or cut in half by the inclusion or exclusion of individuals with certain conditions. It is consequently not possible to determine how many cases of youngsters with orthopedic impairments exist currently or how many of these may be expected to be found in the regular school, the special school, or the hospital.

The orthopedic conditions presented in this chapter are those found among school-age students. The discussion is divided into three sections: disorders that immobilize lower limbs, disorders that limit ambulation, and disorders that affect other body movements. This organization allows specific orthopedic disabilities that cause similar movement problems to be brought together under one heading, permitting emphasis to be placed on the movement potential of students with similar limitations rather than on the disabilities and restrictions imposed by each type of orthopedic disability. Before discussing the specific orthopedic conditions, needs and adjustments as well as program planning will be presented.

Needs and Adjustments of Those with Orthopedic Disabilities

When normally active human beings find their usual movements restricted by disease or accident, they face the necessity of changing many of the patterns of their daily living. The degree to which they are able to make these changes determines to a large extent how satisfactory their adjustment will be. The age and the suddenness with which the incapacitating disability strikes appear to have considerable effect upon the adjustment that individuals make. Very intense emotional reactions usually follow, for example, a sudden loss of limb by amputation, but these usually subside as the individuals discover they are still capable of many of the activities of former life. Students with disabilities are likely to make a satisfactory adjustment as they acquire compensatory motor skills. Youngsters with a limb missing from birth or early infancy may have a deep-seated but less easily detected emotional disturbance as the result of the continual frustration they experience in attempting to do the things that other children do. On the other hand, they may have made an entirely adequate adjustment as the result of having acquired such satisfactory compensatory skills that they and those with whom they associate do not think of them as different. If students have not made this kind of adjustment, they need help in overcoming their fears and frustrations so that better adjustment will be possible.

The incapacitation produced by an infectious disease like spondylitis is usually much less sudden than that resulting from amputation. Nevertheless, a strong emotional reaction is usually evidenced during the early stages of the disease, which increases as the disease progresses and the movement limitations become more evident. It is likely to continue even after the disease has been terminated if the limitation to normal locomotion remains. The most common emotional reactions are withdrawal, hostility, and aggressiveness.

The age of the child presents certain other problems in adjusting to the disability. Children and adolescents are particularly susceptible to the reactions of others to the cosmetic appearance of their disabilities. They may worry unduly about how they look and become overly sensitive to the responses of others to their appearance. The anxieties thus aroused are not easily relieved.

Orthopedic disorders occurring early in life frequently limit the child's opportunities for play and other social contacts and greatly restrict the development of satisfactory social growth. Courage, resourcefulness, and initiative fostered in the vigorous exchanges of childhood play activities are commonly deficient in children with physical disabilities who are deprived of opportunities to engage in play.

These desirable characteristics are also frequently lacking in adults with orthopedic disabilities, stemming from their inability to participate in the normal patterns of living. In addition, many of them have inferiority feelings or have excessive anxieties usually related to their inability to support themselves economically. On the whole, a change of any kind is more difficult as age advances, owing to the force of daily habits. Consequently, unless the adult is given a good deal of help, satisfactory adjustment is very difficult.

The lack of active play in the lives of these youngsters and adults has detrimental physiological, as well as psychological, results. General body fitness is lacking. Coordination is poor. There is increased susceptibility to injury and hypokinetic diseases.

To achieve satisfactory adjustment, individuals with orthopedic disabilities must compensate for their lack of success in physical performance or they must seek satisfying substitutions. Some people compensate by achieving superiority in intellectual endeavors; in the development of musical, artistic, or literary talents; or in the creativity of crafts. Some measure of compensation can be achieved by nearly everyone, but compensation is not enough—satisfactory substitutions for the loss of motor skills must also be found.

Physical activity can make one of its most significant contributions to the welfare of those who have disabilities by enabling them to enjoy the pleasures of active participation in activities and sports through the teaching of substitute motor skills. This is, of course, only part of the role of physical education for those with orthopedic disabilities. Play provides the incentive for the improvement in motor skills, and as locomotion increases, morale receives a needed lift. When more complex game skills are achieved or former skills are reacquired, the youngster's self-esteem reestablishes itself and he or she looks forward with greater confidence and reassurance to achieving satisfactory substitutions for lost skills.

As participation becomes more active, physical fitness is increased and body mechanics are improved. The individuals become more skilled in the use of previously unused portions of the body and in the use of the assistive device, if one is required. Because they can play better and longer, owing to the improved conditioning and better playing skills, they enjoy themselves more and others enjoy playing with them. In such an atmosphere of social acceptance, the first steps may be taken toward a more satisfactory adjustment.

Planning the Program

In some cases, during the early stages of treatment, it is necessary to confine youngsters with orthopedic impairments to a hospital setting. Although these stays are usually short, it is imperative that an educational program, including physical education services, be provided for these students. The physical education program in this situation should be concerned with those big-muscle activities used for leisure-time play and the promotion of body conditioning, rather than with the correction of the handicap for the purpose of increased motor function. This latter and important aspect of the child's program must be left to the discretion of the related services personnel, primarily the physical and occupational therapists. Consequently, the physical education program should be carefully planned in consultation with the medical authorities so that muscles will not be used incorrectly, thus negating the therapeutic treatment.

The Hospital or Special Program

During the hospital stay or active treatment stage, the physical education teacher must consider the medical problems that are related to specific types of disabilities. Weakened muscles must not be strained by overwork; the muscles of the set antagonistic to the weaker ones must be protected from overdevelopment, which would produce muscular imbalance; the hip joints in Legg-Calvé-Perthes disease must bear no weight; an injured joint in the spinal column must be protected from all movement. In most cases of crippling diseases, after the disease is arrested and muscular reeducation is nearly complete, the physical education activities need be limited only by the structural limitations of the student.

One of the important objectives of the physical education program for children in special schools and hospitals is to provide play opportunities that encourage them to try the motor skills that they are acquiring or relearning under the care of the physical therapist. Consequently, the program must be carefully planned to provide good progression of skills and experiences. When the very simple skills are satisfactorily mastered, more complex ones can be introduced, and finally very complex skills can be taught. The variety of skills required by the games should be as wide as possible.

The students should be prepared for the great amount of practice that may be necessary to accomplish a skill. If they understand this, they will not become discouraged when they compare their present rate of skill acquisition with their rate before their disabilities. Words of encouragement and praise should be spoken often by the instructor. Students with mental retardation or emotional disturbance in special programs will need extra encouragement in overcoming the limitations in movement imposed by their orthopedic disability. They must be helped in setting realistic goals for themselves and in accepting the fact that improvement in motor skill, however small, is very worthwhile.

The Regular School

A student returning to school after hospitalization with an orthopedic disability may display no apparent aftereffect; others may exhibit a mild or even severe movement disorder. Although there may be no visible debility, the physical education teacher should not automatically include the student full time in the regular physical education curriculum. Possible muscular weakness or lack of endurance may not be observable. The teacher should not attempt to include the student in the activities until he or she has received medical recommendations as to the amount of activity in which the student should engage and the kinds of activities that will prove most beneficial, as well as those that should be monitored carefully. With this knowledge the teacher will be able to plan the kind of program that will help students increase their general level of fitness and motor efficiency so that they will be better able to meet the physical demands of daily life.

The returning student who has a moderate or severe disability may need considerable help in achieving maximum physical efficiency. Upon receipt of the medical report, the teacher should work out a carefully planned, graduated program of exercises and activities to meet the special needs of the student. It is advisable to secure medical approval of the planned program. Students who have considerable residual paralysis or a limb amputation are also likely to need a great deal of help in making a satisfactory adjustment to their disability. Because of their possible concern about their appearance and their inabilities to perform motor skills, they may experience more anxieties about physical education class than about other phases of their school life. The teacher can help alleviate their fears by assisting them to find a solution that is satisfying to them concerning dressing and showering in the presence of others, and by preparing them to meet the challenges of their restrictions with good humor rather than with fear of embarrassment or ridicule. These concerns should be addressed in the Individualized Education Program (IEP) meeting, at which time parental input can be obtained.

Many students who have had their orthopedic disability for much of their lives achieve a high level of motor efficiency by the time they enroll in physical education. Special instruction for them may need only be directed toward refinement of movement patterns and the introduction of new skills. Other youngsters, however, require the same kinds of physical education programming considerations as those with recently acquired orthopedic disabilities.

The activities of the special program for those with orthopedic disabilities will be determined by the nature and extent of the impairment and the general debility. The early phases of the program for the returning student will be largely exercises and games to increase physical fitness and improve posture and body awareness. As the physical condition and motor performance improve, modified games, dances, and team sports can be introduced into the adapted program. Specific suggestions are made following the discussion of the orthopedically disabling conditions in each of the three sections of this chapter. When the situation warrants it and to the maximum extent possible, the student with a disability should be included in the activities of the regular class.

Disorders That Immobilize Lower Limbs

Many types of orthopedic disorders can cause such severe paralysis of the lower limbs that the use of a wheelchair or similar device is required to achieve locomotion. The two types of such disorders the physical educator most frequently encounters are traumatic spinal cord injuries and spina bifida. The two conditions are similar in that they both produce lesions in the spinal cord and result in subsequent paralysis of the lower limbs.

The spinal cord is housed in the spinal or vertebral column. It is cylindrical in shape, but it does flatten out at certain segments of the spinal column. Its circumference is approximately the same throughout the length of the cord, except for an enlargement in the area giving rise to the nerves that innervate the upper limbs. Another enlargement occurs at the lumbar (small of the back) segment of the spine where nerves leave to innervate the lower limbs. The spinal cord begins where the skull and spinal column meet; it terminates between the last thoracic (upper back) vertebra (T-12) and the second lumbar vertebra (L-2). (See figure 9.1.) Nerves from the spinal cord pass down into the lumbar and sacral (tail bone) segments of the spinal column.

Sensory and motor nerves emerge from the spinal cord and exit the spinal column through foramina (openings) in the vertebrae. Motor nerves emerging from different levels of the spinal column innervate different muscles (figure 9.2).

Injury to the spinal cord in turn affects the innervation of muscles. The higher the level of injury, the less will be the amount of muscle movement available to the affected person. Because groups of muscles are innervated from nerves emerging at particular levels of the spinal column, it is possible to specify the limits of muscle action remaining to individuals who suffer cord injury at a specific vertebra.

Injury to the Spinal Cord

When the cord is severed at or above the third cervical vertebra, death results. Partial lesion in this area creates weakness over the entire body. Complete severance of the cord above the second thoracic vertebra (T-2) results in involvement of the upper and lower limbs; the term for this condition is quadriplegia, meaning all limbs are affected. Complete severance at the second thoracic vertebra (T-2) or below results in paraplegia, a term used to indicate involvement of only the lower trunk and legs. In both conditions, the degree of paralysis may vary from partial to complete.

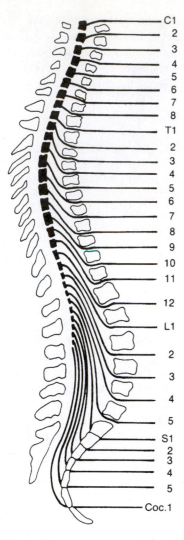

Figure 9.1 Nerves emerging from different levels of the column.

Fourth Cervical Level (C-4)

The person with injury just below the fourth cervical vertebra has use of only the neck muscles and the diaphragm (the main muscle of respiration). Upper limb function is possible only with an electrically powered assistive device, described in the previous chapter, that moves the arm and opens and closes the hand. Complete assistance is needed in transferring to and from the wheelchair.

Fifth Cervical Level (C-5)

Those who sustain injury below the fifth cervical vertebra retain use of the neck muscles, diaphragm, deltoid muscles of the shoulder, and biceps of the arms. The arms can be raised but gravity must be relied upon to lower them; likewise the elbow can be flexed but gravity must be utilized to extend it. A substitute is required for the nonfunctioning hand and wrist musculature and may be either a fixed

support of the wrist and fingers or the electrical device described earlier. Persons with this type of injury can perform many activities with their arms; for example, they are able to groom themselves, help apply their braces, and push their wheelchair for short distances if it is equipped with a special projection on the rims of the wheels. They will need complete assistance in transferring to and from their wheelchairs.

Sixth Cervical Level (C-6)

A person with a functional sixth cervical vertebra has the use of the wrist extensors in addition to the movements retained by those with higher levels of injury. With the ability to extend the wrist and with the use of gravity for flexion, considerable utilitarian movement is possible. Small instruments can be attached to a leather cuff worn on the arm. Wrist extension is possible through use of a special mechanism that makes the finger flex, providing a grip and release.

Those with injuries at this level can, in addition to all the activities performed by those with higher lesions, push the wheelchair for long distances and make use of the overhead trapeze (a bar hung overhead to be grasped with the hands as an aid in moving the body). A person injured at this level can also transfer his or her body by holding the extended arms close to the body and adducting the shoulders to stabilize the elbows. Some very adroit individuals with this injury are able to drive a car with hand controls.

Seventh Cervical Level (C-7)

When the injury is below the seventh cervical vertebra, the major additional functions that remain are extension of the elbow and flexion and extension of the fingers. Movement of the hand is not completely normal because the intrinsic muscles of the hand do not function. The person with this level of injury can do pullups, pushups, and grasp and release. Consequently, he or she can be fairly independent in manipulating the wheelchair and in transferring from one place to another.

Upper Thoracic Levels (T-1 to T-9 Inclusive)

Individuals with lesions in the first through the ninth thoracic vertebrae have total movement capacity in the arms but none in the legs; the term given to this condition is paraplegia. Control remains of some of the muscles of the upper back, the abdominal muscles, and the muscles of the ribs. Complete control of the wheelchair is possible, as are self-feeding and grooming. Although standing is possible by use of long leg braces with pelvic bands, ambulation is very limited.

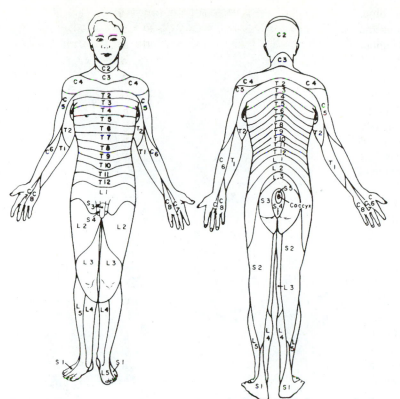

Figure 9.2 Cutaneous distribution of spinal nerves.

(Source: Barr, M.L., & Kieman, J. A. (1988). *The human nervous system: A medical viewpoint* (5th ed.). Hagerstown, MD: Harper & Row; reprinted by permission.)

Lower Thoracic Levels (T-10 to T-12 Inclusive)

Those with a separation of the spinal cord in the lower thoracic upper lumbar level have the movement potential of all types described above and possess complete abdominal muscle control as well as control of all the muscles of the upper back. Complete innervation of the abdominal muscles makes walking feasible with the support of long leg braces.

Lumbar Levels (L-1 to L-5 Inclusive)

The lumbar levels one through three innervate the muscles of the hip joint that flex the thigh. The fourth level of the lumbar also innervates the muscles of flexion of the hip and, together with the fifth level, innervates all the muscles of the lower leg and the muscles that extend the hip.

Those with the lesion at the upper lumbar levels have fairly good walking ability. The hip can be flexed but it is necessary to depend on gravity to extend it. With injuries below the fifth level, the voluntary muscles of the lumbar region are not affected.

Sacral Levels (S-1 to S-5 Inclusive)

The sacral level supplies nerves to the muscles of the pelvic floor, the bladder, the anal sphincter (muscle that controls the anus), and the external genitals. Those with

the lesion in this area or at any level above it do not have bladder or bowel control.

Traumatic Spinal Cord Injuries

When one first encounters traumatic spinal cord injuries, the tendency is to assume that the major consequence of the injuries is lack of motor movement. Unfortunately, many other serious problems are brought about by destruction of the spinal cord. Most of these are not noticeable to the casual observer, but they are of important consequence and should be understood by the physical education teacher working with students who have spinal cord injuries.

A condition called *hyperreflexia* (exaggeration of reflexes) occurs when the spinal column is severed. It is more common in individuals with quadriplegia than paraplegia. The symptoms vary, ranging from whitening of the area around the mouth and mild sweating to severe hypertension, excruciating headaches, profuse sweating, and feelings of impending doom. It is thought that hyperreflexia is caused by the indiscriminate release of a hormone into the body, the result of the sympathetic nervous system's inability to control the spinal cord. The release of the hormone is stimulated by a full bladder.

A condition called *contractures* (abnormal shortening of muscles) occurs frequently. It is the result of allowing joints to remain in one position for long periods of time. Contractures can be avoided by moving and stretching the muscles around the joints at periodic intervals throughout the day.

Still another problem that may occur is heterotopic bone formation. This is a laying down of new bone in soft tissue around joints, especially at the hip joints. During the process of formation, the area may become inflamed and swollen. It is not known what causes the problem or how it can be prevented. Such formation is usually self-limiting; and if the condition interferes with joint movement, removal by surgery is possible.

Urinary infections are common among those who have spinal cord injuries. All persons with separated spinal cords lack bladder control and must use a catheter and bag, at all times. The most frequently used catheter is a tube inserted into the urethra (the canal conveying urine from the bladder to the exterior) that empties into the bag attached to the leg. The presence of the catheter and the difficulty of excreting the urine create conditions in which infection is very likely to occur. Also, because the bag may cause irritation to the skin, it must be moved from one leg to another at least once a day. Another type of catheter, used by males, is not inserted into the urethra; instead it covers the external genital organs. Drainage flows directly into the bag. The possibility of urinary infection is less with the use of this catheter (figure 9.3). Many individuals with paralegia develop some control of their bladder without the insertion of a tube. This requires the exertion of manual pressure in a downward direction on the lower abdomen. This procedure, known as the Credé maneuver, can be taught to children to encourage them to empty the bladder completely at each diaper changing.

For many individuals with paralysis, defecation is difficult; however, proper scheduling of bowel movements and ingestion of sufficient bulk in the diet can usually alleviate the problem. If the problem is severe, a surgical procedure known as ileostomy or colostomy is necessary to create an opening in the small or large intestine through which the fecal matter can move into an attached bag. Like the urine bag, the ileostomy bag must be moved from leg to leg to avoid irritation. It is removed for swimming; a water-tight bandage is placed over the stoma (opening) to retain the fecal material and to prevent infection. Any students with an ileostomy or colostomy should have the approval of their physician before taking part in swimming.

Because their condition requires them to remain seated or lying on the back for long periods of time, persons with spinal cord injuries commonly develop decubitus ulcers (bed sores) on the back and buttocks. The major cause is pressure of the body weight on these areas. Pads placed to relieve the pressure help to prevent the ulcers from developing.

Almost all persons who have spinal cord injuries become spastic; that is, they experience spasms of the muscles, to some degree. The condition may last for years or may gradually disappear over the course of time. Spasticity

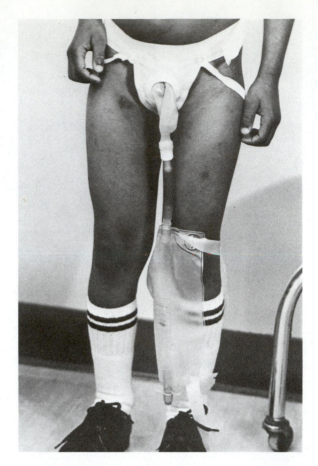

Figure 9.3 External collection device.

(Courtesy of Bigge, June L., & O'Donnell, Patrick A.: *Teaching Individuals With Physical and Multiple Disabilities.* Columbus, OH, Charles E. Merrill Publishing Co., 1976.)

is a problem because it prevents any effective movement in those parts of the body over which partial control is possible.

Spasms can occur at any time and can be violent enough to awaken the person from sleep or even throw him or her from the wheelchair. The condition can be controlled to some extent by medication. In some cases, surgery is necessary. All muscles that are spastic must receive daily passive stretching to maintain full range of motion in all involved joints and to prevent contracture.

A weight control problem is also likely to plague those with spinal cord injuries. Low expenditure of energy due to lack of physical activity results in fat being stored rather than burned. Consequently, unless they are very careful to avoid foods high in calories and to remain as active as possible, individuals with paralysis tend to become obese relatively easily, exposing them to the serious problems commonly associated with obesity.

The fitness level of individuals in wheelchairs is generally low (Shepard, 1990; Davis, 1993). This is often attributed, in part, to the unnecessary activity restrictions placed on individuals with spinal cord injuries. There is also evidence that individuals with lower limb disabilities have a reduced maximum heart rate and lower stroke volume. Some of the abnormal physiologic findings would be expected due to the nature of the disability. For example, the loss of vasomotor regulation below the level of the lesion reduces venous return, restricting the central blood volume, and thus leads to poor cardiac performance. Unfortunately, the use of the wheelchair in performing the activities of daily living does not impose a sufficient demand on the system to generate a training effect. Fitness programs, therefore, must be designed to improve important variables such as maximal oxygen intake and heart rate. Wheelchair users must recognize that normal wheelchair activity is not sufficient to produce a favorable cardiovascular response. In general, interval training programs have been found to be effective in producing desirable training effects for individuals with spinal cord injuries. Additional information about the design of a fitness program for this population will be presented in chapter 27, *Physical Fitness*.

Spina Bifida

Spina bifida is a congenital anomaly (deviation from normal) resulting from nonfusion of the dorsal arch in one or more vertebrae. The lumbar vertebrae are the most often affected, but incomplete development can occur at any level of the spine.

The exact cause or causes of this neural tube development failure have not been identified. Both environmental and hereditary factors have been cited (Williamson, 1987). The occurrence risk for spina bifida and related anomalies in siblings and offspring of those with spina bifida is slightly higher than the expected occurrence in the general population; also, the incidence is higher among the Welsh and Irish. A relationship between the occurrence of the disease and maternal age has been noted in some surveys (Holmes, Driscoll, and Alkins, 1976), as well as between the occurrence of the disease and environmental factors (socioeconomic and seasonal factors, for example). Environmental factors probably interact with multifactorial genetic determinants to produce spina bifida.

Classification

Classification and terminology regarding spina bifida will vary with authors. The classification and definitions offered by Freeman (1974) will be utilized in this discussion. Essentially there are two clinical forms: spina bifida occulta (no external manifestations or signs) and spina bifida manifesta (a demonstrable abnormality). Spina bifida cystica is a term often applied to the most common anomalies found under spina bifida manifesta.

Spina bifida occulta is a common abnormality in which incomplete formation of the vertebral column occurs without external manifestations. In the great majority of cases there is no disability associated with the bony maldevelopment, and treatment is not required. Occasionally, a clump of dark hair or a dimple may appear on the infant's back: in these cases the condition is referred to as spina bifida occulta with skin manifestations (figure 9.4).

There are two types of spina bifida cystica; in both, a lesion and a herniation (protrusion) are present on the back of the newborn infant at the location of the defective

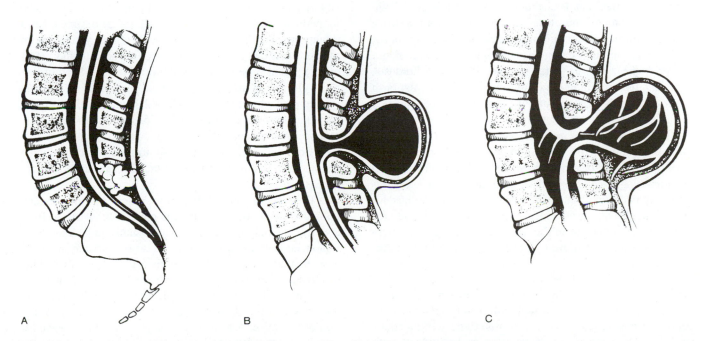

Figure 9.4 Three types of spina bifida. (*A*) Spina bifida occulta, (*B*) meningocele, and (*C*) myelomeningocele.

(Source: Williamson, G.G. (1987). *Children with Spina Bifida: Early Intervention and Preschool Programming* (p. 2). Baltimore, MD.: Paul H. Brookes Publishing Co.; reprinted by permission.)

vertebra. The protrusion, or sac, varies in size and appearance. It may be covered by skin or a transparent membrane. In one type, meningocele, the sac contains the meninges (membranes that envelop the brain and spinal cord) and spinal fluid but does not involve the spinal cord. This type, which is rare, is generally not accompanied by motor or sensory deficiencies. The only necessary procedure is surgery to reduce the herniation, close the lesion, and prevent infection. Prognosis is excellent.

When the neural tissue of the spinal cord is attached to the sac, the condition is called meningomyelocele or myelomeningocele. This type is much more common than meningocele, so subsequent discussion primarily concerns this type.

Myelomeningocele

Myelomeningocele is a very severe anomaly in which some degree of neurological impairment is inevitable. The extent of involvement depends on the location of the lesion and the degree of spinal cord damage. Sacral lesions may cause only muscular flaccidity (weakness or softness) in the lower legs and feet. The abdominal and leg muscles will be involved in persons with lesions located in the third to fifth vertebrae. Complete paraplegia will generally occur from lesions located in the first and second lumbar and thoracic vertebrae. Lesions located on the cervical region are often meningoceles and generally show no paralysis, though some have involvement of the arm muscles. The loss of sensation invariably accompanies paralysis.

Muscle imbalance occurs and joint deformities may result when there is partial or unequal paralysis in the lower limbs. Most frequent is the unopposed action of the hip flexor and adductor muscles, causing hip dislocation. Knee joint deformities (recurvation, or backward bending) occur but are less common. Pes cavus and equinovarus (see figure 9.9 on page 183) are often present. Scoliosis, lordosis, kyphosis, or a combination of these may be present at birth or may appear later as a result of rapid growth accompanied by the absence of a complete vertebral column.

Innervation of the muscles concerned with micturition (urinating) comes from the sacral level of the spine; therefore, bladder paralysis is almost universal in persons with myelomeningocele. This means incontinence (lack of control) may occur, with resultant urine buildup in the bladder that eventually reaches the kidneys and causes hydronephrosis (cystic enlargement of the kidney). Anal sphincter muscles may become paralyzed so that bowel incontinence also occurs.

Myelomeningocele lesions predispose the meninges to immediate and serious infections. Urinary tract and renal (kidney) infections due to urine buildup and stagnation constitute serious and continuous hazards. Repeated infections are most often the cause of fatalities in individuals with spina bifida.

The most common and most serious complication associated with myelomeningocele is hydrocephalus. It is present in more than 80 percent of persons with myelomeningocele and is caused by the accumulation of excessive amounts of cerebrospinal fluid within the cranial cavity, frequently causing an enlarged head. When present with spina bifida, it is generally brought about by obstruction of the cerebrospinal canal. Unchecked, hydrocephalus may cause brain damage and subsequent mental retardation.

Individuals with myelomeningocele are, as are all those paralyzed, very susceptible to skin ulcerations (sores) because of the loss of sensation in the skin. Obesity may also become a problem, and the incidence of congenital heart disease seems to be higher in children with spina bifida.

Treatment

Prior to the 1950s, myelomeningocele infants were left untreated and the vast majority died within a few months. Today improved surgical techniques and drug treatments can lead to prolonged life in many patients. Unfortunately, however, paralysis and other serious problems present at birth are not reversible and treatment is not completely ameliorative. Extensive and continuous medical treatment of a child with a poor prognosis places heavy emotional, social, and economic burdens on the family. Thus, even today, selective treatment is advocated (Anderson and Spain, 1977). Complete evaluation is made and a decision for treatment is reached based on economic, social, familial, and medical factors.

Because of the number of complications and the diversity of clinical manifestations, each person must be treated individually and only general procedures are outlined. Most infants are taken to myelomeningocele clinics where a team of specialists can give intensive care. Immediate and vigorous treatment is necessary for optimal success. Prompt surgical closure of the skin defect is performed to prevent infection. Hydrocephalus is treated by surgical drainage, with the insertion of a shunt to provide a permanent drainage system. A shunt consists of a plastic tube with a valve that runs from the ventricle in the brain to the heart or abdomen (figure 9.5). Often the bulge behind the ear caused by the tube is visible.

The tube and shunt valve do not require special care and normally the child with a shunt is not overly restricted from activity. The only movement that is usually to be avoided is prolonged hanging upside down (this position may interfere with the flow of fluid and disrupt the valvular function of the shunt) and sports such as soccer, where the head might be hit.

Periodically the shunt may have to be replaced due to the growth of the child, obstruction in the tube or malfunction of the valve. Teachers and parents need to be aware of warning signs that may indicate possible problems with the shunt. The warning signs indicated that follow should be brought to the attention of the child's physician.

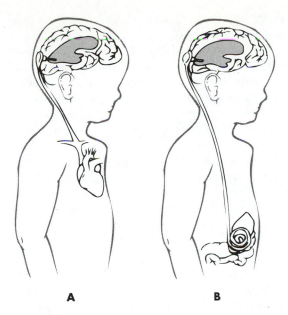

A   **B**

Figure 9.5 (A) Ventriculoatrial shunt. (B) Ventriculoperitoneal shunt.

1. Increase in head size
2. Behavioral changes such as extreme irritability or fussiness
3. Increase in sleepiness
4. Seizures
5. Diminished reaction to the environment, or lethargy
6. Forceful vomiting
7. Swelling or redness of the skin in the area of the shunt
8. Headaches
9. "Setting sun" eyes (iris only partially visible due to a downward gaze) (Williamson, 1987, pp. 83–84)

Correction of skeletal deformities, especially in the hip and spine, is extremely difficult. Orthopedic surgery may be required but must be performed in conjunction with other operations. Deformities of the foot and knee are more easily treated, and braces or casts may be used.

There are two important urological considerations. One is the prevention of infection and renal dysfunction and the other is the prevention of socially unacceptable incontinence. Controversy exists as to which is the best of the several treatment methods available. As yet, none seems to be satisfactory in all cases. Treatment varies with the individual and depends on urinary tract involvement, the sex and age of the person, and the preference of the family and physician.

Successful micturition may be brought about by manual pressure on the lower abdomen (Credé maneuver) for some persons or by a catheter from the bladder for others. The use of the catheter, known as catheterization, requires inserting a catheter (a tube) through the urethra into the bladder for the withdrawal of urine at set intervals. For young children, catheterization must be done by a teacher or aide, but later students learn to perform this procedure without assistance (figure 9.6).

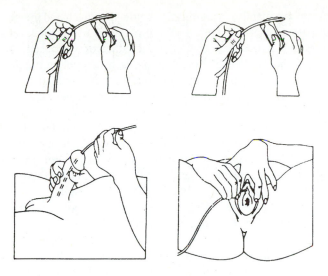

Figure 9.6 Catheterization, a means of withdrawing urine from the bladder, is used by persons with spina bifida, spinal cord injuries, and other conditions that cause urinary incontinence. The catheter is lubricated and then inserted about 6 inches into the penis or about 3 inches into the female opening. Parents can generally instruct teachers as to the correct procedure.

(From Claudine Sherrill, *Adapted Physical Activity, Recreation and Sport*, 4th ed. Copyright © 1993 Wm. C. Brown Publishers, Dubuque, Iowa. All Rights Reserved. Reprinted by permission.)

For boys, a urinal bag with penile attachment may be used. When progressive upper urinary tract damage is evident, surgical diversion is recommended. The most common is the ileal loop. In this diversion the ureters are brought into a loop of the bowel, which is opened to the outside through the abdominal wall, thus eliminating the bladder as a collection bag. Antibiotic drugs are used to combat infections.

Bowel management through diet, medication, and the use of suppositories and enemas when necessary is relatively successful. Further treatment is generally not necessary.

Prognosis for the myelomeningocele infant is more encouraging today than fifteen years ago because of advances in treatment. Mortality rates have decreased from 50 to 90 percent (Tecklin, 1989). Those who survive may still face paralysis, continued threats of infection, and genitourinary problems. Concurrent with improved treatment practices are new methods of screening and detection of spina bifida during the fetal period that provide the possibility of prevention through early identification. Genetic counseling is available for parents in danger of producing spina bifida offspring.

Suggested Activities

The kinds of motor activities in which a student in a wheelchair can engage depend upon the specific nature of the disability. For those with spinal injuries, including spina bifida, the activity choices depend on the severity and level of the lesion. (It will be recalled from the discussion of the nature of such injuries that complete destruction of the cord at a given level paralyzes all muscles below that level, and injury or partial severance creates partial paralysis below the level at which it occurs.) The physical educator will need to assess the movement potential of each student, utilizing knowledge of the level of injury and actual observation of the student. Careful attention when observing the ways in which the student manipulates his or her body to perform daily routine will provide possible clues as to the potential for movement. Teachers will notice, for instance, that children with spina bifida frequently have visual-motor problems requiring special assistance when teaching games that involve balls and objects that are thrown or struck.

Persons with paraplegia, after recovery from the initial injury, can perform most physical education activities from the wheelchair. For younger children, catching and throwing games are easily devised; target games using bean bags are also readily developed. Bouncing balls off walls is another activity possible for the child in a chair. Even a game of modified handball is possible; the child bats the ball so that it returns to him or her or to a partner, who in turn bats it to the wall. A ball suspended from the ceiling with a heavy cord makes an excellent piece of equipment for teaching catching and throwing skills to the child who needs a wheelchair (figure 9.7). In addition, the suspended ball can be used for various activities, such as throwing at a target drawn on a board or at empty milk cartons or plastic bottles standing on a table.

The child in a wheelchair can also take part in parachute play. There is no reason why he or she cannot engage in all of the common activities of parachute play, including exchanging places with another player while the parachute is in the air, by substituting locomotion of the chair for walking and running. The same substitution is possible in most basic skill games.

Older students can be offered many of the activities included in the regular program, with only such modifications as are necessitated by the need to remain in the chair. The way in which the skills are performed usually requires some adaptations; specific suggestions for these are made in the chapters on various activities. In some instances, the regulations and equipment must also be modified. The playing area for games and sports is usually reduced in size, playing equipment is lighter, and frequently the handles of rackets and mallets are extended to increase the range of the reach. In team games, the area that each player must cover is reduced, the assignment of duties is made on the basis of the players' abilities, or two people with different abilities share an assignment. For rhythm and dance activities, the size of the formations is increased to accommodate the wheelchair in the maneuvers.

For individuals with paraplegia and quadriplegia, special attention should be given to providing exercises to achieve and maintain physical fitness. Especially important for the person with paraplegia are activities that strengthen the arms and shoulder girdle, because optimal strength in these muscles will make propelling the wheelchair and transferring to and from it easier and less exhausting (Glaser, 1989; Coutts et al., 1993). Emphasis should also be given to activities that encourage a full range of motion in the spastic muscles to aid in the prevention of contracture (Jeffrey, 1986).

Swimming is an especially good activity for total physical conditioning. Students with bowel- and bladder-control problems can use waterproof pants to eliminate the possibility of embarrassment while in the water. For individuals with paraplegia, weight training can be used to develop muscular strength. Persons with quadriplegia can also engage in conditioning with weights if certain adaptations are made. In total quadriplegia, a head harness attached to wall pulleys is supplied. For those with partial quadriplegia who have some arm movement, special weight resistance exercises are possible.

Several organizations promote competition on local, national, and international levels for persons with paraplegia and quadriplegia. Events include archery, bowling, basketball, table tennis, swimming, weightlifting, shooting, and tennis. Classification systems, based on the levels of injury, have been developed so that no player or team will have an unfair advantage over another. More information on this can be found in chapter 30, *Competitive Sport for Athletes with Disabilities*.

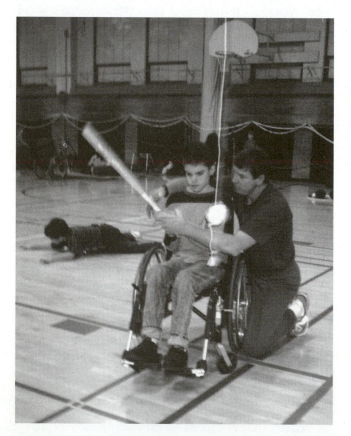

Figure 9.7 After each hit, the suspended ball returns to the student in the wheelchair, eliminating problems of retrieval.

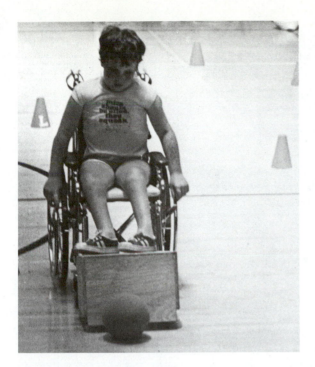

Figure 9.8 Requiring a student in a wheelchair to use a scoop attached to the front of the chair to move a ball around obstacles is a fun and valuable mobility training skill.

Disorders That Limit Ambulation

Many orthopedic disorders affect ambulation, the ability to walk. This section includes a discussion of the disabilities that make walking difficult. However, these disabilities may, in severe cases or cases of multiple disabilities, require the person to use a wheelchair.

Tuberculosis of the bone, rickets, osteomyelitis, and poliomyelitis were once very common causes of orthopedic disabilities in children; this is no longer true, owing to the effectiveness of prevention and treatment methods. Congenital hip dislocation, talipes, certain types of osteochondrosis, epiphysiolysis, and leg amputation are still relatively prevalent disorders affecting ambulation.

Congenital Hip Dislocation

Congenital dislocation of the hip refers to a partially or completely displaced femoral head (in relation to the acetabulum of the hip) that is present at birth. Defective development of the acetabulum, termed dysplasia of the hip, accompanies the condition. Because the acetabulum is much shallower than normal, it allows easy displacement of the head of the femur. In time, with continued dislocation, the acetabulum changes in shape, becoming triangular or oval rather than flat, and may become filled with fibrous tissue.

Congenital hip dislocation occurs more commonly among girls than boys. It is more often unilateral than bilateral, and the left hip is affected more often than the right. It

is the fourth most common congenital defect. Prolonged malpositioning of the hip joint produces a chronic weakness of the leg and hip muscles. If the condition is left untreated, ambulation becomes difficult; however, if adequate medical treatment, consisting of bracing and surgery, is received early in life, the prognosis for normal locomotion is very good.

Talipes

Talipes (commonly called clubfoot) is the most common orthopedic deformity. In this condition, the foot is twisted out of shape or position (figure 9.9). In most cases, the condition is congenital, but it can be acquired as the result of certain neuromuscular diseases—spastic paralysis, for example.

The limitations and capabilities of anyone with talipes depend upon the extent of derangement of the foot or feet. With only moderate derangement, one can perform with minimum limitation. In more severe cases, walking may be very difficult, and standing for any length of time impossible.

Braces, when used in the early years, are effective in remedying talipes in which deformity is mild. Surgery is necessary when the foot is extremely malformed.

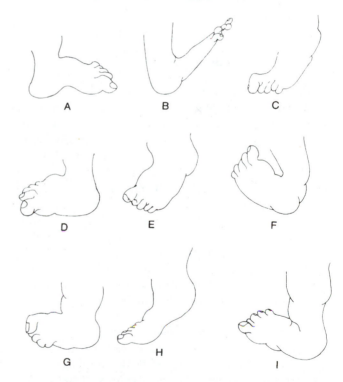

Figure 9.9 Talipes. (*A*) Cavus—hollow foot. (*B*) Calcaneus—heel lower than toes. (*C*) Equinus—toes lower than heel. (*D*) Valgus—toes and sole of foot turned out. (*E*) Equinovarus—combination of talipes varus and talipes equinus. (*F*) Calcaneovarus—combination of talipes calcaneus and talipes varus. (*G*) Varus—toes and sole of foot turned in. (*H*) Equinovalgus—combination of talipes valgus and talipes equinus. (*I*) Calcaneovalgus—combination of talipes calcaneus and talipes valgus.

Equinovarus is the most common form of talipes. With this condition the foot is inverted, the heel is drawn up, and the forefoot adducted, forcing the child to walk on the outer border of the foot.

Osteochondrosis

Osteochondrosis, also known as osteochondrosis deformans juvenilis and growth plate disorder, is a disorder of the epiphysis (growth center) of the bone. The exact cause is not known. Some authorities suspect that trauma to the bone that interferes with the normal blood supply to the epiphysis may be the basic reason for development of the disorder. The bone area around the epiphysis becomes softened and undergoes partial necrosis (death) and is consequently liable to deformity if pressure is applied to the bone. In time, new bone replaces the dead tissue and the bone returns to normal. The bone retains its original shape unless it has come under stress or strain such as occurs in weight-bearing. The period of time from the beginning of the disease until the dead tissue is replaced varies according to the bone involved.

Although there are several sites where osteochondrosis can occur, three of the most common forms of osteochondrosis are Legg-Calvé-Perthes disease, Osgood-Schlatter disease, and Scheuermann disease.

Legg-Calvé-Perthes Disease

Legg-Calvé-Perthes disease, named for the three physicians who first identified this condition in the early 1900s, is a condition in which the capitular epiphysis (growth center of the head of the bone) of the femur is affected. The condition is most commonly found in boys between the ages of four and ten. Very seldom does it occur in girls. The cause of the disease has not been definitely established, but it has been postulated that the probable cause is a circulatory disturbance arising from strain on or trauma to the hip area.

In Legg-Calvé-Perthes disease, the epiphysis of the femoral head disintegrates and is absorbed and replaced by other bone tissue (figure 9.10). Collapse of the head of the femur may occur, causing it to flatten. In this case, when the new bone is formed, the shape of the normal epiphysis is not regained. Treatment consists of attempting to prevent the collapse of the femoral head by limiting the strain of bearing weight. This is achieved by utilizing ambulation and non-weight-bearing devices, such as the Newington ambulatory splint, during the later stages. If weight-bearing is prevented during the acute stages of the disease, function may return to normal. However, in many cases a slight limp persists and there is some restriction of hip motion.

The first signs of Legg-Calvé-Perthes disease in a child are often a slight limp and complaints of pain along the inner side of the thigh or knee. As the disease progresses, the limp becomes more noticeable. Usually the limp is not severe and there is no extensive limitation of motion in the hip area. Examination by X ray will verify the presence of the disease.

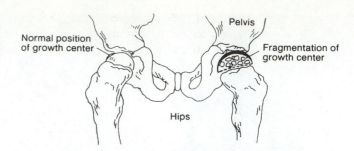

Figure 9.10 Legg-Calvé-Perthes disease. Destruction of the growth center may be partial or complete.

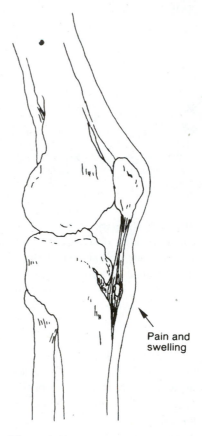

Figure 9.11 Osgood-Schlatter disease. Pain and swelling in the area of the insertion of the tendon into the tibia is the common complaint of those affected with this condition.

Osgood-Schlatter Disease

This syndrome, independently described by Osgood and Schlatter in the early 1900s, is manifested by the separation of the tibial tubercle (a prominence on the top of the tibia to which the kneecap is attached) from the tibia (figure 9.11). Normally, the individual will complain of tenderness in the knee area accompanied by swelling. If the medical examination, including X ray, does not show any other disorder, then the diagnosis of Osgood-Schlatter disease is made.

This disease was once more common among young boys, ages ten to fifteen, than among girls. Because of the increased activity levels of girls, an increasing number of females are now experiencing discomfort from Osgood-Schlatter disease. Most authorities believe that this disease is the result of trauma that may produce major changes in the area as a result of one isolated event or the accumulation of several smaller injuries to the knee.

The disease responds well to treatment. Usually vigorous use of the knee is contraindicated for a period of six to nine months. During this time the student is restricted from activities that involve running, jumping, climbing, and bicycling. In some cases, particularly when the X ray shows damage or displacement of the bone at the tendon, the extremity may be placed in a cast for six weeks to limit knee motion. After the cast is removed, the patient must be limited in activity for a period of three to six months. Generally, with good treatment, the symptoms will subside by about age fifteen to eighteen.

Scheuermann Disease

Scheuermann disease, also known as juvenile kyphosis, is a disturbance of the normal vertebral growth in the cervical and upper thoracic region. The epiphysis or cartilage of one or more vertebra may be inflamed, resulting in fragmentation of the vertebra(e). Similar to Legg-Calvé-Perthes, the etiology is generally unknown and the disease appears to have an active phase in which activity is contraindicated. The recommended treatment is bracing designed to avoid forward flexion. The use of the brace will also ensure that the weight is taken by the neural arches rather than the affected vertebral bodies.

The amount of pain and discomfort associated with Scheuermann disease varies from individual to individual. Some complain of no pain and insist that they be allowed to participate in any activity of their choosing. If the student's activity level is not restricted, particularly forward flexion, the kyphotic slump may increase. Some physicians will insist that the student wear a cast, brace, or body jacket for an extended period of time to alleviate any concern they might have about the youngster's activity patterns.

Epiphysiolysis

Epiphysiolysis (slipped epiphysis) is a condition in which there is a separation of the epiphysis from the bone itself. As the separation occurs, the epiphysis slips to the side of the shaft of the bone. Slipping epiphysis may occur at any bone growth center. However, by far the most common location is in the head of the femur and, unless otherwise designated, the term epiphysiolysis is assumed to refer to a slipped epiphysis in the femur.

When slipping occurs in areas other than the femur, the probable cause is acute trauma. Although some of the cases that involve the femur are caused by trauma, the vast majority are not. In these cases the cause of the slipping is not known, but a very large percentage of them also have Frölich's syndrome, a condition associated with endocrine dysfunction marked by obesity and underdevelopment of the genitals.

Epiphysiolysis begins with a widening of the epiphyseal line, the space between the bone and epiphysis. At this time mild pain is experienced in the groin area. As the slip progresses, a change occurs in the relationship of the femur to the pelvis that causes the thigh to rotate outwardly; the hip becomes slightly flexed and the leg shortened. As this occurs, the child develops a slight limp. The limp becomes more prominent and the pain may increase as the epiphysis slips downward.

The course of the disorder from the active through the healing stage is one to three years. If not treated, the deformity becomes fixed. In a few cases, the limp may disappear, but usually it becomes progressively worse. The bones of the hip may atrophy, and later osteoarthritis may develop.

The treatment usually requires surgery. Pins are inserted across the epiphyseal line to help correct the displacement. After surgery the student is usually allowed, if involvement is unilateral, to walk using crutches to keep the weight off the affected hip. In a case of bilateral involvement, the individual must use a wheelchair for a time.

Leg Amputation

Amputation, the loss of all or part of a limb, may be due to several factors. Among these are congenital conditions in which the infant is born with all or part of a limb missing. Other reasons for amputation are tumor, trauma, and disease. Amputation may be performed to arrest a malignant condition. Traumatic amputation may occur as the result of accident, or the damage may be so extensive as to require surgical removal of the limb. The diseases responsible for most amputations are those, like diabetes and arteriosclerosis, that cause circulatory problems. Such problems occur more often in the legs than in other parts of the body. The terms that are used to identify amputations are presented in figure 9.12. This information is valuable in helping the teacher to interpret medical information and its educational relevance to the affected student.

The person with a leg amputation can be readily fitted with a prosthesis. The problems of ambulation will vary with the specific level of amputation. Those with below-knee amputations can readily learn the use of the prosthesis in locomotion. Many young individuals with an amputation learn to use their prostheses so well that walking effectiveness is altered very little.

Those with amputations above the knee but below the hip may have difficulty in developing a proper walking gait because the gait pattern is drastically changed due to the loss of the knee joint. Steps are shortened to prevent a movement that would tend to flex the artificial knee as it is swung forward. The individual must lean forward at the hips and when

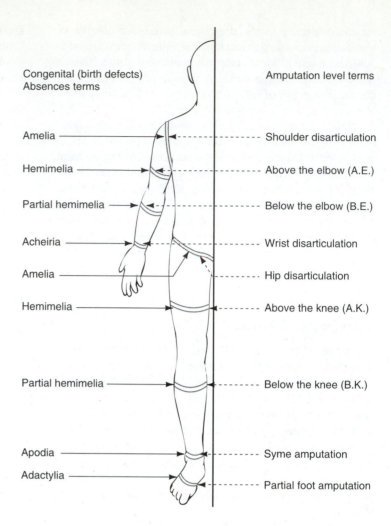

Congenital (birth defects) Absences terms	Amputation level terms
Amelia	Shoulder disarticulation
Hemimelia	Above the elbow (A.E.)
Partial hemimelia	Below the elbow (B.E.)
Acheiria	Wrist disarticulation
Amelia	Hip disarticulation
Hemimelia	Above the knee (A.K.)
Partial hemimelia	Below the knee (B.K.)
Apodia	Syme amputation
Adactylia	Partial foot amputation

Figure 9.12 On the left, terms used to describe deficiencies of limbs from birth defects. On the right, terms used for amputation levels.

the foot strikes the ground, the hip must be extended to prevent bending of the knee. As the weight passes over the artificial leg, the thigh is flexed and the artificial limb flexes at the knee, owing to the weight of the lower part. The hip is then extended to bring the body weight over the artificial foot as it is planted on the ground.

A common fault in walking for the person with above-the-knee amputation is the abduction or rolling gait. As weight is borne on the good leg, the opposite side of the body is raised, elevating the hip and causing the prosthesis to swing out from the body as well as forward.

Amputation of both lower extremities obviously adds serious problems. However, the basic technique in walking is approximately the same. The chief difference is the need to manipulate two artificial limbs rather than one.

Poliomyelitis

Poliomyelitis is a condition that is caused by a virus that attacks the anterior horn of the spinal cord. The motor cell becomes inflamed, resulting in muscular weakness.

Although the introduction of the Salk vaccine has greatly reduced the likelihood that this disability will affect students, occasionally a youngster with polio will be found within the public school setting.

Disabilities resulting from poliomyelitis vary with the extent of residual paralysis and its location. Those who have severe lower extremity involvement may be required to use wheelchairs, leg braces, or crutches. Common deformities in the lower extremities are: pathological dislocation of the hip following paralysis of the gluteus maximus; flexion deformity of the knee following paralysis of the leg muscles; and foot-drop as a result of the persistent contraction of the gastrocnemius. In the upper extremities, contracture of the shoulders may develop as the result of paralysis of the abductors. There may also be deformities of the elbow, wrist, and hand resulting from unbalanced muscle pull.

Because of the inability of the muscles to control a joint, the joint is sometimes fused by surgery to achieve stability. Joints frequently fused are the hip, knee, and ankle. Bones of the foot are also fused to give greater stability to the foot.

The severity of the disability caused by polio varies according to the individual and the type of medical treatment received. Approximately 6 percent of those affected die, with 44 percent suffering mild to severe paralysis. Fifty percent recover completely.

Suggested Activities

A student with an orthopedic disorder affecting ambulation may or may not use an assistive device to aid locomotion. If the assistive device is a cane or crutches, few problems arise to hinder participation in physical education. Many of the activities suitable for students in wheelchairs are also appropriate for these children. The chief difference is that those with canes or crutches need to learn to balance themselves in such a manner as to free one hand for use (figure 9.13). The kind of crutches as well as the manner of use will vary from one situation to the next. In most cases it is easier to use the arms in activities if crutches with cuffs are used. The balance can be maintained by one crutch while the other arm is free. The crutch does not fall to the ground because it is anchored to the forearm. Activities such as volleyball, throwing a ball, and striking with one hand can all be readily accomplished.

All students whose ambulation is impaired are at a disadvantage when speed of locomotion is required. Such activities should be adapted so that the distance the player has to travel is limited. For example, in badminton the regulations can be changed so that the objective becomes to hit the bird back to the opponent with a disability rather than to place it where he or she cannot return it, or the court of the player with a disability can be reduced in size to compensate for his or her movement limitation. Decreasing the speed needed to move from one place to another also allows more efficient participation by these students. Using a balloon for a ball in a game of toss is an example of a way in which the requirement for fast movement can be modified, since a balloon when thrown moves at a slower rate through the air than does a ball.

Activities for young children can be adapted from some of the basic skill games described in chapter 21. For example, children who have difficulty moving can participate in games such as circle ball, wonder ball, or target toss from a sitting position in a chair. Children with some degree of functional leg movement can play softball, bowling, driving pig to market, partner toss, and similar games in which leg agility is not essential. These children can also participate in singing games like Here We Go Over the Mountain, and Way Down Yonder in the Paw-Paw Patch by substituting walking for skipping.

The student with a leg prosthesis has a problem in maintaining balance. The individual with a unilateral amputation should practice maintaining his or her balance on the

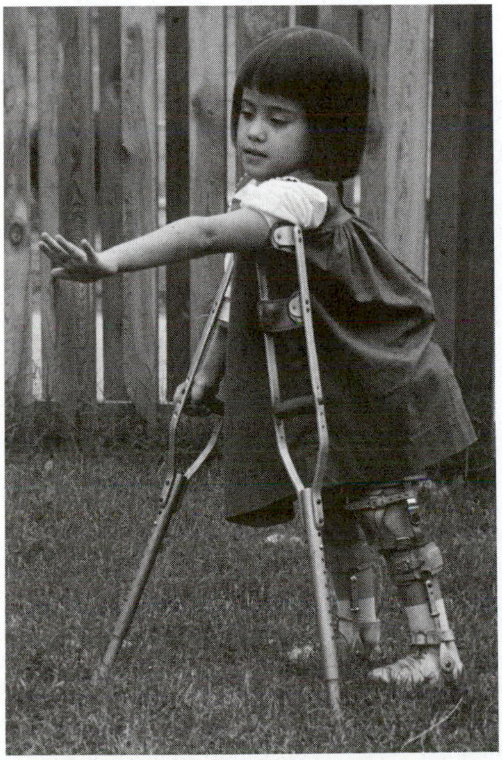

Figure 9.13 To achieve balance and free an arm for activity, a crutch must be appropriately propped.

Figure 9.14 Activities can be modified for the enjoyment of all students.

prosthetic limb so as to be able to use the sound foot for other purposes in game situations, for example, kicking a football or trapping in soccer. Balance on stairs is easier to maintain if the sound limb leads when ascending and if the prosthesis leads when descending.

Certain devices can be used to help persons with leg amputations to perform various skills. Poles of wood or metal to lean against can be erected in playing areas for players who require support while using their hands. Tables that permit players with disabilities to stand by supporting themselves within recessed areas are available but are better suited to indoor than outdoor play. Those who cannot stand but are able to sit unsupported in a straight chair can perform many activities while so seated.

In most cases, individuals with single-leg prostheses can develop balance and other locomotion skills so that they are able to participate in all physical education activities. Many become active in athletic competition such as football or baseball, both as amateurs and as professionals. These athletes usually train in the same manner as others. Strengthening exercises are done while wearing the prosthesis, thus strengthening the muscles that control the device.

The prosthesis is not worn in the water, and a missing leg will cause a change in the center of gravity in swimming. Consequently, the swimmer experiences difficulty in maintaining a prone or back position because the body tends to turn in the water toward the heavier side (away from the missing limb). Proper stroking can eliminate the problem (chapter 26, *Swimming*).

The student with an orthopedic disability enjoys movement in the water that is not possible out of the water. Even individuals with Legg-Calvé-Perthes disease, who are denied participation in weight-bearing activities, can enjoy the pleasures of swimming. Although not encouraged to stand erect in the water, they can do so without much risk because the buoyancy of the water reduces the pressure of body weight on the head of the femur. For others, the water buoyancy makes control of the body easier by minimizing the effects of weak muscles and the lack of balance and stability that hinders or restricts movement out of the water. Assistive devices that must always be worn otherwise can usually be removed for swimming.

Many individuals with unilateral leg amputations have been very successful in skiing. Those with below-the-knee amputations can usually wear regular skis with their prostheses. Skiers who have a single above-the-knee amputation employ a three-track ski technique, in which one regular ski and two handheld outriggers are used. The outrigger consists of a Löfstrand crutch attached by a hinge to a short ski (figure 9.15). The outrigger is constructed to allow only limited movement at the hinge. A moveable spike is inserted at the rear of the ski. The spike is lifted when skiing downhill and can be lowered to sink into the snow when skiing over flat terrain or moving uphill.

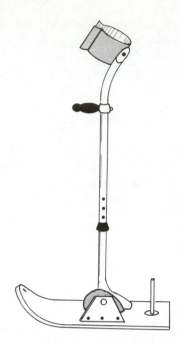

Figure 9.15   Outrigger ski.

Disorders That Affect Other Body Movement

The first two sections of this chapter have been directed toward orthopedic disabilities that prevent or impede ambulation. This section will discuss other orthopedic disorders that affect body movement but do not necessarily impose limitations on locomotion to any great extent; included are wryneck, scoliosis, spondylitis, spondyloses, and arm amputation. Under certain conditions, some of these disabilities indirectly affect walking gait because the resultant deformity causes problems in body balance that, in turn, disturbs the normal gait.

Wryneck

Wryneck is also called torticollis. In this disorder the neck is persistently held at a tilt, with the chin pointing in the opposite direction. This is caused by a contracted sternocleidomastoid muscle. This disorder may be congenital or hysterical, or it may be caused by pressure on the nerves, by muscle spasm, or by inflammation of the glands in the neck. Treatment is symptomatic; that is, it differs depending on the symptoms.

Scoliosis

When a body with a normal spinal column is viewed from the back, the right and left sides of the body are symmetrical, both shoulders and both hips are at the same level, and the spinal column is straight. Most individuals will show a very slight deviation in the spinal column. A slight deviation is usually not noticeable to casual observation and, if it does not become progressively worse, is of no consequence. However, a lateral curvature that is obvious must be considered an abnormal condition.

The lateral curvature of the spine is accompanied by a twisting of the vertebrae and takes its name, *scoliosis,* from the Greek word *skolios,* meaning twisting or bending. The lateral curve may be to the right or left or a combination of both. If it is to the right or left, it is called a C curve. An S curve is one in which the lower part curves in the opposite direction. In the latter condition, one of the curves is usually the primary curve while the other is a secondary curve developed to compensate for the first in restoring equilibrium to the trunk as a whole. An uncorrected C curve will eventually encourage the development of an S curve.

The C curve takes its name from the direction of convexity of the curve. A left C curve is to the individual's left and causes the right shoulder to be lowered and right hip to be raised (figure 9.16 *A*). The reverse is true of the right C curve. A condition of convexity of the curve, present at birth, is usually a left C curve. A curve that develops after birth is usually to the right.

In most S curves the primary curve is to the left, in the upper portion of the spine. The right shoulder will be held lower than the left, while the left hip will be raised higher than the right (fig. 9.16 *B*).

Scoliosis may be functional or structural in nature. If the curve tends to disappear when a hanging or prone position is assumed, it is probably functional. The causes of scoliosis are varied. A shortened leg, disease, injury, congenital conditions, and faulty postural habits, often due to hearing and vision problems, are the most frequent causes. Seldom

does scoliosis in its early stages cause pain or noticeable fatigue. However, in the later stages the muscular pull necessitated by the abnormal condition of the spine may cause back fatigue and frequent pains. It is, moreover, a definite cosmetic concern.

Because scoliosis is a common problem affecting 10 percent of the school-aged population, with 2½ percent requiring some form of medical attention, it is important that the school initiate a screening process. Students should be periodically checked for evidence of scoliosis until growth is complete. A simple screening checklist has been developed by the Scoliosis Association to assist teachers and parents in checking students for possible signs of scoliosis (figure 9.17). Questions 9 and 10 require that the student assume the Adam's position with the legs straight, hips flexed, and arms hanging freely in line with the toes. This position enables the teacher to look down the student's back to check for symmetrical muscle development. Mandatory screening programs for scoliosis now exist in several states with other states utilizing a voluntary screening program.

Treatment consists of bracing and muscle reeducation. Among the commonly used orthopedic devices are corsets, adjustable frames, and casts. However, one of the most effective devices is the Milwaukee brace (shown in figure 8.31). Several studies of the effectiveness of the Milwaukee brace have been reported. Generally these studies suggest that the Milwaukee brace is effective in the treatment of scoliosis if the brace is applied early and for a long period of time, particularly with children who have a curve of less than thirty degrees. The value of prescriptive exercise, both in and out of the brace, has also been found important in the total treatment program (Nash, 1980).

As discussed in chapter 8, the Boston-Hall brace, a modular prefabricated plastic girdle, has also been widely used in the treatment of mild forms of scoliosis.

A new form of treatment for scoliosis, the electrical muscle stimulator, became available in 1983 following approval by the Food and Drug Administration. This technique, used with patients with moderate scoliosis, uses electrical stimulation to contract muscles near the spine several times a minute during the night while the patient sleeps. These muscles, located on the outer or convex side of the spinal curve, provide a counteracting force against other muscles that are pulling the spine out of line. Use of the electrical stimulator, similar to various braces that are used with scoliosis, must be continued until the patient reaches bone maturity.

Spinal curves that measure forty to forty-five degrees and greater may require surgery to prevent further curvature and related health problems. The most common surgical procedure involves attachment of a thin stainless steel rod to straighten the spine, along with fusion to hold the spine in a corrected position. The rod is referred to as the Harrington rod (figure 9.18) in honor of its inventor. The fusion of the

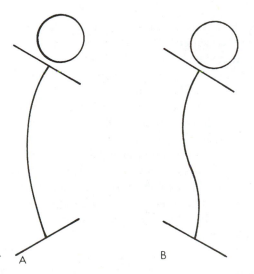

Figure 9.16 Diagrammatic illustration of the slant of shoulders and hips in scoliosis. (*A*) C Curve to left. (*B*) S curve to left.

	Yes	No	
1.	____	____	Is one shoulder higher than the other?
2.	____	____	Is one scapula (shoulder blade) more prominent than the other?
3.	____	____	Does one hip seem higher or more prominent than the other?
4.	____	____	Is there a greater distance between the arm and the body on one side than on the other, when the arms are hanging down loosely at the sides?
5.	____	____	Does the child have a "swayback" (lordosis)?
6.	____	____	Does the child have "round shoulders" or "humpback" (kyphosis)?
7.	____	____	Is there a larger "crease" at one side of the waist than at the other side?
8.	____	____	Does the child seem to "list" or lean to one side?
9.	____	____	Is there a hump in the rib area?
10.	____	____	Is there a hump in the lumbar region (near the waist)?

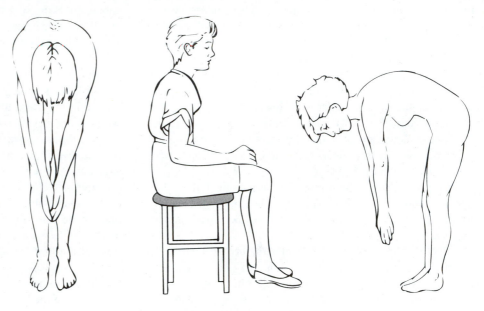

Figure 9.17 Simple test for early detection of scoliosis.

Forward bending position for screening

spine is achieved by grafting small strips of bone, usually taken from the pelvis, over the affected vertebrae.

Muscle reeducation is vitally important in the treatment of scoliosis. It is carried out only after careful examination by a doctor. Actual exercises, other than symmetrical (exercise of both sides; see chapter 28), should be under the supervision of medical personnel. Basically, the exercises consist of stretching the muscles that have pulled the spinal column into the curve and strengthening those muscles that straighten the column, along with general physical fitness exercises. Learning which muscles to contract and to relax to straighten the spine is effected through constant repetition of the use of those muscles. Appropriate exercises also contribute to the prevention of scoliosis. (For special exercises that help to strengthen muscles that maintain efficient posture, refer to chapter 28.)

Spondylitis and Spondylolisthesis

Spondylitis and spondylolisthesis are disorders of the spinal column. The latter is a deformity, usually inherited, in which a vertebra slips forward over another vertebra, usually the fourth or fifth (lumbar) vertebra. As a result, motion in bending forward is restricted and often painful. The pain may be aggravated by lordosis (swayback). Treatment consists of maintaining proper posture. In more advanced cases, surgery is usually performed to stabilize the joint.

Spondylitis is an inflammation of the vertebrae. It is almost always serious and is frequently associated with infectious diseases such as tuberculosis of the bone and brucellosis. The infection may destroy the affected vertebra, resulting in permanent stiffening of the back. Drugs are used to control the inflammation. If the cause is an infectious disease, the disease must be treated. Surgery is often used to fuse the affected vertebrae.

Arm Amputation

Arm amputation may occur at various levels (see figure 9.12). Causes of upper limb amputations are the same as those discussed earlier in this chapter under the heading *Leg Amputation*. The prosthesis of the individual with an arm

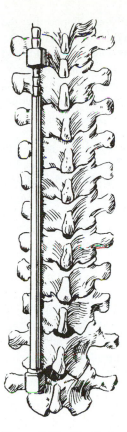

Figure 9.18 The Harrington rod in place.

(From Bleck and Nagel, *Physically Handicapped Children: A Medical Atlas for Teachers* (2d ed.) by Grune and Stratton. Reprinted by permission.)

amputation does not substitute as well as the prosthesis of the person with a leg amputation. It is almost impossible to develop a mechanical device that substitutes for the human hand and fingers in both function and appearance. Nevertheless, it is possible to achieve considerable dexterity with the utility arm and split hook in performing manual tasks, including racquet and paddle games in physical education.

The motor limitations of a person who has lost his or her arm(s) are obvious. However, a problem that is not readily apparent until the individual attempts certain kinds of activities is that of balance. Maintaining an erect position both in everyday activities and in games and sports is difficult because of the body imbalance created by the missing segment(s). Attempts to maintain proper balance in the erect position often result in lateral spinal curvature. In the water, the body imbalance creates difficulty in maintaining effective positions while performing the various strokes.

Suggested Activities

Physical education activities for those with orthopedic disorders that affect other body movements must be selected to meet the students' special needs and limitations, with consideration for their interests and movement potential.

Students with wryneck and scoliosis are usually not greatly restricted in movement. Those with wryneck are able to perform all activities except those that place an undue stress upon neck muscles. Some, because of spasms in the neck muscles or limited movement in the neck, cannot participate in the forward roll, the headstand, or similar activities.

Scoliosis does not interfere with the normal performance of motor activities unless there is extreme deformity. Locomotion may be affected to some degree, as may movements of the body that require extreme flexibility, such as tumbling. Activities that place undue stress on the spinal column, such as football, may be contraindicated.

Weight-lifting programs for those with scoliosis should be initiated only with the approval of the doctor. All exercise that affects the muscles on only one side of the spinal column should not be attempted without approval by the physician. Most symmetrical exercises can be participated in without adding further to the imbalance of the body. Chin-ups, passive hanging from a bar, and pushing or pulling equally with both hands are examples of suitable exercises.

Activities for those who have spondylitis should be suspended until the inflammation is brought under control. If there is no permanent damage to the spinal column, the student can resume normal activity. If damage does occur, the activities selected must not cause undue twisting or stress and strain on the spinal column. The congenital arm amputee or student who has had a single arm since early life usually has made sufficient motor adaptation by the time he or she reaches school and will require little assistance in making adaptations in motor skill performance. Students with a recent amputation, in contrast, will need to relearn some skills before they are able to participate in most activities. Also, they must adjust to their disability. Many individuals, after losing a limb, become self-conscious and tend to withdraw from activity. The physical education teacher can be of great assistance to such students by encouraging them to try the suggested modifications of the activities. When they find that they can perform many skills that they thought they could never engage in again, they are very likely to begin to accept their loss and adjust more successfully.

Those who have lost a single arm, if it is not the dominant arm, can play most basic skill games and participate in more advanced physical education activities without significant modifications, except in the technique of catching. If the dominant hand is lost, the student can learn to use the other hand. Performing the skill with this hand will at first seem awkward, but practice will overcome this. The development of arm dexterity should be initiated with simple throwing activities such as throwing beanbags or darts at a target. Devices can be specially built by an orthotist to fit into the arm prosthesis for the purpose of holding sports equipment such as gloves. Students having difficulty in learning to catch with one hand may wish to have such a device made. How to catch a ball with a glove and one arm is described in chapter 25, in the section on softball.

Most racquet games are not affected by single-arm amputation. In the case of the double arm amputee with sufficient stump, a paddle or racquet can be attached to the stump to enable play of many racquet games (chapter 24). Swimming, as mentioned previously, is a good activity for single or double amputees and others with orthopedic disorders affecting body movement.

Of course, students who have use of their feet can participate in activities that chiefly require foot action, such as soccer, goal kicking, and various running events.

It is possible for the student with double-arm amputation to play volleyball by using parts of the body to play the ball; the head and knee are the most effective for this.

Soccer handball, a game developed at the University of Connecticut for those with limited use of their arms, can be played by participants who have upper-limb involvement in both arms. It is played in a handball court with a soccer ball. The ball is kicked against the wall. The serve, to be good, must be kicked against the front wall and must return behind the service line. The ball is allowed to bounce once. It may hit any wall or combination of walls and remain in play. The ball may be played with any part of the body.

Thermal Injuries

Two million people sustain burn injuries each year; 100,000 seriously enough to require hospitalization. The exact number of children who are affected by a serious or life-threatening thermal injury each year is difficult to estimate but is not insignificant. The effect of a thermal injury can be devastating, including the loss of an extremity, disfigurement, and severe contractures.

Burns may be caused by several things including fires, chemicals, and scalding from extremely hot water. Recent efforts to treat burns and other thermal injuries have been so successful that today many individuals survive what were life-ending injuries a few years ago. This means that educators, including physical educators, must be sensitive to this disability population and specific instructional needs they may require.

Rehabilitation for the burn victim begins the first day after the accident. One of the primary goals of treatment is to maintain joint motion and to avoid, where possible, contractures. Deformities caused by contractures can be prevented or minimized by proper positioning of the patient both in bed and in a chair, appropriate splinting and bracing, performing selected exercises, and participating in a general conditioning program.

Active, passive, and resistive exercises of both the burned and unburned area should be performed frequently. The purpose of the exercise program is to:

1. Prevent or minimize functional and cosmetic deformities.
2. Prevent deconditioning.
3. Prevent complications of prolonged bed rest and immobilization.
4. Enhance the individuals's self-worth and confidence by preserving the ability to perform activities of daily living.

These programs, while normally developed by the physical therapist, can be implemented by the physical educator in consultation with the medical team. In addition, rehabilitation specialists recommend that burn victims participate in a program of fitness and conditioning activities as soon as possible. This is done to ensure that the individual maintains an appropriate level of fitness and to emphasize a positive outlook toward an active life.

The child with a thermal injury should be encouraged to return to school as soon as possible. The physical education program for the youngster should be similar to that of any other youngster, with modifications as necessary. Because the child may be wearing a splint or brace, the physical educator may need to assist the child in removing, cleaning, and reapplying the device. Some children may wear a jobst, an elastic support made to fit a particular area of the body. The jobst applies pressure to the burned area to help minimize the amount of scarring.

Physical education teachers will need to be sensitive to the burn-injured child's reaction to sun and to chlorine in swimming pools. Normally, activities in the pool and in sunlight are not contraindicated but consultation with the youngster's physician may be appropriate.

Summary

Significant strides have been made in the past twenty-five years in the treatment and rehabilitation of individuals with orthopedic impairments. Injuries that only a few years ago would have resulted in certain death are now treatable. This has created opportunities and challenges for medical personnel, including therapists, to develop effective treatment programs. Contrary to past practice, effective treatment requires that all aspects of the individual's life be considered, including school for children and adolescents. In addition, greater attention is now paid to the quality of the individual's life, including his or her level of fitness. Recent studies have indicated, for example, that the fitness levels of individuals in wheelchairs are lower than expected but that training programs can be effective in increasing important variables such as oxygen consumption.

The implications, therefore, for physical educators are clear. Programs should be developed that contribute to functional health and fitness. The medium through which this may be accomplished includes all of the activities commonly engaged in by individuals without disabilities. Modifications can be made, where necessary, to accommodate the individual with orthopedic impairment in regular physical education classes. Separate classes may be scheduled as appropriate to accommodate any special activity needs that may exist.

The athletic accomplishments of some athletes with orthopedic impairments have helped to dispel the myth that those with spinal cord injuries and other bone and joint disorders are incapable of high performance levels. Those with orthopedic impairments, similar to the nondisabled, enjoy and benefit from participation in physical activity. While the activity may initially be therapeutic in nature (e.g., increasing the range of motion for a severely burned individual), the ultimate goal is to contribute to and enhance the quality of life.

Selected Readings

Adams, R.C., & McCubbin, J.A. (1991). *Games, sports, and exercises for the physically disabled* (4th ed.). Philadelphia: Lea and Febiger.

Anderson, E.M., & Spain, B. (1977). *The child with spina bifida*. London: Methuen and Co., Ltd.

Bartshaw, M.L., & Perret, Y.M. (1986). *Children with handicaps: A medical primer* (2d ed.). Baltimore: Paul H. Brookes Pub. Co.

Bigge, J., & O'Donnell, P.A. (1976). *Teaching individuals with physical and multiple disabilities*. Columbus, OH: Charles E. Merrill Publishing Co.

Bleck, E.E., & Nagel, D.A. (1982). *Physically handicapped children: A medical atlas for teachers* (2d ed.). New York: Grune and Stratton.

Brewer, E.J., Jr. (1970). *Juvenile rheumatoid arthritis*. Philadelphia: W.B. Saunders Co.

Cratty, B.J. (1976). *Developmental games for physically handicapped children*. Palo Alto, CA: Peek Publications.

Cratty, B.J. (1989). *Adapted physical education for handicapped children and youth* (2nd ed.). Denver: Love Publishing Co.

Coutts, K., McKenzie, D., Loock, C., Beauchamp, R., & Armstrong, R. (1993). Upper body exercise capacity in youth with spina bifida. *Adapted Physical Activity Quarterly, 10,* 22–28.

Davis, G.M. (1993). Exercise capacity of individuals with paraplegia. *Medicine and Science in Sports and Exercise, 25*(4): 423–432.

Davis, G., & Glaser, R. (1990). Cardiorespiratory fitness following spinal cord injury. In L. Ada and C. Canning (Eds.), *Key issues in neurological physiotherapy* (pp. 155–196), London: Butterworth and Heinemann.

Dibner, S., & Dibner, A. (1973). *Integration or segregation for the physically handicapped child*. Springfield, IL: Charles C. Thomas.

Freeman, J.M. (Ed.). (1974). *Practical management to meningomyelocele*. Baltimore: University Park Press.

Garwood, G.S. (1979). *Educating young handicapped children: A developmental approach*. Germantown, MD: Aspen Systems Corporation.

Glaser, R.M. (1989). Arm exercise training for wheelchair users. *Medicine and Science in Sports and Exercise, 21,* 5149–5157.

Holmes, L.B., Driscoll, S.G., & Alkins, L. (1976). Etiologic heterogeneity of neural-tube defects. *New England Journal of Medicine, 29,* 365.

Jeffrey, D.L. (1986). The hazards of reduced mobility for the persons with a spinal cord injury. *Journal of Rehabilitation, 52,* 59–62.

Lockette, K.F., & Keyes, A.M. (1994). *Conditioning with physical disabilities*. Champaign, IL: Human Kinetics Publishers.

Michael, J.W. (1989). New developments in prosthetic feet for sports and recreation. *Palaestra, 5*(2), 21–22; 32–35.

Nash, C.L., Jr. (1980). Current concepts review scoliosis bracing. *The Journal of Bone and Joint Surgery, 62A,* 848–852.

Nicosia, J.E., & Petro, J.A. (1983). *Manual of burn care*. New York: Raven Press.

Sawisch, L. (1990). Strategic positioning in the disabled sports community: A perspective from the new kids on the block. *Palaestra, 6*(5), 52–54.

Schaller, J., & Wedgewood, R.J. (1972). Juvenile rheumatoid arthritis, a review. *Pediatrics, 50*(9), 40–53.

Shepard, R.J. (1990). *Fitness in special populations*. Champaign, IL: Human Kinetics Publishers.

Sherrill, C. (1993). *Adapted physical activity, recreation and sport* (4th ed.). Dubuque, IA: Wm. C. Brown Publishers.

Scoliosis. (1979). New York: The Scoliosis Association, Inc.

Taylor, H., Haskell, S.H., & Barret, E.K. (1977). *The education of motor and neurologically handicapped children*. New York: John Wiley and Sons, Inc.

Tecklin, J.S. (1989). *Pediatric physical therapy*. Philadelphia: J.B. Lippincott.

Williamson, G.G. (Ed.). (1987). *Children with spina bifida*. Baltimore: Paul H. Brookes Publishing Co.

Enhancing Activities

1. Draw a diagram of the spinal column and the nerves emanating from the column. Label the nerves and the area of the musculature that the nerves innervate.

2. Obtain permission to observe and assist a parent or teacher in helping a child who uses a catheter.

3. Attend an athletic event such as a track and field meet for athletes with spinal cord injury and note the various techniques used by individuals with different levels of spinal cord injury.

4. Volunteer to serve as a helper in a school district conducting a school-wide screening for spinal deviations or, with the assistance of your teacher and classmates, organize and conduct a scoliosis screening for a local school.

5. Visit the orthopedic section of the local hospital and observe the treatment and rehabilitation programs conducted by various professionals.

6. Compare and contrast the resting and exercise heart rate of an individual with orthopedic impairment (e.g., one with a spinal cord injury) to that of a person with no disabilities. Discuss the findings with your professor and/or an exercise physiologist.

7. Develop a short survey of selected questions related to physical education and activity programs and ask students with and without orthopedic impairments to respond. Questions such as, "How often do you exercise?" "Where do you exercise?" and "Why do you/do you not exercise?" will generate some interesting observations.

CHAPTER 10

Cerebral Palsy

◆ **CHAPTER OBJECTIVES** ◆

After studying this chapter, the reader should be able to:

1 Recognize the various types of cerebral palsy and their characteristics.

2 Understand the importance of the primary reflexes and the role that they play in controlling and/or inhibiting the movement of the individual with cerebral palsy.

3 Identify various treatments for cerebral palsy, including physical therapy and orthopedic surgery.

4 Appreciate the importance and limitations of physical therapy in the treatment of cerebral palsy.

5 List and discuss the secondary disabilities, such as epilepsy and mental retardation, that sometimes accompany cerebral palsy.

6 Recognize and discuss important objectives and features in developing a physical activity program for individuals with cerebral palsy.

7 Analyze activities and their appropriateness for the student with cerebral palsy.

8 Appreciate the importance of the psychosocial aspect of physical activity to the overall development of the student with cerebral palsy.

9 Understand the physical and motor characteristics of cerebral palsy and the importance of physical activity, body-image activities, breathing exercises, and physical fitness to the development of the student with cerebral palsy.

Based on what we know today about the causes and prevalence of cerebral palsy, it would be safe to say that this condition has probably affected people for many centuries. However, until relatively recently, cerebral palsy has received little significant attention from those in medicine, education, or the social services. The great strides of medical science over the past century have been largely responsible for stimulating attention to and concern about those with cerebral palsy.

W.J. Little, an English orthopedic surgeon, is credited with being the first physician to document and analyze the condition of cerebral palsy. His published reports on sixty-three children, describing the manifestations of their condition, appeared in the early 1860s, and the disorder became known as Little's disease. The term was changed to spastic paralysis in the 1930s and finally to cerebral palsy in the 1940s.

In spite of improved medical treatment, those with cerebral palsy face many difficulties. Lack of public understanding of the condition hinders opportunities for personal development. Because of the distortion of speech and facial expressions, the disorder may cause many misconceptions and stigmas to become attached to the affected individual, producing social isolation. Other physical manifestations of the various cerebral palsy conditions may make movement difficult, giving rise to problems in performing motor skills including the activities of daily living.

Through the efforts of such groups as The United Cerebral Palsy Association, the educational, occupational, and social opportunities for persons with cerebral palsy are continually improving. The extent to which individuals with cerebral palsy can avail themselves of these new opportunities will depend, in part, on the amount of independence they can attain in their motor behavior. It is in the achievement of this objective that the physical educator's expertise is needed.

The Nature and Causes of Cerebral Palsy

Cerebral palsy is a condition resulting from brain damage that is manifested by various types of neuromuscular disabilities. These disabilities are characterized by the dysfunction of voluntary motor control. The lesion causing the brain damage is found in the upper motor neurons of the cerebrum and brain stem, thus affecting the functions of the central nervous system.

To date, cerebral palsy is incurable. However, the condition is amenable to therapy and training, and the motor functions of those with this impairment can be improved. In addition, cerebral palsy is nonprogressive; that is, the extent of the lesion will not increase, so the condition will not worsen or result in death. A major characteristic of this condition is that it interferes with the development of the central nervous system. The degree of this interference is related to the extent of the lesion and the age at which it occurs. Generally, the earlier the occurrence, the more extensive will be the interference. Thus, because approximately 90 percent of all those affected contract cerebral palsy early, either at birth or during the prenatal period, many of those with cerebral palsy have multiple disabilities.

Cerebral palsy may be incurred before or during birth or at any time in later life. Approximately 30 percent of all cerebral palsy cases have a prenatal cause, while 60 percent have a natal cause and 10 percent a postnatal cause. Major causes of cerebral palsy before birth are maternal infection such as rubella (German or three-day measles), metabolic malfunctions, toxemia (toxic products in the blood), or anoxia (deficiency of oxygen). During the birth process cerebral palsy is usually caused by anoxia or trauma to the head. Postnatal occurrences are caused chiefly by severe head injuries or infections such as encephalitis (inflammation of the brain) or meningitis (inflammation of the covering of the brain and spinal cord).

Estimates of the incidence of cerebral palsy range from .6 to 2.4 cases per 1,000 births and vary little across industrialized countries (Paneth and Kiely, 1984). Cerebral palsy does not appear to be related in any way to socioeconomic structures; however, it is more prevalent among Caucasians, the firstborn and males. Of those affected, about 10 percent will be so severely disabled that they will require intensive care for the rest of their lives. The remaining 90 percent can be found in various educational settings, ranging from regular public school classes to special education classes.

Types of Cerebral Palsy Conditions

There are five major types of conditions: (1) spasticity, (2) athetosis, (3) ataxia, (4) rigidity, and (5) tremor. Various combinations of these conditions can be found in many cases. Physical education instructors should know the manifestations of each condition so that they can better understand the effect each type has upon the movement capabilities of the individual with cerebral palsy.

Spasticity

Spasticity results from a lesion in the motor cortex. The motor cortex is the area in the central nervous system composed of motor neurons grouped together to form tracts. These tracts originate in the upper central portion of the cerebrum and proceed downward through the brain into the spinal column. It is in this area that voluntary motor actions originate. Because the damage is to the motor cortex or to the pyramidal tract of the brain, some authorities use the term pyramidal cerebral palsy rather than the expression spastic cerebral palsy (Kurtz, 1992).

Spasticity is the most prevalent type of cerebral palsy, occurring in 50 to 60 percent of all cases. It is characterized by a persistent and increased hypertensity of muscle tone.

The continuous hypertensity results in contractures (abnormal shortening) of the affected muscles, usually leading to postural deviations.

Voluntary control of movements in the affected limbs is limited for the person with spasticity. Movement is usually restricted, jerky, and uncertain. Inconsistent control of movements is also present. On any given occasion, a movement may be very slow and deliberate or very explosive. In addition, the individual with spasticity tends to respond to the slightest stimulation, be it visual, verbal, or tactile, with a muscular reaction.

Another common characteristic of the individual with spasticity is a hyperactive stretch reflex. The stretch reflex, which is monosynaptic (passing through a single nerve junction), serves as a protective agent for the skeletal muscles. When a muscle is stretched too quickly, the reflex causes the antagonist muscles to contract to prevent the stretching muscle from being injured by a violent overstretch. This reflex is elicited by muscle spindles located throughout the skeletal muscles. The proper stimulation of these spindles is controlled by various motor centers in the brain.

When the normal neurologic controls of a healthy muscle are greatly reduced, the stretch reflex is disturbed both in timing and in strength. Any sudden stretch will result in a strong contraction. A frequent result of the hyperactive stretch reflex is a sudden contraction followed by repeated jerks. This reaction is known as clonus.

Spasticity tends to affect the flexor muscle groups; thus, the maintenance of proper posture becomes very difficult. In addition, the individual with spasticity may have pathological reflex problems that also affect movement ability. If the lower limbs are spastic, they may be rotated inward and flexed at the hip joint, and the knees may be flexed and adducted, while the heels are lifted from the ground. These characteristics force a crossing of the legs through the midline during the walking gait, producing a scissors-type movement called the scissors gait (figure 10.1). When the upper limbs are involved, the person may have pronated forearms with flexion at the elbows, wrists, and fingers (figure 10.2). Mental impairment is more frequently associated with spasticity than with any other type of cerebral palsy.

Athetosis

Athetosis is caused by a lesion in the area of the basal ganglia called the globus pallidus. This area is composed of large masses of neurons located deep within the center of the cerebrum. It is this part of the brain that controls purposeful movement. Because the damage to the brain occurs outside of the pyramidal tract, the athetoid type of cerebral palsy is sometimes referred to as extrapyramidal.

Athetosis, the second most prevalent type, is seen in approximately 30 percent of all individuals with cerebral palsy. The condition is characterized by constant involuntary movements that are uncontrollable, unpredictable, and purposeless. At times the movements are slow and rhythmical, whereas on other occasions they are jerky and fast. In addition, the athetoid individual is hampered by a problem known as overflow. This is manifested by extraneous movements that accompany voluntary motion. The combination of overflow and involuntary movement produces a situation in which the body position is constantly in a stage of change.

The muscles of the head and upper limbs are commonly affected. Frequently seen movements of the upper limbs

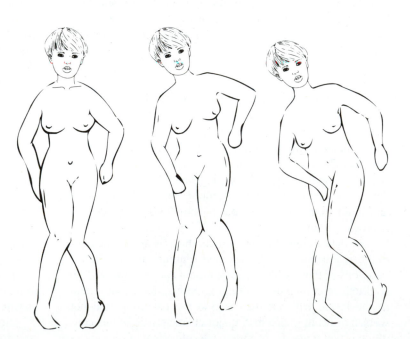

Figure 10.1 Typical scissors gait of individual with cerebral palsy.

(Redrawn from Ducroquet, R., Ducroquet, J., and Ducroquet, P.: *Walking and Limping.* Philadelphia, Lippincott, 1968.)

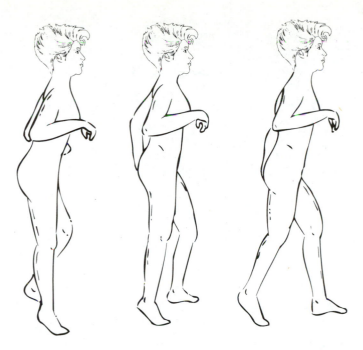

Figure 10.2 Typical walking pattern of individual with spastic hemiplegia.

(Redrawn from Ducroquet, R., Ducroquet, J., and Ducroquet, P.: *Walking and Limping.* Philadelphia, Lippincott, 1968.)

include constant flexion and extension of the fingers, wrists, and elbows, plus the drawing of the arms backward while palms are held downward. Lack of head control is a major problem. In many cases the head is continually drawn back and the face turned to one side. Accompanying this are facial contortions in which the mouth is frequently open; this produces drooling and makes eating and speaking very difficult. Other individuals may be affected by inward rotation of their feet.

There are several clinical types of athetosis, the most common characterized by rotary movements. The amount of athetoid-type movements is reduced when the person is relaxed and calm and increased when the person is nervous and tense. Athetosis is not commonly characterized by mental retardation.

Ataxia

A third type of cerebral palsy, ataxia, is the result of a lesion in the cerebellum, the area located below the cerebrum and posterior to the brain stem. The cerebellum acts as the feedback mechanism of the brain and organizes the information to coordinate muscular functions.

The major manifestations of ataxia are a reduced sense of balance, which results in frequent falls, and a reduced sense of kinesthesis, which produces uncoordinated movements. Examples of ataxic problems are inconsistent foot placement in locomotion, overshooting when reaching for objects, and a general loss of manual dexterity. The person with ataxia usually exhibits a very awkward gait.

Although this is the third-most common type of cerebral palsy, ataxia accounts for less than 10 percent of the cases. The condition is usually acquired rather than congenital.

Rigidity

Rigidity is the most severe type of cerebral palsy, accounting for 2 to 5 percent of cases. It is characterized by hypertensity of both agonist and antagonist muscles, making movement very difficult. Because of the relative absence of the stretch reflex, hyperextension of body parts is common.

The muscles of the affected limbs usually atrophy, and postural defects are present. Rigidity is a result of a diffused brain lesion that affects both the motor cortex and the basal ganglia. Severe mental retardation is usually present.

Tremor

Of the five major types of cerebral palsy, tremor occurs least frequently. It results in uncontrolled, involuntary, rhythmic motions. The motions may appear only upon attempting movement, or they may be present at all times. This condition can be caused by a lesion of the cerebellum or basal ganglia.

If the damage is to the cerebellum, the tremor is usually manifested in the arms. The tremor is accentuated during movement and reaches its peak as the body part approaches the end of the movement. If the basal ganglia is damaged, the symptoms are less severe and may disappear during sleep or relaxation. The cranial and digital muscles are the most affected.

Mixed Type

In some individuals it is apparent that more than one type of cerebral palsy is evident. In these cases the term *mixed type* is used. Although not a pure form of cerebral palsy, the term is applied as a classification term when more than one type is prevalent and no single type predominates. Those with the most frequent combination of types of cerebral palsy exhibit both tenseness of movement associated with the spastic type and lack of control associated with the athetotic type. Obviously, the student with the mixed type of cerebral palsy experiences significant problems with motor control. Although it is generally recognized that the frequency of the mixed type of cerebral palsy is small, studies suggest that the percentage is higher than previously thought.

Major Reflex Problems

Many of the movement problems of persons with cerebral palsy are reflexive in nature. These movements depend solely upon the proper stimulus and cannot be controlled. All individuals are born with certain reflex patterns which are the foundations upon which motor behavior is developed (discussed in chapter 2). These reflexes are present within the first few months of life and then are suppressed by higher brain centers as the infant develops control of its movements. In many persons with cerebral palsy, several reflex patterns persist for a longer-than-normal period and, in effect, retard motor development. Winnick and Short (1985) explain the importance of this information: "If reflexes, when elicited, are uneven in strength, too weak or too strong, or inappropriate at a particular age, neurological dysfunction may be suspected. Various reflexive behaviors are quite predictable and are expected to appear at particular ages and to be inhibited, disappear, or be replaced by higher order reflexes at later ages. Failure of certain reflexes to disappear, be inhibited, or be replaced may inhibit the development of voluntary movement" (1985, p. 50). There are three reflexes—the asymmetrical tonic neck reflex, the tonic labyrinthine reflex, and the positive support reflex—that significantly affect the posture and movement of the child with cerebral palsy (figure 10.3).

The asymmetrical tonic neck reflex (ATNR), stimulated by the active or passive rotation of the head, causes an increase in extension in the arm and leg on the same side as the chin while the opposite arm and leg increase in flexion. The presence of the ATNR causes an increase in muscle tone and may bring about a change in position as well. The presence of this reflex inhibits the child's ability to control the arm and interferes with early efforts to crawl and sit without support.

The tonic labyrinthine reflex is initiated when the head is moved. Flexion of the head causes extension in the legs, whereas extension of the head is accompanied by flexion of the legs. In some instances the reflex is not strong and

Full-term infant resting position   Asymmetrical tonic neck reflex

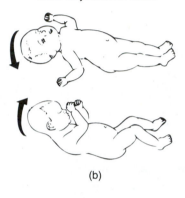

(a)

Tonic labyrinnthine reflex

(b)

Positive support reflex

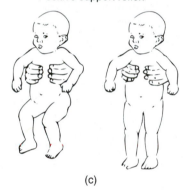

(c)

Figure 10.3 (*a*) The asymmetrical tonic neck reflex, or fencer's response. As the head is turned, the arm and leg on the same side as the chin extend, and the other arm and leg flex. (*b*) In the tonic labyrinthine reflex, extension of the head backward leads to retraction of the shoulders and extension of the legs. The opposite occurs if the head is flexed forward. (*c*) The positive support reflex. As the baby is bounced, his legs straighten to support his weight.

(Printed with permission of the authors: Mark L. Batshaw, MD and Yvonne M. Perret, MSW. *Children with Handicaps: A Medical Primer,* 2d edition. Baltimore: Paul H. Brookes Publishing Co., 1986.)

changes in muscle tone may occur without any changes in the position of the limbs. The presence of the tonic labyrinthine reflex creates major challenges in the infant's ability to sit independently. Movement of the head causes postural responses that are difficult to control (Batshaw and Perret, 1986).

With the positive support reflex, the infant extends the legs when the balls of the feet come in contact with a surface. For the child with cerebral palsy, the extension of the legs leads to a rigid position of the legs accompanied by adduction and internal rotation of the hips. Unfortunately this response interferes with rather than helps with walking and standing.

Topographical Classification

Cerebral palsy affects different parts of the body. To describe the portion involved, the topographical classification utilized for paralysis of the body due to any cause may be applied. The classification is as follows:

1. Monoplegia: only one limb is involved.
2. Paraplegia: only the legs are involved.
3. Diplegia: primarily, legs are involved; arms are slightly affected.
4. Hemiplegia: limbs on one side of the body are involved.
5. Triplegia: three limbs are involved, usually the legs and one arm.
6. Quadriplegia: all four limbs are involved.

Quadriplegia is more frequently found in athetotic cerebral palsy; the other types occur more often in the spastic condition. Spastic hemiplegia is the most common involvement (see figure 10.2). In figure 10.4, the topographical classification system and its relationship to the area of the brain affected is presented.

Treatment

Treatment to help alleviate the motor dysfunction of cerebral palsy is conducted primarily by physicians and physical therapists. It is upon the ability level developed through the treatment that the physical educator will attempt to build motor patterns to be utilized in play, leisure, and health related activities. Some understanding of the medical treatment and of the techniques utilized by the physical therapist in the muscular treatment of cerebral palsy is important to physical educators because such knowledge enables them to plan a better program of supplementary skills.

Medical Treatment

Medical treatment for the motor dysfunction of cerebral palsy is conducted by orthopedic surgeons and, when applied, usually involves bracing or surgery, or both. Over the past quarter century, physicians have become more conservative in their treatment, and the use of these medical procedures has greatly decreased.

When bracing is used it is almost exclusively done with the lower limbs. There are two major objectives in the use of braces: (1) to keep spastic muscles stretched to prevent contractures and structural deviations, and (2) to give support to weak muscles. A person wearing a brace should in most instances keep the brace on during physical education (swimming not included); however, it is advisable to check with the physician.

The objectives in performing surgery fall into three categories: (1) as a cosmetic procedure to improve the appearance of the individual, (2) to reduce contractures and prevent structural deviations, and (3) to improve the performance of a movement pattern. The procedure will involve muscle transfers, tendon lengthenings, or neurectomies (severing of nerves). Surgery is usually performed on young children and is done only if a thorough evaluation suggests a reasonable amount of improvement can be expected.

Many surgical procedures involve improving the function of the lower limbs. There are three common procedures

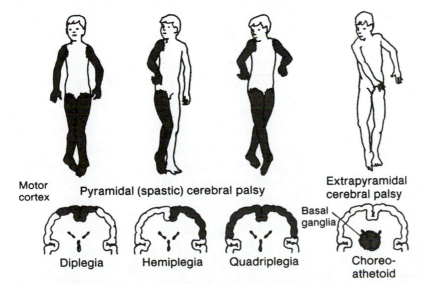

Motor cortex

Pyramidal (spastic) cerebral palsy

Extrapyramidal cerebral palsy

Diplegia   Hemiplegia   Quadriplegia

Basal ganglia

Choreo-athetoid

Figure 10.4   Different regions of the brain are affected in various forms of cerebral palsy.

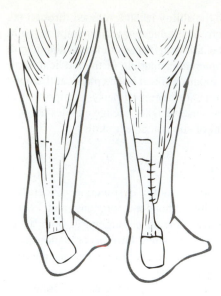

Figure 10.5 The Achilles tendon is lengthened by surgically removing some of it. Approximately six weeks after lengthening, the gap between the tendon ends is filled with new tendon tissue.

(Adapted from Bleck, Eugene E., and Nagel, Donald A.: *Physically Handicapped Children: A Medical Atlas for Teachers,* 2d ed. New York, Grune and Stratton, 1982.)

utilized in this area: (1) lengthening of the Achilles tendon to allow the heel to rest on the ground (figure 10.5); (2) the Eggars' procedure, which involves transferring the insertion of the hamstrings to the femur to reduce the flexion deformity of the knee and to help extend the hip; and (3) the Sharrod procedure, which involves transferring the insertion of the iliopsoas (muscle of the thigh) through a hole in the ilium (hip bone) to the greater trochanter of the femur, a point near the head of the upper leg, for the purpose of improving abduction at the hip joint. When instructing students who have had these operations, the physical educator should consult with the physician to develop a thorough understanding of the movement potentials and limitations of the body parts involved.

Individuals with cerebral palsy must have sufficient strength and endurance to perform the functional skills of daily living as well as participate in recreational sport activities (Fernandez, Pitetti, and Betzen, 1990). Although most of the concepts used in strength-development programs for the nondisabled can be applied to programs for individuals with cerebral palsy, there are some unique characteristics of cerebral palsy that require careful attention. Some guidelines are suggested below:

1. Strive for muscle balance. Because many individuals with cerebral palsy have overdeveloped flexors in relation to extensors, normally the program for the student with cerebral palsy should be developed to strengthen the muscle extensors. The goal is to achieve as much balance as possible between muscle groups.

2. Emphasize range of motion. Programs designed to improve muscle strength and endurance will be successful if efforts to improve the range of motion in a particular joint are also emphasized. This means that stretching activities should be included in the strength-development program.

3. The type of resistance utilized may affect development. A resistance training program, when properly applied, can improve the strength of the extensor muscle while helping to normalize the tone in the opposing muscle group through reciprocal inhibition. In general, isokinetic exercises that hold constant the speed and resistance applied to the muscle are preferred over isotonic exercises. However, isotonic exercises in which the muscle is moved through a range of motion at a variable speed and resistance (the use of barbells, for example) have been found as effective as isokinetic exercises in subjects with nonhandicapping conditions (Sanders, 1980). Equipment used in isotonic training is also more readily available than that used in isokinetic programs. McCubbin and Horvat (1990) provide guidelines for resistance exercise training for persons with cerebral palsy.

4. Progression is important. In initiating a strength-development program, it is important that the program be individualized. This means that the amount of weight and type of exercises selected should be appropriate to the youngster. It is also essential that light weights be selected initially and that the focus be on executing the exercises slowly and correctly. Adequate time must be allowed before and after the strength program to allow for stretching exercises. The length and intensity of the program should also be modified for the individual with cerebral palsy. The amount of energy expended by some students with cerebral palsy in performing an exercise contrasted to that of the nondisabled is much greater (Rose et al., 1990).

5. The position of the individual is important. Because of the difficulties some individuals with cerebral palsy have counteracting the forces of gravity, it may be advisable for the individual to perform the weight exercises in a seated or supine position. The role of the uninhibited reflexes and their effect on movement must be considered in selecting the best position.

6. Explain the movement pattern. As the youngster engages in different weight-training exercises, explain what is happening to the muscles and joints and the sensations the individual should be experiencing. Many individuals with cerebral palsy have a difficult time differentiating a normal from an abnormal movement sensation.

7. Recognize unique needs. For some students with cerebral palsy, participation in an active weight-resistance training program may not be possible.

A passive exercise program in which the various joints and muscles are moved with the assistance of an aid or therapist may be necessary. Overcoming gravity or working on moving from one side to the other side may be the appropriate and necessary level of strength development for some students. The use of isometric exercises in which the child lifts and holds the head off of a mat for a few seconds is effective in enhancing the functional levels of strength for a youngster with more severe disabilities.

An excellent example of a progressive-resistance training program for an individual with spastic cerebral palsy has been reported by Horvat (1987). The program used both free weights and weight machines to perform a variety of exercises. Initial weights were set at 30 percent of body weight to allow the subject to complete at least ten repetitions of each exercise. Prior to each session, fifteen minutes were devoted to stretching various muscle groups. As a result of the eight-week training program, improvement was found in strength, endurance, and range of motion on both sides of the body. The program demonstrated that a common-sense approach to training in which stretching, low amounts of weight, and a high number of repetitions are combined can produce desirable outcomes.

Exercises and activities to increase flexibility should be an essential aspect of the physical fitness program for individuals with cerebral palsy. As previously described, these youngsters experience contractures, which limits their range of motion. The lack of flexibility affects overall physical performance.

Generally, activities to improve flexibility should be scheduled daily with the length of time devoted each day to flexibility exercises dependent upon the individual's needs. A particular stretch may be held from a minimum of six seconds to several minutes. In severe cases it may be necessary to use weight or temporary braces to assist the individual with selected stretches. In cases where outside forces are needed, consultation with a physician or therapist is recommended. The goal of the stretching program is to teach appropriate flexibility exercises and to encourage individuals to incorporate the program into their daily activities. Self-monitored programs will help to ensure that these needed but time-consuming exercises are performed daily but not to the detriment of other important aspects of the physical education program.

The type of stretching that is recommended for individuals with cerebral palsy is static rather than ballistic stretching. In static stretching the movements are slow and deliberate with the muscles stretched to the point of discomfort but ordinarily not to exceed 10 percent overstretch.

Physical Therapy

Without question, physical therapy is the primary source of movement education for the individual with cerebral palsy.

There are many different theories and methods employed, but in a generic sense they can be divided into those methods developed to treat spasticity and those developed to treat athetosis. Today, many physical therapists do not adhere to a pure system, but use procedures from various methods in order to accomplish their objectives. Physical educators working with students who have cerebral palsy should become familiar with current procedures.

For athetosis, it is recommended that the procedures of conductive education (Cotton and Parnwell, 1967) and sensory training be investigated (Harris, 1971); for spasticity, sensory stimulation (Rood, 1954), and neurodevelopmental treatment (Bobath, 1959) should be reviewed.

Until the 1970s, many physical therapists followed what has become known as the traditional approach in the treatment of spasticity. In this approach, spastic cerebral palsy was viewed as predominantly a muscular problem that manifested itself in the muscle imbalance of opposing groups. Treatment involved the following: (1) conscious relaxation of spastic muscles, (2) passive stretching of spastic muscles, (3) strength-building exercises for the antagonistic muscles, and (4) motor-pattern training for afflicted segments. Now that the neurological basis of cerebral palsy has become known, new therapeutic treatment methods have been developed.

Of the new methods developed, the one originated by Karl and Bertha Bobath (1959) will be of the most interest to physical educators. Not only does their description of the method explain the neurological basis of the cerebral palsy condition but it also provides a very good explanation of motor development during infancy (Bobath, 1971; Bobath and Bobath, 1975).

The Bobaths view cerebral palsy as a neurological problem and the spastic condition as one that produces a retardation of normal development with a retention of primitive motor behavior along with the manifestation of abnormal motor patterns. The Bobaths believe a person with spastic cerebral palsy should be helped to attain proper postures in order to develop more efficient movement. They recommend that the individual start receiving treatment in the first few months of life and that this training be continued until adolescence. Their treatment involves reducing the effects of the pathological reflexes by manipulation and proper positioning, followed by teaching motor patterns for everyday life and self-help.

Frost (1972) contends that no treatment has been developed that can totally alleviate the problems of spasticity. Thus, he believes that, although motor training for individuals with this condition is important, the primary goal in the treatment and education of individuals with spastic cerebral palsy should be the development of the total person. Physical education can definitely contribute to this goal by offering quality programs to help the child with spasticity to develop motor patterns that can be used in play and leisure activities. Bleck and Nagel (1982) caution that therapy should not be viewed as a magical method for overcoming a permanent motor disorder. They add that "Passive 'hands-on' therapy in cerebral palsy has not been effective and has been given up in favor of active programs that emphasize functions, fun, games, and sports for the school aged child" (1982, p. 81). In this light they recommend that the expertise of therapists be used as consultants in developing and modifying motor programs.

Medications are sometimes prescribed in the treatment of cerebral palsy. Valium and Dantrium are the two most commonly used drugs. Valium affects both the muscle fibers and the central nervous system to decrease tone. Dantrium acts on the muscle fibers and the neuromuscular junction to reduce spasticity. Young and Delwaid (1981) report that about half of the children they studied who were taking Dantrium showed modest improvement. Because of the side effects (drooling, drowsiness) associated with these medications they are used cautiously.

Physical therapists recognize that sustaining the interest of the child with cerebral palsy in therapy can be very challenging. In an attempt to address this need, various therapeutic methods and approaches have been developed, including the use of horseback riding as a therapeutic modality. In this approach the horse is used as a treatment modality similar to the use of therapy balls and other equipment found in pediatric physical therapy clinics. The goal is to facilitate particular postural responses by placing the rider in various positions on the horse such as prone, side lying, side sitting or sitting (figure 10.6). The horse is usually led at a walking pace by a therapist, who is a skilled rider. Frequently the therapist rides behind the child to ensure that proper positioning and desired responses are facilitated.

Although the scientific support for therapeutic horseback riding as a treatment modality is limited, Bertoti (1988) reported significant improvements in postural control of children with cerebral palsy following participation in a therapeutic horseback riding program. Clinical improvements were noted also in muscle tone and balance as evidenced by improved functional skills.

The treatment of cerebral palsy with biofeedback has generated some interest. In this approach, through the placement of surface electrodes over groups of muscles, the individual is provided information about the electrical patterns of normal and abnormal muscle contractions. The goal is to help the individual recognize muscle contractions and gain control over selected movements. Although some success has been achieved with biofeedback, the application of the technique is limited to the treatment of single muscle groups. For example, helping an individual to relax the jaw muscles, allowing the mouth to close. The technique does not appear practical when several muscle groups are involved. Thus its usefulness in the treatment of cerebral palsy is limited.

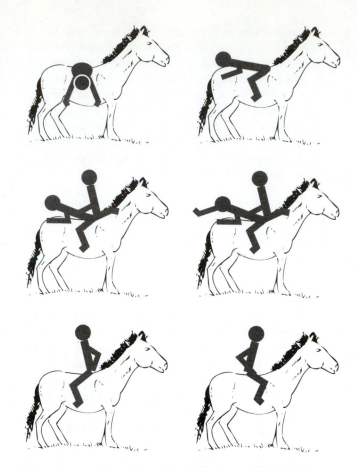

Figure 10.6 Examples of some positions used for therapeutic horseback riding.

Needs and Adjustments of Those with Cerebral Palsy

In addition to motor dysfunction, many individuals with cerebral palsy have concomitant problems. These problems or disturbances all are associated with the common group of syndromes related to brain damage. As illustrated in figure 10.7, these disturbances include the motor dysfunction found in cerebral palsy as well as associated problems of intellectual functioning, sensory loss, speech and/or language disorders, and disturbances of communication or behavior. Although the reported percentage of individuals with cerebral palsy with secondary disabilities varies as shown in table 10.1, the figures do support the view that the student with cerebral palsy is frequently a student with multiple disabilities.

The incidence of mental retardation in the cerebral palsy population has been estimated to be as high as 76 percent. The highest incidence of retardation appears in the spasticity and rigidity conditions. Because of the problems

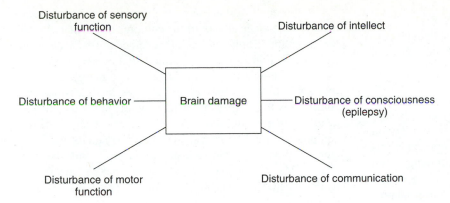

Figure 10.7 Group of syndromes related to brain damage.

(Courtesy of Best, Gary A.: *Individuals with Physical Disabilities.* St. Louis, C.V. Mosby Co., 1978, p. 28.)

Table 10.1 *Secondary disabilities to cerebral palsy*

	Percentage of Total Reported Population*				
Source of Data	Mental Retardation	Speech/Language Defects	Visual Handicaps	Auditory Defects	Seizures (Epilepsy)
California survey, 1965–1966 (Gore and Outland, 1966)	32 (IQ unspecified)	38	6	5	9
Ingram, Jameson, Errington, and Mitchell (1964)	62–76 (IQ 50–90)	27–58	NR**	NR	30–42
Bleck (1975)	75	48	NR	NR	NR
Jones (1975)	NR	NR	60–80	33	33

*All figures are approximates based on calculations, estimates, or reports from the reported sources.
**Data not reported—may be unavailable or not conducive to present table categories.
Courtesy of Best, G.A. (1978) *Individuals With Physical Disabilities* (p. 36). St. Louis: C.V. Mosby Co.

in accurately measuring the IQ of these individuals, estimates of the incidence of mental retardation are not totally reliable; however, the academic performance of many is below the level of their peers.

Perceptual deficits are another problem of the individual with cerebral palsy. Some of these deficits are a result of delayed development due to an inadequate foundation of motor functions; others are probably neurological. Many of the perceptual problems are in the visual or haptic (tactile) modalities.

A majority of individuals with cerebral palsy have sensory deficiencies, with a major portion of these being visual problems. Convulsions (which may be due to epilepsy) and learning disabilities also occur. In addition, nearly all of these individuals have speech defects caused by their inability to control the muscles of speech. Their problems in communicating are a great barrier to social and academic adjustments. The need for speech therapy by this population must not be minimized.

In spite of the movement and learning problems individuals with cerebral palsy must cope with, probably their greatest adjustment needs have to do with their emotional well-being. Because of their motor inadequacies, communication problems, and, in some cases, differences in appearance, they often experience social rejection or excessive sympathy. The acceptance that all persons seek is often denied them. Many must also deal with the rejection and shame of their parents and relatives. Without a proper atmosphere of acceptance, these individuals have a very difficult time developing a good self-concept and consequent feelings of adequacy and contentment. Instead, tremendous frustration, which may be coupled with excessive fears, is a common occurrence.

A number of professionals in the field believe that some of the emotional problems observed in individuals with cerebral palsy are a result of specific brain damage. This opinion is substantiated to some extent by the observation of several pronounced behaviors with certain types of cerebral palsy. For example, those with spastic cerebral palsy often exhibit withdrawal traits and are not usually overresponsive to affection. However, regardless of the influence of structural damage on their emotional stability, it can reasonably be assumed that most of their emotional problems are environmentally related.

Planning the Program

The program for students with cerebral palsy should be governed by two primary objectives: (1) to enhance physical development and muscular control, and (2) to assist psychosocial development. The primary needs of each student will determine where the emphasis should be placed. If the student is receiving adequate physical therapy and displaying satisfactory motor improvement, the greater contribution can be made in the psychosocial realm. Development in this area can be accomplished not only by encouraging social interaction but also by promoting acquisition of sport and leisure activity skills that can add enjoyment to life and provide an avenue for further social endeavors. If the individual's greater need is to develop basic motor skills, then the program should emphasize the first objective. Through assessment and consultation with the physical therapist or physician, or both, the teacher can discover which skills need additional work. Activities can then be planned within the program that require the student to practice these skills (figure 10.8). For example, if there is a need to develop some skill in manual manipulation, activities such as placing objects in a container, rearranging blocks, and striking with rackets can be offered.

Figure 10.8 Physical education experiences for the student with cerebral palsy contribute to motor and physical fitness and psychosocial development.

A thorough evaluation of the facilities and equipment must also be made as part of the comprehensive planning of the program. Ramps to help the student reach elevated teaching stations should be provided. Lockers should be assigned that will not require the student to maneuver a narrow aisle. Certain areas of the shower facilities must be equipped with benches and hand supports under the shower heads to make safe showering available. In addition, the equipment should be investigated to determine its appropriateness. When possible, special equipment should be purchased. Many times, special equipment can be constructed by the teacher or other school personnel. This is an excellent alternative when budgets are restricted. As with all other programs, the scope of the program that can be offered is, to a large extent, dependent upon the facilities and equipment available. Thus, adequate attention to these factors will greatly enhance the program.

Two additional items that must be considered in planning the program are scheduling and placement. Whenever possible, these students should be integrated with their peers. For a small minority this may not be realistic and, therefore, placement in a special class may be necessary.

Special classes should be scheduled in facilities that can be utilized adequately by the students. Consideration should also be given to the extra time needed by the students to prepare for class, to change afterward, and to move to and from the facilities.

It is important to ensure that the program is challenging and offers a genuine learning experience. Individuals with cerebral palsy can learn, and it is the responsibility of the physical education teacher to recognize their motor potentials and to develop these abilities through physical education.

Suggested Activities

As is true in program planning for all individuals with disabilities, the Individualized Education Program meeting is the key to the quantity and quality of educational and related services. Maximum benefits for the student with cerebral palsy will be realized through the concerted efforts of educators and therapists working cooperatively to respond to the individual's educational, social, psychological, and physical needs.

Because programming for students with cerebral palsy is individualized, the activities selected should be determined by the type and severity of the disability, the amount of muscular training that has occurred, and the interest level of the student. Thus, the physical educator looks at what the student *can* do and builds the program from there. Facts that are important to ascertain are:

1. What body parts are affected and what is the type of cerebral palsy?
2. What surgery has been performed and what are the effects of these operations?
3. What reflex problems are present?

Figure 10.9 The objective of this adaptation of the obstacle course is to develop skill in moving through small spaces by walking with crutches between closely placed furniture without touching it.

4. What is the person's level of emotional stability?
5. What medication is being used and what are the effects of the drugs?

In addition, the physical educator should attempt to learn if there are any perceptual-motor deficits or learning difficulties. The physical educator should also know the verbal ability of the student and the kind of physical education and recreation experiences he or she has had.

The type of cerebral palsy will determine the adaptations that are needed. When working with individuals with spasticity, activities requiring great agility and fast-moving actions should be avoided. The environment should be structured to minimize external stimuli (loud noises and sudden movements will cause the person to become tense). If the student has reflex problems, movements that elicit the unwanted responses must be avoided. When instructing those with athetosis, the emphasis must be on creating a relaxed atmosphere; they need to remain calm because body tension and excitement tend to increase the athetoid symptoms. To reduce tension, frequent rest periods should be planned.

An important aid in the performance of motor skills is an apparatus that can be utilized to create distal stabilization, which is the stabilization of an opposite limb during the performance of a movement. This procedure tends to reduce involuntary movements. For those with ataxia, adjustments must be made for severe balance and coordination problems; for example, (1) conducting balance activities on the floor instead of on a balance beam, (2) using very soft balls to reduce the possibility of injuries in catching, and (3) creating wider spaces between objects in the agility run.

Carry-over leisure activities are an important aspect of the program. Community activities that the individual can engage in should be taught. Examples of activities that have been successfully taught to these students include bowling, table tennis, horseshoes, and swimming.

Swimming is an excellent activity. The buoyancy of the water allows students with cerebral palsy to have a freedom of movement that they cannot have out of water. The water also provides a superb environment for the student to practice walking. Special techniques for the teaching of swimming skills to students with cerebral palsy are presented in chapter 26.

It is also recommended by some authorities that muscular relaxation training be given to these students. There is considerable disagreement, however, as to the effects of such training. More research is still needed to determine its appropriate use. Chapter 29 explains the techniques of such training.

Thanks to the United States Cerebral Palsy Athletic Association (USCPAA), opportunities now exist for individuals with cerebral palsy to participate in organized sports programs. USCPAA's purpose is to promote competitive sport programs and recreational opportunities for persons disabled by cerebral palsy and similar disorders. Local, state, national, and international meets are held to allow athletes with cerebral palsy to demonstrate their skills in various dual and team sports. An eight-category classification system is used to ensure that individuals compete fairly and equitably with athletes who have a similar type of cerebral palsy, degree of involvement, and mode of ambulation. Additional information on the USCPAA will be presented in chapter 30, *Competitive Sport for Athletes with Disabilities.*

In addition to these general suggestions, there are some specific activities that should be incorporated into the physical education program of a student with cerebral palsy. These include experiences designed to enhance body image, breathing capacity, and physical fitness.

Body Image

Children with cerebral palsy frequently lack a complete understanding or awareness of the movement capability and location of their body parts. Activities, therefore, should be designed to help the student overcome this difficulty. For young children, this will require simple games designed to help the students name and identify body parts. As they progress, more attention can focus on helping them become aware of the body's position in basic movements such as rolling over or throwing a ball. It is very important to help students focus on their movement patterns by questioning them as they participate in various games. For example, questions such as, "Which hand are you using?" and "Which way are you moving?" help the student become more aware of the body's capability and its relationship to space and other objects. For some students, the teacher may find it necessary to provide nonverbal cues, such as touching the student's arm while emphasizing, "*This* is your right arm."

Breathing Exercises

As discussed earlier, some individuals with cerebral palsy find it very difficult to speak in a manner that is easily understood. It is not surprising that speech impairments are a part of the cerebral palsy syndrome, because speech production is, in part, a motor act and, hence, susceptible to impairment due to damage to the motor-control areas of the brain. There are, however, other conditions such as respiration problems that may also interfere with the ability of a student with cerebral palsy to speak. For instance, some individuals are unable to articulate properly because they have an insufficient amount of air volume available during exhalation. Efforts, therefore, must be undertaken to help students become more aware of the diaphragm and to design programs to help students increase their air intake so that they will have sufficient volume to speak with a pattern that is more discernible.

Asking students to assume different postures, such as lying supine or sitting in a chair, and having them breathe deeply with the hands on the diaphragm, helps the student to become more sensitive to deep breathing in contrast to shallow breathing. Various breathing games such as asking two students to blow a ping-pong ball back and forth across a table can also be developed to help students increase their lung capacity. The specific breathing program should be developed in consultation with the speech pathologist.

Rothman (1978) found that the vital capacity of youngsters with cerebral palsy could be improved significantly when following a breathing exercise program for as short as eight weeks. The exercises used by Rothman include the following:

1. *Diaphragmatic breathing.* Have the youngster assume a seated or back-lying position and breathe through the nose as the abdomen pushes out like a balloon. Breathe out and pull in the abdomen. Have the child place the hands on the diaphragm and abdomen so that the child can get the "feel" of the chest expanding. The breathing should be slow, controlled, and rhythmic. As the child progresses, weight can be applied to the abdominal area to add resistance to the movement of the diaphragm.

2. *Expiratory exercise using abdominal muscles.* While seated, the child blows the ping-pong balls across the table for different distances.

3. *Inspiration and expansion of the chest.* In the supine position, the child inhales while elevating the arms above the head and exhales while lowering the arms.

4. *Stimulation of inspiration.* While the child is seated, place a belt around the lower ribs and crossed in the front. As the child exhales the belt is tightened and as the child inhales the belt is loosened.

5. *Strengthening anterior abdominal musculature, especially rectus abdominous.* (a) In a supine position, the child exhales while bringing the knees to the chest and inhales as the knees are lowered. (b) The child performs a sit-up with the knees flexed and feet flat on the floor.

6. *Strengthening lateral abdominal muscles and internal and external obliques.* With knees flexed and feet flat on the floor, the youngster performs a sit-up by bringing one elbow to the opposite knee. On each sit-up alternate elbows and knees.

Physical therapists and speech pathologists should be consulted for additional ideas and suggestions for breathing exercises.

Physical Fitness

The level of physical fitness for many individuals with cerebral palsy is such that special efforts should be undertaken to help students improve their performance in this important area (Rintala, Lyytinen, and Dunn, 1990). Cardiovascular endurance, in particular, is a physical fitness component about which there is a growing body of literature to support the contention that individuals with cerebral palsy can improve the efficiency of their heart and lungs, thereby increasing their stamina. To do this, however, requires that a systematic program be developed in which students are provided opportunities to stress their cardiorespiratory system. Individuals in wheelchairs, those who walk with the aid of an assistive device, and those who walk unaided but with an imperfect gait can all undertake activities that stress the cardiorespiratory system gradually over time. The basic premise of the program is that the student is asked to move greater and greater distances, with a gradual reduction in the amount of time taken for a given distance. Monitoring the individual's pulse rate can be used as an informative way to help the student appreciate the benefits of a systematic cardiorespiratory fitness program (see chapter 27).

Motor Characteristics

There are motor characteristics unique to the student with cerebral palsy that the physical educator must consider in teaching various movement skills. For instance, the individual may exhibit abnormal reflexes that can impede success in physical education activities. As an example, the presence of the symmetrical tonic neck reflex can interfere with the catching of a ball. With this reflex, as discussed earlier, when the individual extends the head, the arms flex and the legs extend; conversely, as the head flexes, the arms extend and the legs flex. The presence of this reflex and its implications for the teaching of a skill such as ball catching is very clear. In the early stages of skill development, the ball should be presented to the student at eye level, eliminating the need for either head extension or flexion. This can be accomplished by keeping the ball in a flat plane by rolling it on a surface level with the student's head. Once the student masters this initial task and experiences success, then the height of the ball can be varied.

Some students with cerebral palsy may also have problems because of the presence of the asymmetric tonic neck reflex. With this pattern, as the head turns, the extremities on the side to which the student looks extend while the extremities on the opposite side flex. For this individual, the teacher must give instruction from the side opposite to the way the head usually faces in the abnormal reflex position. Using our earlier example of ball catching, the ball would be rolled slightly to the student's left rather than to the right if in the abnormal reflex behavior the head normally turns to the right. This technique increases the probability of student success because as the student prepares to trap the ball, the head will move to the left into a favorable midline position. How far to the side the ball should be rolled and the speed with which the ball should be rolled are factors that must be adjusted for each individual.

Movements that are continuously repeated are easier for those with spasticity. However, individuals with athetosis achieve their best performance if rest and relaxation occur between movements. Ataxic persons do not perform well in skills requiring balance and kinesthesis; they are able to move the body successfully but have difficulty responding to objects, as in the instances of picking up or catching or kicking objects in a game situation. Because of their poor kinesthesis, they often move too far or not far enough in executing the required movement. Success will be more likely if the skill can be performed in a stationary position. Kicking the ball while running will be very difficult for those who are ataxic, but if they can stop and then make the kick the chances of performing the skill successfully are immeasurably better.

For the nonambulatory student who uses a wheelchair, it is very important that the individual be removed from the chair periodically during the day to prevent excessive contractures. The physical education period provides an excellent opportunity for the student to learn and explore new movement skills while on a mat. It is essential, however, that the teacher employ correct lifting and handling techniques with children with cerebral palsy. For example, when the student is on a mat and the teacher wants to place the individual back into the wheelchair, it is best to first roll the child on his or her side, bend the head and shoulders forward, thus facilitating the bending of the hips. Physical therapists can provide additional information to help the teacher learn other valuable lifting and handling techniques.

The motor characteristics of the student with cerebral palsy require that the teacher not only adapt activities but select alternative experiences when necessary. For example, if the class is working on the skill of ball throwing, various adaptations of the skill can be utilized, like using a ball of different weight or size, or changing the size and distance of the target. Any adaptation of an activity must be done carefully, recognizing the unique needs of the student with cerebral palsy. For instance, using a lightweight ball to help a child learn how to kick a ball is considered an acceptable teaching technique. However, this approach for the individual with hemiplegic cerebral palsy may not be appropriate. As illustrated in figure 10.11, the use of a light, small ball with this child increases extension in the leg and flexion of the arm with a backward body lean as the kick is performed. Using a heavier, larger ball, however, forces the student to keep the leg flexed and body weight over the ball. This improves overall body balance and position, thus increasing the probability of success.

For some, however, adaptations of the skill may not be helpful. In these cases an alternative experience may be necessary. A skill becomes an alternative activity when the skill is modified to such an extent that the traditional skill may not be easily recognized, or the child is unable to assume the physical posture required by the traditional skill. An example of a traditional, adapted, and alternative objective is presented in table 10.2. For some students with cerebral palsy,

Figure 10.10 Students with movement disorders can participate successfully in physical education and sport activities.

Figure 10.11 Children who are hemiplegic benefit from opportunities to kick large heavier balls. Heavier balls add resistance, whereas lighter balls encourage a backward lean that increases stiffness in the leg and in the bending of the arm.

(Adapted from Finnie, Nancie: *Handling the Young Cerebral Palsied Child at Home,* New York, E.P. Dutton and Co., Inc., 1975, p. 267.)

Table 10.2 *An example of a traditional, adapted, and alternative objective*

Goal: Participation in games involving throwing
Skill: Throwing
Objective (traditional): Given a softball, the child will assume a stride position and employ the overhand method to throw a given distance of 20 feet with 80% success.
Objective (adapted): Given a Nerf ball, the child will throw a distance of 20 feet with 80% success. The child will be stabilized at the hips by an assistant.
Objective (alternative): Given a wheelchair with foot pedals, the child will balance an 8-inch ball on the lap and placing one hand, fisted or open, between the legs and under the ball, lift the ball up, and at the same time push it forward. The ball must travel 10 feet in the air with 80% success.

Courtesy of Joan Kelly, Adapted Physical Education Specialist, Eugene, Oregon, Public Schools.

successful physical education experiences require a teacher who can adapt and, when necessary, design alternative experiences.

There is much that is not known or understood about the motor characteristics of cerebral palsy. For example, there is some uncertainty about the amount of time these individuals require to process information prior to the execution of a motor task. Parks, Dunn, and Rose (1989), in a study of adolescents with mild spastic hemiplegia, found that the premotor component of a fractionated reaction time task with these students was longer than that of their nondisabled counterparts. These findings suggest that teachers will need to allow for additional processing time when instructing students with spastic cerebral palsy, including those who do not have a cognitive deficit. Sensitivity to this need will help to create a favorable and positive learning environment. Future research will help to confirm some of these findings and to shed new light on methods of teaching those with cerebral palsy.

Summary

Cerebral palsy is a condition resulting from brain damage that may be incurred before or during birth or at any time in later life.

There are various types of cerebral palsy; the spastic and athetoid conditions are the most prevalent. Cerebral palsy affects different parts of the body with the topographical classification of hemiplegia being the most common.

The major problem confronting the individual with cerebral palsy is learning to move the body as efficiently and effectively as possible. Treatment for cerebral palsy includes physical therapy, orthopedic surgery or bracing, medication, and to a lesser extent biofeedback. While treatment for cerebral palsy can be helpful, no cure for this disorder exists. The goal of the treatment program is to minimize the effect of selected reflexes while helping the individual acquire functional skills that can be used in daily life. Bracing or surgery will sometimes be employed to stretch selected muscles or to reduce contractures that might cause structural deviations.

In addition to the obvious neuromuscular problems, many individuals with cerebral palsy have secondary disorders. Concomitant problems may include mental retardation, speech and language disorders, sensory disabilities, and epilepsy. While not all individuals possess all or even some of these secondary disorders, many do. This suggests that the population with cerebral palsy is significant and varied. Treatment programs today, therefore, emphasize a multidisciplinary approach in the delivery of medical treatment and educational programs.

Physical education is an important and essential service for individuals with cerebral palsy. Modern treatment of cerebral palsy emphasizes the importance of helping the individual function effectively in the activities of daily life. This requires, among other things, that the person be healthy and physically fit. Physical educators can be effective in helping young students with cerebral palsy develop appropriate levels of cardiorespiratory fitness, muscular strength and endurance, and flexibility.

Furthermore, efforts must be directed toward teaching motor skills essential to successful participation in sports, games, and play activities. There is a growing awareness that the individual with cerebral palsy can perform physical feats that only a few years ago were thought to be impossible. Organizations such as the United States Cerebral Palsy Athletic Association have been helpful in dispelling myths about cerebral palsy while promoting a realistic and positive image of individuals with this disorder.

Selected Readings

Batshaw, M.L., & Perret, Y.M. (1986). *Children with handicaps: A medical primer* (2d ed.). Baltimore: Paul H. Brookes Publishing Co.

Bertoti, D.B. (1988). Effect of therapeutic horseback riding on posture in children with cerebral palsy. *Physical Therapy, 68,* 1505–1512.

Best, G.A. (1978). *Individuals with physical disabilities.* St. Louis: C.V. Mosby Co.

Bigge, J.L., & O'Donnell, P.A. (1976). *Teaching individuals with physical and multiple disabilities.* Columbus, OH: Charles E. Merrill Publishing Co.

Blackman, J.A. (1984). *Medical aspects of developmental disabilities in children birth to three.* Rockville, MD: Aspen Systems Corporation.

Bleck, E.E. (1979). *Orthopedic management of cerebral palsy.* Philadelphia: W.B. Saunders Co.

Bleck, E.E., & Nagel, D.A. (1982). *Physically handicapped children: A medical atlas for teachers* (2d ed.), New York: Grune and Stratton.

Bobath, B. (1971). Motor development, its effect on general development, and application to the treatment of cerebral palsy. *Physiotherapy, 57,* 526–532.

Bobath, B., & Bobath, K. (1975). *Motor development in the different types of cerebral palsy.* London: William Heinemann Medical Books Ltd.

Bobath, K. (1959). The neuropathology of cerebral palsy and its importance in treatment and diagnosis. *Cerebral Palsy Bulletin, 1*(8), 13–33.

Bobath, K. (1980). *A neurophysiological basis for the treatment of cerebral palsy.* Philadelphia: J.B. Lippincott.

Brown, A. (1975). Review: Physical fitness and cerebral palsy. *Child: Care, health, and development, 1,* 143–152.

Cotton, E., & Parnwell, M. (1967). From Hungary: The Peto method. *Special Education, 56*(4), 7–11.

Cruickshank, W. (1976). *Cerebral palsy: A developmental disability* (3d ed.). Syracuse, NY: Syracuse University Press.

Denhoff, E. (1976). Medical aspects. In W.M. Cruickshank (Ed.), *Cerebral palsy: A developmental disability.* Syracuse, NY: Syracuse University Press.

Edgington, D. (1976). *The physically handicapped child in your classroom.* Springfield, IL: Charles C. Thomas.

Eichstaedt, C.B., & Kalakian, L.H. (1987). *Developmental/adapted physical education* (2d ed.). New York: Macmillan Publishing Co.

Fernandez, J.E., Pitetti, K.H., & Betzen, M.T. (1990). Physiological capacities of individuals with cerebral palsy. *Human Factors, 32,* 457–466.

Finnie, N. (1975). *Handling the young cerebral palsied child at home.* New York: E.P. Dutton.

Frost, H. (1972). *Orthopedic surgery in spasticity.* Springfield, IL: Charles C. Thomas.

Harris, F. (1971). Inapproprioception: A possible sensory basis for athetoid movements. *Physical Therapy, 51*(7), 761–770.

Harris, S.R. (1990). Therapeutic exercises for children with neurodevelopmental disabilities. In Basmajian, J.V. & Wolf, S. (Eds.), *Therapeutic exercise* (5th ed.), 163–176. Baltimore: Williams and Wilkins.

Heward, W.L., & Orlansky, M.D. (1988). *Exceptional children* (3d ed.). Columbus, OH: Charles E. Merrill Publishing Co.

Holland, L.J., & Steadward, R.D. (1990). Effects of resistance and flexibility training on strength, spasticity/muscle tone, and range of motion of elite athletes with cerebral palsy. *Palaestra, 6*(4), 27–31.

Horvat, M. (1987). Effects of a progressive resistance training program on an individual with spastic cerebral palsy. *American Corrective Therapy Journal, 41*(1), 7–11.

Jones, J.A. (1988). *Training guide to cerebral palsy sports* (3d ed.). Champaign, IL: Human Kinetics Publishers.

Kurtz, L.A. (1992). Cerebral palsy. In M. Batshaw and Y. Perret (Eds.), *Children with medical disabilities: A medical primer* (3d ed.), 441–469. Baltimore: Paul H. Brookes Publishing Co.

Levitt, S. (1985). *Treatment of cerebral palsy and motor delay* (2d ed.). Boston: Blackwell Scientific Publications.

Lugo, A.A., Sherrill, C., & Pizarro, A.L. (1992). Use of a sport socialization inventory with cerebral palsied youth. *Perceptual and Motor Skills, 74,* 203–208.

McCubbin, J.A., & Horvat, M. (1990). Guidelines for resistance exercise training for persons with cerebral palsy. *Palaestra, 6*(2), 29–21; 47.

Mullins, J.B. (1979). *A teacher's guide to management of physically handicapped students.* Springfield, IL: Charles C. Thomas.

Paneth, N., & Kiely, J. (1984). The frequency of cerebral palsy: A review of population studies in industrialized nations since 1950. *Clinics in Developmental Medicine, 87,* 46–56.

Parks, S., Rose, D.J., & Dunn, J.M. (1989). A comparison of fractionated reaction time between cerebral palsied and non-handicapped youth. *Adapted Physical Activity Quarterly, 7,* 379–388.

Pitetti, K.H., Fernandez, J.E., & Lanciault, M. (1991). Feasibility of an exercise program for adults with cerebral palsy: A pilot study. *Adapted Physical Activity Quarterly, 8,* 333–341.

Rintala, P., Lyytinen, H, & Dunn, J.M. (1990). Influence of a physical activity program on children with cerebral palsy: A single subject design. *Pediatric Exercise Science, 2,* 46–56.

Rood, M. (1954). Neurophysiological reactions as a basis for physical therapy. *Physical Therapy Review, 34*(9), 444–449.

Rose, J., Gamble, J.G., Medeiros, J., Burgos, A., & Haskell, W.L. (1990). Energy expenditure index of walking for normal children and for children with cerebral palsy. *Developmental Medicine and Child Neurology, 32,* 333–340.

Rothman, J.G. (1978). Effects of respiratory exercises on the vital capacity and forced expiratory volume in children with cerebral palsy. *Physical Therapy, 58*(4), 421–425.

Sanders, M. (1980). A comparison of two methods of training on the development of muscular strength and endurance. *Journal of Orthopedic Sports Physical Therapy, 1*(4), 210–213.

Sherrill, C. (1993). *Adapted physical activity, recreation and sport* (4th ed.). Dubuque, IA: Wm. C. Brown Publishers.

Sugden, D.A., & Keogh, J. (1990). Problems in movement skill development. Columbia, SC: University of South Carolina Press.

Winnick, J.P., & Short, F.X. (1985). *Physical fitness testing of the disabled.* Champaign, IL: Human Kinetics Publishers.

Winnick, J.P., & Short, F.X. (1991). A comparison of the physical fitness of non retarded and mildly retarded adolescents with cerebral palsy. *Adapted Physical Activity Quarterly, 8,* 43–56.

Young, R.R. & Delwaid, P.J. (1981). Drug therapy and spasticity. *New England Journal of Medicine, 304*(1), 28–33.

Enhancing Activities

1. Attend an athletic event sponsored by the United States Cerebral Palsy Athletic Association. Observe the various athletes and the differences in movement capability and performance by classification.

2. Interview an adult with cerebral palsy. Through discussion, obtain the individual's perception of the disability and the effectiveness of various treatment techniques.

3. Develop a physical fitness program for an adolescent with cerebral palsy. If possible, implement the program under the guidance of your professor.

4. Confer with a physical therapist to obtain his or her view of cerebral palsy and the effectiveness of various treatment techniques.

5. Write a paper defending the importance of physical education as an essential aspect of the education of the child with cerebral palsy.

Muscular Weakness and Other Movement Disorders (Les Autres)

◆ ──────────────── **CHAPTER OBJECTIVES** ──────────────── ◆

After studying this chapter, the reader should be able to:

1 Describe and discuss each of the following conditions: muscular dystrophy; juvenile arthritis; growth disorders and short stature; arthrogryposis; osteogenesis imperfecta; Friedreich's ataxia; multiple sclerosis; myasthenia gravis; and poliomyositis.

2 Define the term *les autres* and explain the origin and rationale for the use of this expression.

3 Identify the factors that should be considered in developing appropriate programs for individuals with the movement disorders described in this chapter.

4 Explain the progressive stages observed in the development of muscular dystrophy.

5 Analyze the similarities and dissimilarities among the conditions classified under the heading *les autres*.

6 Recognize the role that sport has played in helping those with les autres conditions demonstrate their health and vitality.

There are several disorders that, although they differ in many respects, share the common effect of interfering with normal patterns of movement. Some of the disorders are diseases that bring about abnormal weakness in the muscles. The four most common of these diseases affecting young people are muscular dystrophy, multiple sclerosis, myasthenia gravis, and polymyositis. They occur most frequently during the late teens and early adult years; however, children of younger ages do get the diseases. One type of muscular dystrophy, unfortunately the most common type, affects only young children, often in their second or third year of life.

These disorders and others, including osteogenesis imperfecta, arthritis, arthrogryposis, and Friedreich's ataxia, are commonly grouped together today under the heading of *les autres,* a French term meaning "the others." This expression was coined by sport enthusiasts to denote the other locomotor disabilities not eligible to compete in the Wheelchair Sports, USA or United States Cerebral Palsy Athletic Association (USCPAA) athletic events. The U.S. Les Autres Sports Association (USLASA) was organized in 1986. It serves all conditions except dwarfism. The Dwarf Athletic Association of America (DAAA) was also founded in 1986 and sponsors its own events. Through these efforts a new sense of appreciation for individuals with special disorders such as arthritis and short stature is developing. Physicians, therapists, physical educators, and other professionals are becoming unified in their belief that students with les autres conditions can and should benefit from physical activity and sport opportunities. Their ability levels range from novice to highly skilled performance levels. Within this chapter information will be provided to highlight the importance of activity and exercise programs for populations with les autres conditions, including those with progressive muscular weakness, and the many benefits to be derived from these experiences.

Muscular Dystrophy

The term *muscular dystrophy* applies to a group of related muscle diseases that are progressively incapacitating because the muscles gradually weaken and eventually atrophy. Muscular dystrophy, or the propensity for the disease, is inherited. Females who may not themselves have the disease transmit the sex-linked trait to their children, particularly to their sons. Consequently, the incidence of muscular dystrophy is much higher among males than among females. It is estimated that there are more than a quarter of a million cases of the disease in this country.

The exact cause of the disease has not been fully determined. It is known that muscle protein is lost and is gradually replaced by fat and connective tissue, causing increasing degeneration of the voluntary muscle system.

Childhood Muscular Dystrophy

The most prevalent type of muscular dystrophy, accounting for about 65 percent of all dystrophies, affects young children. It is known as Duchenne, or progressive, muscular dystrophy. The disease is also called pseudohypertrophic muscular dystrophy, because the hypertrophy of the muscles produced by replacement of lost protein with fat, particularly of those in the calves of the legs, creates the deceptive appearance of a healthy, well-developed musculature.

The symptoms make their appearance in the second or third year of life. Prominent among the early signs are difficulty in running, climbing stairs, and rising from a sitting position. The walking gait resembles a side-to-side waddle. Falls are frequent, and regaining the feet is performed in abnormal fashion by placing the hands and feet on the floor to raise the hips to a forward-leaning position and then elevating the trunk by pushing the hands against the legs along the length of the legs. This method of rising is called Gower's sign (figure 11.1).

As the disease progresses, contractures form in the muscles of the legs and hips and the early symptoms become more pronounced. Within a few years, dystrophic children become so weakened that they must rely on a wheelchair for locomotion (figure 11.2). Later, these individuals will stay in bed for much of the time. Death frequently occurs before the age of twenty and results from a secondary cause, usually respiratory or cardiac in nature.

Figure 11.1 Gower's sign. Children with the Duchenne type of muscular dystrophy experience muscle weakness in the legs and calves, making it difficult for them to rise from a seated position.

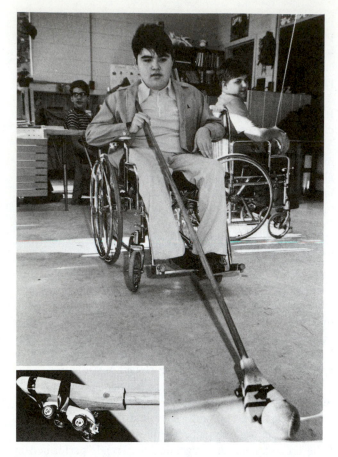

Figure 11.2 The child with muscular dystrophy is characteristically weak and needs modifications to be made in activities. For example, to play a game of shuffleboard, wheels must be attached to the cue and a tennis ball used in place of the puck.

Eight stages in the development of the disease have been identified by the Muscular Dystrophy Association of America (Muscular Dystrophy Association of America, Inc., 27th floor, 810 7th Avenue, New York, NY 11019). These stages, from the early, less severe stage to the more involved levels, are as follows:

1. The child walks with a mild waddling gait and lordosis but can mount curbs and stairs without assistance.
2. The child walks with a moderate waddling gait and lordosis but needs some assistance to mount curbs and stairs.
3. The child walks with a moderate waddling gait and lordosis. The individual is unable to negotiate curbs and stairs but can assume an upright posture from a standard height chair.
4. The child walks with a severe waddling gait and lordosis. No longer can the individual rise from a chair of standard height. This is the critical stage at which it is too soon to place the child in a wheelchair. Instead, these children should be encouraged to use their functional skills to walk, stretch, and engage in deep breathing exercises.
5. The child relies on a wheelchair for ambulation and is able to perform successfully the activities of daily living.
6. The child can propel the wheelchair but needs assistance with some bed and wheelchair activities.
7. The child can move the wheelchair only a short distance. Back support must be provided for good chair position.
8. The child stays in bed and requires assistance for all activities of daily living.

Other Types

Another type of muscular dystrophy occurs most frequently during the teens and twenties, although it sometimes appears in younger children. Unlike progressive muscular dystrophy, this type affects girls as frequently as boys. The disease can take one or both of two forms that closely resemble one another.

One form is called limb-girdle, deriving its name from the area of the body in which the symptoms first manifest themselves. Difficulty is experienced in the use of the thigh and hip muscles and is caused by weakness in the musculature of the pelvic girdle. The shoulder girdle muscles are involved less frequently. The rate of deterioration varies, but severe crippling occurs in most cases.

Another form of the disease, known as facioscapulohumeral, afflicts the muscles of the face, shoulders, and upper arms. Its first symptom is a very slight weakening of the facial muscles followed by subsequent involvement of the muscles of the shoulders and upper arms. The degree of weakening varies among individuals; in some it is very slight. The disease progresses slowly over many years and may be arrested at any time.

Characteristics of the disease in its more advanced stages are sagging cheeks, pouting lips, inability to close the eyes completely, and a lack of facial expression caused by weakness of the muscles of the face. Lack of strength and awkwardness in movements of the shoulder and arm muscles are other symptoms. Less frequently affected are the muscles of the thigh and hip; symptomatic of the presence of the disease, when these areas are involved, are frequent falling and a waddling gait.

Other types of muscular dystrophy have been identified, but they occur so rarely that discussion of them here is not warranted. Sometimes a person may have two or more forms of the disease.

To date, no treatment has been discovered to halt the progress of the disease. However, some hope is held out as the result of recent experiments with medications that help to build up protein in the muscle cells or that prevent the loss of excessive protein from the cells. Secondary infections, which so often cause complications and lead to death, can be largely controlled by the use of antibiotics. Programs that include stretching exercises and deep breathing exercises can, in some cases, retard muscle shortening. Braces worn to compensate for muscle weakness sometimes help to delay the need to use a wheelchair.

Juvenile Rheumatoid Arthritis

Arthritis, inflammation of the joints, is a condition that affects more than 12 million people in the United States. The precise cause of this disease is unknown, but it is believed that the inflammation of the joints is caused by an immunologic attack on normal body materials. Abnormal antibodies mysteriously appear in the blood, destroying protein needed for protection against joint inflammation. The appearance of these antibodies does not seem to be related to diet, climate, or pattern of living. Arthritis is not considered to be an inherited disease.

A specific form of arthritis that can afflict children as young as six weeks is known as juvenile rheumatoid arthritis. There are several important differences between this disease and rheumatoid arthritis found in adults. Fortunately, the prognosis for children who have juvenile rheumatoid arthritis is very positive, with approximately 60 to 70 percent recovering from this disease after a period of ten years. With proper medical care, only about 10 percent of the children with this disease will experience any functional problems later in life.

Juvenile rheumatoid arthritis usually takes one of three forms with children. The greatest portion, 50 to 60 percent, of those who have this disorder have the type known as *polyarticular*. Most of these children have five or more severely inflamed joints. The knees, ankles, wrists, neck, fingers, elbows, and shoulders are frequently involved. This disorder is very painful, with children normally assuming a flexed position of the joints to relieve the pain. Without exercise and treatment the joints will lose their range of motion and flexibility and develop contractures. If the disorder occurs early in life, the child will likely be small, with a delayed sexual maturation.

A second form of juvenile rheumatoid arthritis that affects approximately 20 percent of children who have an arthritic disorder is known as the *systemic* type. Unlike children who have the polyarticular type, arthritis is a minor part of the illness for individuals with the systemic type. These children suffer from extremely high temperatures that occur once or twice a day. General fatigue, enlarged spleens, and a pink rash are other signs that accompany this disorder. The long-term outlook for these children is good, although a few do also develop polyarticular arthritis.

Children who have four or fewer swollen joints are generally assumed to have a type of arthritis known as *pauciarticular* rheumatoid arthritis. Children with this disease do not have any systemic signs or symptoms, nor do they look or feel ill, except for soreness in the involved joints. An inflammation of the iris of the eye is an associated problem frequently seen with this type of arthritis. This visual problem, which can lead to blindness, occurs independently of the arthritis and develops so slowly that it may go undetected unless there are regular eye exams.

Although juvenile rheumatoid arthritis is rarely fatal, it does cause severe to mild crippling in approximately 50 percent of the affected children. The primary treatment for this disorder is medication, usually aspirin, to control the inflammation; exercise to help maintain range of motion; and in a few extreme cases, surgery to correct deformities due to contractures. During the acute stages of the treatment, children should not bear weight on the inflamed joint. This may require, therefore, the use of a wheelchair or splints to immobilize joints. Although rest is extremely important as part of the treatment prescription, exercise is also considered essential. Even during the acute stages of the disease, the child with rheumatoid arthritis should move the affected joints through the greatest range of motion possible. As the joints become less swollen, greater amounts of exercise may be undertaken. The optimal program requires a careful balance between maximum joint movement and strength development without causing additional joint inflammation.

Physical education teachers should be particularly sensitive to the special needs of the student with arthritis. It is not uncommon, for instance, for these children to have fluctuations in their mood depending upon the amount of pain and stiffness they experience from day to day. A phenomenon known as "jelling" is a characteristic of this disorder. This causes abnormal stiffness after a night of rest or after sitting for prolonged periods of time. For this reason, it is important that teachers encourage children with rheumatoid arthritis to move frequently within the classroom setting.

Teachers should also be aware that children such as these who require large doses of aspirin as part of their medical treatment may experience a high-tone hearing loss. This is a temporary problem that will disappear when the aspirin treatment is stopped. Prior to initiating a physical education program for the student with arthritis, it is important that the teacher meet with the therapist and physician to develop some specific guidelines for the student. Normally it will be recommended that a program of passive stretching be initiated. The physical educator's efforts, then, would be directed toward games and activities that stretch the child's flexor and adductor muscle groups while strengthening the extensor and abductor groups as a complement to the therapeutic program of passive stretching exercises.

Activities that jar or produce unusual stress on the joints should be eliminated from the program for children with arthritis. Thus, many of the locomotor activities such as jumping and leaping should be avoided as well as many of the contact activities such as football, volleyball, and soccer. This is not to suggest, however, that individuals with juvenile rheumatoid arthritis should be overly restricted in their activity level. Goldberg (1990) argues that physicians should advocate for these individuals and their right to engage in whatever level of activity will help them to reach their potential.

Swimming and water activities are particularly desirable forms of exercise for the student with arthritis. Other activities that encourage full range of motion without undue stress on the joints include creative dance, relaxation exercises, and games such as quoits, horseshoes, shuffleboard, and pool.

Short Stature and Growth

There are many individuals who, for a variety of reasons, are considered to be short or small in stature. These individuals historically have been referred to as dwarfs or midgets. The accepted terms today are "dwarf" and "little people." The little people have formed an organization, Little People of America, dedicated to ensuring that those small in stature are recognized as real people and treated accordingly. Little People of America is dedicated to eradicating the use of inappropriate terms such as "midget" and helping the general public to accept little people.

There are many reasons why individuals may be short in stature. These include malnutrition, the effect of chronic diseases, intrauterine growth retardation, chromosomal anomalies, and endocrine disturbances. Most of the causes of growth disorders relate in some way to the growth hormone secreted by the pituitary gland in response to stimulation by the hypothalamus, the part of the brain that stimulates growth. If the skeleton is unable to convert cartilage within its growth centers into bone, the disorder known as *chondrodystrophies* or *skeletal dysplasia* occurs. This condition results in a disproportionate ratio between the trunk and limbs (figure 11.3). Two of the most common forms of disproportionate growth are *achondroplasia* (those with predominantly short limbs) and the *Morquio syndrome* (those with a short trunk). In both of these disorders the intelligence of those affected is well within the normal range.

Physical education experiences for those with growth disorders must be modified to ensure that the individual will be successful. This will require, for instance, that care be taken to assess the height and length of equipment, such as basketball hoops and golf clubs, and make modifications as necessary. Many of the modifications that should be made in physical education activities for individuals who are dwarfs are the same common sense modifications that should be made for students in general who are small in stature in comparison to classmates. Selected rule changes may also be necessary to help the little person to be an asset to his or her team. Specific suggestions on activity modifications are found in chapter 21, *Activities and Games for Young Children*.

Special care will also need to be taken to understand and accept the associated disabilities that accompany disorders such as achondroplasia and Morquio syndrome. Frequently, these individuals experience spinal disorders, ambulate with a waddling gait, and are susceptible to hip joint dislocations. In disproportionate dwarfism, achondroplasia being by far the most common, joint defects of the shoulder, elbow, hip, and knee joints, limit range of motion and contribute to a high incidence of dislocations and trauma (Knudsen, 1993). Swimming, therefore, is recommended as a highly desirable activity because of its overall contribution to fitness and limited stress to the joints. Close articulation with the medical community will help in designing appropriate and enjoyable exercise and activity programs.

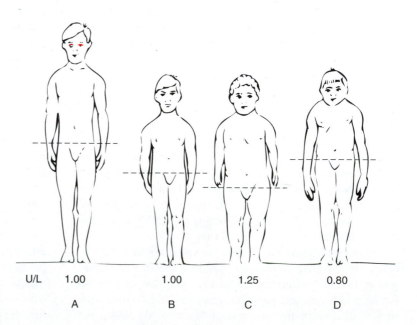

Figure 11.3 Four children aged approximately 10 years. (*A*) Normal. (*B*) Proportionate dwarfism. (*C*) Disproportionate short limb dwarfism. (*D*) Disproportionate short trunk dwarfism. Upper segment to lower segment (U/L) ratio is given for each child.

U/L	1.00	1.00	1.25	0.80
	A	B	C	D

Efforts should also be made to assist those who are athletically gifted and desire to participate in regional and national competitions for dwarfs. The Dwarf Athletic Association of America (DAAA) sponsors and promotes various sports, including basketball, volleyball, powerlifting, swimming, and bowling. Basketball is played using a regulation court and basket height. The basketball dimension is that used by women. In volleyball, the height of the net is lowered slightly so that the players can spike. As additional experience is gained in providing sport experience for individuals short in stature, it is highly likely that further adaptations will be made in sports such as swimming and track and field to create equitable opportunities for this population.

Arthrogryposis

Arthrogryposis is a very rare congenital disease in which children are born with stiff joints and weak muscles. Although the exact cause is unknown, the contracture and resultant bone deformity may be observed early in fetal life. With this disease, normally the shoulders are turned in, elbows are straightened, forearms are turned with the palm down, wrists are flexed and deviated inward, and fingers are curled into the palm. The hips are bent upward and turned outward, with the feet usually turned in and down. There is also frequently a curvature of the spine and joints are large with limited range of motion.

Children with arthrogryposis must also deal with associated conditions including congenital heart disease as well as urinary tract and respiratory problems.

Surgical treatment combined with plaster casts and braces is the usual treatment for correcting deformities, particularly those of the lower limbs. Treatment efforts are directed toward helping the child walk, although some will function more effectively with the use of a wheelchair.

The educational program for students with arthrogryposis is similar to that provided for all students. They usually have normal intelligence with average to above average academic achievement. Because the condition does not deteriorate and little pain is felt, children with this disease are encouraged to participate in games and play activities to the limit of their abilities.

Osteogenesis Imperfecta

Osteogenesis imperfecta, also known as brittle bone disease, derives its name from the fragile bone structure that children with this disorder exhibit. Unlike normal bone, the bone structure of children with this inherited disease is deficient in protein and bone salts. The bones become weak and the extremities break easily, often healing in a deformed, shortened, and bowed position.

There are two types of osteogenesis imperfecta: congenital (present at birth) and tarda (onset later in life). In the former condition, the infant is born with deformed limbs, broken bones, and a soft skull that tends to grow in a triangular shape, broad at the forehead and narrow at the chin. Many infants, severely disabled from this condition, die at birth or at a very early age. Children who survive the first few years of life, and those who develop the tarda type, experience fewer fractures as they grow older. Both types, however, experience other associated problems such as scoliosis and teeth that are easily broken and prone to cavities.

Surgery is the most effective treatment for this disease. The procedure involves removing the bone, cutting it into segments, and then rethreading the pieces onto a steel rod positioned between the ends of the bone (Bleck and Nagel, 1982). Surgery combined with bracing enables some children with osteogenesis imperfecta to walk. Many, however, will still require the assistance of a wheelchair. Teachers who handle or lift the student with this disease should do so carefully, with support under the buttocks and behind the child's back.

Although children with this disorder frequently have normal academic performance, they do require special assistance in physical education. Gentle range of motion exercises and aquatic activities are normally recommended as desirable activities for the child with osteogenesis imperfecta. Care must be taken to ensure that all exercises are done on padded exercise mats. Games that use soft or padded equipments, such as balls made out of foam, allow these students to practice fundamental motor skills (e.g., throwing and catching) and to enjoy the experience of movement. As the individual grows older, normally after age fifteen, the incidence of fractures decreases allowing for greater involvement and exploration with a wide range of sport activities. Many individuals with osteogenesis imperfecta, beginning as young adults, engage in sport programs sponsored by dwarf or les autres organizations.

Friedreich's Ataxia

Friedreich's ataxia is an inherited disease characterized by progressive degeneration of the sensory nerves of the limbs and trunk. Individuals with this disorder experience poor balance (ataxia) of the extremities and trunk, sometimes leading to frequent falling or a wide-base, side-to-side gait that resembles that of an intoxicated person. Associated difficulties may include general problems with agility, slurred speech, lack of coordination, and tremors of the upper extremities. In addition, individuals with Friedreich's ataxia usually experience spinal deformities (kyphosis or scoliosis) and heart problems. Electrocardiographic changes occur in over 90 percent of those with Friedreich's ataxia. These heart irregularities include problems with heartbeat, heart murmurs, and enlargements of the heart. Eye disorders including nystagmus and lack of visual acuity may also be found.

The incidence of mental retardation and epilepsy, while greater than that found in the nondisabled population, is not high with individuals with Friedreich's ataxia.

Friedreich's ataxia normally becomes evident during the first or second decade of life, although symptoms may be present in early infancy (figure 11.4). Progression of the disease may be rapid or slow with most individuals finding it necessary to rely on the use of a wheelchair in their late teen years. The life span of the individual with Friedreich's ataxia is short, with death occurring in the twenty-five to forty-five age range.

The therapy for Friedreich's ataxia is designed to maintain the alignment of the spinal column and to control for any cardiac complications. This will require that the individual take selected prescriptions and work closely with a physical therapist.

Because most individuals with Friedreich's ataxia will be educated in regular educational settings, it is essential that the physical educator coordinate closely with the student's physician. This contact will help to ensure that the activities selected are appropriate in light of this population's high prevalence of cardiac disorders. In addition, care will need to be exercised in selecting activities that do not overtax the system or place the individual in an unsafe position, such as activities involving height, in light of the associated balance problems.

While it cannot be denied that Friedreich's ataxia is a serious disease, there is every indication that individuals with this disorder perform at an exceptionally high level. The role of the physical educator is to ensure that the negative effect of the progressive muscular disorder is minimized. A program that teaches functional skills such as strength for activities of daily living in a positive and reinforcing environment will go a long way in developing a successful experience for these individuals.

Multiple Sclerosis

Multiple sclerosis is one of our country's most common chronic diseases of the nervous system, affecting several hundred thousand people. The disease attacks females more frequently than males. The peak period of onset is approximately age thirty, but youngsters of high-school age do contract the disease; young children are very seldom affected. Multiple sclerosis does not cause early death. Those who are afflicted may live up to 75 percent of the normal life span; deaths of younger people are almost always due to the complications of secondary infections to the lungs or bladder.

During the course of the disease, hardened patches of varying size appear in random areas of the brain and spinal cord, interfering with the function of the nerves in these

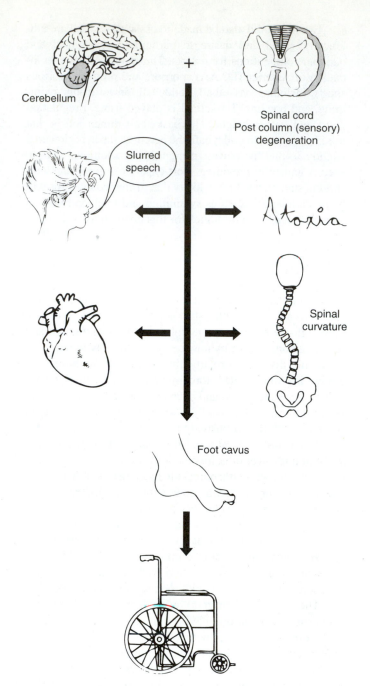

Figure 11.4 Friedreich's ataxia. Representation of the location of the disease process in the sensory nerves and of the progressive signs and symptoms leading to eventual severe disability.

(From: Bleck and Nagel, "Friedreich's Ataxia," *Physically Handicapped Children: A Medical Atlas for Teachers* (2d ed.), by Allyn & Bacon, Inc.)

areas. The patches are actually scar tissue resulting from the disintegration of the thick white covering of the nerve fibers. The covering is called myelin and the process of its disintegration is known as demyelination.

The effects of multiple sclerosis vary according to the portion of the nervous system in which the patches appear; consequently, symptoms differ considerably among those with the disease. Often, however, an early indication of the presence of the disease is a problem with vision, such as double vision or reduction of the field of vision. Unusual weakness, fatigue, and numbness are other common early symptoms. Slurred or monotonous speech, stiff or staggering gait, and tremors or shaking of the limbs may occur as the disease progresses. Eventually there may be paralysis.

The frequency of the attacks varies in different individuals. During the course of the disease, especially in the early stages, attacks are followed by periods of remission during which the symptoms largely disappear. These are followed by periods of exacerbation in which the symptoms return. As the scar tissue proliferates on the central nervous system, the symptoms become more prominent and the periods of remission occur less frequently and finally cease to occur. However, in some cases, even after several attacks, the symptoms permanently disappear.

The cause of the demyelination from which the symptoms of multiple sclerosis rise is not known. Much of the search for the cause has centered on environmental factors, since the disease occurs most frequently in the temperate zones and very seldom in the tropics. Possible causes that also are being investigated include malfunctioning of the biochemistry of the myelin virus, and the presence of an autoimmune disease in which antibodies attack the normal tissue of the myelin.

The treatment of multiple sclerosis includes the use of drugs. However, their benefits have been found to be limited to the first few weeks of treatment. After that, the symptoms return as before. Adherence to good health practices is important in the treatment, because multiple sclerosis appears to become worse after any illness. Emotional distress also seems to have an adverse effect on the disease, so promotion of good mental health is important. Physical therapy usually includes massage and exercise to retard weakening of the affected muscles to the greatest extent possible.

Myasthenia Gravis

Myasthenia gravis is a relatively common chronic disease characterized by progressive muscular weakness. Onset can occur at any age, although young children incur the disease less frequently than do other age groups. The incidence is highest in females between the ages of fourteen and thirty-five and in males between the ages of forty and seventy. Obviously, then, the physical education teacher may expect to encounter some students, particularly high-school-age girls, who have myasthenia gravis.

Specific symptoms vary depending upon the muscles involved; all of the voluntary muscles can be affected. The onset of the disease seldom occurs all at once; rather, the symptoms are more likely to appear over a long period of time and go unrecognized initially. Muscular contraction becomes gradually less forceful; but for a time, rest after muscular exertion restores the former strength of the muscles. The muscles do not become painful as they do in physiological fatigue.

The disease may begin with a characteristic weakness in a single set of muscles or in several sets. Most commonly, the muscles that are initially affected and most severely involved are those of the face and throat, causing difficulty in chewing and swallowing. Other symptoms produced by the weakness of muscles in this area are a drooping of the upper eyelids and a nasal quality of the voice. As the disease progresses, the back, abdomen, arms, and legs may be affected. In advanced cases, the muscles used in respiration may be involved, producing complications that are often fatal.

The cause of myasthenia gravis is not known. It has been postulated that a block occurs, owing to formation of an abnormal chemical compound, that hinders the nerve impulses at the end-plates (terminal ends of a nerve that contract a muscle fiber).

Recent advances in the treatment of myasthenia gravis have effected a reduction in the death rate and in the severity of the disease. Among the improvements in treatment have been such emergency and support measures as the utilization of tracheotomy to open the windpipe, the use of respirators to assist breathing, and the administration of antibiotics to prevent infection. The symptoms can be fairly well controlled with drug treatment. According to the National Institute of Neurological Diseases and Stroke, myasthenia gravis is one of the most successfully managed neuromuscular disorders.

It has been noted that the disease may worsen suddenly when there is emotional stress or when a cold or other infection is present. Consequently, treatment is also directed toward maintaining good physical and mental health.

Polymyositis

There are several types of polymyositis. All are characterized by inflammation of the voluntary muscles, resulting in diminished muscular strength and reflex action. Both children and adults may experience the disease; the incidence is higher among females than among males.

The disease may be acute or chronic. In its acute form, the symptoms are high fever and weakness and severe pain in the muscles. The attacks frequently result in death. Symptomatic of the chronic form is a progressive weakening of the muscles. All of the voluntary muscles may be affected, but most frequently the involvement is in the muscles of the legs and trunk. Disturbance of the walking gait and of other movements utilizing the muscles of the legs and trunk can be observed. Muscle contractures occur in both the acute and the chronic forms, but are more common in the latter.

Polymyositis may also involve other systems. The most frequently involved of these is the skin; the disorder in this case is called dermatomyositis. It is characterized not only by muscular weakness but also by scaling, atrophy, and a pinkish discoloration of the skin.

Some types of polymyositis are remittent. Periods when the health of the affected person improves are followed by periods of attack. Between the attacks the weakened and contracted muscles do not regain their functional efficiency.

The exact cause of the disease is unknown. Medical investigators have hypothesized that it is allergic in nature, which refers to the body's characteristic response to invasion by a foreign substance.

Treatment involves the administration of drugs; however, their effect on the course of the disease is difficult to assess because spontaneous remission does occur. General systemic measures, such as a well-balanced diet high in protein and prompt attention to infectious and respiratory ailments, are important in the treatment. Braces may be used to support the body and assist in movement.

Needs and Adjustments of Those with Muscular Disorders

Maintenance of the best possible physical and mental health is, as we have seen, important in the treatment of those with any of the diseases characterized by muscular weaknesses. Because exercise plays an essential role in physical conditioning, a logical assumption would be that participation in selected physical education activities is highly recommended by physicians who specialize in the treatment of these disorders. This is not entirely the case. Various kinds of exercise are prescribed for those who have muscular dystrophy, and these can be supplemented with appropriate physical education activities. For individuals with multiple sclerosis, most physicians believe that inactivity leads to secondary complications and so they advocate exercises that help to retard incapacitation and loss of fitness. These exercises can be supplemented in the physical education program. With respect to myasthenia gravis and polymyositis, the value of special exercises in the treatment program has not been given significant attention by the medical profession. Consequently, there is little information to guide the physical education teacher who has students with these disorders. More frequent communication with the doctors of these students will be necessary to develop a suitable program to serve their special needs.

In helping students with muscular weakness to maintain a level of physical fitness consistent with their capacity to engage in physical activity, the physical education teacher is likely to encounter apathy or resistance. Students who are experiencing considerable muscular weakness and pain usually prefer not to make the effort required to do even mildly taxing motor activities. They see little value in working to delay the general deterioration and incapacitation that they know, or suspect, is their inevitable fate.

Motivating such students requires planning and patience. Discovering and utilizing their interests to make participation appealing will help to provide the basis for acceptance of the program. Praise and encouragement are essential in motivating effort; it may be necessary to offer extrinsic rewards as well. Goals must be short term so that results can be seen as immediate benefits.

The debility that is characteristic of the diseases discussed in this chapter is distressing to those affected. Inability to perform physical tasks with the same vigor and control as previously is frustrating and bewildering. Disturbances in walking gait and of the facial features are particularly distressing because they create problems of social acceptance and often give rise to ridicule.

When youngsters become progressively weakened such that they must use wheelchairs to move about, the difficulty in adjusting is increased. While others in their peer group are expanding their activities and experiences, the world of students with movement deficiencies becomes more challenging. Without supportive and caring teachers, these youngsters would be denied the adventure and excitement that accompany each new stage of growth and development in the years of childhood and young adulthood. Awareness of their present state and of the unlikelihood of future improvement produces feelings of depression and anxiety.

Perhaps the greatest contribution the physical education teacher can make to these children is to serve their need to feel part of the group. In physical education more than in any other school situation, students can be brought into activities from which they would otherwise be excluded. Because the activities in which they are able to participate are limited, the teacher must exercise great ingenuity in modifying activities to allow some type of participation with the group. Whatever the level of participation, the youngster with movement disorders must feel a part of the group and that he or she is making a worthy contribution.

Program Planning for Those with Muscular Disorders

Probably no two students, even with the same disorder, will have the same kind and degree of movement limitations, so the activity program will need to be planned on an individual basis. The selection of appropriate motor activities requires careful preliminary analysis of the movement potential of the student. Consultation with the student's physician is recommended to ensure that the activities and planned modifications will have no adverse effects and that they will complement the student's physical therapy program.

In general, the activities selected should provide moderate exercise to the unaffected muscles. Such exercise is needed not only to maintain physical efficiency but also to consume calories to assist in weight control, almost always a difficult task for the sedentary person. The use of specific exercises to increase the strength of the affected muscles should be done only after consultation with the medical team. While the use of resistance exercises for students with muscular dystrophy should be done cautiously and in consultation with medical personnel, there is some evidence that strength training may be a potentially useful therapeutic option in the management of selected neuromuscular disorders (McCartney et al., 1988).

If the student is mature enough to understand the principles of movement, the teacher should describe these. Preferably such discussion would occur in connection with the learning of movements to which the principles apply. The purpose is to give the student enough information and insight into movement to make the necessary adjustments needed to perform the skills of other activities without the teacher's assistance; or if the student is going to become progressively weaker, so that he or she can accommodate skill techniques to counteract diminishing capability.

Suggested Activities

Activities for students who are only mildly affected or whose conditions are not yet advanced may be chosen from among the less vigorous activities of the regular physical education sports, games, and dances. Possibilities are unlimited and include basic skill games of shuffleboard, table tennis, archery, softball, and volleyball. Modification of these and other activities will be required for students who suffer greater deterioration of muscular strength and reflex action. The kind of adaptation made is largely determined by the degree of mobility of the participant.

The activities described here are generally suitable for those who are very restricted in locomotion or who use wheelchairs. They may be used in the form in which they are presented or modified to meet special needs. Similar games or activities can be readily developed by the teacher after initial experience with students who have progressive muscular weakness.

All activities should be integrated to include children with and without disabilities.

1. The children form a circle and pass the ball to one another. The ball may be passed in various ways—one hand, two hands, overhand, or underhand. Balls of different sizes may be used, and more than one ball may be used at one time. Another possibility is the assignment of numbers at random around the circle; the ball is then passed in numerical order. Reassignment of numbers should be made frequently to keep interest high.

2. A ball suspended from the ceiling affords several activity possibilities. It may be batted with a plastic bat, thrown to a target on the wall, or used for a game of catch by two or more children.

Figure 11.5 Students with muscular disorders may require special assistance in learning motor skills.

3. An inflated balloon of heavy rubber may be used for catching and throwing by students who are too weak to handle the heavier weight of a regular ball.

4. The attachment of a long cord to a bean bag enables its easy retrieval by students with restricted movement. The bean bag can be used for throwing at a target or for throwing between students. In both situations, the thrower retains a hold on the cord after the bean bag leaves his or her hand.

5. A bowling game is simulated with plastic bowling pins and a heavy ball. Milk cartons that have been filled with beans to give them weight may be substituted for the pins. The ball is rolled toward the pins to knock down as many as possible. Score may be kept if desired. If the player is unable to roll the ball, a cue may be used. A player in a wheelchair may need to use a special ramp on which the ball is placed and guided toward the pins.

6. A game may be made of bouncing a ball beside the wheelchair for the student who uses a chair. A basketball or lighter rubber ball is used. The student

explores different heights of the ball in the dribble, various ways of striking the ball with the hand, and so forth. Another possibility is dribbling the ball while moving the wheelchair.

7. Batting activity is possible from a sitting or standing position with the use of a batting tee and a ball attached with a string to the tee. The ball is retrieved by pulling on the string.

8. With a special paddle that hangs from a frame, the student can engage in a game of hitting a table tennis ball over the net, to the left or right court. A modified game of table tennis is also possible.

9. Exploration of motor movements in unaffected parts of the body provides a suitable activity. For example, the student whose leg is not involved may explore to discover how slowly and how rapidly it can be moved and the various heights to which it can be raised.

10. Exercises of contraction and relaxation (described in chapter 29, *Relaxation*) are other possible activities, as are rolling, crawling, and similar movements performed on a mat. The choices of relaxation exercises and movements on the mat are dictated by the areas of the body affected by the disease.

Because physical therapy to retain flexibility is usually prescribed for those with muscular dystrophy early in the course of the disease, complementary exercises can be offered in the physical education program. Examples of these are given:

Throwing—encourage full range of motion from the ready position to the follow-through.
Reaching for and picking up objects—encourage the extension of the body as far as possible in the bend and reach.
Batting and striking—encourage a full swing.
Kicking—encourage full extension of the leg in the kick.
Stepping up and over objects—encourage taking the longest possible step consistent with good balance.

Swimming is an appropriate activity for most individuals with muscular weakness, regardless of the lack of muscle action. Extremely weak muscles can often function when they are freed from the pull of gravity by the buoyancy of the water. It has been found that those with muscular weakness can master the elementary back stroke more easily than other strokes and, therefore, it is recommended that this be the first swimming stroke taught. Flotation devices are extremely helpful in supporting a segment of the body that is completely restricted in movement. (See chapter 26, *Swimming*, for further discussion.)

There is a special technique for assisting the youngster with muscular dystrophy to rise from a sitting position. The helper stands facing the youngster and puts his or her arms around the lower back and locks the hands. The helper lifts up so that the youngster's trunk can sway backward and the hips can be pulled forward to a balanced position. The lift should not be made under the arms, because putting upward pressure on the arms may cause injury to the shoulders due to the extreme weakness of the shoulder girdle area.

Summary

Within this chapter information has been presented about a variety of disorders categorized under the heading *les autres*. The term *les autres* is a French expression that means "the others." This designation is appropriate and valuable in helping physical educators remember that the label is not as important as the commitment to provide needed services and programs. There are many individuals with unnamed or unfamiliar disorders who need assistance. Care must be taken not to avoid providing special services to individuals because they fail to fit the established categories. For example, many individuals with conditions such as multiple sclerosis and growth disorders were denied the opportunity to participate in athletic competitions, including those developed by organizations for people with disabilities, because their conditions were not recognized as part of the established system for classifying athletes. Without an appropriate classification system, they were denied the opportunity to compete and to derive the benefits associated with the various meets and events. Fortunately, this is no longer true. Athletes with les autres conditions can compete and as a result we have learned much about these individuals. We know that their interests and needs are very much like those of other individuals with and without disabilities. These individuals can participate in many of the programs, activities, and exercises used in physical education and sport programs, with modifications as necessary.

The goal for individuals with les autres conditions is to minimize the effects of the disorder through a well-balanced program that emphasizes physical fitness, skill development, and activities to enhance opportunities for interaction with others. While the les autres disorders have similar features, there are also some unique aspects that will require close interaction and articulation with other professionals including educators, therapists, and physicians.

Selected Readings

Ablon, J. (1988). *Living with difference: Families with dwarf children.* New York: Praeger.

Adams, R.C., & McCubbin, J.A. (1991). *Games, sports and exercises for the physically disabled* (4th ed.). Philadelphia: Lea and Febiger.

Basmajian, J.V., & Wolf, S. (Ed.). (1990). *Therapeutic exercise* (5th ed.). Baltimore: Williams and Wilkins.

Bleck, E.E., & Nagel, D.A. (Eds.). (1982). *Physically handicapped children: A medical atlas for teachers* (2d ed.). New York: Grune and Stratton.

Brooke, M.H. (1986). *A clinician's view of neuromuscular diseases.* Baltimore: Williams and Wilkins.

Cratty, B.J. (1989). *Adapted physical education in the mainstream* (2d ed.). Denver, CO: Love Publishing Co.

Croce, R. (1987). Exercise and physical activity in managing progressive muscular dystrophy: A review for practitioners. *Palaestra, 3*(3), 9–14, 14.

Downey, J.A., & Low, N.L. (1974). *The child with disabling illness.* Philadelphia: W.B. Saunders Co.

Drennan, J. (1983). *Orthopedic management of neuromuscular disorders.* Philadelphia: J.B. Lippincott.

Gershwin, M., & Robins, D. (1983). *Musculoskeletal diseases of children.* New York: Grune and Stratton.

Goldberg, B. (1990). Children, sports, & chronic disease. *Physician and Sports Medicine, 18*(10), 44–50, 53–54, 56.

Greenblatt, M.H. (1972). *Multiple sclerosis and me.* Springfield, IL: Charles C. Thomas.

Knudsen, M. (1993). Flexibility and range of motion of dwarfs with achondroplasia. Unpublished thesis, Texas Woman's University, Denton, Texas.

Krusen, F.H., Kottke, F.J., Stillwell, G.K., & Lehmon, J.F. (1971). *Handbook of physical medicine and rehabilitation* (2d ed.). Philadelphia: W.B. Saunders Co.

Low, L. (1992). Prediction of selected track, field, and swimming performances of dwarf athletes by anthropometry. Unpublished doctoral study, Texas Woman's University, Denton, Texas.

McCartney, N., Moroz, D., Garner, S., & McComas, J. The effects of strength training in route with selective neuromuscular disorders. (1988). *Medicine and Science in Sports and Exercise, 20*(4), 362–368.

Scott, C.I. (1988). Dwarfism. *Clinical Symposia, 40*(1), 2–32.

Skinner, J.S. (Ed.). (1987). *Exercise testing and exercise prescription for special cases.* Philadelphia: Lea and Febiger.

Swaiman, K.F., & Wright, F.S. (1970). *Neuromuscular diseases of infancy and childhood.* Springfield, IL: Charles C. Thomas.

Tecklin, J. (1989). *Pediatric physical therapy.* Philadelphia: J.B. Lippincott.

Walton, J.N. (1969). *Disorders of voluntary muscles.* Boston: Little, Brown, and Co.

Enhancing Activities

1. Interview a person of short stature to obtain his or her view of the terms "midget," "dwarf," and "little people."

2. Develop a game or activity that would be appropriate for individuals with one of the disorders described in this chapter. Describe the game, rules, suggested age of players, and modifications, where appropriate.

3. Review the results of the 1996 Paralympics. Identify and list those activities in which individuals with the les autres conditions competed.

4. Assist in conducting a local or regional meet sponsored by the United States Les Autres Sports Association. Analyze the performance of the athletes competing in the les autres events.

5. Develop a list of the agencies or organizations that provide information and material on the disorders described in this chapter.

6. With the assistance of your professor and/or local school system, locate a youngster with a les autres condition and offer to assist in the physical education program for the student. Analyze the activities taught, the method(s) used to present the information, adaptations, and procedures to evaluate the student's progress.

CHAPTER 12

Sensory Impairments

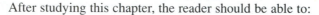

CHAPTER OBJECTIVES

After studying this chapter, the reader should be able to:

1 Appreciate the historical and changing perspective of the importance of physical activity and its contribution to the well-being of students with sensory impairments.

2 Recognize the various communication techniques utilized to help those with auditory and visual impairments benefit from educational programs and activities.

3 Analyze various games and activities commonly played by children and suggest modifications in these experiences to accommodate the special needs of those with sensory impairments.

4 Identify and describe the common causes of sensory impairment and the degree of sensory loss associated with each.

5 Identify adaptations made to games such as soccer, volleyball, tennis, and horseshoes for individuals with sensory impairment.

6 Explain the classifications systems used to describe the magnitude of the visual or hearing loss.

7 Identify the special equipment and instructional techniques used to teach physical education to those with visual and/or hearing impairments.

8 Describe the following terms used to describe programs and services for the visually and hearing impaired: congenital, adventitious, legal blindness, myopia, hyperopia, nystagmus, astigmatism, strabismus, Braille, mobility orientation, beep baseball, goal ball, hearing impaired, blind, deaf, decibel, hertz, AMESLAN, finger spelling, speech reading, and deaf-blind.

9 Identify and describe general guidelines that can be employed to develop appropriate programs for students with sensory impairments.

10 Identify the different sports and recreation associations available for individuals who are sensory impaired.

The term *sensory impairment* describes a condition in which one or more of the senses are diminished in their effectiveness to respond to stimuli. Such a condition may be present from birth or may develop at any time during life as the result of injury or disease. The lack of sensory response to stimulation may be total or partial. Difficulties for the person involved are created by any sensory impairment regardless of the time of incurrence or the degree of severity.

The discussion in this chapter will be limited to visual and auditory handicaps and to a combination of the two, or dual sensory impairment. Much of the information presented concerning the causes, special needs, and adjustment problems of persons with either of the disabilities also applies to those with dual impairment and can serve as a foundation for a fuller understanding of the presentation of the dual sensory disability.

Visual Impairments

Physical education for those with visual impairments has a long and interesting history. In the 1830s three schools for blind children were founded in the United States, providing the first educational opportunities for such children. One of these schools, Perkins Institute in Boston, had as its director a medical doctor who was an enthusiastic advocate of the benefits of physical exercise. He organized a program of vigorous physical activity that included playing outdoors, swimming in the ocean, and working on gymnastic apparatus. His program was far in advance of the physical education in the public schools of his day.

Gradually other schools for the visually impaired were established. Some of these made provisions for physical training classes in which gymnastics constituted the chief activity. Military training, which received emphasis in the public schools following the Civil War, displaced gymnastic training in schools for the visually impaired. The consequence was that marching and military exercise or formal gymnastics have served as the core of physical education for students with visual impairments in many schools until very recent times. In other schools, the play movement that swept the country in the early part of this century encouraged administrators to begin athletic programs in wrestling and track and field. Intramural teams in these sports became prevalent, and soon varsity teams entered into interschool competition.

Today physical education programs at the special schools offer a balanced variety of activities, including intramural and interscholastic sports. Dr. Charles Buell, a physical educator who is blind and former Athletic Director at the California School for the Blind, was instrumental in formulating many of the ideas used in physical education classes for the visually impaired throughout the United States. Many students with visual impairments who in former years would have been enrolled in special schools now attend public schools where they participate in regular physical education or special physical education as their needs require.

The Nature of Visual Impairments

Approximately one child out of every four or five has some significant deviation from the accepted norm of good vision. A large majority of these have such slight deviations that they are not extremely detrimental to the child or are remediable either medically or by wearing prescribed lenses. For these children no special educational provisions need be made. However, about one out of every fifteen hundred has such severe deviations from normal vision that he or she cannot read books printed in regular type and so require materials printed in large type or Braille.

Visual acuity, the ability to clearly distinguish forms or discriminate details, is commonly measured by the use of a chart having several lines of progressively smaller letters or symbols. The person being tested reads the chart from a specific distance. Visual acuity, as determined by the number of lines the individual is able to read, is expressed in a numerical ratio. For example, a ratio of 20/200 indicates that the person being tested had to stand twenty feet from the chart (the first number in the ratio) in order to see what someone with normal vision can see from two hundred feet (the second number).

The degree to which students are impaired is determined largely by how greatly their vision deviates from normal. Although for purposes of classification those with visual acuity of 20/200 or less with glasses are considered legally blind, most of those so classified have some useful sight. They may be able to perceive light, form, or movement and are, consequently, considered to be partially sighted (table 12.1). The partially sighted have traditionally been enrolled in schools for the blind along with the totally blind because their visual impairments require special educational methods and equipment. However, the enrollment

---

Table 12.1   *Degrees of visual acuity*

Legal Blindness.   Visual acuity of 20/200 or less or a field of vision less than 20°. Students so designated are eligible to receive special assistance from state and federal sources.

Travel Vision.   Visual acuity from 5/200 to 10/200 inclusive. Enough sight is present to allow moving or walking without extreme difficulty.

Motion Perception.   Visual acuity from 3/200 to 5/200 inclusive. Movement can be seen but usually not the still object.

Light Perception.   Visual acuity less than 3/200. A bright light can be distinguished at a distance of three feet or less but movement cannot.

Total or Complete Blindness.   Inability to see light.

Tunnel Vision.   A field of vision of 20° or less. The field of vision is so drastically narrowed that the person sees as though looking through a tube.

of partially seeing students in regular school systems, with some special arrangements made for their needs, is now common practice. Sometimes their instruction is provided in special classes with a teacher trained in methods of instructing the partially sighted and with equipment designed especially for their needs. In other situations they are accommodated in the regular classroom.

The age at which individuals lose sight has as much bearing on their educational needs as the degree to which their vision is affected. Blindness at birth is more challenging than blindness that occurs later in life, because it prevents the individual from establishing visual concepts of any kind.

Causes of Visual Impairments

The primary function of the eye is to receive visual input and to transmit this information to the brain via the optic nerve. This is a complicated procedure in which the eye collects light reflected from objects in the visual field and focuses these objects on the retina. The visual information is then transmitted from the retina to the optic nerve. In a normal eye, refraction occurs when a ray of light is deflected from its course as it passes through various surfaces of the eye (figure 12.1).

First, light focuses on the cornea; then it passes through a watery liquid known as the aqueous humor. Next, light passes through the pupil, a circular hole in the center of the eye that contracts or expands according to the amount of light reaching the eye. The light then enters the lens, which is curved to reflect the light more before it enters a jelly-like fluid known as the vitreous humor. A clear image finally reaches the retina and is transmitted to the brain via the optic nerve.

The ability to see normally is a very complex process involving various intricate parts of the eye. It is understandable, therefore, that problems can develop that interfere with normal sight. Although there are many causes of visual impairments, only those that more commonly occur will be presented here.

Visual impairments may be due to congenital problems or to difficulties that occur later in the student's development.

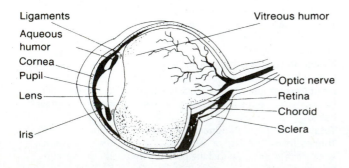

Figure 12.1   Diagram of the human eye.

Those who are born with visual disorders are referred to as *congenitally blind;* those who develop problems later are referred to as *adventitiously blind.* Causes of visual impairments may be classified as refractive errors, eye muscle disorders, or diseases and genetic defects.

Refractive Errors

Refractive errors occur when the visual image is blurred due to improper focus of the light rays. Myopia, hyperopia, and astigmatism are three common refractive errors. Myopia occurs when the eyeball is too long from front to back, causing the visual image to focus in front of, rather than on, the retina. Myopic, or nearsighted, individuals have to hold objects close to their eyes to see them clearly. In hyperopia, or farsightedness, the eyeball is too short, causing the visual image to focus in back of, rather than on, the retina. People who are farsighted have difficulty seeing close objects clearly but perceive distant objects with no problem. Astigmatism is due to an irregularly shaped cornea, causing blurred vision for both far and near objects. Fortunately, refractive problems can be corrected for most individuals through the use of prescription glasses or contact lenses.

Muscle Imbalance

Some students experience visual problems because the eyes do not work together. Although each eye's retina sees a separate visual image, normally the brain coordinates the eyes so that one visual image is perceived. For some, however, the muscles that surround each eye are not synchronized, resulting in vision that is distorted. Normally this condition is characterized by nystagmus, rapid side to side or up and down movement of the eye; strabismus, misaligned vision in which the eyes either cross or turn out; or amblyopia, domination by one eye due to the inability of the two eyes to focus clearly on an object.

Genetic Disorders and Diseases of the Eye

Infectious diseases cause many cases of vision loss. The secondary infection of a contagious disease that has attacked the body, such as smallpox, scarlet fever, or typhoid fever, may cause eye difficulties, or the problems may be caused by infectious diseases that primarily affect the eyes.

Among the infectious diseases that affect the eyes and frequently cause loss of sight are trachoma and ophthalmia. Trachoma is a chronic inflammation of the conjunctiva believed to be conveyed mechanically to the eye through the use of common washcloths, towels, and handkerchiefs or by the fingers. Ophthalmia is an inflammation of the conjunctiva occurring most often during the first two weeks of a baby's life. It is the result of infection by any one of several pathogenic organisms contracted by the baby during birth, or from the presence of contaminated objects near the eyes.

Another cause of visual impairment in infants is the infection of the mother by rubella (German or three-day measles) during the first trimester of pregnancy. During the rubella epidemic of 1963 to 1965, a large number of children were born with vision problems as the result of their mothers' having contracted the disease in early pregnancy. Since that time a vaccine to prevent rubella has been discovered and marketed. With the widespread use of the vaccine, rubella, like gonorrhea and retinopathy of prematurity (ROP), may cease to be a major factor in the development of childhood vision impairments.

Glaucoma, a disease of the eye characterized by increased intraocular (within the eye) pressure, is the second leading cause of blindness in the United States and the leading cause of blindness in African Americans (Danyluk and Paton, 1991). Although glaucoma can occur at any age, it is more prevalent in older persons, affecting approximately 2 percent of the population over the age of forty. Glaucoma, if not treated, results in progressive and irreversible contraction of the visual field that may lead to total blindness.

Conditions of a hereditary nature that produce blindness are cataract, atrophy of the optic nerve, and retinitis pigmentosa (deposits of pigment on the retina of the eye).

Gonorrhea, once a common cause of prenatal blindness, has been brought under effective control by state legislation requiring doctors delivering babies to use silver nitrate or other effective medicinals in the eyes of newborn babies. Another cause of blindness, occurring in premature infants, is also being successfully controlled. This is a condition known as retrolental fibroplasia, which was discovered to be related to the administration of excessive amounts of oxygen to premature babies.

Figure 12.2(A) Glaucoma: A disease where tissues are damaged by increasing pressure inside the eye. If not treated soon enough, glaucoma can destroy side vision, leaving "tunnel vision"—a small central area in which the person still sees.

Figure 12.2(C) Retinitis pigmentosa: An inherited disease which affects vision due to a breakdown of retinal tissues. Characterized by night blindness, retinitis pigmentisa frequently results in tunnel vision. Central vision can also be affected.

Figure 12.2(B) Cataract: A clouding of the lens which causes a general loss of detail in what a person sees. The field of vision is unaffected, but glaring light conditions, distortion, and double images can prove annoying.

Figure 12.2(D) Detached retina: Retinas detach for a variety of reasons and many can be surgically repaired. When active, the hole or tear involved fills with liquid, lifting the retina from its normal position, and causing a defect in the field of vision.

Figure 12.2(*E*) Macular degeneration: The most common eye disease, macular degeneration causes loss of vision in the central field, making it difficult to read or do close work.

Needs and Adjustments of Those with Vision Impairment

Children with impaired vision have the same needs for physical activity as other children, but their lack of normal vision does in numerous instances restrict their play activities to such an extent that they are noticeably retarded in their physical development. Fear of injury instilled in them by protective parents reduces their natural interest in big-muscle movements such as running, climbing, and jumping, which are an inherent part of most children's play and contributes to their muscular growth and the development of coordination. As a result, physical vitality and resistance to certain diseases are low and excess weight is often a problem. Posture may be poor both because of the lack of strength in the postural muscles and because of the lack of visual examples of good posture to emulate.

Because the urges of children who are blind to move and play are frustrated, they often develop certain mannerisms known as blindisms. These are physical movements through which, it is thought, the child who is blind seeks to fulfill the need for muscular movement without moving about through space. Rocking back and forth, twitching of the head, and jerking of the limbs are characteristic blindisms. It is desirable to overcome these mannerisms, because they set children with visual impairments apart from their seeing peers. Moreover, in working to eliminate the blindisms a greater sense of security in moving about in space will be developed. Teaching children who are blind physical and recreational pursuits will give them alternative activities during idle time other than blindisms or self stimulation.

Those who are visually impaired may have personality problems as well as physical incapacities. Because of their fears of activity, those who are visually impaired tend to pursue solitary and sedentary occupations. This limits their social contacts, which may in turn feed a feeling of inferiority. Frustrations experienced in attempting normal activity or normal social relations contribute to maladjustment. Fantasies and daydreaming are common among the visually impaired who have made unsatisfactory adjustments to their circumstances. The age at which individuals lose their sight has considerable effect upon their social adjustment. Children who have been without sight since birth have more difficulty in social adjustment than those who had achieved some degree of social maturity before losing their sight. However, the latter may experience anxieties and fears about their future, resulting in extreme cases of despondency and depression.

The age at which the impairment occurs likewise influences the movement patterns. These are also governed by the degree to which the person can see. Those who have gained assurance from previous experiences or from their ability to see slightly will move about with less awkwardness and with more confidence than others whose fears are heightened by lack of such assurance.

Individuals who are visually impaired tend to develop their other senses to a higher degree than sighted people to compensate for their lack of sight. Some believe the visually impaired to have a "sixth sense" because they have developed such an awareness of their environment that they appear to perceive things that their sighted associates cannot perceive. There is no evidence to support the concept that those with visual impairments have an unnatural or mystical gift that enables them to perform activities that would seem possible only for the seeing. The adroitness with which a person without sight walks down the crowded sidewalk avoiding other walkers and obstacles, negotiates the curb, and crosses with the light seems almost superhuman to the fully visioned, who cannot conceive of doing this themselves without the use of eyes. Behind the skill of the walker who is visually impaired is a highly developed kinesthetic sense, the ability to listen closely to auditory clues, and experience in the interpretation of the various stimuli to the other senses. The person's "sixth sense" is actually the acute development of the other senses.

Planning the Special Program

There are several effective teaching procedures that may be utilized to integrate a student with a visual impairment into the regular physical education class. Before these procedures can be used, of course, the teacher must ascertain the degree to which the student can perceive and how well he or she has developed compensatory skills. Of fundamental importance is for the teacher to ascertain how well the student can see. For example, the teacher should question the student as to his/her visual abilities (e.g., can the student see light, shadows, outline of faces, and colors such as white versus red). With this knowledge about the student, the teacher can make simple modifications in the activities to accommodate the youngster in the games of the class.

An example should suggest many more similar possibilities to the physical education teacher. Assume that a student with partial vision is to be integrated into a softball unit with sighted students. The teacher, in consultation with the student, must devise a system to help the individual learn the fundamentals of softball. As presented in chapter 6, the teacher would first identify the tasks involved in the game of softball and then systematically explore ways the various tasks could be modified. The game of softball, for instance, requires students to hit, run bases, pitch, field, catch, and throw. Modifications for the task of hitting might include having the student hit using a batting tee; hit with a larger bat; use a larger, brightly colored ball; swing at a pitched ball with the verbal assistance of the teacher or a classmate; or use an audible ball. Each of these modifications must be studied carefully by the teacher with a view to identifying the one most closely approximating the original task that can be performed successfully by the student. Use of a substitute batter should be made only if none of the other options were successful. Modifications for other softball skills are given in table 12.2 and offer an example of the way in which games can be adapted for participation by players with visual impairments.

The ultimate aim is to have the students without disabilities recognize the student who is visually impaired as an asset rather than a liability for their team. Utilization of modifications like those suggested before promotes the development of such recognition. However, the teacher sets the tone for how the student with visual impairments is received. If the teacher is overly protective and solicitous of the student in the class, such will be the general attitude displayed by the class. Acceptance of the students for who they

are, with an appreciation of the talents and abilities they display, will be the response of the class if this is the attitude demonstrated by the instructor.

The discussion that follows identifies several factors that physical educators must consider in teaching movement experiences to students who are visually impaired. The information applies to students taught in the regular program as well as students enrolled in special classes or special schools for the blind.

Play Areas

The play area, indoors and out, should be a large, uncluttered space. As a safety precaution the play area should be free of nonessential equipment and unnecessary obstructions. For outdoor playing fields, hedges and shade trees are considered desirable boundaries rather than walls or fences, which present a certain element of danger for all students, including those who are visually impaired. Boundaries for games can be indicated by varying the composition of the court as, for example, having the in-bounds area composed of asphalt or an all-weather surface and the out-of-bounds area of sand or grass. Players will then be able to tell by foot sensitivity when they have stepped out of bounds. Newspaper tightly secured to mark the out-of-bounds area on a floor or field is an inexpensive method to achieve this effect.

Boundaries in the indoor playing area should be painted in white for the benefit of those students able to distinguish white. The gymnasium should be well lighted to present the best possible seeing conditions for those who are able to perceive light. A contrast in playing surfaces in the gymnasium can be achieved with wood and concrete or the composition surface, which is becoming increasingly popular. Rope taped to the floor is also a cheap and safe way to distinguish boundaries.

Students who are blind should be thoroughly introduced to an unfamiliar playing area before they are allowed to play. They should know the size and shape of the area and the nature of the boundaries before they engage in activity in the area. To orient the students, the teacher should walk with them around the area, including the locker room facility, describing the essential details. Specific areas, such as entrances and exits and other permanent fixtures, should be identified for the student. These permanent fixtures, commonly referred to by individuals who are blind as anchor points, serve as valuable reference points for orientation. A few simple games or contests might be played to help the students gain familiarity with the playing area before engaging in strenuous play.

To guide children with visual impairments in running activities and to give them greater security, ropes and rings that are grasped in the hands may be suspended from wires strung across the gymnasium well above the heads of the participants. For outside running events, ropes can be placed along the path of the runners to guide them. The runners will

---

Table 12.2 *Sample modifications for the game of softball*

Task	Modification
Hitting the ball	Use a larger, bigger bat
	Use a larger, brightly colored ball
	Use a batting tee
	Use an audible ball
	Swing at a pitched ball with the verbal assistance of the teacher
Running the bases	Follow a guide rope
	Use the natural contrast of worn base path to grass field
	Shorten the distance between bases
	Run with a partner
	Run to sound provided by audible device or teammate's coaching
Fielding a ball	Use the buddy system for assistance
	Modify rule so that if player who is visually impaired picks the ball up before runner reaches base, the runner is out
	Modify the rule to allow for put out when ball is thrown to closest player or base
	Use an audible ball

need some type of warning at the finish line; this may be a knot tied at the end of the rope, or some sort of auditory signal such as a whistle may be sounded.

Special Equipment

Playground equipment for younger children may be the same type found on any playground, including swings, jungle gyms, and teeter-totters; however, greater care must be exercised in locating them to avoid possible injury to the nonseeing participants. Swings should be constructed with no more than two swings on the stand; a third swing in the center is difficult to reach without danger when the other two swings are occupied. The use of guard rails or ground markers is a necessary safety precaution to prevent youngsters from bumping into equipment or being hit by flying swings.

It is recommended that balls to be used by students who are blind be larger in size and softer than regulation balls and that they be yellow or white to make them more easily seen by those with some vision. Bells, rattles, or buzzers inside the balls help to indicate their location to players who are blind.

A portable aluminum rail is a useful aid to the blind in bowling (figure 12.3). The rail may be used on bowling alleys or on the gymnasium floor when plastic bowling sets are being used. Stationary bicycles, common equipment in physiology of exercise laboratories, are excellent for use by the blind in physical conditioning. Information concerning the purchase of the previously mentioned special equipment can be obtained by writing to the American Foundation for the Blind, Inc., Aids and Appliances Division, 15 West 16th Street, New York, NY 10011.

Only such playing equipment as is actually in use should be permitted in the playing area to ensure maximum safety. Children who are blind can memorize the location of the permanent fixtures but cannot avoid superfluous equipment that has been left in their way. The youngsters also can memorize the place in the storage closets where each item of equipment is kept and are capable of securing the needed items and returning them at the end of the play period.

Communication Aids

Instruction in physical education, similar to other curricular areas, requires that students read assigned material, take tests, and complete class reports. For the student who is blind, this usually requires some special considerations when disseminating written material. For some, such as those who can read printed material with the aid of a magnifier, the modifications will be minor. Others may need printed material that is enlarged with the use of fonts found in many computer software programs. In figure 12.4, the large print is illustrated. The American Printing House for the Blind (1839 Frankfort Avenue, Louisville, KY 40206) publishes books with enlarged print.

For students unable to read printed letters that are one-quarter inch high, reliance on the Braille system is an alternative means of written communication. Braille is a tactile alphabet system developed in the nineteenth century by Louis Braille, a blind Frenchman. The Braille alphabet is a code system consisting of raised dots arranged in various positions within a six-dot cell. Letters, numbers, mathematic symbols, and abbreviated words are represented in the Braille system by various configurations of raised dots (figure 12.5). Braille may be written by the use of a Braille writer, a device similar to a typewriter, or a slate and stylus to produce the raised dots.

In many schools, resource teachers for the visually impaired are common. Cooperative planning with these professionals will assist the physical education teacher in selecting the best system for preparing written material. These experts also can help transfer assignments and tests into Braille or enlarged type. Some material may also be recorded, enabling the student to complete reading assignments and tests by listening to tapes.

Figure 12.3 A special rail that helps the player with a visual impairment to determine direction when releasing a bowling ball can be used for practice in the gymnasium or for play at a regular bowling alley.

Large-print books for the visually impaired use type

of the size shown in this sample. Fewer characters fit on each line; so the width of the line

Figure 12.4 Sample of large print type size.

Braille Alphabet and Numerals

The six dots of the Braille cell are arranged
1 •• 4
2 •• 5
3 •• 6
and numbered thus: The capital sign, dot 6, placed before a letter makes it a capital. The number sign, dots 3, 4, 5, 6, placed before a character, makes it a figure and not a letter.

1	2	3	4	5	6	7	8	9	10
a	b	c	d	e	f	g	h	i	j

k	l	m	n	o	p	q	r	s	t

u	v	w	x	y	z	Capital Sign	#	.	,

:	;	!	(	)	'	-	"	"	?

Figure 12.5 The braille system for representing numbers and letters.

(Courtesy of American Foundation for the Blind, Inc., 15 West 16th Street, New York, NY, 10011.)

Instructional Approach

The introduction of new skills requires a kinesthetic approach. The teacher and perhaps a few of the students who have learned the skill may demonstrate it while those without sight examine the parts of the body involved with their hands. In teaching the golf swing, for example, the student can stand behind the instructor with arms around the instructor and with hands on the instructor's hands. (An inspection of people and objects with the hands is called "brailling" in the vernacular of the blind.) At times it may be helpful for the teacher to place the student's hands and feet and other parts of the body into the desired positions. Lengthy verbal explanations should be avoided. However, clear and concise descriptions that accompany the kinesthetic approach may be used with great effectiveness. In planning the teaching of a skill, sighted instructors may gain greater insight into the problems that the skill will present to their students who are visually impaired if they close their eyes while performing the skill.

A whistle is an essential piece of equipment for the instructor of students who are visually impaired, and it may be blown to identify for the students the teacher's location, to signal for attention, or for other purposes. A meaningful set of signals may be worked out with the students. Because of the noise found in most gymnasiums, a megaphone is useful to teachers in making their voices heard to the players. The players will need to be given a great many details of the progress of the game that players with normal vision would observe naturally. For example, if a kickball game is in progress, the players will need to be told which players are on which bases, who will kick next, the placement of players on the field, and when an out or a score is made. Here again, if teachers will try to empathize with players who are blind when choosing what facts the students need to know as the game progresses, they can select the most useful information to give to the players.

Nearly all the varieties of activities offered to sighted students in the physical education curriculum can be presented to youngsters who are blind. Some require more adaptation than others, but children who are blind enjoy and need participation in the same games, sports, and physical activities as other children. In addition, the activities can help them overcome some of the problems, physical and emotional, that are the direct result of the visual impairments. Students with visual impairments should participate with their sighted peers. If special instructional assistance is needed, it should be in addition to regular instruction in physical education.

Mobility and Orientation

The ability of a student with visual impairments to move about independently is one of the primary goals of his or her total educational development. Orientation refers to the ability of nonsighted students to use their remaining senses to relate their body position to other objects. Mobility refers to the ability to move from one point to a second point. Obviously, both skills are important if the student who is visually impaired is to be independent.

Although the specific techniques used in mobility training are provided by professionals with specialized preparation, physical educators can reinforce many of these concepts in games and play experiences. For instance, asking students to locate a sound (a radio or metronome, for example) in the gymnasium provides not only a useful experience but also one that reinforces the basic concept of direction taking. Blindfolding students who are sighted and having them engage in similar experiences offers them an opportunity to appreciate the mobility skills some students who are blind develop. Relay races with sighted, blindfolded students and nonsighted children also can be conducted with the use of a sound device at the end of each line or the aid of teammates' voices. For older students, more advanced games can be developed in which the sighted and the nonsighted students are asked to follow first a constant, and then an intermittent, sound. Measures can then be taken to compare how far the sighted students veer from the path compared to their classmates who are visually impaired. Such comparisons may help sighted students understand how adept many students with visual impairments are in moving efficiently toward a sound or signal.

Teachers also can help reinforce the student's skill in walking with a sighted guide. This technique requires that the nonsighted individual grasp a sighted person's arm just above the elbow. With the hand on the guide's arm, the student who is blind then walks about one-half step behind the guide. The person who is visually impaired must learn to follow the guide and to "read" movement or changes in the guide's body position (figure 12.6). The guide must learn to provide verbal cues such as "step up," "step down," "turn to the right," and so on when leading a person who is blind. Other students in the class should be shown the proper way to walk with their visually impaired classmates. This will

not only provide the nonsighted individual an opportunity to practice trailing with a number of different guides, but also will develop a skill that sighted students can employ to assist others with visual impairments outside the school.

Free Play

Although children should be encouraged to use the playground equipment on their own during the leisure hours, they should be given explicit instruction in the use of the play equipment for their own safety and for that of others. All children should be taught the skills involved in the use of the apparatus and the safety measures that must be observed. This is especially true of children with visual impairments.

The teacher may find some hesitancy on the part of some children who are blind to play on the equipment. This is most likely to be true of those who have led extremely sheltered lives. The teacher must begin with the children at their level of motor skill development and their level of self-confidence and strengthen both by encouraging participation at the tempo they will accept. In very young children and very timid ones, it may be necessary to inspire a desire for carefree play on the equipment.

Chair seats on swings and teeter-totters require less balancing skill and promote confidence and security. In introducing these pieces of equipment, the teacher should tell the children something about how they look and how they are used while the children explore them with their hands. Each child may be assisted in sitting on the equipment and trying it with the help of the teacher. A reassuring grasp on the shoulders or arm promotes confidence during the first attempts. When a certain amount of confidence has been developed, mounting and dismounting and safety precautions can be taught to the children.

The safe and enjoyable use of the slide requires careful instruction by the teacher. The children must be taught to wait their turn at the bottom of the ladder and not to climb the steps until the one who is having a turn signals by clapping the hands that he or she is going down the slide. Upon reaching the bottom of the slide, the child must inform the one who is waiting at the top that the slide is clear.

To encourage reluctant children the teacher may first have to help them sit on the slide near the end and hold them as they slide down. This may be done several times at increasing heights. Children should be shown how they may slow down the speed of the slide by forcing their feet against the sides.

Jungle gyms and parallel ladders can be dangerous if improperly used by either sighted or nonsighted children. Children often have sufficient confidence to get on the bars but do not have sufficient skills and strength to perform with safety. A low single bar can be utilized to develop sufficient arm and hand strength and to develop skill in hanging or swinging the body through space. Or a child may be started out very low on the jungle gym where the danger of falling

Figure 12.6 Technique for walking with a visually impaired student.

would be minimal. On the parallel ladders, a thick board may be placed between the rungs of the two upright ladders of a very high ladder. This lessens the distance of the drop and the board can also be used as a bouncing board to spring up and down on, which is an excellent exercise in itself.

Special Considerations

The student who wears glasses for corrected vision may present a safety problem in vigorous sports participation. If the glasses cannot be removed during play, the student should either wear the special type of rugged glasses made to withstand rough treatment or wear glass guards. Many glasses today are plastic and designed to be shatter proof. While these improvements are excellent, they do not necessarily lessen the need for protective eyewear. It may be necessary to give the glasses protection and support in some instances by placing adhesive tape over the stems of the glasses at the temples.

Another problem with which the teacher must be concerned is a condition of retinal detachment. Individuals with partial sight who suffer from progressive myopia sometimes have this condition, in which there is partial detachment of the retina from the choroid. It will be necessary to safeguard such individuals from situations that might produce a blow to the head, as such a jar may cause further detachment that can result in total blindness. Contact sports and diving are contraindicated for them. However, persons with corrected myopia can participate in contact sports with safety.

Suggested Activities

Primary Grade Activities

In the primary grades, physical education activities and games are often utilized as tools in the learning of reading, number concepts, and other areas of study. There are many methods of doing this, and each primary school teacher has worked out numerous ways that might be employed in teaching children who are blind. Many activities suggest themselves, and the suggestions made in subsequent paragraphs are given only as a foundation from which other ideas will spring.

For teaching number concepts, the turns taken in certain activities may be counted, such as the number of times a ball is bounced or the steps taken on a balance beam. In developing reading readiness the background of meaningful experience is expanded, and toward this end numerous physical activities may be utilized. Exploration of the surrounding areas, following paths and sidewalks, going up and down hills, and climbing trees are a few possibilities.

Many of the singing games and mimetic games of the primary grade level need no adaptation for those who are blind. A game such as London Bridge does not need any modification. Other games may need only slight modifications to offset the disadvantage of being unable to see the other players. In the game Red Light and Green Light, which is recommended for children who are blind because it encourages them to run freely and swiftly, the teacher should name those who are moving on the call of "red light," because the children who are blind will not be able to tell which runners should be brought back.

Because persons who are blind need to develop greater spatial awareness, activities in physical education should promote learning to move the body through space and to relate the body's location to other people or objects that share the space. Motor exploration activities are an excellent vehicle for such learning. In motor exploration, students are not trying to find the most effective way to make a movement; rather they are experimenting with a number of different ways of moving to discover the one that is most efficient for and most satisfying to them. In the process they learn a great deal about moving the body through space. Suggested motor activities for exploration of space are as follows:

Movement While Stationary

The objective in these activities is to learn how the body can be moved without locomotion.

1. Starting with the arms at the sides, move them up and down. (If the arms are bare, the wind currents created by the movements can be felt on the arms.)
2. Move any part of the body except the arms but do not move from the original space.
3. Lift up one leg and then try to lift up the other. (Because this is impossible to do, it teaches the concept of motor limitations.)

Exploring Locomotion

Elementary skills of locomotion are rolling, crawling, walking, running, jumping, and variations of these. Exploration of these skills helps children to learn the variety of ways the body can be moved from place to place. In teaching locomotor skills to children who are blind, it is important to clearly identify a stationary point where all movement skills begin and end. This will help students to feel secure and confident as they engage in various movement activities.

1. Move from one place to another, not allowing the feet to touch the floor.
2. Move about the play area, trying to create an impression of being tall, small, wide, flat, round, and so on.

Communication through Movement

In this phase of exploratory movement, children learn the ways in which the body may be used to communicate emotions and ideas.

1. Move like, and make noises like, a dog. (Previous to this activity, children will need an opportunity for brailling a dog and listening to it bark and to have been given an idea of how it moves.)
2. Move in a manner to show fear, anger, happiness, and so on. This also helps the children learn to display emotion.
3. Move to depict a gentle rain, a hot sunny day, and a snowstorm. Important concepts about weather can also be taught through this activity.

Manipulation of Objects

Having discovered movements that can be made with the body, the child is ready to explore the use of the body in the manipulation of objects. The ball is the most common object of manipulation in physical education and so it will be used in the sample activities.

1. Make the ball move, using the hand, foot, head, shoulders, and so on.
2. Move the ball so that it makes different sounds.
3. Throw a ball (suspended from the ceiling by a cord) at different speeds.

Relaxation

Muscular relaxation is another activity that lends itself to exploration. Learning to relax is not always easy, and participation in the exploratory activities helps to develop an understanding of the process. Suggestions for such activities are made in the discussion of relaxation in chapter 29.

Spatial Awareness

Excellent activities for teaching spatial awareness also can be presented by the direct or traditional method. Possibilities include the following:

1. Walk in a straight line. (Children who are blind have a tendency to veer to the side of their dominant hand or weave back and forth.)
2. Follow sounds; for example, a drum beat, a voice, footsteps.
3. Slide a hand along a rope that encloses a small area while walking around it; retrace the steps without touching the rope.
4. While walking, turn on command to make a ninety-degree turn, a forty-five-degree turn, and so on.
5. Follow a cord stretched between two points. At the farther point, release the hold on the cord and return to the starting point.

Activities for Older Children

There are many games suitable for elementary and high school students that need no modification. Many dual competitive games such as arm wrestling or leg wrestling can be presented without modification. In tag games and other games in which the players need to make their location known to the one who is "It," the players may make vocal sounds. When sighted players are participating in the game, these students may join hands with a nonsighted player and play as a couple. Certain games with balls such as dodge ball and wall ball are easily modified by slight rule changes that prevent seeing players from having undue advantage and provide for the calling out by players so that opponents who are blind can locate them by the sound of their voice.

Some games lend themselves more easily than others to adaptation for playing by students who are blind or have limited vision. As a guide for the selection of those games that can be readily used without much modification, Buell (1974) suggests these eight characteristics:

1. Blindfolding one or two players
2. Sounds whereby the sightless know what is happening
3. Different duties for students who are blind and partially seeing
4. Running to a goal easily found by those who are totally blind
5. Limited playing area such as gymnasium or tennis court
6. Direct contact as in wrestling
7. Line or chain formations
8. The possibility of players pairing up in couples

Because individuals who are blind rely so much on sound to receive their impressions, they are particularly receptive to the rhythm not only of music but also of the human activities that surround them. The knowledge thus gained of rhythm patterns is a valuable asset in learning to dance. All types of dance may be taught to those who are blind: musical games, folk dances, modern dance, and social dancing. The musical games such as Farmer in the Dell are limited to young children. All other types of dance can be taught at almost any age level as soon as children have learned to move freely, with confidence and skill, through space.

Although the needs of those with visual impairments are similar to that of the sighted, special attention must be directed toward the physical fitness of these students. Winnick and Short (1985) reported that the fitness level of students who are visually impaired was inferior to that of their nonimpaired peers. The reason for this is generally attributed to the restricted activity level of the visually impaired. Because of their visual limitations these children do not experience some of the natural movement and play associated with an active childhood. Special efforts, therefore, must be directed toward ensuring that those who are visually impaired participate in programs that encourage the development of physical fitness. Without such a program, the lack of physical activity will lead to further losses of stamina, strength, and flexibility. Weitzman (1985) advocates that walking programs, if done with sufficient intensity, are very effective in helping those who are visually impaired improve their cardiorespiratory levels of fitness. Equally important is the observation that for some students who are visually impaired the "high" associated with being physically active leads to an improved self-concept. Rowing, cycling, dance aerobics, and cross-country skiing are all activities high in endurance that students who are visually impaired, with modifications, can engage in successfully. Programs should be structured with goals so that change in performance can be documented and reinforced.

Sports

Students who are blind participate in many team and individual sports. The type and the modification depend upon the extent of the student's visual impairment. Some students who are visually impaired, for instance, have sufficient residual vision that they can participate in various sports with their sighted peers. For those with more serious visual impairments, however, the modifications are more extensive and require careful planning on the part of the teacher.

Popular team sports include basketball, football, and volleyball. Students who are partially sighted adapt well to basketball; those who are legally blind will require major modifications of this activity. For instance, the player without sight will find shooting baskets and playing such games as Around-the-World and Twenty-one enjoyable. Students with severe visual impairments may find participating in the game as their team's free-throw shooter a fulfilling activity and one that allows them to be a part of a team experience.

Football is a popular sport in which many visually impaired students can successfully participate. Those with limited vision can play on the line as a center or guard. Rule modifications are simple, including having the player who is carrying the ball shout to identify his or her position. Some partially sighted players have become so proficient at football that they have participated on regular high school teams.

Volleyball, particularly the lead-up game of newcomb, is an enjoyable activity that many partially sighted students can play. In this game, the ball is played on the first bounce or may be caught and thrown rather than hit while in the air. Students also may be allowed to move toward the net, feel the top of the net and throw the volleyball over the net. Time limits can be imposed on how long the ball may be held and the number of consecutive throws limited.

There are many individual sports that students who are visually impaired have found enjoyable. Some of these include track and field, bowling, golf, wrestling, gymnastics, and swimming.

Track and field is such a popular sport among the blind that many of the residential schools sponsor interscholastic teams. The competitive events usually included are the 50- and 100-yard dashes, the mile and two-mile run, the standing high jump and long jump, the triple jump, and the throwing events.

In training for running events in track, the participant who is totally blind can run with a partially seeing partner by using the partner's footsteps as a guide or by running at his or her side, lightly and intermittently brushing the partner's arm. Overhead wires with drop cords that slide along the wire that runners can grasp in their hands will aid them in keeping a steady course. Guide wires about hip high along one side of the track, which students can slide their hands along as they run, are good for the training period. Later, as confidence and skills develop, another wire is placed on the other side so that runners run between and are guided by them without placing their hands on the wires. This permits greater speed in running, and if the runners swerve off the course, the wires brush against them and remind them to adjust their position. A less elaborate but effective system for assisting the visually impaired runner is to use a rope instead of the guidewire. In this system large knots are tied toward the ends of the rope to warn the runner that the end of the rope is near. To avoid rope burns, a relay baton can be placed over the rope and held by the runner while running. In running events, teammates or coaches, are stationed at the end of the run to serve as callers. Their task is to call the runners name, thus providing a constant cue to guide the runner. Some investigators have reported that use of sighted guides and guide wires are less restrictive and generate faster times than using a caller.

Bowling and golf are very popular individual sports for students who are blind or visually impaired. Bowlers who are blind orient themselves by feeling the sides of the alley or by using the guide rail if it is available. With golf, the only adaptation is the necessity of playing with a sighted person who locates the ball and provides verbal feedback. Swimming offers an unusually fine activity for the person who is visually impaired. The nature of the confined environment combined with the availability of lane markers makes this activity one that many students who are blind have participated in with little modification. An audible locator such as a buzzer or battery-operated radio may be placed at the ends of the pool lane to assist swimmers who are visually impaired with their turns. Many swimmers who are visually impaired count the number of strokes per lap and use this as a guide for marking the end of the pool and for making turns. Diving may also be successfully undertaken by individuals who are blind. The only modification necessary here is helping the person who is blind locate the end of the board. Most prefer to hold onto the diving board rail and then crawl on hands and knees to the end of the board.

Wrestling is the sport in which students with visual impairments have most distinguished themselves. Athletes who are blind have successfully competed against sighted opponents at the high school, university level, and the Olympics. The only rule modification that is necessary is that wrestlers who are blind begin the match in a standing position with a hand-touch start and initial contact must be from the front.

Unfortunately, students who are visually impaired have only recently been introduced to winter sports. Skiing is rapidly becoming a very popular sport among the blind. This activity requires that the person ski with a partner. Some ski instructors prefer to ski in front of the blind skier, leading them down the slope, whereas others prefer to ski behind, providing the visually impaired skier with verbal directions. Likewise, many students who are blind are finding ice skating enjoyable. Orientation to the skating surface and boundaries is the only necessary modification.

Two sports—goal ball and beep baseball—have been specifically developed for participation by individuals who are visually impaired. In goal ball, three players compose a team. The objective of the game is to roll a large ball with a bell in it across the opponent's goal while the other team tries to stop it. The defensive team may stop the ball from a sitting, lying, or standing position. Each player must wear a helmet, mouth piece, elbow pads, and blindfold. The team that scores the most total goals in two five-minute halves wins the match. Because all players wear blindfolds, this is an excellent activity to encourage interaction between sighted and nonsighted players.

Beep baseball, which was introduced in 1975, is governed by the National Beep Baseball Association. Similar to baseball, this game is played on a regulation size diamond. Each team has five players who are blind plus a sighted catcher and pitcher. The ball, which is available through an organization known as the Telephone Pioneers (call your local phone company for further information), is a regulation sixteen-inch softball with an audible device inside. Only two bases are used, first and third. Each base is a thirty-six-inch tall plastic cone with a speaker in the top. The sighted players serve as the pitcher and catcher for their own team and as spotters when their team is in the field. The role of the spotters is to help their nonsighted peers locate the ball. Each batter is allowed seven pitches with fouls counting as strikes except on the last strike. When a fair ball is hit, one of the two bases is activated by the umpire and emits a buzzing sound. The batter must run to the buzzing base. The concept of running to either first or third as randomly determined by the umpire is designed to equate the reaction time of batter and fielder. If the batter reaches the base before being tagged, a run is scored. The team who scores the most runs in six innings with three outs per inning wins the game.

Deaf and Hard-of-Hearing

Auditory losses of varying degrees of severity constitute as a group one of the most common disabilities affecting children and adults. Statistics show that approximately 9 percent of the American population experience some hearing loss (The National Center for Health Statistics, 1994). These hearing losses range from slight deviation from normal hearing to total loss of sound perception. Less than 10 percent of the children and youth enrolled in schools for the deaf are totally devoid of hearing.

Too often in the past a hearing loss has been considered to be a "handicapping" condition in much the same way as the loss of sight and to affect the individual in much the same way—socially and psychologically. Such thinking was to be expected in view of the fact that both conditions arise from a complete or partial loss of one of the senses. However, this tendency to regard a visual and hearing loss as similar has retarded a true consideration of the implications of a hearing loss. Helen Keller reflected on her own life and declared that deafness was a far greater hardship than blindness. She observed that blindness cuts people off from things, deafness cuts people off from people (Dolnick, 1993). Despite this dire perception of hearing loss as a condition that isolates people, deaf individuals argue that deafness is not a disability. They offer that deaf people constitute a subculture and that they comprise a linguistic minority. The deaf argue that treatment and educational programs should not focus on "fixing" them but rather they should be recognized and accepted as unique and culturally different. While this view of the deaf as an ethnic minority is not universally accepted, the movement has led to some rethinking of educational and treatment programs for the deaf and hard-of-hearing. This includes important questions of where, what, and how to teach this population. Strident supporters of the deaf culture movement suggest, too, that deaf individuals are best reared and educated in settings with members of their own culture. Given that 90 percent of deaf children are born to hearing parents, this creates some challenging questions for parents and educators in developing and delivering the desired educational programs and activities. The goal is not only to assist the deaf and hard-of-hearing in learning but to recognize their unique sociocultural perspective.

The Nature and Causes of Hearing Loss

Individuals with hearing loss may be referred to as deaf or hard-of-hearing depending on the degree of loss and, to some extent, on the communication ability of the individual. The term deaf may be used to encompass all forms of hearing loss as is common among groups such as the American Athletic Association for the Deaf (AAAD). Within educational settings, primarily for funding or school purposes, it is common to make a distinction between the terms deaf and hard-of-hearing.

In 1975, the Executives of American Schools for the Deaf defined the terms "deaf," "hard-of-hearing," and "hearing impairment (Larson and Miller, 1978)." A *deaf* person is recognized as one who is unable, with or without a hearing aid, to process linguistic information through audition. The *hard-of-hearing* are defined as those who, with the assistance of a hearing aid, have sufficient residual hearing to process linguistic information. Individuals who are hard-of-hearing, therefore, have hearing that is deficient but functional. Deaf persons, on the other hand, have nonfunctional hearing. The term *hearing impaired* is a generic term used by some individuals to identify individuals with hearing impairments, including those who are deaf or hard-of-hearing. The deaf community rejects the term impaired, arguing that: (1) they are not impaired, and (2) the term impaired suggests that they are deficient and in need of medical treatment.

Modern educational methods for students with hearing loss make the maximum use of the residual hearing that they possess. Consequently, it is important that educators teach students who are hard-of-hearing more nearly like hearing students than like students who are deaf.

Hearing loss may also be described in terms of its age of onset. Hearing impairments may be either congenital, present at birth, or adventitious, occurring later in life. The child who is deaf from birth will not be able to learn to speak spontaneously. The needs of this youngster are very different from those of a child who acquires a hearing loss after the age of seven, when speech and language are well developed. Frequently, the term prelingual and postlingual are used to distinguish the impact of a hearing loss on the ability of the student to speak. Those with a postlingual hearing loss normally, with special assistance, retain the ability to speak.

Like the eye, the ear is a complex organ, capable of discriminating the intensity and frequency of various sounds. Sound is first received by the outer ear and transmitted to the middle ear before it finally reaches the inner ear, where it is transferred to the brain via the auditory nerve. As illustrated in figure 12.7, the function of the outer ear is to collect sound waves and transmit them via the auditory canal to the middle ear. In the middle ear, the sound passes from the tympanic membrane to the ossicular chain, where the vibrations created by the motion of the stapes, incus, and malleus move the sound from the outer to the inner ear. The inner ear is divided into two sections, the vestibule and the cochlea. The latter part, the cochlea, is the critical element in hearing. As the stapes bone moves, the oval window moves, transmitting the sound from the middle ear to the fluid-filled cochlea. Inside the cochlea are thousands of tiny hair cells that are set in motion. Movement of the hair cells in turn causes electrical impulses to be sent to the brain.

Also located in the inner ear are three small loops called the semicircular canals. Although the semicircular canals do not contribute to the hearing process, they are extremely important in helping individuals maintain balance.

Hearing disabilities are usually structural in origin, and damage to any part of the ear, outer, middle, or inner, can result in a hearing loss. The three types of hearing loss are classified as conductive, sensorineural, or mixed.

Conductive Hearing Loss

This disorder is caused by a physical obstruction to the conduction of the sound waves to the inner ear, such as impacted wax or a middle ear infection. Although the nature of the obstruction may be severe and the hearing seriously impaired, deafness is never total. Impacted wax can be readily removed by a physician, and infection can be treated medically with relatively good chances for arresting or improving it, particularly in its early stages. A hearing aid is very useful in improving a hearing loss due to conduction difficulties.

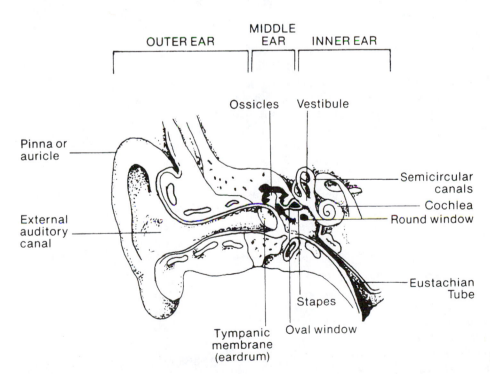

Figure 12.7 Diagram of the human ear.

Two causes of conductive hearing loss that are of particular interest to the physical educator include external otitis and otitis media. In external otitis, there is an inflammation of the auditory canal due to infection. Although a hearing loss does not occur with this condition unless there is severe swelling, students with external otitis should not swim until the infection subsides.

Otitis media, infection of the middle ear, accounts for more conductive hearing losses than any other condition. Although this is a common disorder with young children, without proper medical treatment, otitis media can damage the ossicles, preventing the normal transmission of sound.

Some young children have artificial tubes inserted into their ears. This is done to alleviate blockage of the Eustachian tube, thereby reducing the unequal pressure on the two sides of the tympanic membrane. Insertion of the tubes permits the middle ear to heal. Swimming is usually contraindicated during the period of time the tubes are worn.

Sensorineural Hearing Loss

Sensorineural loss is usually a more serious condition and less likely to be improved by medical treatment. It is caused by damage to the cells or nerve fibers that receive and transmit the sound stimuli. The loss of hearing may range from mild to total disability. Some degree of sensorineural deafness is common among the aging. A certain amount of high-tone nerve deafness appears to be part of the natural process of aging in many people, just as many of advanced years suffer hardening of the arteries and deterioration of eyesight. This condition is in fact so prevalent that the most common cause of nerve deafness is attributed to aging.

In children and young adults the most frequent cause of sensorineural deafness is congenital, the nerve having been injured or destroyed before or during birth. However, research into the causes of deafness in children has shown that a number of cases heretofore classified as hereditary were actually associated with certain contagious diseases that the mother contracted during the early months of pregnancy. Rubella, mumps, and influenza all have been indicated as causes of deafness in infants whose mothers were afflicted during early pregnancy.

Cases of sensorineural deafness that have a noncongenital origin are classified as acquired deafness. Among the common causes are brain infections such as meningitis, brain fever, and sleeping sickness and communicable diseases such as scarlet fever, measles, influenza, and others.

At one time it was considered that hearing aids were of little value to those with sensorineural hearing loss, but with the improvement of the quality of hearing aids, it has become possible to successfully fit more and more persons with this type of hearing loss. Many cochlear implants have been performed successfully, allowing deaf people to hear.

Prolonged loud sounds of any spectra can produce a temporary threshold shift (auditory fatigue); recovery usually takes place within a day. The more intense the sound, the shorter the exposure time necessary before a temporary fatigue takes place. Continual exposure eventually produces a permanent hearing loss. As a general rule, the ears should not be exposed to sounds over 130 decibels (units of loudness) longer than momentarily. There is some evidence to suggest that prolonged listening to amplified music is causing hearing losses in young men and women, especially among the musicians themselves. In these cases, the hearing loss occurs in the higher frequency ranges. The combined sounds of the environment, such as street noises in a city, often reach levels of intensity that may cause hearing loss.

Mixed Loss

When both conductive loss and sensorineural loss are present, the result is classified as a mixed loss. Individuals who experience this disorder may have what is referred to as a significant air conduction/bone conduction gap. If the conductive aspect of the hearing loss is stabilized, the probability of receiving assistance through the use of a hearing aid is good. The individual then functions similarly to those who experience only a conductive loss.

Measurement and Classification of Hearing Loss

An audiologist is a professional who specializes in assessing hearing loss. With the use of an instrument known as an audiometer, the audiologist measures hearing acuity, the sharpness or clarity with which sound is received. The audiologist uses the audiometer to present tones that vary in intensity (loudness) and frequencies (pitch). The results of the hearing examination are recorded on a graph called an audiogram (figure 12.8).

Two units of measurement are noted on the audiogram. A decibel (dB) refers to loudness of sound. A loud shout at a distance of one foot is measured at 110 decibels, whereas ordinary conversation is about 60 decibels. The expression hertz (Hz) refers to the frequency or pitch at which sound may be heard. Hearing losses are noted in decibels; the higher the number value, the more significant the loss. Frequency measures are used to determine whether the hearing loss is constant at different levels of pitch. As noted in figure 12.8, the student has a decibel loss in the right ear of 60 at 500 Hz but a loss of 70 at 2000 Hz.

Degrees of hearing loss are classified differently by various authorities, but the classification most frequently used in educational circles divides the losses into five categories. These include:

Slight	27 to 40 dB
Mild	41 to 55 dB
Marked	56 to 70 dB
Severe	71 to 90 dB
Profound	91 dB or more

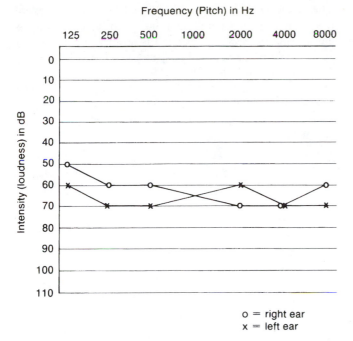

Frequency (Pitch) in Hz

o = right ear
x = left ear

Figure 12.8 Example of an audiogram.

A person with a slight hearing loss (27 to 40 dB) may have difficulty hearing faint or distant speech. Although some students with slight hearing loss will require speech reading instruction as well as speech correction, normally these individuals will not have difficulty in school and will experience no disadvantages in the physical education class.

Students with a moderate loss (41 to 55 dB) can understand conversational speech at a distance of three to five feet. Obviously, these individuals are unable to follow much of the conversation and instruction in the physical education class without special assistance. Several forms of help—including hearing aids, speech reading, and favorable seating or roving privileges can be utilized to improve communication with students who have a moderate hearing loss. (The use of the latter in physical education is discussed later in this chapter.)

In those with a marked hearing loss (56 to 70 dB), conversation must be loud to be understood. Students with this degree of loss have difficulty following group discussion. It is also likely that these individuals have a limited vocabulary and speech is affected. The aids identified for students with mild hearing loss also benefit those with this greater degree of hearing loss.

A severe hearing loss (71 to 90 dB) means that the individual may not hear loud voices one foot from the ear. The student with a severe hearing loss may be able to discriminate vowels but not all consonants. Like the student with a marked loss, this individual has difficulty with speech and needs the assistance of aids and special instructional techniques in those subjects that require a high level of language skills.

Students with a profound hearing loss (91 + dB) cannot rely on hearing as their primary channel for communication. Although these individuals may have some residual hearing and, therefore, hear loud noises, they are more aware of vibrations than of tonal patterns. It is probable that children with a profound hearing loss will need the assistance of an interpreter. Most of these students, however, are capable of participating in the regular physical education class if they have not been deprived of these experiences earlier in their development.

Needs and Adjustments of Those with Auditory Disabilities

The most obvious adjustment that the deaf must make is to the loss of the normal means of communication. A new way of receiving messages must be found if the disability is acquired after speech has been learned. If the loss of hearing is congenital or acquired before speech has been learned, a means of conveying as well as receiving communications must be learned. Deaf persons who could not speak were once taught signing as the sole means of communication, but deaf children are now being taught to speak by the technique of properly utilizing the mouth and vocal cords in the production of sounds. They also receive speech reading and usually signing instruction.

Considerable controversy exists among those who work with the deaf as to the extent to which deaf people should be taught to communicate by speech, speech reading, and signing. One faction contends that signing should not be taught at all and that the educational efforts should be directed entirely toward learning to speech read and to speak because such communication skills are closer to normalcy. This approach is known as the oral method.

Opponents say that signing, speech reading, and speech should all be taught to give the deaf child the widest possible communication skills. Their approach is referred to as the total communication approach and is frequently referred to as a philosophy rather than an educational method. The emphasis with total communication is placed on maximizing the student's ability to communicate using the best of both systems.

Educators should recognize, however, that students who speech read do not read every word, but rather they follow conversation by observing the speaker's lips, mouth, and facial expressions for clues to determine the essence of what has been said. Obviously, this is a difficult skill and one that requires considerable effort, practice, and training to master. In tests using simple sentences, deaf people recognize perhaps three or four words in every ten (Dolnick, 1993). Not all students with hearing impairments speech read.

For those students who are taught to communicate manually, the American Sign Language (ASL) system is frequently used. With this approach, hand gestures and body positions are used to represent words and concepts. For many words, the gesture is closely related to the action being described. Physical education teachers, therefore, may find that some communication with ASL is possible even without formal training. For example, the sign for throw is the arm motion of overhand throwing. Figure 12.9 presents other signs frequently used in the physical education setting.

A second form of manual communication is finger spelling, in which there is a distinct hand position for each letter in the alphabet (figure 12.10). In this system each word is spelled letter by letter. Total reliance on finger spelling as the sole means of communication is not feasible because of the amount of time required to spell each word. This system, therefore, is frequently combined with other methods. Finger spelling is particularly helpful for spelling words and proper names for which no sign exists. Deaf-blind persons also can make use of finger spelling by feeling the user's hand to decipher the letters.

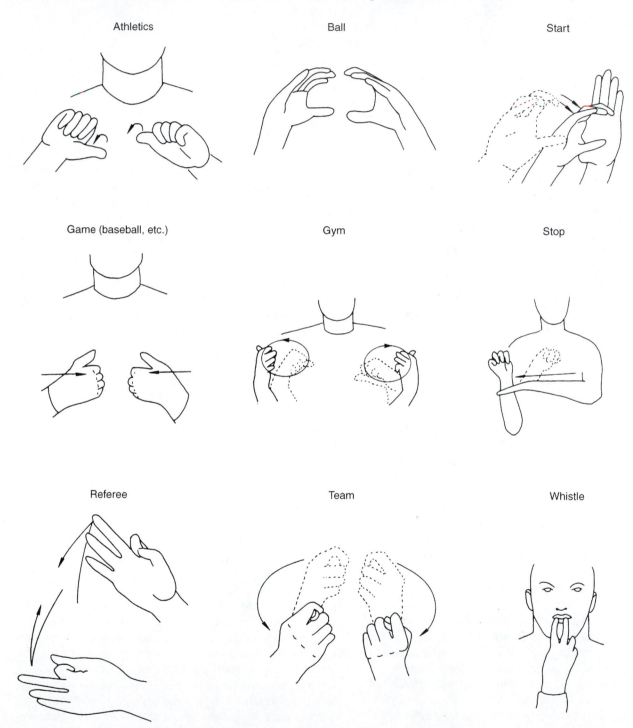

Figure 12.9 Example of signs commonly used in physical education instruction.

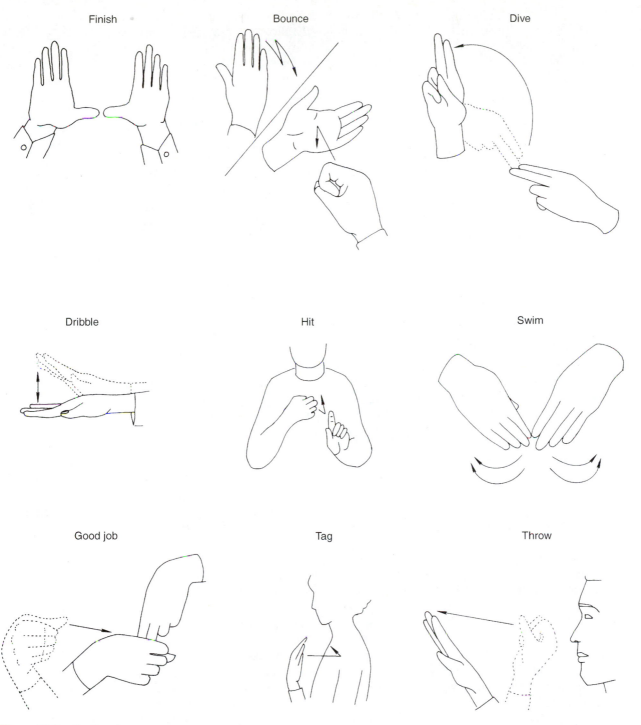

Finish   Bounce   Dive

Dribble   Hit   Swim

Good job   Tag   Throw

Figure 12.9—*Continued*

Cued speech (Cornett, 1982), a supplement to speech reading and a substitute for signing, is a communication approach used by some individuals who are deaf. It consists of eight signs or shapes of the hand and four hand positions that signify all the vowels and consonants in the English language (other positions apply to other languages). These hand shapes and positions are used by a speaker to enable the deaf person to know which specific vowel or consonant sound is being made by the speaker in cases where the difference between the vowels or consonants cannot be distinguished by watching the lips and mouth of the speaker, because of the great similarity in the way the sounds are formed. For example, the words "bat," "mat," and "pat" are similar enough to appear to the speech reader to be the same; cued speech eliminates the confusion by informing the speech reader which of the consonants is being used.

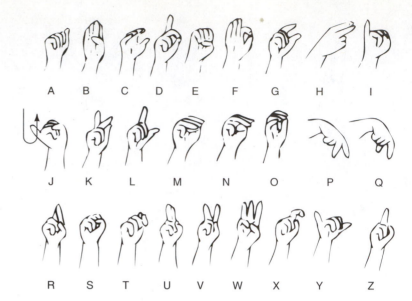

Figure 12.10 Finger spelling alphabet.

Some argue that all of the communication systems for the deaf, including total communication, have serious limitations and thus the search continues for alternative approaches. A new approach, known as the bilingual/bicultural system, has generated considerable controversy. In this approach, deaf students are first taught ASL and then eventually build on that knowledge to learn English as a second language. Critics of this approach fear that too much time will be devoted to ASL and not enough to the fundamentals of learning to write and read English. Hearing parents of deaf children fear, too, that the bilingual/bicultural movement will be too oriented toward a deaf culture and, therefore, potentially isolating the child from them and other hearing children and adults.

Students who are hard-of-hearing often have residual hearing, and, therefore, many find a hearing aid an invaluable assistance in achieving total development. The purpose of the hearing aid is to amplify sound. Contrary to the generally held concept, hearing aids do not make speech and sound clearer; those who hear distorted sounds will still experience distortion with a hearing aid. The value of hearing aids lies in enabling children with severe hearing impairments to learn to recognize the sound of their own name or in assisting those with a moderate loss to hear their own speech.

Although there are many different types of hearing aids, they are usually worn in one of three places: behind the ear, on the chest, or in eyeglasses. Each aid is composed of three primary components: an amplifier, a microphone, and a receiver. The microphone collects the sound; it is then amplified and transmitted to the ear. Students should be encouraged to wear their hearing aids throughout the day. It is important that they learn how to use the aid to help them interpret conversation. This cannot be done with proficiency if the student refuses to wear the aid or turns it off periodically. In the physical education setting the hearing aid should be worn as much as possible. Given the noise level in the gymnasium, and the inability of the hearing aid to selectively filter certain sounds, some students may choose to remove the hearing aid on occasion. Students also will need to remove the hearing aid for selected activities, such as swimming and team sports that involve body contact. The physical education teacher should be cognizant of when the student is or is not wearing the hearing aid and adjust the process for communicating accordingly.

The hearing aid should be periodically checked to ensure that it is properly functioning. Two common problems are batteries that are low and an ear mold that needs to be cleaned. Occasionally, the cord that connects the microphone to the receiver will be broken or defective. The hearing-impaired specialist or resource teacher can quickly teach the physical education teacher to detect and fix many of the minor problems associated with hearing aids, so that children need not be put at a disadvantage due to an easily remedied problem.

Individuals with profound bilateral deafness may benefit from implantation of a cochlear device. The cochlear implant consists of an external speech processor, and implanted electrodes. A small wire runs from the receiver via the implant to the cochlea. Sounds are picked up by a microphone worn near the ear and transmitted through a wire to the speech processor, which converts the sound into an electrical signal sent to the cochlear implant. In selected patients the implant has produced excellent results. The cochlear implant enhances speech reading, recognition of sound, and allows for the discrimination of some words (Silverstein, Wolfson, and Rosenberg, 1992). Some deaf advocates argue that the cochlear implant is an invasion of the ear and a denial of deafness and its associated culture (Dolnick, 1993).

In addition to their loss of the usual conversational method of communication with others, those with severe deafness experience other losses that cause difficult problems of adjustment. The personal and social development of deaf children and youth is frequently reported as unusual. Keane et al. (1992) cite several studies indicating that the deaf, as a group, manifest higher degrees of impulsivity, egocentricity, and rigidity than the population at large. Teachers and parents (Strika, 1989), too, report that deaf children appear to have more social and emotional problems than hearing children of the same age.

There are several factors that might help to explain the reported high frequency of social and emotional adjustment problems of deaf children and youth. These include: level of parental acceptance; availability of appropriate role models; reduction in level of communication and interaction; and limited school and extracurricular activities. Solutions to help eradicate some of the reported social and emotional problems include: parent education and counselling programs; greater involvement of deaf individuals in programs for young deaf children; increased fluency in sign language on the part of parents, teachers, and other adults important in the life of a deaf child; and expanded and enriched educational and social opportunities (International Encyclopedia of Education, 1994).

The early childhood literature recognizes that play is critical to the development of a healthy personality and physical education teachers are in a unique role to foster the social and emotional development of deaf and hard-of-hearing children and youth. First and foremost is the need to create an educational environment in which the deaf feel that they are part of and welcome in the physical education setting. Second, it is essential to develop success experiences so that deaf and hard-of-hearing students feel that they are progressing and enjoying the opportunity to participate in and learn various concepts related to movement. Third is the need to expand the ability of the teacher to communicate so that the student recognizes that his or her form of communication is accepted and valued. Additional tips for teaching students who are deaf and hard-of-hearing will be found later in the chapter.

Without the orientation of the auditory background and the symbols and warnings that are customarily provided by sound perception, the deaf are prone to frustrations and anxieties. This is particularly true in cases in which hearing is lost in adolescence or adulthood. The longer a person has had full powers of hearing, the more difficult is the adjustment to a severe hearing loss. The loss of background sounds contributes also to inaccuracy in the recognition of space and motion, and, as a consequence, the movements of the deaf are often vague and distorted.

Motor Performance of the Deaf and Hard-of-Hearing

Studies have been conducted since the 1930s to examine the motor performance of the deaf and hard-of-hearing. These investigations have focused primarily on measures of balance, fine and gross motor skills, and motor ability. Efforts have also been made to compare the performance level of the deaf and hard-of-hearing to those without a hearing loss. For the most part, the studies that have been conducted are not definitive because of the failure to control for factors such as cause of the hearing loss and level of hearing loss. A comprehensive review of studies which have been conducted to examine the motor performance of students with hearing losses has been reported by Goodman and Hopper (1992). The following generalizations, however, may be made about the motor performance of the deaf and hard-of-hearing:

1. Some deaf students may have balance problems, depending upon the cause of the hearing loss. If the cause results in an inner-ear problem, it is also probable that the vestibular system, particularly the semicircular canal, where the sense receptors for balance are found, will also be affected.

2. The extent of the hearing loss may have an influence on motor performance. Some deaf students, therefore, may be less proficient in some motor skills than those who are hard of hearing. This difference, however, may be due to previous experience with game and movement skills rather than to the extent of hearing loss. The deaf students' greater difficulty in receptive and expressive communication skills may also contribute to these differences.

3. Compared to hearing students, some deaf and hard-of-hearing individuals appear to perform at a lower level on many motor tasks.

4. In general, the deaf and hard-of-hearing were found to be more similar in motor performance, with the exception of balance. Where differences were noted, much of the variance may be due to: (1) the extent of previous opportunities to participate in physical education activities and (2) inadequate communication in assessing the motor performance of deaf students (Pontecelli and Dunn, 1988).

Generally, these findings suggest that although much remains unknown about the motor performance of the deaf and hard-of-hearing, involving these students in physical education programs is highly desirable. Successful experiences will require teachers who are empathetic and willing to develop sufficient communication skills to assist the deaf student to benefit from the instruction offered. For students whose motor skills or communication skills, or both, are seriously limited, special physical education classes may be necessary. Most deaf and hard-of-hearing students, however, can successfully participate in regular physical education classes with minimal modifications.

The setting in which deaf and hard-of-hearing students are to be educated has generated considerable attention. Some have argued that the least restrictive environment for this population is a special class or special school placement. Butterfield (1991) summarizes this position eloquently by stating that the regular class placement lacks (a) cultural foundations unique to deaf individuals and essential for their optimal development and (b) appropriate support services vital for the education of such students. Decker (1993) believes that deaf students have more to gain than to lose by receiving their education with hearing peers.

Both Butterfield and Decker acknowledge that deaf students will not be successful in integrated settings unless there are adequate support services. In this respect, the Individuals with Disabilities Education Act (IDEA) emphasizes that deaf students should be provided interpreters, if this level of assistance is needed. The interpreter plays an essential role in helping the deaf student benefit from instruction. It is important to emphasize that the interpreter should be with the deaf student for all class periods, including instruction in physical education. The idea or suggestion that the active nature of the physical education class will not need the services of an interpreter should be challenged.

Planning the Program in the Regular School

It is estimated that approximately 4 to 5 percent of the school population actually experiences some hearing loss. Children with a slight auditory deficiency will not be readily noticed in the classroom; or, if noticed because of their behavior, their actions may not be attributed to hearing loss. Students may be inattentive, fail to answer questions, and require frequent repetition of directions. They may watch those who are speaking very closely in order to grasp something of the meaning of the speech from the movements of the mouth or gestures of the body, or they may incline their head when spoken to so their ear is directed toward the speaker. Evidence of such mannerisms or behavior patterns may be more quickly revealed in the physical education class than in the regular class, for in the vastness of the gymnasium or playing field students are even less likely to hear directions and explanations, particularly when these are given in game situations and they are some distance away or have their head turned away from the instructor. Consequently, teachers should be alert to the possibility that a child who fails to grasp the instructor's directions or fails to respond well may have a hearing loss and should take steps to see that the child is adequately tested.

Most children with hearing loss are enrolled in the regular schools, and generally speaking, such children are successfully included in the regular physical education class. Winnick and Short (1985) reported, for instance, that individuals with auditory loss compared very favorably to the hearing students on selected tests of physical fitness. However, if the child's hearing loss has prevented normal participation in play activities to the extent that marked physical needs or personality problems are evident, the teacher should consider the case more carefully to determine if the child could profit more from participation in the special class. Children who have experienced recent hearing loss and are still in a period of adjustment may well profit from individualized instruction in a special physical education program, as may those with subnormal strength and coordination.

Students who need special help might benefit best by participation in both the regular and special class. This approach will allow the students to benefit from additional instructional time and provide opportunities to work on selected skills. Deaf students, too, will enjoy the advantage of having class time with other deaf students. This should help to increase opportunities for socialization with other deaf students and increase the probability of participating in sport programs sponsored by the American Athletic Association for the Deaf (Stewart, McCarthy, and Robinson, 1988).

Many students who are hard-of-hearing wear hearing aids that may be removed during physical education classes for some types of activities. Without this assistance to the individual's auditory perception, the student will again be disadvantaged in the amount of verbal direction he or she can comprehend. The teacher must anticipate this and be prepared to help the student make the necessary adjustment.

For calling roll or giving preliminary instruction to the class before the activity begins, the teacher should place the student with a hearing loss where the student will be in the best position to watch the instructor's face. During actual play, when the need to comment arises, the teacher may move close to those students who cannot hear well before speaking. Or the students may be granted "roving" privileges so that they may move about freely to a position at which they are better able to hear the speaker.

Other students in the class are usually very cooperative in helping those who cannot hear to make the right responses in game situations once they recognize that the student has a hearing loss. As long as the hearing students are unaware that deaf students respond the way they do because of a hearing loss and not because of personal peculiarities, they sometimes ignore or ridicule those with a hearing loss. Consequently, the physical education instructor must set the pattern for the class. The teacher's kindness and patience in directing and explaining the class activities to the student with a hearing loss will be imitated by the others. Soon the teacher will find that when such a student has muffed a play by being out of position, a teammate will quietly step over to indicate what was wrong.

Students with a hearing loss may demonstrate a lack of cooperation in class activities and undesirable behavior in competitive play. Such tendencies are related largely to their failure to have understood the directions or rules of the game. In the lower grades where the play is less dependent upon vocal directions and rulings, the deaf child is usually a considerably more successful participant than in later years when games become more dependent upon the comprehension of spoken words. Clear explanations directed at the student and careful demonstrations of the skill to be performed should do much to alleviate the misunderstandings that prompted the undesirable behavior. It is the teacher's responsibility to make sure that students understand what is expected, including how to play selected games and sports.

Students with hearing losses need to be taught more factual information about a game than hearing children whose ears as well as their eyes have given them insight into the activity. The vocabulary of the game as well as the rules and playing strategy must be conveyed with greater care and exactness than is necessary for the student who can hear. Well-described and illustrated written materials may be used to good advantage for this purpose with students who read.

Visual aids have greater significance as a teaching technique in the instruction of the hard-of-hearing and deaf than in perhaps any other situation. Their use can substitute for considerable amounts of verbal instruction. Videotapes, movie films, and slides can be used to good advantage, although slides will frequently require more explanation than moving pictures. However, the required explanation can be shown on the screen in written form if the students are old enough to be good readers. The videotapes chosen should show performances of the skills in such a way that they are largely self-explanatory. Frequently, reruns of the demonstration will help to make it more clear to those who are trying to learn the correct techniques from the picture. Captioning on television has been well received by the deaf community and provides another important system that can be used to enhance instruction.

A visual system for assisting the deaf and hard-of-hearing to participate successfully in physical education classes has been proposed by Schmidt and Dunn (1980). In their approach, movement symbols have been developed to help the student who is deaf or hard-of-hearing associate various movement responses with standard symbols. For example, in figure 12.11, the symbols for body awareness and space awareness are presented. A student learns, therefore, that a straight line centered on a nine- by twelve-inch card means stretch. Individual cards can also be combined to write movement sentences. For example, in figure 12.12, the movement sentence requires that the student do a stretch, curl, twist, and stretch without stopping. The movement cards can also be used with various apparatus such as the balance beam, or the cards may be placed around the room to permit the student to work independently at various stations.

Creativity is encouraged through the use of the movement symbols. Students quickly learn, for instance, that there

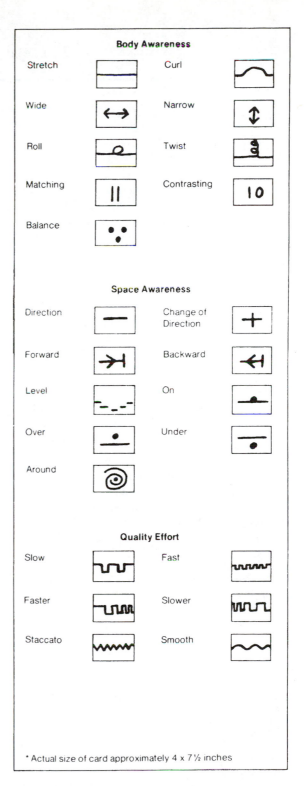

Figure 12.11   Symbols for fundamental movement.

are many ways to stretch. With a traditional approach in which the teacher relies primarily on demonstration, some deaf students associate the image of the teacher standing on tip-toes with arms raised above the head with the correct way to stretch. The movement symbol system helps the student to understand that the word stretch may be associated with many

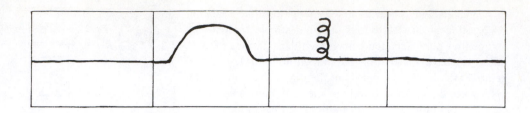

Figure 12.12 "Do a stretch, curl, twist, stretch movement sequence without stopping."

different movement patterns. Hearing students will find the movement symbol system fun and helpful as will other disability populations. The symbols may be made out of felt to accommodate the needs of students who are visually impaired to receive tactile information.

General Guidelines

General guidelines that teachers of physical education should consider in providing appropriate physical education experiences for the deaf and hard-of-hearing include:

1. Good eye contact must be maintained. This means that the teacher will need to be in a position that enables the student to see the instructor's face. With young children, it may be necessary for the teacher to kneel or sit down on the floor when talking with them.

2. The teacher must speak clearly but avoid talking slowly or overemphasizing words. When it is apparent that the student did not understand the teacher's directions, repeat the instructions but use different words and phrases.

3. Sport terms are frequently difficult for the young deaf student to follow. For example, the meaning of the word touchdown is to "touch" "down." This word, however, takes on a very different meaning in the game of football. Instructors must make a special effort to explain sport jargon to the student with a hearing loss.

4. An overhead projector is a necessary visual aid in physical education classes that include students with hearing loss. This aid allows the instructor to speak facing the class while drawing diagrams and putting key words on the overhead. The teacher's ability to maintain eye contact while speaking and making notes helps both those with and those without a hearing loss to follow directions.

5. When outside, teachers should avoid standing in the shadow of buildings or trees or stationing themselves so that students must face the sun during group instruction. Shadows that descend over the face of the instructor interfere with the deaf student's ability to speech read or follow instructions. Having the student facing into the bright sun creates the same difficulty.

6. Some students with hearing loss find long verbal instructions very fatiguing. This is attributed to the intense listening effort that some have to maintain to follow the class discussion. Teachers, therefore, should recognize this special need and provide for frequent rest periods as well as employ alternative methods of providing information to the deaf.

7. When teaching the profoundly deaf student, it is important that the teacher ask frequent questions to ascertain whether the student is following the specific lesson. It is also important that only one question be asked at a time to avoid confusion.

8. Other students must be reminded that they should look at the deaf student when asking or answering a question. The teacher may need to repeat the student's statement so that it is clear to the deaf student as well as others in the class.

9. If possible, a hearing student should be assigned to serve as a peer aide for the student with a hearing loss. The aide's responsibilities include taking notes for communication purposes, helping in the orientation to new activities, and providing visual signals when required during play in team games. Weekly or monthly rotation of the peer aide is recommended to avoid overdependence. Caution must be exercised, too, to ensure that the aide provides assistance only when it is necessary. Lieberman (1995) found that deaf and hearing students benefitted when paired as peers in integrated physical education classes.

Planning the Program in the Special School

Children who have had extreme hearing loss or have been totally deaf since birth or early infancy are sometimes enrolled in special residential schools for the deaf. Schools directed entirely toward the education of the deaf are located in nearly every state, and many of them provide special daily instruction to children who have less severe disabilities but can profit from the speech training, language instruction, manual communication, and speech reading offered to the students in residence. The physical education teacher employed by these special schools will, then, find students in his or her classes who have considerable sound perception in addition to those who have very little hearing, or none.

The students are best instructed in relatively small groups of perhaps seven to ten. The instructor should be placed so that his or her face can be well seen by all the students in the group. A circular or straight-line formation is undesirable because not all the students will be able to face the instructor. A staggered line or horse-shoe shaped formation or informal grouping is very effective.

Some type of signal will need to be arranged to assemble the class. Many students even with very limited hearing are able to hear very low tones, so that some type of percussion instrument producing low tones might be sounded as a signal. Those who cannot hear it will take their cue from watching the others. The switching on and off of lights is another signal that can be used to attract the attention of the students.

Children with hearing problems are reluctant to leave the old games in which they are comfortable and confident to learn new games and activities. Small children enjoy solitary play on playground apparatus such as swings and bars and usually prefer this to the seeming hazards of group play. But deaf students of every age need the socialization and physical exercise provided by group games and competitive play. With careful and patient instruction they can learn new activities and experiences with the same pleasures as other children.

Suggested Activities

There are few restrictions on the activities that may be offered to students with hearing loss in the regular or special physical education class in the usual school or in the physical education program of the special school. The limitations imposed on these students are of a social rather than physical nature. To help these students in their adjustment to their hearing loss and in their relationship with others takes precedence in planning the program to meet their greatest need.

Students who have sustained damage to the semicircular canal of the ear may have poor balance and experience dizziness. Certain limitations in activities are necessary for the safety of these students: Activities that require climbing on high equipment or demand acute balancing are usually prohibited.

Games and Sports

All the individual and team sports may be learned by the deaf and hard-of-hearing. Many special schools field basketball, baseball, and football teams that compete successfully against teams of hearing players. Deaf students enjoy competitive play and play to win, but more important than the winning or losing are the social contacts provided by the game and the acceptance of their worth by opponents with good hearing.

There are, of course, some hazards to the safety of the deaf and hard-of-hearing in competitive play because they are unable to hear signals and other warning sounds. As a precautionary measure, certain visual signals such as the waving of colored flags should be arranged. The instructor should be sure that each participant understands the meaning of each signal before play begins. If the opponents are also nonhearing, the signals should be agreed upon and understood by both teams. If the opponents can hear, they should be alerted to the need for the visual signals and for their cooperation in preventing accidents to hard-of-hearing players.

Fencing, archery, bowling, tennis, golf, and badminton are other sports with demonstrated appeal for students in both deaf schools and regular schools. Activities such as archery and bowling that can be participated in without others have great value as leisure-time activities for those who cannot hear, for whom some avenues of recreation are closed due to their hearing loss. Because listening to records, radio, concerts, and similar recreational pursuits that require normal hearing are lost to them, many deaf and hard-of-hearing people do not have adequate recreational outlets and their leisure hours are boring and depressing as a consequence. They should be taught some individual sports that they can participate in during leisure time; however, these should not be emphasized to the detriment of team play, which encourages the give and take of social intercourse so extremely vital to these students.

Swimming

Water play and swimming are enjoyed by the deaf and hard-of-hearing as much as by other active people. Although some may experience balancing difficulties in the water, nearly all progress similar to other children in learning the swimming skills. A modified stroke that permits the head to remain above water will be necessary for those who must not get water in the ears or who become disoriented when their heads are submerged.

Rhythmic Activities and Dance

Students of all ages with hearing loss take pleasure in rhythmic movement, even though their hearing of the rhythm in music is totally or partially restricted. For successful performance in musical games and dancing, the students must be taught the pattern of movement, with emphasis upon the length of time each phase of the movement is held before it is changed. To students with hearing this is evident in listening to the musical accompaniment, but for those who cannot hear adequately the teacher must accentuate the rhythm with hand movements so that the students can perceive visually what they cannot perceive by hearing. Some students will, of course, hear some of the music, and even those who do not hear melody experience musical vibrations. For this reason a percussion instrument is helpful in establishing rhythms.

Students should be taught simple tap or folk dances first. The basic steps may be presented in demonstration with the back to the students so they will not become confused as to which foot is being used, as is often the case when the teacher faces the class. Dances and musical games that are performed in circles or squares and involve complex formations are best taught in a straight-line formation and in short parts that are later put together in the required formation.

Motor Exploration

Motor exploration and the use of problems in motor movement to be solved through experimentation help the deaf and hard-of-hearing to lose their fears and inhibitions about moving freely in space. Because students proceed at their own pace and their own level of competence in motor movement, they are relieved of the pressures that they usually experience in more formal activities. With each small gain of confidence in their ability to move the body and to control it will come an increased willingness to expand movement experience. Eventually, the student's fears and inhibitions will diminish entirely.

Physical Fitness

Those who are deaf and hard-of-hearing may be underdeveloped physically, owing to their withdrawal from vigorous play activities; they may also be poorly coordinated and purposeless in their movements because of their lack of sound orientation. The physical education program at all levels should include a variety of activities for well-rounded physical development as well as specific exercises that develop cardiorespiratory endurance, flexibility, and muscular tone.

Balance

Although their value is questioned by some, balancing stunts and activities should be included for those students who have difficulty maintaining good balance because of damage to the semicircular canal. Such dysfunction is irreversible, but the kinesthetic sense can be developed and the eyes trained through practice to aid in maintaining body balance in compensation for the loss of semicircular canal control. Young children will enjoy such stunts as walking a line and performing the stork stand (standing on one foot). For older children, work on the pogo stick or on a low balance beam is effective in improving balance. Training in all sport activities encourages the development of better balance in those who lack it. The goal of any balance training that may be required should be to supplement and not supplant the regular instruction in physical education. Students who are deaf need opportunities to be included in activities along with hearing students; programs that pull students out of the mainstream should be discouraged and kept to an absolute minimum.

Dual Sensory Impairment

Individuals with dual sensory impairment experience the loss of both sight and hearing. The United States Office of Special Education defines the deaf-blind child as one "who has both auditory and visual impairments, the combination of which causes severe communication and other developmental and educational problems so that he cannot be properly educated in special education programs for the hearing impaired child or the visually impaired." The degree of loss of visual and auditory acuity that cannot be accommodated in special educational programs varies from situation to situation. However, a student with a visual ratio of less than 20/200 or a field of vision of twenty degrees or less who has a hearing loss of twenty-five decibels or more is usually unable to be educated in such programs and so is considered deaf-blind.

Concern for the education of the deaf-blind has been relatively slow in developing despite the well-publicized success in teaching Helen Keller to read and communicate. Prior to the 1950s, education of the deaf-blind was confined to a very small and select group; most other such children were given little more than custodial care. During the 1950s interest in and efforts to provide for the educational needs of the deaf-blind gradually gained momentum. The endeavors were given impetus by the sudden increase in the number of children born with dual sensory impairments during the 1963 to 1965 rubella epidemic. In the wake of this disaster, many schools for the blind expanded their curricula to include programs directed toward the education of deaf-blind children. In 1968, ten original centers were established, each serving from one to seven states, to provide educational services for the deaf-blind. In 1975 a conference of physical educators and recreationists convened at the University of Iowa to assess needs and recommend recreation programs for the deaf-blind, giving considerable attention to physical recreation.

The Nature and Causes of Dual Sensory Impairment

The most common causes of dual sensory impairment are congenital defects. Other causes are linked to accidents and infectious diseases such as meningitis (inflammation of the membrane covering the brain and spinal column). Of the congenital causes, a large percentage of the cases are the result of the pregnant mother's infection by rubella during the first trimester of pregnancy. Until the 1963 to 1965 rubella epidemic, the number of cases of dual sensory impairment due to rubella amounted to less than one-third of the total number of cases; the figure rose to one-half with the widespread outbreak of rubella. In recent years, Usher's syndrome has become the leading cause of deaf-blindness. Usher's syndrome is a genetic condition resulting in congenital deafness and is accompanied by a progressive blindness known as retinitis pigmentosa. Although the exact number of individuals with deaf-blindness is not known, it is estimated that there are approximately 2,000 individuals age six to twenty-one who are deaf and blind.

Unfortunately, children who are deaf-blind as the result of rubella often have other disabilities as well. Among these are other physical disorders and mental and emotional problems.

Needs and Adjustments of Those Who Are Deaf-Blind

The child who is deaf-blind has challenges similar to those of blind children and those of deaf children. However, the effects of dual sensory deprivation are multiplicative rather than additive. The effects of both blindness and deafness are much more serious than the effects of either deafness or blindness alone, for where these disabilities occur separately, the healthy sense organs can be trained to compensate for the deficient one.

One of the great problems for the person who is deaf-blind is that very little foundation exists for the development of communication skills. The deaf individual is able to see communications between people, and the blind person is able to hear them, but the deaf-blind person has only limited resources for even knowing that people do communicate.

There is, of course, a great need to develop a means of communication for the deaf-blind. Residual hearing, residual sight, or both can be the basis for communication if the child retains either or both. If there is no residual sight or hearing, communication will depend upon body contact using touch signs, signing in the hands, or both of these. In the former, the person who is teaching works with the student to establish certain interpretations of specific touches made on the body. Signing in the hands refers to the use of a manual alphabet in which words are signed or spelled out on the hand of the receiver. Many deaf-blind persons also learn to talk by use of the vibration technique, in which the hands are placed on the face and mouth of the talker to feel the vibrations created by the voice, the movements of the mouth, the control of the breath, and to some extent the placement of the tongue.

Like the blind and the deaf, the child who is deaf-blind needs to develop the unimpaired senses as well as learn to utilize fully any residual sight or hearing. Students who are deaf-blind must rely heavily on their tactile, kinesthetic, vestibular (inner ear balance), and olfactory sensations as stimuli for movement. The educational environment should provide opportunities for experiences that encourage such use.

Without the ability to communicate, children who neither see nor hear are isolated from the world around them. In their isolation they experience little of the social interaction required to develop a sense of well-being and to fulfill the basic need of belonging. Consequently, such children urgently need assistance in learning to relate to others, especially to their peers.

Figure 12.13 Activities designed to help students who are deaf-blind achieve an understanding of their body and its location in space are important.

The formation of a positive self-concept is important to normal social development. Knowledge of one's physical self, the body image, is necessary for the development of a concept of the self. Because they have great difficulty in learning to move about in their world, deaf-blind children have limited opportunities to develop an awareness of their body and to integrate their observations with other information to form a concept of themselves as persons. One of their most essential needs, therefore, is to have greatly expanded opportunities to utilize their bodies in movement.

Movement-related activities should be encouraged from birth with the goal of associating cues (visual, auditory, tactile) with various forms of movement. Van Dijk (1966), developed a system of teaching communication through movement. In this system, which consists of several stages, the teacher uses close body contact with the student to imitate various movements. As the student progresses, the amount of body closeness between teacher and student can be reduced. Throughout the instructional program, the goal is to introduce language by associating movement with cues that can be understood by the student.

Experiences that create tactile and social awareness and control of the body in gross and fine motor movements need to be provided. The total movement experience for deaf-blind children must be varied enough to help them understand their potential in movement and to provide the means to realize this potential.

Program Planning

The physical education activities that can be presented to students who are deaf-blind depend upon their age and also upon the degree of deafness and blindness and the extent to which movement has been learned. Movements that are taught should be presented in such a manner that they contribute to the communication skills of the person. To accomplish this the physical education teacher must learn body signs for general communication from the teacher who works with the student so that the same signs can be used in physical education. Other signs will need to be developed to convey certain concepts of movement peculiar to physical education. The signs developed for this purpose should be used consistently, and additional signs should be introduced only when the previously learned signs are inadequate in instructing the child in a new motor movement.

One system that has been successfully employed with students who are deaf-blind mentally retarded is to rely on kinesthetic cues to communicate. For instance, in teaching a young deaf-blind student to reach for a ball, the teacher, with the student in a seated position, would tap the student's elbows as a signal to reach for the ball. If the student fails to reach, as requested, the instructor would then take the deaf-blind student's hands and physically assist the child to retrieve the ball. Additional feedback would be provided by moving the student's head up and down to indicate yes or side to side to indicate no.

The teacher must also develop a daily routine so that the deaf-blind student will know what to expect each day. The lesson should begin with the teacher identifying himself or herself to the child. A watch or ring that is normally worn every day is useful for this purpose; the child can feel it and know which person this teacher is. Following the introduction, a review of previously taught movements is desirable. The same order should be used in each review. After practice of the previously taught movements, a new movement can be introduced and the child allowed to experiment and practice it. The lesson may end with a familiar activity or game that the child particularly enjoys. Although the idea of sameness might appear boring or limiting to some teachers and students, it is essential that the program for deaf-blind students follow a consistent routine.

Suggested Activities

Sample activities and teaching suggestions are given in the subsequent paragraphs. Each should be given a specific body sign. The teacher should give the sign each time before an activity starts, so that the student can become aware that this sign refers to the activity that follows. The activities are listed in order of difficulty of performance for most children. However, because of past experience or interest, some children may perform the most difficult skills more easily than the skills preceding them. The order also reflects the increased communication skill that will be developed as the activities progress.

Angels in the Snow

Place the child in a prone position on the floor. Touch arms, legs, and head one at a time, helping the child to move the parts touched.

Walking

Help the child to a standing position. Lead child gently forward by the hands until a step is taken. (A helper may be needed to push against the legs.)

Rocking in a Chair

Seat the child in the chair. Help child to rock, indicating the need to shift weight.

Rocking on Back

Lay the child on his or her back. Raise the child's legs to a pike position (knees to chest). Clasp your hands around the child's knees. Lift head and rock body gently back and forth. Help child shift weight to rock alone.

Rocking on Stomach

Place the child on his or her stomach. Raise legs and indicate they are to be held erect. Elevate head and shoulders and indicate that they are to be held up. Help the child to shift weight to rock the body.

Crawling

Help the child assume the position for crawling. Move limbs in the proper order to move forward in a crawl. (A helper is generally needed.)

Kneeling

Help the child take a position on knees with buttocks resting on the back of the legs. Lift buttocks off the legs to raise the trunk to the upright position.

Finger Play

Move the fingers of the child into various positions; for example, cross one finger over another, touch the thumb to each finger on the same hand, squeeze and release soft objects.

Rolling Down

Place the child on an incline mat and move the body so that it rolls forward and down the incline. Help child shift weight so that body rolls without assistance.

Rolling on the Level

Help the child to take a prone position. Move one leg over the other. Cross the arm on the same side over the body. Push the child over onto the stomach. Move the leg that was moved when the child was on the back over the other leg; pull the same arm across the back until the body turns onto the back.

Pushing and Pulling

Put the child's hands on the object to be pushed or pulled (for pulling, the fingers are placed around the object). Push or pull the arms until the object moves.

Rolling over a Medicine Ball

Place the ball on the mat. Position the child to lie on the stomach across the ball. Push on body to start the ball moving forward. Tuck the child's head so that the back of the head will land on the mat as the ball moves forward. Lift the hips and push them over the ball, lowering the hips to the mat.

Running

Pull the child along by the hand at a slow run. As the child gains confidence, run together, each holding opposite ends of a short length of rope.

Running Unaided

The child holds the guide rope while running (see discussion of this technique in the section on suggested activities for the blind).

Rebounding

Help the child to balance on an inner tube or a jouncing board. Lift at the waist or under the shoulders. Move the legs from flexion to extension in coordination with the lift and return. (A helper will be needed.)

Jumping

Put the child in a standing position and indicate that knees are to be flexed. Lift up and down, simultaneously helping the legs to flex or extend as in rebounding. (A helper will be needed.)

Tossing

Place the child's fingers in a grip around an object to be thrown (a bean bag is the simplest to handle). Lead the arm through tossing movements with one hand; with the other hand pull the object from the grasp. When the object is released without aid, move arm through the toss more vigorously to achieve forward movement of the object.

Striking

Set a large ball on a batting tee. Place a bat in the child's hands with the proper grip. Move the bat to within a few inches of the ball. Move the arms through the batting motion to strike the ball. As skill improves, move the bat farther from the ball. When introducing new equipment, such as the ball and bat, it is essential that the student be provided an opportunity to orient to the equipment by feeling and touching it.

Catching

Place the child's hands in the proper position for catching. Drop a ball onto the hands and immediately bring the arms up to entrap the ball between the arms and chest.

Moving to Drum Beat

Place a large drum near enough to the child to enable the vibrations to be felt. Beat the drum with one hand and move parts of the child's body in time to the beat.

Children with more advanced communication and motor skills will be able to participate in more complex activities than those just described. Possibilities are pullups, scooter-board riding, hula hoop play, bean-bag tossing at various targets, rebound tumbling on the trampoline, bouncing a ball, catching and rolling a ball, goal kicking, and moving through an obstacle course.

Older students will be able to participate with assistance in many activities, among them bowling, golf, shuffleboard, archery, weight training, track and field events, rhythms, dance, wrestling, and swimming. Adaptations of these are described in the chapters in which the activities are discussed.

Summary

Information in this chapter focused on sensory impairment, specifically those individuals with visual impairments or hearing loss or a combination of the two. Although the loss of sight or hearing is a major impairment, the focus of this chapter was to highlight that most individuals with sensory impairments function at a very high level and that they enjoy the same activities as individuals who are not disabled. Information about hearing loss and visual impairments were discussed separately.

Visual disabilities range from common eye disorders such as myopia (nearsightedness) to diseases such as trachoma which cause loss of sight. The causes of visual impairments may be classified as refractive errors, muscle imbalance, or genetic disorders and diseases of the eye. The degree of visual acuity is expressed in a numerical ratio such as 20/200, where the first number indicates that the person being tested had to be twenty feet from the chart in order to see what someone with normal vision can see at 200 feet from the chart. Legal blindness is defined as visual acuity of 20/200 or less or a field of vision less than twenty degrees.

In developing physical education programs for those with visual impairments, emphasis must be placed on developing an effective form of communication. Depending on the student's prior experience with activity and the nature of the visual impairment (for example, congenital versus adventitious), the exact approach will vary. Many, however, have found a physical assistance approach in which the student is guided through the movement to be very effective. Some have also found the technique of allowing those with visual impairments to touch the teacher while the skill is being performed effective in helping the student to get the feel of the skill. Communication aides—for example, Braille and special equipment—also can be used to assist the student who is visually impaired. The type of physical education activities used for those with visual impairments are basically the same as those used with the sighted. Some activities such as beep baseball and goal ball are unique sport forms for those with visual impairments. Modifications in activities will need to be made to accommodate the child with a serious visual impairment. Special effort must be made to encourage these youngsters to explore their environment and to participate in creative movement experiences.

Individuals with auditory loss, similar to those with visual impairments, vary considerably in their motor and physical fitness performance levels. Those students whose hearing loss is mild participate successfully with hearing children in play activities. Individuals with profound hearing losses require special modifications in the instructional environment for communication. Hearing losses may be classified according to the type of loss—conductive, sensorineural, or mixed, a combination of the two. Major importance is also placed on whether the hearing loss was congenital or after birth. Those individuals born deaf experience major problems in developing speech. Another factor that must be considered prior to developing physical education programs is to assess the degree of hearing loss, measured in decibels, as well as the hertz or pitch at which sound may be heard. Finally, the method of communication that the person is utilizing must be known. This can range from manual language including gesture (known as ASL) to finger spelling or speech reading. Many deaf and hard-of-hearing individuals use a combination of these methods.

Motor and physical fitness programs for the deaf and hard-of-hearing are very similar to those for the student who hears. The same activities, games, and sports are taught with modification in instruction as appropriate. Similar to the visually impaired, special effort should be made to encourage the student with a hearing loss to engage in creative movement. These experiences add considerably to the student's background and avoid the all too common reliance on demonstration as the only teaching technique. Throughout the chapter, guidelines for creating successful and favorable learning experiences were emphasized.

Information was also presented concerning the special needs of the deaf-blind population. Although the challenges of this population are similar to those with hearing or visual losses, the negative effects of dual sensory deprivation are multiplicative rather than additive. A major problem is the limited foundation that exists for establishing a communication system with this population. Physical assistance and kinesthetic cues have been successfully used in the physical education class. Efforts of this nature, while slow, have produced positive gains in both the physical and motor fitness levels of deaf-blind students.

Fortunately today there is an acceptance and understanding that individuals with sensory impairments enjoy and benefit from participation in physical and motor fitness activities. With proper instruction and adaptations as appropriate, their students can successfully and safely participate with their hearing and sighted peers in a variety of games and sports.

Selected Readings

Best, G.A. (1978). *Individuals with physical disabilities: An introduction for educators.* St. Louis: C.V. Mosby Co.

Birch, J. (1975). *Hearing impaired children in the mainstream.* Reston, VA: The Council for Exceptional Children.

Buell, C.E. (1974). *Physical education and recreation for the visually handicapped.* Washington, DC: American Alliance for Health, Physical Education, and Recreation.

Butterfield, S. (1991). Physical education and sport for the deaf: Rethinking the least restrictive environment. *Adapted Physical Activity Quarterly, 8,* 95–102.

Collins, M.T., & Zambone, A.M. (1994). Deaf-blind children and youth, Education of. *International Encyclopedia of Education.* 1398–1402.

Corbett, E.E., Jr. (Ed.). (1975). *The future of rubella—deaf/blind children proceedings.* Dover, DE: Department of Public Instruction.

Corliss, E. (1978). *Facts about hearing and hearing aids.* Washington, DC: U.S. Department of Commerce, National Bureau of Standards.

Cornett, R.O. (1982). Center for Studies on Language and Communication, Washington DC: Gallaudett College. Personal communication.

Danyluk, A.W., & Paton, D. (1991). Diagnosis and management of glaucoma. *Clinical Symposia, 43–44.*

Decker, J. (1993). Least restrictive environment programming for individuals with hearing impairments: A response to Butterfield. *Adapted Physical Activity Quarterly, 10,* 1–7.

Dolnick, E. (1993). Deafness as culture. *The Atlantic Monthly,* September, 37–53.

Fischgrund, J. (1994). Deaf and hearing impaired youth, Education of. *International Encyclopedia of Education.* 1398–1402.

Goodman, J., & Hopper, C. (1992). Hearing impaired children and youth: A review of psychomotor behavior. *Adapted Physical Activity Quarterly, 9,* 214–236.

Heward, W.L., & Orlansky, M.D. (1988). *Exceptional children* (3d ed.). Columbus, OH: Charles E. Merrill Publishing Co.

Keane, K., Tannenbaum, A., & Krapf, G. (1992). Cognitive competence: Reality and potential in the deaf. In H.C. Haywood and D. Tzuriel. (Eds.), *Interactive assessment,* Berlin, Germany: Springer and Verlag.

Kratz, L.E. (1973). *Movement without sight.* Palo Alto, CA: Peek Publications.

Larson, A.D., & Miller, J.B. (1978). The hearing impaired. In E.L. Meyen (Ed.), *Exceptional children and youth: An introduction* (p. 431). Denver: Love Publishing Co.

Lieberman, L.J. (1995). The effect of trained hearing peer tutors on the physical activity levels of deaf students in integrated elementary school physical education classes. (Unpublished doctoral dissertation). Corvallis, OR: Oregon State University.

Mandell, C.J., & Fiscus, E. (1981). *Understanding exceptional people*. St. Paul, MN: West Publishing Company.

McGuffin, K., French, R., & Maestro, J. (1990). Comparison of three techniques for sprinting by visually impaired athletes. *Clinical Kinesiology, 44*(4), 97–100.

Meyen, E.L. (Ed.). (1978). *Exceptional children and youth.* Denver, CO: Love Publishing Company.

Nesbitt, J., & Howard, G. (1975). *Proceedings of the National Institute on Recreation for Deaf-Blind Children, Youth, and Adults.* Iowa City, IA: University of Iowa Press.

National Center for Health Statistics (1994). National Health Interview Data, Series 10, Number 188, Washington, DC: U.S. Department of Health and Human Services.

Pontecelli, J., & Dunn, J.M. (1988). The effect of two different communication modes on motor performance test scores of hearing impaired children. The national convention of the American Alliance for Health, Physical Education, Recreation and Dance. Poster Presentation.

Rosenthal, R. (1978). *The hearing loss handbook.* New York: Schocken Books.

Ryan, K. (1979). *Adapting physical education and recreation for the visually handicapped student.* New York: American Foundation for the Blind.

Schmidt, S., & Dunn, J.M. (1980). Physical education for the hearing impaired: A system of movement symbols. *Teaching Exceptional Children, Spring,* 99–102.

Silverstein, H., Wolfson, R.J., & Rosenberg, S. (1992). Diagnosis and management of hearing loss. *Clinical Symposia, 44*(3), 32.

Strika, C. (1989). Empathy and its enhancement in hearing impaired children. (Unpublished Dissertation). Syracuse, NY: Syracuse University.

Stewart, D.A., McCarthy, D., & Robinson, J. (1988). Participation in deaf sport: Characteristics of deaf sport directors. *Adapted Physical Activity Quarterly, 5*(3), 233–244.

Vander Kolk, C.J. (1981). *Assessment and planning with the visually impaired.* Baltimore: University Park Press.

Van Dijk, J. (1966). The first steps of the deaf-blind child towards language. *International Journal for the Education of the Blind, 15*(4), 112–114.

Weitzman, D.M. (1985). An aerobic walking program to promote physical fitness in older, blind adults. *Journal of Visual Impairment and Blindness, 79*(3), 97–99.

Wilson, G.B., Ross, M., & Calvert, D.R. (1974). An experimental study of the semantics of deafness. *The Volta Review, 76,* 408–414.

Winnick, J., & Short, F.X. (1985). *Project Unique.* Champaign, IL: Human Kinetics Publishers.

Enhancing Activities

1. While blindfolded, and with the assistance of a sighted partner, participate in a number of activities including walking on campus, visiting the student union, participating in a class, and going to a movie and exercise class. Keep notes on your reaction to performing these activities without sight. What was the reaction of your guide and others to your performance?

2. While blindfolded, participate in a game of goal ball with some players who are visually impaired.

3. Practice communication skills with a deaf student by using some simple signs or finger spelling. While wearing earplugs, watch others speak and try to follow their conversation.

4. Select a favorite skill or sport and modify the activity for a student who is visually or hearing impaired. Try the modifications with an appropriate student and make additional changes as necessary.

5. Visit a local school to observe the educational program employed with a deaf-blind student. Observe the various techniques used to communicate with the student.

6. Interview a deaf educator, a parent of a deaf child, and a deaf person to obtain their views on the various communication systems used with the hearing impaired. Do they agree or disagree on the value of ASL compared to speech reading? Do they agree that deaf students should be mainstreamed?

7. Using the system developed by Schmidt and Dunn, develop some movement sentences to use with deaf and hard-of-hearing students. This same approach can be used with the visually impaired if felt is placed on the cards that contain the symbols.

8. Attend a beep baseball game and/or a goal ball match. Identify similarities and differences in these activities compared to sport experiences for the nondisabled.

CHAPTER

13

Cardiopathic Conditions

 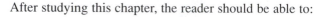
After studying this chapter, the reader should be able to:

1 Comprehend the nature and causes of heart disease.

2 List and describe the most common types of heart disease found among young children.

3 Recognize that cardiovascular disorders associated with adulthood, namely hypertensive heart disease and coronary heart disease, may begin in childhood.

4 Describe the symptoms of heart disease and the recommended emergency procedures for students with heart disorders.

5 Explain that heart murmurs are very common among children and in most cases do not require medical treatment or activity restrictions.

6 Understand the concepts and principles used in developing a graded exercise program.

7 Develop a program for the youngster with a heart disorder using input from parents and family physician.

8 Recognize that the student with a cardiovascular disorder is entitled to a physical education program under the provisions of Federal Legislation.

9 Appreciate that the attitude toward children with heart disorders is changing from that of caution and pessimism to one of optimism, with few activity restrictions and increased attention on exercise programs.

Long before scientists understood the physiological function of the heart, they were concerned with its influence upon the body. The ancients at various times considered the heart the source of love, courage, and kindness; and the association of the heart with these virtues still fills our present-day language with such descriptive phrases as "stout-hearted," "queen of my heart," "sweetheart," and "kindhearted." Actual knowledge of the heart dates from the early seventeenth century, when William Harvey, an English medical doctor, through animal experimentation and observation of his patients, determined its true function. He recorded his findings in a book, which is today acknowledged as the first accurate description of the heart's function.

With the discovery of the X ray, a fairly generally held belief that excessive exercise was injurious to the heart appeared to be substantiated. Through the use of X rays it was determined that pathological hearts were frequently enlarged hearts; it was also determined that athletes had larger hearts than nonathletes. From this evidence the conclusion was made that strenuous exercise worked to the disadvantage of the heart. It was many years before this theory was completely invalidated by physiologists investigating the effects of exercise upon the heart. They discovered that the heart subjected to strenuous exercise over a period of years probably did become larger, but this increase in size resulted from increased strength of the heart muscle rather than from a pathological condition.

Other recent studies have found a relationship between a lack of muscular activity and heart disease. It has been shown that those engaging in sedentary occupations are more prone to heart disease than those whose jobs require muscular activity. Although evidence is not complete, most experts are inclined to agree that exercise throughout one's life is to the advantage of the heart (American College of Sports Medicine, 1995; Frazee, Brunt, and Castle, 1984).

Increased participation by junior high schools in varsity athletics during the 1940s gave rise to considerable concern about possible damage that might be inflicted on the immature heart by the strenuous activity of competitive play. Many physical educators and medical personnel voiced the opinion that excessive strenuous activity could affect the young heart detrimentally. However, the preponderance of evidence accumulated since then indicates that if the heart of the young participant is not predisposed to cardiac disturbance, strenuous activity cannot injure it.

Students with cardiac problems are identified under Public Law 101-476 as individuals with disabilities. This means that all of the provisions of special education, including physical education programs, must be provided for the student with a cardiac condition. Providing appropriate motor and physical fitness programs requires that teachers and medical personnel work cooperatively to plan realistic goals and objectives for each student. Within this chapter, information will be provided to assist teachers in understanding the various cardiovascular problems. Suggestions that teachers can use to improve the functioning level of students with cardiovascular conditions will also be presented.

The Nature and Causes of Heart Disease

Over the past few years, deaths in the United States due to heart disease have been on the decline. This is largely the result of the better care people are giving their bodies. Routine exercise, better diet, and less cigarette smoking are big contributors to the decrease of deaths for individuals over the age of thirty. However, heart disorders are still the primary cause of deaths in the adult population.

Most heart disorders that occur in the younger age group are of a congenital nature or are acquired with illnesses such as rheumatic fever. It has been estimated that there are about 500,000 children in this country suffering from rheumatic fever. Approximately 18,000 to 20,000 new cases are added each year. Of these, approximately one-half show some sign of cardiac damage.

Heart disorders are of two classifications—organic and functional. In an organic disorder a definite lesion exists in the heart or other parts of the cardiovascular-renal system. No lesion is present in a functional heart disorder, but there is some disturbance in function. The symptoms are: irregular or accentuated heartbeat, weakness after physical effort, shortness of breath, dizziness, fatigue, and considerable concern and anxiety.

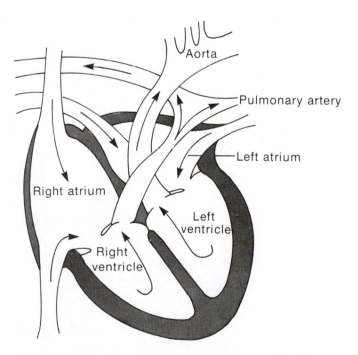

Figure 13.1 Blood enters the right atrium and passes into the right ventricle, where it is pumped to the lungs. Returning from the lungs, the blood enters the left atrium and passes into the left ventricle. It is then pumped through the body by way of the aorta.

Medical research has discovered many different kinds of organic heart diseases. Of these the most commonly occurring, and consequently the most important health problems, are rheumatic heart disease, hypertensive heart disease, coronary heart disease, and congenital heart diseases. Two of these are prevalent among school-age children—rheumatic heart disease and congenital heart disease.

Rheumatic Heart Disease

Rheumatic heart disease begins most often in children between the ages of six and twelve as the result of rheumatic fever. Early signs of rheumatic fever, which may occur singly or in combination, are pain in joints and muscles, twitching of muscles, frequent nosebleeds, pallor, poor appetite, fever, and present or recent streptococcal infection. Evidence of these symptoms does not necessarily mean that a child has rheumatic fever; a period of medical observation and special tests are necessary to determine the presence of rheumatic fever.

Rheumatic heart disease is the result of an attack of rheumatic fever, but the exact cause is not known. Two factors appear to be involved in its development—allergy and a particular kind of streptococcus infection. Rheumatic fever develops only in certain people who have suffered infection of the throat, respiratory tract, or middle ear caused by hemolytic (blood-destroying) streptococcus organisms and who have developed an allergic and inflammatory reaction to the infection. The rheumatic reaction usually occurs a few weeks after the initial attack of the infection but may not be evident until some time later. Rheumatic fever is not communicable, and there is no danger of contracting it by exposure to one who has it.

Rheumatic fever does not always cause heart disease, and the heart is the only organ that may be seriously affected. During the course of the disease the valves of the heart may become inflamed, and subsequent scarring of the valves and surrounding tissue may result. The valves most frequently affected are the mitral and aortic. The scars may prevent their proper function. When the valves cannot close correctly, a back flow of blood is permitted; this is called regurgitation. If the valves do not open correctly to allow the blood to flow easily, the condition is called stenosis (figure 13.2).

Immunity from rheumatic fever does not develop from an attack; on the contrary, the disease tends to recur. Repeated attacks are more likely to damage the heart. For as long as the disease is active and for a period of convalescence it is important to spare the heart unnecessary work. Children with the disease must remain in bed for a given time, after which they may participate in motor activity at a gradually accelerated pace.

Teachers, particularly those of students with disabilities, must be aware of any symptom that might be indicative of streptococcal infection. To assist in identifying a potentially harmful infection, the American Heart Association has listed the following guides:

1. Did the sore throat come on suddenly?
2. Does the youngster complain that the throat hurts most when he or she swallows?
3. Does the child feel pain under the angle of the jaw when that area is pressed gently with the fingers? Are the lymph glands swollen?
4. Does the child have fever? How much? (Streptococcal infections bring on fever between 101° F and 104° F.)
5. Does the child complain of headache?
6. Is the child nauseated?
7. Has the child been in contact with anyone who has had scarlet fever or a sore throat?

Effective treatment to prevent the reccurrence of rheumatic fever is possible through the administration of antibiotics that destroy the streptococcus bacteria. Without proper medication, second attacks occur in more than half of the children initially affected. Additional attacks may permanently damage the valves of the heart, causing them to

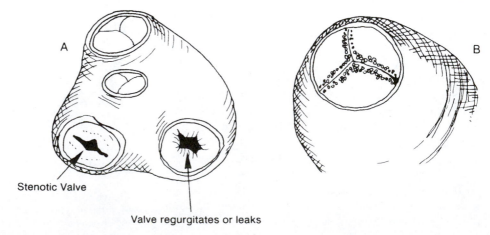

Stenotic Valve

Valve regurgitates or leaks

Figure 13.2 (A) Rheumatic disease of heart valves. (B) Rheumatic disease.

function improperly. Fortunately, the probability of rheumatic fever recurring during adolescence becomes less likely.

Congenital Heart Disease

Children with heart disease are more likely to have a congenital problem than an acquired condition. Some form of congenital heart defect occurs in approximately 8 of every 1,000 live births (Vargo, 1985). Many of these problems will result in early death, normally within the first few months of life, if the disease is not detected and treated.

The cause of most congenital heart defects is not known. Chromosomal abnormality accounts for less than 5 percent of the conditions with Down syndrome, the most widely recognized syndrome. Forty percent of the children with this condition have congenital heart defects.

Three common congenital heart disorders account for more than 50 percent of all congenital heart defects. These are patent ductus arteriosus, ventricular septal defects, and tetralogy of Fallot. These and other common congenital heart defects are described as follows. Please refer to figure 13.3 for illustrations.

Patent Ductus Arteriosus

Patent ductus arteriosus is a failure of an opening between the aorta and the pulmonary artery to close prior to birth. This opening, the ductus arteriosus, is open during prenatal life, allowing most of the blood of the fetus to bypass the lungs, but normally it closes shortly before birth. When the ductus arteriosus remains open, an undue stress is placed upon the heart. In early life, the symptoms often go undetected. As

Atrial Septal Defect

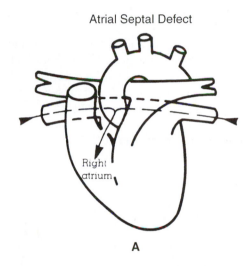

A

Tetralogy of Fallot

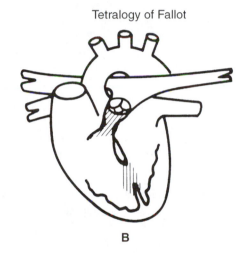

B

Transposition of the Great Vessels

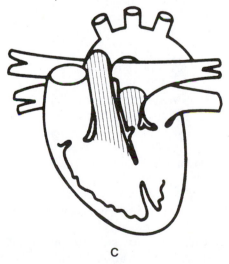

C

Aortic Stenosis

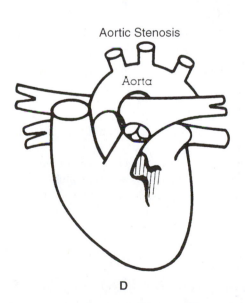

D

Figure 13.3   Common congenital heart defects.

Coarctation of the Aorta

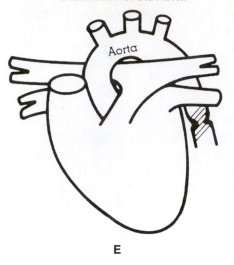

Pulmonary Stenosis

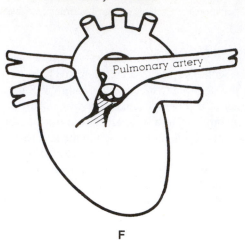

E

F

Figure 13.3—*Continued*

children with this disability grow older and more active, symptoms of dyspnea (shortness of breath) are noticed when they exert themselves. Surgery can correct the defect and is usually performed when the child is four to ten years old. Prognosis is excellent, and the child can often participate in activities without restrictions.

Ventricular Septal Defects

The seriousness of this condition is determined by the size of the opening between the left and right ventricles. If the opening is large, both ventricles will have to pump large amounts of blood at high pressure. Eventually, the heart will hypertrophy (enlarge). With proper medical treatment, the student may do well except for slow growth and undernutrition. The possibility of pneumonia and lung infection is also more likely with children who have a large opening between the ventricles. If a young infant with a large defect has pneumonia, heart failure can result. Treatment normally calls for corrective surgery if the symptoms, including repeated infections, persist.

Atrial Septal Defect

As is true with the ventricles, holes or openings can also occur in the septum separating the two atria. This condition, however, is usually not as serious as patent ductus arteriosus or ventricular septal defects. Rarely does an opening between the atria result in heart failure, persistent problems with pneumonia, or stunted growth. In some children, bypass surgery will be necessary depending upon the size of the shunt.

Tetralogy of Fallot

This disorder produces cyanotic or so-called "blue babies." It combines four structural abnormalities: narrowing of the

pulmonary artery, ventricular septal defect, enlarged right ventricle, and an abnormal positioning of the root of the aorta that causes it to receive blood from both the right and the left ventricles. This, the most serious and most common of the congenital heart disorders, responds well to surgery in a large number of cases. Without corrective surgery the prognosis is extremely poor.

Transposition of the Great Vessels

As the name implies, with this congenital condition the location of the aorta and pulmonary artery are reversed or transposed. This is a serious condition that requires immediate attention. Without surgery, 90 percent of those affected will die within the first year of life. Although the surgical procedures for the condition have improved, they are not entirely satisfactory and it is likely that students with this condition will have to restrict their activity levels throughout life.

Aortic Stenosis

Aortic stenosis occurs when there is an obstruction in the region of the aortic valve. With this condition a narrowing, or stenosis, of the valve occurs. If the narrowing is in the valve itself, the condition is referred to as valvular aortic stenosis. Narrowing above the valve is referred to as supravalvular aortic stenosis while that just below the valve is known as subvalvular aortic stenosis. The obstruction forces the left ventricle to pump at higher pressures to force the blood to the aorta. If the stenosis is severe, the demand on the heart may be too severe, resulting in congestive heart failure.

The youngster with aortic stenosis is usually asymptomatic with the first warning occurring during strenuous exercise. Many youngsters with this disorder have difficulty understanding or accepting the condition. Without discomfort or any other warning signs it is difficult to convince the youngster or the family that there is a heart disorder. Depending on the severity of the condition, activity levels vary from a normal routine, including physical education participation, to programs that must be carefully monitored. In some instances participation in any competitive sport is contraindicated. A general guideline is to allow youngsters with aortic stenosis to rest when they experience chest discomfort. This also encourages the child to develop an appreciation for the necessity and value of self-monitoring.

In some cases of aortic stenosis, surgery may be performed to relieve the obstruction. This decision must be weighed carefully because of the residual deformity which may occur. For example, opening the valve may result in some degree of leakage of blood from the aorta back into the left ventricle. In some cases stenosis may recur following surgery.

Coarctation of the Aorta

Coarctation of the aorta refers to a constriction in the region where the large arterial branch to the left arm arises. If severe, this narrowing, or coarctation, interferes with delivery of blood to the branches of the aorta. This results in elevated arm blood pressure with rapid brachial and radial pulses and a diminished pulse in the legs. Unless the coarctation is severe, surgical repair is normally not performed until after age five but before ten.

The level of activity and decisions about intensity and contraindications must be reviewed carefully with the child's physician. In some cases, the blood pressure readings and other clinical signs are such that the child can engage in normal activities. For some, however, the coarctation may be so severe that the blood pressure is elevated to very high levels. Exercise programs must be carefully developed and monitored. In these cases, close articulation with the medical community is essential.

Pulmonary Stenosis

The pulmonary valve assists blood to flow from the right ventricle into the pulmonary artery. Pulmonary stenosis occurs when there is an obstruction to the outflow from the right ventricle. If the obstruction is severe enough to cause high blood pressure, surgery is required to open the valve. Fortunately, the postoperative results are usually very positive, allowing the individual to engage in activity and exercise programs without restrictions. In some individuals, surgery may not be necessary. Cumming (1993) advises that in these cases there may be some reduction in aerobic capacity but this should not preclude participation in sport and exercise programs. In general the prognosis for individuals with pulmonary stenosis is very positive.

Hypertensive Heart Disease

Hypertension, or high blood pressure, and changes in the arteries are often associated with heart disease affecting both young people and adults, although more prevalent in the latter. When the blood pressure is consistently high, the heart is forced to work harder. Arteriosclerosis (hardening of the artery walls) frequently accompanies hypertension, further increasing the work of the heart. When the heart begins to show the effects of this strain, hypertensive heart disease develops.

The causes of arteriosclerosis are not clearly understood and are classified as: primary or essential (cause unknown) and secondary (cause can be linked with specific disorders or pregnancy). Some authorities feel that an upset in cholesterol (fat) metabolism is a contributing factor; others attribute the disease to hereditary factors. Still others are inclined to blame a mode of living in which excessive anxiety, worry, and fear, and insufficient amounts of rest, relaxation, and exercise, as well as too much eating and smoking, are common. Such factors are known to increase the work of the heart, thereby placing an added burden on it. Some hardening of the arteries does occur as one grows older as part of the natural process of aging. In males, arteries begin to harden about ten to fifteen years before the process begins in women. The reason for this is not known, although it is believed to be related to hormone differences.

Childhood hypertension, specifically the severe form, is associated with kidney disease, obesity, or coaction of the aorta. In recent years, increased emphasis has been placed on the early identification of children at risk for cardiovascular disease. Physicians are now classifying children whose blood pressure over time exceeds the 95th percentile for their age and sex as having primary hypertension. Kaplan (1990) has emphasized the high correlations between large body mass and hypertension and recommends that the best treatment for primary hypertension in children is loss of weight.

Coronary Heart Disease

Coronary heart disease is most prevalent in middle and old age but sometimes occurs in school-age children. The most serious accident that may occur in coronary heart disease is occlusion (closure) of a coronary artery or a rupture of one of the blood vessels, which hemorrhages into the muscle tissue of the heart. Severe pain in the chest often, but not always, accompanies a heart accident or attack. Weakness, pallor, and sweating may also be present. This condition is known as angina pectoris and is due to anoxia of the myocardium (lack of oxygen to the heart). Excitement, fear, and effort make the condition worse. Bed rest of from two to four weeks is usually advised for a moderately damaged heart before convalescent exercises are begun. A longer bed rest is needed if there has been more extensive damage to the heart.

Stroke

Stroke, also commonly referred to as a cerebrovascular accident, is associated with any major disruption of the blood circulation to the brain. The primary sign of a stroke is complete paralysis of one side of the body (hemiplegia) or partial paralysis of one side of the body (hemiparesis). Recognizing that the right side of the brain controls the left side of the body and vice versa, the side of the brain affected can be identified. The disruption of the blood flow to the brain can be the result of a cerebral thrombosis, hemorrhage, or embolism. A thrombosis is a clot that forms within a major blood vessel of the brain, gradually reducing or stopping the flow of blood to a particular area. A cerebral hemorrhage results when a blood vessel, usually an artery in the brain, bursts or ruptures creating additional pressure within an area of the brain. An embolism is a blood clot or fatty material that originates somewhere in the bloodstream and eventually lodges in a vessel in the brain, thus reducing blood supply to that area of the brain.

Although a stroke can occur at any age, the frequency increases with age, becoming much more common after age sixty. Individuals who experience a stroke will respond in various ways depending on the location of the stroke and the immediacy of medical attention following the stroke. Some individuals make excellent recovery and others may be faced with serious debilitating conditions for the remainder of their lives. Common problems that one might see in patients who have recently had a stroke include: incontinence of bowel and bladder, partial memory loss, and depression. Voluntary motor responses might also be impaired, causing a delay or hesitancy in making a voluntary motor response. This, of course, is an area where the physical educator working with young individuals recovering from a stroke can develop innovative programs to enhance proprioception and perceptual motor skills.

Conduction Abnormalities

The activity of the heart is regulated by electrical impulse. Disruption or abnormalities in the heart's electrical conduction system results in various kinds of dysrhythmia (i.e., irregular heartbeats) and blocks interruption or delays in conduction. Electrocardiograms (ECG) are used by physicians to detect abnormalities in the electrical impulse. For a detailed explanation of electrocardiogram tests and procedures used to interpret the test the reader is referred to the American College of Sports Medicine's *Guidelines for Graded Exercise Testing and Exercise Prescription* (1995). The ECG provides a visual reading of the function of the heart over a specified period of time at rest and with varying workloads. As noted in figure 13.4, the waves of electrical activity recorded on the ECG are designated by letters (P, QRS, T). Individuals skilled in reading the ECG monitor these letters to detect any abnormalities that might be

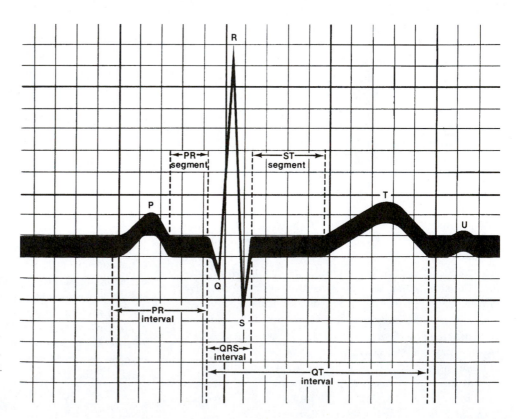

Figure 13.4 Example of wave intervals and segments associated with an electrocardiographic vending.

(Adapted from Scheidt, S. and Netter, F. N. (1986). Basic Electrocardiography, Ciba-Ceigy Pharmaceuticals, West Caldwell, NJ.)

present. For example, two readings that would suggest an exercise contraindication include an ST depression and T-Wave inversion.

Some common terms and problems associated with heart rate and electrical conduction include:

Chronotropic Incompetence: This condition which is noted in individuals with severe developmental disabilities is associated with a slow heartbeat that fails to rise normally in response to vigorous activity.

Sick Sinus Syndrome: This is a generic term that is used to refer to irregular heartbeat problems associated with the sinus node, autonomic nervous system, and hypothalamus. Fatigue and dizziness may be associated with this condition.

Fibrillations: These are caused by incomplete contractions of heart fibers caused by problems with electrical conduction. While in fibrillation, the heart is unable to pump blood. Ventricular fibrillation is the cause of most cardiac arrests and deaths in adults (Wilmore and Costill, 1988). The defibrillator is a device used by trained personnel to provide electrical stimulation to the heart in life-threatening situations.

Tachycardia: This term refers to an excessively fast resting heart rate. There are many different types of tachycardia, all caused by conduction disorders. Healthy individuals can experience temporary bouts of tachycardia as a result of diet (caffeine, alcohol), smoking, or illnesses accompanied by high fever.

Bradycardia: A slow heartbeat can be either a sign of cardiovascular wellness or pathology. For example, it is not uncommon to find well-trained adult endurance athletes with resting heart rates of less than forty to fifty beats per minute. However, an excessively slow heart rate could also be an indicator of a serious health condition such as anorexia nervosa or acute myocardial infarction.

Heart Block: The rhythm of the heartbeat can be blocked or delayed due to an interruption in the electrical impulse. There are many types of block and some that would lead to exercise contraindications (American College of Sports Medicine, 1995). Attempting to monitor exercise by use of heart rate is a problem, for example, with individuals who have an atrioventricular block.

Symptoms of Heart Disease

As discussed earlier, a normal heart makes certain characteristic sounds, which can be heard when the ear or stethoscope is placed in a specific area over a person's chest. There are definite variations in these sounds that accompany certain pathological conditions of the heart. These variations are known as murmurs. Some murmurs are caused by a structural deviation such as valvular incompetence (leaky valves). Frequently, however, adolescents have functional heart murmurs not caused by a structural deviation. Such a murmur has little significance and should not become the focus of worry and concern. It will very likely disappear as the youngster grows older. Restriction of activity is not necessary.

The important danger signals of heart disease are related to the failure of the heart to perform properly. The following symptoms may indicate heart disease: pain in the chest; shortness of breath; edema (swelling) in the feet, ankles, or abdomen; dizziness; fatigue; indigestion; and double vision. People who experience a disturbance in heart rhythm (skipping a beat) often become greatly concerned, but there is usually no reason for concern, as a very large percentage of these cases show no presence of heart disease. Chest pain may result from many different causes. A sharp pain accompanying deep breath inhalation is very seldom due to heart disease. The pain that accompanies heart disease is of a stifling, crushing nature. Dizziness, fatigue, indigestion, double vision, and shortness of breath also frequently come from other causes than heart disease. Individuals should not assume they have heart disease because they have any, or even all, of the symptoms until they have had a thorough medical examination; in many instances the symptoms are not related to heart diseases.

Emergency Care for Heart Cases

A basic premise of the physical activity program for cardiac patients is that the program must be safe. Within the school setting, certain precautions must be taken to ensure that the physical education program is both beneficial and free from possible dangers to the student. In addition to developing an exercise program in cooperation with the medical team, the teacher must be aware of any emergency procedures that should be followed. The steps in emergency care include the following:

1. Let the student assume the most comfortable position—this will usually be a sitting position.
2. Loosen tight clothing.
3. Give the individual plenty of air and avoid drafts.
4. Seek medical assistance immediately. Reassure the individual. The teacher's manner will affect the entire class as well as the student, so the teacher should strive to remain calm and unemotional.
5. Administer cardiopulmonary resuscitation, if necessary. Cardiopulmonary resuscitation is indicated if the carotid pulse is absent, the pupils of the eyes are dilated, and the chest is not moving.

In addition, any specific medical information such as emergency drugs and the procedure for administering them, should be known for each student with a history of heart problems.

Classification of Patients with Cardiac Conditions

The physical limitations imposed by cardiac conditions vary depending upon the degree and amount of malfunction of the heart. Patients with heart diseases are classified by the American Heart Association according to their tolerance to exercise as follows:

Class I, No Restrictions

Patients with heart disease, but without resulting limitation of physical activity. Ordinary physical activity does not cause undue fatigue, palpitation, dyspnea, or anginal pain.

Class II, Mild

Patients with cardiac disease resulting in slight limitation of physical activity. They are comfortable at rest. More than ordinary physical activity results in fatigue, palpitation, dyspnea, or anginal pain.

Class III, Moderate

Patients with cardiac disease resulting in moderate limitation of physical activity. They are comfortable at rest. Less than ordinary activity causes fatigue, palpitation, dyspnea, or anginal pain.

Class IV, Limited

Patients with cardiac disease resulting in inability to carry on any physical activity without discomfort. Symptoms of cardiac insufficiency or of the anginal syndrome are present even at rest. If any physical activity is undertaken, discomfort is increased.

Heart Murmurs

Eighty percent of children four to ten years of age have a heart murmur (Cumming, 1987). In most of these cases, the murmur is normal or innocent and attributed primarily to the slow development of the circulatory system. The consequences are minimal and most children outgrow these murmurs, known as functional murmurs, in adolescence.

Heart murmurs are detected by the physician with the aid of a stethoscope. Murmurs are so named because of the gurgling or hissing sound the physician hears while listening to the heart. Although these sounds may be associated with heart disease, usually an imperfection in the heart valve is the cause, and they are frequently found to be normal following closer examination. In some cases other tests such as electrocardiography or echocardiography are used to rule out any concern about serious heart disease.

The child with a normal murmur should participate without restriction in all physical education activities. If there is a diagnosis of a borderline murmur, consultation with a physician is essential. Cumming (1987), a Canadian pediatrician and researcher, believes that too many children with a murmur have been needlessly restricted in their activity program. His views appear to be shared by a growing number of physicians who recognize the contribution of physical activity to overall health and development of the child.

Two conditions which generally preclude participation in strenuous physical activity of a competitive nature include Marfan syndrome and hypertrophic cardiomyopathy (Adams and McCubbin, 1991). Marfan syndrome is a congenital condition associated with individuals that are slender with long thin extremities, joints that hyperextend, and chest deformity. The primary heart-related problems with this disorder include aortic dilation and mitral valve failure. Although recently there has been considerable interest expressed in Marfan syndrome with the "lay person" perspective that all tall, thin individuals are at risk, this is not the case. Tall individuals with long extremities should not be discouraged from participation in strenuous activity unless there is clinical diagnosis by a physician that suggests the prevalence of a heart disorder.

Hypertrophic cardiomyopathy is the most common cardiac disorder associated with the unexpected death of a young athlete (Adams and McCubbin, 1991). This condition is associated with family history, including the likelihood of a history of sudden death in adolescents or young adults. The primary clue to this disorder is a heart murmur and abnormal electrocardiogram. The nature of this condition requires good medical treatment and close communication with the medical community in developing an appropriate physical education experience.

Needs and Adjustments of Those with Cardiopathic Conditions

The outlook of children with heart disease and that of their parents should be filled with optimism. Medical treatment and recent studies have demonstrated that most youngsters with heart disorders can participate in most if not all of the activities enjoyed by other children including participation in physical education and sport experiences (Cumming, 1993). Even following recent heart surgery, children can be active. For example, children who have undergone surgery for pulmonary stenosis, aortic stenosis, or coarctation are encouraged to walk three days after surgery, return to school within two to three weeks, and walk, swim, or cycle within a month of surgery. Participation in regular physical education can usually be expected following recovery from surgery (Cumming, 1993).

Parents and teachers are becoming more aware that children with heart disorders benefit from activity and unnecessary restrictions may pose additional threats to normal development. Physical activity is valuable not only in maintaining the fitness of the heart, but also in promoting total body fitness. A certain amount of muscular activity is necessary to maintain strength and endurance of the skeletal muscle system. Moreover, exercise is an important factor in digestion and the elimination of wastes, as well as a factor in the feeling of well-being. Exercise programs have helped many individuals with heart disorders reduce anxiety and depression, and accept a more positive attitude toward the future (Kavanagh, 1990).

Many parents and professionals recognize that children with heart disorders can be helpful in determining their own appropriate level of activity. Young children, in particular, seem to be very good judges for establishing an appropriate level and intensity of exercise. Some have recommended that children are very accurate in assessing their exercise capacity. In some cases, however, the medical condition or the age of the student may warrant a more structured and prescribed program. In such cases, it may be necessary to conduct tests and develop a graded exercise program.

Graded Exercise Program

A graded exercise program is sometimes recommended by physicians to increase the efficiency of the cardiorespiratory system of patients with heart problems. Longmuir and associates (1983) found that when children with heart disorders and their parents were given formal instructions regarding exercise programs, improvements in fitness test results were obtained. Before the program is set up, an evaluation of the individual's tolerance for exercise is made; for this purpose, a stress test or graded exercise test is administered. Basically this test consists of the application of a gradually increased workload over a short period of time during which the heart is monitored by an electrocardiograph. The test provides information about the functional capacity of the heart and about its reaction to exercise. The functional capacity of the heart is expressed in the number of pulse beats per minute or the amount of work that the person can perform expressed in a unit known as a MET.

In the latter system a MET is the amount of oxygen the body requires while sitting quietly. One MET equals 3.5 milliliters of oxygen per kilogram of body weight per minute. Normally, it is recommended that the individual with a heart condition work at 60 to 70 percent of his or her functional capacity. For a student with a maximum MET capability of 6.0 this would require an activity program with a workload of approximately 3.6 to 4.2 METs. Given this information, the physical educator can refer to activity charts that identify the energy required of various activities (table 13.1).

Table 13.1   *Leisure activities in METs: sports, exercise classes, games, dancing*

	Mean	Range		Mean	Range
Archery	3.9	3–4	Horseshoe Pitching	–	2–3
Backpacking	–	5–11	Hunting (Bow or Gun)		
Badminton	5.8	4–9+	small game (walking, carrying light load)	–	3–7
Basketball			big game (dragging carcass, walking)	–	3–14
game play	8.3	7–12+	Judo	13.5	–
nongame	–	3–9	Mountain Climbing	–	5–10+
Billiards	2.5	–	Music Playing	–	2–3
Bowling	–	2–4	Paddleball, Racquetball	9	8–12
Boxing			Rope Jumping	11	–
in-ring	13.3	–	60–80 skips/min	9	–
sparring	8.3	–	120–140 skips/min	–	11–12
Canoeing, Rowing and Kayaking	–	3–8	Running		
Climbing Hills	7.2	5–10+	12 min per mile	8.7	–
Conditioning Exercise	–	3–8+	11 min per mile	9.4	–
Cricket	5.2	4.6–7.4	10 min per mile	10.2	–
Croquet	3.5	–	9 min per mile	11.2	–
Cycling			8 min per mile	12.5	–
pleasure or to work	–	3–8+	7 min per mile	14.1	–
10 mph	7.0	–	6 min per mile	16.3	–
Dancing (Aerobic)	–	6–9	Sailing	–	2–5
Dancing (Social, Square, Tap)	–	3.7–7.4	Scuba Diving	–	5–10
Fencing	–	6–10+	Shuffleboard	–	2–3
Field Hockey	8.0	–	Skating, Ice and Roller	–	5–8
Fishing			Skiing, Snow		
from bank	3.7	2–4	cross country	–	6–12+
wading in stream	–	5–6	downhill	–	5–8
Football (Touch)	7.9	6–10	Skiing, Water	–	5–7
Golf			Sledding, Tobogganing	–	4–8
power cart	–	2–3	Snowshoeing	9.9	7–14
walking (carrying bag or pulling cart)	5.1	4–7	Squash	–	8–12+
Handball	–	8–12+	Soccer	–	5–12+
Hiking (Cross-country)	–	3–7	Stairclimbing	–	4–8
Horseback Riding			Swimming	–	4–8+
galloping	8.2	–	Table Tennis	4.1	3–5
trotting	6.6	–	Tennis	6.5	4–9+
walking	2.4	–	Volleyball	–	3–6

Courtesy of American College of Sports Medicine. (1995). *Guidelines for graded exercise testing and exercise prescription* (5th ed., pp. 164–165). Philadelphia: Lea and Febiger.

Table 13.2 *Approximate energy requirements in METs for horizontal and grade walking*

mi•h⁻¹ᵃ	1.7	2.0	2.5	3.0	3.4	3.75
% Grade m•min⁻¹ᵇ	45.6	53.7	67.0	80.5	91.2	100.5
0	2.3	2.5	2.9	3.3	3.6	3.9
2.5	2.9	3.2	3.8	4.3	4.8	5.2
5.0	3.5	3.9	4.6	5.4	5.9	6.5
7.5	4.1	4.6	5.5	6.4	7.1	7.8
10.0	4.6	5.3	6.3	7.4	8.3	9.1
12.5	5.2	6.0	7.2	8.5	9.5	10.4
15.0	5.8	6.6	8.1	9.5	10.6	11.7
17.5	6.4	7.3	8.9	10.5	11.8	12.9
20.0	7.0	8.0	9.8	11.6	13.0	14.2
22.5	7.6	8.7	10.6	12.6	14.2	15.5
25.0	8.2	9.4	11.5	13.6	15.3	16.8

Courtesy of American College of Sports Medicine (1991). *Guidelines for graded exercise testing and exercise prescription* (4th ed., p. 298) Philadelphia: Lea and Febiger.
ᵃMiles per hour
ᵇMeters per minute

Original Linear Scale		Updated Ratio Scale	
6		0	Nothing at all
7	Very, very light	0.5	Very, very weak
8		1	Very weak
9	Very light	2	Weak
10		3	Moderate
11	Fairly light	4	Somewhat strong
12		5	Strong
13	Somewhat hard	6	
14		7	Very strong
15	Hard	8	
16		9	
17	Very hard	10	Very, very strong (maximal)
18			
19	Very, very hard		
20			

Figure 13.5 Borg RPE Scales for Measuring Exercise Intensity.

(Source: G. Borg. Psychophysical basis of perceived exertion, *Medicine and Science in Sports and Exercise*, 14, 371–381, 1982, © by The American College of Sports Medicine.)

METs may also be determined by analyzing the amount of work that a student can perform at a given workload (table 13.2).

Pulse rate may also be used as a technique of monitoring an exercise program for the student with a heart condition. In this system, the student's maximum pulse rate is determined during a graded exercise or submaximal stress test.

The exercise program is then established with the objective of providing a workload that will produce a pulse rate of approximately 70 percent of the functional capacity. As the individual becomes conditioned by the exercise, pulse rate decreases when performing the same amount of work. When this occurs, the workload is increased to again bring the pulse rate up to 70 percent of the functional capacity. Students may be taught to count their own pulse rates, thus helping them to monitor their own exercise levels. Activities included in the graded exercise program are those that allow great control over intensity; that is, they are self-paced and performed in a stable environment. Examples are walking, jogging, cycling, swimming, and calisthenics.

A technique for determining exercise intensity that some find easier to understand and apply is the Borg Rating of Perceived Exertion. In this system, developed by Borg (1982), the individual "grades" or rates the level of exertion using a numerical scale. As noted in figure 13.5, Borg has developed two RPE scales. The first is a 15 point scale with numbers ranging from 6 to 20 and the second scale consists of numbers 0 to 10. Carton and Rhodes (1985) report that the rating of perceived exertion has a strong linear relationship with heart rate.

The American College of Sports Medicine has determined that a perceived exertion rating of 12 to 13, using Borg's 15 point scale, corresponds to approximately 60 percent of target heart rate. Corresponding ratings using the 10 point scale are between 4 and 6. When a person exercises at this intensity level, he or she should be able to carry on an intermittent conversation with a friend and exercise strenuously enough to achieve a training effect. The rating of perceived exertion has been used successfully with various individuals, including those with mental retardation. The value of this system, of course, is the ease with which the approach can be explained and implemented.

Using the MET or pulse-rate system helps to monitor the *intensity* of the activity program. It is also important that the *duration* and *frequency* of the exercise regimen be carefully structured, recognizing it is difficult to develop specific guidelines that apply to various people. According to the American College of Sports Medicine (1995), the recommended frequency varies from several daily sessions, to three to five periods per week according to the needs, interests, and functional capacity of the participants. Environmental factors including temperature, humidity, wind, altitude, and pollution must also be considered in developing programs. Given the nature of the disability and the numerous variables that must be considered, the specific intensity, duration, frequency, and mode of exercise should be cooperatively developed with qualified professionals, including a physician. An example of a suggested program developed for an individual with a maximum threshold of six METs is found in table 13.3.

Planning the Program

Teachers should work cooperatively with physicians, parents, and other school personnel to develop appropriate physical education programs for the student with a cardiac condition. Information about the student's functioning ability is particularly helpful in establishing a safe and worthwhile program. Target heart rate as well as the student's maximal levels of oxygen intake are particularly helpful

Table 13.3 *Example of a walking program developed for a person with a maximum MET score of six*

Period	Intensity (MET)	Intensity (ml/O₂/ kg min.)	Equivalent Exercise
Warm-up	2–3	7–11	Walk .25 mile in 7.5 min. (2 mph)
Training	3.5–4.5	11–16	Walk 1.0 mile in 20 min. (3 mph)
Cool-down	2–3	7–11	Walk .25 mile in 7.5 min. (2 mph)

facts (chapter 27). In some cases, this information may not be known and the individual's condition may be classified according to one of the categories described earlier in this chapter. Based on all the available information, an Individualized Education Program with realistic goals and objectives can be developed consistent with the student's functioning ability. The final program must, of course, have the approval of the student's physician.

When selecting activities, it must be kept in mind that the strenuousness of an activity is not determined solely by its type but by how vigorously and how long it is performed. Some individuals may play table tennis at such a rapid pace that the activity might be classified as moderate, whereas others may play much more slowly and deliberately so that the activity would be only mild in nature.

Age, personality, drives, and attitudes all determine the strenuousness with which a person performs an activity. Some may be more tense and work harder under the pressure of the learning situation with a teacher, while in free play they are much more relaxed. There are also those players, particularly among children, who in free play without the guidance of the instructor will not set a wise course in their play. There is a general tendency for children to overwork in muscular activity, while adults are generally too sedentary. All such factors must be given consideration in planning the program.

Competitive play with its emphasis on winning is contraindicated for most heart patients. The emotions involved may speed the action of the heart so that the overall work of the activity is beyond the tolerance level for the patient. Moreover, when there is an overemphasis on winning there is always a possibility that the participant may ignore safety precautions that he or she would otherwise heed.

The physical education teacher must be sure that the medical information needed to provide suitable activity at the appropriate level of intensity for those students who have been placed by their doctors on a graded exercise program is available. Frequent monitoring of the pulse is necessary to enable the participant to adjust the exercise level. Older students are capable of taking their own pulse or may have learned from experience to predict the level of intensity from subjective feelings. The teacher may need to take the pulse count of younger participants. This is readily done by counting the palpitations at the brachial (wrist) or carotid (neck) pulse points. Exercise heart rate can be determined with reasonable accuracy by making either ten- or fifteen-second pulse counts immediately upon the completion of exercise and multiplying by either six or four, respectively, to obtain the per-minute count.

Students' exercise tolerance level should be discussed with them, and they should have a clear understanding of their capacity and the amount of activity that constitutes an adequate work load. To help participants keep within their tolerance level, they should understand that as long as they can perform the activity without breathing through the mouth or without forced breathing through the nose, they are not overexerting. Activity should stop at once if any cardiac distress or shortness of breath is evidenced.

Short periods of activity are usually best. Rest periods should be provided about halfway through an activity and should equal in length the time devoted to activity.

Some special consideration will need to be given to the influence of weather conditions and certain features of the activity area on the planned program. In extremely hot weather or on damp, rainy days, special precautions may be required. If activity is to take place on rough or hilly playing areas, the expenditure of energy is likely to be greater, and consideration of this fact should be made in regard to the cardiac patient.

Flexibility exercises designed to extend the range of movement in the various joints of the body are desirable for total fitness and do not appear to tap the cardiovascular system greatly. They should be included in an exercise program, particularly as warm-up activities, because they maintain complete movement potential. In general, slow stretching with a short period of holding at the extreme range appears to be the best way to develop flexibility with minimal risk of muscle pulls.

Suggested Activities

Individuals with a heart disorder can participate in most of the activities taught in a physical education class. The intensity of the activity can be determined by using as a guide table 13.1. If there are any questions about the medical condition or physical capabilities of the students, the child's physician should be consulted. Although generally few restrictions will apply, there may be some activities or intensity levels that the physician will recommend avoiding. Occasionally competitive sports may be contraindicated. Almost any sport can be modified, if necessary, to reduce the strenuousness of the activity. For example, tennis may be played with the court width cut in half and with the elimination of the drop shot to modify the demands on physical exertions.

For very young children, many of the basic skill games described in chapter 21 are applicable, depending upon the

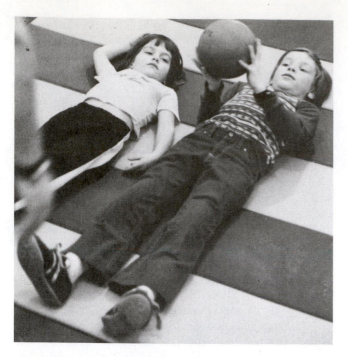

Figure 13.6 The strenuousness of throwing and catching can be modified by lying down to play.

ability and functioning level of the child. Singing games may be used, but the child should not attempt to perform both the singing and the activity at the same time, as this may be too strenuous. The teacher or the others in the class may sing while the child performs. Games that do not require sustained periods of running, such as Red Light and Call Ball, are very good for children with moderate functional capacity, as they enable the player to rest for short periods between action. Games such as Wonder Ball and Circle Ball, which utilize body activities other than running, are fine exercises. The work load may be further minimized by having the children seated to pass the ball around, or the children may lie down in line and a balloon may be substituted for the ball. Another popular activity is modified volleyball. For this game a badminton net is stretched across the playing area three or four feet above the floor; the students sit on each side of the net and volley a balloon back and forth as in volleyball.

Summary

The information in this chapter focuses on cardiovascular disorders with primary emphasis on those heart diseases found in children. Heart murmurs were discussed with emphasis on how frequently they occur, usually without any harm. Rheumatic fever, an acquired disorder, was discussed as well as the common congenital heart diseases including patent ductus arteriosus, ventricular and atrial septal defect, tetralogy of Fallot, pulmonary and aortic stenosis, and coarctation of the aorta. Implications of these diseases for physical activity programs were also discussed.

There is a growing awareness that some of the restricted practices used with these children in the past are no longer accepted from a child-development or medical perspective. The prognosis for many children with heart disease, including those who have experienced heart surgery, is excellent. While close articulation with the family and child's physician is prudent, physical educators should understand that children with cardiovascular disorders will probably engage in the same physical education activities as all other children. If modifications are necessary, individualized programs should be developed using input from the family, physician, and child to develop an appropriate activity program. In some cases it may be necessary to follow a graded exercise program using the guidelines described in this chapter. The overwhelming evidence suggests, however, that the restrictive practices common in the past are unnecessary and represent an overreaction for many children with cardiovascular heart disease. Current treatment and programs emphasize that children with heart disease should be encouraged to be active, including those who have undergone recent heart surgery. Every effort should be made to assist these children in developing a full and active life.

Selected Readings

Adams, R.C., & McCubbin, J.A. (1991). *Games, sports and exercise for the physically disabled* (4th ed.). Philadelphia: Lea and Febiger.

American College of Sports Medicine. (1995). *Guidelines for graded exercise testing and exercise prescription* (5th ed.). Philadelphia: Lea and Febiger.

American Heart Association. (1970). *If your child has a congenital heart defect*. New York: American Heart Association.

Baum, D. (1982). Heart disease in children. In E.E. Bleck and D.A. Nagel (Eds.), *Physically handicapped children: A medical atlas for teachers* (2d ed.) (pp. 313–324). New York: Grune and Stratton.

Borg, G. (1982). Psychophysical basis of perceived exertion. *Medicine and Science in Sports and Exercise, 14*, 371–381.

Burch, G.E. (1977). *A primer of cardiology* (5th ed.). Philadelphia: Lea and Febiger.

Corbin, C. (1980). Cardiovascular fitness of children. In C. Corbin (Ed.), *A textbook of motor development* (2d ed.) (pp. 107–114). Dubuque, IA: Wm. C. Brown Publishers.

Carton, R.L., & Rhodes, E.C. (1985). A critical review of the literature on rating scales for perceived exertion. *Sports Medicine, 2*, 198–222.

Cumming, G.R. (1987). Children with heart disease. In J.S. Skinner, *Exercise testing and exercise prescription for special cases* (pp. 241–260). Philadelphia: Lea and Febiger.

Fletcher, G., & Cantwell, J. (1974). *Exercise and coronary heart disease*. Springfield, IL: Charles C. Thomas.

Frazee, R., Brunt, D., & Castle, R.F. (1984). Exercise tolerance of a young child with congenital heart disease associated with asplenia syndrome. *Adapted Physical Activity Quarterly, 1*, 332–336.

Kaplan, N.M. (1990). Clinical hypertension (5th ed.). Baltimore: Williams and Wilkins.

Kavanagh, T. (1990). Exercise and coronary artery disease. In J. Basmajian and S.L. Wolf (Eds.), *Therapeutic exercise* (5th ed.) (pp. 548–564). Baltimore: Williams and Wilkins.

Kavanagh, T. (1984). Exercise and coronary artery disease. In J. V. Basmajian (Ed.), *Therapeutic exercise* (4th ed.) (pp. 565–586). Baltimore: Williams and Wilkins.

Longmuir, P., et al. (1983). The benefits of a postoperative exercise program for children with congenital heart disease. *Clinical Investigative Medicine, 5*(45).

Pollock, M. L. (1979). How much exercise is enough? In D. E. Cunliff (Ed.), *Implementation of aerobic programs*. Washington, DC: American Alliance for Health, Physical Education, and Recreation.

Rimmer, J. (1994). *Fitness and rehabilitation programs for special populations*. Dubuque, IA: Brown and Benchmark.

Ross, J., & O'Rourke, R. (1976). *Understanding the heart and its diseases*. New York: McGraw-Hill Book Co.

Scheidt, S., & Netter, F.N. (1986). Basic electrocardiography. Ciba-Ceigy Pharmaceuticals, West Caldwell, NJ.

Sherrill, C. (1993). *Adapted physical education and recreation* (4th ed.). Dubuque, IA: Wm. C. Brown Publishers.

Vargo, T.A. (1985). Congenital heart disease. In R.B. Conn (Ed.), *Current diagnosis 7* (4th ed.). Philadelphia: W.B. Saunders.

Wilmore, J.H., & Costill, D.L. (1988). *Training for sport and activity* (3d ed.). Dubuque, IA: Wm. C. Brown Publishers.

Enhancing Activities

1. Interview a pediatrician to obtain his or her views on whether the medical community's treatment and attitude toward the child with heart disease has changed.

2. Utilizing table 13.1, compute some MET values using hypothetical data. Convert the MET values into some suggested activity programs.

3. Visit a setting in which a graded exercise test is being performed.

4. Obtain a copy of one of the references listed in this chapter or a book on cardiovascular disorders and read additional information on one of the heart diseases identified in this chapter.

5. Conduct a survey of your friends to determine how many of them may have been diagnosed as having a heart murmur. What were their reactions to the murmur and that of their parents? Were any unnecessary activity restrictions imposed?

CHAPTER 14

Respiratory Disorders

CHAPTER OBJECTIVES

After studying this chapter, the reader should be able to:

1 Recognize and describe the most commonly occurring disorders of the respiratory system.

2 Identify the various treatment strategies used in the management of asthma, bronchitis, and cystic fibrosis.

3 Define selected terms and phrases including *dyspnea, exercise induced asthma (EIA), forced expired volume in one minute (FEV1), vital capacity,* and *chronic obstructive pulmonary disease (COPD).*

4 Appreciate the value of exercise programs in the treatment of asthma and cystic fibrosis and its effects on the overall health and well-being of individuals with these disorders.

5 Suggest activities and exercises, including breathing programs, for individuals with respiratory disorders.

6 Explain that programs for individuals with respiratory disorders should be progressive in nature and emphasize aerobic activities.

7 Understand the role of disability grading systems and perceived-exertion scales in developing individualized fitness programs for students with respiratory disorders.

The respiratory disorders discussed in this chapter will be those that prevent adequate ventilation of the lungs, a condition that leads to an insufficient supply of oxygen and the retention of carbon dioxide in the body. The causes of respiratory disorders may be the loss of elasticity of the breathing mechanism, muscular weakness, increased resistance to the flow of air through the connecting tubes of the respiratory system, increased thickness or destruction of the air sacs of the lungs, or a combination of these.

As a background for understanding the nature of respiratory disorders, a brief review of the anatomy of the respiratory system is useful. The respiratory system may be thought of as having an upper and a lower level. The upper level includes the head and throat and is made up of the nasal cavity, pharynx, and trachea. These act chiefly as passages for the air, allowing the air to warm before entering the lungs. The diaphragm and the two lungs, which lie on either side of the heart, make up the lower level (figure 14.1). The left lung has two lobes (divisions); the right lung has three. The lungs consist mainly of bronchi, bronchioli, and alveoli. The bronchi are tubes branching from the trachea; the bronchioli are branches of the bronchi that transport the air to the alveoli, which are small saclike structures in which oxygen and carbon dioxide are exchanged.

Various muscles are also involved in the work of the respiratory system. The most important of these, because it is the primary muscle used in breathing, is the diaphragm, a dome-shaped muscle separating the chest and abdominal cavities. In contraction it flattens and loses its domed appearance, thereby enlarging the chest cavity and allowing expansion of the lungs. This results in inspiration of air into the lungs. When the diaphragm relaxes, the chest cavity diminishes in size and air is forced out of the lungs.

When the airflow restriction is severe, the expression *chronic airflow obstruction* is used. This condition may be described functionally by using a spirometer, an apparatus that measures the flow of air into and out of the lungs. Two useful but easy-to-obtain measures with the aid of the spirometer are *forced expired volume in one second (FEV1)* and *vital capacity (VC)*. The forced expired volume is the amount of air that can be forcibly expired in one minute. Vital capacity is the change in pulmonary volume between a maximal inspiratory effort followed by a maximal expiratory effort. These values can be compared to normative data to assess the degree to which the individual may have an airflow obstruction.

Certain muscles of the neck, chest, and abdomen assist the diaphragm in the breathing process; they also have other functions. If weak, these muscles can be strengthened by exercises of the trunk. The muscles[1] referred to are the

---

[1]The location of the muscles below the surface are identified by their relationship to the surface muscles. See Appendix VI for location of the surface muscles of the body.

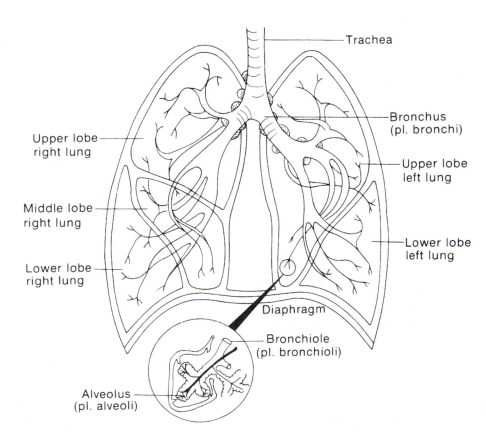

Upper lobe
right lung

Middle lobe
right lung

Lower lobe
right lung

Trachea

Bronchus
(pl. bronchi)

Upper lobe
left lung

Lower lobe
left lung

Diaphragm

Bronchiole
(pl. bronchioli)

Alveolus
(pl. alveoli)

Figure 14.1 The lower level of the respiratory system.

iliocostalis lumborum and iliocostalis dorsi (both located under the ligamentous band, which is the tissue at the small of the back into which the latissimus dorsi inserts); the external and internal oblique muscles (the internal lies beneath the external); and the rectus abdominus.

Individuals suffering from respiratory disorders are frequently lumped together into the medical classification *chronic obstructive pulmonary disease (COPD)*. Unfortunately, this title suggests that there is only one disease and that asthma, cystic fibrosis, and bronchitis are all the same disorder. As will be indicated in this chapter, this is not true.

The most familiar and most commonly occurring disorders of the respiratory system are asthma, hay fever, cystic fibrosis, chronic bronchitis, and emphysema. (Tuberculosis, although well known, is no longer a common disease, owing to the effectiveness of treatment and preventive measures.) Asthma, hay fever, and cystic fibrosis affect both children and adults. Emphysema is much more prevalent among adults. There are two types of bronchitis: acute and chronic. The acute form attacks both children and adults, but the chronic form is more common among adults. Even though chronic bronchitis and emphysema primarily affect adults, the basis for their development is laid during childhood and youth. It is generally agreed in the medical profession that these two disorders are insidious; that is, they develop over a long period of time, as the result of inhalation of irritants such as smoke in the heavy use of tobacco, dust, and fumes. Because the kind of air that is breathed in earlier years affects the possibility of incurring chronic bronchitis and emphysema at a later date, educators have a responsibility to make young people aware of the latent dangers of air pollution and smoking, and to teach them the means of prevention. Students with disabilities, particularly, need to know how to avoid adding another health problem to the difficulties they are already experiencing.

Asthma

Asthma is the common term used for the condition of bronchial asthma. It is a disease of the bronchi characterized by swelling of the mucous membrane lining the bronchial tubes, excessive secretion of mucus, and spasms of the bronchial tubes. Symptoms of asthma are dyspnea (breathlessness), coughing and wheezing, and a feeling of constriction in the chest. Typically an attack of asthma is characterized by a coughing stage, followed by dyspnea and wheezing. The attack usually terminates with the coughing up of a large amount of thick sputum.

People afflicted with asthma tend to overuse the intercostal muscles in breathing, at the expense of the diaphragm. Also, there is a tendency to tighten the abdominal muscles during inspiration, which further reduces the action of the diaphragm. The reduction in action causes a decrease in the amount of air that is inhaled. Continual reliance on the upper chest muscles for breathing results in a gradual loss of flexibility of the diaphragm.

Asthma is a chronic disease in which periodic attacks are followed by periods of remission of the symptoms. Attacks vary greatly in severity and duration; they may range from a slight period of wheezing to a prolonged period of coughing accompanied by severe dyspnea. An attack that persists for days is referred to as status asthmaticus. Attacks can be triggered by breathing very cold air or air that has a high content of moisture or by respiratory tract infections.

Extrinsic asthma is caused by the reaction of the body to the introduction of a foreign substance to which the body is sensitive. Usually this substance, called an allergen, is suspended in inhaled air; however, the offending substance may also be ingested in the form of food or drugs. The most common allergens are plant pollen, dust, molds, and animal fur.

Asthmatic attacks may be induced by exercise. This condition is frequently referred to as exercise-induced asthma (EIA). Fatigue and emotions are also factors in attacks. The tolerance level for exercise of those subjects to exercise-induced asthma varies from person to person but is related to physical condition; those who are in good physical condition usually have a higher tolerance than those who are not. Attacks also strike different people at different times. In some people, the symptoms occur during exercise; in others, the symptoms manifest themselves several minutes after the end of the activity.

An as-yet-undefined relationship exists between asthma and the emotions. Some cases are thought to be due chiefly to emotional stress, because they have no extrinsic causes and the symptoms disappear when the emotional tension subsides. Because extrinsic asthmatic cases often become worse in times of emotional distress, this type of asthma is generally considered to be psychosomatic.

Asthmatic attacks that are neither extrinsic in nature nor primarily caused by emotional reaction are thought to be related in some way to a deficient cellular function that affects the sympathetic nervous system, which, in turn, alters the tonus of the bronchial tube linings.

The greatest incidence of asthma occurs among young children and is reported to be the most important cause of school absenteeism (Hill, Britton, and Tattersfield, 1987). Fortunately, many young sufferers no longer have asthmatic attacks after puberty. Approximately 10 million Americans, or 4 percent of the nation's population, are asthmatic—3.5 million adults and 6.5 million children (U.S. Department of Health and Human Services, 1989). The incidence of asthma is slightly higher among males than among females (Partin, 1989) and is more common in blacks than whites (Weiss and Wagener, 1990).

Treatment

The treatment of asthma begins with attempts to determine the cause. The cause may be an allergen, which must be identified so that it can be avoided. If avoidance is not possible, medication is administered.

During the past twenty years many new and effective drugs for the treatment of asthma have been developed. Some of the new drugs are designed to prevent asthma; others have the effect of reversing bronchospasms. Because of these developments, many asthmatics now can participate in activity programs without fear of an asthmatic attack. A list of the drugs commonly used to treat asthma and their effectiveness in preventing EIA is found in table 14.1. Although drugs may be taken orally or by aerosol, the aerosol dispersion is preferred. This is due to the superior protection provided and the speed with which the aerosol form works compared to oral administration. Students must be cautioned, however, to use the aerosol as prescribed. If not carefully monitored, some students will use the inhaler at the slightest feeling of discomfort. Use of the inhaler more frequently than once every three hours can be harmful and should be avoided.

Teachers should also be aware that some side effects may be associated with the various medications prescribed for asthma. For example, headaches, tremors, apprehension, faintness, and dizziness have been reported with the use of several of the medications found in table 14.1. The student's parents and physician should be consulted if the teacher notices any unexpected or unusual responses in the student's behavior or motor performance.

The American Academy of Pediatrics issued a statement that recommended that asthmatic children should be encouraged to participate in physical education and sport programs. Its statement is as follows:

> Physical activities are useful to asthmatic children. The majority of asthmatic children can participate in physical activities at school and in sports with minimal difficulty, provided the asthma is under satisfactory control. All sports should be encouraged, but should be evaluated on an individual basis for each asthmatic child, depending on his tolerance for duration and intensity of effort. Fatigue and emotional upheaval in competitive athletic contests appear to be predisposing factors in precipitating asthmatic attacks in

some instances. This may depend to some extent on the duration and severity of the disease. As a general rule, every effort should be made to minimize restrictions and to invoke them only when the condition of the child is necessary. (American Academy of Pediatrics, 1982)

Recent studies have supported the value of physical activity for the asthmatic and have concluded that the benefits of regular aerobic exercise are similar for the asthmatic and nonasthmatic. In a practical sense this policy statement was reinforced in recent Olympics where approximately 11 percent of the U.S. Olympians suffered from asthma and related disorders. The same percentage of athletes with asthma won Olympic medals as athletes without the disease (Afraisiabi and Spector, 1991). They obviously were successful in the management of their asthma and, with the exception of ensuring that their medication was approved by the Olympic committee, participated at a high level of achievement without modification.

Unfortunately, many asthmatic individuals are unaware of the value of exercise and avoid vigorous activity because of the initial discomfort many experience as they exercise. Uninformed parents, teachers, and physicians also add to the problem by encouraging the child with asthma to avoid vigorous activity programs. Consequently, some asthmatic children have low physical fitness and motor fitness levels. Exclusions from physical education programs must be avoided for the student with asthma. As indicated in Public Law 101–476, individualized physical education goals and objectives must be developed for health-impaired children, including those with asthma. In more severe cases, consultation with the parents, physician, child, and other school personnel within the format of an Individualized Education Program meeting is essential. In table 14.2, some guidelines for promoting exercise for asthmatics are presented.

Hay Fever

Hay fever is an allergic disease caused by a sensitivity to specific substances in the air. The most common allergens are pollen and the spores of mold. Spores of mold are not commonly found in the air; however, pollen, especially ragweed pollen, is frequently present, depending upon the geographic area and the time of year when plants release their pollen.

A milder disorder than asthma, hay fever involves only the upper level of the respiratory system. It is characterized by sneezing, watery eyes, and a runny nose. Often these symptoms are accompanied by a burning sensation in the throat and the roof of the mouth.

Hay fever often interferes with sleep and appetite and can lower the body's resistance to disease. It may lead to inflammation of the ears, sinuses, throat, and bronchi. In some cases it may even be a precursor of asthma.

Table 14.1   *Drugs used for treating asthma*

Drug	Route of Administration	Effectiveness
Ephedrine	Oral	Uncertain
Isoproterenol	Oral	Slight
	Aerosol	Fair
Metaproterenol	Oral	Fair
	Aerosol	Good
Atropine	Aerosol	Slight
Glucocorticosteroids	Oral	Uncertain
	Aerosol	Uncertain
Theophylline	Oral	Good
Cromolyn sodium	Aerosol	Good
Beta-2 agonists terbutaline sulfate	Aerosol	Excellent

Table 14.2 Guidelines for promoting exercise for asthmatics

Warm-up	Low-level activity such as stretching, walking, and general strength exercises prior to vigorous activity is necessary. The warm-up should continue until a mild sweat occurs.
Warm-down	A low-level activity such as walking for five minutes after activity or until the pulse rate returns to within 20 beats per minute of resting should be undertaken.
Duration	Sessions should last 30 to 40 minutes. For the very low fit it may be necessary to begin with 15-minute sessions.
Frequency	Four to five times a week.
Intensity	Exercise levels should be gradually increased to a level of 70 percent of heart rate during interval work to a maximum of 90 percent. Rest intervals should be of sufficient length to reduce the heart rate to 50 percent to 60 percent of maximum. With continuous training techniques, the work intensity should progress slowly to a maximum heart rate of 85 percent.
Age	Regular exercise should be continued throughout life.
Mode	Activities that promote aerobic fitness are encouraged. Swimming is particularly desirable because it causes less bronchospasm than does running. Consideration must be given to those activities valued by the student.
Exercise loading	If students regularly experience EIA they should start with a low-level walking program of 10 to 30 seconds, followed by rest periods of 30 to 90 seconds, and then progress to higher levels. Asthmatics who can "run through" their asthma by using suitable pre-exercise medication may perform long-distance continuous activities. With suitable medication, either continuous or interval training is well tolerated by most asthmatics.
Pre-exercise medication	This is essential for most asthmatics. Aerosol beta-2 agonists or cromolyn sodium are the preferred agents.
Medication to reverse EIA	If EIA occurs during the activity, it may be reversed by the appropriate aerosol agent.

Adapted from Morton, A.R., Fitch, K.D., & Hahan, A.G. (1981). Physical activity and the asthmatic. *The Physician and Sports Medicine, 9*(3),51–64.

There is no permanent cure for hay fever, although the symptoms may be relieved. Avoiding the allergen is the most effective preventive measure. Desensitizing injections given in a series have proved to be a helpful preventive for many sufferers. The severity of attacks can be effectively reduced by the use of antihistamines and other drugs.

Cystic Fibrosis

Cystic fibrosis is also called mucoviscidosis. It is inherited as a Mendelian or recessive trait; both parents must carry the trait. Although not clearly established, the cause is generally assumed to be an abnormality or inadequacy of some hormone or enzyme of the body that affects the excretion of mucus, saliva, and perspiration. The disease is characterized by the excretion of excessively thick mucus and abnormal amounts of sweat and saliva.

The most serious effect of cystic fibrosis is the presence of thick mucus that interferes with breathing and digestion. Mucus of normal consistency flows easily, carrying with it foreign substances, bacteria, wastes, and dirt that will be eliminated from the body. The mucus of the person with cystic fibrosis does not flow readily but adheres to surfaces with which it comes in contact. As the mucus adheres to the lungs, it creates breathing problems because it blocks the bronchioli. Infection follows, causing damage to the lung tissue. Also, the thick mucus can block the ducts of the pancreas, a gland whose excretion is vital to digestion. When this blockage occurs, digestion is hindered because the pancreatic excretion cannot reach the small intestine. Fats become especially difficult to digest. Consequently, a child with cystic fibrosis may have a good appetite and eat well and yet fail to grow or gain weight. The most marked symptom of a blocked pancreas duct is the production of bulky, fatty, foul smelling feces. Most individuals with cystic fibrosis manage to consume only 80 percent of the recommended dietary allowance (Jankowski, 1987).

The presence of the disease can be confirmed by use of a sweat test in which the perspiration is analyzed for concentration of sodium and chlorides (constituents of salt). Chlorides and sodium are released in perspiration; the detection of a large amount of either in the perspiration indicates the presence of the disease.

It is estimated that the incidence of cystic fibrosis is about one in every one thousand births. As high as 3 to 4 percent of the population of the United States may carry the gene that produces the disease. The frequency of the disease is greater among whites than among blacks; it is rare among Orientals, Puerto Ricans, and American Indians.

The child with cystic fibrosis, in almost every respect looks and acts normal. Frequently only the child's parents and closest relatives are aware of the disease until its final stages. Thompson (1990) has observed that many individuals with cystic fibrosis, even with severe respiratory disease, perform well above average in tests of muscle power, endurance, and agility.

The prognosis of cystic fibrosis is unpredictable. More than 60 percent of children with the disease die before they reach puberty, and more than 75 percent die before the age of eighteen; but some live well into adulthood.

Treatment

Treatment involves procedures to aid in the removal of the thick mucus from the lungs and the manipulation of the diet to avoid fatty foods and to ensure ingestion of large amounts of proteins. In addition, extracts of animal pancreas are given with meals to compensate for the pancreatic deficiency.

Various procedures utilized to aid the drainage of thick mucus in the lungs are use of a mist tent to dilute the secretion in the lungs, aerosol therapy in which medication is introduced directly into the lungs, oral expectorants that induce ejection of the mucus, and postural drainage, in which different lying postures are assumed to encourage the draining of the lobes of the lungs so that the mucus will be coughed up and expelled. To help dislodge mucus, some therapists employ the technique of clapping on and vibration of the chest while the individual is in the drainage position.

Harvey (1982) suggests that the youngster with cystic fibrosis should be treated as much as possible like other children. Other observations offered by Harvey (1982) for teachers of children with cystic fibrosis include the following:

1. It is important that children with cystic fibrosis cough out the mucus in their lungs, so they should be encouraged not to hide their cough. Other children will need to be taught that cystic fibrosis is not a communicable disease.

2. The diet of the student may be altered in such a way that more frequent requests to visit the restroom may be necessary.

3. Although children with cystic fibrosis may have less stamina, it is essential that they participate as fully as possible in all activities.

4. Because some students with cystic fibrosis may be on multiple medicine for the pancreatic and lung involvement, they may need to take medication during class time.

5. The intelligence of children with this disease compares favorably to their peers.

Bronchitis

Bronchitis is an inflammation of the bronchi of the lungs. The condition may be either acute or chronic. It is possible for acute bronchitis to develop into chronic bronchitis.

Acute bronchitis, which is common among small children, also occurs frequently among adults. In mild cases the disease is sometimes referred to as a cold in the chest. However, acute bronchitis can be a serious disease if it progresses downward into the bronchioli. In its milder form the disease is not a serious concern to the physical education teacher, as it usually runs its course in about ten days. Students returning to school after severe acute bronchitis should be given the same considerations in physical education as are given the convalescent. (See the section on convalescence in chapter 16.)

Chronic bronchitis is a serious disease that interferes with breathing, resulting in dyspnea. Along with shortening of the breath, the sufferer coughs and frequently expels phlegm from the bronchial tubes. The disease may follow a series of attacks of acute bronchitis, or it may appear abruptly or insidiously with no apparent cause. Its chief cause is the long-term inhalation of irritants, such as dust and tobacco fumes. The "smoker's cough" is, in most cases, chronic bronchitis.

Chronic bronchitis usually affects older adults. The incidence is greater among men than among women; however, with the increasing prevalence of smoking among women, the difference in the number of cases is diminishing. Also, as the age of becoming a smoker decreases, the frequency of the disease in young people increases.

Administration of antibiotics and medications to loosen the phlegm in the bronchi is the chief treatment of the disease. Postural drainage, referred to in the discussion of cystic fibrosis, is also effective with chronic bronchitis.

Emphysema

Like chronic bronchitis, emphysema is a disease more common among adults than among children. In the course of the disease destruction of the alveolar walls occurs. Small holes appear in the alveolar membrane, and the lungs as a whole lose their elasticity. The symptoms of emphysema are dyspnea, coughing, and wheezing. The wheezing is usually not as prominent as it is in asthma. Often the individual with emphysema develops a barrel-shaped chest as the result of repeated overexpansion of the lungs and excessive use of upper chest muscles in an attempt to provide sufficient oxygen to the body.

It is known that a relationship exists between the incidence of emphysema and air pollution and smoking. As smoking and air pollution increase, there is a dramatic rise in the number of cases of emphysema. Currently, chronic emphysema kills more than 10,000 people in the United States each year. The disease occurs more frequently in males than in females and is more common among Caucasians than among African Americans. It is thought by some medical specialists in respiratory diseases that a defect in the elastic tissue of the lungs may make certain individuals more susceptible than others.

Bronchodilators are drugs used in the treatment of emphysema to enlarge the bronchi and provide better pathways for the air. Expectorants are administered to aid in the removal of mucus from the lungs. Postural drainage and breathing exercises may also be prescribed. In more severe cases a respirator (a machine that assists breathing) may be used.

Bronchial Hygiene for Respiratory Disorders

There are various procedures and practices that help to alleviate the health problems of persons having respiratory disorders. Two of the most effective of these bronchial hygiene measures are belly, or diaphragmatic, breathing and postural drainage.

Persons who have poor breathing habits usually do not use the diaphragm sufficiently in breathing; rather, they rely chiefly on the chest, rib, and back muscles to expand the lungs. Hence, these muscles become very tight and tense. Inefficient breathing can be improved through specially designed exercises. Basically, the exercises assist in relaxing spasmodically contracted muscles and in decreasing the tension in rib, chest, and back muscles (the intercostals, pectoralis major and minor, and trapezius). (See the muscle chart in Appendix VI.)

The basis of the exercises for diaphragmatic breathing is learning to empty the lungs more efficiently and effectively so that new air can be inhaled. The emphasis is placed upon exhalation, because if sufficient air is expelled, an adequate amount of air will automatically return when the respiratory muscles relax. The exhalation takes place over a long period of time, taking approximately twice as long as inhalation. In the inhalation, the muscles of the abdomen are relaxed and the belly is protruded so the diaphragm can descend. The importance of extending the belly cannot be exaggerated.

With the use of the correct procedures, less effort is expended in breathing. All of the muscles are less tense. Muscles that add little to increasing the air flow in and out of the lungs, like the scalenes (neck muscles), which are frequently used in forced breathing, are not utilized. Contraction of the abdominal muscles in forced inspiration, another common error, is avoided. The net effect is improved efficiency and comfort in respiration and conservation of energy for use in other body functions.

Postural drainage is the term given to a bronchial hygienic procedure in which specific positions of the body are assumed to aid in the removal of secretion from the lungs. The procedure is prescribed in conjunction with the use of bronchodilators, drugs that reduce the swelling in the bronchial tubes.

The positions for postural drainage place the chest and head lower than the rest of the body to allow the force of gravity to pull the mucus from the lungs so that it can be coughed up more easily. Recommended positions and the portion of the lungs drained in each position are shown in figure 14.2. The treatment, which occurs three times daily, lasts for twenty to thirty minutes with three or four minutes spent in each position. It is generally recommended that the treatment sessions occur just before the three meals are taken in order to reduce the possibility of regurgitation.

Clapping on and vibration of the chest with the hands help dislodge the mucus during postural drainage. Use of these procedures requires special training and should not be practiced by the physical educator without instruction from a physician or physical therapist.

Although many physicians believe that physical therapy emphasizing bronchial drainage is helpful, there is little objective evidence in support of such treatment (Jankowski, 1987). Lorin and Denning (1971) found a slight improvement in sputum production after postural drainage. Given that most individuals with respiratory disorders dislike the postural drainage procedure and regimen, the use of this technique requires additional study. Until evidence to the contrary is available, it appears likely that the bronchial drainage procedure will continue to be recommended and/or prescribed.

Needs and Adjustments of Those with Respiratory Disorders

Youngsters with the more severe types of respiratory disorders are unable to participate normally in vigorous group play. Exclusion from the active games of childhood tends to produce feelings of isolation and doubts about self-worth, which if prolonged and intensified can cause serious problems of adjustment. The physical education teacher is particularly well placed to provide opportunities to fulfill these youngsters' need for social interaction by integrating them into group activities.

Lack of participation in vigorous play, which is necessary for a high level of physical fitness, produces a great need among these children for general body conditioning. Increase in strength is important, particularly the strength of the muscles of the chest and abdomen that aid in breathing. Deep breathing exercises that strengthen the muscles of respiration and develop efficient patterns of breathing can be of special benefit.

Motivating students with asthma to engage in activities that are sufficiently vigorous to promote physical fitness presents a serious problem. The exertion of physical effort, particularly if accompanied by anxiety about doing well, tends to heighten the symptoms of respiratory diseases—breathing is more difficult, and wheezing and coughing are more pronounced. A severe attack can be a terrifying experience. Rather than risk an attack that is either frightening or embarrassing or both, the youngsters prefer not to engage in the activity. The more frequent the withdrawals from activity, the greater is the loss of tolerance for exercise. A vicious circle can become established in which the lower level of tolerance intensifies the avoidance of physical exertion that further lowers the exercise tolerance level, and so on.

For students caught in this cycle, a positive attitude toward participation in physical activity must be promoted. A good first step for the teacher is to develop social acceptance of the nose blowing, expectorating, and wheezing and coughing necessitated by the respiratory disorder. The teacher should be sure that there are paper towels or tissues (or even a receptacle for spitting) readily available and

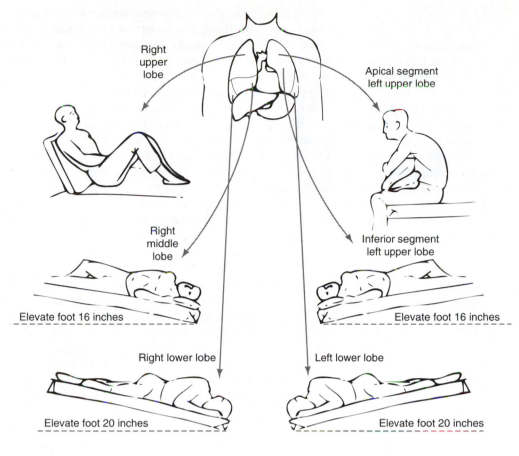

Right upper lobe

Apical segment left upper lobe

Right middle lobe

Inferior segment left upper lobe

Elevate foot 16 inches

Elevate foot 16 inches

Right lower lobe

Left lower lobe

Elevate foot 20 inches

Elevate foot 20 inches

Figure 14.2 Postural drainage positions for draining various portions of the lungs. The bottom figure is in a less specific, though commonly used, position.

should treat the need to use them as entirely ordinary. An attitude of acceptance on the part of the teacher will do much to reassure both the youngsters with respiratory disorders and their classmates that the conduct required to attend to an ailment or a disability is neither repulsive nor impolite.

Other steps the teacher may take depend largely upon the individual student—his or her interests, abilities, and adjustment. Ensuring success in early efforts to perform an exercise or activity is, of course, the keystone of any motivational strategy. Youngsters with a severe respiratory disorder often experience tension, owing to anxiety about performing

a motor activity or owing to other causes. Consequently, it is very beneficial to them to learn the techniques of conscious relaxation. Most of the exercises for relaxation suggested in chapter 29 make minimal demands on strength, endurance, and skill ability and so can be successfully performed by students in poor physical condition and with low tolerance for exercise. The satisfaction these students find in doing the exercises, as well as the pleasure they experience from relaxing, can provide the impetus for attempting other physical education activities.

Planning the Program

For the most part, students with respiratory disorders will be able to participate in the regular physical education class. However, it may be necessary to provide rest periods of four to five minutes after several minutes of participation or to adapt the activities so that they will be less strenuous. All but a very few students can engage in nonendurance activities without modification. The few who cannot must be given special consideration.

The evidence is very clear that students with respiratory disorders benefit from individualized exercise programs. Although a common-sense approach to exercise is what is needed, there are some helpful guidelines that can be employed. Some have found, for example, that it is very desirable to grade the individual's difficulty on a scale of one to four. In table 14.3, a disability grading system for an individual following a walking program is indicated. This information, when combined with selected respiratory measures including forced expired volume in one minute and vital capacity, is very helpful in developing an appropriate program.

The program for Grade 1 individuals is very similar to that for individuals who are not disabled, with the student working at a specified target rate for thirty to sixty minutes daily, or at a minimum, every other day. The program for the grade 2, 3, and 4 individuals is progressively milder due to the individual's level of ability. Every effort, however, must be made to ensure that the program does elicit some training effect, regardless of how small.

One very helpful technique for providing valuable feedback to the student, parents, and other members of the IEP team is to develop a perceived exertion scale for selected tasks. Using this approach, the student with a respiratory disorder is asked to indicate the rating of a symptom such as shortness of breath during or immediately after a given task. An example of such a scale and form is presented in figure 14.3. The type of tasks used may vary from those of daily living, such as walking to the bus or mowing the lawn, to physical education tasks such as running a specified distance or playing tennis for thirty minutes. The scale provides a means of assessing the functioning level of the individual.

When possible, the usual type of aerobic training activities (jogging, cycling, swimming) is recommended. For those who are more severely impaired, greater reliance on interval training bouts may be necessary—for example, fast walking for three minutes followed by rest. The goal is to progressively increase the individual's tolerance for aerobic activity. Exercise programs must be adjusted to accommodate dyspnea and feelings of anxiety that may occur when breathing becomes difficult. Belman and Wasserman (1982) indicated that the following can be expected to occur if a progressive and ongoing program is developed and properly implemented: (1) improved aerobic capacity, (2) increased motivation, (3) desensitization to sensation of dyspnea, (4) improved muscle function, and (5) improved technique of performance.

Specific breathing exercises to increase the efficiency of respiration may be provided for those who require or may benefit from them. Because such exercises are of very little value to those who do not have breathing difficulties, they should be planned only for those who need them; the other students can spend the time more productively in other activities.

Students with breathing problems will also benefit from exercises that strengthen the muscles involved in respiration and those that generally improve physical fitness. Conditioning must be approached cautiously, however. It must be a very gradual process, beginning with mild activity and slowly increasing in strenuousness as the student is able to tolerate a greater workload. Any activity planned for the student should be approved by his or her physician.

It is important in planning physical education activities for students with respiratory disorders that their participation not exceed their level of tolerance for exercise. A rule-of-thumb guide for the teacher to use in deciding when to terminate an activity is a noticeable increase in the performer's breathing rate. Extensive breathing of air through the mouth is a good indication that the rate has increased and the activity must stop.

In program planning, consideration must also be given to the possibility that air pollution may reach a level dangerous to health. In this event, exercises and activities requiring deep breathing should be discontinued for *all*

Table 14.3 *Guide to grading disability (based on 40-year-old man)*

Grade	Cause of Dyspnea	FEV_1 (% pred)	Max V_{O_2} (ml • min^{-1} • kg^{-1})	Exercise Max V_E (L • min^{-1})	Blood Gases
1	Fast walking and stair climbing	>60	>25	Not limiting	Normal PCO_2, SaO_2
2	Walking at normal pace	<60	<25	>50	Normal $PaCO_2$; SaO_2 above 90% at rest and with exercise
3	Slow walking	<40	<15	<50	Normal $PaCO_2$; SaO_2 below 09% with exercise
4	Walking limited to less than one block	<40	< 7	<30	Elevated $PaCO_2$; SaO_2 below 90% at rest and with exercise

From Skinner, J.S. (1993). *Exercise testing and exercise prescription for special cases* (2d ed.) (p. 235). Philadelphia: Lea and Febiger.

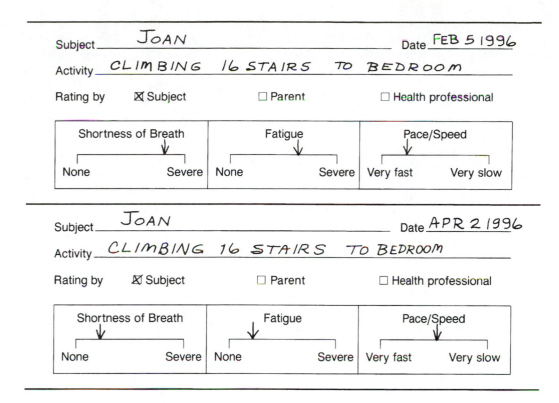

Subject _____ JOAN _____ Date FEB 5 1996

Activity _____ CLIMBING 16 STAIRS TO BEDROOM _____

Rating by   ☒ Subject   ☐ Parent   ☐ Health professional

Shortness of Breath	Fatigue	Pace/Speed
None Severe	None Severe	Very fast Very slow

Subject _____ JOAN _____ Date APR 2 1996

Activity _____ CLIMBING 16 STAIRS TO BEDROOM _____

Rating by   ☒ Subject   ☐ Parent   ☐ Health professional

Shortness of Breath	Fatigue	Pace/Speed
None Severe	None Severe	Very fast Very slow

Figure 14.3   Example of a rating scale for a daily activity completed on two occasions.

students. Outdoor physical education classes should be terminated. If the classes are continued indoors, only those activities and games that do not require strenuous effort should be offered. Table tennis, shuffleboard, bowling, ring toss, and volleyball are among the possibilities. Students with respiratory disorders should be excused from outside activity, because their condition is particularly endangered by air pollution.

Suggested Activities

For older children and youths with respiratory disorders who can tolerate only minimal stress on the respiratory system, activities such as golf, archery, bowling, shuffleboard, table tennis, and weight training are usually appropriate. Of the suggested activities, weight training needs the most adaptation; the others require only the interspersion of occasional rest periods of about five minutes after every fifteen or twenty minutes of participation.

Golf, archery, weight training, and cardiovascular endurance activities provide exercise to strengthen the chest muscles that aid the process of breathing. Weight training is of special value in accomplishing this objective, because the specific muscles that assist inhalation can be isolated and strengthened, applying the progressive overload principle (see chapter 27).

Swimming is an activity in which nearly everyone can participate, and it is frequently recommended as an excellent mode of exercise for those with asthma. Swimming may be contraindicated for persons with ear, nose, and throat disorders and those whose exercise-induced asthma cannot be adequately controlled with medication. For the latter, frequent rest periods during swimming and termination of the activity before fatigue sets in are often sufficient to prevent an attack.

The benefits of swimming for children with cystic fibrosis were supported in a study by Edlund and associates (1983). These investigators reported that following a twelve-week aquatic training program, the clinical status and exercise tolerance of children with cystic fibrosis were significantly improved. Jankowski (1987) cautions that some youngsters with cystic fibrosis have insufficient adipose to remain buoyant and warm in the water. This problem can be alleviated by wearing a neoprene jacket or three-quarter length wetsuit to provide both insulation and floatation.

Trampolining is suggested, in spite of its strenuousness, as an activity for persons with cystic fibrosis or asthma. Adams and Adamson (1973) have found trampolining beneficial for children with accumulations of secretions in the bronchial tree; the rebounding improved drainage of the respiratory tract. However, the amount of time the participant spends on the trampoline should be strictly limited as a control on the strenuousness of the activity. The rule-of-thumb guide for cessation of exercise is useful in deciding when the activity should be terminated.

Some students with severe breathing disorders that require special consideration may be able to participate in strenuous team games with a slight modification that provides for substitute players to relieve them after two or three minutes of participation for periods of rest of five or more minutes. Volleyball and softball can often be played without adaptation, although those who are severely affected may need to have someone run bases for them until the effect of their training program reduces this need.

Younger children are generally able to participate in regular physical education activities. If the class is taught by the indirect method that utilizes movement exploration or problem solving, it is relatively easy to control the strenuousness of activity to the level of exertion most appropriate for each student. Many basic skill games like Pussy Wants a Corner, Circle Ball, and Red Light can be played by children with respiratory disorders because periods of rest after brief periods of movement are inherent in these games.

Other basic skill games are easily adapted to control the amount of energy used and so lessen, when necessary, the stress upon the lungs. In most games energy requirements can be reduced by decreasing the distance required to move, slowing the tempo of movement, and interspersing milder activities or rests between periods of more strenuous play as, for example, clapping the hands or keeping time with the foot at intervals during a square dance. In the game of Red Light, any of the following suggestions may be used to control the strenuousness of the play: reducing the distance the players must travel, requiring players to walk rather than run, and stipulating that when the player who is Red Light turns, he or she must lead the group in clapping slowly in unison five to ten times to provide a rest period. Stunt activities such as leap frog, measuring worm, and seal walk are easily modified by working with the child to set limits for himself or herself as to how long and vigorously he or she performs the stunt.

These efforts to control or reduce the strenuousness of the activity should not be used as a substitute for vigorous activity programs. The goal is to employ a program that is challenging but sensitive to the discomfort children with respiratory disorders may experience, particularly if they have not been exercising. The benefits of exercise to overall general health and as a means to improved pulmonary function are of sufficient value that they should be established as a high priority in the lives of children with respiratory disorders.

Children with breathing problems should begin their physical education program with breathing exercises. The techniques developed in these exercises should be learned so thoroughly that they become automatic and can be used at all times, most particularly when performing motor activity.

Children who are not accustomed to breathing exercises should be warned that in the first few seconds of the exercise, when the diaphragm is forced to do most of the work

of exhaling the air, they may expect to cough and wheeze. Each child should be provided a mat to lie on, a receptacle for spitting, and a box of tissues. The children should be encouraged to cough up phlegm and to blow their noses whenever necessary. Clothing that binds the chest and waist should be loosened.

Sample exercises for improving the breathing pattern are given here:

1. Lie on the back and, employing imagery (see chapter 29), relax the neck muscles; follow with relaxation of the chest muscles, and then the abdominal muscles.

2. Relax the neck and chest muscles and then tighten the abdomen, using any relaxation technique suggested in chapter 29.

3. Take a supine position, with the knees bent and feet on the floor. Place the hands on the stomach just below the rib cage, fingers touching. Breathe in to the count of three. The belly should be expanded to raise the hands. Then release the air slowly through puckered lips to a count of six, contracting the stomach muscles very slowly and pushing gently down with the fingertips. The neck muscles should be relaxed at all times.

4. Take a sitting position, with the shoulders, rib cage, and head lifted; the abdominal and neck muscles are relaxed. Inhale to the count of three. During a count of six, depress the shoulders, lower the head, tighten the stomach muscles, and expel air through puckered lips.

Examples of Games to Develop More Efficient Breathing

For younger children with inefficient breathing patterns, games that assist in the development of control of expiration and encourage diaphragmatic breathing are recommended. The games described in the following may be used as models for the development of similar games.

1. One student is selected to be blindfolded. The other members of the class are divided into two groups, the membership of which is not known to the blindfolded child. One group begins to laugh and continues laughing while the child who is blindfolded calls out the name of a particular child. If the child named is in the group that is laughing, he or she must stop laughing; if not, the child must begin laughing. The object is to stop all laughter by naming all those who are laughing.

2. A balloon is tossed into the air. As it descends, everyone whistles a low note until the balloon touches the floor. The player who first stops whistling before the balloon hits the floor must toss the balloon into the air for the next round.

3. Jugs and bottles of different sizes are secured as instruments for a jug band. Sound is created by blowing across the opening of the container. The children are encouraged to blow low, long, steady sounds rather than short, loud ones. Homemade drums and rhythmic devices may be added to the band; these could be played by children who do not need the breathing exercises.

4. Two players stand at opposite ends of a short table. A table tennis ball is placed in the center of the table. Each player tries to blow it off the other end.

5. Two or more teams of three or four students are formed. Each team has a table tennis ball. Two lines are marked on the floor ten to thirty feet apart, depending upon how well the ball rolls on the surface of the floor. The teams form a line behind the first player, who blows the ball to the other line and back. Each successive player in line repeats this action. The first team to complete the race is the winner.

6. Several players group around a circular table. A balloon is placed in the center and all the players try to blow it off the table, while attempting to prevent the balloon from going off the table on either side of them. No one is allowed to touch the balloon.

Muscles that assist in expiration can be strengthened by trunk exercises rather than breathing exercises. The iliocostalis lumborum and iliocostalis dorsi, when contracted separately, abduct and rotate the spinal column; when contracted simultaneously, they extend the spinal column. Hence, any movement that rotates, abducts, or extends the trunk will strengthen these muscles if the progressive overload principle is applied.

Examples of exercises that might be used are given here:

1. Lie in the prone position on a bench with the trunk extended over the end. Lower the trunk toward the floor and return to the original position. Weights may be held behind the head to increase the difficulty.

2. Stand with the feet spread and the arms raised at the sides. Twist the trunk from one side to the other and back.

3. Stand with the feet apart and the hands on the hips. Move the trunk from side to side, lowering it as far as possible to each side.

The external and internal obliques and rectus abdominus are the muscles that bend the spinal column and the pelvis. Any exercise that flexes the spinal column or the pelvis is suitable for strengthening these muscles, applying the progressive overload principle. Two suitable exercises are given as follows:

1. Lying in the supine position on the floor, raise the head and shoulders four or five inches off the floor and return to the original position. To increase the difficulty, weights may be held on the forehead.

2. Lying supine on the floor, with the knees bent and the feet on the floor, move to a sit-up position and return. Weights held behind the head increase the difficulty.

Summary

The purpose of this chapter was to provide information concerning selected respiratory disorders and the relationship of physical activity and exercise programs in the treatment of these disorders. Primary emphasis was placed on asthma and cystic fibrosis, the most common and troubling respiratory disorders for children. The treatment for these disorders was discussed including medication, its value, the potential overuse of bronchodilators, and the pros and cons of postural drainage programs. Breathing programs and activities, including games to develop the control of expiration and encourage diaphragmatic breathing, were identified.

The important contribution that exercise makes in the lives of individuals with respiratory disorders was emphasized. Authorities recognize that a progressive program that emphasizes aerobic activities contributes to the overall health of those with respiratory disorders. In addition, exercise programs can be extremely beneficial in the treatment of cystic fibrosis. Studies report that as a result of participation in physical activity programs, students with cystic fibrosis enjoy a greater degree of general health and suffer fewer and milder respiratory complications than their sedentary counterparts. Some of the suggested exercise guidelines for students with respiratory disorders discussed in this chapter include the following: (1) programs should be individualized and developmentally progressive; (2) clinical information, including forced expired volume in one minute (FEV1) and vital capacity, can provide valuable information in the development of an effective program; (3) aerobic activities should be emphasized; (4) techniques such as perceived exertion scales and graded disability systems can be effective in establishing an appropriate exercise level; and (5) individuals should exercise daily. There is every reason to believe that students with respiratory disorders can safely and successfully participate in regular physical education programs. When and if modifications in the intensity of the program are necessary, the modifications will be minor. The most important variable is the presence of a caring and sensitive teacher who can recognize and appreciate the discomfort associated with a respiratory disorder such as exercise-induced asthma. In severe cases, physical educators have at their disposal the IEP team, including parents and medical personnel, if necessary, to assist them in their program planning.

Selected Readings

Adams, R.C., & Adamson, E. (1973). Trampoline tumbling for children with chronic lung disease. *JOHPER, 44*(4), 86–87.

Adams, R.C., & McCubbin, J.A. (1991). *Games, sports, and exercises for the physically disabled* (4th ed.). Philadelphia: Lea and Febiger.

Afrasiabi, R., & Spector, S.L. (1991). Exercise-induced asthma: It needn't sideline your patients. *The Physician and Sports Medicine, 19*, 49–62.

American Academy of Pediatrics. (1970). The asthmatic child and his participation in sports and physical education. *Pediatrics, 45,* 150–151.

American Academy of Pediatrics, Committee on Sports Medicine. (1982). The asthmatic child and his participation in sports and physical education. Mimeographed.

Belman, J.J., & Wasserman, K. (1982). *Respiratory care, 27,* 724–731.

Dennis, W. (1979). *What every physical educator should know about asthma.* New York: American Lung Association.

Edlund, L.L., French, R.W., Herbst, J.J., Ruttenberg, H.D., Ruhling, R.O., & Adams, T.D. (1983). *Effects of a swimming program on children with cystic fibrosis.* Paper presented at the Southwest Chapter of the American College of Sports Medicine.

Ghory, J.E. (1975, November). Exercise and asthma: Overview and clinical impact. *Pediatrics, 56,* 844–846.

Guyton, A.C. (1984). *Physiology of the Human Body* (6th ed.). Philadelphia: W.B. Saunders Co.

Harvey, B. (1982). Asthma. In E.E. Bleck and D.A. Nagel (Eds.), *Physically handicapped children: A medical atlas for teachers* (2d ed.) (pp. 31–42). New York: Grune and Stratton.

Harvey, B. (1982). Cystic fibrosis. In E.E. Bleck and D.A. Nagel (Eds.), *Physically handicapped children: A medical atlas for teachers* (2d ed.) (pp. 255–263). New York: Grune and Stratton.

Hill, R.A., Britton, J.R., & Tattersfield, L.E. (1987). Management of asthma in schools. *Archives of Diseases in Childhood, 62,* 414–415.

Jankowski, L.W. (1987). Cystic fibrosis. In J.S. Skinner (Ed.), *Exercise testing and exercise prescription for special cases* (pp. 189–203). Philadelphia: Lea and Febiger.

Jones, N.L., Berman, L.B., Bartkiewicz, P.D., & Oldridge, N.B. (1987). Chronic obstructive respiratory disorders. In J.S. Skinner (Ed.), *Exercise testing and exercise prescription for special cases* (pp. 229–240. Philadelphia: Lea and Febiger.

Lorin, M., & Denning, C. (1971). Evaluation of postural drainage by measurement of sputum volume and consistency. *American Journal of Physical Medicine, 50,* 215.

Morton, A.R., Fitch, K.D., & Hahn, A.G. (1981). Physical activity and the asthmatic. *The Physician and Sports Medicine, 9*(3), 51–64.

Orenstein, D.M., Franklin, B.A., Doershuk, C., Hellerstein, H., Germann, K., Horwits, J., & Stern, R. (1981). Exercise conditioning and cardiopulmonary fitness in cystic fibrosis. *Chest, 80,* 392–398.

Orenstein, D.M., Henke, K.G., & Cerney, F.J. (1983). Exercise and cystic fibrosis. *Physician and Sports Medicine, 11*(1), 57–63.

Partin, N. (1989). Exercise induced asthma. *Athletic Training, 24,* 250.

Skinner, J.S. (1993). Exercise testing and exercise prescription for special cases (2d ed.). Philadelphia: Lea and Febiger.

Thompson, K. (1990). Cystic fibrosis—Update on exercise. *Physician and Sports Medicine, 18*(5), 103–106.

U.S. Department of Health and Human Services. (1989). Asthma Statistics. Washington DC: U.S. Government Printing Office.

Weiss, E.B., & Segal, M.S. (Eds.). (1976). *Bronchial asthma: Mechanisms and therapeutics* (pp. 537–546). Boston: Little, Brown, and Co.

Weiss, K.B., and Wagener, D.K. (1990). Changing patterns of asthma mortality: Identifying target populations at high risk. *Journal of the American Medical Association, 264,* 1683–1687.

Winnick, J.R. (1977). Physical activity and the asthmatic child. *American Corrective Therapy Journal, 31,* 148–151.

Zadai, C.C. (1990). (5th ed). Exercise in pulmonary disease and disability. In J.M. Basmajian (Ed.), *Therapeutic exercise.* Baltimore: Williams and Wilkins, Co.

Enhancing Activities

1. Schedule a visit to an exercise physiology laboratory to observe lung capacity measures being collected. If possible, have selected measures, including forced expiratory volume in one minute and vital capacity, taken on yourself.

2. Develop a chart, similar to that found in table 14.3, that grades your performance on a selected task such as a twelve-minute run. Compare your perceived level of effort after a scheduled interval of time.

3. Interview a physical therapist or respiratory therapist to obtain an additional perception as to the importance of a postural drainage program.

4. Obtain an anatomy book and review the anatomy of the cardiopulmonary system.

5. Obtain a copy of the *Physicians' Desk Reference* and review the list of drugs cited in table 14.1, which are used in the treatment of asthma.

6. Suggest a game or exercise that might be helpful in assisting an individual improve his or her breathing pattern.

CHAPTER 15

Nutritional Disturbances

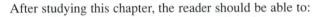

CHAPTER OBJECTIVES

After studying this chapter, the reader should be able to:

1 List and discuss various tools that can be used for nutritional planning.

2 Identify the dietary goals for the United States.

3 Describe some of the common nutritional problems including those that are pertinent to students with severe disabling conditions.

4 Recognize the inherent danger in some of the common eating disorders including anorexia nervosa and bulimia.

5 Discuss various weight control strategies including the value of behavior modification in altering dietary habits.

6 Explain the important and critical relationship between diet and exercise in the prevention and treatment of obesity.

7 Define various terms including obesity, body fat, lean body mass, skinfold, overweight, hyperplasia, and hypertrophia.

8 Describe techniques used to determine the percentage of body fat and the rationale for using these measures.

9 Apply selected criteria and guidelines to assess the potential effectiveness of selected weight control programs for children.

10 Recognize some of the unique dietary and exercise needs of selected disability populations.

11 Identify the components of a well-designed exercise program for the student who is obese.

The era of narrowly defining nutrition in terms of the nutrient requirements necessary for the maintenance of health and fitness has passed with the recognition of the complexity of human behavior in the ingestion of food. Food behavior is so complex because it is influenced by both biological and cultural factors. Biologically, food satisfies hunger and provides the needed nutrients for growth or maintenance and energy. The choice of foods, however, is culturally determined; that is, an individual's culture establishes a set of customs, traditions, and beliefs about food that influences the selection of foods to be eaten. Consequently, the study of human nutrition has expanded to encompass consumption as well as utilization of food by the body; and in the search for knowledge, analysis of socially determined food behavior has become as important as scientifically controlled biological research.

Some understanding of the complex nature of nutrition and of the nutritional problems common to children and young adults is valuable to the physical educator working with students who have disabilities, because of the relationship between health and fitness (as determined by proper nutrition) and motor performance. Poor health and lack of energy reduce the efficiency and effectiveness of motor skill performance. Those whose abilities to perform are already limited by disabling conditions experience even greater difficulty if their diet is not supplying their bodies with the proper nutrients. Of particular concern is the effect of exercise on the expenditure of energy as related to caloric intake.

Tools for Nutrition Planning

Attempting to translate the body's needs for particular nutrients to foods commonly consumed is not an easy task. Furthermore, the average diet in the United States has not improved during the last fifty years; for the most part, the average American still consumes too much fat, sugar and salt. The overconsumption of one or more of these foods has been associated with heart disease, some types of cancer, stroke and hypertension, diabetes, arteriosclerosis, and cirrhosis of the liver.

The Federal government has on several occasions attempted to provide general nutrition guidelines and direction for the United States. In 1977, the Select Committee on Nutrition and Human Needs of the U.S. Senate published the *Dietary Goals for the United States*. Recent efforts have focused on the goal of improving the overall health of Americans by the year 2000. Nutritional goals for the year 2000 are extensive and focus on objectives presented in three broad categories: Health Status, Risk Reduction, and Service and Protection (Nutrition in Healthy People 2000, 1991). Selected objectives for each of the categories include:

1. Health Status Objectives

   —Reduce the overweight population to no more that 20 percent among adults aged twenty years and older and no more than 15 percent among adolescents aged twelve through nineteen years.

   —Reduce growth retardation among low-income children aged five years and younger to less than 10 percent.

2. Risk Reduction Objectives

   —Reduce dietary fat intake to an average of 30 percent of calories or less and reduce average saturated fat intake to less than 10 percent of calories among persons aged two years and older.

   —Increase complex carbohydrates and fiber-containing foods in the diets of adults to five or more daily servings for vegetables (including legumes) and fruits, and to six or more daily servings of grain products.

   —Increase to at least 50 percent the proportion of overweight persons aged twelve years and older who have adopted sound dietary practices combined with regular physical activity to attain an appropriate body weight.

   —Decrease salt and sodium intake so that at least 65 percent of those who prepare home-cooked meals do so without adding salt, at least 80 percent of persons avoid using salt at the table, and at least 40 percent of adults purchase food modified or low in sodium.

   —Reduce iron deficiency to less than 3 percent among children aged one through four years and among women of childbearing age.

3. Service and Protection Objectives

   —Achieve useful and informative nutrition labeling for virtually all processed foods and for at least 40 percent of fresh meats, poultry, fish, fruits, vegetables, baked foods, and ready-to-eat carry-out foods

   —Increase to at least 90 percent the proportion of restaurants and institutional service operations that offer identifiably low-fat, low-calorie food choices, consistent with the nutrition principles in the *Dietary Guidelines for Americans*.

   —Increase to at least 75 percent the proportion of schools in the United States that provide nutrition education from preschool through 12th grade, preferably as part of quality school health education.

The Nutritional Objectives for the Year 2000 offer a foundation for promoting dietary and service changes that must be achieved if the general population is to improve its overall health status. The objectives, combined with other tools for good nutrition, help educators and other concerned youth service providers reinforce and promote good nutritional practices. This is especially important for personnel who work with individuals with disabilities because of the higher percentage of individuals who may require special dietary considerations.

Food Guide Pyramid

One of the most practical and useful systems for helping individuals identify the right kind and amount of food to eat is the Food Guide Pyramid (figure 15.1). The pyramid illustrates the research-based food guidance system developed by the United States Department of Agriculture and supported by the Department of Health and Human Services (USDA, 1992). The pyramid is based on research conducted by the USDA as to the foods Americans eat, what nutrients are in these foods, and how to make the best food choices. The pyramid focuses on fat because most Americans' diets are too high in fat. Following the pyramid will help to keep intake of total fat and saturated fat low. The pyramid is an outline of what to eat each day. It is not a rigid prescription, but a general guide that allows for choices to achieve a healthful diet. As noted in figure 15.1, the Food Guide Pyramid emphasizes foods from the five major groups shown in the three lower sections of the pyramid. Each of the food groups provides some, but not all of the daily nutrients needed. Foods in one group can not replace those in another. No one food group is more important than another. Good health requires access to all five food groups. A brief description of the pieces of the pyramid follows:

The small tip of the pyramid shows fats, oils, and sweets. These are foods such as salad dressings and oils, cream, butter, margarine, sugars, soft drinks, candies, and sweet desserts. These foods provide calories and little else nutritionally.

On the second level of the pyramid are two groups of foods that come mostly from animals: milk, yogurt, and cheese; and meat, poultry, fish, dry beans, eggs, and nuts. These foods are important for protein, calcium, iron, and zinc.

On the third level are foods that come from plants—vegetables and fruits. Most people need to eat more of these foods for the vitamins, minerals, and fiber they supply.

At the base of the pyramid are breads, cereals, rice, and pasta—all foods from grains. The greatest number of daily servings is required from this level.

The USDA and HHS have also identified seven guidelines for a healthful diet for individuals from age two years up. By using the pyramid for food selection and following the Dietary Guidelines (USDA, 1992), the chances for a healthy life free of disease is increased.

The Dietary Guidelines for Americans, as developed by the USDA and HHS are reported below:

1. *Eat a variety of foods* to get the energy, protein, vitamins, minerals, and fiber needed for good health.

2. *Maintain healthy weight* to reduce the chances of having high blood pressure, heart disease, a stroke, certain cancers, and the most common kinds of diabetes.

3. *Choose a diet low in fat, saturated fat, and cholesterol* to reduce the risk of heart attack and certain types of cancer. Because fat contains over twice the calories of an equal amount of carbohydrates or protein, a diet low in fat can help to maintain a healthy weight.

4. *Choose a diet with plenty of vegetables, fruits, and grain products* which provide needed vitamins, minerals, fiber, and complex carbohydrates, and can help lower the intake of fat.

5. *Use sugars only in moderation.* A diet with lots of sugars has too many calories and too few nutrients for most people and can contribute to tooth decay.

6. *Use salt and sodium only in moderation* to help reduce the risk of high blood pressure.

7. *If you drink alcoholic beverages, do so in moderation.* Alcoholic beverages supply calories, but little or no nutrients. Drinking alcohol is also the cause of many health problems and accidents and can lead to addiction (USDA, 1990).

The pyramid offers a relatively simple and quick guideline for selecting the foods that should be included in the daily diet. The food groups are easy to understand and follow, and most students can be readily taught to utilize the pyramid in assessing what they need to eat on a daily basis.

Recommended Dietary Allowances

The Recommended Dietary Allowances (RDAs) are standards by which nutrient intakes can be compared. They represent levels of nutrient and energy intake thought to be adequate for nutritional needs of virtually all healthy Americans. The RDAs, which have been revised many times since their inception in 1943, are based on surveys, controlled feeding experiments, and metabolic studies on animals. Because these allowances are set high enough to provide a margin of safety, the actual needs of most healthy individuals are easily met.

In format, the Recommended Dietary Allowances include categories by age and gender and for the pregnant and lactating female. Allowances for protein, calories, and several vitamins and minerals are listed. No RDAs are set for carbohydrates and fats but their omission is not intended to indicate that these nutrients are not needed in the daily diet.

The RDAs are not intended for use by individuals in planning a proper diet but instead represent a range within which the nutrients in the food intake of most healthy persons should probably fall. They may be used as a guide by most individuals with disabilities; however, certain medical problems, which will be addressed later in this chapter, may alter the nutrient needs.

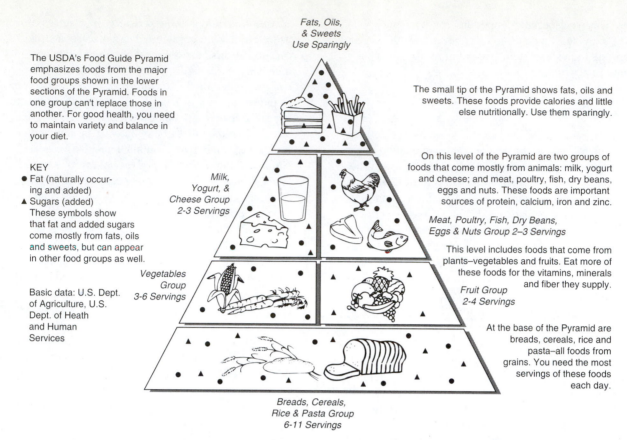

The USDA's Food Guide Pyramid emphasizes foods from the major food groups shown in the lower sections of the Pyramid. Foods in one group can't replace those in another. For good health, you need to maintain variety and balance in your diet.

Fats, Oils, & Sweets
Use Sparingly

The small tip of the Pyramid shows fats, oils and sweets. These foods provide calories and little else nutritionally. Use them sparingly.

KEY
● Fat (naturally occurring and added)
▲ Sugars (added)
These symbols show that fat and added sugars come mostly from fats, oils and sweets, but can appear in other food groups as well.

On this level of the Pyramid are two groups of foods that come mostly from animals: milk, yogurt and cheese; and meat, poultry, fish, dry beans, eggs and nuts. These foods are important sources of protein, calcium, iron and zinc.

Milk, Yogurt, & Cheese Group
2-3 Servings

Meat, Poultry, Fish, Dry Beans, Eggs & Nuts Group 2–3 Servings

This level includes foods that come from plants–vegetables and fruits. Eat more of these foods for the vitamins, minerals and fiber they supply.

Vegetables Group
3-6 Servings

Basic data: U.S. Dept. of Agriculture, U.S. Dept. of Heath and Human Services

Fruit Group
2-4 Servings

At the base of the Pyramid are breads, cereals, rice and pasta–all foods from grains. You need the most servings of these foods each day.

Breads, Cereals, Rice & Pasta Group
6-11 Servings

How many servings do you need each day?

Be sure to eat the minimum number of recommended servings from the five major food groups listed below.

	Many women, older adults	Children,* teen girls, active women, most men	Teen boys, most men
Bread Group Servings	6	9	11
Vegetable Group Servings	3	4	5
Fruit Group Servings	2	3	4
Milk Group Servings	2–3**	2–3**	2–3**
Meat Group Servings	2, for a total of 5 ounces	2, for a total of 6 ounces	3, for a total of 7 ounces
Total Fat (grams)	53	73	93
Total Calories	1,600	2,200	2,800

* Young children may not need as much food. They can have smaller servings from all groups except milk, which should total two servings per day. No restrictions should be placed on fat and cholesterol in the diet of infants from birth to age 2.
** Women who are pregnant or breastfeeding, teenagers and young adults to age 24 need three servings.

Basic data: U.S. Dept. of Agriculture

The amount of food that counts as one serving is listed below. If you eat a larger portion, count it as more than one serving.

Milk, Yogurt and Cheese

1 cup of milk or yogurt	1 1/2 ounces of natural cheese	2 ounces of process cheese

Meat, Poultry, Fish, Dry Beans, Eggs and Nuts

2–3 ounces of cooked lean meat, poultry or fish	1/2 cup of cooked dry beans, 1 egg, or 2 tablespoons of peanut butter count as 1 ounce of lean meat

Vegetables

1 cup of raw leafy vegetables	1/2 cup of other vegetables, cooked or chopped raw	3/4 cup of vegetable juice

Fruit

1 medium apple, banana or orange	1/2 cup of chopped, cooked or canned fruit	3/4 cup of fruit juice

Bread, Cereal, Rice and Pasta

1 slice of bread	1 ounce of ready-to-eat cereal	1/2 cup of cooked cereal, rice or pasta

Figure 15.1 Food Guide Pyramid.

with this condition include short attention span, easy distractibility, impulsive behavior, overactivity, restlessness, and learning disabilities (see chapter 18).

In the classroom and at home, the child who is hyperactive or hyperkinetic is frequently disruptive and difficult to control. Treatment has usually included the use of medication such as amphetamines, which produce a calming effect on the child. Feingold (1973) reported behavioral improvement of hyperkinetic children when fed special additive-free diets. Since that time, several researchers have attempted to test the effectiveness of such additive-free diets under more scientifically controlled conditions. Results of these studies have not been conclusive and have not supported the same degree of success achieved by Feingold.

The one problem associated with the original Feingold diet is the omission of foods containing salicylates in natural form. Oranges, strawberries, and tomatoes are examples of such foods, and strict adherence to a diet from which they are omitted may result in ascorbic acid deficiency. Therefore, parents willing to follow the Feingold diet are advised to seek nutrition counseling and vitamin supplementation.

Obesity and the Student with a Disability

The student with a disability requires exercise and activity programs similar to other individuals. Unfortunately, the desired level of activity is not always attained. The reasons for this include overprotective parents and other adults, lack of program accessibility, and limited understanding of the physiologic and health-related benefits of activity for those who are disabled. The lack of activity and a sedentary lifestyle contribute to a pattern that can lead to obesity for many individuals with disabilities. This pattern can only be broken if there is an increase in activity or a decrease in food intake. Given that most youths with disabilities, similar to their nondisabled peers, find restricting their diet very difficult, a program that includes general fitness and aerobic activities must be undertaken. Fortunately, there are some excellent role models who are demonstrating that individuals with disabilities can be active and healthy.

There are, of course, some individuals who have specific disabilities that interfere with their movement and activity levels. The prevalence of obesity is greater in these individuals. Individuals with Duchenne muscular dystrophy, for example are particularly vulnerable to obesity. As this disease progresses it destroys muscle tissue, which is replaced by fat and connective tissue. Movement becomes more difficult as the condition increases resulting in an imbalance in the calorie-energy system. Shepherd (1984) advises that these students are directly affected by the principal causes of obesity: overeating, inactivity, improper diet.

The prevalence of obesity in individuals who are mentally retarded has been well documented (Fox and Rotatori, 1982; Kelly, Rimmer, and Ness, 1986). Some have speculated that this is attributed to the cessation of their growth

period at approximately sixteen years of age. This results in a short stature of approximately five feet for boys and four feet, seven inches for girls. The problem is further compounded if the diet is not adjusted accordingly. Other complicating factors include the hypotonicity evident in the Down syndrome population. There is a general looseness of the joint ligaments resulting in a shuffling gait and fallen arches. Many of these problems could be avoided if activity programs were incorporated into the lives of these youngsters at very early ages. This would help to alleviate large weight gains, and discomfort associated with activity programs in later years. Effort should also be directed toward managing the diet of the Down syndrome population. In a study of institutionalized adolescents with Down syndrome, Caveny (1986) found that when given a specific low-fat diet of 1200 calories, these individuals were able to lose weight and eventually maintain weight on an 1800-calorie diet.

The tendency toward obesity is evident in any population that tends to overeat and be sedentary. This problem is particularly pronounced in those individuals who become disabled after birth. If proper adjustments are not made in the caloric intake and output, weight gains will occur. Even the participant who uses a wheelchair and is active will need to recognize that the energy expenditure generated with the arms and hands propelling the chair will not equal that associated with running and jogging. An appropriate adjustment in the diet will be necessary.

In developing an appropriate activity and nutrition program for students with disabilities, consultation with other professionals such as physicians and nutritionists is necessary. The input of the home is essential to ensure that an effective and manageable program is developed.

Nutrition and Individuals Who Are Severely Disabled

There is growing awareness that the nutritional needs of those who are severely disabled present some unique challenges. Sobsey (1983) suggests that four factors must be considered in analyzing the diet and nutrition of the individual with a severe disabling condition. The first factor, type of condition, is related to the specific disability syndrome. For example, as presented earlier, there are studies that indicate that the child with spasticity requires fewer calories while the individual with athetosis, due to extraneous involuntary movement, may require extra calories. Children with certain syndromes will require special dietary treatments. For example, the importance of a diet void of protein is essential for the child with phenylketonuria. Likewise, special dietary treatments are necessary for selected disorders including galactosemia, cystic fibrosis, and Wilson's disease. Individuals with spina bifida (myelomeningocele) may have an acid ash diet prescribed to help avoid urinary infections. Given these special diet and nutrition needs, it is very

Common Nutritional Problems

There are several problems associated with poor or inadequate nutrition. Although it is beyond the scope of this chapter to list all of the problems, information will be presented on some of the more common nutritional disorders.

Vitamins have long been recognized as important in the efficient functioning of the human body. Vitamins are generally classified as fat soluble or water soluble. Fat-soluble vitamins are so named because they are dissolved and stored in the fat and the fatlike compounds within the body. Four fat-soluble vitamins have been identified: vitamins A, D, E, and K. Each of these vitamins plays an important role in regulating the body. Vitamin A, for example, is helpful in preventing night blindness. Water soluble vitamins are transported in the watery medium of tissues and cells. Because of their solubility in water, these vitamins are not stored in the body to any appreciable extent. Excess amounts are usually excreted in the urine on a daily basis. Without the proper diet, including sufficient vegetables, meats, fruits, and plants, vitamin deficiencies may occur. In table 15.1 the vitamins, their functions, and symptoms associated with vitamin deficiencies are reported. In some instances, the vitamin deficiency can produce serious long-term health problems.

Rarely do people who eat balanced meals require vitamin supplements. Unfortunately, some individuals have taken to megavitamins or doses of at least ten times that of the Recommended Dietary Allowance. Excessive amounts of vitamins can be harmful. Parents who express concern

about their child and vitamin deficiencies should be encouraged to consult with a physician.

Similar to vitamins, minerals are essential for maintaining optimum health and sustaining life. Minerals are part of enzymes, hormones, and vitamins, and are found in muscles, connective tissues, and the various body fluids. Calcium, phosphorous, and iron are some of the important minerals. An insufficient amount of minerals can result in serious health-related problems. Calcium, for instance, is essential in maintaining the normal function of muscles as well as for blood clotting and the transport of fluid across cell membranes.

Overweight and underweight are problems frequently observed in students with disabilities. *Underweight* is defined as 10 percent below desirable weight and *overweight* is 10 percent above desirable weight. When weight is 20 percent or more above desirable weight, the term *obese* is used.

Obesity is considered by many health experts to be the number one health problem in America. Estimates suggest that 25 to 40 percent of the population over the age of thirty may be affected (Friedman, 1988; Kissebah, Freedman, and Peiris, 1989). Leung and Robson (1990) estimate that 20 percent of the children in this country can be classified as obese. Obesity in populations with a high incidence of disability is likely to be higher than is true among individuals with more typical sensory, emotional, and intellectual capabilities (Cratty, 1989). The consequences of overweight and obesity are frequently associated with such debilitating

Table 15.1 *Vitamins—their functions and symptoms of their deficiency*

A (Retinol)	Vision, growth	Poor vision (night blindness), failure of bones to grow in length, skin and respiratory infections, failure of tooth enamel
D	Bone calcification	Bone diseases
E (Tocopherol)	Not clear in humans	Unclear, possibly anemia
K	Blood clotting and coagulation and energy metabolism of the cell	Prolonged blood-clotting or coagulation time
B-1 (Thiamine)	Metabolism of nutrients in cells	Bereberi—the degeneration of nerves and muscles, loss of appetite, mental depression, and neurological dysfunction
B-2 (Riboflavin)	Reactions that release energy in the cells	Lesions of the skin, eye, mouth, and retardation of growth
Niacin	Release of energy from the breakdown and synthesis of carbohydrate, fat, and protein	Diseases of the skin, gastrointestinal tract, and nervous system, resulting in dermatitis, diarrhea, and depression
B^6 (Pyridoxine)	Synthesis and breakdown of amino acids	Usually no deficiency because this vitamin is so readily available in foods
Pantothenic acid	Metabolism of carbohydrates, fats, and proteins, important in the formation of cholesterol	Subclinical symptoms such as irritability, restlessness, easy fatigue, muscle cramps
Folacin	Formation of normal red blood cells and of DNA and RNA	Toxemia of pregnancy and anemia and retarded production of white blood cells
B^{12}	Normal growth, maintenance of neural tissue, and formation of blood	Pernicious anemia (sore tongue, weight loss, mental and nervous disorders, degeneration of the spinal cord)
Biotin	Removal or addition of carbon dioxide in chemical reactions and metabolism of carbohydrate and protein	Dermatitis, such as scaling or hardening of skin, loss of appetite, nausea, muscle pains, high blood cholesterol levels

Katch, Frank I., & McArdle, W. (1989). *Nutrition, weight control, and exercise* (3rd ed.). Philadelphia: Lea and Febiger.

conditions as heart disease, diabetes, and stroke. While it was commonly accepted in the past that overweight and obesity were simply a problem of overeating, recent evidence indicates clearly that the problem is an imbalance between the number of calories consumed and the number of calories expended. Numerous studies confirm that children who are obese participate in less physical activity than their nonobese peers (Bar-Or, 1983).

Underweight is a significant nutritional problem, but it is far less prevalent than overweight. In some cases the cause is poor eating behavior or other poor health habits such as insufficient sleep and rest. In other cases the tendency to thinness appears to be hereditary. Underweight may also be the indirect result of chronic infection, such as tuberculosis or diseased tonsils, or other conditions and diseases such as hyperthyroidism diabetes. Loss of appetite may be a possible contributing factor in weight loss, or it may be an indication of some underlying difficulty, usually of psychogenic origin.

Although the reasons why certain individuals become overweight are many and complex, overeating may result from unusual sensitivity to such external clues as smells, sights, and sounds of food even when hunger is not an issue. Or it may be that these individuals learn to overeat or to be less active than is necessary for maintenance of energy balance. Observations of individuals who are obese have supported the finding that overweight people are generally inactive and spend more time sitting, standing, or lying about when compared to individuals of normal weight.

The etiology of obesity is a complex subject. Data of the Ten State Nutritional Survey (TSNS) suggest that patterns of obesity may be established early in life, but that socioeconomic and cultural factors also influence both energy expenditure and weight control (Garn and Clark, 1976). It was found that although white females were fatter than black females in adolescence, during adulthood black females were heavier than white females. Girls from higher-income families also had thicker fat-fold measurements through childhood and early adolescence, but in late adolescence and adulthood reversed this trend by becoming leaner. A recent study confirmed these findings, noting that 48 percent of black women can be classified as obese (Wadden et al., 1990).

Interestingly, other studies have shown that obese individuals see themselves as minorities and apart from the mainstream of daily life. So-called normal children who develop into obese children run the risk not only of increased health problems but also of becoming children who, avoiding participation in sports and physical activities and shunning social events and relationships, gradually retreat into the world of television and fantasy.

Genetics versus Environment

Although there are many theories about the cause of obesity, much of the debate on whether genetics or the environment is the primary contributor to obesity (figure 15.2). Those who support the pull theory of obesity believe that

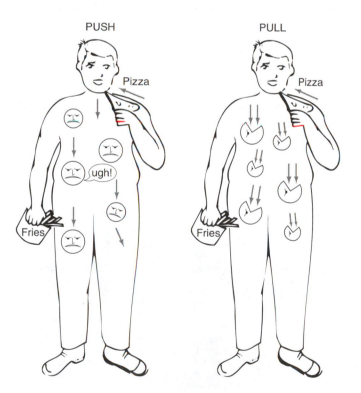

Figure 15.2 The *push* and *pull* theories of obesity. In the *push* model, obesity is *caused* by voluntary pushing of excess nutrients into the body. In the *pull* model, internal alterations lead to increased eating, but the increased eating is *secondary* to the internal disorder.

obesity is attributed primarily to inborn metabolic errors that lead to increased eating (Rimmer, 1994). Hirsch, in a *New York Times* editorial (1988), argues, for example, that overweight people are born with a handicap and like other people with a disability, they must learn to live with the disorder.

Those who support the environment as the primary cause of obesity believe that obesity is a behavioral disorder (i.e., people are excessively fat because they eat too much). Proponents of this view label the overeating as the push theory of obesity—the voluntary pushing of excess food into the body. Many speculate, too, that overeating is related to socioeconomic status. Garn (1986), for instance, argues that women of lower socioeconomic status are heavier than expected and that this finding advances the environment as more important than genetic composition as the cause of obesity.

Conclusive support for either genetics or the environment as the primary cause of obesity is not possible at this time. It may be that the physiologic, metabolic, and psychological structure of the individual is so complex that future studies will continue to emphasize that both heredity and environment are important in fostering an understanding of obesity.

Hyperplasia and Hypertrophia

Hirsch relates obesity to the number and size of adipose cells. This theory has led to the classification of obesity into hyperplasia or hypertrophia (Hirsch and VanHallie, 1973).

Hyperplastic obesity is early onset or childhood obesity caused by an increased number of fat cells. *Hypertrophic* obesity is caused primarily by an increased fat cell size and is associated with late onset or adult obesity. Cell numbers tend to increase in the last trimester of pregnancy, the first three years of life, and adolescence. It is believed that once the number of fat cells in the body is established, only the

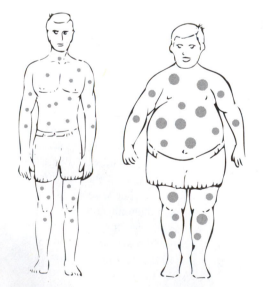

Figure 15.3 Comparison of fat cells of thin and obese individuals.

amount of fat stored within the cells and not their number can be increased. Thus, it appears that once the fat cells have been established, it becomes more difficult to lose weight.

As Smith explains, "The fat cell is uniquely adapted for its function to store energy as triglyceride in the cell and to release the stored lipids as fatty acids when needed by the body. The cell is capable of changing its diameter at least 10-fold to accommodate the stored triglyceride" (1983, p. 245). Pollock, Wilmore, and Fox (1984) estimate that the mature obese individual has 90 to 150 billion fat cells compared to the nonobese individual, who has only 20 to 30 billion. Unfortunately, the time of greatest growth of the fat cells occurs during the early childhood years.

Delayed Growth

Improper nutrition frequently results in delayed growth in both children with and without disabilities. Diagnosing the cause of delayed growth in children with disabilities is more complex because of the lack of information on the effects of condition-related factors on growth rate. In children with inborn errors of metabolism such as phenylketonuria (PKU), delayed growth is more clearly understood. But studies on children with mental retardation have indicated that such factors as dietary intake, appetite, activity level, medication, parental stature, health, and economic status may be important factors in the potential size and growth pattern of the child.

Inactivity

Overweight may be observed in children with Down syndrome or Prader-Willi syndrome and is frequently related to low activity level, hypotonia, overeating, or, in limited cases, inability to distinguish true hunger. Hammar and Bernard (1966) have identified activity level (excessive or insufficient), inappropriate parent care, and disturbed interpersonal relations between the child and mother as the primary causes of abnormal weight in these children.

The effects of physical or mental disabilities on the nutrient and energy needs of the individual must be given appropriate consideration. Muscular impairments, as in the case of children with cerebral palsy, may vary from the high energy need of an extremely active athetonic to a spastic whose palsy permits very little activity (see chapter 10). It is, therefore, difficult to generalize about their dietary needs when the former could possibly burn up 6,000 calories a day compared to 1,500 calories needed by the latter. Students with disabling conditions will need evaluation regarding caloric intake and energy expenditure.

Hyperactivity

A recently identified problem frequently associated with nutrition is hyperactivity. Although confusion about definition continues to exist, the behavioral characteristics associated

important that a nutritionist or dietician be consulted when establishing programs for children with selected disabilities.

Medications prescribed for the treatment of children who are disabled may also influence nutrition. Several of the anticonvulsant medications, for instance, have been found to increase ascorbic acid (vitamin C), which may decrease ascorbic acid requirements (Butterworth and Weinser, 1980). Palmer and Kalisz (1978) report that dilantin, mysoline, primidone, and phenobarbital have all been found to deplete folic acid and cause anemia in some individuals. In addition to the anticonvulsant drugs, many of the common drugs can significantly influence nutrition. For example, the absorption of fat-soluble vitamins A, D, E, and K is decreased when mineral oil is taken. Other laxatives generally reduce the absorption of all nutrients. The excretion of vitamin C is increased with the use of the common aspirin.

Even vitamins that are sometimes used in the treatment of children with behavior disorders, if used in large dosages, may create nutritional needs. Large doses of some vitamins may increase the breakdown of other vitamins; for example, high dosages of vitamin C will increase the need for vitamin B^{12} (Springer, 1982). Sudden decreases in vitamin treatment may also generate additional nutritional problems even though the dietary intake remains at or above the recommended allowances.

Clearly, many drugs have nutritional side effects and for those who are severely disabled the probability of this occurring is high. Consultation with nutritionists, pharmacists, and physicians is recommended. Their input can add significantly to the overall health and wellness plan.

A third factor that affects the nutritional needs of those who are severely disabled relates to special diets. For example, special diets are sometimes recommended to make eating easier, to prevent allergic responses, or to respond to unique metabolic requirements. When these adjustments are made, care must be taken to avoid secondary nutritional problems. To make eating easier, many individuals with severe disabilities are given pureed diets. Pureed diets are frequently found lacking in fiber, protein, ascorbic acid, and certain vitamins. In addition, these diets have been found to be of questionable value and may, in fact, make eating more difficult (Sobsey, 1983). Many nutritionists are recommending that those who are severely disabled progress as quickly as possible to semisolid and solid foods. Changing from pureed to whole foods has been shown to improve intake of several important nutrients (Palmer, Thompson, and Linscheid, 1975).

There are, of course, some children who will require a pureed diet and there are some whose allergies and metabolic disorders are such that special diets will need to be established. In these cases it is essential that the diet is structured to provide the necessary nutritional requirements.

Behavioral influences also serve as a factor that can affect nutrition. For example many children who are severely disabled follow behavior management programs that require the use of foods and drinks as reinforcers. These primary reinforcers are usually necessary as bridges to more desirable secondary reinforcers such as praise and attention. The food reinforcers are frequently high in sugar and contribute little to the child's diet. Even substitutes such as cereals and raisins are high in calories. The use of food as reinforcers can lead to undesirable weight gain and nutrient deficiencies because some of the foods replace other, more desirable foods.

Some children with severe disorders exhibit strong preferences for foods of a specific taste or texture. The reason for this is unknown, although it is thought to be related to hypersensitive oral facial structure or possibly parents who are too tolerant of their child's disinterest in new foods. Some speculate that parents of children who are severely disabled are unwilling to try new foods because of their uncertainty as to how the child will handle the new food. Obviously, when the child's diet is restricted to just a few foods, balanced nutrition is difficult to achieve. Care, therefore, must be given to the diets of these children, and every effort must be made to have these children accept new foods and textures.

Although it is impossible to develop specific recommendations for each child with a severe condition, some helpful guidelines have been proposed by Sobsey (1983):

1. Dietary and nutritional assessments should be considered in the evaluation of every child with a severe disability.
2. Individuals with expertise in diet and nutrition should contribute to the total service plans for children with severe disorders.
3. Whenever practicable, efforts should be made to normalize the texture of children's diets.
4. Efforts should be made to eliminate restrictive food preferences of some children and to provide a widely varied diet.
5. When medications are prescribed, especially for extended durations, their nutritional effects should be considered.
6. When foods must be eliminated from a child's diet due to allergy or metabolic abnormality, a specific plan should be made and carried out to compensate for its absence.

Dietary Habits and Intakes

Research on the dietary habits and intakes of students and adults with disabilities has not been widely reported in the literature. Most of the reported research has been on institutionalized persons and was completed many years ago. In one such study, it was reported that children with cerebral palsy had a lower intake of calories than would be expected (Eddy, Nicholson, and Wheeler, 1965). A study of noninstitutionalized individuals, ranging in age from four to twenty-one, with disabling conditions of mental retardation, neuromuscular deficiency, and epileptic disorder revealed inadequate calorie and nutrient intake by all subjects. The author accounts for these inadequate diets by describing some of the eating-related problems. These include inability of the individuals to feed themselves, inability to chew normally, poor appetite, and difficulty in swallowing (Nowak, 1977). All of these problems contribute to lengthy feeding times that may tire or discourage individuals with disabilities from eating enough of the right foods. In such cases, it is strongly advised that the diet be of high quality and that foods be chosen with care to meet the requirements for growth, maintenance, and energy.

In Sweden, a study of the dietary intakes of forty-two residents with physical disabilities between the ages of fifteen and twenty-four showed that the caloric intake was low, 1200 to 1300 calories per day (Bergstrom and Lundberg, 1969). Although the authors admit this is low, they believe the requirement for calories is met based on the marked inactivity of this population. They state that a large number of sweets are consumed and account for one third of the total calorie intake by these young people. Iron deficiency anemia was a problem in this population. In the United States, when caloric intakes drop to such low levels, it is almost universally assumed that nutrient deficiencies will occur.

Eating Behavior in Adolescence

During adolescence, social pressures and the growing desire for independence and peer acceptance may influence eating behaviors. For most adolescents this will likely mean more meals away from home, more fast foods, and observable changes in food selection. In the teen years, snacking accounts for a third of the total energy intake. When more nutritious foods are unavailable, easy-to-obtain, high-calorie fast foods are consumed. Teenagers in the United States are not particularly well nourished, as several recent surveys indicate.

The adolescent, whether male or female, disabled or nondisabled, faces many problems related to nutrition. Adolescence is the time of rapid growth and sexual maturation, which necessitates a high-quality diet. For the female, her health and nutritional status in adolescence may affect her ability to bear a healthy child.

Vegetarian Diet

New-found interest in health-related and social issues may lead the adolescent to try new ways of eating. The vegetarian diet may be an example of this independence that eventually leads to a new eating pattern and alternative food choices. There are many different kinds of vegetarian diets. These include the *lactovegetarian* of milk and vegetables; *ovovegetarian* of eggs and vegetables; *lactoovovegetarian* of milk, eggs, and vegetables, and the *pure vegetarian* or *vegan* diet that includes only plant foods. The person with a disability who is considering a change to a vegetarian diet must first become knowledgeable about nutrition and the appropriate balance of one food with another in meeting the requirement for essential amino acids.

Nutritional studies on a specific group of persons who are vegetarians for religious reasons have shown them to be well nourished and of normal or below-average weight (Hamilton and Whitney, 1979). No nutritional problems have been observed in milk and egg-type vegetarian diets. Problems, generally related to a lack of the nutrients calcium, iron, zinc, riboflavin one, and vitamin B^{12}, have been observed in all-plant diets.

Anorexia Nervosa

The emphasis on slimness, fostered by television and diet-related commercials, has produced a host of weight-conscious people. As a consequence, eating disorders have become common, and a specialty within the fields of nutrition and psychiatry has begun to emerge in response to their prevalence.

The most common eating disorder now recognized is anorexia nervosa or willful self-starvation. This disease occurs primarily in adolescent girls and is not recognized until it is well advanced. The American Psychiatric Association (1994) associates the following characteristics with anorexia nervosa: (1) intense fear of becoming obese, which does not diminish as weight loss progresses; (2) disturbance of body image; (3) weight loss of at least 25 percent of original body weight or, if under eighteen years of age, weight loss from original body weight plus projected weight gain expected from growth charts may be considered to constitute the 25 percent; (4) refusal to maintain weight over a minimum normal weight for age and height; and (5) no known physical illness that would account for weight loss. The first clinical sign is weight loss. Other symptoms include hyperactivity, drive for academic attainment, and self-induced vomiting. As weight loss continues, the biochemical characteristics of protein-calorie malnutrition can be observed. Treatment is more effective in the early stages.

Bulimia, a process used to rid the body of food before it is digested, is commonly associated with anorexia nervosa. This disorder is most commonly observed in young women, with an estimated 15 to 20 percent of college-age women practicing forced vomiting or using laxatives. Bulimia is a serious disorder that can lead not only to obvious nutritional deficiencies but can be life threatening.

Although an obsession with thinness is similar in both anorexia and bulimia, there are differences in these two disorders. The anorexic eats almost nothing while the bulimic compulsively overeats and resorts to purging to keep from gaining weight. Both conditions require psychological assistance and counseling. The physical activity program for these individuals must be carefully structured. An overemphasis on strenuous activity may deplete the limited energy reserve.

Lifetime activities such as golf and tennis may be helpful in assisting the individual to focus on desirable goals and outcomes. Giles (1985) recommends that yoga classes be scheduled following lunch to assist the anorexic in relaxing and reducing any guilt that may be associated with eating.

Nutritional Planning and Energy Expenditure

Overweight and obesity may be the result of certain disabling conditions that restrict activity. In other cases, obesity is in itself a disability in that the condition creates social and physical problems that put the individual at a disadvantage. It is also important to keep in mind that both underweight and overweight are problems frequently observed in, but not limited to, children with disabilities. Although the discussion that follows focuses on weight control for students who are overweight and obese, the basic information is applicable to the problem of underweight, with the exception of the suggestions for weight reduction.

The quality of life among individuals with disabilities can be improved through helping them to understand and regulate their diet and exercise, a fact that is also true of the general population. Schools have the opportunity to provide the necessary help by offering a carefully planned nutrition and exercise program for students who need to control their weight. Establishing an environment conducive to the development of positive lifelong attitudes about eating and exercising should be the goal.

A team effort involving the physical educator, dietitian, home economist, health educator, parents, physician, school administrators, and interested peers can be effective in creating opportunities for influencing eating behavior. Team members can use their respective media to give students with problems of weight control appropriate information and motivation to utilize exercise, menu planning, food selection, and caloric values to deal with their weight problems in a practical and meaningful way. For the physical educator this means helping students to understand the influence of good nutrition and weight control on successful and enjoyable motor performance; promoting enthusiasm for participation in motor activities; and developing an appropriate individualized exercise program. Information about the amount and types of exercise scheduled for the week in physical education should be given to the parents along with the weekly school menus so that family physical activities and menus can be planned accordingly. The reinforcement and support of the parents is very important in the team effort to establish the best possible environment for successful weight control.

Determining Ideal Weight

One of the major questions facing physical educators is deciding what an appropriate or ideal body weight should be for the overweight or obese student. This question is particularly critical when attempting to establish realistic or meaningful goals as part of a weight reduction program. There are several procedures used for determining body fat. Some of these techniques—underwater weighing, ultrasound, Xray, computed tomography—are helpful but require facilities, equipment, and expertise not readily found in the school setting. Two procedures, circumference scores and skinfold measures, have been found useful as indirect measures of body fat with children who are nondisabled (Hastad, Marett, and Plowman, 1983) and those with disabilities (Winnick and Short, 1985). Both of these procedures are useful, practical, and easily adapted to the school setting.

Figure 15.4 The quality of life for individuals with disabilities can be improved through programs designed to maintain a proper balance between diet and exercise.

Skinfold Measures

Skinfold measures are based on the premise that one-half of the body's total fat content is located in the tissues beneath the skin. With the assistance of special pincer-type calipers, measures of this fat can be taken at representative sites on the body with relative accuracy. The triceps plus subscapular or triceps plus calf skinfolds are the sites normally used with children. In table 15.2 are body fat norms proposed by Lohman and Lohman (1987) for children and young adults from six to eighteen years of age. Their estimates take into account that children have a lower bone-mineral content and higher body-water content in their lean body mass. By using table 15.2, minimal and maximal weight ranges can be generated. A software program is available that generates a two-page report that includes a chart showing the child's percent body fat (Lohman and Lohman, 1987). The computer report is based on the skinfold measures and considers the child's age, weight, and height. For boys, minimal weight is that

---

Table 15.2 *Body fat norms for boys and girls, 6-18 years of age*

Triceps plus subscapular skinfolds—Boys

Skinfolds, mm

5	10	15	20	25	30	35	40	45	50	55	60

Very Low 6%–	Low	Optimal Range	Moderately High	High	Very High

% Fat: 2, 6, 8, 13, 18, 23, 26, 29, 32, 35, 38, 41

Triceps plus subscapular skinfolds—Girls

Skinfolds, mm

5	10	15	20	25	30	35	40	45	50	55	60

Very Low	Low	Optimal Range	Moderately High	High	Very High

% Fat: 4, 10, 15, 20, 24, 28, 30, 33, 35.5, 38, 40

Triceps plus calf skinfolds—Boys

Skinfolds, mm

5	10	15	20	25	30	35	40	45	50	55	60

Very Low	Low	Optimal Range	Mod. High	High	Very High

% Fat: 6, 10, 13, 17, 20, 24, 28, 31, 35.5, 38, 40

Triceps plus calf skinfolds—Girls

Skinfolds, mm

5	10	15	20	25	30	35	40	45	50	55	60

Very Low	Low	Optimal Range	Mod. High	High	Very High

% Fat: 7, 11, 14, 18, 21, 25, 29, 32, 36, 39, 43

Note: From *Software program on body composition in children* by Tim Lohman and Mike Lohman, Champaign, IL: Human Kinetics Publishers.

weight at which a child is 6 percent fat. The corresponding value for girls is 11 percent. The gender difference is due to the higher fat tissue found in the female population. Optimal weight for boys is that weight at which a child is between 10 percent and 20 percent fat. The corresponding values for girls are 15 percent and 25 percent. Maximal weight is 25 percent fat for boys and 31 percent for girls. Children whose weight exceeds their maximum should be encouraged to lose weight. Skinfold norms for selected disability populations may be found in *Physical Fitness Testing of the Disabled,* by Joseph P. Winnick and F. X. Short (see Selected Readings at end of chapter).

The accuracy of the skinfold measures is very important and requires that the techniques be standardized with periodic review and practice sessions. Some have cautioned that the potential for error when using skinfold measures alone is very high (Katch, 1985). A viable solution to this concern is to incorporate body circumference measures into the process for determining body fat.

Body Part Circumference Measures

One of the difficulties in taking skinfold measures is that the procedure is obtrusive and embarrassing for some individuals. This problem is compounded in extremely large individuals who may be sensitive to their overweight condition. Circumference measures of selected body parts is one way to overcome this problem. The measure is achieved by measuring the girth or circumference of various body sites. A cloth tape is used with duplicate measures taken and averaged for each site. Katch and McArdle (1983) recommend that the following anatomical sites be used according to the age and gender of the individual.

Young women	Older women
1. Abdomen	1. Abdomen
2. Right thigh	2. Right thigh
3. Right forearm	3. Right calf

Young men	Older men
1. Right upper arm	1. Buttocks
2. Abdomen	2. Abdomen
3. Right forearm	3. Right forearm

The site for each of these measures is identified below:

Abdomen—one inch above the umbilicus

Buttocks—maximum protrusion with the heels together

Right thigh—upper thigh just below the buttocks

Right upper arm—arm straight, palm up and extended in front of the body (measure at the midpoint between the shoulder and elbow)

Right forearm—maximum circumference with the arm extended in front of the body with palm up

Right calf—widest circumference midway between the ankle and knee

An example of the procedure for measuring body circumference is found in figure 15.5. Charts such as these can be useful in maintaining records on an individual over a period of time.

Katch and McArdle (1983) suggest that the following formula should be used to determine desirable body weight:

desirable body weight = lean body weight/1.00-percent fat desired

Using this formula, a 180 lb teenage boy who has 25 percent body fat decides to lower his body fat to 20 percent. The computation would be:

$$\text{fat weigh} = 180 \text{ lb} \times .25 = 45 \text{ lb}$$
$$\text{lean body weight} = 180 \text{ lb} - 45 \text{ lb} = 135 \text{ lb}$$
$$\text{desirable body weight} = 135 \text{ lb}/1.00 - .20 = 135 \text{ lb}/.80$$
$$= 169 \text{ lb}$$
$$\text{desirable fat loss} = \text{present body weight} - \text{desirable} = \text{body}$$
$$\text{weight} = 180 \text{ lb} - 169 \text{ lb} = 11 \text{ lb}$$

Given the above, the boy would have to lose 11 lbs to achieve a fat content equal to 20 percent. Because these

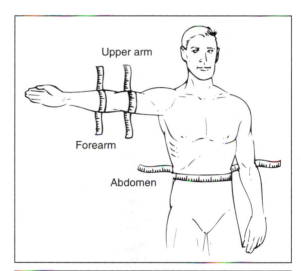

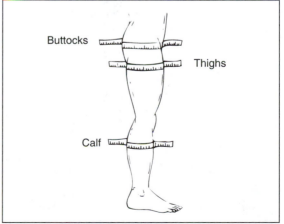

Figure 15.5 Measurement of circumferences with a tape.

measures are not precise, the physical educator should always indicate a range rather than a specific number of pounds to lose. In this example, we might suggest that the student lose between nine and twelve pounds. These values should be discussed with the youngster, his parents, and the family physician, where appropriate.

Body Mass Index

Another technique which has been employed by some to determine obesity is the Body Mass Index (BMI). This measurement system, also known as the Quetelet index, can be calculated using the following formula:

$$BMI = \frac{Body\ Weight\ (kg)}{Height^2\ (m)}$$

Where 1 kg = 2.2 pounds and 1 m = 39.37 inches

The Body Mass Index, which minimizes the effect of height, has been found to be highly correlated to other measures of obesity (Frankle, 1988). It is commonly accepted that a BMI value of greater than 27 suggests that the individual is overweight; a BMI value of 30 suggesting an obese condition. The primary value of the BMI is that it is another tool that can be used to provide assurance that an individual is indeed obese. The National Institute of Health has developed a convenient table that can be used to determine a person's BMI based on height and weight (table 15.3).

Weight Control Strategies

Numerous strategies have been used by adults and children to control their weight. For the obese individual the battle is a continual struggle with a common pattern of weight loss followed by weight gain. A successful approach for some

Table 15.3 *Body Mass Index for any given weight and height*

| Weight (pounds) | Height (inches) | | | | | | | | | | | |
	56	57	58	59	60	61	62	63	64	65	66	67
80	17.9	17.3	16.7	16.2	15.6	15.1	14.6	14.2	13.7	13.3	12.9	12.5
85	19.1	18.4	17.8	17.2	16.6	16.1	15.6	15.1	14.6	14.2	13.7	13.3
90	20.2	19.5	18.8	18.2	17.6	17.0	16.5	16.0	15.5	15.0	14.5	14.1
95	21.3	20.6	19.9	19.2	18.6	18.0	17.4	16.8	16.3	15.8	15.3	14.9
100	22.4	21.7	20.9	20.2	19.5	18.9	18.3	17.7	17.2	16.7	16.2	15.7
105	23.6	22.7	22.0	21.2	20.5	19.9	19.2	18.6	18.0	17.5	17.0	16.5
110	24.7	23.8	23.0	22.2	21.5	20.8	20.1	19.5	18.9	18.3	17.8	17.2
115	25.8	24.9	24.1	23.2	22.5	21.7	21.0	20.4	19.8	19.2	18.6	18.0
120	26.9	26.0	25.1	24.3	23.5	22.7	22.0	21.3	20.6	20.0	19.4	18.8
125	28.0	27.1	26.1	25.3	24.4	23.6	22.9	22.2	21.5	20.8	20.2	19.6
130	29.2	28.2	27.2	26.3	25.4	24.6	23.8	23.0	22.3	21.6	21.0	20.4
135	30.3	29.2	28.2	27.3	26.4	25.5	24.7	23.9	23.2	22.5	21.8	21.2
140	31.4	30.3	29.3	28.3	27.4	26.5	25.6	24.8	24.0	23.3	22.6	21.9
145	32.5	31.4	30.3	29.3	28.3	27.4	26.5	25.7	24.9	24.1	23.4	22.7
150	33.7	32.5	31.4	30.3	29.3	28.4	27.5	26.6	25.8	25.0	24.2	23.5
155	34.8	33.6	32.4	31.3	30.3	29.3	28.4	27.5	26.6	25.8	25.0	24.3
160	35.9	34.7	33.5	32.3	31.3	30.3	29.3	28.4	27.5	26.6	25.8	25.1
165	37.0	35.7	34.5	33.4	32.2	31.2	30.2	29.3	28.3	27.5	26.7	25.9
170	38.1	36.8	35.6	34.4	33.2	32.1	31.1	30.1	29.2	28.3	27.5	26.6
175	39.3	37.9	36.6	35.4	34.2	33.1	32.0	31.0	30.1	29.1	28.3	27.4
180	40.4	39.0	37.6	36.4	35.2	34.0	32.9	31.9	30.9	30.0	29.1	28.2
185	41.5	40.1	38.7	37.4	36.2	35.0	33.9	32.8	31.8	30.8	29.9	29.0
190	42.6	41.1	39.7	38.4	37.1	35.9	34.8	33.7	32.6	31.6	30.7	29.8
195	43.8	42.2	40.8	39.4	38.1	36.9	35.7	34.6	33.5	32.5	31.5	30.6
200	44.9	43.3	41.8	40.4	39.1	37.8	36.6	35.5	34.4	33.3	32.3	31.3
205	46.0	44.4	42.9	41.4	40.1	38.8	37.5	36.3	35.2	34.1	33.1	32.1
210	47.1	45.5	43.9	42.4	41.0	39.7	38.4	37.2	36.1	35.0	33.9	32.9
215	48.2	46.6	45.0	43.5	42.0	40.7	39.4	38.1	36.9	35.8	34.7	33.7
220	49.4	47.6	46.0	44.5	43.0	41.6	40.3	39.0	37.8	36.6	35.5	34.5
225	50.5	48.7	47.1	45.5	44.0	42.5	41.2	39.9	38.7	37.5	36.3	35.3
230	51.6	49.8	48.1	46.5	45.0	43.5	42.1	40.8	39.5	38.3	37.2	36.1
235	52.7	50.9	49.2	47.5	45.9	44.4	43.0	41.7	40.4	39.1	38.0	36.8
240	53.8	52.0	50.2	48.5	46.9	45.4	43.9	42.5	41.2	40.0	38.8	37.6
245	55.0	53.1	51.2	49.5	47.9	46.3	44.8	43.4	42.1	40.8	39.6	38.4
250	56.1	54.1	52.3	50.5	48.9	47.3	45.8	44.3	42.9	41.6	40.4	39.2
255	57.2	55.2	53.3	51.5	49.8	48.2	46.7	45.2	43.8	42.5	41.2	40.4
260	58.3	56.3	54.4	52.6	50.8	49.2	47.6	46.1	44.7	43.3	42.0	40.8

Source: B. T. Burton, W. R. Foster, and T. B. Van Itallie. Health implications of obesity: An NIH consensus development conference. *International Journal of Obesity, 9,* 155–169., 1985. As reported in Rimmer, J. H. (1994). *Obesity in Fitness and Rehabilitation for Special Populations.* p. 128–129, Dubuque, IA: Brown & Benchmark.

individuals is to follow a behavioral therapy program. Proponents of this approach believe that the excessive eating that leads to obesity is a habit. The desire for food is triggered by events in the immediate environment and is tied to numerous internal and external controls. If eating is perceived as a desirable way to reduce stress or eliminate boredom, the need for food will become associated with stress and boredom. A learned association or habit thus forms, which is very difficult to break.

The first step in behavioral modification techniques is to help the individual who is overweight to become aware of his or her eating habits and patterns and not to immediately change the diet. The individual is asked to keep meticulous answers to questions such as:

Where are meals eaten?
When are meals eaten?
What is the mood, feeling, or psychological state
    during the meal?

How much time was spent at the meal?
What activities were engaged in during the meal?
    (watching television, etc.)
Who was present during the meal?
What and how much food was eaten?

While questions such as these are appropriate for teenagers, parents will have to assist young children in analyzing their eating patterns and habits. The purpose of having individuals respond to these questions is to provide the individual who is obese with objective information concerning his or her eating behaviors. A young girl, for example, may come to realize that she is eating an excessive amount of food while watching television. Once the analysis of eating behaviors has been established, the next step is to substitute alternative behaviors for the inappropriate use of food. In figure 15.6, a list of techniques people have employed to gain control over eating habits may be found.

Table 15.3—*Continued*

Weight (pounds)	Height (inches)										
	68	69	70	71	72	73	74	75	76	77	78
80	12.2	11.8	11.5	11.2	10.9	10.6	10.3	10.0	9.7	9.5	9.3
85	12.9	12.6	12.2	11.9	11.5	11.2	10.9	10.6	10.4	10.1	9.8
90	13.7	13.3	12.9	12.6	12.2	11.9	11.6	11.3	11.0	10.7	10.4
95	14.5	14.0	13.6	13.3	12.9	12.5	12.2	11.9	11.6	11.3	11.0
100	15.2	14.8	14.4	14.0	13.6	13.2	12.8	12.5	12.2	11.9	11.6
105	16.0	15.5	15.1	14.7	14.3	13.9	13.5	13.1	12.8	12.5	12.1
110	16.7	16.3	15.8	15.4	14.9	14.5	14.1	13.8	13.4	13.1	12.7
115	17.5	17.0	16.5	16.1	15.6	15.2	14.8	14.4	14.0	13.6	13.3
120	18.3	17.7	17.2	16.7	16.3	15.8	15.4	15.0	14.6	14.2	13.9
125	19.0	18.5	17.9	17.4	17.0	16.5	16.1	15.6	15.2	14.8	14.5
130	19.8	19.2	18.7	18.1	17.6	17.2	16.7	16.3	15.8	15.4	15.0
135	20.5	20.0	19.4	18.8	18.3	17.8	17.3	16.9	16.4	16.0	15.6
140	21.3	20.7	20.1	19.5	19.0	18.5	18.0	17.5	17.1	16.6	16.2
145	22.1	21.4	20.8	20.2	19.7	19.1	18.6	18.1	17.7	17.2	16.8
150	22.8	22.2	21.5	20.9	20.4	19.8	19.3	18.8	18.3	17.8	17.3
155	23.6	22.9	22.3	21.6	21.0	20.5	19.9	19.4	18.9	18.4	17.9
160	24.3	23.6	23.0	22.3	21.7	21.1	20.6	20.0	19.5	19.0	18.5
165	25.1	24.4	23.7	23.0	22.4	21.8	21.2	20.6	20.1	19.6	19.1
170	25.9	25.1	24.4	23.7	23.1	22.4	21.8	21.3	20.7	20.2	19.7
175	26.6	25.9	25.1	24.4	23.8	23.1	22.5	21.9	21.3	20.8	20.2
180	27.4	26.6	25.8	25.1	24.4	23.8	23.1	22.5	21.9	21.4	20.8
185	28.2	27.3	26.6	25.8	25.1	24.4	23.8	23.1	22.5	22.0	21.4
190	28.9	28.1	27.3	26.5	25.8	25.1	24.4	23.8	23.1	22.5	22.0
195	29.7	28.8	28.0	27.2	26.5	25.7	25.1	24.4	23.8	23.1	22.6
200	30.4	29.6	28.7	27.9	27.1	26.4	25.7	25.0	24.4	23.7	23.1
205	31.2	30.3	29.4	28.6	27.8	27.1	26.3	25.6	25.0	24.3	23.7
210	32.0	31.0	30.2	29.3	28.5	27.7	27.0	26.3	25.6	24.9	24.3
215	32.7	31.8	30.9	30.0	29.2	28.4	27.6	26.9	26.2	25.5	24.9
220	33.5	32.5	31.6	30.7	29.9	29.0	28.3	27.5	26.8	26.1	25.4
225	34.2	33.3	32.3	31.4	30.5	29.7	28.9	28.1	27.4	26.7	26.0
230	35.0	34.0	33.0	32.1	31.2	30.4	29.6	28.8	28.0	27.3	26.6
235	35.8	34.7	33.7	32.8	31.9	31.0	30.2	29.4	28.6	27.9	27.2
240	36.5	35.5	34.5	33.5	32.6	31.7	30.8	30.0	29.2	28.5	27.8
245	37.3	36.2	35.2	34.2	33.3	32.3	31.5	30.6	29.8	29.1	28.3
250	38.0	36.9	35.9	34.9	33.9	33.0	32.1	31.3	30.5	29.7	28.9
255	38.8	37.7	36.6	35.6	34.6	33.7	32.8	31.9	31.1	30.3	29.5
260	39.6	38.4	37.3	36.3	35.3	34.3	33.4	32.5	31.7	30.9	30.1

Many alternate acceptable behaviors can be used to replace a particular set of environmental cues associated with eating. Below is a list of some examples of existing behaviors associated with eating, as well as possible substitute behaviors.

Established behavior patterns	Replacement behavior
1. Eating candy while driving	1. Singing along with the radio while driving
2. Eating snacks while watching television	2. Sewing, painting, or writing letters while watching television
3. Feeling hungry at 4:00 P.M.	3. Going for a walk at 4:00 P.M.
4. Eating ice cream after an argument	4. Doing 10 repetitions of an exercise after an argument
5. Never eating breakfast or lunch at the kitchen table	5. Eating breakfast and lunch only at the kitchen table

While we can give numerous other examples, the major aim of this approach is clear: *to create new associations to replace the old established patterns of behavior.*

Figure 15.6 Substituting alternative behaviors.

The long-term goals of the weight control program are threefold: (1) improvement in personal appearance, (2) subtle but observable changes in psychological behaviors, and perhaps (3) better health because of physiological changes (Katch and McArdle, 1983). Achieving these goals requires that incentives and positive reinforcements be an integral aspect of the weight control program. Young children, for instance, might find a new toy or game a desirable reinforcer for a five-pound weight loss. Teenagers might find money or clothes to be more reinforcing. The purpose of the reinforcer is to communicate in a very visible way encouragement for adhering to the weight control program.

Peck and Ulrich (1985) have proposed that the following criteria should apply to prevention and intervention weight control programs for children. The programs should:

1. Be capable of being individualized.

—No single preventive or treatment measure will work for all because of multiple causation and cultural differences.

2. Be nutritionally sound.

—contain adequate calories, protein, and other nutrients to support increase in height and muscle mass.

—tailor weight loss, if any, to child's growth needs.

—encourage child to develop sound, sensible eating patterns that reflect the Dietary Guidelines.

3. Be psychologically sound.

—help child to build a positive self-image and self-acceptance.

—use an educational approach.

—involve the parents and/or child in decision-making.

—not cause a control problem between parents and child.

—bring about positive behavior modification.

—not raise undue expectations.

4. Supportive of social needs.

—for young children, involve family.

—for older children, involve peer group support as well as family.

—help children to participate in normal social activities.

5. Include an activity portion

—include a physical activity or exercise component

—encourage the development of positive attitudes toward physical activity, which can be continued through life.

6. Be coordinated with medical care.

7. Continue over a long enough period for attitude and behavioral changes to occur.

8. Be reasonably priced.

9. Be judged by changes in knowledge, attitudes, and practices that permit the child to grow normally and develop a positive attitude toward life and self, not merely in weight loss.

10. Be based on an attitude that there is a wide range of acceptable body sizes and shapes. Heritability is an important variable to consider in establishing appropriate weight. Stunkard (1987) warns

against unreasonable weight goals for persons with a family history of obesity.

Students seeking to modify or change eating behavior can utilize several strategies that have proved helpful in eliminating the stimuli and conditions conducive to eating too much and eating the wrong kinds of food. The strategies include (1) removing all food, including that in fruit bowls and candy dishes; (2) serving smaller portions and using smaller plates to make the portions appear larger; (3) establishing one place for all eating to discourage random snacking and eating while watching television; (4) providing foods that require extensive chewing, such as raw vegetables; and (5) extending the eating time by chewing slowly and allowing a set period of time for eating. It has also been suggested that twenty minutes be allowed upon completion of a meal before a decision is made as to whether the ingestion of additional food is needed to assuage hunger. Usually, during the time lapse, a feeling of satisfaction occurs and no more food is required.

Family and teachers, too, when the occasion arises, can help students by encouraging them in the practice of these strategies. They can also help by guarding against their own use of food for purposes other than nourishment. When food is used to reward or to substitute for love and affection, values become associated with food that are difficult to change. With children who are disabled, the temptation to use food in inappropriate ways is often hard to resist in moments of sympathy with their problems or admiration for their efforts to cope. It is wise for parents and teachers to avoid all use of food as prizes and rewards to children, disabled and nondisabled alike. Food, particularly candy, is often recommended as a reinforcer in behavior modification of students with mental retardation; but in the interest of good nutritional practices, efforts should be made to find other effective substitutes.

Commercial Weight Reduction Programs

Several weight reduction programs have been so effectively publicized in the national media that their names are familiar to nearly everyone. Less well known are their nature and potential danger to health. Some information on these aspects of the programs may be helpful to the teacher who is asked for advice by prospective dieters. *Weight Watchers*. Uses a nutritionally adequate standardized meal plan. Provides for encouragement in weekly group meetings. *Stillman's*. Utilizes a high-protein, low-fat, low-carbohydrate diet. Provides for rapid weight loss. May be medically risky for some individuals. *Scarsdale*. Primarily a fourteen-day high-protein diet plan. Fosters short-term rapid weight loss. Medically risky for cardiac patients. Low in calories. *Liquid Protein*. High-protein, low-carbohydrate, low-fat diet. Fosters short-term rapid weight loss. May be medically risky and is nutritionally imbalanced. *Beverly Hills*. Utilizes the "conscious combining" technique, which means that common food types are eaten together—proteins are eaten with other proteins, but not with carbohydrates or fats. The diet is dangerous and physicians have warned that lack of natural salt combined with large amounts of fruit may cause serious water loss.

Exercise

A program of appropriate exercise must accompany the efforts to change eating behavior in the interest of developing a positive life-style of diet and exercise that produces a gradual and lasting weight loss. The first step in planning an exercise program is to analyze the caloric intake and caloric expenditure. The intake can be determined by use of charts that show the number of calories in specific sizes of servings of various foods. By keeping a daily record of the quantity of each food consumed and its caloric content, the individual can determine the total caloric intake for each day over a period of time and from these totals arrive at an average that can be taken as an indicator of general caloric intake. Caloric expenditure can be similarly assessed using charts like the one in Appendix V that show caloric expenditure per minute for the common forms of exercise.

The number of calories needed to maintain body weight is a highly individual matter, determined by such factors as size, gender, work output, and metabolic rate. For people who could be said to be average in respect to these factors, the daily caloric intake to maintain the body's weight is in the range of 1,600 to 2,800, with females at the lower end of the range and males at the upper end. Twenty-eight hundred to 3,500 calories are required to add a pound of body fat; hence, loss of a pound necessitates a reduction of the same number of calories either by lowered consumption or increased expenditure of calories. Ideally, the weight loss is effected through both increased work output in exercise and reduction in intake of foods with high caloric content.

The exercise program should be planned, then, to expend more calories than are taken into the body; in this way calories stored in the body in the form of fat will be burned, resulting in weight reduction. Weight loss of one half to one pound per week can be achieved by careful adherence to a well-planned program. More rapid weight reduction may cause medical risks and should not be attempted except at the direction of a physician.

Exercise periods should be planned to last long enough to burn up the designated number of calories; therefore, the vigorousness of the activity must be taken into account. Some other suggestions for the physical educator in planning and conducting the program follow:

1. Involve all participants in the selection of the activity and setting the goal for calorie consumption.
2. Ensure a vigorous workout.
3. Keep the activity exciting and enjoyable.

4. Offer a variety of activities that may be incorporated into each period according to interest and attention span.
5. Promote pride in self and performance.
6. Encourage students to support and praise each other's performance.
7. Conduct each session with enthusiasm and give group and individual reinforcements.
8. If the activity involves skill learning and drills, make them interesting and fun.
9. Make suggestions about activities that can be done individually by students over weekends or vacations. Teach or demonstrate these activities in the regular sessions.
10. Have students keep their own records of daily activity and caloric expenditure as well as calories consumed and a weekly weight record.
11. Take advantage of interest in activities that are in vogue (rope jumping, aerobic dance, jogging, and so on).
12. Make safety a prime consideration, especially for those with disabilities in addition to weight problems.

Suggested Activities

Activities for students who are overweight must be those that utilize energy but do not require more strength and agility than the students possess. Activities in which the body weight must be lifted (for example, rope climbing and high jumping) are generally contraindicated both because the heavy students will probably not have sufficient strength to perform them and because of the chances of injury should they fall.

Physical educators must be sensitive to the reduced energy level of the student who is obese. Many obese students perform at a lower level because the metabolic cost of exercise is greater for them. Bar-Or offers the following explanation for the obese child's reduced performance: "In physiologic terms, obese children require a higher O_2 uptake to perform a given task. Their maximal O_2 uptake, in contrast, is often lower than that of leaner children . . . a high submaximal O_2 uptake might reflect either reduced mechanical efficiency at the muscle subcellular level or mechanical 'wastefulness' due to the carrying of excessive weight and to their clumsy execution of movement. Based on current knowledge, the latter seems to be true" (1983, pp. 199–200). These findings were supported by DeMeersman et al. (1985), who reported that girls who are obese between the ages of seven and twelve were significantly less efficient than nonobese girls in maximal oxygen consumption. Students who are obese are working harder and moving less efficiently. Programs for these students, therefore, must be structured to encourage aerobic development with a recognition that "perceived" nonstrenuous activities can be effectively used in the early stages to achieve desirable outcomes.

Guidelines for developing an appropriate fitness program are found in chapter 27, *Physical Fitness*. Successful programs for obese children utilize a variety of physical activities that appeal to different children. The goal is to develop exercise habits that can be used throughout life.

Summary

The purpose of this chapter was to focus on common nutritional problems and to draw attention to the serious health-related problems associated with obesity. Information was also presented concerning the relationship between diet and exercise. Procedures for determining ideal body weight were described, with emphasis on skinfold and body circumference measures. The importance of a balanced diet was stressed along with guidelines for modifying dietary habits. Some of the fad diet programs were identified and guidelines for selecting an appropriate weight control program were presented. Underweight as a nutritional problem was also discussed with emphasis on anorexia nervosa and bulimia.

The unique nutritional needs and factors that affect the nutrition of students who are severely disabled were described. Medication, special diets, nature of the disability, and activity pattern all have the potential to affect the diet of the individual with a disability. The tendency toward obesity in this population is influenced by the reduced activity patterns commonly observed. Sedentary lifestyles may be attributed to several factors including limited program availability, the effect of the disability, and overprotective parents.

Sound nutritional practices and an active life-style are the keys to maintaining proper body weight. This statement applies to individuals with and without disabilities. The concept is very simple; the amount of calories consumed must equal the amount expended. If more is taken in than expended an increase in weight will occur. Large weight gains lead to obesity and increase the probability of debilitating illnesses. Many individuals who are obese experience emotional problems and tend to withdraw. Obesity is a serious problem, a disability in its own right. Educators must strive to help students with and without disabilities to understand the importance of proper diet and activity in maintaining good health.

Selected Readings

Allsen, P.E., Harrison, J.M., & Vance, B. (1980). *Fitness for life: An individualized approach* (2d ed.). Dubuque, IA: Wm. C. Brown Publishers.

American Psychiatric Association. (1987). *Diagnostic and statistical manual of mental disorders (DSM-III-R)*. Washington, DC: Author.

American Psychiatric Association. (1994). *Diagnostic and statistical manual of mental disorders (DSM-IV)*. Washington, DC: Author.

Bar-Or, O. (1983). *Pediatric sports medicine for the practitioner*. New York: Springer-Verlag.

Beal, V. A. (1980). *Nutrition in the life span*. New York: John Wiley and Sons, Inc.

Bergstrom, S., & Lundberg, A. (1969). Dietary intake in physically disabled students. *Nutritio et Dieta, 11,* 173–183.

Boskind-Lodahl, M. (1976). Cinderella stepsisters: A feminist perspective on anorexia nervosa and bulimia. *Signs: Journal of Women in Culture and Society, 2*(2), 342–356.

Bruch, H. (1973). *Eating disorders: Obesity, anorexia nervosa, and the person within.* New York: Basic Books, Inc.

Butterworth, C.E., & Weinser, R.L. (1980). Malnutrition in hospital patients: Assessment and treatment. In R.S. Goodhart and M.E. Shills (Eds.), *Modern nutrition in health and disease* (6th ed.) (pp. 667–684). Philadelphia: Lea and Febiger.

Caveny, P.A. (1986). In C.B. Eichstaedt & L.H. Kalakian (1987) *Developmental/Adapted Physical Education* (p. 249). New York: Macmillian Publishing Co.

Cratty, B.J. (1989). *Adapted Physical Education in the Mainstream* (2nd ed.). Denver: Love Publishing Company.

DeMeersman, R.E., Stone, S., Schaefer, D.C., & Miller, W.W. (1985). Maximal work capacity in prepubescent obese and nonobese females. *Clinical Pediatrics, 24*(4), 199–200.

Eddy T.P, Nicholson, A.L., and Wheeler, E. (1965). Energy expenditures and dietary intakes in cerebral palsy. *Developmental Medicine and Child Neurology, 7,* 377–386.

Eichstaedt, C.B., & Kalakian, L.H. (1987). *Developmental/adapted physical education.* New York: Macmillan Publishing Co.

Fomom, S.J. (1977). *Nutritional disorders of children.* Available through U.S. Department of Health, Education, and Welfare, Public Health Service, Health Services Administration, Bureau of Community Health Services, 5600 Fishers Lane, Rockville, MD 20857. (DHEW Reprint, No (HSA) 77–5104)

Fox, R., & Rotatori, A.F. (1982). Prevalence of obesity among mentally retarded adults. *American Journal of Mental Deficiency, 87,* 228–230.

Frankle, R.T. (1988). Weight control for the adult and elderly. In R.T. Frankle and M. Yang (Eds.), *Obesity and weight control* (pp. 361–389). Rockville, MD: Aspen.

Friedman, R.B. (1988). Helping the patient fight fat. *Postgraduate Medicine, 83,* 106–111.

Garn, S.M. (1986). Family-line and socioeconomic factors in fatness and obesity. *Nutrition Reviews, 44,* 381–386.

Garn, S.M., & Clark, D.D. (1976). Trends in fatness and the origins of obesity. *Pediatrics, 57,* 443–456.

Giles, G.M. (1985). Anorexia nervosa and bulimia: An activity-oriented approach. *The American Journal of Occupational Therapy, 39*(8), 510–517.

Grant, A. *Nutritional assessment guidelines.* Available from A. Grant, Box 25057, Northgate Station, Seattle, WA 98125.

Hamilton, E.M., & Whitney, E. (1979). *Nutrition, concepts and controversies.* St. Paul: West Publishing Company.

Hammar, S., & Bernard, K. (1966). Mentally retarded adolescents: A review of characteristics and problems of 44, noninstitutionalized retardates. *Pediatrics, 38,* 845.

Harper, A.E. (1974). Recommended dietary allowances: Are they what we think they are? *Journal of the American Dietetic Association, 64,* 151.

Hastad, D.N., Marett, J.R., & Plowman, S.A. (1983). *Evaluation of the health related physical fitness status of youth in the state of Illinois.* DeKalb, IL: Northern Illinois University, Human Performance Laboratory.

Hirsch, J., & VanHallie, T.B. (1973). The treatment of obesity. *American Journal of Clinical Nutrition, 26,* 1039.

Katch, V.L. (1985). Body composition and sports medicine: Clinical considerations. In *Body composition assessments in youth and adults,* report of the Sixth Ross Conference on Medical Research. Columbus, OH: Ross Laboratories.

Katch, F.I., & McArdle, W.D. (1983). *Nutrition, weight control, and exercise* (2d ed.). Philadelphia: Lea and Febiger.

Kelly, L.E., Rimmer, J.H., & Ness, R.A. (1986). Obesity levels in 553 institutionalized mentally retarded adults. *Adapted Physical Activity Quarterly, 3,* 167–176.

Kissebah, A.H., Freedman, D.S., & Peiris, A.M. (1989). Health risks of obesity. *Medical Clinics of North America, 73,* 111–138.

Lawson, H.A., & Placek, J.H. (1981). *Physical education in the secondary schools: Curricular alternatives.* Boston, MA: Allyn and Bacon, Inc.

Leung, A.K., & Robson, W.L. (1990). Childhood obesity. *Postgraduate Medicine, 87,* 123–133.

Lipman, A.G. (1981). Interactions between diet and drugs. In the American Dietetic Association, *Handbook of clinical dietetics.* New Haven: Yale University Press.

Lohman, T., & Lohman, M. (1987). *Software program on body composition in children.* Champaign, IL: Human Kinetics Publishers.

Lowenberg, M.E., Todhunter, E.N., Wilson, E.D., Savage, J.R., & Lubowski, J.L. (1974). *Food and man.* New York: John Wiley and Sons, Inc.

Marley, W.P. (1982). *Health and physical fitness.* Philadelphia: Saunders College Publishing.

Martin, E.A., & Beal, V.A. (1978). *Roberts' nutrition work with children.* Chicago: University of Chicago Press.

Mayer, J.M. (1968). *Overweight causes, cost and control.* Englewood Cliffs, NJ: Prentice-Hall, Inc.

McArdle, W.D., Katch, F.I., & Katch, V.L. (1991). *Exercise physiology: Energy, nutrition and human performance* (3rd ed.). Philadelphia: Lea and Febiger.

McArdle, W.D., Katch, F.I., & Katch, V.L. (1991). *Exercise Physiology* (3d ed.). Philadelphia: Lea and Febiger.

McNutt, K.W., & McNutt, D.R. (1978). *Nutrition and food choices.* Chicago: Science Research Associates, Inc.

New York Times. (1988). No-fault fat (editorial), February 29, p. 26.

Nowak, A.J. (1977). Effect of dietary and brushing habits on dental caries in non-institutionalized handicapped children. *Journal of Dentistry for the Handicapped, 3,* 15–19.

Palmer, S., & Kalisz, K. (1978). Epilepsy. In S. Palmer and S. Ekvall (Eds.), *Pediatric nutrition in developmental disorders* (pp. 61–72). Springfield, IL: Charles C. Thomas.

Palmer, S., Thompson, R.J., & Linscheid, T.R. (1975). Applied behavior analysis in the treatment of childhood feeding problems. *Developmental Medicine and Child Neurology, 17,* 333–339.

Peck, E.B., & Ulrich, H.D. (1985). *Children and weight: A changing perspective.* Berkeley, CA: Nutrition Communications Associates.

Pollock, M.L., Wilmore, J.H., & Fox, S.M., III. (1984). *Exercise in health and disease.* Philadelphia: W.B. Saunders Co.

Rimmer, J.H. (1994). *Obesity in fitness and rehabilitation programs for special populations.* Dubuque, IA: Brown and Benchmark, 113-151.

Shepherd, R.B. (1984). *Physiotherapy in pediatrics* (2d ed.). London: William Heinemann Medical Books Limited.

Shils, M.E., Olson, J.A., & Shike, M. (1994). *Modern Nutrition in Health and Disease* (8th ed.). Philadelphia: Lea and Febiger.

Smith, N.J. (1976). *Food for sport.* Palo Alto, CA: Bull Publishing Co.

Smith, U. (1983). Regional differences and effect of cell size on lipolysis in human adipocytes. In A. Angel, C.H. Hollenberg, & D.A.K. Roncari (Eds.), *The adipocyte and obesity: Cellular and molecular mechanisms.* New York: Raven Press.

Sobsey, R.J. (1983). Nutrition of children with severely handicapping conditions. *The Journal of the Association for Persons with Severe Handicaps, 8*(4), 14–17.

Springer, N.S. (1982). *Nutrition casebook on developmental disabilities.* Syracuse, NY: Syracuse University Press.

Stunkard, A.J. (1987). An adoption study of human obesity. *New England Journal of Medicine, 314,* 193–198.

United States Department of Agriculture and Department of Health and Human Services. Nutrition and Your Health: Dietary Guidelines for Americans (1990) (3rd ed.). Home and Garden Bulletin No. 232, Hyattsville, MD, Human Nutrition Information Service, United States Department of Agriculture.

U.S. Senate. (1977, February). *Select committee on nutrition and human needs, dietary goals for the United States.* Washington, DC: U.S. Government Printing Office.

Wadden, T.A., Stunkard, A.J., Rich, L., Rubin, C.J., Sweidel, G., & McKinney, S. (1990). Obesity in black adolescent girls: A controlled clinical trial treatment by diet, behavior modification, and parental support. *Pediatrics, 85,* 345–352.

Winnick, J.P., & Short, F.X. (1985). *Physical fitness testing of the disabled.* Champaign, IL: Human Kinetics Publishers.

Enhancing Activities

1. Obtain a copy of one of the commercial weight control programs identified in this chapter. Review the program to determine if its claims are consistent with good dietary practices.

2. Keep a log of your dietary habits for three days. Record what you eat, where you eat, your mood during the meal, who ate with you, and what you did during the meal, such as reading or watching television.

3. Using the procedure described in this chapter, determine your ideal body weight.

4. Given the information presented in this chapter, identify some of the principles that should be used in developing a weight control program for a student with a disability.

5. Visit a local school or community recreation program to observe children participating in a physical activity program. Analyze the movement patterns and energy levels of overweight students compared with the other students.

6. Interview a dietician or nutritionist to obtain his or her views on nutrition and exercise for the student with a disability.

7. Using the information on caloric expenditures for various activities, estimate the number of calories you expend daily through exercise. If possible, do the same activity for someone who has a disabling condition.

CHAPTER
16

Other Conditions Requiring Special Consideration in Physical Education

---

◆ ──────── **CHAPTER OBJECTIVES** ──────── **◆**

After studying this chapter, the reader should be able to:

1 Identify the causes and characteristics of various conditions, including nephritis, diabetes, epilepsy, anemia, hemophilia, and AIDS, and modifications, if any, in physical activity programs that may be necessary for students with these disorders.

2 Explain why it is important for individuals with the conditions listed above to engage in activity and exercise programs.

3 Comprehend that Public Law 94-142 mandates that students with health impairments are entitled, if necessary, to the provisions of special education, including physical education.

4 Discuss why students with health impairments are entitled to appropriately designed physical education programs.

5 Apply selected concepts to the development of physical activity programs for individuals with diabetes, epilepsy, and those convalescing from injury, illness, or surgery.

6 Discuss the following concepts in relation to students with various health impairments: excuses from physical education; activities, if any, that may be contraindicated; integration versus segregation; and the design of individualized educational programs in physical education.

7 Identify selected journals and references, including organizations, that can be used to obtain additional information regarding students with the conditions described in this chapter.

Public Law 101-476 and its predecessor, P.L. 94-142, identify "Other Health Impaired" as one of the categories of disabling conditions. This category was defined to mean "limited strength, vitality, or alertness due to chronic or acute health problems which adversely affect a child's education performance" (*Federal Register,* August 23, 1977, p. 42478). Examples of conditions included in this category are disorders previously discussed such as heart and respiratory conditions as well as nephritis, hemophilia, diabetes, and epilepsy, which will be discussed in this chapter. The reasons for providing information regarding these conditions is clear: students with health impairments are entitled to the privileges of special education including physical education. For some disorders, such as diabetes, the only special instructional arrangements that may be necessary are in physical education. When this occurs, special education funds can be used to support these services. Regardless of the funding amount or source, every effort should be made to ensure that appropriate physical education experiences are provided for students with health impairments. As will be discussed in this chapter, the need for physical activity and the benefits to be derived from these services will justify the expenditure of funds and energy.

Nephritis

Nephritis (Bright's disease) is an inflammation of the renal capillaries (filters of the kidney responsible for the formation of urine). The inflammation may damage the renal capillaries, impairing the filtering process so that blood and proteins, such as albumen, are excreted with the urine.

The disease is classified as either acute nephritis or chronic nephritis. Acute nephritis is largely a disease of childhood and youth and is the most common form of nephritis among the early age groups. The disease is apparently a reaction to an infection elsewhere in the body. Although the infection occasionally affects the skin, it is almost always in the upper respiratory tract. Common examples are scarlet fever, "strep throat," and other infections caused by streptococci. The relationship between the infection and the development of nephritis is not clearly understood; however, the disease is thought to be an antigen-antibody reaction (immune response) by the kidney to the infection. Nephritis may occur from one to three weeks after the initial infection.

Acute nephritis may vary from a very mild case to a severe attack. In milder cases, the symptoms may be unnoticeable or there may be edema (accumulation of fluid in the tissue) around the eyes, low-grade fever, hematuria (passing of blood in the urine), and back pain. In severe cases, symptoms also include headaches, malaise (feelings of uneasiness), fever, hypertension (excessive pressure of the blood against blood vessels), diminution of urine excretion, and

general edema. In extremely severe cases, cardiac disturbance may occur, possibly resulting in death.

Bed rest and a carefully controlled diet are the chief procedures used in treating acute nephritis. Antibiotics are frequently administered to control the streptococcal infection if it is still present. Recovery is usually complete. However, in a very few cases the disease may subside only to reappear again or to develop into chronic nephritis.

Chronic nephritis may develop from acute nephritis immediately or after the symptoms of acute nephritis have disappeared. It may also occur in those who have never had acute nephritis. Chronic nephritis differs from acute in that there is steady progressive damage of a permanent nature to the kidneys.

In most instances there are three stages of chronic nephritis. In the first stage, very few overt symptoms manifest themselves; however, blood and urine tests do reveal the presence of the disease. No special treatment is prescribed during this period except the avoidance of excessive fatigue and the maintenance of a diet that is low in sodium and high in protein.

In the second stage, general edema occurs, affecting especially the legs, arms, and face. Steroid hormones may be used to treat the disease, but maintaining a high-protein, low-sodium diet is the best treatment. Also, strenuous exercise is to be avoided.

In the third state, uremia (poisoning of the blood by waste products of the body) occurs. At this stage, damage to the kidneys is so great that death will result unless the kidneys are aided by the use of an artificial kidney, or unless a single kidney is removed or a transplant is accomplished.

Suggested Activities

In developing a physical education program for those with kidney disorders, extreme care should be exercised to avoid any activities strenuous enough to cause stress to the kidneys when eliminating waste products. In severe cases all exercise is contraindicated. Those with mild acute nephritis may take part in physical education, avoiding any excessively strenuous activities. Competitive situations in which the student would be likely to extend himself or herself beyond the level of activity that can be comfortably tolerated should not be offered.

For students who have the disease more severely, the expenditure of energy must be drastically reduced. Because of the nature of the disease, the development of physical fitness by application of the progressive overload principle (see chapter 27) must be severely limited. Concentration should be on motor skill development to decrease the use of energy in motor movement. For this purpose, the basic principles of movement and how they are utilized to make movement more efficient should be emphasized for all students old enough to comprehend their significance.

Another important goal is to provide students with severe cases of nephritis an opportunity to play with peers and to develop a feeling of belonging. Many of the less strenuous games, such as table tennis, catching and throwing, and archery, will allow the student with nephritis to integrate readily with nonaffected students. In other games and activities, the regulations can be adapted to allow the student with nephritis to play with his or her peers. Having a teammate run the bases for the batter is one example of an appropriate modification that can be readily made.

Diabetes Mellitus

Diabetes mellitus, a disease in which the body exhibits an inability to properly use the starches and sugars that it ingests, is a major health problem that affects more than 7 million Americans (Etzwiler, 1991). The prevalence of the disease is increasing, with some estimates suggesting that the number of people affected by this disorder will double every fifteen years. Diabetes is found in both children and adults with approximately two children affected for every eight adults. The disease is more common in females than males and accounts for 50 percent of the lower limb amputations. Historically, diabetes has been divided into two types—juvenile and adult or maturity onset. Today, the classification system receiving the most common use refers to these as insulin-dependent diabetes mellitus (IDDM), also known as Type I or juvenile onset diabetes, and non-insulin-dependent mellitus (NIDDM), also known as Type II or adult on-set diabetes. As the names imply, the IDDM affects young individuals normally before the age of twenty-four and the NIDDM is more common among those over the age of forty but may be found in young children, which is one reason that the term "adult-onset diabetes" is becoming less commonly used.

As table 16.1 indicates, there are other differences between these two types of diabetes. IDDM individuals normally require insulin and are lean. In this type the pancreas lacks the ability to make sufficient amounts of insulin. IDDM is the most difficult type to control and is sometimes referred to as brittle diabetes because those affected are susceptible to wide blood-glucose swings and insulin reactions. NIDDM diabetes generally occurs in later life in older, overweight individuals. NIDDM is different from IDDM in that the pancreas produces insulin, but the body's cells lack receptor sites to receive the available insulin. NIDDM generally develops slowly and with symptoms so mild that it may be undetected for years (Duda, 1985). While it is true that individuals with Type II diabetes (NIDDM) normally do not require insulin, a significant number are taking insulin for optimal management of their disease. While not dependent on insulin the same way that Type I individuals are, they benefit from insulin therapy to maintain adequate glucose levels (Henry and Eddelman, 1992; Rimmer, 1994).

Cause

The cause of diabetes mellitus is known to be related to an improper supply of insulin, secreted by the islets of Langerhans in the pancreas and responsible for the breakdown of sugars for utilization and storage by the body. This lack of proper function is not caused by an organic defect; consequently, medical investigation of its cause is being directed toward other possible causes, such as the factors that control the production of insulin in the pancreas. In juvenile diabetes mellitus, considerable interest has focused on the likelihood that the disease may be inherited. Falconer (1967) reported that heredity is a factor in the history of 70 to 81 percent of young diabetics. Some, however, have suggested that the disease is complex and that heredity is not a satisfactory explanation for the cause for all Type I

Table 16.1   *Comparison of major clinical types of diabetes mellitus*

	Juvenile Growth-Onset Type I Insulin-Dependent (IDDM)	Maturity Adult-Onset Type II Non-Insulin-Dependent (NIDDM)
Usual occurrence	Between early childhood and age 24 years (only 24% are older)	After age 24 years (only 5% are younger)
Familial frequency	Higher	Lower
Prevalence	Around 15%	Around 85%
Usual cause	Failure of insulin production	Cellular resistance to insulin action
Circulating plasma insulin	Greatly reduced or not detectable	Normal or elevated
Body weight	Non-obese (often thin)	Usually obese
Method of control	Exogenous insulin required	May be controlled by weight loss, diet, oral hypoglycemic agents, or stable low doses of insulin
Ketosis	Tendency to develop	Nonketotic

From Skinner, J. (1987). *Exercise testing and exercise prescription for special cases* (p. 118). Philadelphia: Lea and Febiger.

diabetics. Other explanations suggest that the cause may be due to a virus because some viruses are known to destroy pancreatic beta cells. Another factor may be related to the process of autoimmunity—when the body destroys its own cells in response to selected viruses. Researchers also have investigated the relationship between obesity and prevalence of adult-type diabetes. Cantu (1982) reported, for instance, that the prevalence of diabetes among Sumo wrestlers was approximately 60 percent compared to the Japanese average of 5 percent. Sumo wrestlers are revered for their large size, which is made possible through a daily diet of up to six thousand calories, 80 percent of which is carbohydrate. This same phenomenon, to a lesser degree, is observed in the Type II diabetic. Over 90 percent of individuals with this type of diabetes are overweight.

In diabetics an improper supply of insulin to act upon carbohydrates permits an excessive accumulation of sugar in the blood that is eventually eliminated from the body in the urine. The body is consequently denied the heat and energy that might have been produced by the lost sugar, and the individual begins, in severe cases, to exhibit such symptoms as loss of weight, lack of energy, and continual hunger. Other frequently experienced symptoms are unusual thirst, excessive urination, intense itching, and slow healing of injuries.

Treatment

Joslin, one of the early leading figures in the treatment of diabetes, recognized from the outset that the effective management of diabetes required careful attention to three factors: diet, insulin, and exercise. Recent and modern practice research supports Joslin's early contention with increased attention directed toward the relationship among these three factors. The amount of exercise and physical exertion of the diabetic influences the insulin requirements because of the amount of sugar burned by the body in physical activity. Modenard reported, for example, that young diabetic children were able to reduce their insulin intake by 75 percent as the result of participating in an exercise program. A carefully established balance among food intake, insulin requirement, and physical activity must be established.

Some individuals with the adult type of diabetes can successfully manage the disease through careful control of their diet. As indicated earlier, a significant number of the Type II diabetics are obese. For these individuals reduction of excess body weight often results in satisfactory regulation of the disease (Krall, 1978; Leon, 1993). This implies that effort must be made to reduce the total number of calories to obtain a more ideal weight. The type of food eaten is also important. Recent evidence suggests that a diet high in complex carbohydrate, usually in the form of starchy, high fiber foods, helps to improve tolerance for carbohydrates and reduces the amount of required insulin (Leon, 1987).

Diet is also important for the Type I diabetic. These individuals should follow a nutritionally balanced diet with meals eaten at regularly scheduled intervals of time with a mid-morning and mid-afternoon snack. Teachers will need to be sensitive to the dietary needs of the diabetic child and allow time to take the necessary snacks. In table 16.2 some dietary goals for individuals with diabetes are listed.

Injections of insulin will be required by the Type I diabetic and some Type II diabetics. Insulin is needed to treat or avoid ketoacidosis and to control symptoms associated with elevated blood sugar levels. The student with diabetes will usually receive a single dose of long-acting insulin each morning. Additional quantities of fast acting insulin are given when the blood glucose level rises too high, such as immediately after meals. The specific program of insulin treatment must be individualized for each individual with the guidance of a physician. There are several different types of insulin preparations including some that can be taken orally. Unfortunately, the oral forms have not been found effective with Type I diabetics. One advance that has the potential to lessen the dread associated with insulin injections is the use of insulin pumps. These devices, which are operated by a small battery, deliver insulin through a tube inserted under the skin. Some units can operate for a period of time without being refilled. One type of pump administers insulin continuously under the skin, into the muscle, or directly into the blood stream. Some pumps administer insulin on demand similar to the pancreas.

Exercise is an essential component in the effective treatment of diabetes. Some of the advantages of a vigorous exercise program have been outlined by Leon (1993). He reports that an exercise program can be helpful in the following ways:

1. *Improved Diabetic Control.* Regular exercise decreases insulin requirements for individuals with insulin-dependent diabetes. Exercise training likewise reduces insulin secretion in response to a glucose challenge in non-insulin-dependent diabetic individuals.

2. *Skeletal Muscle Adaptations.* The effects of training on skeletal muscle can make significant contributions to

---

Table 16.2 *Recommended dietary goals for diabetic patients*

If obese, reduce calories and increase physical activity to obtain and maintain ideal weight gradually
Liberalize intake of complex carbohydrates
Reduce intake of total fat, saturated fat, and cholesterol
Minimize simple sugars, except those that naturally occur in fruits and vegetables
Eat nutritionally sound meals
For insulin-dependent diabetic individuals, spread food intake throughout waking part of day and keep amount stable
Limit use of salt and alcohol

From Skinner, J. (1993). *Exercise testing and exercise prescription for special cases* (p. 164). Philadelphia: Lea and Febiger.

the control of diabetes, as well as to the improvement of work capacity.

3. *Reduced Risk of Coronary Heart Disease.* Given the risk factors associated with the obese condition found in adult-onset diabetes, it appears logical that this population is more susceptible to coronary heart disease. An exercise program can be helpful in controlling weight and reducing associated risk factors.

4. *Increased Work Capacity and Endurance.* Similar to the nondiabetic population, individuals with diabetes benefit from exercise programs that improve work capacity.

5. *Psychosocial Benefits.* Individuals with diabetes, particularly those with Type I diabetes, benefit from the sense of well-being generated by exercise programs. Riley and Rosenbloom state, "An important aspect of physical exercise is the 'good' feeling, the increased self awareness, self assertiveness, and self confidence that accompanies physical fitness. These benefits are enormously valuable to young people whose self images are damaged by this serious chronic disorder. This aspect of physical exercise is as important in the therapy of insulin dependent diabetes as the metabolic improvement" (1980, p. 393). Similar benefits have been noted in the adult-onset, Type II diabetic.

There are some exercise precautions that should be considered when working with the student who is diabetic. The muscle site in which the student injects insulin is important because the absorption rate of working and nonworking muscles is very different. Some have reported that the absorption rate of working muscles might be twice as fast as that of the nonworking muscles. Therefore, if the legs and arms are to be heavily used (such as in long-distance running), the preferred injection site might be the abdomen. This decision requires careful articulation with the youngster's physician.

The amount of insulin required is also related to the amount and intensity of the exercise. If the exercise is intense and the insulin has already been injected, additional carbohydrates must be taken before and during exercise to avoid insulin reaction. If the student is aware that a strenuous exercise program is planned, then he or she can reduce the amount of insulin. The decision as to how much of an insulin reduction is possible is difficult to determine and will require a trial and error process. Knox offers the following advice: "When activity is expected to be less than normal, insulin is increased. For greater than normal activity, prior ingestion of carbohydrates is advised. If exercise is strenuous and prolonged, hourly snacks should be taken" (1975, p. 389).

Leon (1993) advises that the individual who is diabetic should not exercise alone and should make certain that a partner is aware of the possibility of a hypoglycemic response. Adequate fluid during and after exercise is also important to avoid dehydration. Proper footwear and good foot hygiene are important to the diabetic involved in an exercise program. Care must be taken to avoid blisters and other foot problems, which can become serious problems with this population because of the frequent association of peripheral vascular disease and tendency for infection.

In developing an exercise program for the individual who is diabetic it is important to emphasize activities that are interesting and enjoyable and utilize the large muscles of the body. Aerobic activities such as walking, jogging, bicycling, swimming, and cross-country skiing are particularly desirable. The intensity of the activity should be such that a desirable training effect can be achieved (70 percent of maximal heart rate). The intensity, frequency, and duration of each exercise session should be recorded so that food intake and insulin can be adjusted accordingly.

There are few activities that should be contraindicated for the student who is diabetic. These students need to be encouraged to be active and to learn early in life the important relationship between diet, medication and exercise. Some have expressed concern that scuba diving may impose some risk to the diabetic. When questions of possible limitations arise, the Individualized Education Program planning process can be effectively utilized to ensure that the input of all parties is received before imposing unnecessary restrictions.

Individuals with diabetes, including children, are frequently required to conduct periodic tests to ascertain the amount of sugar in the blood. Normally, the person with diabetes conducts a test before breakfast as well as before other meals if the case is severe. A negative test, one in which no sugar is evident, is the desired result. Although urine samples were once the accepted source for determining the presence of sugar, new techniques rely on directly measuring the sugar in the blood. This requires that the individual prick the finger to obtain a drop of blood. The blood can then be applied directly to a chemical strip indicator. After waiting for a designated period of time and rinsing or wiping the end of the strip, its color is then compared to a chart. Each color represents a specific blood glucose level. Electronic blood sugar kits (glucometer) are also available and may be used instead of the chemical strip indicators. Teachers need to assure young children that blood sugar testing is an essential and acceptable practice.

Insulin shock or hypoglycemia (table 16.3), may occur if the individual with diabetes receives too much insulin, if the intake of food is too little, or if participation in exercise has been too great. Feelings of hunger, trembling, perspiring, and muscular contractions are symptomatic of insulin shock. If these symptoms are recognized in time, the reaction can be reversed by providing the body with more sugar through the eating of candy or a lump of sugar or through drinking orange juice or carbonated drinks. Administering sugar, normally, will end the reaction. If the individual, however, continues to experience sluggish thinking,

Table 16.3 *Comparison of hypoglycemia and hyperglycemia*

Hypoglycemia	Hyperglycemia
Weakness	Excessive urination
Sweating	Excessive thirst
Blurred vision	Nausea and vomiting
Mood change	Abdominal pain
Hunger	Drowsiness
Pallor	Sweet (acetone) breath
Rapid, labored respirations	Rapid pulse
Seizures	Coma
Shock	
Coma	

muscle weakness, unconsciousness or convulsions, or both, an injection of glycogen may be necessary. This substance causes the liver to break down liver glycogen and release free glucose into the bloodstream. Teachers should consult with the parents and family physician to determine the specific procedure that should be followed for each individual.

Diabetic coma (hyperglycemia), which results from too little insulin, is an uncommon but more severe condition. This condition is caused by an increase in acids (ketone bodies) resulting from a too-rapid breakdown of fat in the bloodstream. Diabetic coma, also known as ketoacidosis, is characterized by uncontrollable drowsiness or muscular pain, possibly resulting in unconsciousness. In some cases, the most significant symptom that a teacher can recognize is a "fruity" odor to the diabetic's breath. A diabetic in coma requires the immediate attention of a physician for the administration of insulin. Individuals under medical care are not likely to experience coma.

Sherrill (1993) has listed some of the causes of diabetic coma as: (a) insufficient insulin; (b) neglecting to take injection; (c) onset of infection or mild illness; (d) diarrhea, vomiting, and mild stomach upsets; (e) overeating or excessive drinking of alcoholic beverages; and (f) emotional stress. In general, most diabetics recognize that any deviation from the regular eating, exercise, and medication pattern must be monitored carefully.

Program Considerations

Individuals with diabetes are normal in appearance and motor function and so do not usually experience the severe emotional problems that those with more obvious disabilities frequently have. Whenever unsatisfactory adjustment is found in those with diabetes, the cause can usually be found in overprotection or overindulgence by the parents during childhood.

Many doctors emphasize the importance of muscular activity in the lives of diabetics. Exercise is important not only because it decreases the need for inulin but also because it contributes to general body health. Moreover, it helps to keep the body weight under control, an important

problem with older diabetics, who have a tendency toward obesity. Exercise also improves glucose tolerance even in the absence of insulin. The only concern associated with physical activity programs is that the individual must learn to regulate the amount of insulin required in relation to the amount of exercise. Most persons who are diabetic learn to make this adjustment easily, particularly if the intensity and duration of exercise is monitored on a regular schedule. Some find it helpful to eat a snack prior to exercise and at regular intervals throughout the exercise period.

Other aspects of teaching students with diabetes that school personnel, including physical education teachers, should consider include the following:

1. Teachers should be aware that they have a student with diabetes in their class. Pertinent information that should be obtained from the parents and provided to teachers is presented in the sample form found in figure 16.1.

2. Individuals with diabetes are expected to test their blood for the presence of sugar. Blood sugar testing is normally carried out four times per day: in the morning, before lunch, before dinner time, and at bedtime. Teachers should be prepared to assure the child that sufficient time and privacy will be provided to conduct the necessary tests. A positive recording, the presence of sugar, may also account for a mood change in the student. The teacher must be sensitive to this possibility and provide support when necessary.

3. Efforts must be extended to assure other students that diabetes is not an infectious disease. Explanations that the individual with diabetes is capable of participating fully in all of life's activities may also help others better understand this condition.

4. Teachers should have dextrose tablets, candy bars, or soft drinks available to them to administer in case a student experiences an insulin shock.

5. The individual who is diabetic, when engaging in vigorous activity, will on occasion find it necessary to stop activity to eat candy or sweets to compensate for the increased metabolic state, thus avoiding an insulin reaction. Fortunately, many individuals with diabetes recognize the early signs of a low glucose level. Teachers should reinforce a student's decision to stop his or her activity rather than to "tough it out."

6. The diabetic is particularly susceptible to infection and great care must be practiced to avoid cuts, abrasions, blisters, and fungus infection. The physical education teacher can help students monitor this important aspect of their health.

7. Individuals with diabetes have excelled in every conceivable sport and activity. Many, such as Ty Cobb, Jackie Robinson, and Scott Verplank have achieved superstar status as professional athletes.

Student's Name			Date

Name of Parent or Guardian	Street	City	Zip

Phone Numbers	(home)	(work)

Alternate Person to Call in Emergency	Relationship	Phone

Name of Physician

Signs and symptoms commonly exhibited prior to insulin reaction:

_____

_____

Time of day reaction most likely to occur: _____

Kind of sweets to be administered to reverse insulin shock:

_____

Figure 16.1 Example of a diabetic survey card.

For the young diabetic this means that the physical education program should be well-rounded and include all of the same activities participated in by other students. The positive effects of physical activity upon total health throughout life should be stressed as well as its unique value for the individual with diabetes. The ultimate aim of the physical education experience is to foster within students who have diabetes an appreciation for the value of exercise as an important factor in the total treatment of diabetes.

Convulsive Disorders—Epilepsy

The incidence of convulsive disorders, also commonly referred to as epilepsy and/or seizure disorders, cannot be accurately determined for the general population or the school population because only severe and uncontrolled cases come to the attention of medical and school personnel. It has been estimated that as many as 1 of every 200 people has some form of epilepsy; a large number of these cases are so mild as to go undetected. Many persons whose epilepsy is diagnosed respond so effectively to treatment that they live completely normal lives, and the fact that without medication they could suffer seizures is known only to their families. In others, however, the seizures are not entirely controlled. This appears to be particularly true of those with severe disabilities or multidisabilities. The cause may be failure to follow a proper schedule in taking the medication, ineffectiveness of the medication itself, or some other as-yet-undetermined reason.

In ancient times, epilepsy was known as the sacred disease, a disorder that was widely misunderstood and believed to be due to the presence of evil spirits. Even today in modern society there is a great deal of misunderstanding about epilepsy. Those with epilepsy are considered by some to be different. Teachers must be knowledgeable about epilepsy so that they can respond to the students' needs and communicate with others about this disorder. Epilepsy is a phenomenon that can be explained and should be accepted in the same way as any health condition that requires medical attention.

Cause

Epilepsy is not a specific disorder but rather a result of an electrical-chemical imbalance within the regulatory mechanism of the brain. The abnormality of brain function causes seizures. Although attention has focused on the role of heredity in the cause of epilepsy, insufficient data are available to substantiate this relationship. Epilepsy is prevalent among individuals with neurological problems, primarily those with mental retardation or cerebral palsy, or both. The term "developmental disabilities," for instance, is frequently used to describe those who have cerebral palsy, epilepsy, mental retardation, or a combination of these conditions.

The seizures that accompany epilepsy may begin very early in life or they may not commence until adulthood. In about half of the cases in which seizures do occur, they begin before the age of twenty. As age increases, the number of seizures often decreases.

Types

Several different classifications are used for the various types of epilepsy. The international classification system adopted by the World Health Organization divides seizures into two major categories: partial or generalized. This classification system is endorsed by the Epilepsy Foundation of America. The traditional clinical classification system, commonly utilized by physicians, classifies epilepsy into four types: grand mal, petit mal, focal, and psychomotor. The relationship between these two classification systems is found in table 16.4.

The most severe type is the generalized motor seizure, or grand mal. It is characterized by loss of consciousness, rigidity, and falling. Fortunately, some individuals are aware that they are about to have a seizure. This warning, or **aura**, as it is frequently referred to, is described by some as a sensation they have prior to the seizure, such as a sick feeling, unpleasant taste or odor, or simply a "funny" feeling. In cases in which the aura is well defined, the student with epilepsy may have time to move to a quiet area or a more comfortable position prior to the seizure.

The seizure itself includes a tonic phase, clonic phase, and sleep phase. During the tonic phase, the individual will stop all activity, lose consciousness, experience a generalized body stiffening, and fall to the ground. As the muscles tighten, air may be forced from the lungs resulting in a piercing and sometimes frightening cry. Bowel and bladder control may also be affected.

Following the tonic (stiff) phase, the individual will experience a clonic (jerking) phase during which various uncontrolled body movements will occur. Frothing of the mouth may also occur as excessive saliva builds up due to the interference with the mechanics of swallowing. Regular respiration is also inhibited, resulting in a temporary cyanotic state, characterized by blueness of the skin as the result of lack of oxygen.

After the tonic and clonic phases, the individual's respiration quickly returns to normal. Postseizure responses may include a general sense of confusion and headache symptoms. Some persons with epilepsy will, for a period of time ranging from a few minutes to several hours, sleep after the seizure.

The petit mal (generalized seizure) should not be interpreted as simply a minor form of grand mal, for the difference is in the kind of seizure rather than degree. It results in unconsciousness for a short duration of approximately five to fifteen seconds. Mental processes cease during the attack and conscious physical activity is suspended, although automatic action may continue. Muscular twitching and rolling or blinking of the eyes or the fixing of the eyes upon some object are characteristic of this type of attack. Recovery is immediate. This type of epilepsy is very difficult to recognize and some students with this disorder have been identified as daydreamers or students with poor attention spans.

Of the many kinds of partial seizures, the Jacksonian is the most common. The Jacksonian seizure originates on one side of the body, usually an arm or leg, and moves to the rest of the body, although it may not encompass the entire body. The focal seizure resembles the grand mal although there is no aura or tonic phase. Although individuals who experience a focal seizure do not lose consciousness, their conscious state is altered. Despite the fact that they may recognize their surroundings, their ability to speak or respond normally is impaired.

Psychomotor attacks constitute another type of epilepsy affecting a small number of those with epilepsy. Consciousness is not lost during the attack but there is no recall of the attack afterward. The attack is characterized by extremely odd behavior in which the individual may have a temper tantrum or otherwise demonstrate unsocial behavior. Although students with this disorder seldom remember the happenings surrounding their unusual and sometimes disruptive behavior, they are frequently punished as if they were in complete control of their psychological processes. Efforts are being extended today to improve the procedures for identifying students with psychomotor epilepsy so that these students will be spared punishment for behavior beyond their control.

As indicated in table 16.4, seizures sometimes occur that are either clonic or tonic.

Myoclonic seizures are sudden and violent contractions in some part of the body or to the entire body. There may be a loss of consciousness but the duration of the myoclonic seizure is very brief.

Atonic seizures are similar to absence or petit mal seizures except there is a momentary loss of posture control in which the person tends to sag or collapse.

Akinetic seizures are frequently referred to as sudden-drop attacks, because the person loses consciousness and muscle tone and falls to the ground.

Table 16.4 *Two commonly used classification systems in epilepsy: A comparison of terms*

International Classification System (Gastaut, 1970)	Traditional Clinical Classification System
I. Partial seizures	Focal epilepsy
A. Without impairment of consciousness	Motor (Jacksonian) or sensory
B. With impairment of consciousness	Psychomotor or temporal lobe epilepsy
II. Generalized seizures	
A. Absence	Petit mal
B. Tonic-clonic	Grand mal
C. Tonic only	Limited grand mal
D. Clonic only	
E. Myoclonic	Atypical petit mal *or* minor motor
F. Atonic	seizures *or* Lennox-Gastaut
G. Akinetic	syndrome
H. Infantile spasms	Jackknife or Salaam seizure
III. Unilaterial seizures	
IV. Unclassified seizures	

Source: Sherrill, C. (1993). *Adapted physical education and recreation* (4th ed., p. 493). Dubuque, IA: William C. Brown Publishers.

Infantile spasms, as the name implies, occur between the ages of three and nine months, after which other types of seizures may occur. This disorder, characterized by a doubling-up of the body, is associated with severe mental retardation.

Unilateral seizures, which may be associated with any of the convulsive disorders, attack only one side of the brain and therefore only one side of the body is affected.

Unclassified seizures include those disorders that do not meet existing criteria or appear to be of a mixed type. Approximately 35 percent to 40 percent of epilepsy is a combination of absence and tonic-clonic seizures.

Factors Associated with Seizures

There are several factors that trigger seizures in students with epilepsy. The factors identified below should be helpful to teachers in analyzing the classroom environment for the student with epilepsy.

1. Hyperventilation or excessive breath-holding, as sometimes occurs in endurance activities or underwater swimming.

2. Menstrual period. The probability of seizures increases in female students during this time.

3. Emotional stresses including fright, anger, frustration, and similar responses.

4. Alcohol in excessive amounts. The probability of a seizure increases when large amounts of alcohol have been consumed.

5. Subtle changes in the acid-alkaline balance of the blood. This variable may be influenced by changes in diet. Some diets have high-acid foods such as cream, butter, and eggs, which are thought to be valuable in protecting against a seizure. The accumulation of lactic acid in the blood as a byproduct of exercise is believed to be beneficial in the control of seizures.

Aid During a Seizure

Drugs, primarily phenobarbital and Dilantin (phenyltoin sodium), are very effective in preventing seizures. Seizures in public places, including the school setting, are becoming less frequent. Nevertheless, every teacher should be familiar with the emergency care measures to be taken in the event of a seizure. Basic guidelines to follow include:

1. Be calm. The teacher's ability to respond calmly but quickly to the student experiencing a seizure will reassure other members of the class that their classmate will be all right. Ask the other students to continue their activities away from the affected student.

2. Place the student on the floor in a back-lying position and put something soft under the head. Some students, as indicated earlier, will experience an aura prior to the seizure and will assume a comfortable position in a quiet area of the room.

3. Move all obstacles away from the student. This is done to ensure that the student will not bang his or her head against various objects. In some instances, it may be necessary to pad the area around the student with a shirt or towel if the student is too close to an immovable object such as a set of bleachers.

4. Loosen any restraining clothing such as a belt or shirt collar, if this is possible without the use of force.

5. If there is breathing difficulty, keep the airway open by tilting the head back.

6. Once the convulsions have stopped, place an item such as a blanket or shirt over the student to eliminate the possibility of embarrassment if the individual has soiled him- or herself.

7. If the student is hazy following the seizure, move him or her to a quiet place to rest or sleep. The student should be kept warm and be permitted to rest as long as necessary.

8. Explain matter-of-factly to other members of the class what has happened.

9. After the class, the teacher should report the seizure to the appropriate school official. In some school systems this may be the nurse, a health officer, or the principal. Reporting the incidence to a central source assures that the total number of seizures within a day or specified time period will be accurately recorded. This is particularly important for those students who are experiencing a change in the dosage of their medication.

Graff et al. (1990) recommend that the teacher should record the student's activity during the seizure. Important information would include the following:

1. When did the seizure begin?
2. In what area of the body did the seizure begin?
3. Did the seizure begin in one area of the body and move to another area?
4. What were movements of the head, face, eyes, arms, and legs?
5. Was the student's body limp or rigid?
6. Were the student's eyes rolled back, to the right or to the left?
7. Did the student stop breathing?
8. Did the student bite his or her tongue?
9. Was the student's skin pale, blue, or reddened in color?
10. When did the seizure end?

Suggested Activities

Students whose seizures are under control need no special consideration and can participate in the activities of the regular program without modification. At one time the medical profession recommended that children with epilepsy not participate in sports in which head injuries may occur. However, that attitude has been undergoing a change. Many physicians now claim that the possibility of head injury poses no special threat to children with epilepsy. It is argued that the social stigma attached to exclusion from participation is more serious than any medical problem that may be incurred.

The American Medical Association's (1974) position is that collision sports (basketball, soccer, wrestling) and contact sports (football, ice hockey, lacrosse) can be played by students whose epilepsy is under medical control. Some activities that involve direct blows to the head such as boxing should be avoided. Activities that involve repeated blows to the head such as heading a soccer ball also should be eliminated.

Certain activities are contraindicated for students who are subject to seizures. These include rope climbing and similar activities in which there is danger of injury from falling a great distance during an attack. Because of the danger of seizure underwater, diving and underwater swimming should be avoided and swimming permitted only under close supervision.

Poor development of the cardiorespiratory system from lack of exercise appears to have some relationship to the frequency of seizures. Activities that improve physical conditioning are therefore important to such students because of the possibility of reducing the number of seizures.

Youngsters with a history of seizures are generally in poor physical condition and need special attention to the development of physical fitness. For these students the special programs of exercise suggested in chapter 27, *Physical Fitness*, will be extremely beneficial. In addition, games that provide varied and vigorous big-muscle activity are of great value.

Side Effects of Drug Therapy

Drug therapy is the most common treatment for epilepsy. Antiepileptic drugs are effective in the treatment of 90 percent of the students who experience seizures, with 50 percent of these individuals free of seizures while taking the prescribed medication. As discussed in chapter 6, different medications are prescribed for the various types of epilepsy. Students who experience grand mal seizures are normally administered phenobarbital and Dilantin, whereas Zarontin is the preferred drug in the treatment of the petit mal type. Tegretol is the commonly prescribed drug for the psychomotor type of epilepsy. Each of these medications can cause possible side effects, as described in table 6.2. Teachers must be sensitive to these side effects, particularly those that might impair the student's motor performance. Dilantin, for example, a commonly prescribed antiepileptic drug, may produce dizziness, ataxia, and mental confusion in some individuals. These possible side effects not only interfere with the student's motor performance but can be detrimental to the student's safety in certain activities. Information about the student's drug therapy program must be discussed at the Individualized Education Program meeting. Pertinent information can then be incorporated into the student's physical education program.

Anemia

Anemia is a common defect of the blood in which there is a reduction in erythrocytes (red corpuscles) or the amount of hemoglobin they contain. Because hemoglobin carries oxygen throughout the body, a decrease in its ability to perform this function affects the amount of oxygen in the blood.

Anemia may be the result of several different conditions. The most common of these are loss of blood and nutritional deficiency. Two other conditions that are fairly prevalent in young people are defective hemoglobin synthesis and disease of the bone-forming tissue. The former is the condition responsible for sickle cell anemia, and the latter for aplastic anemia and pernicious anemia. Pernicious anemia is not a common disorder among children, occurring most often after age thirty-five. Symptomatic of the presence of anemia are chronic fatigue that results from a lack of oxygen in the blood, and pallor caused by the lack of hemoglobin.

Chronic blood loss, such as may occur in excessive menstruation, bleeding ulcer of the stomach, or parasitic diseases such as hookworm or malaria, is treated by removing or treating the cause and by prescribing iron tablets or a diet high in foods containing iron to rebuild the hemoglobin.

Iron is the main constituent of hemoglobin, and the ingestion of a small but constant amount of iron is needed to replace the red blood cells that are destroyed by natural processes. Besides iron, vitamin B_{12} and protein are needed in the production of hemoglobin. Insufficient quantities of these in the food intake may result in anemia. Treatment consists of a diet high in the deficient nutrients.

Sickle Cell Anemia

Chicago physician James E. Herrick was the first individual to describe the disorder that is today known as sickle cell anemia. Intense efforts have been extended since 1970 to more fully understand this phenomenon and to develop effective procedures for treating young children with sickle cell anemia.

To comprehend sickle cell anemia it is necessary to understand the physiology of red blood cells and their important function in transporting oxygen from areas of high concentration, such as the lungs, to areas of low concentration, such as the muscles, liver, and brain. In normal red blood cells, the transportation is facilitated by the round, doughnut shape of the cells and the ability of the hemoglobin within the cells to hold on to oxygen. With sickle cell anemia, the red blood cells are long, thin, and angular in design and shaped like the sickles used to cut grain.

The fast removal from the body of the sickled red cells because of their abnormal shape causes a rapid destruction of hemoglobin that in turn creates a jaundice condition of the whites of the eyes. The bone marrow attempts to compensate for the anemia by manufacturing new red blood cells but, unfortunately, an insufficient number can be produced. Individuals with sickle cell disease have only one-half or one-third as many red blood cells as do those who are not affected. The shape and fluid state of the sickled red cells also creates a situation in which the red blood cells "jam up," depriving tissue of their normal blood supply. A vaso-occlusive episode is a term used to refer to this serious state of oxygen deprivation. This is obviously a critical situation that causes pain and sometimes death.

Specific sites that are most likely to experience a vaso-occlusive episode include the bones (usually the hands and feet of children under three), intestines, spleen, liver, gallbladder, brain, and lungs. Treatment varies depending on the site affected, but surgery and an analgesic are frequently recommended. The symptoms experienced by the youngster also vary but usually include pain and discomfort associated with the affected site. Other symptoms include fatigue, shortness of breath, pale color, loss of appetite, and a yellow cast to the eyes. Usually, those with sickle cell disease do not grow and develop as fast as they should. The life span of those affected is usually short.

Figure 16.2 An activity such as swimming can be modified to accommodate the energy level of the student.

Sickle cell disease is an inherited disorder with approximately one out of ten African Americans carrying the gene for sickle cell disease, which is referred to as sickle cell trait. For children of parents with sickle cell trait, the probability is two out of four that a child will have sickle cell trait, one out of four that a child will have sickle cell anemia, and one out of four that the child will not be affected. Some Caucasians, particularly those whose ancestors come from the Mediterranean area, the Middle East, and parts of India, may also have the disease.

There is no drug therapy for sickle cell anemia. Treatment is symptomatic. Anticoagulants have had some success in dislodging the clumps of sickle cells, and ice packs can relieve swelling of the joints. Some physicians recommend blood transfusions to relieve the symptoms, but relief is only temporary. Those suffering from sickle cell anemia must avoid high altitudes and other situations in which there is less oxygen available in the air than normal.

Aplastic Anemia

Aplastic anemia is a disease of the bone marrow, where red blood corpuscles are formed. In addition to the general symptoms of anemia, aplastic anemia results in frequent bleeding from the nose and the appearance of black and blue spots on the skin. The bone marrow's failure to effectively produce red blood cells may be caused by cancerous growth of the bone marrow or by destruction of the marrow by chemical agents, such as certain weed killers, industrial poisons, radiation, and some antibiotics.

Aplastic anemia is a serious disease and often the affected person is hospitalized until the cause has been isolated and removed. Cortisone has been effectively used to treat some cases. Blood transfusions at regular intervals are usually required. The prognosis is poor, and death often occurs at an early age.

Suggested Activities

Generally, children with sickle cell trait can participate fully in all school activities including vigorous physical education activities. However, most physicians recommend that the student not swim underwater and avoid breathholding for long intervals. These precautions are necessary to eliminate the possibility of a severe depletion of oxygen.

The NCAA Committee on Competitive Safeguards and Medical Aspects of Sports has issued a statement on the athlete with sickle cell trait. Its position is that the likelihood of a sickling crisis is very remote and that the athlete with sickle cell trait should not be restricted or limited in his or her participation in sport. It does caution, however, that athletic trainers and others should carefully monitor athletes with sickle cell trait to ensure that they do not become dehydrated during early practice sessions or while playing or practicing at high altitude (Adams and McCubbin, 1991).

Children with sickle cell disease must be monitored very carefully during participation in physical education. It is possible that these students could experience a vaso-occlusive crisis by lowering the oxygen level slightly. Physical education teachers must offer experiences, therefore, that require a minimal supply of oxygen. Motor skill activities should be provided to develop agility, coordination, balance, and the ability to manipulate objects. Physical fitness, particularly cardiovascular, activities must be developed cooperatively with the assistance of qualified medical personnel.

Hemophilia

A blood disorder resulting in the inability of the blood to coagulate (clot) properly, hemophilia affects approximately one of every ten thousand people. Although there are many different forms of hemophilia, the most common forms are hereditary deficiency of coagulation factor VIII (hemophilia A) and lack of coagulation factor IX (hemophilia B). A deficiency in these factors results in a poor-quality clot, which can be easily dislodged. When the person with hemophilia experiences a wound, either internal or on the body's surface, bleeding is prolonged.

Cause

Hemophilia is a genetic, sex-linked disorder that primarily occurs in boys. The condition is carried by the female, who has a 50 percent chance of passing on the disorder to her male offspring. A female may also pass the disorder to a female, who will then become a carrier but who will not herself experience hemophilia.

Clotting of the blood normally occurs in one of three ways: vascular contraction, platelet plug formation, and fibrin formation. These reactions can occur singularly or in an interactive fashion. When a blood vessel is injured, the small bundles of muscle fiber that surround the vessel will contract and decrease in size. The blood flow will immediately decrease or stop if the muscle contraction is strong enough. Platelets, small bodies found in blood, will adhere to the tissue, forming a plug to slow the blood flow. Platelets also release enzymes that cause further contractions, as well as attracting more platelets, and aid in the formation of a firm fibrin clot. For individuals with hemophilia, this normal blood clotting process does not occur, resulting in poor quality clots that can be easily dislodged.

Treatment of Hemophilia

A hemophilic disorder is not always obvious at birth. The signs and symptoms may not become evident until the youngster becomes more active. Early warnings are the relative ease with which a child bruises or the profuse bleeding of a small cut. Many bleeding disorders, however, go undetected because they occur internally around the stress joints such as knees, elbows, and ankles. If not treated, the individual will experience increased swelling and pain, making movements such as walking very difficult. Further damage to the articular surface through additional bleeding episodes will lead to joint degeneration.

Hemophilia was once treated through the administration of whole blood or plasma. This process frequently required hospitalization and in many instances resulted in circulatory overload and death prior to adulthood. Today, fortunately, clotting factor concentrates that can be easily administered are available. In some instances, depending on the site and severity of the wound, treatment is rather simple, consisting of a pressure dressing, ice packs, and oral medication. More serious bleeding usually requires hospitalization and replacement of the deficient clotting factor. Efforts in treatment today are also directed toward teaching individuals with hemophilia how to administer concentrates to themselves. Early recognition and treatment with concentrates can prevent bleeding episodes.

Suggested Activities

Individuals with hemophilia should take part in regular physical education as much as possible. These students should be encouraged to participate in activities that maintain their strength and endurance. While students with hemophilia vary widely in their response to physical activity, the National Hemophiliac Foundation and the American Red Cross have developed a system for categorizing traditional physical activities.

> Category 1: Activities recommended for most pupils with hemophilia.
> Category 2: Games and sports in which the physical, social, and psychological benefits may outweigh the risks. Most physical activities are in this category.
> Category 3: Activities in which the risk outweighs the benefits from individuals with hemophilia and are considered dangerous.

Table 16.5 lists several activities and their classifications.

Exercise is essential to develop strong muscles and joints. Students who are active also appear to have fewer bleeding episodes than those who are inactive. Swimming is a highly recommended exercise, as are walking, rhythmic activities, and sport activities that do not involve the possibility of joint trauma (leaping, jumping, and so on). Contact sports such as football must be avoided, as well as activities in which hard objects are thrown, such as baseball. Individual differences among students with hemophilia require, as they do for all students, attention to specific motor and physical development needs. Once developed, the physical education objectives and the program to accomplish them for

Table 16.5	Classification of selected activities according to criteria from the National Hemophiliac Foundation

Activity	Category
Baseball	2
Basketball	2
Bicycling	2
Bowling	2
Boxing	3
Football	3
Frisbee	2
Golf	1
Gymnastics	2
Hockey	3
Horesback riding	2
Ice skating	2
Motorcycling	3
Racquetball	3
Roller skating	2
Running and jogging	2
Skateboarding	3
Skiing:	
Downhill	2
Cross-country	2
Soccer	2
Swimming	1
Tennis	2
Volleyball	2
Waterskiing	2
Weight lifting	2
Wrestling	3

Source: Jansma, P., & French, R. (1994). *Special physical education: Physical activity, sports, and recreation*. Englewood Cliffs NJ: Prentice-Hall, p. 324.

the student with hemophilia should be reviewed by the parents and family physician for their recommendations. Discussions of this kind can usually best be accommodated within the format of an Individualized Education Program meeting.

Adams and McCubbin (1991) have identified four primary reasons why the student with hemophilia should participate in physical activity and exercise programs. These include:

Development of coordination. The student with hemophilia needs to attain as much coordination as possible at the earliest possible age.

Strengthening muscle groups. If muscle groups that surround joints can be strengthened, this may help to protect joints against bleeding due to trauma.

Development of a healthy attitude toward the body. Because individuals with hemophilia and their families worry about injury and bleeding episodes, special efforts must be undertaken to help the student recognize and enjoy the positive aspects associated with physical activity and movement.

Relationship to rehabilitation. For individuals who are more severely involved and require the use of a wheelchair or mobility device, participation in modified sports can contribute significantly to the overall rehabilitation program.

The probability that an individual with hemophilia will experience an injury at school, although no greater than for other students, should be discussed and a plan developed to cover this emergency. Teachers, in particular, must be sensitive to any signs of internal bleeding, such as limping due to a swollen knee joint, a large fresh bruise, or urine that may be dark brown or red. Fortunately, many children with hemophilia as young as seven are capable of discriminating the first symptoms of hemorrhage and some, having learned from experience, can administer the doses of factor concentrate necessary to control their own bleeding. When bleeding involves the joints or soft tissues, ice or cold compresses should be applied and the affected body part elevated. This technique helps the blood vessels to constrict, thus reducing the flow of blood. Teachers should not administer aspirin or aspirin compounds to hemophiliacs because these agents increase the severity of bleeding in individuals with clotting disorders. These and other first-aid procedures should be thoroughly discussed with the student's physician and parents.

Hernia

A hernia is the protrusion of a loop of an organ or tissue through an abnormal opening in the body. Hernias may occur in many different areas of the body, but the abdominal region is the most frequent site. The most common hernia involves the inguinal canal, which is located in the groin and serves as the passage for the spermatic cord in the male and the round ligament in the female. In the male embryo, the testes move down from the abdomen to the scrotum. This canal normally closes early in life but undue pressure or exertion may reopen it, resulting in a hernia or a loop of the intestine protruding through the opening.

If the protrusion remains in the canal, the hernia is called incomplete. If it leaves the canal and enters the scrotum, it is a complete hernia. A complete hernia faces the danger of becoming strangulated. The loop of the intestine becomes constricted, shutting off the blood supply to the area, which may result in the development of gangrene.

Cause and Treatment

The frequency of inguinal hernia is higher in the male than in the female and higher among those who are obese. Inguinal hernia may occur where there is abdominal pressure against weak abdominal muscles. Lifting heavy weights with the epiglottis closed is a frequent cause. Blows to the abdominal region are another cause. Surgery is indicated in the cure of hernia.

Suggested Activities

Students who have hernias should avoid activities such as weight lifting, boxing, wrestling, or football, which may cause increased pressure on the abdominal area or in which a blow to that area is likely to occur. For severe hernia cases, running games are also contraindicated. Rope climbing and activity on the bar and parallel ladders are not recommended. Games in which students may safely participate are horseshoes, swimming, bowling, casting, golf, table tennis, volleyball, and basic skill games that are not chiefly running.

Exercises to strengthen the abdominal walls are of value and offer some protection until surgery can be performed. They are also of great benefit to the patient after surgery. Added protection may be given the hernia during exercise by placing the hand over the hernia area. The breath should not be held during exercises.

Dysmenorrhea, Menorrhagia, and Amenorrhea

Dysmenorrhea, or painful menstruation, occurs most frequently at the beginning of the menstrual cycle, and is sometimes referred to as premenstrual syndrome (PMS). At this time the abdominal cavity is gorged with an additional amount of blood. This produces increased pressure upon nerves and hence pain. The changes that take place during the cycle within the body may lower the threshold of pain and increase irritability. Dysmenorrhea is often due to lack of exercise, fatigue, constipation, chilling of the body, and poor posture. Sometimes an organic condition such as a displaced uterus may be the cause.

Menorrhagia is a condition of unusually heavy flow during the menstrual period. Because of the large amount of blood that is lost, the individual is likely to be tired and somewhat anemic. Exercise, which is helpful to dysmenorrhea because it increases the flow, is not desirable in cases of menorrhagia. Consequently, in the physical education program for such girls all activities should be modified unless permission for them to participate has been given by their physicians.

Amenorrhea, a condition which describes the absence of menstruation, can be a serious disorder if ignored. This condition can be caused by several factors, including emotional stress, anemia, hormonal disturbance, or abnormal organs. Amenorrhea is relatively common in women who exercise strenuously. It is important, therefore, that physical educators be aware of the seriousness of the condition and help young women obtain assistance, as needed. Fortunately, in many cases amenorrhea is a temporary disorder with menstruation becoming possible when the emotional conflict has been resolved or after the body has adapted to stress.

Activities and Special Exercises for Dysmenorrhea

Dysmenorrhea is frequently given as a reason by girls seeking excuse from physical education during menstruation.

Most of these girls are unaware that their condition may be relieved by participation in physical education activities that are not extremely strenuous in nature. These girls should be encouraged not only to take part in their physical education classes but also to participate regularly in a program of special exercises that are known to be of value in preventing and alleviating dysmenorrhea. These exercises, known as the Mosher, Billig, and Golub exercises (figure 16.3), are beneficial because they improve circulation in the abdominal area, increase abdominal muscle tone, increase lumbopelvic flexibility, and encourage muscular relaxation.

The Mosher exercise is designed to relieve abdominal congestion by "abdominal pumping." To perform the exercise, a supine position is taken with the knees bent and the feet resting on the floor. One hand is placed on the abdomen. The abdominal area is then retracted or pulled in, and a deep breath is taken. The hand massages slowly and heavily from the symphysis pubis up to the sternum (approximately from the region of the pubic hair to the ribs). The abdominal area is relaxed, and the air is expelled entirely. The exercise is repeated several times.

The Billig exercise is designed to stretch the fascial ligamentous bands through which the sensory nerves pass. (The fascial ligamentous bands are bands of ligaments that attach the fascia, which covers the muscle, to the bone.) It is theorized that the stretching of these bands relieves the pressure on the nerves and so reduces pain. To perform the exercise, the subject stands with one side of the body toward the wall, with the feet together and approximately eighteen inches from the wall. With the knees locked and the hips rotated forward, the forearm is placed horizontally against the wall at shoulder height (the palm of the hand, the forearm, and the elbow should be in contact with the wall). The other hand is placed against the hollow of the hip and slowly and deliberately pushes the hips forward and toward the wall as far as possible. The return to the original position is made slowly. The exercises should be performed over a period of two or more months three times a day, three repetitions on each side.

The Golub exercise stresses systematic twisting and bending of the trunk, activities that were found to be effective in reducing the pain of dysmenorrhea in a study by Golub (1959). The first part of the exercise is done from a standing position with the arms extended straight out from the sides. The body is bent while the knees are kept straight. One hand is lifted up, and with the other an attempt is made to reach around the outer side of the opposite foot until the heel can be touched. The exercise is repeated on the other side. In the second part of the exercise, the individual stands with the arms at the sides. The arms are then swung forward and upward, while the left leg is simultaneously raised backward vigorously. Then the exercise is repeated on the opposite foot. Each phase of the exercise is performed four times on each side.

Figure 16.3 (*A*) Mosher, (*B*) Billig, and (*C*) Golub exercises for prevention of dysmenorrhea.

Convalescence

Students, like adults, frequently experience serious injury, illness, or surgery that may require them to be absent from school for an extended period of time. In these situations, it is the school's responsibility to provide the student with an appropriate education consistent with the guidelines of P.L. 101-476. The school's intervention normally occurs during that period of time referred to as convalescence.

Convalescence is a period of recovery from illness or injury. It can be said to begin when the acute stage of the disability has passed and to end when the patient is physically, mentally, and emotionally ready to resume the activities that were part of daily existence prior to the illness or injury. The nature of the convalescence depends largely upon the nature of the illness or injury, and the types of convalescence are consequently divided into five general areas, depending upon the nature of the initial illness. The five areas are surgery, infectious disease, constitutional disease, accidental trauma, and obstetrics.

The early stage of the convalescent period is characterized by general body weakness and low vitality that stem not so much from the illness or injury itself as from the forced inactivity during this stage. In extended bed rest, deterioration of the body functions is evident most conspicuously in the muscles. Considerable loss of muscular strength, endurance, and power occurs and there is some muscle atrophy. The patient's heart and blood vessels become less efficient in maintaining good circulation, which decreases cardiorespiratory endurance. Lack of good circulation and constant pressure on areas of the back of a patient confined to lying on the back causes bed sores. Bones decalcify from lack of muscular activity, and in very long periods of bed rest bone deterioration may be so great that strenuous muscular contraction can cause a bone to break. Appetite is affected by bed rest. Although less energy foods are required, the patient may become so finicky about eating that it becomes difficult for the patient to ingest sufficient amounts of the nutrients needed by the body. Defecation is difficult for inactive persons. Postoperative patients confined to complete bed rest are frequently bothered with distressing gas pains and difficulty in urination. Moreover, evidence indicates that postoperative patients confined to complete bed rest are more susceptible to pneumonia and thrombophlebitis (inflammation and clotting of blood in the veins).

A rehabilitation program of exercises can offset these undesirable consequences of extended confinement to bed. Participation in adapted exercises and games helps to maintain good circulation and prevent the deterioration of muscular strength, endurance, and coordination. Susceptibility to disease is decreased. Appetites are more likely to be stimulated because the patient is hungrier and more interested in food. Difficulties in elimination are reduced because of the beneficial effects of the exercise.

Special education programs, including physical education experiences, as mandated by Public Law 101-476 must be provided for the convalescing student. The physical education experience should, of course, be appropriate to the health needs of the individual and consistent with the overall medical plan for the student. Those students confined to a hospital bed and unable to participate in an exercise program can benefit from physical education instruction by receiving information about various aspects of physical fitness and motor fitness. Instructions and assignments can be developed to assist convalescing students to improve their understanding of the importance of exercise and its relationship to total well-being. Special efforts also can be extended to help students appreciate the importance of rehabilitative exercises for improving the function of injured muscles and joints. Individuals who have experienced damage to a joint, for instance, can benefit from information about the structure and function of the damaged area. In consultation with the medical team, specific rehabilitative exercises and an overall plan of general physical conditioning can be developed.

In the late stage of convalescence, the patient is no longer confined to bed and is able to resume many former activities, including returning to school if of school age. The convalescent will experience fatigue sooner and will have less strength and endurance than before confinement;

appetite and capacity for restful sleep also may be less. However, all of these aspects of the person's health will be much improved over what they were in the early stage of convalescence, particularly if the patient has been engaging in an exercise program. Full recovery can be hastened by a carefully planned program of exercise and activities.

Some convalescing students who are able to return to school will have had such serious injuries or illnesses that adaptation of the physical education activities is needed not only during convalescence but also for the remainder of their time as physical education students. Others will have less lasting effects but may require frequent rest periods and participation in mild forms of activities until endurance and strength begin to return.

There are some disorders that may interfere only temporarily with participation in regular physical education and so require special consideration just for the duration of the condition. Among the most common of these are athletic injuries, contagious and infectious diseases, and skin disorders.

Common Athletic Injuries

Certain injuries, resulting particularly from sports participation, occur more frequently than others among the school population. Because they are so common, it is desirable for the physical education teacher to have specific knowledge about these.

Ankle and Foot Injuries

The most common ankle injury is a hyperinversion sprain caused by excessive inward turning.[1] In this type of sprain, the lateral collateral (situated at the side) ligaments are stretched or torn, and immobilization of the ankle by strapping is usually necessary. The area around the ankle is tender and the individual finds it difficult to walk. As the injury heals, walking becomes easier but the injured area remains highly vulnerable to further injury from running or sudden twisting and turning.

Fractures to the ankle usually occur to the lateral malleolus. This type of fracture is often called a sprain fracture (figure 16.4). In the foot the most common fracture occurs to the anterior portion consisting of the metatarsals (small bones in the front of the foot) and phalanges (toes) of the foot. In almost all cases, foot or ankle fractures are immobilized by a cast. The individual may be provided with a walking cast that will bear his or her weight, or the cast may be such that the use of crutches is required for walking. After the cast is removed, the area needs protection from severe stress for some time.

---

[1]A sprain refers to the tearing or stretching of ligaments and tendons, whereas a strain refers to the tearing of muscles.

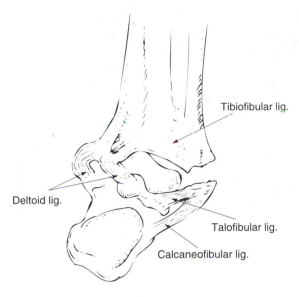

Figure 16.4 Sprain fracture of lateral malleolus.

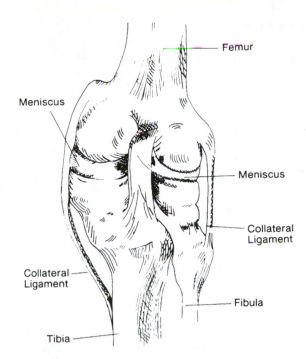

Figure 16.5 Posterior (rear) view of right knee joint.

Knee and Leg Injuries

Knee injuries that are most common are medial collateral ligament sprain, cruciate ligament sprain, and meniscus tear (figure 16.5). The ligament injuries result in an unstable knee; that is, the ligaments may not hold the femur and the tibia in proper relationship to each other. A meniscus tear may cause an inability to move the knee if the cartilage becomes displaced, causing the joint to lock.

If severe, these injuries to the knee cause the quadriceps (extensor muscle of the thigh) to atrophy and become weaker. Atrophy and accompanying weakness also occur after surgery to the knee. A specific conditioning program is necessary to prevent atrophy and weakness and to restore strength.

Sprains and Strains of the Spinal Column

The discussion here is concerned only with those injuries of the spine that involve muscles, ligaments, and tendons; injury to the spinal nerves is discussed in chapter 9.

The neck area is highly vulnerable to sprain and strain. Those with a history of neck injury often experience a recurrence as the result of a sudden twist, forced hyperextension, or a quick snap of the head. Those who have experienced a lower spinal injury are also subject to a recurrence produced by suddenly twisting the trunk, bending violently from the waist, or lifting a weight while the back is bent. Youngsters with weak abdominal muscles and tight hamstring muscles that result in faulty vertebral alignment are susceptible to low back injury and low back pain, a subject discussed in chapter 28, *Posture and Body Awareness*.

Shoulder Girdle, Arm and Hand Injuries

Common injuries to these areas are strains to the rotator cuff (four muscles that cover the head of the humerus and attach to the scapula) in the shoulder joint, dislocation of the joint, fracture of the clavicle (collarbone), and fractures of the ulna and radius (bones in the forearm) and of the small bones of the wrist. The fractures are usually immobilized by a cast for a period of time while the strains and sprains may be partially immobilized by strapping. The injured area is tender for a period of time; and even after the cast or strapping is removed, it is highly vulnerable to reinjury by excessive force. Each time a shoulder dislocation occurs, the ligaments and tendons are stretched so that the possibility of a recurrence of the dislocation is greater. An individual with recurring dislocation must avoid strenuous activities that necessitate raising the elbow higher than the shoulder.

Contagious and Infectious Diseases

There are several contagious and infectious diseases that school children are likely to contract. Among them are influenza, pneumonia, streptococcal diseases, and infectious mononucleosis. Students returning to school[2] after the acute stage of illness has passed exhibit extreme fatigue and lack of endurance and strength for some time. During the completion of their convalescence, they should engage in developmental activities selected for their special needs.

---

[2]No student who has had a contagious disease should be allowed to return to school until the disease is no longer contagious and permission for return has been given by the attending physician.

Skin Disorders

There are several types of skin disorders that may require adaptation of the physical education activities while the student is suffering from them.

Blisters

Blisters on the foot or certain other parts of the body may become so severe that withdrawal from certain types of physical education activities is necessitated. In a blister, pinching or continual irritation causes the epidermis to separate from the dermis, and the area between the two layers fills with fluid. If only the epidermis is involved in the injury, the area fills with the water-like fluid of the blood to produce a water blister. If, however, the dermis is also injured, the area fills with blood, resulting in a blood blister.

Blisters occurring on the feet, usually water blisters, may cause temporary difficulty in activity participation. First aid measures to open the blister are usually not desirable unless there is indication that the blister will be caused to break open by further irritation of the area. The opening of the blister should be done with a sterile instrument and the wound kept as sterile as possible. Proper padding around the broken or unbroken blister to reduce the pressure on the area will permit the student to participate without further irritation.

If participation in regular physical education is contraindicated because of the additional stress and strain that would be placed on the blistered area by the nature of the activities, the students may engage in activities that require little foot movement, such as ring toss, table tennis, and shuffleboard. The shoes may be removed for these activities, but other activities in which running is an element should not be permitted without proper shoes because of the danger of slipping.

Corns, Calluses, Warts, and Bunions

Students with corns, calluses, warts, or bunions may require medical attention before they are able to participate without pain in unrestricted activities. Securing better-fitting shoes or a better adjustment of the old shoes may relieve the condition sufficiently to permit participation. Padding to take the pressure off the area is also possible. In situations where such remedial action cannot be taken, the student may be placed in the special class for adapted activities of the same nature as those recommended above for students with blisters.

Contagious Skin Diseases

Some communicable diseases and disturbances of the skin require dismissal from school until the condition is no longer contagious. Among these are impetigo, a dermatitis with small blisters that break and crust; pediculosis, an infection with head, body, or crab lice; and scabies, commonly called the seven-year itch, due to infestation of the skin with a very small mite that buries itself in the skin.

Athlete's Foot

Ringworm of the foot, commonly called athlete's foot, once believed to be highly communicable, is not readily transferred. Students affected with ringworm need not be excluded from the use of the shower room and swimming pool as was once a common practice. The disease responds readily to treatment and usually does not interfere with participation. However, a severe case may be very painful, and in this event the student should be placed in activities that do not require much foot movement.

Boils

Boils are caused by an infection produced by bacteria entering the hair follicle. Boils are readily transmitted from one part of the body to another. They should be protected with a sterile dressing in order to prevent spreading the infection. If a boil occurs in an area such as the groin or axillary region where movement might tend to irritate it, the student should not be required to participate in activities requiring the movement of the involved area but should instead participate in modified activities. Running activities are contraindicated for boils in the groin area, and arm movements for boils in the axillary region.

The Program for Convalescing Students

Convalescing students who have recuperated sufficiently to return to school should participate in specially designed programs; during this time they may be given physical fitness or posture exercises and adapted activities as their special needs require. Participation in physical education that is suited to their special needs and abilities during the last stage of convalescence will help the students regain more quickly their former level of physical fitness, strengthen the weakened area if a particular part of the body was affected, continue their general improvement of motor skills, and achieve the feeling of well-being that is so important to complete recovery.

The physical education teacher may expect to plan activities for students in all five classifications of convalescence, including obstetrics (adolescent girls who are returning to school after giving birth or having an abortion). In all cases, medical consultation with the student's physician about the adapted activities should be sought before the student begins activity. Under no condition, however, should the student be removed from physical education. If the physician feels that all activity should be contraindicated, a clarification should be sought as to whether this includes modified activities of low intensity, such as a program of relaxation and rhythmic activities. The forum in which these discussions should occur is the Individualized Education Program meeting. There are very few instances in which an informed group of professionals will recommend no physical education activity. Modifications can and should be made including, if necessary, a program that emphasizes concepts and understanding about exercise, fitness, and sport rather than activity per se.

Physical education encompasses many activities and methods of instruction; modifications in activity and appropriate programs can be developed for all children. Most students who have been confined to bed in their homes will return to school with a very low level of fitness and should not attempt the same amount of activity as they engaged in before their confinement. If there was no injury to a specific area, the exercises and activities described in chapter 27 for low physical fitness may be used with these students. Some mild and easily regulated games in which older students may participate are volleyball, bowling, shuffleboard, deck tennis, table tennis, archery, horseshoes, and bowling on the green.

In situations where there has been injury to a specific area, a special exercise may be given to strengthen that part and to develop total body fitness. The first seven to ten days that a student is on crutches, the activity of walking is in itself sufficient overload for the upper arm area. Isometric muscular contractions can be used to exercise the muscles of the limb that is immobilized in a cast. Students with limbs in casts will want to avoid excessive perspiration in their workouts, because perspiration collects in the cast. If the activities can be performed in a cool area, undue perspiration usually can be avoided.

Games recommended for students with orthopedic disabilities are suitable for grade school and high school students with legs and arms in casts. Students in whom a specific area of the body has been weakened by injury or infection require special precautions to protect the area from further injury during exercises that build up the strength of the area or increase general body strength. When bones have been broken, joints sprained, or other parts of the body have suffered injuries, activities chosen for participation should be those that will not place undue stress and strain upon the area. In the cases of shoulder dislocation, knee instability, and ankle sprains, the muscles of the areas involved can be strengthened by exercise to prevent the recurrence of the injury.

To increase strength through exercise, the muscles involved must be given an overload. For a continuous increase in muscular strength, an overload must be applied to the muscle systematically. In doing so, it must be recognized that even an area of the body that may ultimately benefit from exercise may not tolerate activity during the acutely painful stage of recovering from an injury. Consequently, exercise should not be started until it is recommended by the physician of the convalescing student. The exercises, when they are initiated, must be moderate. They should not be done when the muscles are very tired and should be terminated at any time that a sharp pain occurs. If weights are used in the exercises, the load to be carried should be of an amount that is easily lifted by the injured part and yet provides a small overload.

Exercise that increases the strength of the muscles of the shoulder and shoulder girdle, especially the rotator cuff, tends to stabilize a shoulder that is susceptible to dislocation. The rotator cuff tends to hold the head of the humerus in the glenoid fossa, thus preventing displacement during abduction. It abducts and rotates the humerus. Resistance applied to the arm while abducting and laterally rotating the arm increases the strength of the muscles. All exercises that require raising the arm over the head creating a possibility of pressure on the arm, as in basketball, overhand swimming, and volleyball, are contraindicated. A type of belt and arm strap, shown in figure 16.6, may be used to prevent extreme abduction of the arm and yet permit the student to engage in regular activities. An example of a developmental exercise program is presented in the following:

Phase I Move the shoulder through a wide range of motions, stopping when pain is felt. With the waist bent and arms hanging loosely at the side (pendular exercise position), perform shoulder movements in all directions. Apply light resistance as progress is made.

Phase II In an upright position, continue to work on increasing the shoulder's range of motion. Two exercises that are excellent for increasing range of motion are the use of the shoulder wheel and a towel routine. The shoulder wheel improves flexibility while increasing rotary movement. A rolled up towel held by its ends in the hands, is helpful in stretching the shoulder muscles as various movements are made.

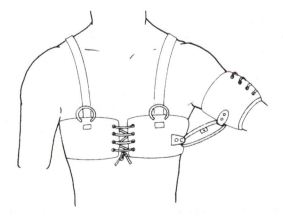

Figure 16.6 A belt with arm straps prevents extreme abduction of the arm.

Phase III Apply resistance to improve the strength of the shoulder. Some exercises using dumbbells that are helpful include shoulder shrugs, pushups, alternate press, double side-arm lift, shoulder extension, and shoulder flexion. Abduction and lateral rotation should be stressed.

Activities that do not place undue stress upon an injured shoulder include:

> weight lifting (avoid all lifts that raise the arm
>   overhead)
> pulley weights (same precaution as above)
> table tennis
> shuffleboard
> golf
> track
> swimming the side stroke
> racquet games, if the weak shoulder is not involved
> exercise on the shoulder wheel
> all basic skill games and activities that do not require
>   lifting the arm above the shoulder

Exercises that increase the strength of the quadriceps femoris of the leg tend to stabilize the knee by exerting more pull upon the patella, which in turn holds the tibia in closer contact in the joint with the femur. An exercise that is frequently used to strengthen the quadriceps femoris uses a knee exercise machine. Using light resistance, the subject sits on the table, straightens the knee, and returns the leg to the original position. Other exercises that are helpful include isometric muscle contraction known as "quad setting." As the student's condition improves, straight leg raises, from both a sitting position with hip flexion and a prone position, should be used. Exercises such as toe raises should also be performed to strengthen the gastrocnemius and hamstring muscles. These muscles are very important in supplying support and stability to the knee. Individuals with unstable knees may participate in activities and games that do not place undue stress upon the knee. Among these are the following:

> jogging (increasing the speed and sharp turns slowly)
> horseshoes
> shuffleboard
> table tennis
> bowling
> swimming

As the initial soreness of an ankle sprain decreases and walking is permitted, exercises may be given to promote healing and increase the strength of the muscles involved (peroneus longus and peroneus brevis) in preventing the foot from inverting accidentally. Forced inversion causes the majority of ankle sprains. Suggested exercises are the following:

> ankle circumduction
> gripping and spreading toes
> standing and walking on tiptoes
> walking on heels
> walking on inside of foot
> walking on outside of foot
> toe raises against resistance
> rope jumping

The kind of exercise recommended for the back that has suffered a sprain or strain depends upon the nature and degree of injury sustained. In almost all cases in which exercise is not contraindicated, muscular activity designed to improve the relationship of the pelvis and the sacrum with the lumbar spine—that is, to flatten out the small of the back—is appropriate. This is of special value to those with low back pain due to poor alignment of the pelvis and sacrum with the lumbar spine. The exercises are graded according to severity. In starting an exercise program for the back, the first two exercises should be given over a period of days before progressing to the more difficult ones.

1. The student assumes a supine position on a hard surface with the hips and knees flexed. The chin is tucked to the chest by placing a pillow under the head, and the small of the back is pressed hard against the floor.

2. The same position as before is taken. One knee is brought up to the forehead in an attempt to make contact with it. The hands are wrapped around the knee to help pull it toward the forehead. The other leg maintains its original position. The exercise is repeated with the opposite knee.

3. The same position as before is assumed. One leg is straightened and raised straight into the air. The leg is held in this position a few seconds and then returned. The exercise is repeated with the other leg. Caution must be taken by anyone with a ruptured disc.

4. A supine position is taken on a hard surface with the legs straight. The head and shoulders are lifted slightly off the floor and held for a few seconds and then returned. To increase the strenuousness of the activity, the hips can be flexed and the feet placed flat on the surface. While the feet are held down by a helper, the student executes a sit-up. This exercise should not be performed by one who has had a recent compression fracture or who has osteoporosis (abnormal rarefaction of bone) of the spine.

Resistive exercises to the arms and shoulders for one who has had a back injury should be performed with the back in an upright position. To supply added support to the back, the individual can be seated with his or her back resting against a support.

Activities for Young Children

Elementary school children returning to school after illness or injury can be readily accommodated in the physical education program if the problem-solving method is being utilized, for each can work at his or her own capacity. This does not mean, however, that the children will not need some help from the teacher in setting up guidelines as to the kind of movement and the amount of exertion that are appropriate for their individual cases. The teacher should construct the problems to be solved in such a way as to avoid overexertion and possible harm to the area of the body that is recovering from injury. Also, the problems may be designed so that in solving them, conditioning exercises are applied to the weakened area; however, it is necessary in this situation to prevent experimentation or exploration that is likely to involve contraindicated movements.

Many of the basic skill games can be played with or without adaptation by convalescing children. The games that require only moderate expenditure of energy, such as target toss, balancing a beanbag on the head, and Circle Ball, can be performed by those who cannot engage in strenuous exercise but need moderate conditioning activity. For youngsters who require protection of an injured area, the selection of games can be made from among those that do not involve that part of the body; for example, a child recovering from a broken clavicle can participate in Line Relay or Cross Tag.

Acquired Immune Deficiency Syndrome (AIDS)

One of the most recent and most serious health problems confronting the United States is the acquired immunodeficiency syndrome, commonly referred to as AIDS. First diagnosed in 1981, AIDS is caused by a virus that can destroy the body's ability to combat infection. Without the protection of the immune system, individuals with AIDS can acquire diseases that lead to death. The virus which causes AIDS has been given different names. The shortened form of some of the names are HIV, HTLV-III, or LAV[3] with HIV now the preferred term of many scientists.

When the AIDS virus enters the bloodstream, it begins to attack certain white blood cells. Antibodies produced can be detected by a simple blood test given two weeks to three months after infection.

Once an individual is infected, there are several possible outcomes. Some people may remain well but are able to infect others. Others may develop a disease referred to as AIDS Related Complex (ARC). Signs and symptoms of ARC include loss of appetite, weight loss, fever, night sweats, skin rashes, diarrhea, tiredness, lack of resistance to infection, or swollen lymph nodes. In some individuals infected by the AIDS virus, the protective immune system

may be destroyed by the virus and then other germs and cancers use the lowered resistance to infect and destroy. These diseases are referred to as the "opportunistic diseases" because they use the opportunity created by the defective immune system to cause serious damage, resulting in death. The most common illnesses of those with AIDS are a lung infection called pneumocystis carinii pneumonia and a cancer, Kaposi's sarcoma. Evidence shows that the AIDS virus may also attack the nervous system, causing damage to the brain.

Estimates now place the number of individuals in the United States infected with the AIDS virus to be about 1 million (Surgeon General's Report, 1993). While all of these individuals are assumed to be capable of spreading the virus through sexual activity or the sharing of needles and other paraphernalia used by drug abusers, it is estimated that 100,00 to 200,000 will come down with AIDS Related Complex (ARC). In the United States, over 25,000 individuals have been diagnosed with AIDS; half have died of the disease. Since there is no cure, the other half are also expected to eventually die from the disease. Most disturbing is the realization an estimated 179,000 deaths will have occurred within the decade since the disease was first recognized. The number of young children with AIDS is also alarming. In table 16.6, the number of AIDS cases for children 13 years of age and younger is summarized.

Transmission of the AIDS Virus

AIDS is transmitted by contact with certain body fluids, mainly semen and blood. A person gets the virus by exposure to these infected body fluids. There are three primary ways the AIDS virus can be transmitted.

Table 16.6 *New AIDS cases each year among children 13 years of age and younger, United States, 1982–1992*

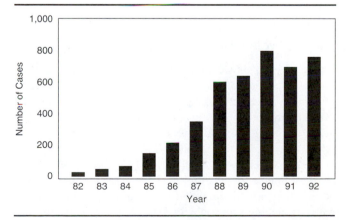

Source: Surgeon General's Report to the American Public on HIV Infection and AIDS (1993), p. 3.

---

[3]human immunodeficiency virus (HIV)
human T-lymphotropic virus type III (HTLV-III)
lymphadenopathy-associated virus (LAV)

1. Sexual contact. Intimate sexual contact is the most common way the AIDS virus is transmitted. If an infected person exchanges blood or semen during anal or vaginal intercourse, he/she can pass the virus. Oral-genital or oral-anal sex may also be ways the AIDS virus is transmitted. Contrary to popular thought, anyone heterosexual, homosexual, or bisexual engaging in risky sexual or drug abusing behavior with an infected person can acquire the AIDS virus.

2. Exchange of blood. Blood to blood contact between an infected person and someone else is the second most common way to contract AIDS. This method of transmission is normally associated with the use of illicit drugs through the sharing of IV drug needles and syringes.

   Unfortunately before much was known or understood about AIDS, some individuals with hemophilia became infected when undergoing blood transfusions. Today, the screening of donated blood is such that the chances of getting AIDS from blood transfusions is about one in a million (Yarber, 1987).

3. Mother to child. One of the tragedies of the AIDS epidemic is that innocent children can get the AIDS virus from their infected mothers. This can occur during pregnancy, childbirth, or breast feeding. Approximately 1 percent of AIDS cases in the United States occur in children. Not every child of an infected mother acquires the virus.

The major risk groups for contracting AIDS are homosexual and bisexual men (74 percent), heterosexual IV drug abusers (17 percent), heterosexual sex partners of persons with AIDS or at risk for AIDS (4 percent), and recipients of transfused blood or blood-clotting factor (3 percent). Future predictions suggest that the number of infected heterosexual men and women will increase gradually. Infection due to blood transfusions will decrease dramatically due to the safer and more rigorous monitoring of donors and the testing of donated blood.

Students with AIDS

There has been considerable controversy generated concerning the education of students with AIDS. Some school districts have argued that these children pose a health threat to teachers and other students. These worries are unfounded. Scientific evidence has repeatedly demonstrated that the AIDS virus is hard to transmit and is passed only during intimate sexual behavior, the sharing of IV drug needles, and from an infected woman to her fetus. The AIDS virus cannot be transmitted through casual contact such as eating with or touching a person with AIDS. While it is true that the AIDS virus has been found in tears and saliva, the amount of virus in these fluids is very small and there have been no reported cases where the virus was passed through these fluids. For these reasons, students with AIDS are covered under the provisions of PL 101-476 and should be enrolled in school and encouraged to participate in all activities of which they are capable. Consultation with the student's physician will assist in the development of an appropriate individualized educational plan.

Program Planning

There is very little known about physical activity programs for students with AIDS. Because the disease is fatal, close articulation and coordination with the student's family and physician is essential. In general, these students should be encouraged to participate to the extent their medical condition will permit. Swimming is an appropriate activity and one which most students with AIDS will find enjoyable. Contrary to what some might argue, no one has caught AIDS from the water in the swimming pool. In addition, these students should be encouraged to participate in normal childhood activities, with modifications as appropriate.

The needs of students who have been infected but who do not have AIDS varies. Some of these individuals remain healthy with no apparent symptoms of illness. Others may develop the AIDS-related complex (ARC) and may develop symptoms such as loss of appetite, weight loss, fever, night sweats, skin rashes, diarrhea, lack of resistance to infection or swollen lymph nodes. The needs of each student must be carefully weighed and appropriate modifications in activities made. The ultimate goal is to include these students in as many activities as possible. Because of the possibility of injury and blood loss in a physical education class, many questions have surfaced concerning first aid procedures. Although the risk of contracting the AIDS virus from giving first aid is extremely small, the risk can be further minimized by adhering to the following guidelines when giving first aid to a person with a bleeding injury.

> Wear disposable plastic or latex gloves.
> Clean any blood spills with soap and water and use a disinfectant, such as bleach, afterwards.
> Put any blood-soaked items that need to be laundered or thrown away in a plastic bag.
> Wash your hands with soap and water when finished.

Several authorities have articulated that students with AIDS should be received positively in educational programs. Surburg (1988) cautions that these students should not be viewed as a potential problem, but as pupils who deserve an appropriate physical education program. Based on current knowledge, participation in sports carries virtually no risk for getting HIV (Surgeon General's Report, 1993). The only real concern, of course, is when bleeding occurs as a result of contact in a sport. In these instances, proper measures should be taken, including removing the injured student from the activity until the bleeding stops. It is unnecessary, however, to develop more restrictive policies. One authority, recognizing the poor prognosis for children with AIDS, aptly stated "AIDS patients have little time to enjoy life. Let's not waste this time of theirs by forgetting that they are still living" (Buckingham, 1989, p. 117).

Because new information is being generated daily and there is so much that is not known about AIDS, teachers should make frequent use of the numerous resources which have been established at the federal and state levels to assist professionals in understanding AIDS. To locate these and other sources of helpful information, readers should use the AIDS national hotline 1–800–342–AIDS.

Summary

Several disorders collectively classified as "other conditions" or "other health impairments" including nephritis, diabetes, epilepsy, anemia, hemophilia, and AIDS were discussed in this chapter. In addition, minor or temporary problems such as athletic injuries, illnesses, and dysmenorrhea were presented. Emphasis was placed on the importance of physical activity in the lives of individuals with permanent as well as temporary health impairments. Public Law 101-476 is very clear that children with conditions such as diabetes, epilepsy, and hemophilia are entitled to all of the educational provisions provided by this law. Therefore, these youngsters should receive physical education programs with modifications as necessary. The intent of the law is consistent with recent studies that have found that students with health impairments benefit from regular exercise and activity programs. Improvements in overall health as well as an enhanced sense of self-worth have been reported. The medical community, too, has indicated that children with health impairments should be encouraged to participate in activity programs to the extent possible. There is a growing awareness that denying these youngsters the opportunity to participate in physical activity programs may interfere with their overall health as well as eliminate one of the important aspects of child development. All children deserve the opportunity to learn to play and exercise and participate in game, exercise, and sport activities with other children.

Much remains to be done, however. Some educators and school systems still have very restrictive policies concerning students with selected health impairments such as epilepsy and hemophilia. There is an implied message: "We would prefer you not participate." Some physicians, too, have discouraged children from leading active lives by recommending that they be excused from physical education classes. Some physical educators, too, have implied that they are not willing to modify or make special arrangements for students with health impairments. These attitudes, beliefs, and inappropriate practices must be eliminated, and they will be. The change will be brought about by professionals who are current in their thinking and knowledge regarding students with health impairments and by students who will demonstrate by action that a health impairment need not be a delimiting condition.

Selected Readings

Adams, R., & McCubbin, J. (1991). *Games, sports, and exercises for the physically disabled* (4th ed.). Philadelphia: Lea and Febiger.

American Medical Association. (1974). Epileptics and contact sports: Position paper. *Journal of American Medical Association, 229,* 820–821.

Berg, K.E. (1986). *Diabetic's guide to health and fitness.* Champaign, IL: Life Enhancement Publications.

Biermann, J., & Toohey, B. (1977). *The diabetic's sports and exercise book.* Philadelphia: J.B. Lippincott.

Billig, H.E., Jr. (1943). Dysmenorrhea: The result of postural defect. *Archives of Surgery, 46,* 611.

Boshell, B. (1971). *The diabetic at work and play.* Springfield, IL: Charles C. Thomas.

Boshes, L.D., & Gibbs, F.A. (1972). *Epilepsy handbook* (2d ed.). Springfield, IL: Charles C. Thomas.

Buckingham, R.W. (1989). *Care of the dying child.* New York: Continuum.

Cantu, R.C. (1982). *Diabetes and exercise.* New York: E.P. Dutton Inc.

Department of Health, Education, and Welfare, Office of Education. (1987, August 23). Education of handicapped children, part II, implementation of part B of the Education of the Handicapped Act. *Federal Register,* 42478.

Duda, M. (1985). The role of exercise in managing diabetes. *The Physician and Sports Medicine, 13,* 164–170.

Etzwiler, D.D. (1991). Diabetes: The light grows brighter. In M.J. Franz, D.D. Etzwiler, J.O. Joynes, and P.M. Hollander (Eds.), *Learning to live with diabetes.* Minneapolis: DCI.

Falconer, S.D. (1967). The inheritance of liability to diseases with variable age of onset with particular reference of diabetes mellitus. *Annals of Human Genetics, 31,* 1–20.

Golub, L.J. (1959, July). A new exercise for dysmenorrhea. *American Journal of Obstetrics and Gynecology, 78,* 152–155.

Graff, J.C., Ault, M.M., Guess, D., Taylor, M., & Thompson, B. (1990). *Health care for students with disabilities.* Baltimore: Paul H. Brookes Publishing Co.

Henry, R.R., & Eddelman, S.V. (1992). Advances in treatment of Type II diabetes mellitus in the elderly. *Geriatrics, 47,* 24–30.

Jette, D.U. (1984). Physiological effects of exercise in the diabetic. *Physical Therapy, 64,* 339–342.

Jung, K. (1982). Physical exercise therapy in juvenile diabetes mellitus. *Journal of Sports Medicine, 22,* 23–31.

Klafs, C.E., & Arnheim, D.D. (1981). *Modern principles of athletic training* (5th ed.). St. Louis: C.V. Mosby Co.

Knox, K.R. (1975). Management of the diabetic child. In H.F. Conn (Ed.), *Current therapy 1975.* Philadelphia: W.B. Saunders Co.

Krall, L.P. (1978). *Joslin diabetes manual* (11th ed.). Philadelphia: Lea and Febiger.

Leon, A.S. (1993). Diabetes. In J.S. Skinner (Ed.), *Exercise testing and exercise prescription for special cases* (2nd ed.) (pp. 115–133). Philadelphia: Lea and Febiger.

Love, H.D., & Walthall, J.E. (1977). *A handbook of medical, educational, and psychological information for teachers of physically handicapped children.* Springfield, IL: Charles C. Thomas.

Marlow, D.R. (1973). *Textbook of pediatric nursing.* Philadelphia: W. B. Saunders Co.

Mosher, C.D. (1914). Dysmenorrhea. *Journal of the American Medical Association, 62,* 1297.

Mullins, J.B. (1979). *A teacher's guide to management of physically handicapped students.* Springfield, IL: Charles C. Thomas.

National Hemophilia Foundation and American Red Cross. (n.d.). *Hemophilia and sports.* New York.

O'Donoghue, D.H. (1970). *Treatment of injuries to athletes* (2d ed.). Philadelphia: W.B. Saunders Co.

Richter, E.A., Ruderman, N.B., & Schneider, S.H. (1981). Diabetes and exercise. *The American Journal of Medicine, 70,* 201–209.

Riley, W.J., & Rosenbloom, A.L. (1980). Exercise and insulin dependent diabetes mellitus. *Journal of Florida Medical Association, 67,* 392–394.

Rimmer, J. (1994). *Fitness and rehabilitation programs for special populations.* Dubuque, IA: Brown and Benchmark.

Sherrill, C. (1993). *Adapted physical education and recreation* (4th ed.). Dubuque, IA: Wm. C. Brown Publishers.

Song, J. (1971). *Pathology of sickle cell disease.* Springfield, IL: Charles C. Thomas.

Surburg, P.R. (1988). Are adapted physical educators ready for students with AIDS? *Adapted Physical Activity Quarterly, 5,* (4) pp. 259–263.

Surgeon General's Report to the American Public on HIV Infection and AIDS. (1993). Rockville, MD: Centers for Disease Control and Prevention, National Institute of Health.

West, K.M. (1978). *Epidemiology of diabetes and its vascular lesions.* New York: Elsevier North-Holland, Inc.

Yarber, W.L. (1987). *Aids education: curriculum and health policy.* Bloomington, IN: Phi Delta Kappan Educational Foundation.

Enhancing Activities

1. Identify national and state organizations that promote and advocate for individuals with the health impairments discussed in this chapter. Select one of the organizations and write to it to obtain information about its position concerning physical activity.

2. Obtain a copy of the local school district's policy regarding excuses from physical education. Is the policy consistent with the intent of P.L. 101-476? Are health-impaired youngsters receiving instruction in physical education?

3. Interview a person with diabetes or one of the other health impairments discussed in this chapter and, based on the information provided, develop a recommended exercise and activity program for the individual.

4. Develop a list of noteworthy people (celebrities, politicians, athletes, etc.) who have one of the health impairments described in this chapter. For some of the individuals, determine, if you can, what effect the disorder has played in their lives.

5. Obtain and review a copy of the American Medical Association's position paper on epilepsy, diabetes, and hemophilia.

6. Ask a person with epilepsy to share his or her feelings about this condition and the effect it has had on the individual's life. What positive or negative effect, if any, has sport and physical education had on the person's life?

CHAPTER
17

Mental Retardation

CHAPTER OBJECTIVES

After studying this chapter, the reader should be able to:

1 Recognize and understand the nature of mental retardation, its causes, classification systems, and prevalence.

2 Identify the learning, social, and emotional characteristics of individuals with mental retardation, appreciating the similarities and differences associated with this disorder.

3 Plan and implement a physical education program that is sensitive to and consistent with the needs of people who are mentally retarded.

4 Appreciate the diversity of talent and ability among individuals with mental retardation.

5 Comprehend the importance of utilizing a systematic instructional process when teaching physical education to those with mental retardation.

6 Explain the unique physical and motor characteristics of the Down syndrome population, including the propensity toward obesity, atlantoaxial instability, and congenital heart defects.

7 State the definition of mental retardation and the criteria for identifying someone as mentally retarded.

8 Evaluate the needs of students with mental retardation and identify selected motor learning concepts that can be applied to this population.

9 Explain why it is essential that there be close coordination between the school-based physical education program and services offered by other agencies such as the community park and recreation departments and sport organizations such as Special Olympics.

10 Defend the statement that most youngsters with mental retardation should receive their physical education program with nondisabled youngsters.

It is well documented that physical activity can make a major contribution in the lives of children and adults with and without mental retardation (Bar-Or, 1983; McCubbin, Frey, and Lavay, 1992; Savage et al., 1986; Seefeldt and Vogel, 1987). This includes participation in sports, recreation, and physical activities that lead to physical, psychological, and social development. Yet until recently, individuals with mental retardation were left on their own for physical activity or worse, excluded from it altogether (Eichstaedt and Lavay, 1992).

In 1970, Rarick and colleagues reported only 25 percent of students who were educably mentally retarded received more than an hour of physical education each week while 45 percent received no physical education. Since this time there have been many legislative, vocational, academic, and favorable attitudinal gains toward individuals with mental retardation. Today, opportunities for individuals with mental retardation to learn with their nondisabled peers, participate in structured recreational programs, hold jobs, and even marry are commonplace. Unfortunately, societies have not always accepted individuals with mental retardation.

Throughout history, individuals with mental retardation were persecuted, punished, enslaved, and frequently punished until death. It wasn't until the end of the eighteenth century that the work of Itard began what is today Special Education. More recently, the end of World War II saw individuals with mental retardation given the opportunity to participate in physical education. Finally, in 1965 physical education for students with mental retardation became a special interest to the profession. At this time the American Association of Health, Physical Education and Recreation (AAHPER[1]), in cooperation with the Joseph P. Kennedy, Jr., Foundation, established the Project on Recreation and Fitness for the Mentally Retarded to provide assistance and encouragement to schools and community agencies in the development of programs of recreation and fitness activities for those with mental retardation. The Special Olympics program, sponsored by the Joseph P. Kennedy, Jr., Foundation, also has contributed significantly to increased awareness of educators and the public to the value of physical activity for individuals with mental retardation.

Early researchers such as Cratty (1969), Fait and Kupferer (1959), and Rarick and his colleagues (1970) investigated the impact that participation in physical activities played on the lives of individuals with mental retardation. Since this time, considerable advances have been made in our understanding of the importance of training and participation in physical activities for this population. Today, individuals with mental retardation participate in Little League Baseball, run in the Boston, Portland and other famous marathons, and participate in their own World Games (formerly Special Olympics International Games) in which more athletes and countries participate than in the "regular" Olympics. Recognition that persons with mental retardation can learn is attributed to a large extent to the work of Jean Itard, a French physician. In 1799, Itard undertook a five-year program to educate an animal-like boy of twelve who was found in the forest of Aveyron, France. Although Itard considered his program a failure, others familiar with the boy observed definite improvement in the youngster's behavior. The ideas of Itard were introduced to the United States by one of his pupils, Edouard Seguin, who became superintendent of a Pennsylvania institution for the mentally retarded. During the 1800s many of the progressive ideas proposed by Seguin, such as emphasis on the whole child, individualized teaching, and good rapport between teacher and child, were incorporated into the programs of other publicly supported institutions, which were growing rapidly in number.

Defining Mental Retardation

No one definition of mental retardation has been constructed that will satisfy all the professional disciplines (medical, psychological, educational, social, and legal) concerned with this population. Throughout the world, the term mental retardation has many different meanings and definitions. Even within the United States terms such as idiot, imbecile, moron, feeble minded, and subnormal were once commonly acceptable. The phrase "individuals with mental retardation" is now used to describe this group.

Like society's changing acceptance of individuals with mental retardation, revisions have been made to the definition. Originally produced by the American Association on Mental Deficiency (AAMD), the definition of mental retardation has undergone many changes. For example, since the 1950s the definition was revised in 1959, 1972, 1983 and most recently in 1992. The most widely employed contemporary definition of mental retardation is that established by the American Association on Mental Retardation (AAMR), formerly AAMD (Luckasson et al., 1992):

> Mental retardation refers to substantial limitations in certain personal capabilities. It is manifested as significantly subaverage intellectual functioning, existing concurrently with related disabilities in two or more of the following applicable adaptive skill areas: Communication, self care, home living, social skills, community use, self direction, health and safety, functional academics, leisure and work. Mental retardation begins before the age of eighteen years.

A careful analysis of the definition clarifies some of the important considerations that must be met before classifying students as mentally retarded. Various terms used in the statement are defined as follows:

> *Limitations in personal capabilities*—These include limitations in functional, social, and cognitive capabilities.

[1]Now the American Alliance for Health, Physical Education, Recreation, and Dance (AAHPERD)

Significantly subaverage—Intellectual functioning is determined by one or more of the standardized tests developed for that purpose. Two of the most frequently used tests include the Stanford-Binet and the Wechsler, the results of which yield an intelligence quotient (IQ). The mean IQ score for the population on both tests is 100 points with a standard deviation of approximately 15 points. Performance on a standardized intelligence test of greater than two standard deviations below the mean is required before a score can be considered significantly subaverage. According to the definition, therefore, persons with mental retardation possess an intelligence quotient (IQ) of less than 68 if using the Stanford-Binet or less than 69 on the Wechsler test. Due to the arbitrary nature of these numbers, scores less than 70 also qualify under this definition.

Before the age of 18—Due to the ambiguity of the term "developmental period," as described in the earlier definition, this most recent definition clarifies this period by specifically identifying mental retardation beginning before the age of 18 years.

Adaptive skill areas—Adaptive skills are defined as the ability to meet the standards of social responsibility for a particular age group based on the level of support required in any adaptive skill. Levels of support include: (1) continuous, (2) substantial, (3) minimal, or (4) no support necessary. Because these expectations vary for different age groups, the defects in adaptive behavior vary according to age as well. During infancy and early childhood significant delays in the maturation areas of communication, self-help skills, and sensory-motor activities are potential indicators of mental retardation. During childhood and early adolescence, primary focus is centered on the ability to learn the basic academic skills. The ability to make a living and to handle oneself and one's affairs with the prudence ordinarily expected of an adult in our society is the important determinant of the presence of mental retardation. The ten adaptive skill areas identified include: (1) communication, (2) community use, (3) functional academics, (4) health and safety, (5) home living, (6) leisure, (7) self care, (8) self direction, (9) social skills, and (10) work.

Due to the dynamic concept of mental retardation, a person may meet the criteria at one point in life but not at some other time or in different environments. As explained by Grossman (1973), "A person may change status as a result of changes or alterations in his intellectual functioning, changes in his adaptive behaviors, changes in the expectations of the society, or for other known or unknown reasons." As a result, IQ is no longer the determinant of the severity of mental retardation, rather, it is determined environmentally. For example, an individual might experience significant deficits in academic abilities throughout childhood but can successfully accomplish vocational skills which find that individual functioning "normally" during adulthood.

Classification of individuals with mental retardation is made with tests which measure intelligence and adaptive skill areas. The American Association on Mental Retardation classifies mental retardation as: (1) mild, or (2) severe. This is a departure from previous definitions in that IQ scores are now not used to determine classification. Previously, mental retardation was defined as: (1) mild, 52–69; (2) moderate, 36–51; (3) severe, 20–35; and (4) profound, below 19.

Standardized tests of adaptive behavior such as the Vineland Social Maturity Scale and the American Association on Mental Deficiency Adaptive Behavior Scales are frequently employed to determine extent of impairment in adaptive skills. However, Reiss (1994) suggests that more research is "required to develop measures of the 10 adaptive behavior skills and to evaluate the effects of the new definition on schools and on various support systems" (p. 7). Although the relationship is not perfect, persons who score low on the intelligence tests often score low on the adaptive skill scales and vice versa.

Severe Classification

Individuals with severe mental retardation are almost always identified at birth or shortly thereafter. The nature of their condition is usually attributed to a central nervous system defect with associated disabling conditions. The severeness of their mental retardation is such that training will focus on the self-care and functional life skills of toileting, dressing, eating, and drinking. Assistance in helping these individuals develop language and communication skills is typically provided. An individual with severe retardation may require complete supervision and care throughout life. Recent developments in instructional technology and vocational education have provided substantial improvements in self-sufficiency for this population.

The range of movement to be found in those who are totally dependent varies from random, meaningless movements to the intricate and controlled movements required by such skills as walking, running, catching, throwing, and climbing. The kinds of movements of which they are capable depend upon mental ability, absence or presence of physical disabilities, general level of physical fitness, and past experiences in physical education. With the downsizing of traditional state hospitals and institutions, many individuals with severe mental retardation are relocated into community-based residences and group homes that allow a greater level of independence than previously thought possible.

Mild Classification

Students with mild mental retardation have difficulty learning at a rate equal to that of their peers but are capable of learning basic academic skills. They can acquire from second- to sixth-grade achievement in reading, writing, and arithmetic by the age of sixteen. Their development is approximately one-half to three-fourths as fast as the average child; consequently, their academic progress is also at one-half to three-fourths the rate of the average child. Although their communication skills may be limited, they can adequately develop skills for most situations. Most students can learn to get along with others and can acquire enough skills to support themselves economically in adulthood. Many achieve a level of self-sufficiency such that they are not recognized as having mental retardation once they leave the school setting. Frequently they hold jobs, obtain a driver's license, and live independently with no supervision. The majority of these individuals are able to participate in the same motor activities as their nondisabled peers.

The Extent of Mental Retardation

It is difficult to formulate a precise estimate on the prevalence of individuals with mental retardation. The normal distribution of intelligence (figure 17.1) shows a value of approximately 3 percent of the population, or according to the U.S. Bureau of Census report (1992), there are nearly 8 million individuals with mental retardation. However, basing prevalence estimates on IQ scores alone neglects the most important criterion for mental retardation—deficits in adaptive skills.

Recent data on the prevalence of school-age individuals with mental retardation are reflected in the findings of the United States Department of Education report for the 1989–1990 school year. It reports that nearly 2 percent or approximately 600,000 students between the ages of 6–21 were provided services by public schools and identified as having mental retardation. This figure does not include students with multiple handicaps or those enrolled in non-categorical early intervention programs. Of the nearly 5 million school children identified with disabilities, approximately 13 percent were classified with mental retardation (U.S. Bureau of Census, 1992).

With the reauthorization of P.L. 99-457, IDEA (1990) has allowed early intervention programs to identify a significant number of at-risk children who may have been previously overlooked or not properly diagnosed. The mortality rate in this group is known to be high but is difficult to document. Frequently, a baby with mental retardation may not show significant signs for months or even years after birth. Usually, however, when parents of children with mental retardation look back, they can recognize that signs were present from infancy.

At the turn of the century, the life expectancy of individuals with mental retardation was approximately nine years (Thase, 1982). Today, the life expectancy of individuals with mild retardation is probably about the same as that of other people. It is difficult to document since many individuals with mental retardation achieve a satisfactory degree of adaptive behavior and attain economic and social independence, and no longer are recognized as having mental retardation. For this reason they are often not identified and counted when community surveys are made, although most of them remain potentially vulnerable to adverse social or economic pressures. For individuals with severe mental retardation, life expectancy is substantially less, although they have been known to live to age seventy to eighty.

With the establishment of advanced medical technologies it is likely that the life expectancy of individuals with mental retardation will continue to increase. Statistics on

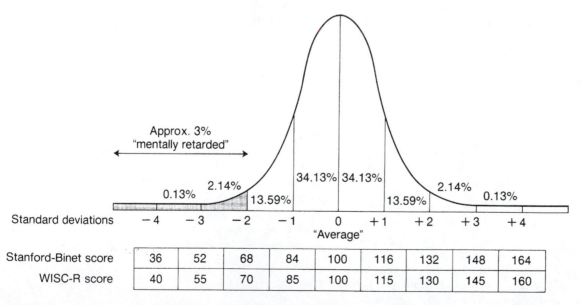

Figure 17.1   Theoretical normal distribution of intelligence.

survivorship among persons with Down syndrome, for example, indicate a much greater life expectancy for this group today than twenty or thirty years ago. As a result, the number of adults who may require help because of varying degrees of mental retardation probably is no more than 1 million to 1.25 million. Many of these persons are receiving disability or general welfare assistance or are dependent on relatives and friends. Thus, as a cause of lifetime disability and as a medical, social, and educational problem of unique extent and complexity, mental retardation today presents an outstanding challenge to science and society in the United States and throughout the world.

The Causes of Mental Retardation

Mental retardation can be caused by any condition that hinders or interferes with development before birth (prenatal), during birth (natal), or in the early childhood years (postnatal). While well over 300 causes have been identified, educators should note that teaching strategies are based on the characteristics of the student and not the cause of mental retardation.

Grossman (1973) identified ten separate etiological classifications of mental retardation, including:

Infection and Intoxication This grouping includes maternal and child infectious diseases and intoxication. Specific causes include: sexually transmitted diseases (syphilis), rubella (German measles), infections after birth (encephalitis), or anytime before or during birth (meningitis); intoxications due to alcohol (fetal alcohol syndrome), tobacco, or other drugs (cocaine). Less frequent is plumbism (lead-based poisoning) which had been the most common source of intoxication among children.

Trauma or Physical Agent Physical trauma or injury to the brain may occur prenatally, perinatally, or postnatally. This includes exposure to X rays, anoxia (lack of oxygen) during birth, or trauma to the skull due to accidents and/or child abuse causing excessive swelling, hematomas, or thrombosis.

Metabolism or Nutrition Disorders directly due to metabolic, nutritional, endocrine, or growth dysfunction should be classified under this category. More specifically, lipid storage (fatty acid) disorders such as Tay-Sachs; mineral (hypercalcemia), endocrine (thyroid dysfunctions), and carbohydrate disorders (idiopathic hypoglycemia); protein disorders such as phenylketonuria (PKU); and nutritional deficiencies (malnutrition, calorie deprivation) are found in this category.

Gross Brain Disease (Postnatal) This category includes new growths and a large number of hereditary disorders in which the cause is unknown or uncertain. Examples include von Recklinghausen's disease (a nervous disorder), multiple tumors of the skin and peripheral nerves, and tumors in the central nervous system and other organs.

Unknown Prenatal Influence This division is intended only for conditions for which no definite cause can be established but that existed at, or prior to, birth. Macrocephaly (accumulation of fluid within the cranium causing enlargement of the head), and microcephaly (insufficient skull growth) are two of the primary examples found within this category.

Chromosomal Abnormality Syndromes associated with chromosomal errors are included in this category. These disorders may be in the number or structure of chromosomes, or in both. Examples include Down syndrome, Fragile X, Prader-Willi, and Turner.

Gestational Disorders There is a high incidence of defects related to atypical gestation. Prematurity, low birth weight, and postmaturity are the primary subdivisions within this category.

Following Psychiatric Disorder Cases of retardation occurring after serious mental illness when there is no evidence of cerebral disorder due to disease fall in this category.

Environmental Influences This category is for cases in which retardation is caused by a sensory disability or by adverse environmental conditions (e.g., cultural deprivation or mistreatment) when there is no cerebral disorder due to disease. Examples include sensory disabilities such as blindness and deafness and situations such as maternal deprivation.

Other Conditions Included in this classification are cases in which there is no evidence of a physical cause or structural defect, no history of subnormal functioning in parents and siblings, and no evidence of an associated psychosocial factor.

As time goes on, more people are found to have specific diagnosable causes of their mental retardation that fit neatly into the first eight categories just discussed. Nevertheless, even today, in the majority of cases, no clear diagnosis of cause can be made, and in most of these there is no demonstrable pathology of the nervous system. Therefore, most cases of mental retardation are attributed to environmental influences and other conditions. Undoubtedly among those with mental retardation there are many people whose development has been adversely affected by nonspecific influences, such as inadequate diet, inadequate prenatal and perinatal care, and lack of adequate stimulation toward growth and development through learning opportunities. Mental development, like physical development, is promoted by the right kinds of activity and stimulation and is retarded when these are lacking. Indeed, mental and physical development tend to interact. In the developmental process, the years of early childhood when the nervous system is maturing and language is developing, are certainly very critical.

Gross Brain Disease and Mental Retardation

The term "brain damage" has not been adequately defined and is used differently by different people. Destruction of brain tissue or interference with brain development in the infant or young child frequently produces mental retardation as well as cerebral palsy, convulsive seizures, hyperactivity, and perceptual problems. Such damage accounts for a substantial percentage of severe mental retardation. Although it may be definitely shown in some cases of mild mental retardation, the extent of its contribution is not known and expert opinion is divided. Several factors may be at work in the same individual. For example, the premature infant is more vulnerable to brain damage, prematurity is more common among mothers who receive inadequate prenatal care, and inadequate prenatal care in turn is more common in the disadvantaged groups in our society; these same children are more apt to have inadequate postnatal opportunities for growth and development and to be subject to psychological and cultural deprivation.

The extent of psychomotor, perceptual, and sensory handicaps among those with mental retardation points to common causation in many cases. Most individuals with severe mental retardation have pronounced motor handicaps or impairment of hearing, vision, or speech, or a combination of several of these. Although the majority of those with mild retardation would not be readily identified as physically disabled, their general level of motor coordination is below average, despite the occurrence among them of a few remarkable athletes.

Prevention of Mental Retardation

Progress is being made in the prevention of mental retardation, but it is proceeding, as might be expected, through a succession of small advances across the broad front rather than by any spectacular breakthrough. Each of the many contributing causes must be analyzed individually, with specific preventive measures devised when the cause has been found. Steps can be taken before conception, at birth, and during childhood.

Before conception, the education of parents has perhaps had the greatest impact on the prevention of mental retardation and other disabilities. This includes the passage of federal and state laws and nationwide advertising efforts which require warning labels on medications, tobacco and alcohol products, and the implementation of mandatory seat belt laws. In addition, progress is being made in identifying the characteristics of mothers most likely to give birth prematurely, so that this indirect cause of mental retardation may

be reduced. Recent advances in science have helped physicians to identify certain genetic factors strongly associated with mental retardation. These breakthroughs have led to genetic counseling, which provides information to prospective parents about the possibility that they may give birth to a child with a disability. Other tests such as amniocentesis detect the presence of selected genetic disorders, including Down syndrome, prior to birth.

Early intervention within the United States began with President Johnson's policies on funding programs which would promote intellectual and physical development in children of lower socioeconomic backgrounds. The program began as a cost-cutting effort to minimize future costs of caring for individuals with and without disabilities. The idea being that, if a child can be provided with a positive developmental trajectory, this will allow the child opportunities to be successful earlier and hopefully over the lifespan. As a result of these policies, legal mandates have since been introduced which help identify children at risk or developmentally delayed. This includes P.L. 99-457 the Handicapped Infants and Toddlers Act of 1986.

The implementation of P.L. 99-457 follows a noncategorical approach and includes children who show delays in one or more of the following: cognitive development, physical development, psychosocial development, speech and language, and self-help skills. The focus of this legislation is to identify children at risk and to ensure they are provided educational opportunities they might not otherwise receive. This law also focuses on empowering families to get involved with the establishment of the Individual Family Service Plan (IFSP) and mandates educational programs for children ages three to five. Financial incentives are also provided to encourage services for the child and family as early as the first day of life. This law ensures that every effort is made to identify and provide needed services as early as possible. The law may have far-reaching implications for minimizing some of the deficits associated with mental retardation. Progress is being made against some of the more serious forms by such techniques as corrective surgery for malformations of the skull and the diversion of excess fluid in the brain through various shunting techniques. Infants who have inadequate blood sugar in the first few critical days after birth are now more readily identified and given corrective treatment. Damage resulting from Rh factor incompatibility can be prevented by treatment of the mother after the birth of her first child (the firstborn is not vulnerable to damage). Quick treatment in cases of lead poisoning or, better yet, action to prevent children from eating paint containing lead can undoubtedly prevent some cases. Further preventative measures include the removal of environmental contaminants, immunization of children for all preventable diseases, using bicycle helmets, seat belts, and car seats.

While all of these steps have been effective in eliminating only a relatively small fraction of mental retardation, increased attention to relevant basic and applied research and to the prompt application of new discoveries is essential in carrying forward this initial progress. Unfortunately, even with these advances, there are disturbing trends which still need to be addressed. A 1993 Centers for Disease Control report showed that the number of babies born with fetal alcohol syndrome (FAS) tripled between 1979 and 1992. Reported cases leapt from 1 per 10,000 births in 1979 to nearly 4 per 10,000 in 1992 (Facts on File, 1993) and FAS is known to contribute to health problems, including mental retardation.

Needs and Adjustments of Those with Mental Retardation

Students with mental retardation exhibit certain common characteristics, but, like their nondisabled counterparts, they vary greatly in the extent to which they demonstrate specific characteristic behaviors. This appears to be the result of the idiosyncratic characteristics of this population. Students with mental retardation may exhibit unique problems, which in the educational setting, make progress challenging. For example, secondary health problems and sensory or physical impairments may influence educational outcome. Educators must learn to recognize these common behavioral patterns while remembering, too, to search for the individual qualities that are unique to each human being.

Students with mental retardation have the same basic needs, including recreational, vocational, educational, social, and others as do their nondisabled peers. In addition, frequently these students need additional services beyond those normally provided students with mental retardation. While educational outcomes may be different, the goal should be to promote activities which are safe, functional, and age appropriate for the student.

Learning Characteristics

Essentially, the learning characteristics of students with mental retardation are similar to those of their nonretarded peers in that they follow the same developmental sequence. Primary differences are noted in the total amount of information gained and in the rate at which this material is learned. Other learning characteristics of individuals with mental retardation include a short attention span, difficulty in dealing with abstracts, and a limited ability to generalize information. It is widely recognized that individuals with mental retardation have attention deficiencies (Bergen and Mosley, 1994).

Since traditional educational programs have required students to sustain continuous attention for relatively long periods of time, teachers need to be sensitive to the unique needs and abilities of students with these learning traits. Research would suggest that attention training can significantly improve the performance of students with mental retardation but may not be transferrable (Del Rey and Stewart, 1989).

While teaching students with mental retardation, it remains imperative that information be presented in a way which is easily understood. Merrill (1990) reports it takes longer for individuals with mental retardation to encode and process information than their normal peers. Educationally, this requires providing students with the opportunity to rehearse and frequently repeat the same activities. Burger and colleagues (1980) suggest that when individuals with mental retardation are afforded opportunities to rehearse specific strategies, they are able to significantly improve performance.

Perhaps as challenging for the student with mental retardation is to generalize the information he or she learns and transfer those skills. This includes the inability to solve problems in different situations and effectively employ problem-solving strategies. Therefore, educators must use instructional strategies so that students with mental retardation not only attend to relevant stimuli, but be given the opportunity to rehearse and practice those skills in a variety of settings. Students who distract easily and/or have short attention spans may need additional visual cues and modeling as much as possible. Instruction should be designed which affords students opportunities to be successful.

Although the inability to transfer material learned, academic or social, from one situation to another is a major learning difficulty for students, the primary learning deficiency may be the failure of persons with mental retardation to effectively employ problem-solving strategies. Educators, therefore, must use procedures to present information in such a fashion that youngsters attend to relevant stimuli.

Applied behavior analysis is the instructional approach that has produced the most consistent educational improvements in students with mental retardation. Gains with this approach are attributed to its emphasis on the direct and continuous measurement of selected behaviors that have been systematically task-analyzed.

Social and Emotional Characteristics

The failure of students with mental retardation to keep intellectual pace with other students contributes to personality maladjustment and the development of undesirable behavior patterns. Much of the normal individual's social maturity and satisfactory adjustment is acquired in play situations throughout the formative years. This is not so with children with mental retardation, who frequently find themselves rejected by their nonretarded peers, or who, because of their low mentality, have no interest in group play. As a result, these students often feel inferior and then tend to devalue their skills and talents, resulting in further withdrawal and regression in ability. Understandably, these individuals are frustrated and develop an attitude of "I can't," which means

"I have tried, I have failed, and I do not want to try again." Researchers have reported that individuals with mental retardation have significantly lower levels of self-esteem than their normal peers (Chiu, 1990), but historically, a greater emphasis has been placed on the cognitive, and not the social or emotional functioning of children with mental retardation (Koop, Baker, and Brown, 1992).

Relatively few studies have investigated the effects of participation in physical activities on self-concept (Riggen and Ulrich, 1993). Anecdotally, teachers, coaches, and parents have long praised the numerous benefits of sports participation for children with mental retardation, including changes in self-esteem. Rarick (1971), and later Bell, Kozarv, and Martin (1979) not only examined self-concept, but the influence of Special Olympic participation on physical fitness, social interaction, and community awareness. Both studies found significant improvements for athletes who participated in these events. More recently, Wright and Cowden (1986) and Gibbons and Bushakra (1989) found significant gains in feelings of self-concept and self-worth, respectively, with participation in Special Olympics training.

Conversely some individuals with mental retardation, placed in circumstances in which more is expected of them than they can deliver, exhibit expressions of fear and aggression. Aggressiveness on the part of the child with mental retardation may be an attempt to cover weaknesses, to demonstrate worth, to attract attention, or to relieve tensions. Rebellious acts and other undesirable behavior are similarly motivated. On occasions those who have mental retardation may use their disability as a protective shield or in an outright bid for sympathy to compensate for their lack of social acceptance.

Physical and Motor Learning Characteristics

Comparative studies of children with mental retardation have shown they consistently score lower than other children on measures of strength, endurance, agility, balance, running speed, flexibility, and reaction time. Generally, the motor performance of youngsters with mental retardation tends to be two to four years behind their non-mentally retarded peers. These differences have been attributed to developmental lags and variability in performance (Porretta, 1985; Moss and Hogg, 1981). Dobbins and his associates (1976; 1981) caution, however, that the motor performance of many boys with mental retardation compares favorably with their nondisabled peers when allowances are made for differences in body size. Some differences may be attributed to failure to understand the movement skill task rather than the inability to execute the skill. Newell (1985) believes that the motor deficiency in populations with mental retardation lies not in the coordination of the action but in its control. This line of reasoning suggests that the problem may be due to a deficiency in the biodynamic system—force, mass, and stiffness of muscles and joints.

Those with Down syndrome possess some unique physical characteristics worthy of a separate discussion. These individuals are often inappropriately referred to as mongoloids because of the resemblance of their facial features to those of the Mongol race. Although these similarities have been exaggerated, children with Down syndrome do tend to have a flat nose with eyes that appear to slant upward. Other visible characteristics include reduced head and ear size, a small mouth with abnormal teeth, and a protruding tongue. Small, square hands, and hair that is usually sparse, fine, and straight are other noticeable characteristics. Impairments in speech are quite common among this population. Physical educators should be particularly cognizant that these individuals are usually short and stocky with a tendency toward obesity. In the area of physical fitness, the Down syndrome population performs at a lower level than that of other individuals with mental retardation (Connolly and Michael, 1986). These differences may be due to their generally short stature and hypertonia, lack of muscle tone (Share and French, 1982), or inability to respond cardiovascularly (Piteti et al., 1992). However, these individuals do well and improve through physiological training programs (Dyer, 1994). In addition, those with Down syndrome have a tendency to gain weight in their early teens after they have reached their maximum height (Glaze, 1985). Winnick (1979) has listed major physical and motor characteristics of Down syndrome children and the movement implications associated with these characteristics (table 17.1). Upper respiratory infection, heart defects, and poor muscle tone are also very prevalent among individuals with Down syndrome. A medical history is essential in developing physical education programs for this population.

Individuals with Down syndrome may suffer from a condition known as atlantoaxial instability, a malalignment of the first two cervical vertebrae. This condition exists in approximately 17 percent of all Down syndrome individuals. Because individuals with this disorder do not indicate any symptoms, X rays of the vertebral column are necessary. If the condition exists, but is not detected, forceful forward or backward bending of the neck, which is common in some sports such as gymnastics, may dislocate the axis, causing damage to the spinal cord (figure 17.2). School officials should follow the lead of Special Olympics (1983) and require all students with Down syndrome to have medical clearance before they can be allowed to participate without restrictions in physical education and sports programs. In the absence of medical clearance, Down syndrome students should be restricted from participating in gymnastics, diving and butterfly stroke in swimming, high jump, pentathlon, and any warm-up exercise placing pressure on the head and neck muscles. This restriction should be temporary until the necessary clearance is obtained. If the diagnosis confirms atlantoaxial instability, the individual should be permanently restricted from these activities. In these situations other activities can be selected that are enjoyable and pose minimal risk to the student.

Table 17.1 *Characteristics of the child with Down syndrome*

Characteristics	Movement Implications
Lag in physical growth. (Growth ceases at an earlier than normal age and generally results in shorter height and smaller overall stature.) Lag is evident in motor development.	The child may need to participate in activities geared for younger age groups.
The circulatory system is less well developed. Arteries are often narrow and thinner than normal, and less vascular proliferation is evidenced. Many children (especially boys) exhibit congenital heart disorders, with heart murmurs and septum defects being the most common.	Although there is a need for the development of endurance, youngsters will have difficulty in endurance activities. It is necessary for all children to have a medical exam and for the instructor to develop a program with medical consultation.
Poor respiration and susceptibility to respiratory infections. (Underdeveloped jaw causes mouth to be too small for normal-sized tongue, inducing mouth breathing.)	Poor respiration may impede participation in endurance activities.
Perceptual handicaps.	Children may be clumsy and awkward. Activities to develop perceptual abilities should be emphasized.
Poor balance.	Since balance is important in most physical and motor activities, lack of balance will affect performance ability. Children need balance training.
Enjoyment of music and rhythmic activities.	The instructor should include rhythmic activities in the program to provide successful and enjoyable experiences and should use music as an aid in teaching.
Obesity.	General overall participation in activities that enhance weight reduction are recommended.
Flabbiness. (Hypotonicity, particularly associated with newborn infants.)	The instructor should provide opportunity for movement experiences at early ages and activities to increase strength at later ages.
Protruding abdomen, lack of muscle and ligament support around the joints, and pronated ankles.	Activities to enhance body alignment, increase muscle and ligament support around the joints, and abdominal exercises are recommended.
Ability to mimic.	Instructor should demonstrate activities and ask children to imitate them.

Source: Reprinted with permission from Winnick, J. P. (1979). *Early movement experiences and development: Habilitation and remediation* (p. 229). Philadelphia: W. B. Saunders Co.

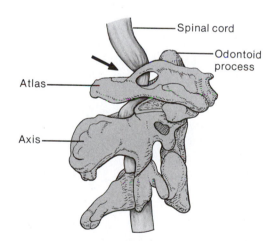

Figure 17.2 Alantoaxial instability. Dislocation of the atlas may injure the spinal cord.

Recognition of these characteristics points to the need of students with mental retardation for successful experiences in group play. Although youngsters who have mental retardation cannot generally acquire the high degree of skill of nonretarded players, they can acquire sufficient skills to participate in enough different muscular activities to increase their physical fitness and improve their body

mechanics. In addition to the physical benefits, play provides many opportunities for social development and emotional growth. Adherence to the rules of the game and to the sportsman's code of fair play provides incentive for self-discipline and self-control. Respect for one's own abilities and limitations and those of others is stimulated in the cooperation and sharing necessitated by the game situation. Many desirable learnings are claimed for sports in the training of nondisabled youngsters. However much these have been exaggerated for other children, they are essentially acceptable for those with mental retardation, whose other opportunities for learning to work and play with others are considerably restricted.

Students with severe and progressed mental retardation are in great need of personal attention in physical education; because of their physical and social limitations, they do not respond well in group play. They even experience difficulty in relating to just one person. Serving these children effectively requires a very low teacher-pupil ratio, usually one to one.

Planning the Program

Directing the play of the student requires careful organization on the part of the instructor. The ultimate goal is a

Figure 17.3 Children with Down syndrome enjoy participating in movement activities.

physical activity program in which students can enjoy the experience while improving their movement proficiency. Additional planning considerations must focus on creating a program that can be conducted in an appropriate environment with suitable activities presented in a manner so that students can succeed.

In planning any program, particularly one funded by federal, state, and local taxes as many such programs are, it is essential that a clear statement of the rationale of the program be developed. The essential question to be answered in the statement is, "Why this program with these activities for this group of students?" This question is legitimate, and it deserves a straightforward answer that can be understood by participants, their parents, school officials, and the public.

Those who support physical education for students with mental retardation often justify this support by stating that movement experiences improve intelligence, enhance self-concept, improve motor ability, and develop physical fitness. Although research evidence is extremely limited, support, to some extent, may be given to each of these and it would seem logical to suggest that physical education may be one of the few disciplines that contributes to all three learning domains: psychomotor, cognitive, and affective.

Nevertheless, it must be emphasized that the unique contribution physical education provides to those with mental retardation is in the area of motor development. It has been established clearly that these youngsters are deficient in motor ability and in physical fitness. Furthermore, data supports conclusively the argument that improvements can be made in these areas if appropriate programs are provided (Eberhard and Eterradossi, 1990; Horgan, 1983).

As students experience success in physical education, they often improve in self-concept and in general emotional development. Emphasis on motor skill development also provides opportunities to reinforce the youngsters' understanding of certain important concepts, such as shape, size, and color. It is important that the physical education teacher be aware of the activities that children are doing in the classroom. A coordinated curriculum involving special education personnel is necessary for the most efficient presentation of material to those with mental retardation.

Emphasis on motor skill instruction is a must in programs for students with mental retardation. Tasks such as reaching and grasping, which normally develop with maturation, will need to be taught to many of these youngsters. The value of psychomotor skills and their relationship to affective and cognitive learning will be apparent to all who work with students who are severely retarded. For these reasons, school officials and parents of the children will actively seek assistance from motor development specialists. Unfortunately, in the past too many professionals teaching those students have not had a sufficient background in motor skill development.

Class Placement

In recent years, classroom placement, and more specifically, issues of inclusion, mainstreaming, integration, least restrictive environment, and segregation have come to the forefront within educational systems in the United States and Europe (Downs and Williams, 1994). Public Law 94-142, The Education for All Handicapped Children Act of 1975 and its succesor, P.L. 101-476, IDEA, emphasize that students with disabilities, including those with mental retardation, should be educated in the least restrictive environment. Although educators are in general agreement with this concept, means to implement this requirement have generated a great deal of controversy. Specifically, some feel that youngsters with mental retardation should be taught in separate special classes and others feel that these children should receive instruction in the regular educational setting, the mainstream of education. In the field of physical education there are few studies available to support either position. It is apparent, though, that youngsters with mental retardation are capable of successfully participating in regular physical education classes. The topic of inclusion has become an emotional and controversial topic for many educators, parents, and students with and without disabilities. Block and Krebs (1992) have challenged previous thinking relating to a continuum of placements for least restrictive environment in special physical education. They offer a continuum of placement from a local school setting with no classroom support to a fully supportive residential school setting with reversed mainstreamed peers. Craft (1994) suggests that "inclusion can be successful when all children are not required to follow the same curriculum" (p. 23), and Block and Vogler (1994) support that "students with disabilities can receive an appropriate, individualized education within the regular class setting" (p. 43). While this continuum provides numerous placement opportunities, it fails to include full-time special physical educators in the regular or residential facility. Furthermore, they suggest that regular physical education is the only environment which allows students enough flexibility to provide opportunities for interactions with a group of peers while still providing individual instruction.

While special physical education is not the LRE for all children with mental retardation, it is a necessary part of many students IEP's. Often times, regular physical educators are ill-prepared to adequately address the needs of students with mental retardation. This may be due to a lack of training, inadequate facilities and equipment, or perhaps personal misbelief or fear.

Others, including Block and Krebs (1992), feel that placement decisions into special physical education are frequently made on categorical labels rather than on systematic decision making. While labeling has drawn criticism from many parents, teachers, and administrators, labels are frequently necessary to receive adequate support services from federal, state, or local educational offices. In a study by Rarick and his associates (1981), data have been obtained to suggest that youngsters with mental retardation can benefit from placement in the regular physical education class. Children with severe mental retardation will require classes that are specifically designed to meet their unique movement needs. It must not be assumed, however, that all youngsters fit these general guidelines. Occasionally, low functioning children with mental retardation have the competency to participate in some or all of the regular physical education activities. Similarly, not all students with mental retardation will find success in the regular class program. Therefore, placements must be individualized to respond to the unique needs of each student.

Placement flexibility is extremely desirable in movement programs for students with mental retardation. Some students may be placed in special classes; others may be placed with regular classes for a small portion of every period. Some students may have sufficient skill to completely integrate for an entire physical education period. Placement consideration must be based on a careful evaluation of motor skill and physical fitness performance coupled with other factors such as the child's social maturity level, the level of support and modifications needed, and curricular considerations. Remember, too, that no placement decision is final, and periodic reviews should be made at least semiannually.

Teaching Environment

Educators often assume that physical education activities must be taught in a gymnasium. For many children, particularly those with mental retardation, this is an incorrect assumption; conducting classes within such a large space may actually interfere with their skill development. These youngsters are easily distracted and the presence of permanent or temporary equipment usually found in the gymnasium will compete with the teacher's ability to hold the attention of the students. It is recommended, therefore, that instruction be confined to a small area when introducing a new skill. A distraction-free corner of the classroom will often be suitable for this purpose. As the participants become proficient in the skill, opportunities should be provided to utilize the new skills within the larger environment of the playground or gymnasium.

Physical education teachers should strive to maintain a class size conducive to learning. The ratio of teacher to student will vary according to the motor skill level of the youngster and the ability of the teacher. Children with severe mental retardation will often require a one-to-one student-teacher ratio. For higher-functioning students, the class size may reach as high as one teacher to ten or twelve youngsters. As a general guide, it is strongly suggested that the physical education teacher not be asked to teach more youngsters with mental retardation per class than is the classroom teacher. Early indications suggest that using trained peer tutors can provide an invaluable resource to the classroom teacher and provide beneficial experiences for students with and without mental retardation (Houston-Wilson, 1993).

Student Interest

In organizing any activity designed to assist students, it is essential to consider the interest level of the participants.

Many students with mental retardation will come to the physical education class with high initial interest because the change to another type of class activity is interesting in itself. Moreover, if previous physical education periods have been fun, interest is high in anticipation of more fun. If natural initial interest does not exist among the students, as is often true when new skills are introduced, it can be aroused in various ways. Students with mild mental retardation can be introduced to a new game with simple, colorful pictures. Through cooperation with the classroom teacher, a short story related to the activity to be presented may be told. Or, if a song or music is to accompany this activity, it may be introduced in an interesting way before the actual activity is presented. Although considerable student interest may be generated, it is usually not sustained because the interest span of these students is relatively short. A change to an alternate activity, designed to achieve the same purpose as the initial activity, is indicated when interest lags.

Children with severe mental retardation do not always respond well to the use of pictures or stories as a means of motivation for desirable behavior. Generally, children require individual attention and continuous stimulation and encouragement by the teacher.

The technique of behavior modification has been a most successful method for reaching these children.

Equipment

To maintain the interest of the students, a wide variety of play equipment is desirable (figure 17.4). Using a dynamic systems approach, one should ask: (1) Does the equipment take into account the ability and/or size of the student?, (2) Will the equipment stimulate interest and imagination?, (3) Is the equipment safe?, (4) Does the equipment stimulate social, locomotor, and manipulative activities?, (5) Can the novelty of the equipment be easily manipulated?, and (6) Does the equipment provide feedback on how well the movement was made? There should be enough physical education equipment for each specific activity, so that no child need sit around idly waiting for a turn. An insufficient amount of equipment interferes with learning by reducing the maximum number of practice trials available to the student. Opportunities to explore with different items designed to achieve the same purpose, such as teaching students to throw using objects of various shapes, sizes, and substances, should be used to renew stimulation and interest.

In addition to the conventional equipment and supplies found in good physical education programs, many ordinary items can be adapted to offer variety and stimulate interest. Old tires, logs of various sizes, barrels, large pipes, boards and planks, saw horses, wooden and paper boxes, balloons, steps, and parachutes are some examples. An innovative teacher will discover many other items that can be used effectively in the program.

Figure 17.4 Play equipment can be used to stimulate interest.

Teaching Methods and Techniques

Prior to the onset of the actual lesson, the instructor should ask several important questions:

1. What is the purpose of the activity?
2. Is the activity age appropriate?
3. Is the activity safe for individuals and/or groups?
4. How will the activity benefit students?
5. Is the teacher adequately prepared to teach the activity?
6. Is the activity meaningful (functional) and fun?

The problem-solving method has limitations in teaching motor skills to students with mental retardation because of their need for structure and direction; nevertheless, exploration can be rewarding for some students with cognitive dysfunction.

To increase the possibility that problem-solving will be successful as a method of teaching students with mental retardation, the following suggestions are offered:

1. Select problems that have a simple solution.
2. Keep the problems few in number and related to the same area of motor skill.
3. Explain and demonstrate how moving one part of the body while in motion can change the nature of the movement. For example, in solving the problem "Can you hop like a rabbit?" demonstrate a hop on two legs and then show how, by lifting one leg in hopping, or by raising the hands to the head to simulate bunny ears, the nature of the movement can be changed.
4. Repeat the same problem frequently, encouraging some small change in movement.

Modifying instruction to meet the individual's needs is a starting point toward successful learning. Throughout a student's education, parents should be an integral part of the planning and teaching team. While teaching individuals with mental retardation it is important to:

1. Use concrete materials that are interesting, age-appropriate, and relevant to the student.
2. Present information and instructions in small sequential steps and review each step frequently.
3. Provide prompt and immediate feedback.
4. Stress and provide opportunities for success.
5. Teach tasks or skills that students will use frequently in such a way that students can apply the tasks or skills in settings outside the school.
6. Break down activity and instruction into small steps or segments.

The direct method is generally very successful for helping students with mental retardation learn motor skills. Of the various techniques utilized in the method, demonstration appears to be the most effective for teaching students with mild mental retardation. These students are great mimics, and much can be accomplished by encouraging them to imitate the demonstrated skill. The demonstration must be adapted to the intellectual abilities of the students. It is usually less successful when the students attempt the activity at the time it is being demonstrated. In some cases, it may be desirable to use physical assistance at the time the demonstration is being made; this may require manually moving the child's body parts through the desired movements. To avoid confusion, the instructor and child should face in the same direction when a new skill is to be demonstrated. This technique, known as mirroring, does not require the youngster to reverse the visual image. Similarly, when giving physical assistance, the teacher should stand behind the student, reaching around him or her, if necessary.

Physical assistance is effective in many situations, such as when teaching a child to ride a tricycle. Here the child may not be able to perceive the nature of the action required to pedal the tricycle until the teacher moves his or her feet alternately through proper movements. Physical assistance may be successfully used for teaching motor movement to the low-functioning student. When working with students of this level it is important that the teacher move the parts of the body in the same way each time to avoid confusion. The hold taken on the child should be firm and reassuring to promote confidence in attempting the movement.

Verbal cues and prompts can be utilized when teaching students with mental retardation in much the same way as with nondisabled youth. However, overreliance on the use of verbalization with students who are severely retarded, many of whom have communication disorders, has definite limitations. It is possible to teach these students to understand and respond to a limited number of words related to the skills they are learning. Examples of such words are "sit," "grasp," and "step over." Only one or two words should be taught during a given period. The word that is being taught should be repeated over and over as the action it describes is being demonstrated by the teacher or being performed by the student. The word should be used alone rather than in a sentence. This does not preclude speaking in sentences. Rather, it is highly desirable that such communication take place because hearing sentences is important to the potential language development of the students.

Care must be exercised not to provide students with mental retardation with more information than they can process during a given period of time. It is not uncommon to observe a response delay of several seconds in students with mental retardation, similar to that observed in very young children. During this interval of inaction, it is important that the teacher not become impatient and provide additional visual or verbal cues. This extra instruction interferes with information still in the processing system, thereby confusing the student.

Efforts must be made to assist students in recalling and retaining information. Consistency in the instructional environment—using similar cues or requests—is helpful in establishing efficient and effective gains in physical education. Likewise, in the teaching of any task it is essential for the teacher's directions to be as specific as possible. The instructor's failure to provide good visual, verbal, or manual cues often results in the student not performing the task because of their inability to understand what is expected of them. For example, many students with mental retardation have difficulty learning the hand and foot placement required in the sprint start. Hand and foot prints cut out of cardboard or other material and placed on the floor can be invaluable aids in teaching this skill, especially if the prints are actual tracings of the student's own hands and feet. The use of various colored lines painted on the floor can help in-class organization by providing the teacher and students with several specific common points of reference. One can well appreciate the confusion that can arise from an inexperienced teacher's nonspecific command of "over there."

Instructional efforts should be directed toward providing success-oriented experiences for the participants. Recognition of this principle is especially critical for teachers of students with special needs, since so many of these individuals have failed in tasks for which they were ill-prepared. To overcome this difficulty, instructors of these students should recognize the importance of breaking skills down into minute components and listing them in a hierarchical sequence (task analysis). For each component, behavioral statements with criterion levels may then be developed so that teacher and student will know when to advance to the next step. An analysis of skill in this manner provides a means for the student to recognize success. The teacher, too, will become more cognizant that small but important improvements are being achieved.

An excellent example of a developmental approach applied to a motor skill has been proposed by Roberton and DiRocco (1981). These investigators established that their overarm-throw-for-force sequence, initially developed for students without mental retardation, was comprehensive enough to include the overarm throw movements exhibited by students with mental retardation. This finding suggests that much of the motor development work that has been conducted to establish developmental sequences for the nonretarded may be appropriate for those with mental retardation.

Participation in play activities by everyone should be actively encouraged by the teacher. There should, of course, be no resort to pressure tactics. Students need and seek approval, and they can be led to cooperate and participate if they know that this is what the teacher wants and gives approval for. Teacher participation, when possible, in the play and fitness activities of these students is also encouraged. Students react favorably when they see that what is asked of them is good for all, including their teacher. Because students with mental retardation are easily distracted, class observers should be kept to a minimum or, perhaps best, be included in the class activities.

Praise should be offered generously for the efforts of the youngster. The attempt may not result in successful performance, but the effort that is exerted should be commended by the teacher. Sincere praise can be one of the teacher's most effective motivators and helps to create the kind of learning situation most conducive to progress.

The teacher should exercise firm discipline without resorting to threats and corporal punishment. The disciplining must take a form that the group is capable of comprehending, such as withholding approval. Those who present a disruptive influence may be temporarily removed from the class and dealt with in a small group or on an individual basis.

Individuals with mental retardation perform best the first few times they do a skill. Consequently, it is to their advantage to end the practice of any one skill before frustration at inability to master the skill sets in. After the skills of a game have been mastered over a gradual period of time,

they should be reviewed briefly each time before the game is played. These drill periods should be just long enough to refresh the students' memories.

Because many individuals who are mentally retarded have low physical vitality, they fatigue easily. This has important implications for the teaching situation. First, it means that new and complex activities should be planned for the early part of the period while the students are fresh and alert. Then, too, a greater chance of injury exists after fatigue sets in, so it is extremely important for the instructor to watch for signs of fatigue. However, the teacher should also incorporate fitness activities into each lesson. Research supports that fitness levels can be significantly improved if opportunities and proper training supervision takes place (Pitetti and Tan, 1991; Lavay and McKenzie, 1991).

Special efforts may be required to evoke responses from torpid youngsters. Such students are particularly in need of physical activity but show no interest in play. The physical education teacher must endeavor to arouse interest and awaken their sensibilities. To do this it may be necessary to force a physical response; for example, tossing balloons at the student so that he or she will raise the arms for protection or will attempt to catch or dodge the balloons. From the use of balloons, the instructor may progress to beanbags and large soft balls that would not cause serious hurt if they were not warded off. Eventually the child can be taught catching, throwing, and other simple motor skills.

In some instances, physical education teachers have obtained the assistance of outstanding high school students on a volunteer basis in providing individual attention for youngsters with mental retardation. This has proven to be a worthwhile learning experience for students with and without a disability. Parents of students with mental retardation are often willing to volunteer their services. When this occurs in the school setting it is to the benefit of both parent and child to assign to the parent a child other than the parent's own. Maguire (1985) found that parents can be effective implementors of instruction in physical education if properly trained and provided with periodic feedback. In his approach the parents were asked to supplement through home instruction programs that were conducted at school. The rate at which skills were acquired was faster in this approach than a school-based program alone. To utilize program volunteers effectively, they must be trained and the teacher and parents must provide a daily written program for each student emphasizing the skills to be learned. A concerted effort must be made to monitor the efforts of the volunteers, correcting and reinforcing them when appropriate.

The physical educator also has the opportunity of teaching the student with mental retardation certain health and safety facts and of encouraging the development of habits pertaining to personal care and protection and in the wise use of leisure time. Specifically in the area of health are such personal hygiene matters as showering after activity, care of the feet to prevent athlete's foot, and cleanliness of gym clothes and socks. Good safety practices, such as not throwing the bat, should be clearly and firmly established so that they will be observed not only in supervised play but also in free play. By providing in the physical education curriculum opportunities to learn games that can be played during leisure hours, the wise use of such time can be encouraged. Because of their generally restricted interests and recreational opportunities, individuals with mental retardation often pursue undesirable leisure activities or idle the time away, which has a negative impact from the standpoint of their development and may become harmful to themselves and to society.

For the low-functioning youngster, the health and safety habits to be taught are simple and more fundamental in nature. Examples are when and where to go to the toilet, how to wash the hands, and being aware that a shoe is untied.

Suggested Activities for Students with Mild Mental Retardation

The physical education program must present a variety of activities directed toward the special needs of children with mental retardation. These experiences, depending on the functioning ability of the individual, range from basic motor skills to leisure activities. The discussion that follows applies primarily to the youngster who, although not severely retarded, possesses movement deficiencies serious enough to require modification or adaptations in some or all of the activities of the regular physical education class. For a more complete discussion of the motor skills, games, sports, and other activities discussed within this section, the reader is referred to the chapters within this text devoted to those topics. An excellent example of a comprehensive physical education curriculum developed for students with mental retardation is the I CAN materials prepared by Janet Wessel and her associates (1976).

Basic Motor Skills

For very young children and those who cannot participate with success in more complex exercises and games, a variety of simple activities that will achieve the goal of desired physical development should be introduced. Among the very simplest of these activities are the basic motor skills of everyday living: walking, balancing, twisting, turning, bending, and climbing stairs. Slightly more involved are the basic play skills: running, hopping, jumping, skipping, kicking, hanging, catching, and throwing. Perceptual motor skills such as visually tracking a suspended ball and stepping over and under obstacles placed at various heights should also be emphasized.

The skills must be presented to students so that they will take pleasure in performing them. Variety in presentation is also vital to achieving interest in their performance.

Figure 17.5 Teaching students basic motor skills such as walking up and down steps is an important aspect of programs for children with special needs.

The following suggestions are ways in which this may be accomplished:

1. Walking at varied tempos and with different sizes and kinds of steps, such as short, quick steps; slow giant strides; tiptoeing.
2. Running at varied tempos.
3. Jumping on both feet, alternating feet, one foot; attaining various heights.
4. Hopping on one foot and on alternate feet.
5. Skipping at varied tempos.
6. Marching at varied tempos; alternating with running, skipping, and jumping; accompanied by hand clapping.
7. Climbing stairs, alternating the feet.
8. Catching and throwing a large balloon.
9. Catching and bouncing a ball.
10. Throwing the ball for distance and at objects; throwing the ball to a catcher.
11. Kicking, with the leg swinging freely, at a large ball, at a small ball.

12. Hanging from a bar or the rung of a ladder, with both arms, with one arm; climbing the ladder with the hands only.
13. Balancing on a balance beam or log; walking along a chalked line; stepping on the rungs of a ladder placed on the floor.
14. Springing up and down on a jouncing board,[2] leaping from the board to the ground.
15. Walking on and jumping on and off tires.
16. Crawling through and over barrels or large pipes.
17. Walking on a balance beam while focusing on a fixed point at the end of the beam.
18. Walking on a balance beam while focusing on a fixed point to the side of the beam.
19. Jumping and turning to the right and then the left side.
20. Rolling on a large inflated ball.

The possibilities for emphasizing the basic motor skills through mimetic play are practically limitless. Pretending they are animals, the children can waddle like ducks, hop like bunnies, leap like frogs, and walk softly (on tiptoes) like kittens. Imitating the actions of people, they may vigorously chop wood, march in a band, sweep the floor, or iron clothes. At times the mimetic activities may be done to musical accompaniment, both for the added interest provided by the music and for the introduction it provides to instruction in dance.

Figure 17.6 Emphasis on basic motor skills such as jumping is important for later skill development.

Basic Skill Games

Activities such as relays, parachute play, and simple games may be introduced to those who have acquired some basic skill movement and can follow simple directions. The following guide is offered for the selection of simple activities. The more capable the students are of participating in complex activities, the less necessity there will be for the games to meet all of the suggested criteria. A very simple game is one in which

1. All children do the same thing.
2. The space is relatively small.
3. Choices that must be made are few in number.
4. Positions are fixed.
5. Quality of performance brings no penalties or privileges.
6. The possible directions of movement are restricted.
7. Personnel remain the same.
8. Motor skill requirements are limited.

Whenever possible, games that reinforce cognitive concepts such as letter, color, and symbol recognition should be incorporated into activities. In addition to the obvious value of these experiences, they are also highly motivating and are enjoyed by the children. Physical education activities designed

to reinforce cognitive concepts also will help the student generalize material taught by the special educator to other settings.

For the higher-functioning adolescent who has successfully participated in activities meeting the previous criteria, opportunities to learn lead-up games, such as kickball, keep away, line soccer, twenty-one, and newcomb, should be provided.

Rhythmic Activities

Like most children, individuals who are mentally retarded enjoy music and respond respond well to dance and rhythmic activities. Such activities are valuable in improving coordination, flexibility, and body carriage (figure 17.7). Improvement in rhythm may also lead to improvement in the smooth performance of skilled movements (Liemohn, 1984). Extensive dance activities, ranging in complexity from simple movements to musical accompaniment to folk dances of complex patterns, should be included in the physical education program. Moreover, they provide a release from tensions and anxieties, which is in itself extremely valuable for these students. The listening experience also heightens auditory perception.

Efforts at teaching rhythmic patterns should initially focus on having children learn to keep time with one hand,

---

[2]A board one inch thick, six to eight inches wide, and six feet long, balanced on two supports.

Figure 17.7 Dance activities contribute to the development of coordination and flexibility.

then two hands, and finally, for the more advanced, incorporating the feet into the sequence as well. Children unable to master this sequence should be encouraged to let their bodies sway from side to side with the music. Making and utilizing their own instruments to play along with the music is also an activity from which all children, including those with mental retardation, can derive much pleasure.

Physical Fitness

Individuals with mental retardation, as a group, are deficient in all of the components of physical fitness. To a great extent this poor performance is due to a lack of opportunity to participate in play activity. Therefore, if programs are well designed and administered by an enthusiastic teacher, noticeable improvements in physical fitness can be achieved. The total amount of physical education time devoted to fitness activities for students who are mentally retarded need not be extensive. However, a developmental program of from twenty to thirty minutes that contributes to strength, flexibility, and endurance should be provided daily.

Children with mental retardation enjoy doing exercises with their teacher. Included in the program may be such simple activities as bending, squatting, twisting the trunk, and rotating the arms. Students can achieve considerable skill in the performance of more complicated calisthenics, such as the push-up and jumping jack. Circuit training, in which different exercises are performed at various stations in the room, is highly motivating for the student and has been successfully implemented for this population (Horvat, Croce, and McGhee, 1993; Rimmer and Kelly, 1991). Charts should be provided at each station with pictures

depicting the exercises to be performed and the number to be executed. Aerobic activities such as fast walking, jogging, cycling, and swimming are essential if improvements in cardiorespiratory fitness are to be obtained. For all of the physical fitness activities, records simple enough for the students to understand should be maintained to help teacher and student "see" progress.

Moon and Renzaglia (1982), in a comprehensive review of fitness of individuals with mental retardation, suggest that there is little empirical evidence to indicate the activities and instructional techniques best suited for this population. There is every reason to believe that significant gains in fitness levels can be obtained with this population. Future efforts, however, must be directed toward documenting these changes and to ensuring that opportunities to maintain fitness levels are available. Many of the techniques and strategies that have been developed and successfully utilized with nonretarded youth can be implemented with students with mental retardation. Careful attention, however, must be directed toward the use of systematic instructional techniques if desirable gains are to be achieved. Instruction in fitness programs, similar to academic and motor skill activities, requires the use of task analysis, daily data keeping, reinforcement, and the use of a prompt hierarchy from verbal through modeling to physical assistance as necessary.

Team Sports

As students with mental retardation achieve success through lead-up games, additional instructional time should be directed toward teaching the various team sport activities. Most of these youngsters will be familiar with sporting events as a result of attending local contests, watching television, or looking at pictures in books describing sport activities. Individuals who are mentally retarded, like most others, thoroughly enjoy these exposures. Teachers of students with mental retardation often marvel at the number of their students who can recall the names of local and national sport heroes. Because of this high interest level, the physical education program should provide as many of these sports and games as possible. They provide the vigorous muscular activity essential to improving physical fitness in these youngsters. Besides the physical benefits are the recreational and socializing values, which have already been stressed.

Capable teachers have been able to teach the skill of team play well enough to students who are mentally retarded that they have been able to compete against other teams. Some schools field special baseball and basketball teams. Many individuals have been provided extensive opportunities to participate in competitive athletics under the auspices of the Special Olympics program sponsored by the Joseph P. Kennedy, Jr., Foundation and directed by Eunice Kennedy Shriver. Individuals with mental retardation enjoy competition of this nature and desire it for the personal satisfaction and social approval that it brings them. An in-depth discussion of the organization and structure, including sponsored events of the Special Olympics, may be found in chapter 30, *Competitive Sport for Athletes with Disabilities.*

Competition for some, however, may promote undesirable aggressive behavior on the one hand or cause them to lose interest entirely on the other. The teacher coaching a competitive team should attempt to prevent these reactions through careful development of the best possible attitudes toward competitive play. This is accomplished by emphasizing the competitive opportunities as an outgrowth of well-developed and implemented instructional programs.

Leisure Skills

Within recent times the schools' responsibility for teaching students skills that they can use in later life has gained wide acceptance. Recent federal legislation, specifically P.L. 101-476 (IDEA) recognizes the need to teach functional skills such as leisure activities, that can be used throughout life. These needs should be included in transition plans, which are required in the IEP beginning at age sixteen. For individuals with mental retardation, acquisition of leisure skills is particularly critical because many will have excess time available. Most important, however, is the awareness that use of these skills is a vehicle by which many can lead a more normal life within the community. For the physical education teacher this means that skills such as roller skating, bicycle riding, bowling, and swimming need to be taught. Providing some of these experiences in a school district with limited equipment and facilities will require the efforts of a dedicated and resourceful teacher. One need only

experience the enthusiasm and pride generated by the successful completion of a first wobbly solo on a bike to make any inconveniences seem well worth the effort. Parents, seeing their children achieve vital skills such as learning to swim, also will respond favorably to the school program. For these parents, enjoyable and relaxed "family" outings to the beach can now become a reality.

The development of leisure skills should involve close articulation and cooperation with other community agencies such as the local park and recreation department, and youth organizations such as Campfire and scouting organizations. If opportunities are created early to use community resources, it is likely that generalization of play and leisure skills to other settings will occur and continue throughout life.

Body Mechanics

The prevalence of postural deviations among those who are mentally retarded appears to be quite high. Common body alignment abnormalities include forward head, sagging shoulders, and swayback and its accompanying protruding abdomen. Correcting these problems and keeping the body in balance are difficult because of the subconscious attempt to overcompensate in the other direction. This can be overcome if students are encouraged to practice good postural positions in front of full length mirrors. Pictures and videotapes of the children as they walk and perform other dynamic movements also can be quite helpful in communicating information to youngsters about correct and incorrect body positions. Activities in which students pair up and trace their partner's upright and supine body positions are also helpful in providing a visual image of their appearance.

Although many postural problems are directly related to inadequate amounts of strength and flexibility, frequently the key to improving the student's posture lies in improving his or her body awareness. Many times as the person learns the names of the various body parts and their functions, and then is taught motor skills through which this information can be successfully used, changes in body awareness and hence improvement in posture occur. It is recommended that programs designed to remedy functional deviations be initiated prior to maturation of the skeletal system at about age fifteen. After this time permanent changes tend to occur in the bone structure and the postural problems become structural in nature. Postural exercises usually have no influence on such problems.

Suggested Activities for Students with Severe Mental Retardation

The range of activities in a physical education program for those who are severely retarded is necessarily limited. These individuals, if not properly stimulated, often sit or lie for hours and appear to be totally unaware of their environment.

Until recently, little attention has been devoted to the educational and motor development needs of individuals with severe retardation. Confined to an institution, they were frequently permitted to exist in a vegetable-like state. The lack of suitable programs may be attributed to inadequate staff-resident ratio as well as to the belief of many that the most severely retarded were incapable of learning. Changes in this attitude are evident today, and an increasing number of professionals are focusing on this forgotten population. Because those with severe retardation exhibit numerous motor deficiencies, it is essential that attention be directed toward remedying these problems. Although little research has been conducted to provide evidence to support the choice of program content, physical education experiences for this population have consisted primarily of sensory-motor experiences and the fundamental motor skills of everyday living. In addition, Croce (1990) and Tomporowski and Ellis (1984) have successfully implemented well-structured physical education classes for institutionalized individuals which have resulted in positive physiological and behavioral changes.

Sensory-Motor Experiences

Based on information gathered from the study of infant development, sensory-motor experiences usually consist of activities to increase awareness of stimuli and to improve manipulative activity. Experiences designed to raise the awareness of those severely involved should be developed for all of the senses. Stimulation of the tactile senses may include vigorously rubbing the skin with towels and brushes of various textures to obtain a motor response. Lights and sounds of various intensities may be moved from one side to the other to elicit head turning responses. Providing opportunities to discriminate between various tastes, odors, and temperatures is useful for developing avoidance (turning away) and approach (turning toward) motor responses. Combinations of various sensory stimuli may also be presented. For many individuals who are severely retarded, an extensive time allotment should be provided for sensory awareness activities. Without the ability to attend to relevant stimuli, further educational experiences for this population will be seriously impeded.

The skills of reaching, grasping, holding, and releasing do not develop normally for individuals with severe mental retardation. Therefore, opportunities for these individuals to play with toys of various colors and textures should be provided. Finger, hand, and arm movements may also be obtained through the use of materials such as water, sand, and clay. Efforts also should be directed toward teaching self-help skills that emphasize manipulative activities, such as eating and dressing.

Figure 17.8 Popping soap bubbles is a fun activity to help children develop eye-hand coordination.

Fundamental Motor Skills

In addition to the sensory-motor experiences, the physical education curriculum for individuals who are severely mentally retarded should include activities that develop basic everyday skills, such as lifting the feet over objects and up steps. Additional examples of the basic activities that can be included in the program and the techniques most frequently used for teaching them are listed below. Because of the individual variation found within this population, the techniques listed are suggestions and do not preclude the use of others.

1. Crawling (arms, chest, belly, legs): demonstration, physical assistance (use crawler, if necessary)
2. Creeping (hands and knees): demonstration, physical assistance
3. Rolling: demonstration, physical assistance
4. Sitting: demonstration, physical assistance (external supports such as straps, if necessary)
5. Standing (with and without assistance): demonstration, physical assistance
6. Walking: demonstration, physical assistance (use parallel bars and weighted cart, if necessary)
7. Bending at the waist to pick up a favorite toy: demonstration, physical assistance

8. Bending at the knees to pick up a favorite toy: demonstration, physical assistance
9. Stair climbing: demonstration, physical assistance
10. Balancing: physical assistance (use wide beam; assist student along beam)
11. Stepping over and into objects: physical assistance (use tires, boxes, beams)
12. Bouncing: physical assistance (use trampoline; start pupil by bouncing on bed; later a jouncing board may be used)
13. Jumping from object: physical assistance (use object or beam no higher than one foot in the beginning; start by pulling student off balance)
14. Climbing: physical assistance (use a ladder or Swedish box)
15. Running: demonstration, physical assistance (pull by the hand or use rope around the waist)
16. Throwing: physical assistance (use eight-inch or larger ball and a tire as a target; have student start by dropping the ball and gradually increase the distance from the tire)
17. Catching: physical assistance (use eight-inch ball; in the beginning use short distances and place the ball into the hand)
18. Kicking: demonstration, physical assistance (use large, soft rubber balls or heavy cardboard boxes)

The way in which these activities are presented by the teacher is extremely important in achieving good results. As pointed out above, teaching low-functioning individuals requires a very low teacher-to-pupil ratio—in most cases, one to one.

No more than two or three activities should be presented during any one class period. Anyone who refuses to participate in one kind of activity may take part in another. Participation should be of short duration. After leaving one activity the teacher may return to it in a few minutes or at some time before the period is over. The same activities should be presented every day until learned. After the skills of one activity have been mastered, new activities may be introduced; but the skills already learned should be reviewed briefly from time to time. An obstacle course in which students climb stairs, duck under bars, step over ropes, and step into and out of tires provides a good warm-up and a means of quickly reviewing important activities.

Teaching these students requires great patience and kindness. The teacher should never resort to pressure tactics to achieve improvement. The instructor's attitude must be that improvement may come very slowly, and he or she must work patiently with the student until it comes. All genuine effort by the student should be acknowledged with indications of approval. Heward and Orlansky (1992) recommend that a behavioral approach with the following elements be employed with individuals who are mentally retarded:

1. Require the student to perform the target behavior repeatedly during each session.
2. Provide immediate feedback, usually in the form of positive reinforcement.
3. Use cues and prompts that help the student respond correctly from the very beginning of the lesson and systematically withdraw these as appropriate.
4. Help the student generalize the newly learned skill to different, nontraining environments (1992).

Additional suggestions for developing programs for those with severe disabilities are presented in chapter 20.

Behavior Modification

Verbal praise has its limitations with those who are severely and profoundly retarded because many of these students do not comprehend the spoken word; therefore, other means of rewarding successful behavior have been experimented with. One of the most effective of these is a procedure known as behavior modification.

Behavior modification is defined as the systematic use of selected reinforcers to weaken, maintain, or strengthen behaviors. Although there are several behavior modification techniques, the two most successfully employed with those who are severely mentally retarded are positive reinforcement and modeling. Combining these two techniques provides a system in which a skill is demonstrated and modeled, and the student is reinforced for initiating any movement that resembles or approximates the skill. It may be necessary to shape the behavior of some totally dependent individuals by isolating and reinforcing very basic responses, such as the turning of their heads and eyes toward the demonstration. Reinforcing those who are functioning at a lower level while they are manually guided through the skill may also develop within them a sense of pleasure that over a period of time may gradually be associated with the movement. Several types of reinforcers may be employed. These include manipulatables such as toys, trinkets, and hobby items; visual and auditory stimuli such as films, records, and animations; and social stimuli such as verbal praise and attention (Dunn, 1975). Selection of the appropriate reinforcer must be determined for each person. For some students, praise or knowledge that the attempt was successful is sufficient reinforcement. For others, especially the more severely involved, a reward of food is effective. The time between the reinforcement and the desired behavior must be as short as possible; otherwise the student is not always certain what he or she is being rewarded for. The reward should be given consistently and only for performance at maximum capacity.

A movement that is made up of two or more parts must be broken into its components and each taught separately. For example, the movement pattern of reaching for and picking up a ball may be broken down into these components: (1) a movement in the direction of the ball, (2) touching the ball, (3) placing the fingers around the ball, and (4) lifting the ball up. The student is first encouraged to reach for the ball; any effort to do so is rewarded with a reinforcer, and words of praise. Thereafter, the reward is given when the student reaches the same distance or a greater distance than in the initial effort. Whenever the student reaches a greater distance, bringing the hand closer to the ball, the new distance becomes the point of reinforcement. When the student finally touches the ball, this becomes the point of reinforcement; the same applies when he or she grasps it and when he or she picks it up. After the individual has mastered the skill, the reinforcer is slowly withdrawn by offering it only periodically. Praise and approval continue to be given for successful effort. Often, they can eventually be used entirely as the reinforcer.

Summary

Information concerning individuals with mental retardation was presented in this chapter. An overview of the nature and needs of this population and the classification systems used in mental retardation were described. In discussing the emotional, social, learning, and motor characteristics of these students, emphasis was placed on the significant variability found within this population, including the unique physical and medical needs of the Down syndrome population. Modern views of mental retardation recognize that individuals with cognitive disorders are capable of contributing to society and benefiting from interactions with other nonretarded individuals. The emphasis today is on deinstitutionalization and normalization. The progressive view of mental retardation is reflected in the definition of mental retardation, which emphasizes that the intelligence quotient is only one factor in determining mental retardation. Adaptive behavior is recognized as essential in determining the presence or absence of mental retardation. This view is also evident in schools, where the traditional segregated class for students with mental retardation has been replaced by resource rooms where students who are mentally retarded obtain assistance as needed. Instructional integration is the norm, with segregated experiences provided for more involved students who need the structure and individualization offered in special classes.

In physical education there is increasing awareness that individuals with mental retardation as a group do not compare favorably with nonretarded students on measures of physical and motor fitness. These differences to a large extent may be attributed to the lack of activity and structured programs provided for these students. If programs are properly presented, significant gains will occur. This means that motor and fitness skills must be task-analyzed with appropriate cues and consequences utilized. Data must be maintained with positive reinforcement provided when learning occurs. Efforts must also be directed toward ensuring that skills learned are maintained. Parents therefore should be encouraged to reinforce selected skills at home. In addition schools should coordinate with other community agencies to help students make the transition from the gymnasium to other play and recreational settings. The outlook for individuals with mental retardation is very positive. Given properly trained professionals with progressive attitudes it is probable that significant gains will be made in the overall health and physical performance level of individuals with mental retardation.

Selected Readings

Baroff, G.S. (1982). Predicting the prevalence of mental retardation in individual catchment areas. *Mental Retardation, 20,* 133–135.

Bar-Or, O. (1983). *Pediatric sports medicine for the practitioner: From physiologic principles to clinical applications.* New York: Springer.

Bell, N., Kozav, W., & Martin, A. (1979). *The impact of Special Olympics on participants, parents and the community.* Lubbock, TX: Texas Tech University.

Bergen, A.M.E. & Mosley, J.L. (1994). Attention and attentional shift efficiency and individuals with and without mental retardation. *American Journal on Mental Retardation, 98,* 688–743.

Beuter, A. (1983). Effects of mainstreaming on motor performance of intellectually normal and trainable mentally retarded students. *American Corrective Therapy Journal, 37,* 48–52.

Block, M.E., & Krebs, P.L. (1992). An alternative to least restrictive environments: A continuum of support to regular physical education. *Adapted Physical Activity Quarterly, 9,* 97–113.

Block, M.E., & Vogler, E.W. (1994). Inclusion in regular physical education: The research base. *Journal of Physical Education, Recreation and Dance, 65,* 40–43.

Bruininks, R. (1974). Physical and motor development of retarded persons. In N.R. Ellis (Ed.), *International review of research in mental retardation* (Vol. 7, pp. 209–261). Ellis, NY: Academic Press.

Burger, A.L., Blackman, L.S., & Tan, N. (1980). Maintenance and generalization of a sorting and retrieval strategy by EMR and nonretarded individuals. *American Journal of Mental Deficiency, 84,* 373–380.

Chiu, L.H. (1990). Self-esteem of gifted, normal, and mildly mentally handicapped children. *Psychology in the Schools, 27,* 263–268.

Connolly, B.H., & Michael, B.T. (1986). Performance of retarded children, with and without Down syndrome, on the Bruininks Oseretsky Test of Motor Proficiency. *Physical Therapy, 66,* 344–348.

Craft, D. (1994). Inclusion: Physical education for all. *Journal of Physical Education: National status-update.* Northern Illinois University.

Cratty, B.J. (1969). *Motor activity and the education of retardates.* Philadelphia: Lea and Febiger.

Croce, R.V. (1990). Effects of exercise and diet on body composition and cardiovascular fitness in adults with severe mental retardation. *Education and Training in Mental Retardation, 25,* 176–187.

Del Rey, P., & Stewart, D. (1989). Organizing input for mentally retarded subjects to enhance memory and transfer. *Adapted Physical Activity Quarterly, 6,* 247–254.

DiRocco, P.J., Clark, J.E., & Phillips, S.J. (1987). Jumping coordination patterns of mildly mentally retarded children. *Adapted Physical Activity Quarterly, 4,* 178–191.

Dobbins, D.A., Garron, R., & Rarick, G.L. (1981). The motor performance of educable mentally retarded and intellectually normal boys after covariate control for differences in body size. *Research Quarterly for Exercise and Sport, 52*(1), 1–8.

Dobbins, D.A., & Rarick, G.L. (1976). Separation potential of educable retarded and intellectually normal boys as a function of motor performance. *Research Quarterly, 47*(3), 346–356.

Downs, P. & Williams, T. (1994). Students' attitudes toward integration of people with disabilities in activity settings: A European comparison. *Adapted Physical Activity Quarterly, 11,* 32–43.

Dummer, G. (1988). Teacher training to enhance motor learning by mentally retarded individuals. In C. Sherrill (Ed.), *Leadership training in adapted physical education* (pp. 349–359). Champaign, IL: Human Kinetics Publishers.

Dunn, J.M. (1975). Behavior modification with emotionally disturbed children. *Journal of Physical Education and Recreation, 46,* 46–70.

Dunn, J.M., & French, R. (1982). Operant conditioning: A tool for special physical educators in the 1980s. *Exceptional Education Quarterly, 3,* 42–53.

Dyer, S.M. (1994). Physiological effects of a 13-week physical fitness program on Down syndrome subjects. *Pediatric Exercise Science, 6,* 88–100.

Eberhard, Y., & Eterradossi, J. (1990). Effects of physical exercise in adolescents with Down syndrome. *Adapted Physical Activity Quarterly, 16,* 281–287.

Eichstaedt, C.B., & Lavay, B.W. (1992). *Activity for individuals with mental retardation: Infancy through adulthood.* Champaign, IL: Human Kinetics Publishers.

Ellis, D.N., Cress, P.J., & Spellman, C.R. (1993). Training students with mental retardation to self-pace while exercising. *Adapted Physical Activity Quarterly, 10,* 104–124.

Feingold, B. (1975). *Why your child is hyperactive.* New York: Randam House.

Fryers, T. (1993). Epidemiological thinking in mental retardation: Issues in taxonomy and population frequency. In Norma W. Bray (Ed.), *International review of research in mental retardation* (Vol. 19, pp. 97–127). San Diego, CA: Academic.

Gibbons, S.L., & Bushakra, F.B. (1989). Effects of Special Olympic participation on the perceived competence and social acceptance of MR children. *Adapted Physical Activity Quarterly, 6,* 40–51.

Glaze, R.E. (1985). *Height and weight of Down syndrome children as compared to normal children aged ten to eighteen.* Unpublished masters study. Illinois State University, Normal, IL.

Grossman, H.J. (1973). *Manual on terminology and classification in mental retardation.* Washington, DC: American Association on Mental Deficiency.

Haywood, K.M. (1993). *Life span motor development* (2d ed.). Champaign, IL: Human Kinetics Publishers.

Heward, W.L., & Orlansky, M.D. (1992). *Exceptional children* (4th ed.). Columbus, OH: Charles E. Merrill Publishing Co.

Hoover, J., & Wade, M. (1985). Motor learning theory and mentally retarded individuals: A historic review. *Adapted Physical Activity Quarterly, 2*(3), 228–252.

Horgan, J.S. (1983). Mnemonic strategy instruction in coding, processing and recall of movement related cues by the mentally retarded. *Perceptual and Motor Skills, 57,* 547–557.

Horvat, M., Croce, R., & McGhee, T. (1993). Effects of a circuit training program on individuals with mental retardation. *Clinical Kinesiology, 47,* 71–77.

Houston-Wilson, C. (1993). The effect of untrained and trained peer tutors on the Opportunity to Respond (OTR) of students with developmental disabilities in integrated physical education classes. Unpublished doctoral dissertation. Oregon State University. Corvallis, Oregon.

Johnson, L., & Londeree, B. (1976). *Motor fitness testing manual for the moderately mentally retarded.* Washington, DC: American Alliance for Health, Physical Education, Recreation, and Dance.

Koop, C.B., Baker, B.L., & Brown, K.W. (1992). Social skills and their correlates: Preschoolers with developmental delays. *American Journal on Mental Retardation, 96,* 357–366.

Lavay, G., & McKenzie, T. (1991). Development and evaluation of a systematic run/walk program for men with mental retardation. *Education and Training in Mental Retardation, 26,* 333–341.

Liemohn, W. (1984). *Rhythmicity and timing in special populations.* Paper presented at the American Alliance for Health, Physical Education, Recreation, and Dance Annual Convention. Anaheim, CA.

Lindgren, G.W., & Katoda, H. (1993). Maturational rate of Tokyo children with and without mental retardation. *American Journal on Mental Retardation, 98,* 128–134.

Londeree, B., & Johnson, L. (1974). Motor fitness of TMR vs EMR and normal children. *Medicine and Science in Sports,* 247–252.

Luckasson, R., Coulter, D.L., Pollaway, W.A., Reiss, S., Schalock, R.L., Snell, M.E., Spitalnik, D.M., & Stark, J.A. (1992). *Mental retardation: Definition, classification and systems of support* (9th ed.). Washington D.C.: American Association on Mental Reatardation.

Maguire, P. (1985). *The effects of supplemental home instruction by parents utilizing the data based gymnasium instructional model on the performance of selected motor skills with moderately and severely mentally retarded children.* Unpublished doctoral dissertation. Oregon State University, Corvallis, OR.

McCubbin, J., Frey, G., & Lavay, B. (1992). Fitness assessment of persons with disabilities: Past, present, and future. Presentation at the International Federation of Adapted Physical Activity Conference. Miami, FL.

Merrill, E.C. (1990). Attention resource allocation and mental retardation. In Norma W. Bray (Ed.), *International review of research in mental retardation,* (Vol. 16, pp. 51–88). San Diego, CA: Academic.

Moon, M.S., & Renzaglia, A. (1982). Physical fitness and the mentally retarded: A critical review of the literature. *Journal of Special Education, 16,* 269–287.

Moss, S.C., & Hogg, J. (1981). The development of hand function in mentally handicapped and nonhandicapped preschool children. In P. Mittler (Ed.), *Frontiers of knowledge in mental retardation* (pp. 35–44). Baltimore, MD: University Park Press.

Newell, K.M. (1985). Motor skill orientation and mental retardation: Overview of traditional and current orientations. In J.E. Clark & J. H. Humphrey (Eds.), *Motor development: Current selected research* (Vol I). Princeton, NJ: Princeton Book Co.

Pitetti, K.H., Climstein, M., Campbell, K.D., Barrett, P.J., & Jackson, J.A. (1992). The cardiovascular capabilities of adults with Down syndrome: A comparative study. *Medicine and Science in Sports and Exercise, 24,* 13–19.

Pitetti, K.H., & Tan, D.M. (1991). Effects of minimally supervised exercise program for mentally retarded adults. *Medicine and Science in Sports and Exercise, 23,* 594–601.

Porretta, D.L. (1985). Performance variability of educable mentally retarded and normal boys on a novel kicking task. *Adapted Physical Activity Quarterly, 2*(1), 76–82.

Rarick, G.L. (1971). Evaluation of local Special Olympics programs. Unpublished study. University of California, Berkeley, CA.

Rarick, G.L. (1973). Motor performance of mentally retarded children. In G.L. Rarick (Ed.), *Physical activity: Human growth and development* (pp. 225–256). New York: Academic Press.

Rarick, G.L., Dobbins, P.A., & Broadhead, G.D. (1976). *The motor domain and its correlates in educationally handicapped children.* Englewood Cliffs, NJ: Prentice-Hall, Inc.

Rarick, G.L., & McQuillan, J.P. (1979). *The effects of individualized physical education instruction on selected perceptual motor and cognitive functions of institutionalized and home reared TMR children.* Final Report, U.S. Office of Education, Bureau of Education for the Handicapped (Grant No. G007601432).

Rarick, G.L., McQuillan, J.P., & Beuter, A.C. (1981). *The motor, cognitive, and psychosocial effects of the implementation of Public Law 94-142 on handicapped children in school physical education programs.* Final Report, Department of Education (Grant No. G007901413).

Rarick, G.L., Widdop, J.H., & Broadhead, G.D. (1970). The physical fitness and motor performance of educable mentally retarded children. *Exceptional Children, 36,* 509–519.

Reid, G. (1980). Overt and covert rehearsal in short-term memory of mentally retarded and nonretarded persons. *American Journal of Mental Deficiency, 85,* 69–77.

Reis, S. (1994). Issues in defining mental retardation. *American Journal on Mental Retardation, 99,* 1–7.

Riggen, K., & Ulrich, D. (1993). The effects of sport participation on individuals with mental retardation. *Adapted Physical Activity Quarterly, 10,* 42–51.

Rimmer, J.H., & Kelly, L.E. (1991). Effects of a resistance training program on adults with mental retardation. *Adapted Physical Activity Quarterly, 8,* 146–153.

Roberton, M.A., & DiRocco, P. (1981). Validating a motor skill sequence for mentally retarded children. *American Corrective Therapy Journal, 35,* 148–155.

Savage, M.P., Petratis, M.M., Thomson, W.H., Berg, K., Smith, J.L., & Sady, S.P. (1986). Exercise training effects on serum lipids of prepubescent boys and adult men. *Medicine and Science in Sports and Exercise, 18,* 197–204.

Seefeldt, V., & Vogel, P. (1987). Children and fitness: A public health perspective. *Research Quarterly for Exercise and Sport, 58,* 331–333.

Share, J., & French, R. (1982). *Motor development of Down syndrome children: Birth to six years.* Sherman Oaks, CA: J.B. Share.

Sheppard, R.J. (1990). *Fitness in special populations.* Champaign, IL: Human Kinetics Publishers.

Special Olympics Bulletin. (1983). Participation by individuals with Down syndrome who suffer from the atlantoaxial dislocation. Washington, DC: Joseph P. Kennedy Jr. Foundation.

Sugden, D.A. (1978). Visual motor short-term memory in educationally subnormal boys. *British Journal of Educational Psychology, 48,* 330–339.

Thase, M.E. (1982). Reversible dementia in Down syndrome. *Journal of Mental Deficiency Research, 26,* 111–113.

Tomporowski, P.D., & Ellis, N.R. (1984). Effects of exercise on the physical fitness, intelligence and adaptive behavior of institutionalized mentally retarded adults. *Applied Research in Mental Retardation, 5,* 329–337.

Tomporowski, P.D., & Hager, L.D. (1992). Sustained attention in mentally retarded individuals. In Norma W. Bray (Ed.), *International review of research in mental retardation* (Vol. 18, pp. 111–136). San Diego, CA: Academic.

Wehman, P. (1977). *Helping the mentally retarded acquire play skills.* Springfield, IL: Charles C. Thomas.

Wessel, J.A. (1976). *I CAN.* Northbrook, IL: Hubbard Publishing Company.

Winnick, J.P. (1979). *Early movement experiences and development: Habilitation and remediation.* Philadelphia: W.B. Saunders Co.

Wolfensberger, W. (1991). Reflections on a lifetime in human services and mental retardation. *Mental Retardation, 29,* 1–16.

Wright, J., & Cowden, J.E. (1986). Changes in self-concept and cardiovascular endurance of mentally retarded youths in a Special Olympics swim training program. *Adapted Physical Activity Quarterly, 3,* 177–183.

Zittel, L.L. (1994). Gross motor assessment of preschool children wtih special needs: Instrument selection considerations. *Adapted Physical Activity Quarterly, 11,* 245–260.

Enhancing Activities

1. Volunteer to participate as a coach or official for the local Special Olympic organization. Write a paper describing your reaction to this experience.

2. Attend a local meeting of the Association for Retarded Citizens. Compare this meeting, including the agenda, to a meeting of the local Parent Teacher Association.

3. Interview an adolescent who is mentally retarded. Obtain his or her views on physical education and recreation. Is physical activity an important aspect of the individual's life? What recommendations does he or she have for improving the way programs are conducted?

4. Visit a group home or special facility for those who are mentally retarded. Record your impressions and compare those to the living arrangements—meals, activities, routine—found in other homes.

5. Observe a physical education class in which a student with mental retardation enrolled. What adaptations in instruction and/or activity were made for the student? Suggest other adaptations or modifications that might be made.

6. Select one of the tests described in chapter 7, *Evaluation,* and administer the test to a student who is mentally retarded. Given the test results, recommend a goal and objectives that should be included as part of the student's IEP.

7. Visit a local school and review curricular materials used to teach basic skills to students who are mentally retarded. Identify ways in which the physical education experience for those students could be structured to complement instruction in the classroom. Identify changes that could be made in the classroom that might facilitate learning in the gymnasium.

CHAPTER

18

Learning Disabilities

◆ _____ **CHAPTER OBJECTIVES** _____ ◆

After studying this chapter, the reader should be able to:

1 Define the expression _learning disabilities_ and discuss the areas in which discrepancy between actual and expected levels of achievement normally occur in this population.

2 Identify the common causes of learning disabilities and the relationship of these to educational programs for students with this disorder.

3 Discuss the learning and behavioral characteristics of individuals with learning disabilities and the relationship of these to instruction in physical education.

4 Define and explain the various perceptual disorders and terms associated with learning disabilities including hyperactivity, dissociation, perseveration, distractibility, laterality, directionality, visual discrimination, auditory discrimination, and apraxia.

5 Analyze the term _perceptual-motor_ and the relationship of perceptual-motor programs to instruction in physical education.

6 Develop guidelines for the implementation of appropriate physical education programs and experiences for students with learning disabilities.

7 Recognize and appreciate the importance of a multidisciplinary team approach toward the assessment and implementation of effective learning environments for students with learning disabilities.

8 Appreciate what is known and not known about the nature, cause, and treatment of individuals with learning disabilities.

9 Suggest activities and instructional procedures for teaching physical education to students with learning disabilities.

10 Explain what is meant by the expressions: _Attention Deficit Disorder (ADD)_; _Attention Deficit Hyperactivity Disorder (ADHD)_; and _Undifferentiated Attention Deficit Disorder (UADD)_.

11 Recognize that not all students with ADD and ADHD are learning disabled.

Learning disabilities represent a field of special education that has experienced a tremendous amount of growth and interest since the early 1960s. Attention has been directed toward students with learning disabilities by scientists, educators, allied health personnel, media representatives, and the general public. This interest has helped to foster an environment in which our understanding of the meaning and significance of learning disabilities has improved dramatically. Although there is still much that is unknown about the causes of this disorder, as well as the procedures for identifying and treating students with learning disabilities, the future for these individuals is encouraging.

Dr. Samuel Kirk is generally recognized as the originator of the term *learning disabilities*. In 1963, while addressing a group of parents with children who were experiencing serious difficulties in learning to read, who were hyperactive, or who could not solve math problems, Dr. Kirk commented that recently he had been using the term "learning disabilities" to describe children who had learning problems but who were not mentally retarded or emotionally disturbed. Parents and educators quickly adopted this term as an acceptable label and an appropriate alternative to such terms as brain damaged, neurologically impaired, minimal brain dysfunctions, and perceptually disabled.

Today, most states and communities have formed chapters as part of a national group known as the Association for Children With Learning Disabilities (ACLD). The ACLD is an advocacy group dedicated to improving educational services for students with learning disabilities. This group, in joint effort with the Council for Exceptional Children's Division for Children With Learning Disabilities (DCLD), has been responsible for persuading the federal government to recognize the needs of those with learning disabilities. Learning disabilities are recognized as a handicapping condition identified by Public Law 101-476. Students with this disorder are eligible for federally funded special education programs.

Learning Disabilities Defined

There is considerable discussion among professionals and parents concerning the definition of learning disabilities and the students who should be included within this special population. For some, the term "learning disabled" should be applied to any student who experiences a problem with learning. According to proponents of this philosophy, the term would include any student whose learning is disabled by conditions not classified under other special education categories such as mental retardation and blindness.

Some, however, have argued that learning disabilities is a specific disabling condition and that this term should be applied only to those students whose underachievement is directly attributed to a specific learning disability. Kirk (1978) believes that the term "specific learning disabilities" should be used to differentiate the truly learning disabled from the much larger group of students who have various learning problems. Although the discussion as to the precise definition of learning disabilities continues today, a definition has been proposed for nationwide use by the federal government. Under this law, "specific learning disability" means a disorder in one or more of the basic psychological processes involved in understanding or in using language, spoken or written, which may manifest itself in an imperfect ability to listen, think, speak, read, write, spell, or to do mathematical calculations. Such disorders include conditions such as perceptual disabilities, brain injury, minimal brain dysfunction, dyslexia, and developmental aphasia. Such terms do not include children who have learning problems that are primarily the result of visual, hearing, or motor disabilities; of mental retardation; of emotional disturbance; or of environmental, cultural, or economic disadvantages.

Under the guidelines of Public Law 101-476 (IDEA, 1990, Section 1401) a multidisciplinary team must be used to establish that a severe discrepancy exists between the student's actual and expected levels of achievement based on the individual's age and ability. Areas in which the severe discrepancy between ability and achievement may be found are as follows:

1. oral expression
2. listening comprehension
3. written expression
4. basic reading skill
5. reading comprehension
6. mathematics calculation
7. mathematics reasoning

To certify a student as learning disabled requires that the individual evidences learning difficulties in one of these seven areas. Additionally, the evaluation team must determine that the reason for the severe discrepancy between achievement and ability cannot be attributed to other conditions or sociological factors. Hallahan and Kauffman (1988) emphasize that there remains much controversy about the definition of learning disabilities offered by the federal government. They note, for instance, that the Association for Children and Adults with Learning Disabilities argues that the scope of potentially affected areas goes beyond academics, including self-esteem, vocation, socialization, and daily living activities. Using the criteria under Public Law 101-476, it is generally accepted that approximately 4 to 5 percent of the nation's school-age children meet the criteria to be identified as learning disabled. The prevalence of learning disabilities is much more common with boys than girls. The total number of children with learning disabilities comprise better than 40 percent of all children with disabilities in the United States and it appears that this number is growing. Among the reasons cited by the U.S. Department of Education (1994) to explain the increase in the growth of children with learning disabilities are "eligibility criteria that permit children with a wide range of learning problems to be classified as learning disabled; social acceptance and/or preference for the learning-disabled classification; the reclassification of some children with mental retardation as learning disabled; and the lack of general education alternatives for children who are experiencing learning problems in regular classes."

Kirk and Gallagher (1989) attribute the increase in students classified as learning disabled to five primary factors:

1. The concept of learning disabilities is becoming more accepted by parents, professionals, and schools.
2. Children who were once misdiagnosed as mentally retarded are now being recognized as learning disabled.
3. Children whose academic problems stem from environmental conditions are now being classified as learning disabled.
4. Remedial programs, formerly a provision of the federal government for the education of the disadvantaged, are receiving less support.
5. Learning disability programs have expanded to include preschool children and adolescents.

Although it is clear that the definition of learning disabilities proposed by the federal government does not specifically address students with motor learning disabilities, such as awkward or clumsy children, many authorities recognize that students with learning disabilities do evidence motor deficiencies. For example, S. Tarver and D. P. Hallahan (1976) identified the following ten characteristics of learning-disabled students as those most frequently mentioned in the literature:

1. hyperactivity
2. perceptual-motor impairments
3. emotional lability (moodiness, anxiety)
4. general coordination deficits
5. disorders of attention (distractibility, perseveration)
6. impulsivity
7. disorders of memory and thinking
8. specific academic problems in reading, writing, spelling, and arithmetic
9. disorders of speech and hearing
10. equivocal neurological signs

A review of these characteristics suggests that specially designed physical education programs may be necessary for some children with learning disabilities.

Causes of Learning Disabilities

The specific cause of learning disabilities is unknown. Generally, educational specialists attribute learning problems to one of four primary causes. These include brain damage, biochemical imbalance, environmental factors, and genetics.

Some students with learning disabilities are referred to as "minimally brain damaged." This term implies that through a neurologic assessment process involving an electroencephalogram, the student exhibits some responses that suggest the possibility of brain damage. The term *minimal* is used to emphasize that the impairment is slight and specific to certain intellectual processes in contrast to mental retardation, which is a broad-based impairment interfering with all intellectual development. Research studies have not been conclusive, however, in support of the once widely accepted proposition that all students with learning disbilities are brain damaged (Smith and Robinson, 1986).

Investigations on the relationship between learning problems and biochemical disturbances suggested that artificial flavoring and coloring in the food that children eat can cause learning disabilities and hyperactivity (Feingold, 1975). Some have argued that the learning problems are caused by the inability of the child's bloodstream to produce a normal amount of vitamins. Supporters of this theory propose that the treatment for learning disabilities should consist of minimal daily doses of vitamins (mega vitamin therapy) to compensate for the suspected vitamin deficiency. Although the discussion of biochemical factors and their effect on learning has created a great deal of interest, there is little research evidence at this time to suggest that students with learning disabilities experience biochemical deficiencies (Spring and Sandoval, 1976; Kennedy, Terdal, and Fusetti, 1993).

The third category identified by some professionals as a potential cause of learning disabilities relates to the student's learning environment. Some have proposed that the combined variables of poor teaching and inadequate curricular offerings contribute to learning problems. These factors lead to frequent absences from school that may be compounded by lack of student motivation attributed to poor parental and professional attitudes toward education in general and the student in particular. Learning problems also may be caused by family strife, social adjustment difficulties, cultural deprivation, and behavioral disorders. Remedial learning programs for these students will not be successful unless those factors that interfere with the learning environment receive attention.

Various investigators have tried to study the relationship of genetics to reading, writing, and language disabilities. While some have suggested that learning disabilities "runs in families," this is difficult to state conclusively, given the interaction between heredity and environment. DeFries, Fulker, and LaBuda (1987) examined sixty-four pair of identical twins and fifty-five pair of fraternal twins. At least one member of each pair had a reading disability. They found that approximately 30 percent of the reading problems stemmed from genetic factors; the rest were due to environmental influences.

The relationship between learning disabilities and motor impairments has not been clearly established. Some researchers (Bruininks and Bruininks, 1977; Kendrick and

Hanten, 1980; Kerr and Hughes, 1987) have reported that the child with a learning disability often has difficulty acquiring and performing motor skills. It appears to the authors that the perceptual deficit that causes learning problems may also cause problems in motor learning. For example, it seems reasonable that a perceptual problem, such as a deficit in visual figure-ground discrimination, that interferes with the child's ability to identify a specific word from among the other printed words on a page could also hamper the child's ability to distinguish a target at which a ball is to be thrown from other nearby targets. If a connection of this kind does exist, it might be assumed that improvement in one area affects improvement in the other. (Early theorists, as noted in chapter 3, did make this assumption and developed perceptual-motor programs in efforts to improve academic skills through improvement of motor skills.) However, the preponderance of research evidence shows the assumption to be unfounded: no direct transfer of learning occurs between the remediation of learning problems and motor skills (Cratty, 1979). An accepted alternative procedure is to identify the motor skills in which the youngster is experiencing problems, task-analyze the skill into small units, provide direct instruction and reinforcement, and allow for sufficient repetition and practice.

Additional research is needed to identify more precisely the real cause of learning disabilities. The present evidence is more speculative than factual. Until such time as hard evidence is available as to the cause of learning disabilities, educators will be required to assess many factors in the student's life to provide answers helpful toward the development of an appropriate educational program.

Learning and Behavioral Characteristics

Learning disabilities usually fall at the level of symbolization, and hence they affect conceptualization. Symbolization is defined as the ability to communicate or translate visual and auditory images into meaningful symbols. It includes all of the tasks requisite to successful reading, writing, spelling, arithmetic, and speaking. Conceptualization, regarded as the highest form of intellectual activity, refers to the ability to categorize, to abstract, to critically analyze, to generalize, and to create.

The potential contributions of physical educators to the remediation of difficulties in symbolization and conceptualization are still largely unacknowledged. Movement, although widely recognized as a means of communication, is usually excluded from discussions of symbolization and conceptualization in special education textbooks.

However, for many years classroom teachers have availed themselves of the assistance of physical education specialists in using movement exploration as a means of enabling young children to kinesthetically feel language concepts related to form, size, height, distance, time, and other qualitative aspects of experience. Using the body as an instrument for making and testing initial judgments about large and small, fast and slow, high and low, circular and rectangular, and other concepts is thought by many practitioners to enhance the child's competence in symbolization and conceptualization with respect to the use of words. In addition, motivation to learn the verbal tasks is enhanced by the great interest most children have in motor movement.

Learning disabilities are usually classified into the following categories: (1) inner language, (2) receptive language, and (3) expressive language. Because effective teaching is based upon adequate communication, it is imperative that physical educators be cognizant of individual differences among children in understanding and using language. Classroom teachers should be able to expect physical educators to coordinate motor activities with the teaching strategies they are employing to remedy language disorders.

Inner language processes are those that permit the transformation of experience into symbols. The first and most fundamental aspect of language to be acquired, it is greatly dependent upon the breadth and depth of experiences in infancy and early childhood. Sensory deprivation, or insufficient opportunities to see, hear, touch, smell, taste, and move in a variety of environments, is a major cause of inner language deficits. Children who read well but cannot grasp the meaning of the sentence or paragraph have inner language problems.

Receptive language is the ability to comprehend words and to remember sequences. Problems of receptive language may be either auditory or visual in nature. Students who seem to ignore or fail to follow directions often have deficits in receptive auditory language. Such youngsters find sounds in the environment confusing and frustrating. Their inability to discriminate between relevant and irrelevant sounds often helps to explain such behavioral aberrations as hyperactivity, distractibility, and short attention span. Instructing such children to "Listen" or "Pay better attention" will do little good; alternative ways of giving directions must be found. Students whose difficulties in reading are manifested by a lack of memory for words, the inability to divide words into syllables, or the inability to blend sounds into words are usually suffering from receptive visual deficits. Such individuals learn more effectively through listening than through reading.

Expressive language, or the ability to communicate, may also be either auditory or visual in nature. Auditory expressive language deficits, of course, refer to speaking and are sometimes labeled as expressive aphasias. Visual expressive language deficits encompass problems in writing and are sometimes called dysgraphias. Problems of expressive language are more easily identified and remedied than those of inner language and receptive language. Characteristics that classroom teachers often report are (1) inability to reproduce simple geometric forms; (2) persistent reversals of words, syllables, or letters; (3) rotation or inversion of letters; (4) reversed sequence of letters and syllables; (5) mirror writing, and (6) transposition of numbers.

Some students with learning disabilities exhibit behavioral characteristics such as distractibility, hyperactivity, dissociation, and perseveration. The management of these problems is largely controlled by physicians, often through drug therapy.

Distractibility is the inability to concentrate attention on any particular object or person in the environment. Distractible children have a short attention span and may forget completely what they were doing. These children are distracted by any movement, sound, color, or smell and lack the ability to block out irrelevant stimuli. It does little good to admonish them to "Pay attention"; they would if they could. Their distractibility is of neurological origin.

Hyperactivity, or hyperkinesis, is the inability to sit or stand quietly. Hyperactive children appear driven to react to everything within an arm's reach; hence, they are always touching, bending, pulling, or twisting objects in the environment. Such children seem to have an uncanny amount of energy, and it is virtually impossible to tire them out, even through endurance-oriented big-muscle activity. Estimates as to the existence of hyperactivity in youngsters with learning disabilities range from a low of 33 percent to a high of 80 percent (Shaywitz and Shaywitz, 1987).

Dissociation is the inability to see things as a whole. These children visualize parts of things but cannot conceptualize the whole; they therefore often react only to parts, making their behavior seem inappropriate or bizarre.

Perseveration is the inability to shift with ease from one activity to another. Often mistaken for stubbornness, perseveration is of neurological origin. The child would like to follow directions but he or she simply cannot respond immediately and appropriately to "stop and start" activities.

It is interesting that children with learning disabilities may exhibit any of these behavioral characteristics on some days but not on others. Inconsistency of behavior should be expected and allowances made.

Disorders of Attention and Hyperactivity

During the reauthorization of the Education for All Handicapped Children Act of 1975, now known as the Individuals with Disabilities Education Act, 1990, many parents, professionals, and members of congress questioned whether or not the term Attention Deficit Disorder (ADD) should be added as a separate disabling condition. This, of course, raised several questions, including the observation that problems focusing or maintaining attention are frequently noted in individuals with learning disabilities. Some also noted that a related disorder, attention deficit hyperactivity disorder (ADHD) is also frequently observed in individuals with learning disabilities. It was finally concluded that individuals with ADD and ADHD should receive special education

services, if qualified. The appropriate classification would vary depending upon the nature of the primary cause, but could include the P.L. 101-476 category of other health impaired, learning disability, or serious emotional disturbance.

Estimates suggest that 3 to 5 percent of the school-aged population has an attention deficit disorder. According to many professional groups, approximately 50 percent of the students with ADD do not require special education, but rather appropriate modification to the regular program of instruction. Recent evidence indicates that about one-third of the children identified as having a specific learning disability also have an attention deficit disorder, and that anywhere from 30 to 65 percent of children identified as having a serious emotional disturbance also have attention deficit disorder (Council for Exceptional Children, 1992).

In addressing ADD and ADHD, the *Diagnostic and Statistical Manual of Mental Disorder* (DSM IV, 1994), lists fourteen behaviors thought to be prevalent among children with ADD, and it specifies that the child must exhibit, prior to age seven, at least eight of the fourteen behaviors at a greater frequency than observed among others at the same mental age. (See table 18.1.) In addition, the characteristics must have been present for at least six months. Many of these characteristics can be summarized as developmentally inappropriate degrees of inattention, impulsiveness, and/or hyperactivity. Hallahan and Kauffman (1988) believe that these problems fall into three categories: coming to attention, decision making, and maintaining attention. In coming to attention, the problem seems to be an inability to select

Table 18.1 *Behaviors prevalent among children with ADD*

1. Often fidgets with hands or feet or squirms in seat (in adolescents, may be limited to subjective feeling of restlessness)
2. Has difficulty remaining seated when required to do so
3. Is easily distracted by extraneous stimuli
4. Has difficulty awaiting turn in games or group situations
5. Often blurts out answers to questions before they have been completed
6. Has difficulty following through on instructions from others (not due to oppositional behavior or failure of comprehension); e.g., fails to finish chores
7. Has difficulty sustaining attention in tasks or play activities
8. Often shifts from one uncompleted activity to another
9. Has difficulty playing quietly
10. Often talks excessively
11. Often interrupts or intrudes on others, e.g., butts into other children's games
12. Often does not seem to listen to what is being said to him or her
13. Often loses things necessary for tasks or activities at school or at home (e.g., toys, pencils, books, assignments)
14. Often engages in physically dangerous activities without considering possible consequences (not for the purpose of thrill-seeking); e.g., runs into street without looking

From: *Diagnostic and Statistical Manual of Mental Disorders*, Fourth Edition, Washington, DC, American Psychiatric Association, 1994.

the important information to which ADD students should be attending. Decision making is related to impulsivity. The ADD student seems to choose one of the first alternatives they come upon rather than considering other possibilities before responding or acting. Maintaining attention is a problem for students with ADD; therefore lists or learning tasks must be short to avoid a deterioration in performance.

It also is important to note that while ADHD is a major category under ADD, the DSM IV also contains a second category, undifferentiated attention deficit disorder (UADD), which refers to children who display significant inattentiveness, but without hyperactivity. Such children tend to be underactive, rather than overactive (Council for Exceptional Children, 1992). Children with UADD are frequently described as daydreamers, confused, and lethargic. Studies indicate that children with UADD are at high risk for academic failure and they may have a higher rate of associated learning problems than children with ADHD (Parker, 1992).

While it is clear that ADD, ADHD, and UADD individuals should not be routinely classified as learning disabled, there is overlap and many of these individuals will exhibit characteristics similar to those with learning disabilities. The goal, of course, is to ensure that students with ADD are recognized as individuals who may need special assistance and to provide the appropriate intervention, as necessary. Many of the ideas and suggestions presented in this chapter as well as the chapter on Behavior Disorders will provide useful information in developing meaningful and positive physical activity programs for students with ADD.

Perceptual-Motor Disorders

Students with learning disabilities who experience problems with motor skills frequently exhibit problems related to perception, imagery, and memory. Included in this category are such characteristics as (1) nonspecific awkwardness or clumsiness, (2) problems of laterality or directionality, (3) generalized inadequacy of perceptual-motor function, (4) poorly developed body awareness, (5) poorly developed kinesthesis, and (6) fine motor incoordination.

Deficits in learning motor skills are often observable in preschool children, who are incapable of tying shoes, cutting with scissors, buttoning clothes, and performing other daily living tasks. A lack of ability to perform these common tasks that continues into the years when most other children can perform them, if not caused by loss of sensory function or paralysis, is called apraxia. Children with apraxia may demonstrate inadequacies in visual perception, auditory perception, kinesthesis, and touch and pressure perception.

Visual Perception

Faulty visual perception may be due to deficiency in one or more of the following: visual discrimination, figure-ground discrimination, depth perception, object constancy, and object identification (visual agnosia).

Children whose visual perception is affected by inadequate visual discrimination have difficulty in determining the size, shape, color, and texture of an object. Very young children begin to use size, shape, and texture as aids in identifying objects. Texture is the last of these characteristics children learn to use in visual discrimination. Without special instruction in utilizing the various identifying characteristics of objects, children with impairment show little improvement in visual discrimination.

Students with faulty visual discrimination are not very successful in physical education. They are likely to be unable to distinguish a large ball from a small ball, a square block from a rectangular block, a blue bean bag from a red bean bag, or rough ground from smooth ground. There are very few games and activities that do not require some degree of discrimination in size, form, color, and texture. Consequently, success and pleasure in play are largely denied these children.

The ability to visually differentiate a specific object from a complex background is minimal in young children and develops slowly to reach its peak during adolescence. In children with faulty visual perception due to poor figure-ground discrimination, this development is retarded. Such children lack the ability to identify and focus attention upon a single object or figure in a cluttered or complex background. They may, for example, become so confused by the various players that form the background for a game of tag that they cannot locate the one who is "it." Inability by some children to follow the aerial path of a thrown ball is another illustration of the figure-ground problem. Obviously, such children will have difficulties in the performance of many activities in the physical education program.

Depth perception is the term given to the ability to judge distances between near and far objects. Those who have problems determining how close or far away an object is have difficulty placing their bodies in the proper relationship to the object. In catching a ball, for example, they overreach or do not reach far enough and miss the ball. Any activity that requires judgment of distances is difficult, if not impossible, for students with this visual perception deficit.

The ability to identify an object regardless of the direction from which it is viewed is termed object consistency. Youngsters without this ability become lost in a maze of unrecognizable objects as they move about. For example, such children will not be able to recognize an item of play equipment when viewed from any side other than the one from which they learned to identify it. Such a deficit in visual perception obviously creates many difficulties in physical education and in all other areas of endeavor.

Visual agnosia is a disorder that prevents the identification of objects. The underlying cause for the disorder appears to be a lesion in the cortex. As a result, the visual process is incomplete; affected children appear to be unable to synthesize all of the visual stimuli into a unified whole, so that what they see may lack color, form, or size. Students with this disorder have serious problems in learning motor skills.

Auditory Perception

Like visual perception, auditory perception can be broken down into various factors: auditory discrimination of different pitches, intensities, and tonal qualities; figure-ground discrimination; directionality of sounds; and temporal or rhythmic reception. Deficiency in one or more of these detracts from successful learning but is not as detrimental to coordination of motor movement as faulty visual perception can be. The influence of faulty auditory perception will be most noticeable in rhythmic activities and in other motor activities that necessitate adequate sound perception.

Kinesthetic Perception

Kinesthetic perception is multifaceted, including such attributes as balance and laterality, orientation of the body and its parts in space, arm positioning, leg positioning, and awareness of force and extent of muscular contraction. Two of the most widely discussed aspects of kinesthesis are laterality and directionality, terms innovated and made popular by Kephart (1971) in the late 1950s. Laterality, defined as the internal awareness of the two sides of the body and their difference, normally develops in early childhood. Well-developed laterality is considered necessary by many reading specialists for success in reading and writing when left-to-right progressions across the page must be sustained. It is thought to be the vital factor underlying the ability to discriminate between such letters as *b* and *d* or *p* and *q*. Laterality is also postulated to be essential to the maintenance of balance.

Directionality, a term often used in conjunction with laterality, involves not only kinesthetic perception but also visual and auditory perception as well as higher functions of the brain such as imagery, symbolization, and conceptualization. Not only must children be able to feel where their bodies are in space, but they must remember the meanings that society has attached to such words as up, down, over, under, high, and low and acquire the ability to assign proper labels to them. Moreover, they must learn to recognize the sounds of such words and to respond correctly to instructions with respect to moving the body through space. Furthermore, it may not be assumed that a student who can recognize the meaning of words such as over and under can generalize the meaning of these terms into various movement activities, such as responding to a request to step over the rope.

It is important to note that there is no general kinesthetic sense. The coordination problems of children must be analyzed in terms of the specific factors that compose kinesthesis.

Figure 18.1 Engaging in interesting and challenging activities such as wall climbing encourages the development of kinesthetic perception.

Students with perceptual-motor deficits often have a poorly developed body awareness that is manifested by difficulties in the identification of body parts and discrimination between right and left. It should be noted that an inability to identify body parts does not necessarily indicate a lack of body awareness but may be due to failure to learn the meaning of the words used for the parts of the body. The normal development of body image entails mastery of the following tasks at approximately the ages cited.

Age 3
Ability to name one's own body parts. Somewhat later the child learns to identify the body parts of dolls, animals, and other human beings. Last in the developmental sequence, the child learns to recognize body parts depicted in pictures and other unidimensional media.

Ages 6–7
Ability to understand right-left concepts as they relate to one's own body.

Ages 8–9
Ability to understand right-left concepts in terms of other persons.
Ages 11–12
Ability to understand right-left concepts in terms of inanimate objects.

Children with perceptual-motor disorders may be slow in the acquisition of these abilities and may manifest confusion with respect to right-left concepts throughout life.

Needs and Adjustments of Students with Learning Disabilities

Repeated failure on the part of the student with learning disabilities may lead to the development of severe anxieties, frustrations, loss of self-confidence, and a tendency to either withdraw from or rebel against the educational system. Children with learning disabilities have repeatedly been found to have significantly lower self-concepts than nondisabled peers (Martinek and Karper, 1982). Levy and Gottlieb (1984) observed that students with learning disabilities tend to play alone more often and have lower social status than other students. They also noted that students with learning disabilities tend to follow game rules well and are not more aggressive than their nondisabled peers. However, these students do demonstrate difficulty entering and remaining in activity groups, which in turn, leads to some isolation. Gresham and Reschley (1986) found that students with learning disabilities demonstrate deficits in peer acceptance and social skills. These children need desperately to achieve. Children whose learning disabilities affect their ability to learn movements are often hesitant to attempt new motor skills in front of their peer group. Moreover, they generally shy away from such competitive activities as relays and softball batting in which their lack of competence may contribute to the whole team's loss.

To meet the needs of these individuals, the physical education setting should be structured so as to guarantee success in the initial stages of learning. It may be necessary to enrich the regular education physical experience by providing alternative physical education experiences and utilizing volunteers, paraprofessionals, and peers to provide individualized instruction. Arrangements should be made so that the student can practice alone or with a small, understanding group in school facilities. Emphasis even in the primary grades should be upon the mastery of skills that the child will use and feels a need to acquire, such as catching, throwing, and kicking.

Because the traditional physical education or academic class rarely meets their needs, children with learning disabilities often develop a variety of strategies for coping with the instructional environment, many of which are self-defeating. Foremost among these strategies are (1) attention-getting, (2) helplessness, (3) destructiveness or antisocial acts, and (4) stubbornness. Attention-getting may take the form of asking many questions, dropping objects on the floor, cute sayings, or picking on others. On the other hand, the child may seek attention by being sweet and cooperative, shadowing the teacher, and assisting with noninstructional chores. Helplessness may be real or professed; the child who says, "I can't" generally elicits the teacher's sympathy, thereby placing the teacher in the student's service. Destructiveness or antisocial acts often serve to build up the ego; the class bully is seldom ignored and often gains a small following of admirers. Stubbornness, or passive resistance, initiates a power struggle between the child and the adult. Students using this strategy purposely forget assignments, lose or hide their papers, and inevitably move at an infuriatingly slow pace. Other classroom behaviors associated with behavioral and personal characteristics of students with learning disabilities are summarized in table 18.2.

Children with learning disabilities, like their nondisabled counterparts, have the capacity to understand and show insight into the meaning of their own behavior. It is important that teachers recognize self-defeating strategies for what they are. Individual or group counseling should be made available to those who exhibit problems in classroom adjustment.

Students with learning disabilities need assistance in forming meaningful and satisfactory relationships with others. Their characteristic social immaturity often makes them victims of teasing, playful gossip, and ultimately isolation and loneliness. Both boys and girls need special guidance

Table 18.2 *Classroom behaviors associated with behavioral and personal characteristics of students with learning disabilities*

Characteristic	Student's Classroom Behavior
Hyperactivity	
Attention deficits	Apparently has greater difficulty attending than peers
	Is easily distracted
Impulsiveness	Blurts out responses
	Reacts physically
Problems with rule-governed behavior	Has poor self-control
	Fidgets, shifts about in seat
	Has difficulty following directions
	Has difficulty applying problem-solving strategies
Self concept	
Poor self-esteem	Is related to limited family support
	Makes negative self-statements
Lowered autonomy and increased dependence	Requests feedback
Poor social skills	Asks questions seeking confirmation
	Is not included in social activities with peers
	Has few friendships
	Plays alone usually

Source: Bauer, A.M., & Shea, T.M. (1989). *Teaching exceptional students in your classroom.* Needham Heights, MA: Allyn and Bacon, p. 149.

with respect to grooming, the development of many and varied hobbies, and the improvement of conversational skills.

Medication and Hyperactivity

Medication is frequently prescribed for acute hyperactivity with estimates suggesting that 75 percent of students with ADHD can be helped with medication (Kennedy, Terdal, and Fusetti, 1993). The type of medication used is a stimulant which provides a calming and quieting effect on some students. The most frequently prescribed medication of this type include Ritalin, Dexedrine, and Cylert. Ritalin is most frequently used because of its safety record, even for young children. Dexedrine is a stronger medication, and Cylert is reserved for older, school-aged children. The main treatment effects of the stimulants are to: improve attention span; reduce impulsive behavior; reduce disruptive behavior; and increase compliant behavior (Kennedy, Terdal, and Fusetti, 1993).

While stimulant medications for the treatment of children are considered safe, there are some side effects, including difficulty sleeping, stares or daydreams, decreased appetite, and increased irritability (Barkley et al., 1990). Physical education teachers, classroom teachers, and other personnel who work with children on medication need to coordinate their observations to ensure that any negative side effects are reported. For additional information on medications and their use with students with hyperactivity, the reader is referred to *The Hyperactive Childbook* (Kennedy, Terdal, and Fusetti, 1993) for an informative discussion of medication and hyperactivity from the perspective of a parent, physician, and psychologist.

Planning the Program

Students with learning disabilities demonstrate a wide range of abilities in the performance of physical education activities. Although some children, particularly the younger boys and girls, are characterized by being uncoordinated and awkward, others reach levels of excellence in their chosen activities. The casual observer generally cannot distinguish between individuals with learning disabilities and their nondisabled counterparts in the gymnasium setting, providing they have had equivalent instruction and opportunities for practice.

With few exceptions, the student with a learning disability should participate in the regular physical education class. Modifications in instruction may be necessary, depending upon the activity, the specific type of learning disability, ability level of the student, number of students in the class, and the setting. Of course, decisions about instructional placement, goals, and objectives for physical education are the responsibility of the student's IEP team. Occasionally a student's needs will be so great that the IEP team

will recommend specialized motor skill experiences in small group instruction and participation in large group experiences to enhance the student's social interaction with others. This apparent dilemma in placement can be resolved in a positive way by creating flexible placement alternatives in which the student's special physical education needs are met through small group instruction and the student's need for social interaction with his or her nondisabled peers is met through integration into those activities in which he or she can be successful.

The student with a learning disability may or may not also have a motor learning disability. Many children with verbal learning problems show no signs of deficiencies in motor learning, and some may actually demonstrate superior motor ability. Whether or not the child with a learning disability has a deficit in motor learning, he or she may benefit from participation in selected motor activities. Cratty (1969) has found that for some children, "games and game-like problem-solving situations are effective in motivating the learning of some academic competencies." The games utilized must integrate motor activity with conceptualization of selected academic skills, such as word recognition, spelling, and number combination. The physical education teacher should work closely with the classroom or special education teacher in selecting and introducing the integrated games to ensure that the motor experiences will be appropriate and successful.

Facilities and Equipment

The first, and perhaps the most important, requirement in adapting the instructional environment to the special needs of the student with severe learning disabilities is the reduction of stimuli within the gymnasium to a minimum. Reduction of extraneous stimuli may be achieved by covering windows and using artificial light. All equipment, except that which will be immediately used, can be removed from sight. Whenever possible, noise should be minimized by soundproof walls and ceilings. Many modern gymnasiums designed as instructional centers now have wall-to-wall carpeting.

The number of lines on the floor and markings on the wall should also be minimized. It is recommended that "floor spots" in the form of simple geometric shapes or other relevant symbols be placed on the floor to assist young children in finding "their own space" and to assure that the distance between students is sufficient to eliminate body contact.

The second requirement in adapting facilities is the reduction of space in the gymnasium through the use of cubicles or partitions or the identification of small rooms within the school that can be used for physical education purposes. Placing sturdy tumbling mats vertically on end creates an easily designed but effective cubicle instructional setting for students easily distracted (figure 18.2). When

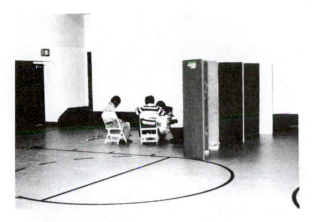

Figure 18.2 Smaller, less distractive teaching areas can be created by placing mats vertically.

children play outdoors, it is especially important that small areas be roped off and that space boundaries be carefully defined. Ideally the outdoor area should be surrounded by a high wooden fence to exclude irrelevant stimuli.

The third requirement in adapting facilities is consistency from day to day in the organization of teaching stations and the placement of equipment. Because these children are often described as "lost in space," it is recommended that the instructional environment be highly structured with as little as possible left to chance.

In addition to the requirements of stimuli control, space reduction, and consistency in placement of equipment, the facilities for students with learning disabilities should include an adequate number of teaching stations and sufficient equipment for individualized instruction. A Learning Resources Center with high tech equipment, including video camcorders, computers, and hypermedia resources should be established to provide opportunities for students to view themselves and others in the performance of motor skills.

Perceptual-Motor Activities

In the 1960s and 1970s many professionals argued that the learning problems experienced by children with learning disabilities could be remediated through various perceptual-motor programs. Kephart (1971) believed, for instance, that reading difficulties could be overcome through programs designed to enhance eye-hand coordination. The basic premise was to correct or remediate the underlying processes or abilities so that improvements in achievement would occur. Perceptual-motor programs were developed to provide children training in the motor bases of behavior, such as balance in different positions and the development of laterality and directionality; training in perceptual skills, such as space discrimination, form perception, and recognition of texture, size, color, and structure; and training in visual perception, auditory perception, and kinesthetic perception. At the present time well over forty perceptual-motor theories with accompanying programs of remediation

have been proposed in professional literature. Those of Barsch, Cratty, Frostig, Getman, and Kephart are probably best known to physical educators who utilize an eclectic approach in planning their perceptual-motor programs, selecting the best from each school of thought.

In the perceptual-motor program, regardless of the type of activity or instructional approach, it is basic that children develop awareness of the nature of the sensations they are receiving and of the results that occur from responses to the stimuli. Once such consciousness has been developed, children can begin to replace the unsuccessful responses with substitutes that will result in satisfactory performance. For example, children who have difficulty in balancing on a beam must be helped by the teacher to achieve awareness of the sensations that occur when they are losing their balance and to recognize the elements in their response to the sensations that prevent them from regaining balance. Then, with assistance from the teacher, these students must analyze the motor skills involved to determine the adjustments in muscular movements they need to make in order to regain and maintain balance. As they attempt the new movements, they must consciously associate the new responses with the stimuli. Frequent repetition of the process is required to enable

Figure 18.3 Work on a balance beam helps a child become aware of the sensation of losing and regaining balance.

the children to develop the new responses to the point that they use them automatically in substitution for the old unsuccessful ones.

Professionals have questioned the effectiveness of perceptual-motor programs and training. Kavale and Mattison (1983), following a comprehensive review of studies that investigated the effectiveness of perceptual-motor programs, concluded that it is "not effective and should be questioned as a feasible intervention technique for exceptional children." In a similar vein, Myers and Hammill (1982) observe: "As a consequence of our reviews of these systems, we would recommend that perceptual-motor training in the schools be carefully reevaluated. Unlike a decade ago, when research on the topic was sparse, one can no longer assume that these kinds of activities will be beneficial to the children who engage in them. In fact in the long run they may even be somewhat harmful because (1) they may waste valuable time and money and (2) they may provide a child with a placebo program when the child's problem requires a real remedial effort. We would suggest that when these programs are implemented in the schools, they be considered as highly experimental, nonvalidated services that require very careful scrutiny and monitoring."

Until further evidence is available to either support or refute the value of perceptual-motor programs, physical educators should be cautioned against using this approach as a substitute for a well-developed and well-designed, success-oriented physical education program. Children with learning disabilities profit from activities that are task-analyzed and presented in a sequential order. These children need success and positive reinforcement, even when the achievement appears small. Activities based upon a careful diagnosis of each person's needs, the use of carefully planned teaching progressions, and the avoidance of excessive competition all contribute to success.

Teaching Hints

Good teaching is based upon careful diagnosis of individual needs. With the growing popularity of the multidisciplinary approach to learning disabilities, several disciplines may share responsibility for the evaluation of the motor and cognitive development of the child. Depending upon the expectations of the other academic disciplines with which the instructor is working, the physical educator may administer standardized specific tests to assist in identifying children in need of special motor training. Some of these tests were discussed in chapters 3 and 7. However, the most important diagnostic technique remains careful, conscientious observation of the student's motor performance over long periods of time. It cannot be overemphasized that no single test is valid and reliable enough to determine a child's needs. Nor is it possible for someone with learning disabilities to be entirely consistent in his or her motor performance. The student may lack motivation on one day, be affected by

medication on the next, and be convalescing from a cold on the next. It is important to remember that children view their motor acts as an extension of themselves and as a measure of their own worth. Therefore, the process of diagnosis and evaluation, like that of instruction, should be so presented that children feel they are succeeding.

Effective diagnostic techniques enable the physical educator to teach to the level of involvement. It is essential to determine whether the major learning disability is auditory, visual, or kinesthetic. The accepted practice seems to be to emphasize the use of those senses that are unaffected rather than to attempt to remedy the disability. This implies that some individuals must be taught mainly through the visual and kinesthetic modalities while others must receive instruction chiefly via the auditory and kinesthetic modalities.

It is equally important to ascertain the level at which the child's learning is breaking down: perception, imagery or memory, symbolization, or conceptualization. The following list of questions demonstrates the application of this technique to teaching a forehand drive in tennis.

1. *Visual perception.* In viewing a demonstration, can the student discriminate between open and closed positions of the racquet face? Does the student see what you think he or she sees? Can the student organize all visual sensations of head, arms, and legs into the meaningful whole we call a forehand drive?

2. *Auditory perception.* In hearing an explanation or analysis of a skill, can the student discriminate among sounds? Does the student hear what you think he or she hears? Can he or she organize all auditory sensations (words, words, and more words) into a meaningful whole?

3. *Proprioceptor perception.* Is the student aware of what the body is doing? Does he or she respond to the stimuli from the proprioceptor?

4. *Memory.* Is the student capable of mental practice? Can the student remember the positions of joints, the rhythm of the movements, and the exact sequence in which the movements occur? Two days later is the student still able to visualize the correct movements? Can he or she still recall the verbal analysis of the skill?

5. *Symbolization.* Can the student make the body do what the mind tells him or her? Can the student translate visual and auditory memory into an accurate reproduction of the movements viewed in the demonstration?

6. *Conceptualization.* Can the student discriminate between accurate and inaccurate reproduction in movement? Can he or she analyze errors in movement? Can he or she use problem solving to decrease the discrepancy between perceived movement, intended movement, and the actual motor performance?

One of the fundamental principles in adapting instruction is that of *structure,* a form of conditioning used with distractible children to assure appropriate responses to stimuli. Structure in the teaching situation refers to a planned routine or activity, with as little as possible left to chance, so that children can anticipate the sequence of events and know what is expected of them. In a highly-structured physical education program, the children always enter the gymnasium through the same door, go to the same floor spot, participate in warm-up activities, and start individualized instruction at the same teaching station. The direction of rotation between stations is uniform from day to day, as are the stop and start signals employed by the teacher. The structured teaching environment is adult-dominated; children are not asked to make choices and demonstrate competence in self-direction because they lack the readiness to cope with freedom and the exposure to unessential stimuli that freedom brings.

It is important to understand that in the large majority of cases some educational objectives, like the development of creativity, that are important for children without disabilities are entirely inappropriate for boys and girls with severe motor or verbal learning disabilities. If, or when, the child learns to control his or her distractibility, structure is gradually lessened. The physical educator should discuss the concept of structure with the classroom teacher and ascertain that the amount of structure imposed in the gymnasium is equal to and consistent with that imposed in the classroom.

Many practices in physical education that traditionally have been thought of as desirable are contraindicated for children with learning disabilities. Some of these follow:

1. Opportunities to develop leadership-followership qualities through membership on many different kinds of teams with different students serving as leaders each time. Frequent changes in group structure confuse children with learning disabilities. They should be allowed to play with the same small group throughout the year with as few changes in leadership as feasible.

2. Opportunities to "let off steam" and to develop fitness through freedom to run, jump, and shout in an optimal amount of space. Despite the fact that this practice may meet the needs of some children with learning disabilities, particularly those with hyperactivity, it tends to heighten the hyperactivity of others. Many special educators feel strongly that noise, as in cheering on teammates and clapping when a game is won, should be discouraged. Time should be spent on the mastery of neuromuscular skills that have carry-over value and activities designed primarily for cardiovascular development. Rather than rule out certain types of activities for *all* hyperactive students, it is desirable to experiment with variations in speed

and distance to determine which kinds of fitness activities are best for each individual.

3. Emphasis upon the development of speed through awards for track and field events and the association of winning with the fastest team. Many children with learning disabilities need assistance in deceleration. For them it is recommended that the emphasis be changed to "How slowly can you dribble the ball?" "How slowly can you do a crab walk?" "How slowly can you go up and down in pushups?" Because hyperactive children exhibit considerable muscular tension, they must be taught specific techniques for relaxation, for slowing down, and for maintaining a stationary position. Sherrill and Pyfer (1985) advocate that each physical education class period for the student with a learning disability should incorporate three to five minutes of conscious relaxation instruction.

The key to successful instruction of children with learning disabilities is individualization. It is possible that no two children in the gymnasium will ever be doing the same thing simultaneously. To facilitate implementation of this principle, each child, upon entering the gymnasium, may pick up a card on which his or her activities for the day are printed. The nature and sequence of these activities should not change radically from week to week.

Suggested Activities

The program of physical education activities varies with age, degree of involvement, and specific type of learning disability. If the students have verbal learning disabilities, the program should be planned cooperatively by the physical educator and classroom teacher to ascertain that needs are met and that methodology is consistent.

In the primary grades, attention must be focused upon the development of basic movement patterns—running, jumping, hopping, throwing, catching, striking, and kicking. Children should explore their capability for movement on different surfaces—wood, cement, sand, pebbles, high and low grass, both wet and dry. Opportunities to experiment with different sizes, shapes, and weights of balls and sports implements should be provided. Ample time should be spent on climbing and hanging activities as well as creeping and crawling activities. Balancing activities are important provided they are varied and interesting and the child can achieve some measure of success. The gross motor activities that promote basic skill development and physical fitness often can be combined with sensory experiences to promote perceptual-motor learning; some examples may be found at the end of the chapter.

Instruction in individual and dual sports, with appropriately modified equipment, should begin as early as grade three. Competence in such activities as bowling, ballet, and swimming helps to win the admiration of the peer group, many of whom may not yet have had the opportunity to try these activities. Most important, competence in individual and dual activities enhances self-esteem and serves to compensate for any inability to participate successfully in team activities. Early acquaintance with lifetime sports also contributes to family unity and may lead to closer parent-child relationships when, for instance, parents and children can bowl or swim together.

In the primary grades physical education may play a major role in the development of inner language and the enrichment of vocabulary. When this is a concern, the teacher should plan contrasting activities, such as up and down, over and under, below and above, forward and backward, to enable students to experience kinesthetically the words they must recognize on paper. Likewise, appropriate time should be devoted to learning the names of body parts and the terms for different kinds of movements and positions in space.

In the intermediate and secondary grades, emphasis upon individual and dual activities should continue. Students should be introduced to mechanical principles and given special assistance in problem solving and generalizing with respect to similarities and differences in basic movements, such as, for instance, the overarm throw, the tennis serve, and the badminton smash. Because of their characteristic deficits in symbolization and conceptualization, it cannot be assumed that they will learn anything through incidental exposure.

Perceptual-Motor Activities

Although there appears to be general agreement that perceptual-motor programs should be implemented carefully and monitored closely to determine outcomes, there is agreement that instruction in selected concepts with which children with learning disabilities struggle, such as discriminating between large and small, can be provided in the physical education class. The intent is not to replace or duplicate instruction in the classroom; rather the intent is to supplement and reinforce these experiences. The concept of over and under, for example, can be introduced in the classroom and reinforced in the gymnasium through the use of activities where the body and body parts are placed over or under selected objects—for example, the arm is "over" the head, the body is "under" the rope. In the following section various activities are suggested to assist teachers in working with youngsters who experience problems in visual and auditory discrimination, balance, and body awareness. These activities can be incorporated into the physical education program for use in the teaching of various basic skills.

Activities Focusing on Visual Discrimination (size):

1. Tossing balls of various sizes into receptacles of appropriate size to hold them. Several receptacles of different sizes and a ball that will fit into each size will be needed. The child selects the ball that is the most appropriate size (neither too large nor too small) for the container and tosses it in.

2. Running around circles of various sizes marked on the floor. Circles of progressively larger size are painted or drawn on the floor inside a large circle. The child runs around the circle that is the size indicated by the teacher.

3. Selecting a particular-size object and running a designated distance. Needed will be an object so large that running with it is difficult, an object so small that it can be easily held in the hand, and an object of a size between these two. The child is then instructed to run to the teacher (or to run some easily defined distance) with the object with which he can run the fastest; with the one that is largest, the one of middle size, and the smallest one.

4. Crawling through circular objects of various sizes. Hoops, tubes, or similar objects of various circumferences will be needed. The child crawls through the object of the size indicated by the teacher.

5. Running zigzag between chairs that are various distances apart. Several chairs are set three and five feet apart, as shown in figure 18.4. The child runs between the chairs that are closer or farther apart as directed by the teacher.

Activities Focusing on Visual Discrimination (color):

1. Throwing balls or bean bags of different colors into containers of matching color. Balls or bean bags of various colors with receptacles to match will be

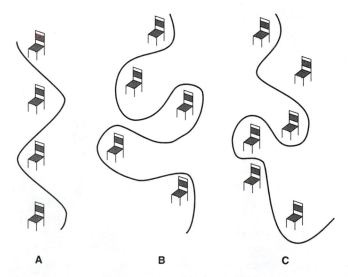

A   B   C

Figure 18.4 Zigzag run uses chairs set various distances apart. The complexity of the task can be determined by changing the distance and spacing of the chairs.

needed. The child matches the colors and throws the object into the appropriate receptacle.

2. Selecting an object of designated color from among others and running with it to another group of objects to pick the object of matching color. Two objects of each color are needed. In response to the teacher's instructions, the child picks up an object, runs with it to the location of the other objects, and matches it to one of like color.

3. Kicking balls into goals of the corresponding color. Several large balls of different colors and goals to match will be needed. (Goals can be improvised from suitably sized paper cartons from which one side is removed to allow the ball to enter.) The child kicks each of the balls into the appropriate goal.

4. Jumping into hoops of different colors after seeing a model of the color. Two hoops of each color will be needed; one set is held by the teacher and the other laid on the floor. The child is shown a hoop of a certain color and must jump into the hoop of the corresponding color. The activity can be varied by placement of other parts of the body in the hoop.

Figure 18.5 Hoops and other objects can be used to create interesting and challenging paths to follow.

5. Striking balls with bats of the corresponding color. Several bats and balls of matching color are needed, or the bats may be tied with ribbons in matching colors. The child chooses a bat and then selects a ball of the same color for "batting practice."

Activities Focusing on Visual Discrimination (shape and form):

1. Reproducing in movement a specific shape. Several plastic, wood, or cardboard shapes will be needed. The teacher holds up a shape and the child must reproduce it by drawing in the air or walking on the floor.

2. Selecting matching shapes. Two sets of objects of various shapes will be needed. One set is placed in various locations in the room; the other remains with the teacher. When the teacher holds up one of the shapes, the child must find the one like it and run back to the teacher with it.

3. Choosing from among several objects the one best suited to an activity. Several objects such as a large block, large ball, and bean bag are needed. In response to instructions from the teacher, the child must select the object most suitable for sitting, rolling, and throwing, and then use the object in the appropriate activity.

4. Matching paper shapes with objects of similar form. Shapes that resemble several of the items of furniture or equipment in the room should be cut from heavy paper. Upon being handed one of the paper shapes by the teacher, the child must locate the item that has a similar form and carry it to a designated spot. (The items will need to be ones that the child is able to carry.)

5. Reproducing shapes with the body. A child who knows the letters of the alphabet can attempt to form such letters as c, l, and y with his or her body, or several children may work together to reproduce in a lying position on the floor most of the letters of the alphabet.

Activities Focusing on Visual Discrimination (distance):

1. Throwing at a goal from various distances. The goal may be a box or container for younger children and a basketball hoop for older ones. Three marks are made on the floor at various distances from the goal, and the child is instructed by the teacher to shoot a ball at the goal from the mark nearest the goal, farthest from the goal, and from the mark between the two.

2. Throwing at targets of various heights. Targets are placed or drawn on a wall at three different distances

from the floor. The teacher instructs the child to throw a ball or bean bag at the highest target, the lowest target, and the one at the middle distance.

3. Judging distance of an object from a given point. Several objects are placed around the room at different distances from the point where the child will stand. The student is asked to estimate how many steps away each object is from him or her. Then he or she checks the accuracy of the estimates by stepping off the distance.

4. Rolling a large ball different distances. A large ball, such as a medicine ball, will be needed. Two or more sets of marks, each set placed the same distance from the starting point, but in different directions from it, are drawn or painted on the floor. From the starting point, the child must roll the ball to a set of marks that are the same distance away.

5. Tossing an object into the air at various distances. A ball or bean bag will be needed. The teacher instructs the child to throw the object a long distance into the air, a short distance, and an intermediate distance. For more acute discrimination, the child may be asked to throw the object at distances between the three; for example, to a height higher than the lowest distance but lower than the middle distance.

Activities Focusing on Visual Discrimination (speed):

1. Running at different speeds. In response to directions from the teacher, the child runs slowly, moderately, and fast.

2. Throwing objects of different kinds to compare speed of movement. Needed for the activity will be balls of various sizes, a bean bag, and a balloon. The teacher throws the objects and the child determines which ones move more slowly and which ones faster and which is the slowest and which the fastest.

3. Swinging a suspended ball at different rates of speed. A ball of medium size is suspended by a cord from the ceiling. The child puts the ball in motion by hitting it with his or her hand so that it will swing slowly, moderately, or fast in response to the instructions of the teacher.

4. Rolling a ball various distances to judge the speed of movement. Objects that will serve as backstops are placed at various distances from the starting point. The teacher rolls a ball toward each object, and the child judges the speed at which each ball travels.

5. Moving the body in various forms of locomotion to determine the speed of each. The child moves over a designated distance by hopping, crawling, jumping, and so forth, and decides which form of movement is

the fastest and which the slowest, and which is faster or slower than some other one.

Activities Focusing on Figure-Ground Phenomenon:

1. Catching a ball suspended in front of a distracting background. A brightly colored ball is hung from the ceiling so that it is suspended in front of other objects. When the ball is swung, the child concentrates on following it with his or her eyes in order to catch it.

2. Rolling a ball between objects. A tennis ball or ball of similar size will be needed, as will several objects that cannot be easily knocked over with the ball. The child rolls the ball toward the objects in an attempt to place it between two of them.

3. Locating and kicking a moving ball in a group of stationary balls. Several balls of medium size are placed on the floor a short distance from the child. One is put into motion by the teacher, and the child must move to it in order to kick it.

4. Throwing a ball at a target. A target of any kind is placed against a wall on which there are pictures or other objects. The child concentrates on the specific target and attempts to hit it with a ball thrown from several feet away.

5. Playing tag in a small space. Confining the game to a small space will make it easier for the child to keep his or her attention focused on the person he or she is trying to catch.

Activities Focusing on Auditory Discrimination:

1. Responding to different tones and frequencies with a specified motor movement. Various objects that create different tones and frequencies will be needed. The teacher works out the motor movement with the children, such as nodding the head or waving the hand, that will be used to respond when a certain tone or frequency is produced.

2. Identifying the direction of a sound. Two children work together in this activity. One child bounces a ball in various directions; the other child must determine the direction from which the sound is coming. Sight may be used to help locate the right direction.

3. Differentiating the sounds made by a ball. The child bounces a ball and describes the difference between the sound that is made when the ball is struck with the hand and that made when the ball strikes the floor.

4. Differentiating sounds made by striking objects. A short, thin piece of wood or drumstick is used to strike against various objects in the room. The

child listens to the sounds and tries to match each sound with its source.

5. Isolating a sound from background noise. This activity requires that there be a number of sounds emitted from various sources in the room, such as from the play activities of several children. The teacher helps the child to isolate some of the sounds and then encourages him or her to try to isolate others. The child may use vision to locate the source and identify the sound.

Activities Focusing on Balance:

1. Standing on one foot. While standing, the child lifts one foot and tries to balance. The difficulty of the activity can be increased by moving the raised leg to various positions and by moving one or both arms to various positions.

2. Standing on the balance beam. The child stands with one foot behind the other on the balance beam. The activity can be made more difficult by balancing only on one foot, walking on the beam, reversing direction, squatting, and so forth.

3. Walking the line. Strips several inches wide are applied or painted on the floor. The student walks along the strips, placing one foot in front of the other.

4. Balancing objects. A book or similar object is placed on the head to be balanced while walking or is placed on the feet to be balanced while holding the legs straight up from a supine position. Other parts of the body might also be used in various positions.

5. Walking on a resilient surface. The child walks around the top of a large inner tube, maintaining balance. The trampoline may be substituted in this activity and may be used for other simple balancing stunts.

Activities Focusing on Identity of Body Parts:

1. Touching parts of the body. This activity is like a game of Simon Says, with all the activity consisting of touching parts of the body.

2. Tossing a balloon and allowing it to land on a part of the body. Each child is supplied with an air-filled balloon. The balloons are tossed into the air and the children maneuver so that the balloons land on the part of the body the teacher designates.

3. Moving a part of the body in response to its being named. The teacher or a child chosen as the leader calls out a part of the body, such as foot, arm, head, and the group responds by moving that part.

4. Naming the body part used to produce a movement. The child performs a leap or squat or picks up or throws an object and names the parts of the body involved in the action.

5. Using parts of the body to form a shape. Children are divided into pairs for this activity. One child directs the other to form his or her body into a certain shape by telling the child which parts of the body to move.

Activities Focusing on Body Awareness:

1. Observing reflections of movements in the mirror. The child observes in a mirror the movements made with various parts of the body. The child is encouraged to talk about what he or she is doing, such as by saying, "My arm is moving up over my head."

2. Analyzing different kinds of locomotion. The child moves across the floor by crawling, rolling, sliding, hopping, skipping, or running. He or she is asked to describe the movements made in the particular locomotion skill.

3. Describing positions of the body. The child takes a position such as the stork stand. He or she identifies the shape and describes the movements and parts of the body involved.

4. Performing movements of different quality. The child makes a movement that has a certain quality, such as a languid swing of the arm, and then explores other ways of making the movement to achieve other qualities, such as strength, fluidity, tenseness.

5. Performing one part of a movement pattern without engaging the rest of the parts. The child isolates one movement of a total movement pattern and performs it without moving any other part of his body.

Activities Focusing on Laterality:

1. Sliding to right and left. In response to the teacher's direction, the child slides his foot to the left or right.

2. Walking and retracing steps on the balance beam. The child walks on the balance beam and turns left or right, as indicated by the teacher, and retraces the steps.

3. Following footprints. Footprints are drawn or painted on the floor in such a manner that the child must, in stepping on them, cross one foot over the other (figure 18.6).

4. Crawling on alternate hands and feet. The crawl is made with the hand and the leg of opposite sides extended forward at the same time.

5. Combining arm movements with a zigzag run. The student follows a zigzag pattern, and as he or she turns to the left or right, holds up the arm on that side of the body.

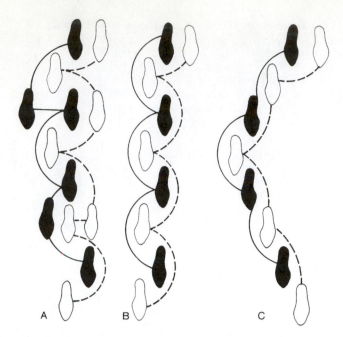

Figure 18.6 Patterns of footprints for an activity to promote laterality. (*A*) Simple, (*B*) moderately complex, (*C*) complex.

Activities Focusing on Directionality:

1. Passing to the left or right. The child walks toward the teacher and passes to the left or right side of the teacher as directed.

2. Matching the movements of another child. Two children work together, facing each other. One child performs a movement, such as lifting the left foot or raising the right arm, and the other child matches the movement with the same side of the body.

3. Identifying the left and right sides of objects. The teacher directs the child to touch one or the other side of an object in the room, such as a chair, and the child runs to it and places his or her hand on the correct side.

4. Walking between objects. Large objects, such as big blocks or chairs, are placed in a row with enough space between them to allow a child to pass through. The child walks to the right or left of each chair in the row in response to the direction given by the teacher.

5. Touching the corresponding hand or foot of another child. The students work in pairs, facing each other. One child touches his or her right or left hand or foot to the corresponding hand or foot of the other child.

Activities Focusing on Rhythm and Tempo:

1. Marching to a cadence. The teacher beats a drum, increasing and decreasing the tempo to enhance the experience.

2. Keeping time with a swinging ball. A ball is suspended from the ceiling by a cord. It is swung at various speeds by the teacher, and the child swings his or her foot, arm, leg, head, or trunk to match the swinging of the ball.

3. Moving various parts of the body to a cadence. The cadence is supplied by a strong beat on the drum, or piano. The child responds by keeping time with different parts of the body—fingers, head, arms, legs, and so forth.

4. Jumping in rhythm to a swinging rope. The teacher and a helper swing a jump rope back and forth (not a full turn of the rope). The child jumps over the rope as it passes near his or her feet.

5. Performing various movements to a beat. This activity is like number one except that the difficulty is increased by having the child skip, jump, or hop to the cadence.

Summary

There are more children identified as learning disabled than any other disabling condition in the United States. Significant gains have been made in the last twenty years to define the term *learning disability* and to understand some of the causes of this disorder. There is general agreement that a learning disability occurs when there is a major discrepancy between an individual's actual and expected levels of achievement that cannot be attributed to other handicapping conditions or sociological factors. People with learning disabilities are normally bright people who can excel in many areas if provided proper instruction and a positive learning environment. Although there is much that is not known about the reasons for a learning disability, many attribute the condition to one of three primary causes; brain damage, biochemical imbalance, and environmental factors.

Persons with learning disabilities have difficulty translating visual and auditory images into meaningful symbols. This is evident in the classroom when the child is unable to understand the symbols (letters and words) essential for success in reading or numbers used for success in mathematics. Some of these same challenges are evident in the physical education class where the child is unable to differentiate the colors or geometric symbols (triangles and circles) used in many games. In addition to these problems, some students with learning disabilities have motor impairments such as balance and coordination problems that require special instruction in physical education. There is also evidence, however, that some students with learning disabilities have excelled as athletes.

Although students with attention deficit disorder (ADD) and attention deficit hyperactivity disorder (ADHD) may or may not be learning disabled, information on these disorders was provided in this chapter because of the prevalence of hyperactivity among children with learning disabilities. It should be understood, however, that students with ADD and ADHD may or may not qualify under P.L. 101-476 and if they do qualify could be classified as other health impaired, learning disabled, or seriously emotionally disturbed.

As is true with all disabling conditions, the physical education program must be based on the individual needs of the child with the learning disability. Cruickshank (1967) identified the following concepts that are generally accepted today as effective in the education of students with learning disabilities: Establish a highly structured program; reduce environmental space; eliminate irrelevant auditory and visual stimuli; and enhance the stimulus value of the instructional materials. These concepts, combined with the general practice of creating a successful and positive experience, should be used in teaching students with learning disabilities. Skills should be task-analyzed and students given the opportunity to practice skills with reinforcement provided as learning occurs. Although many have recommended that specific perceptual-motor programs be developed for students with learning disabilities, there is evidence that questions the effectiveness of these programs in remediating specific learning problems. Such programs, when used, should function as a supplement to the physical education program.

Although much is not known about students with learning disabilities, specific gains have been made in the past few years that indicate that those with learning disabilities, if provided with a positive and skill-oriented curriculum, can be successful in schools and make major contributions to society. Where would we be without Albert Einstein, generally recognized as having a learning disability, and his work in helping to understand the nature of the universe?

Selected Readings

Amerikaner, M., & Summerlin, M. (1982). Group counseling with learning disabled children: Effects of social skills and relaxation training on self-concept and classroom behavior. *Journal of Learning Disabilities, 15,* 340–343.

Arnheim, D.D., & Sinclair, W.A. (1979). *The clumsy child* (2d ed.). St. Louis: C.V. Mosby Co.

Barkley, R.A., McMurray, M.B., Edelbrock, C.S., & Robbins, K. (1990). The side effects of methylphenidate in children with attention hyperactivity disorder: A systemic, placebo-controlled evaluation. *Pediatrics, 86,* 184–192.

Bauer, A.M., & Shea, T.M. (1989). *Teaching exceptional students in your classroom.* Needham Heights, MA: Allyn and Bacon, Inc.

Bruininks, V.L., & Bruininks, R.L. (1977). Motor proficiency and learning disabled and non-disabled students. *Perceptual and Motor Skills, 44,* 1131–1137.

Children with ADD: A shared responsibility (1992). Reston, VA: Council for Exceptional Children.

Churton, M. (1989). Hyperkinesis: A review of literature. *Adapted Physical Activity Quarterly, 6*(4), 313–327.

Cratty, B.J. (1975). *Physical expressions of intelligence.* Englewood Cliffs, NJ: Prentice-Hall, Inc.

Cratty, B.J. (1975). *Remedial motor activity for children.* Philadelphia: Lea and Febiger.

Cratty, B.J. (1979). *Perceptual and motor development in infants and children* (2d ed.). Englewood Cliffs, NJ: Prentice-Hall, Inc.

Cratty, B.J., & Martin, M. (1969). *Perceptual-motor efficiency in children.* Philadelphia: Lea and Febiger.

Cruickshank, W. (1967). *The brain-injured child in home, school, and community.* Syracuse, NY: Syracuse University Press.

DeFries, J., Fulker, D., & LaBuda, M. (1987). Evidence for a genetic aetiology in reading disability of twins. *Nature, 329,* 537–539.

Feingold, B.F. (1975). Hyperkinesis and learning disabilities linked to artificial food flavors and colors. *American Journal of Nursing, 75,* 797–803.

Gresham, J.F., & Reschley, D.J. (1986). Social skill defects and low peer acceptance of mainstreamed learning disabled children. *Learning Disability Quarterly, 9*(1), 23–32.

Hallahan, D.P., & Kauffman, J.M. (1988). *Exceptional children* (4th ed.). Englewood Cliffs, NJ: Prentice-Hall, Inc.

Haubenstricker, J.L. (1983). Motor development in children with learning disabilities. *Journal of Physical Education, Recreation, and Dance, 53,* 41–43.

Kavale, K., & Forness, S. (1985). *The science of learning disabilities.* San Diego, CA: College-Hill Press.

Kavale, K., & Mattison, P.D. (1983). One jumped off the balance beam: Meta-analysis of perceptual-motor training program. *Journal of Learning Disabilities, 16,* 165–173.

Kendrick, K.A., & Hanten, W.P. (1980). Differentiation of learning disabled children from normal children using four coordination tasks. *Physical Therapy, 60,* 784–788.

Kennedy, P., Terdal, L., & Fusetti, L. (1993). *The hyperactive childbook.* New York: St. Martin's Press.

Kephart, N.C. (1971). *The slow learner in the classroom* (2d ed.). Columbus, OH: Charles E. Merrill Publishing Co.

Kerr, R., & Hughes, K. (1987). Movement difficulty and learning disabled children. *Adapted Physical Activity Quarterly, 4,* 72–79.

Kirk, S.A. (1978). An interview with Samuel Kirk. *Academic Therapy, 13,* 617–620.

Kirk, S.A., & Gallagher, J.J. (1989). *Educating exceptional children* (6th ed.). Boston, MA: Houghton Mifflin.

Levy, L., & Gottlieb, J. (1984). Learning disabled and non-learning disabled children at play. *Remedial and Special Education, 5*(6), 43–50.

Martinek, T., & Karper, W. (1982). Entry-level motor performance and self-concepts of handicapped and nonhandicapped children in mainstreamed physical education classes: A preliminary study. *Perceptual and Motor Skills, 55,* 1002.

Morris, P.R., & Whiting, H.T.A. (1971). *Motor impairment and compensatory education.* Philadelphia: Lea and Febiger.

Myers, P.I., & Hammill, D.D. (1982). *Learning disabilities: Basic concepts, assessment practices, and instructional strategies.* Austin, TX: Pro-Ed Publishers.

Parker, H. (1992). *The ADD hyperactivity handbook for schools.* Plantation, FL: Impact.

Shaywitz, S.E., & Shaywitz, B.A. (1987). Attention deficit disorder: Current perspectives. Paper presented at the national conference on Learning Disabilities. Bethesda, MD: National Institutes of Child Health and Human Development (NIH).

Sherrill, C., & Pyfer, J.L. (1985). Learning disabled students in physical education. *Adapted Physical Activity Quarterly, 2,* 283–291.

Smith, D.D., & Robinson, S. (1986). Educating the learning disabled. In R. J. Morris & B. Blatt (Eds.), *Special education: Research and trends* (pp. 222–248). New York: Pergamon Press.

Spring, C., & Sandoval, J. (1976). Food additives and hyperkinesis: A critical evaluation of the evidence. *Journal of Learning Disabilities, 9,* 560–569.

Tarver, S., & Hallahan, D.P. (1976). Children with learning disabilities: An overview. In J.M. Kauffman & D.P. Hallahan (Eds.), *Teaching children with learning disabilities: Personal perspectives.* Columbus, OH: Charles E. Merrill Publishing Co.

U.S. Department of Education. (1994). *Sixteenth annual report to Congress on the implementation of the Education of the Handicapped Act.* Washington, DC: Author.

Wallace, G., & Kauffman, J.M. (1978). *Teaching children with learning problems.* Columbus, OH: Charles E. Merrill Publishing Co.

Wallace, G., & McLoughlin, J.A. (1979). *Learning disabilities: Concepts and characteristics* (2d ed.). Columbus, OH: Charles E. Merrill Publishing Co.

Wiederholdt, J.L. (1974). Historical perspectives on the education of the learning disabled. In L. Mann & D.A. Sabatino (Eds.), *The second review of special education.* Philadelphia: JSE Press, Division of Grune and Stratton.

Enhancing Activities

1. Many famous and distinguished people such as Thomas Edison, Woodrow Wilson, Winston Churchill, and Albert Einstein are believed to have had a learning disability. Develop a list of other well-known figures who have a learning disability.

2. Review the reference list at the end of this chapter and obtain a copy of one of the articles of interest to you. Upon completion of the article develop a list of the major points discussed by the author.

3. Engage in a debate with a person who opposes your views concerning the value of perceptual-motor programs. Upon completion of the debate, identify the major areas of agreement and disagreement.

4. Write to the Division of Learning Disabilities of the Council for Exceptional Children to obtain general information from it concerning learning disabilities.

5. Develop some activities that could be used in physical education to help students with learning disabilities improve their ability to understand selected concepts such as left and right or over and under. What recommendations could be made for a student who, because of his or her poor visual discrimination, is unable to strike a tennis ball?

6. Develop a list of suggested activities that could be used to encourage students to move "slowly." Example: Who can take the longest time to walk between point *x* and point *y*? In this example the students would have to walk the designated route and not be permitted to come to a complete stop.

7. Observe two or three students with learning disabilities in a physical education class. Explain why these and similar students would benefit from instruction in integrated settings with nonhandicapped youngsters—or why they wouldn't. What other placement options might be recommended?

8. Seek permission to attend an IEP meeting for a student with a learning disability. Observe the various professionals and the interaction that occurs in a multidisciplinary setting. Did you find the session helpful in identifying the type of physical education program to be provided for this student?

CHAPTER
19

Behavioral Disorders

◆ CHAPTER OBJECTIVES ◆

After studying this chapter, the reader should be able to:

1 Define behavior disorders and comprehend the various terms used to describe this population.

2 Recognize the characteristics of students with serious emotional problems and the importance of analyzing the frequency, intensity, and duration of behavior in assessing the seriousness of the problem.

3 Appreciate the classification systems used to identify those who have a mental disorder and the important role mental health specialists play in developing appropriate treatment and education programs.

4 Identify characteristics associated with conduct and personality disorders and other behavior disorders that affect children and youth.

5 Suggest activities and physical education program considerations for students with behavior disorders.

6 Provide physical education instruction for students with behavior disorders that is based on selected behavioral practices and concepts developed by various professionals.

7 Appreciate the important role physical educators must assume in helping students to overcome fears or apprehensions sometimes associated with activities such as swimming, contact sports, and experiences involving height.

8 Recognize the significance of recent research that suggests activity and exercise programs help to reduce behavior problems and contribute to greater academic production.

There is a growing awareness of the need to provide educational programs for students whose conduct at school and home deviates to a marked extent from what is generally accepted as appropriate behavior. These are youngsters whose lives appear to be in constant turmoil. They show their unhappiness in a variety of ways ranging from violent and destructive acts at one extreme to withdrawn and sullen behavior at the other end of the spectrum. Making friends, accepting themselves, and cooperating with teachers and parents are all very difficult for these individuals.

Students with serious behavioral problems are referred to by a variety of names such as "socially maladjusted," "emotionally handicapped," "emotionally disturbed," or even "psychotic" if their behavior is significantly abnormal. In recent years, the term *behavior disorder* has become generally accepted as the preferred term for describing youngsters whose actions and conduct are considered socially unacceptable. The acceptance of this description is due to the growing awareness among educators that the identification and treatment of behavior problems is an integral part of the educational community's responsibility. Physical educators, too, are becoming more acutely aware of their role and responsibility in providing quality experiences for students with serious behavior problems. Physical education experiences that incorporate skill development, exercise, and fun through games, dancing, and sport activities are an integral part of the comprehensive program for students with behavior disorders.

Within this chapter, a definition of behavior disorders will be provided. Information about the causes and a classification system for this disability will also be presented. The last section will focus on teaching considerations and implications for program development. Although educational programs for those with behavior disorders have improved dramatically, much is still unknown about the learning characteristics and instructional methodology most appropriate for these students, particularly those whose behavior is highly unusual.

Defining Behavior Disorders

There is not a commonly accepted definition among professionals for the term *behavior disorders*. Much of the confusion is due to the lack of understanding of what constitutes good mental health. The orientation of the professionals involved—for example, psychologists, psychiatrists, and educators—also adds a new and sometimes different dimension to the definition. Educators, for instance, have generally found the following definition originally proposed by Kauffman (1977) as acceptable: individuals with behavior-disorders are "those who chronically and markedly respond to their environment in socially unacceptable and/or personally unsatisfying ways but who can be taught more socially acceptable and personally gratifying behavior" (p. 23).

Unlike other definitions that have been proposed by medical and allied health personnel, this statement indicates clearly that students can be taught to respond and act in more socially acceptable ways. Kauffman's definition also underlines the importance of the student's environment as both a potential cause of conflict and an important variable in the development of a successful instructional program. This realization is in contrast to the belief of some professional personnel in medicine and health who have traditionally viewed behavior problems as inherent within the student's personality composition.

In an effort to provide guidelines for the identification and educational treatment of students with behavior disorders, the federal government under Public Law 101-476 uses the term "seriously emotionally disturbed" and defines it as a condition exhibiting one or more of the following characteristics over a long period of time and to a marked degree, which adversely affects educational performance:

1. an inability to learn that cannot be explained by intellectual, sensory, or health factors;
2. an inability to build or maintain satisfactory interpersonal relationships with peers and teachers;
3. inappropriate types of behavior or feelings under normal circumstances;
4. a general pervasive mood of unhappiness or depression;
5. a tendency to develop physical symptoms or fears associated with personal or school problems.

The term includes children who are schizophrenic and have a serious personality disorder. The term does not include children who are socially maladjusted, unless it is determined that they are seriously emotionally disturbed.

The definition accepted by the federal government was first proposed by Bower in 1969. A clarification of the characteristics inherent within the definition is necessary to fully comprehend the intent of the definition. First, students classified as emotionally disturbed are individuals with average to above average learning capabilities, and their school-related problems are not the primary result of any intellectual inadequacy. If learning problems are evident, they are attributed to the student's behavioral patterns rather than to the individual's ability to comprehend information. Additionally, the student's difficulty relates to an inability to interact positively with peers and teachers, and to respond appropriately in various settings. Although most authorities recognize that all children and adults have difficulty responding appropriately at various times, the difference for students with behavior disorders is found in the frequency, duration, and intensity of their behavior patterns. In essence, the most effective way to describe students with behavior problems is to actually define those behaviors that seem unusual and then to specify the frequency, duration, and intensity of the behavior.

Frequency refers to how often the particular behavior is performed. All children cry, get into fights, and at times respond aggressively. Exhibiting these behaviors, however, does not constitute a behavior problem unless the specific behavior—fighting, for example—occurs frequently. Although the student who is disturbed exhibits inappropriate behaviors similar to those of other children, he or she makes the undesirable responses much more often.

Duration, which is closely related to frequency, is a measure of how long a student engages in an activity. The amount of time students with behavior disorders act unacceptably is different from that of their peers. For example, although all children experience temper tantrums lasting a few seconds to a few minutes, the student with severe behavior problems may have a tantrum for a period of time approaching one hour or longer. Occasionally the problem involves exhibiting a behavior for too short a period of time, such as paying attention or attending to a task.

The third variable that helps to explain behavior disorders relates to the magnitude of a given behavior. Magnitude refers to the intensity of the behavior. Although many people may occasionally respond angrily in a loud voice, individuals with behavior disorders frequently rely on a high-pitched voice as the medium to express all of their demands. There are also students with behavior problems who express themselves too softly to be heard. The concept of magnitude may be applied to many behaviors, such as the intensity with which a youngster fights, slams a door, or picks on others.

Defining behaviors by focusing on their frequency, duration, and magnitude helps in the identification and treatment of students with serious behavior problems. This technique also adds meaning to the definition of emotional disturbance proposed by the federal government.

There continues to be disagreement and confusion as to the "best" definition or term to identify and describe students with behavior disorders. Most authorities agree, however, that having a behavior disorder involves the following: (1) behavior that goes to an extreme—behavior that is not just slightly different from the usual; (2) a problem that is ongoing—one that does not disappear, and (3) behavior that is unacceptable because of social or cultural expectations (Hallahan and Kauffman, 1991).

Prevalence

The U.S. Department of Education has historically used the value of 2 percent when referring to that portion of the school-age population that is behavior disordered. National child count data, however, suggests that this percentage is double the number actually receiving services. It is generally acknowledged that the government's estimate and the number actually served are very conservative. Studies conducted by several investigators, including Juul (1986) and Kauffman (1986) believe that at least 6 to 10 percent of

children and youths of school age exhibit serious and persistent behavioral problems. Some of the confusion relates to the status of students who are juvenile delinquents. While some argue that these students qualify as emotionally disturbed, others counter that most juvenile delinquents are socially maladjusted, not emotionally disturbed.

Although there may be differences as to the actual number of children who are behavior disordered, there is general agreement that the number is large and that many with emotional problems may not be receiving the special education services they need. Other areas of agreement suggest that there are more boys with behavior disorders than girls. Mendelsohn and Jennings (1986) found that greater than 80 percent of the children referred for emotional problems in a large metropolitan area were boys. Overall, boys tend to exhibit more aggression and conduct disorder patterns than girls do (Kazdin, 1987).

With respect to age, the middle school years appear to be the time of greater incidence with a decline in reports during junior high and high school. The exception to this statement are conduct disorders, one form of emotional disturbance, which tends to increase in junior-high and the early high school years. Among juvenile offenders, boys tend to be identified as conduct problems for committing aggressive acts such as assault, whereas girls are normally associated with truancy and sexual promiscuity.

Classification of Behavior Disorders

There are many systems that have been proposed to classify those with mental illness. The American Psychiatric Association relies, for instance, on a collection of categories catalogued in its *Diagnostic and Statistical Manual for Mental Disorders* (DSM-IV). Although this system assists psychiatrists, its application in the educational setting is complicated by many problems, including its emphasis on labels without application to individual treatment. In addition, earlier editions of the system were not very reliable. Even with the more precise language found in the 1994 revision, mental health professionals vary in their use of the categories in classifying individual children. Nevertheless, familiarity with aspects of the system is important so that physical educators will be able to communicate with the various mental health specialists.

The DSM-IV disorders are grouped into fifteen major diagnostic classes and one additional section, "Other Conditions That May Be a Focus of Clinical Attention" (table 19.1). A brief explanation of each of the categories follows:

Disorders Usually First Diagnosed in Infancy, Childhood, or Adolescence Although there are many disorders in this category, including mental retardation and learning disorders, the primary behavior disorders of concern include: autistic disorder, conduct disorder, oppositional defiant disorder, and disruptive behavior disorder. Although this category title suggests that these disorders are first diagnosed in infancy, childhood, and adolescence, this is for convenience only and is not meant to suggest that there is any clear distinction between "childhood" and "adult" disorders. Additional information and diagnostic criteria for autistic disorder, conduct disorder, and oppositional defiant disorder are found in tables 19.2, 19.3, and 19.4. Also included in the category of disorders in infancy, childhood, or adolescence are various tics, including Tourette's Syndrome, which has received much attention through the media. Mahmoud Abdul-Raue, a talented National Basketball Association player, has Tourette's Disorder. The criteria for diagnosis of Tourette's Disorder requires that the condition be recognized before age eighteen. The anatomical location, number, frequency, complexity, and severity of the tics change over time. The tics normally involve the head and, frequently, other parts of the body, such as the torso and upper and lower limbs. Vocal tics include the various words and sounds, including grunts, yelps, barks, snorts, and coughs. Coprolalia, the uttering of obscenities, is present in a few individuals (less than 10 percent) with this disorder (DSM-IV, 1994).

Delirium, Dementia, and Amnestic and Other Cognitive Disorder The predominant disturbance in the disorders in this category is a significant deficit in cognition or memory that represents a significant change from a previous level of functioning. In the earlier DSM III-R, disorders in this category were placed in a section titled "Organic Mental Syndromes and Disorders." The term organic mental disorders is no longer used because it incorrectly implies that "nonorganic" mental disorders do not have a biological basis. Impairments of memory, dementia, and delirium, a disturbance of consciousness, are examples of disorders included in this category.

Mental Disorders Due to a General Medical Condition Disorders in this category are characterized by the presence of mental symptoms that are judged to be the direct physiological consequences of a general medical condition. While this is a very broad category, it does permit the classification of mental disorders, even in young children, that appear to be directly related to a significant physiological consequence of a general medical condition.

Table 19.1 *DSM-IV disorders*

Disorders Usually First Diagnosed in Infancy, Childhood, or
  Adolescence
Delirium, Dementia, and Amnestic and Other Cognitive Disorders
Mental Disorders Due to a General Medical Condition
Substance-Related Disorders
Schizophrenia and Other Psychotic Disorders
Mood Disorders
Somatoform Disorders
Factitious Disorders
Dissociative Disorders
Sexual and Gender Identity Disorders
Eating Disorders
Sleep Disorders
Impulse-Control Disorders Not Elsewhere Classified
Adjustment Disorders
Personality Disorders
Other Conditions That May Be a Focus of Clinical Attention

Table 19.2 *Diagnostic criteria for 299.00 Autistic Disorder*

A. A total of six (or more) items from (1), (2), and (3), with at least two from (1), and one each from (2) and (3):
  (1) qualitative impairment in social interaction, as manifested by at least two of the following:
    (a) marked impairment in the use of multiple nonverbal behaviors such as eye-to-eye gaze, facial expression, body postures, and gestures to regulate social interaction
    (b) failure to develop peer relationships appropriate to developmental level
    (c) a lack of spontaneous seeking to share enjoyment, interests, or achievements with other people (e.g., by a lack of showing, bringing, or pointing out objects of interest)
    (d) lack of social or emotional reciprocity
  (2) qualitative impairments in communication as manifested by at least one of the following:
    (a) delay in, or total lack of, the development of spoken language (not accompanied by an attempt to compensate through alternative modes of communication such as gesture or mime)
    (b) in individuals with adequate speech, marked impairment in the ability to initiate or sustain a conversation with others
    (c) stereotyped and repetitive use of language or idiosyncratic language
    (d) lack of varied, spontaneous make-believe play or social imitative play appropriate to developmental level
  (3) restricted repetitive and stereotyped patterns of behavior, interests, and activities, as manifested by at least one of the following:
    (a) encompassing preoccupation with one or more stereotyped and restriced patterns of interest that is abnormal either in intensity or focus
    (b) apparently inflexible adherence to specific, nonfunctional routines or rituals
    (c) stereotyped and repetitive motor mannerisms (e.g., hand or finger flapping or twisting, or complex whole-body movements)
    (d) persistent preoccupation with parts of objects
B. Delays or abnormal functioning in at least one of the following areas, with onset prior to age 3 years: (1) social interaction, (2) language as used in social communication, or (3) symbolic or imaginative play.
C. The disturbance is not better accounted for by Rett's Disorder or Childhood Disintegrative Disorder.

From: *Diagnostic and Statistical Manual of Mental Disorders, Fourth Edition.* Washington, DC. American Psychiatric Association, 1994.

Table 19.3 *Diagnostic criteria for 312.8 Conduct Disorder*

A. A repetitive and persistent pattern of behavior in which the basic rights of others or major age-appropriate societal norms or rules are violated, as manifested by the presence of three (or more) of the following criteria in the past 12 months, with at least one criterion present in the past 6 months:

Aggression to people and animals
(1)   often bullies, threatens, or intimidates others
(2)   often initiates physical fights
(3)   has used a weapon that can cause serious physical harm to others (e.g., a bat, brick, broken bottle, knife, gun)
(4)   has been physically cruel to people
(5)   has been physically cruel to animals
(6)   has stolen while confronting a victim (e.g., mugging, purse snatching, extortion, armed robbery)
(7)   has forced someone into sexual activity

Destruction of property
(8)   has deliberately engaged in fire setting with the intention of causing serious damage
(9)   has deliberately destroyed others' property (other than by fire setting)

Deceitfulness or theft
(10)   has broken into someone else's house, building, or car
(11)   often lies to obtain goods or favors or to avoid obligations (i.e., "cons" others)
(12)   has stolen items of nontrivial value without confronting a victim (e.g., shoplifting, but without breaking and entering; forgery)

Serious violations of rules
(13)   often stays out at night despite parental prohibitions, beginning before age 13 years
(14)   has run away from home overnight at least twice while living in parental or parental surrogate home (or once without returning for a lengthy period)
(15)   is often truant from school, beginning before age 13 years

B. The disturbance in behavior causes clinically significant impairment in social, academic, or occupational functioning.
C. If the individual is age 18 years or older, criteria are not met for Antisocial Personality Disorder.

Specify type based on age at onset:
Childhood-Onset Type: onset of at least one criterion characteristic of Conduct Disorder prior to age 10 years
Adolescent-Onset Type: absence of any criteria characteristic of Conduct Disorder prior to age 10 years

Specify severity:
Mild: few if any conduct problems in excess of those required to make the diagnosis **and** conduct problems cause only minor harm to others
Moderate: number of conduct problems and effect on others intermediate between "mild" and "severe"
Severe: many conduct problems in excess of those required to make the diagnosis **or** conduct problems cause considerable harm to others

From: *Diagnostic and Statistical Manual of Mental Disorders, Fourth Edition.* Washington, DC. American Psychiatric Association, 1994.

Table 19.4 *Diagnostic criteria for 313.81 Oppositional Defiant Disorder*

A. A pattern of negativistic, hostile, and defiant behavior lasting at least 6 months, during which four (or more) of the following are present:
(1)   often loses temper
(2)   often argues with adults
(3)   often actively defies or refuses to comply with adults' requests or rules
(4)   often deliberately annoys people
(5)   often blames others for his or her mistakes or misbehavior
(6)   is often touchy or easily annoyed by others
(7)   is often angry and resentful
(8)   is often spiteful or vindictive

Note: Consider a criterion met only if the behavior occurs more frequently than is typically observed in individuals of comparable age and developmental level.

B. The disturbance in behavior causes clinically significant impairment in social, academic, or occupational functioning.
C. The behaviors do not occur exclusively during the course of a Psychotic or Mood Disorder.
D. Criteria are not met for Conduct Disorder, and, if the individual is age 18 years or older, criteria are not met for Antisocial Personality Disorder.

From: *Diagnostic and Statistical Manual of Mental Disorders, Fourth Edition.* Washington, DC. American Psychiatric Association, 1994.

Substance-Related Disorder   As implied in the name, this category refers to abusing a drug, or to the side effects of a medication, or a toxin. Eleven classes of substances including alcohol, nicotine, and cocaine are discussed. With the incidence of substance abuse among children and adolescents on the rise, and the association of substance abuse to other forms of emotional and behavioral problems, the likelihood of a student falling into this category is high.

Schizophrenia and Other Psychotic Disorders   The term psychotic has been defined differently by various authorities. The DSM-IV acknowledges this and suggests that it is best to define psychoses by referring to specific disorders such as schizophrenia. For example, schizophrenia is a disturbance that lasts for at least six months and includes evidence of two or more of the following symptoms for a period of at least one month: delusions, hallucinations, disorganized speech, grossly disorganized or catatonic behavior, and negative symptoms. The onset of schizophrenia typically occurs between the late teens and the mid-30s, with onset prior to adolescence rare. There are various types of schizophrenia. These include:

Paranoid Type. The essential feature of this disorder is the presence of prominent delusions or auditory hallucinations. The delusions and hallucinations are usually persecutory or grandiose, or both. Because the cognitive functioning of these individuals does not appear impaired, the prognosis for this type is believed better than other sub-types.

Disorganized Type. The essential features of this type are: disorganized speech, disorganized behavior, and a flat, lifeless response. The behavioral disorganization is such that activities of daily living may be disrupted for this individual.

Catatonic Type. This catatonic type of schizophrenia is marked by various disturbances that may include motor immobility, negativism, and peculiar movements. Some individuals appear to have excessive motor activity and echolalia (repeat words phrases spoken to them).

Undifferentiated Type. A type of schizophrenia which meets the general criterion for schizophrenia, but does not meet the criteria for any specific subtype.

Residual Type. This type is reserved for those instances when there has been an episode of schizophrenia, but the clinical picture is not clear. It may be that the individual is in transition to one of the other types or possibly to remission.

Mood Disorders   As indicated in the name, the disorders included in this section have as their predominant feature a disturbance in mood, for example, depression. In children and adolescents with depression, the mood may be irritable rather than sad. Some of the signs that may be evident include problems with concentration, including a precipitous drop in grades for children. Another form of mood disorder is a manic expression where there is a distinct period in which the mood is abnormally elevated or expansive, a euphoric state. Panic attacks and disorders are also included in this category. Children may fear a particular activity (e.g., swimming) or competition in the physical education setting. Various phobias—obsessive-compulsive behavior, and anxiety disorders—are classified under the heading of Mood Disorders.

Somatoform Disorders   This disorder is characterized by physical symptoms which suggest a general medical condition which is not supported by medical examination. The physical symptoms are not intentional and are not under voluntary control. An example of one of the disorders in this category is hypochondriasis which is the fear of having a serious disease based on the person's misinterpretation of bodily symptoms. Another example which is sometimes encountered by physical educators is body dysmorphic disorder or the preoccupation with a defect in appearance.

Factitious Disorders   Unlike somatoform disorders where the physical symptoms are not under voluntary control, factitious disorders are characterized by physical or psychological symptoms that are intentionally produced or feigned in order to assume the sick role.

Dissociative Disorders   The essential feature of the dissociative disorders is a disruption in the usually integrated functions of consciousness, memory, identity, or perception of the environment. Dissociative amnesia, the inability to recall important personal information, is one of the disorders included in this category. The DSM-IV cautions that amnesia is very difficult to assess in preadolescent children, because of its confusion with inattention, anxiety, oppositional behavior, etcetera. Dissociative identity disorder, formerly known as multiple personality disorder, is one of the better known dissociative disorders, due to the general fascination with the idea that one can possess several different and distinct personalities.

Sexual and Gender Identity Disorders   Although most of the disorders included in this category do not apply to children, gender identity disorder is sometimes noted in children. Although difficult to diagnose, in young boys the cross-gender identification is manifested by a strong desire to participate in generally feminine activities. Young girls, on the other hand, display intense negative reaction to parental expectations or attempts to have them wear dresses or other feminine attire. Frequently what is perceived by parents as a "problem" is only a phase that does not lead to a gender identity disorder. About three-quarters of adolescent boys who had a childhood history of gender identity disorder report a homosexual or bisexual relationship without concurrent gender identity disorder (DSM-IV, p. 536).

Eating Disorders   Anorexia nervosa and bulimia nervosa are the two specific diagnoses included in this category. Both conditions were described in chapter 15. Anorexia nervosa is most commonly found in females (90 percent of all cases) and in countries where food is abundant and thinness is viewed as an ideal for women. The group most at risk is girls between the ages of thirteen to eighteen. Bulimia, or binge eating, is characterized by obsessive eating followed by purging by means of self-induced vomiting or laxatives. This practice has serious health implications, including impaired liver and kidney function and tooth decay.

Sleep Disorders   There are various disorders that can occur while sleeping or attempting to sleep. These include various dyssomnias, which are primary disorders of initiating or maintaining sleep or of excessive sleepiness. Some of the common lay terms used to describe these include insomnia and narcolepsy (prominent daytime sleepiness). The ability to monitor sleep and to determine the various stages of sleep, shallow to deep, has improved dramatically in recent years bringing medical attention and relief to individuals affected by various sleep disorders.

Impulse-Control Disorders Not Elsewhere Classified
This section includes disorders of impulse control that are not classified elsewhere in the DSM-IV. The essential feature of impulse-control disorders is the failure to resist an impulse, drive, or temptation to perform an act that is harmful to another. Examples include kleptomania (impulse to steal) and pyromania (impulse to set fire to objects).

Adjustment Disorders   This disorder is used primarily to identify individuals who, following a significant stress in life, are unable after a period of time (e.g., three months) to make the necessary and appropriate adjustments. The disorder may occur in any age group and may be evident in children following the loss of a loved one, divorce, or move to a different community.

Personality Disorders   The DSM-IV identifies a personality disorder as ". . . an enduring pattern of inner experience and behavior that deviates markedly from the expectations of the individual's culture, is pervasive and inflexible, has an onset in adolescence or early adulthood, is stable over time, and leads to distress or impairment" (p. 629). The ten types of personality disorders include three that are noted in tables 19.2, 19.3, and 19.4. Diagnostic information is presented on these three disorders—autistic disorders, conduct disorders, and oppositional defiant disorder—which are frequently observed in the school setting.

Autistic disorder, also known as early infantile autism, childhood autism, and Kanner's autism, was recognized in the revision of the Individuals with Disabilities Education Act (IDEA) as a disability with its own separate category. As noted in table 19.2, this is a serious disorder with many characteristics similar to schizophrenia. In most cases, there is an associated diagnosis of mental retardation, commonly in the moderate range.

Children with autism respond chiefly to their inner thoughts and cannot relate to others around themselves or to their environment as a whole, and thus often give the appearance of mental retardation. Frequently they are mute and do not attempt communication of any kind and give no indication of recognizing the presence of others. Other common characteristics that children with autistism may demonstrate at one time or another are unusual body movements and peculiar mannerisms, abnormal responses to stimuli, resistance to change, emotional outbursts, and excessive preoccupation with objects and procedures without regard to their social acceptability. Children with conduct disorders (see table 19.3) are frequently referred to as "tough" kids because of the persistent pattern of violating societal rules and norms. These are usually children, who at very young ages begin to challenge both school and home rules, are a problem in school, and are well known to the larger community by around thirteen years of age. Although the exact number of individual with conduct disorders is unknown, it is estimated that 6 to 16 percent of males and 2 to 9 percent of females qualify. Most disturbing is the observation that the number of individuals with this disorder is increasing and conduct disorder is one of the most frequently diagnosed conditions in outpatient and inpatient mental health facilities for children.

Although oppositional defiant disorder (see table 19.4) includes some of the features observed in conduct disorder, it does not include the persistent pattern of the more serious forms of behavior disorder found with conduct disorder. The primary feature of oppositional behavior is persistent negative, defiant, and disobedient behavior toward adults. Because many children exhibit transient behavior that might be classified as oppositional behavior, care must be exercised to avoid unfairly speculating or classifying some children as suspected of having an oppositional defiant disorder.

Some of the major conditions included in the DSM-IV are also included in a classification system proposed by Quay (1972). Quay's four dimension classification system (table 19.5) has proved useful to educators because of its specific focus on behavior disorders.

In this system, four types or dimensions of behavior problems were identified by analyzing teacher and parent behavior ratings, life histories, and interviews with children who are emotionally disturbed. The four dimensions identified by Quay include: conduct disorder, personality disorder, immaturity, and socialized delinquency. Students with conduct disorders are frequently described as disobedient, disruptive, and bossy. Personality disorder, on the other hand, generally involves withdrawal and is usually characterized by feelings in the student of anxiety and fear. The immature student classified with an attention defect disorder is identified as a daydreamer and passive with a short attention span. The behaviors of these dimensions persist even though they are inappropriate to the child's chronological age. The last dimension, socialized delinquency, is characterized by gang membership, truancy, and illegal activity.

Table 19.5 *Selected behavior traits of behavior disorders using Quay's four dimensions*

Dimensions

Conduct Disorder	Personality Disorder (Anxiety-Withdrawal)	Inadequacy-Immaturity	Socialized Delinquency (Socialized Aggression)
Behavior Traits:	Behavior Traits:	Behavior Traits:	Life History Characteristics:
Disobedience	Feelings of inferiority	Preoccupation	Has bad companions
Disruptiveness	Self-Consciousness	Short attention span	Engages in gang activities
Fighting	Social withdrawal	Clumsiness	
Destructiveness	Shyness	Passivity	Engages in cooperative stealing
Temper tantrums	Anxiety	Daydreaming	
Irresponsibility	Crying	Sluggish	Habitually truant from school
Impertinent	Hypersensitive	Drowsiness	
Jealous	Seldom smiles	Prefers younger playmates	Accepted by delinquent
		Easily led	subgroups
Shows signs of anger	Chews fingernails		
Acts bossy	Depression, chronic sadness	Masturbation	Stays out late at night
Profanity	Fails to attempt new tasks	Giggles	Strong allegiance to selected
			peers
Attention seeking		Easily flustered	
Boisterous		Chews objects	
		Picked on by others	
		Plays with toys in class	

Adapted from Mandell, C.J., and Fiscus, E. (1981). *Understanding exceptional people* (p. 357). St. Paul, MN: West Publishing Co.; and Bauer, A.M., & Shea, T.M. (1989). *Teaching Exceptional Students in your Classroom*. Needham Heights, MA: Allyn and Bacon, Inc. p. 172–173.

A third classification system used by some educators is to categorize students with behavior disorders as either aggressive, acting-out, or withdrawn. Edelbrock uses (1979) the terms *overcontrolled* and *undercontrolled* to describe these students. Overcontrolled is applied to students who are shy and anxious with personality problems; the term undercontrolled is reserved for students with behavior patterns such as fighting, acting-out, tantrums, and conduct problems.

Causes of Behavioral Disorders

An effort to identify the causes of behavior problems is considered essential if appropriate intervention techniques are to be employed. Unfortunately, however, although various theories have been proposed to explain behavior disorders, there is still little known about the causes of emotional problems. Some have argued that the problem is biophysical; others support a psychoanalytical or sociological premise. Most of the explanations that have been proposed attribute the disorders to either a psychological or a physiological factor.

Some students who are severely disturbed, primarily those with autistic disorders, show signs of biochemical imbalance. To suggest, however, that this imbalance is the cause of behavior disorders cannot be stated with certainty. Some have suggested that there is a genetic or heredity link for some selected behavior disorders, including schizophrenia. The evidence for the genetic influence on behavior has been traced through the study of identical twins, adopted children, and statistical analyses of certain families or populations. Research suggests that there is a genetic influence on the development of temperament characteristics that can create a favorable or unfavorable environment in which individuals must function (Plomin, 1986). For many individuals with behavior disorders, there is no evidence of organic disturbance. Students with emotional disturbance frequently appear to be very normal, healthy individuals. Although there is continued interest in analyzing the physiologic composition of those with behavior problems, there is little evidence at the present to support a physiologic premise as the cause of behavior disorders.

Many theorists, including behavioral psychologists and psychoanalysts, have proposed that psychological factors in the lives of people affect the way they act. However, the suggested treatment procedures for children with behavior problems are different among supporters of a psychological orientation.

Psychoanalysts, for instance, believe that children become behaviorally disordered because they have not successfully dealt with the problems they encountered as they developed. For these theorists, the underlying problems are more important than the behavior exhibited by the individual.

Behaviorists argue, however, that searching for the cause is wasteful of time and effort. Instead, behaviorists contend that educational programs should focus on the student's behavior and his or her interaction with peers, teachers, and parents. Supporters of this view also emphasize that behaviors are learned and thus, inappropriate behaviors can be remediated. Teachers also find this approach positive because the focus is away from labeling students as bad, emphasizing instead that it is their actions that are unacceptable.

The role of the school and family in contributing toward behavior problems has also been examined. The structure of the family, increasing divorce rate, and one parent families have been the focus of recent attention. Although findings are not definitive, some authorities have concluded that divorce is a difficult transition, and life in a single-parent family can be a high-risk situation for both parent and child (Kirk and Gallagher, 1989, p. 415). The social environment, including the prevalence of crime and its depiction on television, has been the object of study. Some of Bandura's early work (1977) indicates clearly that models, including those on television, do affect behavior and some believe that the influence is greater on high-risk students. The increasing prevalence of substance abuse among school-age children is also reason for concern. Johnson (1988) theorized that there is a relationship between behavior disorders and chemical dependency and that students with behavior disorders and selected personality traits are vulnerable to substance abuse.

Although there is no basis to say with certainty that school and family environments cause emotional problems, it must also be emphasized that these two social institutions have a responsibility to help prevent the development of behavior problems. This means that students should be treated fairly, recognizing and accepting their individual differences. Teacher and parent expectations must be reasonable, not too high or too low. Most importantly, teachers and parents should reward students for good behavior and withhold reinforcement for inappropriate behavior. The breakthrough in furthering our understanding of the causes of behavior disorders may come from a recognition of ways to prevent the occurrence of emotional problems.

The Program for Students with Behavior Disorders

Physical education experiences contribute in many ways to enhance the total well-being of the student who is emotionally disturbed. Obvious benefits of a well-designed program include improvement of the student's motor and physical fitness performance. Some research has indicated that students with behavior problems experience deficiencies in these important areas. These differences have generally been attributed to the lack of appropriate programs rather than to an inherent motor deficiency in those who are emotionally disturbed.

Exercise programs also have been studied to determine their effect on the behavior patterns of children who are emotionally disturbed. Allan (1980) reported a 50 percent decrease in the disruptive behavior of children who participated in a ten-minute daily jogging program. The effect of exercise on boys with austism was found by Watters and Watters (1980) to decrease self-stimulatory behavior, such as rocking back and forth and hand flapping, by 32 percent. Their study also indicated that vigorous activity such as jogging does not interfere with the student's ability to concentrate following an exercise program. Evans and associates (1985) found that jogging and touch football resulted in fewer talkouts and increased academic production in the classroom. Findings such as these help to dispel a common myth that exercise programs tend to excite students with behavioral disorders and in turn inhibit their performance upon returning to the classroom after participating in physical education activities.

The specific physical education objectives for those with behavior disorders should be developed and specified in the student's Individualized Educational Program. As with all students with physical education deficiencies, the program should be based on the student's needs as identified through formal and informal assessment techniques. Given this information, the activities selected for the program should include those with which the student has had some preliminary success. As part of the motivating process, a wide variety of instructional equipment can be displayed for the students to look at and handle. When an interest in a particular piece has been kindled, the instructor may talk to the student about it and show him or her how to use it. As the student tries it out, he or she is encouraged to continue to play with it. Instructions should be simple but structured.

Group participation in play activities is highly desirable because it makes social contacts possible. Some students may experience considerable strain in social adjustment, so it may be necessary to work gradually toward group activities, progressing from spectatorship to one-to-one instruction and eventually to small group activity. As the youngsters become accustomed to small group play, more peers can be taken into the group to increase the scope of social contacts. Their inclusion in the activity also provides an incentive for approved social conduct, but the instructor should monitor carefully to ensure that the nondisabled students do not dominate the game or detract in any way from the successful performance of the student with the behavior disorder.

Basic motor skill games and exercises that do not require fine coordination are usually the most suitable. Individuals who are very regressed or experience motor disturbances due to medication are easily frustrated by activities requiring numerous movement patterns and detailed directions. Activities of limited responses and simple structure that may be successfully used with the older school-age group are shuffleboard, casting, croquet, horseshoes, ring toss, bowling, weight lifting, bag punching, and the basic sport skills of throwing, catching, dribbling, and striking a ball. A certain element of competition in the games usually is acceptable. For most students, contact sports and highly competitive games that tend to encourage the expression of aggression directly toward others are contraindicated.

For younger children, the elementary activities utilizing the basic skills (running, throwing, catching, jumping, and so forth) are appropriate and are readily taught. More competitive activities often encourage antisocial conduct, either withdrawal or aggression; therefore, their use in the curriculum should be limited. Children who are aggressive may benefit from participation in strenuous games and activities, as vigorous exercise is helpful in reducing aggressive conduct in some persons. Some aggressive students act as they do because of a subconscious desire for attention, and it is possible to modify their behavior by giving them recognition. Making such a child a squad leader or putting him or her in charge of an activity can often reduce the aggressiveness. Special efforts should be made to get students with behavior disorders to interact. Activities must be planned that promote group interaction. Neel (1986) suggests that simply by varying methods used with traditional activities, opportunities for interaction can be created. For example, in the game of musical chairs, when the music stops, the child left without a chair must approach each of the other children in the group and say "hi" or "hello," give his or her name, and shake hands. There is no need to remove a chair as the game continues until each child has had the opportunity to initiate contact.

Shy children need special help in developing self-confidence. The teacher can help by showing confidence in the child's ability and setting goals that realistically can be achieved. Such children should not be forced into any activities they fear. This also holds true for overanxious children. Both kinds of students should be brought to accept an activity that causes them fear and worry by very gradual exposure to parts or elements of the activity until the emotional reaction subsides.

Not all play activities should be organized for the students. They should be given access to equipment so they may play on their own; they should also have the chance for passive and spectator participation in sport activities. Those engaging in impromptu play must be made to understand the regulations that have been established in regard to their use of the equipment and facilities during unsupervised periods. Strict adherence to safety precautions should be expected and received. If a student must be denied permission to use the equipment or refused any other request made of the physical education instructor, this should be done on an impersonal basis so the student will not feel hurt or discriminated against.

Co-recreational activities in which the two sexes can mingle socially should be given appropriate attention in the program. Because of the appeal of music to the emotions, one of the most successful co-recreational activities is social dancing. Square and folk dances are usually too complicated in structure for most students who are severely disturbed, although they are greatly enjoyed by some. Those who cannot participate in these forms of dance can be encouraged to perform simple rhythmic activities to music. Modern or interpretive dance has interesting possibilities as a therapeutic aid for persons who are mentally ill whose other means of expression are blocked. Because of the strong emotional involvement in this type of dance expression, it is recommended that this form of dance be approached only with the consultation of a psychologist and a dance therapist.

Swimming should be included among the activities of the program because of the desirable effects that water produces. It frequently acts as a stimulant to the depressed and encourages movement in the extremely withdrawn. Persons who are hyperactive are often greatly relaxed by the water, particularly if it is warmer than normal.

The instructor must plan for successful participation in the activities by the students. Success is extremely important to them. To be successful does not necessitate being a winner, but it does require that the activity be fun and self-satisfying. To ensure success the instructor must consider the special needs and interests of each person; give friendly, patient instruction in the skills; and continually encourage a wider interest in play and in the people who play.

Above all, the instructor must treat the student with a behavior disorder as an individual who is deserving of respect and consideration. There is still in our society a great stigma attached to being publicly recognized as mentally ill; those who have a mental illness are regarded by far too many as misfits and failures. Of course, students with behavior disorders are well aware of these attitudes and anticipate being degraded in their dealings with others. This obviously interferes with establishing social relationships. Peers tend to reject students with behavior disorders more than youth without behavior disorders (Sabornie and Kauffman, 1985), and, not surprisingly, youth with behavior disorders report feelings of extreme loneliness (Asher and Wheeler, 1985). Because most students with behavior disorders are not socially adept, having generally spent withdrawn and aloof lives, failure to treat them as deserving of the dignity accorded other human beings is defeating to them and defeating to the success of the physical education program.

In trying to institute programs with such people, it should also be borne in mind that many of them are extremely concerned about their personal problems (some students who are severely disturbed may even be pondering the desirability of death over their present life), so that games of any sort are of little interest to them. Although they may participate, if forced to do so, because of their passivity, they will not enjoy the activity and will probably feel degraded and silly doing it. Such a response is, of course, detrimental to the objectives of the program.

Students with behavior disorders need help and it is the responsibility of all professionals, including physical educators, to create success-oriented programs. The environment must be structured but sensitive to the needs of these at-risk youth. For some students, the physical education teacher and the emphasis on physical activity may make the difference in enhancing their lives.

Instructional Placement

The appropriate instructional placement for the student with behavior disorders will vary according to the nature and severity of the disability. As specified in P.L. 101-476, the desired goal is to place students with disabilities in the educational environment which is least restrictive and will allow for the greatest educational gain. Students who have severe behavior disorders may need separate educational experiences, but for many students with behavior disorders, placement, with modification, in the regular physical education program is appropriate. Critical decisions about placement, including the appropriate physical education environment, reside with the student's IEP team. One of the primary reasons that it is highly desirable, if possible, to include students with behavior disorders in the regular physical education program is based on research demonstrating that the most effective way to teach students behaviors they are lacking is to expose them to others who demonstrate the appropriate behaviors (CEC, 1991). Placement alone, however, does not ensure that the student will necessarily model or emulate the desired behavior. Direct instruction on target behaviors is often required to help students master them. Consultation with other specialists, including the special education teacher, school psychologist and others may prove helpful in devising an effective strategy. To most effectively address the student's needs in regular physical education, as well as ensure a positive experience for other students, the following suggestions have been proposed by the Council for Exceptional Children (Lewis, Heflin, and DiGangi, 1991).

1. Keep an organized classroom learning environment.
2. Provide an abundance of success for all students.
3. Hold high expectations.
4. Devise a structured behavior management program.
5. Maintain a close working relationship with the special education teacher and other staff members.
6. Collect data so that the effects of instruction-based decisions can be evaluated and modified.

As an aid in using data to make instructional decisions, figure 19.1 provides a very simple example of how graphing data will be helpful in assessing the effectiveness of a particular program or strategy. As noted in figure 19.1, the steps involved in developing the graph include:

Step One. Establish baseline data. As an example, the physical education teacher might want to graph the number of times the student is verbally rude to other students. It is recommended that the baseline include at least three data points (e.g., number of occurrences per day for three days) (figure 19.1*A*). In consultation with others, the teacher should determine a target (A), representing the desired reduction in the target behavior (verbally rude to other students). The baseline might include total number of

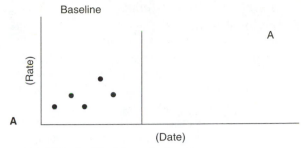

Establish aim (A), date and rate.

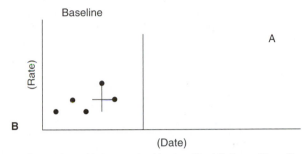

Determine mid-date and mid-rate of last 3 days of baseline.

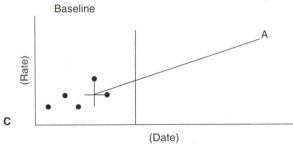

Draw an aim line to aim star.

Figure 19.1 Plotting data on a graph helps teachers make wise instructional decisions.

occurrences per the entire period or some time sample. This will depend on the amount of time and instructional support available.

Step Two. Determine the mid-date and mid-rate of the last three days of baseline data points (figure 19.1*B*). Mid-date and mid-rate are the median or middle-most points. For the mid-date, count left to right. For the mid-rate, count bottom to top.

Step Three. Draw an aim line through the mid-date/mid-rate intersection to the aim star (figure 19.1*C*).

Step Four. Formulate data decision rules. The goal is to assess how the treatment is working and to know when to consider alternative approaches if the plan is not working (e.g., if the data fall above the aim line for three consecutive days, consult with the others to determine if a change in strategy is needed).

Instructional Considerations and Behavioral Ecologies

Although many different educational approaches have been used to teach students with behavior disorders, the two techniques that are widely acclaimed to be effective are the behavioral and ecological approaches.

The behavioral model assumes that the behavior exhibited by students has been learned. Providing appropriate educational experiences requires, therefore, that the teacher use behavior modification techniques to teach appropriate responses and eliminate inappropriate ones.

An ecological approach stresses the importance of the student's interaction with his or her peers, teachers, and parents. Treatment is directed toward teaching the child to function within the home/school setting. This approach requires that all those who relate with the individual respond to his or her behavior in a consistent manner.

The behavioral and ecological approaches can effectively be used together if teachers, parents, and peers are taught to employ some basic reinforcement techniques. Basic concepts that need to be stressed include the following:

1. Reinforcers should be those rewards that are desired and enjoyed by the students. Some teachers identify appropriate reinforcers by observing the students to determine their likes and dislikes. Talking with the student about favorable reinforcers is also possible with some individuals.

2. If possible, the reinforcers should be ones that are most natural and closely associated with the social reinforcers that work with most individuals. Some children who are severely disturbed, however, may not respond to social reinforcers, and it may be necessary to select more primary reinforcers such as toys and food.

3. Rewards should be given immediately following the desired behavior. A delay of longer than a few seconds can create a situation in which the student is reinforced for some unacceptable acts that followed the appropriate response. Many teachers have successfully used a token economy system with students with behavior disorders to facilitate the process of immediate reinforcement. Check marks, stars, and pluses are examples of tokens that may be given in the gymnasium and used later in exchange for a particular reward.

4. Social rewards should always be paired with primary reinforcers, with the ultimate goal of helping the student to eventually respond to the natural reinforcers.

Many of the concepts used in behavior modification systems are simply good common sense application of the laws of learning. Unfortunately, however, too few physical educators use this approach in their interaction with children who are emotionally disturbed. As indicated in an article by Dunn and French (1982), behavior modification is one of the tools that special physical educators must understand and employ with students with disabilities, particularly those who are emotionally disturbed.

In addition to skills in the application of behavior modification principles, the teacher of students with behavior disorders must have an unusual capacity to witness extreme acts of anger, hate, and aggression from youngsters without in turn responding in a similar manner. This means that the teacher must accept such outbursts as very visible signs of the students' frustration with others and themselves. The teacher's role is not to condone such acts but to accept the behavior in an empathetic manner, stressing to the student that there are more appropriate ways to express feelings of frustration and anger.

Teachers must also realize that they serve as models for the students who are emotionally disturbed. Their actions, therefore, must be consistent, mature, and controlled. Emotional outbursts and angry shouting exchanges with students inhibit rather than create a healthy educational environment.

Specific suggestions that the teacher working with children who are emotionally disturbed can apply are indicated in the following (Fried, 1980):

1. Ignore inappropriate behavior. This technique, frequently referred to as extinction, is used to communicate that the *behavior* is unacceptable, not the child.

2. Catch the student doing something positive. Search for opportunities to reinforce the child by acknowledging good behavior or quality efforts to learn a new skill.

3. Use closeness and touching. Teachers can sometimes avoid a potential problem by moving closer to a student or touching a child.

4. Tell the student how you feel. Frequently it is best to appeal directly to the child by explaining that a particular behavior is annoying to you and to others in the class.

5. Use physical restraint when necessary. Occasionally a student may lose control so completely that restraint or removal is required to avoid harm being done to the student or to others. The exact restraint procedures to be used should be discussed by the student's IEP team. It is very important to emphasize that when a student is restrained or removed, the teacher should be firm but not punitive. Unfriendly remarks by the teacher and other children should be avoided.

6. Learn to say no. Teachers of students with behavior disorders must establish clearly defined limits and expectations. Students accept a "no" response more easily if they realize that the denial is consistent with

the established guidelines. Therefore, the behavior guidelines, not the teacher, become the object of the students' dislike.

7. Help the student build a positive self-image. Frequently, students who are emotionally disturbed devalue their true worth. Teachers must strive to create positive self-concept builders. Physical educators who employ a problem-solving teaching approach can create many situations in which children can be successful.

8. Encourage students to express themselves verbally. Many youngsters who are emotionally disturbed find talking about their anger an effective means of maintaining their composure. Teachers must be prepared to be good listeners. Students must also be taught to express their anger in an acceptable manner.

Other suggestions or tips for helping teach the student with behavior disorders are summarized in table 19.6. These tips, developed by Cullinan and Epstein (1986), apply equally to the classroom or gymnasium setting.

Extreme Hate or Fear of Physical Education

Extreme hate or fear of physical education manifest themselves at all educational levels, from elementary school to college. Hatred of muscular activity can usually be traced to unfavorable experiences in physical education. Fears are most

---

Table 19.6 *Tips for helping students with behavior disorders*

1. Provide a carefully structured environment with regard to physical features of the room, scheduling and routines, and rules of conduct. If there are to be unstructured activities, you must clearly distinguish them from structured activities in terms of time, place, and expectations.
2. Let your pupils know the expectations you have, the objectives that have been established for them, and the help you will give them in achieving those objectives. When appropriate, seek input from them about their strengths, weaknesses, and goals.
3. Reinforce appropriate behavior; inappropriate behavior should be ignored or mildly punished. Model appropriate behavior and refrain from behavior you do not wish students to imitate.
4. Do not expect students with behavior disorders to have immediate success; work for improvement on a long-term basis. Reinforce approximations to or attempts at the desired behavior. Continue with the intervention strategy being used when a student is making progress toward an objective; try another way if there is no progress.
5. Be fair, be consistent, but temper your consistency with flexibility.
6. Be sensitive to your students as individuals and as a class; balance individual needs with group requirements.
7. Try to understand the frustrations, hopes, and fears of your students and their parents.

Source: Haring, N., & McCormick, L. (1986). *Exceptional children and youth* (4th ed., p. 199) Columbus: Charles E. Merrill Publishing Co.

---

often stimulated by particular types of activities that are associated with danger in the minds of certain students, swimming being the most common. Fear of swimming ranges from a more or less normal reaction to water, because of lack of swimming skill, to aquaphobia, in which there is extreme fear of water. If the student exhibits abnormal and persistent fears and/or unrealistic worries, the DSM-IV classification Anxiety Disorder may apply. Contact sports elicit great fear in some students, whereas activities such as rope climbing, tumbling, and apparatus work may evoke fears in others.

In young children a reaction of dislike usually stems from fear of the activity or factors inherent within the situation itself. Overprotectiveness of parents and inexperience in play activities are chiefly responsible for abnormal emotional reactions to physical education activities. In older children the fears are usually more deep-seated than in younger children. Lack of experience may be the reason, although unsatisfactory experience in such activities is the more usual cause. Fear of ridicule and continual defeat in achievement of physical performance are important contributing factors. Fear of physical injury is yet another factor.

Dislike and hate in older students may develop from a long history of continual fear as well as from experiences in poor physical education programs that promoted none of the values inherent in well-planned programs. This reason for dislike is more prevalent among upper level high school and college students. In the majority of cases this dislike does not result in any great deviation in behavior; however, some students go to great lengths to avoid class participation. Malingering is the method most frequently used, in the hope of being excused from participation for physical reasons.

Students who experience extreme dislike, fear, and hate for physical education need special help in overcoming their strong emotional reactions to muscular activity. If circumstances permit, they should be placed for a time in the special program, where attention can be given to seeking out the cause of the emotion and overcoming it. When it is not possible to accommodate these students in the special program, individual conferences with the students can achieve the same objectives.

In either situation, the student should be guided toward an understanding and appreciation of the values of physical education. The facts of the physiological benefits of exercise should be described dramatically and in a vocabulary appropriate to the student's educational level. The fun of playing and the social benefits to be derived from it should be given special emphasis. If fear of injury is the basis of the strong emotional reaction, the student should be given every reassurance that the possibility of injury is minimal. All the various precautions that are exercised to ensure the safety of the players should be demonstrated. The student should also be given instruction in falling to avoid injury, to help him or her realize that there is little danger of personal injury even in vigorous activity. Exposure of such students to actual participation should be very gradual (figure 19.2). The

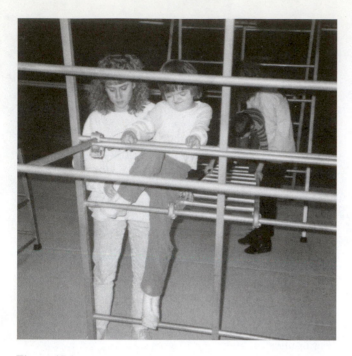

Figure 19.2 Overcoming fear or anxiety about performing a motor activity necessitates building self-confidence by a careful process of gradual exposure.

technique of helping a student overcome a fear will be described here in detail, in order to suggest ways in which a student can be led gradually into an activity that is feared.

Perhaps the most common fear of students in physical education is that of water. Unless the student has an actual water phobia, he or she can usually overcome fear of the water through a careful process of introduction to it. A student with a phobia cannot as a rule be persuaded even to enter the pool area and will require special help from a psychiatrist or psychologist. Others whose fear is not as great should be requested to come to the pool and sit on the edge with their feet in the water. They are informed that nothing else is expected of them, but if they feel like getting into the water they may do so. After a day or two of sitting on the pool's edge it is likely that even the most reluctant student will venture into the water. From that point on, the techniques are much the same as those recommended for introducing any beginner to the water; however, progress may be considerably slower and the instructor should never force or rush the students. It may, for instance, take much longer before a student who is mastering fear of the water will splash water into his or her face than for the normal beginner. Care must be taken to prevent splashing and commotion by experienced swimmers who may be in the pool at the same time; and, above all, no ridiculing remarks should be tolerated. It is easier, of course, if those with water fears can be alone in the pool until they overcome their fears, but this is not usually possible. Hence it is very important that careful control be exercised over the other students who are present.

Lack of success in performance and generally unfavorable physical education experiences are the usual underlying causes of extreme dislike of physical education activities. Students who hate physical education class because they are always last in the race and repeatedly in error when playing the ball are numerous. Subnormal strength, endurance, and flexibility are the usual basis of failure to perform well, and work in the developmental program on fitness exercises will greatly benefit these students. The instructor also should encourage these students to practice skills during their free hours. He or she might also refer them to visual aids and reading materials that may be used to learn more about the techniques of skill performance. The teacher should give them as much individual instruction as possible in analyzing and overcoming skill faults. Those whose dislike stems from former poor physical education experiences may need to be convinced of the values of physical education. Every effort should be made to arouse the interest of these students in a special game or sport that they will learn to perform with success and pleasure, and which can then be used as a springboard to broader participation.

Summary

Information was provided in this chapter concerning students with behavior disorders. Within Public Law 101-476, the term *seriously emotionally disturbed* is used to identify these students. As is true with the other disabilities, specific criteria are applied to differentiate those youngsters who are seriously emotionally disturbed from those whose behavior is within the range of normalcy. For a given behavior problem, the intensity, frequency, and duration of the problem must be considered in differentiating more permanent disorders, such as autism, from temporary problems.

Various classification systems are employed to identify and classify those with mental disorders. The American Psychiatric Association's *Diagnostic and Statistical Manual of Mental Disorders* is widely used by mental health specialists. In the field of education, systems such as those proposed by Bower and Quay have received favorable review because of their emphasis on classification as well as procedures for educational intervention. Students included under the term *behavior disordered* range from those with severe schizophrenic disorders to children who are disruptive and disobedient (conduct disorders) to those who are members of gangs and juvenile offenders (socialized delinquents). Why students have behavior disorders is not clearly known. Some have attributed the cause to psychological, sociological, or physiological problems including biochemical imbalances. Psychoanalysts argue, for instance, that children are behaviorally disordered because they have not successfully dealt with problems as they have developed. While behaviorists might concur with this premise, the intervention strategy they promote doesn't emphasize determining the cause but stresses helping the youngster to interact positively with peers, teachers, and parents.

In developing educational programs for students with behavior disorders, there is consensus that certain educational practices should be followed. These include: structure the learning environment; clearly establish student expectations and consequences;

provide success-oriented experiences; use behavior modification concepts with an emphasis on positive reinforcement; analyze tasks into small steps and recognize gains even when very small. Teachers must be patient, sensitive, good listeners, fair and consistent in their treatment of the student with a behavior disorder.

There is increasing evidence that physical education programs play a significant role in treatment and intervention programs for students with behavior disorders. Programs that emphasize skill development contribute to a positive self-image. Exercise programs that emphasize cardiorespiratory endurance decrease disruptive behavior and increase academic production. Physical educators recognize, too, that care must be taken to assist students who are fearful of participation in some or all physical education activities. The emphasis must be placed on positive learning experiences with special efforts directed toward avoiding unnecessary emotional stress in the physical education class.

The outlook for students with behavior disorders is very encouraging. Physical education can and should play a significant part in helping these students enhance their quality of life.

Selected Readings

Allan, J.I. (1980). Jogging can modify disruptive behaviors. *Teaching Exceptional Children,* 66–70.

American Alliance for Health, Physical Education, and Recreation. (1976). *Physical education, recreation, and related programs for autistic and emotionally disturbed children.* Washington, DC: Author.

American Psychiatric Association. *Diagnostic and Statistical Manual of Mental Disorders (DSM-IV).* (1994). Washington, D.C.: Author.

Asher, S.R., & Wheeler, V.A. (1985). Children's loneliness: A comparison of rejected and neglected peer status. *Journal of Consulting and Clinical Psychology, 53,* 500–505.

Bandura, A. (1977). *Characteristics of children's behavior disorders.* Columbus, OH: Charles E. Merrill Publishing Co.

Bauer, A.M., & Shea, T.M. (1989). *Teaching exceptional students in your classroom.* Boston: Allyn and Bacon, Inc.

Bower, E. (1969). *Early identification of emotionally handicapped children in school* (2d ed.). Springfield, IL: Charles C Thomas.

Connor, F. (1990). Physical eductaion for children with autism. *Teaching Exceptional Children, 23*(1), 30–33.

Cullinan, D., & Epstein, M.H. (1986). Behavior disorders. In N.G. Haring & L. McCormick (Eds.), *Exceptional children and youth* (4th ed.) (pp. 160–199). Columbus, OH: Charles E. Merrill Publishing Co.

Davis, K. (1990). *Adapted physical education for students with autism.* Springfield, IL: Charles C. Thomas.

Dunn, J.M., & French, R. (1982). Operant conditioning: A tool for special physical educators in the 80s. *Exceptional Education Quarterly, 3,* 42–53.

Edelbrock, C. (1979). Empirical classification of children's behavior disorders: Progress based on parent and teacher ratings. *School Psychology Digest,* 355–369.

Epstein, P.B., Detwiler, C.L., & Reitz, A.L. (1985). Describing the clients in programs for behavior disordered children and youth. *Education and Treatment of Children, 8,* 265–273.

Evans, W.H., Evans, S.S., Schmid, R.E., & Pennypacker, H.S. (1985). The effects of exercise on selected classroom behaviors of behaviorally disordered adolescents. *Behavioral Disorders, 11,* 42–51.

Fried, H. (Ed.). (1980). *Plain talk about dealing with the angry child* (DHHS Publication No. ADM 80–781). Rockville, MD: National Institute of Mental Health, United States Department of Health and Human Services.

Hallahan, D.P., & Kauffman, J.M. (1991). *Exceptional children: Introduction to special education* (5th ed.). Englewood Cliffs, NJ: Prentice-Hall, Inc.

Heward, W.L., & Orlansky, M.D. (1992). *Exceptional children* (4th ed.). Columbus, OH: Charles E. Merrill Publishing Co.

Hewett, F.M., & Taylor, R.D. (1980). *The emotionally disturbed child in the classroom: The orchestration of success.* Boston: Allyn and Bacon, Inc.

Johnson, J. (1988). The challenge of substance abuse. *Teaching Exceptional Children, 20*(4), 29–31.

Juul, K.D. (1986). Epidemiological studies of behavior disorders in children: An international survey. *International Journal of Special Education, 1,* 1–20.

Kauffman, J.M. (1977). *Characteristics of children's behavioral disorders.* Columbus, OH: Charles E. Merrill Publishing Co.

Kauffman, J.M. (1986). Educating children with behavior disorders. In R.J. Morris and B. Blatt (Eds.), *Special education: Research and trends.* New York: Pergamon Press.

Kazdin, A.E. (1987). *Conduct disorders in childhood and adolescence.* Beverly Hills, CA: Sage Publishing.

Kirk, S.A., & Gallagher, J.J. (1989). *Educating exceptional children* (6th ed.). Boston, MA: Houghton Mifflin.

Kugelmass, N.I. (1974). *The autistic child.* Springfield, IL: Charles C. Thomas.

Lewis, T.J., Heflin, J., & DiGangi, J.A. (1991). *Teaching students with behavioral disorders.* Reston, VA: Council for Exceptional Children.

Mandell, C.J., & Fiscus, E. (1981). *Understanding exceptional people.* St. Paul, MN: West Publishing Co.

Mendelsohn, S.R., & Jennings, K.D. (1986). Characteristics of emotionally disturbed children referred for special education assessment. *Child Psychiatry and Human Development, 16,* 154–170.

Neel, R.S. (1986). Teaching functional social skills to children with autism. *Focus on Autistic Behavior, 1,* 1–8.

Plomin, R. (1986). Behavior genetics and intelligence. In J. Gallagher & C. Ramey (Eds.), *The malleability of children.* Baltimore, MD: Paul H. Brookes Publishing Co.

Quay, H.C. (1972). Patterns of aggression, withdrawal, and immaturity. In H.C. Quay & J.S. Werry (Eds.), *Psychopathological disorders of childhood.* New York: John Wiley and Sons, Inc.

Reid, G., Collier, D., & Morin, B. (1983). Motor performance of autistic individuals. In R.L. Eason, T.L. Smith, and F. Caron (Eds.), *Adapted physical activity: From theory to application* (pp. 201–218). Champaign, IL: Human Kinetics Publishers.

Reinert, H.R. (1976). *Children in conflict.* St. Louis: C.V. Mosby Co.

Ross, A.O. (1974). *Psychological disorders of children: A behavioral approach to theory, research, and therapy.* New York: McGraw-Hill, Inc.

Sabornie, E.J., & Kauffman, J.M. (1985). Regular classroom sociometric status of behaviorally disordered adolescents. *Behavioral Disorders, 10,* 268–274.

Swanson, H.L., & Reinert, H.R. (1979). *Teaching strategies for children in conflict.* St. Louis: C.V. Mosby Co.

Watters, R.G., & Watters, W.E. (1980). Decreasing self-stimulatory behavior with physical exercise in a group of autistic boys. *Journal of Autism and Developmental Disorders, 10,* 379–387.

Webster, C.D., Konstanteres, M.M., Oxman, J., & Mack, J.E. (1980). *Autism: New directions in research and education.* New York: Pergamon Press.

Enhancing Activities

1. Obtain a copy of the American Psychiatric Association's *Diagnostic and Statistical Manual of Mental Disorders* (DSM-IV) and review the various disorders included in the manual.

2. Review the studies of Allan; Watters and Watters; and Evans, Evans, Schmid, and Pennypacker. Analyze these studies and their positive findings concerning the effects of exercise programs with students with behavior disorders.

3. Observe a physical education class and chart the number of behavior problems or incidences that occur during a specified time frame (one period, several periods, etc.). Note the frequency, intensity and duration of the problem(s). Develop a baseline and projected target.

4. Interview the parents of a child with a conduct disorder. Obtain their perceptions of this disorder and their views concerning the importance of physical activity programs for youngsters similar to theirs.

5. Discuss the following question with some of your classmates. If you were hired as a physical education teacher, what would your reaction be to knowing that a student with a behavior disorder would be mainstreamed into your regular physical education class?

6. Visit a program for students with behavior disorders. Record your perceptions as to the program, students, teachers, and curriculum. Did you find the program to be structured with rules and consequences clearly established? How was the program similar to or different from that provided for non-behavior-disordered youth?

CHAPTER

20

Physical Education for the Student with Severe Disabilities

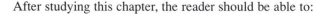

CHAPTER OBJECTIVES

After studying this chapter, the reader should be able to:

1 Appreciate the needs and rights of students with severe disabilities and the important contribution physical activity makes in the lives of these individuals.

2 Recognize the social, cognitive, language, and motor characteristics of individuals with severe disabilities.

3 Identify successful practices that have been used in developing appropriate education programs for individuals with severe disabilities.

4 Recognize that structured learning experiences, including the use of appropriate cues and consequences and task analysis, are essential in developing success-oriented, positive experiences for students with severe disabilities.

5 Apply the principles and suggestions presented in this chapter to the teaching of physical education skills to students with severe disabilities.

6 Appreciate the importance of group instruction to the overall development of students with severe disabilities, including helping them generalize skills and make successful transitions to the community.

7 Understand the need for data-based instruction in assisting the teacher to make informed decisions concerning future instructional and program needs.

8 Serve as an informed advocate for persons with severe disabilities, emphasizing that these individuals can learn if structured learning experiences are provided.

One of the exciting recent trends in the field of special education is the development of appropriate learning experiences for students with severe and profound disabilities. Until very recently those who deviated significantly from the accepted societal norm were frequently committed to institutions, where they would reside for their entire lives. Those with severe disabilities were segregated, set apart, and hidden from the mainstream of public life. Unfortunately, the institutions into which individuals with severe disabilities were placed were usually underfunded and understaffed. The conditions in many of these institutions were dehumanizing and without the necessary resources to provide treatment, rehabilitation, and educational programs.

Fortunately, today there is a new national commitment to accept those who are severely disabled as citizens with the same basic needs and rights as all citizens. Within public schools, for instance, it is common to find students who have significant impairments, and who require unique educational programs and instructional approaches.

Support for the educational rights of persons with severe disabilities was spearheaded by professional organizations such as the National Association for Retarded Citizens and the American Association on Mental Deficiency. Members from these groups banded together to inform the public that those with severe disabilities could benefit from education and training programs. The federal government, too, through the Office of Special Education and Rehabilitative Services, supported the cause of these individuals by funding projects designed to develop curricular materials and instructional techniques for those with severe disabilities. The formation in 1974 of The Association for Persons with Severe Handicaps (TASH), formerly known as the American Association for the Education of the Severely/Profoundly Handicapped, and its rapid membership enrollment attest to the number of professionals and parents committed to improving the educational opportunities available for individuals with severe disabling conditions.

The efforts of concerned citizens, parents, and professionals on behalf of the severely disabled was rewarded in 1975 when Public Law 94-142, the Education for All Handicapped Children Act of 1975, was signed into law by President Gerald R. Ford. This law not only mandated that appropriate educational programs must be provided for *all* students with disabilities, but specified that priority consideration should be given to those with severe disabilities and those with unmet needs. Public Law 94-142 also stipulated that special education students are to be educated in the least restrictive environment. This implies that placement of children with severe disabilities in public schools is more desirable than placement in an institution.

Although the future for individuals with severe disabilities is more encouraging than in the past, much work remains in developing educational programs that are responsive to their unique needs. In the field of physical

education more personnel who are committed to working with individuals with severe disabilities are needed.

Defining Severely Disabled

In earlier chapters of this book, a variety of disability populations have been discussed. It is possible that within each of these populations a certain segment could be classified as severely disabled—the severely mentally retarded, the deaf-blind, and the multiply disabled. However, in combining the severely disabled segments within these groups it becomes apparent that this population or any population of students labeled severely disabled is very heterogeneous. The only commonality found within this group is that their educational needs are such that, compared with peers of similar disability, they require greater assistance. *In essence, students with severe disabilities are individuals who are divergent in degree, not kind.* Sontag and his associates (1977) explain that the severely disabled are those whose needs are so great that they are *functionally retarded*. This phrase emphasizes that students with severe impairments need special assistance to help them function at a level consistent with their ability level. For students who are deaf-blind this may mean special instruction to assist them to develop necessary communication skills. Students with orthopedic disabilities, unable to stand or sit, will require educational techniques that recognize the mobility limitations with which they must deal. Programs must be developed and instruction individualized to assist those with severe disabilities to overcome, to the extent possible, their functional deficits.

If services are not provided, maladaptive behavior is likely to prevail (Snell and Renzaglia, 1986). Recognizing the degree of the disability and the need for specialized services, the United States Office of Special Education has proposed the following definition: "Severely handicapped children are those who because of the intensity of their physical, mental, or emotional problems, or a combination of such problems, need educational, social, psychological, and medical services beyond those which are traditionally offered by regular and special education programs, in order to maximize their potential for useful and meaningful participation in society and for self-fulfillment."

The underlying theme of this definition is that children with severe disabilities can learn if provided with the necessary educational and support services.

The Association for Persons with Severe Handicaps (TASH) suggests that the term severely disabled should include "individuals of all ages who require extensive ongoing support in more than one major life activity in order to participate in integrated community settings and to enjoy a quality of life that is available to citizens with fewer or no disabilities" (Meyer, Peck, and Brown, 1991, p. 19). Block

(1992) acknowledges that while the TASH definition is useful, it does not adequately address the profoundly disabled. He suggests that there is a difference between those with *profound* as contrasted to *severe* disabilities. Block contends that the phrase "students with profound disabilities" should refer to those with ". . . very limited skills in terms of awareness, movement, and communication. In addition, these students are prone to health disorders that can lead to medical complications" (Block, 1992, p. 199).

A major challenge in trying to identify or define those whose disability would be classified as severe or profound is directly related to the number of individuals with more than one disability. A few of the more common disabilities that tend to be found in combination include:

Mental Retardation. While the nature of mental retardation in and of itself creates challenges for the person who is mentally retarded and his or her teacher, the challenges become even greater when there is a secondary disability, such as cerebral palsy, hearing impairment, or behavioral problems. The concern, of course, is that the instructional adaptations required for an individual who is mildly mentally retarded may not work and or need further adaptations when a secondary disability is present. Depending upon the nature of the secondary disability, the individual may require services and treatments more commonly reserved for those who are severely disabled.

Autism. Although there have been significant improvements in the understanding and educational treatment of individuals with autistic disorders (see chapter 19), this population continues to challenge many special and regular educators. Autism is really a combination of disabilities—speech and communication delays, inappropriate behavior, sensory disabilities, and significant learning delays. The syndrome of disorders associated with autism, collectively place these youngsters in a high risk situation such that their disability is frequently viewed as severe or profound.

Deaf-Blind. The individual who loses one of the major senses (hearing or vision) is at a major disadvantage for many of life's activities, including the process of acquiring an education. For the individual who is without functional vision and hearing, the loss is devastating and much greater than the summative loss of two senses (i.e., the dual sensory loss is much more like a three or four sensory loss in terms of life and educational impact). It is known, however, that individuals who are deaf and blind (e.g., Helen Keller) are capable of great gains and contributions if needed family and educational support is provided. Due to the nature of the disability and the specialized skills and instruction required (see chapter 12), teachers who work with these students may find some of the suggestions and instructional approaches described in this chapter helpful.

The discussion in this section provides some examples of the type of individual who because of the severity of a single disability or a combination of disabilities might be viewed as someone with a severe disability. It must be emphasized, however, that this is not a complete description of all the children who might be viewed as having severe or multiple disabilities (e.g., there are many individuals who might be classified as medically fragile such that their condition would qualify as a severe or profound disability). The important point to remember is that our recent breakthroughs and educational gains with even the most severely and profoundly involved individuals is encouraging and a tribute to teachers who focus not on the educational challenges presented by these children, but the opportunity to help them learn and live.

Prevalence

Because of the absence of a uniform definition, the number of children with severe disabilities cannot be accurately identified. Ludlow and Sobsey (1984) report that estimates of the number of persons in the population with severely disabling conditions have ranged from .1 percent to 1 percent of the population. Snell (1987), a leading authority in the education of students with severe disabilities, believes the prevalence figure to be approximately .05 percent. The wide discrepancy in figures may be attributed to the various definitions utilized and the procedures for identifying students who are severely disabled. For example, Sims-Tucker and Jensema (1984) estimate that there are six thousand individuals who are deaf and blind and that this number has increased due to federally mandated child-find activities.

Regardless of the number of children with severe disabilities, it is clear that school systems across the United States are now providing programs and services for these students. Given the influence of P.L. 94-142, P.L. 101-476, and the recent emphasis on early intervention stressed by P.L. 99-457, it appears likely that the number of children with severe disabilities enrolled in the public schools will increase dramatically in the future.

Characteristics of Those with Severe Disabilities

Discussing the characteristics of individuals with severe disabilities is difficult, if not impossible. As indicated previously, those with severe disabilities are a heterogeneous population and the differences among the members of this population are greater than their similarities. What will be presented here, therefore, are those behaviors or conditions that are more commonly found in students with severe disabilities. It must be emphasized, however, that not all students with severe disabilities possess the characteristics described in this section and no two individuals exhibit the same behavior patterns.

Social Development

Many students with severe disabilities have difficulty interacting with others. Frequently, it appears that they are oblivious to the presence of others. Some students with severe disabilities neither initiate interactions with others nor respond when others try to interact with them. This type of behavior is more commonly observed in individuals who are severely mentally retarded and those with extreme behavior disorders.

Deficiency in performing many self-help skills is a characteristic found in some students with severe disabilities. The ability to perform functions such as dressing, feeding, and grooming oneself may be totally absent, or present in varying degrees. Many students with severe disabilities also are unable to be toilet trained. For some individuals, such as students with spina bifida and meningomyelocele, the neurologic damage they have sustained precludes developing the necessary sphincter control. Other students with severe disabilities, however, are unable to perform self-help skills because they are developmentally delayed and have not yet mastered these essential skills.

Abnormal behaviors are also evident with some individuals with severe disabilities. These include self-abusive acts as well as behaviors that are injurious to others. Examples of self-abusive behaviors include head banging, pinching, biting, scratching, and excessively rubbing the eyes. Fortunately, the prevalence of self-abusive acts is not common, and when they do occur they are more frequent at younger ages and more common to those who are severely mentally retarded and emotionally disturbed (Corbett, 1977).

Stereotyped behaviors are also seen in some students with severe disabilities. These include bizarre acts such as rocking back and forth, waving the hands in front of the eyes, spinning objects, and making strange sounds with the mouth. Students who are deaf-blind and those with serious cognitive dysfunctions are most likely to exhibit these behaviors. Some speculate that stereotyped behaviors are caused by the individual's need for self-stimulation.

Cognitive Development

Students with severe disabilities exhibit a great deal of variation in their cognitive development. If the student's primary disability relates to an orthopedic or health impairment, it is likely that the individual's cognitive development is progressing normally, assuming that his or her education has not been interrupted for surgery and other medical reasons. Although students who are deaf-blind may experience academic problems, the difficulty may be attributed in many cases to communication problems rather than to any inherent cognitive dysfunction.

Students who are severely mentally retarded and seriously emotionally disturbed have obvious problems in cognitive development. Many of these students will be unable to respond to simple commands, identify shapes and colors, or recognize symbols and words. Some may also have difficulty recognizing family pictures and familiar surroundings. The ability to apply generalized skills learned in one setting to a different environment is also very difficult for many students who are severely mentally retarded. This does not mean, however, that essential pre-academic skills are beyond the reach of these students. Given a well-defined curriculum, qualified instructors, and a well-designed instructional format, many educational gains can be made with any students.

Language Development

Students who are severely disabled frequently experience some problems in language development. Common problems include delays in speech and language, lack of speech clarity, and unusual speech patterns.

One of the greatest frustrations experienced by many students with severe disabilities is their inability to communicate clearly with others. For many of these individuals, speech patterns are not developed to the point that they can be easily understood. This creates a frustrating situation for the student as well as for teachers, parents, and peers. Major strides, however, have been made in technological advances to develop systems enabling those with speech impairments to communicate.

Some students with severe disabilities, particularly those with cognitive deficiencies, understand little of what is said to them. Teachers, therefore, must communicate using simple statements and gestures and observe these children closely to anticipate their needs.

Unusual speech patterns are noted in some individuals with severe disabilities. For example, some will continuously repeat certain phrases or passages that they have memorized. Students with severe mental retardation may also speak out of turn or interject a statement that is inappropriate to the topic of discussion. Some individuals may tend to repeat what is said to them. This phenomenon, which is observed in those who are severely mentally retarded and emotionally disturbed, is called echolalia. As the term implies, students repeat or echo questions or statements directed toward them.

Motor Development

Motor development delays are very common among students who are severely disabled. Specific problems that may be observed include difficulty in walking or sitting without support. Many children are unable to perform such basic tasks as rolling over, grasping objects, or holding their head up. Developmental delays are sometimes so significant that the primitive reflexes discussed in chapter 2 are either nonexistent or persist for an abnormal period of time.

Other motor development problems frequently observed in individuals with severe disabilities include deficiencies to varying degrees in the performance of motor tasks that involve strength, flexibility, agility, coordination, and reactions. With those who are more severely involved, problems in gross motor development are usually attributed to central nervous system damage.

An increasing number of universities with teacher education programs in the area of the severely disabled require courses in the field of motor development. There is also evidence that some departments of physical education recognize that course work in the field of physical education for individuals with severe disabilities is necessary if quality movement experiences are to be provided for this unique population.

Heward and Orlansky (1992) have summarized the characteristics of children with severe disabilities as follows:

1. Little or no communication
2. Delayed physical and motor development
3. Frequent inappropriate behavior
4. Deficits in self-help skills
5. Infrequent constructive behavior and interaction

While the above may paint a picture of those with severe disabilities as negative, it is important to emphasize that significant gains can be made when appropriate educational services and programs are provided. Given the right educational, medical, and family treatment, the positive attributes of this population become very apparent.

Teaching Physical Education to Students with Severe Disabilities

The need to provide appropriate physical education experiences for those who are severely disabled is readily acknowledged by most educators. Desire, concern, and care, however, are not enough to respond to the unique problems evident in this population. Likewise, placing these students in the traditional physical education class and expecting them to respond in an appropriate fashion to the instruction provided is inadequate. What is needed are structured learning experiences to help them benefit from instruction. This means that what is to be taught, how the material is to be presented, why something is taught, and when the skill is to be achieved must be carefully developed and structured by the teacher. Several investigators (Dunn, Morehouse, and Fredericks, 1986; Jansma, 1982; Stainback et al., 1983) have emphasized that those with severe disabilities can benefit from physical activity programs if instruction is provided in a systematic and consistent manner.

Principles of Program Development

The following are general principles that should be adhered to in the development of quality physical education experiences for students with severe disabilities. Many of these concepts were developed at Oregon State University after extensive field testing with students enrolled in the National Model Program for Severely Handicapped Children conducted by Teaching Research in Monmouth, Oregon (Dunn, Morehouse, and Fredericks, 1986).

1. Every student, regardless of disabling condition, can learn. This is an important principle that must be continually emphasized in educational programs for those with severe disabilities. Occasionally the educational gains may be so small as to appear insignificant, but as long as there is progress the student is benefitting from the program. If the student is not learning, then the teacher must experiment by (a) changing the method used to present material, (b) employing a different technique to reinforce the student, or (c) reducing the task to be learned to smaller steps.

2. Physical education is an integral component of the educational curriculum for students with severe disabling conditions. As an important area, it is essential, therefore, that physical education programs adhere to the same standards expected of other areas. Instructional programs should be sequenced, task-analyzed, and data-based so that performance changes in physical education skills can be determined.

3. Students with severe disabilities learn at a slower rate than other students. This means that they will require more extensive and intensive education to compensate for their slower learning rates. Because it is generally impossible to extend the time of the school day, maximum use of the time available will require that parents and volunteers assume responsibility for conducting part of the instruction.

4. There is no way of determining the extent to which a student with severe disabilities will progress. Therefore, no ceiling is placed on the physical education curriculum. The teacher must be prepared to take the student as far and as rapidly as possible. Physical education curricular materials should extend from very basic skills such as executing various body movements while standing to more advanced game skills such as catching and throwing.

5. Effective instruction for those who are severely disabled frequently requires that programs be conducted in a one-to-one relationship. This is necessary because of the heterogeneous nature of the population and the behavior problems sometimes evident with this population. The utilization of trained volunteers is necessary, therefore, to provide individualized instruction in the gymnasium.

6. Physical education experiences for students with severe disabilities must be designed to ensure student success. Many students with severe disabilities have found previous educational experiences very frustrating. Teachers must be sensitive to this possibility and the

all-too-common attitude of "I can't." This can best be dealt with by structuring educational experiences in such a way that success is guaranteed.

Employing the above principles requires that educators, in cooperation with parents and surrogates as part of the IEP process, review carefully a few overriding issues related to the education of the individual who is severely or profoundly involved. Some of these important issues include:

Placement. It is generally acknowledged that the educational needs of individuals with severe disabilities are such that a highly structured, specialized program taught by a specialist is required. This may or may not be true. As Block and Krebs (1992) have emphasized, the goal of all educational programs is to make as many adaptations as possible within the regular program such that no student, regardless of his/her disability, would be excluded automatically from contact with peers in regular physical education. Within this chapter, many of the educational concepts, even one-to-one instructional approaches, have been employed with students who are severely involved in the regular physical education program. While this approach does not necessarily lead to direct interaction with nondisabled peers and involvement in the activities engaged in by other children, it does ensure that the student is part of the regular educational program. Such an approach, as is emphasized later in this chapter, requires that the teacher develop skills as an instructional manager and undertake the training of a cadre of volunteers, including peers, to serve as instructional assistants. While these "extras" require teacher time and energy, more and more teachers and schools recognize that direct interaction between students who are severely involved and their peers is beneficial to the entire school and community.

There are, of course, times when students with severe disabilities will benefit from instruction outside of the regular physical education program. For example, the use of specialized instructional or health-related equipment may lead to temporary separate placements. Also, many students with severe disabilities will benefit from supplementary or intensive instruction. Even in these situations, however, it is difficult to justify total isolation from peers for an extended period of time. As Block (1992) has emphasized, the principle of partial participation suggests that through the use of available technology and creative teachers, all students can enjoy some participation in natural environments.

Age-Appropriate and Functional Curriculum. One of the challenges of teaching and working with those who are severely and profoundly disabled is to avoid the trap of teaching concepts, games, and activities that are not age appropriate or functionally appropriate. For example, using musical chairs as an activity with fifteen and sixteen-year old individuals who are severely mentally retarded would not be an age-appropriate activity.

Proponents of a developmental approach to physical education will need to exercise care in how programs to teach selected concepts are sequenced. For example, some

developmentalists will not introduce an activity (e.g., roller skating) unless all of the prerequisite balance skills are demonstrated. For some individuals with severe disabilities, this can be devastating (i.e., they may have some success with the activity without having all of the prerequisite skills in place). For additional examples of chronologically age-appropriate activities, please refer to table 20.1.

Functional skills refer to those skills used frequently in natural settings, including the work and play environment (e.g., recreational settings). Unfortunately, many individuals with severe and profound disabilities are frequently taught essential skills using inappropriate props or in inappropriate settings. For example, it does little good to teach an individual to go up and down fabricated steps if the goal is to use stepping up and down in functional settings (e.g., going up and down the steps in the school, home, or for purposes of boarding a bus). In physical education activities, the goal is to use meaningful activities that are as close to the functional skill as possible. Having the student who is deaf-blind substitute throwing the ball when "batting" is far less functional than using a batting tee or learning to swing when given some appropriate cue or prompt.

Community-Based. One of the essential goals of any good instructional program for students with severe and profound disabilities is to use the skills learned in natural community-based settings. In earlier years, many thought that this could be accomplished by first teaching the skill in a non-natural setting and then transferring the skill to the real setting (e.g., teaching individuals to bowl in the gymnasium and then expecting them to transfer these skills to the community bowling lane). This approach entailed much relearning and has proved to not be very efficient. The challenge, of course, is developing a strategy that will provide access to community-based settings with minimal cost and interruption in the daily school or instructional schedule. Some have overcome this problem by simulating to the greatest extent possible the community setting in teaching the skill (e.g., roller skating with intermittent trips to the "real" setting when possible). Coordinated planning with parents and surrogates can help to move in the direction of an exciting community-based approach to instruction.

Choice-Making. The concept of choice-making in its simplest terms suggests that everyone should be allowed to make decisions and to have input in the activities planned for him or her. One of the most refreshing advances in the education of students with severe and profound disabilities addresses the concept of choice-making. And it is now clear that everyone should have some control and choice in daily activities. In the physical education setting, this might mean allowing the individual to choose the ball to be thrown or allowing the individual to indicate whether he or she wishes to continue or to stop an activity. Effective instructional strategy, of course, will structure the choices (e.g., limit the number of balls from which to choose) such that the desired educational goals and objectives can be reached.

Table 20.1 *Chronological age-appropriate activities and sample modifications for elementary-age students with profound disabilities*

Age-Appropriate Activities	Modifications
Manipulative patterns	
Throwing	Pushing a ball down a ramp, grasp and release
Catching	Tracking suspended balls, reaching for balloons
Kicking	Touching balloon taped to floor, pushing ball down ramp with foot
Striking	Hitting ball off tee; hitting suspended ball
Locomotor patterns	
Running	Being pushed quickly in wheelchair while keeping head up
Jumping/hopping	Lifting head up and down while being pushed in wheelchair
Galloping/skipping	Moving arms up and down while being pushed in wheelchair; also, student can use adapted mobility aids such as scooterboards and walkers
Perceptual-motor skills	
Balance skills	Propping up on elbows, balancing prone over wedge
Body awareness	Accepting tactile input, attempting to imitate simple movements
Spatial awareness	Moving arms in when going in between, ducking head under objects
Visual-motor coordination	Tracking suspended objects, attempting to touch switches that activate visually stimulating toys
Physical fitness skills	
Endurance	Tolerate continuous activity, move body parts repeatedly
Strength	Use stretch bands, use isometric exercises
Flexibility	Perform range-of-motion activities as suggested by PT

Note: In all activities, utilize the principle of partial participation to ensure that the student is successful.
Taken from Block, M. E. (1992). What is appropriate physical education for students with profound disabilities? *Adapted Physical Activity Quarterly, 9*(2), p. 201.

Block (1992), in emphasizing many of the above points, has suggested that the ideal curriculum for the student with a severe or profound disability would be based on a functional, life-skills curricular model. This approach would include age-appropriate and functional activities, taught in natural settings, adhering to the principles of partial participation and choice-making, and using data-based instructional strategies.

Instructional Procedures

Educators generally recognize that students with severe disorders will benefit from instruction designed to improve their physical and motor fitness levels. One could even argue that because the motor needs of those with severe disabilities are so great, they will benefit more than their higher-functioning peers from specially designed movement experiences. However, there is little information available in the physical education literature that focuses on teaching strategies for working with this population. More is known about ineffective educational strategies than about procedures that have been found to be helpful. For example, it is clear that individuals who are severely and profoundly disabled will not be successful in the regular physical education program without needed support and services. Serious motor deficiencies and failure to respond cognitively to basic game and activity structure present challenges that require special instructional techniques and approaches.

The technique most frequently employed to teach those who are severely disabled is known as behavior modification (see chapter 6). The essence of this approach is that the instructor makes maximum and efficient use of the environment to assist a student in learning a behavior (defined skill). Physical educators are becoming more aware of this instructional strategy and the positive manner in which behavior modification or reinforcement strategies can be employed to assist the severely disabled learn basic movement skills. Dunn and associates (1986) have successfully utilized a modified behavioral approach to teach physical education to individuals with severe disabilities. In this section, selected components of their approach will be presented.

Preliminary Considerations

Throughout this chapter it has been emphasized that educational programs for the severely involved must be systematically designed. An important element in achieving this goal is to develop a curriculum that specifies the individual functional life skills or behaviors considered essential. Each behavior must be presented in a task-analyzed format so that elements of the task from least to most difficult can be identified. For example, in the *Oregon State University Data Based Curriculum for the Severely Handicapped,* skills have been divided into four broad sections. The first section, Movement Concepts, deals with movement through space in one's immediate personal environment to movement skills in more complex environments. Section 2 includes skills found in many of our popular elementary games. Physical fitness skills essential for survival in modern society are included in section 3. The last section focuses on age-appropriate leisure skills, including activities such as those enjoyed by young children, such as tricycle riding and swinging.

An important preliminary consideration related to curriculum development is the critical decision of what to teach. Obviously, this decision is determined by the educational needs of each individual student. This implies, therefore, that some type of educational assessment be utilized. In choosing an appropriate test to use with those who are severely disabled, Jansma (1982) recommends that the test should be (a) developmentally low with respect to comprehension and performance, (b) observational in nature, and (c) accompanied by curriculum/programming ideas. Given these guidelines and the heterogeneous nature of this population, criterion-referenced tests are the preferred evaluation method for determining the students' functioning levels. If the curricular materials are sequentially developed, the criterion for each behavior or skill in the curriculum can be used as a means of determining students' abilities. This would necessitate that students be evaluated on selected behaviors within the curriculum to determine areas of strength and weakness and, ultimately, to make decisions about where educational programming should begin. For additional information concerning the psychomotor assessment of individuals with disabilities, the reader is referred to Jansma (see Selected Readings).

A qualified teacher is needed to implement the curriculum and to respond to the educational needs of students with severe disabilities. Although the person selected to fulfill this assignment will vary from school to school, the professionals chosen most frequently are either special educators or physical educators. Preferably, the individual selected should also have additional training in the area of working with individuals with disabilities. The best approach is one in which the special educator and physical educator cooperatively develop the student's motor and physical fitness program. The special educator can contribute information about the student's behavior patterns and language capabilities. The physical educator would assume responsibility for the design of the physical education program and the instructional procedures to be utilized.

The physical education teacher also must be prepared to serve as an instructional *manager,* making decisions about the student's physical education program but not providing all of the direct teaching. Students with major disabilities require educational settings in which they are instructed individually or in small groups. This requires, therefore, that the teacher be provided time to recruit, train, and supervise volunteers to provide the needed one-to-one instruction.

The utilization of parents is also an essential part of the instructional team. Effective instruction can be carried out by parents at home. Parents can serve to not only maintain skills learned in physical education, but also actually accelerate learning. Maguire (1985) found that parents of children with severe disabilities could be taught to provide home-based instruction in physical education. Children who received instruction from their parents as a supplement to the school physical education program progressed more rapidly than those children who received only the school program.

Thus, coordination with parents is an important element in enhancing the motor and physical fitness of students with severe disabilities. For additional information about how parents and volunteers may be trained to teach children with severe disabilities, *Physical Education for the Severely Handicapped* by Dunn and associates (1986) should be consulted.

Educational Approach

Educators generally agree that the learning and behavior needs of those with severe disabilities are such that structure and careful planning are essential in developing educational programs. Ludlow and Sobsey observe that "Precise behavioral objectives, task analysis, and other individualized instructional techniques combine to form a powerful teaching process" (1984, p. 22) for students with severe learning needs. Heward and Orlansky (1992) believe that the following components must be given careful consideration in the development of instructional programs for students with severe handicaps.

1. The student's current level of performance must be precisely assessed.
2. The skill to be taught must be defined clearly.
3. The skills must be ordered in an appropriate sequence.
4. The teacher must provide a clear cue or instruction to the child.
5. The child must receive feedback and reinforcement from the teacher.
6. The teacher should include strategies to facilitate generalization of learning.
7. The child's performance must be carefully measured and evaluated.

These principles have been applied successfully to physical education programs for students with severe disabilities by Dunn, Morehouse, and Fredericks (1986). The procedure used to implement some of these principles are described in the following section.

The basic learning approach requires that careful attention be given to three important variables: (1) the method used to present material, (2) the complexity of the behavior the student is asked to perform, and (3) the procedure used to reinforce or correct the student. Each of these variables will be discussed in the following paragraphs.

Cuing Students with Severe Disabilities

The cue is the sign, signal, request, or information that calls for the occurrence of a behavior. It is synonymous to the instructions or materials presented to the student. Cues are those things in the environment that "set the occasion" for the student to behave. For instance, "Come to me, Johnny" is a cue for the student to respond to verbal instructions and to move toward the teacher. The presentation of a ball that

Figure 20.1 Physical assistance is an instructional technique frequently used with students who have special needs.

the student is to throw is a cue. Thus, a cue can take the form of any instructional materials, verbal, printed, or gestural, that are presented to a student. The concept of cue includes all the verbal instructions by the teacher. It includes the gestures of the teacher as well as the way in which objects or materials are presented.

Cues may be ordered according to their level of complexity. Although many students with disabilities respond to verbal cues, this is very difficult for individuals with severe disorders. The cues used by teachers must be specific and easily understood. The following sequence has been found to be effective in teaching those with severe disabilities:

1. Verbal cue is given—student is told what to do. If the student does not respond or responds incorrectly, go to step 2.

2. A demonstration of the skill (visual cue) is combined with the verbal cue. If the student does not respond or responds incorrectly, go to step 3.

3. A demonstration of the skill (visual cue) is combined with the verbal cue and the student is given help in the form of manual physical assistance (see chapter 6). Gradations in the amount of physical assistance

provided (e.g., heavy—manually moving a body part, to light—touching or tapping the body part) are also possible.

Obviously, the intent of this hierarchy is to help students perform physical tasks at the highest cue level possible. Special care must be taken to utilize verbal cues that are sensitive to the age of the individual. With verbal cues, the tone of voice, inflections, and terms should be appropriate to the individual's age. For example, using "pet" terms such as "tiger" "sweetie" etc., while questionable for use at any time, are entirely inappropriate for older students.

Analyzing the Behavior to Be Taught

The second variable that must be considered in teaching students with severe disabilities is to analyze carefully the behaviors to be taught. A behavior is anything a person does. It includes lifting a little finger, blinking an eye, kicking a ball, or climbing a rope. In the teaching of students, a behavior is a particular task that the student is to learn. Behavior can be something as simple as having the student extend the arms or as complex as having the student bat a pitched ball.

When teaching a behavior, however, the teacher should constantly keep in mind that most behaviors can be divided into smaller behaviors or pieces of behavior. It is these pieces of behavior that make up the teaching sequence. Take, for instance, riding a tricycle. Riding a tricycle is called a terminal behavior. Yet, it is comprised of a number of small behaviors—mounting the tricycle, placing the feet on the pedals, pushing the pedals, turning the tricycle, stopping, and so on step by step until the tricycle can be ridden. The smaller or less difficult behaviors are called *enabling* behaviors. The learning of them enables the student to learn the terminal behavior.

This process of breaking down a terminal behavior into the enabling behaviors is called analysis of behavior or task analysis (see chapter 6). Breaking the behaviors or tasks down into smaller steps helps the physical education teacher to create instructional settings geared toward student success. As additional behaviors are learned, these are combined so that ultimately the student performs the terminal behavior. Nietupski, Hamre-Nietupski, and Ayres (1984) report that there is ample evidence to support the use of task-analytic procedures as effective in the instruction of leisure skills, including physical fitness tasks, to those who are moderately and severely disabled.

Consequences

Consequences are the third major variable that must be considered in developing effective instructional programs for students with severe disabilities. Consequences can be likened to a feedback system. After the student performs a particular behavior, feedback or a consequence for that performance is provided. This consequence tells students that what they did was correct or incorrect. In a school setting one might think of the student taking a motor fitness test and having the test score interpreted as a consequence of the way the individual performed. The consequence can either be pleasing or displeasing to the person receiving it. A consequence that is pleasing to a person is called a reinforcer; a consequence that is displeasing is called a punisher. The basic concept underlying utilization of consequences is that the reinforcers delivered following a behavior increase the probability of the behavior occurring again; punishers delivered following a behavior decrease that probability.

A reinforcer must be pleasurable to the person experiencing it. Because it is pleasurable and because the person desires that pleasure and associates a particular behavior with the receipt of the reinforcer, a reinforcer by definition increases the probability of a behavior recurring. The student who enjoys social praise may increase the quality or quantity of his or her performance after being told, "You're doing a nice job!" Consequently, reinforcers by definition must be individualized because what is pleasing and, therefore, reinforcing to one person may not be pleasing and reinforcing to another. The principle of individualization also applies to punishers. A verbal reprimand may be severely punishing (displeasing) to one student whereas another student may not perceive that same reprimand as punishing. Therefore, punishers, like reinforcers, must be individualized.

A basic rule in the use of consequences is to rely, if at all possible, on the natural consequences of the environment. Fortunately, in the physical education environment there are many activities and experiences that in themselves are reinforcing, such as watching the movement of a ball after it is rolled. For some, however, the natural consequences of the environment are not sufficient and it may be necessary to identify other types of reinforcers to utilize with the student. This may be accomplished by exchanging ideas with the special education teacher and the student's parents, and subsequently coordinating the use of types of reinforcers decided upon.

Maintaining Data

The effectiveness of the instructional process is determined by reviewing data maintained on each student. For example, in the Oregon State University system, data are initially kept on each instructional trial. Therefore, every time a student is cued, an X indicating the student performed the skill correctly or an O indicating the student did not perform the skill correctly is recorded on the data sheet. A daily review of the data helps the teacher to update the student's program for the next day. If, for example, it is apparent that after ten trials (or another designated number) the student has yet to do the skill correctly, the teacher must review the elements of instruction (cue, behavior, and consequences) and make the appropriate changes. Frequently, the problem relates to a need to further analyze the behavior into smaller steps. It is

also possible that the cue or method of "consequating" the student should be modified. The ultimate criterion of a successful program is whether the student is learning. Morehouse (1988), in employing the Data Based Gymnasium Model, reported that using three consecutive executions of physical activity tasks was an effective criterion standard. Using the three consecutive criteria as a rule of thumb provides the physical education teacher with guidance in determining when to advance to the next step in the task analysis. Maintaining data provides the teacher with an excellent opportunity to make informed decisions about student progress. Focusing on the elements in the instructional process—the cue, behavior, and consequences—helps the teacher to make adjustments, when necessary, in a systematic manner.

Managing the Instructional System

The instructional elements described previously must be coordinated into a system that is practical and efficient for the teacher to manage. This requires that information on each student in the program be readily available and in a format that is easy to use. In the Oregon State University system, a clipboard record is developed for each student, on which pertinent information related to instructional procedures is maintained (figure 20.2). The clipboard describes in detail what to do with each student, where to record the information (data), and how to interact with the student. It is the "communication channel" through which information to volunteers is provided by the teacher. The clipboard also provides a mechanism whereby feedback comes to the teacher so that the student's individualized program can be modified.

Each student's clipboard contains the weekly cover sheet specifying all programs, including the physical education programs in which the student is currently engaged (figure 20.3). A student may be engaged in as many as five to

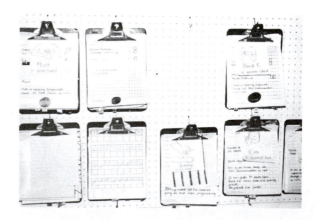

Figure 20.2 Clipboards with information similar to that found in figures 20.3 to 20.7 serve as an effective tool to help individualize instruction.

Weekly Cover Sheet

Name ___John Q.___

Program	M	T	W	Th	F
1. Game Skills Basic—underhand roll					
2. Personal Space—move arms up and down					
3. Self-Help Skills—button coat					
4. Writing—reproduce shapes					
5. Color—recognize primary colors					
6. Language—recognize prepositions					
7.					
8.					
9.					
10.					

Figure 20.3 Weekly cover sheet.

twelve programs, such as physical education (underhand roll), eating (finger foods), and writing (reproduced shapes). The number of programs will be determined by the student's capability and number of volunteers available to conduct each program.

Immediately following the weekly cover sheet on the clipboard is the consequence list and language file (figure 20.4). The consequence list identifies things that are reinforcing to the student. This list provides the teacher and volunteer with information about reinforcers for the student. On the sheet with the consequence list is a section for general comments. Included here are instructional tips that the teacher has found successful in working with the student.

The language section is divided into three parts: (1) receptive language, (2) expressive language, and (3) new vocabulary. The receptive language section defines the degree of understanding the student has of spoken language. The expressive language section describes the degree of language capability to be expected of the student. The new vocabulary section includes new words or sounds the student has acquired that need to be reinforced. In all programs, including physical education, the consequence and language sheet are used by all teachers and volunteers. Whether in the gymnasium or in the classroom, consistency in behavior treatment and communication procedures is essential for successful programming.

Following the consequence file and language sheet are three sheets (a behavioral sequence sheet, a program cover sheet, and a data sheet) for each program listed on the weekly cover sheet. The behavioral sequence sheet (figure 20.5) contains an example of a task analysis of one skill and

the program cover sheet (figure 20.6) describes how a sample program is to be run. The latter enables the volunteer to see what the verbal and nonverbal cues are, materials to be used, the reinforcement ratio, and the criterion level of success. This information helps the volunteer conduct the program as designed by the teacher. The last form is the data sheet (figure 20.7). Taking data assists the teacher in reviewing the student's performance so that an informed decision can be made to update the program appropriately for the following day.

Once criterion for a skill has been reached, it is essential that the skill be used if it is to be retained. The effectiveness of efforts to help students with severe disabilities maintain skills can be monitored by making periodic checks to evaluate the degree to which students perform the skill. In the Oregon State University system, this is accomplished by placing all skills that have been learned by each student into a maintenance file. The student is then asked to demonstrate the skill at scheduled times during the six-month period following the date on which the student reached the desired criterion level.

Group Process

Students with severe disabilities, as previously discussed, frequently require an instructional setting of one teacher to one student. Insufficient motor and physical fitness levels necessitate an approach in which students with severe disabilities can receive intense instruction to offset their movement deficiencies. As the basic foundational skills are

Language File, Consequence File, and General Comments

Child's Name: John Q.

Reinforcement File

PRIMARY / TANGIBLE:

- Swinging on a rope
- Playing with a ball
- Turning a kaleidoscope
- Rubbing a stuffed animal

SOCIAL: (Examples)

- "Give me five"
- "Nice going"
- "Super job"
- "Right on"
- Smile

Receptive Language

- Be sure John is attending prior to giving cue
- Make eye contact with John
- John responds to two concept commands

Expressive Language

- John will emit one and two word responses
- Require John to respond verbally to questions
- If John wants something have him ask for it

General Comments

- John must keep his hands to himself before delivering a new cue
- John is right handed
- Conduct the behavior treatment program if John strikes someone

Figure 20.4 Language and consequence files.

gained, however, the student should be provided the opportunity to generalize the skills learned to instructional situations involving more students. When several students share equipment, take turns, and receive group directions, new opportunities are created to allow those who are severely involved to respond to experiences similar to those found in many physical education activities.

Indicated in the following paragraphs are some suggested developmental stages for helping students to progress from individual instruction to group instruction. Not all students with severe disabilities will be able to progress to Stage VI. The student should be taken as far as possible consistent with the individual's needs and ability to be successful.

GAME SKILLS, BASIC

A. Underhand Roll

Terminal Objective: Student, from a standing position, will perform an underhand roll by swinging the arm backward and then forward while stepping forward simultaneously with the opposite foot and releasing the ball at the end of the swing in the direction of the target.

Prerequisite Skills: Gross Motor, DD; Fine Motor Skills, A and G.

Phase I   Sitting in a chair, swing arm backward and then forward, releasing ball.

Phase II   Standing with knees bent, swing arm backward and then forward, releasing ball.

Phase III   Standing with one foot forward and one foot back, and knees bent, swing arm backward and then forward, releasing ball.

Phase IV   Standing with knees bent, swing arm backward and then forward, releasing ball while simultaneously stepping forward with the opposite foot.

Teaching Notes:
1. For those students in wheelchairs, the underhand roll can be performed with the student sitting in the wheelchair, thus eliminating the need for the above prerequisite body positions.

2. For nonambulatory students who are not in a wheelchair, ball rolling could be taught from a supported sitting position.

3. When students have problems with timing the step and throw, the teacher may choose to physically assist, and/or prompt the foot during the throw.

Suggested Materials: A tennis ball and a 3-foot x 3-foot target placed on the floor. Any type or size of ball may be used to facilitate learning.

Figure 20.5   An example of one skill from the Oregon State University *Game, Exercise, and Leisure Sport Curriculum.*

PUPIL: John Q. DATE STARTED: October 3, 1996 DATE COMPLETED:	PROGRAM: Game Skills, Basic—A. Underhand Roll

SETTING (NONVERBAL CUE):
   Establish eye contact with John
     prior to delivering the cue.
	MATERIALS:
	   Clipboard
	   Pencil
	   Chair
	   Ball
	   3-foot x 3-foot target

INSTRUCTIONAL PROCESS:
  Verbal   John, roll the ball
  Cue   underhand.
  Model   Demonstrate if the
          response to the verbal
          cue is incorrect.
  Physical Provide assistance if the
  Assistance response to the verbal
          cue and demonstration
          is incorrect.
	CRITERION:
	   Three consecutive responses before
	     moving to the next phase.

Figure 20.6 Example of a program cover sheet.

Reinforcer	Phase	Step	Trials											Comments	Date
Social	I		0	0	0	X	X	0	0	0	X	0	Has trouble attending	3/8
Social	I		0	0	X	X	0	(X	X	X)			Seems to have the idea	3/9
Social	II		0	X	0	X	0	0	X	0	X	X	Needs help with backward swing	3/10
Social	II		X	0	(X	X	X)						Good day	3/11
Social	III		0	0	X	0	X	0	(X	X	X)		Has the idea	3/12
Social	IV		0	X	0	0	0	X	0	0	X	0	Has difficulty with step	3/15
Social	IV		X	0	X	0	(X	X	X)					3/16
Maintenance															

Figure 20.7   Example of a program data sheet for the underhand roll.

Stage I (Individual)   As described in the previous section, the basic intent of this stage is to ensure that students can learn in a systematic way given that appropriate cues and consequating procedures are used. One teacher or volunteer is necessary for each student.

Stage II (Advanced Individual)   This stage is similar to stage I but two or three students are assigned to each teacher. Again the attempt is to provide systematic instruction, with the teacher conducting programs, alternating from student to student. This stage allows for early peer interaction and creates opportunities for students to observe the skill performance of others.

Stage III (Transition)   The ultimate goal of this stage is to advance students from the instructor-directed individual setting in which specific cues are used to a generalized instructional format. The students are given general directions and are then assigned an area within the gymnasium to practice specific skills. Each student is expected to function independently at the assigned station, with the teacher assisted by volunteers providing direct instructional cues when needed.

Stage IV (Skills with Peer Interaction)   Stage IV is an advancement over stage III because at this level students interact with one another through the medium of various skills; in other words, students practice skills together. One student, for instance, may practice rolling a ball while another student practices trapping the ball. The important element in this stage is the emphasis on creating opportunities for peers to interact. If the student can successfully perform at this stage, it is possible that the individual will be able to achieve success and to participate more fully in the regular physical education program.

Stage V (Basic Games)   In this stage, students are provided an opportunity to play basic games using two sequenced skills, such as hitting and running to first. The fielder in this example would field and then throw to first. Many elementary games could be introduced at this level. The primary point to remember is that no more than two skills should be sequenced. Students with severe disabilities need opportunities to learn phases of a game before they are introduced to the complexity of the total activity. Some may never progress beyond learning certain aspects of the game.

Stage VI (Intermediate Games)   This stage is an advancement over stage V because students are now asked to sequence three skills. A student, for example, might be asked to hit a ball, run to first, and then return to home plate. Another example might be to catch a pass, dribble the basketball to the basket, and then shoot the ball. Obviously, sequencing three skills requires not only an advanced skill level but also high receptive and expressive abilities.

The appropriate stage for each student may change from day to day depending upon the skill to be learned and the ability of the student. It must be emphasized, however, that a student who is severely disabled must experience some success at stages I and II before the individual is faced with the challenges inherent in the more advanced stages.

The key to group experiences for students with severe disabilities is to allow for as much independence as possible. For example, some students will respond very well to stage III (transition), where the teacher provides general cues (directions) to the class and then assigns each student to a particular station to practice a specific skill. In this situation, the student is expected to respond to very natural cues. For example, the presence of a bucket of balls means to throw the balls one at a time at a target using an overhand throw. When the teacher notices an error in performance or behavior, a nondirective cue can be used. For example, if the student is not throwing with the correct arm, the teacher might ask, "Mary, which arm do you throw with?" If the response is correct a mild positive social reinforcer should be used, such as saying, "okay." If Mary continues to throw with the wrong arm, then a direct verbal cue is necessary such as, "Mary, throw with the *other* arm." Occasionally, it may be necessary to move to the next cue level, the use of a model, or demonstration. If this is not successful, physical assistance should be used to ensure that the student experiences success and comprehends the verbal information. The ultimate goal is to use natural cues when possible and move as necessary to teacher-directed cues. An overview of the cue hierarchy system is presented in figure 20.8.

During group programming, data must be maintained to determine the effectiveness of the program. The emphasis on trial-by-trial data found in stages I and II is replaced in the more advanced stages by taking data only on two of the student's trials. For example, in the Group Data Sheet for five students participating at a stage III instructional level (figure 20.9), the students are working on the same motor skill—kicking. It is quite acceptable, however, for the teacher to create situations in which students work on different skills, having the students rotate from station to station. In this situation, the teacher has a separate data sheet with the name of each student listed for each specific skill. For the more advanced stages, V and VI, the data sheet is very similar to that used in stage III except for the name of the program and the identification of the phase. As indicated in figure 20.10, the students are at stage V, working on a two-part motor skill sequence, kicking a ball and running to a base. The phases and steps of the skills are not identified. The focus of the instruction and, therefore, the data collection is to ensure that the student can sequence the skill,

Program Presentation Levels

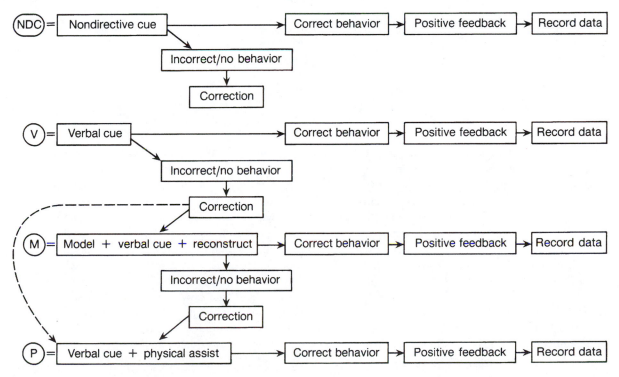

Figure 20.8 Cue hierarchy system.

(Source: Dunn, J. M., and Morehouse, J. W.: *Leadership Training.* Corvallis, OR: Oregon State University, Department of Physical Education.)

Group Data Sheet

Skill: Kicking

Stage: III

Names

Sam	Date	3/10/96	3/11/96	3/12/96			
	Phase/Step	VI 1	VI 1	VI 1			
	Data	O | X	O | X				
Jenny	Date	3/10/96	3/11/96	3/12/96			
	Phase/Step	VI 1	VI 1	VI 2			
	Data	X | O	X | X				
Paul	Date	3/10/96	3/11/96	3/12/96			
	Phase/Step	VI 1	VI 1	VI 1			
	Data	O | O	X | O				
Dick	Date	3/10/96	3/11/96	3/12/96			
	Phase/Step	VI 1	VI 1	VI 1			
	Data	X | O	O | X				
Ann	Date	3/10/96	3/11/96	3/12/96			
	Phase/Step	VI 1	VI 1	VI 2			
	Data	O | X	X | X				
	Date						
	Phase/Step						
	Data						
	Date						
	Phase/Step						
	Data						

Figure 20.9 Group data sheet, stage III.

(Source: Dunn, J. M., Morehouse, J. W., and Fredericks, H. D. (1986). *Physical Education for the Severely Handicapped.* Pro-Ed Publishers, Austin, TX, p. 122.)

successfully relying on natural cues. It cannot be emphasized too strongly that each of the stages used in group instruction can be implemented in the regular physical education class. In many instances, this approach will resemble a side-by-side instructional environment, where the student or students with severe disabilities would occupy an area in the gymnasium along with the students participating in the regular instructional activities. To do this successfully, however, requires the use of volunteers, including appropriately trained peers. These individuals can be assigned by the teacher to assist students with severe learning needs who require systematic instruction, including the use of carefully developed individualized cues and consequences. The goal, of course, is to maximize, to the extent possible, the interaction between individuals with severe disabilities and their nondisabled classmates.

The purpose of developing physical education skills is to use them in game or leisure activities. Higher-functioning students who have received one-to-one programming with sufficient opportunities to practice these skills in small group settings are capable of successfully participating in modified forms of popular games and thus achieving the goal of partial participation. Students who have mastered the skill of hitting should be challenged to sequence this skill into an activity such as hit and run. Only through opportunities like these will students make the transition from successful mastery of an isolated skill to the use of the skill in a meaningful context.

Group Data Sheet

Activity: Kick ball

Skill: Kicking and running to a base

Stage: V

Names

Sandra	Date	5/21/96							
	Data	O	X						
Danny	Date	5/21/96							
	Data								
Peter	Date	5/21/96							
	Data								
Joel	Date	5/21/96							
	Data								
Michael	Date	5/21/96							
	Data								
Jenny	Date	5/21/96							
	Data								
	Date	5/21/96							
	Data								

Figure 20.10 Group data sheet, stage V.

(Source: Dunn, J. M., Morehouse, J. W., and Fredericks, H. D. (1986). *Physical Education for the Severely Handicapped.* Pro-Ed Publishers, Austin, TX, p. 122.)

Summary

Although there is no universally accepted definition of severely disabled, it is generally recognized that students with severe disabilities need assistance in self-help, motor, cognitive, social, and communication skills. Usually these are students with multiple disabilities who look and act differently than other children. However, there is much individual variation in these children with no two being identical in their needs and/or abilities.

In recent years educators have demonstrated rather convincingly that individuals with severe disabilities can learn if provided an appropriate instructional environment. This means that educational experiences should be structured with the skills to be taught task-analyzed. In addition, the educational approach for students with severe disabilities requires precise teaching techniques with appropriate cues and consequences. A system approach, in which data are taken on individual trials, should also be incorporated so that informed decisions can be made about the individual's educational progress. Dunn, Morehouse, and Fredericks (1986) have demonstrated that these principles can be effectively utilized to teach physical education skills to those with severe disabilities.

Efforts should be made to include, to the extent possible, students with severe disabilities in group experiences. This will require the assistance of parents and the availability of appropriately trained volunteers and aides. Significant gains can be made in physical education classes with students who are severely disabled if support personnel are available.

Future directions in the education of those with severe disabilities will focus on the need to generalize skills to a variety of settings including community recreational centers. The emphasis will be, as it should be, on the need to develop age-appropriate, functional, leisure, and work-related skills. This will require close articulation and cooperation between physical educators and community recreators. Federal legislation makes it clear that educational programs and services must be provided for those who are severely disabled. The legislative emphasis has helped educators demonstrate what many knew—persons with severe disabilities can learn if given the opportunity. This observation is true whether applied to the classroom or gymnasium. Greater efforts must be directed toward assisting these individuals realize their full human potential. Physical educators can play a significant role in making this possible. In some instances this will mean teaching a youngster to roll a ball or helping a child to learn to swim or to use playground equipment. Given dedicated and caring professionals, the future for persons with severe and profound disabilities is very promising with much of the potential in this population yet to be realized.

Selected Readings

Bender, M., & Valletutti, P.J. (1976). *Teaching the moderately and severely handicapped: Vol. I. Behavior, self care, and motor skills.* Baltimore: University Park Press.

Bigge, J.L., & O'Donnell, P.A. (1976). *Teaching individuals with physical and multiple disabilities.* Columbus, OH: Charles E. Merrill Publishing Co.

Block, M.E.(1992). What is appropriate physical education for students with profound disabilities? *Adapted Physical Activity Quarterly, 9*(3), 197–213.

Block, M.E., & Krebs, P.L. (1992). An alternative to least restrictive environments: A continuum of support to regular physical education. *Adapted Physical Activity Quarterly, 9*(2), 97–113.

Browder, D.M. (1987). *Assessment of individuals with severe handicaps.* Baltimore, MD: Paul H. Brookes Publishing Co.

Cleland, C.C. (1979). *The profoundly mentally retarded child.* Englewood Cliffs, NJ: Prentice-Hall, Inc.

Corbett, J. (1977). Aversion for the treatment of self-injurious behavior. *Journal of Mental Deficiency Research, 19,* 79–95.

Croce, R.V. (1990). Effects of exercise and diet on body composition and cardiovascular endurance in adults with severe mental retardation. *Education and Training in Mental Retardation, 25,* 176–187.

Dunn, J.M., Morehouse, J.W., & Dalke, B. (1981). *Game, exercise, and leisure sport for the severely handicapped.* Corvallis, OR: Oregon State University, Department of Physical Education.

Dunn, J.M., Morehouse, J.W., & Fredericks, H.D. (1986). *Physical education for the severely handicapped.* Austin, TX: Pro-Ed Publishers.

Fredericks, H.D.B. (1976). *The teaching research curriculum for moderately and severely handicapped.* Springfield, IL: Charles C. Thomas.

Geddes, D. (1974). *Physical and recreational programming for severely and profoundly mentally retarded individuals.* Washington, DC: American Alliance for Health, Physical Education, Recreation, and Dance.

Heward, W.L., & Orlansky, M.D. (1992). *Exceptional children* (4th ed.). Columbus, OH: Charles E. Merrill Publishing Co.

Jansma, P. (1980). Psychomotor domain tests for the severely and profoundly handicapped. *Journal of the Association for the Severely Handicapped, 5,* 368–381.

Jansma, P. (1982). Physical education for the severely and profoundly handicapped. *Exceptional Education Quarterly, 3,* 35–41.

Jansma, P. (Ed.). (1993). *The psychomotor training and serious disabilities.* Lanham, MD: University Press of America, Inc.

Ludlow, B.L., & Sobsey, R. (1984). *The school's role in educating severely handicapped students.* Bloomington, IN: Phi Delta Kappa Educational Foundation.

Maguire, P. (1985). *The effects of home instruction by parents utilizing the data based gymnasium instructional model on the performance of selected motor skills with moderately and severely mentally retarded children.* Unpublished doctoral dissertation, Oregon State University, Corvallis, OR.

Meyen, E.L. (1978). *Exceptional children and youth.* Denver, CO: Love Publishing Co.

Meyer, L.H., Peck, C.A., & Brown, L. (Eds.). (1991). *Critical issues in the lives of people with severe disabilities.* Baltimore, MD: Paul H. Brookes Publishing Co.

Morehouse, J.W. (1988). *The effect of trials-to-criterion on the retention of a discrete motor skill by moderately and severely mentally retarded individuals.* Unpublished doctoral dissertation, Oregon State University, Corvallis, OR.

Nietupski, J.A., Hamre-Nietupski, S., & Ayres, B. (1984). Review of task analytic leisure skill training efforts: Practitioner implications and future research needs. *Journal of the Association for Persons with Severe Handicaps, 9,* 88–97.

Sims-Tucker, B.M., & Jensema, C.K. (1984). Severely and profoundly auditorially/visually impaired students: The deaf-blind population. In P.J. Valletutti and B.M. Sims-Tucker (Eds.), *Severely and profoundly handicapped students.* Baltimore, MD: Paul H. Brookes Publishing Co.

Snell, M.E. (Ed.). (1987). *Systematic instruction of persons with severe handicaps* (3d. ed.). Columbus, OH: Charles E. Merrill Publishing Co.

Snell, M.E., & Renzaglia, A.M. (1986). Moderate, severe, and profound handicaps. In N.G. Haring and L. McCormick (Eds.), *Exceptional children and youth* (4th ed.), (pp. 271–310). Columbus, OH: Charles E. Merrill Publishing Co.

Sontag, E., Smith, J., & Sailor, W. (1977). The severely/profoundly handicapped: Who are they? Where are we? *Journal of Special Education, 11,* 5–11.

Stainback, S., Stainback, W., Wehman, P., & Spangiers, L. (1983). Acquisition and generalization of physical fitness exercises in three profoundly retarded adults. *Journal of the Association for the Severely Handicapped, 8,* 47–55.

Webster, C.D., Konstantareas, M.M., Oxman, J., & Mack, J.E. (Eds.). (1980). *Autism.* New York: Pergamon Press.

Wehman, P., Renzaglia, A., & Bates, P. (1985). *Functional living skills for moderately and severely handicapped individuals.* Austin, TX: Pro-Ed Publishers.

Enhancing Activities

1. Observe a class for students with severe disabling conditions. In your observation note the heterogeneity of the students and the instructional techniques used by the teacher.

2. Select a physical skill and task-analyze the skill. Make sure that the steps and progressions are small enough so that the students with severe disabilities can experience success.

3. Observe various settings (college classes, shopping, sporting events, etc.) and note the variety of cues and consequences employed. Is feedback (consequence) frequently or infrequently used? Is the level of cue appropriate? Contrast the use of cues and consequences used with those that might be appropriate for individuals with severe learning difficulties.

4. Review the list of nondirective cues reported in figure 20.8. Identify other nondirective cues that would be appropriate for the physical education class.

5. Select a skill and develop a program cover sheet (see figure 20.6). With the assistance of your teacher and using the principles identified in this chapter, implement the program with a student who is severely disabled.

6. Write to The Association for Persons With Severe Handicaps and request information regarding their organizations and services provided by their group.

Activities and Programs

The section is designed to help the reader to:

1 Modify lifetime activities, individual and dual sports, and dance forms so students with disabilities can successfully and safely participate in activity.

2 Appreciate the value of teaching relaxation and posture in the special physical education program and their contribution to the total well-being of persons with disabilities.

3 Utilize methods and techniques to teach persons with disabilities to swim effectively and safely.

4 Provide competitive sport experiences for students with disabilities consistent with their needs, interests, and abilities.

The focus of this final section is on activities and programs for students with disabilities. Some of the chapters provide comprehensive descriptions of adaptations for a wide variety of physical education activities to permit participation by students with disabilities. Ideas are included for modifying rules and regulations, adapting playing techniques and equipment, and devising new versions of the activities. Other chapters describe special program offerings that are particularly beneficial to students with disabilities.

CHAPTER 21

Activities and Games
for Young Children

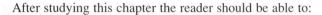

CHAPTER OBJECTIVES

After studying this chapter the reader should be able to:

1 Appreciate the contributions of early intervention programs toward the development of individuals with disabilities.

2 Recognize that recent federal legislation (P.L. 99-457 and P.L. 101-476) addresses the need for motor and physical activity programs for infants, toddlers, and young children.

3 Understand that young children with and without disabilities benefit from the opportunity to participate together in movement related experiences.

4 Identify gross motor assessment instruments and procedures commonly used with young children ages three to five.

5 Develop movement and activity programs that can be used to address the locomotor, non-locomotor, and manipulative skills needs of young children with disabilities.

6 Appreciate the significance of games and their contribution to the cognitive, affective, and psychomotor development of children.

7 Select games on the basis of their ability to enhance the basic motor and physical fitness skills.

8 Identify numerous games played by children and be familiar with the structure and strategy of various games.

9 Adapt and modify games so that children with disabilities can participate with their nondisabled peers.

10 Organize the instructional environment so that children can learn to participate in games successfully and safely.

11 Assist children, including those with disabilities, in creating new games and activities.

12 Structure games and play activities so that the experience is enjoyable and beneficial to all children, including those with disabilities.

13 Recognize the need for games that encourage cooperation and maximum participation, as contrasted to those that are competitive and designed to minimize participation.

In recent years a growing number of authorities have concluded that intervention activities and educational services for individuals with disabilities must begin as early as possible following the identification of a disability. The support and evidence for early intervention services have resulted in federal legislation that stipulates the provision of appropriate services for infants age birth to two years and young children, beginning at age three. The focus of recent legislation (P.L. 99-457 and P.L. 101-476) emphasizes clearly that early intervention services will be provided, parents will play an integral part in the delivery of services, schools and others will cooperate in providing programs, and personnel from various disciplines will be involved in delivering appropriate programs (Dunn, 1991). Title I of P.L. 99-457 mandates that states develop a statewide plan that will ensure that all children with special needs, birth through thirty-six months, receive a comprehensive evaluation, individualized family service plan (IFSP, see chapter 2), and access to procedural safeguards (Eichstaedt and Lavay, 1992). Title II of P.L. 99-457 makes it clear that children between three and five must receive the same services and protection now provided to school-age children. These services include, in part, full and appropriate education, due process, and the development of an Individualized Education Program (IEP). The Individuals with Disabilities Education Act (IDEA) reinforces P.L. 99-457 and reaffirms the commitment to provide educational services for infants, toddlers, and young children.

Motor and physical activity programs are essential in the education of infants and young children with disabilities (McCubbin and Zittel, 1991). Cowden and Eason (1991) have reinforced this need, arguing that early motor programs are so critical that a new cadre of specialists with training as pediatric adapted physical educators should be developed. As discussed in chapter 2, infants and toddlers who experience deviations from normal development benefit from early movement experiences, including programs with a sensorimotor emphasis. For more information regarding this population, the reader is referred to chapter 2. Within this chapter, the emphasis will focus on activities and programs for young children three to eight years of age.

Assessing Young Children with Disabilities

As described in chapter 7, there are several instruments that can be used to assess the motor performance of young children with disabilities. One of the most popular tests, the Test of Gross Motor Development (Ulrich, 1985), is widely used because the test includes locomotor and object control items commonly found in quality movement programs for young children. Zittel (1994) conducted an extensive analysis of tests that have been used with young preschool children, including tests frequently used to assess the gross motor performance of children with disabilities. In assessing the merit

of tests to use with young children, Zittel suggests that the following criteria should be employed: test purpose; technical adequacy; nondiscriminatory items; administrative ease; instructional link; and ecological validity (table 21.1). In applying these criteria to tests commonly used with young preschool children, Zittel suggests that the instruments most closely meeting all of the criteria include the Peabody Developmental Motor Scales, Test of Gross Motor Development, and the Battelle Developmental Inventory. Summary information about these tests and other instruments rated highly can be found in table 21.2.

As noted in chapter 7, *Evaluation,* it is essential that sound evaluation procedures be used in physical education programs for individuals with disabilities. Eason (1991) has identified assessment as one of the essential components in an effective physical education program for preschool children with disabilities. Federal legislation mandates that special programs be provided for young children, ages three to five, who are "at risk" or with a developmental delay. While it may be difficult at times to find the "best" test to use with preschool children with disabilities, this should not be used as an excuse to avoid evaluating the students and their educational gains. If necessary, physical educators should employ other procedures to determine educational progress, such as task analyses and checklists as described in chapter 7. Baganto and Neisworth (1990) proposed that clinical

Table 21.1 *Key features for selecting an appropriate preschool gross motor assessment instrument*

Criteria	Selection Features
Purpose	Resource materials state: What the instrument is designed to provide How the measurements can be used The type of reference
Technical adequacy	Evidence for validity Evidence for reliability Standardized population
Nondiscriminatory	Adaptations permitted Multisource information permitted Standardized sample sensitive to culture and disability
Administrative ease	Scoring more than pass/fail Interpretation includes a raw score summary, comments related to performance, or level of mastery indicated Administration time clearly stated or flexibility in test component administration allowed
Instructional link	Curriculum-referenced Test items sequenced to provide low inference for instructional objectives Ability to monitor progress
Ecological validity	Familiar materials Familiar setting Caregiver present

From: Zittel, L.L. (1994). Gross motor assessment of preschool children with special needs. *APAQ, 11*(3), p. 247.

Table 21.2 *Summary of nine gross motor assessment instruments*

Name	Age (Years)	Type of Reference	Component Areas	No. Items	Publisher
I CAN Preprimary Motor and Play Skills	Preprimary	Criterion	Locomotor Object control Body control Health/Fitness Play equipment Play participation	31 total 26 gross motor	Michigan State University Instructional Media Center
OSU Scale of Intra-Gross Motor Assessment	2½–14	Criterion	Gross motor	11	Ohio Motor Assessment Associates
Peabody Developmental Motor Scales	Birth–7	Norm Criterion	Gross motor Fine motor	282 total 170 gross motor	DLM Teaching Resources
Test of Gross Motor Development	3–10	Norm Criterion	Gross motor: locomotor object control	12	Pro-Ed, Inc.
Battelle Development Inventory	Birth–8	Norm Criterion	Personal/Social Adaptive Motor Communication Cognitive	341 total 82 motor 44 gross motor	DLM Teaching Resources
Brigance: Inventory of Early Development	Below the developmental age of 7 years	Norm Criterion	Motor Self-help Speech/language General knowledge/ comprehension Early academic skills	98 total 13 gross motor	Curriculum Associates
Denver Development Mental Screening Test	Birth–6	Norm	Gross motor Language Fine motor/adaptive Personal/Social	125 total 32 gross motor	Denver Development Materials
Developmental Indicators for the Assessment of Learning—Revised	2–6	Norm	Motor Conceptual Language	24 total 8 motor 2 gross motor	Childcraft Education Corp.
Miller Assessment for Preschoolers	2.9–5.8	Norm	Sensory Motor Cognitive	27 total 8 motor 3 gross motor	The Psychological Corp.

From: Gross motor assessment of preschool children with special needs: Instrument selection considerations, by Laurice L. Zittel, *Adapted Physical Activity Quarterly* (vol. 11, No. 3), p. 247–252, 253, Copyright © 1994 by Human Kinetics Publishers. Reprinted by permission.

judgment is a highly representative form of assessment and provides a broad description of behavior. Using this approach, the teacher is asked to use subjective checklists to evaluate the child over time and in various settings. Sherrill (1993) believes that the best way to evaluate young children is to observe them in informal play settings as they engage in natural movement. Collecting and sharing observational data with other professionals, including special educators and related services personnel, will provide a rich source of information on which to base a determination of the child's developmental status and future progress.

Placement and Programming

The education of young children has received increased attention since the mid-1980s. Much of this concern has been driven by the recognition that an increasing number of young children, ages three to five, are receiving services in child-care centers and preschool programs. As more and more young children have been placed together in educational centers and settings, organizations such as the National Association of the Education of Young Children have developed position papers and statements which describe developmentally appropriate practices for the education of young children. The Council on Physical Education for Children (COPEC), an organization within The American Alliance for Health, Physical Education, Recreation, and Dance, also has identified appropriate and inappropriate practices in the education of young children with disabilities. COPEC's (1994) guidelines provide educators and parents a starting point from which to evaluate the quality of movement programs and experiences offered young children. Developmentally appropriate practices for young children are based on a number of important premises, including the value and benefit of interacting with children of various abilities, including those with disabilities.

There is an extensive body of literature to support the value of including young children with disabilities in programs with nondisabled peers. Block (1994) has articulated the benefits of inclusion for children with and without disabilities (table 21.3). It is important to note that young children with and without disabilities are enriched as a result of the opportunity to engage in programs together. History has revealed time and time again that individuals who do things together at early ages have the best opportunity to develop positive attitudes toward one another. Young children without disabilities will need guidance and direction from teachers and adults to help them understand and appreciate peers who are disabled. If this is done properly, however, nondisabled peers can be effectively utilized to help or assist learners who have special physical education needs (Houston-Wilson, 1994).

The majority of activities and games that are developmentally appropriate for the nondisabled also are appropriate for young children with disabilities. This would include activities that emphasize health-related fitness as well as movement skills commonly found in well-designed programs for young children. The goal, of course, is to ensure that the educational program is leading to desired changes for students with and without disabilities. For the student with a disability to experience success, it may be necessary, depending on the level of severity, for the teacher to modify the instructional approach.

There are numerous modifications that can be made to ensure that the young child with a disability can be successful in a regular setting. Chief among these is the manner in which information is presented. For example, a verbal cue, while appropriate for many young children, will need to be modified for the student with a hearing, visual, or processing disability. Block (1994) has succinctly captured many of the modifications that may need to be made in the instructional approach to working with young children with disabilities (table 21.4). Numerous other examples may be found in earlier chapters devoted specifically to a particular disability.

In employing a physical education curriculum for the young child with a disability, it may be necessary to modify various movement experiences such that the child can experience success. In the section on Adaptations, found later in this chapter, information is provided about various modifications that can be made in conventional games to

---

Table 21.3 *Benefits of inclusion*

To children with disabilities:
- Opportunity to learn social skills in integrated, more natural environments.
- More stimulating, motivating, normalized environment.
- Availability of age-appropriate, nondisabled role models and peer supports.
- Can participate in a variety of in-school and extracurricular activities.
- Potential new friendships with peers who live in same neighborhood.
- Improved self-esteem.

To children without disabilities:
- With guidance from adults, can improve attitudes towards children with disabilities.
- With guidance from adults, can learn how to interact with, be friends to, assist, and advocate for peers with disabilities.
- Availability of special resource personnel, instruction, and equiment that may be beneficial to children without disabilities
- Perspective—having a hurt knee, acne, or losing a friend suddenly seems somewhat trivial compared to the daily challenges faced by children with disabilities.
- Future parents of children with disabilities, future taxpayers, future teachers, and future business persons have greater personal knowledge of disability and thus are less prejudiced.
- Improved self-esteem.

From: What is appropriate physical education for students with profound disabilities? by Martin Block, *Adapted Physical Education Quarterly* (vol. 9, No. 3) p. 201, Copyright © 1992 by Human Kinetics Publishers. Reprinted by permission.

Table 21.4 *Suggested modifications in activity for young children with specific needs*

Does the student have limited strength?

THINGS TO CONSIDER
- ❑ shorten distance to move or project object
- ❑ use lighter equipment (e.g., balls, bats)
- ❑ use shorter striking implements
- ❑ allow student to sit or lie down while playing
- ❑ use deflated or suspended balls
- ❑ change requirements (e.g., a few jumps, then run)

Does the student have limited speed?
- ❑ shorten distance (or lengthen for others)
- ❑ change locomotor pattern (allow running v. walking)
- ❑ make safe areas in tag games

Does the student have limited endurance?
- ❑ shorten distance
- ❑ shorten playing field
- ❑ allow "safe" areas in tag games
- ❑ decrease activity time for student
- ❑ allow more rest periods for student
- ❑ allow student to sit while playing

Does the student have limited balance?
- ❑ provide chair/bar for support
- ❑ teach balance techniques (e.g., widen base, extend arms)
- ❑ increase width of beams to be walked
- ❑ use carpeted rather than slick surfaces
- ❑ teach students how to fall
- ❑ allow student to sit during activity
- ❑ place student near wall for support
- ❑ allow student to hold peer's hand

Does student have limited coordination and accuracy?
- ❑ use stationary balls for kicking/striking
- ❑ decrease distance for throwing, kicking, and shooting
- ❑ make targets and goals larger
- ❑ use larger balls for kicking and striking
- ❑ increase surface of the striking implements
- ❑ use backstop
- ❑ use softer, slower balls for striking and catching
- ❑ in bowling-type games, use lighter, less stable pins

Modified from Block, M. E. (1994). *A teacher's guide to including students with disabilities in regular physical education.* Paul H. Brookes Publishing Co., P.O. Box 10624, Baltimore, MD 21285-0624. Used with permission.

accommodate the needs of the young child with a disability. Many of these suggestions represent good common sense such as altering or reducing the activity space for individuals unable to move with the same ease as their classmates.

One of the highly desirable features of teaching activities and games to young children with and without disabilities is that the content can be varied to respond to individual needs. Teaching the movement skills found in table 21.5 using a movement concepts approach (table 21.6) creates exciting opportunities to permit all students to learn and to experience success. For example, in teaching static balance using a movement concepts approach, the skill can be varied according to duration (time) of the balance, the body part to be balanced, the body in relation to an object (i.e., balancing on something, etc.). For a young child with a disability, the nature of the balance task can be varied in numerous ways (e.g., the time to balance reduced, the number of body parts to use in the balance activity increased, use two or three contact points instead of one, etc.). For students who use assistive devices such as walkers and wheelchairs, movement skills that emphasize dynamic or static balance can be modified in many ways, permitting the young child to experience success by incorporating the assistive device into the balance activity. For example, in a dynamic balance task emphasizing space and the use of pathways (straight, curved, zigzag), the child who walks with the aid of a crutch

Table 21.5 *Fundamental movement skill themes*

Skills

Locomotor ⇒	walking
	running
	jumping
	galloping
	sliding
	hopping
	leaping
	skipping
Stability ⇒	stretching
	curling
	bending
	twisting
	body rolling
	dodging
	balancing
	inverted supports
Manipulative ⇒	dribbling
	throwing
	catching
	kicking
	punting
	trapping
	volleying
	striking

This article is reprinted with permission from the *Journal of Physical Education, Recreation, and Dance*, Aug. 1994, p. 29. JOHPERD is a publication of the American Alliance for the Health, Physical Education, Recreation, and Dance, 1900 Association Drive, Reston, VA 22091. This permission applies to printed materials only and is expressly forbidden in any electronic medium without additional request for permission.

Table 21.6 *The movement concepts*

Effort	Space	Relationships
Force	*Levels*	*Objects/People*
strong	high/medium/low	over/under
light		in/out
	Directions	between/among
Time	forward/backward	in front/behind
fast	diagonally/sideways	above/below
slow	up/down	through/around
sudden		
sustained	*Pathways*	*People*
	straight	mirroring
Flow	curved	shadowing
free	zigzag	in unison
bound		together/apart
	Ranges	solo
	body shapes	partner/group
	body spaces	
	body extensions	

This article is reprinted with permission from the *Journal of Physical Education, Recreation, and Dance*, Aug. 1994, p. 29. JOHPERD is a publication of the American Alliance for the Health, Physical Education, Recreation, and Dance, 1900 Association Drive, Reston, VA 22091. This permission applies to printed materials only and is expressly forbidden in any electronic medium without additional request for permission.

or uses a wheelchair can participate fully in the activity with minimal modifications and, most importantly, benefit from the unit on balance.

In addition to the teaching of movement skills and concepts, the familiar games of childhood have a definite place in educational programs for young children with and without disabilities. Participation in game activities contributes in many ways to the growth and development of children. Games promote development of students' motor and physical fitness levels. By virtue of their structure, games provide unique opportunities for learning to share, take turns, and cooperate. Reinforcement of academic skills related to language, mathematics, science, and social studies can be accomplished with appropriate adaptations of games, such as those described by Humphrey (1976), Cratty (1970), and Werner (1994). In addition, most games have a folk origin and so offer children a chance to learn about different cultures as well as to expand their understanding of their country's heritage and the importance that game experiences have played in the history of the world.

Significant as these contributions of game activities are, of even greater importance is the role that games play in developing the basic locomotor and manipulative skills discussed in chapter 2, *Developmental Patterns*. Young Children find games to be an exciting environment in which to utilize the basic motor skills they have acquired, and so they are motivated not only to improve the quality of their skills but also to apply them in new experiences. Observing children in game activities also provides teachers with a unique opportunity to assess the skill level of students and to evaluate their performance.

For example, the teacher closely watches for the performance errors as the child executes the basic skills indigenous to the game during play. When it is observed that the child is making an error in movement, that is, inappropriate muscular contractions are producing inefficient movement, the teacher provides information and assistance to the individual to correct the error and then offers them opportunities to practice the correct movement by itself and in game situations. In the case of a child with a disability, the limitations and potentiality of movement must be carefully considered in assessing the efficiency of skill performance: The most efficient and effective movement for a child with a disability may not be the same as that for a child without a disability. The information acquired through informal evaluation can, if desired, be recorded after class to provide a permanent record to be utilized in reporting progress or for the development of specific lessons to improve deficiencies in the basic skills. To fail to provide children with the opportunities for development engendered by play in the basic skill games is to deny them entrance to one of the best avenues to optimum growth and development.

Organizing for Game Instruction

Because the space required for playing the basic skill games need not be large, the games can be organized for play almost anywhere—on the playground, in the classroom, in the gymnasium or all-purpose room, even in hallways. Equipment is relatively simple and inexpensive: balls, beanbags, boxes, batons, and plastic bowling pins. Most of these items are easily obtained or readily improvised. Beanbags, for example, can be made from scrap cloth sewn into a bag and filled with dried beans or rice. Wood scraps of suitable size and free of splinters may be substituted for batons and empty milk cartons or plastic jugs for bowling pins.

The strategies for including the child with a disability into game activities will vary according to the disability, severity level, and the nature of the game. If the student has sufficient skill, but the nature of the game itself is restrictive (for example, a student in a wheelchair playing dodge ball), the activity should be modified to accommodate the special needs of the student. A discussion of strategies useful in modifying activities to permit the integration of children with disabilities with their nondisabled peers will be presented in the last section of this chapter. Indicated below are some instructional guidelines teachers should observe when teaching games to children. The following have been modified from Dauer and Pangrazi (1986).

1. The teacher should study the game before attempting to teach it. This will require not only knowledge of the game itself (rules and equipment) but also an understanding of how to modify or adapt the game as various situations unfold.

2. When presenting a new game to a class, the teacher should have the youngsters sit or stand in the formation that they are going to use. The directions should be well organized and presented clearly in a concise and succinct manner. Efforts should be made to ensure that students with disabilities understand the directions. For example, the student with a hearing loss may need to be reminded to sit close to the front so that he or she can hear and observe the teacher.

3. Allow students to try the game early before all of the rules and strategies of the game are introduced. This will generate student interest without requiring the students to listen to a long presentation. This approach is particularly beneficial to many students with disabilities who rely on visual rather than verbal cues.

4. Games provide excellent opportunities for children to learn selected social skills. For example, youngsters may be asked to call infractions or penalties on others as well as themselves. This will help them develop a sense of ethics and fair play as well as learn to accept the judgment or ruling of others. This approach also allows the child with a disability to be a judge as well as to be judged. Some children, too, learn quickly that it is "okay" to modify the rules for some youngsters. For example, a child with a congenital hip dislocation may be allowed to run a shorter distance in a relay game or be permitted a head start.

5. Every effort should be made to ensure that all children play an equal amount of time in games that require the taking of turns. The teacher should make a special note to minimize the use of elimination games so that children, particularly youngsters with disabilities, do not sit out for an extended period of time.

6. Games tend to be most enjoyable when they are novel. A variety of games should be used to stimulate and maintain interest. In addition, it is effective to stop games at the height of interest. Children will consequently look forward to playing the game again in the near future.

Figure 21.1 Language concepts such as "into" can be reinforced through movement activities.

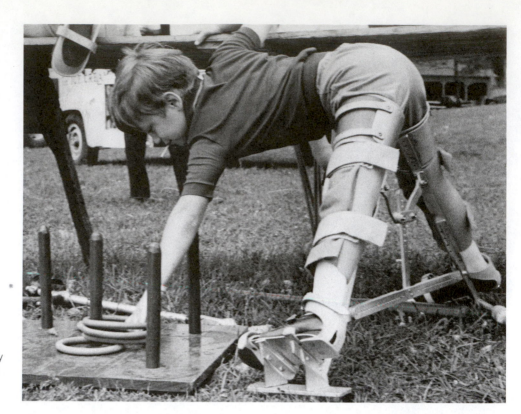

Figure 21.2 Target games usually require little adaptation for students who have the use of their upper limbs.

Choosing Appropriate Games

The selection of games for use in the program for any given class depends upon the objectives being sought; the number and abilities of the children; and the space, time, and equipment available (figure 21.3). An analysis of the nature of a game indicates which of the basic skills of running, throwing, catching, kicking, and so forth the game may be expected to accomplish. The locomotor and manipulative skills essential to growth and development were discussed in chapter 2, *Developmental Patterns.* The abilities of the children can be determined both by observation and testing. Procedures for the latter are discussed in chapter 7, *Evaluation.*

To facilitate the selection of appropriate games for various ages, the games that follow, which are only representative of the vast number of existing games and stunts, have been labeled according to the levels for which they are most suited as determined by the abilities, interests, and needs of

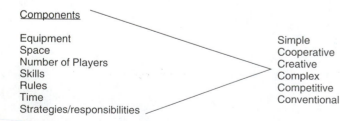

Components

Equipment
Space
Number of Players
Skills
Rules
Time
Strategies/responsibilities

Simple
Cooperative
Creative
Complex
Competitive
Conventional

Figure 21.3 Variables to consider in selecting games.

young children. It must be remembered, however, that the manner in which a game is presented has a direct bearing on its acceptance by any age group. In the case of individuals who are mentally retarded, the chronological age cannot always be relied upon as an effective guide for choosing appropriate games. Games for younger children may be considered too babyish and many individuals with mental retardation will refuse to play them or be so embarrassed while playing them that the potential value of the game is lost. Care must be exercised in selecting games that these children, particularly the older ones, are willing to accept as fitting for their age. The basic skills each game emphasizes are identified in table 21.7.

Ringmaster (Grades Preprimary–1)

Players form a circle, with one player called the *Ringmaster* in the center. The Ringmaster pretends to snap a whip and calls out the name of an animal. All those in the circle imitate the animal named. This procedure continues with different animals. Finally the Ringmaster calls, "We will all join in the circus parade," and everyone moves around the circle imitating any animal. Ringmaster then picks another player to take his or her place.

Bouncing Ball (Grades Preprimary–1)

Children choose partners, with one becoming a *ball* and the other the *bouncer.* The one who is the bouncer pushes on the

Table 21.7 Basic motor skills emphasized in various games

Game	Crawling	Walking	Running	Jumping	Hopping	Galloping	Skipping	Throwing	Catching	Kicking	Striking
Ringmaster	X	X	X	X	X	X	X				
Bouncing Ball					X						
Pussy Wants a Corner			X								
Circle Ball								X	X		
Spider and Flies		X		X							
Jouncing on Jouncing Board				X							
Circle Relay			X								
Magic Carpet		X					X				
Elephant Walk		X									
Bronco Relay						X					
Midnight			X								
Farmer and the Chickens		X	X								
Jumping Jack				X							
Walking, Balancing Beanbag on Head		X									
Target Toss								X			
Line Relay			X								
Skunk Tag			X								
Eagle and Sparrows			X								
Partner Ball Toss								X	X		
Cats and Mice		X	X								
Call Ball								X	X		
Hop Tag					X						
Red Light			X								
Post Ball								X	X		
Driving Pig to Market			X								X
Measuring Worm	X										
Fire on the Mountain			X								
Chain Tag			X								
Circle Weave Relay			X								
Cross Tag			X								
Wall Ball								X	X		
Beat Ball			X					X	X	X	
Bat Ball			X					X	X		X

Table 21.7—*Continued*

Game	Crawling	Walking	Running	Jumping	Hopping	Galloping	Skipping	Throwing	Catching	Kicking	Striking
Circle Kick Ball										X	
Line Soccer			X							X	
Hot Potatoes						X					
Crows and Cranes			X								
Line Dodge Ball								X			
Dodge Ball								X			
Parachute Play	X	X	X	X	X	X					

partner's head as if bouncing a ball. The partner does a deep knee bend and returns to standing position.

Pussy Wants a Corner (Grades Preprimary–1)

Circles are drawn on the floor for each player. One player, called *Pussy*, walks to different circles saying, "Pussy wants a corner." The player in the circle answers, "Go to my next-door neighbor." Meanwhile, as Pussy is at other circles, the remaining players signal each other and attempt to exchange places. Pussy tries to occupy a circle left by another player. The one left without a circle becomes the new Pussy. A player who continues as Pussy too long may call "All change" and quickly find a vacant circle as everyone changes circles.

Circle Ball (Grades Preprimary–1)

Players form a circle with a leader in the center. The leader tosses the ball to each player in the circle, who then tosses it back. (The teacher may serve as the leader in order to give the children practice in catching the ball at different levels, since most young children cannot throw well enough to control the heights at which the ball is to be received.)

Spider and Flies (Grades Preprimary–2)

Mark off two goal lines forty feet apart. Draw a circle between the goal lines large enough to hold all the players. One player is a *Spider* and squats in the circle while the rest of the players are *Flies* and stand behind the goal lines. All Flies advance toward the circle and walk around to the right. When the Spider jumps up, all Flies run toward a goal while the Spider tags as many Flies as possible before they get back behind either goal line. Those tagged join the Spider in the circle and help catch the remaining Flies. The last Fly caught is the Spider in the next game.

Jouncing on Jouncing Board (Grades Preprimary–2)

A two- by eight-inch board several feet long is supported by two sturdy uprights. Participant stands in the middle of the board and jounces.

Circle Relay (Grades Preprimary–2)

Players form circles of six to eight players. Number one in each circle is given a handkerchief. He or she runs counter-clockwise around the circle and gives the handkerchief to number two, who repeats the same procedure. The relay continues until each person has had a turn. The first circle finished is the winner.

Magic Carpet (Grades Preprimary–2)

Large circles called poison spots are drawn in the play area. On signal, eight to twenty players march or skip to the right, stepping in each spot. When "stop" is called, players stop promptly in position. Players attempt to move quickly to avoid being caught on a spot.

Elephant Walk (Grades Preprimary–2)

Each child stands and bends forward at the waist, clasping the hands together and letting the arms hang in imitation of an elephant's trunk. The arms are swung from side to side as the child walks with back rounded and knees slightly bent.

Bronco Relay (Grades Preprimary–2)

Players form lines of even numbers of players. Each line divides into partners. The first couple, one behind the other, straddles a broomstick at the starting line. On the signal, they gallop with the broomstick to a specified turning line and back to the starting point, where they give the broomstick to couple number two, who repeat the same action. The line in which all the couples complete the relay first is the winner.

Midnight (Grades Preprimary–2)

For this game two players are designated as *Mr. Fox* and *Mother Hen* and all the other players are called *Chickens*. The Hen and Chickens have a goal line thirty yards away from the Fox. Mother Hen leads the chickens to Mr. Fox and asks, "What time is it?" Mr. Fox may give any time in reply, but when the answer is "Midnight," the Hen and Chickens run toward their goal with Mr. Fox chasing them. Those tagged become Mr. Fox's helpers.

Farmer and the Chickens (Grades Preprimary–2)

One player, the *Farmer,* pretends to toss out seed and to lead other players, the *Chickens,* away from their safety area, or *Pen*. When Farmer has taken them far enough from the Pen, he or she calls, "Today is Thanksgiving," and chases the Chickens, who run for the Pen. Chickens caught become Farmer's helpers.

Jumping Jack (Grades Preprimary–2)

Children squat down and cross arms on chest and then jump to standing position with arms out to the sides. The movements are repeated to create jumping jacks. Legs may also be spread in the jump to increase the difficulty of the exercise.

Walking, Balancing Beanbag on Head (Grades Preprimary–2)

Players form even-numbered teams into lines about four feet apart. The first person in each line, balancing a beanbag on the head, walks to a line twenty feet away, touches the marking, walks back to the starting line, and gives the beanbag to the second player, who repeats the same procedure. Players dropping the bag must start over. The first team finished is the winner.

Target Toss (Grades Preprimary–2)

Players form groups of four to eight players. Each group has a beanbag and a circle drawn on the floor. The children in each group stand in a straight line ten feet from the circle. Each child tosses the beanbag at the target and receives one point for getting it in the circle. The group with the greatest number of points at the end of the playing time wins.

Line Relay (Grades Preprimary–2)

Players form teams in parallel lines and number off. A leader calls a number, and this player steps out to the right and runs counterclockwise completely around the team,

back to his or her original position. The player who returns first scores a point. The team with the highest score wins.

Skunk Tag (Grades Preprimary–2)

Eight to ten players spread around the playing area. One person who is *It* runs around trying to tag someone. To avoid being tagged, children must hold their nose with their right hand and hold their left foot with their left hand. Anyone tagged before getting into this position becomes the new It.

Eagle and Sparrows (Grades Preprimary–3)

One player is chosen as the *Eagle*. Other players, six to eight, are *Sparrows*. Sparrows stretch their arms to the sides and circle them up, back, down, and forward. The Eagle chases the Sparrows as they run while rotating arms in the described fashion. Sparrows, when tagged, become Eagles.

Partner Ball Toss (Grades Preprimary–3)

Players choose partners. Each pair throws the ball back and forth. Each time the ball is caught, the partners move farther apart, attempting to get as far from each other as possible. If the ball is missed, they start over at the original positions.

Wring the Dish Rag (Grades Preprimary–3)

Partners stand facing each other and join hands. One raises his or her left hand, elevating the right hand of the other. Partners lower the other arms and turn under the raised arms, ending in a back-to-back position. They then raise the other pair of arms, turning under them to face each other again. Repeat several times.

Cats and Mice (Grades Preprimary–3)

Players divide into two teams called *Cats* and *Mice,* which stand sixty feet apart on their respective goal lines. Each team chooses a leader. All Cats, except the leader, turn around. The Mice walk up, and when the leader of the Cats thinks they're close enough he calls, "The Mice are coming!" The Cats chase the Mice, attempting to tag them before they reach their goal line. All Mice tagged become Cats. The procedure is reversed for the next game. The team having the largest number at the end of the playing time wins. If leaders are caught, the teams pick new ones.

Call Ball (Grades Preprimary–3)

Players form a circle of six to ten players. One player who is *It* stands in the center of the circle and, while tossing the ball into the air, calls a player's name. This player must catch the ball before it bounces more than once. If the player succeeds, he or she becomes the new It. If not, the one in the center remains until a player successfully catches the ball.

Hop Tag (Grades Preprimary–3)

Eight to ten players spread around the playing area. One player who is *It* hops around trying to tag another player who is also hopping. Any player who is tagged becomes the new It.

Simon Says (Grades Preprimary–4)

The leader performs simple activities, such as putting hands on shoulders, which the children imitate if the leader prefaces the activity with the words "Simon says do this." However, if the leader says only the words "Do this," the children must not execute the movement.

Red Light (Grades Preprimary–3)

Eight to twenty players form a line standing side by side. One player who is *It* stands about twenty yards in front of the line and facing in the opposite direction. The one who is It rapidly counts to ten, during which the line of players runs forward to try to tag It before the count is completed. Upon reaching ten, It calls "Red Light" and all players must stop running before It turns around. Anyone seen moving by It must return to the starting point. The first one to tag It becomes the new It.

Post Ball (Grades 1–4)

Two or more teams participate. They form parallel lines with each player about three feet behind the other. A leader stands facing each line twelve feet away. On signal, the leader tosses a ball to the first player in line, who catches it, throws the ball back, and squats in line. The leader repeats the same procedure with each one in the line. The team finishing first and dropping the ball the least number of times wins.

Driving Pig to Market (Grades 2–3)

Players form even-numbered lines. The first person in each line is given a wand, and a ball is placed in front of the feet. On signal, the player pushes the ball, by sliding the wand back and forth, around a stool twenty feet away and back to the starting line. Here the equipment is passed to the next one in line, who repeats the same action.

Stork Stand (Grades 2–4)

Child places hands on hips, raises one foot and places it against the inside of the opposite knee. To eliminate the role of the eye in achieving balance, the participant may close the eyes while attempting to maintain balance.

Measuring Worm (Grades 2–4)

Child bends over and places hands on the floor and extends legs to take a front leaning position. With the hands in place, the child walks toward the hands. Keeping the feet in place, the child walks on the hands away from the feet. The elbows and knees remain straight as the actions are repeated several times.

Fire on the Mountain (Grades 2–4)

Players form two circles with one circle, called the *Trees*, standing inside the other circle, called *Children*. In the center is one player who is *It*. The one who is It begins clapping and calls, "Fire on the Mountain. Run, Children, run!" The Trees remain standing while the Children run to the right behind the Trees. When It stops clapping, he or she and the Children run to stand in front of a Tree. The one who does not find a Tree is the new It. In the next game, the Trees and Children change roles.

Chain Tag (Grades 2–4)

One player, who is *It*, tags another player, and the two join hands and run to tag other players. Each player who is tagged joins the chain at the end. Hands must remain joined and only the first and last players in the chain are allowed to tag.

Circle Weave Relay (Grades 2–4)

Players form circles, six to eight players to a circle. One player from each circle starts the relay by running to the outside of the player to the right, to the inside of the next, and continues weaving in this pattern around the circle to the starting position. The player tags the next child on the right, who similarly runs to the right around the circle. The relay continues until everyone in the circle has had a turn. The first circle to complete the relay is the winner.

Cross Tag (Grades 3–4)

Eight to ten players scatter around the playing area. One player who is *It* runs and tries to tag another player. If another player crosses between the chased player and It, It must change and chase the crossing player.

Wall Ball (Grades 3–4)

Players divide into groups of four to six players. Groups form lines about four feet apart, perpendicular to a wall. Distances are marked off every foot, beginning at three feet from the wall and ending at eight. Starting at the three-foot mark, the first player in each line makes three throws and catches of the ball off the wall. Upon successful completion of the three catches, the player may move back to the next mark. Any time the catch is missed, the player must go to the end of the line, and the next player in line takes a turn, beginning at the three-foot mark. Each player in the line does likewise. A player who successfully completes the catches at each mark is through. Others must repeat the throws and catches, beginning at the mark of their previous miss. The team with all of its players completing their catches first is the winner.

Beat Ball (Grades 4–5)

Two teams of five to ten players are formed. Bowling pins used as bases are set up in a softball or kickball formation. One team is at "bat," the other in the field. The pitcher rolls a soccer ball to the batter, who kicks it and runs to first, second, third, and home. The fielding team catches the ball and throws it to the first baseman, who knocks over the pin, throws the ball to the second baseman, who knocks over the pin, and so on. If the batter gets home before all the pins are knocked down, one run is scored—otherwise, the batter is out.

Outs: ball at home plate before runner; fly ball caught; batter misses kick and ball knocks over pin at home; runner knocks over any pin while running bases; or kicked ball knocks over any pin not touched by fielder first.

Runs: ball not thrown in correct order of bases; or baseman fails to knock over pin with ball before throwing to next base.

Bat Ball (Grades 4–5)

Players divide into two teams, one at bat and one in the field. A volleyball or soccer ball is used. The first player at bat hits the pitched ball into the field and runs to a base and home. If the player makes the complete trip without the fielder catching the fly or hitting the player below the waist with the ball, one run is scored. Three outs and teams change. The team with the most runs wins.

Circle Kick Ball (Grades 4–5)

The players form two teams. One team stands in one half of a twenty-five-foot circle, the other team in the remaining half. The leader rolls a ball to one team, which kicks the ball toward the opposite team, which kicks it back. One point is scored for each ball kicked out of the circle past the opponents at waist height or below. A ball kicked out above the waist scores for the opposite team. The team having the highest number of points at the end of the playing time wins.

Line Soccer (Grades 4–5)

Two even-numbered teams form lines facing each other. Players stand side by side in each line. Teams count off from diagonal ends so that number one of one line faces the last number in the opposite line. A leader places the ball between the lines and calls out a number. The two players with that number rush into the center and attempt to kick the ball through the opposite line. Players in line may stop the ball from going through. A ball kicked through the line scores a point.

Hot Potatoes (Grades 4–5)

Players form a circle with six to twenty players in each circle. Players all sit crosslegged and roll or punch balls across the circle. Three or four balls are kept going at once. Players try to knock the ball past other players through the circle. The player permitting the least number of balls to go through the circle wins. An extra player retrieves all the balls going out of the circle. No ball higher than the shoulders counts. Balls may not be bounced or thrown.

Crows and Cranes (Grades 4–5)

Players divide into two groups of eight to twenty players. One group is called *Crows* and the other *Cranes*. The playing area is divided with a line in the center and a goal line at each end of the area. Crows and Cranes stand facing each other at the center. The leader calls "Crows" or "Cranes." The group called runs to the goal line behind it with the other group chasing. Players tagged go to the other group. Crows and Cranes return to the center line. The leader gives the call again. The group with the larger number of players at the end of the playing time wins.

Seal Walk (Grades 4–5)

Child puts weight on the hands on the floor and extends legs backward. Child walks forward on the hands, dragging legs behind.

Rocker (Grades 4–5)

Children lie on their stomachs and arch their backs to grasp the raised legs at the ankles with their hands. In this position, they rock forward and backward.

Crab Walk (Grades 4–5)

Children take a squat position. They reach back and place hands flat on the floor without sitting. Distributing the weight equally on all fours, they walk forward in this position.

Stand-Up (Grades 4–5)

Partners stand back to back and lock elbows with each other. They push against each other's back and with small steps walk forward and sit on the floor. To stand up, the partners keep arms locked and bend the knees with the feet close to the body. They brace their feet, push against each other's backs, extend legs, and come to a standing position.

Stand-Up Wrestle (Grades 4–5)

Partners stand facing opposite directions beside each other. The outsides of the right feet are placed together. Right hands are joined. The two players push and pull until one partner's right foot is lifted from position. The one whose right foot remains in position wins.

Line Dodge Ball (Grades 4–5)

Players standing side by side form two lines twenty feet apart with a four foot square drawn in the middle. One person stands in this box, and the other players take turns trying to hit him or her below the waist with the ball. The player may dodge the ball but must keep one foot in the box. When hit, the player changes places with the one who made the hit.

Wheelbarrow (Grades 4–5)

Partners stand one behind the other facing the same way. The one in front places hands on floor while the one behind lifts the partner's legs at the ankles. The first child walks forward on the hands with the legs supported by the partner in wheelbarrow fashion.

Parachute Play (Grades 5–8)

To start parachute play, the chute is spread out on the floor and the students take positions around it, equidistant from each other. Twenty to thirty students can participate when a regulation-size parachute is used. The students kneel on one knee and grasp the chute by its edge with both hands in any one of three ways: palms up, palms down, or one palm up and one palm down. The palms-down grasp is generally the most effective. Some parachutes have handles that make holding the chute easier for the children.

In lifting the chute into the air, height is achieved by everyone simultaneously raising the chute to the maximum of his or her reach. As the parachute fills with air, it rises to form a canopy above the children. A small aperture in the center of the chute permits enough air to escape in order to stabilize the parachute as it slowly descends.

Various actions are possible during the rise and descent of the parachute. Students may move to the right or to the left or in alternate directions. Their movement may be at various tempos: walking, running, galloping, skipping. Musical accompaniment may be used, if desired. Another possibility involves the use of a light ball. The chute is raised with the ball resting on top. The class attempts to bounce the ball or otherwise maneuver it about on the parachute.

Interesting possibilities exist for creative play. The parachute can be held at waist height, and different patterns of waves and billows can be created by each child shaking the chute in independent action. Unusual patterns can be created also by small groups working together to achieve a specific motion. To facilitate this activity, the children can be separated into groups of three or four to plan the movement they will contribute to the total pattern.

Adaptations

Games or activities that have been designed by others and taught without modification are usually referred to as conventional games. Many of the games described in the

Figure 21.4 The creative possibilities of parachute play are not limited by restrictions on mobility.

preceding section would be classified as conventional games. While the use of conventional games is widely accepted and encouraged, there is general recognition that many games when modified or adapted create new and exciting challenges and allow for the successful inclusion of children with disabilities. In the following section, general guidelines for the adaptations of the games will be presented. These adaptations can apply to the games previously discussed as well as many other games.

Modify the Rules of the Game

Many games that children play have intricate rules that require a high level of comprehension and reasoning ability. Children who are mentally retarded or those with learning problems frequently find the structure and rules of some games too complex. For instance, the game of Call Ball requires that a player must respond when his or her name is called by catching a ball that has been thrown into the air before it bounces more than once. This game requires quick reaction, good motor skills, and the ability to process information quickly. For young children with learning problems the game can be modified in several ways. For example, the child who is to throw the ball into the air could call the special child's name *before* the ball is thrown into the air, permitting a longer time to respond to the command. In addition, some students may require two, three, or even four bounces instead of the specified one bounce before they retrieve the ball. A ball of a different size, color, or texture may also be helpful to some children.

Many games emphasize the skill of running. For children with limited mobility, these games can be discouraging unless some provision is made to accommodate their special needs. In relay races, for instance, the distance the student who is orthopedically impaired has to run can be reduced. It is also helpful to modify running games by structuring experiences to encourage slow rather than fast movements: for example, substituting walking for skipping and running. The size of targets, balls, and other equipment also can be easily adapted to accommodate the special needs of children with disabilities.

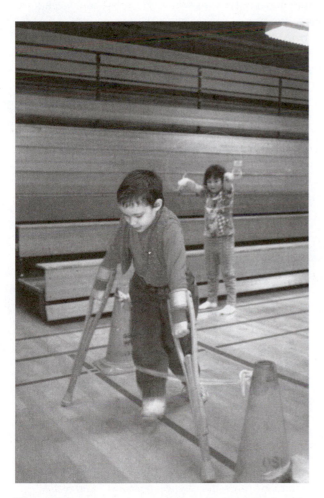

Figure 21.5 Students who are orthopedically impaired can be integrated into regular physical education experiences if the rules of traditional activities are modified.

Avoid Elimination Games

Many elementary games are designed to eliminate players, such as in tag games. These activities are particularly discouraging to students with disabilities who find that they are frequently eliminated first because of the effects various disabilities have on their movement capabilities. Elimination games can be modified to provide success-oriented experiences for students with disabilities. The game of Dodge Ball, for instance, can be changed so that those who are hit become throwers rather than sideline spectators. The activity could also be modified so that children who move slowly and are most likely to be hit first become throwers only if hit in a designated body region, such as the right foot. Such an adaptation forces throwers to focus on accuracy. In addition, the slower student is not always the first hit and quickly eliminated. Changes such as these can be disguised to avoid embarrassing the special student by designating all players wearing shirts with a particular color or players whose names begin with the letter *J* as the individuals who must be hit on the right foot.

Most activities in physical education can be structured to include rather than exclude children. Even the simple task of asking children to jump over a rope held parallel to the floor can be altered by holding the rope higher at one end than the other. This modification provides children an opportunity to select an appropriate jumping height and avoids the common problem of children eliminating themselves by jumping and missing or avoiding the activity entirely because the rope is too high. Developing activities that include rather than exclude children only requires a teacher who cares and is sensitive to the needs of children.

Accommodate the Special Needs of Children

Children with orthopedic and sensory impairments will find it impossible to participate with success in some games unless their special needs are considered. For instance, the game of line soccer will require special adaptations for children who are visually impaired or who are unable to move their lower limbs. Students who are blind could be accommodated in this activity by having their opponent on the opposite team serve as their helper. For example, when the student who is blind number is called, the student in the opposite line with the same number could run to the ball and use his or her voice to guide the nonsighted player from the opposite team to the ball. If the sighted player was successful in helping the student who is visual impaired locate the ball within a designated time period the team could be awarded a point. The nonsighted player's team would earn its points in the usual manner, by having the visually impaired student kick the ball past the opposing team.

In some games it may be necessary to change the skill for students with disabilities. For example, some individuals with orthopedic impairments are unable to use the lower extremities, so a throw will have to be substituted for a kick in games involving the skill of kicking. Similarly, in the game of Bat Ball the students who are visually impaired could hit the ball from a batting tee, run to first base using a rope, an aide, or the sound of a coach's voice. The same youngster could field a ground ball with the verbal assistance of a teammate. A rule modification that a runner going to first is out if the fielder with a visual impairment locates, picks up, and brings the ball to waist level could be made. A throw to first would not be necessary, thus creating a situation in which a student with a disability becomes an asset for a team and not a liability.

Alter the Activity Area

Children with disabilities sometimes experience movement limitations that require the activity area in some activities to be altered. For example, in games in which students with limited mobility serve as goalies or protectors of a certain area, the designated goal should be reduced in size, thereby enhancing the player's success as a goalie. In throwing and kicking activities the distance to the target might be changed, permitting closer action. Enlarging the target likewise will ensure a success-oriented experience for children whose skill level requires this modification. All students find adaptations such as these acceptable if efforts are made to explain the rationale for the alterations in the activity.

Encourage Creativity

Teachers can structure games so that children are asked to respond to challenge questions such as, "Make a bridge with your body," "Balance on five body parts," "Move forward," and "Now show me another way to move forward." Such an approach permits students with various disabilities to respond in ways that allow for success. Students in wheelchairs, for instance, could respond successfully to each of the previous questions by bending forward with their arms or arching their arms to the side to make a bridge; balancing on five body parts by placing their foot or a stick on the floor (four wheels on the chair plus the foot or stick); and successfully moving forward two ways using the conventional manner plus using one arm rather than two arms for the second method.

Games such as Ringmaster are excellent for encouraging students' creativity. The children are asked to move as they think a particular animal moves. All students can be successful in this experience regardless of their physical or mental limitations. One of the authors was pleased to encounter a young child who, although completely paralyzed, participated successfully in this activity by making the sounds of the various animals.

Children, too, can be very effective in creating new games. The extent of their effort can range from a modification of an activity to creating an entirely new activity. Having children create new games can be a particularly effective strategy in helping youngsters with and without disabilities interact. Both groups can learn to accept and appreciate the skills and abilities that are unique to each person.

Graham et al. (1980) has suggested the following guidelines for helping students create their own games:

1. Begin gradually. More structure will be needed at the beginning; however, as students become more adept, the teacher should slowly decrease the structure.

2. Limit your interference. If students are to learn to make significant decisions, they must be responsible for the consequences.

3. Always be aware of safety. Regardless of the level of decision making given the child, a safe environment is the teacher's responsibility. An unsafe situation is one of the few times that the teacher must interfere. When possible, unless the situation calls for an immediate

Figure 21.6 Integrated experiences for students with and without disabilities are possible when the rules and activity area are modified.

change, make the students aware of the potential hazard and allow them to decide on an alternative.

4. Allow students to enforce their own rules. If students are given the opportunity to make rules, they should enforce them as well. Keep the control in their hands and act only as a facilitator.

5. Remind students of the creative concept—the only rule is that the game can always be changed. Remind them to be flexible; if they are unhappy or can create another aspect, encourage them to make a change!

6. Be patient! The creative process is often time-consuming. The process is as important as the product. Once the general idea of game components and how to manipulate them is mastered, the quality of response will increase.

Emphasize Cooperative Games

Fortunately, greater emphasis today is placed on cooperative play experience. Games like Walking Chairs, for example, impress upon children that success is frequently dependent upon a planned, coordinated group effort. This provides the teacher a unique opportunity to help students understand more about the capabilities and limitations that everyone experiences. Cooperative games also help nondisabled students better understand and accept those with disabilities.

Games in which the student's disability becomes an asset are also excellent opportunities for students to experience cooperative group activities. Blindfolding students and asking them to walk to a designated sound affords the student who is visually impaired a chance to assist sighted classmates. Students in wheelchairs find helping their nondisabled friends move a wheelchair in and out of an

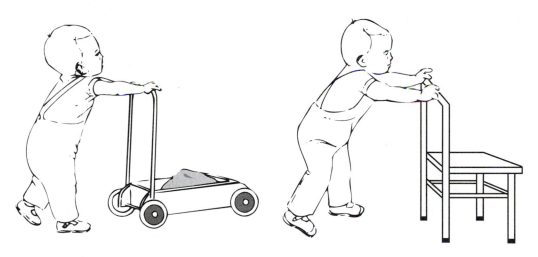

Weighted wagons and chairs can be used as walking aids for some children with cerebral palsy. These are most useful for children who have low muscle tone.

Rolling walkers are used for some school-aged children who have difficulty getting around.

Figure 21.7 Examples of simple aids that assist in walking.

obstacle course fun and rewarding. Through cooperative experiences, individuals learn to be considerate of others, to be aware of an individual's feelings, to practice sharing, and to perform with another's interest in mind.

Change the Method of Communication

Students with disabilities sometimes require communication systems that are specific to their needs. For example, verbally explaining a task may not match up well with some children's information processing systems. Information that is more specific might be provided in other ways. The instructor or a peer helper, for example, could demonstrate the game or activity. Also, the teacher could permit a student to "feel" a specific component of a game by encouraging the child to hold onto the teacher's hand as together they explore the equipment used in various games. Some students need not only to hear about or to see a game but also to read a description or a story about the game. This need can be met for poor readers or nonreaders through the use of poster board to which stick figures are attached to show the sequence of a game such as Post Ball.

Summary

In recent years an increasing number of educators, therapists, and allied health personnel have stressed that infants, toddlers, and young children with disabilities should receive early intervention services as soon as the disability becomes apparent. For some individuals the disability might be evident at the time of birth or soon thereafter. The literature offers substantial evidence that early intervention services for young children with disabilities can make a difference in how these individuals develop. Federal legislation, namely P.L. 99-457 and P.L. 101-476, requires that early intervention services be provided for individuals "at risk" or those with developmental delays. Because of the important role movement plays in early development, it is obvious that programs for young children with disabilities must include programs that emphasize locomotor, non-locomotor, and manipulative skills.

Within this chapter information is provided about approaches to assessing young children with disabilities as well as ideas for developing appropriate movement-based programs. It is clear that young children with disabilities should be educated, to the extent possible, with their nondisabled peers. Programs based on the concept of inclusion benefit all young children, including those with and without disabilities. Programs that focus on fundamental movement skills (locomotor, non-locomotor, and manipulative) taught using a movement concepts approach provide exciting opportunities for all young children, including those with disabilities, to benefit from positive and enjoyable learning experiences.

Games have long been recognized as an important aspect in the development of young children. Participation in games contributes to growth and development and helps children to learn the essential affective skills of taking turns, sharing, and cooperating. In addition, games can be used to reinforce selected cognitive concepts such as shapes, sizes, and colors and to teach children about their heritage and the culture of other individuals. Most importantly, games can be used to enhance basic motor skills such as running, throwing, jumping, and kicking.

Games can be structured so that they are fun and challenging yet designed to elicit desirable movement patterns. In selecting games to use with young children, attention must be given to the number, age, and ability of the youngsters. Games can be played in any environment, including the classroom and gymnasium. Equipment need not be elaborate, and the necessary items can be made inexpensively.

Within this chapter information is presented about the importance of adapting and modifying activities so that young children with disabilities can participate in games with their nondisabled peers. The integration of children with disabilities can be accomplished if special efforts are made to modify rules as appropriate, encourage inclusion rather than exclusion activities, and emphasize games that promote cooperation. In addition, teachers should be creative in the development of new games and should encourage children to participate in the design and modification of games. There is a growing awareness that young children with special needs can participate with other children in game activities if a proper attitude and creative efforts are employed. The ultimate value is establishing at the earliest of ages that individuals with disabilities can and should enjoy a lifetime of participation in activity with their nondisabled peers.

Selected Readings

Avery, M. (1994). Preschool physical education: A practical approach. *Journal of Physical Education, Recreation, and Dance,* 65(6), 37–39.

Baganto, S.J., & Neisworth, J.T. (1990). *SPECS: System to plan early childhood services.* Circle Pines, MN: American Guidance Service.

Block, M.E. (1994). Including preschool children with disabilities. *Journal of Physical Education, Recreation, and Dance,* 62(6), 45–49, 56.

Block, M.E. (1994). *A teacher's guide to including students with disabilities in regular physical education.* Baltimore, MD: Paul H. Brookes Publishing Co.

Cowden, J.E., & Eason, R.L. (1991). Pediatric physical education for infants, toddlers, and preschoolers: Meeting IDEA H and IDEA B challenges. *Adapted Physical Activity Quarterly,* 8(4), 263–279.

Cratty, B.J., et al. (1970). *The effects of a program of learning games upon selected academic abilities in children with learning difficulties.* Washington, DC: U.S. Office of Education.

Cratty, B.J. (1973). *Intelligence in action.* Englewood Cliffs, NJ: Prentice-Hall, Inc.

Dauer, V., & Pangrazi, R. (1986). *Dynamic physical education for elementary school children* (8th ed.). Minneapolis: Burgess Publishing Co.

Dunn, J.M. (1979). *Adaptive physical education: A resource guide for teachers, administrators, and parents.* Salem, OR: State of Oregon Mental Health Division.

Dunn, J.M. (1991). (Feature Editor). P.L. 99–457: Challenges and opportunities for physical education. *Journal of Physical Education, Recreation, and Dance* 62(6), 233–34, 47.

Eason, R.L. (1991). Adapted physical education delivery model for infants and toddlers with disabilities. *Journal of Physical Education, Recreation and Dance, 62*(6), 41–43, 47–48.

Eichstaedt, C.B., & Lavay, B. (1992). *Physical activity for individuals with mental retardation: Infant to adult.* Champaign, IL: Human Kinetics Publishers.

Gabbard, C., LeBlanc, E., & Lowy, S. (1987). *Physical education for children—Building the foundation.* Englewood Cliffs, NJ: Prentice-Hall, Inc.

Graham, G., Holt-Hale, S.A., McEwen, T., & Parker, M. (1980). *Children moving: A reflective approach to teaching physical education.* Palo Alto, CA: Mayfield Press.

Houston-Wilson, C. (1994). *The effect of untrained and trained peer tutors on the motor performance of students with developmental disabilities in integrated physical education classes.* Unpublished doctoral dissertation, Oregon State University, Corvallis, OR.

Humphrey, J.H. (1976). *Improving learning ability through compensatory physical education.* Springfield, IL: Charles C. Thomas.

Ignico, A. (1994). Early childhood physical education: Providing the foundation. *Journal of Physical Education, Recreation, and Dance, 65*(6), 37–39.

Marlowe, M. (1980). Games analysis: Designing games for handicapped children. *Teaching Exceptional Children,* 48–51.

McCubbin, J.A., & Zittel, L. (1991). P.L. 99-457: What the law is all about. *Journal of Physical Education, Recreation, and Dance, 62*(6), 35–37, 47.

Morris, G.S.D. (1980). *How to change the games children play* (2d ed.). Minneapolis: Burgess Publishing Co.

Orlick, T. (1982). *The second cooperative sports and games book.* New York: Pantheon Books.

Sherrill, C. (1993). *Adapted physical activity, recreation, and sport* (4th ed.). Madison, WI: Brown and Benchmark.

Ulrich, D.A. (1985). *Test of gross motor development.* Austin, TX: Pro-Ed Publishers.

Werner, P. (1994). Whole physical education. *Journal of Physical Education, Recreation, and Dance, 65*(6), 40–44.

Wessel, J.A. (1976). *I CAN program.* Northbrook, IL: Hubbard Scientific Co.

Zittel, L.L. (1994). Gross motor assessment of preschool children with special needs: Instrument selection considerations. *Adapted Physical Activity Quarterly, 11*(3), 245–260.

Enhancing Activities

1. Select one of the activities identified in this chapter and modify the activity so that it would be possible for a youngster with a disability such as a visual or hearing impairment to participate in the activity.

2. Meet with a group of children and have them create a game or activity that is designed to include children of various ability levels, including those with disabilities.

3. Observe a group of young children playing. Do they understand the nature of the game and enforce the rules fairly? Observe to see if the children naturally modify the activity in any way to accommodate the special needs of their peers.

4. Meet with children and have them review a popular game such as kick ball. Have them generate ideas as to how the activity could be modified to become more of an inclusion activity rather than exclusion activity.

5. With a group of young children, organize an activity in which the form of communication must be other than talking. Note the children's responses and discuss with them later their reactions. Observe the creative efforts used to help others understand the rules and strategy.

6. Given a child who is having difficulty kicking a ball with accuracy and distance, select or design a game(s) that could be used as a fun activity to help the child improve his or her performance.

7. Interview a teacher of young children ages three to five as to the importance of movement experiences in the development of young children.

Rhythms and Dance

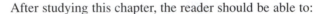

CHAPTER OBJECTIVES

After studying this chapter, the reader should be able to:

1 Appreciate the importance of dance and rhythmic activities in the lives of students with disabilities.

2 Comprehend the structure and content of the dance program including the relationship between creative rhythmic activity and traditional dance forms.

3 Understand the meaning of dance elements and terms such as *tempo, beat, measure, phrase, meter, accent, intensity,* and *mood.*

4 Utilize movement concepts such as flow, balance, and time in rhythmic programs with individuals with disabilities.

5 Adapt creative and traditional dance activities so that students with impairments can successfully enjoy these experiences.

6 Recognize the importance of folk, modern, and social dance as cultural and aesthetic experiences that can serve to enhance the life of an individual with a disability.

7 Appreciate the similarities and differences between dance education and dance therapy.

Rhythm permeates the universe, and all children are capable of responding to rhythmic activity provided the stimulation exists. Basic rhythm yields simple movement patterns. Dance itself is an accumulation of various forms of movement and may be thought of as a formal composition or as a vehicle of emotional expression. Dance contains elements that can satisfy the individual's need for recognition, satisfaction, and creativity and can provide opportunities to develop a sense of belonging and of adequacy.

Rhythms and dance play an essential role in the physical education program for students with disabilities. Many such youngsters have a basic need to develop freedom of self-expression, skill in social interaction, and fundamental movement patterns. Dance provides a medium through which these needs may be realized.

It is frequently observed that children with disabilities must adjust not only to problems that they have in common with other students but also to individual difficulties that stem more directly from their own disabilities. The teacher must continually keep in mind that these youngsters are, first, children in the dance class and, second, persons who have a disability. Given the opportunity, each will benefit from, as well as contribute to, the school dance program.

Content of the Dance and Rhythm Program

The dance and rhythm program for children with disabilities should be similar to that offered to nondisabled youngsters. In this respect the following objectives, developed by the Task Force on Children's Dance in Education, provide a framework for the variety of dance and creative activity that should be provided. The task force emphasized that movement-centered dance activities and other movement experiences should assist children to:

Realize their biological urges to experience primal patterns of movement.

Develop an adequate degree of satisfaction in and mastery of their body movements for their own pleasure, confidence, and self-esteem.

Greatly expand their movement resources by offering them many opportunities to explore, discover, invent, and develop different ways of moving and to structure sequences.

Increase their aesthetic sensitivity by emphasizing the expressive and imaginative potential of their movements, as well as the physical and athletic aspects.

Develop their appreciation of dance as art, by relating it to appropriate experiences in music, literature, painting, and sculpture.

Relate their movements effectively to accompanying sounds and to music.

Participate with others in recreational folk and ethnic dances by helping them learn traditional dance

steps and understand the different ways these steps have been used through centuries of people dancing together.

Make dances for themselves and others and, when they seem ready for the experience, to perform them for peer audiences.

These objectives encompass a variety of dance and rhythmic activities including traditional forms of dance such as folk, square, and social dance as well as the creative expressions inherent in much of rhythmic movement. Children with disabilities can enjoy and participate successfully in all of the dance forms with modifications as appropriate. Creative movement to music, in particular, offers those with disabilities the opportunity to express themselves as individuals. Encouraging children to express their feelings through music allows them to demonstrate and explore the creative dimensions of their personality.

Dance and rhythmic activities are dependent on the use of locomotor and/or nonlocomotor skills and movement concepts. The locomotor skills of walk, run, leap, hop, jump, gallop, skip, and slide can be incorporated in various ways into dance and rhythmic activities. These skills can be used singly or in combination as created by the teacher or student. The locomotor skills are also used in the execution of many of the common dance steps as in the polka and two-step. The nonlocomotor skills also play an important role in dance activities. These include the ability to bend, swing, sway, twist, turn, push, and pull. Similar to the locomotor skills, nonlocomotor skills may be used singly or in combination. They also are combined frequently with locomotor skills.

Movement concepts play an important part in the dance and rhythm program. Through participation in dance activities, students have the opportunity to enhance their understanding of movement qualities such as force, balance, and time. Dance also helps them develop an awareness of the body and the relationship of body parts. An understanding of the following rhythmic elements will assist students in their understanding of dance and movement activities:

Tempo: Tempo is the speed of the music. The music can be fast, moderate, or slow.

Beat: The beat is the underlying rhythm of the music. The beat can be even or uneven.

Measure: A measure is the number of underlying beats that comprise a unit. The number is dependent upon the meter.

Meter: Meter refers to the number of beats in a measure such as ¾, ¼, ¼, ⅝. The upper number represents the number of beats per measure, the lower number the type of note that equals one beat.

Accent: An accent is the emphasis put on a beat. Usually the accent is applied to the first beat of a measure.

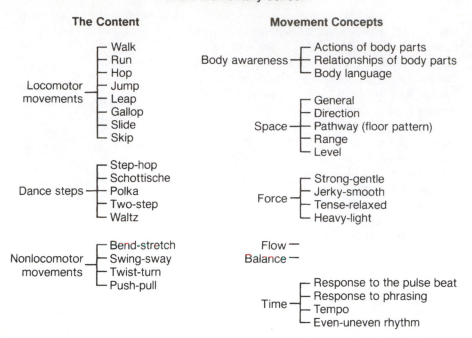

**Dance and Rhythmic Activities
in the Elementary School**

The Content		Movement Concepts	
Locomotor movements	Walk Run Hop Jump Leap Gallop Slide Skip	Body awareness	Actions of body parts Relationships of body parts Body language
Dance steps	Step-hop Schottische Polka Two-step Waltz	Space	General Direction Pathway (floor pattern) Range Level
Nonlocomotor movements	Bend-stretch Swing-sway Twist-turn Push-pull	Force	Strong-gentle Jerky-smooth Tense-relaxed Heavy-light
		Flow	
		Balance	
		Time	Response to the pulse beat Response to phrasing Tempo Even-uneven rhythm

Figure 22.1 Content of a dance and rhythm program for an elementary school.

(Source: Nichols, B. (1986). *Moving and Learning.* St. Louis: Mosby, p. 76.)

Phrase: A phrase is a natural grouping of measures that constitutes a musical thought or rhythmic pattern.

Intensity: The intensity of music can be loud, soft, light or heavy.

Mood: The mood of music refers to the human feeling associated with the music such as happiness, sadness, joy, or gaiety.

In figure 22.1, an overview of the content of a dance and rhythmic program for elementary children is found. There is every reason to believe that the rhythmic program for children with disabilities should be the same, with modifications as appropriate. In the following sections, suggestions for organizing and modifying the program for students with special needs will be presented.

Equipment

Elaborate equipment is not necessary to provide dance activities for the student with a disability; the materials available for regular dance instruction are more than adequate. Musical accompaniment, while not essential, is certainly helpful. If a well-tuned piano is not at the disposal of the dance instructor, a cassette player is an excellent substitute. The recent availability of electronic keyboards also has been found to be very helpful.

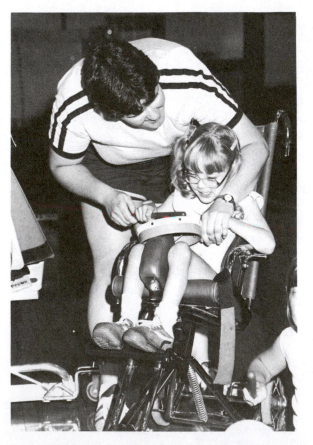

Figure 22.2 Using simple equipment such as a tambourine can be a satisfying rhythmical experience for the student with a disability.

Figure 22.3 Accenting a rhythmic pattern on a drum is helpful to the performance of other students and is a personally satisfying experience for the drummer with a disability.

Figure 22.4 The piano is helpful for children with disabilities to enjoy rhythmic effects.

Specially prepared compact disks or tapes ranging from pieces with simple and definite rhythms to intricate folk and square dance melodies are available through special firms. Marking each compact disk or tape alphabetically and keeping a small index card file on the recordings eliminate needless disorganization.

To obtain satisfying results in various dance activities, the use of individual pieces of equipment is strongly recommended. The drum, in particular, accentuates basic accents in rhythmic patterns and is a valuable dance instrument for the student who is hard of hearing. Rhythm is recognizable in terms of what it does, and its real significance on an elementary level can only be grasped by actually experiencing it. Maracas, tambourines, rhythm sticks, triangles, and homemade musical instruments are helpful. Individuals who are mentally retarded, particularly, respond to the "feel" of the muscle sensations and activity aroused within their bodies through the use of this equipment. Movements are often awkward efforts at first, but after timing and values of intensity are understood, efficient and more skilled movement results.

The individual with orthopedic impairments, when not involved in group-oriented activity, finds great pleasure in rhythmic exercises at the dance barre. Mirrors help stimulate self-awareness in those who are emotionally disturbed as well as aid the growth of poise and unison of dance movement in other students with special needs. Heavy equipment such as the piano should be located where it will not have to be moved often; smaller instruments and dance materials should be put away after use. This allows the student who is blind or partially sighted full freedom of the dance area.

Equipment that provides additional expression and interpretation movement plays a vital role in rhythmic activity for those with disabilities. However, it will not take the place of the structuring and dynamic role of the dance teacher. The teacher must use these materials as tools toward a better understanding of rhythm and basic movement.

Organizing the Instruction

The development and application of teaching techniques in dance for students with disabilities are much the same as in teaching nondisabled children, because the learning process is basically the same for all individuals. However, in teaching those with disabilities, rate of learning and extent of adaptation are more important considerations than with nondisabled students.

Specific disabilities have been discussed in previous chapters. An understanding of the capabilities and limitations of each individual is most valuable when considering various teaching techniques. The instructor cannot safely assume that dance fundamentals will have been previously acquired. The type and extent of the disability provide an individual guide to instruction.

Mental Retardation

Students with mild and moderate levels of mental retardation should be included, with support as appropriate, in regular dance and rhythmic activities. It is well documented that individuals with mental retardation enjoy dance and expressive movement and some exhibit unique talent in creative movement activities.

Students who are more severely mentally retarded will need additional assistance and support to develop the skills necessary to participate in various dance forms such as square and folk. In many instances the complexity of the step or dance can be modified to allow the individual to be successful and to enjoy the experience. While full inclusion of individuals who are more severely and profoundly mentally retarded with nondisabled peers in dance and rhythmic activities is challenging, the teacher should look for and structure opportunities to include these students with their peers as much as possible.

Students with cognitive loss will need special assistance to benefit from the dance and rhythmic activities. The teacher should recognize that many of these individuals have a short attention span. Dance periods, therefore, should be short and repetitive to allow for reinforcement. Techniques in teaching should be widely diversified, using among other things, mirror image, physical assistance, prompts, and specific learning cues. Teachers also will need to demonstrate and use peers as demonstrators to make things concrete, rather than rely on verbal directions, which are too abstract.

Behavior-Disordered

Students with behavior disorders often have good mental ability but are unable to integrate their intellectual efforts and direct them toward realistic goals. Erratic behavior, insecurity, hostility, and withdrawal are characteristic. Rigidity of thought and insecurity of self-expression severely constrict the emotional growth of many of these children. Dance may prove most helpful in developing appropriate social adjustment and in encouraging these students to creatively express their feelings.

Under the supervision of trained personnel, the teacher should focus the program on stimulating interaction with the environment. The child who is disturbed may find satisfactory emotional experiences through the medium of the dance. By identifying with objects, the youngster finds gratification in rhythmic movement. Later, the learning process will involve interaction with an authority figure, such as the dance instructor. Dance is then introduced in formal step sequences. Students with behavior disorders should be included in dance classes with nondisabled peers to the extent possible. The amount of integration will vary depending upon the level of the disorder (i.e., whether the student's behavior is under control) and the ability level of the individual. Some students with behavior disorders find integrated settings extremely frustrating and depressing if their skill level is markedly different from their peers. The teacher, therefore, will need to work with the student to develop the appropriate dance and rhythmic skills and integrate the student in classes or activities where a high level of success is predictable.

Blind and Partially Sighted

Today most blind and partially sighted youngsters are attending regular public school classes. Their acute auditory skill as well as their ability to follow directions proves to be extremely helpful in various dance experiences.

Students who are blind often develop an early awareness of music and rhythmic movement because they must use auditory cues. "Blindisms," or unique mannerisms, which may take the form of rocking, twisting, or waving of the arms or fingers, are characteristic of many young children who are blind. These habits, not particularly socially acceptable, are often best controlled by calling them to the attention of the child. Interestingly enough, these very characteristics are self-expressive and almost always have a rhythmic pattern. Thus, the next obvious means of control is to convert these forms of expression into acceptable patterns of movement.

Teachers find working with individuals who are blind enjoyable because the visually impaired rely on their kinesthetic sense and rhythmic sensations when learning to dance. Some of the early difficulty experienced by sighted dancers may relate to their reliance on the visual aspect of movement rather than on their inner sensation of moving to a rhythmic sound or music.

Precise verbal instruction and physical assistance are good teaching techniques. After a basic understanding of position and formation, the student who is blind or partially sighted can be successfully included as an active and enthusiastic member of many folk and square dance groups. Teachers must remember, however, that in integrated settings, using a verbal expression such as "spin like a top" may not be helpful to the blind student whose concept of a top and the motion of spinning has not been fully developed. Using peers effectively will pair the blind student with peers so that the peer can help the blind person and respond to visual signals (e.g., stop, turn, change partners, etc.) that may be inherent in the activity itself.

Deaf and Hearing Loss

Many students in the public school program have auditory deficiencies. A prime objective for these individuals is the utilization of residual hearing. The dance teacher is in an excellent position to provide experiences in gross discrimination through rhythm instruments and dance recordings. The child may be taught to feel vibrations from instruments and to use rhythm to develop inflection and timing in dance quality. Rhythm may be expressed in clapping activities as well as visually in an integrated group dance situation. It may first be necessary for students who are deaf to be conditioned by the beat of a drum or to sit close to the record player or cassette and familiarize themselves with the basic rhythm being introduced.

With support, the deaf are able to participate with their peers. Whenever possible, these youngsters should be placed in a regular dance class. Teachers should position themselves in such a manner that the student with a hearing loss can see their face during the learning experience. Group dancing will prove beneficial and enjoyable if the child is appropriately placed near the music and, if necessary, accompanied by a child with normal auditory skills.

Those who are totally deaf also benefit from participation in various dance forms. Their dependence on visual images serves to underline the importance that movement plays in the lives of deaf individuals. Creative dance and movement experiences serve as an effective means of communication for the deaf. The dance program at Gallaudet University, located in Washington DC, provides an excellent example of the creative expression and dance talent found within the deaf community.

Orthopedically Impaired

Many disabling conditions have been found to be relative to cultural expectations. Through dance activities, children with orthopedic disabilities can successfully fulfill various basic needs that might not be met in other areas of motor activity. Students with a disabling condition formulate their own response to their disability. The dance teacher may stimulate proper adjustment by providing avenues of self-expression and group interaction.

Basic rhythmic activity acts as a stimulus to control otherwise involuntary movement; however, this stimulus may also release emotional expression in free activity.

Students with orthopedic impairments can participate and will benefit from group dance experiences with their nondisabled peers. Frustration can be minimized by adapting dance activities to meet the needs and capacities of these students. The teacher must use ingenuity to determine the benefits the student may gain from dance experiences. Individuals in wheelchairs enjoy folk and square dances and can easily learn to move their chairs in intricate patterns or be propelled by other members of the class. Creative exploration utilizing upper trunk and arm movement instills physical poise and reassurance. Students with hand deficiencies can be frustrated unnecessarily when working with rhythm toys. By manipulating instruments with the knees and upper arm, these children can successfully enjoy rhythmic experiences.

Adapting Dances and Rhythms

When introducing a dance step or a new dance, it is important that the students be familiar with the various positions and formation used in dancing (figure 22.5). In selecting the formation and position, it is best to make choices that will be easily understood by the participant. For example, single-circle formations are easier than double-circle formations and dances without partners are normally easier than those with partners. Exceptions to these principles, however, can and should be made when the needs of a student dictate otherwise. Students who are blind, for example, benefit from dances that include a partner.

With modification, rhythmics and dancing will usually prove to be an enjoyable experience for students with special needs. The major objective in the adaptation of dance for persons with disabilities is to provide experiences that allow them to perform on a common ground with their peers. The dance instructor must select those activities that remain within the intellectual comprehension and work tolerance level of the individual. The aim of instruction is to enable the individual to find pleasurable and rewarding activity rather than master intricate dance techniques. The following items concerning procedure should be considered:

1. Demonstration by teacher or pupil provides the visual picture of rhythmic movement. Demonstration sets the pattern when predetermined steps are to be learned; it illustrates and stimulates the imagination when creative expression is the goal.

2. Explanations should be brief and precise. Motivation may be increased by stating a brief history of the activity. Performance should immediately follow demonstration and explanation.

3. The instructor should analyze performance and vary the method of explanation when necessary.

4. Each person should experience success. All must feel that they are dancing rather than preparing for a later performance.

5. Ample opportunity for individual practice should be provided.

6. Listening, clapping, stamping, and beating to music stimulate an understanding of tempo, accent, and phrasing.

7. For beginners in partner dancing, frequent partner change in mixer-type activities is advisable.

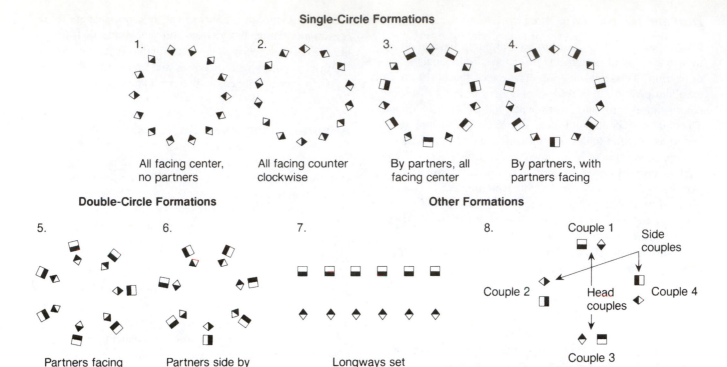

Figure 22.5 Dance formations.

(From: Pangrazi, R.P., & Dauer, V.P. (1995). *Dynamic Physical Education for Elementary School Children* (11th ed.). Minneapolis: Burgess Publishing Co.)

8. Integrating the dance program with academic and extracurricular opportunities enriches the school experience of the students.

Liemohn (1985), after extensive research in the area of rhythmic activity for special populations, has concluded that rhythm is important to performance in many gross and fine motor skills. His findings also suggest that the rhythm of children with special needs can be improved through the use of special training activities. In addition to those already described in this chapter, Liemohn advocates the use of a rebound tumbler (a minitrampoline) in which students are taught to synchronize their bounce with that of a strobe light or bass drum. The goal is to eventually have the youngster bounce in rhythm to a particular piece of recorded music. Balloons are another tactile device that Liemohn has found beneficial. Students who are deaf, for example, can feel the rhythmic pulsations that the balloon receives from loud music or a bass drum.

Special methods of instruction are made necessary by the limitations imposed by specific disabilities. As pointed out in chapter 6, verbal and visual cues and physical assistance are vital teaching techniques in any adapted program.

Brief and precise verbal explanations are beneficial to all individuals with disabilities and are essential for the blind or partially sighted.

Demonstrations and "do-as-I-do" activities are invaluable when working with those who are mentally retarded, and the student who is deaf or hard of hearing also must be given opportunities to watch the skill being performed.

By leading a student's arm or part of the body involved in the activity through the movement, wide avenues of understanding are opened to the individual with a disability. Directing the student in this manner permits skills to be mastered and difficulties to be overcome in a pleasant and nonthreatening atmosphere. Only when the association is made between the desired result and the appropriate form will the student begin to "feel right" about the performance.

Creative Rhythmic Activity

Rhythms are the basic skills of the dance. They should be an essential part of the elementary school program and should occur repeatedly throughout subsequent dance activity.

With fundamental rhythms to an accompaniment, children walk, run, jump, hop, skip, and leap. In informal rhythmic "do-as-I-do-and-say" games, children experiment with space, focus, direction of movement, levels, varying tempo, and different qualities of movement.

With interpretive rhythms, children—including children with various disabilities—can express themselves as animals, sounds, paintings, and fairy tale and story book characters. For example, children can assume the identify of a familiar character, creature, or object. The following ideas have been adapted from Pangrazi and Dauer (1995).

Animals—dogs, rabbits, lions, bears, deer, chickens, ducks, etc.

People—firefighter, nurse, teacher, cowboy and cowgirl, scientist, construction worker, farmer, etc.

Play objects—swing, slide, tricycle, scooters, and many other toys with which children play

Machines—tractors, trains, bulldozer, lawn mower, car, trailer truck, plane and many others

Natural phenomena—wind, fire, flowers, clouds, hurricanes, rain, snow, fluttering leaves, etc.

Performers—magicians, various circus performers, musician, singer, dancer, juggler, clown, gymnast, etc.

Adapted teaching hints: Activities may be stimulated by listening to the basic beat and clapping to the rhythm. The child with a disability learns best by doing, and each student must make an effort to perform the movement to the extent permitted by the disability. Many dance and music teachers suggest that it is best initially to watch a child move and then match the prescribed beat to the child's movements. A high degree of motivation produced and maintained by the teacher is essential. Students who use a wheelchair can clap the basic rhythm with the class while being pushed in the chair during locomotor activity or, when possible, keep time by moving the chair. Those with impaired hearing must use visual cues and experience the vibration of the instruments. Students who are blind may find great joy in marking the rhythmic beat through sound and touch.

Most children, with or without disabilities, particularly enjoy creative activity and spend much of their leisure time in imaginative play. Students who are mentally retarded are sometimes the exception. For them, various stimuli such as musical instruments and other toys that are easily manipulated reinforce their concentration and lead to self-expressive motor activity.

Many children with a disability find the use of equipment motivating when first exposed to rhythmic activities. These include easily obtained items such as flags and flowing streamers. Children enjoy watching the motion of the flag and streamers as they trail behind and the variation in patterns that they can create with these items in response to a change in their body movements. Hula hoops, balls, and balloons also can be easily incorporated into a unit on rhythms to emphasize that rhythm relates not only to body movements but to other items as well. Older students, for instance, may discover that dribbling a ball does have a beat. Using a familiar item such as a basketball is also an excellent way to introduce a unit on rhythms to students who may feel somewhat inhibited about moving their bodies in response to a prescribed beat. Likewise, jumping a swinging rope to the beat of a bass drum assists children to time their jumps so they can be successful and more aware of the important relationship between movement and rhythm.

Traditional Dance Steps

There are several forms of dance frequently referred to as traditional or conventional dance. These include folk, social, and square dance. Children with disabilities benefit from these dance forms because they are fun and provide cultural and historical information about our heritage.

Traditional dance steps have their foundation in fundamental rhythms. Folk dancing and much social dancing involve one or more traditional dance steps.

Step Point

The *step point* is a step on the left foot, pointing the right foot in front. This action is repeated, stepping on the right foot.

count 1	count 2	count 3	count 4
step left	point right	step right	point left

Adapted teaching hints: Floor markings prove beneficial. Teach the step first in a stationary position without music. Do the step in a circle formation, and later alone or with partners.

Step Hop

The *step hop* is a step on the left foot and a hop on the same foot. This action is repeated, using the right foot.

count 1	count 2	count 3	count 4
step left	hop left	step right	hop right

Adapted teaching hints: Practice entirely with one foot at first, and later alternate feet. Students in wheelchairs can enjoy the activity by moving arms on counts one and three and clapping on counts two and four or by moving the chair forward on counts one and three and to the left on count two and to the right on count four.

Step Swing

The *step swing* is a step on the left foot followed by a swing of the right foot across in front of the left. This action is repeated, stepping on the right foot.

count 1	count 2	count 3	count 4
step left	swing right	step right	swing left

Adapted teaching hints: This step is an excellent follow-the-leader activity. The use of the dance barre as well as manual assistance should be considered when introducing the "swing" technique to students who are visually impaired.

Balance Step

The balance step can be done in any direction. The dancer steps left and closes right foot to left, rising on the balls of both feet.

count 1	count 2	count 3
step left	close right	rise on toes, lower

count 1	count 2	count 3
step right	close left	rise on toes, lower

Adapted teaching hint: Some individuals with disabilities will have considerable difficulty coordinating this movement. The teacher should suggest that they gaze at a distant object at eye level to attain balance initially.

Polka

The simple polka is a step on the right, close left to right, step on right, hold. The action is repeated, using the opposite foot.

count 1	and	count 2	and
	heel		toe
count 1	and	count 2	and
step	close	step	hold

Adapted teaching hints: After listening to the music and viewing the demonstration, all students should verbally recite the action words, "heel and toe," and so forth. The steps should be practiced informally in front of the mirror to a familiar recording. The teacher can then give individual attention to each student by taking his or her hand and walking through the dance pattern.

Waltz

The waltz step is a step forward left, step sideward right, and close left to right; then a step backward right, step sideward left, and close right to left.

count 1	count 2	count 3
step left (forward)	side right	close left

count 1	count 2	count 3
step right (backward)	side left	close right

Adapted teaching hints: The step should be first introduced in a line formation. Marking individual "boxes" on the floor with tape gives the students an outline to follow for a better understanding of the waltz pattern. Students who are blind may pass their hands over the markings on the floor to gain tactile cues.

Two-Step

The two-step is a step forward on the left, close right to left, step left and hold. The action is repeated, beginning right.

count 1	count 2	count 3
step left	close right	step left

count 1	count 2	count 3
step right	close left	step right

Adapted teaching hints: The two-step is the foundation of social dancing and can be introduced in partner formation. The tempo should start out slowly and increase as proficiency is acquired. Practice in parallel lines, placing those having difficulty in the back line, where they can watch the successful performers in the front line, helps to promote a better understanding of the step sequence.

Folk Dances

Folk dancing has a fascinating history that belongs to all people including those with disabilities. Many of the dances done today originally stemmed from various rites that celebrated important events in people's lives—the planting of crops, weddings, and even religious sacrifices. Our heritage is rich in its variety of movement qualities, styles, and patterns. Yet with all these differences, there is a lasting universality in the social satisfaction that people derive when they move together in rhythmic harmony.

Folk and square dancing afford excellent opportunities for individuals with disabilities to learn desirable social skills and attitudes. Much of the vigorous activity provided in this type of social dancing may be modified, if necessary, for the student with special needs without losing its authenticity or original sequence.

A firm understanding of basic formation and specific skills involved in various patterns are foundations for enjoyable dance experiences. Repetition and enthusiasm are tools for success. The child who is deaf will learn by listening to the accompaniment and by seeing the formation in movement. The student who is blind may be placed with a seeing partner. With a group of students who are partially sighted students, in dances calling for "crossing over," arch formations, or grand right and left, steps can be worked out going forward and backward instead.

The following dances are but a few examples that are easily adaptable.

The Muffin Man (English)   This is an old English singing game that children enjoy greatly.

Adapted teaching hints: Walking may be substituted for skipping around the circle. Those in wheelchairs may be pushed by others or may propel themselves.

Troika (Russian)   *Troika* means "three horses." The dance symbolizes the three horses that traditionally drew sleighs for noble Russian families.

Adapted teaching hints: This dance makes use of fundamental rhythms. In a formation of three, a student with an arm that is disabled can choose the side on which he or she wishes to dance. The student with behavior disorders may find security in the middle position of the formation.

Chimes of Dunkirk (French) Here is a folk dance that delights young children. It was brought to this country by the French masters many years ago.

Adapted teaching hints: This simple activity is an enjoyable experience for many children, including the child who is mentally retarded. If the group is small, each student should be given the opportunity to dance with the teacher. This may stimulate the slow repetitive learning process.

Square Dances

Folk, in the literal sense, means people. Folk dancing, therefore, is the "dance of the people." With the steady influx of people from many lands to the United States, there slowly emerged an array of international dance figures. The basic formation was the "drill of four" or the quadrille, thus leading to the name *square dance*. The following square dances can be easily adapted.

Head Two Ladies Cross Over The four ladies are active in this exchange partner dance. A child in a wheelchair could easily be the stationary partner.

Duck for the Oyster Duck for the Oyster is one of the oldest and most popular square dances in this country. While the square performs allemande left, grand right and left, the child with limited locomotion can circle or stamp in the center.

Virginia Reel This contradance is an old favorite. Extensive right- and left-hand instruction may be necessary for students who are mentally retarded. With children who are partially sighted, particularly, clapping should be restricted to the child in the contraline who is waiting to be swung. This will enable the child with a visual disorder to more easily find the one he or she is to swing.

Adapted teaching hints for square dances: Because of the frequent partner changes, square dancing provides unique opportunities in the school program for developing an appreciation and respect for others. It is an activity those with disabilities can participate in throughout their adult years.

When students who are deaf or hard of hearing are included, dancers should refrain from loud clapping when the dance is in progress, so that those with impairments may better follow instruction and tempo.

The walk-through method of teaching is the most profitable. Frequent repetition and an exaggeration of directional cues are necessary. Allow the children to listen to the music at first; then demonstrate, using one couple or square; complete the entire pattern with music. Those with visual impairments are more successful when taught in musical phrases rather than in count. Those who are mentally retarded achieve success when the continuity of the dance has been preserved.

The following substitutions are suggested as ways in which the regular movements of the square dance may be modified for those who must use crutches:

Honor your partner. Bow heads.

Swing your partner. Hold out one hand while balanced on crutches to partner who dances around. If both are on crutches, touch bottom parts of one crutch of each partner, forming a pivot which both partners go around.

Allemande left. Walk around to the left.

Right and left grande. Walk around first to the left and then to the right.

Promenade. Partner whose mobility is not impaired places hand on partner's shoulder. If both are on crutches, they move their crutches in unison as they walk.

Do-si-do. Partner whose mobility is not impaired may do most of the movement if it is difficult for the other partner to perform. If both are on crutches and movement is difficult, the swing may be substituted.

Balance. One crutch is placed forward. If the partner with a disability has sufficient strength and skill to balance on the crutches with the feet raised, as some do, this movement may be substituted for the balance.

Social Dance

Social dance is an activity that can be engaged in with pleasure throughout life. It is a popular recreational activity among nondisabled as well as teenagers with disabilities. The courtesies and standards of social dancing can best be taught in school. Mastering these social graces will provide the student who is disabled with the poise that is so important to adjustment. Self-confidence is also encouraged by the use of familiar, currently popular songs with a definite rhythm.

Modern Dance

This type of dance derives its name from its effort to portray significant ideas of current life through movement. Modern dance represents ideas or emotions rather than some standard and traditional dance form. It is a medium of dynamic movement that releases anxieties and frustrations in a socially acceptable fashion. Modern dance is founded on techniques that develop maximum muscular strength, joint flexibility, and body coordination.

The student who is disabled has a pervasive need for self-expression and harmonious utilization of the entire body that modern dance offers. The child who is blind dances to abstract impressions and finds a means of expressing these through movement of the arms and hands as well as other parts of the body. The child with cerebral palsy can release frustrations by freely engaging in gross rhythmic movement and can actually benefit from concentrated movement, which leads to greater control of disabled limbs. The deaf or hard-of-hearing child seeks continuity in muscular activity. The student with a behavior disorder finds self-expressive movement a relaxing adventure. Creativity and self-awareness are developed in the child who is mentally retarded with the use of modern dance activities.

The program may be structured or nonstructured; the teacher must have a purpose for all activities. Scarves, pieces of rope, costumes, chairs, or other accessible materials can stimulate activity. Musical accompaniment should clearly represent various tempos or moods; many popular recordings can accomplish this goal. Narrative stories and recent happenings also provide interesting stimuli for movement.

Creative movement concepts can be taught in a variety of ways through modern dance experiences. Some suggested activities include the following:

1. Exploring the contrast in feelings between soft and hard. This can be done through activities such as having children clap their hands versus bringing them together slowly and softly; walk with light steps in contrast to stomping; and jump and land softly rather than making a hard or heavy landing.

2. Developing an understanding of the ways in which space can be used. For example, doing movements that are in a horizontal plane compared to movements done in a vertical plane. Some teachers have found it helpful to encourage students to alternate movements between the horizontal and vertical as part of a dance routine. Students in wheelchairs find this request a challenging experience but one they can successfully accomplish by using the motion of the wheelchair for the horizontal actions and the arms or neck and head to make movements in the vertical plane.

3. Encouraging slow as well as fast movements. Modern dance experiences should encourage a full range of movement speeds from very slow to very rapid. Many students, particularly those who are hyperactive, benefit from experiences that are designed to encourage them to move slowly. Some children who are lethargic find dance experiences that encourage fast, repetitive movements motivating.

4. Promoting exploration of movements with parts of the body as well as the total body. Many students fail to recognize the intricate and creative movement patterns that can be done with a single extremity such as the hand. Students who are orthopedically impaired frequently excel at this activity.

There are many other modern dance variations that may be used to encourage students to be creative. The ultimate goal is to help the student with a disability become less rigid and more free in his or her movement patterns. The results achieved in the dance experience ideally can be transferred to the movement patterns utilized throughout the student's life activities.

Movement Songs

Movement songs, sometimes referred to as singing games, are rhythmic activities in which children sing verses that provide directions or cues as to how they should move. This is a very popular activity with children, including those with disabilities, because the songs are fun and the verses allow the children to interpret the movement. Considerable latitude is therefore possible as to what constitutes a correct movement. A movement song can be a poem, fable, or any verse that can be set easily to music. In movement songs it is important that adaptations, as necessary, be made for students with special needs. For example, students who are deaf will need extra help to ensure that they understand the words to the song. Students who are mentally retarded may need physical assistance or prompts to help them associate the correct action with a verse. Two popular movement songs are indicated below.

Looby Lou In this song, the children skip around the circle during the chorus and move the body parts as they are named. The chorus and verses are as follows:

Chorus:	Here we go looby lou. Here we go looby light. Here we go looby lou. All on a Saturday night.
Verse 1:	I put my right hand in. I put my right hand out. I give my right hand a shake, shake, shake. And turn myself about.
Verse 2:	I put my left hand in. I put my left hand out, etc.
Verse 3:	I put my right foot in. I put my right foot out, etc.
Verse 4:	I put my left foot in. I put my left foot out, etc.
Verse 5:	I put my head in. I put my head out, etc.
Verse 6:	I put my whole self in. I put my whole self out, etc.

Adaptations: Students who are orthopedically impaired or in a wheelchair can substitute other body parts or use the chair or an assistive device in lieu of the specific body part. Children who are mentally retarded can be asked to name a body part with the class instructed to follow their lead.

Hokey Pokey In this song the children act out the words during the first four lines. During lines 5 and 6, they hold their hands overhead with palms forward and do a kind of hula while turning around in place. During line 7, they stand in place and clap their hands three times.

Line 1: You put your right foot in,
Line 2: You put your right foot out,
Line 3: You put your right foot in
Line 4: And you shake it all about;
Line 5: You do the hokey pokey
Line 6: And you turn yourself around.
Line 7: That's what it's all about.

The basic verse is repeated by substituting, successively, the left foot, right arm, left arm, right elbow, left elbow, head, right hip, left hip, whole self, and backside. The final verse finishes off with the following:

You do the hokey pokey,
You do the hokey pokey,
You do the hokey pokey,
That's what it's all about.

Adaptations: Students should feel free to substitute any body part for any of the parts identified in the song. This is important for the student with a missing limb or whose movement is limited due to paralysis. Students in wheelchairs can do the movements in a wheelchair, including those parts which require the performers to turn around in place. Those who are blind will be able to do the movements without modification. The Hokey Pokey is a favorite activity of many students who are mentally retarded.

A Hunting We Will Go   In this song the long way formation (see figure 22.5) is used. During the verse, the head couple joins inside hands and skips between the lines to the end of the set. They change hands and return to the head of the set. All other children clap while the head couple is active. During the chorus, the head couple skips around the left side of the set, with all couples following. When the head couple reaches the end of the set, they form an arch by facing each other, joining two hands and holding them high in the air. All other couples proceed through the arch reforming the set with a new head couple.

Verse: Oh, a hunting we will go. A hunting we will go. We'll catch a fox and put him in the box. And then we'll let him go.
Chorus: Tra, la, la, la, la, la, la. Tra, la, la, la, la. Tra, la, la, la, la, la, la. Tra, la, la, la, la, la.

Adaptations: The locomotor pattern used in this action song can be modified as necessary. Some students may find it easier to walk or slide. Students with limited movement may substitute a stationary movement instead of the specified locomotor activity.

Dance Therapy

As noted in the foregoing discussion, dance activities help individuals with disabilities to achieve poise and confidence, to relate to others in a group, and to give expression to latent feelings. Such therapeutic benefits, although extremely important, are not the specific goal of the dance program in physical education. The utilization of dance for the promotion of mental health is the focus of the separate profession of dance therapy.

Dance therapists are primarily concerned with establishing a relationship with those in the program, one that permits therapeutic intervention to improve mental health. The medium for this purpose is a wide variety of dance activities adapted in style, content, form, and method of presentation to meet individual needs. Obviously, the teacher of dance for students with disabilities and the dance therapist have much in common regarding knowledge of dance, information about disabling conditions, and utilization of special teaching techniques. The important difference between the two is one of purpose: the teacher utilizes dance as a motor activity to enhance total education while the therapist seeks to improve mental health through the teaching of dance. Dance therapists work closely and cooperatively with psychiatrists, psychologists, and other medical and allied health personnel. Careful attention is focused by therapists on the psychodynamic needs and recovery process of individual participants. Dance therapists are certified by the American Dance Therapy Association. Special training and study is required before a person can achieve the high standards required by this national association.

Summary

Rhythm and dance are an integral part of the physical education program for children with disabilities. All children, regardless of the level of disability, can participate in creative rhythmic activity. This can take the form of following a simple beat to executing a sophisticated move or dance step found in a traditional dance form such as folk dance. Procedures for ensuring that all children enjoy dance and creative rhythms require that the teacher modify or adapt activities as necessary. Because dance is a creative experience, the setting and movement form naturally lend themselves to a process that encourages participation and acceptance.

The content of the dance program for children with disabilities is similar to that of their nondisabled peers. Early attention is given to the teaching of basic rhythms using various pieces of equipment such as drums and tambourines. Movement songs and games in which children move creatively to music or a verse are very popular. These activities also can be used to practice locomotor and nonlocomotor skills. Asking children, for instance, to gallop like a horse while following the rhythm of a song is an enjoyable and self-motivational experience. Children who have movement difficulties or sensory impairments can utilize a different locomotor pattern or, if necessary, move a different body part such as a hand or foot. Movement concepts of flow, balance, and time also can be incorporated into these early experiences.

Conventional dance forms such as folk, square, and social dance should be included in the dance program for older elementary students. These experiences reinforce desirable movement patterns and provide valuable information about our culture and heritage. In addition, traditional dances are fun and provide a meaningful social experience for the student with special needs. All dance forms, including modern dance, can be adapted or modified for individuals with disabilities. Many wheelchair users have participated successfully as members (dancers as well as callers) of square dance clubs. The use of partners, which is common in dance, is an asset to students with sensory impairments. Valuable cues, for example, can be gleaned from the sighted or hearing partner.

Dance can be educational or it can be used as a therapy to improve mental health. Professionals known as dance therapists receive special training that allows them to use dance as an intervention therapy. Dance therapists work closely and cooperatively with psychiatrists, psychologists, and other medical and allied health personnel.

Rhythm and dance play an essential role in the physical education program for students with disabilities. Many such youngsters have a basic need to develop freedom of self-expression, skills in social interaction, and fundamental movement patterns. Dance provides a medium through which these needs may be realized.

Selected Readings

Bernstein, P.L. (1975). *Theory and methods in dance-movement therapy* (2d ed.). Dubuque, IA: Kendall/Hunt Publishing Co.

Fitt, S., & Riordan, A. (1980). *Focus on dance IX: Dance for the handicapped.* Washington, DC: American Alliance for Health, Physical Education, Recreation, and Dance.

Gabbard, C., Leblanc, E., & Lowy, S. (1987). *Physical education for children.* Englewood Cliffs, NJ: Prentice-Hall, Inc.

Hill, K. (1976). *Dance for physically disabled persons.* Washington, DC: American Alliance for Health, Physical Education, and Recreation.

Kovach-Long, S. (1980). *Adapting dance: Folk, social, creative, spontaneous.* Cupertino, CA: De Anza College Learning Center Press.

Liemohn, W. (1985). *Rigors and rhythms.* Knoxville, TN: The University of Tennessee.

Nichols, B. (1986). *Moving and learning.* St. Louis: Times Mirror/Mosby.

Pangrazi, R., & Dauer, V. (1995). *Dynamic physical education for elementary school children* (11th ed.). Minneapolis: Burgess Publishing Co.

Schoop, T. (1974). *Will you, won't you, join the dance?* Palo Alto, CA: National Press Books.

Werner, P.H., & Burton, E.C. (1979). *Learning through movement.* St. Louis: C.V. Mosby Co.

Winters, S.S. (1975). *Creative rhythmic movement for children of elementary school age.* Dubuque, IA: Wm. C. Brown Publishers.

Enhancing Activities

1. Using the library or instructional media center, obtain and view a copy of the film *A Very Special Dance,* by Anne Riordan.

2. Write to the American Dance Therapy Association (ADTA) and request information concerning the profession of dance therapy. The address is Suite 216E, 1000 Century Plaza, Columbia, MD 21044.

3. With the assistance of your teacher, organize and conduct a rhythmic or dance activity for a group of children, including those with disabilities.

4. Using a rhythmic instrument (drum, tambourine, triangle, etc.), create a rhythm that can be used to incorporate various locomotor and nonlocomotor skills.

5. Develop a file of dance and rhythmic activities, including movement songs, in which children with and without disabilities can participate.

6. Discuss the value of creative dance (e.g., creative rhythms and modern dance) in contrast to traditional dance forms such as folk and square.

Individual Lifetime Activities

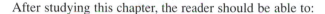

CHAPTER OBJECTIVES

After studying this chapter, the reader should be able to:

1 Recognize what is meant by the term *lifetime activities* and identify the more common activities engaged in by children.

2 Modify the following activities so that individuals with disabilities can participate safely and successfully in them: archery, bicycling, boating, bowling, downhill skiing, frisbee disc, golf, roller skating, ice skating, and track and field.

3 Appreciate the importance and contribution of lifetime activities to the life of individuals with disabilities.

4 Organize the instruction in physical activity so that lifetime activities can be provided for students with disabilities.

5 Identify resources, including adaptive equipment, that can be used to help the student with a disability to participate in lifetime activities.

6 Recognize that the participation of those with disabilities in lifetime activities is limited only by the imagination and willingness of the human spirit to overcome obstacles.

"Lifetime activities" is a term used to designate those activities that generally can be played for enjoyment and exercise throughout life. When the activities are ones in which a person may participate alone or against opponents, they are usually referred to as individual sports. Among the most widely played individual lifetime sports are archery, bowling, and golf. Participation in certain track events is also enjoyed by many long into their adult years.

Because these activities are designed for individual participation, they can be readily adapted to individual restrictions and capacities. For this reason alone they are excellent choices for the special physical education curriculum. However, there are other important reasons for including them in the program for people with disabilities. One of the most obvious of these reasons is their contribution to the physical fitness of the participants. Although individual lifetime activities are not considered to be vigorous, they do place sufficient demands upon the body to encourage desirable development for players with disabilities in such fitness factors as strength, flexibility, and cardiorespiratory endurance. Then, too, individual lifetime activities have high carry-over value. Because they require less organization than most other active games, they are among our most popular leisure activities. Consequently, participation in these activities virtually ensures that the individual with a disability has opportunities for good fellowship with nondisabled players who enjoy these activities as recreation. In this sense, the individual lifetime activities are functional skills that can be used by the individual to enjoy and participate more fully in the life of the community.

Many persons with disabilities find other lifetime activities, in addition to sport experiences, enjoyable and beneficial. These include basic activities, such as cycling, to more complex skills, such as roller skating and skiing. Although some of these experiences may be beyond the traditional physical education curriculum, there are community agencies, such as the public recreation department, youth organizations, the YMCA, or the YWCA, that may provide these activities independently or cooperatively with school systems. Parents, too, may take the initiative for providing these special experiences but will frequently look to teachers for suggestions about how to structure the experiences so that their children will be successful. For this reason, some special lifetime activities are included in this chapter.

Organizing the Instruction

Instruction in the individual activities requires considerable planning and organization on the part of the teacher. Because these are individual activities, each student requires considerable individual instruction, and the planning of class time must provide for this. Moreover, equipment is required by each participant, and there may not be sufficient equipment for all members of the class to practice simultaneously.

Fortunately, most students can be successfully placed in the regular physical education classes. The nature of individual lifetime activities is such that participants can move at their own pace. Students who are extremely skilled and have mastered the techniques may be used by the teacher to assist in the instruction of the individuals with disabilities. If the class must be paired because of lack of equipment, it is wise to have a more skilled student with a less skilled one in the early practice sessions. Later it will prove more stimulating to the participants if they are evenly matched.

Nearly all students with disabilities will require considerable experimentation to determine the best method of performing the skills of the various individual activities. It is important to help the learners with disabilities to analyze the mechanics of each skill in the activity. Toward this end, audiovisual aids and textbooks that describe the performance of the skills in detail are extremely useful because, although in many instances the descriptions are not directly applicable, they do help the students to gain insight into the mechanics of performing the skills and thereby make possible a better understanding of how an adaptation may be made successfully. Information about suitable films and other audiovisual aids are included in appendix II.

Few schools will have their own golf courses and bowling alleys. Many aspects of golf and bowling can be taught, however, without actual use of these facilities. By utilizing plastic golf balls, golf cages, and indoor and outdoor putting areas, most of the skills of golf can be introduced to the students in the school setting. Bowling skills can be taught very successfully with sets of polyethylene bowling balls and pins. If necessary, empty milk cartons and a soccer ball can be used satisfactorily as substitutes in teaching the fundamental skills of bowling. It is, of course, desirable to give students opportunities to play in actual game situations if at all possible. Frequently, arrangements can be made with commercial bowling alleys and golf courses to use their facilities at certain slack hours for a nominal fee. If such arrangements are to be made, they should be worked out well in advance of the teaching period and should, of course, have administrative approval.

In presenting adaptations that can be made for those who have disabilities in the activities discussed in this chapter, very brief descriptions of the specific skills are given to enable the reader to make a better comparison of the adaptation with normal performance and so gain a better understanding of the process of adapting skills for participants with disabilities. It is not the intent to provide instruction for learning to perform the skills. Those who wish this information are referred to the books in Selected Readings at the end of the chapter. Readers are reminded that the safety equipment, with or without modifications, should be used by all who participate in lifetime activites.

Archery

Of the several forms of archery activity, shooting arrows at an upright target is the most easily adapted for most persons with disabling conditions. Archery does not require vigorous movement, nor is it excessively fatiguing; consequently, it is very suitable for those who cannot participate in strenuous activities and for those with lower-limb disabilities. It is also a good activity for people with visual impairments, who are able to participate with sight changes in the procedure of sighting and with help in locating arrows that miss the target.

General Adaptations: For archers who use wheelchairs or crutches the target should be located where there is no rise behind it to stop the arrows, because these students will have too much difficulty retrieving arrows from an elevated area. Moving from the shooting area to the target can be made easier for archers with visual impairments by stringing a wire from one area to the other.

At the shooting area, a stick eight to twelve inches long should be placed on the ground, pointing in the direction of the target, to orient the archers with visual impairments. To help in determining the correct amount of pull on the bow, two poles are placed in the ground and aligned with the target; one pole indicates the place at which the hand of the extended arm should be, and the other where the back of the wrist of the hand drawing the string should be.

Stance, Nocking, and Drawing the Bow

In taking the stance, the feet are comfortably spread, with the left side of the body facing the target if the archer is right-handed. The head is turned towards the target. The bow is grasped in the left hand at the handle. It is held parallel to the target with the string toward the body and the back of the hand up. The arrow is picked up at the nock between the forefinger and thumb and placed across the bow at the arrow plate at right angles to the string. The cock feather is up. The thumb and forefinger encircle the string and hold the end of the arrow and place the nock over the bowstring.

To assume the position for shooting, the fingers of the right hand are placed under the bowstring to grasp the string with the tips of the first three fingers. The arrow is held between the first and second fingers. The bow is raised with the left arm and extended toward the target.

The elbow is straight but not locked. The other arm, with fingers bent to hold the string, is raised so the arm is bent at the elbow and is parallel to the ground. The bowstring is pulled back with the right arm so that the arm, wrist, and arrow make a straight line toward the target. The bowstring is pulled back against the chin. The hand is anchored under the jaw and against the neck with the forefinger up against the chin.

Adaptations: An archer in a wheelchair will turn the chair to the side and reach over the side of the chair to draw

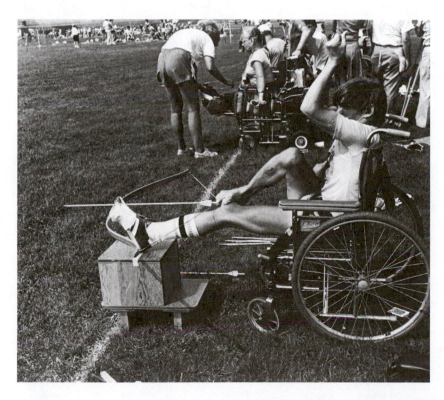

Figure 23.1   For some individuals with disabilities, success in archery may require the use of the legs and feet rather than the arms and hands.

the bow. Those on crutches will need to prop themselves with the crutches so as to free their arms. This can be accomplished by tilting the body toward the target and putting most of the weight on the front crutch. This will hold the crutch in place, and the arm can be used to hold the bow. The other arm will have to squeeze slightly on the rear crutch to hold it in place, but the arm is freed sufficiently to draw the bowstring parallel to the ground. Another method is to maintain equal weight on both crutches and bend the extended arm at the elbow so the front crutch can be cradled in the arm pit. The back crutch is cradled in the armpit by lowering the bowstring arm. Those who have difficulty in balancing may sit in a chair for shooting.

Sighting and Releasing

For any given bow there is a certain distance from each target at which the center can be hit by sighting over the point of the arrow to the center of the target. When closer to or farther back from the target, the archer must aim above or below the target to hit it.

When the bow is sighted correctly, the arrow is released by straightening the fingers quickly. No other movement of the body should occur.

Adaptations: For the archer who has a visual impairment, the two poles already described as an aid in drawing the bow may be wound with tape at the places where the hands should be for sighting accurately. The correct location of the tape is determined by trial and error. In shooting, the archer with a visual impairment knows the sighting is correct when the backs of the hands touch the taped areas.

For those who have the use of only one arm, the bow may be anchored to a standard of the type used for supporting a volleyball net. The bow is attached in the correct position for the correct range. If the standard is portable rather than permanently fixed, it must have a sufficiently large base to enable the archer to place a foot on it to help hold it securely. Sturdy poles might be substituted for standards. If the archer with one arm uses a wheelchair, the bow may be strapped to the chair. Several types of mouth pieces have been used by individuals with various upper extremity hemiplegia impairments to assist in drawing the bowstring with the mouth.

There will be little need for adaptation for those with finger amputations if at least two functional fingers remain. These fingers can then be made to perform the work ordinarily performed by the missing fingers.

The crossbow may be substituted for the standard bow for those with limited movement of the arms. The bow is cocked by the teacher and sighted and shot by the student.

The recurve bow, however, is the only bow that may be used in competition sponsored by the National Archery Association or the American Wheelchair Archers.

In recent years, there has been growing interest in the sport of archery by individuals with disabilities, including those who have severe physical impairments. Some of these individuals have minimal hand and wrist strength. This necessitates, therefore, that they be equipped with some type of hand and wrist support similar to that developed at the Courage Center in Golden Valley, Minnesota, and pictured in figure 23.2. Lyn Rourke advocates that the best wrist position is obtained by attaching to the bow a metal brace that fits into a reinforced cuff. Some archers may also require the assistance of an elbow brace to support the forearm (figure 23.3). For additional information on these and other innovative equipment aides, the reader should contact Courage Center, 3915 Golden Valley Road, Golden Valley, MN 55422.

Archery is a lifetime activity in which a person with a disability may participate for recreation or competition. Participation may be an independent activity or with a group, and

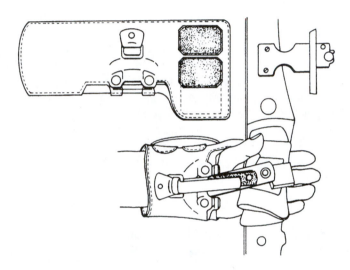

Figure 23.2 Reinforced wrist support for archery.
(Courtesy of *Sports 'n Spokes*.)

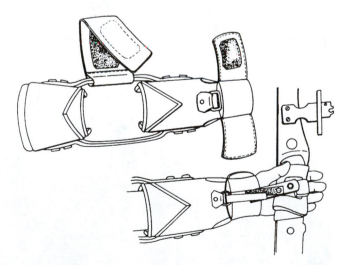

Figure 23.3 Elbow/wrist support for archery.
(Courtesy of *Sports 'n Spokes*.)

may be enjoyed with others who may or may not have a disability. New Zealand resident Neroli Fairhall qualified to compete in the Olympics while shooting from her wheelchair.

Bicycling

Bicycling is one of the most useful skills that a person with a disability can learn. Not only is riding a bike fun, it is an activity that promotes leg strength and cardiovascular endurance. Transportation to and from work, shopping, and leisure activities are other values associated with this skill. Learning to ride a bike has enhanced the quality of life for many individuals with disabilities. It is a skill that can be used throughout one's life.

General Adaptations: Some individuals with disabilities will not have sufficient balance and coordination to ride a two-wheel bicycle. Fortunately, today there are many bicycles available commercially that have been adapted for children and adults with disabilities. These include cycles with three and four wheels and some equipped with hand cranks rather than the standard foot cranks. For additional information on modified bicycles and mobile rowing machines, the reader is referred to periodic evaluations in *Sports 'n Spokes* magazine.

A couple of the new, innovative designs are pictured in figure 23.4. Individuals with lower leg involvement, in particular, find the three-wheel hand crank cycles to be valuable. The ever-popular tandem bicycle enables cyclists with visual impairments to enjoy the experience of biking.

Cycling Technique

The technique of teaching an individual with a disability to ride a bike is the same as that used in instructing young children. This involves breaking the skill down into its component parts—mounting, dismounting, pedaling, turning, and stopping—and then structuring appropriate learning experiences. Many instructors find the use of a stationary bicycle an indispensable aid in helping individuals learn the rhythm necessary to maintain a pedal cadence. Bicycles with training wheels can also be used to integrate the skills of pedaling, turning, and stopping.

Adaptations: Safety must always be identified as an essential component of any instructional unit on cycling. An ANSI or Snell approved helmet is mandatory for all who participate in bicycling, mobile rowing machine, or other human-powered vehicle activities. Students who are mentally retarded and those with hearing impairments in particular, must be monitored carefully to ensure that they can respond to signals, warning signs, and traffic patterns. The use of a tandem bicycle enables the instructor to practice traffic skills with the student in a safe and controlled manner.

Some students with visual impairments have found it possible to cycle with the aid of another cyclist who rides either to the side or front, providing information concerning direction and terrain. This technique has allowed athletes to successfully participate in road races and triathalons.

Boating

The United States Coast Guard estimates that there are more than 100,000 boaters with physical disabilities in the United States. This large number should not be surprising, because boating offers many beneficial and pleasurable experiences to all, including individuals with disabling conditions. The feeling of independence generated by moving a boat or canoe through the water is perhaps the number one reason many individuals with disabilities enjoy boating activities. Although

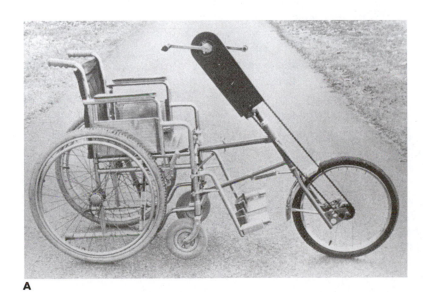

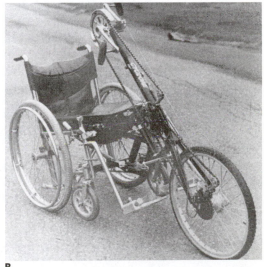

A

B

Figure 23.4 Hand-crank cycles. (*A*) The unicycle. (*B*) Access Designs Cycle-one.

the term *boating* covers a variety of water activities, canoeing and rowing will be discussed here. Both of these activities require the use of the upper extremities, making this a particularly beneficial activity for individuals with lower body paralysis.

General Adaptations: In canoeing and rowing the major adaptations relate to the manner in which the person gets into the canoe or boat. Although there is much individual variation and preference, the most common method used by boaters with mobility disabilities is to transfer into the canoe or boat from a mat placed on the deck next to the canoe. The boater with a disability then leans back and using the arms for support, drops the buttocks into the boat landing on a soft mat. Next, the legs are lifted by pulling on the pant cuffs and then placed into position one leg at a time.

Rowboats and canoes require little modification for individuals with disabilities. Some individuals will utilize a shorter paddle or oar to compensate for their limited shoulder and arm mobility. Seats that are contoured are also desirable for those who require support while sitting.

Safety is a critical factor in the design and implementation of a boating program for all participants, including those with disabling conditions. The American Red Cross requires that participants with physical disabilities perform the following skills prior to participation in one of the organization's courses:

1. Be able to pitch or fall, fully clothed, into the water and recover to the surface.
2. Swim one minute without a personal flotation device.
3. After being thrown a United States Coast Guard–approved personal flotation device, remain afloat an additional four minutes, progressing a minimum of twenty feet through the water.

It is recommended that boaters with disabilities, particularly those with orthopedic impairments, make a checklist of any special needs they should prepare for while boating. In addition to their personal flotation device, some may require special medication. Care should also be taken to analyze and prepare for the effects of weather on specific disabilities prior to long boating trips.

Rowing and Paddling Techniques

The individual with a disability uses the same basic bow stroke taught to all beginning canoers. With this stroke, the upper arm pushes forward and across the front of the body while the lower arm pulls. The paddle should be pulled backward until the bottom hand reaches the hip and the upper arm is fully extended with the hand over the water. An effective technique for teaching individuals with paralysis proper stroke technique is to have them practice paddling in shallow water while seated in their wheelchair.

Rowing Technique

Although there are many different types and styles of rowing, the information presented here will focus on the techniques most commonly used by pleasure rowers. In this system, the hands should be placed on the oar handle so that the handle is held in the fingers with the thumb over the end of the handle, not under it. The rowing stroke is divided into the catch, pull, finish, and recovery phases. In the catch phase, the wrists are dropped to bring the ends of the oars, the blades, to a near horizontal position. At the same time, the rower should rock forward from the hips and simultaneously extend the arms. The catch is made by straightening the wrists and allowing the blades to drop to their edgewise floating depth. During the pull phase, the body moves back toward the vertical. The back and arms remain straight as the trunk goes to a layback position of approximately twenty to twenty-five degrees. At the end of the pull, the blades will glide from the water if a slight downward pressure is applied to the handles. The last phase, recovery, is accomplished by moving the trunk forward as the hands are thrust toward the front of the boat. The blades remain feathered (parallel to the water) during the recovery until the point for the catch is reached, initiating a new rowing cycle.

Adaptations: Rowers with limited shoulder mobility may require oars that have been shortened and adjusted to ensure proper balance. Rowers with visual impairments should be provided an opportunity to examine the oar or paddle with the hands as it is taken through several complete cycles of the stroke. This can be accomplished with the assistance of a sighted partner and the placement of the boat in shallow water. In the open water, the paddler with visual impairments will assume the front position with the sighted partner in the rear, or stern, responsible for controlling the general direction of the canoe.

Depending on the nature of a person's disability, some modification to the canoe may be necessary. A person with lower body amputations or atrophy needs some bracing to prevent him or her from sliding forward in the seat. Individuals with poor trunk balance may need additional support for balance and padding to prevent pressure sores or other injuries. Individuals with cardiorespiratory problems should be taught to monitor their pulse rate to establish an oar or paddle cadence consistent with their functioning level.

Bowling

Bowling is an extremely popular game among people who use wheelchairs and have the use of at least one arm. Like archery, bowling is not a vigorous game and therefore is very appropriate for those for whom strenuous activity is contraindicated. Bowlers with visual impairments are usually more successful in their efforts at bowling than at archery; they do need someone to tell them which pins are left standing after the first ball and to record their scores when automatic scoring is not used.

General Adaptations: In addition to providing equipment for bowling instruction when regular alleys are not available, the polyethylene pins and balls discussed in the introduction are excellent for those students who, because of their disabilities, lack the strength and coordination to use the heavier regulation bowling balls. The grip on the ball is taken at the first joints of the fingers rather than the second joints, which are used in gripping a regulation bowling ball.

Students with muscular weakness in the arm and hand may find the use of a specially designed bowling ball with a retractable handle a valuable piece of equipment. The handle enables the bowler to grasp the ball with all of the fingers of the hand similar to the action used to carry a bucket. As the ball is released, the handle retracts completely so that the ball rolls smoothly. A bowling ball holder, a ring that attaches to the chair (figure 23.5), is a helpful device for the wheelchair user who prefers not to have the ball rest in the lap when positioning or moving to the line.

A useful piece of equipment for bowlers with strength or mobility limitations is a light metal rack that provides a track for the ball to travel down from the lap of the holder to the floor of the alley. The ball is placed on the track and the track is aimed toward the pins. The ball is released, and it rolls down the track and onto the alley toward the pins (figure 23.6C).

Approach and Delivery

The four-step approach is generally preferred. The ball is held chest high with both hands. Then, as the approach begins, the left hand (for a right-handed bowler) is withdrawn and the hand with the ball starts downward and into the backswing. The backward swing should be straight back. As the left hand is withdrawn, the first step in the approach is taken with the right foot. The second step is taken as the ball swings down. As the ball reaches the height of the backswing, the third step is taken. With the final step, the arm swings forward. The last step is a longer stride than the others. After planting the foot, the feet are allowed to slide forward just back of the foul line. On the last step, the body is crouched over the lead leg to enable the bowler to deliver the ball on the floor smoothly so it will not bounce.

Adaptations: To bowl from a wheelchair when the metal rack need not be used, the bowler must place the chair to face the pins. The body is moved as far as possible to the side of the chair from which the ball will be released. The player leans over the side of the chair to permit the arm to swing freely in delivering the ball. To compensate for the lack of approach in the delivery, a preliminary swing may be taken. The ball swings back, then forward without touching the floor, back again, and in the forward swing the body is leaned farther to the side so that the ball can be released smoothly on the floor. Unlike ambulatory bowlers, the arm swing for the bowler in a wheelchair must be a straight, pendulum-like swing. A firm grip on the nonthrowing side of the wheelchair will prevent the bowler from falling out of

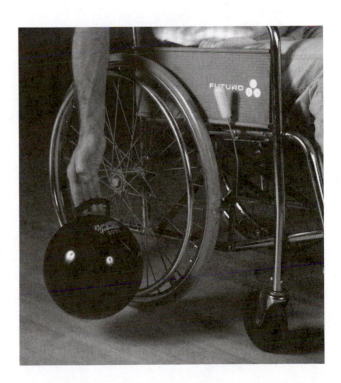

Figure 23.5 Bowling ball ring holder and handle are used.

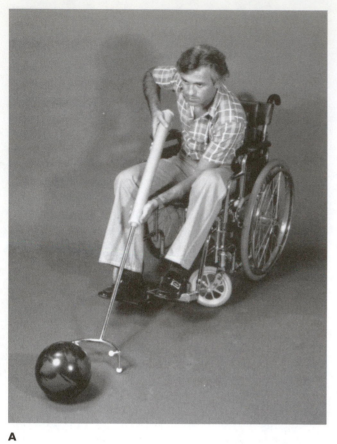

A

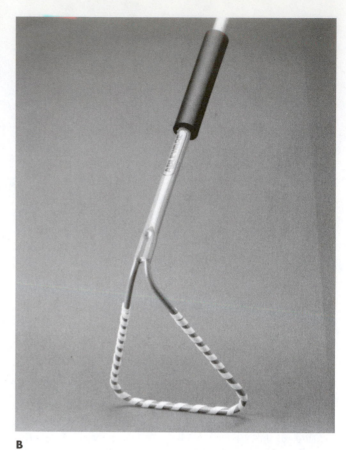

B

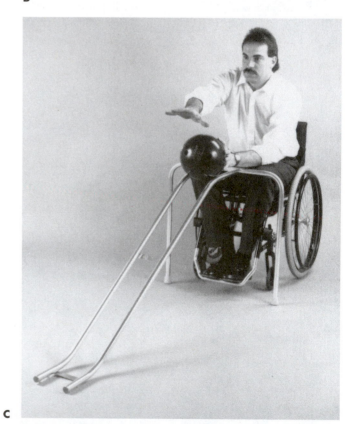

C

Figure 23.6 Devices that involve both upper and lower limbs and assist a bowler's ball delivery.

the chair. Some bowlers equip their chairs with a reinforced brake to increase the holding power of the brake during the release phase.

If the wheelchair is too high for the bowler, a chair without arms may be used. A chair might also be used by bowlers on crutches or others with limited locomotion. An adaptation for those able to stand but unable to make the necessary steps in the approach is to permit them to stand at the foul line to make the delivery.

All bowlers who lack strength in the arm and shoulder should use the lighter polyethylene ball and pins. In using this ball, only the straight ball may be thrown, because the ball is not easily controlled in a spin; otherwise the ball responds similarly to the regulation bowling ball.

Bowlers with visual impairments orient themselves by feeling the sides of the alley or using a rail if one is provided. The accuracy of the aim may be determined by the number of pins knocked down, which is told to the bowler by a sighted person.

Bowlers who have mental retardation will need special assistance and additional practice to ensure that they perform the approach, delivery, and release correctly. The use of footprints to remind them of the proper foot placement can be a very helpful aid. For some students it may be best to teach and practice the release first, then the release and one step, etc., before introducing the full approach with four steps. In essence the skill is taught in a backward sequence. This technique has been found to be valuable with students who are mentally retarded (Hsu and Dunn, 1984).

Downhill Skiing

Downhill skiing was once considered to be too rugged a sport for people with disabilities. This myth has been disproved in recent years, as evidenced by the number of individuals with disabilities who successfully participate in this activity, including those with orthopedic and visual impairments.

Instruction in the technical aspects of skiing are beyond the scope of this book. Some of the fundamentals of skiing are presented and specific methods that have been employed will be discussed.

Stance, Walking, Side Step, and Turning Around

Beginning skiers should strive to develop a well-balanced, relaxed ski stance. To achieve this objective it is essential that the skis are parallel, with the knees flexed, back straight, and weight evenly distributed on both skis. The hands should be at waist level in front of the skier with the pole baskets behind. The head should be over the shoulders with the eyes pointed straight ahead.

Walking on skis is very easy if the skier will remember to keep the skis parallel and about hip width apart. From this position the skier should slide one ski forward and then the second. Pushing with the poles will make sliding the skis forward easier. The push with the pole is made on the side opposite to the ski that is being pushed forward.

Climbing up a slope requires that the skier learn to side step. To employ this technique, the skis should be perpendicular to the slope, with the knees rolled into the hill. This position forces the skis to be edged into the snow. With the poles to the sides, a small uphill step should be taken by resetting one ski into the snow, followed by the second ski. The procedure is repeated up the slope. The poles should be used for balance, with the uphill pole at arm's length and the downhill pole close to the skis.

Turning around is a procedure used to change the direction of the skis without sliding. This move is executed with the skis across the slopes and the poles placed down the hill so that a straight line is formed from the shoulders to the basket of the poles. The hands should be on top of the poles with the elbows locked and arms straight. From this position, the skier moves one ski at a time, taking small steps until the desired change in direction is reached.

Adaptations: The most notable advancements in assisting those with disabilities to ski have been in the development of specialized equipment. For example, three-track skiing, whereby a skier uses one ski and two outriggers, has been employed successfully by individuals with various disabilities, including those with leg amputations. The outrigger is a short ski (sixteen inches) attached to a Canadian crutch by a hinge that allows the crutch to move forward or backward without tipping the ski. The arm band is reinforced to stand the pressure exerted against it while skiing. An outrigger is held by the hands on each side of the body to help the skier balance.

A "four-track" technique has made it possible for individuals with cerebral palsy to ski. In this system, the skier maneuvers with the aid of a walker attached to its own pair of skis. A clamp referred to as a ski bra (figure 23.7) is

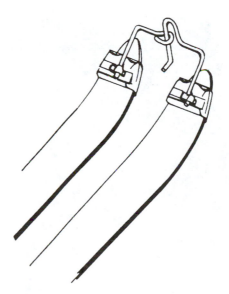

Figure 23.7 A ski bra.
(Source: NHSRA of Michigan)

placed across the tips of the skis to hold them together. In the initial stages of instruction, the ski instructor skis behind the skier with cerebral palsy, controlling the skier's speed and direction by hooking the handles of the poles onto the disabled skier's skis (figure 23.8).

The mono-ski (figure 23.9 and 23.10) offers the skier with a disability a basic trunk support and upper-arm strength with the ability to rival the speed, control, and maneuverability of stand-up skiing. The mono-ski provides seat and back cushions and a nylon cover to keep the skier dry and comfortable. A single or dual alpine ski is mounted on a bump-absorbing suspension that attaches under the seating shell. Skiers have reported faster times and better control using the mono-ski compared to other sit-ski devices.

McCormick (1985) advises that safety precautions be taken to avoid injury while sit-skiing. For example, the

Figure 23.10 Shadow Mono Ski by Quickie lets an individual hit the slopes in competition or recreational skiing.

Figure 23.8 To assist students with cerebral palsy, skis are attached to a walker.

Figure 23.9 Skier, riding on a mono-ski, or single ski, uses poles equipped with short skis for balance.

probability of a thumb fracture can be minimized by holding the pick with the thumb on the same side of the grip as the fingers (figure 23.11).

Skiers with visual impairments ski with the assistance of a sighted partner. Normally the sighted individual skis behind the skier with limited vision, providing helpful cues for direction changes and ensuring safety. A bright vest is worn by the skier with a visual impairment to notify other skiers of his or her presence.

Frisbee Disc

In a recent Gallup poll of leisure activities in the United States, Frisbee disc was identified as one of the most rapidly growing sport activities. More people play this sport than other popular sports including tennis, softball, and golf. The reason for this is that the plastic flying disc, the Frisbee, is inexpensive and can be enjoyed by a variety of people of various sizes, shapes, and abilities. Participants with disabilities enjoy the sport because the activity can be easily adapted to their needs.

There are three basic throws used to fly the disc. These are the backhand, underarm, and sidearm throws. The backhand requires that the disc be held in the dominant hand with the thumb on top of the disc, the index finger along the rim, and the other fingers underneath. To throw the Frisbee with the right hand, the student stands in a sideways position with the right foot toward the target. The student steps toward the target and throws the Frisbee in a sideways motion across the body, hyperextending the wrist and trying to keep the disc flat on release. The underhand throw uses the same grip as in the backhand throw, but the child faces the target and holds the disc at the side of the body. The Frisbee is thrown by stepping forward with the leg opposite the throwing arm. When the throwing arm is out in front of the body, the Frisbee is released. The sidearm throw, as the name implies, is it cleanly with one hand. Time is measured from the moment of release to the moment of the catch. The wind plays a big factor in this game with the ideal throw being made directly into the wind with the wind helping to hold the disc aloft. A variation of this game is to throw the disc and do some movement, such as a forward roll, and catch the disc before it hits the ground.

Disc golf is a game patterned after the popular game of golf. The primary difference is that disc golf uses a Frisbee, which must be thrown into a basket-like device (figure 23.12).

Ultimate Frisbee is a game similar in structure to soccer. The game is fast-paced, highly competitive, exciting, and fun to watch.

General Adaptations: Because Frisbee is a sport that uses the arms and emphasizes skill rather than strength, it is an easy activity to adapt for individuals with various disabilities. Users of wheelchairs, for instance, will find that they can perform the basic Frisbee throws without modification. For those with limited strength or paralysis, a Frisbee known as the Quad-Bee has been designed. With this disc, two adaptive clips are mounted where the thumb would be naturally placed. The thumb is placed between the clips so that the player can pick up the Quad-Bee, hold it, and throw. In participating in games such as disc golf, rules may need to be adapted to compensate for the terrain. Some of the holes may be difficult to play from a wheelchair unless the course has been designed to be accessible. In playing maximum time aloft, the rules may need to be modified to provide for the more limited mobility imposed by the chair.

Students with visual and hearing impairments will find Frisbee an enjoyable activity. Discs that emit a sound have been designed so that the individual who is visually impaired can easily retrieve the disc. An activity such as

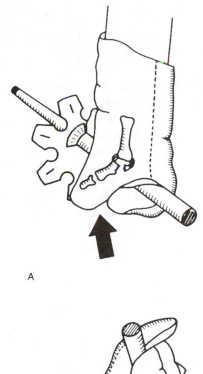

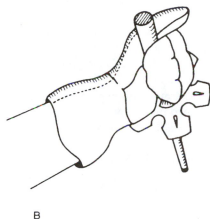

Figure 23.11 (*A*) When force against snow or ice drives the thumb outward as the pick handle comes up into the web space between thumb and hand, a thumb fracture occurs. (*B*) Technique to prevent thumb injury. Thumb is held up and away from snow surface. The hand grip at the pick does not penetrate the web space.

(Courtesy of *Sports 'n Spokes.*)

initiated by holding the disc in the dominant hand with the arm extended to the side. The disc is thrown by keeping the throwing arm straight and releasing the Frisbee with a snap of the wrist as the arm passes in front of the body. Novice throwers are encouraged to keep the disc flat and to work on accuracy.

Several games can be played with the Frisbee. These include *throwing for distance,* which requires that the disc be thrown cleanly to minimize resistance. Usually the backhand throw is best for this game. Contrary to many games that use distance as a criterion, skill and not strength is the critical factor for determining success.

Another popular game is *maximum time aloft.* In this game the objective is to throw the disc into the air and catch

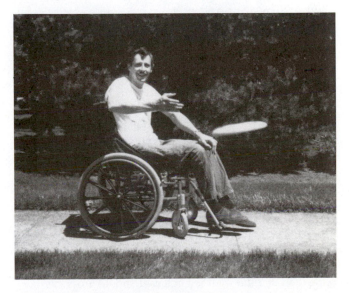

Figure 23.12 Disc golf is a popular sport among users of wheelchairs.

throwing for distance allows youngsters with visual impairments to participate on equal terms with nondisabled peers. Students with hearing impairments will not require modifications other than preliminary cues to ensure that they are watching when the disc is tossed to them.

Golf

Golf is an excellent activity for most individuals with disabilities. The vigor with which the game is played is easily modified for those whose conditions do not permit strenuous workouts. Anyone with extreme limitations can play an adapted form of the game that consists of hitting balls into a golf net. Golf also can be played with considerable success by those who use wheelchairs and crutches. Players with only one arm can become proficient enough to compete on nearly equal terms with other players. Golfers with visual impairments are able to play without modification of the game except for the need for help in locating their golf balls.

It is not necessary to have a full set of clubs in order to play the game. A short set composed of the number-one and -three woods and the three, five, seven and nine irons plus the putter will serve adequately.

General Adaptations: Golf can be played by many people with disabilities without modifications if they have sufficient stamina. Because weather conditions and the hilliness of the course are related to the physical demands of the game, special consideration must be given to these factors if the players are convalescing, have kidney disorders, or have cardiac, asthmatic, or anemic conditions.

Some golfers with disabilities, although able to execute the strokes, are unable to do the amount of walking required by the game. The use of motor-powered or electric carts can solve this problem if the cost of their purchase is not prohibitive. Some carts have been designed with a swivel seat, enabling the golfer with paralysis to turn the seat and hit the ball from a seated position without leaving the golf cart. The height of the seat can be adjusted so that when the golfer addresses the ball, the action of the swing is similar to that used by golfers—back straight and knees flexed—so that the golfer assumes a natural position to address the ball. When carts cannot be provided for them, the players with disabilities will need to restrict their playing to putting or shooting plastic golf balls on an available grassed area, or shooting into a golf cage.

Grip

The most commonly used grip on the golf club is the overlapping grip. To take this grip, the handle of the club is placed across the fingers of the left hand (for a right-handed player) so that the shaft is angled. It should cross the index finger at the second joint and extend up to the lower part of the palm. The hand is then closed over the handle with the thumb on the top of the shaft. The right hand is placed under the shaft, with the little finger overlapping the first finger of the left hand and the left thumb fitting into the palm of the right hand. The thumb of the right hand is slightly on the left side of the shaft.

Adaptations: Students with hand or arm disabilities may require considerable adaptation of the grip on the golf club. Those with finger amputations or hand deformities may need to do extensive experimentation with gripping the club to find the grip that provides the greatest stability. For example, if the thumb is missing on the left hand of a right-handed player, instead of taking a regular grip where the palm of the right hand covers the left thumb, the right-hand grip may be taken so that the palm will come in firm contact with the base of the thumb. The interlocking grip, in which the little finger of the right hand interlocks with the forefinger of the left hand, will bring the fists closer together to make a better contact with the base of the thumb and palm.

Missing fingers other than the little finger on the right hand and forefinger on the left hand require little, if any, adjustment in the grip for a right-handed player. If the little finger of the right hand or the forefinger of the left hand is missing, the next finger may be used to make contact with the opposite hand. In this case the overlapping grip is likely to give greater stability.

A player whose left arm is missing or incapacitated must use golf clubs designed for use by left-handed players; in the use of a missing or disabled right arm, regular clubs will be used in the left hand.

With a missing hand, the remaining arm is utilized to stabilize the club during the swing by placing it against the shaft of the club or against the arm of the hand that is grasping the club. The United States Golf Association (USGA) permits golfers with upper arm amputations to use selected prosthetic devices. The *Amputee Golf Grip and Robins Aids Golfing Device* meet the USGA regulations and make use of a flexible device that attaches to the prosthesis and does not necessitate modifying the club (figure 23.13).

Players with one arm or limited function may find that the affected arm can be used in some manner of grip to stabilize the club in the swing. Experimentation will determine if the affected arm has a functional use in holding and swinging the club or if it will be necessary to rely entirely on one arm.

Stance, Address, and Swing

In all strokes, the weight is distributed equally on the feet, which are spread about shoulders' width apart. The body is held partially bent at the hips with the knees flexed. There are three general types of stances used when addressing the ball prior to stroking it: the open stance, the closed stance, and the square stance. Each type of stance will affect the flight of the ball. In the square stance, both feet are perpendicular to the line of flight of the ball. In the open stance, the

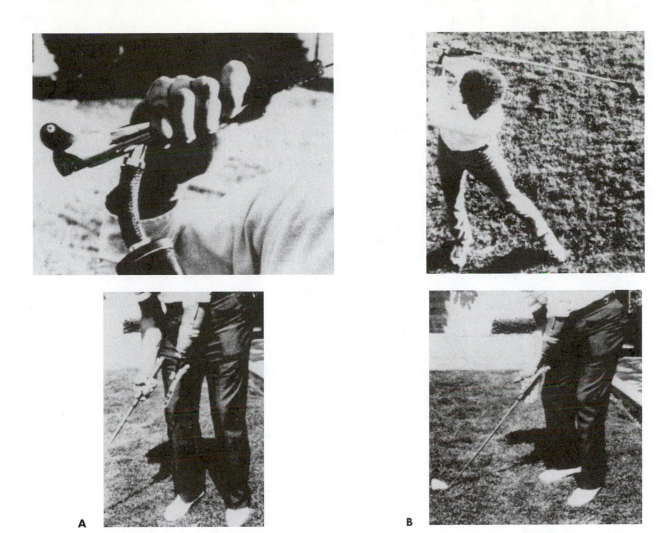

Figure 23.13 *(A)* The *Amputee Golf Grip* is a standardized manufactured product that meets USGA requirements (Courtesy of TRS). *(B)* The *Robins Aides Golfing Device* (Courtesy of TRS).

(As presented in Paciorek, M.J. and Jones, J.A. (1989). *Sports and recreation for the disabled.* Indianapolis IN.: Benchmark Press, Inc., p. 155.)

front foot is placed farther back from the intended flight; this will normally cause the ball to curve to the right. In the closed stance, the rear foot is dropped back, which causes the ball to curve to the left. The square stance is the one most frequently used.

In most shots the ball is placed in position in front of the body in line with the heel of the forward foot. The body is positioned so that the head of the golf club rests behind the ball. The swing begins by a preliminary waggle of the club head to emphasize the point of contact followed by moving the club head, hands, and arms backward in unison. The arms swing close to the body. The left arm is held straight but not rigid. The club head is carried back by rotating the body and shifting the weight to the right foot. The wrists are allowed to cock as the club reaches the waistline. The club is brought over the shoulder to a horizontal position. The head is held still throughout the swing, and the eyes are kept on the ball.

The forward swing starts with a rotation of the left hip; simultaneously the weight is transferred from the right to the left foot. This is followed immediately by a rotation of the body back to its original position. The arms are kept close to the body, and the wrists are held in the cocked position until the hands reach the level of the waist. Then wrists uncock as the club follows its arc to and through the ball. The club head should swing out along the intended line of flight, while the body rotates to permit a complete follow-through of the hands and arms.

Adaptations: For those with limitations in movement, the stance must be adjusted to create the balance necessary for swinging correctly. The distance of the feet from the ball will generally depend upon body structure (length of arms, trunk, and legs). However, players who, because of hip disabilities, cannot bend forward easily at the hips will need to stand closer to the ball or use extra-long clubs.

In the case of leg impairment, the stance may need to be modified. The leg spread may be lengthened to provide a wider base for balance in the case of unilateral weight distribution caused by wearing a brace or by unequal leg lengths.

Players with crutches who cannot stand and swing a club without support can brace themselves on their left crutch, disposing of the right crutch; then, using a left-handed club in the right hand, they execute the swing with one arm. A little experimentation will determine where the left crutch should be placed on the ground to maintain the best balance for swinging; usually this will be achieved by placing the crutch slightly behind and out from the left leg.

Players who cannot maintain their balance on one crutch or who are unable to stand may sit in a sturdy, straight chair with a wide base to prevent tipping for such activities as driving balls into a golf cage or putting on a practice green. Those playing from a chair, as well as those in wheelchairs, must have the chair turned so they are facing the ball, with the left side (for right-handed players) in the direction of intended flight. Extra-long clubs may be needed by some golfers who use wheelchairs in order to reach over the foot of the chair. The wheels of the chair should be locked or blocked to prevent rolling during the swing.

Contrary to what would appear to be the case, a player with only a right arm should use left-handed clubs and one with only a left arm should use right-handed clubs. The former must make the back swing and the swing forward like a nondisabled left-handed player, whereas the latter makes the swing like a right-handed player who has both arms.

Those with leg disabilities who cannot shift the weight readily from one foot to the other will need to cut down on the length of the backswing and secure force more from the rotation of the hips than from the total body, as would normally be the case.

Those seated in chairs or wheelchairs will shift their weight to the right of the buttocks on the backswing if they are right-handed players. The trunk will twist to the right. The head will be over the left shoulder with eyes on the ball at the end of the backswing, as in the regular stance. The head remains stationary in the swing until after contact with the ball. As the swing is brought down, the weight is shifted to the left side and the trunk is twisted back. A follow-through is made, the trunk is twisted to the left, and the weight comes to rest on the left side.

The golfer with visual impairments need make no adaptation of grip, stance, or swing but may be permitted to place the ball on the ground with one hand and with the other, place the head of the club beside it. The stance is assumed without moving the head of the club. The preliminary waggle before stroking is sometimes eliminated because this may throw off the alignment of the club with the ball.

Most errors in stroking are the result of improper movement that causes a change in the radius of the swing. If, then, golfers with disabilities cannot make the necessary correction of their swing, they will need to make some compensation in the swing to overcome the difficulty. If the nature of the disability necessitates keeping the weight on the left leg in the backswing, conscious effort must be made to control the arms so that, at the bottom arc of the swing, the head of the club will come where the ball is resting. A shift of the hips to the right may help to compensate for the inability to shift the weight to the right leg. In cases of an abnormal alignment of the legs, hips, or trunk the position of the left foot cannot perhaps be moved as required. Consequently, the angle of the foot will have to be adjusted so that it will allow the trunk to be parallel to the ball when addressing it.

Putting

The grip for putting differs from the grip used in other strokes. In the most commonly used grip, the whole right hand (for right-handed players) is placed on the handle and the index finger of the left hand covers the little finger of the right hand. The thumbs of both hands run straight down the top of the shaft. The left thumb is in the palm of the right hand, as in the regular grip. After the grip is taken, the head

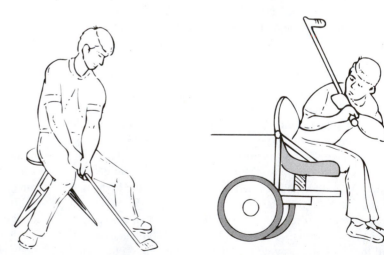

Figure 23.14 Seat supports for golfers with balance difficulties and/or lower extremity impairments can be portable or fixed directly to a golf cart.

of the club is placed directly behind the ball and the stance is adjusted to center the weight opposite the ball with the eyes directly above the ball. The ball is stroked by keeping the face of the club perpendicular to the line of the putt throughout the swing. The distance of a putt is governed by the amount of backswing. The club is swung toward the cup, imparting an overspin or roll. The club should follow through for a distance greater than the backswing.

Adaptations: In cases where the thumb on either hand is missing, the forefinger may be substituted for the thumb in taking the proper grip to give stability to the club in the swing. Golfers using wheelchairs may find the use of one arm more effective than both arms in putting. Because the tires may cut into the greens, wide-wheeled chairs should be used; if these are not available, wide boards may be placed under the wheels while on the greens. Precautions against cutting into the grass are not necessary on the fairways or grassed playing fields on which wheelchair players may wish to practice. For additional information concerning golf adaptations for special populations, the reader should review an excellent reference by Owens (1985), *Teaching Golf to Special Populations.*

Roller Skating

Roller skating is an activity that can be enjoyed throughout life. Today, many schools are providing instruction in this activity as part of their physical education curriculum. The use of rubber-wheeled skates makes skating on gymnasium floors possible without harming the floor's surface. Children and adults can continue to skate for pleasure through the availability of public and private roller skating rinks. Individuals with disabilities find this to be an enjoyable experience because of the skill involved and the opportunities for social interaction with peers and adults fostered through participation in roller skating activities.

General Adaptations: Skaters with visual impairments find skating an enjoyable activity but one in which a sighted partner is essential. Generally, the sighted skater will skate behind the individual with a visual impairment to provide verbal cues about when to turn and stop. Some skaters with visual limitations prefer to skate by holding onto the partner's arm or to a short rope held by both skaters. Students with muscular disorders or orthopedic impairments may find it necessary to use a wide, more stable skate to maintain balance.

Start, Glide, Turn, and Stop

When first beginning to skate the most critical phase is learning to maintain balance while standing on two skates. Many individuals accomplish this phase successfully by using a bar or rail to hold on to until they perfect the skill of standing on skates. The glide phase of skating involves stepping with one skate while pushing with the second skate.

During the glide the weight is borne on the lead foot with the upper body leaning forward while balancing on one leg. The second foot comes forward to complete the recovery process of the glide phase and continues forward to initiate a new step with the supporting leg shifting to provide the push necessary to maintain momentum.

Most novice skaters find turning on skates to be difficult at first. The turn is accomplished by stepping with the lead foot at a slight angle in the direction of the turn and shifting the body weight slightly to the same side. As the trail foot comes forward, each successive step is made in the direction of the turn until the turn is complete.

Stopping on skates may be accomplished in several ways. Most beginners prefer to stop by coasting into a wall, railing, or some other support. This primitive stop is subsequently replaced by learning to drag the toe of one foot while maintaining balance on the second foot. To stop quickly, greater pressure is applied to the toe.

Adaptations: For students who have balance problems, several adaptations in roller skating can be made to accommodate their special needs. These include the following:

1. Have students wear only one skate and place a block with a strap on it on their other foot. This adaptation enables the student to get used to the feel of the skate.

2. Increase the skate's friction, thus slowing the wheels, by having students skate on rugs. Indoor-outdoor carpet works well for this purpose. Some carpet outlet stores will donate carpet remnants to schools or provide them for a very reasonable price.

3. Reduce the free wheel roll of the skate. This adaptation can be accomplished by keeping older skates that have defective, rusty ball bearings. Special students will find these skates easy to walk on, permitting them to get the feel of having something on their feet.

4. Use an assistive device such as a bar or chair to help the students maintain their balance while standing on their skates. Coaster wheels can be easily attached to a chair to serve as an effective support while skating.

Ice Skating

Similar to roller skating, ice skating is a skill that requires a great deal of balance and coordination. Although this activity has been recommended for people with disabilities since before World War II, ice skating has not received the attention it deserves. Individuals with physical limitations, in particular, can benefit from this activity because it emphasizes many of the skills associated with the proper alignment used in walking. In 1974, the International Council on Therapeutic Ice Skating was founded in Charlottesville, Virginia, to emphasize the values associated with this experience. For more information about this organization contact the International Council on Therapeutic Ice Skating, P.O. Box 396, Goldenrod, FL 32733.

General Adaptations: Most people with disabilities will be able to ice skate without major modifications. Close articulation with the student's physician and therapist is necessary to determine the appropriateness of ice skating for individuals with certain disabling conditions, primarily cerebral palsy, myelomeningocele, muscular dystrophy, spinal cord injuries, cardiovascular disease, and amputations. Students with visual impairments can be successful at ice skating if paired with a sighted skater. This activity also has been used successfully with students who have learning disabilities, mental retardation, and emotional disturbances.

Ice Skating Techniques

The Oppelt Standard Walking Method of Ice Skating, developed by Kurt Oppelt at Pennsylvania State University, is generally recommended as an effective technique for teaching individuals with disabilities to ice skate (Adams, Hakala, and Oppelt, 1978).

The Oppelt technique uses the following steps (Oppelt and Ward, 1980):

1. Skaters first practice standing on dry land with their skates on. The feet should be parallel, with the blades upright and perpendicular to the floor.

2. Walking on dry land is practiced next. A total walking motion with a pendular swing from the hip over the knee to the feet is used. The blades should be kept upright and perpendicular while walking. As the step is completed, the blade is set down slightly forward and to the side. The position of the shoulders should be directly over the hips with the head erect and eyes looking forward. Arms should be raised to the sides of the body with the hands held waist high, palms facing down. With each step the body should be balanced over the center of the blade to attain the desired edge control.

3. After mastering steps 1 and 2 on dry land, skaters are placed on ice and taught to discover their center of balance while walking forward on ice using the same method as practiced on land.

4. With practice, skaters gain confidence, relax, and begin to walk on the ice at a more rapid pace. Soon they find themselves skating/sliding and picking up speed with each step.

Adaptations: Various assistive devices are sometimes necessary. Students with visual impairments can be aided by a volunteer who gives support by grasping the upper arm and holding the hand of the skater. Students with orthopedic impairments sometimes find the Hein-A-Ken and an outrigger skate aid useful devices (figure 23.15).

Individuals who use a wheelchair can enjoy the sensation of ice skating by using wheelchair runners

Figure 23.15 The Hein-A-Ken is a useful device to help students with disabilities learn to ice skate.

(figure 23.16). This device, designed by the National Capital Commission of Ottawa, can be easily constructed by using steering skis from a snowmobile. The wheels of the chair rest within the channel-like structure of the skis.

Track and Field

Track and field events offer many opportunities for individuals with disabilities to participate on equal terms with their nondisabled counterparts. Some of the events require little or no adaptation for the less disabling types of disabilities; others are readily modified to enable those with more restricted movement to participate. Even those who are prevented by their limitations from entering competition can enjoy the personal satisfaction of achievement in competition against themselves to better their previous time or to increase the distance of their earlier effort.

Track and field events, especially running events, are good activities for general body conditioning, which most people with disabilities need. Although it is not a track event, jogging should be mentioned in this connection because of its popularity as a conditioning activity.

General Adaptations: In some instances the teacher's job will be one of finding an event in which students with disabilities can participate rather than adapting the performance of the skills of the event to their capabilities. For example, those with upper-limb disabilities can participate in running and jumping events; those with lower-limb disabilities are able to participate in throwing events. Students with visual impairments will be able to take part in throwing events without much modification, but some modification will be needed to enable them to participate in the running events. Students who perform track and field activities from a wheelchair may need additional modifications. In order to participate in jumping events, slight modifications in style are necessary for individuals with upper arm amputations.

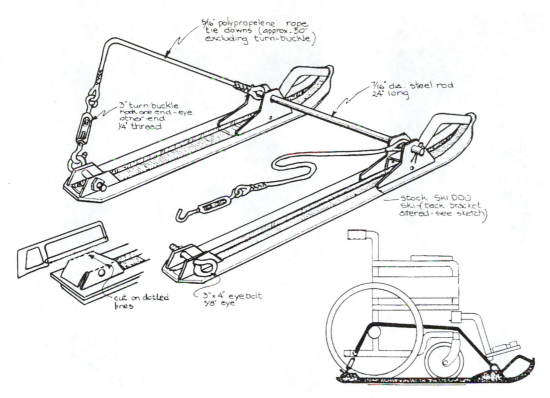

Figure 23.16

Specifications for construction of wheelchair runners. An able-bodied skater pushes the wheelchair; however, the person with disabilities receives the unusual sensation of gliding over a smooth surface.

(Adams, R.C., Daniel, A., McCubbin, J.A., Rullman, L: *Games, Sports, and Exercises for the Physically Handicapped.* (4th ed.) Lea and Febiger, Philadelphia, 1991.)

Running Events

Common running events in track and field meets in school competition include: 100-meter dash, 200-meter run, 400-meter run, 800-meter run, 1500-meter run, 3000-meter run, low hurdles, high hurdles, the 800-meter relay, and the mile relay.

Adaptations: Wheelchair "running" events consist of the 50-meter and 5000-meter events and a slalom race in which the racers must negotiate an obstacle course that tests their strength and ability to maneuver the wheelchair.

Competitive track events for runners with visual impairments include distances from 100 to 10,000 meters as well as marathons. In the dashes, the runner with a visual impairment uses guide wires stretched one-hundred meters along the track without intervening supports; or, as an alternative method of guiding them, a continuous sound is made by someone standing at the finish line to guide the runner in the right direction. In sanctioned meets sponsored by the United States Association for Blind Athletes (USABA), the international caller system is used for athletes with limited vision (B-1 and B-2) in the 100-meter dash. Runners compete individually against the clock, following an auditory signal, usually a number representing the lane in which they are running. If the runner swerves off-course, the number being yelled is changed to represent that the runner is off-course. USABA participants with greater sight (B-3) are not allowed any modifications. For races of longer distance, the runner who is blind runs with a sighted partner using a tethered rope of less than 50 centimeters which is held by both runners. Sighted runners are not permitted to run in front of their partner. Some below-the-knee amputees are now using prosthetic devices designed to improve running technique. Some of the devices such as the Flex-Foot (figure 23.17) help to recreate normal heel-to-toe action thus allowing the serious athlete to maximize performance.

When jogging is used for conditioning by those for whom strenuous activity is contraindicated, the student's physician should be consulted to determine the recommended distance and speed of the jog. Joggers with visual impairments can be accompanied by sighted partners as just suggested for track events. If a partner is not available, jogging in place may be substituted.

Jumping Events

The two most popular events in field competition are the long jump and high jump. However, in some schools the triple jump or hop, step, and jump is also included.

Adaptations: The participant with a visual impairment and the student with a single leg can perform both the high jump and the long jump from a stationary position. The former can also execute the triple jump from a stationary start.

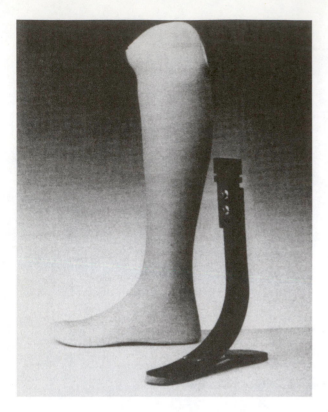

Figure 23.17 The *Flex-Foot* (*left*) stores and releases energy, recreating normal heel-to-toe action for super-active lower extremity amputees who participate in rigorous high-energy activities (Courtesy of Flex-Foot, Inc.). World's fastest amputee Dennis Ohler (right), *Flex-Foot* user, awaits the handoff in the 4 × 100 meter relay at the 1988 Paralympics in Seoul, South Korea (Courtesy of Specialized Sports Unlimited).

(As presented in Paciorek, M.J., and Jones, J.A. (1989). *Sports and recreation for the disabled.* Indianapolis IN: Benchmark Press, Inc., p. 325.)

The blind participant performing the high jump stands at the point of take-off, swings the lead leg back and forth to gain momentum, and then springs from the take-off leg. A jumper with one leg performs in the same way without the swinging of the leg to generate momentum.

Participants missing or without the use of one or both arms must alter the style of the high jump to compensate for the lack of the use of the arms in maintaining balance as they go over the bar. The take-off point for the standing long jump and triple jump would be the start of the long jump or triple jump for athletes with visual impairments or leg amputations.

Throwing Events

The shot put, discus, and javelin are the main field events of most track and field meets.

Adaptations: Athletes who use wheelchairs and whose limitations affect only the lower body can participate in all three of the previously mentioned field events. Each participant must adapt a style of throwing based on personal capabilities. If trunk maneuverability is possible, the participant can use the twisting of the trunk to help generate power in the throw; otherwise he or she must rely completely on the arm and shoulder. In throwing events, the wheelchair must be made secure to prevent its turning over.

Figure 23.18 Shot-putting from a wheelchair requires the assistance of an aide to maintain the stability of the chair.

Throwing events require little modification for participants with limited vision. In the javelin event, they must usually decrease the distance they run before making the throw to a few steps so they will not run over the foul line; or they throw from a stationary position.

Several unique throwing events have been developed for athletes with cerebral palsy. As explained by Paciorek and Jones (1989), it is generally recognized that many individuals with cerebral palsy have severe disabilities requiring a need to create meaningful and unique athletic competition to allow this population to participate successfully. The events include:

Distance Throw: The distance throw involves throwing the soft shot as far as possible.

Soft Discus: Similar to the conventional discus event, a round implement is thrown for distance.

Precision Event: In this event a beanbag is thrown at an eight-ringed target placed on the ground. The objective is to accumulate the highest score by means of six throws.

High Toss: This event involves throwing a soft shot over a progressively higher bar, usually a pole vault bar. Competitors are given three tries at each height with the athlete throwing the highest declared the winner.

Club Throw: The club throw involves throwing an Indian Club for distance.

Kicking Event: This event was designed for more involved individuals with cerebral palsy who have lower extremity dominance. The event consists of two separate activities. In the thrust kick, the athlete places his/her foot on a six pound medicine ball and "thrusts" or moves the ball as far as possible. In the kick, the athlete "kicks" a thirteen-inch rubber utility ball as far as possible.

The United States Cerebral Palsy Association (USCPA) has guidelines regarding these specialized field events and their use with the athlete, depending upon level of ability. For additional information the reader is referred to the USCPA.

The Special Olympics Sports Rules and Medicine Committee (Paciorek and Jones, 1989) has prohibited athletes in Special Olympic competition from participating in several field events. The events include: javelin throw, discus throw, hammer throw, and pole vault.

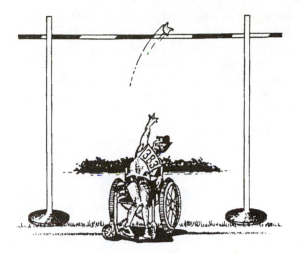

Figure 23.19 The high toss, a unique sport form for individuals with cerebral palsy.

(Adapted from Paciorek, M.J., and Jones, J.A. (1989). *Sports and recreation for the disabled.* Indianapolis IN: Benchmark Press, Inc., p. 102.)

Walking

Walking is an individual lifetime activity with worldwide participants. Noncompetitive walking events and permanently established walking courses can be found in most communities. The American Volkssporting Association conducts periodic events, typically ten kilometer walks, during which the participants walk from checkpoint to checkpoint. Beginning and ending times are established for the day of the event, but the walker may choose any starting time as long as the course is completed by ending time. There is typically a window of six to ten hours when walkers will be on the course. Some participants prefer a solitary walk while others walk in groups and stop for lunch or to sightsee. Avid participants keep a log book and commemorative pins or patches for each walk. The organization will provide log books for a small fee, but it is not necessary to be a member or to keep a log to participate.

In some cities and rural areas the courses are permanently marked, and may be completed at any time. Many of the courses are suitable for strollers and wheelchairs, so the entire family may participate. For detailed information contact the American Volkssporting Association, Suite 101 Phoenix Square, 101001 Pat Booker Road, Universal City, TX 78148, 210/659–2112.

General Adaptations: There are few adaptations which need to be made to assist individuals with various disabilities in engaging successfully in walking events. The course may need to be modified for individuals who use assistive devices such as wheelchairs and walkers. Course and event organizers should identify walking areas that are accessible so that individuals who use assistive devices can participate successfully. Individuals who are obese or have limited vitality due to health conditions will need to monitor carefully their level of activity. A buddy system, in which walkers walk with someone, should be utilized at all times, particularly for those with health impairments.

Individuals who are visually impaired enjoy the opportunity to walk with others. Although many of these individuals walk independently, the opportunity to be with others in group outings is particularly enjoyable.

Walking is a good family and group activity. For individuals who are mentally retarded, the opportunity to be with others while engaging in a healthy activity provides many benefits. Care, of course, will need to be taken to ensure that basic safety practices are followed (e.g., crossing streets on signal, etc.), but the advantages of "moving" and being with others outweighs the inconvenience of planning for any special precautions that may be required.

Summary

Lifetime activities refer to those activities that can generally be played for enjoyment and exercise throughout life. When the activity is one in which a person may participate alone or against an opponent, the activity is referred to as an individual sport. Some of the more traditional popular lifetime activities include archery, golf, bowling, and track and field. Individual lifetime activities that are growing in popularity include boating, bicycling, downhill skiing, roller skating and ice skating. Within this chapter information about these lifetime activities and adaptations that can be made to allow the student with disabilities to enjoy these and similar experiences was presented.

The values of lifetime activities for individuals with disabilities are numerous. In addition to their contribution to physical fitness, engaging in lifetime sports allows the student with disabilities to participate with nondisabled peers. Because the activities are designed for the individual, they can easily be modified for the student with a disability. The modifications can be designed in such a way as to create enjoyable, integrated experiences for participants with and without disabilities. In addition, due to their high carryover value, lifetime activities can be enjoyed for many decades beyond the school years. Lifetime activities and sports, therefore, play a significant role in enhancing the life of the individual with a disability.

Although several lifetime activities were discussed in this chapter, it must be emphasized that there are many activities beyond those presented that can be enjoyed by individuals with disabilities. What was deemed impossible only a few years ago— for example, downhill skiing by those with visual impairments—is now accepted as the norm. The quality of the performances are also improving at a dramatic rate. While some of this is attributed to better equipment, improved technique, and an increased number of participants, much of the improvement is due to the determination and courage of individuals with disabilities, persons who demonstrate by their action that it is *ability,* not disability, that counts.

Selected Readings

Adams, R.C., Daniel, A., McCubbin, J.A., & Rullman, L. (1991). *Games, sports, and exercises for the physically handicapped* (4th ed.). Philadelphia: Lea and Febiger.

Adams, R., Hakala, M., & Oppelt, K. (1978). Ice skating therapy. *The Physician and Sports Medicine, 6*(3), 71–81.

American Alliance for Health, Physical Education, and Recreation. (1970). *Physical education for high school students* (4th ed.). Washington, DC: Author.

American National Red Cross. (1977). *Canoeing* (rev. ed.). Garden City, NY: Doubleday Publishing Co.

Cheatum, B.A. (1975). *Golf* (2d ed.). Philadelphia: Saunders College Publishing.

Cordellos, H.C. (1976). *Aquatic recreation for the blind.* Washington, DC: American Alliance for Health, Physical Education, and Recreation.

Cottrell, J. (1980). *Skiing—everyone.* Winston-Salem, NC: Hunter Publishing Co.

Crase, N. (1986). Springtime snow show. *Sports 'n Spokes, 12*(1), 40–43.

Crase, N., Schmid, R., & Robbins, S. (1987). Pedal power. *Sports 'n Spokes, 12*(5), 27–30.

Evans, V. (1981). *Physical education activities for lifetime sport participation.* Winston-Salem, NC: Hunter Publishing Co.

Hedley, E. (1979). *Boating for the handicapped.* Albertson, NY: Human Resources Center.

Heer, M. (1984). Elements of archery, part I, getting started. *Sports 'n Spokes, 10*(2), 17–19.

Heitman, P., & Roddick, D. (1985). Flying disc sports: A special opportunity for wheelchair play. *Sports 'n Spokes, 10*(6), 13–16.

Hsu, P.Y., & Dunn, J.M. (1984). Comparing reverse and forward chaining instructional methods on a motor task with moderately retarded individuals. *Adapted Physical Activity Quarterly, 1*(3), 240–246.

McCormick, D.P. (1985). Skiing injuries among sit-skiers. *Sports 'n Spokes, 10*(6) 20–21.

McKinney, W.C. (1980). *Archery* (4th ed.). Dubuque, IA: Wm. C. Brown Publishers.

Mood, D., Musker, F.F., & Rink, J.E. (1987). *Sports and recreational activities for men and women* (9th ed.). St. Louis: Times Mirror/Mosby College Publishing.

Oppelt, K., & Ward, M. (1980). Ice skating. *Journal of Physical Education and Recreation, 5,* 32–33, 59–60.

Owens, D. (Ed.). (1985). *Teaching golf to special populations.* New York: Leisure Press.

Paciorek, M.J., & Jones, J.A. (1989). *Sports and recreation for the disabled.* Indianapolis, IN: Benchmark Press, Inc.

Rourke, L., & Heer, M. (1985). Elements of archery, part II, equipment. *Sports 'n Spokes, 10*(3), 11–13.

Rourke, L. (1985). Elements of archery, part III, instruction. *Sports 'n Spokes, 10*(6), 18–19.

Schunk, C. (1983). *Bowling* (3d ed.). Philadelphia: Saunders College Publishing.

Shivers, J.S., & Fait, H.F. (1982). *Therapeutic and adapted recreational services* (2d ed.). Philadelphia: Lea and Febiger.

Special Olympics. (1981). *Basketball: Sports skills instructional program*. Washington, DC: Joseph P. Kennedy, Jr., Foundation.

Special Olympics. (1981). *Track & field: Sports skills instructional program*. Washington, DC: Joseph P. Kennedy, Jr., Foundation.

Enhancing Activities

1. Contact the local school system or community recreation program to identify opportunities for individuals with disabilities to participate in lifetime activities.

2. Obtain one of the resources identified at the end of this chapter and review the article or book to obtain additional ideas for programs and activity modifications.

3. Develop a scrapbook to include information found in popular magazines and newspapers regarding the accomplishments of individuals with disabilities as they participate in various lifetime leisure or sport activities.

4. Select a lifetime activity not discussed in this chapter and develop a paper describing the modifications that could be made in the activity to allow individuals with various disabilities to participate in the activity.

5. Select one of the lifetime activities discussed in this chapter and teach the activity to a student with a disability.

Dual Lifetime Sports

◆ ━━━━━━━━━━━━━━━━━━━━━━━━━━━━━ ◆
CHAPTER OBJECTIVES

After studying this chapter, the reader should be able to:

1 Appreciate the significant role that dual lifetime sports play in the life of an individual with a disability.

2 Identify the values associated with participation in dual lifetime sports for individuals with disabilities.

3 Adapt some of the more popular lifetime sports, including tennis, badminton, table tennis, racquetball, fencing, shuffleboard, and horseshoes, so that individuals with disabilities can participate successfully in these activities.

4 Recognize that through thought and creative effort, unique sport forms such as corner ping-pong and loop badminton can be created for individuals with disabilities.

5 Organize the instructional environment so that students with disabilities can enjoy and benefit from participation in dual lifetime sports.

6 Identify resources, including adaptive equipment, that can be used to help the individual with a disability to participate in dual lifetime sports.

Dual sports are all those games in which one player engages in play with a single opponent or two players engage in play with a pair of opponents. Among the better known and most widely played dual games are tennis, badminton, and table tennis. A lesser known but increasingly popular activity is fencing. Suitable areas are required for tennis, badminton, and fencing, and a special table may be required for playing table tennis. Some other dual games, however, require much less space or special equipment; among these are loop badminton, corner ping pong, horseshoes, and shuffleboard. All can be considered lifetime sports, because all these sports can be played throughout life.

Some proficiency in playing all of these games can be acquired by most students with disabilities, even those with severe limitations. The more simple games can, of course, be learned more easily and require less adaptation. Tennis, badminton, and table tennis require greater physical effort on the part of the learner and, consequently, usually necessitate more adaptations; but the rewards to the participants with disabilities are so great that the games should be included in the special physical education program if at all possible.

The most obvious reward is the physiological benefit to the body resulting from the vigorous workout afforded by playing the dual games. There are other important but less tangible rewards. Because a certain amount of prestige is attached to participation in such games as tennis, playing them gives the individual a sense of achievement and the feeling of being like others. Then, too, the playing of these games opens up opportunities for social contacts with both sexes, an important consideration in selecting activities for students with disabilities.

Organizing the Instruction

Those dual games played on large courts can become strenuous, and because of this they are sometimes overlooked as possibilities for adaptation for play by those whose disabilities limit the area through which they are able to move when playing. It is possible, however, to modify these games to decrease the amount of necessary locomotion.

Most of the other games can be played with few or no adaptations by those with limited movement or by those who use wheelchairs. All of the games discussed in this chapter can be readily modified for those with limited use of one arm and for single-arm amputees; adaptation for these, as well as for those who have a weak shoulder subject to dislocation on the side of the dominant arm, consists of learning to play with the other arm.

Double-arm amputees can play all the games presented here if a functional partial limb remains on one arm to which the racquet or cue may be taped. In taping, padding should be placed between the handle of the equipment and the arm to prevent chafing and to ensure comfort. Enough of the handle should extend up the arm to allow two straps to encircle the arm and handle. The handle may be placed on the inside or outside of the arm, but usually the inside is preferable. The position in which the piece of equipment is taped should simulate that in which it would be held by a nondisabled player. Two leather or cloth straps may be used to hold the handle in place. Taping makes the equipment more secure, but because this cannot be done by double-arm amputees, they may prefer to use straps that they can learn to put on themselves, using the stumps and mouth, or prostheses and mouth. Participants with amputations who regularly play dual sports may want to invest in a prothesis to attach an implement for play. Repeated taping breaks down the skin and can be very time consuming. With the help of a prosthetist and occupational therapist, a safe, effective and easily installed prosthesis may be formed which will permit multiple attachments—a tennis racquet, a badminton racquet, or a foil.

When the disability of the student is such that considerable adaptation of the playing skills is required, as in the case of the double-arm amputee, extensive experimentation is usually necessary to discover the most effective way to perform the skills. Because the process of experimenting is likely to be emotionally frustrating and physically uncomfortable, the teacher should be particularly generous with praise and encouragement during this phase of instruction.

Like the individual lifetime activities, the dual sports require careful organization of class time to permit as much individual instruction as possible. Equally important is planning the use of the facilities to ensure as much playing of the game as possible. This is particularly applicable in games such as tennis and table tennis, where only a limited number of players can be accommodated at any one time. It is important to ensure that instructional time is not wasted by having students wait idly. Construct practice to be performed while waiting for a facility, within the stamina limits of the participants.

In presenting adaptations that can be made for those with disabilities in the sports discussed in this chapter, very brief descriptions of the specific skills are given to enable the reader to make a better comparison of the adaptation with normal performance and so gain a better understanding of the process of adapting skills for participants with disabilities. It is not the intent to provide instruction for learning to perform the skills. Those who wish this information are referred to the books in Selected Readings at the end of the chapter.

Tennis

Tennis is a relatively strenuous game, but the amount of activity can be modified considerably by decreasing the size of the court. This enables those with limited leg movement and those who cannot engage in vigorous activity to play.

A smaller court also allows less mobile players to participate with nondisabled players.

General Adaptations: For individuals whose skills are inadequate to keep the ball in play for any length of time, regulation scoring may be dispensed with. As a substitution the score may be counted as the number of times the ball is successfully returned during a given period of time. The objective in this case is playing the ball so that the opponent is able to return it rather than playing so that the opponent cannot return it, as in regulation tennis. Those who have insufficient strength to hold the racquet at arm's length with a proper grip may choke up on the handle—that is, move the hand up the handle toward the head of the racquet a few inches. Shorty racquets for children and beginners, as well as racquets with a larger face may be used for tennis players with a disability.

Forehand and Backhand Strokes

Basic to both forehand and backhand strokes is footwork. The player must be ready to move in any direction as the ball is returned by the opponent. In returning the ball, the player must place his or her body to the side of the ball to achieve the best possible swing with the racquet. The racquet is swung back while the player is moving into position, with the side of the body turned toward the net while stroking the ball.

In the forehand stroke, the left foot and shoulder are forward. When the racquet head is swung back in the backswing, the elbow is slightly bent. The weight of the body is carried well on the rear foot. A slight hesitation occurs at the end of the back swing. As the swing starts forward, the weight is shifted to the forward foot. The ball should be stroked at about waist height. The wrist is held firm as the ball is hit. After the ball is hit, the racquet continues to follow through, first following the path of the ball and then swinging in a wide arc in front of the body.

The flight of the ball is determined by how the ball is stroked and the direction the face of the racquet is at the moment of impact. With the face tilted upward the ball bounces higher into the air than if it is tilted downward. A ball going to the right or left of the intended flight may be caused by the direction the face was pointing on contact with the ball.

The backhand stroke is similar to the forehand and is used to return balls that are on the opposite side of the body from the arm that holds the racquet. For a right-handed player the right foot and the right shoulder are facing the net. The backswing is brought across the body as the weight shifts to the rear foot. Before the backswing is made, the backhand grip is taken. There is a slight pause at the end of the backswing before the racquet is brought forward in a wide arc to meet the ball at hip level just opposite the forward foot. The racquet follows through in the direction of the ball's flight and then swings wide in front of the body.

Adaptations: By reducing the size of the court for those with some limitations in locomotion or reaction time, the movement to place the body in the proper position for stroking may be achieved in no more than a single step. Reducing the court size even further enables those who cannot make the proper leg movement to achieve a satisfactory stroke by placing the body in the proper position by twisting at the hips.

Tennis players who use wheelchairs and have novice chair handling skills or limited endurance may require a modification of court size. This adaptation permits them to be successful in the activity while focusing their efforts primarily on returning the ball with good forehand and backhand strokes. A reduced court also equalizes the player's opportunities in tennis matches with able-bodied players. As illustrated in figure 24.1, the less mobile player's court is modified to include only one-half of the width of the court while the opponent's court remains the regulation size. This adaptation is a challenging experience for both players and, in particular, an excellent opportunity for the nondisabled player to work on shot selection and accuracy. Another simple adaptation is to allow the tennis ball to bounce twice for players who are less mobile or use a wheelchair.

Wheelchair players with good back and lateral muscle support may elect to use a chair with the back removed or shortened in height. This wheelchair modification permits the player a full range of motion when performing the basic strokes.

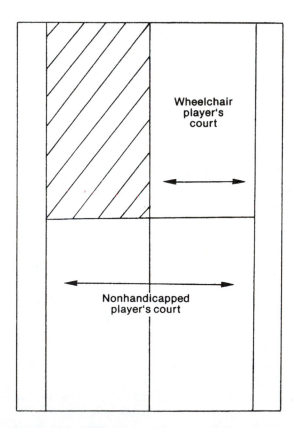

Figure 24.1 Example of a tennis court modified to accommodate the special needs of a player who uses a wheelchair.

Figure 24.2 Polyethylene-type material used to help grip a tennis racquet.

A player who has the racquet strapped to the arm cannot change the position of the racquet for the backhand stroke. Therefore, the ball will be stroked in the same way as in making the forehand stroke.

There have been several modifications employed by players with quadriplegia to assist them in gripping the racquet. These include using an Ace bandage and tape as well as specially designed hand molds that enlarge the handle of the racquet (figure 24.2). One of the simplest methods is to tape the hands to the racquet and use a two-handed stroke to hit both forehand and backhand shots.

Serve

In the serve, the body is turned with its side to the net as in the forehand stroke. The ball is carried in the opposite hand to that which holds the racquet. The ball is tossed at arm's length from the body high enough in the air so the racquet arm is fully extended when the ball is hit. The weight is shifted to the rear foot as the ball is tossed into the air. As the toss is begun, the racquet is swung back behind the head. As the ball drops to the correct height, the weight shifts to the forward leg and the racquet is brought up with the wrist hyperextended. The racquet is brought down upon the ball, driving it over the net into the opponent's appropriate service court. The follow-through is made with complete swing, the racquet coming to rest near the opposite knee.

Adaptations: Individuals who lack coordination and the ability to execute the regulation serve may perform the service by bringing the racquet up in front of the body as the ball is tossed into the air. The ball is stroked as it falls within reach of the racquet head. Served in this way the ball will lack speed and will make a higher arc over the net, but many players are able to learn to serve in this way who may never develop the necessary skill to serve in the usual way.

Players with double arm amputations who have the racquet taped to their arms may serve by balancing the ball on the face of the racquet. The ball is tossed into the air by a short, quick upward movement of the racquet and stroked as it bounces. Players who are quadriplegic will use the bounce drop serve because the overhand serve is difficult due to their limited range of motion. A loose rolling ball is brought under control by placing the racquet over the ball and pressing it to the ground. It is picked up by placing the racquet under the rolling ball and gradually brought under control by bouncing it on the face of the racquet. A stationary ball may be picked up on the racquet by placing the face of the racquet (near the handle) on the ball, drawing the racquet quickly toward the body to start the ball rolling, and slipping the head of the racquet under the rolling ball, which is brought to balance on the racquet face. A loose bouncing ball is brought under control by catching it on the racquet face and bouncing it up and down on the face until it is under control. Velcro placed on the racquet may also be used to assist in picking up the ball.

Players with only one arm serve by carrying the ball in the racquet hand. A regular grip is taken, and the thumb and forefinger are extended beyond the handle. The ball is grasped between these extended fingers and rests against the handle. The ball may be tossed into the air and stroked as described for players who lack coordination, or it may be tossed into the air and stroked as it bounces.

Basic Strokes and Strategy

Volley is the term used for the act of hitting the ball after it comes over the net but before it bounces on the court. A volley is made chiefly in the forecourt position. The smash or kill is a stroke used on a high bouncing ball or a short lob. The ball is hit hard and at a sharp angle so that it will bounce above the opponent's reach. The smash can be made effectively between the serving line and the net. The lob is a stroke in which the ball is hit so that it is lifted above the opponent's head and falls near the base line. It is used as a defensive shot to force the opponent back to the rear court.

In singles, as soon as the ball has been stroked, the player should move to one of two places: the center of the court, three or four feet from the net, or about two feet behind the base line in the center of the court. The net position is taken when it appears that the opponent will have a difficult time returning the shot. The back court position is safer but does not allow the advantage that can be had from handling balls at the net.

The doubles game requires less speed and endurance than singles. The lob becomes one of the most important strokes to keep the opponent away from the net. It is desirable to force one of the opponents far back into the back court so that a net position can be taken by the other two players. Players should always come to the net on each serve to gain the attack. The return of the service should usually be to the deep middle court. In rallying, partners should play parallel positions. The volley and smash are used whenever possible. All lobs should be hit before they bounce, if possible, in order to keep the offensive.

Adaptations: In using one half of a single court with chops and drop shots eliminated, the player stands in the middle of the court about two feet behind the base line. The body can be positioned properly by taking one or two steps in either direction.

In the doubles game three or four players may be used on each side to decrease the amount of movement necessary to get the body or, in the case of a player in a wheelchair, the wheelchair into the proper position to stroke the ball. If three people are playing on a side, one plays at the net, the other two near the base line on each side of the court. Two players are placed on the net if four people are playing on a side.

There are some excellent resources and organizations committed to assisting individuals with disabilities enjoy the game of tennis. Chief among these is the United States Tennis Association (USTA). Through its publications and exposure, the USTA is making a focused effort to bring the game to all populations regardless of ability. The USTA publication, *Tennis Programs for the Disabled*, serves as an excellent guide for individuals wishing to offer tennis activities for individuals with disabilities. The National Wheelchair Foundation, founded in 1976 by Brad Parks, also has played a significant role in promoting tennis for players with disabilities.

Badminton

Badminton is a popular racquet game that is being used increasingly for family recreation in back yards. This is one of the important reasons for promoting it for students with disabilities; having acquired the skills of the game, players with disabilities can take part in one more active recreational activity with family and friends. The game is easily adapted for individuals with various disabling conditions.

General Adaptations: To decrease the amount of movement required by the game, play may be limited to half the singles court or to half the doubles court, using the back serving line of the doubles court as the back line in either case. If half the singles court is used, the players will not have to move to either right or left to return the bird. Only one or two steps will be required to return all possible placements of the bird when half a doubles court is used. To avoid the necessity of movement to and back from the net, the

drop shot may be made illegal. In doubles play, a player in a wheelchair may partner with a nondisabled player on each team. Normally, it is better to place the player with the greatest mobility in the backcourt. In some instances, depending upon the ability of the players, three players (triples play) may be recommended. When using two or three players, the rules can be resolved by the players before the match begins. For example, most will prefer to impose a rule that makes it a fault if the front court player moves to the back court or vice versa.

The reach of the player in a wheelchair can be extended by lengthening the handle of the racquet by splicing a length of wood to the center of the shaft as shown in figure 24.3. To facilitate retrieval of the bird, a strip of Velcro is attached around the rim of the racquet face and around the base of the bird, so that the bird adheres to the racquet on contact and can be lifted up to the hand (figure 24.4).

If a player with a double arm amputation is using a strapped-on racquet, the handle should be taped or strapped to the stump six to eight inches up the arm. The best location must be determined for each individual through mechanical analysis combined with experimentation. Even though a large portion of the badminton stroke is made by the wrist, those with strapped-on racquets can achieve considerable success in playing the game because the racquet is relatively light. Furthermore, a good defensive game can be built around drop shots that are made effectively without wrist action.

Outdoor badminton is never very satisfactory for class work because breezes even of light velocity blow the shuttlecock off course. However, if badminton is scheduled for an outdoor court, the bird to be used can be made more stable in slight breezes by weaving copper wire between the feathers at the base.

Figure 24.3 Splicing the handle of a badminton racquet extends the reach of a player who has limited locomotion.

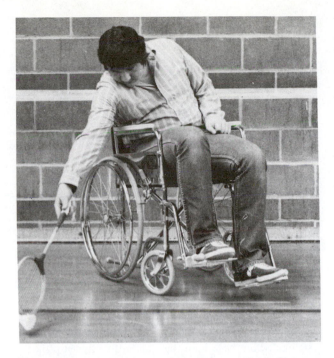

Figure 24.4 Use of Velcro on the racquet and bird facilitates retrieval of the bird.

Two players with limited mobility may work as a team to keep the bird aloft as long as possible. Consequently, instead of attempting to make the opponent miss the shot, they must attempt to place the bird so it can be stroked. Balloons may be used in place of a shuttlecock to allow players with slower movements to ahieve success in keeping the bird aloft.

Grip

The racquet handle is grasped as if one were shaking hands with the racquet. The fingers are spread slightly. When the racquet handle is held toward the body and the racquet head is vertical to the floor, the V formed between the thumb and the forefinger is on top of the handle. The grip is taken so that the heel of the hand is flush with the end of the handle.

Adaptations: Because of the lightness of the racquet, very few players will be unable to control the racquet with the regular grip. However, in extreme cases of grip weakness, the grip may be taken higher on the handle. Although gripping a racquet will be difficult for those who have lost both upper limbs, some have experienced success by using a racquet attached to the remaining limb. The game is modified to encourage the use of drop shots rather than overhead shots.

Serve

The serve is made from the short service line into the service area diagonally across the net from the server.

The right-handed server stands with the left foot forward. The bird is held low in front and to the right of the body by the feathers with the thumb and forefinger. The racquet is swung back with the wrist hyperextended. The racquet is brought forward and the wrist is flexed just before contact with the shuttlecock. The left hand releases the shuttlecock just before it is hit.

Adaptations: Those individuals who cannot use wrist action in serving may be allowed to serve in front of the service line so that the high serve to the back court will be effective.

Players who are unable to place their feet in the correct position for serving may manipulate the body into the proper position by twisting at the hips. Players in wheelchairs serve from the side of the chair. The serving tray (figure 24.5) is an assistive device that enables the unilateral above- or below-elbow amputee to actively use his or her prosthesis when serving the shuttlecock (Adams and McCubbin, 1991). The tray may be held by the terminal device or supported by the use of a cuff that slips over the forearm. With the shuttlecock placed in the serving tray, feathers down, the player can release the bird by lifting and rotating the artificial arm.

When playing doubles, the rules can be modified to allow two attempted serves before a fault is declared. The decision as to where to serve the bird and the service area can also be modified as necessary. For example, some students with limited mobility, including students in wheelchairs, will prefer to serve from the front court.

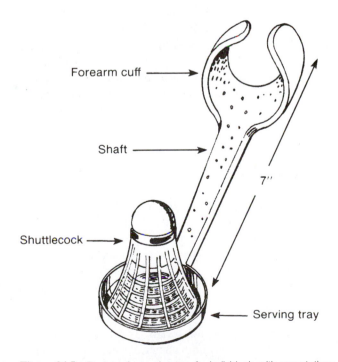

Forearm cuff

Shaft

7″

Shuttlecock

Serving tray

Figure 24.5 Design of a serving tray for individuals with amputations.

Basic Strokes, Flights, and Strategy

The overhead, forehand, backhand, and underhand lift strokes are the basic strokes in badminton. The stroke used depends upon the position of the bird, the position of the opponent, and the flight or shot to be made.

The common flights are the high clear, smash, and drop shot. The high clear is a shot that is driven high and deep into the opponent's back court. The smash is a "kill" shot executed from the overhead position. The stroke is made so that the bird is driven down into the opponent's court. In the drop shot the bird is struck lightly so that it drops immediately after passing over the net.

The flight that is used will depend on the situation. The high clear is used most frequently. It is a defensive stroke used to force the opponent back. It can be used anywhere on the court. The drop shot is used when the opponent is not expecting it and is away from the net. The underhand lift is used only when the bird is falling too close to the net for any other shot. The shot is more effective if the bird is stroked so that it goes to the other side of the court as it goes over the net from where it was played. The smash is used whenever the bird is higher than the net and in the forecourt.

Adaptations: The ability to use different strokes will vary according to the nature of the disability. Those players with limited wrist action will not be able to employ the smash as effectively as they do the drop shot. Strategy for these players will be to use chiefly the high clear and the drop shot. Those who are playing on half a singles court with the drop shot declared illegal will necessarily have to rely upon the smash and high clear. Playing on the modified court, the player stands in the center of the court and merely moves the appropriate foot forward to get into position for a backhand or forehand stroke.

Students with visual impairments will be unable to react to the flight and direction of the bird with sufficient speed to be successful in badminton. An adapted version of the game, in which a balloon with a bell inside is substituted for the bird, has been used with success by some players with limited vision.

Loop Badminton

Loop badminton is an adaptation of badminton developed by Hollis Fait that is played with a badminton shuttlecock, table tennis paddles, and an upright metal loop. It is an active game, requires considerably less space than badminton, and is more adaptable to play by those who are restricted in movement than is badminton. Two players engage in play with the objective of hitting the cock legally through the loop to score.

The playing area is ten feet by five feet with a metal loop twenty-four inches in diameter placed in the center of the area. The loop is strapped on an upright pole such as a badminton or volleyball standard so that the pole bisects the

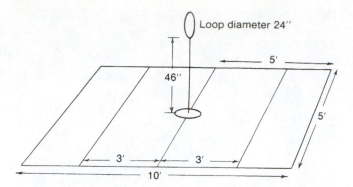

Figure 24.6 Loop badminton court.

loop. The bottom of the loop is forty-six inches from the floor. A restraining line is drawn across the court three feet from each side of the loop (figure 24.6).

Adaptations: The size of the loop may be increased to enable the less skilled to return the bird through the loop successfully. For those who have very poor skills, the loop may be placed on the side of the standard so that it projects from the side and is not bisected by the standard.

If a standard is not available, the loop may be hung from the ceiling with a cord. To keep it from swinging, another cord must anchor it to the floor. For those who are seated either in a chair or a wheelchair while playing, the loop may be placed lower than the recommended forty-six inches.

The loop may be constructed from heavy wire or from small flexible branches. The ends are brought together to form the loop and secured with wire or tape.

Playing the Game

The game starts with an underhand service, as in badminton, behind the end line. The serve must pass through the loop without touching the loop or standard. If the bird touches the loop or standard, a let serve is called and the server serves again. The bird must land beyond the opponent's restraining line and in the opposing court. The receiver can stand anywhere behind the restraining line to receive the serve. The bird must be returned through the loop. After the serve the bird may be struck so that it lands anywhere in the opponent's court, including in front of the restraining line, as long as it passes through the loop. A bird that touches the loop or standard and goes through the loop is considered fair if it is not the serve. The bird must be struck sharply and cannot be carried momentarily on the paddle. If a player touches the loop or reaches through it or around it, he or she loses either a point or the serve. A player may not play the bird while standing in front of the restraining line or hold the paddle in front of the loop to prevent the bird from passing through.

Scoring is as in badminton. Only the server can score a point. If a fault is committed, the serve is lost. The winner of the game is the first player to get fifteen points in a game. When the score has reached thirteen all, the first person to reach thirteen has the option of setting the game to five more points or allowing it to remain at two more. When the score is fourteen all, the first player to reach the score has the option of setting the game to three more points.

Adaptations: If players are playing from wheelchairs or crutches, the serve is made from in front of the service line. If the player is playing from a chair that is not mobile, it is placed in the center of the court. The serve is made from this position. When the players' mobility is limited, any bird that does not land beyond the opponent's restraining line is considered a fault. Those who are subject to chronic shoulder dislocation can usually play loop badminton using the involved arm without adverse effect, since all strokes can be made with the arm held lower than the shoulder.

Table Tennis

Table tennis resembles the game of tennis, but may be less strenuous. Consequently, many kinds of persons with disabilities are able to play table tennis. By learning the skills of the game, they can participate in a popular recreational activity that provides needed exercise the year around.

General Adaptations: For play by students in wheelchairs, the table should be situated in an area with sufficient room to accommodate the movement of the chairs and the table must be high enough to provide adequate knee clearance. The table should be made stationary by nailing or screwing the legs to the floor. This enables players with limited mobility to use the table for support.

A paddle that is useful to players with limited vision may be constructed from a rectangular board 2 or 2½ feet by 1½ feet in size with handles attached at each end. A Space Ball net, which is made of a rectangular frame and netting and designed to be held in the hands, may also be substituted for the regulation paddle.

For novice players with visual impairments, play may be limited to a portion of the table on each side of the net. Paper is placed on the parts of the court not being used so that players will be able to tell by the difference in the sound of the ball striking the surfaces if the ball is good or out of bounds. If a sighted player is the opponent for the beginning player with limited vision, the former may be required to play the full court while the latter plays half the court. Sections of plywood or finely meshed nets attached to standards may be placed along the sides of the table to help keep the ball on the table where it can be more easily located by players with visual limitations.

Another adaptation of the game for those who are blind is playing the ball by pushing it with a paddle so that it rolls beneath a string that is used in place of the net. Boards are attached along the sides of the table to prevent the ball from rolling off the table.

Grip

The tennis grip is the preferred grip for table tennis. The paddle is grasped as if shaking hands with the handle. The thumb and forefinger are placed on either side of the surface of the paddle. The side of the thumb rests gently on the paddle where the handle and the face meet. The forefinger is separated slightly from the rest of the fingers and

Figure 24.7 Sides erected on a table and a Space Ball net, substituted for the paddle, enable a blind player to engage in modified table tennis. Paper placed on her side of the court provides auditory cues.

extends across the face at its base. The rest of the fingers are closed around the handle.

Adaptations: Players with visual impairments using the special paddle described previously will grasp a handle in each hand and hold the paddle in front of the body ready for play.

The pen holder grip, in which the handle is gripped as if holding a pen with the head of racquet pointing down, is preferred by some players who play from a sitting position. For those individuals who have difficulty holding or grasping the paddle, the table tennis paddle can be strapped to the forearm (figure 24.8). The strap-on paddle described by Adams and McCubbin (1991) uses a webbed strap attached to the paddle by a nail or screw. Velcro is sewn on the strap to keep the paddle tight. The player using the strap-on paddle will be restricted to striking the ball with the backhand.

Serve

For the serve the ball is held in the open flat palm of the hand; the fingers must be held straight. The server puts the ball into play by tossing it into the air. The ball is struck with the paddle so that it bounces first into the server's court, then passes over the net and lands on the receiver's side. When the ball is struck in serving, it must be completely free of the

Figure 24.8   Strap-on paddle.

serving hand. At the moment of impact the ball must be behind the end line and between the side lines (if they were extended beyond the end line).

Adaptations: Players who are on crutches and use the table for support are allowed to serve in front of the end line if it is necessary to maintain body balance. Players with one hand serve by grasping the ball between the extended forefinger and thumb after the grip has been taken. The ball is tossed into the air and served either before or after it bounces. The serve by a single-armed player with taped-on paddle is accomplished by balancing the ball on the face of the paddle and then tossing it into the air with an appropriate movement of the paddle. The ball is stroked after it bounces. Beginners may be permitted to hit the ball over the net without its bouncing again; skilled players may be required to allow the ball to bounce on their side of the table after it is hit and before it passes over the net.

A ball can be picked up on the face of the paddle by placing the face of the paddle on the ball. The paddle is then drawn quickly toward the player. In the same movement, the paddle is slipped under the rolling ball, which is brought to balance on the face. If the ball is resting on the table, it may be picked up by pushing it close enough to the edge of the table to be reached by the player's head. The paddle is placed parallel with the table and the ball rolled onto its face with the forehead. The ball may be carried by pressing it between the forehead and the paddle.

Players with visual impairments who use the special paddle may start the game by gently tossing the ball over the net to the opponent.

Individuals whose ability to use the upper arms is limited will find it easier to throw the ball upward from the palm of the free hand or bounce the ball on the table before serving. Both of these adaptations are permitted in wheelchair table tennis competition for players in the quadriplegic classes.

Forehand and Backhand

The forehand is employed for all balls that are driven more than one foot to the right side of the player (for right-handed players). As soon as it can be determined that the ball is going to land so it can be played by a forehand stroke, the backswing is made: the paddle is brought to the right side about table height, the wrist is slightly hyperextended, and the paddle is held so that the handle is parallel to the table and the head faces the right. As the swing forward is made, the weight shifts to the left foot. The paddle is brought forward and upward to strike the ball at its highest bounce. If top spin is desired, the face of the paddle is slanted slightly downward as it makes contact with the ball and is dragged over its top. In either case the paddle follows through forward and upward.

The backhand is used on balls that bounce on the left side of the body, in front of the body, or within one foot of the right side of the body (for a right-handed player). The paddle is turned so that the opposite face from that used in the forehand is facing the ball. If the ball is on the left side of the player, the arm crosses the body. If the ball is in front or not over one foot from the right side, the paddle is held in front of the oncoming ball. In all cases the head of the paddle points to the left and the handle is parallel to the ground. The backswing is very short, but the wrist is flexed to add power to the stroke. The backswing should bring the paddle in front of the approaching ball slightly above table height. The paddle is brought forward and upward; at the same time the wrist is hyperextended to meet the ball at the height of its bounce.

For a forehand or backhand chop the paddle is held above the point where the ball will reach the height of its bounce. With the paddle tilted slightly upward, the head is dragged downward on the ball as it is hit forward.

Adaptations: Beginners and those who have difficulty in making coordinated arm movements will depend chiefly upon forehand and backhand strokes without spin. If the paddle head is not dragged on the ball, the tilt of the paddle face will dictate how high the ball will go into the air. A player who consistently knocks the ball into the net will need to tilt the face up, whereas one who knocks the ball too high into the air will need to tilt it down.

The player with a visual impairment who is using the two-handled paddle will hold the paddle in front of the body with both hands and move it to the right or left upon hearing the ball bounce. If the ball consistently goes into the net, the player will need to tilt the face of the paddle upward. Conversely, if the ball bounces too high, the board must be tilted downward. Beginners should be encouraged to bounce the ball high to make its return easier.

Some individuals with limited strength due to disabilities such as muscular dystrophy will find the use of a ball-bearing feeder arm support (figure 24.9) helpful. This device allows for a full range of motion while providing support and reducing fatigue so that the player with limited strength can play for a longer period of time.

Playing the Ball

After moving to play a ball, the player should return to a position near the center of the table two to four feet (depending upon ability to play the ball) from the end line. The weight should be carried on the balls of the feet, and the knees should be slightly flexed so that the body may move readily in either direction to play the ball. The ball cannot be hit until after it bounces in the receiver's court, so it is undesirable to be too close to the table as this makes it difficult to return a hard-hit ball that bounces off the table.

Adaptations: The player in a wheelchair will keep the center position as just described but will stay closer to the table. One hand is placed on the rim of the wheel to maneuver the chair into position to play the ball. Some players

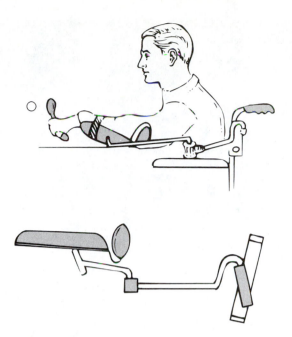

Figure 24.9 The arm support moves freely through use of a ball-bearing mechanism.

prefer office chairs with free-rolling casters to wheelchairs because they are more maneuverable.

A fault is not called if a player with a visual impairment inadvertently holds the two-handled racquet in such a way that the ball is struck before it bounces. However, if there is intent to hit the ball, the act becomes a fault. The width of the playing surface should be reduced for players who, due to their disability, move slowly from one side of the table to the other. This modification will force their opponents to hit the ball in the center of the table thus encouraging longer rallies and more equitable competition. This technique has been used successfully with students who have visual impairments or spastic hemiplegic cerebral palsy.

Racquetball

The popularity of racquetball as a recreational activity has grown tremendously in the past two decades. Racquetball, a variation of handball and paddleball, is also gaining popularity as an activity for individuals with disabling conditions. The National Wheelchair Racquetball Association (NWRA) and its sponsorship of clinics as well as regional and national competition has done much to help promote the sport of racquetball. Racquetball, unlike paddleball or handball, uses a stringed racquet which allows for early success in contacting and placing the ball. As additional racquetball courts and facilities become accessible it is probable that more and more individuals with disabilities will participate in this activity.

Figure 24.10 Integrated table tennis player in a wheelchair.

Playing Equipment and Area

The equipment for the game of racquetball consists of a racquet, usually with a lightweight metal or plastic frame, a specially designed ball about the size of a tennis ball, and goggles to prevent eye injuries.

Racquetball is normally played on a court with hardwood floors and four smooth walls constructed of plaster, tile, concrete, glass, or brick. The court should measure twenty by twenty by forty feet. The game also can be played on a court with one wall. The length of the one-wall court is thirty-four feet with the wall measuring sixteen feet high and twenty feet wide.

Playing the Game

A racquetball match consists of the best two of three games. The first player or team to score twenty-one points wins a game. The game is begun by a serve from within a designated service zone. In serving, the ball must be bounced on the floor and struck on the rebound from the floor. The receiver of the service must stand five feet behind the short line on the court. After the ball has been served, the opposing side makes a legal return by striking the ball on the fly or first bounce, causing it to hit the front wall before hitting the floor. The ball may hit ceiling, back wall, and either one or both side walls before it hits the front wall. The serving and receiving sides alternate in attempting to make legal returns until one side fails. If the serving side fails, it scores an out; if the receiving side fails, a point is scored for the server.

The game may be played by two (singles), three (cutthroat), or four (doubles). In cutthroat the players alternate returning the ball where as in doubles the teams alternate.

General Adaptations: Individuals with limited or restricted mobility enjoy racquetball if the rules are modified. The NWRA allows two bounces between returns for wheelchair players and multibounces for players who are quadriplegic. Allowing two bounces between returns is suggested for novice players or those with limited mobility. In addition, a rule can be imposed that the ball may only be played off the front wall. This will allow the novice wheelchair players, in particular, to experience early success. Integrated doubles with players (disabled and nondisabled) forming a team encourages cooperative play and allows the player with a disability to be responsible for a smaller area of the court.

Players who have mental retardation will benefit from the use of an oversize racquet similar to those used by some players in tennis. The handle of the racquet can be modified by reducing the length of the shaft.

Using a softer, larger ball such as a Nerf ball or tennis ball will also benefit some players with a disability. The Nerf ball will require less force to hit and will move at a slower rate.

While players with visual impairments will have difficulty with a quick action game such as racquetball, some will be able to play the game depending upon the amount of residual vision. Efforts should be made to use a yellow or orange ball so that the contrast from the white wall may be as dramatic as possible. Because of the speed at which the ball travels, the student's ophthalmologist should be consulted regarding the potential of additional eye damage. While protective goggles should always be worn, some may not offer sufficient protection.

While most players with hearing impairments enjoy racquetball without modification, care must be exercised to avoid serving or hitting the ball when the hearing impaired player is not ready.

Serve

In the serve the ball is dropped with the nondominant hand and hit on the return bounce from the floor. The position of the player when the ball is bounced prior to the serve is with the nondominant shoulder and foot at right angles to the front wall. As the ball is served, the player steps with the opposite foot, extends the hand with the racquet to the side, contacts the ball, and follows through with the racquet passing in front of the body. The server may elect to hit the ball with power, use a high lob serve, or position the ball so it caroms off the front wall to one of the side walls.

Adaptations: The recommended serve for the novice player is to concentrate on making good, firm contact with the ball. Players with only one arm will drop the ball with their racquet hand and, if necessary, play the ball on the second rather than the first bounce. Some prefer to balance the ball on the racquet before dropping the ball for the bounce and subsequent serve.

Players using wheelchairs will serve with the chair facing the wall at an angle. The ball may be dropped with either the serving or nonserving hand. There are many variations that can be used depending upon the functional ability of the player. For example, similar to table tennis, some players may need to have the racquet strapped to the hand for additional support and stability.

Strokes

There are three basic strokes used in racquetball—the over arm, sidearm, and underarm. With the overarm stroke, the body position is very similar to that used when throwing an overhand fast ball. The arm swings back so that the racquet begins the stroking action from behind the ear. In reaching high for a ball, the arm is usually held almost straight while stroking. A quick wrist snap is desirable.

The sidearm stroke is similar to the sidearm motion used to throw a ball. If possible, the foot opposite the racquet side should be in front and turned toward the front wall.

The underarm stroke is similar to that used in tennis when reaching for a low shot. This stroke is not used very much in racquetball play because many players prefer to hit low shots by bending at the knees and using the sidearm stroke.

Adaptations: In racquetball, the use of the wrist to impart speed to the ball is critical. For some players with impairments in the upper extremities, primary effort must be given to proper position and placement on the court so that the need for quick reaction shots that require a lot of wrist action will be reduced. Some may have to accept that their game of racquetball will be a game of straight, forward contact shots rather than attempts at shots where the ball is played at various angles off the wall. Players in wheelchairs should maintain a position in the center of the court, eight to ten feet away from the back wall.

The underarm stroke will be very helpful in the overall game of those who play from a wheelchair. Whereas ambulatory players are able to bend at the knees and hit low shots with a sidearm stroke, this is not always possible for the player in a wheelchair. The underarm stroke can be used effectively to keep the ball in play and occasionally to drive the opponent back to retrieve a high lob.

Corner Ping-Pong

Corner ping-pong was developed at the University of Connecticut by Fait for use in the special physical education program by those who are limited in movement of the legs. The game utilizes the skills of table tennis and might be used as a practice drill as well as an adapted game.

Playing Area and Equipment

A corner area with smooth walls for a height of six feet by six feet on each side of the corner is needed. The floor and wall markings are shown in figure 24.11. Table tennis paddles and ball are used.

Adaptations: If smooth walls are not available, plywood may be cut the required size and placed over rough walls or attached to the floor to create a corner for playing. To decrease the amount of movement required of the players, the court size may be reduced, with the size of the wall surface kept in the same proportion to the floor area.

Playing the Game

One player stands on each side of the center line. The ball is dropped by the server and stroked against the floor to the forward wall. The ball must rebound to the adjacent wall, then bounce onto the floor of the opponent's area. If the server fails to deliver a good serve, one point is recorded for the opponent.

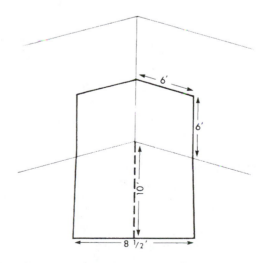

Figure 24.11   Corner ping-pong court.

The ball may bounce only once on the floor before the opponent returns it. The ball must be stroked against the forward wall within the opponent's section of the playing area so that the ball rebounds to the adjacent wall and onto the floor in the server's playing area. Failure to return the ball is scored as a point for the server.

Scoring is similar to table tennis. Each player gets five serves. A ball that is stroked out of bounds is scored as a point by the other player. Game is twenty-one points, and the winner must win by two points.

Adaptation: To decrease the speed of play, the served ball is required to strike the floor before it hits the wall. In each subsequent play, the ball must be hit so as to strike the floor first before it hits the wall.

Fencing

Fencing, a sport long popular in European countries, has received considerable attention in the United States during the past few years. Many individuals with disabilities have found this activity to be enjoyable and beneficial to their long-term physical and motor fitness needs. Additionally, some recognize fencing as an ideal activity for tension release.

General Adaptations: The most striking adaptations made in the sport of fencing for individuals with disabling conditions relates to the design of the fencing court. Participants using wheelchairs find, for instance, that a circular court with a twenty-foot diameter is preferable to the traditional six feet by forty feet rectangular court design. In international competition, participants fencing from wheelchairs are required to remain in a stationary position and execute movements by rapidly extending and retracting the sword arm. Movement of the wheelchair for defensive maneuvers is not permitted. Fencers with visual impairments will require the use of a smaller, narrower court equipped with a special guide rail.

Fencing Technique

The objective of fencing is simply to score by touching the opponent's target and to avoid being touched. This requires that the fencer learn basic offensive and defensive techniques. Offensive moves include the lunge, which is a forward movement in which the front foot advances forward and the back leg straightens; the thrust, which is a smooth but rapid extension of the sword arm to a position higher than the shoulder; a disengage, which consists of moving the blade's point around the opponent's guard into an open line; and a beat-lunge, which is a sharp slap on the opponent's blade in an effort to deflect it, followed by a thrust or lunge. The primary defensive technique is known as a parry. This is a defensive motion made to deflect the opponent's blade by a direct or circular movement of the blade.

Equipment and Rules

The basic equipment used in fencing is the sword. There are three different types of swords: foil, saber, and épeé. Each sword consists of several parts, including the tip, blade, guard, handle, and pommel (figure 24.12). Fencers also use a face mask, jacket or vest, and gloves.

Prior to the actual start of the match, the referee is responsible for calling certain commands. These commands, known as *distance point, salute,* and *en garde,* are given prior to the command *fence.* In the distance point, the

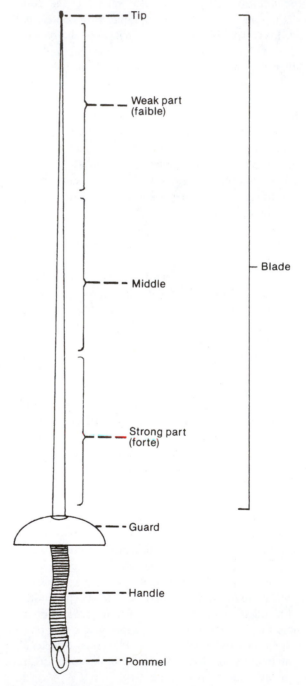

Figure 24.12 Parts of the French foil.

fencers stand at right angles to each other. With the foil arm straight, each fencer raises the foil so that the tip touches the guard of the opponent. The command *salute* requires that each fencer bring the tip of the foil up to chin level in front of the face mask in a salute position. The last position taken prior to the command to fence is the en garde position. In this position, the foil arm is raised until the hand is level with the chest with the fencers' foils crossed.

In each match five points are needed to be declared the winner. Points are awarded for making a direct hit upon the opponent's jacket. If a player makes an illegal move such as hacking (bringing the foil above shoulder level and slicing down on the opponent) a point is awarded to the opponent. Players must also stay within the boundary lines. Two warnings are permitted before awarding the opponent a point for infractions of the boundary lines.

Adaptations: Many individuals with disabilities will participate successfully in this activity without major modifications. Students with mental retardation, hearing-impairments, learning-disabilities, and behavior disorders will require only well-designed and individualized instruction. Care also will be necessary to ensure that matches do not become opportunities for emotional outbursts potentially harmful to others.

Students in wheelchairs will require extra practice time and teacher's assistance to learn how to use the trail hand (opposite the hand with the foil) to move the chair forward and backward rapidly. This is obviously an important skill and one that should transfer to other settings in which the chair must be moved in and out of small, awkward places.

Orr and Sheffield (1981) recommend that the épée (dueling sword) be used rather than the foil or saber with persons who have disabilities because the latter swords require more leverage and leg strength. The rules governing épée fencing also can be easily modified for fencers with disabilities. In épée fencing, the whole body is regarded as a target and a point is awarded to the fencer who touches first. Awarding points is thus very easy and does not require technical decisions. The same rules used in épée fencing apply to fencers with disabilities with one exception. For students in wheelchairs, touches to the chair are regarded as a floor or wall touch. However, the wheelchair may not be used to shield the target area. A point is awarded after two warnings when this rule is violated. Fencers using wheelchairs also can fence against nondisabled opponents. In this system, the nondisabled fencers attack first, with the wheelchair opponent providing the counter.

Because of the vigorous nature of fencing and the implications of certain conditions such as cardiorespiratory disorders, congenital hip disorders, rheumatoid arthritis, and muscular disorders, consultation with the student's physician about necessary precautions and limitations is essential prior to participation in this activity.

The International Committee on Sports for the Disabled has created special rules and competitive opportunities for athletes with spinal cord injuries and those with cerebral palsy (Paciorek and Jones, 1989). For additional information about various rule modifications, including safety procedures, the reader is referred to the United States Fencing Association in Colorado Springs, CO.

Shuffleboard

Shuffleboard is readily adapted to nearly all kinds of disabling conditions. Like the other dual sports, one of its great values is in the social contacts that it affords individuals with disabilities, whose opportunities for social interaction are so often limited.

General Adaptations: The length of the court may be shortened for those who do not have sufficient strength to propel the disks the total distance on the regulation court. It may also be shortened for students with disabilities who are poorly coordinated, to ensure success in scoring.

A strip of tape placed on the floor to show the direction of the court is helpful to students with visual impairments. By feeling the tape, they are able to locate the court and to adjust their aim accordingly. The doubles game is, of course, preferable for players with limited locomotion. If there are not enough players for a doubles game, singles may be played with opponents stationed at opposite ends. The opponent, in this case, counts the score and returns the disks by pushing them back to the other player for the next turn. Playing the game this way eliminates the challenge and excitement of preventing the opponent from scoring, but it does provide fun and exercise for those whose range of locomotion necessitates adaptation of the game.

Playing the Game

A player in a singles game uses disks of one color only, and in doubles the partners use the same disks of one color. At the start of the game the four disks of each player are put on the side of the 10-off area. Players play the disks alternately from the 10-off area.

To shoot, the player faces the disk, with the head of the cue resting on the court squarely behind the disk, the cue forming a straight line with the disk and the target. The player stands slightly at the side so that the arm is in a straight line with the cue. The cue is grasped in the fist with the V formed by the forefinger and thumb on top.

The delivery is made (by a right-handed player) by taking a step forward on the left foot as the arm with the cue swings forward, pushing the disk evenly and smoothly forward. The head of the cue slides along the floor. In the follow-through the arm is fully extended, with the cue pointing in the direction of the moving disk.

Adaptations: Players using wheelchairs should place their chairs facing the court and slightly to the side so that the arm with the cue can be dropped to the side of the chair to make the shot.

Players on crutches must shift the body weight to the crutch of the opposite arm to free the playing arm to make the shot.

For those seated in straight chairs for playing, it may be easier to move the disks along the 10-off line to put them in the proper position than to move the chair to place the player in the proper position for shooting.

Players who have spastic movements may achieve better results in playing the disk by making several repetitive movements with the cue behind the disk before actually pushing it forward. Players with athetoid movements, on the other hand, have greater success if no preliminary movements are made. They should place the cue behind the disk and push forward immediately.

To simplify scoring for players with cognitive deficits, the score may be based on the number of disks that land within the scoring area of the court; each disk then counts one point.

Horseshoes

Horseshoe pitching is a very old activity that continues to be popular in the United States and many foreign countries. Its continued popularity may well be due to the ease with which the game can be played and enjoyed throughout one's lifetime. The game may be played in two ways, singles and doubles. In singles, one person pitches against another from one stake to the other and back again. In doubles, one player of each team stands at a stake and faces his partner, who is at the other stake. The two opponents standing by a stake pitch against each other, and the shoes are pitched back by their partners.

The only equipment needed to play horseshoes are horseshoes and two stakes driven into the ground forty feet apart.

General Adaptations: Horseshoe pitching is an excellent activity for people with disabling conditions. It is one of the few activities that can be performed from a stationary position. This in and of itself is an attractive feature for students whose impairments interfere with their ability to move easily and skillfully. Students with cardiorespiratory problems also can partake of this activity without modifications.

Shoes and stakes made of rubber or plastic allow students who have limited shoulder and arm strength to enjoy a game of horseshoes. Participating in this game indoors is also possible with the use of the lightweight shoes and stakes.

Grip

Although there are five basic grips utilized for the purpose of pitching horseshoes, the most commonly used, the one-turn, will be described here. With this grip the open end of the shoe is away from the pitcher. The thumb is on top and in line with the right shank (the portion of the shoe from the tip to the curved end). The other fingers are flexed and under the shoe with the index finger extended beneath the right shank to support the weight of the shoe. As the name implies, with the one-turn grip, the shoe makes one complete clockwise revolution before striking the stake.

Adaptations: Students with limited strength in their hands will find the use of a lightweight rubber shoe necessary. Some individuals with limited hand dexterity may prefer a variation in the grip just described. For example, the over-under grip, in which the shoe is held by four fingers extended over the top of the shoe with the thumb underneath, is a natural grip for those unable to extend the fingers.

Delivery

The delivery begins with the pitcher standing with feet together, both hands in front of the body with the arms slightly flexed. The dominant hand should be gripping the shoe properly, with the nondominant hand giving support to the shoe. To begin the delivery the supporting hand is dropped. The pitching hand carries the shoe backward in an arc to a point parallel to the ground. As the shoe nears its height on the backswing, the foot opposite the pitching hand steps forward. The shoe is then brought forward in a downward arc while the foot completes its step. The arm continues its forward movement after the step to approximately a forty-degree angle. At this point the shoe is released and the arm follows through upward and across the body line.

Adaptations: Variations in the delivery approach will be necessary for students in wheelchairs and those who use assistive devices. Horseshoe pitchers who use wheelchairs normally prefer to position their chair so that they are facing the stake. This allows the arm to follow a natural forward and backward swinging motion with the arm parallel to the wheelchair. Students who use walkers and crutches may prefer pitching from a chair rather than standing and using one arm on the assistive device for support.

Because of the motion used in horseshoe pitching, physicians of students with scoliosis or other spinal deformities should be contacted prior to introducing this activity to these youngsters.

Some students with visual impairments will find a sound device, such as a radio, placed parallel to and even with, but safely away from the stake, helpful in determining the distance to pitch the shoe. Many individuals with visual impairments become excellent horseshoe pitchers. The immediate auditory feedback received from a shoe striking or ringing the stake is very reinforcing.

Boccia

Boccia is an indoor version of the Italian game of lawn bowling. Boccia is increasing in popularity because it is an enjoyable activity in which modifications can be made easily to allow individuals of varying ability, including those who are severely disabled, to participate in the activity (Jones, 1988).

Boccia is played in national and international competition by individuals with cerebral palsy. However, the game is used in many recreational programs for individuals with and without disabilities. The game can be played one on one (individual boccia) or three against three (team boccia).

The object of the game is similar to lawn bowling, with a white target ball being thrown onto the court and opponents alternating attempts to get their ball as close to the target as possible. Points are awarded on the basis of proximity to the target ball. Individual boccia is played with six balls per player for four rounds, while team boccia is played using two balls per player for six rounds.

The boccia ball is normally hard and about the size of a baseball. The ball used in international competition for those with cerebral palsy is handmade of leather and slightly smaller than a baseball. This adaptation allows for the ball to be grasped more easily.

The boccia court consists of two areas, the player's boxes and the playing area (figure 24.13). The playing area consists of two parts, the nonvalid target area and the valid target area. Each player must stay completely within his or her box during play.

The player may use various means to release or roll the ball. Most will use a technique similar to that of bowling. The strategy of course is to develop sufficient touch or "feel" to gauge accurately the speed and direction of the throw.

General Adaptations: One of the primary reasons that boccia is increasing in popularity as a sport for individuals with disabilities is because of the many adaptations which can be made in the sport. For example, many participants with limited movement can participate in the sport by using a chute or ramp to aid in releasing and guiding the ball. The ramp can be constructed of various materials and modified to meet the specific need of the player (figure 24.14).

In selecting the best method to throw the ball, several factors should be considered including ability to grasp, release the ball, and see the target. Players with cerebral palsy, for example, might find it most efficient to push or release the ball using the lower extremities (figure 24.15). Individuals who are visually impaired will benefit from having a sound device placed near the target to aid in determining direction and distance. Players with mental retardation

Figure 24.14 Boccia ramps can be easily made from materials found in most local hardware stores.

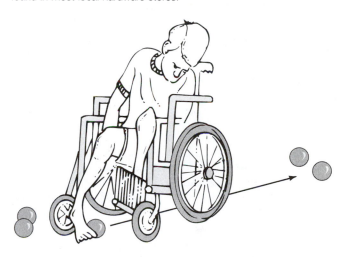

Figure 24.15 A number of cerebral palsy athletes will choose to use their feet to compete in boccia.

will enjoy the activity if the ball and target sizes are modified to increase the probability of success.

Boccia is one of the newer sports that is attracting interest because it allows many individuals of varying ability to participate, with modifications, on equal terms.

Summary

Dual sports are those games in which one player engages in play with a single opponent or two players engage in play with a pair of opponents. Although there are many sports that fit this description, some of the most popular are the racquet sports of tennis, table tennis, badminton, and racquetball. Other popular dual lifetime sports include fencing, shuffleboard, horseshoes, and boccia. The values of lifetime dual activities are numerous. They enhance physical fitness levels, increase opportunities for social interaction, and because they can be played throughout life, add significantly to the overall quality of life.

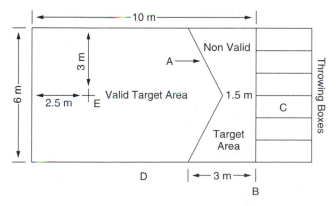

Figure 24.13 Boccia court dimensions. A = First throwing line; B = Throwing line; C = Sidelines; D = Border lines; E = the cross.

Within this chapter the racquet sports of tennis, table tennis, badminton, and racquetball were discussed. Information was also provided about horseshoes, fencing, shuffleboard, boccia and two unique games, loop badminton and corner ping-pong. The intent of the chapter was to offer suggestions and examples of how each of these activities can be adapted to meet the needs of individuals with disabilities. For some sports the primary focus is on the modification of the rules or equipment used to play the sport. Depending on the disability or the sport, the changes can be minor or major. This is also true with respect to the specific adaptations that may be needed in the form or technique used to execute a specific sport skill. Throughout the chapter the primary message is that individuals with disabilities can be successful participants in dual lifetime sports. The instructional effort must be devoted to exploring a variety of possible adaptations to ensure success for all students. In some instances the "best" way has yet to be developed and will require a creative teacher and a patient student.

Teachers also should be encouraged to develop new games similar to the games of corner ping-pong and loop badminton described in this chapter. Activities that are specifically developed for individuals with disabilities can be structured to ensure success, building on individual ability rather than disability. Many nondisabled students find these activities of interest and will want to learn to play them. This will lead to new opportunities for mainstreaming where nondisabled students are challenged to learn an activity in which students with special needs are already comfortable.

Every effort must be made to help students with disabilities benefit from the opportunity to participate in dual lifetime sports. People with disabilities have demonstrated rather convincingly that they enjoy lifetime sports and with training and effort perform very well in a variety of activities. As additional opportunities are created and restrictions such as inaccessible facilities are removed, there is little doubt that more individuals with disabilities will find and participate in dual lifetime sports.

Selected Readings

Adams, R., & McCubbin, J. (1991). *Games, sports, and exercises for the physically handicapped* (4th ed.). Philadelphia: Lea and Febiger.

Auxter, D., Pyfer, J., Huettig, C. (1993). *Adapted physical education and recreation* (7th ed.). St. Louis: C.V. Mosby Co.

Bower, M. (1985). *Foil fencing* (5th ed.). Dubuque, IA: Wm. C. Brown Publishers.

Crase, N. (1976). 40/Love. *Sports 'n Spokes, 2*(2), 5–6.

Crase, N. (1987). Charging the net. *Sports 'n Spokes, 12*(5), 9–12.

Gensemer, R. (1985). *Intermediate tennis.* Englewood, CO: Morton Publishing Company.

Gensemer, R.E. (1985). *Tennis* (3d ed.). Philadelphia: Saunders College Publishing.

Johnson, M.L., & Hill, D.L. (1980). *Tennis.* Winston-Salem, NC: Hunter Publishing Co.

Jones, B.J., & Murray, M.J. (1978). *Softball concepts for coaches and teachers.* Dubuque, IA: Wm. C. Brown Publishers.

Jones, J.A. (1988). Wheelchair boccia. In J.A. Jones (Ed.), *Training guide to cerebral palsy sports.* Champaign, IL: Human Kinetics Publishers.

Kneer, M.E., & McCord, C.L. (1980). *Softball, slow and fast pitch* (3d ed.). Dubuque, IA: William C. Brown Publishers.

Lasko-McCarthey, P., & Knopf, K.G. (1992). *Adapted physical education for adults with disabilities* (3d ed.). Dubuque, IA: Eddie Bowers Publishing, Inc.

Miller, A.G., & Sullivan, J.G. (1982). *Teaching physical activities to impaired youth.* New York: John Wiley and Sons, Inc.

Mills, R. (1979). *Badminton.* New York: Sterling Publishing Co. Inc.

Mood, D., Musker, F.F., & Rink, J.E. (1991). *Sports and recreational activities for men and women.* St. Louis: Times Mirror/Mosby College Publishing.

Orr, R.E., & Sheffield, J. (1981). Adapted épeé fencing. *Journal of Physical Education, Recreation, and Dance, 52*(6), 42, 71.

Paciorek, M., & Jones, J. (1989). *Sports and recreation for the disabled.* Indianapolis, IN: Benchmark Press, Inc.

Pelton, B.L. (1986). *Tennis.* Glenview, IL: Scott, Foresman and Company.

Sklorz, M. (1979). *Table tennis.* New York: Sterling Publishing Co., Inc.

Smith, F.J. (1980). *Physical education activities handbook.* Winston-Salem, NC: Hunter Publishing Co.

Thompson, G. (1984). Tennis tips: Quadriplegic tennis? You bet!!! *Sports 'n Spokes, 10*(2), 8.

Verner, B. (1985). *Racquetball: Basic skills and drills.* Palo Alto, CA: Mayfield Publishing Company.

Enhancing Activities

1. Conduct a survey of the public and private recreational and sport facilities within the community to determine where individuals with disabilities can participate in dual lifetime sports. Attention should be directed toward the management philosophy of the facility director and issues such as accessibility.

2. Obtain one of the resources identified at the end of this chapter and review the book/article for additional ideas concerning activity adaptations.

3. Select a dual lifetime sport not discussed in this chapter, such as handball, and develop a paper describing the activity and suggestions regarding modifications for persons with disabilities.

4. Select one of the dual lifetime sports discussed in this chapter and with the assistance of your instructor teach the activity or some phase of the sport to a youngster with a disability.

5. Locate a wheelchair and use it to play your favorite dual lifetime sport. Develop a list of the modifications you used while playing the sport. Describe how your list might be similar/different to that of an athlete who regularly uses a wheelchair.

CHAPTER

25

Team Games

◆ CHAPTER OBJECTIVES ◆

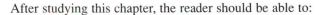

After studying this chapter, the reader should be able to:

1 Appreciate the value of team games, specifically basketball, softball, football, soccer, volleyball, and floor hockey, to the overall development of individuals with disabilities.

2 Identify various modifications that can be made in the popular team games to accommodate the needs of students with various disabling conditions.

3 Recognize some of the team games such as wheelchair basketball, wheelchair softball, beep baseball, goal ball, and quad rugby that have been developed for specific disability populations.

4 Adapt team games so that students with disabilities can safely and successfully participate with nondisabled peers.

5 Organize the instructional environment so that positive learning experiences are created in team games for students with and without disabilities.

6 Identify other resources that can be used to provide valuable information regarding team games for individuals with disabilities.

Team games are important in the physical education program because they provide big-muscle activity necessary for developing and maintaining a desirable level of physical fitness. Because students with disabilities are likely to have a low level of physical fitness, their participation in team games is especially important. Team games are important, too, for the opportunities they provide students to demonstrate their ability to contribute to the group effort. Their fellow team members are likely to gain an understanding and respect for people with disabling conditions they would not otherwise develop. Individuals with impairments are likely to acquire greater confidence in their abilities and to accept themselves as they really are. That some of the team games are among our most popular spectator sports is still another reason to include team games in the curriculum; in learning to play them, students become more intelligent spectators. Students with disabling conditions should also be provided the opportunity to participate in competitive athletic experiences. This right was guaranteed by the passage of Section 504 of the Rehabilitation Act of 1973. A discussion of the rationale and efforts to organize competitive sport activities for athletes with disabilities is presented in chapter 30.

Organizing the Instruction

Team games, because of their vigorous nature, cannot be adapted to all types of players with disabilities. However, even though the game as a whole may not be adaptable, specific skills can be adapted for play by nearly all individuals with special needs. For example, those whose locomotion is restricted because of leg disabilities may still engage in popular activities, with modifications, such as basketball and soccer.

In the school situation, then, the teacher may plan to include students with disabilities in the drills that are used for improving the skills of the team sports. Some slight modifications may need to be made, as, for example, in a drill requiring rapid movement from one position to another; students who are incapable of moving rapidly may modify this phase of the drill and continue on to their place in line.

Unless severely restricted in arm and leg movements or greatly lacking in physical fitness, students with disabilities also may be included in the lead-up games and in the actual competitive play of the team sports, subject to the adaptations required by the physical condition. Frequent rest periods should be planned because the strenuousness of competitive team play may tax even the most physically fit player, and, as noted elsewhere, youngsters with disabilities are likely to be lacking in physical fitness. For students unable to participate in these phases of the class instruction, the teacher may plan continued work on the drills. The drills should be varied whenever interest wanes. Injecting a competitive element into a drill makes performing the drill more interesting and often more satisfying to students with impairments, because it

provides them with a tool for evaluating their progress. Rather than drilling on passing by throwing the football to a receiver, for example, a competitive element may be introduced by drawing a target on the field at which the thrower may aim in the hope of scoring a bull's-eye. Cooperative activity also can be used to enhance skill development; for example, in softball the pitcher can be required to pitch the ball so that the opposing batter can hit it.

If students will be working on drills and drill-like games while the teacher is engaged in instructing and supervising the rest of the class in team play, the teacher must organize student helpers to retrieve balls and otherwise assist players who cannot work entirely on their own. No student should be allowed to serve so frequently as a helper, however, that he or she is deprived of a personally beneficial physical education experience.

In presenting adaptations that can be made for those with disabilities in the sports discussed in this chapter, very brief descriptions of the specific skills are given to enable the reader to make a better comparison of the adaptation with nondisabled performance and so gain a better understanding of the process of adapting skills for participants with disabilities. It is not the intent to provide instruction for learning to perform the skills. Those who wish this information are referred to the books in Selected Readings at the end of the chapter.

Basketball

Because basketball is a strenuous game requiring speed and endurance, some modifications in the activity will be required for students with disabilities. For those with limited stamina or whose activity patterns must be restricted, use only a portion of the basketball court. The number of players per team may also be increased to reduce the physical demands upon individual players. If the game is too strenuous for some individuals, even with these modifications, they usually can engage in drills and games of passing, catching, and shooting.

General Adaptations: The baskets may be lowered and enlarged for modified activities designed for students with restricted arm movement and for students who must shoot from a sitting position in a chair or wheelchair. A light string hung from the back side of the hoop so that it is low enough to be reached with the hand and yet high enough to be above the head is of great assistance to the player with a visual impairment in determining the location of the hoop before shooting the ball. A bell attached to a length of twine may be hung from the hoop so that it will ring when the ball enters the hoop and notify the shooter of a successful basket. The rules of basketball may need to be modified to accommodate the special needs of some students. For example, children with severe coordination problems should be allowed three or even four steps between dribbles. As will be discussed later, creative rule modifications have been developed for players in a wheelchair.

Catching the Ball

In catching, the fingers are spread to receive the ball. When catching a high ball (above the waist), the thumbs are together. If the ball is below the waist, the little fingers are together. The ball is caught on the cushions of the finger tips, not with the heels of the hands. As the ball is caught, the arms give with the ball as the elbows are flexed. The ball is brought back toward the body. The eyes follow the ball throughout the catch.

Adaptations: A player with one hand may catch the ball by trapping it between the lower portion of the arm and the body, with the upper arm cradling the ball as it is brought into the body.

Those on crutches may find it easier to bring the ball to the side of the body rather than toward the body when catching the ball, as this permits balance to be maintained more easily.

Players with limited vision will catch the ball by extending both arms forward, with elbows slightly flexed. The passer must throw the ball into the open arms. The ball is cradled in the arms as the fingers come in contact with the ball to control it. Students who have difficulty learning this skill might find it helpful if a foam ball or rubber ball is used instead of a basketball.

Passing

The passes most commonly used are the two-handed chest pass, two-handed bounce pass, and overhand pass.

In the two-handed chest pass, the ball is brought chest high with the elbows flexed. The arms are extended sharply and the ball is released from both hands with an outward snap of the wrists. As the pass is made, the weight is brought forward.

The two-handed bounce pass requires that the ball be held with both hands on the sides of the ball with the thumbs up and fingers spread. The ball is brought to the chest and released by extending the arms and wrists, and turning the palms downward and outward. As the ball is released the player should step in the direction of the pass with the non-dominant leg. The ball should be aimed at a spot approximately half the distance to the teammate.

For the overhand pass, the ball is brought back behind the shoulders about head high, with one arm, as in throwing a baseball. Then the arm is brought forward, and the ball is released with an abrupt snapping of the wrist. The ball should be thrown without imparting a spin, because a spin makes it difficult to catch.

Adaptations: Players with one arm will make their passes with one arm. In long passes the overhand pass will be used, whereas in short passes the ball will be thrown underhand.

Players using crutches will have to have a greater wrist snap than others in making the two-handed chest pass. Generally the most effective pass for those on crutches will be the one-hand pass.

The easiest pass for the player using a wheelchair is the two-handed chest pass. The basic technique is the same as used by any player with the exception that the distance the pass can be thrown is shorter.

In the early stages of learning this skill it may be necessary to use a different type of ball, such as a rubber playground ball, and to physically guide the student so that he or she can get a feel for the proper execution. In the bounce pass, a mark on the floor halfway between the player and a teammate will provide an effective target for where to bounce the ball.

When passing the ball to a player with a visual impairment, the name of the student should be called before the pass is thrown. This information will help the player prepare for the pass by properly positioning the body. The bounce pass is effective with students who are visually impaired because the sound of the bounce provides an additional auditory cue.

Shooting

The two shots most used are the one-hand push shot and the two-hand set shot.

In the one-hand push shot (with the right hand), the ball is brought up in front of the body with both hands. The right hand is under and in back of the ball, and the left hand is under the ball. The right arm is extended up and in the direction of the basket, with the left hand holding the ball against the fingers of the right hand. As the ball is brought to shooting position in front of the right shoulder, the ball is rolled onto the right hand. The right arm is extended full length, and the left hand is removed from the ball. The ball is released with a wrist snap and leaves the hand from the fingertips. The ball must go high enough, with sufficient arch, to drop straight into the basket.

In the two-hand set shot, the ball is held chest high with the fingertips covering its upper portion. The knees are flexed, with the weight brought forward. The elbows are held close to the body. The wrists are straightened, the knees and the elbows extended, and the ball released toward the basket with a snap of the wrists.

Adaptations: Players using crutches are more successful with one-hand shots than with two-hand shots. Most of the body weight must be taken on the crutch to free the shooting arm. A combination of one regular crutch and one Löfstrand crutch often provides sufficient means of getting around on the floor, and, with the use of the latter on the shooting arm, that arm is freed for shooting while the weight is borne on the other crutch.

Players using wheelchairs are usually able to make both types of shots, although the novice player prefers the two-hand shot because of the additional force that can be generated by two arms rather than one. Skilled players, however, prefer the use of the one-hand push shot. The techniques of shooting for the wheelchair player are basically

Figure 25.1 The game of basketball may be modified in many ways to ensure student success.

the same as those used by other players. One difference has to do with the position of the body in relation to the basket. When shooting from a wheelchair, players prefer to position the wheelchair in front of but at a slight angle to the basket. A right-handed shooter would place the chair slightly to the left of center. The use of a frame and net device that attaches to a basket is helpful in retrieving basketballs during shooting practice (figure 25.2).

Shooters with visual impairments use both shots and can shoot with considerable accuracy if a buzzer or sound device is placed behind the goal.

Modifications in the rules to permit walking with the ball and double dribble may be necessary to create a challenging but enjoyable experience for players with mental retardation.

Dribbling

Dribbling should be done with the fingers spread comfortably apart and with the fingertips pushing the ball toward the floor with a little wrist flexion-extension. The ball should be dribbled in the front and to the side of the player. When the skill is first introduced, the players will want to watch the ball and then look up, alternating back and forth. The goal, of course, is to develop sufficient kinesthetic and tactile skill that the player can dribble the ball under control without having to watch the ball. As players become more proficient, they will be able to dribble the ball under control while moving at a rapid pace. When this occurs, the ball will be dribbled further out in front so that the player may maintain control.

Adaptations: Players with one arm, including some players with cerebral palsy, will need to learn to shoot from the dribble. This can be accomplished by stopping the dribble, placing the hand under the ball, and moving the ball to a one hand push-shot position.

Players with visual impairments will need some audible cues to help them orient while dribbling. This initially is challenging because of the concentration required to dribble the ball and the noise generated by the bouncing ball.

Some players with limited upper-arm movement may find it easier to dribble the ball with the back of the hand or the back of the wrist. This technique is used by players who have limited use of the wrist muscles.

As stressed earlier in this chapter, it may be necessary to modify the rules of basketball so that novice players do not become overly discouraged. This might mean, for instance, allowing additional steps between each dribble and double dribbling.

Wheelchair Basketball

Wheelchair basketball has emerged as the most popular team sport among people who have mobility impairments, with more individuals participating in it than in any other team sport. Some of this success is attributed to the long history associated with this sport. Wheelchair basketball was first played in 1946 at veterans hospitals in New England and California. The veterans hospital team from Birmingham, California, helped to popularize the sport by playing other wheelchair teams in annual tours, which it conducted for several years. Today there are more than 200 teams participating in tournament play compared to six in 1949.

The rules for wheelchair basketball are the same as those of regular basketball, except for a few changes to accommodate the use of the wheelchair and the disability of the players. A traveling violation is called when a player takes more than two pushes on the rims of the wheelchair with the ball sitting on the player's lap. After dribbling one or two times, the player may shoot, pass, or wheel the chair two additional pushes. Players must remain seated at all times in the chair and are charged with a technical for rising out of the chair. One of the most interesting rules of wheelchair basketball is the requirement that in the course of a game the players, based on their functional classification, may not exceed twelve total points for five players. Three classes of players (I, II, and III) are possible. An explanation of the classification systems is presented as follows:

Figure 25.2 Basketball return device allows wheelchair player to practice shots without assistance from others.

Figure 25.3 Bouncing the ball in a stationary position is an important development skill and is used extensively in wheelchair basketball.

Class I: Complete motor loss at the seventh thoracic vertebra or above or comparable disability that severely limits trunk mobility, balance, arm strength, and range of motion.

Class II: Complete motor loss from eighth thoracic to second lumbar vertebra or comparable disability (including double-leg hip amputee) that limits forward, backward, and sideward trunk mobility and balance.

Class III: Complete motor loss from the third lumbar vertebra downward or comparable disability that limits sideward trunk mobility and balance and/or ambulatory speed and power compared to nondisabled peers. This classification includes persons who ambulate with a limp or who have an impaired gait.

In competitive games, the players on the floor may not collectively exceed twelve points nor can there be more than three class III players. The points assigned to the classes are equal to the specific classification: class I players are assigned one point, class II, two points, and class III, three points. This rule was instituted to encourage players with various degrees of ability to participate and to make competition more equitable. The United States Amputee Athletic Association also uses a classification system that assigns a point value to each competitive class (i.e., above- or below-the-knee amputee, etc.) (Paciorek and Jones, 1989). Many have suggested that similar rules applied to team sport for the nondisabled should be seriously considered.

An excellent reference on wheelchair basketball, *Playing and Coaching Wheelchair Basketball* by Ed Owen, is available for the reader who wishes additional information

Figure 25.4 Wheelchair basketball is an exciting sport played on a regulation size court.

on this exciting sport. This book provides a wealth of valuable information on wheelchair basketball including fundamentals, drills, offensive and defensive strategies, the rules of the game, and other important information.

Students in wheelchairs also can participate in regulation games with nondisabled players if a few simple rule modifications are followed. In a game of five players to a side, each team should have an equal number of players per side, even if it means having a nondisabled player use a wheelchair for the game. Generally, it is best to have one wheelchair player per team. The basketball court should be modified by designating a lane in which the players using wheelchairs must stay. A second set of baskets is placed at the end of each lane at a height appropriate to the skill level of the wheelchair participant. Designating baskets made from a sitting position as worth four points makes the student with a disability an asset to the team and encourages nondisabled players to attempt playing from a wheelchair. When the players who use wheelchairs progress beyond novice skill, they should be permitted the option of using the modified or regulation basket. This change adds a new challenge both offensively and defensively for the wheelchair participants.

Softball

Softball can be played with only slight modification by all except those who are most severely disabled. Because this is the case, players with mild to moderate disabilities are easily integrated with nondisabled players. Students with visual or orthopedic impairments may require major changes in the game to participate.

Adaptations: The size of the diamond may be reduced and the distance of the pitching box from home plate

decreased as needed to accommodate the abilities of the players.

More fielders and more bases may be added to reduce the work and the amount of movement required of any one fielder.

Play might be modified as needed for students with visual impairments. These modifications might include playing in a gym or fenced area, reducing the number of bases to one, and substituting a larger ball for the regulation softball.

Playing the Game

A game is divided into innings. An inning is completed when both teams have been up to bat and have been retired after three outs. An out is made at bat when:

1. The batter has three strikes (except on the third strike when the catcher fails to catch the ball and there is no one on first base).
2. A foul ball is hit and caught.
3. An infield fly is hit and there are runners at first and second base with fewer than two outs.

A strike is a ball, legally thrown above home plate in the strike zone, that the batter either fails to strike at or strikes at and misses. The strike zone is the area over the plate between the batter's knees and shoulders. A batter becomes a runner upon hitting a fair ball. An out is made when:

1. An opposing player reaches first base with the ball before the runner touches the base.
2. A runner is touched with the ball while going to and from any base.
3. A runner leaves the base before the ball leaves the pitcher's hand in a pitch to the batter.
4. A runner runs to the next base on a fly ball that is caught, if the runner leaves before the ball is caught.

Pitched balls that do not legally enter the striking zone and are not struck at are called balls. After four balls the batter is permitted to advance to first base.

Adaptations: Strikes may be called only when the batter strikes at the ball and misses. Balls are not called, and the batter is not permitted to advance on balls.

If a batter is able to bat but unable to run bases, a teammate may do the base running. Where the runner starts from will depend upon the ability of the batter. If the batter is especially good, the runner should be required to start on the opposite side of home plate from first base. For weaker batters, the runner may start closer to first base.

A player who has partial sight might bat from a batting tee and run the bases with assistance from the basemen, who are required to make sounds to guide the runner toward the base. The teammates of a runner who is visually impaired may hold a rope between bases to guide that player to the next base. The rope should be used only when the player with limited vision is batting or baserunning. Tie a knot in

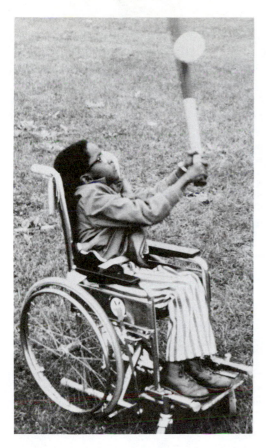

Figure 25.5 Softball play becomes possible for a player in a wheelchair when a teammate does the base running.

the rope two strides before each base so the baserunner is reminded of the proximity of the base. If there is only one player with visual limitations playing in a group of nondisabled teammates, the player with the visual impairment should bat for both teams to equalize play. A verbal cue "swing" or "ball" timed with the delivery of the pitch will allow some players with visual impairments to develop commendable batting skills.

When using one base and a large ball to ensure the success of players with visual impairments, the pitch should be rolled so it bounces on the way to homeplate. If a fair hit is made, the first baseman makes an intermittent sound loud enough to be heard by the fielders and the runner with a visual impairment heading for first base, yet not so loud as to interfere with the ability of the fielders to hear where the ball is rolling. If the ball is fielded successfully, the fielder rolls the ball to the first baseman. If it comes into the first baseman's possession before the runner gets to first base, the runner is out. If the runner gets safely to first base, the run scores and the player returns to the batting line-up. Three outs retire the side. A version of baseball known as "beep baseball" is designed especially for play by those who have visual impairments. This exciting game will be described later.

Catching

Softball can be played without a glove, but a glove does provide protection to the hand and makes catching easier. In catching the ball, the body should be placed in line with the ball. The player should watch the ball throughout the catch. If possible, the ball should be caught in both hands. If the ball is above waist level, the thumbs will be together; if it is below the waist, the little fingers will be together. If a ball is far to the side, it may be necessary to reach with one hand to catch the ball. In either case, the ball is caught in the palm of the left hand (for right-handed players). As the ball strikes the hand, the hand should give slightly to cushion the ball. If both hands are used in catching, the dominant hand is brought over the top of the ball to hold it in the palm as the ball strikes the palm of the nondominant hand, e.g. the right handed player would catch the ball with the left hand.

Adaptations: In most cases, players who lack skill in catching should be provided with gloves to increase their efficiency and protect their hands.

Players with one hand can catch the ball without a glove and so be ready immediately to throw the ball; however, these players can learn to use a glove if a functional joint at the shoulder and a portion of the upper arm remains on the disabled arm. In this case, as soon as the ball is caught with the one hand, the glove with the ball in the pocket is placed under the opposite arm and the hand slipped out of the glove so that the ball stays in the pocket. In one continuous movement, the ball is grasped with the hand and thrown.

The ball may be caught by players who use crutches or wheelchairs with a little practice of the proper techniques. On crutches the body is propped in position by the crutches, with one arm bearing most of the body's weight, thereby freeing the other arm to catch the ball. The participation of players on crutches may be limited to throwing and catching and perhaps batting.

Students with visual impairments playing modified softball will face the direction from which the ball is coming as determined by hearing it move along the ground. The feet are spread apart to cover as much ground as feasible. The hands, with fingers spread, are placed between the legs. As the ball rolls forward, the hands are positioned to grasp the ball. To provide information about the location of the ball while fielding and to ensure safety, a sighted player should be paired with each player who has a visual impairment.

Adapting the rules so the runner is out when the fielder with a visual impairment fields the ball and raises it waist high will make that player an asset to the team. If the ball is to be thrown through the air by seeing or partially seeing players, the catcher turns toward the thrower and extends the arms with the palms up to make a basket to catch the ball. The thrower aims for the "basket," letting the catcher know by a verbal cue when the ball is thrown.

Throwing

Pitching in softball is done underhanded. However, the overhand throw is used almost exclusively in the rest of the game. In making an overhand throw, the player holds the ball with the first and second fingers on top of the ball and the thumb under it. The arm is raised to the back of the head at about ear level. The wrist is hyperextended, and the elbow is held back on the level of the shoulder. The left foot is placed forward in the direction of the throw (for a right-handed player). The ball is brought forward past the ear until the arm is fully extended at about shoulder height. In a continuous motion, the wrist is flexed and the ball is released. The trunk is simultaneously rotated to the left. The arm follows through, coming to rest down near the knee on the opposite side of the body. The body weight shifts from the back foot to the front foot as the throw is made.

Adaptations: Very young children may need to grasp the ball by placing three fingers on top of the ball. Individuals with missing fingers will need to adjust the grip so they are able to place at least the thumb or one finger on one side of the ball and one finger on the other side.

Those players who are throwing from a sitting position or from a propped position on crutches will, of course, use the upper part of the body in throwing. The twist of the trunk will come from the hips only. Those who are unable to or should not twist in this manner will make the throw completely with the arm, keeping the body relatively motionless.

To develop catching skills, players with visual impairments should have the ball rolled to them along the gound so that the bounces can be heard as the ball approaches. An audible ball that emits a continuous sound is used successfully by some players who are visually impaired.

Batting and Base Running

The (right-handed) batter should grip the bat firmly near the end with the left hand, placing the right hand above and as close to the left as possible. The top hand should be aligned with the bottom hand so that the third joint of the little finger rests between the second and third joints of the index finger of the lower hand as it encircles the bat. The batter takes a position at the plate with his or her left side toward the pitcher; the nearest corner of the plate splits the center of the batter's body. The distance from the plate should be such that, when the bat is swung, the heavy part of the bat will come over the center of the plate. The bat is held in back of the body and not rested on the shoulders. Both elbows and right wrist are flexed. The elbows are held away from the body, with the left elbow in line with the wrist and hand. The batter watches the ball as it leaves the pitcher's hand and continues to watch it until it is hit or has passed by the batter.

When the player swings to strike the ball, the front foot moves forward in a shuffle step. The step is completed before the ball is hit. The bat is swung parallel to the path of the oncoming ball. The ball is contacted in front of the plate, and the bat should follow the ball after it is hit until the swing of the body at the hips changes the direction of the bat. After the ball is hit, the first step toward the base is taken by the right foot with a short step. This is followed by one or two short steps to speed the acceleration, and then the runner goes into full stride toward first base. The player runs through the base rather than attempting to stop exactly on it.

Adaptations: Batters on crutches will need to depend more on their arms for power in hitting than on the twist of their bodies. Consequently, they should probably concentrate more on placement than on distance. For those who are unable to run to first base, a substitute runner may be provided as described earlier in this chapter.

Batters with visual impairments in the adapted game take a stance with the left side to the pitch (if right-handed). Kneeling on the left knee, the player takes the weight partially on the right foot. The left hand grasps the bat near the end. The right hand is four to five inches above the left. The bat is brought back in preparation for the swing. It is parallel to the ground and two or three inches above it. Before the pitch, the batter indicates readiness to bat by signaling to the pitcher. Upon hearing the ball roll into the striking zone, the batter swings the bat forward to strike the ball, keeping the bat parallel to the floor. Traditionally batters and catchers have used protective equipment while playing softball. It may be necessary to have additional masks, batting helmets, and padding to prevent injuries when players are unable to detect the approach of other players, the ball, or the bat regardless of the position being played.

Wheelchair Softball

The National Wheelchair Softball Association (NWSA), founded in 1977, promotes softball events and programs primarily for athletes with spinal cord injuries. Individuals with other disabilities, including those with amputations, cerebral palsy, and several les autres conditions also compete in the NWSA on a regular basis. Indicated below are some of the rule modifications which have been made by the NWSA to accommodate athletes in wheelchairs.

1. All participants must be in wheelchairs; all chairs must have foot platforms.

2. The playing field shall be a smooth level surface of blacktop or similar material with 150 feet on the foul lines and from 180 feet to 220 feet to straight center.

3. The official diamond shall have 50 feet between all bases and 70 feet 8½ inches from home to second base.

4. A pitching stripe extending perpendicularly 1 foot on either side of the diagonal from home to second base shall be located 28 feet from home plate.

5. At first, second, and third bases, in fair territory shall be located a 4-foot diameter circle around and centering on a 1-foot square flat base; the defensive

baseman has only to have one or more wheels touching within this defensive circle while the base runner must either cross over or touch the base with one or more wheels in order to tag the base.

6. If at any time a fielder should leave the chair in order to gain an advantage in catching or stopping a hit ball or to field a thrown ball, all base runners will be awarded two bases.

7. If a throwing error occurs and the ball leaves the playing area, all base runners shall be awarded one base beyond the last base each had reached before the error.

Beep Baseball

Beep baseball is played on a regulation field with special markings as shown in figure 25.6. If possible, the field should be a grassy area so that the ball can be more easily heard and located. As noted in the figure, a semicircle forty feet from home plate designates the foul line. A batted ball must travel over this line to be considered fair. The bases in beep baseball are ninety feet from home plate, the same distance used in regulation baseball. The bases differ, however, in that they are located five feet outside of the baseline. In addition they are forty-eight inches tall, with the bottom part a pliable plastic cone and the remaining twelve inches a long cylinder of foam rubber. Each base contains a speaker with one of the speakers activated to make a buzzing sound when a fair ball is hit.

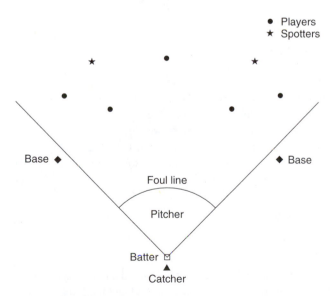

Figure 25.6 Playing field for beep baseball. The semi-circular foul line between first and third bases is a constant distance of forty feet from home plate. A batted ball must travel over this line to be considered *fair*. The pitcher stands twenty feet from home plate. The distance between home plate and each base location is ninety feet. The base is five feet outside the baseline.

A team is composed of seven players, two of whom are sighted and five who have visual impairments. The sighted players act as spotters when their team is in the field. Their responsibility is to call out the name of the player to whom the hit ball is coming closest. For safety reasons, only the name of one player is called. The role of the spotters, when their team is at bat, is to serve as the pitcher and catcher.

The game is played by having the pitcher, using an underhand throw, pitch the ball from a distance of twenty feet to the batter. The ball is a regulation sixteen-inch softball with a battery operated electronic sound device inside. Batters must attempt to hit all pitched balls with the option of letting two pass without penalty. Five strikes are allowed with a foul ball on the last strike considered an out. A run is scored if the runner reaches the base before being tagged out. To ensure that the runner does not have an advantage over the fielder, the rules require that the base to which the batter should run is not known until the ball is hit. The base is activated by the umpire. Three outs are allowed per inning with a game consisting of six innings.

Football

Football is a strenuous competitive game in which only the people who are most physically fit and skilled in the use of their bodies can participate. However, the skills of football—catching, throwing, and kicking—can be learned and enjoyed for their own sake by many types of persons with disabling conditions.

General Adaptations: Because football is a sport that requires body contact, its strenuousness cannot be modified by reducing the size of the playing area or by increasing the number of players, as is possible with the other games presented in this chapter. Consequently, only those whose disabling condition does not impose restrictions on the range or amount of movement, such as people with deafness[1] or mild mental retardation, can participate in regulation football. For others, modifications must be made in the way the game is played. Positions on the line or place kicking may be played by students who have arm amputations if blocking is substituted for tackling.

Players with visual impairments cannot compete successfully against sighted teams but do well against other teams whose players have limited vision. End runs must be eliminated for successful play. Players who are completely without vision play center, guard, and tackle positions while those with partial vision play back and end positions. The linemen play their positions by meeting force with force. If the opponent attempts to block from a certain direction, this is taken as a cue by the linemen that the play is going in the

---

[1]There is a slight modification for the deaf in that the signals are made with hand signs.

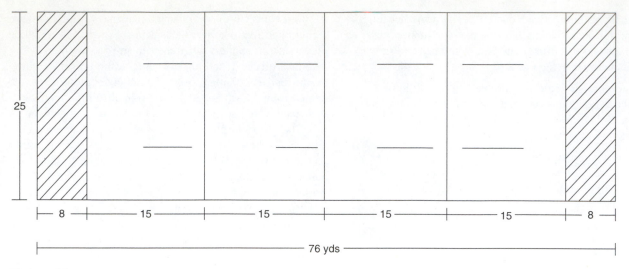

Figure 25.7   Wheelchair football field dimensions.

opposite direction; they fight their way in that direction. They grab any opponents who attempt to run by them.

The game of football has been adapted for use by players in wheelchairs. Although rule modifications vary, wheelchair football is normally played on an asphalt surface with six players per team. The field will vary in size, but the field dimensions recommended by the Santa Barbara Recreation Department have been adopted widely (figure 25.7).

The game consists of four 15-minute quarters, with a 10-minute halftime period. Play is similar to flag or touch football. Players advance the ball by running or passing. The quarterback may pass, but not run without handing the ball off. All players are eligible as receivers.

Passing

In a forward pass, the ball is grasped so that the index finger is about two inches from the tip. The thumb is placed opposite the index finger, with the fingers spread. The ball is brought up and back near the ear with the end that is being grasped pointing back over the shoulder. For a right-handed thrower, the right shoulder is thrown back and the left foot is placed forward with the weight on the back foot. The arm is then brought forward close to the head. A step is taken forward in the direction of the throw. The weight is brought forward on the front foot as the arm is brought forward. The ball is released with a wrist snap, making the ball spiral as it goes forward.

Adaptations: Short passes of four to five feet are most effective for players with limited vision. This enables the receiver to tell where the ball is by the movement of the thrower. Passes should be thrown to the midsection of the receiver. Many novice players will find throwing a football made of foam much easier to grip and control than a standard size and composition football.

For those players who because of limitations cannot participate in football but are able to throw the ball, games of accuracy can be devised for participation. Tires hung by ropes can be used as targets. The tire may be swung to increase the difficulty of the game. A pass receiver may be used to create another game of throwing accuracy. The passer's accuracy is measured by how far the receiver has to move in order to catch the ball. Throwing for distance can be used as another competitive activity.

Receiving Passes

Passes are caught on the fingers. Both hands should be used in catching the ball. The fingers are spread wide and the hands give as the ball comes in contact with the fingers. As in all catching, the ball is watched until it is caught.

Adaptations: Players with one arm should catch the ball with the palm and fingers. As the ball comes in contact with the hand, it is drawn to the body and trapped between the body and hand.

To ensure success for players with little or no vision, short and accurate passes aimed at the player's midsection are the most effective. Cueing the player that the ball is coming and passing without excessive force allows the receiver to place the arms across the midsection parallel to the ground, palms facing each other in preparation to receive the ball. The player with partial sight watches the thrower, which helps in judging when the ball will arrive, even though the flight of the ball cannot be seen.

Kicking

In punting, the ball is held by both hands. For a right-handed kicker, the right hand is under the ball and the left hand is on the left side. A step is taken forward with the left foot. The right foot starts the swing with the knee slightly bent. The ball is dropped so that in kicking, the ball will be partially on the instep and partially on the toe. The toe is pointed slightly inward. The foot meets the ball about knee high, continues to follow through, and rises above the head.

In the place kick, the ball is held by another player, who is in a kneeling position. For a pass from center the holder should be back ten to twelve yards from the center. A mark should be made by the holder at the place where the ball will be held. If the kicker is kicking with the right foot, the holder will be on the kicker's right side. Upon receiving the ball, the holder places the point of the ball on the ground, with the fingers of the right hand on the top of the ball. The kicker stands in front of the ball. As the ball is placed on the ground, the kicker steps forward with the left foot so that it is six to eight inches behind and slightly to the left of the ball. Keeping the eyes on the ball at all times, the kicker then swings the right foot forward so the toe meets the ball slightly below its center. The leg follows through, and the head remains down to watch the ball until completion of the follow-through.

Adaptations: Punting may be accomplished by players with a single arm by grasping the ball at the point with the finger and thumb before kicking. Place kicking may be learned by players who have had double arm amputations.

Students who because of physical limitations cannot play football or touch football may participate in kicking-for-distance contests. Contests of kicking accuracy also can be devised for these students. For this purpose, several concentric circles are laid out on the field, with each circle given a number value, much like an archery target. The points achieved by each of a designated number of kicks are totaled to determine the winner.

Soccer

One of the most rapidly growing sports in the United States is soccer, possibly because it is an experience that may be enjoyed by players of various ages, ability levels, and sizes. Participation in soccer enhances the player's cardiorespiratory endurance and specific types of agility and eye-foot coordination. Students with disabling conditions enjoy the challenges afforded by this unique game. Because of the various skill positions in soccer, most students with impairments can be successfully integrated into this sport.

General Adaptations: Students in wheelchairs will find playing soccer outdoors difficult unless the surface of the field is of the all-weather composition design. Because the primary skill emphasized in soccer is kicking, a rule modification permitting players using wheelchairs to use their hands, if necessary, is allowed. Students with visual impairments will benefit from the use of a brightly colored yellow or orange ball. Those without vision or who have limited residual vision will be most successful in playing the position of goalie. Reducing the size of the goal and providing the goalie with a face mask will help ensure that the goalie is successful and safe.

Athletes with cerebral palsy play a modified form of soccer in which the size of the field and goal are reduced. The number of players is seven rather than the standard of eleven. In figure 25.8 the soccer field dimensions recommended by the United States Cerebral Palsy Athletic Association (USCPAA) are identified. The USCPAA also uses a classification system to ensure that players are representative of the various ambulatory classifications used by the USCPAA (Roper and Roberts, 1988)

Many athletes with lower limb amputations find playing three-legged soccer with the use of crutches an enjoyable and exciting activity. Normally in this game the field is reduced in size and a team is composed of eight players. (Paciorek and Jones, 1989).

Individuals with visual impairments can enjoy the game of soccer with the aid of a few modifications. In addition to the use of a brightly colored ball mentioned above, other modifications for students with visual impairments include the use of: a beeper ball, flags or cones to mark the sidelines, sighted guides, an audible goal locator, and goalposts wrapped in brightly colored tape.

Kicking

There are several different methods that can be used to kick the soccer ball. The kick most frequently used to achieve distance and accuracy is the instep kick. As the name implies, the player strikes the ball with the instep of the foot (shoelaces). Prior to striking the ball, the nonkicking foot should be placed next to the ball with the toes pointed in the intended direction of the kick. The kick is initiated by balancing on the nonkicking foot with the knee of the kicking leg positioned over the ball. The arms should be held away from the body parallel to the ground. The head remains down as the ball is struck with the instep. A full follow-through of the leg is necessary to kick the ball with distance and accuracy.

The most popular kick used to pass the ball is the push pass. This kick is executed by turning the foot out and striking the ball with the inside of the foot. A quick jab with the kicking foot is usually all that is required to execute this pass quickly and with accuracy to a teammate.

Adaptations: Students in wheelchairs should be permitted to pass the ball with the hands. Kicking is accomplished by the student with a single leg amputation by balancing on the prosthesis and kicking with the nondisabled foot. Because people with visual impairments may walk with a slight backward lean, it may be difficult to execute the instep kick which requires a forward lean. These individuals may find greater success kicking with the toe instead of the instep. Students with crutches may use the crutch to strike the ball. Balls of various colors and sizes may also be used to assist students whose movement capabilities require special help.

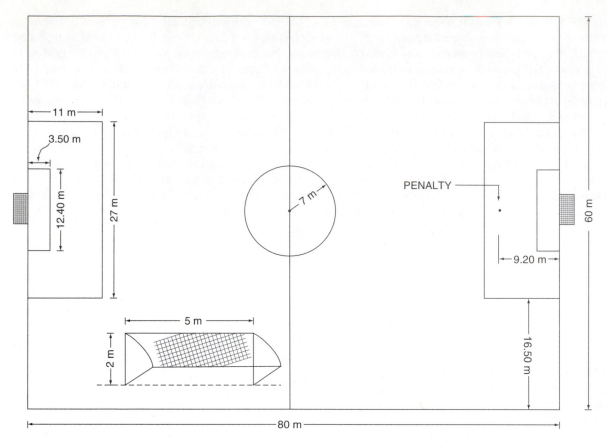

Figure 25.8 USCPAA soccer field dimensions.

Figure 25.9 Students with cerebral palsy participate in soccer, one of the team activities conducted by the United States Cerebral Palsy Athletic Association.

Dribbling

Dribbling involves the use of short kicks to move the ball down the field while running. The objective of dribbling is to keep the ball under control by moving it in front of but close to the body. The toe, inside of the foot, and outside of the front part of the foot are all used to dribble the ball. Good soccer players learn to dribble while maintaining an awareness of their teammates and opponents.

Adaptations: Students with assistive devices such as crutches and canes will find the skill of dribbling possible but difficult to do well. For this reason, in regulation soccer these players are normally encouraged to play the forward, fullback, or goalie's positions rather than serving as a halfback.

The dribble may be performed by players using wheelchairs by pushing the ball along the ground with the footrests of the wheelchair. Foot protection is necessary for this technique. This technique works particularly well with students who require the use of a motorized wheelchair as described in the section on Power Wheelchair Soccer. Air dribbling by repeatedly tossing the ball into the air and catching it is another option for the player who uses a wheelchair.

Trapping

The technique used to stop a ball that is passed to a player is known as trapping. Any part of the body except the hands, arms, and shoulders may be used to trap the ball. Most traps are executed by using the head, trunk, or feet. Traps with the feet are executed by stopping the ball with the inside of the foot. As the ball strikes the foot, it is important that the player move the foot back to absorb the impact of the ball. Trapping the ball with the abdominal area requires that the player flex at the hips, squatting slightly so that the abdomen moves backward in preparation for the impact of the ball.

Adaptations: Students who are fearful of the ball will find trapping a difficult skill to learn. For these students the use of foam balls or soccer balls that are deflated may help them overcome their concern.

Players who use a wheelchair will also find trapping difficult. The concept of this skill, however, can be taught by using a soft ball and tossing it gently so that the student can trap the ball by leaning forward with the head and shoulders and cushioning the ball into the lap.

Throw-In

When the soccer ball crosses the sidelines, it is put back into play by a throw-in. This skill is executed by throwing the ball with two hands from behind the back over the head to the intended player. During the throw, the player performing the throw-in may use a stride position but must keep both feet on the ground. As players perfect this skill, they quickly learn that the ball can be thrown for greater distance if they learn to use their spine and back muscles when throwing.

Adaptations: The throw-in of soccer provides a unique opportunity for some students to be an integral part of the game without any modifications. Players in wheelchairs who have good upper mobility skills can throw the ball in very well. Students with visual impairment, too, can quickly learn to recognize the voice of a teammate and throw the ball to the intended player. Students who are restricted from many activities because of a severe heart problem can normally, with their physician's approval, participate in this aspect of the soccer match.

Adaptations in the throw-in must, however, be made for some students. Those without any arms can kick rather than throw the ball. Players with only one arm can throw the ball with a one-arm motion similar to that used when throwing a baseball. A basketball push technique may be necessary for some students who find raising the arms over their head not functionally possible.

Goalie

The goalie, like any other player, may play anywhere on the field. Normally, however, goalies will position themselves in close proximity to the goal being defended. As long as the goalie is within the penalty area, use of the hands to pick up the ball is permitted. Once the goalie stops the ball after a goal or shot, the ball must be returned to play by throwing or punting it to one of the goalie's own teammates. No more than four steps may be taken before the goalie must pass the ball.

Adaptations: Because the goalie uses skills different from those of the other players, many students with disabling conditions find playing as their team's goalie the ideal position for them. Students in wheelchairs and those who use lower extremity prosthetic devices enjoy the goalie position because it enables them to use their hands. For these students, the position of goalie provides a unique opportunity to be part of a regular game in which their disability does not necessitate major modifications in the activity. Reducing the size of the goal, however, is recommended to ensure that students with limited mobility are successful in covering the assigned area. Occasionally, students who use wheelchairs and other assistive devices will find, with their physician's approval, that playing goalie in a seated or lying position is preferable to playing with the use of their assistive device.

Students with limited vision also can serve as effective goalies. Reduction in the height and width of the goal enables these students to use auditory cues to locate and retrieve soccer balls that are low and bounce along the ground. Players with experience in Goal Ball find playing soccer goalie an easy transition.

Power Wheelchair Soccer

In recent years considerable interest has focused on modifying team games so that individuals in wheelchairs can participate in these activities. With few exceptions, these modifications have been made for those who are mildly and moderately impaired and capable of propelling a wheelchair. There are many individuals, however, who are so severely disabled that they require the assistance of power wheelchairs. Until recently, there have been few team games specifically developed for this population.

Recognizing this need, Cowin, Sibille, and O'Riain (1984) introduced a team sport called motor soccer for individuals who use power wheelchairs. This game is played on a basketball court with four players on a team. The objective of the game is to use the wheelchair to push the ball over the opponent's goal line, which is three meters (approximately ten feet) wide. The game consists of two 30-minute halves with a 10-minute halftime period. Some of the rules of this activity include the following:

1. A coin toss determines which team will start play with the ball at center court. When a goal is scored, the opposing team initiates play at center court.

2. The ball is to be propelled only by the chair. The player is not permitted to use the arms or hands to play the ball. If this occurs, the other team is granted possession of the ball.

3. If a ball becomes lodged between two players for longer than three seconds, the ball is declared dead and a face-off between the two players follows.

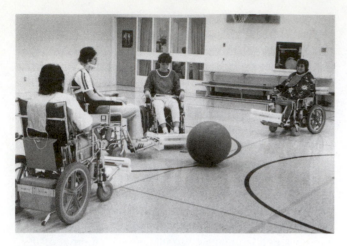

Figure 25.10 Wheelchair bumper used for motor soccer.

4. If the ball goes out of bounds, the opposing team is awarded the ball at the point where the ball left the playing area.

5. Although incidental contact between chairs is allowed, players are not permitted to charge another player with the wheelchair. If this occurs, a two-minute penalty is assessed. The rule applies whether the act was intentional or accidental.

The game's inventors emphasize that some form of foot protection is desirable to avoid injury to the feet and shin. They have proposed the use of a wheelchair bumper (figure 25.10). The bumper is designed to fit directly into the footrest where rubber tips are usually found. Combined with specific rules about wheelchair contact, the bumper seems to provide adequate foot and lower leg protection (Paciorek and Jones, 1989). The Gymnastik ball used to play this game is available from the Equipment Shop, P.O. Box 33, Bedford, MA 01730. Power wheelchair soccer is an excellent example of a team game that has been specifically developed for a particular population. Similar experiences will be developed in the future as more and more professionals become aware of the value of team games and the various modifications that can be made by creative and thoughtful teachers.

Volleyball

Volleyball is perhaps the most easily modified of all the team games for play by individuals with disabilities. Even those for whom strenuous activity is contraindicated can participate if the pace of the game is moderate. Those with limited locomotion also can be successfully accommodated.

General Adaptations: The net may be lowered to less than the standard height if the abilities of the players indicate the need for this. However, the net should be high enough so that no player is able to reach over the top of it.

On a regulation court, it is possible to increase the size of the teams to eight or ten players. If some of the players are on crutches, they can be assigned a smaller area to defend.

For players in wheelchairs, the court may be increased or decreased in size, depending upon the number of players. In any case, the area that each wheelchair player defends will need to be small enough to be readily covered.

The game of volleyball has been modified for those with amputations of either upper or lower extremities. Standing volleyball is played according to standard rules. Players with upper extremity amputations usually play without their prosthesis; whereas players with lower extremity amputations normally play with their prosthesis. The game is referred to as standing volleyball to differentiate it from the game of sitting volleyball.

In sitting volleyball, double leg amputees and individuals with spinal injuries, polio, and various other lower extremity disabilities can participate successfully. Sitting volleyball is played according to standard rules with the primary exception that players must sit. In addition, the nets are lower and the court smaller.

Playing the Game

In assuming playing positions, three players on each team are net players. They face the net about an arm's length from it and at equal distances from each other. The other three players are in the backcourt. The players here are directly behind the net players and about two or three strides in from the back line.

The game begins by serving the ball from anywhere behind the back boundary line. In serving, the ball is held in the open palm of one hand and struck with the closed fist of the other hand so that the ball rises into the air and goes over the net.

Each team member serves in turn and may have one trial to serve the ball over the net. The server continues to serve until teammates fail to return the ball; then the serve passes to the opposing team. All offensive players rotate clockwise one position when a new player begins to serve.

In returning the ball, the player must hit it; it cannot be momentarily caught. Each team is allowed three hits to return the ball over the net. No player may hit the ball twice in succession. One point is scored if the receiving team fails to return the ball. The receiving team gets the ball to serve but does not score if the serving team fails to return the ball. Usually the game is played to fifteen points, provided that the winner has won by two points. If such a margin does not exist, the game continues until one team wins two points in a row.

Adaptations: If more than six players are used, the distribution of players may be made so that they will be equally divided between the net and the backcourt, or three players may be placed at the net with three in the backcourt and three others placed in between.

Those who have insufficient power to get the ball over the net in the serve may be permitted to move up a specified distance to the net. A server with one arm must throw the ball high into the air and bat it with the same hand. An overhand stroke is made. Players lacking sufficient coordination to strike the ball to return it over the net may be permitted to catch the ball and return it by throwing it back in bounds on the other side of the net. The net in this case should be higher than usual, and a score is made when the ball is not caught or when it is thrown out of bounds or into the net. Throwing the ball over the net may be substituted for serving, if necessary.

This adaptation may be used also by the player with minimal vision with the addition of permitting the ball to bounce. A point is scored when:

1. The ball rolls out of bounds before it is trapped.
2. The ball is thrown and does not land in the opponents' court.
3. The ball goes into the net.

When a player who is blind or partially sighted is participating with sighted players, the former may be permitted to serve all during the game and to take part in the volleying only if able to see the ball well enough. If necessary, because the ball cannot be seen clearly enough for volleying, the player may be allowed to catch the ball and play it as in the game of newcomb. An audible volleyball, the Aud-a-ball, may also be used.

The deaf can play the game of volleyball without any significant modifications. A red flag is used as a substitute for a whistle in competition sponsored by the American Athletic Association for the Deaf.

Individuals with mental retardation compete in competitive volleyball sponsored by the Special Olympics International. Team competition is played according to standard rules with the understanding that minor rule modifications may be necessary (e.g., lowering the net, using a lighter ball, and moving the serving line forward).

Students with visual impairments or other disabling conditions may enjoy wall volleyball as a game or a drill. Players volley the ball against the wall. The number of times a player volleys the ball successfully constitutes the score. Players with limited vision will need to be allowed to stand closer to the wall than other players. For sighted students, the ball is volleyed above a line six feet high marked on the wall. Players should control the ball on their fingers throughout the volley rather than on the palms.

Students on crutches will need to balance themselves with their crutches in such a manner as to free at least one hand for striking the ball. The ball may be served as described for the one-handed player.

When playing from a wheelchair the player may serve underhand by leaning to the side of the chair, or the ball may be tossed high into the air with one hand and stroked underhand with the other. Returning the ball with one hand is a skill necessary for players who use crutches, wheelchairs, or have only one upper extremity. However, as skill in maneuvering the chair increases, the player will be able to use both hands a large portion of the time. A one-hand return executed on the side of the body, or the side of the chair, can be made by reaching straight out with the arm to the side. The ball is allowed to drop to shoulder height and the ball is struck and lifted into the air by hitting it with the palm or the back of the hand.

Floor Hockey

An activity enjoyed by many young people that offers unlimited valuable experiences for students with disabilities is floor hockey. This game, adapted from the popular sport of ice hockey, is played indoors or outdoors with plastic sticks and pucks. There are two variations of the game with the primary difference being in the type of stick and puck used. In adapted floor hockey, a straight stick is used with a rounded top and bottom. A vinyl sleeve tip is placed on the bottom of the stick to help the stick glide and to avoid marks to the floor. The puck used in adapted floor hockey is a donut-shaped felt puck. The puck is shot or passed by placing the stick in the opening in the center of the puck. In poly hockey, the stick resembles that used in regular floor hockey except it is made of plastic. The puck used in poly hockey is similar to regular hockey except that it is hollow and made of plastic. Both games are safe activities due to the equipment used and the rules followed in playing the game.

The objective of both games is the same: to score a point by getting the puck into the opponent's goal. The number of players on a team is unlimited but usually six players compose a team with one player serving as goalie. As in hockey, the goalie's task is to stop shots on the goal. The goalie, however, may not leave the goalie area. The other team members serve as both offensive and defensive players.

Figure 25.11 Floor hockey is becoming an increasingly popular activity.

Each game is twenty-seven minutes long with three periods of nine minutes each. A two-minute rest period is permitted between periods. Time penalties of five minutes are imposed for roughing fouls, such as striking or pushing an opponent. A penalty shot is awarded to a team when their opponent commits a floor violation, such as touching the puck with the hand or using the wheelchair illegally.

The dimensions of the court vary according to the amount of space available. It is recommended, however, that the goal measure forty-four inches wide by forty-two inches high with a forty-eight-inch area in front of the goal designated as the goalie's restricted area.

General Adaptations: Floor hockey is an excellent activity for many students with disabilities. The flexibility permitted in establishing the court boundaries allows students who require assistive devices because of limited mobility to participate successfully. Students can also be assigned positions consistent with their special needs. For example, students with activity restrictions due to congenital heart problems can serve as their team's goalie. Although many students in wheelchairs have sufficient mobility skills to play floor hockey without any adaptations, it may be helpful for some students to establish designated areas on the floor to which individual players are restricted. A player, therefore, would be responsible for the puck only if it is in his or her area. The concept of restricting players to designated areas is an adaptation that is also highly recommended for students with visual impairments. Placing a device that emits a sound by the goal helps the blind student locate the goal. The size of the goal can be made larger or smaller to accommodate the special needs of individual players.

The tempo of the game may be slowed by modifying the rules so that students must walk rather than run. This modification will assist students with movement limitations as well as those with cardiac impairments. The puck also may be increased in size to assist players who are visually impaired. Adding weight to the puck will be effective in reducing its speed, which will be helpful to players who are unable to move quickly.

A modified form of the game of floor hockey has been adapted for players in electric or power wheelchairs (Paciorek and Jones, 1989). The rules of this game follow closely those of the National Hockey League with a few modifications. A team consists of five players—three forwards, one defensive player, and a goalie. The game is played on a standard gymnasium floor with equipment similar to that used in poly hockey with the exception that a three-inch diameter plastic ball is used in place of a plastic puck.

Skills of Stick-Handling

The basic strokes used with the floor hockey stick are the forehand and backhand pass and shot. Players are instructed to place the hands on the sticks about eight to twelve inches apart with the dominant hand on the bottom. The forehand stroke is executed by pushing the stick forward with a flicking action of the wrist. Hand, wrist, and forearm must work together in a coordinated manner to achieve speed and accuracy. Shots and passes with the backhand stroke are achieved by using the back of the stick with the forearm, hand, and wrist working together to provide the desired speed and accuracy. In both the forehand and backhand strokes, the players may not swing the stick above waist height. Players should use short, controlled jabs at the puck rather than full swings.

Adaptations: Students with only one arm can use it to control the stick. The stick is light enough that this adaptation should not inhibit the student's success. Students in wheelchairs also find using one arm to control the stick a necessary modification. When maneuvering the wheelchair, the stick is normally carried in the player's lap. Players who are unable to hold a stick may advance the puck with the feet. Protective shin and ankle coverings are necessary for these players. These players may also make effective goalies. Reducing the size of the goal may be necessary to enhance success in use of the latter modification. Students who move with the aid of a cane or crutch may use their assistive device in place of the hockey stick to hit the puck. As an alernative, some players may prefer to tape the hockey stick to their assistive device.

Goal Ball

Goal ball is a sport that has been specifically developed for players with visual impairments. The game was created in Europe following World War II and has grown in popularity in recent years. Goal ball, similar to beep baseball and Quad Rugby, is different from the other team games discussed in this chapter. The game is not a modification of a popular team game; it is a unique sport form for a specific disability population. The objective of the game of goal ball is to roll a large ball with a bell in it across the opponent's goal line while the other team tries to stop it. Each team consists of three players, one middle player, two outside players, and two substitutes. In defending the goal, players work as a team trying to stop the ball from a standing, squatting, lying, or kneeling position. The ball may be stopped by any body part or the body as a whole. To score, the ball must be thrown from the team's playing area and must come down in the opponent's throwing area. The ball may not bounce as it enters the team's throwing area. Players are permitted to wear knee, elbow, and hip pads, not to exceed 0.05 meters in thickness. Any player may throw the ball but the ball may only be thrown three times in succession by the same player.

The women's ball is 1,500 grams and 66 centimeters in circumference; the men's is a 2,000 gram medicine ball, 86 centimeters in circumference with eight to twelve 1-centimeter holes. The playing area for goal ball is a

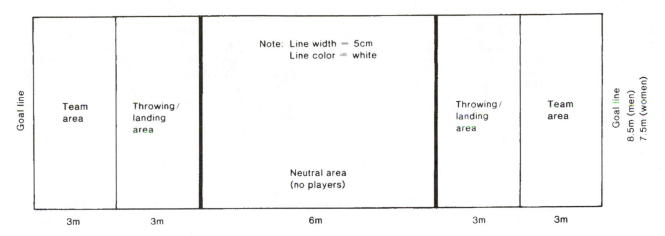

Figure 25.12 Playing area for goal ball.

rectangular field with the dimensions as indicated in figure 25.12. The lines on the field must be of a distinctive texture to assist the players' orientation.

The playing time consists of two periods of 7 minutes. The team scoring the most goals wins the game. If a game ends in a tie, two 3-minute time periods are played. Free throws similar to a soccer match shoot out are used if the game remains tied after the extension. Complete rules for the game of goal ball may be obtained from the United States Association for Blind Athletes. The address for this organization may be found in chapter 30.

Because the rules of goal ball require that all athletes wear blindfolds, sighted and nonsighted players can enjoy this activity. Goal ball is an excellent example of a game that allows the player with a disability to perform extremely well in settings with nondisabled students. Sighted players will quickly learn that goal ball is a vigorous activity and learn to appreciate the talent and skill of their nonsighted friends.

Quad Rugby

The game of Quad Rugby was started in 1976 in Canada by a group of athletes with quadriplegia. Quad Rugby was introduced in the United States in 1982 as part of the National Wheelchair Games. The game is physically challenging and provides a desirable alternative to the faster-paced game of wheelchair basketball.

Quad Rugby combines aspects of basketball and soccer and a penalty system similar to that used in ice hockey. The game, which is played with a volleyball and consists of two 20-minute periods, is based on scoring goals by crossing the opponent's goal line with the ball. The ball is advanced by passing, throwing, batting, rolling, dribbling, or carrying.

A team consists of four players who collectively cannot exceed eight points according to the classification criteria

Figure 25.13 Rugby is a fast-paced game played by women and men. Here Quadzilla's Sun Chan eludes EPVA's Angelo Mongiovi.

used by the National Wheelchair Athletic Associations. The game is played on a basketball court with restricted areas designated with pylons and tapes (figure 25.14).

Strategy used in the game is to score points by penetrating the line of defense to cross the opponent's goal line with the ball. Similar to ice hockey, a player who commits defensive penalties and other violations such as holding or pushing must sit out time in the penalty box. The defense usually employs a zone defense to protect the scoring area with one player designated as a chaser to pressure the opposing player who possesses the ball.

For additional information about the game of Quad Rugby, including the specific rules, the reader is encouraged to write to the United States Quad Rugby Association, 2418 West Fall Creek Court, Grand Forks, ND 58201.

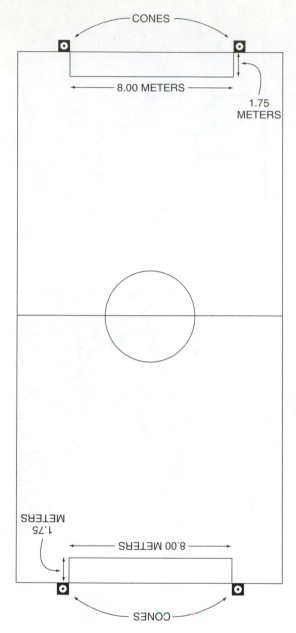

Figure 25.14 Quad Rugby court dimensions.

Summary

The values of participating in team games are numerous—they contribute to physical fitness, provide group experiences, enhance motor skills, and are fun. Knowledge of team games is important for these reasons as well as because of the importance our culture has placed on team sports. Students with disabilities should be provided opportunities to enjoy team games and to benefit from the values associated with organized group experiences.

Within this chapter, information was provided about some of the more popular team games including basketball, softball, football, soccer, volleyball, and floor hockey, and the various adaptations that allow students with disabling conditions to participate in these activities. In discussing each team game, emphasis was

placed on a review of the rules and equipment used in the game to show that with thought and creative effort many adaptations are possible. The goal is to create opportunities for students with disabilities to participate together with their nondisabled peers in the various team games. As demonstrated in this chapter, the modifications can be as simple as teaching a student with one arm how to catch and then throw a ball to more elaborate rule changes that allow a student in a wheelchair to participate in a regular basketball game. Of course for some students the challenge of playing a team game may be very difficult, so the emphasis will need to be placed on the skills that comprise the game and various lead-up activities.

Team games that have been specifically developed for those with disabilities, such as wheelchair basketball, wheelchair softball, wheelchair power soccer, goal ball, beep baseball, and quad rugby also were described and discussed. These games provide excellent opportunities for students with disabilities to participate in exciting and challenging activities. They also provide a forum whereby students with disabilities have been successful in demonstrating the high level of skill and talent that is possible despite the presence of a disabling condition. Many nondisabled students have participated in these activities, finding them enjoyable and challenging and creating new levels of understanding and appreciation for the "ability" of their disabled peers.

As was discussed in chapters 23 and 24, there is a growing awareness that individuals with disabilities enjoy participating in a variety of individual, dual, and team activities. Team games provide a means to contribute to overall health and to enrich the lives of individuals with special needs. Professionals must provide positive learning experiences and to remember that with effort and creative thought the possibilities are unlimited.

Selected Readings

Adams, R.C., & McCubbin, J. (1991). *Games, sports, and exercises for the physically handicapped* (4th ed.). Philadelphia: Lea and Febiger.

Bailey, C.I., & Teller, F. (1971). *Soccer.* Philadelphia: W.B. Saunders Co.

Betts, J.W. (1979). *Football fundamentals for kids and parents.* San Diego: A.S. Barnes and Co., Inc.

Buell, C. (1984). *Physical education for blind children* (2d ed.). Springfield, IL: Charles C. Thomas.

Cowin, L., Sibille, J., & O'Riain, M.D. (1984). Motor soccer, the electric connection. *Sports 'n Spokes, 10*(4), 43–44.

Egstrom, G.H., & Schaafsma, F. (1980). *Volleyball* (3d ed.). Dubuque, IA: Wm. C. Brown Publishers.

Lasko-McCarthey, P., & Knopf, K.G. (1992). *Adapted physical education for adults with disabilities* (3d ed.). Dubuque, IA: Eddie Bowers Publishing, Inc.

McKeeman Hopkins, V. (1981). Physical activities for individuals with spinal cord injuries. In G.R. Roice (Ed.), *Teaching handicapped students physical education* (pp. 41–43). Washington, DC: National Education Association.

Miller, A.G., & Sullivan, J.V. (1982). *Teaching physical activities to impaired youth.* New York: John Wiley and Sons, Inc.

Montelione, T., & Mastro, J. (1985). Beep baseball. *Journal of Physical Education, Recreation, and Dance,* 60–61, 65.

Mood, D., Musker, F.F., & Rink, J.E. (1991). *Sports and recreational activities for men and women.* St. Louis: Times Mirror/ Mosby Publishing.

Nelson, R.L. (1980). *Soccer* (4th ed.). Dubuque, IA: Wm. C. Brown Publishers.

Orr, T. (November/December 1993). Power soccer championships. *Sports 'n Spokes,* 66–67.

Owen, E. (1984). *Playing and coaching wheelchair basketball.* Urbana, IL: University of Illinois Press.

Paciorek, M., & Jones, J. (1989). *Sports and recreation for the disabled.* Indianapolis, IN: Benchmark Press, Inc.

Roice, G.R. (Ed.). (1981). *Teaching handicapped students physical education.* Washington, DC: National Education Association.

Roper, P., & Roberts, P. (1988). Soccer strategies for the beginning coach and team. In J.A. Jones (Ed.), *Training guide to cerebral palsy sports* (pp. 199–204). Champaign, IL: Human Kinetics Publishers.

Slaymaker, T., & Brown, V.H. (1983). *Power volleyball* (3d ed.). Philadelphia: W.B. Saunders College Publishing.

Smith, F.J. (1980). *Physical education activities handbook.* Winston-Salem, NC: Hunter Publishing Co.

Special Olympics. (n.d.). *Basketball sports skills instructional program.* Washington DC: Joseph P. Kennedy, Jr., Foundation.

Special Olympics. (n.d.). *Hockey sports skills instructional program.* Washington, DC: Joseph P. Kennedy, Jr., Foundation.

Special Olympics. (n.d.). *Soccer sports skills instructional program.* Washington DC: Joseph P. Kennedy, Jr., Foundation.

Enhancing Activities

1. Several athletes have participated in competitive team games even though they possessed a disabling condition. Tom Dempsey, for example, was a very successful professional football place kicker despite the absence of a portion of his foot. Identify other examples of athletes with disabilities and write a short paper on one of the athletes to share with your classmates.

2. Obtain a wheelchair and spend some time participating in a team game such as basketball. Identify the skills you need to develop to become proficient in the sport. This same activity could be repeated using a blindfold to simulate a visual impairment.

3. Observe a team game in which a student with a disability participates. Identify the adaptations that have been made. Develop a list of other modifications that should be considered.

4. Organize a group of students to play a game of goal ball. After the game have the students discuss their impressions of the activity.

5. Contact the local chapter of the Special Olympics and volunteer to serve as a coach for one of the teams. Utilize the suggestions provided by Special Olympics and identify other adaptations that might be incorporated.

6. Review the list of resources provided at the end of this chapter. Select one of the books or journals to read for additional information concerning team games for students with disabling conditions.

7. Identify a team game not discussed in this chapter. Develop a list of suggested adaptations that could be utilized to assist an individual with a specific disability to participate successfully in the game.

Swimming

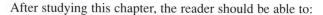

CHAPTER OBJECTIVES

After studying this chapter, the reader should be able to:

1 Appreciate the importance of swimming and water-related activities for individuals with special needs.

2 Modify instruction in swimming so that individuals with various disabilities learn to float, swim, and enjoy the water.

3 Discuss the appropriate use of various assistive devices, including flotation devices, as aids for helping those with disabilities float and swim.

4 Recognize the importance of modifying the pool and locker room to increase the accessibility of these facilities.

5 Select and organize games and activities that can be used to assist students orient to the water.

6 Apply appropriate instructional activities, including task analysis and evaluation procedures, to create effective and efficient swimming experiences for individuals with various disabilities.

7 Recognize when swimming might be contraindicated for some students and the appropriate procedures for helping students with special needs such as epilepsy and incontinence.

8 Analyze the beginning and intermediate strokes used in swimming and modifications that can be made in these strokes for individuals with various orthopedic impairments.

Swimming ranks high among the physical education activities that can be most successfully taught to those who have a disability. The success is due in large part to the buoyancy of the water, which, in providing support for the body, is both helpful and reassuring to the student engaged in learning a new skill. Sustained by the water, an individual with an orthopedic impairment can perform otherwise impossible movements; even those students who are incapable of walking, as is the case with those who have severe cerebral palsy, are frequently able to learn to swim. Students who are mentally retarded find the buoyancy of the water comforting, and this fact is a great help to the teacher in allaying the fears that often prevent successful learning of an activity by individuals with mental retardation.

Swimming is also high among the activities that are most beneficial to individuals with disabilities. Swimming, of course, provides the student with important skills for safety on, in, or near the water. It also makes possible participation in a recreational activity that is popular with the nondisabled and so opens opportunities for socialization and involvement in water-related family activities. In addition, the swimmer with special needs reaps important physiological benefits.

The beneficial effects upon the body result from the amount and nature of the work performed in swimming. Even mild activity in the water has a good effect upon those whose movements are severely restricted. Improved circulation and increased strength are likely to occur in most participants. Those who have restricted movements in the joints caused by pain and stiffness often benefit greatly from the increased movement of the joints made possible in the water. Likewise, those with cerebral palsy often find that because of the water's buoyancy they are able to make movements in the water that they are not otherwise able to make.

Even children with Legg-Calvé-Perthes disease, who are denied participation in so many activities, can enjoy the pleasures of swimming. Although they are not encouraged to stand erect in the water, they can do so without much risk because the buoyancy of the water reduces the pressure of body weight on the head of the femur. For others, the water buoyancy makes control of the body easier by minimizing the effects of weak muscles and the lack of balance and stability that hinder or restrict movement out of the water. Appliances that must always be worn otherwise can usually be removed for swimming.

Organizing the Instruction

Swimming instruction should be scheduled regularly for students who are to be in the swimming program. Class size will vary with conditions. If the students' disabilities are not severe, the teacher will be able to handle larger numbers in a single period. With few exceptions, those with disabilities usually may be included in a regular swimming class for nondisabled students. When the disabilities of students are more severe, the size of the class for one teacher must be reduced proportionately to retain teaching effectiveness and maintain the safety of the participants. For some students with severe disabilities it may be necessary to provide individual instruction. In the school situation, individual instruction may be provided by student helpers. In a community swimming program, volunteers may be recruited from throughout the community.

Before organization of the class and methods of instruction are developed, the instructor must determine each student's present level of skill, movement capabilities, and attitude toward the disability. An example of an evaluation checklist for entering and exiting the water, using a task-analytic format, is presented in figure 26.1. Similar forms should be used to evaluate the individual's performance level. Different kinds of disabilities impose different limitations. The kinds of movements an individual can make will determine the approach used by the instructor. Analysis of movement will provide information for deciding which strokes should be taught and what modifications are necessary. The student's acceptance or lack of acceptance of the disability determines to a considerable extent the way in which the instruction, particularly in its initial phase, is presented.

Consideration must also be given to provisions for those who are incontinent. For example, youngsters with myelomeningocele will have bowel and bladder incontinence. The former is usually managed by appropriate diet and training and, if managed well, is not a problem during activity in water. If the individual has an ileostomy or colostomy and uses an external collection device, the bag should be emptied and cleaned before entering the pool. The bag is not removed for swimming and can be protected from view by the swimming suit to avoid any potential embarrassment. The stoma or opening in the side should be sealed with a watertight bandage. A skimmer should be readily available for dealing with the occasional emergencies when feces are deposited in the pool. Chemicals should be put into the water to prevent such an occurrence from posing a health problem.

As a general rule, swimming is recommended for all individuals with disabilities. There are, however, some conditions that require close articulation with physicians to determine the suitability of swimming and its effect on the safety and health of the affected child as well as others. Some of these conditions include infectious diseases in the active stage (such as when the child has an elevated temperature); chronic ear infections; chronic sinusitis; allergies to chlorine or water; open wounds and sores; skin conditions such as eczema; osteomyelitis in the active stage; acute episodes of rheumatoid arthritis; venereal disease; and severe cardiac conditions.

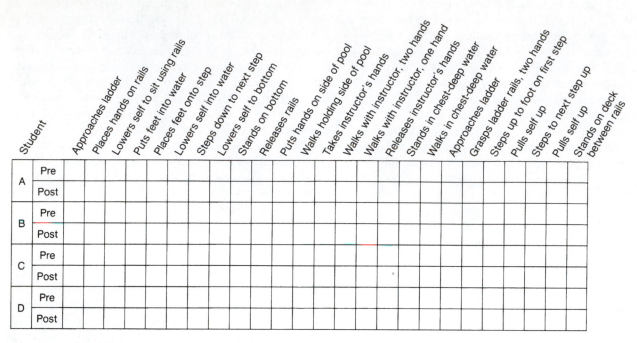

Figure 26.1 Task analysis of entrance into and exit out of the pool.

(Reprinted from *Aquatics for Special Populations.* (1987). YMCA, p. 134.)

The above list does not include children with epilepsy. These children should be encouraged to participate in swimming and other water-related activities. The instructor and lifeguard should be aware of those youngsters who have epilepsy. This is best handled by noting and remembering those who have epilepsy rather than requiring the child to wear a special hat or some other symbol which stigmatizes the youngster. In the event that a child experiences a grand mal seizure in the water, the first aid response is similar to that described in chapter 16. The procedure would call for the instructor or lifeguard to maintain the head above water with the head tilted back to ensure a clear airway and allow the seizure to happen. If time permits, the child should be moved to shallower water; no forced effort, however, should be made to remove the child from the water. In some instances a blanket can be placed in the water under the person to provide additional support. When the seizure is finished, the individual should be removed to a dry and warm room. As discussed in chapter 16, parents and other appropriate officials should be notified so that an accurate record of the frequency of the seizures may be maintained. If the seizure lasts for an extended period of time or a seizure is followed immediately by a second seizure, medical assistance should be obtained. Some authorities recommend, because of the possibility of shock from the ingestion of water, that anyone who has a seizure in the water should be taken to an emergency room for a medical check-up.

Techniques for Getting into and out of the Pool

Locker Room Accessibility

An important consideration in providing swimming instruction for the student with special needs is to ensure that the locker room facilities are accessible. This means, for instance, that the lockers be large enough to accommodate braces and other appliances or orthotics. Some of the lockers should also be opened by a key rather than a combination to assist sudents who are visually impaired. Tables and benches should be available to aid those students who need to dress and undress in a back-lying position. Tables and benches also can be effectively utilized for purposes of transferring to and from a wheelchair. Handrails should be available on some of the walls as well as in the shower and toilet areas. Drinking fountains and showers should be designed to allow the individual with no arms or restricted use of the arms to turn the water on and off.

Priest (1980) suggests that wheelchairs should be permanently stored within the locker room. These chairs could be used to transport nonambulatory students from the locker room to the pool. There are two advantages to this approach: first, the wheelchair would be free of dirt and second, the individual's primary chair would not be subjected to the water and pool chemicals.

The doors into the pool area should be wide enough to accommodate the wheelchair. The locker room floor including the shower area should have a nonskid surface.

Some students, too, may need the assistance of volunteers or peers. These individuals can be very helpful in assisting with dressing and undressing and providing other support as necessary. Volunteers should be cautioned, however, to encourage as much independence as possible and to avoid being oversolicitous.

Students with limited mobility need to develop effective ways of getting into and out of the pool. Ramps and steps with handrails are helpful to those who need only such support as these provide. The techniques for using the ramps and rails need to be worked out by the teacher and the individual student. If these devices, as well as hydraulic lifts, are not available or if they are insufficient, the student will need to be lifted into and out of the pool. Technically, it should be noted that manual lifting of students is considered a violation of the Americans with Disabilities Act (ADA) (1990). The intent of the ADA is not to discourage schools and community centers from offering swimming to students with disabilities, but rather to emphasize that barrier free environments that encourage independence is the desired goal. The ADA and others recognize, however, that until all of the necessary modifications can be made, reasonable accommodations, including lifting individuals to and from the pool, may be necessary.

The usual procedure for lifting students into and out of the pool requires two people. The person who is being assisted may sit on the deck, if able, or be seated in a wheelchair. In the latter case, a helper stands behind the chair and reaches under the student's arms to grasp the wrists and bring them to the chest. The other helper stands in front of the wheelchair and takes hold around the thighs. Together the helpers lift the person free of the chair for seating on a piece of canvas or on a kickboard that has been placed at the edge of the pool. He or she is seated parallel to the pool and supported by one helper while the other enters the water to take a position in front of the student. The helpers turn the canvas so that the student's legs hang over the edge of the pool. The helper on the deck then gently pushes forward on the shoulders of the student while the helper in the pool takes hold at the waist to guide the body into the water. For a student who does not need to be lifted to the edge of the pool, only the techniques for lifting into and out of the water are utilized.

In addition to the above, Adams and McCubbin (1991) emphasize the following points when doing lifts and transfers:

1. Make certain that the brakes on the wheelchair are locked. If additional people are available, have someone hold the wheelchair in addition to locking the brakes.

2. Lifters should use good body mechanics when lifting. The distance the person is lifted should be as small as possible.

3. Explain to the person prior to lifting him or her the plans for the lift and transfer.

4. Lifters should lift the person in unison, with one person giving directions.

5. The swimmer should be lifted from the chair to the deck, then from the deck to the pool. The deck should be nonabrasive. If the deck is abrasive, use a towel or blanket to pad the surface.

6. Ensure that a helper is available to support the person on the deck if necessary.

7. Always have a helper in the pool to help the swimmer into the water.

Special care also will be required when helping the child with a urinary bag transfer into and out of the pool. As indicated in figure 26.2, the hip on the side of the stoma (opening) must be lifted as the child moves from the deck to the water and vice-versa.

A hydraulic lift (figure 26.3) is sometimes available at pools to assist students in wheelchairs into and out of the pool. Although many different systems are available, the goal is to allow the individual to enter and exit the water with as much independence as possible.

If the pool has a ramp, an old wheelchair designated for this purpose is used to wheel the student into the water to chest height. A single helper can then easily transfer the student into the water by placing one arm under the legs and the other behind the back to make the lift. Portable steps into the pool also provide helpful assistance and independence for wheelchair users who are more mobile (figure 26.4)

In all these techniques, the steps for getting students into the pool can be reversed to lift or assist them out. It is assumed, of course, that adjustments are made as required in individual cases.

The choice of techniques used to get someone into and out of the pool is dependent upon the facilities available and the method preferred by the swimmer. For example, although the availability of a hydraulic lift is desirable, some pools may not have this piece of equipment and some swimmers may prefer to be assisted manually.

Pool Accessibility

Generally there are few, if any, modifications that need to be made in the aquatic facility to meet the needs of special students. It is far better to provide swimming instruction for students with disabilities than to argue that the program is not possible because of a poorly designed and somewhat inaccessible pool. Many professionals today realize that creative solutions to problems related to accessibility can be

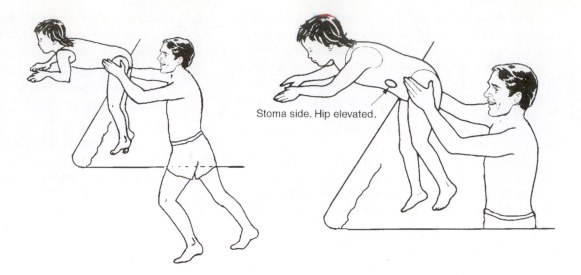

Stoma side. Hip elevated.

Figure 26.2
Modification of over-the-side pool exit for a spina bifida child with stoma and bag.

Figure 26.3 A hydraulic lift is sometimes useful to help the student with a disability get into and out of the water.

achieved given a proper attitude and a desire to make things better. Consumers with disabilities recognize, too, that an inaccessible pool is a serious problem only if the pool manager and instructor are unresponsive and unwilling to seek alternative solutions to help them.

In some school systems and communities that have more than one pool, it may be possible to identify a pool that may be more desirable for use by students with disabilities. Indicated below are some factors that should be considered in checking to determine the appropriateness of the pool.

1. Decks should be wide and slip-resistant. It is also desirable to have a deck that is no more than twelve inches above the water line.

2. The water depth of the pool should be such that a suitable instructional area is available to teach young students with disabilities. An instructional depth of 3½ to 4½ feet is highly desirable. Benches used as resting platforms should be placed in the water to reduce the depth of the pool for paraplegics and double-leg amputees who find a depth of even three feet too deep for them to stand.

3. Higher water temperatures help some individuals, particularly students with cerebral palsy, relax in the water. A water temperature of 80 to 90° F is generally recommended. Indoor pools also should have an air temperature of 4 to 6° F higher than the water temperature.

4. Ramps at the shallow end of the pool are helpful in getting students with orthopedic impairments into and out of the pool. As few older pools are designed with ramps, marine plywood may be used to construct a portable ramp when necessary. Special care must be taken to provide a gradual descent from the ramp into the pool.

5. The bottom of the pool should be as slip-resistant as possible with a gradual slope in the shallow end of one inch per each 1½ feet of horizontal slope.

6. The depth of the pool should be clearly marked on the vertical wall or deck of the pool. The markings

Figure 26.4 Portable steps are helpful for youngsters using and not using a wheelchair and can be easily removed from poolside after use.

should be large and bright so that they may be easily distinguished.

7. Handholds should be provided at depths greater than 3½ feet and spaced no greater than 4 feet apart. Rope fastened to the wall, at or slightly above water level, is an inexpensive adaptation that can be used to assist students with disabilities.

8. Information about accessible dressing rooms, showers, and lockers may be found in appendix VII.

Overcoming Fear of the Water

Most nonswimmers feel some anxiety about entering the water in the beginning. This is especially true of nonswimmers with disabilities because they lack confidence in their movement capabilities. Consequently, the teacher should strive to make the introductory activities to the water as much fun as possible so that the students will begin to feel secure in the water before they have time to be frightened.

The introductory water activities can be fun if the teacher's manner is sincere and friendly, if the instructions are clearly stated and calmly spoken, if the teacher's attitude conveys understanding and appreciation of each student as an individual, and if the instructor's own enthusiasm for water activities is transmitted to the participants.

The teacher should seek to provide experiences that will lead the students from that to which they are accustomed and readily accept to new experiences that will effect complete acceptance of the water. Sitting on the side of the pool splashing with the feet is one example of an activity that is generally accepted without anxiety and that can be directed toward the objective of complete acceptance of the water. Ambulatory students may progress from dangling the feet to standing in waist-deep water and from this to bobbing up and down to their shoulders and eventually to their chins. The final step would be ducking completely under the water and opening the eyes.

For some young students, water adjustment skills are best taught by using a wading pool. The smaller and familiar environment of the wading pool enables the instructor to initiate contact in a setting comfortable to the student. In subsequent sessions the wading pool can be moved closer to the main pool until such time as the trust between student and instructor reaches a point that a successful transfer to the regular pool can be accomplished.

Those who are not ambulatory or have severe limitations in motor movement may need support in the water. Support may be provided by the instructor if this seems necessary or desirable. There are a number of flotation devices (figure 26.5) such as buoyant belts, inflatable vests, arm supports, and swim suits with built-in flotation support that may be used to support or stabilize the body in the water. The students should be held in such a manner as to relieve all fear and anxiety that may develop. Slowly, as their confidence increases, the amount of support can be reduced and finally withdrawn.

With persistent practice almost all children with disabilities can learn to float, or to move in some manner to stay afloat. However, there will be a few who, because of extreme deformity or movement limitations, will always require flotation devices for support in the water.

For students with cerebral palsy it is an absolute necessity that anxiety be kept at a minimum to allow muscular relaxation. For these students, as well as for others who experience difficulty in relaxing in the water, relaxation

Figure 26.5 Various commercially available flotation devices.

exercises such as floating the arms and legs while in a sitting position in shallow water are very helpful. Maintaining the water temperature in the middle eighties, which is somewhat higher than the seventy-eight-degree temperature recommended for normal usage, also aids in muscular relaxation.

Students with visual impairments must be oriented to the pool environment thoroughly to ensure that they have a well-developed mental image of the pool and the surrounding area. The orientation may be accomplished by walking around the pool with the student and explaining concepts

such as pool depth and slope. The location of permanent fixtures such as wall ladders, stairs, diving boards, and lifeguard stands also should be identified for the student who is visually impaired. Opportunities to touch and manually explore pool equipment also assists the blind to develop a meaningful picture of the water environment.

Special care must be taken with the visually impaired and hearing-impaired to ensure their appropriate responses to sensory cues. Establishing a meaningful communication system is particularly desirable for fostering a favorable water environment for student and teacher. For the deaf and hard-of-hearing, this usually requires developing some simple hand signals that communicate concepts such as stop, watch, yes, and so on. Demonstrating the skill to be performed is also effective. With students who are visually impaired, the teacher must promote the desired responses to auditory, tactile, and kinesthetic cues.

During the introductory activities, care should be taken to prevent fearful, cautious individuals from being suddenly and unexpectedly splashed by the more adventurous. A good rule to establish firmly in everyone's mind before entering the water is no deliberate splashing of other people. Care must also be taken to prevent accidents caused by lack of concern for personal safety. Children with cerebral palsy have been observed by swimming instructors to sometimes make no effort to surface for air, after they have become

familiar enough with being in the water to enjoy submerging themselves. These children must be closely watched to avert possible drowning owing to passivity to immersion; their lack of concern gives a false impression of being fully in control.

Individuals who are mentally retarded can be very successful in water-related activities if the various skills, including the orientation phase, are divided into small tasks and sequenced appropriately (figure 26.6). Swimming instructors also should remember that individuals who are mentally retarded need assistance in generalizing skills. Applied to swimming, this means that some orientation activities will be necessary each time the person is exposed to a new water environment. Instructors must emphasize to the student and parents that additional practice will be necessary to ensure success and safety in other water settings.

Walk across the pool holding onto the side with one hand 4 out of 5 times.

Task Analysis

a. Enter pool.
b. Stand next to and face pool wall.
c. Place both hands on wall.
d. Side step the width of the pool.
e. Release one hand and sidestep the width of the pool with support of one hand.
f. Stand with back to pool wall.
g. Hold onto pool wall with one hand (outside hand) and walk from corner to corner in the shallow end.

Teaching Suggestions

• Scatter a large quantity of toys (i.e., balloons, plastic bottles, sponges, etc.) in pool requiring the student to move the toys out of his/her way in order to move about the pool with or without assistance.

Walk across the pool alone 4 out of 5 times.

Task Analysis

a. Enter pool.
b. Stand with back to pool wall.
c. Walk from corner to corner in the shallow end.
d. Walk across the pool in shoulder-deep water.

Teaching Suggestions

• Place hula hoop on top of the water and have students go under the hoop. Once this is accomplished lower the hoop into the water so the students have to go under the water to get through the hoop.
• Have student count your fingers or his/her own while he/she is submerged under the water and his/her face is above the water. Once this is accomplished, student should learn how to open eyes under water and then count fingers.
• Have students search for objects under water, such as rings or large washers. Hands must be used to retrieve objects.

Figure 26.6 Sample task analysis for swimming.

(Source: *Aquatics Sports Skills Program Guide.*)

Figure 26.7 For teaching swimming, a plastic-coated gymnastics mat can serve as a safe and successful platform.

Water Orientation Activities

Students with disabilities frequently require a longer orientation period in the water before they are ready to be taught the basic swimming skills. This longer adjustment time is necessary for several reasons. For some students with disabilities, their previous water experiences have been very limited and they need time to explore the water environment. Some youngsters who are orthopedically impaired find, for instance, that the body movements and positions created by the water buoyancy is exciting, but they need time to explore these new movement sensations. Children who are mentally retarded and neurologically impaired may not have developed the movement concepts, like spatial relationships, that are essential for success in water activities. Regardless of the reason, the time spent in the water in preswimming activities should be structured to create a worthwhile experience for the special student. Some of the water activities that can be used in the early water orientation sessions follow.

Simple Relays

Games in the shallow end of the pool, in which students are asked to walk to and from designated areas, are fun and encourage students to explore the water.

Basic Skill Games

Many motor experiences that children have previously learned can be reinforced in the pool environment. These include simple throwing and catching games. Items such as sponges and Frisbees make ideal objects to throw. The

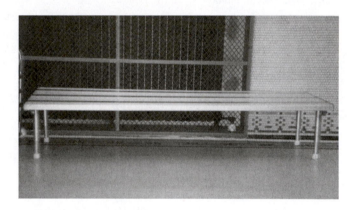

Figure 26.8 A Tot Deck can be placed in the shallow end of the pool for smaller children to gain confidence in the water.

transfer of a familiar skill to the pool environment helps many students in their adjustment to the water.

Circuit Pool

An activity in which children are asked to move around the pool stepping over, around, and under items helps students to associate an enjoyable and familiar land experience with the water while practicing important orientation skills.

Retrieval Games

Children enjoy opportunities to retrieve items that have been placed into the water and around the pool's edge. At first, it is best to have students focus on retrieving objects that do not require them to place the head under water. Later experiences in retrieval of objects with the face in the water can be incorporated into some games students will learn later as they establish their breathing rhythm.

As the students become more accustomed to the water, special group games can be included in the water orientation sessions. These activities will reinforce many of the same concepts, such as taking turns, sharing, and following directions, that students have previously learned. Some popular group water experiences include the following.

Circle Volleyball

This activity requires that the players keep a beach ball in the air for as long as possible without permitting the ball to touch the water. One student is designated as the server to bat the ball into the air to begin the game. Students are encouraged to count the number of consecutive hits they make before the ball touches the water.

Simon Says

This game, with which most children are familiar, is played by having all the students form a circle with one student designated as the leader. The leader calls out movements to be made, prefacing some with the words "Simon says" and others without. Players try to perform only those movements that "Simon says." Various movements such as stepping forward, backward, stooping, bending, and so on, can be incorporated into this activity.

Garbage Clean-Up

Cork balls, ping-pong balls, and other items such as sponges are placed into the pool. The players are divided into two teams. At a given signal, they pick up all the items and place them into buckets placed along the deck. The team collecting the most items is declared the winner.

Movement Relays

Each team is composed of an equal number of players. One member from each team starts the activity by moving to the other side of the pool and back. Upon returning, the player touches a teammate who moves to the other side and returns. The team that has its last player return first is declared the winner. As the name of this relay implies, various movement patterns should be emphasized, such as walking forward, backward, sideways, stooped walking with the chin touching the water, arms over the head, and so forth. Some relays should also be designed to encourage controlled movements such as walking three steps, stop, turn completely around, and move forward again.

Object Relays

Relays in which students move various objects such as kickboards, ping-pong balls, sponges, and plastic balls, around the pool are enjoyable. This activity should be structured so that students have to use various body parts to move the designated objects. Beginners, for instance, might be asked to use their chests to move a beach ball. As the students become better adjusted to the water, this activity can be increased in difficulty by having the students push the ball with the chin. Obviously, this latter experience is an excellent lead-up to placing the face into the water.

Add-Ons

Children enjoy this activity in which one student starts by making a movement that must be repeated by a second student before the latter adds a second movement. The next student performs the first two movements and adds a third. This is an excellent activity because students challenge one another and the instructor is provided an opportunity to observe and assess the quantity and quality of the student's water orientation skills.

One of the concomitant values of the water orientation activities described in this section is that these experiences also reinforce many of the skills taught in the classroom. Specific academic skills that can be supported through water orientation experiences include counting, recognizing letters, and color discrimination. Basic arithmetic and spelling concepts, for example, can be reinforced by having students count the number of plastic letters retrieved from the bottom of the pool and asking them to form words with the letters. The letters could also be sorted by color and size and alphabetized to help students with their color, visual, and language skills. Additionally, children are taught to follow directions, take turns, and develop sequence skills. Although helping the special student orient to the water is in and of itself a worthy objective, other benefits such as reinforcing classroom skills are possible in well-designed water adjustment programs.

Establishing Breathing Rhythm

As soon as the students show sufficient confidence, they may proceed to place their faces in the water while holding their breath. This is done by bending over from a standing position in chest-high water. Students should be encouraged to repeat the action until they are able to hold their face under the water fifteen to twenty seconds.

The next step is to exhale through the mouth while the face is submerged. The final step is to establish a definite rhythmic pattern of breathing. To achieve this the students bob the head up and down in the water, taking air in through the mouth while the head is above the water and exhaling through the mouth while the head is down.

Those who cannot stand may take a sitting position on the bottom of the pool if the water is shallow enough. A steel chair may be used where the water is not sufficiently shallow to permit sitting on the bottom. The seated student performs these activities in the sitting position. If a student must be wholly supported by the instructor or helper, which may be the case in muscular disorders or severe conditions of cerebral palsy, the introduction to the water is made by the instructor holding the student around the waist from the back. If the pool is shallow enough, the teacher sits down in the water while providing support with one hand. In this position the student's arms and legs can be moved alternately by the teacher in the swimming pattern, starting with raising the arms over the head and pulling them to the sides and followed by moving the legs in a kicking fashion. The kinds and amount of movement that can be made by the arms and legs depend, of course, on the limitations of the individual. Later, when progress permits, the student may be held in a prone position to allow lifting the head above and lowering the face into the water at will.

Individuals with cardiac conditions should not be allowed to practice breath holding. For these students, instruction in how to expel air while the face is under water must accompany the instruction in how to place the face in the water. Or, if their conditions are moderate to severe, they may be taught floating and swimming techniques that do not require submersion of the face.

Some children affected by the rubella syndrome appear to have a high sensitivity to certain pool chemicals, even if they have no visual disability. For this reason, a container of clean water should be kept at pool level so that these students can bathe their eyes at regular intervals.

Rhythmic breathing assists students with cerebral palsy to develop their breathing skills as well as improve their breath control and speech pattern. For this reason, some variation of breathing exercises should be incorporated into every lesson for the student with cerebral palsy.

Assistive Devices

There are numerous assistive devices that can be used to help the nonswimmer learn to swim. Swim fins, for example are recommended for children with spastic cerebral palsy. The fins tend to minimize the exaggerated stretch reflex and provide additional power in the kick. Fins are also used to increase the length of a short extremity or serve as a replacement for an extremity. Some students who are quadriplegic, for example, have learned to swim with the assistance of four swim fins serving as the legs and arms. The fins are attached with straps that cross the swimmers' shoulders and lower trunk, simulating the action of the arms and legs. For swimmers with upper extremity amputations, a swimming hand prostheses (figure 26.9) has been suggested as a valuable aid by Radocy (1987).

Goggles, nose clips, and ear plugs can be used to assist some students who experience discomfort in the water. Some physicians will recommend that ear plugs, in particular, be used by certain students. Goggles can be effective in helping the student whose eyes are extremely sensitive to

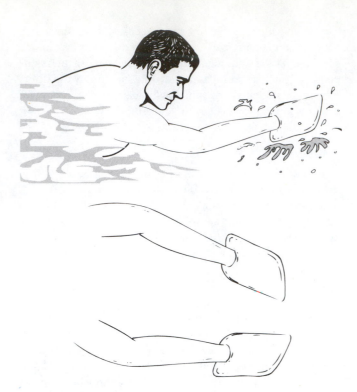

Figure 26.9 The Tabula Swimming Hand prosthesis.

the chemicals used in the water. Generally, swimmers who are blind or visually impaired require few equipment modifications to swim successfully. Some may prefer to use an audible cue, such as a beeper device, to assist them in maintaining a straight line when swimming laps. Tap-sticks, which are used by coaches to signal when to begin the flip turn or to indicate distance from the edge of the pool, are helpful and used by some swimmers with visual impairments (figure 26.10).

While some have questioned the use of flotation devices in swimming programs, they have been found to be invaluable in programs for students with disabilities. They can be used to equalize the body by adding needed buoyancy to one of the sides. In addition, flotation devices allow swimmers with severe impairments to enjoy the water without being held or holding on to an object or another person. Some flotation devices can be made from discarded items such as plastic milk jugs and soda bottles. Kickboards, plastic doughnut rings, and styrofoam buoys are items that can be used and are normally available in most swimming pools.

Personal flotation devices (formerly known as life jackets) also can be a helpful and useful swimming aid for the individual who is severely involved. There are five types of personal flotation devices (PFD) graded according to the amount of buoyancy they provide, with Type I being the most buoyant. Types I, II, and III PFDs are designed to maintain the swimmer in a vertical and slightly backward position in the water. Each swimmer, however, should try the PFD to ensure that the desired fit and action in the water are achieved. Swimmers who are orthopedically impaired including those with neuromuscular disorders, may find that

Figure 26.10 The use of "tap-sticks" allows swimmers who are blind and visually impaired to know when to begin their flip turns.

the PFD does not respond as expected. Bradley et al. (1981) caution that PFDs may not give adequate support if used as a life jacket for some individuals with disabilities. They stress that some of the PFDs available on the market may not provide correct positioning in the water and are difficult to put on.

Heckathorn (1980) recommends that flotation devices be used to regulate body positions. When the following conditions exist, she offers these guidelines:

1. Affected Side Floats Lower in Water
    Life preserver (PFD I, II, or III) around waist, hips, or chest.
    Plastic bottles with velcro strap around waist, hips, or chest.
    Plastic bottles with strap or flotation collar around affected leg(s) and/or arm(s).

2. Legs Sink
    Plastic bottles with velcro strap around legs, hips, or waist.
    Life preserver (PFD I, II, or III) around waist or hips.

3. Hips Sink
    Plastic bottles with velcro strap around hips or waist.
    Life preserver (PFD I, II, or III) around waist or hips.

Adams and McCubbin (1991) believe that the standard Personal Flotation Device works well for those needing support of the head or neck. They caution, however, that the PFD restricts swimming to the supine or backstroke position. The Delta Swim System, developed by Danmark, is a viable alternative and is adaptable to meet various aquatic needs (figure 26.12).

In presenting adaptations that can be made, very brief descriptions of the specific skills are given to enable the reader to make a better comparison of the adaptation with

Figure 26.11 Combo-head flotation device and sectional raft.

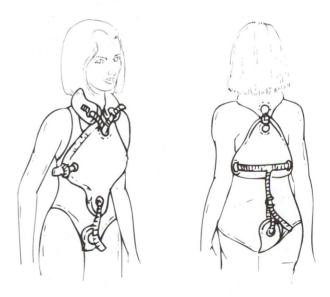

Figure 26.12 The Delta Swim System.

normal performance and so gain a better understanding of the process of adapting skills for those with disabilities. It is not the intent to provide instruction for learning to perform the skills. Those who wish this information are referred to the books in Selected Readings at the end of the chapter.

Beginning Swimming Skills

Teaching a person to float requires an understanding of Archimedes' Principle, which states that a body submerged in a liquid is buoyed up by a force equal to the weight of the displaced liquid. In applying this to swimming, it means that a person will float if the individual's weight does not exceed that of an equal volume of water. This concept is expressed by the following formula:

$$\text{Specific Gravity} = \frac{\text{Weight of Equal Amount of Water}}{\text{Weight of Body}}$$

The specific gravity (also known as relative density) for most adults, after full inspiration, is slightly less than one. The smaller the specific gravity, the easier it is to float. The relative density of the human body varies with age. Young children float easily because their relative density is, on the average, .86. Because muscle weighs more than fat, young athletic individuals, particularly males, experience greater challenges in floating. With age and an increase in adipose tissue, the relative density becomes less, allowing an individual to float with greater ease.

An understanding of the center of buoyancy is also an important concept when teaching a person to float. The center of buoyancy of an individual is that point at which weight is concentrated and serves as a fulcrum about which the body rotates. The center of buoyancy may be thought of as the center of gravity, but applied to the body in water. Only when the center of buoyancy and center of gravity are in the same line can a person float without motion. For some individuals, this will be a position at which the body is parallel to the water. Others, however, will float in almost a vertical position with the legs and feet below the shoulders. Each person must experiment to find that place where the centers of buoyancy and gravity are aligned vertically.

Bloomquist (1992) stresses that the following factors should be considered for all floaters:

1. When any body part is removed from the water, the buoyancy decreases.
2. When the head is lifted during supine floating, the feet sink.
3. When balance is lost, the falling is slowed because of the resistance of the water, allowing for more recovery time.
4. When the head turns to the side, the body tends to follow, causing rotation on the vertical axis.
5. Air held in the lungs increases floating ability.

6. Long, heavy legs lower the center of gravity, causing feet to drop.
7. Bending the knees raises the center of gravity, thereby increasing floating ability.
8. Raising arms over head slowly and underwater raises the center of gravity, thereby increasing floating.
9. People with a greater-than-average amount of fat float more easily.
10. Muscular people and adolescents have more difficulty floating.
11. Children, because of their low density, and the elderly, because of their increased adipose tissue, tend to float more easily.
12. Gripping with hands, holding the breath, or shutting the eyes increases tension and decreases relaxation which is important to successful floating.
13. Fear and cold decrease floating.
14. Because of the need to rotate from prone to supine and return, all swimmers should learn to exhale and blow bubbles as soon as the face enters the water.

In teaching individuals with disabilities to float, the instructor will need to be cognizant of the specific disability and adaptations that may be required. Some examples of factors identified by Bloomquist (1992) to consider when teaching people with disabilities to float include the following:

1. Muscles that are spastic are heavier and tend to decrease floating ability in the affected area.
2. Paralyzed, flaccid muscles are less dense and tend to increase the ability to float in the affected area.
3. A body with a spinal deviation (e.g., scoliosis) will tend to cause body rotation.
4. An individual who is spastic hemiplegic will: (a) have decreased respiration and less buoyancy on the affected side thereby decreasing floating ability and (b) tend to be shorter on the affected side and roll toward that side.
5. Individuals who are blind or visually impaired will have more difficulty floating and following instructions when their main mode of communication (hearing) is lost because of ears being below the water line when floating.
6. A person whose spasticity places elbows, wrists, or knees in flexion may have difficulty keeping body parts in the water, thus reducing buoyancy.

The Tuck Float

Learning to float helps greatly to promote self-confidence in the beginning swimmer. The tuck float is an easy float for the beginner to learn; moreover, in the process of learning it, the student develops the ability to regain the feet in the water. To learn the tuck float, a nonswimmer should stand in water about chest deep. A deep breath is taken and the face is placed in the water; then the knees are pulled up to the chest and gripped with the arms. Holding this position, the body floats to the surface. A return to the standing position is accomplished by releasing the knees and thrusting the feet down. At the same time the head is raised. The hands push down on the water to help regain balance.

The Face Float

The prone face is executed by bending at the hips and placing the face in the water. At the same time the feet are pushed against the bottom of the pool to place the body in a horizontal position face down on the surface of the water. The hands are extended in front. The return to a standing position is made by raising the head and bringing the knees up under the body. The arms are brought forcefully to the sides while at the same time the legs are extended downward into a standing position.

The Back Float

In the back float, a position is taken by extending the head back and pushing slightly with the feet from the bottom. The hips are lifted high and the head is placed back so the ears are under the water. The arms may be held at the sides or extended to the side. A recovery to a standing position is made by bringing the knees toward the chin as the head is brought up and forward. The hands are brought down and past the hips. As the body rights itself, the legs are extended to the bottom.

Adaptations: Tuck and face floats cannot be taught to students who should not hold their breath (for example, those with cardiac disturbances). In these cases the vertical float is used as a substitution.

Some students who are learning disabled also prefer the vertical float position because of the visual field distortion they experience in the back float position.

Students with severe cerebral palsy will often be non-buoyant, and the use of flotation devices may be necessary. These individuals also frequently have difficulty maintaining head control. For this reason it is recommended that the vertical float be emphasized and that each individual be assessed carefully before progressing to a back or front float position. Frequent rest periods are also recommended. Chairs and benches placed in the water can be effectively used as rest stations. The youngster with cerebral palsy who has the spastic hemiplegic condition will have difficulty maintaining the symmetry necessary for effective floating. A technique that can be used to compensate for this is to turn the head away from the side to which the body wants to roll. If this is not sufficient compensation, the affected leg may be crossed over the nonaffected leg, either at the knee or ankle, depending on the amount of roll that requires correcting. In the vertical float, the body is at approximately a seventy-degree angle with the face lifted just enough to clear the water. This will need to be done in water that is chin

deep or deeper. A slight movement of the arms may be necessary to keep the chin above water. A helper may support the body until the swimmer gains confidence and skill in using the arms. To give support, the helper places one hand under the swimmer's chest.

Those who cannot support themselves in the water on their feet should be held by a helper until they have acquired sufficient confidence to use the kickboard or hang on to the gutter for support. A hand placed under the chest in the face float or under the head in the back float will provide sufficient support.

Those who do not have use of the arms will need help at first in regaining their feet from a float position, but they can learn to right themselves by a very forceful extension of the legs while simultaneously lifting the head and shoulders. If the swimmer has the use of only one arm, the arm action used to regain the feet should be executed as near to the center of the body as possible for maximum effectiveness.

Individuals who are visually impaired will have difficulty floating and following instructions when their ears are below the water line. For some this may require the assistance of flotation devices or reliance on the face rather than the back float.

Individuals who are orthopedically impaired will need to experiment with various positions to offset the effect of the displacement of the center of gravity and center of buoyancy. For example, a student who has lost a right leg will tend to roll to the left where the weight of the body is centered.

Where the legs or hands are atrophied due to disease, they are less dense and float easily. Therefore, children with spina bifida and paraplegia will find that their limbs rise to the surface. In the back float position, the swimmer will need to extend the head to depress the feet.

Drownproofing Technique

Regardless of the swimming skill level achieved by students with disabilities, they should eventually be exposed to the water survival skill of drownproofing. This technique, developed during World War II by Fred Lanoue, was used initially to teach servicemen how to remain afloat in water. Today this system of vertical floating is routinely taught as a part of school and community swimming programs. The drownproofing technique can be learned by individuals of various ages and body compositions, including those who are orthopedically impaired.

The basic concept that all good drownproofers must learn is to float face downward in a vertical position. This is the natural position dictated by the buoyant effect of the water. From this position one is taught to breathe about five or six times a minute by lifting the head slightly. Obviously, much energy is conserved by lifting the head only when one wants to breathe. However, the action of lifting the head causes a reaction that tends to send the body downward. This response can be countered by a simple kick of the legs, which assists the body to maintain its relaxed vertical position. People who learn the skill of drownproofing can travel and breathe in the water with only a minimal use of any limbs. This is an important consideration for swimmers with disabilities, particularly those who are orthopedically impaired.

The sequence used in breathing in a vertical float position is as follows:

1. Take a deep breath and assume the vertical face-down position. Relax the entire body with the chin to the chest and the arms hanging freely at the side.
2. Slowly cross the arms in front of the forehead with forearms together.
3. Gently raise the head out of the water to chin level while breathing out at all times.
4. Breathe in normally while gently moving the arms down and out.
5. Let the head descend under water. The arms should assume a relaxed position at the sides of the body. From this vertical rest position, the breathing cycle should be repeated.

Adaptations: Swimmers with paralyzed or amputated limbs will need to modify the drownproofing technique to compensate for their increased buoyancy. For example, a swimmer with only one arm will tend to list to one side in the vertical float position. For this individual a modification will be necessary in the way the head is raised from the water during the breathing cycle. Each adaptation of this nature will have to be individually designed to respond to specific needs.

The student who is ataxic should be watched during attempts to regain the standing position because of a poor sense of balance, particularly when the feet cannot be seen.

The Glide and the Flutter Kick

After beginners have learned the face float, they may be taught how to glide in the prone position. The glide is performed much like the face float except that, instead of lifting the feet off the bottom, the feet push off from the bottom to move the body forward in a prone float position.

The flutter kick is the simplest kick to learn. The student assumes a prone position and thrashes the legs alternately up and down. The kick starts at the hip, followed by extension of the knee. The toes are extended. The feet are spread vertically from fifteen to twenty inches. For younger children, the spread will be less.

Adaptations: If physical abilities permit, the kick may be introduced as a land drill; the student assumes a prone position on a bench with the legs projected beyond the bench. The kick also can be practiced while holding on to the gutter or a kickboard. After the kick is mastered, it is combined with the prone float to propel the body forward.

Those who cannot put their faces in the water should be assisted by helpers who take the swimmers by their extended hands to tow them while they kick.

Swimmers who have lost the use of one leg must learn to use the remaining leg in the flutter kick. If the leg is paralyzed, it may be helpful to put a small float under the thigh of the affected leg.

The Dog Paddle and the Human Stroke

In the dog paddle the head is held above the water. The arms are alternately extended forward and downward and then pulled backward under the chest. At the same time the feet are moved in the flutter kick. The human stroke is executed much like the dog paddle except that the face is in the water as in the prone float and the arms are fully extended in front of the head before pulling down and back. As in the dog paddle, the hands do not leave the water.

Adaptations: Those who are able may practice the arm stroke with the leg kick on a bench before getting into the water. Following this the arm movement is practiced while standing in chest-deep water.

Land practice of swimming strokes is not effective for swimmers with cerebral palsy because of the increased tension in the muscles when they are out of the water. Consequently, all of their practice should be in the water.

Swimmers who have limited movement of their limbs will need to be supported by a helper who passes a hand under the swimmer's chest. Flotation devices also may be used as supports for these students. Those who have difficulty balancing in the water because of amputation or atrophy of a limb must make the necessary movements of the active limbs close to the center of the body to overcome the imbalance. The best placement of the limbs can be determined by movement analysis and subsequent experimentation.

Some youngsters with disabilities will not be able to learn to swim or float in the prone position. For these, the progression in swimming should be from the back float to the elementary back stroke or, if this is not feasible, any movement that propels the body in any direction while supine.

Intermediate Swimming Strokes

The side stroke, the elementary back stroke, and the crawl are strokes that are frequently taught on the intermediate level.

The Side Stroke

The body is turned on its side with the stronger arm on top. The arm under the water is fully extended at right angles to the body while the other arm rests fully extended along the side of the body. The under arm is brought down to a nearly vertical position and then the elbow is bent. At the same time, the top arm is brought up to enter the water near the head. This arm recovers to the starting position with a downward reaching movement. Meanwhile the other arm is recovering with a pulling movement toward the body.

The kick for the side stroke is called the scissors. The legs are bent slightly at the knees as one leg (usually the top leg) is brought in front of the body and the other leg is moved to the rear. The legs are then extended fully and brought together forcefully in a movement resembling the opening and closing of a scissors.

The movements of the arms and legs are coordinated to begin and recover simultaneously. The body glides momentarily in the water before the next stroke begins.

Adaptations: Those who have weak shoulder joints subject to frequent dislocation will find the side stroke the safest stroke for swimming. It will also be the most effective stroke and the most easily learned by those who have lost one limb. When there is a disabled or missing arm, the side stroke is performed with the functional arm on the bottom.

When one leg is missing or disabled, the functional leg may be on either the top or the bottom, whichever proves better through trial and error. If both legs have been lost, the swimmer will probably have to find a suitable modified position through experimentation; this will usually be a partially prone position rather than wholly on the side of the body.

Many students who are visually impaired or blind feel the side stroke is the ideal stroke for them because one ear is always above water, allowing them to listen for and respond to auditory cues.

The Elementary Back Stroke

The arm movement for the elementary back stroke begins with the arms fully extended at a forty-five-degree angle between the head and shoulders. The arms are brought to the sides of the body in a sweeping arc. In the recovery the hands are brought along the sides of the body to shoulder height. They are then fully extended to begin the next downward stroke.

In the kick, the knees are brought up and out to the sides about shoulder width apart. The kick starts when the heels drop below the water surface, then the feet are brought outward with the ankles flexed and toes pointing outward. Finally the legs are extended and feet brought together.

The straightening of the legs occurs at the same time that the arms are being brought down to the sides. The arms recover along the body to the armpits before the legs start their recovery.

Adaptations: Many students with disabilities find it easier to swim on the back than in any other position. In the back position, almost any kind of movement with the arms or legs will move the body in some direction. If the swimmer does not have use of the arms, the legs may be used in a flutter kick to propel the body; conversely, if the legs cannot be used, the arms may be used as in the back stroke.

Finning and sculling movements with the hands may be substituted for the arm stroke if movement of the arms is restricted.

The Crawl

In teaching the crawl, it is necessary only to add the arm movement to the flutter kick and breathing technique introduced in the beginning skills. The arm stroke is made by extending the arm fully in front of the face and pressing downward against the water, with the hand leading the rest of the arm. When the arm is beneath the shoulder, the shoulder is lifted and the elbow is raised until it clears the water. The arm is then brought forward above the water with the fingers near the water, ready for entrance into the water for the next stroke.

The arms stroke alternately, and inhalation should occur as the shoulder is lifted in the recovery. The head may be turned to either side, depending upon which seems more natural for the swimmer. The kick is coordinated with the arms to accomplish a smooth and rhythmical stroke.

Adaptations: The crawl is the most satisfactory stroke for those with loss of movement in the legs. In some cases of leg disability, flexion and extension may be developed to compensate for lack of leg action. Hip impairment may require the swimmer to execute the flutter kick with greater knee bend.

The arm stroke may be modified for those with arm and shoulder limitations by reducing it to less than the full stroke. The crawl should not be swum by those with weak shoulder joints subject to frequent dislocation.

Quad amputees have learned to perform the crawl stroke effectively with the assistance of fins attached to their stumps.

Evaluation

As indicated in chapter 7, *Evaluation,* it is essential that information about student progress be monitored for each instructional unit. In aquatic programs various types of charts may be used, and skills to be included will vary according to the content of the swimming program. An example of an evaluation checklist is found in table 26.1. This form includes preliminary skills such as the student's proximity to the pool as well as more advanced skills such as performing the crawl unassisted. Measuring progress helps students and instructors appreciate the educational gains that are possible through well-designed instructional programs. A record of the skills achieved should be shared with parents and school administrators and filed for subsequent use by other instructors.

Table 26.1 *Swimming checklist sheet*

Name _____   Movements contraindicated _____

Age _____   _____

                                                    Date _____

Skills																							
Enters pool environment																							
Sits on deck																							
Puts feet in water																							
Enters pool																							
Walks across pool																							
Puts face in water																							
Blows bubbles																							
Bobs																							
Floats, tuck																							
Floats, face																							
Floats, back																							
Glides																							
Flutter kick																							
Side stroke																							
Elementary back stroke																							
Crawl stroke																							

Code Symbols: **Instructor's Comments:**
Achieved (unassisted)   +
Achieved (assisted)   1
Practiced   0

Summary

Swimming is a desirable activity for students with disabilities for many reasons. Instruction and programs in swimming improve physical fitness, develop desirable water-related safety skills, provide fun and wholesome recreation, and serve as one more important outlet for individuals with disabilities to interact with the nondisabled. In addition, the water's buoyancy allows individuals with orthopedic impairments and muscular disorders to make movements they are not otherwise able to make.

Most individuals with disabilities can learn to float and swim. The extent to which the individual becomes proficient as a swimmer will vary depending upon the level of disability. Many swimmers with disabilities have achieved at a high level. These successes are attributed to individual effort and the availability of instructional programs. As was emphasized in earlier chapters, good instruction requires that the swimming tasks be broken down and sequenced according to their level of difficulty. An evaluation system should be utilized to help the instructor keep track of student progress. Swimming instructors should be creative in modifying the various strokes and use, when necessary, selected assistive devices. Flotation devices can be very helpful in assisting the swimmer who has a disability in floating and/or supporting the body so that various strokes can be performed.

An important element in the swimming program for swimmers with disabilities is the availability of an environment that is sensitive to their special needs. Emphasis should be placed on the accessibility of the pool and locker room. In addition, the temperature of the water should be higher to help the swimmer relax and to compensate for the slower movements of some of the swimmers. Assistive devices including fins, goggles, ear plugs, nose clips, and various flotation devices should be available as needed.

One of the primary goals of the swimming program is to keep individuals with disabilities safe in the water. Special emphasis, therefore, should be placed on helping the swimmer to understand buoyancy and its effect in relationship to the individual's disability. This will require some experimentation to determine the best floating and swimming position.

Swimming is an excellent activity for its obvious physiological and psychological benefits. Learning to swim is also important as a means of ensuring that a child with a disability is included in water-related activities with other children. Many of the summer activities for children and their families include being in or close to water. The ability to swim will help students with disabilities to be part of the mainstream in a very popular school, community, and family activity. With the assistance of knowledgeable and creative instructors and the availability of accessible facilities, individuals with disabilities will have the opportunity to enjoy the fun and excitement of being in the water.

Selected Readings

Adams, R.C., & McCubbin, J.A. (1991). *Games, sports, and exercises for the physically handicapped* (4th ed.). Philadelphia: Lea and Febiger.

American National Red Cross. (1975). *Swimming for the handicapped—Instructor's manual* (Rev. ed.). Washington, DC: Author.

American National Red Cross. (1977). *Adapted aquatics.* Garden City, NY: Doubleday and Company, Inc.

Bettsworth, M. (1977). *Drownproofing.* New York: Schocken Books.

Bloomquist, L.C. (1992). *University of Rhode Island adapted aquatics program manual* (3d ed.). Kingston, RI: Rhode Island Board of Governors of Higher Education.

Bradley, N.J., Fuller, J.L., Pozcos, R.S., & Willmers, L.E. (1981). PFDs, personal flotation devices. A lifejacket is a lifejacket . . . not necessarily so, especially if you're disabled. *Sports 'n Spokes*, 23–25.

Campion, M.R. (1985). *Hydrotherapy in pediatrics.* Rockville, MD: Aspen Systems Corporation.

Cordellos, H.C. (1976). *Aquatic recreation for the blind.* Washington, DC: American Alliance for Health, Physical Education, Recreation, and Dance.

Council for National Cooperation in Aquatics and American Association for Health, Physical Education, and Recreation. (1969). *A practical guide for teaching the mentally retarded to swim.* Washington, DC: AAHPER.

Grosse, S., & McGill, C. (1979). Independent swimming for children with severe physical impairments. In *AAHPERD Practical Pointers* (p. 3). Washington, DC: American Alliance for Health, Physical Education, Recreation, and Dance.

Heckathorn, J. (1980). *Strokes and strokes.* Reston, VA: AAHPERD Publications.

Newman, J. (1976). *Swimming for children with physical and sensory impairments.* Springfield, IL: Charles C. Thomas.

Paciorek, M.J., & Jones, J.A. (1989). *Sports and recreation for the disabled.* Indianapolis: IN: Benchmark Press, Inc.

Priest, E.L. (1980). *Teaching of adapted aquatics.* Lecture presented at summer workshop, Illinois State University, Normal, IL.

Radocy, B. (1987). Upper extremity prosthetics: Considerations and designs for sports and recreation. *Clinical Prosthetics and Orthotics, 11*(3): 131–153.

Special Olympics Sports Instructional Program. (n.d.). *Swimming and diving.* Washington, DC: Joseph P. Kennedy, Jr., Foundation.

United Cerebral Palsy Associations, Inc. (n.d.). *Swimming for the cerebral palsied.* New York: United Cerebral Palsy Associations, Inc. (321 West 44th Street, New York, NY, 10036).

YMCA of the United States. (1987). *Aquatics for special populations.* Champaign, IL: Human Kinetics Publishers.

Enhancing Activities

1. Using the facility checklist found in appendix VII, conduct a survey of a neighborhood or school swimming pool and the adjacent locker-room area. Suggest modifications that might be made to increase the facility's accessibility.

2. Float and swim with an inflatable ring attached to your leg. Note how the increased buoyancy on one side requires you to compensate and change your technique for floating and swimming.

3. Swim the length of the pool with your legs tied together. Identify the various ways in which the stroke is changed to compensate for the loss of the legs.

4. With the assistance of helpers, transfer from a wheelchair into and out of the pool.

5. Develop a list of water games and water orientation activities that expand upon those identified in this chapter.

6. Volunteer to assist in a swimming program for those with special needs. Apply your knowledge of task analysis to develop appropriate learning activities.

7. Visit the local offices of the YMCA or Red Cross to obtain information and resources concerning swimming for individuals with disabilities.

CHAPTER

27

Physical Fitness

After studying this chapter, the reader should be able to:

1 Define the terms *physical fitness* and *motor fitness* and explain the difference between these concepts.

2 Identify and describe the components of health-related fitness and the importance of these for individuals with disabilities.

3 Describe the various tests of physical fitness including those that have been specifically developed for individuals with disabilities.

4 Develop physical fitness programs for various disability populations utilizing scientific concepts from exercise science.

5 Recognize the need for physical fitness programs that are responsive to the individual needs of special populations.

6 Adapt physical fitness and exercise programs to accommodate the special needs of individuals with various disabilities.

7 Understand that the physical fitness needs of those with disabilities are very similar to those of the nondisabled and that integrated fitness programs should be encouraged.

8 Recognize that for individuals with severe cognitive dysfunction, physical fitness programs must be data based and systematically structured.

Physical education in the United States was founded on the premise that students' health is enhanced through formal exercise. The earliest school programs consisted primarily of group calisthenics designed to exercise the major muscle groups and improve posture and breathing. Early leaders of American physical education included Dr. Edward Hitchcock, Dr. Dudley Sargent, Dr. Edward Hartwell, and Dr. William Anderson, all medical doctors who were convinced of the need for the preservation of health through exercise and knowledge of the laws of hygiene. Though the scope of physical education has expanded beyond that of health maintenance, achievement of healthful levels of physical fitness has remained a major objective of physical education programs in our schools.

Growing public awareness of the relationship of physical fitness to health since the 1950s has produced additional emphasis on physical fitness as a paramount objective of physical education. The focus began with the observations of Hans Kraus and Ruth Hirschland that American children were less fit than many European youths. President Dwight D. Eisenhower reacted by creating the President's Council on Youth Fitness, whose goal it was to promote programs designed to enhance the physical fitness of children. The Council continues today as the President's Council on Physical Fitness and Sports and has been instrumental in promoting school and private physical fitness programs. In 1958 the American Association for Health, Physical Education, and Recreation[1] initiated the Youth Fitness Test, with national norms for school-age children. This test served to foster interest in physical fitness improvement through school physical education programs. A separate Health Related Physical Fitness Test was subsequently developed to emphasize the important distinction between physical fitness and motor fitness. In 1993, the American Alliance for Health, Physical Education, Recreation and Dance (AAHPERD), in an effort to provide the best possible health-related fitness program, developed a partnership with the Cooper Institute for Aerobic Research (CIAR). Under the agreement with the CIAR, AAHPERD accepted responsibility for developing and producing fitness education materials and CIAR agreed to develop the fitness assessment and supporting material. It was further agreed that the Prudential Fitnessgram, a criterion-referenced instrument would be used to measure physical fitness. Using the Fitnessgram, performance is judged with regard to standards which reflect a desirable state of health-related physical fitness. Standards exist for the following components: aerobic capacity, body composition, muscular strength and endurance, and flexibility.

Increased concern over the incidence of heart disease, obesity, and high blood pressure has spurred an interest in cardiorespiratory or aerobic fitness. The current popularity of jogging and other aerobic activities appears directly related to enhanced interest of our populace in healthful life-styles. This acceptance of the importance of exercise to health is producing growing support for physical fitness as a major objective of contemporary physical education programs.

Recent years have also seen a growing recognition for the importance of the health benefits of enhanced physical fitness to the typically less active, including individuals with disabilities. Due to a combination of factors including physical inability, overprotection, self-consciousness, and societal pressures, individuals with disabling conditions often engage in less daily physical activity than do those who are not disabled. This reduced level of daily exercise negatively affects the functional capacity of their neuromuscular and cardiorespiratory systems, producing a generally lower level of physical fitness. One special group, the mentally retarded, have been identified as having significantly poorer scores on some tests of physical fitness and especially on measures of body fatness and cardiorespiratory endurance (Dobbins, Garron, and Rarick, 1981; Moon and Renzaglia, 1982; Fernhall, Tymeson, and Webster, 1988; Rimmer, 1992). Similar findings have been reported for other disability populations including the visually impaired (Jankowski and Evans, 1981), learning disabled (Rimmer and Rosentsweig, 1982), those with cerebral palsy (Short and Winnick, 1986; Winnick and Short, 1991), children with ostomy (Vogler, 1990), and children and adolescents with insulin dependent diabetes mellitus (Kertzer et al., 1994).These findings indicate that those with disabilities, as a group, are less physically fit than the nondisabled. Enhanced opportunity for activity and attempts at motivating individuals with disabilities to be more physically active would serve to improve their general physical fitness status.

The rehabilitative value of exercise has been universally accepted as an adjunct in the return of injured persons to normal functioning as well as in retarding the progress of some diseases. Similar exercise techniques can be used to strengthen alternate muscle groups to aid in compensating for ineffective muscle actions in those with disabilities.

In addition to the direct health benefits, enhanced physical fitness may produce desirable changes in an individual's appearance, self-concept, social relations, and general improvement in the quality of life (Pitetti and Campbell, 1991). A physically fit body is generally associated with a more desirable physical appearance. The body image of individuals with disabilities is often quite negative due to their specific abnormalities. This negative attitude toward the body is often generalized and dominates their ideas of how they look to others. By enhancing the fitness of an individual with a disability, a positive change in body image can result. As the person becomes more capable physically, his or her concept of self in a physical sense is usually improved and may result in greater self-acceptance as well as in acceptance by others. Improved physical fitness will allow the individual with a disability to participate more fully in the

[1]The name of the organization has since been changed to the American Alliance for Health, Physical Education, Recreation, and Dance (AAHPERD).

normal activities of life. This enhanced participation is likely to lead to social development and increased social acceptance.

Most sports and physical games have as a basis some component of physical fitness; that is, some degree of muscular strength, endurance, and flexibility is necessary to perform the skills of the game. Enhancement of the physical fitness components can serve as a means of ensuring sufficient prerequisite physical development to enable mastery of the motor skill. The learning rate of the skill is then accelerated over that of the unfit learner. More rapid learning of the skills has a very positive effect on the motivation of the learner to continue with the activity.

Although it is rare that all forms of exercise are contraindicated for individuals with special needs, often specific activities are inappropriate for an individual and cause aggravation of the condition. In general, these have been noted in the discussion of the specific conditions identified in section 3. The physical educator should guard against the generalization that exclusion from all forms of exercise is necessary for a person for whom one type of exercise is contraindicated.

Simply increasing the amount of total exercise one experiences daily is not sufficient to produce systematic improvement in physical fitness, however. Exercise physiologists have concluded that physical fitness is a multifaceted concept made up of a variety of independent components, each of which responds to specific activities and exercises. Thus the design of exercise programs to improve the various aspects of physical fitness must be carefully undertaken. This is exemplified in the current use of the term "exercise prescription," which denotes an individually designed set of exercises specifying frequency, intensity, and duration of each component of the exercise session. To enable effective design of exercise programs for special students, the professional must be knowledgeable about the essential nature of the fitness components, principles governing fitness enhancement, tests

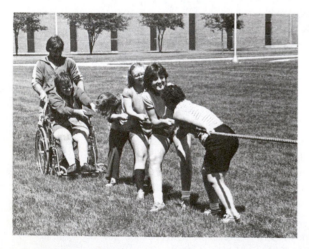

Figure 27.1 Participation in most activities requires some component of physical fitness.

of physical fitness, and appropriate exercise programs for improving physical fitness. These concerns are dealt with in the remaining portions of this chapter.

Physical Fitness Components

There appears to be no universally accepted definition of the term *physical fitness*. Common usage of the term by physical educators, coaches, athletes, and the public varies widely. Because physical fitness has often been linked with athletic ability, some consider any quality that aids athletic ability as a quality of physical fitness. Because this concept encompasses such a large array of possible components, it is now becoming common to separate those qualities that are primarily related to the learning of skills from those qualities that are physiological capacities of the body. Aspects of skill learning (coordination, balance, speed, agility, and so on) are considered motor fitness components, related to learned neuromuscular control patterns. They do not respond to progressive overloading. Physiological capacities including muscle strength, muscle endurance, flexibility, and cardiorespiratory endurance are considered physical fitness components. Given this separation of qualities, physical fitness can be defined as "the functional capacity of the various systems of the body that support exercise, specifically muscle strength, muscle endurance, flexibility, and cardiorespiratory endurance."

Muscle Strength

Muscle strength is the maximal amount of force that a muscle or functional muscle group can exert. It is usually measured in pounds or kilograms of tension. Total strength may be estimated by sampling several of the large muscle groups throughout the body. However, it is quite possible to be strong in one muscle group and weak in another. Consequently, if knowledge of the strength for a particular action is desired, the muscles involved in the action should be specifically tested. The development of muscle strength is particularly important to individuals with disabilities because of the greater independence, freedom from assistive devices, and increased capacity for a variety of physical tasks, including the learning of sport skills, made possible through sufficient strength.

Muscle Endurance

The capacity to sustain repeated muscular contractions with a load representing some percentage of the strength of the muscle is termed *local muscle endurance*. Defined in this manner, muscle endurance depends upon the ability of the muscle to get and use oxygen and to rid itself of waste. Muscle endurance is measured by the number of times a given movement can be performed, carrying a load that is a given percentage of the strength of the muscle(s), before fatigue causes cessation.

A person can possess exceptional muscle endurance without being especially strong. The leg muscles of the marathon runner may not be nearly as strong as those of the football player but they possess far greater endurance capacity. As is true of strength, each muscle possesses a degree of endurance and must be tested separately to determine its capacity to sustain repeated contractions. Improving muscle endurance is especially beneficial to individuals with disabilities in achieving efficient performance of numerous repetitive tasks, such as operating a wheelchair or executing various personal care activities.

Flexibility

The capacity to move a joint through a range of motion is termed *flexibility*. It is usually measured in degrees of joint rotation, 360 degrees being a full circle. The more flexible person can move through a larger range of motion of the major body joints than can a less flexible person. In those conditions in which total movement potential is restricted, maximal flexibility in each functional joint is a definite asset. Additionally, flexibility exercises may retard the loss of movement potential often accompanying a variety of neuromuscular diseases. It is also important to note that a person can be flexible in some joints, but not others. Differences can also be noted from one side to the other (e.g., more flexible in the left shoulder than the right).

Cardiorespiratory Endurance

This quality of physical fitness is determined by the amount of oxygen that the cardiovascular and respiratory systems can deliver to working muscles. The laboratory measurement of *cardiorespiratory endurance* actually measures the amount of oxygen supplied per minute in maximal exercise. Improved cardiorespiratory endurance enables persistence at physically demanding tasks and decreased recovery time, a definite benefit in performing any activities requiring continued large-muscle exercise. In addition, an efficient cardiovascular system offers substantial health benefits.

Body Composition

Body composition, or body fatness, refers to the percentage of the total body weight that is fat. Although not a functional capacity of the body, total body fatness significantly affects the other qualities previously noted and if in excess may be a serious health liability. Although norms vary with age, males should not exceed about 18 percent of their weight as fat; females should not exceed 28 percent. Due to less than normal activity levels, many individuals with disabilities may have excessive body fat percentages. Some individuals with disabilities may not appear overly fat by casual observation. However, when one realizes that their muscle mass may be quite small and their size mainly attributed to fat

content, what appears to be normal size may in fact be substantial extra fat. For these reasons body fatness will be included in this discussion as an important factor affecting physical fitness.

The components of physical fitness—muscular strength, muscular endurance, flexibility, and cardiorespiratory endurance plus body composition—have a relation to healthful functioning of the body. Muscular strength and endurance allow a wide range of activities to be undertaken with decreased incidents of muscle strains and sprains. Flexibility also reduces the chances of the occurrence of these conditions, especially in the low back and hamstring muscle groups. The health benefit of cardiorespiratory endurance is apparent through improved cardiac function, primarily a reduced heart rate and enhanced stroke volume as well as more efficient respiratory patterns. The relationship between the reduced capacity of the cardiorespiratory system and a variety of cardiovascular degenerative diseases is becoming widely accepted by the medical profession. Body fatness has been implicated in a variety of poor health conditions, including high blood pressure, heart disease, and diabetes.

Health-Related Fitness

The increased awareness of the contribution that these components of physical fitness can make in promoting good health was emphasized dramatically in 1994, when AAHPERD joined forces with the Cooper Institute for Aerobic Research (CIAR) and adopted the Prudential Fitnessgram, a criterion-referenced test, as the instrument to assess health-related fitness. The Fitnessgram assesses aerobic capacity, body composition, muscular strength and endurance, and flexibility. A brief overview of the test and items to assess each of the components is presented below:

Aerobic Capacity: The test items used to represent aerobic capacity in the Prudential Fitnessgram are the one-mile run/walk and the pacer. The specific health fitness zones and standards for aerobic capacity as well as other components appear in tables 27.1a and 27.1b.

Body Composition: The sum of triceps and subscapular skinfolds are used as measures of body composition. The sum of these two measures range from 12–33 mm for boys and 20–44 mm for girls. Fitnessgram also provides an estimate of the appropriateness of weight relative to height in the form of a Body Mass Index (BMI). The criterion-referenced BMI standards associated with healthy fitness zones are found in tables 27.1a and 27.1b.

Flexibility: The ability to move muscles and joints through a full range of motion is an indicator of flexibility. On the Fitnessgram, the back saver (see tables 27.1a and 27.1b) is used to measure the flexibility of the hamstrings. A score of 8 inches for boys, ages 5–17+, and scores ranging from 9 to 12 inches for girls, ages 5–17+ are considered acceptable (see tables 27.1a and 27.1b). The Fitnessgram

Table 27.1a *The Prudential FITNESSGRAM Standards for Healthy Fitness Zone**

Boys

Age	One Mile min:sec		Pacer # laps		$\dot{V}O_{2max}$ ml/kg/min		Percent Fat		Body Mass Index		Curl-up # completed	
5	Completion of		Participate in				25	10	20	14.7	2	10
6	distance. Time		run. Lap count				25	10	20	14.7	2	10
7	standards not		standards not				25	10	20	14.9	4	14
8	recommended.		recommended.				25	10	20	15.1	6	20
9							25	10	20	15.2	9	24
10	11:30	9:00	17	55	42	52	25	10	21	15.3	12	24
11	11:00	8:30	23	61	42	52	25	10	21	15.8	15	28
12	10:30	8:00	29	68	42	52	25	10	22	16.0	18	36
13	10:00	7:30	35	74	42	52	25	10	23	16.6	21	40
14	9:30	7:00	41	80	42	52	25	10	24.5	17.5	24	45
15	9:00	7:00	46	85	42	52	25	10	25	18.1	24	47
16	8:30	7:00	52	90	42	52	25	10	26.5	18.5	24	47
17	8:30	7:00	57	94	42	52	25	10	27	18.8	24	47
17+	8:30	7:00	57	94	42	52	25	10	27.8	19.0	24	47

Age	Trunk Lift inches		Push-up # completed		Modified Pull-up # completed		Pull-up # completed		Flexed Arm Arm Hang seconds		Back Saver Sit & Reach** inches	Shoulder Stretch
5	6	12	3	8	2	7	1	2	2	8	8	Passing = Touching the fingertips together behind the back.
6	6	12	3	8	2	7	1	2	2	8	8	
7	6	12	4	10	3	9	1	2	3	8	8	
8	6	12	5	13	4	11	1	2	3	10	8	
9	6	12	6	15	5	11	1	2	4	10	8	
10	9	12	7	20	5	15	1	2	4	10	8	
11	9	12	8	20	6	17	1	3	6	13	8	
12	9	12	10	20	7	20	1	3	10	15	8	
13	9	12	12	25	8	22	1	4	12	17	8	
14	9	12	14	30	9	25	2	5	15	20	8	
15	9	12	16	35	10	27	3	7	15	20	8	
16	9	12	18	35	12	30	5	8	15	20	8	
17	9	12	18	35	14	30	5	8	15	20	8	
17+	9	12	18	35	14	30	5	8	15	20	8	

*Number on left is lower end of HFZ; number on right is upper end of HFZ.
**Test scored Pass/Fail; must reach this distance to pass.

also includes a shoulder stretch, scored pass/fail, to measure upper body flexibility and a trunk lift test to measure trunk extensor strength and flexibility (see tables 27.1a and b). Standards for the trunk lift test are 6 to 12 inches for boys and girls, ages 5–9, and 9 to 12 inches for boys and girls, ages 10–17+.

Muscular Strength and Endurance: The Fitnessgram has selected the upper body and abdominal/trunk regions as areas for testing muscular strength and endurance because of their perceived relationship to maintaining functional health and correct posture, thus reducing possibilities of future low back pain (Cooper Institute for Aerobics Research, 1992). Selected test items used to assess abdominal/trunk strength include the curl-up, and trunk lift test (see tables 27.1a and 27.1b). Upper body strength and endurance is measured by the push-up, modified pull-up, pull-up, and flexed arm hang (see tables 27.1a and 27.1b). Standards for healthy zones for muscular strength and endurance appear in tables 27.1a and 27.1b.

Physical Best, AAHPERD's companion education program to the Prudential Fitness Challenge, provides a highly flexible award system for recognizing the fitness levels of students. Individuals can earn awards for developing and maintaining an active life-style, achieving specified goals (e.g., related to the IEP), or for reaching the standards identified in the Fitnessgram's Healthy Fitness Zone. These awards are officially known as the Participation Award, Personal Goal Award, and Performance Award (table 27.2). Because the award program is based on personal goal setting, all children can participate and be recognized through the program. This feature is particularly desirable for youngsters with special needs and can be included in the individualized education program. It is important to note, too, that developers of the Fitnessgram recognize that adaptations of test items would be necessary for some individuals with disabilities. This might entail, for example, developing alternative test items for students with cerebral palsy or using procedures such as task analysis to address the fitness levels of individuals with severe mental retardation. The goal, of

Girls

	One Mile min:sec		Pacer # laps		VO$_{2max}$ ml/kg/min		Percent Fat		Body Mass Index		Curl-up # completed	
5	Completion of		Participate in				32	17	21	16.2	2	10
6	distance. Time		run. Lap count				32	17	21	16.2	2	10
7	standards not		standards not				32	17	22	16.2	4	14
8	recommended.		recommended.				32	17	22	16.2	6	20
9							32	17	23	16.2	9	22
10	12:30	9:30	7	35	39	47	32	17	23.5	16.6	12	26
11	12:00	9:00	9	37	38	46	32	17	24	16.9	15	29
12	12:00	9:00	13	40	37	45	32	17	24.5	16.9	18	32
13	11:30	9:00	15	42	36	44	32	17	24.5	17.5	18	32
14	11:00	8:30	18	44	35	43	32	17	25	17.5	18	32
15	10:30	8:00	23	50	35	43	32	17	25	17.5	18	35
16	10:00	8:00	28	56	35	43	32	17	25	17.5	18	35
17	10:00	8:00	34	61	35	43	32	17	26	17.5	18	35
17+	10:00	8:00	34	61	35	43	32	17	27.3	18.0	18	35

	Trunk Lift inches		Push-up # completed		Modified Pull-up # completed		Pull-up # completed		Flexed Arm Arm Hang seconds		Back Saver Sit & Reach** inches	Shoulder Stretch
5	6	12	3	8	2	7	1	2	2	8	9	
6	6	12	3	8	2	7	1	2	2	8	9	
7	6	12	4	10	3	9	1	2	3	8	9	
8	6	12	5	13	4	11	1	2	3	10	9	
9	6	12	6	15	4	11	1	2	4	10	9	
10	9	12	7	15	4	13	1	2	4	10	9	
11	9	12	7	15	4	13	1	2	6	12	10	
12	9	12	7	15	4	13	1	2	7	12	10	
13	9	12	7	15	4	13	1	2	8	12	10	
14	9	12	7	15	4	13	1	2	8	12	10	
15	9	12	7	15	4	13	1	2	8	12	12	
16	9	12	7	15	4	13	1	2	8	12	12	
17	9	12	7	15	4	13	1	2	8	12	12	
17+	9	12	7	15	4	13	1	2	8	12	12	

Shoulder Stretch: Passing = Touching the fingertips together behind the back.

*Number on left is lower end of HFZ; number on right is upper end of HFZ.
**Test scored Pass/Fail; must reach this distance to pass.

Table 27.2   *Physical Best Awards*

Participation Award	Recognizes individuals for participation in activity outside the education setting
Personal Goal Award	Awarded to individuals who meet personalized fitness goals and objectives
Performance Award	Awarded to individuals who meet pre-established health-related physical fitness standards or goals

course, is to assess, to the extent possible, the individual's fitness level. Equally important is the need to encourage and promote fitness and not adhere to a specific test item that may be inappropriate for assessing one's fitness level. A team of adapted physical education experts, coordinated by AAHPERD, have developed a manual of useful information on assessing individuals with disabilities (Seaman, 1995). The manual provides extensive discussion and examples of alternative testing ideas and strategies.

Under the direction of Dr. Joe Winnick, State University of New York at Brockport, an extensive research effort is underway to establish and validate criterion-referenced physical fitness test items and standards for adolescents with selected disabilities. This effort will build on the successes of Prudential Fitnessgram. It is hoped that through additional research a new criterion-referenced test, Project Target, will be created. There is a strong belief that Project Target will help extend the current emphasis on health-related fitness criterion-referenced testing and programming to adolescents with disabilities (Winnick, 1994).

Concepts of Fitness Development

Improvement in physical fitness components is accomplished as a result of the body's response to the stresses of exercise. The components of physical fitness are separate qualities, each of which must be attended to if total fitness improvement is desired. This principle of specificity of development states that development will only occur in the specific muscles or organs stressed and that the type of development will be governed by the type of stress experienced. Thus, each exercise causes a very specific developmental response by the body and there is no one exercise or sport that develops all aspects of fitness. Exercises that develop muscular strength in the arms obviously do little for the strength of leg muscles or for the flexibility of those same arm muscles. If both strength and flexibility are desired, both qualities must be provided for in the exercise program. Heavy resistance movements for strength, and movement through a maximal range of motion for flexibility, are required for development of both qualities. Similarly, the development of muscle strength has little effect on cardiorespiratory endurance, yet each can be increased with specific exercises. The following chart identifies the appropriate type of exercises for achieving improvement in each component of physical fitness.

Component	Type of Exercise
Muscle strength:	Heavy resistance exercises that produce fatigue within 10 repetitions.
Muscle endurance:	Light resistance exercises conducted for a prolonged time, producing fatigue in 10 to 100 repetitions.
Flexibility:	Joint movement held at the extremes of the range of motion for 15 to 30 seconds.
Cardiorespiratory:	Continuous large-muscle activity producing rates of 70 to 90 percent of maximum heart rate for at least 15 minutes. (Lower values may be appropriate for very unconditioned individuals.)
Body composition:	Sustained large-muscle activity that causes substantial caloric expenditure. (The total work accomplished as estimated by force × distance will give an approximation of the relative caloric cost of the activity.)

When subjected to the stress of an unaccustomed exercise, the body responds by adapting to enable a higher level of functioning. After repeated exercise bouts using the same intensity, the body will eventually develop to the point where this exercise is easily accommodated. For greater improvement in function to occur, the intensity of the exercise must be further increased. As intensity increases the body will begin to respond, increasing its capacity over the previous level. Thus, continued improvement in any of the fitness components depends upon the exercise program being periodically increased in intensity or duration. This process is commonly known as the principle of progressive

overload, or systematically increasing the strenuousness of the exercise program as one's body responds by increasing its capacity for exercise.

The reverse of the progressive overload principle applies when one reduces or ceases to exercise regularly. The body responds to a lack of stress by becoming less capable of performing. This transitory nature is an important aspect of physical fitness. The various components of fitness can be rapidly improved through systematic exercise but are also rapidly lost when habitual exercise is reduced. This is another way in which physical fitness varies from motor fitness. Generally, motor skills, once learned, are retained at a reasonable level with little or no practice. Physical fitness qualities, however, are developed rather than learned and necessitate continued attention to be maintained.

Strength and muscular endurance losses can also be due to disorders that affect the neuromuscular system. Injury to the motor centers or the peripheral nerves and debilitating diseases such as muscular dystrophy, multiple sclerosis, myasthenia gravis, and polymyositis are some of the disorders that cause muscular weakness and lack of muscular endurance. Muscles that are affected by these disorders may not respond to the progressive overload principle in the same manner as normal muscles, and, in some cases, strength and endurance exercises can even affect the muscles adversely and are, therefore, contraindicated. Joint and bone disorders also can affect the development of strength detrimentally; and for individuals with such disorders, strength and muscular endurance exercises involving the affected parts of the body also may be contraindicated. Although there is evidence to support the use of progressive resistance exercises in programs for individuals with spastic cerebral palsy, further study is needed (Horvat, 1987).

Flexibility exercises generally are of value to all persons with neurological and muscular disorders. In some cases of neurological disorders, such as cerebral palsy, the flexibility exercises should be planned in consultation with medical personnel because of the importance that only certain specified muscles be stretched. Specific stretching or flexibility exercises are done in compliance with the medical prescription.

In light of the foregoing discussion about the specificity of development and realizing the unique needs and interests of each individual, it is apparent that developmental fitness programs should be individually tailored for each participant. It is important that approval of the program be obtained from the student's physician in cases of cardiac problems and muscular and neurological disorders.

The major steps in constructing an individual exercise prescription include:

1. Establishing a desired goal or outcome,
2. Testing current fitness status and assessing limitations imposed by the disabling conditions,
3. Devising the exercise program and periodic reassessment of status resulting in alteration of the prescription, and
4. Assisting the individual in understanding the nature of the program and the benefit from participating. This is

an essential step for success for everyone, but critical for individuals whose mental capacity makes it difficult to internalize the value of good health.

Establishing the goals of the exercise program focuses attention on the specific components of physical fitness to be developed. Although everyone should strive to achieve a modest level of each of the components, unique needs and interests will modify the desired development beyond the minimal healthful level. One student may desire to participate in wheelchair basketball, another to retard flexibility loss, and a third to learn swimming. The specific fitness components important in each of these cases differs greatly. Testing of the appropriate fitness components will identify the current level of functioning and establish the necessary information for the construction of the exercise prescription. The exercise prescription identifies the actual exercises that will be performed, stating intensity (how much resistance or how fast the activity will be performed), duration (how many times or for how long the exercise will last), and frequency (how many times per day or per week it will be performed). For example, one exercise in the workout program for the student who desires to play wheelchair basketball might be a seated press with a barbell, an exercise that strengthens the triceps and deltoid muscle groups used in shooting the ball. The exercise prescription might be:

Intensity: 80 percent of maximum press strength

Duration: three sets of eight repetitions

Frequency: three days per week

A portion of the exercise program for the student who is experiencing loss of flexibility might include a seated low back and hamstring stretch with the following prescription:

Intensity: Stretch to limit of forward flexion

Duration: Hold for twenty seconds, relax, repeat five times

Frequency: Every day

Because swimming involves sustained arm work, one appropriate exercise for a student desiring to learn to swim might be on an overhead pulley done to the following prescription:

Intensity: ten pounds

Duration: two sets of fifty repetitions

Frequency: three days per week

In light of the principle of progressive overload, the intensity or duration of each exercise should be increased regularly, normally about every week or two. Periodic retesting of maximal capacity should be conducted to identify gains, establish new goals, and serve as the basis for revision of the exercise prescription.

General survey tests of physical fitness are valuable in identifying areas of deficiency and can serve as a basis for setting appropriate fitness goals. It may thus be the decision of the physical educator or therapist to begin the process with a general test that samples from all of the fitness qualities. The results of the test can then aid in the selection of appropriate goals and exercises.

Tests of Physical Fitness

Testing of the various components of physical fitness is necessary to identify current functional level and to provide a reference point for determining improvement. Subjective observation of general weakness or lack of movement potential is insufficient information on which to design an exercise program. Reliable, objective measurement is the goal of any physical fitness test. Specific tests for each component of physical fitness have been devised, as well as general survey test batteries that sample from several of the fitness components. The general survey test is useful in obtaining an overview of the person's fitness status and for identifying potential problem areas. Often these tests are given routinely as screening devices. When particular problems are known or identified through screening, more specific testing may then be appropriate to determine the precise nature and extent of the condition.

General Survey Tests

Low physical fitness in students with disabilities sometimes can be identified through observation of their performance in class activities. Although poor performance does not always indicate a lack of physical fitness, this is most often the case. Some types of general physical fitness tests will provide objectivity to this evaluation and will allow for greater quantification than is possible from subjective observation. The test may need to be modified for individuals with orthopedic impairments to protect a specific part of the body from further injury or because of the lack of function in an area of the body.

Several general survey tests are discussed in the following paragraphs. Procedures for test administration and scoring norms are not provided, as that degree of detail is beyond the scope of this text. Rather, the discussion is directed toward the selection of an appropriate test. After the selection process has been completed, a copy of the exact instructions for administering the test should be obtained and carefully followed. This is essential to the use of scoring norms provided with the test. It is possible, of course, for teachers to devise their own tests or modify a standard test based on the limitations of individual students and then simply use gain scores (final score − initial score) achieved on the tests to indicate improvement over time.

The Kraus-Weber Test was designed as a test of minimum muscular fitness. It involves six pass or fail items that evaluate primarily the flexor and extensor muscle groups of the spine and hips. These test items measure muscle strength and endurance at a minimal level. One test of flexibility is included. The large muscle groups of the arms, shoulders, and legs, which are predominate in many sport activities, are ignored by this test and the components of cardiorespiratory endurance and body fatness are not sampled. The pass/fail scoring procedure does not produce a discrimination of different degrees of fitness. This test should thus not be utilized as an indicator of total fitness and may have only limited utility as a screening device for muscular insufficiency of the trunk and hips.

The AAHPERD Youth Fitness Test, an old and somewhat outdated test, is still widely used by many professionals. For this reason, and because several tests specifically developed for special populations have been modified from the Youth Fitness Test, a brief discussion of the test is included here. The AAHPERD Youth Fitness Test provides scoring norms for boys and girls ages ten through seventeen on six test items. The items tested are pull-ups (boys), flexed arm hang (girls), sit-ups for one minute, shuttle run, standing long jump, 50-yard dash, and 600-yard run-walk. Optional distance runs for the 600-yard item include a nine-minute or 1-mile run for ages ten to twelve and a twelve-minute or 1.5-mile run for ages over thirteen.

The pull-up and flexed arm-hang items are a measure of arm and shoulder strength and endurance. The sit-up evaluates muscular endurance of the abdominal muscles. The shuttle run measures agility, speed, and power of the legs. The standing long jump measures explosive leg strength and coordination; the 50-yard dash tests the speed and power of the legs. The 600-yard run/walk and optional distance runs are measures of cardiorespiratory endurance.

Several of the items on this test are motor-fitness measurements. Specifically the standing long jump, the shuttle run, and the 50-yard dash either are highly affected by the skill of the person being tested or are unresponsive to overloading. The performance in these items by persons who have not previously practiced the activities or by individuals who are mentally retarded may produce inordinately low scores that are not indicative of their actual physical fitness. The value of the test lies in its use as a general screening device to identify persons with abnormally low levels of physical fitness. Once areas of weakness are identified, further testing should be undertaken to determine the extent of the limitation.

The obvious omissions within the AAHPERD test are measurements of flexibility and of body fatness. The question of body fatness might be answered, however, by the fact that a person with excess body fat must move that additional weight through all of the test activities, thus hampering achievement in each item. Although this may be true, the test still does not provide a specific measure of body fat content. Thus, uncertainty exists as to whether a low score is indicative of lack of strength or of excess fat. The suggested exercise program for these two conditions might vary considerably.

The deficiencies inherent in the AAHPERD Youth Fitness Test were addressed by AAHPERD's endorsement of the Prudential Fitnessgram, described earlier (see table 27.1a and b). The new test measures those components of physical fitness that directly contribute to health.

Tests for Orthopedically and Sensory-Impaired Children

Some students cannot be given physical fitness tests, either because their disabilities render them incapable of performing the tests or because their conditions may be aggravated in attempting them. However, many individuals with disabilities can be included in the testing if proper precautions are taken. In some instances, this will mean eliminating those tests that involve the part of the body that is injured or disabled. A person subject to chronic shoulder dislocation, for example, would not be required to do pull-ups but could be expected to take the running tests, as these would not be dangerous. In certain cases, the nature of the disability will be such that safety is not a major factor of concern. For example, missing fingers on a hand will not prevent safe participation in the pull-ups. It would not be meaningful, however, to make an evaluation of this subject's score by comparing it to scores achieved by students able to take a normal grip. This individual's score is likely to be lower because of less grip strength and not because of less muscular endurance of the arms, as would be indicated by a nondisabled student's low score.

The application of norms developed on nondisabled populations will misrepresent the true fitness levels of people with disabilities in most cases. A meaningful measurement for each individual with a disability can be devised, however, by using a progress chart on which scores are recorded each time the test is taken.

Figure 27.2 The muscular strength and endurance of students with orthopedic impairments can be assessed if tests are appropriately modified.

Winnick and Short (1985) developed a physical fitness test that can be administered to nonimpaired, sensory impaired, and orthopedically impaired youth ages ten to seventeen. Within this last category, those with cerebral palsy as well as spinal neuromuscular conditions are included. The test, known as Project Unique, was modified from the AAHPERD Youth Fitness Test and the 1980 version of the AAHPERD Health Related Fitness Test. An overview of the test items are included in table 27.3. Norms are provided for individuals with sensory, auditory, cerebral palsy, and spinal neuromuscular conditions. Comparisons can be made within a disability category or with the norms provided for the nonimpaired population. A comprehensive test manual with suggested activities for developing physical fitness in youth with sensory and orthopedic impairments is available from Human Kinetics Publishers.

Tests for Children with Mild Mental Retardation

Physical fitness tests designed for nondisabled youngsters are not valid measurements of physical fitness for students who are mentally retarded because they are, for the most part, too complex, and many times the scores are lowered because of the subjects' inability to comprehend and respond immediately with the proper muscular movements. Additionally, the norms for nondisabled populations probably do not accurately reflect the status of individuals with mental retardation. At least one study on boys classifed as educable mentally retarded has identified lower cardiorespiratory endurance than that for nonretarded children (Maksud and Hamilton, 1974). This contention is supported by studies showing that when physical fitness tests commonly given to nondisabled children are given to children who are mentally retarded, the scores demonstrate a low but positive relationship to the IQ scores of the subject (Rarick and Francis, 1960). Fait and Kupferer (1956) demonstrated that when the physical fitness test items were simplified, the relationship between the scores and the IQ score disappeared or was greatly diminished. The Burpee or squat thrust test serves as a good illustration. The scores of children with mental retardation, when given a modified Burpee test that required them to squat and return without thrusting, fitted a fairly normal curve comparable to normal children, whereas the scores from the performance of the full squat thrust test produced a curve skewed to the left comparable to the curve of their IQ scores. The inability of the subjects with mental retardation to perform well on the Burpee test appears to be caused more by their inability to remember the movement sequence than by poor agility.

Subsequent to this study, Fait adapted physical fitness tests for students with mental retardation from those given to nondisabled children. Although most of the original tests indicated a positive relationship to IQ, the correlations between IQ and the adapted tests were near zero. The adapted tests and the original tests were both given to nondisabled youngsters. A high correlation was shown to exist, indicating that the adapted tests were measuring the same factors of fitness as the original tests. The adapted tests form the basis for a battery of physical fitness tests that are suitable for use with those who are mildly retarded and a majority of individuals with moderate retardation, if the youngsters do not have other handicaps that prevent safe performance of the test (see chapter 17). A description of the test battery is provided in appendix III.

Table 27.3 *An outline of Project Unique physical fitness test items according to major participant groups*

Test Items	Normal, Auditory Impaired, Visually Impaired[a]	Cerebral Palsy[a]	Paraplegic Wheelchair Spinal Neuromuscular[a]	Congenital Anomaly/ Amputee[a]
Body Composition				
Skinfolds	X	X	X	X
Muscular Strength and Endurance				
Grip Strength (Strength)	X[b]	X[c,f]	X[g,h]	X[b,j]
50-Yard/Meter Dash (Power-Speed)	X	X[d]	X[d]	X
Sit-Ups (Power-Strength)	X	—	—	X[i]
Softball Throw for Distance (Power-Strength)	—	X[e]	X[g,h]	X[i]
Flexibility				
Sit and Reach	X	X	—	X
Cardiorespiratory Endurance				
Long Distance Run	X	X	X	X

Winnick, J.P., & Short, F. X. (1985). *Physical fitness testing of the disabled: Project Unique* (p. 7). Champaign, IL: Human Kinetics Publishers.

[a]Items may require modification or elimination for selected group subclassifications (see test administration section).
[b]The broad jump may be substituted for grip strength tests as a measure of strength for these groups.
[c]Grip strengths measure power-strength for males with cerebral palsy.
[d]The dash measures power-endurance for individuals in this group.
[e]The softball throw is recommended for females only as a measure of power-strength.
[f]The arm hang may be substituted for grip tests for males.
[g]The arm hang or softball throw for distance may be substituted for grip strength measures (strength factor) for males.
[h]The softball throw for distance may be substituted for grip strength measures (strength factor) for female participants.
[i]The softball throw for distance may be substituted for sit-ups (as a power-strength factor) in cases where the sit-up would be considered inappropriate.
[j]Males may substitute the arm hang for grip tests (strength factor).

The American Alliance for Health, Physical Education, Recreation, and Dance (AAHPERD) has modified its Youth Fitness Test, discussed previously, for use with students who are mentally retarded. The major changes include: (1) substitution of a flexed arm hang for the pull-up test, (2) restricting the time allowed for sit-ups to one minute, and (3) reducing the distance of the 600-yard run to 300 yards. The most important modification, however, is the provision of norms obtained through testing of approximately 4,200 boys and girls with mild mental retardation. Norms are provided for both sexes within the eight- to eighteen-year age range.

Similarly, Johnson and Londeree (1976) utilized the modified AAHPERD tests and added motor performance measures, including (1) sitting bob and reach, (2) hopping, (3) skipping, (4) tumbling progressions, and (5) target throw, to develop a motor fitness testing manual for males and females aged six to twenty. Roswal, Roswal, and Dunleavy (1986) developed health-related fitness norms for Special Olympic athletes. Their study, based on an analysis of 887 participants ages eight to sixty-eight participating in the Alabama Special Olympic program, provides norms for sit-ups, sit and reach, and body composition. Because these norms are specific to those who are mentally retarded, meaningful comparisons can be made.

Buell (1980) has developed norms for students who are visually impaired based on a modified version of the AAHPERD Youth Fitness Test.

A variety of other physical fitness test batteries have been developed by state public school groups, university physical education departments, and private agencies. All contain similar arrays of test items and usually provide norms developed for some particular population. The previous examples provide a background for evaluating the components measured by these common fitness test items and enable an assessment of the advantages and limitations of any particular test battery. It is quite possible that any agency or program may wish to create a test battery to meet the specific needs of the population it serves.

The following material will identify typical tests useful for evaluation of the components of physical fitness. These can be utilized to further evaluate a weakness noted from a general survey test or for construction of a specialized battery of test items.

Tests of Muscular Endurance and Strength

Any calisthenic in which the weight load can be adjusted to a given percentage of the muscles' strength can be used as a test of muscle endurance by increasing the repetitions to the physical capacity of the individual. Common examples are sit-ups with weights held on the forehead, and bar dips, pull-ups, and jumping jacks with weights strapped to the shoulders.

The measurement of muscle strength requires a setting in which heavy weight equipment can be utilized. Any of the standard weight training exercises can be used as a test item. Care should be taken to select an exercise that directly involves the muscle group for which a measure is desired. (If several large muscle groups are involved and the time period is extended, the test may become a measure of cardiorespiratory endurance.) Through several trials, the maximal weight that can be lifted in each exercise is determined. Sufficient rest between trials must be provided so that fatigue does not limit the expression of strength. A listing of common weight training exercises that can be modified as strength tests is included later in this chapter under the topic of Development of Muscle Strength and Endurance.

More precise measurement of muscular strength and of muscular endurance can be obtained from laboratory testing equipment. Some of this equipment is quite expensive and the tests must be individually administered. The quality of the measurement, however, makes such testing a desirable possibility when the equipment is available.

The most common laboratory strength measuring device is the dynamometer. Dynamometers provide for an isometric muscular contraction, the force of which is indicated on a dial mounted on the instrument. The dial reading provides a direct measure of strength in either pounds or kilograms of exerted force. Muscle endurance testing is done by selecting a percentage of the measured maximal strength and requiring the subject to perform continued contractions at a specific cadence until fatigue prevents continuation. Isometric endurance also can be measured by requesting that the subject hold a percentage of maximum strength as long as possible.

The manuometer is a dynamometer that measures grip strength. A variety of models of manuometers exist, but each requires that the subject squeeze the unit between the palm and the fingers. The force of the squeeze is indicated on a dial in either pounds or kilograms. Some models are adjustable, allowing for differences in hand size; these are highly desirable if both children and adults will be tested. Another model has a rubber ball for the grip, which is very effective for those persons who have a physical problem in gripping with the hand. Since the hands are used in a large number of physical tasks, the hand grip strength has been suggested as a general indicator of overall body strength. This is useful as a very rough screening device; however, considering the specificity of strength, any one measure reveals very little about strength of other muscle groups.

The second most common dynamometer in use is the back and leg dynamometer. It consists of a bar attached to the dynamometer, which is attached to a small bench. The subject stands on the bench and exerts force against the bar, which may be adjusted to allow measurement of leg extension strength, back extension strength, arm flexion strength, and, with an extended chain, arm extension strength.

A cable tensiometer is also often used to measure the strength of various muscle groups. Subjects are positioned for the muscle being tested on a special table that allows for the attachment of a cable to various parts of the table frame. The other end of the cable is connected by a cuff or strap to the body part being tested. As the subject pulls against the cable, the tensiometer is applied to the cable and measures the amount of tension created, which can then be converted to pounds. All of the major muscle groups can be tested by adjusting the subject's position on the table and appropriately attaching the testing cable. This technique is quite valuable in that it allows accurate testing of each functional muscle group.

Other units used in muscle strength and endurance testing are the strain gauge, Cybex Unit, and KinCom. These units are rather expensive but provide very accurate evaluation and a graphic display of the forces of muscular contraction. Strain gauges are similar in concept to the cable tensiometer. They are small electrical devices that respond to the amount of tension on the cable and through an electrical circuit provide graphic recording of changes in the force on the cable. The Cybex Unit is an electrically braked motor that attaches to a solid lever arm. The force the subject exerts against the lever arm is measured electrically and recorded on graph paper. The Cybex allows for dynamic, in addition to static, strength measurements. A preselected speed of movement is set on the instrument and the subject attempts to move through the range of motion as fast and as forcefully as possible. The instrument records the force generated throughout the movement on graph paper. This type of evaluation is especially useful in determining weaker points in the movement. The Cybex can also be used for isometric strength determinations by locking the lever arm in place and allowing the subject to exert force against the immovable arm.

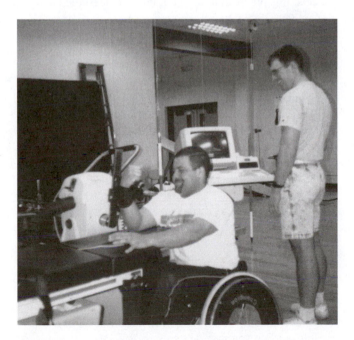

Figure 27.3 Equipment such as the KinCom measures muscle strength.

It should be noted that the majority of the practical testing techniques measure strength dynamically (through a range of movement). Because it is known that maximal strength varies with the position in the range of motion, the dynamic tests usually measure the weakest point in the range. The isometric measures will produce different readings at different angles of joint action, necessitating repeated testing at the same angle if comparisons for improvement purposes are intended. For these reasons it is impossible to compare a dynamic measure of strength directly to one obtained isometrically. Research has shown that isometrically determined strength is substantially greater than dynamically measured strength at the same angle. Because there is a relationship between isometrically and dynamically measured strength, either measurement technique can be used. Repeated measures, however, necessitate using identical testing designs. The KinCom, similar to the Cybex, has helped to alleviate some of this concern by measuring the strength of the muscle through the full range of motion. This is accomplished by using a hydraulic system and load cell arrangement to accommodate the muscular forces so that the muscle contraction speeds can be held at a constant, predetermined speed. This results in a maximal load throughout the full range of joint motion. The KinCom also provides a measure of eccentric contraction or the lengthening of a muscle during contraction. Eccentric contractions are used in resisting gravity, e.g., walking down a hill or steps.

In giving a muscular strength or endurance test, care should be exercised so as not to put undue stress or strain upon disabled or impaired parts of the body. Generally, any part of the body that is diseased or impaired should not be involved in the test. Extreme care should be exercised when administering a muscular strength test to anyone with a cardiac problem because performing feats of muscular strength causes a rapid rise in blood pressure that may be to the disadvantage of a diseased heart. Administration of the test should be done in consultation with the physician of the individual with a cardiac problem.

Tests of Flexibility

Flexibility is often underrated in importance as a component of physical fitness. When a person's range of movement begins to be restricted beyond normal limits, however, increased flexibility quickly becomes a desired quality. This is especially apparent in persons whose conditions restrict flexibility and in the elderly who begin to lose their joint movement potential with advancing age. Except for activities such as diving, gymnastics, and dance, in which enhanced flexibility is obviously desirable, the role of flexibility in motor performance has often been neglected. A wide range of motion can potentially contribute to many activities by giving the participant that extra few inches of reach or allowing that little extra distance through which to accelerate a thrown object. Measurement of flexibility is a common means for identifying the extent of many muscle and joint injuries as well as skeletal or postural abnormalities resulting from defects, diseases, or injuries.

The most familiar measure of flexibility is the toe touch. Unfortunately, this item places undue pressure on the spine and, therefore, should be discouraged as a measure of flexibility. The sit and reach, where the subject is seated on the floor, and asked to reach as far as possible is now the preferred measure of flexibility. It should be noted, however, that the sit and reach, similar to the toe touch, may place undue pressure on the hamstrings. For this reason, recent tests, such as the Fitnessgram, emphasize that the sit and reach test should be conducted with one leg flexed. Other practical tests for flexibility include:

Trunk extension:	From a prone position on a mat the student, whose hips are held down, raises the chest and chin as far off the mat as possible, and a measurement is made from the mat to the top of the sternum.
Shoulder elevation:	Lying prone on a mat with the chin touching the mat, the student raises a wand held at shoulder width and arms' length in both hands as high as possible. Measurement is made from the mat to the bottom of the wand.
Shoulder extension:	In a similar position to the shoulder elevation, except with the wand held at shoulder width behind the back so that the wand rests across the hips, the student elevates the wand as high as possible. Measurement is from the bottom of the wand to the floor.
Hip abduction-rotation:	The student is seated on a mat and the soles of the feet are placed together, knees to the side. The student spreads the knees as far as possible. Measurement is from the bottom of the knee to the mat.

Similar practical tests can be devised using common stretching positions for any body part. In most cases the purpose of testing will be to determine range of movement and to document changes in a particular student. For this reason, differences in body proportions, as they may effect these tests, are of little concern. Caution should be exercised, however, in making comparisons between students.

In all flexibility testing the person should be instructed to move to the extremes of the range of motion slowly, never jerking or bouncing to gain extra distance. Measurements should be made only after the position has been held for at least two seconds. Joint flexibility measurements typically improve with a prior warm-up. Therefore, some general warm-up of the muscles and joints to be measured as well as a preliminary trial or two will yield a more accurate measurement of true movement potential.

The goniometer and the flexometer are the typical instruments used for more exacting measurements of flexibility in the laboratory. The goniometer is a relatively inexpensive device consisting of two movable arms attached to a protractor. The center of the protractor is placed over the joint center being measured and the arms are held along the midline of the limbs or body segments. A reading off the protractor is obtained at each extreme of the range of movement of the joint. The difference between the two readings provides the actual degrees of joint movement. The flexometer is an adaptation of the goniometer principle consisting of a protractor and a weighted needle indicator. The flexometer is attached to the body part being tested by a strap. The subject first moves to one extreme of the range of motion and the dial is set at zero. Then movement through the range is made to the other extreme position. At this point the needle indicator reads the number of degrees through which the body part was moved. Electrogoniometers are also available that attach to the joint and provide a graphic record of the movement. An electrogoniometer is included in the Cybex Unit discussed under Tests of Muscular Endurance and Strength and thus provides an indication of the joint position that corresponds to the strength readings.

For many individuals with disabilities, greater flexibility is highly desirable. Because most work with these individuals will involve personalized testing of physical fitness components, it is practical to use goniometric measurements.

Tests of Cardiorespiratory Endurance

Measurement of cardiorespiratory endurance is performed by three types of test designs: performance tests, heart rate tests, and oxygen consumption tests.

Performance tests require the least equipment and minimize the need for trained test administrators. They consist mainly of distance-run or walk events. Distances from 600 yards to 1.5 miles have been suggested. The longer the distance, the more accurate is the measurement of the cardiorespiratory capacity, assuming the subjects remain motivated to complete the distance. Shorter distances (600 to 1,000 yards) actually measure a combination of cardiorespiratory (aerobic) and anaerobic capacity.

These tests are based on the concept that a person with a more capable cardiorespiratory system will be able to supply greater quantities of oxygen to the working muscles. This continued greater oxygen supply enables these persons to sustain the run at a faster pace than those having less capable cardiorespiratory systems.

There are two methods used in scoring distance-run tests. The first is simply timing subjects over a given distance. This has the drawback of allowing a sprint to the finish line, thus performing part of the test anaerobically. To eliminate this factor, timed runs requiring the subject to run as far as possible in nine, twelve, or fifteen minutes have been designed. The subject is not told of the time remaining and thus cannot cover more distance by sprinting the final few seconds. In these tests distance covered becomes the measured quality. These runs also can be used with participants who use a wheelchair.

All distance-run tests require the subjects to be highly motivated to perform their best. There is no means for determining when a subject has not given a maximal effort. In these cases the subjects are incorrectly scored lower than their actual capacity. Because these tests require maximal effort, they should be used cautiously with those who have any health limitations of the cardiorespiratory system. They should not be used to evaluate subjects with cardiopathic conditions or respiratory impairments. These tests may also be hazardous to typically sedentary individuals and those more than thirty years of age. Some investigators have cautioned that distance-run tests might not be reliable or valid

indicators of aerobic capacity for some populations (Pizzaro, 1990; Baumgartner and Horvat, 1991). This has raised the question of whether a walk test might be more appropriate as a measure of cardiorespiratory fitness with individuals who are mentally retarded. Rintala et al. (1992) found that the Rockport Walking Test was a valid and reliable measure of cardiorespiratory fitness for young adult males with mental retardation.

Heart rate tests of cardiorespiratory endurance require the subject to perform a standardized work load. This is typically done by providing a cadence for stepping up onto and down from a box or bench of a standard height. Work load also can be standardized by riding on a bicycle ergometer at a selected speed and resistance. These tests measure the effect of this standard work load on the heart rate. A more capable cardiorespiratory system will show less increase in heart rate to the work load than a less capable system. Measurement of the heart rate may be taken during the work bout or in recovery immediately following the exercise. Heart rate tests provide for direct monitoring of the cardiorespiratory response to exercise. These tests do not require high levels of motivation because maximal work loads are unnecessary. For this reason they are often more

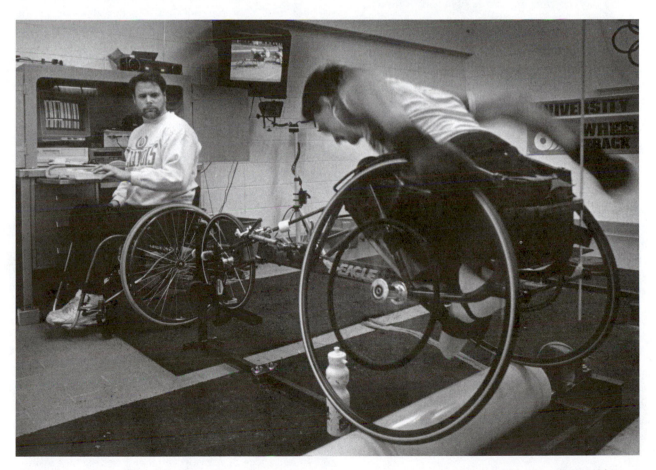

Figure 27.4 Marty Morse works with the computer in the roller room with UI wheelchair athlete Pat Cottini. Morse simulates race with Cottini on the video screen by adding resistance to the computer-interface roller.

appropriate than maximal work performance tests for persons with a questionable health status. However, they must be individually administered by trained testers.

Measures of heart rate also have been applied to those who use wheelchairs. Normally this is done by monitoring the heart rate while using the arms to hand crank a bicycle ergometer. Some investigators have taken direct measure of heart rate while having the subject perform different workloads while propelling the wheelchair. Dreisinger and Londeree (1982), in an extensive review of research, concluded that the heart rate response of the wheelchair user is similar to that of nonimpaired populations. Skuldt (1984) cautions, however, that the maximal heart rate of the individual who is quadriplegic is much less than that of the paraplegic or nonimpaired person. She suggests, therefore, that keeping records of the duration of activity (amount of time exercised) may be a better indicator of fitness for this population.

Oxygen consumption testing requires sophisticated laboratory equipment. The subject usually either rides on a bicycle ergometer or runs/walks on a motorized treadmill. Exhaled air is measured and analyzed to directly determine the amount of oxygen being consumed by the working subject. The rate of work is progressively increased until no further increase in oxygen consumption is obtained or until a preselected submaximal heart rate (one that is less than that obtained in an all-out and sustained exercise bout) is achieved. The more fit individual will be capable of consuming greater quantities of oxygen per minute than the less fit individual.

This direct measure of oxygen consumption is the most accurate means for evaluation of cardiorespiratory endurance. However, the expense in both equipment and time required for this test restricts its use to research, clinical, or highly technical programs.

The normal exercise devices for oxygen consumption testing are the treadmill and the stationary bicycle. For those with lower body disabilities, an arm ergometer has been developed that provides for a pedaling action using the hands and arms. Use of a wheelchair on the treadmill is also satisfactory. Because the amount of muscle mass used in arm cranking or wheelchair propelling is less than that of running, smaller oxygen intake values will be obtained. Comparisons between individuals who use wheelchairs and nondisabled populations must take this factor into consideration.

The necessity for exacting administration of each of the previous tests makes full explanation of the testing protocol too lengthy for inclusion in this chapter. A text dealing specifically with physical fitness testing or the actual test manual must be consulted before giving any of these tests. The discussion here is intended to provide information that will assist in the appropriate selection of the type of test to meet a particular situation.

Tests of Body Composition

Body fatness, though not a functional capacity, directly influences the performance of many bodily movements and has been associated with numerous health conditions. Measurement of body fatness or body composition differs from the typical height–weight table determination of normal body weight. The height–weight tables identify total body weight and thus do not distinguish between the part of that weight due to fat and the part due to lean tissues. Body composition measurement is designed to make this differentiation. The values obtained are in percentage of fat that can be multiplied by the total body weight to obtain pounds or kilograms of fat weight. As an example, a young male may be measured and found to have 16 percent fat and weigh 130 pounds. He thus has $130 \times .16 = 20.8$ pounds of fat. The absolute measure of pounds of fat is often not used because it is meaningless without knowledge of the total weight of the person. When comparisons are to be made, the percentage of the total weight that is fat (16 percent in our example) is most meaningful.

A few simple techniques have been developed for estimating body fatness from circumference measurements of the arms and waist, but the accuracy of these techniques is so poor that they are not much better than using the height–weight tables. A relatively simple and inexpensive technique is the measurement of skinfold thickness. Skinfold calipers are now available at a cost within reason for any program. The caliper is used to measure the thickness of the subcutaneous fat at various standard sites on the body. The most common sites are the triceps, subscapular, iliac crest, abdomen, and thigh. Specific equations for prediction of body fat from skinfold thickness have been developed for men, women, boys, and girls. Accuracy will be enhanced if a prediction equation is selected that was developed on an age and sex group similar to the subject being tested. Rimmer (1994) has produced an excellent text of fitness for special populations. This valuable resource has a comprehensive discussion on procedures for assessing the body composition of individuals with disabilities.

The preferred laboratory measure of body fatness is termed hydrostatic or underwater weighing. For this technique the body's weight in air is compared to the weight when totally submerged in water, with corrections being made for air trapped in the lungs. The rationale for this technique is that body fat is less dense than water, whereas all the lean tissues of the body are heavier than water. Thus, the more fat accumulations in the body, the lighter will be the weight in the water. The relationship of weight in air to weight in water is transformed through an equation to obtain a prediction of total body fat.

Although the underwater weighing technique is preferable from an accuracy standpoint, it requires highly sensitive scales, an immersion tank, and several computations to complete the test. The skinfold test, however, is quickly administered and the results can often be obtained from precalculated table values. For a valid measurement, it is important to practice the skinfold measurement technique and to accurately identify the anatomical sites for measurement. Consequently, students should not be expected to obtain accurate measures of one another in a school setting.

Whether skinfold methods of estimating body fat using norms for nondisabled persons are appropriate for all individuals with disabilities is subject to some doubt. Research is needed to identify specific predictive equations for fat estimations from skinfolds in persons who use wheelchairs and for various amputee groups. Even if the estimate of total fat is inaccurate, changes in local fat accumulation can be measured by the use of the skinfold technique. These changes in regional fat are indicative of total fat gain or loss. Steadward and Walsh (1986) has cautioned that the accuracy of predictions obtained from the use of skinfold measures or underwater weighing are questionable because the formulas are derived from nondisabled populations.

Techniques for Improving Physical Fitness

The popularity of exercise programs to improve physical fitness has increased due to wide acceptance of the ability of these programs to aid in altering body proportions, reducing fat, and gaining enhanced strength, flexibility, and endurance. The rehabilitative value of exercise for many injuries and diseases is becoming as well recognized as the value of exercise training in preparation for athletic participation. Even with populations such as those with spina bifida, ostomy, and multiple sclerosis, where historically little information exists regarding health status and response to exercise, researchers (Coutts et al., 1993; Vogler, 1990; Holland, Bouffard, and Wagner, 1992; Rowland, 1990; and Rimmer, 1992) are providing new insights that will help practitioners develop meaningful programs. While current research suggests that differences exist between the health-fitness status of individuals with disabilities and those without disabilities, the differences may be attributed to many factors, including limited opportunities and expectations that undervalue the potential of many individuals with disabilities. For these reasons, large numbers of boys, girls, men, and women are now exercising regularly to improve their physical fitness. The person with a disability can benefit from these same values as well as specific remediation of some physical conditions.

The section of this chapter dealing with the concepts of fitness development might well be reviewed at this point. The following material will discuss particular means for improving the components of fitness based upon the concepts presented earlier.

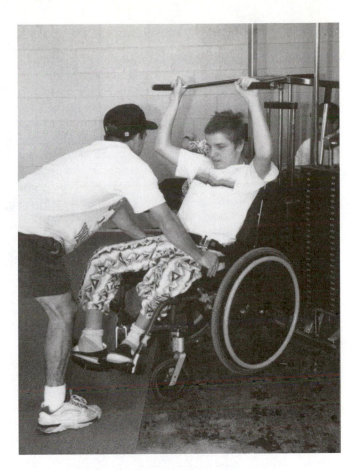

Figure 27.5 Those with lower limb involvement can make lifts while seated in the wheelchair.

Development of Muscle Strength and Endurance

The improvement of muscle strength and endurance is best accomplished through the use of some type of resistive exercise device. The necessary load, or resistance, may be created by springs, elastic cables, friction devices, or, most commonly, by barbell weights. Exercise physiologists recognize resistance training as the most efficient means of enhancing muscle development.

The use of weight training for the improvement of muscular strength and endurance has become a standard practice for all ages and both sexes. Weight training for those with disabilities provides an opportunity for participation with nondisabled peers in a popular activity. In many instances, individuals with disabilities can engage on an equal basis with nondisabled peers when performing exercises not involving their specific impairment. This offers an opportunity for beneficial social acceptance and self-image development. An individual with an amputation may be quite capable of outperforming nondisabled peers on an arm curl or bench press exercise.

Weight training requires very little space; an area as small as one hundred square feet is adequate. The floor must be able to support considerable weight; therefore, a concrete floor is desirable. However, if the floor is wooden, heavy planks may be placed over it.

Equipment consists primarily of barbells and dumbbells. The barbells are used for exercises with two hands, whereas the dumbbells, which are shorter, are used chiefly for one-arm exercises. Weight-lifting machines eliminate the use of barbells and dumbbells; all lifts that are possible with weights can be done with the machine. In addition, some special pieces of equipment have been devised to expand the exercise possibilities; among these are head straps, iron shoes, knee exercisers, wall pulleys, wrist rollers, chest springs, inclined boards, and leg-press apparatus.

Weight training lends itself readily to self-paced programs. After initial instruction in the lifts, students may proceed on their own or in pairs. For those working alone, the use of a personal progress sheet is very helpful; at the end of each class period students should record the amount of weight lifted and the number of repetitions made. This will enable the student to know exactly where to begin at the start of the next class. A sample weight lifting form developed for Special Olympians is found in figure 27.6.

Regardless of the class organization for instruction in weight training, all students, before they begin, should have a clear understanding of the activities they must avoid, the adaptations they must make, and the safety precautions they must observe.

Safety regulations should be stressed emphatically by the teacher. The first one applies when using either the weight-lifting machine or the barbells and dumbbells; the other three apply only to the use of the latter.

1. Warm-up exercises should be performed before attempting a heavy lift. The warm-up may consist of the side-straddle hop exercise or running in place with exaggerated arm movements.

2. In moving a heavy weight from one place to another, the lift should be made with the knees flexed and the back straight. No one, especially those with back difficulties, should ever lift heavy weights by bending at the hips with the legs straight.

3. Collars (the metal pieces that hold the weights to the bar) should be fastened securely. They should be checked before each lift is attempted.

4. A lift should never be made over someone who is sitting, squatting, or lying on the floor.

All exercises that may involve diseased or disabled parts of the body should be reviewed with the student's

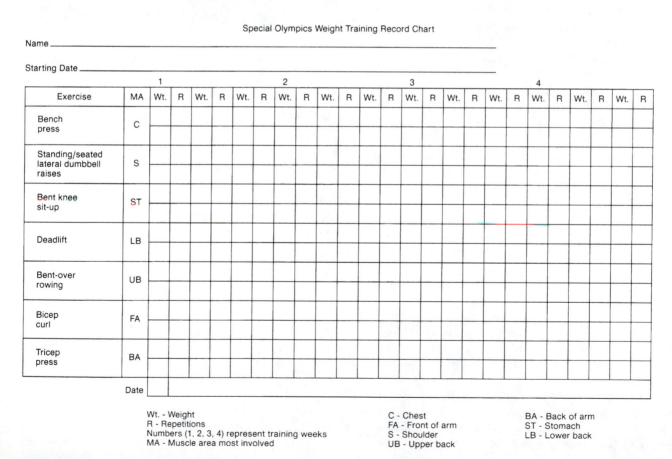

Figure 27.6 Special Olympics weight training chart.

(Source: *Total Conditioning for the Special Olympian* (1986), Lincoln, NE: National Strength and Conditioning Association.)

physician before implementing. Participants with weakened or injured muscles should use light loads as prescribed. When exercising those parts of the body that are not injured, the utmost care must be taken to prevent the injured part from being brought into action inadvertently. Special care must be taken so that the lifter will not slip or allow the load to slip, thereby bringing into action a muscle that was being protected. To be absolutely safe, a lifter with an injury should not make an all-out effort even though the injured part is not involved in the effort.

Those for whom lifting weights is contraindicated for the leg area may do their lifting while sitting or lying down, avoiding all lifts involving the legs. Students who use wheelchairs can perform the lifts while seated in their wheelchairs. Some participants with minor back difficulties may be allowed to take arm and leg exercises if the back is protected against undue stress. To protect the back in such exercises as the two-arm curl, lateral raise, front raise, and military press, these lifts can be made sitting down, with the back held firmly against the back of the chair. Exercises that require heavy weight on the shoulders are contraindicated for those with weak backs. Exercise with the leg machine is a possible substitution for the deep knee bends, which require heavy weight on the shoulder to develop the quadriceps of the legs. Exercises from the prone position do not place undue stress upon the back and therefore need not be adapted. In the supine position those exercises that have a tendency to hyperextend the back, such as the leg raises and the supine pullover, are contraindicated for those with any type of back difficulties or with exceptionally weak abdominals.

In lifting heavy weights, a deep breath is taken and held to stabilize the thoracic region. When this is done, there is an extreme elevation of the arterial blood pressure because the increased pressure in the thoracic region prevents blood from returning to the heart. If the effort is prolonged, the blood

pressure falls after its initial rise. This is known as the Valsalva phenomenon. Because of the increase in blood pressure caused by lifting of weights, the activity is not usually recommended for those with cardiac or circulatory disorders.

The student with the use of only one arm will perform all the lifts involving the use of an arm with this arm. The weights should be sufficiently light so that lifting them with one arm will not produce twisting of the body or bending of the spine laterally, for such movements may produce muscular development that will cause postural difficulties. Students with functional stumps may find it possible to do the lifts with a prosthesis.

In presenting adaptations that can be made for those with disabilities in weight training, very brief descriptions of the specific lifts are given to enable the reader to make a better comparison of the adaptation with normal performance and so gain a better understanding of the process of adapting the lifts for participants with disabilities. It is not the intent to provide instruction for learning to perform the lifts. Those who wish this information are referred to the books in Selected Readings at the end of the chapter.

Lifting Techniques

There are many different types of lifts. Many of them exercise different muscles; others exercise muscles in different groups or exercise the same set of muscles. The muscles that are primarily involved in any given lift can be determined with some degree of accuracy even by someone who does not have a thorough knowledge of anatomy. It must be remembered that a muscle does not push but always pulls to move a joint and that a contracting muscle is harder than a muscle not being worked. Consequently, by examining the direction of movement of the part of the body involved and by palpating the muscle or muscles while the lift is being executed, the muscles being used can be located. Then, by referring to a chart of the skeletal muscles like the one shown in appendix VI, the muscles can be identified.

The lifts presented here are selected to give a fairly complete workout to the major muscle groups in a minimum number of exercises. All lifts using barbells and dumbbells are made from the standing position unless otherwise indicated. Positions for the lifts on the weight-lifting machine will vary according to the kind of machine. The subsequent lifts are described for the barbells and dumbbells, but most of the lifts can be done on the various machines. (For location of muscles listed for each test, see appendix VI.)

Neck Extension and Neck Curl

Neck extension exercises the posterior muscles of the neck (sacrospinalis, cervical muscles, trapezius). A prone position is taken on a bench or on the floor. If a bench is used, the neck extends over the end of the bench. A plate of the barbells is held with both hands on the back of the head. The

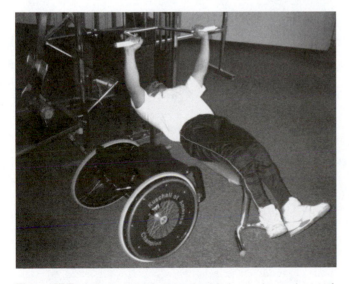

Figure 27.7 Lifts for individuals in wheelchairs can be made out of the chair.

head is lifted backward as far as possible while the chest rests on the bench or floor. The neck is then lowered to the starting position.

The neck curl is performed in the supine position, and the weight is held on the forehead. The head is brought up and forward until the chin touches the chest.

Adaptations: The weights held to the head may be eliminated to decrease the strenuousness of the exercise. If there is extreme muscular weakness or cervical vertebrae injury or malfunction, the neck muscles may be exercised by tightening the flexors and extensors at the same time and holding for approximately six seconds, repeating until sufficient work has been given to the muscles, as a substitute for the exercise with weights.

For those who use wheelchairs, a head harness may be attached to a wall pulley. The medical records of individuals with Down syndrome should be checked to ensure that an anomalous defect know as atlantoaxial instability is not present. If this condition exists, exercises that place undue pressure on the neck would be contraindicated.

Bench Press

The muscles involved in this lift are the pectoralis major and minor, triceps brachia, and the anterior and middle deltoid. This lift is made from a back-lying position on a bench with the buttocks, shoulders, and head in contact with the bench. The feet should comfortably straddle the bench and be in contact with the floor. To perform the bench press, an overhand grip with the hands slightly wider than the shoulders is recommended. The bar is lowered to and touches the chest just below the nipple, and then is pushed upward until the elbows are in an extended position.

Adaptations: A spotter should be used when performing the bench press. The spotter is responsible for assisting the lifter in the event that help is needed. In addition, individuals should be cautioned to avoid arching the back by bringing the buttocks off the bench when performing the lift. Arching the back places tremendous stress and pressure on the lower back region. This can be corrected by using lighter weights and emphasizing that the back must maintain contact with the bench.

Military Press or Standing Press

The muscles involved in this lift are the deltoid, pectoralis major, and triceps. To make the lift, a pronated grip is taken on the bar. The bar is lifted and brought to rest against the chest. The bar is then raised straight over the head until the arms are fully extended. The bar is lowered to the chest position and the exercise repeated.

Adaptations: Care must be taken to keep the back straight as the weight is lifted above the head. This is especially necessary if the lifter has lower back difficulties. To avoid the tendency to hyperextend the back, the participant

may sit in a chair with a high back, holding his or her back firmly against the chair's back.

Two-Arm Curl

The biceps and the brachialis are the primary muscles used in the two-arm curl. The supinated grip is taken. The bar is brought to the thighs. The bar is raised to the shoulders by bending the elbows. The weight is then lowered until the arms are fully extended. The lift may be done by taking a pronated grip. The extensors of the fingers and wrist can be exercised by hyperextending the wrist while lifting the weight to the shoulders.

Adaptations: Lifters with back disorders must take the utmost care to avoid pushing the hips forward to help start the lift upward. This movement hyperextends the back, thereby placing undue stress upon it. To avoid this possibility, the lifter should keep the weight light enough to be handled easily with the arms. As additional protection against hyperextension the lifter may stand with the back against the wall so that movement of the hips is kept to a minimum during the lift. The use of cuff weights or weighted wristbands may be necessary for those who have limited use of the wrists and hands.

Straight-Arm Pullover

The major work in this lift is performed by the pectoralis major and minor, triceps, latissimus dorsi, and serratus anterior muscles. A supine position is taken. The bar is on the floor at arm's length from the head. A grip is taken with the palms up. The bar is pulled and lifted with the arms held straight to a position above the chest. The bar is returned to the starting position and the exercise repeated.

Adaptations: To decrease the difficulty of the lift for those lacking arm strength, the pullover may be done with the arms bent until the bar is above the head, at which time the arms are extended fully. The bar is lowered in a reverse manner.

Those with weak backs should not perform the straight-arm pullover.

Straight-Leg Dead Lift

In this lift the back muscles and upper posterior leg muscles (erector spinae, gluteus maximus, and hamstrings) are used. The bar is placed near the toes. The body is bent at the hips and the upper back held straight. An alternate grip is taken on the bar (one hand pronated and the other supinated), and the bar is lifted by straightening the back. The knees are locked and the arms are kept straight. The bar is then lowered to its original position.

Adaptations: Those with back injuries should modify the lift to reduce the strain on the back muscles and yet exercise the extensors of the back, as follows: A sitting position is taken on a bench, with a light dumbbell in each hand. The shoulders are hunched forward, and the chin rests on the chest. The head is lifted, the shoulders thrown wide, and the back straightened. Return to the original position and repeat the exercise.

Sit-Ups

The major muscles involved in the sit-ups are the abdominals and the iliopsoas. A supine position is taken, with the knees bent to approximately a ninety-degree angle and the toes hooked under the bar. A weight is held to the back of the head with both hands. The head is brought forward until it is approximately thirty degrees off the floor. Movement beyond this range uses the hip flexor muscles and provides little value to the abdominal muscles.

Adaptations: No weight is placed behind the head. The head is brought forward until the chin touches the chest. Then the shoulders start to raise from the floor. The small of the back remains in contact with the floor throughout the lift. The return is made to the supine position.

Knee Bend and Heel Raise

In the knee bend the gastrocnemius, soleus, quadriceps, and gluteus maximus are used extensively. The bar is held across the back of the neck and shoulders, and the body is lowered to a squat position with the upper legs parallel to the floor. The return is made to the original position.

In the heel raise, the gastrocnemius, soleus, and plantar flexor of the feet are developed. The bar is carried on the shoulders as in the deep knee bend. The bar is lifted by raising the heels off the ground until the weight is resting on the balls of the feet. The heels are then lowered.

Adaptations: Some authorities feel that deep knee bends affect the ligaments of the knee to their disadvantage and therefore recommend that only a three-quarter squat be taken.

Those suffering from injured knees should substitute a knee exerciser for the knee bends. Students with back difficulties should not perform the lift with heavy weights on the shoulders. Those with arch problems in the feet should not do the heel raise.

Lateral, Forward, and Backward Lifts

The muscles involved in each of these lifts are: lateral lift—deltoid, supraspinatus, trapezius, serratus anterior; forward lift—deltoid, pectoralis major, coraco-brachialis, serratus anterior, trapezius; backward lift—deltoid, teres major, rhomboids, trapezius.

Dumbbells are grasped in each hand with the hands at the sides of the body. In the lateral raise, the arms are lifted directly sideways to the horizontal level. For the forward raise, they are lifted forward. In the backward raise, the arms are raised backward and upward as far as possible without bending the trunk.

Adaptations: In the lateral and forward lifts, a sitting position may be taken to avoid hyperextending the back. Those with weak shoulder joints subject to dislocation should never raise the arms higher than shoulder level. As an additional safety precaution, the exercise should be performed with one arm at a time. The opposite arm is brought across the chest and the hand grasps the shoulder to pull it in toward the body during the lift. In this way it becomes impossible to raise the arm inadvertently above the desired level.

The backward lift is contraindicated for those suffering from weak shoulder joints subject to dislocation.

Prone Lateral Raise

The deltoid, pectoralis major, infraspinatus, teres minor, and trapezius muscles are brought into play in this exercise. A prone position is taken on a bench, and the hands grasp dumbbells on the floor to each side of the body. The weights are lifted toward the ceiling as far as possible, keeping the arms straight. The dumbbells are then lowered slowly to the floor.

Adaptations: No modification is required except for individuals with missing limbs and those with heart disorders.

Supine Horizontal Arm Lift

The following muscles are used in this lift: deltoid, pectoralis major, coracobrachialis, and serratus anterior. A supine position is taken with the arms extended out from the shoulders. The dumbbells are grasped with the palms facing up. The arms are raised over the chest with the elbows locked and then returned to the original position.

Adaptations: The lift usually will not require adaptation except for individuals with heart disorders and amputations.

Prone Arch Back

The performer lies face down on a bench, with the upper half of the body extended over the end of the bench; the ankles are held securely by a partner. Holding a dumbbell behind the head, the performer arches the back and holds this position for eight to ten seconds.

Adaptations: To reduce the strain on weak extensor muscles of the back, the amount of the weight is decreased. Also a small stool may be placed beneath the lifter's chest to prevent going all the way to the floor. This exercise should not be used for individuals with lower back pain unless specifically prescribed by the student's physician.

Most of the typical exercises used in weight training can be simulated as isometric contractions, thereby making them adaptable for use by those who are unable to engage in isotonic weight training. Isometrics require exerting a muscle against some immovable object. Pushing against a door frame or against stall bars or using ropes or towels to restrict the ability to move can provide isometric contractions. Other body parts can be used as resistance also; for example, one can use the hand to resist head movements or flex one arm while resisting with the other. Isometrics have been criticized for their inability to improve muscle endurance. If repeated contractions are performed, as would be the case in using barbells for muscular endurance, this limitation can be eliminated. One significant advantage of isometrics is that they allow a specific weak point in a movement to be exercised without necessitating the use of the entire range of motion. This advantage may be of special value to a person with a condition for whom stress in one part of the range of motion is contraindicated.

In addition to the typical resistance training exercises, a variety of other games, stunts, and sports can be utilized for the purpose of increasing muscle strength and endurance. Many gymnastics skills performed on the parallel or uneven bars, rings, and side horse will develop significant upper body strength. Floor stunts, hand balancing, and shot putting are also good strength developers. Various types of relay races such as wheelbarrow races, seal walks, one-leg hopping, and medicine-ball passing can provide novelty while stimulating muscular development. Performing calisthenic movements in a swimming pool provides another alternative

form of resistance exercise. The force necessary to move the limbs through the water is much greater than that in air. These aquatic exercises also effectively allow for differences in fitness levels. The stronger individual is instructed to move faster, the water providing increased resistance.

Equipment other than free weights or weight machines can be used to develop muscular strength. For instance, young children will enjoy the use of weighted stuffed animals. Various exercises can be performed with the stuffed animals to encourage the development of appropriate levels of strength. Some have found the use of flexible (surgical) tubing effective for providing resistance through a range of motion. Flexible tubing can be particularly effective when used with individuals who are recovering from serious injury or those who have limited musculature. Tubing or rope also can be held and pulled by two individuals to create a challenging form of resistance.

Circuit training or the use of exercises performed at various stations can also be an effective method for enhancing muscle strength and endurance. Using this approach, students are challenged to perform a certain number of lifts or exercises at a station before moving to the next station. The activity can be individualized for each participant by specifying the number of repetitions at each station and/or the number of times to go through the circuit. The stations should be varied so that different muscle groups are used in adjacent stations. Circuit training can be very effective in motivating students because of the individualized approach used in this system. The individual with a disability will be able to participate with nondisabled peers in the circuit training program.

Development of Flexibility

Flexibility as a component of physical fitness is slower to show gains than are the other components but improvements appear to be retained longer. People attempting to improve flexibility should be made aware of this fact and not become discouraged when rapid improvement does not occur in the first few weeks of exercising. With persistence, dramatic increases are possible in most persons.

A warm-up of the muscles and joints to be involved in the program should be completed prior to starting the flexibility exercises. This will reduce the chance for muscle pulls and muscle cramping and will allow movement through a greater range. Often flexibility exercises are used as a warm-up for other activities. It is not the best practice to perform extreme stretches of cold muscles. Rather, a general warm-up using movements through the middle portion of the range of motion should be completed prior to any stretching to the extreme ranges. In this way greater elasticity of the tissues is produced, which allows the performer to obtain a greater degree of stretch and thereby achieve faster gains in flexibility.

All flexibility exercises should be performed slowly, never using rapid, jerking movements. When the body part

Figure 27.8 Hopping up and down on a rubber ball can contribute to a student's muscular strength and endurance.

reaches the end of the range of motion it should be held for ten to thirty seconds, then slowly returned to a resting position. This "held stretch" is termed static stretching as opposed to the ballistic action of bobbing up and down. Physiologically, the slow, held stretch reduces the activity of the muscle spindle in producing the stretch reflex, which causes an involuntary contraction of the muscle being stretched. Reduction of the stretch reflex by using static stretching reduces the chances for muscle pulls and produces a more relaxed muscle that can be stretched to a greater degree. Each exercise should be repeated three to four times per workout. A large number of specific flexibility exercises can be obtained from most books on exercise or you can create your own by identifying the joint action desired, creating a body position that moves this joint to the limit of the range of motion and holding that position. The most common joint actions included in a comprehensive stretching program would be:

1. Neck: flexion, extension, rotation, lateral flexion
2. Shoulders: flexion, extension, abduction, rotation
3. Upper Spine: flexion, extension, rotation, lateral flexion
4. Lower Spine: flexion, extension, rotation, lateral flexion
5. Hips: flexion, extension, abduction, rotation
6. Knees: flexion, extension
7. Ankles: flexion, extension, rotation

A variety of stunts and games requiring good joint flexibility can be used to enhance range of motion without directly employing calisthenic-like stretching activities. Many skills in gymnastics stress flexibility. Stunts such as the splits, dislocates on the bars, side horse work, and vaults require flexibility. Many dives and most movements in modern, ballet, and jazz dancing can contribute to flexibility. The track and field events of hurdling, long and high jumping, the sport of karate, the butterfly swimming stroke, and various stunts with wands and the limbo stick all can be used to enhance flexibility while practicing skilled movements.

Development of Cardiorespiratory Endurance

Sustained large-muscle activity is necessary to require large amounts of oxygen to be consumed by the working muscles. This type of activity requires the heart, lungs, and vascular system to jointly supply as much as twenty times the resting oxygen delivery. The resultant increases in heart and respiration rates are the necessary stimuli for development of cardiorespiratory endurance.

The heart rate is a convenient guide to the stress being placed on the cardiorespiratory system. A rough estimate of the intensity of the activity can be obtained by counting the pulse rate during or immediately following the exercise. Because heart rate decreases quickly after the conclusion of exercise, it is best to count the pulse for only ten or fifteen seconds and multiply by six or four, respectively. For a conditioning effect to be achieved the exercise heart rate for young, nondisabled individuals should be at least 60 percent of the difference between resting and maximum heart rate added to the resting rate. Resting heart rate should be taken only after at least five minutes of complete rest. Maximum heart rate is estimated to be equal to 220 minus the age of the subject. So for a fifteen-year-old the estimated maximum heart rate is 205 (220 − 15). If the resting heart rate is measured at 63, the minimum exercise heart rate should be:

$$.60 (205 - 63) + 63 = 148$$

It should be noted that recent research has found that as people age the intensity threshold for improving cardiorespiratory efficiency may be only 40 percent. Readers are cautioned to recognize that there are individual differences in maximum heart rate values. There is some evidence to indicate that a similar threshold may apply to extremely sedentary persons, including some individuals with disabilities.

The duration of training necessary for improvement in the cardiorespiratory system has been suggested to be between ten and twenty minutes. Thus for the previous example, the heart rate of 148 or above should be maintained for approximately fifteen minutes at least three times per week for improvement to be achieved. Care should be taken not to elevate the heart rate too high (beyond about 80 percent by the formula) because this will cause fatigue and limit the duration of the exercise. If a choice must be made between intensity and duration, duration should predominate when cardiorespiratory improvement is the goal.

Any type of activity that will produce a sustained elevated heart rate of the magnitude described before is appropriate for obtaining the cardiorespiratory conditioning effect. Jogging has become the most popular. It offers an easy skill that can be done almost anywhere. However, many other activities are equally appropriate, such as swimming, bicycling, rowing, rope jumping, walking, and aerobic and other forms of dancing. Those with orthopedic disabilities may find swimming most appropriate, whereas those who are visually impaired may select stationary or tandem cycling, rope jumping, or dancing in preference to jogging. Persons with joint problems may find that walking or running in waist-deep water does not aggravate their condition but provides a sufficient work load to tax the cardiorespiratory system.

Many of the continuous-type ball games such as soccer and basketball can stress the cardiorespiratory system; however, it is often difficult to regulate the intensity to make the game appropriate for the conditioning needs of all the participants. Additionally, any type of game, stunt, or relay that incorporates large-muscle activity and is sustained for ten to twenty minutes holds the potential for cardiorespiratory development.

Exercise of an endurance nature must be carefully undertaken by anyone having cardiac, respiratory, or vascular insufficiency. The physician should approve the type of exercise to be utilized and very close monitoring of intensity must be practiced. Battery-operated beeper devices are currently available and can be worn by exercising subjects to give a warning when a preselected heart rate is reached. This allows effective monitoring without the necessity of periodic pulse checking.

Reduction of Body Fat

Excessive body fat has been identified as both a significant health hazard and an obstacle to physical performance and skill learning. The great majority of overly fat persons do not have metabolic or glandular disorders; rather, they simply eat more calories than they expend in exercise. For them, weight loss is a simple balance between calories expended and calories consumed. Either reducing caloric intake or increasing caloric expenditure through exercise can accomplish a fat loss. Several studies have indicated that many obese youngsters do not differ significantly in their eating habits from their normal-weight peers, but they do get far less habitual exercise.

Individuals with disabilities, both physical and mental, tend to get less daily exercise than the nondisabled and thus may suffer a greater incidence of obesity. The types of exercise that will facilitate fat loss are those that burn a large number of calories—large-muscle activity undertaken for prolonged periods of time. Heavy exercise with small muscle groups (such as push-ups and sit-ups) may produce feelings of fatigue but provide little total caloric expenditure. Although the type of exercise needed to produce high caloric expenditure is similar to that necessary for cardiorespiratory development, the intensity does not need to be nearly as great. In fact, walking five miles at a slow pace will burn far more calories than running one four-minute mile.

The concept of exercising for spot reduction (losing fat in one part of the body) has remained a popular myth. The exercise performed by a muscle does not use the fat stored in the immediate area as fuel for contraction. Rather the energy for contraction comes from stored glycogen and lipids within the muscle and in circulating blood. Reduction in fat deposits occurs throughout the body, regardless of which muscles may be active, if a negative caloric balance is reached. If this were not true, the legs of an individual who is paralyzed would become extremely large due to fat accumulation around the unexercised leg muscles. Spot exercises will help the toning of muscles utilized and may aid posture, producing a beneficial effect on appearance. They will not, however, produce a greater fat loss in the specific part of the body being exercised.

Special Considerations for Individuals Who Are Mentally Retarded

Recent attention has been focused on those with mental retardation and their low levels of physical fitness. Several investigators have concluded that this population tends to have low levels of physical fitness. Although there may be in some instances of mental retardation a physiologic reason for this, the low levels of physical fitness are probably due to the lack of opportunity and appropriate programs for this population. There is growing evidence to suggest that significant improvements can be made with those who are mentally retarded, including those severely involved, if programs are systematically developed and implemented. Some suggested guidelines are indicated below:

1. Communicate the importance of physical fitness. Many individuals who are mentally retarded have difficulty understanding the "why" of physical fitness—why should someone jog? Halle, Silverman, and Regan (1983) found that a puppet could be used to help children who are mentally retarded focus and listen to information about health and fitness. A valuable communication device for emphasizing the importance of fitness is to perform the exercises with the class. Seeing the teacher "work out" helps the adolescent who is mentally retarded recognize that running and flexibility exercises are not just activities for children.

2. Task analyze the exercise. Many of the fitness activities will require that the activity be broken down into smaller steps and taught to the participants. The amount of instruction required will depend upon the level of retardation and past experience of the individuals. Participants who are mentally retarded will require extended practice to ensure that the exercises are familiar and understood.

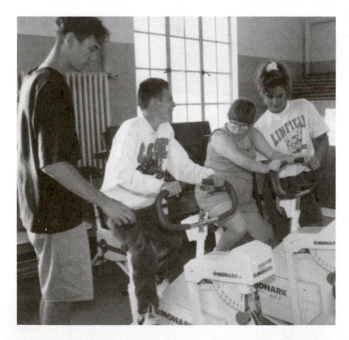

Figure 27.9 Riding a stationary bicycle can aid in the reduction of body fat and increase endurance.

3. Establish goals and criteria for success. During the first week of the program it is essential that baseline measures be taken on the performance capability of the students. For example, the number of sit-ups an individual can perform in sixty seconds should be recorded as well as other indicators such as distance walked/jogged in twelve minutes. Given this information, individual goals and objectives can be developed.

4. Design a motivational system. Because the gains experienced by people who are mentally retarded can sometimes be small, it is essential that a recording system be developed so that the participants can "see" change. This can be accomplished in several ways. For example, a poster with the name of all the students can be displayed and stickers applied for each day that the individual meets or exceeds the prescribed goal. Group or class support can be developed by allowing the class to do something special, such as having a party when all of the participants reach their individual goals. A graphic display of the total number of minutes spent in physical activity can be effective in helping some recognize that it is not necessary to be the fastest or the strongest to be successful.

5. Use peers as tutors to provide for direct and continuous motivation for the students. Rintala et al. (1992) found peers very helpful in encouraging young adult males to walk long distances at a rapid rate. Peers provide constant feedback and help to make the exercise session enjoyable and natural.

6. Probe for change in performance. To determine whether the participants are improving, formal measures of the fitness test items should be conducted at regular intervals of time, such as every two weeks. The level of performance should be compared to the initial score and a graph developed to illustrate change. If the expected gains are not evident, then an effort should be made to determine if the goal or program should be modified. Occasionally the problem may be that the specific exercise has not been learned, resulting in little practice. Frequent testing helps to emphasize that physical fitness is important and that gains will occur when the program is followed.

7. Incorporate the exercise program into the home. Maintenance and generalization of physical fitness and the exercise program will require the support of parents. Individuals with mental retardation require additional time to learn and incorporate selected concepts. Parents can be very effective in helping children to appreciate the importance of fitness and the value of exercise. Teachers should provide frequent feedback to parents about the fitness levels of their children and encourage parents to exercise with their children.

The fitness levels of individuals who are mentally retarded can be improved, but gains will not occur without a systematic training program. In addition, efforts should be made to incorporate fitness and physical activity into the regular daily life patterns of these individuals. Improvements in physical fitness will be maintained if individuals are consistent in their exercise practices.

Individualized Fitness Programs: An Example

In most cases, the program of physical fitness will need to be individualized for the student with a disability. When setting up such a program, consideration must be given to the characteristics, attitudes, and interests of the individual as they relate to the assessment of needs and the selection of activities for the program. The following is a hypothetical example of the fitness evaluation and prescription process.

Description of Subject

Marcia Cox, 152 pounds, fourteen-year-old female, has required the use of a wheelchair since she was hit by an automobile while riding her bike at age ten. Marcia is an above-average junior high school student. Previously, she received no more activity than that required to achieve her mobility from class to class and around her house. Marcia's parents have requested that an assessment be conducted and that fitness be incorporated into Marcia's Individualized Education Program (IEP) in physical education.

Evaluation of Needs

In discussions with Marcia it was clear that she had a rather low self-concept. She indicated a concern over her tendency

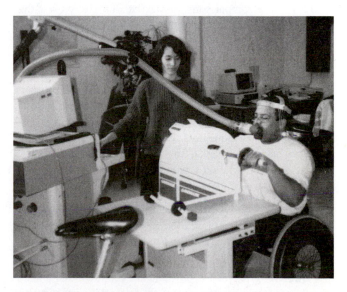

Figure 27.10 Professionals today can help the individual with a disability monitor personal health and fitness.

to be overweight and expressed a desire to be more active. When asked, Marcia responded that she did know how to swim before her accident and had enjoyed it. She commented that she would like to lose some body weight and learn to swim again.

Fitness Testing

Marcia's general fitness was observed to be poor. It was determined that several tests would be appropriate for a fitness evaluation—the results of which would be shared with the IEP team and used as a basis for construction of a specific exercise program. The tests selected were handgrip strength, arm extensor strength, shoulder and neck flexibility, skinfold body fat test, and a modified cardiorespiratory test. This test involved five minutes of a speed-controlled shuttle of fifty feet using her wheelchair with a count of her pulse rate for fifteen seconds immediately following the exercise.

The results of the testing were as follows:

1. Grip Strength: right—18 kilograms, left—16 kilograms
2. Seated Barbell Press: 35 pounds
3. Shoulder Flexibility (flexion-extension): 185°
4. Neck Flexibility (rotation): 130°
5. Skinfold Fat: triceps—27 millimeters, subscapular—29 millimeters
6. Cardiorespiratory Endurance: 15 second pulse count = 47 = 188 per-minute; resting rate = 78

Marcia's grip strength was interpreted as being below that desired. Her barbell press strength was adequate but could be enhanced as an aid to swimming, especially because all her stroke power must come from her arms. Her flexibility was deemed to be adequate but would be increased for the extra value it has for swimming. The measure of her body fat, though it should not be compared to norms, appeared to be rather elevated. The cardiorespiratory endurance task will be used for future comparisons. Subjective observation was that she had rather poor cardiorespiratory endurance.

Exercise Prescription

The following was designed as a beginning exercise program for Marcia with reevaluation to take place in three months. Workouts were scheduled three times per week. She was encouraged to also add some other activity such as accompanying her parents on walks. She was also counseled to follow a moderate diet. Marcia's parents, as members of the IEP team, agreed to help their daughter follow the program.

1. A generalized warm-up consisting of five minutes of continuous laps around the gym in her wheelchair. Moderate speed was suggested and her pulse checked to achieve approximately 125 beats per minute.

2. Stretching exercises for the neck, shoulder, and spine. A variety of exercises were used, each held for fifteen seconds and repeated four times.

3. Weight Training Exercises: (a) barbell press: 20 pounds, 8 to 10 repetitions, 3 sets (b) dumbbell curl: 5 pounds, 10 to 12 repetitions, 3 sets

4. Swimming—total pool time twenty minutes. Combination of various strokes.

Heart rate checked every five minutes—attempting to keep it at approximately 145 beats per minute, working up to 155 beats per minute by the end of the first month.

$$220 \quad 60\% \, (206 - 78) + 78 = 154.8 \text{ target heart rate}$$
$$\underline{- \quad 14} \quad \text{(age of subject)}$$
$$206 \quad \text{(max. heart rate)}$$
$$78 \quad = \text{resting heart rate}$$

The exercise prescription was modified to increase the work intensity periodically as Marcia appeared to be making progress. Marcia enjoyed the workouts. Both the social contact with the physical educator and the activities were enjoyable. She especially liked the swimming and by the second month was feeling quite at home in the water. She expressed that she felt she would be able to enjoy swimming with some friends by summer.

At the end of three months Marcia had improved in all areas of fitness tested. Her second set of test scores was then recorded alongside her initial test results.

This program was deemed a success. Marcia was pleased with her progress and a new set of goals was established with a slightly altered exercise prescription to concentrate more on fat reduction.

Summary

There is increasing awareness of the importance of physical fitness and its contribution toward a healthy life-style. The relationship between inactivity and heart disease, obesity, and high blood pressure are well documented. Many have argued that physical fitness reduces selected health risk factors and contributes toward an overall feeling of well-being. Recognition has also grown in recent years of the importance of the health benefits of enhanced physical fitness to the typically less active, including those with disabilities. Due to a combination of factors including the lack of opportunities, overprotection, and self-consciousness, individuals with disabilities often engage in less daily physical activity than do those who are not disabled. Fortunately, significant efforts are underway to improve the physical fitness of those with disabilities and in turn enhance their overall quality of life.

Within this chapter information was presented on the distinction between physical fitness and motor fitness. Motor fitness has to do with selected factors that lead to the learning of selected motor skills and includes such variables as balance, coordination, and speed. Physical fitness, also known as health-related fitness, consists of five components: cardiorespiratory endurance, muscular strength, muscular endurance, flexibility, and body composition. Each of these components is important in contributing to a healthy and active life. Procedures and tests have been developed to assess physical fitness. Some tests have been specifically developed for special populations with norms that allow for comparisons by disability. Although much work remains to be done in this area, the tests that have been developed have provided needed standards and norms for individuals with disabilities.

Programs to improve the physical fitness of individuals with disabilities follow many of the same guidelines as those for the nondisabled. For example, the principle of progressive overload can be applied, with few exceptions, to individuals both with and without disabilities. Exceptions may be necessary for those with progressive neuromuscular conditions. The endurance of individuals with disabilities can be improved by following a program based on target heart rate and standardized according to the frequency, intensity, and duration of the exercise. Modifications, of course, will be necessary to accommodate those with sensory, neuromuscular, and orthopedic impairments. Users of wheelchairs, for instance, will need to modify their program to ensure that the cardiovascular system experiences sufficient stress to achieve a training effect. Those who are quadriplegic may find the duration of the activity a better guide than heart rate for assessing the intensity of the workout. Fortunately, there are several organizations that are providing leadership and training in this area. The message is very clear. Children and adults with disabilities should be encouraged to lead active lives with an emphasis on maintaining an appropriate level of physical fitness; to do otherwise may place greater emphasis on disability as opposed to ability.

Selected Readings

AAHPERD Fitness and Educational Program. (1987). *ARAPCS Physical Fitness Council Newsletter* (Spring 1988 ed., p. 1). Reston, VA: American Alliance for Health, Physical Education, Recreation, and Dance.

American Alliance for Health, Physical Education, Recreation, and Dance. (1975). *Testing for impaired, disabled and handicapped individuals.* Washington, DC: Author.

American Alliance for Health, Physical Education, Recreation, and Dance. (1975). *Youth fitness test manual.* Washington, DC: Author.

American Alliance for Health, Physical Education, Recreation, and Dance. (1976). *Special fitness test manual for mildly mentally retarded persons.* Washington, DC: Author.

American Alliance for Health, Physical Education, Recreation, and Dance. (1980). *Health related physical fitness test manual.* Washington, DC, Author.

Baumgartner, T., & Horvat, M. (1991). Reliability of field based cardiovascular fitness running tests for individuals with mental retardation. *Adapted Physical Activity Quarterly, 8,* 107–114.

Buell, C. (1980). *Physical education and recreation for the visually handicapped.* Washington, DC: American Alliance for Health, Physical Education, Recreation, and Dance.

Cooper, K.H. (1970). *Aerobics.* New York: Bantam Books, Inc.

Coutts, K., McKenzie, D., Loock, C., Beauchamp, R., & Armstrong, R. (1993). Upper body exercise capacity in youth with spina bifida. *Adapted Physical Activity Quarterly, 10,* 22–28.

Davis, G.M., Tupling, S.J., & Shephard, R.J. (1986). Dynamic strength and physical activity in wheelchair users. In C. Sherrill (Ed.), *Sport and disabled athletes* (pp. 139–146). Champaign, IL: Human Kinetics Publishers.

Dobbins, D.A., Garron, R., & Rarick, G.L. (1981). The motor performance of educable mentally retarded and intellectually normal boys after covariate control for differences in body size. *Research Quarterly for Exercise and Sports, 52*(1), 1–8.

Dreisinger, T.E., & Londeree, B.R. (1982). Wheelchair exercise: A review. *Paraplegia, 20,* 20–34.

Fait, H.F., & Kupferer, H. (1956). A study of two motor achievement tests and its implications in planning physical education activities for the mentally retarded. *American Journal of Mental Deficiency, 60,* 728–732.

Fernhall, B., Tymeson, G.T., & Webster, G.E. (1988). Cardiovascular fitness of mentally retarded individuals. *Adapted Physical Activity Quarterly, 5,* 12–28.

Halle, J.W., Silverman, N.A., & Regan, L. (1983). The effects of a data-based exercise program on physical fitness of retarded children. *Education and Training of the Mentally Retarded,* 221–225.

Holland, L.J., Bouffard, M., & Wagner, D. (1992). Rating of perceived exertion, heart rate, and oxygen consumption in adults with multiple sclerosis. *Adapted Physical Activity Quarterly, 9,* 64–73.

Horvat, M. (1987). Effects of a progressive resistance training program on an individual with spastic cerebral palsy. *American Corrective Therapy Journal, 41*(1), 7–11.

Jankowski, L.W., & Evans, J.K. (1981). The exercise capacity of blind children. *Journal of Visual Impairment and Blindness,* 248–251.

Johnson, L., & Londeree, B. (1976). *Motor fitness testing manual for the moderately mentally retarded.* Washington, DC: American Alliance for Health, Physical Education, Recreation, and Dance.

Kertzer, R., Croce, R., Hinkle, R., & Janson-Sand, C. (1994). Selected fitness and motor behavior parameters of children and adolescents with insulin-dependent diabetes mellitus. *Adapted Physical Activity Quarterly, 11,* 284–296.

Kraus, H., & Hirschland, R. (1954). Minimum muscular fitness tests in school children. *Research Quarterly, 25*(2), 178.

Kraus, H., & Hirschland, R.P. (1954). Muscular fitness and orthopedic disability. *New York State Journal of Medicine, 54,* 212–215.

Lessare, B. (1986). Fitness is for everyone. *Sports 'n Spokes, 11*(6), 35–36.

Maksud, M., & Hamilton, L. (1974). Physiological responses of EMR children to strenuous exercise. *American Journal of Mental Deficiency, 79,* 32–38.

Moon, S.M., & Renzaglia, A. (1982). Physical fitness and the mentally retarded: A critical review of the literature. *The Journal of Special Education, 16,* 269–287.

National Strength and Conditioning Association. (1986). *Total conditioning for the Special Olympian.* Lincoln, NE: Author.

Pitetti, K.H., & Campbell, K.D. (1991). Mentally retarded individuals—A population at risk? *Medicine and Science in Sports and Exercise, 23,* 586–593.

Pizzaro, D.C. (1990). Reliability of the health related fitness test for mainstreamed educable and trainable mentally handicapped adolescents. *Adapted Physical Activity Quarterly, 7,* 240–248.

Rarick, L., & Francis, R.J. (1960). Motor characteristics of the mentally retarded. In *Competitive Research Monograph.* Vol. 1. U.S. Office of Education.

Rasch, P.J. (1982). *Weight training* (4th ed.). Dubuque, IA: Wm. C. Brown Publishers.

Rimmer, J.H. (1992). Cardiovascular fitness programming for adults with mental retardation: Translating research into practice. *Adapted Physical Activity Quarterly, 9,* 237–248.

Rimmer, J.H. (1994). *Fitness and rehabilitation programs for special populations.* Dubuque, IA: Brown and Benchmark.

Rimmer, J., & Rosentsweig, J. (1982). The physical working capacity of learning disabled children. *American Corrective Therapy Journal, 36,* 133–134.

Rintala, P., Dunn, J.M., McCubbin, J.A., & Quinn, C. (1992). Validity of a cardiorespiratory fitness test for men with mental retardation. *Medicine and Science in Sports and Exercise, 24,* 941–945.

Rowland, T.P. (1990). *Exercise and Children's Health.* Champaign, IL: Human Kinetics Publishers.

Roswal, G.M., Roswal, P.M., & Dunleavy, A.O. (1986). Normative health-related fitness data for Special Olympians. In C. Sherrill (Ed.), *Sport and disabled athletes* (pp. 231–238). Champaign, IL: Human Kinetics Publishers.

Seaman, J. (1994). AALF and the alliance: Partners in fitness education. *American Association for Active Lifestyles and Fitness Newsletter.* Reston, VA.: AAHPERD.

Seaman, J.A. (Ed.). (1995). *Physical best and individuals with disabilities.* Reston, VA: AAHPERD.

Short, F.X., & Winnick, J.P. (1986). The performance of adolescents with cerebral palsy on measures of physical fitness. In C. Sherrill (Ed.), *Sport and disabled athletes* (pp. 239–244). Champaign, IL: Human Kinetics Publishers.

Simmons, R. (1986). *Reach for fitness: A special book of exercises for the physically challenged.* New York: Warner Books.

Skuldt, A. (1984). Exercise limitations for quadriplegics. *Sports 'n Spokes, 10*(1), 19–20.

Stainback, S., Stainback, W., Wehman, P., & Spangiers, L. (1983). Acquisition and generalization of physical fitness exercises in three profoundly retarded adults. *The Journal of the Association for the Severely Handicapped, 8*(2), 47–55.

Steadward, R., & Walsh, C. (1986). Training and fitness programs for disabled athletes: Past, present, and future. In C. Sherrill, (Ed.), *Sport and disabled athletes* (pp. 3–20). Champaign, IL: Human Kinetics Publishers.

Vogler, E.W. (1990). Fitness data of children with ostomy: A pilot study. *Adapted Physical Activity Quarterly, 7,* 259–264.

Winnick, J.P. (1994). Personal Correspondence.

Winnick, J.P., & Short, F.X. (1985). *Physical fitness testing of the disabled.* Champaign, IL: Human Kinetics Publishers.

Winnick, J.P. & Short, F.X. (1991). A comparison of the physical fitness of nonretarded and mildy mentally retarded adolescents with cerebral palsy. *Adapted Physical Activity Quarterly, 8*(1),43–56.

Enhancing Activities

1. Select one of the tests referenced in this chapter and give the test to a youngster with a disability. Write up the results of the test with suggestions for program development.

2. Debate with one of your friends the similarities and differences between physical fitness and motor fitness. This activity might be enlarged to include the entire class, utilizing a formal debate approach.

3. Simulate a disability and take one of the physical fitness tests. This could entail wearing a blindfold or using a wheelchair. Write a short paper describing your feelings regarding your performance on the fitness test.

4. Undertake a study of the physiologic response of individuals with paraplegia and quadriplegia to exercise. Describe the similarities and differences in these populations compared with those who are not disabled.

5. Implement a fitness program with an individual with a disability. Establish a baseline that describes the student's initial level of fitness, implement the program, and conduct periodic assessments to determine the amount of progress.

6. Develop a list of strategies that might be employed to motivate students with disabilities to develop and maintain an appropriate level of fitness. Explain how the list might differ depending on the level of disability (severe to mild) and type of disability (such as mental retardation contrasted to paraplegia).

Posture and Body Awareness

CHAPTER OBJECTIVES

After studying this chapter, the reader should be able to:

1. Recognize good posture and the common postural deviations that occur in children.

2. Appreciate that the concept of a perfect posture must be individualized for each child, given the individual differences found in anatomical structure.

3. Discuss various postural deviations including kyphosis, lordosis, scoliosis, genu varum and valgum, and tibial or femoral torsion, and describe the postures associated with these disorders.

4. Apply various screening procedures that can be used as aids in detecting and referring youngsters suspected of having a postural disorder.

5. Explain the difference between a functional and structural postural deviation.

6. Recommend exercises that might be helpful in the treatment of students with functional postural disorders.

7. Comprehend the importance of exercise and activity to the overall health and well-being of students with postural disorders.

8. Apply techniques that have been found useful in helping students to recognize and appreciate the importance of good posture.

Concepts of good posture have undergone numerous changes throughout history. At times the exaggerated styles of women's clothing have influenced the concept of good posture, as in the days of the bustle. The ramrod-straight position of the soldier at attention influenced for many years the idea of good body carriage. There is no doubt that physical education teachers concerned with promoting good posture must take into consideration the aesthetics of certain positions, and these, of course, are dictated by custom and tradition. But they should not ignore the effects that a specific posture will have upon the efficiency of the body.

Mastering efficient walking, sitting, and standing postures makes these movements more beautiful as well as more practical from the standpoint of preventing fatigue. Achieving this efficient, graceful posture involves body mechanics. This term refers to the alignment of the various segments of the body. Achievement of good body mechanics is dependent upon well-developed body awareness, or consciousness of how the body moves in space and what space it occupies. Developing this awareness is a prerequisite to the most efficient use of the muscles to ensure the most effective alignment for the position desired.

Posture cannot be thought of as a single static position, for it changes continually with each movement. Moving the shoulders forward while leaning over from the hips to pick up a small object may be very good posture for that activity, but it is not effective for walking or standing. Consequently, we may say that posture depends upon the type of activity the body is being called upon to perform.

Good posture also depends upon the structure of the body, which is determined by the relationship of the parts of the body to each other—that is, the relationship of the head to the spinal column and shoulder girdle, and so on. The relationship of the parts, how they fit together, is a determining factor in what constitutes good posture for the individual. People are not built alike, and to force everyone into the same mold of a preconceived idea of good posture is useless. Individuals who because of their body structure are more round-shouldered than others should not be forced to stand with their shoulders thrust back to the same extent as one whose bone structure permits them to do this without strain. To do so will lower the body efficiency rather than raise it.

Sheldon (1954) introduced a system of body typing, referred to as somatotyping, which offers a helpful approach for explaining to individuals, including young children, that not everyone's body structure is the same. In Sheldon's classification scheme, three primary body types are identified: Endomorph, Mesomorph, and Ectomorph. For a complete description of the body types, the reader is referred to Sheldon's classic work, *Atlas of Man: A Guide for Somatotyping Adult Males at All Ages*. A brief explanation of the body types follows:

Endomorph: This body type is characterized by roundness and softness of the body; usually associated with the overweight individual.

Mesomorph: This type is associated with solid, well-developed musculature. The bones are usually large and covered with thick musculature.

Ectomorphy: Individuals who have predominantly lean, linear body structure are classified as ectomorphs. The bone structure is small and muscles are thin.

Although most individuals have a predisposition toward one body type versus another, Sheldon emphasized that each person possesses some aspect of each of the body types. To illustrate this point, scores ranging from 1 to 7 were assigned to each body type (figure 28.1)—the 7 representing the endomorphic characteristic, the 4 referring to mesomorphic structure, and the 1 representing little or no endomorphy. The mesomorph would be characterized by a high number in the middle (e.g., 1-7-1.)

The primary value of recognizing variations in body structure is to understand that postural abnormalities are also associated with variations in body structure. For example, the individual who is an ectomorph is predisposed to postural abnormalities such as round shoulders, forward head, and winged scapulae. Endomorphs commonly experience postural problems such as knock knees (genu valgum), pronated and flat fee, round shoulders and round back. Mesomorphs are fortunate in that they seldom experience major postural deviations associated with body structure.

The incidence of poor body alignment is difficult to determine because no standard of good posture can be universally applied. It is estimated that from 75 to 80 percent of the population has some postural deficiency.

Only about 1 percent can be classified as having such good body mechanics that no improvement is possible. Nearly 5 percent have very marked postural deviations. Consequently, the physical education instructor may expect to find a large number of students in the total enrollment who may profit from instruction in good body mechanics and a small percentage in definite need of such instruction.

The teaching unit for developing good posture should stress awareness of how the parts of the body work together to obtain and maintain the relationship that produces the best posture for the individual. Awareness is developed in students by helping them to assume positions of efficient posture and noting how the body segments relate to achieve each position. Practice is afforded by specific corrective exercises, which subsequently become more meaningful to the students because of their awareness of how the body must move in order to achieve efficient posture.

Students with disabilities evidence a higher percentage of postural problems than does the general public. The

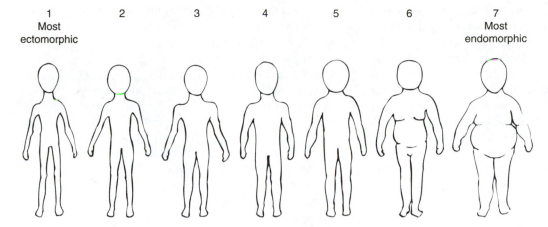

Figure 28.1 The range of body structure using the 7 point classification system developed by Sheldon.

A. Spinal column is flexed in single C curve; arms and legs are flexed—birth to 2 months.

B. Reflex stretching out of arms (Moro) until about 6 months, at which time protective extensor (parachute) reaction appears.

C. Extensor tone increases, reinforced by random limb movements, and cervical curve begins to appear.

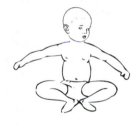

D. Early sitting with head control shows strong cervical extensor muscles—about 6 months.

E. Prone-on-elbows crawling position, combined with labyrinthine and optical righting reflexes, reinforces development of cervical curve.

F. Creeping further strengthens abdominal and lumbar spine muscles—8 months.

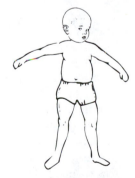

G. Early standing with support shows flat back posture.

H. Lumbar curve appears as back muscles are further strengthened by walking with wide base stance—about 14 months.

I. Knock knees is normal in early walking, especially in endomorphic body types.

Figure 28.2 Normal postural development from infancy through age 2.

explanation for this varies from individual to individual. Frequently, however, the poor posture is associated with the student's impairment: for example, those who are visually impaired tend to walk with a backward lean, and hearing-impaired students tend to turn the head to hear with their better ear. For students who are mentally retarded, some of the postural deviations observed appear to be related to their low self-esteem. In such instances efforts must be made to create positive life experiences for these students. In addition, posture programs for those who are mentally retarded must include sessions on body awareness to help those with low self-esteem obtain a better picture of themselves and the image they portray to others.

Body Structure

The body is held erect by the spinal column. The spinal column of the normal adult is a segmented structure consisting of four curves: the cervical, dorsal or thoracic, lumbar, and sacral (figure 28.3). The cervical curve is the curve at the neck; the convex of this curve is forward. The dorsal curve is the curve of the upper back, and the convex of its curve is backward. The lumbar curve is the curve in the small of the back, and the sacral curve is the curve in the inferior (lower) extremity of the spinal column. The convex of the lumbar curve is forward, whereas in the sacral it is backward.

At birth the spinal column has a single curve, with its convex to the back. During the early months of life, when the baby starts to raise its head and kick its legs, the spine becomes relatively straight. The cervical curvature develops at the time when the infant sits upright. Later, when the child starts to support the weight of the body on the feet and begins to walk, the lumbar curve comes gradually into prominence. This is accompanied by development of the other curves until the spine adopts the normal curves of an adult. The normal development of the curves is dependent in part upon whether the child is well and active during the early years of childhood (see figure 28.2).

Alignment

The upper segment of the body, when in an upright position, must be in alignment with the base of the body (the feet). In perfect alignment the center of gravity of the head, upper trunk, lower trunk, and legs is in a straight line (figure 28.4). Looking at the side view, if a plumb line is dropped even with the lobe of the ear, it will pass through the middle of the shoulder, through the middle of the hip, to the side and slightly behind the patella, and fall in front of the outer malleolus. As seen from the back, a line drawn through the body showing the center of gravity would bisect the head and neck and follow the spinal column down between the cleft of the buttocks. The spine should be straight and the shoulders and hips even, but slight variations will occur, depending upon individual differences. The more the body deviates from this alignment, the more energy is needed to hold the body erect because the postural muscles will have less mechanical advantage in maintaining balance. However, in certain cases the structure of the body may be such that there will be more energy expended in forcing the body into the alignment just described than in a less erect position.

Standing Posture

There has been a tendency to portray good posture as the proper body alignment for the average body build and to expect all "good" posture to resemble this. Such expectation fails to take into consideration the differences in bone structure and body build.

As mentioned previously, most individuals are predominantly of one body type or the other (figure 28.5); however, they can also have characteristics of more than one type. One segment of the body may be predominantly in one classification while another segment will have more characteristics of another type. This sometimes causes individuals to appear to have poor posture when actually their body alignment is the most efficient for their body structure. For example, a person who has a deep, thick chest with a heavy

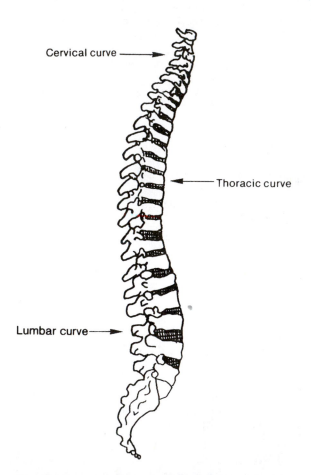

Figure 28.3 Lateral view of vertebral column.

Cervical curve

Thoracic curve

Lumbar curve

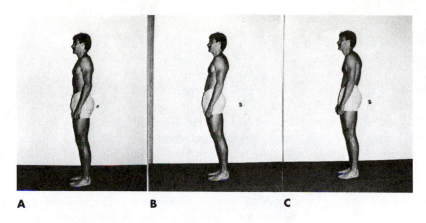

Figure 28.4 *(A)* Well-balanced position. *(B)* Hips forward, shoulders back—strains lower back. *(C)* Zigzag position leads to strain on all joints.

A   B   C

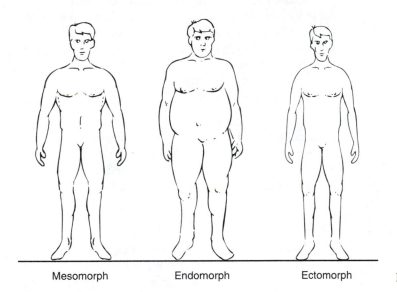

Mesomorph   Endomorph   Ectomorph

Figure 28.5 Traditional body types.

dorsal area (upper back) and relatively slender hip area will appear to have kyphosis (round upper back). To eliminate this condition would require an exaggerated posture that could be maintained only by tremendous contraction of the sacrospinalis muscles (muscles of the lower back). This would entail a considerable expenditure of energy and would therefore be a much less efficient posture than the original one.

The length of the clavicle (collar bone) influences the degree of erectness at which the shoulders will be held habitually by the individual. A relatively long clavicle will force the shoulder girdles back, whereas a relatively short one will require the scapulae (shoulder blades) to lie forward and to the side and will cause the shoulders to be brought forward.

The curves of the spine are also influenced by its structure. If the borders of the body of a single vertebra are thicker on one side than on the other, the curve in that area of the spinal column will tend to be increased. There is considerable variation in the thickness of the borders of vertebral bodies in individuals. The difference in thickness will produce a greater or lesser spinal curve than in the average person. To force a person whose curve deviates from normal to assume a very erect position may actually reduce the efficiency of the support of the spinal column. If the vertebrae are in alignment and the edges of the vertebrae cause a larger curve, an attempt to straighten the curve will spread the vertebrae farther apart, causing a probable instability. This cannot be determined by observation of the back, but it can be shown by X ray.

Differences in the location of the acetabula (cavities in the pelvis receiving the heads of the femurs) influence the degree to which the pelvis is tilted, and the tilt of the pelvis (hip area) determines the size of the angle in the lumbar curve. The acetabula form the pivotal point of balance of the pelvis and the spinal column because of the column's relationship to the pelvis. If the acetabula are situated slightly more to the front than usual, there will be a tendency for the posterior area to drop because of imbalance. The pelvic area rotates upward, causing the lumbar to flatten. If the anterior area drops, the pelvis will rotate downward and the lumbar curve is increased.

Walking Posture

The mechanics of efficient walking involve a basic pattern but, like standing posture, the best pattern for any individual is dictated in part by body structure, particularly leg alignment, and variations within limits may be expressions of individual structure and not actual walking faults. Excessive variations that are caused by improper use of the muscles will, in most cases, warrant efforts to modify them. Common walking errors that are frequently caused by improper use of the muscles are the following:

1. Leaning forward before the lead foot strikes the ground.
2. Carrying the weight on the rear foot until after the lead foot strikes the ground.
3. Exaggerated shifting of the weight to the supporting foot.
4. Swinging the arms in too wide an arc.
5. Exerting force straight up from the rear foot as the step is made.
6. Failing to swing the arms at the shoulders.
7. Looking at the feet.
8. Toeing in or out.

Running Posture

The running posture is similar to the walking posture, except the feet alternate positions more rapidly, the body leans forward, and there is a phase in which both feet are completely off the ground (figure 28.6). The arms are also bent at the elbows, swing in opposition, and are carried comfortably while running. Common running errors include the following:

1. Body lean is backward, rather than forward.
2. Arms are held too high.
3. Elbows are flexed at greater than 90 degrees.
4. Toes strike ground before heel.
5. Eyes look down, rather than forward.
6. Trunk sway or rotation.
7. Excessive pronation or supination of the feet.

Sitting Posture

A good sitting posture should permit some relaxation, whether one is seated for work or for rest. When sitting in a chair for the purpose of resting, as much of the chair as possible should be used to support the body. A slumping posture that does not utilize fully the support of the chair will be more fatiguing than an erect sitting position. Sitting far back in the chair, with the entire back resting against its contours, permits the chair to aid in holding the body, thereby allowing some muscular relaxation (figure 28.7).

For desk work, it is usually necessary to bring the head and eyes over the work; consequently, the back of the chair cannot be used for support. The buttocks are placed far back in the chair, and the weight of the trunk is distributed over the entire area of the buttocks. The trunk leans forward slightly from the hips, and head, neck, and trunk are kept in a relatively straight line. When it is not necessary for the head to be over the working area, the back of the body may be in contact with the back of the chair for support (figure 28.8).

The most common errors in sitting are as follows:

1. Failure to place the buttocks against the back of the chair.
2. Permitting the shoulders and back to slump.
3. Shifting the weight of the body to one side.
4. Sitting on one foot.

Lifting Posture

Lifting heavy objects from the floor or ground incorrectly is a common cause of back strain. When lifting heavy objects, the object should be placed as near to the center of the body as possible, as this increases the mechanical advantage in lifting (figure 28.9). To pick up the load, the legs should be bent and the lift made by extending the legs with the back held relatively straight. If the object being lifted has a handle, it is possible to keep the back entirely straight during the lift. However, when it is necessary to put the hands under the heavy object on the floor, the trunk may be bent while the hold is being taken. The knees will be flexed

Figure 28.6   Correct running pattern.

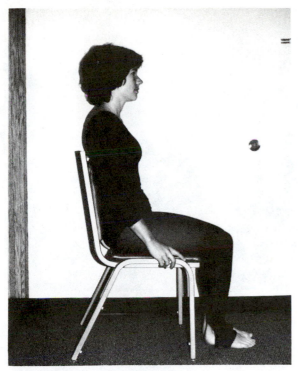

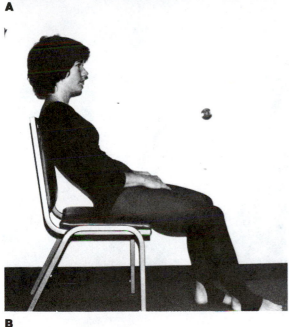

Figure 28.7 *(A)* Good sitting posture—back well supported. *(B)* Poor sitting posture—lower back and thighs unsupported.

during this process. The back is then straightened and the object lifted by extending the knees. In holding a heavy object, the knees should not be locked, as this position has a tendency to cause an exaggeration of the lumbar curve, which may place undue stress upon the muscles of this region.

Light objects may be lifted by bending at the hips. However, anyone who has a history of lower back disorder should use the technique for lifting heavy objects in order to protect the back from possible strain.

Causes of Poor Posture

It is frequently difficult to attribute poor posture to any single cause; in most cases a combination of two or more factors has produced it. For purposes of this discussion, the causes will be divided into two classes: those that are closely associated with fields such as medicine and psychiatry, and those that can be improved by specially designed instruction in physical education. It is recognized that no hard and fast demarcation can be established between the two because of factors that overlap; however, a rough line can be drawn between (1) poor posture attributed to such conditions as illness, infection, injury, malnourishment, a feeling of inadequacy, and deformities that are chiefly medical or emotional; and (2) faulty mechanics caused by poor neuromuscular habits of the postural muscles, weak musculature, overdevelopment of one set of muscles at the expense of another, and lack of body awareness, which can be addressed in physical education programs.

Medical or Emotional Problems

Accidents and illnesses frequently cause deformities that are conducive to incorrect use of the body. Students who suffer from such conditions should be under the care of an orthopedic physician, and postural work with such cases should be under the direct supervision of the physician and the physical therapist. However, in the later stages of recovery, the physical educator may be able to recommend games and activities that will complement the work of the medical team. Such activities need the approval of the physician before the student begins participation.

Injuries that cause a person to shift weight to avoid pain or ease work often encourage the development of poor posture. The treatment of the injury must be made by the physician, but the relearning of postural skills after the healing of the injury may be directed by the physical education teacher in many cases. A missing limb creates problems in aligning the body correctly because of the shift in the body's center of gravity. A student who has lost an arm or a leg will need special assistance in learning to achieve and maintain the most efficient alignment of body parts.

Illness often causes an overall body weakness, which lowers the threshold of fatigue. General fatigue is often a contributing factor to poor posture. Fatigued individuals do not have the energy necessary to hold their body in its proper alignment. The postural muscles are allowed to relax partially, and the various segments of the body gravitate out of alignment (body slump). The longer the fatigue continues, the more habitual the slump becomes. The slumping of the body would appear to be a means of conserving energy. Actually, however, this is not true, for in most cases when the body slumps, the center of gravity is no longer in a straight line; and the force of gravity will make certain muscles work harder to maintain balance.

Figure 28.8 *(A)* Good sitting posture for working at a desk. *(B)* Incorrect posture for desk work.

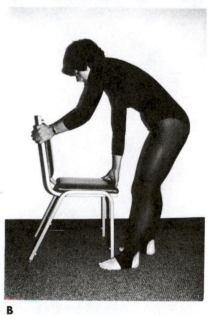

Figure 28.9 *(A)* Correct lifting posture. *(B)* Incorrect lifting posture.

Emotions and attitudes influence muscular movement and postural stance. This is readily observed in the child jumping with joy upon receiving a pleasant surprise or the adolescent slumping in the seat with boredom or dejection. There is evidence to support the contention that a habitual feeling of inadequacy and defeat, especially during childhood, encourages postural slumping. In such cases, if the desired outcome is to be achieved from postural training, it is first necessary to rebuild the individual's self-esteem.

Faulty Body Mechanics

The reasons for neuromuscular habits of the postural muscles that have no pathological basis are difficult to ascertain. It would appear that in some cases the cause is improper use of the muscles: the individual learned to hold his or her body incorrectly in much the same way as one sometimes learns a sport skill wrong through trial and error. Just as the error in the sport skill is corrected by a relearning process, the correction of faulty body mechanics requires a process of relearning.

Lack of use of the postural muscles contributes to their weakness. Weak muscles, because they are weak, will not be used greatly in maintaining posture; this lack of use contributes further to their weakness. If the muscles are weak, there is greater difficulty in maintaining good body alignment. In cases in which the antagonistic muscles are much stronger than the agonists, there is a tendency for the stronger muscles to pull the body out of alignment. It is possible that a contributing factor to the overdevelopment of one set of muscles is an overspecialization in sports that develop this set of muscles. Evidence for this may be seen in athletes who participate exclusively in sports requiring extensive use of the muscles of the chest but little of the back muscles. They may be round-shouldered to some degree because the weak muscles of the back are unable to perform their share of the work in maintaining equilibrium. Baseball pitchers, for example, tend to overdevelop the chest muscles of the dominant throwing side. This is why it is very important that young children divide their playing time among the various positions of a sport and participate in a variety of sports.

Failure to develop body awareness can cause poor posture. Children who do not know how their body moves and what space it occupies as it moves cannot tell when they are utilizing good body mechanics. Consequently, they are likely to develop poor postural habits. For these students the posture improvement program must deal extensively with creating awareness of the body.

Postural Deviations

There is no precise standard of erectness for measuring normal or abnormal posture. The only possible definition of the normal, or most desired, posture is that it is one in which the center of gravity of each segment of the body is kept in an approximately straight line without decreasing the efficiency of the body elsewhere. The frequently heard postural directive to "stand straight" has given rise to some confusion regarding the position of the spine. The spine is, of course, not straight; it has distinct curves. In some cases in which the curves are too marked, it may be advisable to straighten the curves; but a certain amount of curve is normal and natural. Marked increase in the curvature of the spine does not necessarily indicate a serious problem. If the various segments of the body are balanced properly, a spine with moderately increased curves may be considered normal for some individuals.

Postural deviations are classified as structural or functional. In the *structural* deviation, the bony structure has changed. A structural deviation is a permanent condition. Because of the change in the bone structure, the deviation cannot be corrected short of surgery or placing the involved area in a cast. Corrective exercise is of little use in this situation. A *functional* disorder refers to a condition in which only the soft tissue such as muscles and ligaments are primarily involved. Functional disorders respond to exercise,

Figure 28.10 The concept of "good" posture must be adjusted to individual structural differences.

and the disorder can be overcome. It should be remembered that it is not always easy to determine the difference between a structural and a functional disorder. Some cases involve a degree of fixation. In the early stages the disturbance may be in the soft tissues alone, but, as the condition persists, bone changes gradually take place.

Neck Deviations

A condition in which the head tilts toward the shoulder on one side and the chin tilts upward and toward the opposite shoulder is referred to as torticollis. This condition is frequently associated with a shortening of the sternocleidomastoid muscle, which is attached just behind the ear and inserts into the upper border of the collarbone and the sternum. Although there is a sternocleidomastoid muscle on each side of the neck, the shortening normally occurs on only one side. Torticollis, therefore, provides a classic example of muscle imbalance and the importance of identifying a problem early before it shifts from a functional to structural condition. Exercises such as head rotation, and isometric exercises to lengthen the muscle, if started early enough, frequently prove to be very effective. In some cases, surgical intervention may be required.

Forward Head

Forward head is a term used to describe a position in which the neck is flexed and the head is held forward and downward, usually with the chin dropped (figure 28.11*A*). The

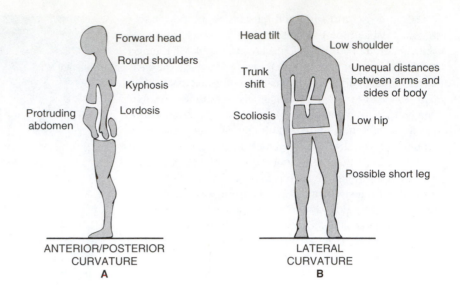

Figure 28.11 Postural deviations.

ANTERIOR/POSTERIOR CURVATURE
A

Forward head
Round shoulders
Kyphosis
Lordosis
Protruding abdomen

LATERAL CURVATURE
B

Head tilt
Low shoulder
Trunk shift
Unequal distances between arms and sides of body
Scoliosis
Low hip
Possible short leg

condition in which the head and chin are not dropped, frequently called "poke neck" or cervical lordosis, has a high incidence among the nearsighted. It is frequently accompanied by the inability to extend the cervical area and hence does not respond well to postural exercise.

In most cases, forward head accompanies an increased thoracic curve. However, if the thoracic curve remains normal, the efficiency of the body will not be decreased to a great extent, although the neck muscles will of necessity do more work to hold the head in position because it is not well balanced on the neck and shoulders. The chief disadvantage is in appearance. Sometimes a twisting of the neck or lateral flexion accompanies the forward head.

Round Shoulders

The term *round shoulders* describes the position that occurs when the scapulae are held to the side toward the axillary area and forward. This is almost always accompanied by an increased thoracic curve. The majority of cases respond well to postural exercises. Some cases of round shoulders, as was pointed out earlier, are not a postural fault in the true sense because they are due to structural differences.

Protruding Shoulder Blades

Protruding shoulder blades or "winged scapula" are common in young children. The condition may accompany round shoulders and back. Lack of muscular strength in the back area is a frequent contributor to protruding shoulder blades. Muscles involved in holding the scapulae flat also aid in pulling the shoulders into correct standing posture. In addition to the exercises prescribed for the correction of round back and shoulders, hanging and climbing exercises and games are excellent activities to strengthen these muscles in children.

Round Upper Back

An increased curve in the upper back causes a round upper back. This is called *thoracic* or *dorsal kyphosis*. It is frequently the result of fatigue or inadequate muscular strength in the extensors of the spine. When the upper back is rounded, the sternum is depressed and the rib cage is lowered, resulting in a decrease of chest cavity that may result in distortion of the normal position of the vital organs. It is not known what effects this may have upon health, although it appears that the normal functions of the vital organs might be restricted. The condition responds well to exercises that strengthen the muscles involved in holding the spine more erect and that stretch their antagonists. It is not uncommon to find the conditions of dorsal kyphosis, round shoulders, and forward head occurring together. This phenomenon is known as the kyphosis syndrome.

Lumbar Lordosis

An exaggeration of the lumbar curve is called lumbar lordosis. A functional exaggeration of this curve is caused by increasing the tilt of the pelvic girdle. The forward tilt of the pelvis is due to a combination of muscle imbalances with weak abdominals, tight hip-flexors and lumbar (lower back area) extensors, and weak gluteals (muscles of the buttocks) and hamstrings (muscles of back of thigh). The tight hip flexors and weak abdominal muscles contribute to the forward tilt while the gluteal muscles and hamstrings are too weak to counteract the anterior tilt. As the pelvic area is tilted, the symphysis pubis (articulation point in the pubic area) is lowered in front, followed by a forward movement of the lumbar area of the spine, causing an increase in the lumbar curve.

Sometimes lordosis accompanies kyphosis, as an attempt to balance the shift of the center of weight caused by the increased thoracic curve. With the increase of the lumbar curve, the center of gravity in that area is shifted to the back, thus compensating for the shifting of the weight forward in the upper trunk caused by the increased thoracic curve. Also accompanying the increased lumbar curve is the hyperextension of the knees. It is thought that this often precipitates the development of lordosis.

When the lumbar curve is increased, the center of gravity is shifted from near the center onto the back part of the vertebrae, bringing the spinous processes (projecting structures of vertebrae) closer together and decreasing the size of the foramina (openings between the vertebrae through which the spinal nerves pass). This decrease in the size of the opening may cause a pressure upon the nerves.

Flat Back

A large decrease in the normal lumbar curve causes a flat back. The action involved in the rotation of the pelvic girdle is the opposite of that in the condition of swayback.

It is difficult to determine just how much a flat back decreases body efficiency. It has been pointed out by some authorities that the extremely straight condition of the back reduces the shock-absorbing mechanism of the spine and causes disturbance in the function of the viscera (organs of the abdominal area) because of changes in the size of the cavity and in the position of the viscera within the cavity. A flat back does decrease the aesthetics of the body.

Scoliosis

When the body is viewed from the back, the right and left sides of the body should be symmetrical, both shoulders and hips at the same level with the spinal column straight. Most individuals will show a very slight deviation in the spinal column. A slight deviation is usually not noticeable in casual observation and, if it does not become progressively worse, is of no consequence. However, a lateral curvature that is obvious must be considered as an abnormal condition (figure 28.11B).

Scoliosis, which is definitely a medical problem, is discussed in detail in chapter 9, *Orthopedic Disabilities*. The special exercises needed by persons with this condition should be prescribed by medical personnel.

Scoliosis may be classified as either functional or structural. Functional disorders refer to disorders that are caused by abnormal postural positions, or muscle imbalance, whereas structural problems are associated with birth defects or bone disease. If not properly treated, functional disorders can result in permanent spinal changes and become structural (Black, 1984).

The age at which the curve develops or appears is also an important consideration in treatment. Curves that develop during the first three years of life are referred to as infantile. If developed between the third and twelfth year in girls and between the third and fourteenth year in boys, the term juvenile is used. If developed after age twelve in girls and after age fourteen in boys but before maturity, the disorder is referred to as adolescent scoliosis. Curves that are moderate to severe (forty to sixty degrees, see figure 28.12) will become more pronounced in adulthood. As indicated in chapter 9, scoliosis, if left untreated, can be a serious medical problem. In addition to the obvious physical deformity, pain, arthritic symptoms, and heart and lung complications can accompany this disorder. Curves that are moderate to severe can be diagnosed and treated by an orthopedic surgeon. Common treatments include orthotic devices (Boston and Milwaukee braces) and surgery. Additional information regarding treatment approaches for scoliosis is found in chapter 9.

The prevalence of scoliosis in children who have selected disabilities is very high. Rinsky (1982) reports that for children with cerebral palsy, the tendency for scoliosis parallels the severity of the condition. Children of short stature and those with quadriplegia are also likely candidates to develop a spinal curvature.

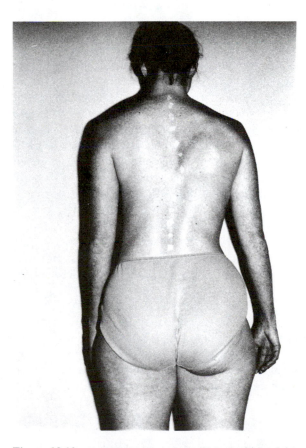

Figure 28.12 Individual with scoliosis. Note the lower right shoulder, the higher right hip, and the distance the right arm hangs away from the body.

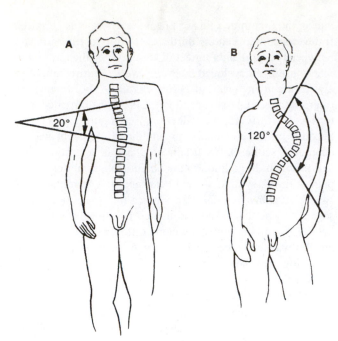

Figure 28.13 *(A)* Mild, 20-degree curvature. *(B)* Severe, 120-degree curvature.

(From Black and Nagel. (1982). *Physically Handicapped Children: A Medical Atlas for Teachers*. Copyright © Grune and Stratton Publishers.)

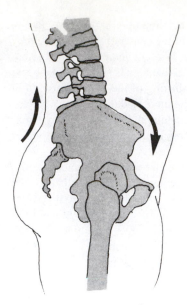

Figure 28.14 Rotating the pelvic area downward results in an increase in the lumbar curve.

Severe Abdominal Muscle Weakness

The abdominal wall comprises four sets of muscles: external and internal obliques, rectus abdominus, and transversus abdominus (appendix VI). The external oblique muscles are closest to the surface; the transversus abdominus is the deepest muscle; the rectus abdominus and internal obliques are in the middle. Some of the muscles run parallel to each other whereas others run obliquely. Together they work to compress the abdomen into its roughly cylindrical shape to maintain body form, to change the intraabdominal pressure in the visceral functions of breathing, defecation, urination, coughing, and vomiting, and to stabilize the pelvis.

Strong muscles tend to shorten, hence strong abdominal muscles tend to flatten the abdomen. Weakness of the abdominal muscles permits the abdomen to protrude, increases the lumbar curve, and, as explained in chapter 14, makes breathing difficult for those with cardiorespiratory problems. Also, weak muscles allow the hip flexors and lumbar extensors to rotate the pelvic area downward, which increases the lumbar curve (figure 28.14). Such an increase causes undue stress to the lumbar spine. In school children, however, an exaggeration is common and is not considered abnormal, because it disappears with maturation.

Tight Hamstrings

The hamstring muscles are three muscles on the posterior of the thigh having a common origin on the tuberosity of the ischium (lower projection of the hip bone) and insertions at different places on the distal (far) end of the tibia. Tightness of these muscles is characterized by the inability to reach down and touch the toes without bending the knees. Otherwise undiagnosed low back pain has been attributed to tightness of the hamstrings. Frequently, if no organic lesion exists, lengthening the hamstrings through stretching exercises eliminates the pain.

Leg Alignment

People do not all walk or stand in the same way because of such differences in basic structure of the body as size, weight distribution, length and shape of the legs, and structure of the pelvic girdle. Leg and foot alignment is said to be proper when a line drawn from the anterior superior iliac spine bisects the knee cap, ankle joint, and second toe. Some variation will occur due to structure. The location of the acetabulum determines to some extent the alignment. If the acetabulum is located to the front of the center of pelvic gravity, there is a tendency for the person to toe in. Often knock knees accompany this tendency. With the acetabulum to the rear, there is a tendency to toe out. To force one with this structure to toe straight ahead would be to decrease the efficiency in the hip area because the head of the femur would have to change from its customary position in the acetabulum.

Bowlegs (Genu Varum)

The Latin word *genu* means "knee." In genu varum the problem relates to the bowed position the legs assume in the standing position with the knees unable to touch (figure 28.15). If the femoral condyles of the knees are five inches

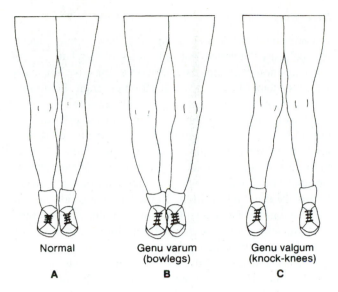

Normal	Genu varum (bowlegs)	Genu valgum (knock-knees)
A	B	C

Figure 28.15 Normal and abnormal knee and leg alignment.

or more apart, the problem is generally considered to be severe. Bowing of the legs is common with young children until the age of two, when the peroneals become strong enough to offset the pull of the tibials.

In most cases the presence of genu varum is structural in origin, with either the shaft of the femur or the tibia being bowed. In these cases exercises are not helpful and the individual should be referred to a physician. Fortunately, slight and even mild cases of genu varum do not impede the affected person's movement capabilities significantly.

Knock Knees (Genu Valgum)

This disorder, in which the lower legs bend outward forcing the femoral condyles of the knees together, is very common in obese persons (figure 28.15). Because of the stress placed on the collateral ligament on the medial aspect of the knee, genu valgum can be painful. Contact activities in which blows to the outer side of the knee may occur are contraindicated. Pronation and weakness in the longitudinal arch of the feet usually accompany knock knees.

Exercises designed to strengthen the sartorius, medial hamstrings, tibials (muscles that rotate the leg), and the outward rotation of the hip may be recommended by orthopedists for students with genu valgum. These exercises must be accompanied by activities to stretch the peroneals and a program designed to help the student lose weight.

Tibial and Femoral Torsion

Occasionally an individual will experience torsion of the leg. This means that either the tibia or the femur is twisted either inward or outward. Torsion of the leg may be due to several reasons, including a congenital condition, the improper setting of a broken leg, or a disorder that prohibited proper weight bearing during early childhood.

Torsion of the tibia or femur is usually corrected in infancy through surgery or various bracing techniques. With the guidance of a physician, special exercises may be undertaken in some cases to strengthen and stretch muscles that aid in normal weight bearing.

Foot Mechanics

The feet are the base of the body and bear the entire weight of the body in an upright position. Because the foot is made up of several segments, it is subject to misalignment. The bones for the foot are so constructed as to form two arches: the longitudinal arch and the transverse arch.

The highest part of the longitudinal arch is on the inner side of the foot. On the inside of the foot the arch extends from the calcaneus (heel bone) to the first, second, or third metatarsal (near the ball of the foot). The longitudinal arch is supported by the shape of the bones that fit together, the ligaments, and the muscles.

The chief factor in the stability of the foot is how well the bones involved fit into each other. For example, the calcaneus gives the best support to the talus (figure 28.16) if its contact point with the talus is flat (horizontal) rather than slanting. If it slopes forward and downward, as it does in some individuals, the body weight pushes the talus down the slope of calcaneus, causing a broken arch or flat foot. Muscles involved in maintaining the longitudinal arch of the foot include the plantar muscles of the foot, which have their origin and insertion on the foot, as well as the deep muscles of the calf that pass under the foot and insert in the toes. Variations in bone structure in individuals account for varying degrees of the height of the arch. The highest arch is not necessarily the strongest arch.

The transverse arch extends across the foot in the area of the ball of the foot. The five metatarsals form the arch. The fifth and first metatarsals are the base for the arch. It is

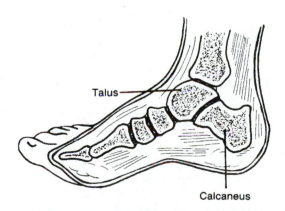

Figure 28.16 A forward sloping of the calcaneus affects foot stability.

thought by some authorities that a dropping of this arch occurs when the second and third metatarsals drop down and become weight-bearing. A callus develops under the second metatarsal as a result. There is some disagreement among authorities about the importance of the transverse arch and the part it plays in creating the callus. Some point out that the callus and pain occur in this area when the second metatarsal is longer than the first and becomes the weight-bearing bone. In either case the problem is accentuated when a person wears high heels, and it occurs less frequently when low heels are worn.

Position of the Feet

The preferred foot position with normal structure of the feet and legs is that in which the toes are pointing straight ahead or only slightly abducted. When the feet are abducted to any great extent, the weight of the body is forced over the longitudinal arch instead of over the outer borders of the feet with their stable structure.

Pronation is a movement in which the ankle rolls inward and the body weight is thrown over the longitudinal arch, causing the depression and lowering of the arch. Pronation is brought about frequently by inadequate muscle strength and improper bony structure. Accompanying this is the abduction of the feet (turning the toes out).

Supination is the opposite condition of pronation. The ankle rolls outward, with the body weight falling on the outer borders of the feet.

Overweight and Flat Feet

Extreme overweight is often a causative factor in flat feet. A person who puts on weight too quickly often overloads foot muscles that have not been strengthened sufficiently over a period of time and cannot do the job of maintaining the arch. Placing a load upon the feet that they are not capable of handling will cause arches to fall. Weak and painful arches are common to the overweight individual.

Inspection of the Achilles tendon from a posterior view is helpful in determining the presence of a flat-foot condition. If the Achilles tendon bows medially (Helbing's sign), the foot is considered flat.

Posture Evaluation

To develop sufficient muscular strength, endurance, and skill in maintaining the best posture for the individual body structure is an objective of the physical education program. Whenever individuals deviate so much they cannot participate in the regular program to their greatest advantage, or require special attention to their needs that cannot be given them in the regular class, individualized activities responsive to their postural needs should be provided.

Screening Tests

In some states, schools are required by law to test students for scoliosis. Screening not only for scoliosis but also for other postural problems is a desirable objective for every school system. The physical education program should provide for some type of screening if at all feasible.

Several different techniques may be used in screening, but subjective evaluation is the most frequently used. It is less expensive and less time-consuming than other methods. Subjective ratings are made by the examiner of anteroposterior and lateral balance and the alignment of the feet and legs in the standing position. To increase the validity of the observation, the body mechanics of walking can be examined. Students should be dressed in swimming suits to provide a view of the spinal column.

Many students find the process of an instructor examining them in a line or column formation for the presence of postural problems to be rather impersonal and somewhat embarrassing. For this reason, it is recommended that students be given information about postural deviations and be involved in the process of screening themselves as well as other students. This can be accomplished by developing individualized charts for each student with the specific screening tests discussed. Each student is then provided an opportunity to first do a self-evaluation. Obviously this may be difficult for some items, such as the plumb bob tests for anterior and lateral views, but the primary reason for this initial evaluation is to help children feel comfortable about the entire screening process. Students are later encouraged to select their best friend and do the complete screening test again, evaluating each other. The emphasis here is on helping students feel secure by working with a classmate and a trusted friend. During this time, the teacher can circulate and provide answers individually or to pairs of students who seek a more authoritative opinion. Teachers will also find that in using this process they will have ample opportunity to make subjective notes about the posture of each student in the class.

Specific screening tests that are recommended include:

1. *Anterior View.* The student stands behind a plumb line. The line should bisect the student's head, trunk, hips, and feet. Special notes should be made on any lateral deviations. Leg alignment and foot mechanics should also be checked for the presence of torsion, toeing in or out, supination, and pronation.

2. *Lateral View.* The student should stand behind a plumb line with the point of the shoulder bisected by the line. The examiner should then check to see if the line passes as follows: from the lobe of the ear, bisect the shoulder, bisect the hip, slightly behind the patella and anterior (1 to 1½ inches) to the lateral malleolus. In this position the student should also be checked for evidence of kyphosis, lordosis, flat back, and hyperextension of the knees.

3. *Posterior View.* From a back view, the plumb line should bisect the student's head and neck, follow the spinal column, and bisect the cleft of the buttocks. The back view should be checked for evidence of hip imbalance, shoulder imbalance, neck and head misalignment, and faulty foot mechanics.

4. *Adams Position.* The feet of the student should be placed with the heels about two inches apart. From this position, the student curls the trunk forward with the head, shoulders, and arms relaxed. The individual reaches down until the fingers are about one foot from the floor. In this position, the examiner should check the student's back from both a front and posterior view to detect any protrusion of one side of the rib cage or a twisting of the back. Either of these indicate muscle imbalance and possible scoliosis.

5. *Walking Mechanics.* Using a piece of tape to make a line on the floor, the examiner should observe the student walking toward, away from, and parallel to him or her. Observations should be made of toeing in or out, leg alignment, use of the foot in heel-ball-toe action, pronation, and movement of the trunk.

6. *Leg Length.* With the student in a supine position, measure the length of both legs with a steel tape. Measurements should be taken from the anterior superior spine of the ilium to the internal malleolus. The tape should also bisect the patella. Differences in leg length of more than one quarter inch may contribute to postural problems, primarily scoliosis.

New York Posture Rating Chart

Posture charts, such as the New York Posture Test, may be effectively used to measure and record posture and postural changes that may occur in students. For additional information about the New York Posture Test and the procedures used to administer the test, the reader should contact the State Education Department, Division of Health, Physical Education, and Recreation, Albany, NY 12224.

In figure 28.17 is an example of a chart that has been adapted from the New York Posture Test. The boxes on the right side of each set of three pictures are spaces for recording the judgment of the examiner over time (e.g., at intervals of six months). Each row of pictures diagrammatically shows the "good" posture and the deviation from that in a specific portion of the body. The examiner is to decide which picture best represents the posture of the child being examined. The teacher then places the number of the picture, which is printed above the picture, in the appropriate box on the right.

Diagnostic Posture Test

Those who are screened as needing postural work beyond that given in regular class should be examined by a physician before the remedial exercises begin. To assist physicians in making their recommendations for the kind and extent of activity, diagnostic posture tests may be administered. There are several types. Two of the most effective are the evaluation of postural photographs or video recordings and anthropometric measurements of the body. Procedures for these tests may be found in test and measurement textbooks. The tests are relatively complex and not recommended for general class testing. Teachers must also ensure confidentiality of pictures and recordings. Consultation with school officials is highly recommended before proceeding.

Some schools make silhouettes of students as a graphic record of their posture. The silhouette, because it shows students so well their own postural errors, can be a very successful motivator for posture improvement. A series of silhouettes make an excellent record of progress.

The teacher may be able to secure the assistance of the school photography club in making the silhouettes. The process is relatively simple. A bed sheet or similar large piece of material is tacked to a frame to form a screen about 7½ feet by 3 feet. In a semidark room a light is placed behind the screen so that it will focus on the back of the screen. The subject stands in front of the screen wearing a swimming suit. The picture is taken against the screen.

A valuable and enjoyable body awareness activity is to see if students can select their own silhouette from among several. Many students have difficulty with this task and are surprised to find that their perceived posture is different from their actual posture.

The Program for Those with Poor Posture

The program for the student with poor posture must be based on good assessment of the individual's postural status and consultation, as appropriate, with others, including physicians and therapists. If the condition is severe (e.g., scoliosis requiring bracing or surgical intervention), obviously the teacher should work cooperatively with the medical team in developing effective intervention strategies. For many students, however, their postural status will emphasize instruction in postural mechanics rather than medical treatment.

In earlier years, physical educators used to adhere to rather rigid approaches to the treatment of postural problems. Frequently, this led to programs that were boring, and for many students, appeared to be punitive rather than helpful. Today's emphasis is on helping students to understand posture, both from a dynamic and static perspective. This suggests, therefore, that the emphasis should be placed on helping the student understand the importance of posture and exercises and techniques that can be used in various settings (school, home, shopping) as an aid to effective posture.

For older age groups, a list of activities can be provided, with descriptions of how the activities are performed. The specific exercises for each individual can be checked on this

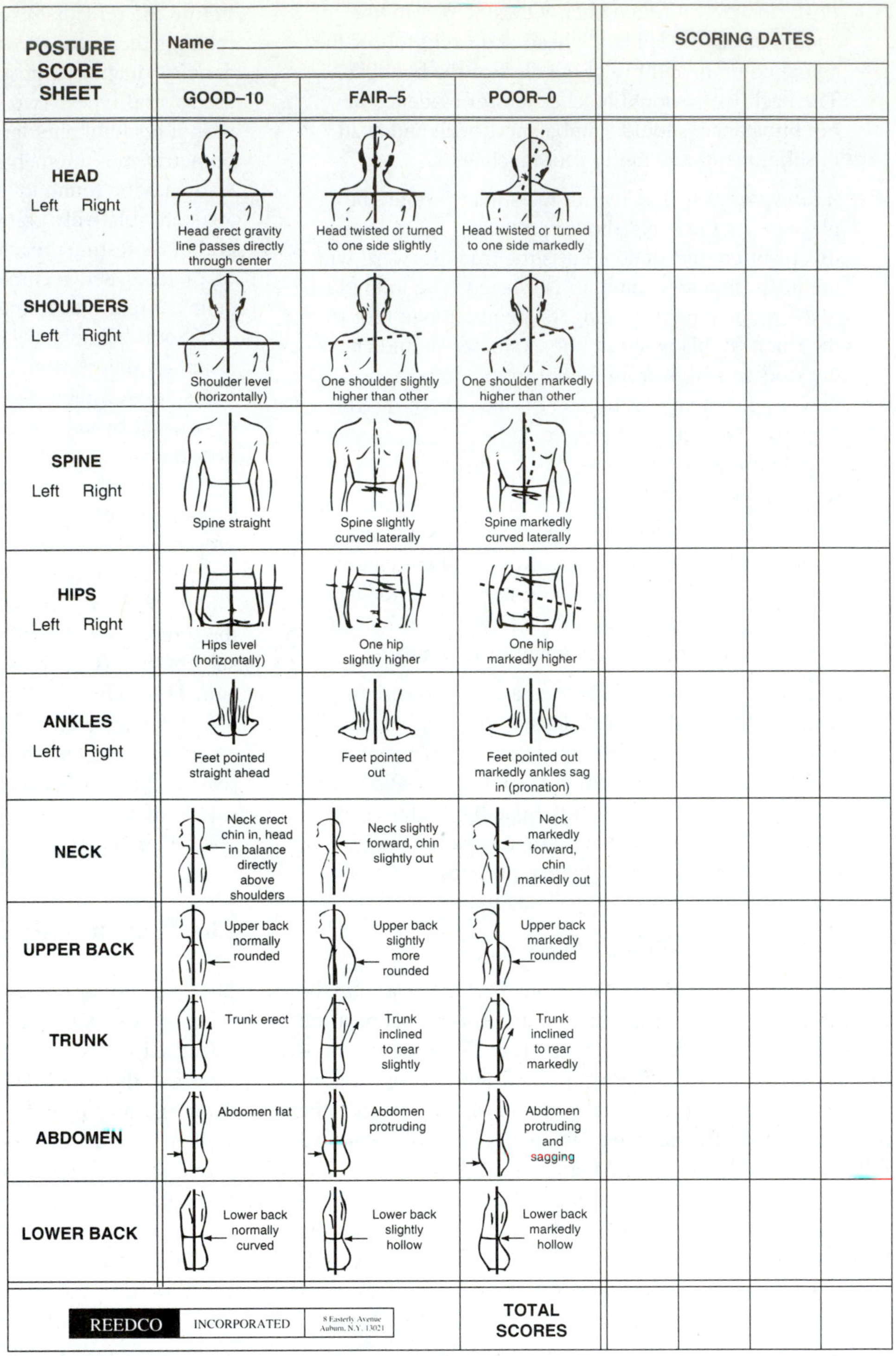

POSTURE SCORE SHEET	Name _____			SCORING DATES				
	GOOD–10	FAIR–5	POOR–0					
HEAD Left Right	Head erect gravity line passes directly through center	Head twisted or turned to one side slightly	Head twisted or turned to one side markedly					
SHOULDERS Left Right	Shoulder level (horizontally)	One shoulder slightly higher than other	One shoulder markedly higher than other					
SPINE Left Right	Spine straight	Spine slightly curved laterally	Spine markedly curved laterally					
HIPS Left Right	Hips level (horizontally)	One hip slightly higher	One hip markedly higher					
ANKLES Left Right	Feet pointed straight ahead	Feet pointed out	Feet pointed out markedly ankles sag in (pronation)					
NECK	Neck erect chin in, head in balance directly above shoulders	Neck slightly forward, chin slightly out	Neck markedly forward, chin markedly out					
UPPER BACK	Upper back normally rounded	Upper back slightly more rounded	Upper back markedly rounded					
TRUNK	Trunk erect	Trunk inclined to rear slightly	Trunk inclined to rear markedly					
ABDOMEN	Abdomen flat	Abdomen protruding	Abdomen protruding and sagging					
LOWER BACK	Lower back normally curved	Lower back slightly hollow	Lower back markedly hollow					
REEDCO INCORPORATED 8 Easterly Avenue Auburn, N.Y. 13021			**TOTAL SCORES**					

Figure 28.17   Postural score sheet.

list. A demonstration of the exercises should be given and the possible errors pointed out. The use of equipment such as mirrors, and weights should be demonstrated and explained. Students above the junior high school level may be permitted to work on their own after this briefing. For younger age groups, more direct supervision should be given.

It should be emphasized that postural exercises do little good if students do not want to improve their posture. The teacher should continually seek ways to motivate them. An understanding by students of their needs and the improvement that may be expected is one of the most effective of all motivators.

It is not expected that the time provided in physical education classes is sufficient to enable much significant change to occur in the quality of the posture. Once students are aware of their problem and know what can be done for it, they should be encouraged to supplement class activity with work outside the class.

Work to improve posture should not be done at the expense of participation in other physical education experiences. Additional work in other physical education activities is a necessity in many cases to ensure optimum development in organic efficiency and social adjustment. The activities must, of course, be selected with care, particularly for those with severe problems.

For students to assume good posture, they must first know what constitutes good posture for them. In attempting to assume good posture, individuals who have poor posture are likely to throw their head and shoulders too far back. This is a strained position, and it is no wonder that students cannot maintain it. Before individuals can achieve a better position, they must first be taught the proper body alignment for their body build. To introduce students to the new position they should be shown how to assume the desired standing posture with the following:

1. The head balanced on neck, neither thrown back nor thrust out, chin slightly tucked in;
2. The shoulders spread as wide as possible, not thrown back;
3. The breast bone held up rather than the chest thrown out;
4. The pelvis placed under the trunk;
5. The knees slightly bent, not locked.

This standing position should be one of ease; it should not be strained or difficult to maintain. This position should be assumed frequently and checked for the ease with which it is held. Students should be encouraged to exercise in front of full-length mirrors so that they can periodically check their body alignment.

Postural exercises are designed to strengthen the muscles that are involved in maintaining the desired posture and in stretching their antagonists. Exercise is, of course, to be undertaken only after determining that the deviation is functional and all pathological causes have been overruled.

Exercise should be moderate in the beginning and the work load gradually increased, until the desired results are achieved or it has become obvious that exercise is not going to be effective. Weak muscles must initially be protected from overwork and their antagonists, which have shortened and so will not allow a wide range of movement, should not be overly stretched in the beginning.

As has been pointed out, the spinal column may compensate for an overcurve by curving in the opposite direction in another area of the spine. In the case of kyphosis, there is usually an increased curve in the lumbar area. When this is so and exercise is given for the round back, care should be taken that the movement does not increase the size of the lumbar curve. The same precaution must be taken with the exercises that are given for forward head and round shoulders and back to avoid increasing the lumbar curve.

The equipment needed to conduct a posture program is readily available in most schools. Equipment items useful in presenting exercises and activities for the improvement of body mechanics include:

1. free wall space (to flatten the back in standing position),
2. full-length mirror,
3. individual mats,
4. padded tables,
5. weights,
6. hanging bars, and
7. benches.

The preventive and corrective exercises that follow are frequently suggested for use in postural work. They are divided into two groups: mild and advanced. These are very broad categories, and some exercises do not belong exclusively to any one group because so much depends on how vigorously the individual performs them. *Those exercises for scoliosis that are asymmetrical (exercising only one side of the body) should not be given without medical consultation; they are identified with an asterisk (*).*

Exercises for Forward Head

Mild Exercises

1. Assume correct standing position and place light object on head. Walk with weight balanced on head and chin held in as much as possible.

2. Rotate head in circle with chin held in. The forward movement is relatively passive; backward movement is more forceful.

3. Lie supine on mat; force head down on mat while chin is held in. Do not increase the lumbar curve.

4. Stand with back to wall, heels two to three inches from the wall. Press the back of the head against the wall with chin held down. Do not increase the amount of curve in the lumbar area.

Advanced Exercises

1. Interlace fingers behind head, pull down with arms, and push back with head.

2. Tighten the muscles of the back of the neck, keeping chin in contact with the chest.

3. Lying in prone position, clasp hands behind the back, raise head as high as possible, keeping chin tucked to chest. (Not recommended when lordosis is present.)

Exercises for Round Shoulders, Round Back, and Protruding Shoulder Blades

Mild Exercises

1. Stand with feet slightly apart and fists clenched. Cross the arms in front and move them upward and backward behind the head. Raise up on toes as arms are moved backward to prevent the arching of the back.

2. Raise the arms at the sides until they are parallel to the floor. Hold the palms up. Move the arms with moderate speed so that the hands describe a small circle backward, downward, forward, and upward.

3. Raise elbows to shoulder level, clasp hands and pull, with each arm resisting the other.

4. Lying supine on a narrow bench with knees bent, feet on floor, grasp dumbbell or weight in each hand. Extend arms sideward, allowing weight of dumbbells to stretch muscles of chest. Bend elbows and return to original position. Do not increase the amount of curve in the lumbar area.

5. Stand in a corner and place a hand on each side of the corner, shoulder height, with arms parallel to floor. Try to touch nose to corner, keeping back straight and feet flat on floor but allowing elbows to bend.

6. On the back, with the knees bent, the feet on the floor, and the hands at the sides, palms up, move the arms horizontally to a position over the head and return to original position. Do not increase the curve in the lumbar area.

Advanced Exercises

1. Lying prone, hands clasped behind the back, raise the head and shoulders off the mat. Keep lower back straight.

2. Lying prone, extend arms over head. Raise head, trunk, and arms, arching upper back. Keep lower back straight.

3. Interlock fingers behind back in lumbar area. Press elbows down and back, trying to bring elbows together. Head is held up. Do not sway lower back.

4. Grasp a wand with hands well spread and raise hands overhead. Wand is moved back over the head as far as possible while the arms are kept straight. Do not sway lower back.

5. Lie supine on mat with pad under shoulders and fingers laced behind neck. Helper kneels at the head, grasps subject's elbows, and presses downward slowly.

6. Standing with arms at sides, move shoulders in circle by first shrugging them, then forcing them backward, and finally dropping them to original position.

7. Lie supine and place the hands under the neck; inhale and raise the shoulders off the floor. The head, elbows, hips, and legs remain in contact with the floor. Avoid arching the small of the back. Exhale and return to original position.

8. Sit on the floor. Place the feet in front and the hands behind the body. Raise the weight of the body on the hands and feet and walk forward, backward, or sideways.

9. Perform straight-arm hang on bar or rings. (Exercise is mild, moderate, or strenuous depending on the length of time position is held.)

10. With a dumbbell or weight in each hand, bend at the waist, extend the arms to the sides, and raise them as far as possible. Return to original position.

Exercises for Lordosis

Mild Exercises

1. Standing with feet spread, bend forward at the hips, keeping knees straight with arms hanging down between legs. Relax with slow, controlled movement; move the trunk up and down.

2. Tilt the pelvis backward; rotate around and around as in hula dancing. Make a rather passive movement in tilting the pelvis forward because this will increase the lumbar curve.

3. Lie in the supine position. Attempt to force the small of the back to the floor by rotating the lower part of the pelvis forward.

4. In hook position on back, contract abdominal muscles and press lumbar region to the floor.

Advanced Exercises

1. Stand as in mild exercise 1 with feet spread. Touch first between legs, return to original position, then touch on the outside of right foot and then outside of left foot.

2. With feet together, bend forward at the hips, keeping knees straight with arms hanging down between the legs. Flexing at hips, touch floor. Hold three seconds.

3. In supine position, raise knees to chest.

4. On hands and knees, tuck pelvic area in so as to flatten the back. Hold for count of five. Return to original position. Avoid extreme arching of the back when returning to original position.

5. Lying in supine position, raise both knees to chest. Stretch both legs into the air. Return to knees-on-chest position.

6. Lying on the back, draw knees up to chest, grasp shins, and pull. Hold for three counts.

7. In a prone position, arms extended to the sides with palms up, raise head and shoulders. At the same time forcibly contract abdominal muscles to prevent lumbar curve from increasing.

Note: Exercises that exaggerate the lumbar curve should be avoided by those with lordosis. Exercises such as back bending, leg raises (lying on the back and lifting both legs), and the straight-arm pullover in weight training are contraindicated for those with weak abdominals who are subject to hollow back.

Exercises for those with low back pain due to poor alignment of the pelvis and sacrum with the lumbar spine are found in chapter 16.

Exercises for Flat Back

Mild Exercises

1. On knees, place forehead on mat on floor; rotate hips to increase lumbar curve.

2. Tilt the pelvis backward; rotate around. Make a rather passive movement in tilting the pelvis forward and forceful in tilting backward.

Advanced Exercises

1. Stand with back against wall; push shoulders against wall and force hips away from wall.

2. Interlock fingers behind back in lumbar area. Press elbows down and back, trying to bring elbows together. Sway in at the back.

3. Lie prone and place the hands behind the neck; raise the shoulders off the floor. Arch the back, keeping hips in contact with floor.

4. Lying on the back with the feet on the floor, arch the back, taking the weight on the shoulders and feet.

Exercises for Scoliosis: C Curve

Note: These exercises are for C curve to the left; if curve is to the right the exercises should be reversed.

Mild Exercises

1. Hang from a bar or rings by the hands with the arms fully extended. (This exercise is mild, moderate, or strenuous, depending upon the time the position is held.)

*2. Standing with hands on hips, raise the right arm forward and overhead; raise the left arm sideward to shoulder height. Then rise on tiptoe and lift leg sideward and stretch the whole body. Return to original position.

*3. Standing with hands on hips, stretch the left arm down at the side and push down hard. Avoid bending body toward left side.

*4. Standing, facing the wall bars, stretch left arm forward and grasp the wall bar that is level with the shoulder. Raise the right arm overhead and stretch.

*5. Standing with hands on hips, stretch the right arm up overhead and press the left hand against ribs at side of body at point that forces the spine into a straighter position.

Advanced Exercises

*1. Stand with feet slightly apart. Trunk should be inclined forward. Place the right hand at back of neck and the left hand well up against ribs. Bend to left and push in with left hand. Avoid letting right elbow come forward.

*2. Sit on stool with hands on hips. Stretch right leg back of stool, resting foot on toes. Stretch right arm up and left arm back. Keep trunk in line with right leg.

*3. Standing with hands on hips, move forward with the left foot, keeping right foot back and slightly turned out. The sole rests on the floor. Raise right arm forward and upward. Stretch left arm back. Do not drop the head. Keep trunk in a line with the rear leg.

*4. Standing with hands on hips, move forward with the left foot. Turn right foot and keep it on the floor. Raise right arm forward and upward. Stretch left arm down and back. Bend forward and touch the floor with the right hand as far out in front of the left foot as can be reached. Keep trunk in a line with the rear foot.

Hint to instructor: Exercise 4 is very much like the preceding one, but the final stretch to touch the floor makes it more difficult. Give exercise 3 first, and when that can be done easily, go on to 4.

*5. Lie on table with right knee bent over end, left knee bent, and left foot on table; left arm is under the back, right arm bent with elbow at waist. Helper grasps wrist of student's right arm pulling sideward while student resists. When arm is up, student must relax and helper stretches to count of five. Student then brings arm to first position while helper resists.

*6. Hanging with back to wall with right arm high, bend and raise left knee.

Exercises for Scoliosis: S Curve

Note: These exercises are for S curve with left dorsal and right lumbar curve; if curves are opposite, exercise positions should be reversed.

Mild Exercises

1. Hang from a bar or rings by the hands with the arms fully extended. (This exercise is mild, moderate, or strenuous, depending upon the time the position is held.)

2. Lying on floor, draw knees up to chest. Clasp hands firmly around knees and hold this position for one minute.

3. With hands on hips, bend forward from hips until back is flat. Hold head up.

*4. Sit astride chair facing back, hands on neck. Bend to left side and come to straight position. Bend only in the dorsal area.

*5. In a supine position with hands on neck, extend right arm upward and at the same time stretch left leg across body.

*6. Lying prone, stretch right arm over head and at the same time stretch left arm downward and across back. Hold this position one minute.

*7. Place hands on hips, shift weight to right leg, and at the same time stretch up as far as possible.

Advanced Exercises

1. Lying prone on table, feet held firmly by helper, clasp hands behind back, straighten arms by sliding the hands down the back; at the same time raise body from the table as far as possible.

*2. Place pad under each knee. Assume position for creeping on hands and knees. Stretch the right arm forward and at the same time slide left knee forward. Stretch left arm forward and slide the right knee forward. Creep in a circle to the left.

*3. Stand erect with feet apart, arms extended sideward. Twist trunk backward to right, trying to touch right toe with left hand. Keep knees straight and return to erect position each time.

4. Stand at bar that comes just to hips. Place hands on bar, push down, stretch spine as much as possible. If possible, lift body weight off floor.

*5. Facing wall bars, grasp bars firmly with both hands, positioning right hand two bars above left hand. Slide feet slowly to right side until body hangs in a curved position.

Exercises for Misalignment of Feet and Weak Arches

In most cases of weak arches, the condition has been developing over a period of time. Poor standing and walking habits may be so thoroughly ingrained into the movement pattern that it will take a period of time to develop the strength of the muscles and relearn proper skills of standing and walking. Furthermore, it is difficult to adequately exercise the plantar muscles of the feet, and so the feet respond slowly to corrective exercise. Any exercise program undertaken must be continued over a period of time to be of any value.

Prevention of foot problems by exercises is much easier than the correction of foot deviation. The following exercises are for strengthening the muscles that aid in maintaining the longitudinal arch. A transverse arch disorder does not generally respond to exercise and should be treated by the proper medical personnel.

Foot exercises that consist of rising on the toes or walking on the toes should not be performed by those who have weak arches because this kind of exercise shortens the calf muscles and throws additional stress on the balls of the feet.

Mild Exercises

1. Stand with feet slightly apart. Press toes against floor, and attempt to rotate the knees inwardly to lift the arches of the feet. (Inside of foot should rise.)

2. In a sitting position, cross one leg over the other. Circle foot, first in, then up, out, and down.

Advanced Exercises

1. In standing or sitting position, curl the toes as if to grasp the floor. Hold in isometric contraction for a brief period of time. The base of the first phalange (big toe) is not lifted off the floor.

2. In a sitting position, place the toes on the edge of a towel. Curl the toes so as to pull the towel under the feet. Do not raise the heel, and keep the base of the big toe on the floor throughout the exercise.

3. Sit on the floor with the knees bent and the balls of the feet touching each other, with the heels slightly apart. Draw the feet toward the body keeping the balls of the feet together and the heels apart.

Note: Exercises should not be given to those with painful feet. These students should be referred to the proper medical personnel.

Exercises for the Cardiopulmonary System

In addition to the muscle strengthening exercises recommended for scoliosis, special emphasis should also be placed on exercises to improve the cardiorespiratory system. Several investigators have noted that the pulmonary capacity of individuals with scoliosis is reduced. This appears to be true for those with severe as well as mild cases. The reduced pulmonary capacity is attributed to the shifting of the spine, which tends to make the thoracic cavity less compliant to respiratory expansion (DiRocco, 1981). As a result of the pulmonary problem, some individuals with scoliosis compound the problem by choosing to further reduce their activity level. A vicious cycle is thus created in which the restricted activity pattern leads to further reductions in the capacity of the pulmonary system. Students with scoliosis, therefore, should be encouraged to participate in a cardiopulmonary training program. The program should be implemented following an evaluation by a physician of the pulmonary system at rest and during exercise. The cardiopulmonary training program should consist of aerobic activities such as jogging, cycling, and/or swimming three times a week for thirty minutes or more. The intensity of the exercise should be at approximately 60 percent of the maximum heart rate. Periodic evaluations should be conducted to monitor the effect of the exercise on the cardiopulmonary system. The goal of the aerobic program is to minimize the impact of scoliosis on the cardiopulmonary system.

Elementary School Activities

Posture difficulties owing to the improper use of muscles are not as prevalent or obvious in children of elementary school age as in older children. However, exercises are much more effective in overcoming postural deviations if they are given before the improper posture becomes well established. Consequently, posture exercises should be included in the physical education program for young children.

As with children who have less than normal physical fitness, it is inappropriate to segregate from the regular class those who need special posture exercises without consultation with other professionals and the students' parents, similar to arrangements followed in IEP meetings. Such students can be accommodated in the regular class by providing special activity designed to meet their special needs. The best method of doing this is through the use of games and activities[1] that require those who need special exercises to perform types of movements that are beneficial to them. Games, contests, and relays have the additional advantage of providing the strong motivation so often lacking in the performance of exercises as such. A few activities are presented here as examples of games or contests that provide beneficial exercises.

1. Mimicking the giraffe. The children stretch their bodies to make them tall like the giraffe by reaching high with the arms and rising on tiptoes. Purpose: to strengthen postural muscles generally.
2. Eagle and mice. One student is chosen as the eagle; the others are mice. The eagle spreads arms to the sides and rotates them back, then up and forward, while running after the mice, trying to catch them. The game may be modified so that all must "fly," in which case the mice become sparrows. Purpose: to strengthen

muscles in upper back and stretch chest muscles.
3. Follow the leader. The leader executes various exercises for improving posture. Purpose: see exercises for specific postural difficulties.
4. Seesaw. Two students face each other in a sitting position with the legs extended. They grasp each other's hands and place their feet together. Keeping the knees straight, one pulls the other until the partner is raised off the floor. Then the procedure is reversed. Purpose: to strengthen muscles of the upper back.
5. Relays using the crab walk (walking on hands and feet with back to the floor), seal walk (walking on hands with legs dragging along floor), or measuring worm walk (walking on hands and feet by first moving forward on the hands and then bringing feet up to hands). The class is divided into two or more separate lines. The first one in each line moves to a specified goal and back, touches the first one in line, and then goes to the end of the line. The one who has been touched takes a turn and so on through the entire line. The line that finishes first is the winner. Purpose: crab walk—to strengthen back muscles; seal walk—to increase lumbar curve in flat back; measuring worm walk—to decrease curve in lumbar area.
6. Crab walk ball. Using the rules of kick ball with the distances between goals shortened, the ball is played with the feet while all players are using the crab walk. Purpose: to strengthen muscles of the upper back.
7. Basketball with the feet. Using a wastebasket or similar receptacle as the basket, the students attempt to toss a basketball or volleyball into the basket with their feet from a sitting position on the floor six to ten feet from the basket. The ball must be grasped by the soles of the feet. Purpose: to strengthen muscles of the longitudinal arch.
8. Ball-passing overhead relay. Two or more teams can participate. Teams form a straight line by sitting cross-legged on the floor. The first player in line passes a basketball overhead with both hands, keeping the elbows as straight as possible. The next one in line receives and passes it on. The last one in the line runs forward with the ball and, sitting down, passes the ball back. When the one who started the game again becomes the first in line, the game is completed. The first team to complete the game is the winner. Purpose: to strengthen muscles of the upper back.
9. Over and under ball-passing relay. Two or more teams can participate. The teams form a straight line. The first one in line passes the ball between the legs to the second person who receives it and passes it overhead to the next one in line. The ball is passed, alternating the over and under pass. The first line to complete the relay is the winner. Purpose: to strengthen muscles of

---

[1] For description of games see chapter 21.

the upper back and decrease curve in lumbar area. (Those with exaggerated lumbar curve should not pass the ball overhead.)

10. Overhead ball-passing with the feet. Two or more teams may be formed, with the members of each team in a straight line, sitting down with the legs extended. The first player in line takes the volleyball between the feet and rolling backward, keeping the knees straight, passes the ball to the person behind, who receives it with the hands and places it between the feet and passes it back in the same manner. The last person in line receives the ball, runs forward to the front of the line, sits down, and passes the ball with the feet to the one behind. The game is completed when the one who started the game returns to the head of the line. Purpose: to decrease curve in lumbar area.

Summary

The concept of good posture has undergone considerable change in recent years. Today, authorities agree that the concept of an ideal or perfect posture is meaningless. Good posture is specific to the individual and must take into consideration the anatomical variations found within children and adolescents. Posture also must be thought of as dynamic and not static. This suggests that some people have good standing posture but not necessarily good sitting posture. Emphasis, therefore, must be placed on not only posture but also body awareness. Students should understand the relationship of various body segments for participation in different activities.

The prevalence of posture problems for students with disabilities is higher than that found in the general population. Frequently, the poor posture is related to the student's impairment: those who are visually impaired tend to walk with a backward lean, and students with cerebral palsy have to make various adjustments to compensate for their neuromuscular condition. In addition to congenital disabilities, posture problems may be caused by accidents, illnesses, or psychological problems and low self-esteem. Activities that contribute to an imbalance in muscle development, such as baseball pitching, also can create postural problems. Efforts must be directed toward ensuring that functional posture problems—those that affect muscle and soft tissue—do not become structural. This is why it is essential that posture screening and education programs be developed. Young people need to understand the long-term negative effects associated with allowing a functional posture problem to become structural. Individuals with scoliosis, for instance, in addition to their obvious problem with the spine, have a reduced cardiopulmonary capacity.

Various screening tests should be given to children and adolescents. These include tests for kyphosis, lordosis, and scoliosis. The alignments of the legs, mechanics of the feet, and strength of the abdominals should also be assessed. Physical educators, in cooperation with allied health personnel, can be very effective in conducting the necessary screening tests. As problems are identified, referral to the youngster's physician should occur and appropriate programs of activities and exercises developed. Although modifications may be necessary, it is highly unlikely that any youngster with a postural disorder should be excused from physical education. Similar to the enlightened thinking regarding the individualized nature of posture, most professionals recognize that activity and exercise, modified as appropriate, should be encouraged for students with postural deviations. The exercise will be utilized for its therapeutic value and contribution toward overall health fitness.

Selected Readings

Auxter, D., Pyfer, J., and Huettig, C. (1993). *Principles and methods of adapted physical education and recreation* (7th ed.). St. Louis: C.V. Mosby Co.

Basmajian, J. & Wolf, S. (Ed.). (1990). *Therapeutic exercise* (5th ed.). Baltimore: Williams and Wilkins.

Black, J.A. (1984). *Medical aspects of developmental disabilities in children birth to three* (Rev. 1st ed.). Rockville, MD: An Aspens Publication.

Dauer, V.P., & Pangrazi, R.P. (1987). *Dynamic physical education for elementary school children* (8th ed.). Minneapolis: Burgess Publishing Co.

DiRocco, P. (1981). Cardiopulmonary effects of scoliosis. *American Corrective Therapy Journal, 35*(2), 38–40.

DiRocco, P.J., Breed, A.L., Carlin, J.I., & Reddan, W.G. (1983). Physical work capacity in adolescent patients with mild idiopathic scoliosis. *Archives of Physical Medicine and Rehabilitation, 64,* 476–478.

Eichstaedt, C.B., & Kalakian, L.H. (1993). *Developmental/adapted physical education* (3rd ed.). New York: Macmillan Publishing Co.

Jansma, P., & French, R. (1994). *Special physical education: Physical activity, sports, and recreation.* Engelwood Cliffs, NJ: Prentice-Hall, Inc.

Rinsky, L.A. (1982). Scoliosis. In E.E. Bleck & D.A. Nagel (Eds.), *Physically handicapped children, a medical atlas for teachers* (pp. 433–443). New York: Grune and Stratton.

Sheldon, W.H. (1954). *Atlas of man: A guide for somatotyping adult males at all ages.* New York: Harper & Row.

Sherrill, C. (1991). *Adapted physical education and recreation* (4th ed.). Dubuque, IA: Wm. C. Brown Publishers.

Shneerson, J. (1978). The cardiorespiratory response to exercise in thoracic scoliosis. *Thorax, 33,* 457–463.

Enhancing Activities

1. With the assistance of a friend, conduct a posture evaluation of yourself and then have your friend do a similar evaluation. Compare notes to see areas of agreement and disagreement.

2. Contact a local school and volunteer to assist as an aid in a screening program for scoliosis.

3. Observe the standing, walking, and sitting posture of students on your campus. Make a list of your observations and discuss these with your classmates.

4. Analyze various sport activities played by children, such as baseball, basketball, and soccer, and develop a list of exercises that should be included as part of the program for these children to ensure that their musculature is symmetrically developed.

Relaxation

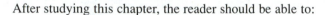

CHAPTER OBJECTIVES

After studying this chapter, the reader should be able to:

1 Recognize the importance of relaxation and its relationship to motor and academic performance.

2 Identify the signs of tension and describe the relationship between tension and relaxation.

3 Describe the various methods used to assist individuals to relax.

4 Plan a program to help students recognize signs of tension and various methods for promoting relaxation.

5 Suggest activities that can be used to improve relaxation.

6 Explain why children should be taught to recognize tension and provide them with skills to help reduce muscle tension.

7 Recognize that students with disabilities have a greater propensity toward muscular tension than students without disabilities.

Muscular relaxation is the opposite of muscular contraction or tension. Muscles contract in response to stimuli from the central nervous system. In muscular relaxation, the muscles receive minimal innervation, and their fibers become longer and less thick than in contraction. In appearance the relaxed muscle is smaller in circumference around its belly (largest part), and to the touch it feels less tense, softer, and more pliable. It is an erroneous assumption that when a muscle is not in complete contraction it is relaxed. A muscle need not be completely tensed to be in a state of contraction. A certain amount of contraction is always present, but more than normal tonus can be detrimental to health and well-being.

The Value of Relaxation

In the relaxation of overly tense muscles, certain positive changes take place in the body. The blood, which is impeded in its flow by the constriction of the blood vessels in tense muscles, circulates more freely, and the work of the heart and the stress on the blood vessels are reduced. It has been reported that the pulse rate can be lowered five beats or more per minute by participation in a specific relaxation program. Because of the salutary effects on the circulatory system, a program of relaxation may be particularly beneficial to those with elevated blood pressure and heart problems.

Because relaxation conserves energy, it prevents undue fatigue. Energy is consumed by muscular contraction, producing waste products that must be removed promptly and efficiently in order to prevent fatigue. The increased consumption of energy brought about by excessive muscular tension produces great amounts of waste that cannot be effectively removed by normal processes, owing to the greater volume of the waste and the impeded circulation of the blood. As a result, fatigue develops more rapidly and is more prolonged. Fatigue usually can be relieved by relaxation; exercises for this purpose are generally helpful to those who tire easily, are chronically fatigued, and have trouble falling asleep.

Another positive effect of relaxation is that breathing becomes easier. Because lung capacity is greater when the chest muscles are relaxed, the breathing rate is decreased. A program of activities to develop slower, more relaxed inhalation and exhalation is often advantageous to those with breathing disorders.

Muscular relaxation has beneficial effects related to such disorders as diarrhea, constipation, stomach upset, nonspecific muscle pain and headaches, and skin irritations. It has been established that frequently at the root of these health problems is an extreme or prolonged psychological response, such as fear, anger, or frustration. Muscular tension caused by an emotional reaction is one of the precursors of all of the disorders just mentioned; other precursors vary according to the nature of the condition. Relaxation tends to restore calm after emotional outbreaks and, of course, decreases the tension within the muscles, which in turn helps to diminish the symptoms of the disorder.

Research provides evidence that training in relaxation can be helpful to children with learning problems. Research studies demonstrate reduced levels of anxiety, increased attentiveness, and possibly higher scholastic achievement (Dunn and Howell, 1982; Denkowski, Denkowski, and Omizo, 1983). Rickard, Thrasher, and Elkins (1984) found that individuals within various IQ ranges were found to benefit from several types of relaxation training, including imagery and suggestions to relax and to control breathing. Eichstaedt and Lavay (1992) believe that individuals with mental retardation can learn through relaxation techniques to deal with stress and tension in a positive and socially acceptable manner, conserve energy, and move with greater efficiency. Evidence is not conclusive on the relationship between relaxation and improvement in scholastic achievement, but it seems likely that freedom from anxiety and tension permits greater concentration on the academic material and, therefore, achievement would be improved.

Because of the positive effects of relaxation on the body, the ability to relax consciously is valuable to nearly everyone. Periods of greater-than-normal tension are experienced by most people, and for many the periods are prolonged and intense. Individuals with disabilities frequently have a high degree of tension, engendered both by the physical pain and problems associated with their condition and by the negative social situation in which they find themselves. For these students relaxation is prophylactic (tending to ward off disease). Moreover, relaxation promotes feelings of well-being and, in some instances, such as in asthma and neurological hyperactivity, provides direct relief from some of the symptoms of the condition. It is important, then, for the physical education teacher to understand the significance of relaxation and to be able to teach the skills of conscious relaxation. Knowledge of the importance of and the means to achieve relaxation in effective performance of motor skills, which is a basic in the training of physical educators, provides a good foundation for teaching conscious total body relaxation to all students, with or without disabilities, who exhibit signs of hypertonicity.

Signs of Tension

Muscular tension can be determined by several simple tests, which will be described later in connection with evaluation for program planning. There are numerous overt signs that indicate hypertonicity. In some people these take the form of displays of excessive annoyance and overanxiousness, inability to remain motionless, or excessive, rapid, and loud conversation, or all of these. Other people display an appearance of great calmness. They seem to be entirely immobile; however, close observation generally reveals signs of muscular tension and physical strain such as rigidity of posture and lack of facial expressiveness. Abnormal perspiration, uncontrollable crying, and irregular breathing (hyperventilation or hypoventilation) are other common signs of neuromuscular tension.

It should be noted that where extreme anxiety and annoyance are evident, it is often difficult to determine if these responses are the results of excessive muscular tension or the causes of it. Actually, they are both cause and result. Individuals with hypertonicity become annoyed or angered by trivial matters that they could ignore if they were not in a state of tenseness. On the other hand, if people are anxious or angry, they become more tense than they would otherwise be. Emotional responses can be controlled to some degree by decreasing the tension in the muscles. The reverse is also true, but more often it is harder to decrease anxiety and anger than to reduce excessive muscular tension, because decreasing anxiety and anger involves discovering the cause from which these emotions spring. The cause may be so obscure and deep-seated as to require professional help in finding and alleviating it.

The Difference between Tension and Relaxation

The process of learning to relax begins with becoming aware of the difference between tension and relaxation. Because relaxation is the opposite of tension, the difference can be perceived in activity that contrasts the two. The muscles in a segment of the body, such as in the arm, are contracted with great force, and thought is concentrated on the contraction. The muscles are then relaxed completely, and the difference between the relaxation and contraction is mentally noted. Alternate contracting and relaxing are continued with an attempt to increase the difference between the two conditions each time.

The contracted muscle is firmer and less flexible and produces a feeling of tenseness and tightness. In contrast, the relaxed muscle is loose and soft. Vigorous contraction followed by relaxation produces a sensation of heaviness and warmth in the muscle. (This phenomenon has significance when using imagery to develop a relaxed state, which will be discussed later in the chapter).

Methods of Relaxation

The program to teach conscious relaxation may be based entirely on the techniques of one of several methods currently favored by sizable groups of adherents, or it may incorporate the techniques of two or more of these. Techniques and activities of several of the widely known methods that appear to be most useful to the physical educator in helping students with and without disabilities to achieve relaxation are described briefly in subsequent paragraphs.

Progressive Relaxation

The method called progressive relaxation was developed during the 1920s and 1930s by Edmund Jacobson, a medical doctor who was greatly concerned about the management of neuromuscular tension. Because Dr. Jacobson tested his method with laboratory procedures, his publications on the subject were, and are, highly regarded, and his method widely practiced in its original and more recently adapted forms.

The basis of the Jacobson method is the development of the ability to "localize tensions when they occur during nervous irritability and excitement and to relax them away" (1983, p. 40). Such ability is achieved, in general, by first learning to recognize muscular contraction and to reduce the tension by relaxing the muscles; this is followed by practice in relaxing major muscle groups, one at a time in a prescribed order. As relaxation of each new group is attempted, all of the groups previously practiced should be relaxed simultaneously. The number of muscle sets included, the duration of the practice, and the specific form of the technique employed depend upon the condition (degree of tension, aptitude, and so forth) of the learner.

When the relaxation techniques are to be used for inducing sleep, Jacobson recommends that auxiliary objects be used to relieve tension at body points where muscular contraction occurs in the supine position. He suggests that a pillow be placed beneath the back of the neck to relieve strain on the shoulders. A pillow also should be placed under the knees to release tension on the hamstring muscles and lower back muscles. When a comfortable position is achieved, the individual consciously relaxes various parts of the body progressively, beginning at the head and going down toward the feet.

Brandon et al. (1986), using a variation of progressive relaxation known as Behavioral Relaxation Training, found their technique helpful in teaching children with learning disabilities to relax. In addition, they reported that children who are in a relaxed state improve their ability to process information and perform attention-demanding motor tasks.

Yoga

Yoga is a system of mental and physical disciplines by which humans seek to attain union with the supreme being or ultimate principle. Originating in ancient India, yoga has had a strong following through the centuries, which continues to the present day. Many Americans practice the physical discipline known as Hatha Yoga, which offers forms of exercise that are particularly effective in learning to relax.

One form is the âsana, which can be described as a held position or pose. The âsana is performed by moving the body slowly into the prescribed position, stretching each segment of the body that is brought into the movement as far as it can comfortably be stretched. No movement is ever forced, and excessive stretching that can cause pain is avoided. The number of repetitions of the âsana exercise is not increased; however, the length of time the position is held may be increased as greater ease is achieved in holding it. The distance over which the body is stretched in the movement increases with practice.

A breathing exercise called pranayama is another form of Hatha Yoga. The objective of the pranayama is to slow the breathing process. This is achieved by gradually increasing the amount of air in each inhalation and exhalation.

Tai Chi

Tai chi chuan, an ancient Chinese system of exercise, is a series of learned movement patterns called forms that provide exercise for each region of the body. Tai chi is effective in helping students to practice slow, controlled movements (Kuo, 1991). Students are taught to concentrate on the movement patterns and to link one pattern or form with a second form. Unlike other dance forms, no posture or pose is held. Instead, each movement flows gently into the next movement. Tai chi also stresses the importance of curved or bent body parts, thus teaching participants to work with rather than against gravity. Because the same slow tempo is maintained throughout the exercises, students with limited experience can participate successfully in tai chi exercises.

Although tai chi is usually taught by a master teacher, the forms can easily be learned by reviewing a text that illustrates the forms (see Selected Readings). Students with disabilities may perform tai chi by following a strict adherence to the prescribed forms or by incorporating the concepts, which stress slow, controlled, sequenced, and rhythmic movements, into other activities.

Static Stretching

One of the earliest proponents of the teaching of techniques of relaxation in physical education and recreation was Josephine Rathbone of Columbia University. Her views on relaxation were influenced by her study of hatha yoga in India during the 1930s, and some of the exercises she recommends for relaxation are adaptations of yogic exercises.

Rathbone (1969) suggests relaxation exercises to increase flexibility in the joints in order to free the muscles of excessive tension. Basically there are two different types of these exercises, one in which a stretch is placed on the muscle and then released, and the other in which a position is held for several minutes. All movements are performed in a slow and deliberate manner. The reason for this manner of movement in the flexibility exercises, and in other exercises that promote relaxation, is that ballistic or jerky movements tend to increase the tension of the muscle.

Rhythmic Exercises

Rathbone (1969) has also suggested the use of rhythmic exercises to encourage the development of a relaxed state. She believed that individuals who were observed to be tense responded well and reported less tension after participating in such exercises. According to Rathbone, the feeling of relaxation is the result of improved circulation brought about by performing the rhythmic activities.

The exercises she developed for this purpose involve the legs, arms, and trunk and consist of swinging and swaying movements. Each exercise is performed for thirty to sixty seconds. Jerky and uncertain movements are avoided. Rhythm is inherent in the natural swinging movements, but music may be used to help establish the rhythmic pattern.

Imagery

Imagery is the formation of mental pictures; the process may be invoked internally without outside stimulation, but often it is encouraged by an external stimulus such as the spoken word or musical mood. Physical education teachers of young children have found imagery extremely helpful in teaching quality of movement. Imagery also can help young children understand the nature of relaxation and how it is achieved. The theoretical basis for the use of imagery to this end is that the formation of certain mental pictures helps students to match movements with their perception of relaxation. Empirical evidence would indicate that mind-set and feelings have a strong influence on the tonus of the muscles; imagery facilitates the process of changing the mind-set or of establishing feelings that are compatible with relaxation.

Imagery is also used to induce autogenous (self-produced) control over certain involuntary functions of the body, such as the heartbeat. The relationship of the use of imagery in relaxation to its use in autogenous control has not been well established. It is recommended that autogenous control not be used with involuntary functions of the body or in conjunction with hypnosis by anyone except a psychiatrist or qualified physician.

Surburg (1989) suggests that mental imagery holds significant promise for use with special populations. He suggests, however, that practitioners need to address several issues before using this approach. These include: (1) the type of imagery technique to be used (e.g., mental rehearsal may prove more beneficial than mental practice for some individuals); (2) the relationship between type of motor task with which imagery is to be used and the cognitive ability of the students; (3) the type of cue (e.g., verbal, visual, or kinesthetic) used to introduce images or mental pictures for relaxation; (4) duration of the imagery lesson (e.g., some individuals may become too lethargic if the session is too long).

Impulse Control

Controlling the impulse to move at a normal rate of speed in the performance of a motor movement has been found to decrease muscular tension in some people. Cratty (1989) has found it a useful relaxation technique for children who are hyperactive.

In impulse control activities the student tries to move as slowly as possible in the performance of a designated motor task. For example, students may be directed to walk as slowly as possible along a line, catch a balloon with the slowest possible movement, or push a large ball across the floor in slow motion. These activities are similar in the quality of movement to those used with the imagery technique. However, the objectives of the activities are different: in imagery the goal is to achieve a quality of movement that is like that of some object, such as a rag doll, while in impulse control the objective is to perform a given movement as slowly as possible. Using peers to mimic or mirror slow movements may prove very helpful with hyperactive children and others who have problems sustaining slow, controlled movements.

Planning the Program

Although a total class period could be used to teach relaxation techniques to students, in most instances the results are better when the instruction is integrated or alternated with the teaching of the regular activities of the program. The way in which the teaching of relaxation is worked into the program depends upon the nature of the physical education activity being presented and the background and experience of the students.

Relaxation activities can be readily integrated with motor exploration activities. Exploration of movement leads easily into discovering the differences between muscular relaxation and contraction. The use of imagery in exploration can lead to an understanding of the quality of the relaxed state and can promote conscious relaxation.

Relaxation activities may be incorporated into warm-up exercises by stressing the difference between contraction and relaxation. Relaxation activities may be done after an active game or at the end of the period to calm the children for their return to classroom work. Use at the end of the period or after any vigorous activity may be of special value to children who are hyperactive. Preferably, the children should lie down in a quiet, semidark environment that is conducive to practicing relaxation techniques on their own. For very young children, such an environment can be provided by placing large paper boxes in the quietest area of the room. It should never appear that the child who goes to the resting place is being set apart from the rest of the class. Because every young child benefits from occasional rest, all children might take a turn resting in the box, thereby avoiding any stigma being attached to the procedure.

Participation in strenuous motor activities provides an outlet for releasing excessive tension for some students. These are generally the ones who are successful in the activities; even though fatigued, they feel relaxed and comfortable after a hard-fought competitive game or other activity requiring physical skill and stamina. However, for many others, especially students who are mentally retarded, hyperactive, or emotionally disturbed who have not experienced success in the activity, strenuous motor effort leads to increased tension that persists long after the activity has concluded. Time devoted to relaxation after the activity is very beneficial to these individuals.

Students who relax with apparent ease will not need extensive work on relaxation, but they should be given some experience in relaxing for possible future use. They may be introduced to the techniques of discovering the difference between muscular relaxation and contraction and have the experience of trying the various techniques on several different muscle groups of their bodies. The students who do show excessive muscular tension will need special help and considerable time in actual practice of relaxation. Contrary to the popular notion, it often takes as much practice to learn to relax the muscles as it does to learn to contract them for proper performance of a motor skill.

The instruction can proceed in a number of ways. Impulse control or imagery may be introduced when students are participating in another activity. For example, if the participants are exploring ways of throwing a ball (overhand, underhand, and so forth), they can also try throwing the ball so slowly that it barely reaches the target or as if it were an egg that must not be broken. Or students may be asked to assume a random formation on the floor to perform relaxation exercises or movements. The teacher may start with the group standing to practice alternate contraction and relaxation of their facial, neck, arm, and finger muscles. Then they sit or lie down to practice relaxing other muscles. The back-lying position is frequently recommended as the preferable position for introducing concepts of relaxation. As indicated in figure 29.1, support in the form of a pillow or rolled-up towel is provided for the cervical and lumbar curves, forearms, and legs. The supports allow for free muscle contraction while the individual is in a comfortable, relaxed position.

The actual teaching of relaxation may commence with evaluation of the students' ability to relax, using both subjective observation and any of the tests described in the following section. If the students are few, testing may be accomplished by the teacher alone. With larger classes the teacher will need to instruct the students in the techniques of giving the tests. Then, with the class divided into pairs, the students can give the tests to one another. If the number who are tested at any time is limited to five or six, the teacher will be able to assist the students who are administering the tests in making a determination of the presence of muscular tension.

Figure 29.1 Basic position for tension reduction exercises.

Arm Test of Relaxation

The subject being tested sits in a chair at a desk with his or her arm resting on the desk. He or she is instructed to relax the arm and shoulder but to maintain balance. The tester lifts the forearm a few inches, with the elbow remaining on the desk. The arm is then released. If the arm drops without control back to the desk, this is evidence of the subject's being able to relax the arm. If, however, the subject contracts the muscles of the arm to assist in raising it, to hold the arm, or to lower the arm when it is dropped, or if he or she resists the lifting action, tension in the arm is indicated.

The test may also be given using the total arm at the shoulder or the hand at the wrist.

Lower Limb Test of Relaxation

The subject sits on a chair with both feet on the floor and the legs comfortably spread. The student is directed by the tester to relax the legs but to maintain balance. The tester pushes the legs to the center and then to the side, one leg at a time and then both together. If the legs are relaxed, they will push easily to the side and then spring back to the original position, bouncing back and forth slightly as they return. Tension is present if the legs remain in the position in which they have been pushed or if they resist the push. Muscular relaxation tests are often performed with the subject lying down. However, this position is not as conducive to detection of muscular tension as a sitting position, because relaxation is more difficult when seated. Greater muscular contraction is required to hold the body in a sitting position, so an inability to relax is more easily detected.

Behavioral Relaxation Scale

A helpful system for evaluating the effectiveness of relaxation training was proposed by Poppen and Maurer (1982). Their system, known as the Behavioral Relaxation Scale (BRS), consists of ten observations that are made while the individual reclines on a lounger. For each BRS item the individual is evaluated to be either relaxed or unrelaxed. The BRS should be administered more than once to increase the accuracy of the observations. The BRS items are:

1. Breathing is scored as relaxed if the breathing is regular and at a slower rate than normal.
2. Quiet is scored as relaxed if no sounds are emitted.
3. Body is scored as relaxed if there is no movement of the body trunk.
4. Head is scored as relaxed if the head is in the midline of the body, supported by the recliner, and with no movement.
5. Eyes are scored as relaxed if the eyes are closed, with smooth eye lids.
6. Mouth is scored as relaxed if the lips are slightly parted at the center of the mouth.
7. Throat is scored as relaxed if there is no noticeable movement within the neck.
8. Shoulders are scored as relaxed if both shoulders are rounded and in the same horizontal plane.
9. Hands are scored as relaxed if the hands are claw-like, with palms down and fingers slightly curled.
10. Feet are scored as relaxed if the feet point away from each other and with the midlines of the feet forming a thirty- to sixty-degree angle with the base of the recliner.

Suggested Activities

The following activities are eclectic, having been chosen from among the various methods for developing the ability to relax the body at will. The activities may be used in the form described or adapted to fit the specific situation as will be required for students with restricted mobility or deficits in motor learning. The activities presented need not be from only one category; some from several categories may be combined for a meaningful lesson in relaxation. The selection of activities should be made in accordance with the age level and experience of the students.

Exercises for Feeling the Difference between Relaxation and Tension

In these exercises students are directed to make a mental note of the difference between relaxation and tension. Each time the students contract or relax the muscles, they are to try to make the difference greater. Muscles not involved should be relaxed during the contraction. The following exercises should be performed in a back-lying position (see figure 29.1). While performing these exercises, tension should be felt only in the specific body part(s) identified. The rest of the body should be relaxed.

1. *Toes.* Curl the toes downward until the toes and feet are pointed toward the end of the mat. Hold this position for a count of ten and then let the toes relax, slowly returning to a resting state. Curl the toes and both feet upward toward the head. Hold the position for a count of ten and then release slowly.

2. *Legs.* Press the legs down toward the mat. Tension should be felt in the back of the legs and buttocks. Hold this position for a count of ten and slowly relax the legs. Straighten the legs to full extension. Tension should be felt in the top of the thighs. Hold for a count of ten and then return slowly.

3. *Thighs.* Forcibly rotate the thighs outward. Tension should be felt in the outer hip region. Hold this position for a count of ten and then return slowly to relaxed state. Rotate the thighs inward. Tension should be felt deep in the inner thigh. Hold for a count of ten and then release slowly.

4. *Buttocks.* Squeeze the buttocks (gluteal muscles) together tightly. Tension should be felt in the buttocks and lower back region. Hold this position for a count of ten and then release slowly.

5. *Abdomen.* Tighten the muscles of the abdomen by pressing downward on the rib cage while rolling the hips backward and flattening the lower back. Tension should be felt in the abdominal muscles and the lower back. Hold this position for a count of ten and then release slowly.

6. *Upper Back.* Tighten the upper back by squeezing the shoulder blades together. Tension should be felt in the back of the shoulders. Hold this position for a count of ten and then release slowly. Raise or shrug the shoulders upward toward the ears. Tension should be felt in the upper part of the back in the trapezius muscle. Hold this position for a count of ten and then release slowly.

7. *Chest.* Lift and roll the shoulders inward so that tension can be felt in the chest area. The arms should remain in the resting position. Hold this position for a count of ten and then release slowly.

8. *Arms.* Tighten the fists and extend the arms so that tension is felt throughout the arm. Hold this position for a count of ten and then release. Repeat the same exercise without tightening the fists. Make a tight fist with both hands and slowly bend the arms at the elbows until the forearms rest against the upper arms. Tension is felt in the front part of the forearms and the biceps. Hold for a count of ten and then release slowly.

9. *Wrists and Fingers.* Make a tight fist with both hands and roll the wrists backward toward the forearms. Tension should be felt in the fingers, wrists, and forearms. Hold for a count of ten and then slowly release. This exercise can be repeated by having the wrists bend to the front and then alternately toward each side.

10. *Neck.* Bend the neck forward, touching the chin to the chest. Tension should be felt in the front of the neck. Hold this position for a count of ten and then release

slowly. This exercise can be repeated by flexing the neck first to one side and then the other. Tension should be felt in the side of the neck not being flexed.

11. *Face.* Lift the eyebrows upward and wrinkle the forehead. Tension should be felt in the forehead. Hold this position for a count of ten and then release slowly. Close the eyelids tightly and then wrinkle the nose. Tension should be felt in the eyes and nose. Hold this position for a count of ten and then release slowly.

Relaxation Exercises Using Imagery

The students are asked to imagine the objects specified in the exercises and then to move as they imagine they would move in the described circumstances. All of the activities are suitable for young children; items 7 through 10 are also appropriate for older students. Because feelings of heaviness and warmth in the muscles accompany relaxation, the imagery related to these feelings suggested in items 7, 8, and 9 is especially helpful in inducing relaxation.

1. Move like a rag doll.
2. Fall slowly to the floor like a balloon that is floating to the ground.
3. Move like a flag waving in a gentle breeze.
4. Be a soft, fluffy kitten curling up its body on the rug.
5. Sway like a slender flower in a gentle breeze.
6. Lie on the floor like a wet towel.
7. Lying on your back, think that your eyelids are getting heavier and heavier; then close the eyelids and relax the entire body.
8. Lying on your back on a mat, think that your arms and legs are heavy like iron and are sinking slowly, slowly into the mat.
9. Lying on your back on the mat, think that your entire body is pleasantly warm and comfortable and is sinking deeper and deeper into a soft, soft mattress.
10. Combine 7, 8, and 9. (Some students may go to sleep if they engage in the combined activity for a sufficiently long period of time.)

Static Stretching of Muscles

All of these activities are performed very slowly and deliberately. Positions obtained should be held for several seconds, followed by relaxation of all muscles involved.

1. Lower the head forward as far as possible, move it to the right and touch the chin to the collarbone and then to the left, touching the collarbone on that side.

2. Bend at the hips and reach to the floor without bending the knees.

3. With the arms hanging loosely at the sides of the body, bend to each side as far as possible.

4. Stand on tip-toes and raise the arms at the sides and parallel to the ground. Move the arms backward as far as possible.

5. Sit on the floor with the legs bent and crossed so that the heel of one foot is under the calf of the opposite leg and the toe of that leg is under the calf of the other leg. Place the hands on the knees and push them toward the floor.

6. Lie on the back and bring the knees to the chest with the arms at the sides, palms on the mat or floor. Holding the palms and shoulders on the floor, lower the legs to one side and then to the other until the thighs touch the floor.

7. Lie on the back with the arms stretched to the sides. Raise one leg in the air and bring it over to touch the opposite hand. Hold the position briefly and then return to the original position. Repeat, using the opposite leg and hand.

8. Stand with one foot on the floor and the other on the seat of a chair. Bring the trunk forward in an attempt to place it on the knee.

9. Stand with the arms raised at the sides. Turn the body to the right as far as possible, then to the left as far as possible.

10. Lie on the back and spread the legs as far as possible.

Rhythmic Exercises

These exercises can be performed to music or counted cadence or without either. The movement should be executed in a smooth and easy manner.

1. Stand and swing one arm back and forth. Swing one arm forward; swing the other backward. Swing both arms together.

2. Move the head in rhythmic motion from side to side very slowly.

3. Sitting in a chair, clench the fist and swing one arm forcibly in a circle. Repeat using the other arm.

4. Sitting either in a chair or on the floor, swing the trunk from side to side in time to a very slow count.

5. Sitting on a high table so the feet do not touch the floor, swing one leg back and forth and then the other. Swing both at the same time.

6. Using the back of a chair for support, stand on one leg and swing the opposite leg back and forth.

7. Select any part of the body and move it back and forth at a slow tempo.

8. Kneel on all fours and sway slowly forward and backward.

9. Walk very slowly forward, moving the arms in an exaggerated swing in rhythm to the walking cadence.

10. With the hands clasped in front of the chest, rock the arms back and forth as if rocking a baby.

Impulse Control Activities

These exercises are done as slowly as possible. The performance of a given activity may be timed with a stopwatch to provide students with a definite goal to match or to better in the next performance of the activity. (In these exercises, a better time is a slower time.)

1. Walk as slowly as possible on a balance beam or along a straight or circular line drawn on the floor.

2. Pretend to throw, bat, or kick a ball in slow motion.

3. Catch a thrown balloon and match the catching movement to the speed of the balloon.

4. Take side-steps as slowly as possible.

5. Sway the body from side to side as slowly as possible.

6. Clap hands in slow motion.

7. Stand on one foot, swing the opposite foot back and forth as slowly as possible; repeat, using opposite feet; swing an arm and leg on the same side of the body.

8. Sit down as slowly as possible; rise equally slowly.

9. Roll over and over on the mat as slowly as possible.

10. Skip as slowly as possible.

Yoga Exercises

The first three of the following activities are âsanas; the last two are pranayamas. The latter are performed to a count by the performer. All movements in both kinds of activities are slow and deliberate.

1. To assume the position, lie on the back with the arms to the sides. Slowly raise the legs, keeping them straight, and bring them over the head until the feet touch the floor above the head. To increase the difficulty, the hands are removed from the sides and locked above the head. This position is called plowshares.

2. To assume the position referred to as the cobra, lie face down with the forehead on the floor or mat. The hands are placed on the floor on either side of the chest. The head is raised with the chest held against the mat. Then the chest is raised. In the first attempts, the hands may be used to help raise the chest, but as skill is increased, the use of the hands is discontinued.

3. A sitting position is taken with the legs straight out. The right leg is bent and turned outward so the thigh

touches the floor or mat. The heel is brought up to the crotch with the sole of the foot touching the left thigh. The left foot is then placed on the right thigh. (This is the lotus position.) The right arm is placed to encircle the knee coming over the top so the right shoulder can be placed on the knee. The right hand extends across the body and grasps the left foot. The right shoulder must be firmly set against the knee to avoid injury to the elbow joint. The reverse position may be taken by starting with the left leg.

4. The pulse is taken at rest to establish the cadence for breathing. A reclining position is taken on the back with the knees slightly bent. Inhale slowly for four counts and then exhale for four counts. The exercise continues for several minutes.

5. Sit on the floor with the legs crossed as in number 5 of the static stretching exercises. Hold the spine erect and take a deep breath and hold for six counts. (The rhythm is the same as in item 4.) Exhale at the count of six. Continue the exercise for several minutes.

Summary

Teaching students to recognize signs of tension and methods of relaxation are essential components of a progressive physical education program. Experts are in agreement that in learning to relax, certain positive changes take place in the body. In the relaxed state, blood circulates more freely and the work of the heart and the stress on the blood vessels are reduced. A relaxed state also conserves energy and prevents undue fatigue. For those who experience psychological disorders, the positive effects of relaxation are well documented. Relaxation tends to restore calm after emotional outbreaks and, of course, decreases the tension within the muscles, which in turn helps to diminish the symptoms of the disorder.

Various methods have been used to teach conscious relaxation. These include ancient practices such as yoga and tai chi as well as more modern techniques such as progressive relaxation developed by Edmund Jacobson in the 1920s and 1930s. Imagery, the formation of mental pictures, and impulse control, where an individual practices moving as slowly as possible, have also received considerable attention because of their effectiveness with small children.

Although relaxation is important for everyone, special efforts should be directed toward helping students with disabilities to learn to relax. Individuals with disabilities often have a high degree of tension, which may be related to their condition and the negative social situations with which they are sometimes confronted. For these students, relaxation promotes feelings of well-being and, in some instances such as with asthma and neurological hyperactivity, provides direct relief from some of the symptoms of the condition. Research indicates that for children who are hyperactive, programs of relaxation lead to improvements in the ability to process information and perform attention-demanding motor tasks.

Relaxation techniques may be taught as a separate special program or integrated into various physical education activities. Both approaches are of value. Some believe that the concepts of recognizing tension and teaching a specific relaxation technique such as progressive relaxation should be done in a series of classes devoted to this subject. Given this foundation, the concepts and techniques can be woven into the daily physical education program. During warm-up activities, for instance, the teacher might reinforce the difference between muscle contraction and relaxation and provide opportunities to experience both. Allowing children to experience some quiet at the end of the class provides an excellent time to emphasize the importance of both activity, with its heightened excitation level, and relaxation, where the emphasis is on tension reduction. Regardless of the approach selected, the teacher must be consistent and conscientious in allowing children to learn and experience techniques for inducing relaxation. Students with and without disabilities will benefit from relaxation programs. The value is immediate, but it also can be incorporated into the person's life and utilized as one more tool that can contribute to an active and healthy life.

Selected Readings

Auxter, D., Pyfer, J., and Huettig, C. (1993). *Adapted physical education and recreation* (7th ed.). St. Louis: Times Mirror/Mosby College Publishing.

Brandon, J.E., Eason, R.L., & Smith, T.L. (1986). Behavioral relaxation training and motor performance of learning disabled children with hyperactive behaviors. *Adapted Physical Activity Quarterly, 3,* 67–79.

Cratty, B.J. (1989). *Adapted physical education in the mainstream* (2nd ed.). Denver, CO: Love Publishing Co.

Denkowski, K.M., Denkowski, G.C., & Omizo, M.M. (1983). The effects of EMG assisted relaxation training on the academic performance, locus of control, and self-esteem of hyperactive boys. *Biofeedback and Self-Regulation, 8,* 363–375.

Dunn, F.M., & Howell, R.J. (1982). Relaxation training and its relationship to hyperactivity in boys. *Journal of Clinical Psychology, 38,* 92–100.

Eason, R.L., Brandon, J.E., Smith, T.L., & Sepas, D.C. (1986). Relaxation training effects on reaction/response time, frontalis EMG, and behavioral measures of relaxation with hyperactive males. *Adapted Physical Activity Quarterly, 3,* 329–341.

Eichstaedt, C.B., & Lavay, B.W. (1992). *Physical activity for individuals with mental retardation.* Champaign, IL: Human Kinetics Publishing.

Greenberg, J. (1990). *Comprehensive stress managment* (3rd ed.). Dubuque, IA: Wm. C. Brown Publishers.

Hittleman, R. (1969). *Introduction to yoga.* New York: Bantam Books.

Jacobson, E. (1983). *Progressive relaxation* (2d ed.). Chicago: The University of Chicago Press.

Jacobson, E.O. (1970). *Modern treatment of tense patients.* Springfield, IL: Charles C. Thomas.

Kuo, S. (1991). *Long life, good health through Tai Chi Chuan.* Berkeley, CA: North Atlantic Books.

Maisel, E. (1972). *Tai chi for health.* New York: Holt, Rinehart and Winston.

Poppen, R., & Maurer, J. (1982). Electromyographic Analysis of Relaxed Postures. *Biofeedback and Self-Regulation, 7,* 491–498.

Rathbone, J. (1969). *Relaxation.* Philadelphia: Lea and Febiger.

Rickard, H.C., Thrasher, K.A., & Elkins, P.D. (1984). Responses of persons who are mentally retarded to four components of relaxation instruction. *Mental Retardation, 22*, 248–252.

Selye, H. (1974). *Stress without distress*. Philadelphia: J.B. Lippincott.

Surburg, P.R. (1989). Application of imagery techniques to special populations. *Adapted Physical Activity Quarterly, 6*(4), 328–337.

Enhancing Activities

1. Review the exercises for impulse control described in the chapter and try these activities. Record your impression of the effectiveness of these exercises.

2. Review the list of impulse control activities. Identify other activities that could be included for impulse control.

3. With the assistance of your instructor, implement a progressive relaxation program with a group of children who are hyperactive.

4. Visit a yoga class and discuss with the instructor the purpose and projected outcomes of the class.

5. Develop a list of the mental pictures (imagery) that you have found helpful in assisting you to relax. Share your list with your classmates and explore with them images that might be helpful to young children.

6. Spend some time observing young children in various settings—at school, engaging in play, participating in sport. Identify various signs of tension and stress and speculate what might be causing this.

CHAPTER 30

Competitive Sport for Athletes with Disabilities

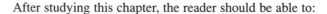

CHAPTER OBJECTIVES

After studying this chapter, the reader should be able to:

1 Recognize important events in the historical development of competitive sport experiences for individuals with disabilities.

2 Understand that federal legislation (P.L. 101-476, Individuals with Disabilities Education Act; P.L. 94-142, The Education for All Handicapped Children Act; P.L. 93-112, Rehabilitation Act of 1973; and P.L. 95-606, The Amateur Sports Act) emphasizes the importance of sport and its contribution to the lives of individuals with disabilities.

3 Describe the value of sport for individuals with disabilities and its evolution from a primarily therapeutic experience to a recognized sport for novice as well as highly skilled athletes.

4 Identify and discuss the various sport associations that promote and govern national and international competition for athletes with disabilities.

Society's awareness, understanding, and acceptance of individuals with disabilities have improved in very significant ways during the past twenty years. Perhaps this evolution is best demonstrated by analyzing the provisions of sport for those with disabilities. For too many years, educators have ignored the potential value of sport opportunities for special education students. This was due to the once common philosophy that education for students with disabilities should focus on the basic educational skills. Little attention, therefore, was given to extracurricular activities such as sport experiences. Some, too, may have felt that students with disabilities would not benefit from sport experiences. An unfortunate but common assumption of the past was that students with orthopedic and sensory impairments would not be able to successfully participate in sport activities. Enlightened school officials recognize today that education for any student is more than the basics, and taking a student's needs or desires for granted is indeed dangerous.

Recent legislation also has reinforced the individual with a disability's right to participate in sport activities. Public Law 94-142, the Education for All Handicapped Children Act of 1975, and Section 504 of the Rehabilitation Act of 1973, Public Law 93-112, specify that physical education experiences, including intramural activities and sports, must be available to students with disabilities to the same extent these opportunities are available to nondisabled students (Dougherty et al., 1994). The law indicates that students with disabilities should not be denied equal opportunity to participate on regular school teams or comparable special teams.

In the following pages, information will be provided about the origins and purposes of sport for people with disabling conditions. Sport organizations and suggestions for developing sport programs for individuals with disabling conditions will also be discussed.

Historical Development

Prior to World War II there is little evidence of organized efforts to develop or promote sport for people with disabilities. Some individuals, due to their own initiative, did achieve success prior to this time. Karoly Tacaczs, a Hungarian marksman who lost his right arm in 1938 after an accident, transferred his skill by intensive training to his left arm, which he had never used previously. He later became a two-time Olympic champion. There are certainly other examples of individuals who overcame many obstacles to achieve success with little, if any, support.

One of the earliest sport organizations for people with disabilities was the Sports Club for the Deaf, founded in 1888 in Berlin, Germany. In 1924, national sport organizations for the deaf were merged into a world organization, *Comite International des Sports Silencieux*. The British Society of One-Armed Golfers is another early sports organization. This group, founded in 1932, holds its annual championships on leading courses throughout England. Today there is also the Association of Disabled American Golfers for golfers with various disabling conditions. Although they represent modest beginnings, these early pre-World War II efforts did illustrate that those with disabilities, too, could grow and benefit from opportunities to participate in sport.

The Effects of World War II

The large number of soldiers injured in World War II posed a great challenge to medical authorities. Traditional methods of rehabilitation did not satisfactorily respond to the medical and psychological needs of the war injured. For instance, those with spinal paraplegia were considered to be hopeless cripples with a short life span of two to three years. Early deaths were attributed to infection of the paralyzed bladder resulting in the destruction of the kidneys.

Recognizing this problem, the British government in 1944 opened the Spinal Injuries Center at Stoke Mandeville Hospital in Aylesbury. The opening of this center under the direction of Dr. Ludwig Guttmann is, perhaps, the most significant event in the history of sport for people with spinal paralysis. Dr. Guttmann recognized from the outset that previous efforts at rehabilitation had failed due to the fragmentation of medical services. Treatment of patients with spinal cord injuries, in Dr. Guttmann's opinion, required a team oriented to all aspects of the injured person's needs. To alleviate boredom and enhance the neuromuscular system, Dr. Guttmann and his staff introduced sport to their patients as a form of recreation.

Early sport forms used at the Stoke Mandeville Center included punch ball exercises, rope-climbing, and wheelchair polo, the first competitive team sport for individuals with paraplegia (Guttmann, 1976). Wheelchair basketball was introduced in 1945 and quickly became the most popular team sport for people with paralysis.

These early attempts to incorporate sport into the medical rehabilitation of people with paralysis soon spread from Great Britain to other countries, including the United States.

Early Efforts in the United States

As in Great Britain, medical personnel in the United States found themselves developing new modes of comprehensive treatment to assist those injured in the war. Veterans Administration hospitals throughout the United States encouraged those with disabilities to become active as sport participants. This effort was assisted in 1946 by the United States tour of the Flying Wheels Team of Van Nuys, California. The Flying Wheels Team, an extraordinarily talented group, assisted all people, disabled and nondisabled to comprehend the value and enjoyment sport holds for athletes with disabilities. Several other wheelchair basketball teams were organized in 1947 and 1948. These included the Brooklyn Whirlaways,

Queen's Charioteers, New York Spokesmen, and the Pioneers of Kansas City, Missouri (Adams and McCubbin, 1991).

The interest of the United States in sport for the wheelchair athlete was enhanced when Dr. Guttmann traveled to New York in the early 1950s to meet with Benjamin H. Lipton, Director of the Joseph Bulova School of Watchmaking. Lipton, along with Dr. Timothy Nugent of the University of Illinois, was responsible for spearheading the growth of sport for individuals with disabilities in the United States. As an outgrowth of the meeting between Guttmann and Lipton, the first National Wheelchair Games in the United States were held in 1958. Although these games were patterned after the Stoke Mandeville Games, new events such as the 60-, 100-, and 220-yard dashes were introduced. These games, which are still a popular annual event, provided a format to train, compete, and eventually select the best athletes to represent the United States in international competition.

Influence of Amateur Sports Act

In 1975 President Gerald Ford formed the President's Commission on Olympic Sports to review the status of Olympic sports and related topics. The commission's findings, published in 1977, formed the basis for the Amateur Sports Act of 1978, P.L. 95-606. This legislation resulted in the reorganization of the United States Olympic Committee (USOC) and reaffirmed the commitment to amateur athletes in the United States. Given the emphasis on physical education and sport found in P.L. 93-112, Rehabilitation Act of 1973, and P.L. 94-142, Education for All Handicapped Children Act of 1975, advocates of sport for people with disabilities were successful in ensuring that the Amateur Sports Act included those with disabilities. Specifically the Act led to the inclusion of the following in the Objects and Purposes Section of the USOC Constitution:

> To encourage and provide assistance to amateur athletic programs and competition for handicapped individuals, including, where feasible, the expansion of opportunities for meaningful participation by handicapped individuals in programs of athletic competition for able-bodied individuals.[1]

To achieve this objective, a special committee, Committee on Sports for the Disabled (COSD), was established by the USOC. The COSD meets semiannually to promote sport for individuals with disabilities. These activities include: coordinating programs and national and international competition for athletes with disabilities, encouraging research and the dissemination of information, and seeking funds and support from the USOC. Several disability sports organizations are affiliated directly with the United States Olympic Committee: American Athletic Association for the Deaf, United States Association for Blind Athletes, Special Olympics, Wheelchair Sports, USA, United States Cerebral Palsy Athletic Association, and Disabled Sports, USA.

The influence of the Committee on Sports for the Disabled has been significant in promoting sport activities for special populations. Through the efforts of the COSD, the 1984 Olympic Games in Los Angeles featured a wheelchair demonstration (800-meter race for women and 1,500-meter race for men); this was the first time athletes with disabilities received recognition in the summer Olympic games. Also for the first time, an athlete in a wheelchair, Neroll Fairhall from New Zealand, qualified to compete in the Olympics. Her success in archery has opened new doors of understanding concerning people with disabilites and their potential as athletes.

Purpose of Sport for Individuals with Disabilities

Society's treatment of those with disabilities has undergone radical changes since the early 1900s. No longer, for instance, is it universally believed that institutionalization is the accepted environment for individuals with disabilities. Efforts have been made to recognize, value, and accept those who deviate from the norm. The ultimate goal is to create an environment in which those with disabilities can achieve a sense of self-realization, a charting of their own course (Dunn and Sherrill, 1996).

Athletes with disabilities and their sport advocates have made great strides in their acceptance of the true meaning of sport. Sport for people with disabilities was initially conceived in a very narrow way as primarily a clinical experience designed to assist the rehabilitative process. Today, athletes with disabilities recognize that sport is broader than this and that sport can contribute to their lives in several ways.

Health and Fitness

Participation in sport makes an important contribution to the health and fitness of individuals with disabilities. Although the amount of information is limited, studies suggest that the fitness levels of youth who have disabling conditions are lower than those of their nondisabled peers. Some of the factors that interfere with the health and fitness of individuals with disabilities are discussed in the following paragraphs.

Nutrition

The nutritional status of some youth with disabilities is affected by several factors including specific disability, medication required, and behavioral influences. The majority of children with developmental disabilities, exhibit nutritional disorders.

---

[1]USOC Constitution, Article II(13), p. 2.

Sedentary Life-Styles

Young persons with disabilities frequently find opportunities to participate in activity outside of their homes or residential settings to be more restricted than for the nondisabled. For many children, youth, and adults, access to mainstream or specialized programs is restricted due to lack of private or public transportation. This results in greater reliance on television and other forms of sedentary entertainment.

Lack of Understanding of the Concept of Fitness

Some youth with cognitive deficits, particularly those with mental impairments, fail to understand the important relationship between health and fitness.

Hereditary Factors

The nature of some disabilities is such that associated health problems can lead to further deterioration in the individual's physical fitness. For example, 40 percent of people with Down syndrome have a congenital heart disorder.

Fear of Failure

For individuals with disabilities, particularly those who are mentally retarded, orthopedically impaired, and sensory impaired, the performance of "routine" exercises can be very difficult. The inability to grasp the technique of the exercise or to possess the coordination to perform the exercise can create a vicious cycle of failure, followed by avoidance.

Program and Facility Accessibility

Unfortunately, the health fitness level of many individuals with disabilities is lower than expected because of the lack of appropriate programs, or programs conducted in accessible facilities.

Young people with disabilities need as many opportunities as possible to improve their health and fitness levels. Sport can play a significant role in developing the desired levels of fitness. Studies indicate that persons with disabling conditions, including those with severe mental retardation, can be taught sport skills, thereby improving important variables such as health and physical fitness.

Psychological Value

Physical activity is an integral part of the function of daily life. Daily tasks such as rising from bed, eating breakfast, and preparing for work all require different forms of movement. For those with disabilities, some of these activities, considered routine by many nondisabled people, require preliminary planning and intensive effort to perform. The

Figure 30.1 Many athletes with disabilities participate in sport because it is fun, exciting, challenging, and provides an outlet for expression and an avenue to recognition.

ability to undertake the activities of daily living and having the stamina to perform part-time or full-time work may be the deciding factor between earning one's own income or being dependent on others for financial resources. Some individuals with disabilities become disheartened when they struggle with basic activities that seem so easy for others. Frequently, this feeling is reinforced by family members and friends who treat the individual with a disability as though he or she is helpless. Some who are disabled begin to develop an inferiority complex, characterized by anxiety with a loss of self-confidence and self-esteem. The result is self-pity, self-centered isolationism, and antisocial attitudes.

Participating in sport often can restore psychological equilibrium, counteract feelings of inferiority, and become a motivating force in the enjoyment of life, which is so necessary to people with disabilities in coming to terms with their ability and disability levels. Sport provides an opportunity for an individual with a disability to express in a very visible way that having an impairment is not synonymous with being helpless or an invalid. Following extensive interviews with more than 300 athletes with disabilities, Sherrill (1986) reported that almost all of the athletes saw sport as a means of affirming their competence, thereby seeking to focus attention on their abilities rather than disabilities. The psychological contribution coupled with the physiological value assists many individuals with disabilities to use sport as a means of enhancing their concept of self.

Normalization

Sport has been recognized by several authorities as an important institution within society. Individuals with disabilities, therefore, striving to be part of society, recognize that participation in sport will help them to integrate more fully into family and community activities. For instance, students with visual impairments who master the art of swimming can use this proficiency not only to compete but, perhaps more importantly, be a welcomed addition to all water activities enjoyed by their families.

Individuals with disabilities also use sport to assure others that, although they have impairments, they are not ill. There is a general tendency for the public, educators, and even some medical personnel to equate the term "disability" and "sickness." This misconception is quickly destroyed when individuals with disabilities are observed strenuously participating in sport forms common to the general public.

The ultimate form of integration for individuals with disabilities is to participate with nondisabled people in activities in which their disabilities do not interfere with their own or the team's performance. Many examples are found in sport where people with disabilities have successfully participated or competed with the nondisabled. Harold Connoly, one of the United States' great Olympians, won a gold medal in the hammer throw although he performed with a disabled left arm. Jim Abbott, a professional baseball player and former Big Ten baseball pitcher, received the Sullivan Award as the United States' top amateur athlete, even though he was born without a right hand. Many other examples could be included here to illustrate that some individuals with disabilities have overcome obstacles to participate successfully with their nondisabled peers.

Sport for Sport's Sake

Although many benefits—including physiological and psychological—accrue to the individual with a disability through sport activities, the primary motivation for many who participate is the need for recognition. This is a common motivation of most participants in sport activities. Athletes with disabilities have become more adamant in recent years in urging others to recognize that they enjoy sport for the same reasons nondisabled individuals do. They stress that sport for them is a "sport" experience, as it is for everyone, and not a therapeutic or rehabilitative program. Similar to the nondisabled, some athletes with disabilities have become very serious in their training programs, emphasizing quality efforts and maximum performance. For these athletes, the ultimate goal is to someday be recognized as an athlete capable of outstanding sport performance. This is an evolutionary goal that builds upon the therapeutic, psychological, and normalizing value of sport to an acceptance of people with disabilities and their right to achieve self-realization through the medium of sport.

Recognition of the last purpose of sport for those with disabilities, sport for sport's sake, suggests, too, that sport participation for all athletes, with and without disabilities, is subject to potentially negative features. Overzealous athletes and coaches can lead to situations in which the desire to win is greater than the desire to compete or cooperate fairly. Some athletes with disabilities are not immune from the plague of winning at all costs, as are some nondisabled athletes. Professionals with strong and ethical value systems are needed to assure that sport for people with disabilities is conducted according to the highest ethical standards. Fortunately, the leaders of sport for athletes with disabilities have made some positive rule changes that differ from the traditional perception of sport. For instance, classification systems that rate athletes according to ability categories are very common in sport for people with disabilities. Examples of this excellent idea that should be incorporated into sport for *all* people will be presented later in this chapter.

Those who have been trained in physical education, or who have competed successfully in sport, have a tendency to believe that all individuals should respond in a positive way to sport competition. It must be recognized, however, that many individuals respond negatively to the direct competition of sport that requires a loser before a winner is produced. Others who enjoy direct competition in other areas of life often shun competition that requires physical strength, speed, and prowess. The variance in responses to sport competition among individuals with disabilities will be no less than in the population as a whole. The educator working with special students in physical education should keep in mind that they need to develop their physical and motor abilities to the optimum but that the process does not necessarily require direct competition with others. It is essential, too, that an atmosphere not be created that encourages an attitude that those who do not wish to participate in sport competition are inferior to those who do and that participation in competitive sports is the most important activity in the program. However, for a large number, *successful* sport competition provides an opportunity to develop an optimum level of physical performance and, additionally, offers the satisfaction of gaining personal recognition and participating with peers. All persons, with and without disabilities, must not be deprived of this experience.

Sport Associations for Individuals with Disabilities

Throughout this chapter references have been made to athletes with paralysis, amputations, and other orthopedic impairments. Although it is true that among special populations those with physical impairments, particularly athletes who use wheelchairs, were the first to benefit from organized sport, there also have been great strides made in recent years to promote sport for other disability populations.

Some of these highlights will be discussed in this section. Organizations have been formed that promote sport for a particular disability group using various sport events. It should be noted that several of the sport for the disabled organizations recognized by the U.S. Olympic Committee offer swimming to the athletes in their group. Each group has a slight variation on the events offered for swimming and slightly different rules; however, the majority of the rules that govern swimming for nondisabled athletes hold true for athletes with disabilities. So in order to conduct a swim meet for athletes with disablities it is necessary to know the rules of the national governing body, *U.S. Swimming,* as well as the rules for the particular sport organization. This is true for track, field (Track and Field USA), skiing (U.S. Ski Association), and all other sports recognized by the U.S. Olympic Committee. Primary emphasis will be given to those groups that are actively promoting national and international games for athletes with disabilities and recognized by the United States Olympic Committee. A selected list of organizations and their addresses is found in table 30.1.

American Athletic Association of the Deaf (AAAD)

This association, organized in Akron, Ohio, in 1945, is composed of approximately 160 member clubs with 20,000 members. The purpose of AAAD is to foster and regulate competition, develop uniform rules, and promote interclub competition. A primary function of this organization is to select a team to participate in the World Summer and Winter Games for the Deaf and the Pan American Games for the Deaf. In 1985, the Summer Games were held for the first time in the United States. The games were very successful with over 2,500 athletes from forty-two nations competing. Team sports consist of soccer, water polo, handball, volleyball, and basketball. The individual sports offered in the Summer Games include cycling, wrestling, swimming, track and field, tennis, table tennis, badminton, and shooting. Annual national tournaments are also held in basketball and softball. Participation in AAAD-sponsored events requires that the individual have a hearing loss of fifty-five decibels or greater in the better ear. There is only one classification, with all athletes with hearing impairments competing together. The organization of the AAAD is somewhat unique among sport organizations for athletes with disabilities because all of the management personnel are hearing impaired.

United States Cerebral Palsy Athletic Association (USCPAA)

Recognizing that athletes with cerebral palsy have movement characteristics different from other athletes with disabilities, the National Association of Sports for Cerebral Palsy was formed in the mid-1970s. The name of this organization was changed in 1987 to the United States Cerebral Palsy Athletic Association (USCPAA). USCPAA's purpose is to promote competitive sport programs and recreational opportunities for persons disabled from cerebral palsy, head trauma, and other conditions resulting from damage to the brain (McCole, 1993). Outstanding athletes from local, state, and regional levels are selected for the national team that represents the United States in international competition. International meets, currently involving more than a dozen nations, are held every two years in such places as Scotland, Holland, and Denmark. The United States was the host for the 1984 International Championships.

USCPAA events include a few team sports such as soccer, but the majority of activities involve dual competition. Currently sponsored events under USCPAA auspices include the following: ambulatory soccer team handball (formerly wheelchair soccer), boccie, archery, bowling, cycle racing, horseback riding, rifle shooting, swimming, table tennis, track and field, and weight lifting. Because of the unique needs of the athlete with cerebral palsy, special field events have been designed to be included with the track and field competition. Some of the events, such as the soft shot distance, precision soft shot, and distance soft shot, use a lighter implement such as a five-ounce bean bag to encourage athletes to compete while recognizing their strength limitations. Athletes who have limited use of their arms, Class 2 Lower, compete in two kicking events, distance kick and thrust kick. In the distance kick a thirteen-inch playground ball is used. For the thrust kick, a six-pound medicine ball is used.

The USCPAA has implemented an eight-category classification system that is sensitive to the participant's type of cerebral palsy, degree of involvement, and mode of ambulation (table 30.2). This system, which requires each athlete to complete a series of functional movement tasks, is used to equate for competition, thus allowing, in the USCPAA's opinion, *sport by ability—not by disability.* The USCPAA offers clinics to advise professionals in coaching techniques, classification of athletes, conduct of meets, and program finances.

Wheelchair Sports USA (formerly NWAA)

Wheelchair sports was founded in 1959 as the National Wheelchair Athletic Association (NWAA) and is the primary organization that promotes competitive sport experiences for amputees and individuals with spinal cord injuries. Wheelchair Sports, USA is the umbrella term for various wheelchair sports organizations including the national governing bodies for: American Wheelchair Archers, American Wheelchair Table Tennis, National Wheelchair Basketball Association, National Wheelchair Shooting Association (air weapons), U.S. Quad Rugby, U.S. Wheelchair Swimming, U.S. Wheelchair Weightlifting, and Wheelchair Athletics (track and field). The recent addition of the National Wheelchair Basketball Association and the name change from

Table 30.1 *Associations for athletes with disabilities**

American Athletic Association of the Deaf
3607 Washington Blvd #4
Ogden, UT 84403-1737
(801)546–2982

American Blind Bowling Association
150 North Bellaire
Louisville, KY 40206

American Hearing Impaired Hockey
Irvin G. Tianhnybik
1143 West Lake Street
Chicago, IL 60607

American Wheelchair Bowling Association
Walter A. Roy
3620 Tamarack Drive
Redding, CA 96003
(916) 243–2696
(916)244–6651 - fax

Amputee Soccer Association
Al Becker
25 North 14th Street #50
San Jose, CA 95112
(408) 293–2342

Amputee Sports Association
George Beckmann, Jr.
P.O. Box 60129
Savannah, GA 31420–0129

Canadian Wheelchair Sports Association
1600 James Naismith Drive
Gloucester Ontario, Canada K1B 5N4
(613) 748–5685
(613)748–5722 - fax

Comite International Des Sports Des Sourds
Jerald Jordan
Gallaudet College
Washington, DC 20002

Disabled Sportsmen of America, Inc.
P.O. Box 5496
Roanoke, VA 24021

Eastern Amputee Athletic Association
Jack Graff, President
Jim Coffey, Vice President
2080 Ennabrock Road
North Bellmore, NY 11710
(516) 826–8340

Handicapped Scuba Association
Jim Gatacre
1104 El Prado
San Clemente, CA 92672
(714) 498–6128

International Foundation for Wheelchair Tennis
Peter Burwash, International
2203 Timberloch Place, Suite 126
The Woodlands, TX 77380
(713) 363–4707

International Stoke Mandeville Games Federation
Stoke Mandeville Sports Stadium
Harvey Road
Alyesbury, Bucks HP 218PP

International Wheelchair Road Racers Club, Inc.
Joseph M. Dowling, President
30 Mayano Lane
Stamford, CT 06902
(203) 967–2231

National Beep Baseball Association
James Mastro
Director of Braille Sport Foundation
7525 North Street
St. Louis Park, MN 55426

National Association of Handicapped Outdoor Sportsmen, Inc.
P.O. Box 25
Carterville, IL 62918
(618) 985–3579

National Foundation of Wheelchair Tennis
Brad Parks, Director
940 Calle Amanecer, Suite B
San Clemente, CA 92670
(714) 361–6811

*These organizations can provide information about local, national, and international programs for athletes with disabilities.

National Wheelchair Athletic Association to Wheelchair Sports, USA will enhance the recognition of accomplishments of athletes who use wheelchairs in the general public (Long, 1993).

Due to the variety of sport offerings, each association classifies athletes according to the demands of the sport, medical evaluation, and in many cases how well the athlete performs the skill. For example, weight lifters are classified by age, gender, and body weight. Basketball has a three point system with class one athletes having the least physical function. Each basketball player is assigned a point value of either one, two, or three; however, the team may only use players whose combined point values do not exceed twelve points at one time. Similarly in quad rugby, seven classifications are possible starting with .5 and ending with 3.5, but the number of players actively participating may not exceed eight points for four players. Recent changes in classification have resulted in a separation of track (five levels) and field (nine levels) and the expansion of swimming classifications to twenty categories. Physical educators and coaches are encouraged to contact the national governing body for complete details about classification systems. Becoming involved in coaching, officiating or sponsoring meets is an excellent way to learn more about classification systems.

Quad Rugby is a fairly recent addition to the growing family of wheelchair sports. The game was designed specifically for athletes with cervical injuries and was formerly known as murderball. Rugby is played on a regulation basketball court, with four players on each side. The object is to score points by carrying the ball over the opponent's goal area on the endline. Players may advance the ball (regulation volleyball) by passing in any direction. Quick play is

Table 30.1—*Continued*

National Handicapped Sports and Recreation Association
Ron Hernley, President
Farragut Station
P.O. Box 33141
Washington, DC 20033
(301) 652–7505

National Wheelchair Athletic Association
Pat Karman, Chairperson
3617 Betty Drive, Suite S
Colorado Springs, CO 80907
(303) 597–8330

National Wheelchair Basketball Association
Stan Lebanowich
110 Seaton Building
University of Kentucky
Lexington, KY 40506
(606) 257–1623

National Wheelchair Softball Association
Jon Speake, Commissioner
P.O. Box 22487
Minneapolis, MN 55422
(612) 437–1792

North American Riding for the Handicapped Association
Leonard Warner, Executive Director
Box 100
Ashburn, VA 22011
(703) 471–1621 or
(703) 777–3540

Ski for Light, Inc.
1455 West Lake Street
Minneapolis, MN 55408

Special Olympics
Joseph P. Kennedy, Jr., Foundation
1350 New York Avenue, NW, Suite 500
Washington, DC 20005

United States Amputee Association
Richard Bryant
149 Abelle Forest Circle
Nashville, TN 37221
(615) 670–2323/2325

United States Cerebral Palsy Athletic Association, Inc.
Grant Peacock, President
34518 Warren Road, Suite 264
Westland, MI 48185
(313) 425–8961

United States Deaf Skiers Association, Inc.
Donald Fields
159 Davis Avenue
Hackensack, NJ 07601

United States Deaf Tennis Association, Inc.
Robbie Carmichael
3102 Lake Avenue
Cheverly, MD 20785

United States Deaf Softball Commissioner
John Miller
7111 Kempton Road
Lanham, MD 20801

United States Deaf Volleyball Commissioner
Bill Davidson
3019 Halsey Avenue
Arcadia, CA 91006

United States Quad Rugby Association
Tommie Willard
811 Northwestern Drive
Grand Forks, ND 58201
(701) 775–0790

United States Wheelchair Racquet-Sports Association
Chip Parmelly
1941 Viento Verano Drive
Diamond Bar, CA 91765
(714) 861–7312

United States Association for Blind Athletes
Dr. Roger Neppl, Executive Director
33 North Institute, Brown Hall
Colorado Springs, CO 80903

encouraged by a ten second rule that demands a pass or bouncing the ball within that time limit. The number of Quad Rugby teams and players more than tripled in the early 1990s, indicating this team sport responded to a previously unfulfilled need (Mikkelson, 1993).

Track has expanded the number of racing events to include every Olympic distance from 100 meters to 10,000 meters. While slalom is no longer an official event for adults, many junior meets offer this obstacle course event to display the unique skills of athletes who use wheelchairs. Weight lifting has two events, the bench press (chest, extended arms, chest) and the powerlifting press (extended arms, chest, extended arms). Each lifter is scored for the bench press, the powerlifting press, and the total of the two presses. Team scoring is now possible in weight lifting, and lifters of unequal body weights may be compared by using the Schwartz index.

Archery, table tennis, and shooting (air weapons), have fewer participants than the well-publicized wheelchair sports. Because many wheelchair athletes are fully integrated into schools and there are a number of athletes, grouping may not be easy. It may be necessary to practice alone, or in sports clubs with able-bodied participants to get ready for competition. For children, novice athletes, and those self-coached, a training camp or technique workshop is highly recommended. Kevin Hansen, who has coached many national and international record holders in wheelchair track and road racing, communicates to skilled athletes such as Craig Blanchette and Eric Neitzel long distance via phone, fax machine, and electronic mail.

Table 30.2 Sport classifications for persons with cerebral palsy

Class	Description
1	Uses motorized wheelchair because almost no functional use of upper extremities. Severe involvement in all four limbs, limited trunk control, has only 25% range of motion. Unable to grasp softball.
2	Propels chair with feet and/or very slowly with arms. Severe to moderate involvement in all four limbs. Uneven functional profile necessitating subclassifications as 2 Upper (2U) or 2 Lower (2L), with adjective denoting limbs having greater functional ability. Has approximately 40% range of motion. Severe control problems in accuracy tasks, generally more athetosis than spasticity.
3	Propels chair with short, choppy arm pushes but generates fairly good speed. Moderate involvement in three or four limbs and trunk. Has approximately 60% range of motion. Can take a few steps with assistive devices, but is not functionally ambulatory.
4	Propels chair with forceful, continuous arm pushes, demonstrating excellent functional ability for wheelchair sports. Involvement of lower limbs only. Good strength in trunk and upper extremities. Has approximately 70% range of motion. Minimal control problems.
5	Ambulates without wheelchair but typically uses assistive devices (crutches, canes, walkers). Moderate to severe spasticity of either (a) arm and leg on same side (hemiplegia) or (b) both lower limbs (paraplegia). Has approximately 80% range of motion.
6	Ambulates without assistive devices, but has obvious balance and coordination difficulties. Has more control problems and less range of motion in upper extremities than Classes 4 and 5. Moderate to severe involvement of three or four limbs, with approximately 70% range of motion in dominant arm.
7	Ambulates well, but with slight limp. Moderate to mild spasticity in (a) arm and leg on same side or (b) all four limbs with 90% of normal range of motion for quadriplegia and 90% to 100% of normal range of motion for dominant arm for hemiplegia.
8	Runs and jumps freely without noticeable limp. Demonstrates good balance and symmetric form in performance, but has obvious (although minimal) coordination problems. Has normal range of motion.

Adapted from: Sherrill, C. (1993). *Adapted physical education and recreation* (4th ed.). Dubuque, IA: William C. Brown Publishers.

United States Association for Blind Athletes (USABA)

In 1976 the USABA was formed to promote opportunities for athletes with visual impairments to participate in regional, national, and eventually international competition. The impetus for forming the USABA began in 1975 when the International Sports Organization for the Disabled (ISOD) announced that the 1976 Olympics for the Physically Disabled would for the first time include athletes wtih visual impairments. Plans were initiated for American participation through the formation of the United States Olympic Committee for the Blind. Through a process of trials and selections, twenty-seven athletes were sent to the 1976 event, the

Table 30.3 Sport classifications for USABA and IBSA

Classification	Description
B1	No light perception in either eye up to light perception and inability to recognize the shape of a hand in any direction and at any distance
B2	Ability to recognize the shape of a hand up to a visual acuity of 2/60 and/or a limitation of field of vision of 5°
B3	2/60 to 6/60 (20/200) vision and/or field of vision between 5° and 20°

first time that men and women with visual limitations from the United States participated in international competition.

Annual national championships have been held for athletes with visual impairments since 1977, when the first competition was conducted at Western Illinois University in Macomb, Illinois. In 1980, more than 500 athletes participated in the annual meet. Two downhill skiers went to the 1994 winter Paralympics at Lillehammer. Sanctioned sports include power and weight lifting, swimming, track and field, wrestling, goal ball, women's gymnastics, downhill and cross-country skiing, tandem cycling, and speed skating. Three classification categories have been established to permit equal competition of participants with similar visual disorders (table 30.3). There are no age limits for USABA participants.

The USABA, in an effort to reach as many athletes with visual impairments as possible, sponsors demonstration teams in sports activities in addition to its eleven fully sanctioned sports. The Carol Center in Massachusetts (617/969–6200) offers a full spectrum of water sports, including sailing.

Special Olympics

In 1968, the Joseph P. Kennedy, Jr., Foundation, with the guidance of Eunice Kennedy Shriver, founded the Special Olympics. This organization is designed to promote and conduct local, regional, national, and international sport experiences for athletes with mental retardation. Individuals eight years of age or older, with an intelligence quotient of less than seventy-five, are eligible to participate. Competition divisions adjusted for age and ability have been established. The official Special Olympics sports include aquatics, track and field, basketball, bowling, gymnastics, floor and poly hockey, figure and speed skating, alpine and cross country skiing, soccer, softball, and volleyball. The Special Olympics also offers clinics on demonstration sports including canoeing, cycling, equestrian sports, racquet sports, roller skating, and weight training. In an effort to reach individuals with mental retardation who are severe and profound, Special Olympics has established a Developmental Sports Skills program to train individuals with mental retardation with low motor abilities in sensorimotor and basic motor skills.

The Special Olympics has conducted international games since 1968. The movement has experienced tremendous growth. In 1968, one thousand participants from the United States were involved. Today, the Special Olympics programs encompass more than one million athletes from the U.S. and sixty other countries, and hundreds of thousands of volunteers and coaches worldwide (Songster, 1986).

The philosophy of Special Olympics supports the belief that striving is more important than success, and determination is more important than winning. The spirit that brings participants to the starting line is more important to the Joseph P. Kennedy, Jr., Foundation than the skill that carries Special Olympic athletes across the finish line.

United States Amputee Athletic Association (USAAA)

A small group of athletes with amputations founded the USAAA in 1981. This organization sponsored national competition annually for athletes with amputations in a variety of events including air pistol, archery, standing basketball, track and field events, sit-down and standing volleyball, swimming, table tennis, and weight lifting. International competition is available through the International Games for the Disabled and other sport-specific competition. The USAAA filed for bankruptcy in 1989, and the athletes are currently being served by Disabled Sports USA (DePauw and Gavron, 1995).

Athletes with amputations are classified according to their level and site of amputation (table 30.4). In swimming, competitions are offered for athletes in each of the classifications. In some sports such as track and field, the classifications are combined. In the field events, those who have bilateral amputations compete together in one class whether the amputation is above or below the elbow, and single-arm amputees comprise one class. In volleyball, a point system, similar in concept to that used by the National Wheelchair

Basketball Association, is enforced. Players are assigned one, two, three, or four points based on their A1 to A9 classification and their muscle strength as determined by certified testers. In competition, the players on the floor must total thirteen or more points.

The USAAA and now National Handicapped Sports have done an excellent job of responding to the needs and ability levels of the athletes. For many sports, athletes with lower limb amputations are permitted the option of using a wheelchair or competing from an ambulatory position. Some sports, such as volleyball, have both standing and sitting competitions. Athletes also may use prostheses and orthoses, depending upon the sport and their classification level.

Disabled Sports USA (DS/USA)

The Disabled Sports USA, founded in 1968, originally was known as the Amputee Skiers Association. As the organization grew and began to serve athletes with disabilities in addition to those with amputations, the name was changed to National Handicapped Sports and later Disabled Sports USA. DS/USA is different than other organizations that promote sport for athletes with disabilities in that it is sport-specific and not disability-specific. Although DS/USA's chapters promote year-round recreational activities and competitive sports, including water skiing and swimming, the organization's primary expertise is in conducting national competition in winter sport programs. For example, DS/USA is responsible for conducting the winter games for athletes with amputations. In addition, the association sponsors a traveling physical fitness team that gives presentations and demonstrations on health and physical fitness for individuals with disabilities. DS/USA now offers clinics and personal fitness trainer certifications for indivduals who wish to coach or provide fitness training for athletes with disabling conditions (Bauer, 1993).

Dwarf Athletic Association of America

The Dwarf Athletic Association of America (DAAA) was formed in 1985 and is now officially recognized by the United States Olympic Committee. The purpose of the DAAA is to develop, promote, and provide quality amateur athletic opportunities for dwarf athletes (less than 4' 10") in the United States. The DAAA sponsors events in track and field, basketball, boccie, powerlifting, swimming, skiing, table tennis, and volleyball. The National Dwarf Games in which athletes compete by age, gender, and functional ability are sponsored by the DAAA. Dwarf athletes can participate in the Paralympics and other international events.

Clinics, developmental events, and formal competitions at local and regional levels are offered by the DAAA. Athletes as young as 7 participate in activities which are used to encourage the enhancement of one's personal best. For children under 7, the DAAA offers wholesome programs that are non-competitive.

Table 30.4   *Nine general sport classifications for persons with amputations*

Class A1 = Double AK
Class A2 = Single AK
Class A3 = Double BK
Class A4 = Single BK
Class A5 = Double AE
Class A6 = Single AE
Class A7 = Double BE
Class A8 = Single BE
Class A9 = Combined lower plus upper limb amputations

Please note:
AK = Above or through the knee joint
BK = Below the knee, but through or above ankle joint
AE = Above or through the elbow joint
BE = Below the elbow, but through or above the wrist joint

Although the organizations discussed previously are the major promoters of sport for people with disabilities, several other associations concerned with sport for people with disabilities exist. No attempt will be made here to discuss all of these groups. Some, however, will be identified to illustrate the magnitude of interest now evident concerning sport opportunities for athletes with disabilities. It is hoped that this information will assist teachers to familiarize themselves, and in turn their students, with these associations.

Additional Sport Associations for Athletes with Disabling Conditions

In recent years, several new organizations promoting specific sport activities for athletes who use wheelchairs have been initiated. For instance, there is now a National Foundation for Wheelchair Tennis (NFWT). This organization sponsors programs for young as well as for older players. Wheelchair tennis is played like regular tennis, with the exception that the ball is permitted to bounce twice.

In response to a strong interest in marathon racing expressed by wheelchair athletes, an association known as the International Wheelchair Road Racers Club, Inc. (213/967–2231) was formed. The general public has been intrigued by the speed at which wheelchair athletes can cover a distance of 26.2 miles, surpassing the times the best marathoners have been able to run this distance. Outstanding performances have been achieved on flat courses as well as courses with hills and rough terrain. It is not unusual for marathon champions such as Jim Knaub to finish a marathon distance in an hour and twenty to an hour and thirty minutes, depending on the course. These efforts have dispelled many of the myths about the frail person who sits in a wheelchair.

For the individual desiring more information on wheelchair sports, the reader is referred to *Sports 'n Spokes,* a very informative periodical found in most university libraries.

Those interested in bowling for people with visual impairments should be aware of the American Blind Bowling Association (ABBA). This organization was formed in 1951 in New York and Philadelphia by a group of bowlers with visual limitations who believed that a national organization was necessary to help other persons with limited vision benefit from this sport. Today the ABBA is the official sanctioning organization for ten-pin bowlers and bowling leagues for athletes with visual impairments in the United States and Canada. An annual tournament is sponsored over the Memorial Day weekend by the ABBA. This tournament normally attracts more than a thousand participants. Competition is held in the five-person team event, doubles event, singles event, and the "all" event (teams are required to include some sighted participants). Cash prizes as well as trophies and medals are awarded to winners. Classification systems are based on the bowler's season average.

A very exciting sport for students with visual impairments is beep baseball. This program is sponsored by the National Beep Baseball Association (NBBA). As the game's name implies, the ball, a regulation 16½-inch-circumference softball, has been equipped with a beeping device. Although the NBBA is a relatively new organization, more than 100 teams from the United States and Canada participate in association-sanctioned regional and national tournaments.

The United States Les Autres Athletic Association has emerged to serve athletes with disabling conditions who have not previously had opportunities to participate and compete. USLAAA serves people with more than fifty disabling conditions associated with deficits in locomotion. Many of the athletes have been affected by muscular dystrophy, multiple sclerosis, or dysmelia and frequently use power wheelchairs. Athletes with Les Autres conditions compete in the full spectrum of summer Olympic events and use an integrated classification system which includes both seated and standing classifications, and takes factors such as strength, range of motion, and spasticity into account. This organization expects to become part of the U.S. Olympic group in the future (Stephenson, 1993).

Teachers also may find organizations within their states that promote or sponsor competition for children with various disabilities. In Oregon, for example, the Oregon Games for the Physically Limited are held annually. In addition to traditional track and field events, the Oregon Games incorporate creative events such as body bowling, obstacle courses, and Velcro darts to ensure that all participants, regardless of disability, have the opportunity to compete and strive to perform at the highest level possible (Dunn, 1987).

Classification Issues

Classification systems have long been used in sports for the nondisabled to promote fairness and equal competition. Boxing has weight classifications matching competitors by body size. Race directors for the ever-popular ten-kilometer road races divide the prize categories by gender, and then further by age. By comparing the age group statistics, each participant can estimate his or her race performance in relation to others of similar age and gender. In the interest of fair competition, it would seem appropriate for sports for people with disabilities to attempt to group competitors by performance similarities. There is little agreement, however, on the mode that should be used to classify participants. Some of the issues surrounding this controversy will be discussed in this section.

Medical Classifications

Medical models have long been used to determine which competitors will vie for medals within a certain class. It was thought that competitors with similar diagnoses would perform athletically in a comparable manner. Early attempts to classify athletes with disabilities were based on medical diagnosis. In sports for athletes with visual impairments, an unusually clear system has been used because the system for diagnosis can be quantified by objective measures. However, with classifications depending on subtle measurements such as muscle testing, dividing the competitors into equitable groups has been extremely difficult. Weiss and Curtis (1986) found that the winners of swimming events and track and field events did not reflect the membership of the Wheelchair Sports, USA (formerly NWAA). They found that certain disability groups were overrepresented compared to their respective percentage of the total membership. Ongoing research must be conducted to determine if classification systems are working as they are intended.

Functional Classifications

More recently organized sport groups such as the National Foundation for Wheelchair Tennis and Special Olympics have taken an approach that is modeled after sport organizations for the nondisabled. Competitors in wheelchair tennis and Special Olympics are grouped by gender, age and previous performances. The value of the functional model is not only its consistency with sport for the nondisabled but also its matching of competitors by sport performance rather than medical diagnosis.

Wheelchair basketball has recently expanded its classification systems to include functional tests and observations of the athlete during competition. Because the NWBA requires that teams be comprised of players of different medical diagnoses to ensure that players with more severe disabilities receive equitable playing time, the traditional medical classification system has been retained and is used in conjunction with the new functional and observation system.

Integrated Classifications

In the past, national governing bodies for each special sports group held autonomous sporting events. This has resulted in some races and events in which the number of competitors is extremely small. Some have suggested that promotion of sport for individuals with disabilities might be best served by combining the games into sports festivities serving more than one disability group. Advocates of integrated sport suggest that athletes, regardless of disability, be selected for heats and events based on previous performances. Therefore, one might see 100-meter races for athletes with visual impairments, developmental disabilities, and orthopedic impairments all competing in the same race. This approach may be welcomed in accuracy sports such as pistol, rifle, and archery, but rejected in sports with locomotor emphasis such as swimming and road racing. Close observation is needed to determine which approach best serves the needs of the athletes and is consistent with the wishes of the participants.

It should be noted that athletes may retain their sport specific classification at local and regional competitions but may be reclassified at national and international competitions. This reclassification may result in a different class within a familiar classification system or a completely unfamiliar classification in an integrated system. Event outcomes may change significantly because of athlete reclassification. Athletes accustomed to finishing near the top of their class may now finish near the bottom of their event. Adults can understand and accept this phenomenon, even though they are not happy about the results; however the effect on children is devastating. Wise coaches will counsel their athletes, particularly the ones new to national and international competition, that classification systems have their limitations and that further revisions are necessary.

Models to Engender Novice and Junior Athletes

Remaining an amateur athlete and earning a living pose numerous obstacles for all athletes, with and without disabilities. There seems to be an increasing discrepancy between entry-level athletes and elite (national and international contenders) in many sports for athletes with disabilities. While participation has increased among highly competitive athletes, there has been a decrease in the number of novice and recreational athletes. Because accumulating enough athletes to host a competition requires extensive travel, many events have been limited to wealthy or sponsored athletes. In addition, some events require specialized equipment that is expensive. It is not uncommon for elite track and field wheelchair athletes to own one racing wheelchair that meets the requirements for international events and one to meet the rules for events held in this country, as well as a wheelchair for everyday use. While some athletes can meet the demands for the latest equipment, many find their daily financial obligations prevent them from investing in sports equipment and meeting the associated costs of travel to national and international meets. Young athletes with disabilities and their families may find the costs prohibitive. Brookes and Cooper (1987) suggested divisions for novice athletes and increased local and regional competitions to foster greater participation. Some sports organizations have responded by offering novice and masters classes within each event. The result for recreational and entry-level athletes has been increased opportunity to participate.

The issue of sport classification systems is particularly critical for young athletes with disabilities. Many times it is necessary to travel a long distance or have a person qualified to classify athletes come to the school in order to determine a youngster's classification. School-sponsored sport programs for athletes with disabilities are few. Some have argued that full inclusion has resulted in students being dispersed among several schools, thus making it difficult, if not impossible, to organize a team of athletes with a specific disability. The numerous and often confusing classification systems have compounded the problem. School administrators recognize, however, that children with disabilities and their parents will press for a solution to this problem. One answer, of course, is cooperative planning among school districts and the fielding of teams that represent a large geographic area, such as a county. This may also require a rethinking of the present systems used to classify students with disabilities. The pooling of students and resources should lead to the formation of leagues and the development of a cadre of coaches, volunteers, and parents committed to serving the sport needs of children with disabilities.

Organizing Sport for the Participant with Disabilities

Extracurricular activities, including sport experiences, have long been recognized as an integral part of the educational process. Most public and private schools sponsor teams for boys and girls in a variety of sport activities. Only recently, however, has it become apparent that these same opportunities must be provided for students with disabilities. This right is guaranteed under the provisions of P.L. 94-142, The Education for All Handicapped Children Act of 1975, and P.L. 93-112, Section 504 of the Rehabilitation Act of 1973. Although both of these acts require generally the same action on the part of schools, Section 504 of the Rehabilitation Act is broader in coverage and includes not only education provisions but also employment, health, welfare, and other social service programs. Concerning the provisions for sport experiences, Section 504 states:

1. In providing physical education courses and athletics and similar programs and activities to any of its students a recipient to which this subpart applies may not discriminate on the basis of handicap. A recipient that offers physical education courses or that operates or sponsors interscholastic, club, or intramural athletics shall provide to qualified handicapped students an equal opportunity for participation in these activities.

2. A recipient may offer to handicapped students physical education and athletic activities that are separate or different from those offered to nonhandicapped students only if separation or differentiation is consistent with the requirements of 84.34 and only if no qualified handicapped student is denied the opportunity to compete for teams or to participate in courses that are not separate or different.

   The task of complying with this mandate causes confusion for many public schools. Therefore, in this section, information will be presented to help school personnel to respond to the sport needs of the student-athletes with disabling conditions.

Preparing the School and Community

The first, and perhaps most important, step in promoting sport for students with disabilities is to meet with school officials, parents, and students with disabilities to enlist their support. This is best accomplished by meeting initially with the Section 504 compliance officer, appointed by the school as required by law. During this meeting the school official can provide information about what has been accomplished and future plans concerning sport opportunities. Appointing a committee comprising parents, persons with disabilities, students, teachers, and administrators to address future plans related to the issue of sport experiences for students with disabilities is an excellent approach used by some schools. The responsibility of this group is to establish a foundation upon which a strong program can be built. Suggested ideas include the following:

1. Prepare a state-of-the-art paper that discusses the importance of sport for all and documents the existence of local school programs, if any, for individuals with disabilities.

2. Identify, with the assistance of the special education coordinator, all students with disabilities within the school system. A chart indicating the number of students, their ages, and their disabilities will be valuable in future planning.

3. Contact the state school athletic association and other school officials to determine if state efforts are now being made to address the sport needs of special students.

4. Communicate with community youth agencies such as the YMCA and YWCA to determine what, if any, programs are available for participants with disabilities.

5. Meet with the school board and key administrators to share the results of all information gathered and to encourage their assistance in promoting equal opportunities.

6. Promote a public awareness program for the community. Activities such as sponsoring a wheelchair basketball game between halves of the local high school game, inviting a well-known athlete to address a school assembly, and staging an event in which public officials play their sport with an imposed disability (playing golf blindfolded, for example) help to generate public support.

7. Write to national associations that promote sport for individuals with disabilities (table 30.1) and ask for films, materials, brochures, and suggestions for helping local schools to promote athletics for students with disabilities.

8. Encourage pay for qualified coaches of youth who provide their services to public school sport programs for youngsters with disabilities. If a physical educator or other qualified individual receives pay for coaching after school sports for nondisabled children, those who coach children with disabilities should receive a comparable stipend. While the coach who works with athletes who have disabilities may not have as many athletes or events as those who coach the nondisabled, they must individualize coaching techniques for each student, learn about special equipment and classification systems, raise money for equipment and travel, and perhaps learn specialized medical procedures. Coaching youth sports has never been for individuals seeking money, but those who coach athletes with disabilities provide no less valuable a human service that those who coach the nondisabled.

9. At school sports banquets or assemblies, recognize athletes with disabilities by showing a slide or two, or a brief video of the athlete in action and a summary of the youngster's accomplishments. If ribbons, medals, and trophies are awarded, insist that all athletes receive comparable recognition.

The primary objective of the committee is to objectively document the sport experiences presently available for individuals with disabilities, recommend improvements where necessary, and communicate this information effectively to the community, thus building a broad base of support for future programs.

Responding to Individual Needs

The educational needs of students with disabilities are so diverse that programs must be individually developed for each student. As discussed in chapter 5, responding to unique learning needs requires the development of Individualized Education Programs (IEPs). The process used to develop the IEP also should be employed to respond to the student with a disability's right to participate in extracurricular activities, including sport experiences. Using the IEP mechanism ensures that this important aspect of the student's educational program will not be overlooked. In addition, the involvement of parents and school personnel on the IEP team, as required by law, plus other invited individuals such as therapists and physicians, enhances the probability of identifying sport programs and placement options appropriate for the student.

The IEP team is charged with the responsibility of insisting that the unique needs of students with disabilities are recognized. Achieving this objective as it relates to equal sport experiences requires team members who are willing to challenge some old assumptions about the nature of sport and its relevance for all students. Some of the more frequently discussed issues will be presented here.

Separate or Integrated Sport

The first consideration in identifying appropriate sport activities for the student with a disabling condition is to analyze the regular sport program. In athletics, for instance, it is not at all unusual for individuals with disabilities to participate fully in regular competition. Therefore, the first consideration is the student's possible participation in the regular program. If after careful study, this placement seems inappropriate, even after minor adjustments have been suggested in equipment, rules, facilities, or some other area, efforts should then be directed toward identifying a special sport program. How this may be accomplished for the small school that has a limited special education population will be discussed later.

Academic Standing

Participation in interscholastic athletics normally requires that a student maintain a minimum grade point average. Although it is certainly desirable to encourage athletes to maintain high academic standards, this rule, if administered inflexibly, discriminates against some students with disabilities. For instance, is it realistic to expect the student with mental retardation, who may possess excellent sport skills, to achieve the desired grade point average? A more equitable basis for determining eligibility might be to monitor the student's progress toward meeting the goals and objectives identified in the student's Individualized Education Program (IEP).

This example reinforces the principle that the law mandates equal opportunity, not equal treatment. Requiring that students with disabilities meet the same grade point average required of nondisabled students may be equal treatment, but it obviously denies equal opportunity. Examples of this same principle also will be seen in the next two sections, which discuss medical and age restrictions.

Medical Implications

A student may not be eliminated from participation in an interscholastic team due solely to a medical disability. To exclude a student on the basis of a disability violates the student's basic constitutional guarantee of due process under Section 504. For example, in the past many students who have lost one of a paired organ, such as an eye or a kidney, have been automatically denied eligibility. Although in some cases this may be a wise and prudent decision, this example illustrates that categorical decisions do not allow for the recognition of individual needs. Important decisions such as these can best be made by the combined wisdom and expertise of the student's IEP team.

Fortunately, the National Federation of State High School Association already has proposed a number of rule changes to facilitate the participation of students with disabilities. In football, for example, rules were changed to allow athletes with prosthetic devices, such as artificial arms, hands, and legs, to compete. This is a significant change that will lead to further rule examinations and the elimination of rules restrictive to the student with special needs.

Age Restrictions

State athletic associations usually impose age restrictions on participants. This rule is designed to protect athletes from unfair competition as well as from potential danger due to size and weight inequities. Although this is certainly a logical rule, it does discriminate against students who have been developmentally delayed due to illness, injury, or congenital birth defects. In such cases it would be more appropriate to consider the individual's developmental level rather than chronological age. Any decision of this nature is, of course, best made by the student's IEP team.

Definitive answers to the various issues that arise concerning the student's participation in sport are not possible. Each athlete with a disability is a unique individual with needs that may not be easily accommodated within the existing state, league, and school athletic codes. Policies, however, that categorically discriminate against individuals with disabilities are no longer acceptable. The student's IEP team is an effective mechanism that can be employed to resolve issues concerning the student's eligibility for athletic participation.

Identifying Special Sport Programs

Educational programs, including extracurricular activities such as athletics, must be provided for students with disabilities in the least restrictive environment. Separate or special programs can be offered only if the student's needs require such a program. Although the primary attempt should be to accommodate the need of an athlete with a disability in regular sport activities, this is not always possible. For instance, some students have such severe disabilities that efforts to participate in the regular athletic program could be detrimental to their physical and mental health. In situations where a special sport program is necessary, the school must respond to this need.

Schools in which few students with disabilities are found can offer special sport programs through a variety of options. Some schools have elected to sponsor regional sport teams. For example, few schools have sufficient populations to field a wheelchair basketball team. Other educational units, however, such as county or district programs, could be used for purposes of designating a regional team. Competition would, therefore, be scheduled in the traditional manner, with cooperating schools sharing program expenses. Several states have recently formed athletic associations to coordinate activities such as this.

Schools also may coordinate special sport programs through community agencies. In some cities, recreation departments have developed comprehensive programs for individuals with disabilities, including competitive sport activities. Other organizations such as YMCAs and YWCAs also can be contacted to assess their present offerings and future plans concerning organized sport for individuals with disabilities. Identifying other agencies to provide special sport experiences does not absolve the school of its responsibility for monitoring the program and evaluating the effectiveness of the services provided. Schools also must be willing to financially assist community organizations when they provide services to public school students.

Selecting and Training Coaches

The selection and training of coaches is certainly one of the most important aspects of a good sport program. In addition to the skills required of all good coach-educators—knowledge of the activity, basic understanding of child development and motor development principles, and recognition of good health and safety practices—the coach of the special athlete should possess some additional expertise. Some of these specialized skills will be discussed in the following sections.

Knowledge of Disabilities

Essentially, all that is required here is that the coach have a basic understanding of the nature of the disability, including some practical information about possible causes and characteristics, and the implications of these for the student's health. For instance, it is important that coaches working with children with Down syndrome realize that congenital heart problems are quite frequent with this population. Discussion with the student's family physician can lead to the development of a program that is safe yet challenging.

Figure 30.2 Many individuals with disabilities, such as Harry James, former tennis coach of the University of Utah, have served as successful coaches.

Regardless of the student's disability, the focus of the program should be centered on developing the student's ability, not analyzing the disability. A very practical exercise for the novice coach is to have the individual list all of the ways in which a student with a disability is like a nondisabled student. Completion of this task will help the coach to quickly realize that the special student has many strengths and that the athlete with a disability needs empathy, not sympathy.

Appreciation of Skill Level

Nondisabled individuals frequently have difficulty appreciating the skill with which athletes with disabilities perform various sport skills. Prospective coaches of athletes with disabilities should take time to experience sport in ways as similar as possible to those with disabling conditions. For instance, many individuals are surprised to learn that shooting a basketball from a wheelchair is quite different from the procedure to which they are most accustomed, or playing volleyball with cotton in their ears is an experience unlike the noisy environment in which they usually have performed. In a contest between nondisabled javelin throwers and those who had spinal paralysis, Guttman (1976) determined that the nondisabled throwers could not project the javelin as far from a seated position as could the trained javelin throwers who had paralysis.

This study illustrates two major points: (1) training for sport performance is specific (one becomes good at tasks one practices), and (2) athletes with disabilities develop through training some musculature and skill proficiency that is unique to them. Some performers with disabilities may never equal the records of their nondisabled peers. This, however, does not negate the relative merit of their effort. Coaches of the athletes with disabilities should recognize and reinforce good performance and help others to appreciate the quality of the athlete's achievement.

Develop Specialized Skills

Coaches who work with athletes who have disabling conditions may also need to learn some special skills. Those coaching the deaf, for instance, should master some of the basic signs used in communicating with people who have hearing losses. Fortunately, many of the signs necessary for communication in the sport setting can be quickly learned because the signed gesture is frequently a demonstration of the sport skill. Examples of some of the signs unique to sport may be found in chapter 12.

Athletes with visual impairments will require a coach who is sensitive to their special needs. For instance, students with visual impairments will require some assistance when they are first introduced to a new environment. The coach also must remember and remind others not to carelessly leave equipment lying around, creating a potentially harmful situation for the student with limited vision. Printed materials such as player handbooks should be available in Braille or audio tape for students who need this assistance. Many of these suggestions are common-sense principles that the enthusiastic coach can easily learn. Specialists, too, such as special educators, speech therapists, and mobility instructors, are available in many schools to help fellow educators respond to the needs of students with disabilities.

Knowledge of Sport Adaptation

Sport for individuals with disabilities requires coaches who are knowledgeable about sport activities and who have the talent to modify these activities, enabling athletes with disabilities to compete successfully. For example, the athlete with cerebral palsy who wants to participate in team soccer, a sport recognized by the United States Cerebral Palsy Athletic Association, must be taught the basics of soccer and the adaptations necessary so that these movement skills can be used efficiently. A thorough understanding of anatomy, physiology, biomechanics, and motor learning is necessary for all coaches, particularly those who work with students who have orthopedic and neurologic impairments. Guttmann's textbook of *Sport for the Disabled* is an excellent reference for the coach who needs additional information about scientifically oriented sport adaptations. A review of chapters 21, 22, 23, and 24 of this text will provide the reader with many examples of methods used to adapt sport for individuals with disabilities.

In addition to knowledge regarding the adaptation of sport activities, the coach also should be thoroughly familiar with the various classifications used in sport for individuals with disabilities. Table 30.5 contains an example of the classification system used by the United States Cerebral Palsy Athletic Assocation. Each of the various sport associations discussed in this chapter has similar systems. Copies of these and the complete rules used by each association may be obtained by writing to the organizations identified in table 30.1.

Facility Accessibility

Many of the challenges associated with physical disabilities are not due to an individual's specific impairment but are

---

Table 30.5 *USCPAA sport classifications*

Class 1 = Motorized Chair
Class 2 = Athetosis; 2L or 2U
Class 3 = Moderate Triplegic or Quadriplegic
Class 4 = Diplegic
Class 5 = Assistive Devices
Class 6 = Athetosis, Ambulatory
Class 7 = Hemiplegic
Class 8 = Minimal Involvement

more accurately attributed to the poorly designed and inaccessible environment in which people with disabilities must work, live, and play. Developing sport skills to high levels of proficiency is less frustrating for some athletes with disabling conditions than attempting to find an accessible building in which the skills may be practiced. Fortunately, federal legislation now requires public agencies, including schools, to survey their facilities and modify buildings that contain programs that cannot be moved to sites more available to students with disabilities. Faced with the reality that transferring athletic programs to alternate sites is difficult and the building of new facilities too expensive to be practical, school officials recognize the necessity of renovating gymnasiums, locker rooms, and training areas. An undertaking of this magnitude requires close cooperation among school administrators, consumers, advocates for persons with disabilities, and architects. Individuals with disabilities should be consulted throughout the remodeling period and asked to try out certain design features to assess their usefulness.

It is beyond the scope of this discussion to cover the kinds of designs, construction, or alteration of facilities that must be accomplished to conform with federal statute. Indicated in appendix VII, however, are some of the items that schools must consider when making athletic facilities accessible. This same survey can be used as a guide for analyzing the accessibility of schools that athletes with disabilities will visit. Complete information containing technical specifications may be obtained by writing the American National Standards Institute, Inc., 1430 Broadway, New York, NY 10018.

Financial Considerations

One of the major problems facing educators today is the task of sufficient funds to cover the many school programs necessary. This is particularly true in athletics, where the impact of Title IX has increased the number of female participants without substantially increasing the funds allocated for athletic programs. Responding to the rights of students with disabilities for equitable sport opportunities also will add to the challenges of an already drained athletic budget. Students with disabilities, however, should not be expected or asked to accept services less than those provided to their nondisabled classmates. The explanation that there are no funds is not a sufficient response. A more acceptable solution, and one that is consistent with the recommendation of Section 504, is to reallocate funds so that *all* students share equally in publicly supported programs. This means that in all budget areas, such as travel, coaching salaries, and equipment, sports for students with disabilities will share equally in the funds budgeted for athletics. This does not mean that athletes with disabilities will receive everything they request

or that they should be exempt from participating in special fund-raising drives. All that the athlete with a disability expects is an equal opportunity.

What follows are some suggestions school administrators may want to explore to generate additional funds for use in support of sport programs for students with disabilities.

1. Public Law 101-476, Individuals with Disabilities Education Act, provides funds to local school systems to assist in the education of students with special needs. These are discretionary funds that can be used by local schools to provide for the educational needs of students with disabilities. Because Public Law 101-476 recognizes sport programs as services that should be available, federal funds could be earmarked for programs for athletes with disabilities.

2. Many private foundations allocate funds annually to public agencies who serve individuals with disabilities. Due to the recent emphasis on "full" services to those with disabilities, the area of sport programs would appear to be worthy of funding. A school's written plan on sport for students with disabilities could lead to fruitful negotiations with a foundation interested in sponsoring a model program.

3. Local business and industrial leaders may find a request to contribute to athletic programs for students with disabilities a new and innovative approach worthy of a contribution. Some company employees with technical backgrounds may desire to volunteer their skills in the design of special equipment.

4. Sponsorship of a basketball game between two experienced wheelchair teams is a good way to generate funds and educate the public about sport programs for students with disablities.

5. Local organizations that advocate for people with disabilities, such as the Association for Retarded Citizens and United Cerebral Palsy Association, might contribute money to a special fund-raising drive for the expansion of sport experiences for those who are disabled.

These suggestions offer some viable solutions for funding a sport program for students with disabilities. Attempts to secure appropriate funds will be a challenge, but if an effort is made to develop a program that emphasizes the fun in participating and competing and deemphasizes expensive uniforms, equipment, and excessive travel expenses, the overall costs can be managed. A healthy attitude by administrators and teachers toward students with disabilities and their sport opportunities is the most important ingredient in a sport program for those with disabilities. Given this variable, a means of funding the program will be found.

Summary

Opportunities for young people with disabilities to participate in sport programs have increased dramatically in recent years. Parents, professionals, and individuals with disabilities all have become more cognizant of the numerous benefits that can be gained through competitive sport. Sport is good therapy; it promotes health and fitness; and most importantly it provides athletes with disabling conditions an opportunity to demonstrate in a visible way that they are capable of training and participating in vigorous activity. Participation in sport helps the athlete and others to recognize that disability is not synonymous with "no ability." Sport also encourages normalization. Children with disabilities understand that sport is an integral part of the fabric of American society.

It is impossible for some athletes with disabilities to integrate by participating with nondisabled players on a "regular" team. Others, however, will find it more reinforcing to compete against children with similar disabilities. Fortunately, there are a number of sport organizations that conduct local, regional, and national meets and help to promote sport opportunities for people with disabilities. Some of these organizations—American Athletic Association of the Deaf, United States Cerebral Palsy Athletic Association, Wheelchair Sports USA, United States Association for Blind Athletes, Special Olympics, Dwarf Athletic Association of America, and the Disabled Sports USA—are members of the United States Olympic Committee. These associations promote national and international competition and serve as valuable resources for information concerning sport for specific disability populations.

Although the sport movement for people with disablities has made significant strides, questions have been raised regarding the procedures used to classify athletes. Some organizations rely primarily on a medical form of classification, while others have adopted a philosophy of classifying athletes on the basis of their performance. Some have extended this philosophy to argue that athletes should not be classified by disability but rather by their performance level. Proponents of this system would have individuals with various disabilities competing in the same race or event. This sensitive issue will continue to receive considerable attention. Federal legislation, P.L. 101-476 and P.L. 93-112, emphasizes the right of students with disabilities to participate in sport programs. Unfortunately, most school districts have not taken this mandate seriously. Some have argued that because their school has too few children with disabilities it is not possible nor financially feasible for them to field a team. Efforts must be undertaken to educate community and school leaders about their responsibility to provide equitable sport programs for individuals with disabilities and to help them identify alternative ways of providing the programs. Creative administrators and empathetic teachers can do much to ensure that children and youth with disabilities are not deprived of the opportunity to participate in sport programs. Given the success of adult athletes with disabilities, such as George Murray's sub-four-minute mile (1985) in a wheelchair, Craig Blanchette's 1993 world record of 3:31, and the notoriety associated with their performances, it is logical that more and more children and youth with disabilities will be inspired to participate in sport (Ball, 1993). As the number of athletes with disabilities increases, individuals with and without disabilities will recognize that "It's ability, not disability, that counts."

Selected Readings

Adams, R.C., & McCubbin, J.A. (1991). *Games, sports, and exercises for the physically disabled* (4th ed.). Philadelphia: Lea and Febiger.

Anderson, L. (Ed.). (1987). *Handbook for adapted competitive swimming.* Colorado Springs, CO: United States Swimming Association.

Ball, M., Athlete (personal communication, December 29, 1993).

Bauer, K., National Handicapped Sports (personal communication, December 23, 1993).

Brookes, P., & Cooper, R. (1987). Plan for equalizing track competition. *Sports 'n Spokes, 13*(3), 13–14.

Bundschuh, E.L. (1979). *Interpreting Public Law 94-142 and Section 504 of the Rehabilitation Act as it relates to athletic participation.* Paper presented at the annual meeting of the National Council of Secondary School Athletic Directors.

Cooper, R.A. (1990). Wheelchair racing sports science: A review. *Journal of Rehabilitation Research and Development, 27*(3), 295–312.

Cooper, R.A., & Bedi, J.F. (1992). An analysis of classification for top 10 finishers in prominent wheelchair road races. *Palaestra, 8*(4), 36–41.

Coutts, K.D., & Schutz, R.W. (1988). Analysis of wheelchair track performances. *Medicine and Science in Sports and Exercise, 20* (2), 188–194.

Curtis, K. (1989). International functional classification systems. *National Wheelchair Athletic Association Newsletter,* Fall, 7–8.

DePauw, K.P., & Clarke, K.S. (1986). Sports for disabled U.S. citizens: Influence of amateur sports act. In C. Sherrill (Ed.), *Sport and disabled athletes* (pp. 41–50). Champaign, IL: Human Kinetics Publishers.

DePauw, K.P., & Gavron, S.J. (1995). Disability and Sport. Champaign, IL: Human Kinetics Publishers.

Dunn, J.M. (1981). History of sport for the disabled. In *Proceedings: National Association for Physical Education in Higher Education* (pp. 158–167). Champaign, IL: Human Kinetics Publisher.

Dunn, J.M. (1987). Sports for disabled children. In V. Seefeldt (Ed.), *Handbook for youth sports coaches* (pp. 311–335). Reston, VA: American Alliance for Health, Physical Education, Recreation, and Dance.

Dunn, J.M., & Sherrill, C. (1996). Movement for individuals with disabilities. *Quest* (In print).

Guttmann, L. (1976). *Textbook of sport for the disabled.* Bucks, England: HM & M Publishers.

Guttmann, L. (1979). The importance of sport and recreation for the physically disabled. In A.S. Leon & G. Amundson (Eds.), *First international conference on lifestyles and health* (pp. 45–52). Minneapolis: University of Minnesota.

Higgs, C., Babstock, P., Buck, J., Parsons, C., & Brewer, J. (1990). Wheelchair classifications for track and field events: A performance approach. *Adapted Physical Activity Quarterly, 7*(1), 22–40.

Howell, R. (1978). History of physical education and sport and the disabled. In J. Hall & J. Stiehl (Eds.), *National Infuse Symposium proceedings* (pp. 37–46). Boulder, CO: University of Colorado.

Jones, J.A. (Ed.). (1988). *Training guide to cerebral palsy sports* (3d ed.). Champaign, IL: Human Kinetics Publishers.

Lindstrom, H. (1986). Sports classification for locomotor disabilities: Integrated versus diagnostic systems. In C. Sherrill (Ed.), *Sport and disabled athletes* (pp. 131–136). Champaign, IL: Human Kinetics Publishers.

Long, P., Executive director, Wheelchair Sports USA (personal communication, December 22, 1993).

Lucas, M., United States Association for Blind Athletes (personal communication, December 29, 1993).

McCole, J., Executive director, Disabled Sport Organization of North Texas, USCPAA affiliate (personal communication, December 26, 1993).

Mikkelson, B., Athlete and president, U.S. Quad Rugby Association (personal communication, December 23, 1993).

Sherrill, C. (1986). Social and psychological dimensions of sports for disabled athletes. In C. Sherrill (Ed.), *Sport and disabled athletes* (pp. 21–33). Champaign, IL: Human Kinetics Publishers.

Sherrill, C., Adams-Mushett, C., & Jones, J. (1986). Classification and other issues in sports for blind, cerebral palsied, les autres, and amputee athletes. In C. Sherill (Ed.), *Sport and disabled athletes* (pp. 113–130). Champaign, IL: Human Kinetics Publishers.

Songster, T.B. (1986). The Special Olympics sport program: An international sport program for mentally retarded athletes. In C. Sherrill (Ed.), *Sport and disabled athletes* (pp. 73–79). Champaign, IL: Human Kinetics Publishers.

Squires, J. (1987). Classification—Can the best means to the fairest end be found? *Palaestra, 3*(4), 45–46, 48.

Stephenson, D., Athlete and volunteer, U.S. Les Autres Athletic Association (personal communication, December 28, 1993).

Stohkendl, H. (1986). The new classification system for wheelchair basketball. In C. Sherrill (Ed.), *Sport and disabled athletes* (pp. 101–112). Champaign, IL: Human Kinetics Publishers.

United States Association for Blind Athletes. (1981). *Athletic handbook.* Beach Haven Park, NJ: Author.

Weiss, M., & Curtis, K.A. (1986). Controversies in medical classification of wheelchair athletes. In C. Sherrill (Ed.), *Sport and disabled athletes* (pp. 93–100). Champaign, IL: Human Kinetics Publishers.

Winnick, J.P., & Short, F.X. (Eds.). (1981). *Special athletic opportunities for individuals with handicapping conditions.* Brockport, NY: State University College of New York at Brockport.

Enhancing Activities

1. Organize a group of nondisabled peers and challenge a group of wheelchair athletes to a wheelchair basketball game.

2. Volunteer to participate as a coach or manager of a youth sport team for individuals with disabilities.

3. Write to one or more of the sport organizations identified in table 30.1 and request information concerning the organization including its purpose, membership criteria, and services available to athletes and coaches.

4. Review the athletic program offered by a local high school. Document the number of students with disabilities participating in the program. Recommend strategies for increasing the sport opportunities for students with disabilities, such as types of sports to be offered, integrated and segregated considerations, and possibilities for coordinating with other school districts.

5. Interview an athlete with a disability. Obtain information regarding the athlete's reason for participating in sport and his or her perceptions concerning the importance of sport in the athlete's life.

6. Observe an athletic event sponsored by one of the sport organizations for athletes with disabilities. Write a summary of your impressions of the event. How was the event similar and/or different than that provided for nondisabled athletes?

7. Review the classification systems used by the various sport organizations for athletes with disabilities. Engage in a debate with your peers as to which system seems to be best and why.

Physical Education for Individuals with Disabilities: Organizations and Related Associations

Adapted Physical Education Academy, c/o American Alliance for Health, Physical Education, Recreation, and Dance, 1900 Association Drive, Reston, VA 22091.

Adapted Sports Association, Inc., Communications Center, 6832 Marlette Road, Marlette, MI 48453.

Alexander Graham Bell Association for the Deaf, 3417 Volta Place NW, Washington, DC 20007.

The Allergy Foundation of America, 801 Second Avenue, New York, NY 10017.

American Alliance for Health, Physical Education, Recreation and Dance, 1900 Association Drive, Reston, VA 22091.

American Anorexia Nervosa Association, 133 Cedar Lane, Teaneck, NJ 07666.

American Association on Mental Deficiency, 5101 Wisconsin Avenue NW, Washington, DC 20016.

American Bar Association Center on Children and the Law, 1800 M St. NW, Suite 300, Washington, DC 20036.

American Blind Bowling Association, 150 N. Bellaire Avenue, Louisville, KY 40206.

American Brittle Bone Society, 1415 E. Marlton Pike, Cherry Hill, NJ 08077.

American Cancer Society, 777 Third Avenue, New York, NY 10017.

American College of Sports Medicine, P.O. Box 1440, Indianapolis, IN 46206.

American Corrective Therapy Association, c/o Kirk Hodges, P.O. Box 485, Boerne, TX 78006.

American Dance Therapy Association, 2000 Century Plaza, Suite 230, Columbia, MD 21044.

American Diabetes Association, Two Park Avenue, New York, NY 10016.

American Foundation for the Blind, 15 W. 16th Street, New York, NY 10011.

American Heart Association, 7320 Greenville Avenue, Dallas, TX 75231.

American Lung Association, 1740 Broadway, New York, NY 10019.

American Medical Association, 535 N. Dearborn Street, Chicago, IL 60610.

American Occupational Therapy Association, 600 Executive Boulevard, Rockville, MD 20582.

American Orthotic and Prosthetic Association, 717 Pendleton Street, Alexandria, VA 22314.

American Physical Therapy Association, 1111 N. Fairfax Street, Alexandria, Virginia 22314.

American Printing House for the Blind, P.O. Box 6085, 1839 Frankfort Avenue, Louisville, KY 40206.

American Psychiatric Association, 1700 18th Street NW, Washington, DC 20009.

American Psychological Association, 1200 17th Street NW, Washington, DC 20036.

American Red Cross, 17th and D Streets NW, Washington, DC 20006.

American Rheumatism Association, Arthritis Foundation, 3400 Peachtree Road NE, Atlanta, GA 30326.

American Schizophrenia Association, Huxley Institute, 1114 first Avenue, New York, NY 10021.

American Speech and Hearing Association, 10801 Rockville Pike, Rockville, MD 20852.

American Therapeutic Recreation Association, P.O. Box 15215, Hattiesburg, MS 39404-5215.

Arthritis Foundation, 1212 Avenue of the Americas, New York, NY 10036.

Association for Children and Adults with Learning Disabilities, 4156 Library Road, Pittsburgh, PA 15234.

Association for Education of the Visually Handicapped, 919 Walnut Street, Fourth Floor, Philadelphia, PA 19107.

Association for Mentally Ill Children, 12 W. 12th Street, New York, NY 10003.

Association for Retarded Citizens, 500 E. Border St., Arlington, TX 76011.

Association for the Aid of Crippled Children, 345 E. 46th Street, New York, NY 10017.

The Association for Persons with Severe Handicaps, 7010 Roosevelt Way NE, Seattle, WA 98115.

Asthma and Allergy Foundation of America, 19 W. 44th Street, New York, NY 10036.

Boys Scouts of America, Scouting for the Handicapped Division, P.O. Box 61030, Dallas/Ft. Worth Airport, TX 75261.

Braille Sport Foundation, 730 Hennepin Avenue S., Suite 301, Minneapolis, MN 55403.

Breckenridge Outdoor Education Center, Programs for Handicapped, P.O. Box 61067, Sacramento, CA 95860.

Canadian Amputee Sports Association, 18 Hale Drive, Georgetown, Ontario, Canada L7G4C2.

Captioned Films for the Deaf Distribution Center, 5034 Wisconsin Avenue NW, Washington, DC 20016.

Center on Human Policy, Syracuse University, 200 Huntington Hall, Syracuse, NY 13244–2340.

Center for Sickle Cell Disease, 2121 Georgia Avenue NW, Washington, DC 20059.

Children's Defense Fund, 122 C. St., NW, Washington, DC 20001.

Clearinghouse on the Handicapped, Office of Special Education and Rehabilitative Services, Room 3106, Switzer Building, Washington, DC 20202.

Coalition on Sexuality and Disability, Inc., 122 E. 23rd St., New York, NY 10010.

Council for Exceptional Children, 1920 Association Drive, Reston, VA 22091.

Cystic Fibrosis Foundation, 6000 Executive Boulevard, Suite 309, Rockville, MD 20852.

Down Syndrome Congress, Central Office, 1640 Rossevelt Road, Chicago, IL 60608.

Education for the Handicapped Law Report, 747 Dresher Road, Box 980, Horsham, PA 19044–0980.

Epilepsy Foundation of America, 1828 L Street NW, Suite 406, Washington, DC 20036.

The Exceptional Parent, 1170 Commonwealth Ave., Boston, MA 02134–4645.

Foundation for Exceptional Children, 1920 Association Drive, Reston, VA 22091.

Friedreich's Ataxia Group in America, P.O. Box 11116, Oakland, CA 94611.

Girl Scouts of the U.S.A., Scouting for the Handicapped Girl Program, 830 Third Avenue and 51st Street, New York, NY 10022.

Goodwill Industries of America, 9200 Wisconsin Avenue, Washington, DC 20014.

Healthy People 2000, U.S. Government Printing Office, Superintendent of Documents, Mail Stop SSOP, Washington, DC 20402–9328 DHHS Pub. No. (PHS) 91-50213.

Hemophilia Research, 30 Broad Street, New York, NY 10004.

Joseph P. Kennedy, Jr., Foundation, 1350 New York Avenue NW, Suite 500, Washington, DC 20005.

Juvenile Diabetes Foundation, 23 E. 26th Street, New York, NY 10010.

Kids on the Block, 1712 Eye Street NW, Suite 1008, Washington, DC 20006.

Leukemia Society of America, 800 Second Avenue, New York, NY 10017.

Little People of America, P.O. Box 633, San Bruno, CA 93901.

March of Dimes Birth Defects Foundation, Division of Health Information and School Relations, 1275 Mararoneck Avenue, White Plains, NY 10605.

Mental Health Law Project, 2021 L St., NW, Suite 800, Washington, DC 20036.

Muscular Dystrophy Association, 810 Seventh Avenue, New York, NY 10019.

National Association for Music Therapy, Box 610, Lawrence, KS 66044.

National Association for Visually Handicapped, 305 E. 24th Street, New York, NY 10010.

National Association of Developmental Disabilities Councils, 1234 Massachusetts Ave., NW, Suite 103, Washington, DC 20005.

National Association of State Directors of Special Education, 1201 16th Street NW, Suite 610 E, Washington, DC 20036.

National Association of the Deaf, 810 Thayer Avenue, Silver Spring, MD 20910.

National Association of the Physically Handicapped, 76 Elm Street, London, OH 43140.

National Beep Baseball Foundation, 512 Eighth Avenue NE, Minneapolis, MN 55413.

National Center for a Barrier Free Environment, 1140 Connecticut Avenue NW, Washington, DC 20036.

National Center for Law and the Handicapped, P.O. Box 477, University of Notre Dame, Notre Dame, IN 46556.

National Committee, Arts for the Handicapped, 1701 K Street NW, Suite 905, Washington, DC 20006.

National Consortium on Physical Education and Recreation for Individuals with Disabilities, Seton Hall, University of Kentucky, Lexington, KY 40506.

National Easter Seal Society, 2023 W. Ogden Avenue, Chicago, IL 60612.

National Federation of the Blind, 1800 Johnson Street, Baltimore, MD 21230.

National Foundation for Asthmatic Children, 5601 West Trails End Road, P.O. Box 5114, Tucson, AZ 85703.

National Foundation for Neuromuscular Diseases, 250 W. 57th Street, New York, NY 10019.

National Hemophilia Foundation, 19 W. 34th Street, New York, NY 10018.

National Information Center for Children and Youth with Disabilities (NICHCY), P.O. Box 1492, Washington, DC 20013.

National Kidney Foundation, Two Park Place, New York, NY 10016.

National Mental Health Association, 1800 N. Kent Street, Rosslyn, NY 22209.

National Multiple Sclerosis Society, 205 E. 42d Street, New York, NY 10017.

National Organization on Disability, 910 16th St., NW, Suite 600, Washington, DC 20006.

National Parent Network on Disabilities, 1600 Prince St., Suite 115, Alexandria, VA 22314.

National Rehabilitation Association, 1522 K Street NW, Washington, DC 20004.

National Society for Children and Adults with Autism, 1234 Massachusetts Avenue NW, Suite 1017, Washington, DC 20005.

National Society to Prevent Blindness, 79 Madison Avenue, New York, NY 10016.

National Spinal Cord Injury Foundation, 369 Elliot Street, Newton Upper Falls, MA 02164.

National Strength and Coaches Association, P.O. Box 38909, Colorado Springs, CO 80939.

National Therapeutic Recreation Society, 2775 S. Quincy St., Suite 300, Arlington, VA 22206.

Office of Special Education, 400 Maryland Avenue SW, Donahoe Building, Washington, DC 20202.

Osteogenesis Imperfecta Foundation, P.O. Box 428, Van Wert, OH 45891.

Paralyzed Veterans of America, 4330 East-West Highway, Suite 300, Washington, DC 20014.

Parents Campaign for Handicapped Children and Youth, Closer Look, Box 1492, Washington, DC 20013.

Parkinson's Disease Foundation, William Black Medical Research Building, 640 W. 168th Street, New York, NY 10032.

People-to-People Committee for the Handicapped, 1522 K Street NW, 1130, Washington, DC 20005.

Prader-Willi Syndrome Association, 5515 Malibs Drive, Edina, MN 55436.

President's Committee on Employment of the Handicapped, 1111 20th Street NW, Washington, DC 20036.

President's Committee on Mental Retardation, Regional Office Building #3, 7th and D Streets SW, Room 2614, Washington, DC 20201.

Rehabilitation International, 432 Park Avenue S, New York, NY 10016.

Spina Bifida Association of America, 343 S. Dearborn Avenue, Suite 319, Chicago, IL 60604.

Team of Advocates for Special Kids (TASK), 100 W. Cerritos Ave., Anaheim, CA 92805.

Telephone Pioneers of America, Beep Ball Information, 195 Broadway, New York, NY 10017.

United Cerebral Palsy Association, 66 E. 34th Street, New York, NY 10016.

United States Department of Education, Office of Special Education and Rehabilitative Services, 400 Maryland Avenue SW, Washington, DC 20202.

U.S. Congress Directory, Capitol Enquiry, Inc., 1228 N Street, Suite 10, Sacramento, CA 95814.

Volta Bureau, 1537 35th Street NW, Washington, DC 20007.

Sports Associations

Access to Sailing, 19744 Beach Boulevard, Suite 340, Huntington Beach, CA 92648.

American Canoe Association, 7432 Alban Station Boulevard, Suite B-226, Springfield, VA 22150.

American Sledge Hockey Association, 10933 Johnson Avenue, So., Bloomington, MN 55437.

American Water Ski Association, Disabled Ski Committee, Adaptive Aquatics, Inc., P.O. Box 7, Morven, GA 31638.

American Wheelchair Archers, 5318 Northport Drive, Brooklyn Center, MN 55429.

American Wheelchair Bowling Association, 3620 Tamarack Drive, Redding, CA 96003.

American Wheelchair Table Tennis Association, 23 Parker Street, Port Chester, NY 10573.

Amputee Sports Association, P.O. Box 60412, Savannah, GA 31420–0412.

Aqua Sports Association for the Physically Challenged, 830 Broadway, Suite 10, El Cajon, CA 92021.

Archery Sports Section, Sister Kenny Institute, 800 E. 28th at Chicago Avenue, Minneapolis, MN 55407.

Association of Disabled American Golfers, 7700 E. Arahoe Road, Suite 350, Englewood, CO 80112.

Canadian Wheelchair Basketball Association, 1600 James Naismith Drive, Gloucester, Ontario K1B 5N4, Canada.

Disabled Sportsmen of America, Inc., P.O. Box 5496, Roanoke, VA 24012.

Eastern Amputee Athletic Association, 2080 Ennabrock Road, North Bellmore, NY 11710.

Freedom's Wings International, 1832 Lake Avenue, Scotch Plains, NJ 07076.

Handicapped Scuba Association, 1104 El Prado, San Clemente, CA 92672.

International Foundation for Wheelchair Tennis, 2203 Timberloch Place, Suite 126, The Woodlands, TX 77380.

International Wheelchair Aviators, 1117 Rising Hill, Escondido, CA 92029.

International Wheelchair Road Racers Club, Inc., 30 Myano Lane, Stamford, CT 06902.

International Wheelchair Tennis Federation, Palliser Road, Barons Court, London W14 9EN, England.

MUSCLES (Michigan United Sports Chair League Endurance Series), 18964 Whitby, Livonia, MI 48152.

National Amputee Golf Association, P.O. Box 1228, Amherst, NH 03031.

National Amputee Summer Sports Association, Ltd., 215 W. 92nd Street, Suite 15A, New York, NY 10025.

National Association of Handicapped Outdoor Sportsmen, Inc., RR. 6, Box 33, Centralia, IL 62801.

National Foundation of Wheelchair Tennis, 940 Calle Amanecer, Suite B, San Clemente, CA 92672.

National Handicap Motorcyclist Association, 315 West 21st Street, Suite 5B, New York, NY 10011.

National Handicapped Sports, 451 Hungerford Drive, Suite 100, Rockville, MD 20850.

National Ocean Access Project, P.O. Box 33141, Farragut Station, Washington, DC 20033–0141.

National Wheelchair Athletic Association, 3617 Betty Drive, Suite S, Colorado Springs, CO 80907.

National Wheelchair Basketball Association, 110 Seaton Building, University of Kentucky, Lexington, KY 40506.

National Wheelchair Billiards Association, 325 Hickory Drive, Cleveland, OH 44017.

National Wheelchair Racquetball Association, 2380 McGinley Road, Monroeville, PA 15146.

National Wheelchair Softball Association, 1616 Todd Court, Hastings, MN 55033.

National Wheelchair Shooting Federation, 102 Park Avenue, Rockledge, PA 19046.

National Wheelchair Softball Association, P.O. Box 22478, Minneapolis, MN 55422.

North American Riding for the Handicapped Association, P.O. Box 33150, Denver, CO 80233.

Physically Challenged Swimmers of America, 22 William Street, #255, South Glastonbury, CT 06073.

POINT (Paraplegics On Independent Nature Trips), 4144 N. Central Expressway, Suite 515, Dallas, TX 75204.

Power Soccer, Bay Area Outreach & Recreation Program (BORP), 830 Bancroft Way, Berkeley, CA 94710.

Sailing for Freedom Foundation, 512 30th Street, Newport Beach, CA 92663.

Ski for Light, Inc., 1400 Carole Lane, Green Bay, WI 54313.

Special Olympics, Joseph P. Kennedy, Jr., Foundation, 1350 New York Avenue NW, Suite 500, Washington, DC 20036.

United States Amputee Athletic Association, 149-A Belle Forest Circle, Nashville, TN 37221.

United States Association for Blind Athletes, 55 W. California Avenue, Beach Haven Park, NJ 08008.

United States Cerebral Palsy Athletic Association, Inc., 3810 W. Northeast Highway, Suite 205, Dallas, TX 75330.

United States Disabled Ski Team, P.O. Box 100, Park City, UT 84060.

United States Organization for Disabled Athletes, 16 Westfield Circle, Danville, CA 94526.

United States Quad Rugby Association, 1605 Mathews Street, Fort Collins, CO 80525.

United States Rowing Association, 201 South Capitol Avenue, Suite 400, Indianapolis, IN 46225.

United States Wheelchair Racquet-Sports Association, 1941 Viento Verano Drive, Diamond Bar, CA 91765.

United States Wheelchair Swimming, 229 Miller Street, Middleboro, MA 02346.

United States Wheelchair Weightlifting Federation, 39 Michael Place, Levittown, PA 19057.

Wheelchair Athletics of the U.S.A., 30 Myano Lane, Stamford, CT 06902.

Wheelchair Motorcycle Association, 101 Torrey Street, Brockton, MA 02401.

Wheelchair Sports, U.S.A., 3595 E. Fountain Boulevard Suite L-1, Colorado Springs, CO 80910.

Selected Sources of Information about Physical Education for Individuals with Disabilities

Selected sources for identifying information about physical education for students with disabilities are presented here to assist college and university students to complete class assignments and to broaden their background in the rapidly expanding field of special physical education.

Periodicals

Ability, U.S. Amputee Athletic Association, P.O. Box 5311, Mission Hills, CA 91345.

Able Bodies, American Alliance for Health, Physical Education, Recreation and Dance, 1900 Association Drive, Reston, VA 22091.

Academic Therapy, 20 Commercial Boulevard, Novato, CA 94947.

Accent on Living, P.O. Box 700, Gillum Road and High Drive, Bloomington, IL 61701.

APAQ, (Adapted Physical Activity Quarterly), Human Kinetics, Box 5076, Champaign, IL 61820.

American Annals of the Deaf, Convention of American Instructors of the Deaf, 814 Thayer Avenue, Silver Spring, MD 20910.

American Corrective Therapy Journal, 4910 Bayou Vista, Houston, TX 77091.

American Journal of Mental Deficiency, American Association on Mental Deficiency, 5101 Connecticut Avenue, Washington, DC 20016.

American Journal of Occupational Therapy, American Occupational Therapy Association, 6000 Executive Boulevard, Suite 200, Rockville, MD 20852.

American Journal of Orthopsychiatry, American Orthopsychiatric Association, 1775 Broadway, New York, NY 10019.

American Journal of Physical Medicine, Williams and Wilkins Company, 428 E. Preston Street, Baltimore, MD 21202.

American Journal of Psychology, University of Illinois Press, 54 E. Gregory, Box 5081, Station A, Champaign, IL 61820.

American Rehabilitation, U.S. Superintendent of Documents, U.S. Government Printing Office, Washington, DC 20402.

American Review of Respiratory Disease, American Thoracic Society, 1740 Broadway, New York, NY 10019.

Amicus, National Center for Law and the Handicapped, P.O. Box 477, University of Notre Dame, Notre Dame, IN 46556.

Annals of Allergy, American College of Allergists, 2117 W. River Road N., Minneapolis, MN 55411.

Archives of Environmental Health, Heldref Publications, 4000 Albemarle Street NW, Washington, DC 20016.

Arthritis and Rheumatism, American Rheumatism Association, 3400 Peachtree Road NE, Atlanta, GA 30326.

Behavioral Disorders, Council for Exceptional Children, CCBD Division, 1920 Association Drive, Reston, VA 22091.

Bulletin on Rheumatic Diseases, Arthritis Foundation, 3400 Peachtree Road NE, Atlanta, GA 30326.

Clinical Notes on Respiratory Diseases, American Thoracic Society, 1740 Broadway, New York, NY 10019.

Deaf American, 814 Thayer Avenue, Silver Spring, MD 20910.

Diabetes in the News, Ames Division, Miles Laboratories, Inc., Box 70, Elkhart, IN 46515.

Education and Training of the Mentally Retarded Child, Council for Exceptional Children, 1920 Association Drive, Reston, VA 22091.

Education of the Visually Handicapped, Association for the Education of the Visually Handicapped, 919 Walnut Street, Philadelphia, PA 19107.

Exceptional Children, Council for Exceptional Children, 1920 Association Drive, Reston, VA 22091.

Exceptional Education Quarterly, Aspen Systems Corporation, 1600 Research Boulevard, Rockville, MD 20850.

Exceptional Parent, P.O. Box 641, Penacook, NJ 03301.

The Exceptional Parent, 605 Commonwealth Avenue, Boston, MA 02215.

Journal of Allergy and Clinical Immunology, C. V. Mosby Company, 11830 Westline Industrial Drive, St. Louis, MO 63141.

Journal of Applied Behavior Analysis, Department of Human Development, University of Kansas, Lawrence, KS 66045.

The Journal of the Association for Persons with Severe Handicaps, 7010 Roosevelt Way NE, Seattle, WA 98115.

Journal of Auditory Research, C. W. Shilling Auditory Research Center, Inc., Box N, Groton, CT 06340.

Journal of Learning Disabilities, 101 E. Ontario Street, Chicago, IL 60611.

Journal of Physical Education and Recreation, American Alliance for Health, Physical Education, Recreation, and Dance, 1900 Association Drive, Reston, VA 22091.

Journal of Rehabilitation, National Rehabilitation Association, 633 S. Washington Street, Alexandria, VA 22314.

Journal of Special Education, Grune & Stratton, Inc., 111 Fifth Avenue, New York, NY 10003.

Journal of Special Educators of the Mentally Retarded, Box 171, Center Conway, NH 03813.

Journal of Speech and Hearing Research, American Speech-Language-Hearing Association, 10801 Rockville Pike, Rockville, MD 20852.

Journal of Visual Impairment and Blindness, American Foundation for the Blind, Inc., 15 W. 16th Street, New York, NY 10011.

Learning Disability Quarterly, The Division for Children With Learning Disabilities (DCLD), Council for Exceptional Children, 1920 Association Drive, Reston, VA 22091.

Mental Retardation, Superintendent of Documents, U.S. Government Printing Office, Washington, DC 20402.

New Outlook for the Blind, American Foundation for the Blind, 15 W. 16th Street, New York, NY 10011.

NWAA (National Wheelchair Athletic Association), 2107 Templeton Gap Road, Suite C, Colorado Springs, CO 80907.

Palaestra, Challenge Publications, LTD, P.O. Box 508, Macomb, IL 61455.

Paraplegia News, 5201 N. 19th Avenue, Suite 108, Phoenix, AZ 85015.

Pediatrics, American Academy of Pediatrics, Box 1034, Evanston, IL 60204.

Perceptual and Motor Skills, Box 9229, Missoula, MT 59807.

The Physical Educator, 9030 Log Run Drive N, Indianapolis, IN 46234.

Physical Therapy, American Physical Therapy Association, 1156 15th Street NW, Washington, DC 20005.

Physician and Sports Medicine, McGraw-Hill Publications Co., 1221 Avenue of the Americas, New York, NY 10020.

Psychoanalytic Quarterly, State Department of Mental Hygiene, Hudson River Psychiatric Center, Poughkeepsie, NY 12601.

Rehabilitation Literature, National Easter Seal Society, 2023 W. Ogden Avenue, Chicago, IL 60612.

Research Quarterly for Exercise and Sport, American Alliance for Health, Physical Education Recreation, and Dance, 1900 Association Drive, Reston, VA 22091.

Schizophrenia Bulletin, Schizophrenia Center, National Institute of Mental Health. For sale by: Superintendent of Documents, U.S. Government Printing Office, Washington, DC 20402.

Sight-Saving Review, National Society to Prevent Blindness, 79 Madison Avenue, New York, NY 10016.

Sportsline, National Association of Sports for Cerebral Palsy, UCP, Inc., 66 E. 34th Street, New York, NY 10016.

Sports 'n Spokes, 5201 N. 19th Avenue, Suite 111, Phoenix, AZ 85015.

Teacher Education and Special Education, Council for Exceptional Children, 1920 Association Drive, Reston, VA 22091.

Teaching Exceptional Children, Council for Exceptional Children, 1920 Association Drive, Reston, VA 22091.

Therapeutic Recreation Journal, National Recreation and Park Association, 1601 N. Kent Street, Arlington, VA 22209.

USABA Newsletter (United States Association for Blind Athletes), Jim Duffield, Managing Editor, R.D. #3, Box 495, Felton, DE 19943.

Volta Review, Alexander Graham Bell Association for the Deaf, 3417 Volta Place NW, Washington, DC 20007.

Young Children, National Association for the Education of Young Children, 1834 Connecticut Avenue NW, Washington, DC 20009.

Indexes and Abstracts

American Doctoral Dissertations. University Microfilms. Complete listing of all doctoral dissertations accepted by United States and Canadian Universities. Author/title listing only; no abstracts given.

Child Development Abstracts and Bibliography. University of Chicago Press. A comprehensive reference source containing abstracts of articles that deal with all aspects of the study of children.

Completed Research in Health, Physical Education, and Recreation. American Alliance for Health, Physical Education, Recreation, and Dance. A compilation of titles and abstracts of theses and dissertations written by graduate students in universities throughout the United States.

Cumulated Index Medicus. Bethsda, MD, National Library of Medicine. Complete listing of reference material related to science, medicine, and unique topics related to disabled populations.

Dissertation Abstracts International. University Microfilms. Compilation of abstracts of doctoral dissertations submitted by cooperating universities.

Education Index. H. W. Wilson Company. Subject index to the major education periodicals. The basic source for location of periodical literature in education.

Educational Resources Information Center (ERIC). Exceptional Child Education Resources. Council for Exceptional Children. Contains abstracts of books, journals, dissertations, and nonprint media dealing with the education of exceptional children.

Medical Literature Analysis and Retrieval System (MEDLARS), a computer-based information network sponsored by the National Library of Medicine in Bethesda, Maryland. Many university libraries can conduct Medline searches, using the computer to identify articles in more than 2,300 worldwide biomedicine journals.

National Institute of Education. A nationwide network for acquiring educational research reports and related documents. Of greatest interest to the special physical educator is the *ERIC Clearinghouse on Handicapped and Gifted Children,* operated by the Council for Exceptional Children.

Physical Education Index. Ben Oak Publishing Company. A subject index to domestic and foreign periodicals that are published in English and relate to Dance, Health, Physical Education, Physical Therapy, Recreation, Sports, and Sports Medicine.

Physical Education/Sports Index. Marathon Press. Quarterly subject index to approximately one hundred journals covering all aspects of physical education.

Physical Fitness/Sports Medicine. President's Council on Physical Education and Sports. Contains citations from more than two thousand selected periodicals including foreign language periodicals that print English abstracts of the articles they publish.

Psychological Abstracts. American Psychological Association. A compilation of abstracts of the world's scientific literature in psychology and related disciplines.

Resources in Education. U.S. Office of Education. Before 1975 called *Research in Education.* Index to publications available through ERIC (Educational Resources Information Center).

Media

Educator's Guide to Free Films, Audio and Visual Material, and Filmstrips. Educators Progress Service, Inc., Randolph, WI. Three separate documents (films, audio and visual materials, and filmstrips) are published annually identifying material that may be obtained free for educational purposes.

National Information Center for Educational Media (NICEM). University of Southern California. An index to 16-mm educational films that contains a directory of publishers and distributors of 16-mm films for all subject areas including special education and physical education.

Other Sources

Clearinghouse on the Handicapped, Office of Special Education and Rehabilitative Services, Washington, DC 20202. This organization, established by the Rehabilitation Act of 1973, is a resource information office designed to answer questions regarding legislation, publications, or programs affecting individuals with disabilities.

The Council for Exceptional Children, Information Services, 1920 Association Drive, Reston, VA 22091. The CEC Information services acts as an information broker for teachers, administrators, students, families, and others bibliographies on topics of current interest and nonprint media available on a variety of topics.

International Association of Parents of the Deaf, 814 Thayer Avenue, Silver Springs, MD 20910. This group acts as a clearinghouse for the exchange of information among family members or persons who are deaf. Information about deafness and raising deaf children, including the deaf-blind, is provided to all inquirers.

International Institute for Visually Impaired, 0-7, Inc., 1975 Rutgers Circle, East Lansing, MI 48824. This organization is a clearinghouse for those concerned with the early development and education of visually handicapped preschool children and with the education of their families.

Let's Play to Grow, Joseph P. Kennedy, Jr., Foundation, 1350 New York Avenue, N.W., Suite 500, Washington, DC 20006–4709. This program is dedicated to bringing the delights of play and shared experiences into the lives of individuals with developmental disabilities, their families, and friends.

National Information Center for Handicapped Children and Youth, 1555 Wilson Boulevard, Suite 600, Rosslyn, VA 22209. Sponsored by the U.S. Department of Education, the center collects and shares information and ideas that are helpful to handicapped children and youth. The center answers questions, links people with others who share common concerns, sponsors workshops, and publishes a newsletter.

Parent Network, 1301 E. 38th Street, Indianapolis, IN 46205. Parent Network is a national coalition of individuals and organizations dedicated to providing a linkage across the country to all those serving individuals with special needs.

Parents' Campaign for Handicapped Children and Youth, 1201 16th Street NW, Washington, DC 20036. The Parents' Campaign for Handicapped Children and Youth works to help parents understand their child's needs, locate appropriate services, obtain their rights, and work with professionals to bring about change. The Parent's Campaign provides technical assistance to groups planning information and referral services for handicapped children and youth, as well as training programs for parents in a variety of areas.

Fait Physical Fitness Test for Mildly and Moderately Mentally Retarded Students*

25 Yard Run (Measures the speed of running short distances). The subject places either foot against the wall (or block) with the foot parallel to it. He or she then takes a semicrouch position with the hands resting lightly on the knees. The forward foot and trunk are turned in the direction to be run. The head is held up so that the subject is looking toward the finish line. At the command of "Ready: go!" the subject begins the run. The watch is started on the "Go" and is stopped as the subject passes the finish line. However, the subject is directed to run to a second line, which is about five feet beyond the finish line, to prevent slowing down during the approach to the true finish line. The time of the run is recorded to the nearest one-tenth of a second.

Bent Arm Hang (Measures static muscular endurance of the arm and shoulder girdle). A horizontal bar or doorway bar may be used for this test. A stool approximately twelve inches high is placed under the bar. The subject steps onto the stool and takes hold of the bar with both hands, using a reverse grip (palms toward the face). The hands are shoulders' width apart. The subject brings his or her head to the bar, presses the bridge of the nose to the bar, and steps off the stool. This position is held as long as possible. The timer starts the watch as the subject's nose presses to the bar and the body weight is taken on the arms. The watch is stopped when the subject drops away from the bar. The tester should be ready to catch the subject in the event of a fall. The number of seconds the subject holds the position is recorded on the score card.

Leg Lift (Measures dynamic muscular endurance of the flexor muscles of the leg and of the abdominal muscles). The subject lies flat on the back with hands clasped behind the neck. A helper should hold the subject's elbows to the mat. The subject raises his or her legs, keeping the knees straight until the legs are at a ninety-degree angle. Another helper, who stands to the side of the subject, extends one hand over the subject's abdomen at the height of the ankles when the legs are fully lifted. This serves as a guide to the

*Test development financed by the Joseph P. Kennedy, Jr., Foundation.

subject in achieving the desired angle and encourages the subject to keep the legs straight. He or she should be instructed to touch the shins against the helper's arm. The subject is to do as many leg lifts as possible in the twenty-second time limit. The test begins on the command of "Go" and ceases on the command of "Stop." The score is the number of leg lifts performed during the twenty seconds.

Static Balance Test (Measures ability to maintain balance on one leg). The subject places hands on hips, lifts one leg, and places the foot on the inside of the knee of the other leg. The subject then closes his or her eyes and maintains balance in this position as long as possible. The watch is started the moment the eyes close. As soon as the subject loses balance, the watch is stopped. The score is the number of seconds to the nearest one-tenth of a second.

Thrusts (Measures the specific type of agility that is measured by the squat thrust or Burpee). The subject takes a squatting position with the feet and hands flat on the floor. The knees should make contact with the arms. At the command "Go," the stopwatch is started. The subject takes the weight upon the hands so that he or she may thrust the legs straight out behind. The legs are returned to the original position. The score is the number of complete thrusts the subject is able to perform in twenty seconds. One-half point is awarded for completing half of the thrust.

300 Yard Run-Walk (Measures cardiorespiratory endurance). If the run is to be given outside on a track, it can be administered to large numbers at one time by placing the runners in one long straight row or in two rows with one behind the other. In taking a starting position, the runners should place one foot comfortably ahead of the other. A semicrouch position with the hands resting lightly on the knees is taken. At the command to go, the stopwatch is started. The subjects run the prescribed course. They are allowed to walk part of the distance if they are unable to run the total distance. As each runner crosses the finish line, the timer calls off the time to a recorder who makes a check beside the corresponding time on a prepared sheet. As the timer continues to call off the times as the runners pass the finish line, the recorder goes down the line of times and checks the times called. If two runners cross the line at the same time, two checks are placed beside the appropriate time on the sheet. As the runners finish, they line up according to the order in which they finished. One person will be needed to help the runners stay in correct order. When the runners are all in line, the name of the runner and the time it took to complete the race can be matched and placed on the score card by comparing the order of runners to the order of times as they appear on the sheet.

A score card for comparison of the results of the test items is presented in a table that appears in appendix IV.

Score Card for Fait Physical Fitness Test for Mildly and Moderately Mentally Retarded Students

25 Yard Run

Boys
(Score in Seconds)

		Trainable			Educable	
Age	Low	Av.	Good	Low	Av.	Good
9–12	7	6	5.2	6.2	5.2	4.4
13–16	6.5	5.5	4.7	5.4	4.7	4.2
17–20	6	5	4.2	5.1	4.4	3.9

Girls

9–12	7.4	6.3	5.3	5.8	5.4	5.2
13–16	6.7	5.6	4.7	6.1	5.2	4.3
17–20	7.3	6.1	5.1	6.4	5.4	4.7

Bent Arm Hang

Boys
(Score in Seconds)

		Trainable			Educable	
Age	Low	Av.	Good	Low	Av.	Good
9–12	2	10	16	3	19	33
13–16	11.2	22	30.2	5	25	43
17–20	23	23	31	8	30	50

			Girls			
9–12	2	8	12	3	9	13
13–16	4	14	22	5	15	23
17–20	3	9	13	4	12	18

Leg Lift   **Boys**

		Trainable			*Educable*	
Age	*Low*	*Av.*	*Good*	*Low*	*Av.*	*Good*
9–12	6	9	12	7	10	13
13–16	6	9	12	8	11	14
17–20	7	10	13	8	11	14
			Girls			
9–12	6	10	14	6	10	14
13–16	7	11	15	7	11	15
17–20	6	10	14	6	10	14

Static Balance   **Boys**
                                                 (Scores in Seconds)

		Trainable			*Educable*	
Age	*Low*	*Av.*	*Good*	*Low*	*Av.*	*Good*
9–12	3	4.4	5.8	4	5	6
13–16	3.1	4.5	5.9	5	6	7
17–20	3.2	4.6	6	5	10	15
			Girls			
9–12	2.2	3.2	4.2	2.5	3.5	4.5
13–16	5.1	6.1	7.1	8.6	9.6	10.6
17–20	4.9	5.9	6.9	5.2	6.2	7.2

Thrust   **Boys**

		Trainable			*Educable*	
Age	*Low*	*Av.*	*Good*	*Low*	*Av.*	*Good*
9–12	4	8	10	6	12	14
13–16	4	8	10	8	14	16
17–20	5	9	11	8	14	16
			Girls			
9–12	4	8	10	5	9	11
13–16	4	8	10	8	12	14
17–20	5	9	11	5	9	11

300 Yard Run-Walk   **Boys**
                                            (Score in Seconds)

		Trainable			*Educable*	
Age	*Low*	*Av.*	*Good*	*Low*	*Av.*	*Good*
9–12	145	115	95	105	80	60
13–16	111	86	66	95	75	55
17–20	104	79	59	74	59	39
			Girls			
9–12	198	148	108	143	113	83
13–16	158	108	65	125	91	61
17–20	159	107	66	142	102	71

APPENDIX

V

Calorie Expenditure
per Minute for
Selected Exercises*

Calorie expenditure per minute for various activities

	Body Weight																					
	90	99	108	117	125	134	143	152	161	170	178	187	196	205	213	222	231	240	249	257	266	275
Archery	3.1	3.4	3.7	4.0	4.5	4.6	4.9	5.2	5.5	5.8	6.1	6.4	6.7	7.0	7.3	7.6	7.9	8.2	8.5	8.8	9.1	9.4
Badminton (recreation)	3.4	3.8	4.1	4.4	4.8	5.1	5.4	5.6	6.1	6.4	6.8	7.1	7.4	7.8	8.1	8.3	8.8	9.1	9.4	9.8	10.1	10.4
Badminton (competition)	5.9	6.4	7.0	7.6	8.1	8.7	9.3	9.9	10.4	11.0	11.6	12.1	12.7	13.3	13.9	14.4	15.0	15.6	16.1	16.7	17.3	17.9
Baseball (player)	2.8	3.1	3.4	3.6	3.9	4.2	4.5	4.7	5.0	5.3	5.5	5.8	6.1	6.4	6.6	6.9	7.2	7.5	7.7	8.0	8.3	8.6
Baseball (pitcher)	3.5	3.9	4.3	4.6	5.0	5.3	5.7	6.0	6.4	6.7	7.1	7.4	7.8	8.1	8.5	8.8	9.2	9.5	9.9	10.2	10.6	10.9
Basketball (half-court)	2.5	3.3	3.5	3.8	4.1	4.4	4.7	4.9	5.3	5.6	5.9	6.2	6.4	6.7	7.0	7.3	7.5	7.6	8.2	8.5	8.8	9.0
Basketball (moderate)	4.2	4.6	5.0	5.5	5.9	6.3	6.7	7.1	7.5	7.9	8.3	8.8	9.2	9.6	10.0	10.4	10.8	11.2	11.6	12.1	12.5	12.9
Basketball (competition)	5.9	6.5	7.1	7.7	8.2	8.8	9.4	10.0	10.6	11.1	11.7	12.3	12.9	13.5	14.0	14.6	15.0	15.2	16.3	16.9	17.5	18.1
Bicycling (level 5.5 mph)	3.0	3.3	3.6	3.9	4.2	4.5	4.8	5.1	5.4	5.6	5.9	6.2	6.5	6.8	7.1	7.4	7.7	8.0	8.3	8.6	8.9	9.2
Bicycling (level 13 mph)	6.4	7.1	7.7	8.3	8.9	9.6	10.2	10.8	11.4	12.1	12.7	13.4	14.0	14.6	15.2	15.9	16.5	17.1	17.8	18.4	19.0	19.6
Bowling (nonstop)	4.0	4.4	4.8	5.2	5.6	5.9	6.3	6.7	7.1	7.5	7.9	8.3	8.7	9.1	9.5	9.8	10.2	10.6	11.0	11.4	11.8	12.2

*Reprinted with permission from Allsen, P.E., Harrison, J.M., & Vance, B. (1980). *Fitness for life* (2d ed.). Dubuque, IA: Wm. C. Brown Publishers. The values reported are based on the work of Consolazio, F.C., Johnson, R.E., & Pecora, L.J. (1963). *Physiological measurements of metabolic functions in man.* New York: McGraw-Hill Book Co. Research completed at the Human Performance Laboratory, Brigham Young University, Provo, UT.

									Body Weight												
	90	**99**	**108**	**117**	**125**	**134**	**143**	**152**	**161**	**170**	**178**	**187**	**196**	**205**	**213**	**222**	**231**	**240**	**249**	**257**	**266**	**275**
Boxing (sparring)	3.0	3.3	3.6	3.9	4.2	4.5	4.8	5.1	5.4	5.6	5.9	6.2	6.5	6.8	7.1	7.4	7.7	8.0	8.3	8.6	8.9	9.2
Calisthenics	3.0	3.3	3.6	3.9	4.2	4.5	4.8	5.1	5.4	5.6	5.9	6.2	6.5	6.8	7.1	7.4	7.7	8.0	8.3	8.6	8.9	9.2
Canoeing (2.5 mph)	1.8	1.9	2.0	2.2	2.3	2.5	2.7	3.0	3.2	3.4	3.6	3.7	3.9	4.1	4.7	4.4	4.6	4.8	5.0	5.1	5.3	5.5
Canoeing (4.0 mph)	4.2	4.6	5.0	5.5	5.9	6.3	6.7	7.1	7.5	7.9	8.3	8.7	9.2	9.4	10.0	10.5	10.8	11.2	11.6	12.0	12.4	12.9
Dance, modern (moderate)	2.5	2.8	3.0	3.2	3.5	3.7	4.0	4.2	4.5	4.7	5.0	5.2	5.4	5.7	5.9	6.2	6.4	6.7	6.9	7.2	7.4	7.6
Dance, modern (vigorous)	3.4	3.7	4.1	4.4	4.7	5.1	5.4	5.7	6.1	6.4	6.7	7.1	7.4	7.7	8.1	8.4	8.7	9.1	9.4	9.7	10.1	10.4
Dance, fox trot	2.7	2.9	3.2	3.4	3.7	4.0	4.2	4.5	4.7	5.0	5.3	5.5	5.8	6.0	6.3	6.6	6.8	7.1	7.3	7.6	7.9	8.1
Dance, rumba	4.2	4.6	5.0	5.4	5.8	6.2	6.6	7.0	7.4	7.8	8.2	8.6	9.0	9.4	9.8	10.2	10.6	11.0	11.5	11.9	12.3	12.6
Dance, square	4.1	4.5	4.9	5.3	5.7	6.1	6.5	6.9	7.3	7.8	8.1	8.5	8.9	9.3	9.7	10.1	10.5	10.9	11.3	11.7	12.1	12.4
Dance, waltz	3.1	3.4	3.7	4.0	4.3	4.6	4.9	5.2	5.5	5.8	6.1	6.4	6.7	7.0	7.3	7.6	7.9	8.2	8.5	8.8	9.1	9.4
Fencing (moderate)	3.0	3.3	3.6	3.9	4.2	4.5	4.8	5.1	5.4	5.6	6.0	6.2	6.5	6.8	7.1	7.4	7.7	8.0	8.3	8.6	8.9	9.2
Fencing (vigorous)	6.2	6.8	7.4	8.0	8.6	9.2	9.8	8.7	11.0	11.6	12.2	12.8	13.4	14.0	14.6	15.2	15.8	16.4	17.0	17.6	18.2	18.8
Football (moderate)	3.0	3.3	3.6	4.0	4.2	4.5	4.8	5.1	5.4	5.7	6.0	6.2	6.5	6.8	7.1	7.4	7.7	8.0	8.3	8.6	8.9	9.2
Football (vigorous)	5.0	5.5	6.0	6.4	6.9	7.4	7.9	8.4	8.9	9.4	9.8	10.3	10.8	11.3	11.8	12.3	12.8	13.2	13.7	14.2	14.7	15.2
Golf, 2-some	3.3	3.6	3.9	4.2	4.5	4.8	5.2	5.5	5.8	6.1	6.4	6.7	7.1	7.4	7.7	8.0	8.3	8.6	9.0	9.3	9.6	10.0
Golf, 4-some	2.4	2.7	2.9	3.2	3.4	3.6	3.9	4.1	4.3	4.6	4.8	5.1	5.3	5.5	5.8	6.0	6.2	6.5	6.7	7.0	7.2	7.4
Handball	5.9	6.4	7.0	7.6	8.1	8.7	9.3	9.9	10.4	11.0	11.6	12.1	12.7	13.3	13.9	14.4	15.0	15.6	16.1	16.7	17.3	17.9
Hiking (40 lb. pack, 3.0 mph)	4.1	4.5	4.9	5.3	5.7	6.1	6.5	6.9	7.3	7.7	8.1	8.5	8.9	9.3	9.7	10.1	10.5	10.9	11.3	11.7	12.1	12.5
Horseback Riding (walk)	2.0	2.3	2.4	2.6	2.8	3.0	3.1	3.3	3.5	3.7	3.9	4.1	4.3	4.5	4.7	4.9	5.1	5.3	5.5	5.7	5.8	6.0
Horseback Riding (trot)	4.1	4.4	4.8	5.2	5.6	6.0	6.4	6.8	7.2	7.6	8.0	8.4	8.8	9.2	9.6	10.0	10.4	10.8	11.2	11.6	12.0	12.4
Horseshoe Pitching	2.1	2.3	2.5	2.7	3.0	3.3	3.4	3.6	3.8	4.0	4.2	4.4	4.6	4.8	5.0	5.2	5.4	5.6	5.8	6.0	6.3	6.5
Judo, Karate	7.7	8.5	9.2	10.0	10.7	11.5	12.2	13.0	13.7	14.5	15.2	16.0	16.7	17.5	18.2	19.0	19.7	20.5	21.2	22.0	22.7	23.5
Mountain Climbing	6.0	6.5	7.2	7.8	8.4	9.0	9.6	10.1	10.7	11.3	11.9	12.5	13.1	13.7	14.3	14.8	15.4	16.0	16.6	17.2	17.8	18.4
Paddleball, Racquetball	5.9	6.4	7.0	7.6	8.1	8.7	9.3	9.9	10.4	11.0	11.6	12.1	12.7	13.3	13.9	14.4	15.0	15.6	16.1	16.7	17.3	17.9
Pool, Billiards	1.1	1.2	1.3	1.4	1.5	1.6	1.7	1.8	1.9	2.0	2.1	2.2	2.4	2.5	2.6	2.7	2.8	2.9	3.0	3.1	3.2	3.3
Rowing (recreation)	3.0	3.3	3.6	3.9	4.2	4.5	4.8	5.1	5.4	5.6	6.0	6.2	6.5	6.8	7.1	7.5	7.7	8.0	8.3	8.6	8.9	9.2
Rowing (machine)	8.2	9.0	9.8	10.6	11.4	12.2	13.0	13.8	14.6	15.4	16.2	17.0	17.8	18.6	19.4	20.2	21.0	21.8	22.6	23.4	24.2	25.0
Running (11-min. mile, 5.5 mph)	6.4	7.1	7.7	8.3	9.0	9.6	10.2	10.8	11.5	12.1	12.7	13.4	14.0	14.6	15.2	15.9	16.5	17.1	17.8	18.4	19.0	19.6
Running (8.5-min. mile, 7 mph)	8.4	9.2	10.0	10.8	11.7	12.5	13.3	14.1	14.9	15.7	16.6	17.4	18.2	19.0	19.8	20.7	21.5	22.3	23.1	23.9	24.8	25.6
Running (7-min. mile, 9 mph)	9.3	10.2	11.1	12.9	13.1	13.9	14.8	15.7	16.6	17.5	18.9	19.3	20.2	21.1	22.1	23.0	23.9	24.8	25.7	26.6	27.5	28.4
Running (5-min. mile, 12 mph)	11.8	13.0	14.1	15.3	16.4	17.6	18.7	19.9	21.0	22.2	23.3	24.5	25.6	26.8	27.9	29.1	30.2	31.4	32.5	33.7	34.9	36.0
Stationary Running (140 counts/min.)	14.6	16.1	17.5	18.9	20.4	21.8	23.2	24.6	26.1	27.5	28.9	30.4	31.8	33.2	34.6	36.1	37.5	38.9	40.4	41.8	43.2	44.6
Sprinting	13.8	15.2	16.6	17.9	19.2	20.5	21.9	23.3	24.7	26.1	27.3	28.7	30.0	31.4	32.7	34.0	35.4	36.8	38.2	39.4	40.3	42.2
Sailing	1.8	2.0	2.1	2.3	2.4	2.7	2.8	3.0	3.2	3.4	3.6	3.8	3.9	4.1	4.3	4.4	4.6	4.8	5.0	5.1	5.3	5.5
Skating (moderate)	3.4	3.8	4.1	4.4	4.8	5.1	5.4	5.8	6.1	6.4	6.8	7.1	7.4	7.8	8.1	8.3	8.8	9.1	9.4	9.8	10.1	10.4
Skating (vigorous)	6.2	6.8	7.4	8.0	8.6	9.2	9.8	9.9	11.0	11.6	12.2	12.8	13.4	14.0	14.6	15.2	15.8	16.4	17.0	17.6	18.2	18.8
Skiing (downhill)	5.8	6.4	6.9	7.5	8.1	8.6	9.2	9.8	10.3	10.9	11.4	12.0	12.6	13.1	13.7	14.3	14.8	15.4	16.0	16.5	17.1	17.7
Skiing (level, 5 mph)	7.0	7.7	8.4	9.1	9.8	10.5	11.1	11.8	12.5	13.2	13.9	14.6	15.2	15.9	16.6	17.3	18.0	18.7	19.4	20.0	20.7	21.4
Skiing (racing downhill)	9.9	10.9	11.9	12.9	13.7	14.7	15.7	16.7	17.7	18.7	19.6	20.6	21.6	22.6	23.4	24.4	25.4	26.4	27.4	28.3	29.3	30.2

										Body Weight											
	90	99	108	117	125	134	143	152	161	170	178	187	196	205	213	222	231	240	249	257	266	275
Showshoeing (2.3 mph)	3.7	4.1	4.5	4.8	5.2	5.5	5.9	6.3	6.7	7.0	7.4	7.8	8.1	8.5	8.8	9.2	9.6	9.9	10.3	10.6	11.0	11.4
Showshoeing (2.5 mph)	5.4	5.9	6.5	7.0	7.5	8.0	8.6	9.1	9.7	10.2	10.7	11.2	11.8	12.3	12.8	13.3	13.9	14.4	14.9	15.4	16.0	16.5
Soccer	5.4	5.9	6.4	6.9	7.5	8.0	8.5	9.0	9.6	10.1	10.6	11.1	11.6	12.2	12.7	13.2	13.4	14.3	14.8	15.3	15.8	16.9
Squash	6.2	6.8	7.5	8.1	8.7	9.3	9.9	10.5	11.1	11.7	12.3	12.9	13.5	14.2	14.8	15.4	16.0	16.6	17.2	17.8	18.4	19.0
Swimming, pleasure (25 yds./min.)	3.6	4.0	4.3	4.7	5.0	5.4	5.7	6.1	6.4	6.8	7.1	7.5	7.8	8.2	8.5	8.9	9.2	9.6	10.0	10.3	10.6	11.0
Swimming, back (20 yds./min.)	2.3	2.6	2.8	3.0	3.2	3.5	3.7	3.9	4.1	4.2	4.6	4.8	5.0	5.3	5.5	5.7	6.0	6.2	6.4	6.6	6.9	7.1
Swimming, back (30 yds./min.)	3.2	3.5	3.8	4.1	4.4	4.7	5.1	5.4	5.7	6.0	6.3	6.6	6.9	7.2	7.4	7.9	8.2	8.5	8.8	9.1	9.4	9.7
Swimming, back (40 yds./min.)	5.0	5.5	5.8	6.5	7.0	7.5	7.9	8.5	8.9	9.4	9.9	10.4	10.9	11.4	11.9	12.3	12.8	13.3	13.8	14.3	14.8	15.3
Swimming, breast (20 yds./min.)	2.9	3.2	3.4	3.8	4.0	4.3	4.6	4.9	5.1	5.4	5.7	6.0	6.3	6.5	6.8	7.1	7.4	7.7	7.9	8.2	8.5	8.8
Swimming, breast (30 yds./min.)	4.3	4.8	5.2	5.7	6.0	6.4	6.9	7.3	7.7	8.1	8.6	9.0	9.4	9.9	10.3	10.8	11.1	11.5	11.9	12.4	13.0	13.3
Swimming, breast (40 yds./min.)	5.8	6.3	6.9	7.5	8.0	8.6	9.2	9.7	10.3	10.8	11.4	12.0	12.5	13.1	13.7	14.2	14.8	15.4	15.9	16.5	17.0	17.6
Swimming, butterfly (50 yds./min.)	7.0	7.7	8.4	9.1	9.8	10.5	11.1	11.9	12.5	13.2	13.9	14.6	15.2	15.9	16.6	17.3	18.0	18.7	19.4	20.0	20.7	21.4
Swimming, crawl (20 yds./min.)	2.9	3.2	3.4	3.8	4.0	4.3	4.6	4.9	5.1	5.4	5.7	5.8	6.3	6.5	6.8	7.1	7.3	7.7	7.9	8.2	8.5	8.8
Swimming, crawl (45 yds./min.)	5.2	5.8	6.3	6.8	7.3	7.8	8.3	8.8	9.3	9.8	10.4	10.9	11.4	11.9	12.4	12.9	13.4	13.9	14.4	15.0	15.5	16.0
Swimming, crawl (50 yds./min.)	6.4	7.0	7.6	8.3	8.9	9.5	10.1	10.7	11.4	12.0	12.6	13.2	13.9	14.5	15.1	15.7	16.3	17.0	17.4	17.9	18.8	19.5
Table Tennis	2.3	2.6	2.8	3.0	3.2	3.5	3.7	3.9	4.1	4.2	4.6	4.8	5.0	5.3	5.5	5.7	6.0	6.2	6.4	6.6	6.9	7.1
Tennis (recreation)	4.2	4.6	5.0	5.4	5.8	6.2	6.6	7.0	7.4	7.8	8.2	8.6	9.0	9.4	9.8	10.2	10.6	11.0	11.5	11.9	12.3	12.6
Tennis (competition)	5.9	6.4	7.0	7.6	8.1	8.7	9.3	9.9	10.4	11.0	11.6	12.1	12.7	13.3	13.9	14.4	15.0	15.6	16.1	16.7	17.3	17.9
Timed Calisthenics	8.8	9.6	10.5	11.4	12.2	13.1	13.9	14.8	15.6	16.5	17.4	18.2	19.1	19.9	20.8	21.5	22.5	23.9	24.2	25.1	25.9	26.8
Volleyball (moderate)	3.4	3.8	4.0	4.4	4.8	5.1	5.4	5.8	6.1	6.4	6.8	7.1	7.4	7.8	8.1	8.3	8.8	9.1	9.4	9.8	10.1	10.4
Volleyball (vigorous)	5.9	6.4	7.0	7.6	8.1	8.7	9.3	9.9	10.4	11.0	11.6	12.1	12.7	13.3	13.9	14.4	15.0	15.6	16.1	16.7	17.3	17.9
Walking (2.0 mph)	2.1	2.3	2.5	2.7	2.9	3.1	3.3	3.5	3.7	4.0	4.2	4.4	4.6	4.8	5.0	5.2	5.4	5.6	5.8	6.0	6.2	6.4
Walking (4.5 mph)	4.0	4.4	4.7	5.1	5.5	5.9	6.3	6.7	7.1	7.5	7.8	8.2	8.6	9.0	9.4	9.8	10.1	10.6	10.9	11.3	11.7	12.0
Walking (110–120 steps/min.)	3.1	3.4	3.7	4.0	4.3	4.7	5.0	5.3	5.6	5.9	6.2	6.5	6.8	7.1	7.4	7.7	8.0	8.3	8.6	8.9	9.2	9.5
Waterskiing	4.7	5.1	5.6	6.1	6.5	7.0	7.4	7.9	8.3	8.8	9.3	9.7	10.2	10.6	11.1	11.5	12.0	12.5	12.9	13.4	13.8	14.3
Weight Training	4.7	5.1	5.7	6.2	6.7	7.0	7.5	7.9	8.4	8.9	9.4	9.9	10.3	10.8	11.1	11.7	12.2	12.6	13.1	13.5	14.0	14.4
Wrestling	7.7	8.5	9.2	10.0	10.7	11.5	12.2	13.0	13.7	14.5	15.2	16.0	16.7	17.5	18.2	19.0	19.7	20.5	21.2	22.0	22.7	23.5

APPENDIX

VI

Surface Muscle Chart

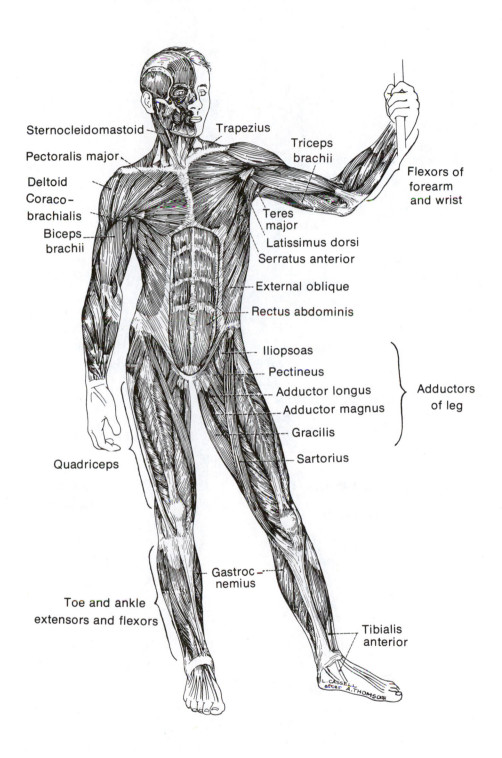

Sternocleidomastoid

Pectoralis major

Deltoid
Coraco-
brachialis

Biceps
brachii

Trapezius

Triceps
brachii

Flexors of
forearm
and wrist

Teres
major

Latissimus dorsi

Serratus anterior

External oblique

Rectus abdominis

Iliopsoas

Pectineus

Adductor longus

Adductor magnus

Gracilis

Sartorius

Adductors
of leg

Quadriceps

Gastroc-
nemius

Toe and ankle
extensors and flexors

Tibialis
anterior

L. CASSELL
after A. THOMSON

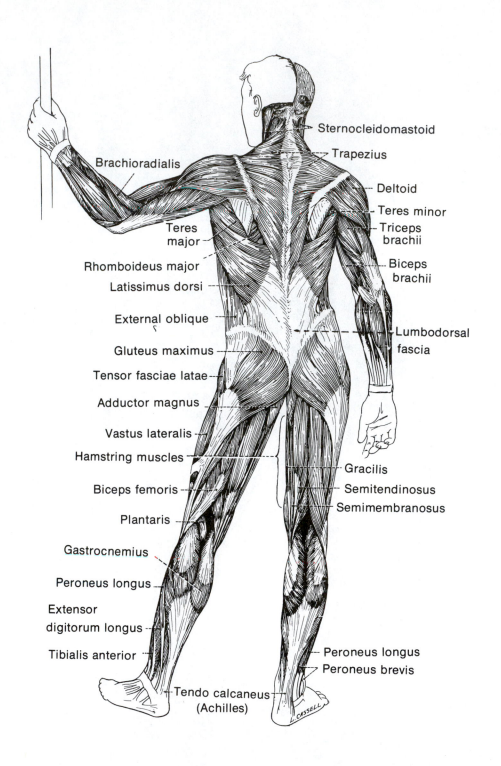

Sternocleidomastoid

Trapezius

Deltoid

Teres minor

Triceps brachii

Biceps brachii

Lumbodorsal fascia

Brachioradialis

Teres major

Rhomboideus major

Latissimus dorsi

External oblique

Gluteus maximus

Tensor fasciae latae

Adductor magnus

Vastus lateralis

Hamstring muscles

Biceps femoris

Plantaris

Gastrocnemius

Peroneus longus

Extensor digitorum longus

Tibialis anterior

Gracilis

Semitendinosus

Semimembranosus

Peroneus longus

Peroneus brevis

Tendo calcaneus (Achilles)

APPENDIX

VII

Facilities Accessibility Chart*

This basic checklist—in the form of questions—provides guidelines for planning facilities for individuals with disabilities. Ideally, the response to each question should be "yes."

I. Site

1. Is the facility easily accessible by foot, wheelchair or vehicle?
2. Is the facility located near the center of student traffic patterns?
3. Is the facility located so the students may go to and from the physical education/sports facility and academic buildings within the typical class-changing time?
4. Is public transportation available, as required, to the facility?

II. Parking

1. Are there on-site, clearly marked parking spaces for individuals with disabilities?
2. Are parking spaces at least 12 feet wide?
3. Is the surface of the parking area firm, smooth, and essentially level?
4. Are parking spaces provided with a cover or canopy?
5. Have steps, curbs, or other barriers between the parking area and facility been adapted to meet the needs of the individual with a disability?
6. Is the parking area lighted for night use?

III. Access to Building

1. Are all walkways leading to the facility at least 48 inches wide?
2. Are all walkways smooth, firm, free of cracks and ruts more than ⅛-inch wide, and without abrupt changes in level?
3. Are motorized vehicles banned from regular use of walkways?

*Reprinted with permission of Bronzan, R.T. (1980, August). Planning facilities for the handicapped: A checklist of guideline questions. *Athletic Purchasing & Facilities*, 16–17.

4. Are street crossings enroute to the facility properly marked and controlled as necessary?
5. Are the main entrances to the facility at ground level?
6. Are all ramps, walkways or other approaches no steeper than a 1"–12" ratio?
7. Are all ramps, walkways or other approaches provided with at least one handrail on one side, 32 inches above surface level, that extends 1 foot beyond the top and bottom? (Recommended: a handrail on each side of the ramp; a handrail in center of ramp if total width allows; or outside ramp with a double-tier rail on each side.)
8. Is a cover or canopy provided at the end of the ramp prior to entering or leaving the building?
9. Are all crosswalk or ramp intersections at the same level?
10. If the entrance door opens outward, is there a level platform of at least 5 feet by 5 feet that extends at least 1 foot beyond each side of the doorway?
11. If the entrance door does not open outward, is there a level platform that is 6 feet deep and 5 feet wide extending at least 1 foot beyond each side of the doorway?

IV. Entrance to Building

1. Does the doorway have at least a 36-inch clearance?
2. Can the door(s) be opened with a single effort?
3. Have two-leaf doors been avoided unless they can be opened with a single effort?
4. Is the door automatically activated?
5. Is the door provided with a delayed closing-time mechanism?
6. Are entrances provided with manually operated emergency doors adjacent to or near the automatically activated door?
7. Are doors provided with both push and pull bars?
8. Are doors provided with a shatterproof glass insert?
9. Do doors allow for a small child or a person in a wheelchair to see through to the other side or be seen from the other side?
10. Are doors provided with kick plates or appropriate materials from the bottom of the door to at least 16 inches from the floor?
11. Are thresholds and doors saddles flush with the floor or no more than ½ inch high?

V. Ramps

1. Is the ramp surface smooth, hard and nonslip?
2. Is the ramp width 5 feet or more so as to allow two wheelchairs to pass safely in opposite directions?

3. Is the ramp no steeper than 1 foot in height for each 12 feet horizontally?
4. Is a 5-foot-long level platform provided at least every 30-foot interval?
5. Are level platforms, each 5 feet long, provided for every turn of the ramp?
6. Is there at least a 6-foot level platform at the bottom of the ramp?
7. Is there at least one handrail, 32 inches above ramp level? (Recommended: handrail on each side of ramp; handrail in center of ramp if width allows; or handrails that are double-tiered.)

VI. Stairs

1. Are risers 7 inches or less?
2. Is nosing of steps slanted?
3. Are all corners on stairs rounded?
4. Is at least one handrail, 32 inches as measured from tread at the face of the riser, provided? (Recommended: dual handrails; double-tiered handrails.)
5. Are treads provided with nonslip surfacing?
6. Is at least a 5-foot level platform provided at the top and bottom of the staircases?
7. Do handrails extend 1 foot beyond the top and bottom of the stairs?

VII. Elevators

1. In all facilities that have more than one level or floor, is there at least one passenger elevator?
2. Is the elevator call button no more than 48 inches above the floor?
3. Is the elevator provided with a delayed-closing door?
4. Is it a relatively easy and quick procedure to adjust elevator heights in relation to the various floor levels?
5. When elevator doors are open, is the clear space at least 36 inches in width?
6. Is the elevator control board button no more than 48 inches above the elevator floor level?
7. Is the elevator emergency telephone not more than 48 inches above elevator floor level?
8. Does the emergency telephone have a cord length of 42 inches?
9. Are emergency instructions located not more than 48 inches above the elevator floor level?

VIII. Restrooms

1. Are restrooms strategically located for the convenience of individuals with disabilities?

2. Are entrances to toilets on the same level as the toilet floor?
3. Is the entrance to the restroom at least 36 inches wide at all points?
4. For entrances that require a change of direction, have dimensions provided for wheelchairs?
5. Is there at least a 5-foot by 5-foot clear area inside the restroom?
6. Is there at least one toilet stall with a door that swings outward, creating at least a 32-inch opening?
7. Is at least one toilet stall 36 inches or more in width and 56 inches deep?
8. Is at least one toilet provided with both easily accessible foot and/or hand flush activators?
9. Is the toilet seat in at least one toilet 20 inches above floor level?
10. Is the toilet wall-mounted with narrow and shallow front, and turning backward more than downward?
11. Are grab rails located on each side of the toilet, made of 1½-inch O.D. stainless steel, mounted securely, with 1½-inch clearance from the wall?
12. Is at least one urinal opening 19 inches above floor level?
13. Are urinals equipped with grip rails?
14. Is the height of at least one lavatory not more than 30 inches above the floor level?
15. Is the bottom height of at least one paper-towel dispenser or hand dryer no more than 40 inches above the floor level?
16. Is the light switch for the restroom located no more than 48 inches above the floor level?
17. Are the lavatories wall-mounted, with narrow aprons?

IX. Water Fountains

1. Are water fountains located conveniently?
2. Do water fountains or coolers have up-front spouts and controls?
3. Can water fountains and coolers be hand and/or foot operated?
4. Are wall-mounted, hand-operated water fountains or coolers mounted 33 inches above the floor?
5. Are water fountains and/or coolers fully recessed?
6. When water fountains and/or coolers are located in an alcove, is the alcove at least 36 inches in width?

X. Telephones

1. Are public telephones located conveniently for use by individuals with disabilities?
2. Are dial and handset heights no more than 48 inches high?
3. Is the handset cord at least 42 inches in length?

4. If the speaker unit is fixed, is it no more than 48 inches above the floor level?
5. Are dial numerals raised for the blind?

XI. Aquatic Facilities

1. Can water temperature be adjusted conveniently to reach 80–90° F?
2. Are dressing/shower/toilet facilities convenient to pool?
3. Are provisions included to facilitate movement by wheelchair from shower room to pool deck?
4. Are provisions included to facilitate the safe, quick and unobtrusive entry into and exit from the pool for the severely involved?
5. Are provisions included to facilitate the safe, quick and unobtrusive entry into and exit from the pool by those with moderate disabilities?
6. Can the air temperature be adjusted conveniently to reach 5–7° F above the water temperature?
7. Are provisions provided to delineate specific pool areas for use by the disabled, as appropriate?
8. Are pool water depths adjustable?

XII. Locker/Shower Rooms

1. Do all entries and exits meet stated dimensional standards?
2. Are horizontal lockers available for people with disabilities?
3. Are locking devices easy to manipulate for the physically or visually challenged?
4. Are shower heads and their controls planned so they may be used while seated in a wheelchair?
5. Are shower facilities equipped with approved grab rails?
6. Are provisions made for the installation and operation of appropriate numbers of hair dryers for people with disabilities?
7. Are lockers free of impediment by benches, etc.?

XIII. Specific Provisions for the Blind and Visually Impaired

1. Are raised letters or numerals and Braille used to identify rooms and offices?
2. Are light-colored characters, numerals, and Braille symbols used on low-reflecting, dark backgrounds to heighten visibility?
3. Are Arabic characters raised at least ½ inch and no more than ¾ inch?

4. Are Arabic characters of a sans serif face type, such as Helevetica?
5. Are standard Grade II six-dot Braille cells raised at least .025-inch?
6. Are the height of characters and numerals markedly different to designate restrooms for men and women and elevator door jams?
7. Are room and office signs placed on the wall to the left (preferably) of the door at a height between 4½ feet and 5½ feet, preferably 5 feet?
8. Are location of tactile signs and location cues standardized so that they are placed on the wall 20 inches to the left of a single door or farthest left-side entranceway door at a height of 5 feet?
9. Is a 2-foot by 1-inch arrow indicator placed 5 inches above the door knob or handle bar on a door, pointing to the location of the tactile information?
10. Are doors free of signs, except arrow indicators?
11. Are buildings identified on the exterior by a building name and address plate placed at a height of 60 inches, 20 inches from left of door farthest to the left?
12. Are blind persons with guide dogs provided entrances other than revolving doors?
13. Is there a tactile orientation map, indicating building location, placed on the nearest wall to the left of the main entranceway or lobby, at a height of 5 feet?
14. Is there a building directory indicating room numbers located on the left wall upon entering the building?
15. Do the public telephones have raised numerals below the coin slot to identify the point of call origination?
16. Do public phones have raised numerals below the coin insert for emergency purposes to call the police or fire department?
17. Do vending machines have tactile signs adjacent to the coin insert that indicates the contents and prices?
18. Is the building provided with other tactile signs that make the facility more usable, convenient, and helpful to the blind?
19. Are the various areas of the building lighted sufficiently to aid the blind?
20. Are regular signs and other amenities painted in colors that aid the blind?

XIV. Emergency Needs

1. Are crash doors adjacent to automated doors adequate for quick evacuation by persons in wheelchairs?
2. In addition to the sound alarm system, is a warning light system available?
3. Are emergency directional signs in tactile symbols?
4. Are emergency directional signs color-coded?
5. Are fire alarms no more than 48 inches above floor level?
6. Are fire extinguishers no more than 48 inches above floor level?

XV. General

1. Are all floors provided with a nonslip treatment?
2. Are all operational devices, such as wall controls, light switches, door knobs, door locks, elevator controls, locker handles, locker locks, telephones, and emergency equipment, no more than 48 inches above the floor level?
3. Have considerations been given to persons in wheelchairs, who have an average unilateral vertical reach of 60 inches, an average horizontal working table reach with both arms extended of 30.8 inches, and an average bilateral horizontal reach with both arms extended shoulder high at 64.5 inches?
4. Are provisions made for the average turning space required for wheelchairs? (Five feet by 5 feet is adequate, although 63 inches by 56 inches is preferred; in an area with two open ends, the space between two walls may be 54 inches.)
5. Are all meeting rooms, dining rooms, restrooms and other public places of assembly or use accessible by a level entrance or proper ramp?

Equipment Suppliers

AMF American, 200 American Avenue, Jefferson, IA 50129.

Athletic Purchasing & Facilities, USPS 360–870, 2038 Pennsylvania Avenue, Madison, WI 53704.

Atlas Athletic Equipment, 2339 Hamptom Avenue, St. Louis, MO 63139.

Blind Sports, Inc., 335 S. Van Ness Avenue, San Francisco, CA 94103.

Cosom Safe-T-Play Products (Catalog of equipment and rule books for "scoop" games, polo games, and hockey), 6030 Wayzata Boulevard, Minneapolis, MN 55416.

Developmental Learning Materials, P.O. Box 4000, One DLM Park, Allen, TX 75002.

Educational Activities, Inc., P.O. Box 392, Freeport, NY 11520.

Flaghouse, Inc. (Motor activity equipment for special populations), 18 W. 18th Street, New York, NY 10011.

J.A. Preston (Materials on exceptional children), 71 Fifth Avenue, New York, NY 10003.

Jayfro Corp., P.O. Box 400, Waterford, CT 06385.

J.E. Gregory Co., Inc. (Mats and ropes of all kinds), W. 992 First, Spokane, CA 99204.

J.L. Hammett Co., 165 Water Street, Lyons, NY 14489.

Kimbo Educational Records (Audiovisual aids, parachute play, and exercise records), P.O. Box 246, Deal, NJ 07723.

LEFLAR Enterprises Inc., 6840 S.W. Macadam Avenue, Portland, OR 97219.

Miracle Recreation Equipment Co., P.O. Box 275, Grinnell, IA 50112.

Rifton (Equipment for the handicapped), Route 213, Rifton, NY 12471.

Voit, Inc. (Catalog of equipment, including rhythm balls and audioballs), 29 E. Rawis Road, Des Plaines, IL 60018.

Wolverine Sports, 745 State Circle, Ann Arbor, MI 48104.

Wheelchair Manufacturers

CBS Cycle Frames Ltd, 1820 Trafalgar St., Vancouver, British Columbia, Canada, V6K 352, (604) 733–0758.

Competitive Engineering, 5494 East Lamona Avenue, Suite 130, Fresno, CA 93727, (209) 251–4403.

E and G Wheelchairs, 2351 Parkwood Road, Snellville, GA 30278, (404) 972–0763.

Everest and Jennings, Inc., 3233 East Mission Oaks Boulevard, Camarillo, CA 93010, (805) 987–6911.

Hall's Wheels, Inc., 11 Smith Place, Cambridge, MA 02138, (617) 547–5000.

Handcrafted Metals, Inc., 4457 63rd Circle, N, Pinellas Park, FL 33565.

Invacare, Inc., 899 Cleveland Street, P.O. Box 4028, Elyria, OH 44036, (216) 329-6000.

Kuschall of America, 15871 Edmund Drive, Los Gatos, CA (408) 438–6508.

Magic in Motion, Inc., 315 10th Street SW, Puyallup, WA 98371, (206) 848–6845.

Magnum Poirer, Inc., 2930 West Central, Santa Ana, CA 92704, (714) 641–9696.

Motion Designs, Inc., 2842 Business Park Avenue, Fresno, CA (209) 292–2171.

Ortho-Kinetics, Inc., W220 N507 Springdale Road, P.O. Box 436, Wukesha, WI 53187, (414) 542–6060.

Quadra Medical Products, Inc., 31166 Via Colinas, Westlake Village, CA 91362 (800) 824–1068.

Sheperd Medical Products, P.O. Box 2249, Charlotte, NC 28211, (800) 833–9962.

Stainless Medical Products, 244 Airport Road, Festus, MO 63028, (800) 238–6678.

Top End, 6551 44th Street N., E.B.P. 5002, Pinellas Park, FL 34605, (813) 522–8677.

Wheel Ring, Inc., 175 Pine Street, Manchester, CT 06040, (203) 647–8596.

XL Wheelchairs, 4950-D Cohasset Stage Road, Chico, CA 95926, (916) 891–3535.

Glossary

abduction   withdrawal of a part from the axis of the body; the act of turning outward.

acetabulum   large cup-shaped cavity on the lateral surface of the os coxae in which the head of the femur articulates.

achondroplasia   those individuals with predominantly short limbs.

acuity   clearness of vision.

Adapted Physical Activity Council   the organization within AAHPERD responsible for providing services to professionals working with the disabled.

adapted physical education   refers to those programs that have the same objectives as the regular physical education program but in which adjustments are made in the regular offerings to meet the needs and abilities of exceptional students.

adduct   to draw toward the median line of the body or toward a neighboring part.

adventitious   acquired after birth through accident or illness; opposite of congenital.

affective   pertaining to an individual's feelings, emotions, moods, temperaments. Used in special education to refer to objectives that deal with attitudes and feelings.

afferent nerves   nerves that convey impulses from the sensory endings toward the never centers or central nervous system.

agnosia   inability to recognize persons or objects. May be restricted to a particular sense modality, as in the following:
auditory agnosia   inability to recognize speech sounds.
spatial agnosia   inability to find one's way about familiar places.
tactile agnosia   inability to recognize objects by touch.
visual agnosia   inability to recognize objects that are seen, or color.

agonistic muscle   a muscle opposed in action by another muscle.

AIDS   acronym for acquired immunodeficiency syndrome. Also referred to as HIV.

allergen   any substance that causes an allergic reaction when it comes in contact with the body.

amblyopia   the inability to focus or coordinate both eyes simultaneously on the same object; commonly referred to as the lazy eye syndrome.

ambulatory   walking or able to walk.

amelia   a condition in which all four limbs are absent.

amelioration   improvement, as of the condition of a patient.

ament   term referring to intellectual subnormality.

Ameslan   slang expression for American sign language. This communication system, used by deaf persons, employs the arms, hands, and parts of the body to represent concepts.

amniocentesis   a medical procedure used to draw amniotic fluid from the uterus to determine certain aspects of fetal development.

amphetamine   a drug with stimulant properties frequently used to treat conditions such as depression, narcolepsy, and obesity; commonly called "uppers."

anemia   a condition of the blood in which the quantity of the hemoglobin or the number of red blood cells is deficient.

angina   spasmodic, choking, or suffocative pain.

ankylosis   abnormal immobility and consolidation of a joint.

anomaly   anything unusual, irregular, or contrary to general rule.

anorexia   a condition that causes a partial or complete loss of appetite; usually related to a psychological disorder.

anoxia   reduction of oxygen content of the blood to a level insufficient to maintain adequate functioning of the tissue.

antagonistic muscle   muscle that acts in opposition to the action of another muscle.

antigen   a substance that stimulates production of antibodies when introduced into the body.

antigravity muscles   muscles that serve to keep the body in an upright position.

aphasia   impaired ability to understand or use language meaningfully.

apraxia   difficulty in carrying out a specific, purposeful movement; a condition in which movements are awkward and slow; inability to determine what the movement shall be and to recognize the movements necessary for the act.

aquaphobia   fear of water.

aqueous humor   fluid occupying the space between the lens and the cornea of the eye.

arteriosclerosis   hardening of the arteries.

arthrodesis   surgical fixation of a joint by fusion of the joint surfaces.

arthrogryposis   a congenital severe crippling disease of children in which the joints become fixed or bend only partially.

asthenis   lack or loss of strength and energy.

ataxia   failure of muscle coordination.

athetoid   a type of cerebral palsy involving involuntary occurrence of slow, sinuous, writhing movements, especially severe in the hands.

atonia   lack of muscle tone; may be due to nervous system disease, as in infantile paralysis, or to muscle disease, as in muscular dystrophy. May also be due to prolonged bed rest or illness.

atrophy   a general wasting away or shrinking due to destruction of the tissue; may be said of any organ, but often used in reference to muscles.

audiogram   a graph of the minimal level of sound a person can hear at least fifty percent of the time measured at several frequencies for each ear.

aura   a subjective sensation that precedes and marks the onset of a paroxysmal intensification seizure, such as an epileptic seizure.

autism   inability to form meaningful interpersonal relationships; characterized by severe withdrawal.

axillary area   hollow formed where arm joins the body at the shoulder; the armpit.

Babinski reflex   extension of the toes when the sole of the foot is touched. This reflex is considered normal in infants but may be a sign of nervous disorder in adults.

barbiturates   a group of drugs that are used medically for relieving tension, anxiety, and pain and as an anticonvulsant in treating epilepsy.

baseline   observational data recorded prior to the beginning of a treatment effect or intervention program.

behavior modification   systematic use of the theories of learning to weaken, strengthen, or maintain a behavior.

bilateral   having two sides.

blindism   mannerism of the blind; purposeless movement.

body image   awareness of the position of the body in space and how the body moves.

bulimia   a self-induced process used to rid the body of food before it is digested.

bursa   a sac or pouch containing fluid useful in reducing friction, such as that found within joints.

calcaneus   heel bone.

cataract   an eye abnormality caused by opacity of the lens, resulting in a visual impairment or blindness.

catatonic   a form of schizophrenia characterized by negative reactions, phase of stupor or excitement, and impulsive or stereotyped behavior.

catheter   a narrow tube that can be inserted into the body to empty the bladder or kidneys.

central deafness   hearing impairment due to damage to the auditory nerve or in the centers of hearing in the brain cortex.

cephalocaudal   used to describe development of the individual that proceeds from the head to the feet.

cerebellum   the lower rear area of the brain responsible for fine motor coordination.

cerebral palsy   a condition resulting from brain damage that is manifested by various types of neuromuscular disabilities.

cerebrospinal fluid   the fluid that surrounds the brain and spinal cord.

cervical   pertaining to the neck.

chemotherapy   treatment of disease by chemical agents.

chorea minor   also called St. Vitus dance or Sydenham's chorea. Acute disease occurring chiefly in children; no specific treatment. Disease of nervous system that causes aimless, wandering movements, especially of the hands and fingers.

choroid   thin, dark brown, vascular coat of the posterior of the eyeball.

chromosome   a chainlike structure found in the nucleus of cells, composed of many genes, responsible for hereditary factors.

cleft palate   a congenital condition that results in an opening in the roof of the mouth (palate), which may extend through the upper lip.

cochlea   the organ of hearing located in the inner ear; shaped like a snail.

cognitive   refers to the mental process of reasoning, memory, comprehension, and judgment.

coma   a state of profound and prolonged unconsciousness usually caused by a disease, such as diabetes.

compensation   an attempt to offset some shortcoming or limitation by developing some special talent or ability.

congenital   condition present at birth.

conjunctiva   the delicate membrane that covers the exposed surface of the eyeball.

continence   the ability to retain urine.

contracture   shortening of a muscle in distortion; a permanent condition.

cornea   the outer coating of the eyeball responsible for the refraction of light rays.

coxa plana   inflammation of the hip joint.

craniosynostosis   premature closures of the sutures in the skull.

cretinism   a form of severe failure of the function of the thyroid gland.

cyanosis   a bluish color of the skin and mucous membranes resulting from insufficient oxygen in the blood.

cybernetics   self-guidance and control of one's behavior.

decibel   a unit of measurement used to record the loudness (intensity) of sound.

delusion   an untrue belief held by an individual that cannot be changed by reasoning or explanation of the true facts.

dementia   deterioration of emotional or psychological functioning.

dermis   innermost layer of skin (beneath the epidermis), consisting of a dense bed of vascular connective tissue.

diabetes   a disease in which the body exhibits an inability to properly use the starches and sugars it ingests.

Dilantin   an anticonvulsant drug frequently prescribed to control convulsive types of disorders such as epileptic seizures.

diplegia   bilateral paralysis; paralysis affecting like parts on both sides of body.

directionality   a perception of direction.

distal   remote; farther from any point of reference.

distractibility   a behavioral characteristic in which the individual is unable to refrain from responding to unnecessary stimuli.

dorsal   pertaining to the back.

dorsiflexion   the act of bending a part backward.

Down syndrome   a specific type of mental retardation resulting from a chromosomal defect or abnormality.

dynamometer   instrument that measures muscular strength.

dysmenorrhea   painful menstruation.

dyspnea   difficult or labored breathing.

echolalia   repetition of words, sounds, or sentences spoken by another person.

ectomorph   a fragile, thin person having a large surface area and thin muscles and subcutaneous tissue.

edema   excessive fluid in the tissue, causing swelling.

educable   term used to suggest that one is capable of learning, of being educated, as in the educable mentally retarded.

efferent nerves   nerves that convey impulses outward from the nerve centers or central nervous system.

electrocardiogram (EKG)   record of electrical impulses produced by contraction of the heart muscle.

electroencephalogram (EEG)   record of brain waves.

electromyogram (EMG)   record of the changes in electric potential of muscle.

embolus   a clot that obstructs a blood vessel.

encephalitis   inflammation of the brain.

encopresis   inability to control one's bowels.

endogenous   describes a condition that occurs from internal rather than external factors, such as hereditary conditions.

endomorph   a person with a soft, round body; large trunk and thighs; and tapering extremities.

enuresis   involuntary discharge of urine, usually during sleep.

epidermis   outermost and nonvascular layer of the skin.

epilepsy   a disturbance in the electrochemical activity of the brain that causes seizures and convulsions.

epinephrine   a hormone secreted by the adrenal medulla; increases blood pressure and cardiac output; accelerates heart rate and stimulates heart muscle.

epiphysis   the growing end of a bone.

etiology   the cause of a condition or disease.

euphoria   an emotional or psychological sense of well-being and optimism; usually describes a temporary mood.

eversion   turning outward, as of the feet (can apply to any part).

exogenous   describes a condition that occurs from external rather than internal factors, such as cultural deprivation.

extinction   a behavior modification technique used to eliminate an undesirable behavior by the removal of reinforcers.

fetus   the developing organism from approximately six weeks after conception to birth.

fibrosis   formation of fibrous tissue; usually in a tumor called a fibroma.

finger spelling   a communication method used by the deaf in which words are spelled out by different combinations of hand and finger motions.

flaccid   flabby.

foramen   a natural opening or passage; especially one into or through a bone.

forced expired volume   the amount of air which can be forcibly expired in one minute.

fovea   the small, central area of the retina in which vision is the most distinct.

Friedreich's Ataxia   an inherited disease in which there is progressive degeneration in the sensory nerves of the limbs and trunks.

genetic   refers to hereditary or features transmitted by chromosomes from parents to children.

geriatrics   branch of medicine that clinically treats problems of the aged, including senility.

gerontology   scientific study of the problems of the aged.

gestation   the period of pregnancy; time in which the fetus is developing within the uterus.

glaucoma   a condition of the eye in which there is excessive internal pressure on the eye; if untreated, will impair vision.

glenoid fossa (of scapula)   socket of the shoulder.

grand mal   major form of epilepsy; characterized by loss of consciousness and convulsions.

handedness   the preference of either the right or the left hand to perform tasks requiring the use of only one hand.

haptic   pertains to the sense of touch as determined by tactile and kinesthetic awareness.

hematoma   a swelling containing blood.

hemiplegia   paralysis of one side of the body.

hemoglobin   the oxygen-carrying transporters found in red blood cells.

hemophilia   a condition, usually hereditary, associated with the inability of the blood to clot following an injury.

hernia protrusion of an organ or tissue through an abnormal opening of a body part.

hertz a unit of measurement to determine the frequency of sound.

Hodgkin's disease a disease of the blood. Pseudoleukemia.

hydrocephalus abnormal accumulation of fluid in the cranial vault (water on the brain); causes mental weakness, convulsions, and enlargement of head.

hyperactivity abnormally increased activity.

hyperextend extreme extension of a limb or part.

hyperglycemia condition in which there is excessive sugar in the blood.

hyperkinetic excessive movement.

hyperopia farsightedness; a condition in which people have difficulty seeing near objects because the image focuses behind the retina instead of on it.

hyperplasia refers to the number of fat cells.

hypertension a condition characterized by abnormally high blood pressure.

hypertrophia refers to the size of fat cells.

hypertrophy enlargement of an organ or part.

hypoglycemia an abnormally low level of blood sugar caused by an increase in metabolism.

hypokinetic showing abnormally decreased mobility or motor function.

hypoplasia cerebral; defective development of the brain.

idiopathic of unknown cause.

ileostomy a surgical procedure for diverting the feces from the normal passage through an opening in the abdomen.

incontinence inability to control bowel or bladder function.

Individualized Education Program (IEP) a written plan of instruction, including goals and objectives, developed for each student receiving special services.

Individualized Family Service Plan (IFSP) a written plan describing the services to be provided infants and toddlers with or suspected of having a disability.

inguinal hernia hernia of the groin.

institutionalization the placement of individuals with disabilities within residential settings.

insulin a hormone produced by the pancreas used in the treatment of diabetes.

integration describes a setting in special education in which youngsters with and without disabilities are educated together.

intelligence quotient an index of intelligence as determined by standardized intelligence tests. The IQ is computed by dividing the mental age by the chronological age and multiplying by 100.

inversion a turning inward, inside out, upside down, or other reversal of the normal relation to a part.

iris the colored portion of the eye; contracts or expands involuntarily depending upon the amount of light entering it.

isometric (exercise) pertaining to a contracture of a muscle when it is not under constant tension.

isotonic (exercise) pertaining to a contracture of a muscle when it is not under constant tension.

Jacksonian seizure a type of epileptic seizure.

jaundice a yellow coloring of the eyes and skin caused by excess bile pigments in the blood and body tissues.

jobst an elastic support made to fit a particular area of the body; helpful in applying pressure to burned area to help minimize the amount of scarring.

kernicterus a condition resulting from blood incompatibility between the mother and developing fetus.

kinesthesia (kinesthesis) the sense by which muscular motion, weight, position, and so on are perceived.

kinesthesis (method of teaching) involves the adjustment of the body segments to achieve successful performance of a skill.

kyphosis condition characterized by an abnormally increased convexity in the curvature of thoracic spine as viewed from the side.

labeling used in special education to refer to the attachment of a generalized name, such as "mental retardation," to a group of children.

larynx structure located in the upper part of the trachea that contains the vocal chords and essential musculature for the production of speech.

lateral flexion to stretch out to the side of the midline of the body.

laterality internal awareness of the two sides of the body.

least restrictive environment an expression used to emphasize the fact that individuals with disabilities should be educated in the environment that provides for them the greatest opportunity to be successful, including the regular educational setting when possible and desirable.

les autres French term for "the others."

lesion any pathological or traumatic discontinuity of tissue or loss of function of a part.

lip reading speech reading; a skill taught to the deaf and hard of hearing that enables them to understand spoken words by observing the context of the situation and the visual cues of speech, such as lip movement and facial expressions.

little people the term used to describe those individuals who are short or small in stature.

lordosis abnormally increased concavity in the curvature of the lumbar spine as viewed from the side.

low-incidence disability those disabilities that are few in number in comparison to other disability populations; for example, deaf-blind.

lumbar pertaining to the lower back.

luxation dislocation.

macrocephaly a condition in which the head is unusually large.

macula the part of the retina that provides the clearest vision.

mainstreaming placement of students with disabilities into regular educational programs with assistance, when necessary, of appropriate support personnel.

malignant virulent; tending to go from bad to worse.

malleolus   a rounded process, such as the protuberance on either side of the ankle joint.

manuometer   an apparatus for measuring the strength of the grip of the hand.

maturation   physical and behavioral changes attributed primarily to the innate process of growth rather than the influence of the environment.

meninges   membrane that surrounds the spinal cord and brain.

meningocele   a saclike pouch that protrudes from the vertebral column that contains cerebrospinal fluid but no spinal nerves.

memingomyelocele   a meningocele pouch protruding from the vertebral column that contains cerebrospinal fluid and spinal nerves.

menorrhagia   excessive uterine bleeding during menstruation; the duration of the flow is also greater than usual.

mental retardation   a term that refers to significantly subaverage general intellectual functioning manifested during the developmental period and existing concurrently with impairment in adaptive behavior. Students who are mentally retarded are generally classified according to their level of severity as mild or severe.

mesomorphic   a body with a relative preponderance of muscle, bone, and connective tissue.

MET   metabolic rate at work divided by resting metabolic rate.

metabolic   pertaining to the nature of all the physical and chemical processes by which a living organism is maintained.

metastasis   transfer of disease from one organ to another.

microcephalus   a condition resulting in an unusually small head and reduced brain size.

mitral valve   left atrioventricular valve in the heart.

mobility training   techniques used with blind individuals to help them to move about in their environment safely and with assurance.

modality   employment of a therapeutic agent; limited usually to physical agents.

modeling   a technique in which the teacher or another student demonstrates a skill or an appropriate behavior.

monoplegia   paralysis of but a single part; as facial, central brachial.

Moro reflex   a startle reflex associated with infants caused by a loud sharp noise or by being dropped gently on their backs; characterized by fanning out of the arms and crying.

Morquio syndrome   those individuals with a short trunk.

motor aphasia   inability to speak because of a lack of muscle coordination to form words.

motor fitness   refers to those components of motor skill learning (coordination, balance, speed, agility, and so on) that are related to neuromuscular control patterns and do not respond to progressive overloading.

multidisabled   possessing two or more disabling conditions at the same time.

multiple sclerosis   a progressive disease in which the myelin sheath surrounding the nerves degenerates and causes failures in the body's neurological system.

muscular dystrophy   a degenerative, noncontagious disease of the muscular system, characterized by weakness and atrophy of the muscles.

mute   unable to speak.

myelin   a white, fatty-like substance that forms a protective sheath around certain nerve fibers.

myopia   near-sightedness; the eyeball is too long from front to back and images are brought to focus in front of the retina.

myositis   inflammation of a muscle.

narcolepsy   a condition in which an individual has uncontrollable episodes of deep sleep at irregular times.

natal   pertaining to birth.

necrosis   local death of tissue.

neonatal   refers to the first month of life of a newborn.

neoplasia   formation of a tumor; a new or abnormal growth.

nephritis   inflammation of the kidney.

nerve plexuses   a network or tangle of nerves.

neuron   structural unit of the nervous system; a nerve cell.

noncategorical   refers to special education programs that do not differentiate between or label the various exceptionalities requiring special services.

normalization   the principle of educating and treating individuals with disabilities in the "normal" environment of the nondisabled to the greatest extent possible.

nystagmus   an involuntary movement of the eyeballs; usually affects both eyes and is associated with impaired vision.

ocular   term that refers to the eye.

olfactory   pertaining to or relating to the sense of smell.

ophthalmia   severe inflammation of the eye or of the conjunctiva.

optacon   an instrument used to convert print into tactile images enabling the blind to "read" print.

optic nerve   a cranial nerve that transmits nerve impulses to the brain, making sight possible.

organic   term used to refer to known structural or neurological abnormality; inherent as contrasted to functional.

orifice   a natural external opening of the body, such as the mouth and nose.

orthopedic   pertaining to the correction of deformities.

orthotics   the field of knowledge relating to orthopedic appliances and their use.

orthotist   an individual skilled in making orthopedic appliances.

Osgood-Schlatter disease   osteochondrosis of the tuberosity of the tibia.

ossification   the formation of bone or of a bony substance.

osteochondrosis   a disease of one or more of the growth or ossification centers in children.

osteogenesis imperfecta   a hereditary condition in which the bones do not grow normally and break easily.

osteomyelitis   inflammation of the bone marrow.

osteoporosis   abnormal diminution of bone density and weight due to failure of osteoblasts to lay down bone matrix.

other health impaired   One of the categories of disability recognized under PL 101-476. The term refers to limited strength, vitality, or alertness due to chronic or acute health problems which adversely affect a child's education performance.

otitis media   an inflammation or infection of the middle ear that can result in a conductive hearing loss.

overt   an action or behavior that can be observed directly.

pancreas   a gland situated behind the stomach that produces digestive enzymes and insulin.

paralysis   refers to loss or impairment of voluntary motion and sensation.

paraplegia   paralysis of the legs and lower part of the body, motion and sensation being affected.

paroxysm   a sudden recurrence or intensification of symptoms.

patella   knee cap.

pathogenic   giving origin to disease or morbid symptoms.

pathological   pertaining to the branch of medicine that treats disease.

pathology   the branch of medicine that deals with the essential nature of disease, especially of the structural and functional changes in tissues and organs of the body that cause or are caused by disease.

perceptual disability   inability to consciously and mentally register a sensory stimulus.

perinatal   refers to the period of time shortly before, during, or immediately after birth.

peripheral nerve   a nerve situated near an outward part of the surface.

perseverate   continuous purposeless repetition of an act or behavior.

petit mal   a form of epilepsy characterized by a brief blackout with only minor rhythmic movements.

phobia   a persistent and unreasonable fear.

physical fitness   the functional capacity of the various systems of the body that support exercise, specifically muscle strength, muscle endurance, flexibility, cardiorespiratory endurance, and body composition.

plantar   pertaining to the sole of the foot.

plexus   a network or tangle.

pneumothorax   an accumulation of air or gas in the pleural cavity.

poliomyelitis   infantile paralysis; disease involving central nervous system.

polydactylism   a congenital condition in which an individual has more than the normal number of fingers or toes.

postnatal   occurring after birth.

prenatal   existing or occurring before birth.

prognosis   prediction of probable result of attack of disease.

pronation   act of assuming the prone position.

prone   lying face down.

prophylaxis   the prevention of disease.

proprioceptors   sense receptors located in the muscles, joints, and tendons that provide information about the location of the body and its parts and whether or not they are in motion.

prosthesis   artificial appliances, such as arms or legs.

proximal   nearest.

proximodistal   term describing the control of body parts developmentally proceeding from the center to the periphery.

psychogenic deafness   deafness having an emotional or psychological origin as opposed to an organic basis.

psychomotor   the interaction of motor behavior and psychological processes, primarily perception.

psychomotor seizure   a type of epileptic seizure in which the individual goes through a period of inappropriate activity of which he or she is not aware.

psychosomatic   illness induced by mental or emotional pressures.

puberty   refers to that period in life when an individual's sex organs become functional and the secondary sexual characteristics appear.

pyogenic   pus forming.

quadriplegia   paralysis of all four limbs.

rationalization   a defense mechanism in which one substitutes a socially acceptable, but not real, reason for some behavior.

regression   returning to an earlier and more immature stage of development in response to frustration.

reinforcement   an event or reward that increases the probability of a behavior it follows.

renal   pertaining to the kidneys or kidney function.

repression   the unconscious inhibition of unpleasant memories.

residual paralysis   paralysis left behind after therapy has remedied as much of the paralysis as possible.

resource room   used in special education to refer to a setting in a school where students with disabilities can go for special assistance with academic or motor skills.

retina   inner layer of the eye that is sensitive to light.

retinitis pigmentosa   a disease, frequently hereditary, marked by progressive hardening and atrophy of the retina.

retrolental fibroplasia   blindness in premature infants attributed to the use of a high concentration of oxygen in their care.

rheumatic fever   a disease, usually following a streptococcal infection, that is characterized by inflammation of the joints, fever, chorea, and abdominal pain.

rigidity   tenseness of movement; inflexibility.

Ritalin   a trademark name that refers to a stimulant drug frequently used to treat hyperactivity.

rubella   German measles. A communicable disease transmitted by a virus; particularly dangerous to pregnant women during the first trimester.

sacral   situate near the sacrum.

sacrum   the triangular-shaped bone formed usually by five fused vertebrae that are wedged dorsally between the two hip bones.

Scheuermann Disease   also known as juvenile kyphosis; a disturbance of the normal vertebral growth in the cervical and upper thoracic region.

schizophrenia   a severe mental disorder in which a person is unable to separate self from reality.

sclera   the tough, protective covering of the eye.

scoliosis   a lateral deviation in the straight vertical line of the spine.

screening in the context of special education, an attempt to locate or identify children who appear to be in need of special help.

seizure a sudden change of consciousness caused by an abnormal brain discharge; associated with epilepsy.

semicircular canal small circular tubes of the inner ear, concerned with balance.

severely disabled a general term used to describe individuals who are experiencing severe physical, emotional, or mental problems, or a combination of these, requiring prolonged and intense treatment.

shaping the gradual molding of desired behavior.

shunt a device used to drain, or provide a bypass, for excess cerebrospinal fluid.

sign language a form of communication, frequently used by the hearing impaired, that involves a systematic use of gestures.

slow learner refers to a student whose academic progress is less than expected for the individual's chronological age.

somatotype a particular category of body build based on physical characteristics.

spasm involuntary muscle contraction.

spastic characterized by sudden, violent, involuntary contraction of a muscle or group of muscles; producing involuntary movement and distortion.

special education specially designed instruction, at no cost to the parent, to meet the unique needs of a disabled child, including classroom instruction, instruction in physical education, home instruction, and instruction in hospitals and institutions

special physical education refers to programs designed to enhance the physical and motor fitness of individuals with disabilities through modified and developmentally sequenced sport, game, and movement experiences individualized for each participant.

specific gravity weight of body divided by weight of equal amount of water.

spina bifida a congenital malformation of the spine characterized by an incomplete closure in the vertebral column; protrusion of the meninges and spinal cord may occur.

spinous process pertaining to the spine or to a spinelike process.

spirometer an apparatus that can be used to measure the flow of air into and out the of lungs.

sprain tearing or stretching of ligaments and tendons.

standard error of measurement the standard deviation of the error distribution around a true score.

static balance balance while at rest or not in motion.

stenosis incomplete opening of a valve that restricts blood from flowing.

sternum breast bone.

stoma an external opening of the body created by surgery.

strabismus a condition in which the eyes cross due to a weakness of the eye muscles.

strain tearing of muscles.

stretch reflex the tendency of a muscle to contract as a reflex when it is extended suddenly.

sublimation the replacement of a desire or impulse that cannot be satisfied with one that can.

subluxation partial dislocation of a joint.

supination act of assuming the supine position.

supine lying on the back, face upward.

syndactylism describes a condition in which an individual is born with webbed fingers or toes, or both.

syndrome a set of symptoms that occur together.

tactile refers to the sense of touch.

talipes a congenital deformity of the foot, which is twisted out of shape or position.

talus the highest of the tarsal bones and the one that articulates with the tibia and fibula to form the ankle joint.

task analysis the breaking down of a skill into smaller, sequentially ordered phases and steps.

tensiometer an apparatus by which the tensile strength of materials can be determined; adapted to measure strength of muscles.

thermal injuries burns caused by several things including fires, chemicals, and scalding from extremely hot water.

thoracic pertaining to the chest.

thrombophlebitis condition in which inflammation of the vein wall has preceded the formation of the thrombus (blood clot).

thrombosis the formation, development, or presence of a thrombus (blood clot) in a blood vessel or heart.

tibia the inner and larger bone of the leg below the knee.

tic an involuntary twitching and contraction of a small group of muscles; frequently occurs in the facial area.

timeout refers to a behavior modification procedure in which a student is removed from a setting for a designated period of time following inappropriate behavior.

token an object given to a student as a secondary reinforcer to be traded later for a primary reinforcer.

torticollis a spasmodic contraction of neck muscles resulting in drawing the head to one side; wryneck.

total communication a communication system used by the deaf or severely hearing impaired that combines the oral (speech reading) and manual (finger spelling and sign language) approaches.

toxoplasmosis infection with, or a condition produced by the presence of organisms of the genus *Toxoplasma*.

trachoma a viral disease of the conjunctiva and cornea producing pain, tearing, redness, and inflammation.

trailing a mobility technique used by the blind with which they trace lightly over a straight surface, such as a wall or table top, with the back of the fingers.

tranquilizer a drug designed to quiet and calm without producing a hypnotic effect.

transverse arch arch in the area of the ball of the foot; the five metatarsals form the arch.

trauma wound or injury.

tremor involuntary trembling or quivering.

triplegia paralysis of three extremities.

tunnel vision a condition in which a person's visual field is severely restricted, producing an effect similar to that of looking through a tunnel.

tympanic membrane the eardrum; a thin membrane between the outer and inner ear.

unilateral   affecting but one side.

valgus   away from the median line.
Valium   the trade name of a tranquilizing drug used as a muscle relaxant and to relieve tension.
varus   bent inward; usually referring to a deformity.

vertigo   a disorder of the sense of balance that causes dizziness.
vital capacity   the change in pulmonary volume between a maximal inspiratory effort followed by a maximal expiratory effort.
vitreous humor   the fluid in the back chamber of the eye that fills the space between the retina and the lens.

Photograph Credits

All photographs unless otherwise credited are the authors.

Page v: © Courtesy of Gladene Fait.

Chapter 1
1.1: Courtesy of Special Population Programs, University of Wisconsin at La Crosse; **1.2:** Courtesy of Oregon State University Special Physical and Motor Fitness Clinic; **1.3:** Courtesy of Oregon State University Special Physical and Motor Fitness Clinic.

Chapter 2
2.1, 2.8: Courtesy of Portland, Oregon, Motor Development Team, Portland Public Schools; **2.13:** Courtesy of Oregon State University Special Physical and Motor Fitness Clinic.

Chapter 3
3.5: Courtesy of Oregon State University Special Physical and Motor Fitness Clinic; **3.7:** Courtesy of Oregon State University Special Physical and Motor Fitness Clinic.

Chapter 4
4.2: Courtesy of American Alliance for Health, Physical Education, Recreation and Dance; **4.3:** Courtesy of Oregon State University Special Physical and Motor Fitness Clinic; **4.4:** Courtesy of Portland, Oregon, Motor Development Team, Portland Public Schools.

Chapter 5
5.10: Courtesy of Oregon State University Special Physical and Motor Fitness Clinic.

Chapter 6
6.2: Courtesy of Oregon State University Special Physical and Motor Fitness Clinic; **6.3:** Courtesy of Special Population Programs, University of Wisconsin at La Crosse; **6.4:** Courtesy of United States Cerebral Palsy Athletic Association; **6.7:** Courtesy of the Portland, Oregon, Motor Development Team, Portland Public Schools; **6.10:** Courtesy of Oregon State University Special Physical and Motor Fitness Clinic.

Chapter 8
8.1(a–d): Courtesy of adaptAbility Products for Independent Living; **8.3c, 8.5c:** Reproduced by permission from Carroll, Norris C.: Wheelchairs and Mobility Aids, In *American Academy of Orthopaedic Surgeons: Atlas of Orthotics,* ed. 2, St. Louis, 1985, The C.V. Mosby Co.; **8.5d:** Courtesy of Rifton: For People with Disabilities; **8.5e:** Reprinted with the permission of Flaghouse, Inc.; **8.7:** Courtesy of adaptAbility Products for Independent Living; **8.8:** Courtesy of Rifton Equipment for the Handicapped Community, Ulster, N.Y.; **8.11–8.14:** Reproduced by permission from Carroll, Norris C.: Wheelchairs and Mobility Aids. In *American Academy of Orthopaedic Surgeons: Atlas of Orthotics,* ed. 2, St. Louis, 1985, The C.V Mosby Co.; **8.17:** Everest and Jennings, Inc., Camarillo, Ca.; **8.21g:** Courtesy of Everest and Jennings; **8.21b,f:** Courtesy of Magic in Motion, Inc.; **8.21c,e:** Courtesy of Motion Design, Inc.; **8.21d,h:** Courtesy of Ortho Kinetics; **8.22:** Courtesy of Sports 'n Spokes; **8.28:** Courtesy of Durr-Fillauer Medical, Inc. Orthopedic Division; **8.10:** Courtesy of Quickie Design/Shadow, 20604 84th, Kent, WA 98032.

Chapter 9
9.3: Courtesy of Bigge, June L., and O'Donnell, Patrick A.: *Teaching Individuals With Physical and Multiple Disabilities.* Columbus, OH, Charles E. Merrill Publishing Co. 1976; **9.7:** Courtesy of Oregon State University Special Physical and Motor Fitness Clinic; **9.8:** Courtesy of Special Population Programs, University of Wisconsin at La Crosse; **9.13:** Courtesy of March of Dimes; **9.14:** Courtesy of Oregon State University Special Physical and Motor Fitness Clinic.

Chapter 10
10.8: Courtesy of the United States Cerebral Palsy Athletic Association; **10.10:** Courtesy of Oregon State University Special Physical and Motor Fitness Clinic.

Chapter 11
11.5: Courtesy of Oregon State University Special Physical and Motor Fitness Clinic.

Chapter 12
12.2: Courtesy of the American Foundation for the Blind; **12.13:** Courtesy of the Portland, Oregon, Motor Development Team, Portland Public Schools.

Chapter 15
15.4: Courtesy of Cheryl Hatch, *Oregon State University Barometer,* Corvallis, Oregon.

Chapter 16
16.2: Courtesy of Oregon State University Special Physical and Motor Fitness Clinic.

Chapter 17
17.3: Courtesy of Oregon State University Special Physical and Motor Fitness Clinic; **17.4:** Courtesy of Oregon State University Special Physical and Motor Fitness Clinic; **17.5:** Courtesy of Oregon State University Special Physical and Motor Fitness Clinic; **17.6:** Courtesy of Oregon State University Special Physical and Motor Fitness Clinic; **17.8:** Courtesy of Portland, Oregon, Motor Development Team, Portland Public Schools.

Chapter 18

18.1: Courtesy of Oregon State University Special Physical and Motor Fitness Clinic; **18.2:** Courtesy of Oregon State University Special Physical and Motor Fitness Clinic; **18.3:** Courtesy of Oregon State University Special Physical and Motor Fitness Clinic; **18.5:** Courtesy of Oregon State University Special Physical and Motor Fitness Clinic.

Chapter 19

19.2: Courtesy of Oregon State University Special Physical and Motor Fitness Clinic.

Chapter 20

20.1: Courtesy of Oregon State University Special Physical and Motor Fitness Clinic.

Chapter 21

21.1: Courtesy of Oregon State University Special Physical and Motor Fitness Clinic; **21.2:** Courtesy of Newington Children's Hospital; **21.4:** Courtesy of Oregon State University Special Physical and Motor Fitness Clinic; **21.5:** Courtesy of Oregon State University Special Physical and Motor Fitness Clinic; **21.6:** Courtesy of Children's Physical Development Clinic, Bridgewater State College.

Chapter 22

22.2: Courtesy of Special Population Programs, University of Wisconsin at La Crosse; **22.3:** Courtesy of March of Dimes.

Chapter 23

23.1: Courtesy of the United States Cerebral Palsy Athletic Association; **23.4:** Courtesy of Access Design Inc.; **23.4:** Courtesy of Unicycle, Montreal, Quebec, Canada; **23.5a:** Courtesy of George Snyder; **23.5b:** Courtesy of Ronnie Van Sickle; **23.6a:** Courtesy of Maddak, Inc.; **23.8:** Courtesy of Fallot Bielefeldt, SOAR Program, Portland, Oregon; **23.9:** Courtesy of Innovative Recreation Inc.; **23.10:** Courtesy of Quickie Design/Shadow, 20604 84th, Kent, WA 98032; **23.12:** Courtesy of Wayne J. Avery; **23.15:** Courtesy of Ron Adams, University of Virginia; **23.13(a–d):** As presented in Paciorek, M.J., and Jones, J.A. (1989) *Sports and Recreation for the Disabled.* Indianapolis: Benchmark p. 155; **23.17:** As presented in Paciorek, M.J., and Jones, J.A. (1989) *Sports and Recreation for the Disabled.* Indianapolis: Benchmark p. 325; **23.18:** Courtesy of United States Cerebral Palsy Athletic Association.

Chapter 24

24.2: Courtesy of Greg Thompson, Rancho Los Amigos Hospital; **24.4, 24.7:** Courtesy of Stephie R. Fine, University of Conn., Storrs; **24.8:** From GAMES, SPORTS, AND EXERCISE FOR THE PHYSICALLY HANDICAPPED by Adams, R., Daniel A., McCubbin, J., and Rullman, L. (1982) p. 211, Fig. 8.9; **24.10:** Courtesy of Children's Physical Development Clinic, Bridgewater State College.

Chapter 25

25.1: Courtesy of the Portland, Oregon, Motor Development Team, Portland Public Schools; **25.2:** Courtesy of John Joseg, Shoot-A-Way; **25.3:** Photo by Curt Beamer. Copyright Sports 'n Spokes/Paralyzed Veterans of America, 1994; **25.4:** Photo by Curt Beamer. Copyright Sports 'n Spokes/Paralyzed Veterans of America, 1994; **25.5:** Courtesy of Newington Children's Hospital; **25.9:** Courtesy of the United States Cerebral Palsy Athletic Association; **25.10:** Courtesy of the Children's Physical Development Clinic, Bridgewater State College; **25.13:** Photo by Delfina Colby. Copyright Sports 'n Spokes/Paralyzed Veterans of America 1994.

Chapter 26

26.4: Courtesy of Oregon State University Special Physical and Motor Fitness Clinic; **26.7:** Courtesy of Children's Physical Development Clinic, Bridgewater State College.

Chapter 27

27.1: Courtesy of Special Population Programs, University of Wisconsin at La Crosse; **27.2:** Courtesy of Jayfro Corporation; **27.3:** Courtesy of Oregon State University Special Physical and Motor Fitness Clinic; **27.4:** Photo by Delfina Colby. Copyright Sports 'n Spokes/Paralyzed Veterans of America, 1994; **27.5:** Courtesy of Oregon State University Special Physical and Motor Fitness Clinic; **27.8:** Courtesy of American Alliance for Health, Physical Education, Recreation, and Dance. Photography by Lyonel Avance, Special Education Branch, Los Angeles City Schools; **27.9:** Courtesy of Oregon State University Special Physical and Motor Fitness Clinic; **27.10:** Courtesy of Oregon State University Special Physical and Motor Fitness Clinic.

Chapter 28

28.10: Courtesy of Oregon State University Special Physical and Motor Fitness Clinic.

Chapter 30

30.1: Courtesy of the United States Cerebral Palsy Athletic Association; **30.2:** Courtesy of University of Utah, Salt Lake City.

Illustrator Credits

Bill Colrus, The Ivy League of Artists: Figures 2.6, 2.7, 10.4, 24.5, 29.1.

Rolin Graphics: Figures 3.1, 3.2, 3.3, 4.1, 6.9, 7.5, 7.6, 14.3, 15.6, 17.1, 20.8, 20.9, 20.10, 22.1, 22.5, 26.1, 27.6.

Name Index

Subject Index

Usher's syndrome, 246–247

Validity of tests
  and conditions/populations, 139
  construct validity, 139
  content validity, 138
  criterion-related validity, 138–139
  ecological validity, 140
Vegetarianism
  nutritional deficiencies, 288
  types of diets, 288
Ventricular septal defects, 256
Verbalization
  and mentally retarded, 335
  as teaching method, 112
Vestibular system, and balance, 47
Vineland Social Maturity Scale, 325
Visual acuity, 46
Visual agnosia, 351–352
Visual aids, for hearing impaired, 243, 244
Visual figure-ground, 47
Visual impairment, 223–234
  adjustments of visually impaired, 226
  congenital, 224
  glaucoma, 225
  gonorrhea, 225
  infectious disease, 224–225
  muscle imbalance, 224
  nature of, 4, 223–224
  and physical fitness level, 232–233
  refractive errors, 224
  visual acuity, degrees of, 223
Visual impairment program
  activities for older children, 232–233
  communication aids, 228
  communication through
    movement, 231–232
  exploring locomotion, 231
  free play, 230–231
  instructional approach, 229
  manipulation of objects, 232
  mobility training, 229–230

movement while stationary, 231
  play areas, 227–228
  playground equipment, 228
  primary grade activities, 231
  program planning, 226–227
  relaxation exercises, 232
  rhythm/dance activities, 422
  spatial awareness, 232
  sports, 233–234
Visualization, as teaching method, 113–115
Visual perception, 46–47
  components of, 46–47
  disorders of, 351–352
Visual perception activities
  for color, 358–359
  for distance, 359–360
  for figure-ground phenomenon, 360
  for shape/form, 359
  for size, 358
  for speed, 360
Visual tracking, 47
Visual training program, Frostig program, 45
Vital capacity (VC), 267
Vitamins
  deficiencies, 283
  functions of, 283
  learning disabilities treatment, 348
  megadoses, 287
Volleyball, 482–483
Volunteers
  and mentally retarded program, 336
  recruiting/training of, 85–86

Walkers, 150–152
  types of, 150–151
Walking
  development of, 23
  as lifetime activity, 449–450
Wall ball game, 410
Warts, 316
Water phobia, 378
  water adjustment activities, 493–495

Weight control, and spinal cord injuries, 178
Weight control programs, 292–295, 528
  alternate behavior substitution, 294
  commercial programs, 295
  criteria for, 294
  exercise in, 295–296, 528
  food reduction strategies, 295
  goals of, 294
Weight training
  for respiratory impaired, 275
  See also Strength-development exercises
Weight Watchers, 295
Wheelbarrow game, 412
Wheelchair basketball, 472–474
Wheelchair bound, physical activities
  for, 181–182
Wheelchairs, 154–161
  guidelines for handling of, 156–158
  lifting person from, 156, 158
  sport chairs, 159, 161
  suppliers of, 607–608
  types of, 154–156, 160
  user's test, 159
Wheelchair soccer, 481–482
Wheelchair softball, 476–477
Wheelchair Sports USA, 11, 577
Winchester Reacher, 152
World Games, 324
Wrestling, for visually impaired, 233
Wring the dish rag game, 409
Written materials, use in teaching, 114
Wryneck, nature of, 188

Y cart, 154
Yoga, 558–559, 563–564
Young disabled children
  game instruction, 405–416
  gross motor assessment of, 401–402
  legislation related to, 401
  movement concepts related to, 404
  movement skills for, 404
  placement of, 402–403